Volume Two from 1865

America

Past and Present

Third Edition

America

Past and Present

Third Edition

Robert A. Divine
University of Texas

T. H. Breen
Northwestern University

George M. Fredrickson
Stanford University

R. Hal Williams
Southern Methodist University

HarperCollins*Publishers*

Sponsoring Editor: Bruce Borland
Development Editor: Charlotte Iglarsh/Marisa L'Heureux
Project Coordination, Text and Cover Design: Proof Positive/Farrowlyne Associates
Cover and Title Page Illustration: *Washington Street, Indianapolis at Dusk* by Theodore Groll, © 1990
   Indianapolis Museum of Art, Gift of a couple of Old Hoosiers.
Photo Research: Nina Page, Leslie Coopersmith
Production: Michael Weinstein
Compositor: Black Dot Graphics
Printer and Binder: R. R. Donnelly & Sons, Inc.
Cover Printer: Phoenix Color Corp

America: Past and Present, Third Edition

Library of Congress Cataloging-in-Publication Data

America, past and present / Robert A. Divine . . . [et al.]. — 3rd ed.
    p. cm.
   Includes bibliographical references and indexes.
   1. United States—History. I. Divine, Robert A.
E178.1.A4895   1991b   90-5040
973—dc20   CIP
ISBN 0-673-38865-4 (Vol. 1)
ISBN 0-673-38866-2 (Vol. 2)
     92 93 9 8 7 6 5 4 3

ontents

CHAPTER 16

The Agony of Reconstruction   460

CHAPTER 17

The West: Exploring an Empire   492

CHAPTER 18

The Industrial Society   524

Appendix A-1

Maps

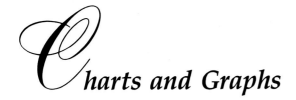

Charts and Graphs

About the Authors

ROBERT A. DIVINE

Robert A. Divine, George W. Littlefield Professor in American History at the University of Texas at Austin, received his Ph.D. degree from Yale University in 1954. A specialist in American diplomatic history, he has taught at the University of Texas since 1954, where he has been honored by the Student Association for teaching excellence. His extensive published work includes *The Illusion of Neutrality* (1962), *Second Chance: The Triumph of Internationalism in America During World War* II (1967), and *Blowing on the Wind* (1978). He is also the author of *Eisenhower and the Cold War* (1981), and editor of *Exploring the Johnson Years* (1981) and *The Johnson Years*, Vol. II (1987). He has been a fellow at the Center for Advanced Study in the Behavioral Sciences and has given the Albert Shaw Lectures in Diplomatic History at Johns Hopkins University.

T. H. BREEN

T.H. Breen, William Smith Mason Professor of American History at Northwestern University, received his Ph.D. from Yale University in 1968. He has taught at Northwestern since 1970. Breen's major books include *The Character of the Good Rule: A Study of Puritan Political Ideas in New England* (1974), *Puritans and Adventurers: Change and Persistence in Early America* (1980), *Tobacco Culture: The Mentality of the Great Tidewater Planters on the Eve of Revolution* (1985), and with S. Innes of the University of Virginia, *"Myne Owne Ground": Race and Freedom on Virginia's Eastern Shore* (1980). His *Imagining the Past* won the 1990 Historic Preservation Book Award. In addition to receiving an award for outstanding teaching at Northwestern, Breen has been the recipient of research grants from the American Council of Learned Societies, the Guggenheim Foundation, the Institute for Advanced Study (Princeton), and the National Humanities Center. He has served as the Fowler Hamilton Fellow at Christ Church, Oxford University (1987–1988) and the Pitt Professor of American History and Institutions, Cambridge University (1990–1991).

GEORGE M. FREDRICKSON

George M. Fredrickson is Edgar E. Robinson Professor of United States History at Stanford University. He is the author or editor of several books, including the *Inner Civil War* (1965), *The Black Image in the White Mind* (1971), and *White Supremacy: A Comparative Study in American and South African History* (1981), which won both the Ralph Waldo Emerson Award from Phi Beta Kappa and the Merle Curti Award from the Organization of American Historians. His most recent work is *The Arrogance of Race: Historical Perspectives on Slavery, Racism, and Social Inequality* (1988). He received both the A.B. and Ph.D. degrees from Harvard and has been the recipient of a Guggenheim Fellowship, two National Endowment for the Humanities Senior Fellowships, and a Fellowship from the Center for Advanced Studies in the Behavioral Sciences. Before coming to Stanford in 1984, he taught at Northwestern. He has also served as Fulbright lecturer in American History at Moscow University and as Harmsworth Professor of American History at Oxford.

R. HAL WILLIAMS

R. Hal Williams is Professor of History at Southern Methodist University. He received his A.B. degree from Princeton University (1963) and his

Ph.D. degree from Yale University (1968). His books include *The Democratic Party and California Politics, 1880–1896* (1973), *Years of Decision: American Politics in the 1890s* (1978) and *The Manhattan Project: A Documentary Introduction to the Atomic Age* (1990). A specialist in American political history, he taught at Yale University from 1968 to 1975 and came to SMU in 1975 as Chair of the Department of History. From 1980 to 1988, he served as Dean of Dedman College, the school of humanities and sciences, at SMU. In 1980, he was a Visiting Professor at University College, Oxford University. Williams has received grants from the American Philosophical Society and the National Endowment for the Humanities, and he has served on the Texas Committee for the Humanities. He is currently at work on a biography of James G. Blaine, the late-nineteenth-century Speaker of the House, secretary of state, and Republican presidential candidate.

Preface

The third edition of *America: Past and Present* is a major revision that strives to achieve the shared goal of the previous editions—to present a clear, relevant, and balanced history of the United States as an unfolding story of national development, from the days of the earliest inhabitants to the present. We emphasize the *story* because we strongly believe in the value of historical narrative in providing a vivid sense of the past. In each chapter, we sought to blend the excitement and drama of the American experience with insights about the social, economic, and cultural forces that underlie it.

In this edition we have gone over each chapter carefully to sharpen the analysis and the prose and to offer new perspectives. Many suggestions proposed by those who used the previous editions in their classrooms have been adopted.

Among the revisions that take account of a growing body of excellent scholarly work are these:

· The opening chapter has been rewritten to provide an extensive discussion of preconquest Native-American culture and a section on African culture and society before American settlement. Students are presented with the necessary information about pre-Columbian, European, and African societies to help them better understand the conjunction of these three cultures in the New World.

· Throughout this revised edition, the roles that Native Americans, as well as African Americans and women, played in the development of American society is emphasized. They continue to appear throughout the text, not as witnesses to the historical narrative, but as principals in its development.

· Chapters 5–7 discuss the Constitution and constitutional issues in greater depth than previous editions. The same chapters also present a fuller explication of republicanism in theory and in practice.

· Chapters 8–20 provide expanded coverage of intellectual and cultural developments of the early and mid-nineteenth century, including illuminating anecdotal material, and a revised section on the Texas Revolution that takes account of Mexican and Mexican-American perspectives of the conflict.

· The chapter on American overseas expansion in the late nineteenth and early twentieth centuries (Chapter 21) includes more material on anti-imperialist thinking; the two chapters on the Progressive Era (Chapters 22 and 23) have had a substantive overhaul; a great deal of new material drawn from the most recent studies has been added and the chapters have been reorganized to achieve greater concept integration and continuity. Chapter 22 now examines the economic and social conditions and the intellectual and cultural currents that gave rise to the Progressive movement; Chapter 23 explores progressivism in terms of political action on all governmental levels.

· The chapters that discuss the post–World War II period and the Cold War have been extensively revised and reordered. Chapter 28 now focuses on the Truman presidency and McCarthyism in the context of the early Cold War; a revised Chapter 29 deals with the domestic developments—mainly civil rights and liberal reform measures—of the Eisenhower, Kennedy, and early Johnson years at the height of the Cold War. Chapter 30 is now devoted exclusively to exploring foreign policy of the 1950s and 1960s with special emphasis on the developing and intensifying Vietnam War. It enables students to see how the Vietnam conflict grew out of the containment policy of the 1950s. Chapter 32 has updated demographics and new material on long-term social trends.

· A greatly expanded and revised final chapter covers the major political developments under Presidents Reagan and Bush, and analyzes the impact of these policies on both the American economy and the world. New sections on major social problems of the decade of the 1980s include discussions of the AIDS epidemic and the "war on drugs." The section concludes with a discussion of the momentous political changes in Europe that may very well mark the end of the Cold War.

APPROACH AND THEMES

As the title suggests, our book is a blend of the traditional and the new. The strong narrative emphasis and chronological organization are traditional; the incorporation of the many fresh insights that historians have gained from the social sciences in the past quarter-century is new. We have used significant incidents and episodes to reflect the dilemmas, the choices, and the decisions made by the people as well as by their leaders. After discussion of the colonial period, most of the chapters examine shorter time periods, usually about a decade, permitting us to view these major political and public events as points of reference and orientation around which social themes are integrated. This approach gives unity and direction to the text.

In recounting the story of the American past, we see a nation in flux. The early Africans and Europeans developed complex agrarian folkways that blended Old World customs and New World experiences; as new cultural identities evolved, the idea of political independence became more acceptable. People who had been subjects of the British Crown created a system of government that challenged later Americans to work out the full implications of theories of social and economic equality.

The growing sectional rift between the North and South, revolving around divergent models of economic growth and conflicting social values, culminated in civil war. In the post–Civil War period, the development of a more industrialized economy severely tested the values of an agrarian society, engendering a Populist reform movement. In the early twentieth century, Progressive reformers sought to infuse the industrial order with social justice. World War I demonstrated the extent of American power in the world. The resiliency of the maturing American nation was tested by the Great Depression and World War II. The Cold War ushered in an era of crises, foreign and domestic, that revealed both the strengths and the weaknesses of modern America.

The impact of change on human lives adds a vital dimension to our understanding of history.

We need to comprehend the way the Revolution affected the lives of ordinary citizens; what it was like for both blacks and whites to live in a plantation society; how men and women fared in the shift from an agrarian to an industrial economy; and what impact technology, in the form of the automobile and the computer, has had on patterns of life in the twentieth century.

Our commitment is not to any particular ideology or point of view; rather, we hope to challenge our readers to rediscover the fascination of the American past and reach their own conclusions about its significance for their lives. At the same time, we have not avoided controversial issues; instead, we have tried to offer reasoned judgments on such morally charged subjects as the nature of slavery and the advent of nuclear weapons. We believe that while history rarely repeats itself, the story of the American past is relevant to the problems and dilemmas facing the nation today, and we have therefore sought to stress themes and ideas that continue to shape our national culture.

STRUCTURE AND FEATURES

The structure and features of the book are intended to stimulate student interest and to reinforce learning. Chapters begin with **vignettes** or incidents, many of them new, that establish direction for chapter themes stated in the introductory sections (which also serve as overviews to the topics covered) and end with **expanded summaries.** Each chapter has a **chronology, recommended readings, bibliography** (redone for this edition), and a **two-page special feature essay** on a topic that combines high interest and instructional value. Nine of the special features are on new topics—some explore the Constitution and landmark cases, immigration, and the culture of the workplace; others relate to historiographical, environmental, and technological issues.

The extensive **full-color map program** has been enhanced to provide a greater global perspective and more integration of information and action. **New charts, graphs, and tables**—many with a capsulized format for convenient review of factual information—relate to social and economic change. The rich **full-color illustration program** bearing directly on the narrative advances and expands the themes, provides elaboration and contrast, tells more of the story, and generally adds another dimension of learning. The illustrations also present a minisurvey of American painting styles. **Five picture essays** explore diverse facets of American life and a **revised and expanded "Growth of America" series** at the front of the book with maps and accompanying narrative includes a **time line of parallel events.** The augmented **Appendix,** with updated presidential, electoral, cabinet, and Supreme Court charts and a statehood admission chart, also features a new chart of U.S. population by state and region with projections to the end of the century.

SUPPLEMENTS PACKAGE

An extensive package of supplements accompanies the Third Edition of *America: Past and Present.*

The *Instructor's Resource Manual* by James Walsh, Central Connecticut State University, includes an essay on teaching American history through maps and a class exercise on teaching writing skills using the rhetoric of the Declaration of Independence. Each chapter includes a brief summary, list of key terms, suggestions for class discussion, examination questions, and annotated film guide.

The *Test Bank* by Carol Brown and Michael McCormick, Houston Community College, contains fifty questions per chapter including multiple choice, true/false, matching, and essay questions. The questions are referenced by topic, difficulty level, cognitive type (factual or conceptual), and text page. The test bank also contains a separate section of map test items designed by James Conrad, Nichols College.

Testmaster Computerized Testing System is available for IBM, Apple, and Macintosh computers. This powerful test-generation system allows the instructor to construct customized test files using questions from the *Test Bank.* In addition, the instructor can add original questions to any test, or even create entirely new test files.

Grades Classroom Management Software records quiz and exam scores for up to 200 students.

The *Student Study Guide* by Donald Smith, Charles Cook, and Jon Garret, Houston Community College, and Richard Bailey, San Jacinto College North, is available in two volumes. Each volume begins with the essay "Skills for Studying and Learning History" and includes a special project: "Applying Your Skills Outside the Classroom." Chapters provide a summary, learning objectives, glossary terms, and study questions in a variety of formats. The *Guide* includes map and chronology exercises, and essay questions.

Supershell Version 2.0 Computerized Tutorial is an interactive program for computer-assisted learning that provides sophisticated diagnostics and feedback including an end-of-session reading assignment based on the student's performance, and tracking of students' performance from session to session. In addition to questions in a variety of formats, *SuperShell* contains comprehensive chapter outlines keyed to the headings and subheadings in the text. A "Flash Card" program helps students learn important terms and concepts. *SuperShell* is available for IBM computers.

American Historical Geography: Computerized Atlas by William Hamblin, Brigham Young University, includes map exercises involving the rise of the Americas, the Revolutionary War, the Civil War, transportation systems, and elections. The program, free upon adoption of the textbook, is available for Macintosh computers.

Mapping American History: Student Activities by Gerald Danzer, University of Illinois, Chicago, features numerous and varied map skill exercises. In addition to increasing students' basic locational literacy, the exercises provide opportunities for map interpretation and for analyzing cartographic materials as historical documents. Each student copy of the text purchased from HarperCollins entitles the instructor to a free student copy of the Map Workbook.

Discovering American History Through Maps and Views by Gerald Danzer, University of Illinois, Chicago, provides 140 four-color transparencies selected from key primary sources. Provided in a 3-ring binder, the collection begins with an essay on teaching history with maps and contains a detailed commentary with each transparency. Free to adoptors of *America: Past and Present* 3/E, the program consists of cartographic and pictoral maps, views, and photos including urban plans, building diagrams, and works of art as well as classic maps.

Audio History Cassettes: "Oral History—American Voices" and "Great Speeches—Words that Made History" are available at no charge to text adopters. The cassettes feature voices from America's past and cover a broad range, from journals of pioneer women to interviews by Studs Terkel and famous political speeches.

The Winner's Circle is a collection of recent prize-winning films and videos relating to American history.

Visual Archives of American History, a new laser disk, provides over 500 stills, including a "portrait gallery" of fine art and photos, and 29 minutes of full-motion film clips from major events in American history. The broadcast quality images, crisp detail and instant remote control access make *Visual Archives* ideally suited for large lecture halls.

The Integrator provides a cross-reference and index to all print, software, and media supplements to help instructors make effective use of this comprehensive supplement package. *The Integrator* also offers teaching techniques for multimedia presentations.

Although this book is a joint effort, each author took primary responsibility for writing one section. T.H. Breen contributed the first eight chapters from the earliest Native-American period to the second decade of the nineteenth century; George M. Fredrickson wrote Chapters 9 through 16, carrying the narrative through the Reconstruction Era. R. Hal Williams is responsible for Chapters 17 through 24, focusing on the industrial transformation and urbanization, and the events culminating in World War I; and Robert A. Divine wrote Chapters 25 through 33, bringing the story through the Depression, World War II, and the Cold War to the present. Each contributor reviewed and revised the work of his colleagues and helped shape the material into its final form.

The Authors

ACKNOWLEDGMENTS

We are most grateful to our consultants and critiquers whose thoughtful and constructive work contributed greatly to this edition:

James Axtell
College of William and Mary

Charles L. Cohen
University of Wisconsin–Madison

Jerald Combs
San Francisco State University

James C. Curtis
University of Delaware

Thomas Dublin
SUNY at Binghamton

William W. Freehling
Johns Hopkins University

Lewis L. Gould
University of Texas at Austin

Steven Lawson
University of South Florida

Herbert Margulies
University of Hawaii at Manoa

James H. Merrell
Vassar College

Joseph C. Miller
University of Virginia

Michael Perman
University of Illinois–Chicago

Kathryn Kish Sklar
SUNY at Binghamton

James P. Walsh
Central Connecticut State University

Rosemarie Zagarri
Catholic University

The following conscientious historians reviewed various drafts of this edition. They were most helpful in offering suggestions that led to significant improvements in the final product.

David Bernstein
California State University, Long Beach

James Border
Berkshire Community College

Mary C. Brennan
Ohio State University

Daniel Patrick Brown
Moorpark College

Raphael Cassimere, Jr.
University of New Orleans

Virginia Crane
University of Wisconsin–Oshkosh

Charles Douglass
Florida Community College at Jacksonville

John P. Farr
Chattanooga State Technical Community College

Richard Frey
Southern Oregon State College

Fred E. Freidel
Bellevue Community College

Gary W. Gallagher
Pennsylvania State University

Sara E. Gallaway
Oxnard College

Louis S. Gomolak
Southwest Texas State University

Edward F. Hass
Wright State University

Richard C. Haney
University of Wisconsin–Whitewater

James A. Hurst
Northwest Missouri State University

Robert M. Ireland
University of Kentucky

Carol E. Jenson
University of Wisconsin–La Crosse

Robert R. Jones
University of Southwestern Louisiana

Henry Louis
Kansas City Kansas Community College

Karen Marcotte
Palo Alto College

Harmon Mothershead
Northwest Missouri State University

John K. Nelson
University of North Carolina at Chapel Hill

Roger L. Nichols
University of Arizona

Marlette Rebhorn
Austin Community College

Andrew W. Robertson
Louisiana State University

David Sandoval
University of Southern Colorado

Howard Schonberger
University of Maine

Ingrid Winther Scobie
Texas Women's University

Paul F. Taylor
Augusta College

Michael E. Thompson
South Seattle Community College

Nancy Unger
San Francisco State University

Donna L. VanRaaphorst
Cuyahoga Community College

Russell Veeder
Dickinson State University

Forrest A. Walker
Eastern New Mexico State University

A large number of instructors, too many to name individually, who used the previous edition were most helpful in reporting on the success of the text in the classroom. We heartily thank them all.

The staff at HarperCollins continued its generous support and assistance for our efforts. We appreciate the thoughtful guidance of Bruce Borland, who was instrumental in initiating the project; Barbara Muller, who carefully paved the way for the development of this third edition; Charlotte Iglarsh and Marisa L'Heureux, developmental editors, who helped us in many ways to augment and enhance the appeal of the text. Project editor Jennifer Kamm and designer Paula Meyers both of Proof Positive/Farrowlyne Associates deftly guided the new edition into production. Others of the HarperCollins staff who gave valuable assistance include photo researchers Nina Page and Leslie Coopersmith and cartographer Paul Yatabe.

Finally, each author received aid and encouragement from many colleagues, friends, and family members. Robert Divine wishes to thank Lisa Divine, Barbara Renick Divine, Ricardo Romo, and George Wright for helpful suggestions, and Brian Duchin, Louis Gomolak, Seth Fein, and Aaron Forsberg for preparing many of the special features. T.H. Breen wishes to thank E. Faber, Susan C. Breen, Chester Pach, and Patty Cleary. Special appreciation goes to Timothy Hall. George Fredrickson wishes to thank Dale Prentiss for help with special features, and maps, tables, bibliography updates, and general research assistance. R. Hal Williams wishes to thank Nan Coulter, Lewis L. Gould, Jane Elder, and Lise and Scott Williams. Special thanks go to Marsha Lewis, Jane Yoder, and John Nicholson.

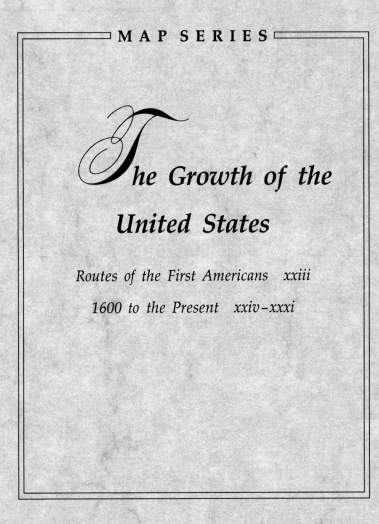

MAP SERIES

The Growth of the United States

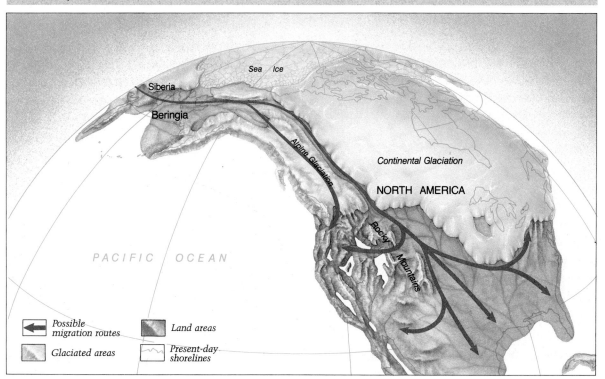

The peopling of North America began about 30,000 years ago, during the Ice Age, and continued for many millennia. Land bridges created by lower sea levels during glaciation formed a tundra coastal plain over what is now the Bering Strait, between Asia and North America. In the postglacial era, the warmer climate supported the domestication and, later, the cultivation of plants. By the first century A.D., intensive farming was established from the southwest to the east coast of what is now the United States. (Ch. 1)

Except for an abortive attempt by Norsemen in the tenth century to settle the New World, contact between North America and Europe was not established until the Age of Exploration at the end of the 1400s. Settlements were founded in Mexico and Florida by Spain in the 1500s, and along the Atlantic littoral by France, England, Sweden, and Holland in the early 1600s.

From the founding of the first colonies along the Atlantic coast to the United States' current involvement in global affairs, the dominant theme in American life has been growth. The pages that follow chronicle the growth of the United States from its colonial origins to the present in 50-year intervals, using maps, narrative, and a chronology of major and parallel events.

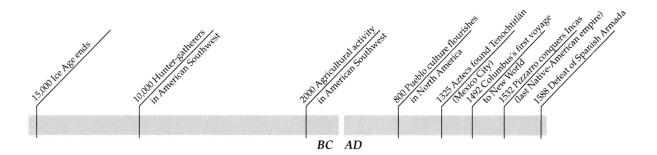

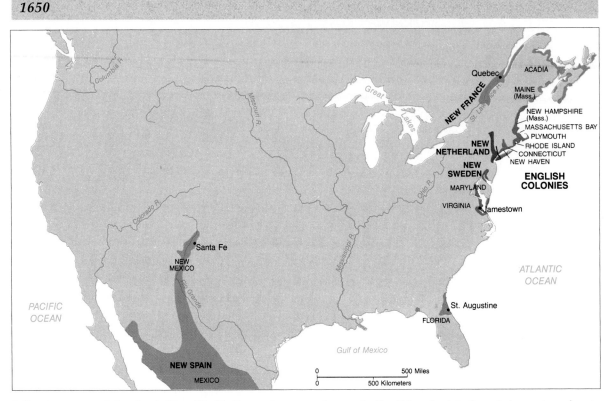

Following up on Columbus's New World discoveries, the Spanish set sail for America and conquered the Native-American Aztecs and Incas in the sixteenth century, establishing a vast colonial empire stretching from Mexico to Peru. The search for gold and silver brought Spanish explorers into the present-day American Southwest, where they established outposts in New Mexico in the early 1600s. Even earlier, Spain had begun the settlement of Florida with the founding of St. Augustine in 1565. Far to the north the French, attracted by the profits of the fur trade with the Indians, began settling the St. Lawrence valley in the early part of the seventeenth century.

Between the Spanish to the south and the French to the north, English colonists founded a series of scattered settlements along the Atlantic coast. Driven by the desire for economic gain, religious freedom, or both, colonists in Virginia and Massachusetts Bay endured severe weather and periods of starvation to establish small but permanent colonies. By mid-century, settlements had sprung up in New Hampshire, Connecticut, and Rhode Island. Along Chesapeake Bay, Maryland was founded as a place of refuge for persecuted Catholics. In the midst of these English colonies, the Dutch established New Netherland and took over a small Swedish settlement. By the middle of the century, the seeds had been planted for a future United States.

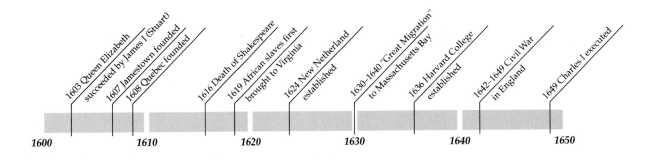

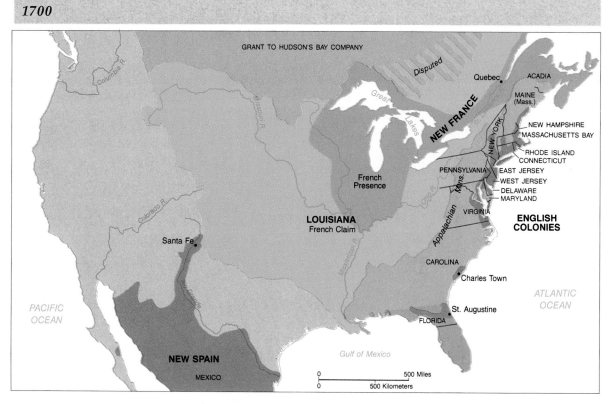

GRANT TO HUDSON'S BAY COMPANY

Disputed

Columbia R.

Great Lakes

NEW FRANCE

Quebec

ACADIA

MAINE
(Mass.)

NEW HAMPSHIRE

MASSACHUSETTS BAY

NEW YORK

RHODE ISLAND
CONNECTICUT

French
Presence

PENNSYLVANIA

EAST JERSEY

WEST JERSEY

DELAWARE

MARYLAND

LOUISIANA
French Claim

Colorado R.

VIRGINIA

ENGLISH
COLONIES

Appalachian Mtns.

Santa Fe

CAROLINA

Charles Town

ATLANTIC
OCEAN

PACIFIC
OCEAN

St. Augustine

FLORIDA

NEW SPAIN

MEXICO

Gulf of Mexico

0   500 Miles
0   500 Kilometers

Having established a precarious foothold, the English settlements slowly began to grow and prosper. The later New England colonies received royal charters, separate from the original Massachusetts Bay charter. William Penn established Pennsylvania as a place of refuge for Quakers, welcoming French, Dutch, German, and Swedish settlers, as well as English and Scotch-Irish. Nearby New Jersey became the home for an equally diverse population. Under English rule, New Netherland became New York. In the south, English aristocrats founded Carolina as a plantation society populated in great part by settlers from the Caribbean island of Barbados. What was most remarkable about these English colonies was not their similarities but the differences between them. Bound together

only by ties to the mother country, each developed its own character and culture.

Meanwhile, intrepid French explorers based in Quebec penetrated deep into the interior of the continent, driven on by the imperatives of the fur trade. Père Jacques Marquette navigated the Mississippi River and Sieur de La Salle journeyed to the Gulf of Mexico, laying claim for the King of France to a vast territory— all the lands drained by the Mississippi and its tributaries. This French initiative alarmed colonists along the Atlantic coast, many of whom believed that France planned to block English settlement on the lands beyond the Appalachian Mountains. About the same time, Spain established missions in Texas as a token presence. (Ch. 1, 2)

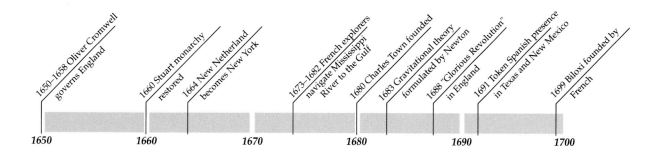

1650–1658 Oliver Cromwell governs England

1660 Stuart monarchy restored

1664 New Netherland becomes New York

1673–1682 French explorers navigate Mississippi River to the Gulf

1680 Charles Town founded

1683 Gravitational theory formulated by Newton

1688 "Glorious Revolution" in England

1691 Token Spanish presence in Texas and New Mexico

1699 Biloxi founded by French

1650   1660   1670   1680   1690   1700

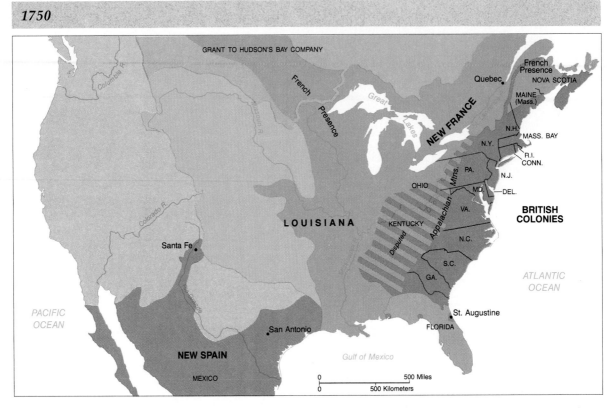

A century-long European struggle for empire between the French and the British led to military confrontation on this side of the Atlantic. Britain's victory in Queen Anne's War changed the map of North America. It gave the British control of the land bordering on Hudson Bay, as well as Newfoundland and Nova Scotia. The French redoubled their efforts to develop Louisiana as a buffer against the westward expansion of the seaboard colonies. Concerned with the Spanish presence in Florida, the British founded the colony of Georgia in 1732 to guard the Carolinas, which had been divided in 1729 into the separate royal colonies of North and South Carolina.

By the middle of the eighteenth century, the American colonists were rapidly moving onto the lands between the Atlantic coast and the foothills of the Appalachian Mountains. Descendents of the original settlers, along with newcomers from England, Northern Ireland, and Germany, filtered into the Shenandoah Valley to settle the backcountry of Virginia and the Carolinas. Other Americans contemplated crossing the mountains to occupy the fertile lands of Kentucky and Ohio. The French, fearful of a floodtide of American settlers, made important alliances with Indian tribes of the Ohio country to strengthen their position, and built a chain of forts to defend the area. Imperial rivalry for control of North America was approaching its climax. (Ch. 4)

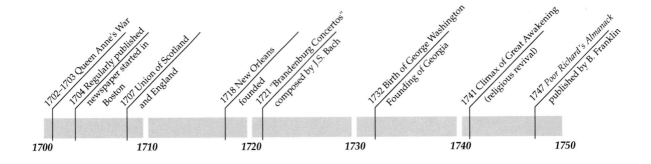

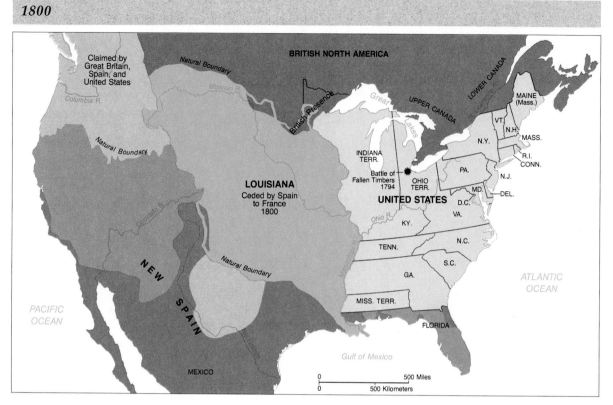

In the half-century between 1750 and 1800, the map of North America underwent extensive political change. First, the British defeated the French and drove them from the mainland of the continent. The Peace of Paris in 1763 called for the French to surrender Canada to Great Britain and transfer Louisiana to Spain. The subsequent British Proclamation Line of 1763, designed to preserve a fur trade with the Indians by blocking settlement west of the mountains, angered the colonists and contributed to the unrest that culminated in the Revolutionary War.

Independence stimulated the westward expansion of the American people. Even while the fighting was in progress, pioneers like Daniel Boone began opening up Kentucky and Tennessee to frontier settlement. In the 1783 treaty that ended the war, Britain granted the United States generous boundaries, stretching from the Great Lakes and the St. Lawrence River on the north to Florida on the south, and the Mississippi on the west. But the young nation found it difficult to make good its claims to this new territory. Indians tried to hold on to their land, with British and Spanish encouragement. In the mid-1790s, however, diplomatic agreements with both nations and a crushing defeat of the Indians at Fallen Timbers opened the way to American settlement of the land beyond the mountains. Kentucky and Tennessee became states in the union before the end of the century, and Ohio would follow just a few years later. (Ch. 4, 5, 6, 7)

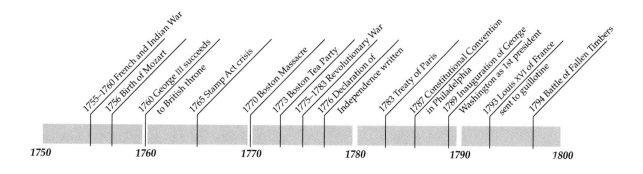

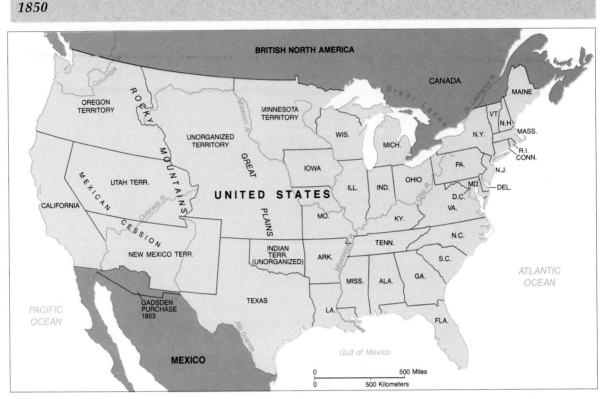

Over the next fifty years, the territory of the United States more than doubled. The purchase of Louisiana from France brought in the vast trans-Mississippi West, stretching across the Great Plains to the Rocky Mountains. From 1804 to 1806, William Lewis and Meriwether Clark and their expedition crossed the continent. Distance, fierce Indian resistance, and an arid climate delayed the settlement of the trans-Mississippi West, but American settlers poured into the area east of the Mississippi. The eastern Indians, their power broken in the War of 1812, were no longer able to resist the tide of settlement; they agreed to evacuate their ancestral homelands and in 1835 the last holdouts, the Cherokees, were forcibly removed to Oklahoma.

The climax of western expansionism came in the 1840s, when the United States extended its boundaries to the Pacific. Proclaiming the nation's "manifest destiny" to occupy the continent, American settlers leapfrogged over the inhospitable Great Plains and rugged Rockies to settle in California and Oregon. Diplomacy with Great Britain secured Oregon to the 49th parallel. Americans moved into Texas in the 1820s, broke away from Mexico in 1836, and joined the union in 1845—a move that led to war with Mexico in 1846. The American victory two years later gave the United States California and the New Mexico territory. The purchase in 1853 of a small strip of southern Arizona from Mexico rounded out the nation's present-day continental boundaries. (Ch. 8, 9, 10, 12)

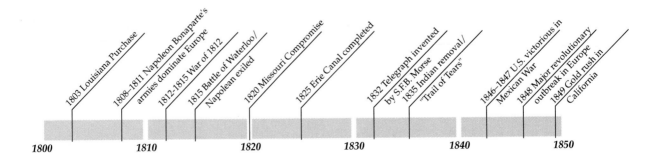

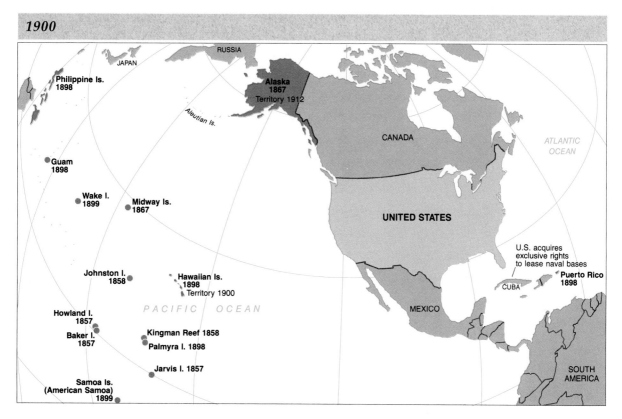

Newly acquired territories brought great opportunities and bitter sectional quarrels. The discovery of gold in California at mid-century was followed by a rush to the Pacific, but the question of extending slavery into the new areas set North against South. That controversy contributed to the outbreak of civil war and the end of slavery. In the three decades following the Civil War, Americans finally settled the last frontier: the Rockies and the Great Plains.

Railroads linked widely separated regions when the first transcontinental line was completed in Utah in 1869. Prospectors flocked to the Rockies, drawn by the bonanza of mineral wealth; ranchers drove cattle through the grasslands of the great open range from the Texas Panhandle to Montana; farmers, using new technology and methods to meet the semiarid conditions, increased the fertility of the soil of the Great Plains. In 1893, historian Frederick Jackson Turner proclaimed that the American frontier was disappearing, signalling the end of an era.

With the continent settled, expansionists looked overseas. William Seward added Alaska to the nation's territory in 1867. Three decades later, victory in the Spanish-American War led to an outburst of enthusiasm for empire. The United States acquired Puerto Rico and the Philippines from Spain, and annexed the Hawaiian Islands. (Ch. 14, 15, 17, 21)

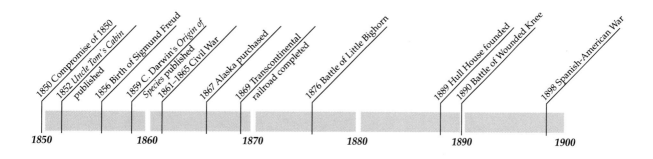

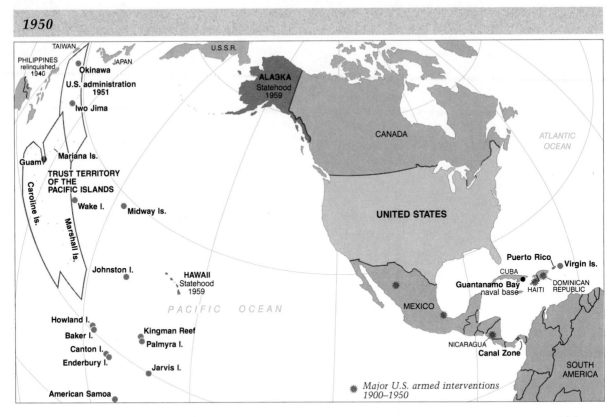

TAIWAN
PHILIPPINES relinquished 1940
JAPAN
Okinawa
U.S. administration 1951
Iwo Jima
U.S.S.R.
ALASKA Statehood 1959
CANADA
ATLANTIC OCEAN
Mariana Is.
Guam
TRUST TERRITORY OF THE PACIFIC ISLANDS
Caroline Is.
Wake I.
Midway Is.
Marshall Is.
UNITED STATES
Johnston I.
HAWAII Statehood 1959
PACIFIC OCEAN
Puerto Rico
CUBA
Virgin Is.
Guantanamo Bay naval base
DOMINICAN REPUBLIC
HAITI
MEXICO
Howland I.
Baker I.
Kingman Reef
Palmyra I.
Canton I.
Enderbury I.
Jarvis I.
NICARAGUA
Canal Zone
SOUTH AMERICA
American Samoa

✳ *Major U.S. armed interventions 1900–1950*

Taking an active role in world affairs led to recurring armed interventions by the United States in distant lands. In 1900, American troops took part in the international effort to put down the antiforeign Boxer Rebellion in China. Over the next decade and a half, the United States intervened in several Latin American countries with armed force, most notably in Panama, where the United States acquired the Canal Zone in 1903, and in Mexico, with the six-month occupation of Vera Cruz in 1914.

America remained neutral for the first three years of World War I in Europe but finally entered the war against the Central Powers (Germany, Austria-Hungary, and Turkey) in 1917, eventually sending more than 2 million men to fight in France. At the war's end, President Wilson played an active role in negotiating

the Treaty of Versailles, even though the United States did not join the League of Nations created by the treaty.

Despite attempts in the 1920s and '30s to limit American involvement in the world, the 1940s found Americans fighting Germany and Japan around the globe. American forces waged World War II in North Africa, on many Pacific islands, and in Europe. Although the United States took the lead in forming the United Nations, the end of the war did not usher in an era of lasting peace. To the contrary, the United States and the Soviet Union faced off in a Cold War that led to the permanent stationing of American troops from West Germany to the Pacific Trust Territory. The Philippines gained their independence in 1946. (Ch. 21, 24, 27, 28)

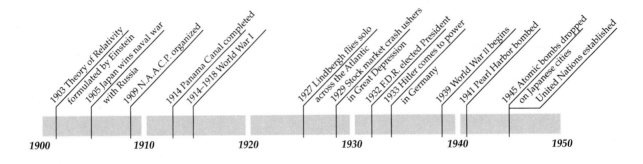

1903 Theory of Relativity formulated by Einstein
1905 Japan wins naval war with Russia
1909 N.A.A.C.P. organized
1914 Panama Canal completed
1914–1918 World War I
1927 Lindbergh flies solo across the Atlantic
1929 Stock market crash ushers in Great Depression
1932 F.D.R. elected President
1933 Hitler comes to power in Germany
1939 World War II begins
1941 Pearl Harbor bombed
1945 Atomic bombs dropped on Japanese cities
United Nations established

1900   1910   1920   1930   1940   1950

The United States took part in two Asian wars after 1950: a stalemate in Korea and a long, frustrating, losing struggle in Vietnam in the 1960s and '70s. Closer to home, Russian ties to Fidel Castro led to a dangerous showdown during the Cuban missile crisis in 1962. In the Middle East, European dependence on Persian Gulf oil and American support for Israel made and continue to make this region an area of vital concern for U.S. foreign policy.

There have been changes in the status of America's territorial possessions: Hawaii and Alaska became the forty-ninth and fiftieth states in the late 1950s; and Puerto Rico was granted commonwealth status in 1952. A new frontier—outer space—was opened up with the Soviet launch of *Sputnik* in 1957. In 1969 came the world's most spectacular space achievement to date when American astronauts landed on the moon. Rock-

ets now launch unmanned probes into the farthest reaches of the solar system, gathering invaluable scientific data. America's space shuttle program—despite setbacks—continues the investigation of space. American horizons, once limited to the confines of thirteen struggling colonies, have expanded over four centuries to embrace the entire world and the nearer reaches of outer space. (Ch. 28, 29, 30, 31; 32, 33)

The greatest changes have come in Europe. The wave of liberation that swept across Central and Eastern Europe in the summer and fall of 1989 was fittingly exemplified by the crumbling of the Berlin Wall. In the Soviet Union, Chairman—later President—Mikhail Gorbachev's new policies of *glasnost* and *perestroika* have led to a series of events that signal the end of the Cold War.

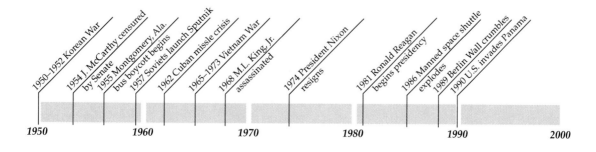

America

Past and Present

Third Edition

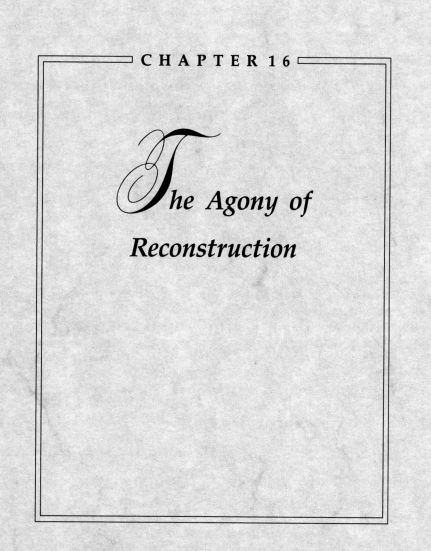

CHAPTER 16

The Agony of Reconstruction

he Yankees who went south immediately after the Civil War and became known as "carpetbaggers" have often been portrayed as vultures preying on the "prostrate South." Some were indeed rogues and swindlers, but a larger number were ambitious men, no less honest than the average, who migrated south just as other people went west, in search of a fair chance to better themselves. Thousands of them leased plantations from grateful Southerners unwilling or unable to make the transition to free labor, and tried growing cotton. Most of these efforts failed by 1868, mainly because of poor crops and a depressed market. Many unsuccessful planters returned to the North, but a minority stayed on, joining other Northerners—former officers of the occupying army and the Freedmen's Bureau for example—to pursue political careers during the period of Republican dominance that lasted from 1868 to the mid–1870s.

Some carpetbaggers were not simply seeking economic and political advantage for themselves but were also sincere champions of equality and opportunity for the newly freed slaves. One such was Albion W. Tourgée, an ex-Union officer from Ohio who settled in North Carolina in 1865. An early proponent of black suffrage and education, Tourgée was a conspicuous advocate of democratic reform at the state constitutional convention of 1868 and was later elected a superior court judge. On the bench, he acquired a reputation for honesty, fairness, and courage. When the Klan rode in North Carolina, he ignored threats against his life and used all the power at his disposal to bring the night-riding terrorists to justice. But the white resistance to Reconstruction was successful; Tourgée and other Republicans were driven from office amid charges of corruption (which in his case, at least, were clearly trumped up).

In 1879, Tourgée returned to the North and wrote a best-selling novel about his southern experiences. Entitled *A Fool's Errand,* it stands as an incisive interpretation of what went wrong during Reconstruction. According to Tourgée, the "wise men" in Washington had blundered badly in the means they used to reconstruct the South. As a member of the ultra-radical wing of the Republican party, Tourgée had favored keeping the South under military rule until its society could be thoroughly reformed and a permanent basis for black equality established. He had warned in 1867 that the Congressional Reconstruction plan of extending suffrage to African Americans and then quickly readmitting southern states to the Union would "deliver the freedmen of the South, bound hand and foot, to their old-time natural enemies." It was not that he opposed black suffrage; it was rather that he regarded the extension of political rights to the freedmen without providing for their economic and social advancement as an invitation to disaster. In *A Fool's Errand,* he described how his prediction had come true. The North had first offended the deep-seated racism of southern whites by declaring that blacks now had "equality of political right." But northern policymakers had failed to establish an effective mechanism to enforce and protect black rights. Instead they had readmitted the "rebellious states" to the Union and left the freedmen to fight for equality "without the possibility of national interference." They told blacks to sink or swim—in the language of the time, to "root hog, or die!"

As the novel makes clear through its vivid depiction of violence and intimidation against black voters, the freedmen were at a great disadvantage in this struggle; their poverty and illiteracy made them no match for the white supremacists who retained control of land and other sources of wealth and power. In Tourgée's view, "Radical Reconstruction" failed to achieve its goal of equality because it was not radical enough. In recent years, historians have begun to echo this judgment. The actions of Congress to overrule the mild presidential policy and set stricter standards for readmission of southern states to the Union may have been a step in the right direction. But guaranteeing equality to the freed slaves required methods that were more thoroughgoing and revolutionary than those that Congress was prepared to accept and sustain.

THE PRESIDENT VERSUS CONGRESS

The problem of how to reconstruct the Union in the wake of the South's military defeat was one of the most difficult and perplexing challenges ever faced by American policymakers. The Constitution provided no firm guidelines, for the framers had not anticipated a division of the country into warring sections. Once emancipation became a northern war aim, the problem was compounded by a new issue: how far should the federal government go to secure freedom and civil rights for four million former slaves?

The debate that evolved led to a major political crisis. Advocates of a minimal Reconstruction policy favored quick restoration of the Union with no protection for the freed slaves beyond the prohibition of slavery. Proponents of a more radical policy wanted readmission of the southern states to be dependent on guarantees that "loyal" men would displace the Confederate elite in positions of power, and that blacks would acquire basic rights of American citizenship. The White House favored the minimal approach, while Congress came to endorse the more radical and thoroughgoing form of Reconstruction. The resulting struggle between Congress and the chief executive was the most serious clash between two branches of government in the nation's history.

Wartime Reconstruction

Tension between the President and Congress over how to reconstruct the Union began during the war. Occupied mainly with achieving victory, Lincoln never set forth a final and comprehensive plan for bringing rebellious states back into the fold. But he did take initiatives that indicated he favored a lenient and conciliatory policy toward Southerners who would give up the struggle and repudiate slavery. In December 1863 he issued a Proclamation of Amnesty and Reconstruction; it offered a full pardon to all Southerners (with the exception of certain classes of Confederate leaders) who would take an oath of allegiance to the Union and acknowledge the legality of emancipation. Once 10 percent or more of the voting population of any occupied state had taken the oath, they were authorized to set up a loyal government. Efforts to establish such regimes were quickly undertaken in states that were wholly or partially occupied by Union troops; by 1864 Louisiana and Arkansas had fully functioning Unionist governments.

Lincoln's policy was meant to shorten the war.

"The Union Christmas Dinner" appeared in Harper's Weekly in 1864. The cartoon illustrates the spirit of forgiveness and reconciliation that marked Lincoln's policy toward the South.

The President hoped that granting pardons and political recognition to oath-taking minorities would weaken the southern cause by making it easy for disillusioned or lukewarm Confederates to switch sides. He also hoped to further his emancipation policy by insisting that the new governments abolish slavery, an action that might prove crucial if—as seemed possible before Lincoln's reelection in 1864 and Congress's subsequent passage of the Thirteenth Amendment—the courts or a future Democratic administration were to disallow or revoke the Emancipation Proclamation. When constitutional conventions operating under the 10 percent plan in Louisiana and Arkansas dutifully abolished slavery in 1864, emancipation came closer to being irreversible.

Congress was unhappy with the President's reconstruction experiments and in 1864 refused to seat the Unionists elected to the House and Senate from Louisiana and Arkansas. A minority of congressional Republicans—the strongly antislavery Radicals—favored protection for black rights as a precondition for the readmission of southern states. These Republican militants were upset because Lincoln had not insisted that the constitution-makers provide for black male suffrage. But a larger group in Congress was not yet prepared to implement civil and political equality for blacks. Many of these moderates also opposed

Lincoln's plan, but they did so primarily because they did not trust the repentant Confederates who would play a major role in the new governments. No matter what their position on black rights, most congressional Republicans feared that hypocritical oath-taking would allow the old ruling class to return to power and cheat the North of the full fruits of its impending victory.

Congress also felt that the President was exceeding his authority by using executive powers to restore the Union. Lincoln operated on the theory that secession, being illegal, did not place the Confederate states outside the Union in a constitutional sense. Since individuals and not states had defied federal authority, the President could use his pardoning power to certify a loyal electorate, which could then function as the legitimate state government.

The dominant view in Congress, on the other hand, was that the southern states had forfeited their place in the Union and that it was up to Congress to decide when and how they would be readmitted. The most popular justification for congressional responsibility was based on the clause of the Constitution providing that "the United States shall guarantee to every State in this Union a Republican Form of Government." By seceding, it was argued, the Confederate states had ceased to be republican, and Congress must set the conditions to be met before they could be readmitted.

After refusing to recognize Lincoln's 10 percent governments, Congress passed a Reconstruction bill of its own in July 1864. Known as the Wade-Davis bill, this legislation required that 50 percent of the voters must take an oath of future loyalty before the restoration process could begin. Once this had occurred, those who could swear that they had never willingly supported the Confederacy could vote in an election for delegates to a constitutional convention. The bill in its final form did not require black suffrage, but it did give federal courts the power to enforce emancipation. Faced with this attempt to nullify his own program, Lincoln exercised a pocket veto by refusing to sign the bill before Congress adjourned. He justified his action by announcing that he did not wish to be committed to any single reconstruction plan. The sponsors of the bill responded with an angry manifesto, and Lincoln's relations with Congress reached their low.

Congress and the President remained stalemated on the Reconstruction issue for the rest of the war. During his last months in office, however, Lincoln showed some willingness to compromise. He persisted in his efforts to obtain full recognition for the governments he had nurtured in Louisiana and Arkansas but seemed receptive to the setting of other conditions—perhaps including black suffrage—for readmission of those states where wartime conditions had prevented execution of his plan. However, he died without clarifying his intentions, leaving historians to speculate on whether his quarrel with Congress would have worsened or been resolved. Given Lincoln's past record of political flexibility, the best bet is that he would have come to terms with the majority of his party.

Andrew Johnson at the Helm

Andrew Johnson, the man suddenly made President by an assassin's bullet, attempted to put the Union back together on his own authority in 1865. But his policies eventually set him at odds with Congress and the Republican party and provoked the most serious crisis in the history of relations between the executive and legislative branches of the federal government.

Johnson's background shaped his approach to Reconstruction. Born in dire poverty in North Carolina, he migrated as a young man to eastern Tennessee where he made his living as a tailor. Lacking formal schooling, he did not learn to read and write until adult life. He subsequently entered politics as a Jacksonian Democrat, and became known as an effective stump speaker. His railing against the planter aristocracy made him the spokesman for Tennessee's nonslaveholding whites and the most successful politician in the state. He advanced from state legislator to congressman to governor and in 1857 was elected to the United States Senate.

When Tennessee seceded in 1861, Johnson was the only senator from a Confederate state who remained loyal to the Union and continued to serve in Washington. But his Unionism and defense of the common people did not include antislavery sentiments. Nor was he friendly to blacks. While campaigning in Tennessee, he had objected only to the fact that slaveholding was the

Nearly insurmountable problems with a Congress determined to enact its own Reconstruction policy plagued Andrew Johnson through his presidency. Impeached in 1868, he escaped conviction by a single vote.

privilege of a wealthy minority. He revealed his attitude when he wished that "every head of family in the United States had one slave to take the drudgery and menial service off his family."

During the war, while acting as military governor of Tennessee, Johnson endorsed Lincoln's emancipation policy and carried it into effect. But he viewed it primarily as a means of destroying the power of the hated planter class rather than as a recognition of black humanity. He was chosen as Lincoln's running mate in 1864 because it was thought that a proadministration Democrat, who was a southern Unionist in the bargain, would strengthen the ticket. No one expected Johnson to succeed to the presidency; it is one of the strange accidents of American history that a southern Democrat, a fervent white supremacist, came to preside over a Republican administration immediately after the Civil War.

Even stranger, some Radical Republicans initially welcomed Johnson's ascent to the nation's highest office. Their hopes make sense in the light of Johnson's record of fierce loyalty to the Union and his apparent agreement with the Radicals that ex-Confederates should be severely treated. More than Lincoln, who had spoken of "malice toward none and charity for all," Johnson seemed likely to punish southern "traitors" and prevent them from regaining political influence. Only gradually did the deep disagreement between the President and the Republican majority in Congress become evident.

The Reconstruction policy that Johnson initiated on May 29, 1865, created some uneasiness among the Radicals, but most Republicans were willing to give it a chance. Johnson placed North Carolina and eventually other states under appointed provisional governors chosen mostly from among prominent southern politicians who had opposed the secession movement and had rendered no conspicuous service to the Confederacy. The governors were responsible for calling constitutional conventions and ensuring that only "loyal" whites were permitted to vote for delegates. Participation required taking the oath of allegiance that Lincoln had prescribed earlier. Once again Confederate leaders and former officeholders who had participated in the rebellion were excluded. To regain their political and property rights, those in the exempted categories had to apply for individual presidential pardons. Johnson made one significant addition to the list of the excluded: all those possessing taxable property exceeding $20,000 in value. In this fashion, he sought to prevent his longtime adversaries—the wealthy planters—from participating in the reconstruction of southern state governments.

Once the conventions met, Johnson urged them to do three things: declare the ordinances of secession illegal, repudiate the Confederate debt, and ratify the Thirteenth Amendment abolishing slavery. After governments had been reestablished under constitutions meeting these conditions, the President assumed that the Reconstruction process would be complete and that the ex-Confederate states could regain their full rights under the Constitution.

The conventions, dominated by prewar Unionists and representatives of backcountry yeoman farmers, did their work in a way satisfactory to the President but troubling to many congressional Republicans. Rather than quickly accepting Johnson's recommendations, delegates in several states approved them begrudgingly or with qualifications. Furthermore, all the resulting constitutions limited suffrage to whites, disappointing the large number of Northerners who hoped, as Lincoln had, that at least some African Americans—perhaps those who were educated or had served in the Union army—would be given the vote. Johnson on the whole seemed eager to give southern white majorities a free hand in determining the civil and political status of the freed slaves.

Republican uneasiness turned to disillusionment and anger when the state legislatures elected under the new constitutions proceeded to pass "Black Codes" subjecting former slaves to a variety of special regulations and restrictions on their freedom. Especially troubling were vagrancy and apprenticeship laws that forced African Americans to work and denied them a free choice of employers. Blacks in some states were also prevented from testifying in court on the same basis as whites and were subject to a separate penal code. To Radicals, the Black Codes looked suspiciously like slavery under a new guise. More upsetting to northern public opinion in general, a number of prominent ex-Confederate leaders were elected to Congress in the fall of 1865.

Johnson himself was partly responsible for this turn of events. Despite his lifelong feud with the planter class, he was generous in granting pardons to members of the old elite who came to him, hat in hand, and asked for them. When former Confederate Vice-President Alexander Stephens and other proscribed ex-rebels were elected to Congress although they had not been pardoned, Johnson granted them special amnesty so that they could serve.

The growing rift between the President and Congress came into the open in December when the House and Senate refused to seat the recently elected southern delegation. Instead of endorsing Johnson's work and recognizing the state governments he had called into being, Congress established a joint committee, chaired by Senator William Pitt Fessenden of Maine, to review Reconstruction policy and set further conditions for readmission of the seceded states.

Congress Takes the Initiative

The struggle over how to reconstruct the Union ended with Congress doing the job of setting policy all over again. The clash between Johnson and Congress was a matter of principle and could not be reconciled. Johnson's personality—his prickly pride, sharp tongue, intolerance of opposition, and stubborn refusal to give an inch—did not help his political cause. The root of the problem was that he disagreed with the majority of Congress on what Reconstruction was supposed to accomplish. An heir of the Democratic states' rights tradition, he wanted to restore the prewar federal system as quickly as possible and without change except that states would no longer have the right to legalize slavery or to secede.

Most Republicans wanted firm guarantees that the old southern ruling class would not regain regional power and national influence by devising new ways to subjugate blacks. Since emancipation had nullified the three-fifths clause of the Constitution by which slaves had been counted as three-fifths of a person, all blacks were now to be counted in determining representation. Consequently, Republicans worried about increased southern strength in Congress and the electoral

According to this cartoon, Congress' program for Reconstruction was a bitter dose for the South, and President "Naughty Andy" urged Southerners not to accept the plan. Mrs. Columbia insisted, however, that Dr. Congress knew what was best.

college. The current Congress favored a Reconstruction policy that would give the federal government authority to limit the political role of ex-Confederates and provide some protection for black citizenship.

Republican leaders—with the exception of a few extreme Radicals like Charles Sumner—lacked any firm conviction that blacks were inherently equal to whites. They *did* believe, however, that in a modern democratic state, all citizens must have the same basic rights and opportunities, regardless of natural abilities. Principle coincided easily with political expediency; southern blacks, whatever their alleged shortcomings, were likely to be loyal to the Republican party that had emancipated them. They could be used, if necessary, to counteract the influence of resurgent ex-Confederates, thus preventing the Democrats from returning to national dominance through control of the South.

The disagreement between the President and Congress became irreconcilable in early 1866 when Johnson vetoed two bills that had passed with overwhelming Republican support. The first extended the life of the Freedmen's Bureau—a temporary agency set up to aid the former slaves by providing relief, education, legal help, and assistance in obtaining land or employment. The second was a civil rights bill meant to nullify the black codes and guarantee to freedmen "full and equal benefit of all laws and proceedings for the security of person and property as is enjoyed by white citizens."

Johnson's vetoes shocked moderate Republicans who had expected the President to accept these relatively modest measures as a way of heading off more radical proposals, such as black suffrage and a prolonged denial of political rights to ex-Confederates. Presidential opposition to policies that represented the bare minimum of Republican demands on the South alienated moderates in the party and ensured a wide opposition to Johnson's plan of Reconstruction. Johnson succeeded in blocking the Freedmen's Bureau bill, although a modified version later passed. But the Civil Rights Act won the two-thirds majority necessary to override his veto, signifying that the President was now hopelessly at odds with most of the congressmen from what was supposed to be his own party. Never before had Congress over-ridden a presidential veto.

*T*his cartoon of Columbia (the personification of a United America) and Robert E. Lee depicts the Radical Republicans' demand for signs of "regeneration" before readmitting Confederate states to the Union.

Johnson soon revealed that he intended to abandon the Republicans and place himself at the head of a new conservative party uniting the small minority of Republicans who supported him with a reviving Democratic party that was rallying behind his Reconstruction policy. In preparation for the elections of 1866, Johnson helped found the National Union movement to promote his plan to readmit the southern states to the Union without further qualifications. A National Union convention meeting in Philadelphia in August 1866 called for the election to Congress of men who endorsed the presidential plan for Reconstruction.

Meanwhile, the Republican majority on Capitol Hill, fearing that Johnson would not enforce civil rights legislation or that the courts would declare such federal laws unconstitutional, passed the Fourteenth Amendment. This, perhaps the most important of all our constitutional amendments, gave the federal government responsibility for guaranteeing equal rights under the law to all Americans. The first section defined national citizenship for the first time as extending to "all persons born or naturalized in the United States." The states were prohibited from abridging the rights of American citizens and could not "deprive any person of life, liberty, or property, without due process of law; nor deny to any person . . . equal protection of the laws."

The other sections of the amendment were important in the context of the time but had fewer long-term implications. Section two sought to penalize the South for denying voting rights to black males by reducing the congressional representation of any state that formally deprived a portion of its male citizens of the right to vote. The third section denied federal office to those who had taken an oath of office to support the United States Constitution and then had supported the Confederacy, and the fourth repudiated the Confederate debt. The amendment was sent to the states with the understanding that Southerners would have no chance of being readmitted to Congress unless their states ratified it.

The congressional elections of 1866 served as a referendum on the Fourteenth Amendment. Johnson opposed the amendment on the grounds that it created a "centralized" government and denied states the right to manage their own affairs; he also counselled southern state legislatures to reject it, and all except Tennessee followed his advice. But, the President's case for state autonomy was weakened by the publicity resulting from bloody race riots in New Orleans and Memphis. These and other reported atrocities against blacks made it clear that the existing southern state governments were failing abysmally to protect the "life, liberty, or property" of the ex-slaves.

Johnson further weakened his cause by taking the stump on behalf of candidates who supported his policies. In his notorious "swing around the circle," he toured the nation, slandering his opponents in crude language and engaging in undignified exchanges with hecklers. Enraged by southern inflexibility and the antics of a President who acted as if he were still campaigning in the backwoods of Tennessee, northern voters repudiated the administration. The Republican majority in Congress increased to a solid two-thirds in both houses, and the Radical wing of the party gained strength at the expense of moderates and conservatives.

Reconstruction Amendments, 1865–1870

Amendment	Main Provisions	Congressional Passage (⅔ majority in each house required)	Ratification Process (¾ of all states including ex-Confederate states required)
13	Slavery prohibited in United States	January 1865	December 1865 (twenty-seven states, including eight southern states)
14	1. National citizenship 2. State representation in Congress reduced proportionally to number of voters disfranchised 3. Former Confederates denied right to hold office 4. Confederate debt repudiated	June 1866	Rejected by twelve southern and border states, February 1867 Radicals make readmission of southern states hinge on ratification Ratified July 1868
15	Denial of franchise because of race, color, or past servitude explicitly prohibited	February 1869	Ratification required for readmission of Virginia, Texas, Mississippi, Georgia Ratified March 1870

Congressional Reconstruction Plan Enacted

Congress was now in a position to implement its own plan of Reconstruction. In 1867 it passed a series of acts that nullified the President's initiatives and reorganized the South on a new basis. Generally referred to as "Radical Reconstruction," these measures actually represented a compromise between genuine Radicals and more moderate elements within the party.

Consistent Radicals like Senator Charles Sumner of Massachusetts and Congressmen Thaddeus Stevens of Pennsylvania and George Julian of Indiana wanted to reshape southern society before readmitting ex-Confederates to the Union. Their program of "regeneration before reconstruction" required an extended period of military rule, confiscation and redistribution of large landholdings among the freedmen, and federal aid for schools to educate blacks and whites for citizenship. But the majority of Republican congressmen found such a program unacceptable because it broke too sharply with American traditions of federalism and regard for property rights and might mean that decades would pass before the Union was back in working order.

The First Reconstruction Act, passed over Johnson's veto on March 2, 1867, did place the South under the rule of the army by reorganizing the region into five military districts. But military rule would last for only a short time. Subsequent acts of 1867 and '68 opened the way for the quick readmission of any state that framed and ratified a new constitution providing for black suffrage. Ex-Confederates disqualified from holding federal office under the Fourteenth Amendment were prohibited from voting for delegates to the constitutional conventions or in the elections to ratify the conventions' work. Since blacks were allowed to participate in this process, Republicans thought they had found a way to ensure that "loyal" men would dominate the new governments. Speed was essential because some Republican leaders anticipated that they would need votes from the reconstructed South in order to retain control of Congress and the White House in 1868.

"Radical Reconstruction" was based on the false assumption that once blacks had the vote, they would have the power to protect themselves

*A*mong the most influential of the radicals was Congressman Thaddeus Stevens of Pennsylvania. He advocated seizing land from southern planters and distributing it among the freed blacks.

against white supremacists' efforts to deny them their rights. The Reconstruction Acts thus signaled a retreat from the true Radical position that a sustained use of federal authority was needed to complete the transition from slavery to freedom and prevent the resurgence of the South's old ruling class. (Troops were used in the South after 1868 but only in a very limited and sporadic way.) The majority of Republicans were unwilling to embrace centralized government and an extended period of military rule over civilians. Such drastic steps went beyond the popular northern consensus on necessary and proper Reconstruction measures. Thus, despite strong reservations, Radicals like Thaddeus Stevens supported the plan of readmitting the southern states on the basis of black suffrage, recognizing that this was as far as the party and the northern public were willing to go.

Even so, congressional Reconstruction did have a radical aspect. Although the program won Republican support partly because it promised practical political advantages, a genuine spirit of democratic idealism gave legitimacy and fervor to the cause of black male suffrage. The principle that even the poorest and most underprivileged should have access to the ballot box was a noble and enlightened one. The problem was finding a way to enforce it under conditions then existing in the postwar South.

The Impeachment Crisis

The first obstacle to enforcement of congressional Reconstruction was resistance from the White House. Johnson thoroughly disapproved of the new policy and sought to thwart the will of Congress by administering the plan in his own obstructive fashion. He immediately began to dismiss officeholders who sympathized with Radical Reconstruction, and he countermanded the orders of generals in charge of southern military districts who were zealous in their enforcement of the new legislation. Some Radical generals were transferred and replaced by conservative Democrats. Congress responded by passing laws designed to limit presidential authority over Reconstruction matters. One of these measures was the Tenure of Office Act, requiring Senate approval for the removal of cabinet officers and other officials whose appointment had needed the consent of the Senate. Another measure—a rider to an army appropriations bill—sought to limit Johnson's authority to issue orders to military commanders.

Johnson objected vigorously to these restrictions on the ground that they violated the constitutional doctrine of the separation of powers. When it became clear that the President was resolute in fighting for his powers and using them to resist the establishment of Radical regimes in the southern states, some congressmen began to call for his impeachment. A preliminary effort foundered in 1867, but when Johnson tried to discharge Secretary of War Edwin Stanton—the only Radical in the cabinet—and persisted in his efforts despite the disapproval of the Senate, the pro-impeachment forces gained in strength.

In January 1868 Johnson ordered General Grant, who already commanded the army, to replace Stanton as head of the War Department. But Grant had his eye on the Republican presidential nomination and refused to defy Congress. Johnson subsequently appointed General Lorenzo Thomas, who agreed to serve. Faced with this apparent violation of the Tenure of Office Act, the House voted overwhelmingly to impeach the President on February 24, and he was placed on trial before the Senate.

Because seven Republican senators broke with the party leadership and voted for acquittal, the effort to convict Johnson and remove him from office fell one vote short of the necessary two-thirds. This outcome resulted in part from a skillful defense. Attorneys for the President argued for a narrow interpretation of the constitutional provision that a President could be impeached only for a "high crime and misdemeanor," asserting that this referred only to an indictable crime. Responding to the charge that Johnson had deliberately violated the Tenure of Office Act, the defense contended that the law did not apply to the removal of Stanton because he had been appointed by Lincoln, not Johnson.

The prosecution countered with a different interpretation of the Tenure of Office Act, but the core of their case was that Johnson had abused the powers of his office in an effort to sabotage the congressional Reconstruction policy. Obstructing the will of the legislative branch, they claimed, was sufficient grounds for conviction even if no crime had been committed. The Republicans who broke ranks to vote for acquittal could not endorse such a broad view of the impeachment power. They feared that removal of a President for essentially political reasons would threaten the constitutional balance of powers and open the way to legislative supremacy over the executive.

Although Johnson's acquittal by the narrowest of margins protected the American presidency from congressional domination, the impeachment episode helped create an impression in the public mind that the Radicals were ready to turn the Constitution to their own use to gain their objectives. Conservatives were again alarmed when Congress took action in 1868 to deny the Supreme Court's appellate jurisdiction in cases involving the military arrest and imprisonment of anti-Reconstruction activists in the South. But the evidence of congressional ruthlessness and illegality is not as strong as most historians used to think. Modern legal scholars have found merit in the Radicals' claim that their actions did not violate the Constitution.

Failure to remove Johnson from office was an embarrassment to congressional Republicans, but the episode did ensure that Reconstruction in the South would proceed as the majority in Congress intended. During the trial, Johnson helped influence the verdict by pledging to enforce the Reconstruction Acts, and he held to this promise during his remaining months in office. Unable to depose the President, the Radicals had at least succeeded in neutralizing his opposition to their program.

RECONSTRUCTION IN THE SOUTH

The Civil War left the South devastated, demoralized, and destitute. Slavery was dead, but what this meant for future relationships between whites and blacks was still in doubt. The overwhelming majority of southern whites wanted to keep blacks adrift between slavery and freedom —without rights, in a status resembling that of the "free Negroes" of the Old South. Blacks sought to be independent of their former masters and viewed the acquisition of land, education, and the vote as the best means of achieving this goal. The thousands of Northerners who went south after the war for materialistic or humanitarian reasons hoped to extend Yankee "civilization" to what they viewed as an unenlightened and barbarous region. For most of them this reformation required the aid of the freedmen; not enough southern whites were willing to accept the new order and embrace northern middle-class values.

The struggle of these groups to achieve their conflicting goals bred chaos, violence, and instability. Unsettled conditions created many opportunities for corruption, crime, and terrorism. This was scarcely an ideal setting for an experiment in interracial democracy, but one was attempted nonetheless. Its success depended on massive and sustained support from the federal government. To the extent that this was forthcoming, progressive reform could be achieved. When it faltered, the forces of reaction and white supremacy were unleashed.

Social and Economic Adjustments

The Civil War scarred the southern landscape and wrecked its economy. One devastated area— central South Carolina—looked to an 1865 observer "like a broad black streak of ruin and desolation—the fences are gone; lonesome smokestacks, surrounded by dark heaps of ashes

Above, a William Aiken Walker painting of a sharecropper's cabin. Too often freed blacks discovered that sharecropping led to a new form of economic servitude.

and cinders, marking the spots where human habitations had stood; the fields all along the roads widely overgrown with weeds, with here and there a sickly patch of cotton or corn cultivated by negro squatters." Other areas through which the armies had passed were similarly ravaged. Several major cities—including Atlanta, Columbia, and Richmond—were gutted by fire. Most factories were dismantled or destroyed, and long stretches of railroad were torn up.

Physical ruin would not have been so disastrous if investment capital had been available for rebuilding. But the substantial wealth represented by Confederate currency and bonds had melted away, and emancipation of the slaves had divested the propertied classes of their most valuable and productive assets. According to some estimates, the South's per capita wealth in 1865 was only about half what it had been in 1860.

Recovery could not even begin until a new labor system replaced slavery. It was widely assumed in both the North and the South that southern prosperity would continue to depend on cotton and that the plantation was the most efficient unit for producing the crop. Hindering

At left, an African-American soldier and his sweetheart are wed by a Freedmen's Bureau chaplin. Many black soldiers asked that the unions they made in slave days be legalized so that their families would qualify for survivors' benefits when they died.

Below is a Freedmen's school, one of the more successful endeavors supported by the Freedmen's Bureau. The Bureau, working with teachers from northern abolitionist and missionary societies, founded thousands of schools for freed slaves and poor whites.

efforts to rebuild the plantation economy were lack of capital, the deep-rooted belief of southern whites that blacks would work only under compulsion, and the freedmen's resistance to labor conditions that recalled slavery.

Blacks strongly preferred to be small independent farmers rather than plantation laborers, and for a time they had reason to hope that the federal government would support their ambitions. General Sherman, hampered by the huge numbers of black fugitives that followed his army on its famous march, issued an order in January 1865 that set aside the islands and coastal areas of Georgia and South Carolina for exclusive black occupancy on 40-acre plots. Furthermore, the Freedmen's Bureau, as one of its many responsibilities, was given control of hundreds of thousands of acres of abandoned or confiscated land

and was authorized to make 40-acre grants to black settlers for three-year periods, after which they would have the option to buy at low prices. By June 1865, forty thousand black farmers were at work on 300,000 acres of what they thought would be their own land.

But the dream of "forty acres and a mule" was not to be realized. President Johnson pardoned the owners of most of the land consigned to the ex-slaves by Sherman and the Freedmen's Bureau, and proposals for an effective program of land confiscation and redistribution failed to get through Congress. Among the considerations prompting most congressmen to oppose land reform were a tenderness for property rights, fears of sapping the freedmen's initiative by giving them something they allegedly had not earned, and the desire to restore cotton production as quickly as possible to increase agricultural exports and stabilize the economy. Consequently, most blacks in physical possession of small farms failed to acquire title, and the mass of freedmen were left with little or no prospect of becoming landowners. Recalling the plight of southern blacks in 1865, an ex-slave later wrote that "they were set free without a dollar, without a foot of land, and without the wherewithal to get the next meal even."

Despite their poverty and landlessness, ex-slaves were reluctant to settle down and commit themselves to wage labor for their former masters. Many took to the road, hoping to find something better. Some were still expecting grants of land, but others were simply trying to increase their bargaining power. "One ob de rights ob bein free," one freedman later recalled, "wuz dat we could move around en change bosses." As the end of 1865 approached, many freedmen had still not signed up for the coming season; anxious planters feared that they were plotting to seize the land by force. Within a few weeks, however, most holdouts signed for the best terms they could get.

One common form of agricultural employment in 1866 was a contract labor system. Under this system, workers committed themselves for a year in return for fixed wages, a substantial portion of which was withheld until after the harvest. Since many planters were inclined to drive hard bargains, abuse their workers, or cheat them at the end of the year, the Freedmen's Bureau assumed the role of reviewing the contracts and enforcing them. But bureau officials had differing notions of what it meant to protect African Americans from exploitation. Some stood up strongly for the rights of the freedmen; others served as allies of the planters, rounding up available workers, coercing them to sign contracts for low wages, and then helping keep them in line.

The Bureau's influence waned after 1867 (it was phased out completely by 1869), and the experiment with contract wage labor was abandoned. Growing up alongside the contract system and eventually displacing it was an alternative capital-labor relationship—sharecropping. First in small groups known as "squads" and later as individual families, blacks worked a piece of land independently for a fixed share of the crop, usually one-half. The advantage of this arrangement for credit-starved landlords was that it did not require much expenditure in advance of the harvest. The system also forced the tenant to share the risks of crop failure or a fall in cotton prices. These considerations loomed larger after disastrous harvests in 1866 and '67.

African Americans initially viewed sharecropping as a step up from wage labor in the direction of landownership. But during the 1870s this form of tenancy evolved into a new kind of servitude. Croppers had to live on credit until their cotton was sold, and planters or merchants seized the chance to "provision" them at high prices and exorbitant rates of interest. Creditors were entitled to deduct what was owed to them out of the tenant's share of the crop and this left most sharecroppers with no net profit at the end of the year—more often than not with a debt that had to be worked off in subsequent years. Various methods, legal and extralegal, were eventually devised in an effort to bind indebted tenants to a single landlord for extended periods, but considerable movement was still possible.

While landless African Americans in the countryside were being reduced to economic dependence, those in towns and cities found themselves living in an increasingly segregated society. The Black Codes of 1865 attempted to require separation of the races in public places and facilities; when most of the codes were set aside by federal authorities as violations of the Civil Rights Act of 1866, the same end was often achieved through private initiative and community pressure. In some cities, blacks successfully resisted being consigned to separate streetcars by appealing to the military during the brief period when it exercised authority or by organizing boycotts. But they found it almost impossible to gain admittance to most hotels, restaurants, and other privately owned establishments catering to whites. On railroads, separate black, or "Jim Crow," cars were not yet the rule, but African Americans were normally denied first-class accommodations. After 1868, black-supported Republican governments passed civil rights acts requiring equal access to public facilities, but little effort was made to enforce the legislation.

Some forms of racial separation were not openly discriminatory, and blacks accepted or even endorsed them. Freedmen who had belonged to white churches as slaves welcomed the chance to join all-black denominations like the African Methodist Episcopal Church, which provided freedom from white dominance and a more congenial style of worship. The first schools for ex-slaves were all-black institutions established by the Freedmen's Bureau and various northern missionary societies. Having been denied all education during the antebellum period, most blacks viewed separate schooling as an opportunity rather than as a form of discrimination. When Radical governments set up public school systems, they condoned de facto educational segregation. Only in city schools of New Orleans and at the University of South Carolina were there serious attempts during Reconstruction to bring white and black students together in the same classrooms.

The upshot of all forms of racial separatism—whether produced by white prejudice or black accommodation—was to create a divided society, one in which blacks and whites lived much of the time in separate worlds. There were two exceptions to this pattern: one was at work, where blacks necessarily dealt with white employers; the other was in the political sphere, where blacks sought to exercise their rights as citizens.

Political Reconstruction
in the South

The state governments that emerged in 1865 had little or no regard for the rights of the freed slaves. Some of their codes even made black unemployment a crime, which meant that blacks had to make long-term contracts with white employers or be arrested for vagrancy. Others limited the rights of African Americans to own property or engage in occupations other than those of servant or laborer. The codes were set aside by the actions of Congress, the military, and the Freedmen's Bureau, but private violence and discrimination against blacks continued on a massive scale unchecked by state authorities. Hundreds, perhaps thousands, of blacks were murdered by whites in 1865–1866, and few of the perpetrators were brought to justice.

The imposition of military rule in 1867 was designed in part to protect former slaves from violence and intimidation, but the task was beyond the capacity of the few thousand troops stationed in the South. When new constitutions were approved and states readmitted to the Union under the congressional plan in 1868, the problem became more severe. White opponents of Radical Reconstruction adopted systematic terrorism as a means of keeping blacks away from the polls. Yet the military presence was progressively reduced, leaving the new Republican regimes to fight a losing battle against armed white supremacists. In the words of historian William Gillette, "there was simply no federal force large enough to give heart to black Republicans or to bridle southern white violence."

Hastily organized in 1867, the southern Republican party dominated the constitution-making of 1868 and the regimes that came out of it. The party was an attempted coalition of three social groups (which of course varied in their relative strength from state to state). One was the same class that was becoming the backbone of the Republican party in the North—businessmen with an interest in enlisting government aid for private enterprise. Many Republicans of this stripe were recent arrivals from the North—the so-called carpetbaggers discussed earlier—but some were scalawags, former Whig planters or merchants who were born in the South or had immigrated to the region before the war and now saw a chance to realize their dreams for commercial and industrial development.

Poor white farmers, especially those from upland areas where Unionist sentiment had been strong during the Civil War, were a second element in the original coalition. These owners of small farms expected the party to favor their interests at the expense of the wealthy landowners and to come to their aid with special legislation when—as was often the case in this period of economic upheaval—they faced the loss of their homesteads to creditors. Newly enfranchised blacks were the third group to which the Republicans appealed. Blacks formed the vast majority of the Republican rank and file in most states and were concerned mainly with education, civil rights, and landownership.

Under the best of conditions, these coalitions would have been difficult to maintain. Each group had its own distinct goals and did not fully support the aims of the other segments. White yeomen, for example, had a deeply rooted resistance to black equality. And for how long could one expect essentially conservative businessmen to support costly measures for the elevation or relief of the lower classes of either race? In some states, astute Democratic politicians exploited these divisions by appealing to disaffected white Republicans.

But during the relatively brief period when they were in power in the South—varying from one to nine years depending on the state—the Republicans chalked up some notable achievements. They established (on paper at least) the South's first adequate systems of public education, democratized state and local government, and appropriated funds for an enormous expansion of public services and responsibilities covered by welfare.

Important though these social and political reforms were, they took second place to the Republicans' major effort—to foster economic development and restore southern prosperity by subsidizing the construction of railroads and other internal improvements. But the policy of aiding railroads turned out to be disastrous, even though it addressed the region's real economic needs and was initially very popular. Extravagance, corruption, and routes laid out in response to local political pressure rather than on sound economic considerations, fostered an increasing burden of public debt and taxation. The policy did not produce the promised payoff of efficient, cheap transportation. Subsidized railroads frequently went bankrupt, leaving the taxpayers holding the bag. When the panic of 1873 brought many southern state governments to the verge of bankruptcy, and railroad building came to an

end, it was clear that the Republicans' "gospel of prosperity" through state aid to private enterprise had failed miserably. Their political opponents, most of whom had originally favored these policies, now saw an opportunity to take advantage of the situation by charging that Republicans had ruined the southern economy.

In general, the Radical regimes failed to conduct public business honestly and efficiently. Embezzlement of public funds and bribery of state lawmakers or officials were common occurrences. State debts and tax burdens rose enormously, mainly because governments had undertaken heavy new responsibilities, but partly because of waste and graft. The situation varied from state to state; ruling cliques in Louisiana and South Carolina were guilty of much wrongdoing, yet Mississippi had a relatively honest and frugal regime.

Furthermore, southern corruption was not exceptional, nor was it a special result of the extension of suffrage to uneducated African Americans, as critics of Radical Reconstruction have claimed. It was part of a national pattern during an era when private interests considered buying government favors to be a part of the cost of doing business, and many politicians expected to profit by obliging them.

Blacks bore only a limited responsibility for the dishonesty of the Radical governments. Although sixteen African Americans served in Congress— two in the Senate—between 1869 and 1880, only in South Carolina did blacks constitute a majority of even one house of the state legislature. Furthermore, no black governors were elected during Reconstruction (although P. B. S. Pinchback served for a time as acting governor of Louisiana). The biggest grafters were opportunistic whites—some of the most notorious were carpetbaggers but others were native Southerners. Businessmen offering bribes included members of the prewar gentry who were staunch opponents of Radical programs. Some black legislators went with the tide and accepted "loans" from those railroad lobbyists who would pay most for their votes, but the same men could usually be depended upon to vote the will of their constituents on civil rights or educational issues.

It was unfortunate, however, that blacks first entered American politics at a time when public ethics were at a low point. If they served or

Changing Views of Reconstruction

A central issue of Reconstruction was the place of blacks in American life after slavery. Changing attitudes on this question strongly influenced later representations of the Reconstruction era, whether in historical writing or in the popular media. Indeed, what later generations imagined had happened in the South in the years immediately after the Civil War is a reliable index of how they viewed black/white relations in their own time.

In the early twentieth century, when white supremacists were in control in the South and northern public opinion was learning to tolerate southern policies of rigid segregation and disfranchisement of blacks, historians played a major role in rationalizing the new order in southern race relations. According to historians like Professor John W. Burgess of Columbia University, writing in 1902, Reconstruction governments represented an unholy alliance of corrupt northern "carpetbaggers" seeking to profit at the expense of the "prostrate South"; southern white opportunists of mean origins, known as "scalawags"; and black demagogues who sought power by putting false and dangerous aspirations for equality into the heads of newly freed slaves. What made this orgy of misrule possible, said Burgess, was the colossal blunder that Congress made when it extended the vote to "ignorant and vicious" blacks. In the eyes of Burgess and a whole school of historians, Reconstruction was "the most soul-sickening spectacle that Americans have ever been called upon to behold . . . here was government by the most ignorant and vicious part of the population for the vulgar, materialistic, brutal benefit of the governing set."

In 1915 the most ambitious film yet made by the fledgling American movie industry—D. W. Griffith's *Birth of a Nation*—popularized this image of Reconstruction and made its racism more lurid and explicit. To underscore the message of this technically brilliant film, words flashed on the screen described Reconstruction as a callous attempt to "put the white South under the heel of the black South." In the film, leering blacks carry signs advocating interracial marriage. Mainly responsible for this state of affairs is a vengeful Congressman meant to represent Thaddeus Stevens, who hatches a devilish plot to oppress and humiliate the white South. One famous scene portrays the South Carolina state legislature as a mob of grinning, barefoot blacks, carousing at the taxpayers's expense. The film's melodramatic plot features the suicide of one southern white maiden to escape the embraces of a black pursuer and the Ku Klux Klan's epic rescue of another damsel from a forced marriage to a mulatto politician.

Birth of a Nation's depiction of the Klan as saving white civilization from bestial blacks inspired vigorous protests from the recently founded National Association for the Advancement of Colored People (NAACP), and censors in a few northern cities deleted some of the more blatantly racist scenes. But

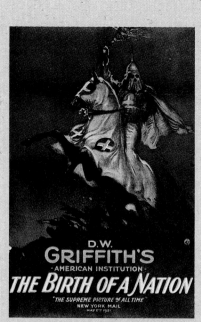

D.W. GRIFFITH'S
- AMERICAN INSTITUTION -
THE BIRTH OF A NATION
"THE SUPREME PICTURE OF ALL TIME"
NEW YORK MAIL
MAY 27, 1921

A scene from The Birth of a Nation. *Note that the role of the black man at right is played by a white actor in dark makeup.*

President Woodrow Wilson endorsed the film. "My only regret is that it is all so terribly true," he announced. Most white moviegoers seemed to agree with the President rather than with the NAACP. Millions of Americans saw and applauded this cinematic triumph.

During the period between 1915 and the 1940s, most historians echoed the judgment of *Birth of a Nation* that efforts to enforce equal rights for blacks after the Civil War had been a grave mistake. One popular work of that era was entitled *The Tragic Era,* and another summed up Reconstruction as "the blackout of honest government." The biases of mainstream historiography served to justify the Jim Crow system of the South by portraying blacks as unqualified for citizenship.

A few black historians of the 1920s and '30s advanced the contrary view that Reconstruction was a noble effort to achieve a color-blind democracy that failed simply because of the strength of white racism and privilege. The most powerful example of this early revisionism was W. E. B. DuBois's *Black Reconstruction in America* (1935).

During the 1950s and '60s another image of Reconstruction emerged. The majority of historians writing about the era finally rejected the exaggerations, distortions, and racist assumptions of the traditional view. The triumph of "revisionism" occurred in 1965 when Kenneth Stampp published his *Era of Reconstruction.* As northern public opinion shifted from tolerance of segregation to support for the black struggle for equality in the South, a more favorable view of earlier efforts on behalf of civil rights became acceptable. White liberal historians like Stampp concentrated on rehabilitating the Radical Republicans by stressing their idealism, while black scholars like John Hope Franklin highlighted the constructive policies and positive achievements of the much maligned black leaders of the Reconstruction South. Previous moral judgments were thus reversed; white and black Republicans became the heroes and the southern whites who resisted and eventually overthrew Reconstruction became the villains. The analogy between these earlier adversaries and the civil rights activists and southern segregationists of the 1960s was clear.

During the 1970s and early '80s, a "postrevisionism" began to develop. As it became apparent that the dream of equality for blacks was still unrealized, historians responded to the changing perceptions and complex cross-currents of black/white relations in their own time by taking another look at Reconstruction. They found, among other things, that those in charge of efforts to make blacks equal citizens in the late 1860s had views that were quite moderate by the standards of the post civil-rights era of the 1970s and early 1980s. "Radical Reconstruction" no longer seemed very radical. The reputations of carpetbaggers and upperclass scalawags went down again as historians emphasized their opportunism and probusiness economic policies at the expense of social justice. Black politicians, too, came in for critical reassessment. It was argued that many worked more for their own interests as members of a black middle class than for the kinds of policies—such as land reform—that would have met the vital needs of their impoverished constituents.

The postrevisionists seem to be agreed that Reconstruction failed because it was inadequately motivated, conceived, and enforced. But the causes of this failure remain in doubt. Some recent historians explain it in terms of an underlying racism that prevented white Republicans from identifying fully with the cause of black equality. Others stress the gulf between the class interests of those in charge of implementing and managing Reconstruction and the poor people of the South who were supposed to be its beneficiaries.

The basic issue raised by Reconstruction—how to achieve racial equality in America—has not yet been resolved. So long as this is the case, we will continue to look at our first effort in this direction for whatever guideposts it provides.

Although African Americans represented a majority in many of the slave states in the Deep South, they constituted a majority only in the South Carolina state legislature (above right). A small number of African Americans were elected to Congress. Among them was Senator Blanche K. Bruce (left) who championed the causes of citizenship for the American Indians and improvement of the Mississippi River.

supported corrupt and wasteful regimes it was because they had no alternative. Although the Democrats, or "Conservatives" as they called themselves in some states, made sporadic efforts to attract African American voters, it was clear that if they won control they would attempt to strip blacks of their civil and political rights. But opponents of Radical Reconstruction were able to capitalize on racial prejudice and persuade many Americans that "good government" was synonymous with white supremacy.

Contrary to myth, the small number of African Americans elected to state or national office during Reconstruction demonstrated on the average more integrity and competence than their white counterparts. Most were fairly well educated, having been free Negroes or unusually privileged slaves before the war. Among the most capable were Senator Blanche K. Bruce of Mississippi—elected to the Senate in 1874 after rising to deserved prominence in the Republican party of his home state; Congressman Robert Brown Elliott of South Carolina—an adroit politician who was also a consistent champion of civil rights; and Congressman James T. Rapier of Alabama,

who stirred Congress and the nation in 1873 with his eloquent appeals for federal aid to southern education and new laws to enforce equal rights for African Americans.

THE AGE OF GRANT

Ulysses S. Grant was the only president between Jackson and Wilson to serve two full and consecutive terms. But unlike other chief executives so favored by fortune and the electorate, Grant is commonly regarded as a failure. Historians used to blame him mainly for the corruption that surfaced in his administration. More recently he also has been condemned for the inconsistency and ultimate failure of his southern policy. The charges are valid, and no one is likely to make the case that he was a great statesman. Faced with the demands of the presidency, Grant found that he had no strong principles to guide him except loyalty to old friends and to politicians who supported him. But the problems he faced were certainly difficult. A president with a clearer sense of duty might have done little better.

Rise of the Money Question

The impeachment crisis of 1868 represented the high point of popular interest in Reconstruction issues. Already competing for public attention was the question of how to manage the nation's currency, and more specifically, what to do about greenbacks—paper money issued during the war. Hugh McCulloch, secretary of the Treasury under Johnson, favored a return to "sound" money and in 1866, he had initiated a policy of withdrawing greenbacks from circulation. Opposition to this hard-money policy and the resulting deflation came from a number of groups. In general, the "greenbackers" were strongest in the credit-hungry West and among expansionist-minded manufacturers. Defenders of hard money were mostly the commercial and financial interests in the East; they received crucial support from intellectuals who regarded government-sponsored inflation as immoral or contrary to the natural laws of classical economics.

In 1868 the money question surged briefly to the forefront of national politics. Faced with a business recession blamed on McCulloch's policy of contracting the currency, Congress voted to stop the retirement of greenbacks. The Democratic party, responding to midwestern pressure, included in its platform a plan calling for the redemption of much of the Civil War debt in greenbacks rather than the gold that bondholders had been anticipating. But divisions within the parties prevented the money question from becoming a central issue in the presidential campaign. The Democrats nominated Governor Horatio Seymour of New York, a sound-money supporter, thus nullifying their pro-greenback platform. Republicans based their campaign mainly on a defense of their Reconstruction policy and a celebration of their popular candidate. With the help of votes from the Republican-dominated southern states, Grant won a decisive victory.

In 1869 and '70 a Republican-controlled Congress passed laws that assured payment in gold to most bondholders but eased the burden of the huge Civil War debt by refunding it, exchanging bonds soon coming due for those that would not be payable for ten, fifteen, or thirty years. In this way the public credit was protected.

Still unresolved was the problem of what to do

The Election of 1868			
Candidate	Party	Popular Vote	Electoral Vote
Grant	Republican	3,013,421	214
Seymour	Democratic	2,706,829	80
Not voted*			23

*Unreconstructed states did not participate in the election.

about the $356 million in greenbacks that remained in circulation. Hard-money proponents wanted to retire them quickly, while inflationists thought more should be issued to stimulate the economy. The Grant administration followed the middle course of allowing the greenbacks to float until economic expansion would bring them to a par with gold, thus permitting a painless return to specie payments. But the panic of 1873, which brought much of the economy to its knees, led to a revival of agitation to inflate the currency. Debt-ridden farmers, who would be the backbone of the greenback movement for years to come, now joined the soft-money clamor for the first time.

Responding to the money and credit crunch, Congress moved in 1874 to authorize a modest issue of new greenbacks. But Grant, influenced by the opinions of hard-money financiers, vetoed the bill. In 1875, Congress, led by Senator John Sherman of Ohio, enacted the Specie Resumption Act which provided for a limited reduction of greenbacks leading to full resumption of specie payments by January 1, 1879. Its action was widely interpreted as deflation in the midst of depression. Farmers and workers, who were already suffering acutely from deflation, reacted with dismay and anger.

The Democratic party could not capitalize adequately on these sentiments because of the influence of its own hard-money faction, and in 1876 an independent Greenback party entered the national political arena. The party's nominee for president, Peter Cooper, received an insignificant number of votes, but in 1878 the Greenback Labor party polled more than a million votes and elected fourteen congressmen. The Greenbackers were able to keep the money issue alive into the following decade.

Retreat from Reconstruction

The Republican effort to make equal rights for blacks the law of the land culminated in the Fifteenth Amendment. Passed by Congress in 1869 and ratified by the states in 1870, the amendment prohibited any state from denying a citizen the right to vote because of race, color, or previous condition of servitude. A more radical version, requiring universal manhood suffrage, was rejected partly because it departed too sharply from traditional views of federal-state relations. States therefore could still limit the suffrage by imposing literacy tests, property qualifications, or poll taxes allegedly applying to all racial groups; such devices would eventually be used to strip southern blacks of the right to vote. But the makers of the amendment did not foresee this result. They believed that their action would prevent future Congresses or southern constitutional conventions from repealing or nullifying the provisions for black male suffrage included in the Reconstruction Acts. A secondary aim was to enfranchise African Americans in those northern states that still denied them the vote.

Many feminists were bitterly disappointed that the amendment did not extend the vote to women as well as freedmen. A militant wing of the woman's rights movement led by Elizabeth Cady Stanton and Susan B. Anthony was so angered that the Constitution was being amended to make gender an explicit qualification for voting that they campaigned against ratification of the Fifteenth Amendment. Another group of feminists led by Lucy Stone supported the amendment on the grounds that this was "the Negro's hour" and that women could afford to wait for the vote. This disagreement divided the woman's suffrage movement for a generation to come.

The Grant administration was charged with enforcing the amendment and protecting black voting rights in the reconstructed states. Since survival of the Republican regimes depended on African-American support, political partisanship dictated federal action, even though the North's emotional and ideological commitment to black citizenship was waning.

Between 1868 and 1872, the main threat to southern Republican regimes came from the Ku Klux Klan and other secret societies bent on restoring white supremacy by intimidating blacks

Susan B. Anthony (left) and Lucy Stone (right), feminist leaders whose adherents split over support for the Fifteenth Amendment. Their differences led to two competing women's rights organizations in the suffrage struggle.

who sought to exercise their political rights. First organized in Tennessee in 1866, the Klan spread rapidly to other states, adopting increasingly lawless and brutal tactics. A grass-roots vigilante movement and not a centralized conspiracy, the Klan thrived on local initiative and gained support from whites of all social classes. Its secrecy, decentralization, popular support, and utter ruthlessness made it very difficult to suppress. As soon as blacks had been granted the right to vote, hooded night riders began to visit the cabins of those who were known to be active Republicans; some victims were only threatened, but others were whipped or even murdered. A typical incident was related by a black Georgian: "They broke my door open, took me out of bed, took me to the woods and whipped me three hours or more and left me for dead. They said to me, 'Do you think you will vote for another damned radical ticket?'"

These methods were first used effectively in the presidential election of 1868. Grant lost in Louisiana and Georgia mainly because the Klan—or the Knights of the White Camelia as the Louisiana variant was called—launched a reign of terror to prevent prospective black voters from exercising their right. In Louisiana political violence claimed more than a thousand lives, and in Arkansas, which Grant managed to carry, more than two hundred Republicans, including a congressman, were assassinated.

Thereafter, Klan terrorism was directed mainly at Republican state governments. Virtual insurrections broke out in Arkansas, Tennessee, North

Carolina, and parts of South Carolina. Republican governors called out the state militia to fight the Klan, but only the Arkansas militia succeeded in bringing it to heel. In Tennessee, North Carolina, and Georgia, Klan activities helped undermine Republican control, thus allowing the Democrats to come to power in all of these states by 1870.

Faced with the violent overthrow of the southern Republican party, Congress and the Grant administration were forced to act. A series of laws passed in 1870–1871 sought to enforce the Fifteenth Amendment by providing federal protection for black suffrage and authorizing use of the army against the Klan. These "Ku Klux Klan" or "Force" Acts made interference with voting rights a federal crime and established provisions for government supervision of elections. In addition, the legislation empowered the President to call out troops and suspend the writ of habeas corpus to quell insurrection. In 1871–1872, thousands of suspected Klansmen were arrested by the military or U.S. marshals, and the writ was suspended in nine counties of South Carolina which had been virtually taken over by the secret order. Although most of the accused Klansmen either were never brought to trial, were acquitted, or received suspended sentences, the enforcement effort was vigorous enough to put a damper on hooded terrorism and ensure relatively fair and peaceful elections in 1872.

In these elections, a heavy black turnout enabled the Republicans to hold on to power in most states of the Deep South, despite efforts of the Democratic-Conservative opposition to woo Republicans by taking moderate positions on racial and economic issues. As a result of this setback, the Democratic-Conservatives made a significant change in their strategy and ideology. No longer did they try to take votes away from the Republicans by proclaiming their support of black suffrage and government aid to business. They began instead to appeal openly to white supremacy and to the traditional Democratic and agrarian hostility to governmental promotion of economic development. Consequently, they were able to bring back to the polls a portion of the white electorate, mostly small farmers, who had not been turning out because they were alienated by the leadership's apparent concessions to Yankee ideas.

Above, members of the Ku Klux Klan, a secret white supremacist organization, in typical regalia. Before elections, hooded Klansmen terrorized blacks to discourage them from voting.

This new and more effective electoral strategy dovetailed with a resurgence of violence meant to reduce Republican, especially black Republican, voting. The new reign of terror differed from the previous Klan episode; its agents no longer wore masks but acted quite openly. They were effective because the northern public was increasingly disenchanted with federal intervention on behalf of what were widely viewed as corrupt and tottering Republican regimes. Grant used force in the South for the last time in 1874 when an overt paramilitary organization in Louisiana, known as the White League, tried to overthrow a Republican government accused of stealing an election. When another unofficial militia—in Mississippi—instigated a series of bloody race riots prior to the state elections of 1875, Grant refused the governor's request for federal troops. As a result, black voters were successfully intimidated—one county registered only seven Republican votes where there had been a black majority of two thousand, and Mississippi fell to the Democratic-Conservatives. According to one account, Grant decided to withhold troops because he had been warned that intervention might cost the Republicans the crucial state of Ohio in the same off-year elections.

By 1876 Republicans held on to only three southern states—South Carolina, Louisiana, and Florida. Partly because of Grant's hesitant and inconsistent use of presidential power but mainly because the northern electorate would no longer tolerate military action to sustain Republican governments and black voting rights, Radical Reconstruction was falling into total eclipse.

Spoilsmen Versus Reformers

One reason Grant found it increasingly difficult to take strong action to protect southern Republicans was the bad odor surrounding his stewardship of the federal government and the Republican party. Reformers charged that a corrupt national administration was propping up bad governments in the South for personal and partisan advantage. An apparent case in point was Grant's intervention in Louisiana in 1872 on behalf of an ill-reputed Republican faction headed by his wife's brother-in-law, who controlled federal patronage as collector of customs in New Orleans.

The Republican party in the Grant era was rapidly losing the idealism and high purpose associated with the crusade against slavery. By the beginning of the 1870s, the men who had been the conscience of the party—old-line radicals like Thaddeus Stevens, Charles Sumner, and Benjamin Wade—were either dead, out of office, or at odds with the administration. New leaders of a different stamp, whom historians have dubbed "spoilsmen" or "politicos" were taking their place. When he made common cause with hard-boiled manipulators like Senators Roscoe Conkling of New York and James G. Blaine of Maine, Grant lost credibility with reform-minded Republicans.

During Grant's first administration, an aura of scandal surrounded the White House but did not directly implicate the President. In 1869 the financial buccaneer Jay Gould enlisted the aid of a brother-in-law of Grant to further his fantastic scheme to corner the gold market. Gould failed in the attempt, but he did manage to save himself and come away with a huge profit.

Grant's first-term vice-president, Schuyler Colfax of Indiana, was directly involved in the notorious Crédit Mobilier scandal. Crédit Mobilier was a construction company that actually served as a fraudulent device for siphoning off profits that should have gone to the stockholders of the Union Pacific Railroad, which was the beneficiary of massive federal land grants. In order to forestall government inquiry into this arrangement, Crédit Mobilier stock was distributed to influential congressmen, including Colfax (who was Speaker of the House before he was elected vice-president). The whole business came to light just before the campaign of 1872.

Republicans who could not tolerate such corruption or had other grievances against the administration broke with Grant in 1872 and formed a third party committed to "honest government" and "reconciliation" between the North and the South. Led initially by high-minded reformers like Senator Carl Schurz of Missouri, the "Liberal Republicans" endorsed reform of the civil service to curb the corruption-breeding patronage system and advocated laissez-faire economic policies—which meant low tariffs, an end to government subsidies for railroads, and hard money. Despite their rhetoric of idealism and reform, the Liberal Republicans were extremely conservative in their notions of

The Election of 1872

Candidate	Party	Popular Vote	Electoral Vote*
Grant	Republican	3,598,235	286
Greeley	Democrat and Liberal Republican	2,834,761	Greeley died before the electoral college voted.

*Out of a total of 366 electoral votes. Greeley's votes were divided among the four minor candidates.

In this Puck *cartoon, U. S. Grant clutches the Whiskey and Navy rings and supports an assortment of bosses, profiteers, and scandals associated with the Grant administration.*

stayed away from the polls. The result was a decisive victory for Grant, whose 56 percent of the popular vote was the highest percentage won by any candidate between Andrew Jackson and Theodore Roosevelt.

Grant's second administration bore out the reformers' worst suspicions about corruption in high places. In 1875 the public learned that federal revenue officials had conspired with distillers to defraud the government of millions of dollars in liquor taxes. Grant's private secretary, Orville E. Babcock, was indicted as a member of the "Whiskey Ring" and was saved from conviction only by the President's personal intercession. The next year, Grant's Secretary of War William E. Belknap was impeached by the House after an investigation revealed that he had taken bribes for the sale of Indian trading posts. He avoided conviction in the Senate only by resigning from office before his trial. Grant fought hard to protect Belknap, to the point of participating in what a later generation might call a "cover-up."

There is no evidence that Grant profited personally from any of the misdeeds of his subordinates. Yet he is not entirely without blame for the corruption in his administration. He failed to take action against the malefactors, and even after their guilt had been clearly established, he tried to shield them from justice.

REUNION AND THE NEW SOUTH

Congressional Reconstruction prolonged the sense of sectional division and conflict for a dozen years after the guns had fallen silent. Its final liquidation in 1877 opened the way to a reconciliation of North and South that some historians have celebrated as a culminating achievement of American nationalism. But the costs of reunion were high for less privileged groups in the South. The civil and political rights of African Americans, left unprotected, were progressively and relentlessly stripped away by white supremacist regimes. Lower-class whites saw their interests sacrificed to those of capitalists and landlords. Despite the rhetoric hailing a prosperous "New South," the region remained poor and open to exploitation by northern business interests.

what government should do to assure justice for blacks and other underprivileged Americans.

The Liberal Republicans' national convention nominated Horace Greeley, editor of the respected New York *Tribune.* This was a curious and divisive choice since Greeley was at odds with the founders of the movement on the tariff question and was indifferent to civil service reform. The Democrats also endorsed Greeley, mainly because he promised to end Radical Reconstruction by restoring "self-government" to the South.

But the journalist turned out to be a poor campaigner who failed to inspire enthusiasm from lifelong supporters of either party. Most Republicans stuck with Grant, despite the corruption issue, because they still could not stomach the idea of ex-rebels returning to power in the South. Many Democrats, recalling Greeley's previous record as a staunch Republican, simply

The election of 1876 pitted Rutherford B. Hayes of Ohio, a Republican governor untainted by the scandals of the Grant era, against Governor Samuel J. Tilden of New York, a Democratic reformer who had battled against Tammany Hall and the Tweed Ring. Honest government was apparently the electorate's highest priority. When the returns came in, Tilden had clearly won the popular vote and seemed likely to win a narrow victory in the electoral college. But the result was placed in doubt when the returns from the three southern states still controlled by the Republicans—South Carolina, Florida, and Louisiana—were contested. If Hayes were to be awarded these three states, plus one contested electoral vote in Oregon, Republican strategists realized, he would triumph in the electoral college by a single vote.

The outcome of the election remained undecided for months, plunging the nation into a major political crisis. To resolve the impasse, Congress appointed a special electoral commission of fifteen members to determine who would receive the votes of the disputed states. Originally composed of seven Democrats, seven Republicans, and an independent, the commission fell under

In the contested presidential election of 1876, Hayes was declared the winner only two days before his inauguration.

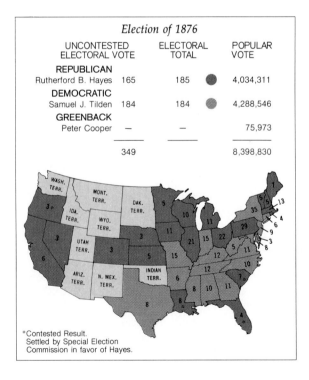

Election of 1876

	UNCONTESTED ELECTORAL VOTE	ELECTORAL TOTAL		POPULAR VOTE
REPUBLICAN				
Rutherford B. Hayes	165	185	●	4,034,311
DEMOCRATIC				
Samuel J. Tilden	184	184	●	4,288,546
GREENBACK				
Peter Cooper	—	—		75,973
	349			8,398,830

*Contested Result.
Settled by Special Election
Commission in favor of Hayes.

Republican control when the independent member resigned to run for the Senate and a Republican was appointed to take his place. The commission split along party lines and voted 8 to 7 to award Hayes the disputed states. But this decision still had to be ratified by both houses of Congress. The Republican-dominated Senate readily approved it, but Democrats in the House planned a filibuster to delay the final counting of the electoral votes until after inauguration day. If the filibuster succeeded, neither candidate would have a majority and, as provided in the Constitution, the election would be decided by the House, where the Democrats controlled enough states to elect Tilden.

To ensure Hayes's election, Republican leaders negotiated secretly with conservative southern Democrats, some of whom seemed willing to abandon the filibuster if the last troops were withdrawn and "home rule" was restored to the South. Eventually an informal bargain was struck, which historians have dubbed "the Com-

promise of 1877." What precisely was agreed to and by whom remains a matter of dispute; but one thing at least was understood by both sides —Hayes would be President and southern blacks would be abandoned to their fate. In a sense, Hayes did not concede anything, because he had already decided to end federal support for the crumbling Radical regimes. But southern negotiators were heartened by firm assurances that this would indeed be the policy. Some were also influenced by vaguer promises involving federal support for southern railroads and internal improvements.

With southern Democratic acquiescence, the filibuster was broken and Hayes took the oath of office. He immediately ordered the army not to resist a Democratic takeover in South Carolina and Louisiana. Thus fell the last of the Radical governments, and the entire South was firmly under the control of white Democrats. The trauma of the war and Reconstruction had destroyed the chances for a renewal of two-party competi-

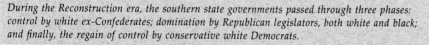

Reconstruction

During the Reconstruction era, the southern state governments passed through three phases: control by white ex-Confederates; domination by Republican legislators, both white and black; and finally, the regain of control by conservative white Democrats.

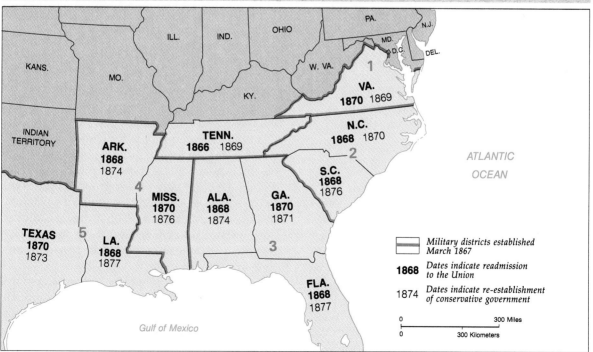

Military districts established March 1867

1868 Dates indicate readmission to the Union

1874 Dates indicate re-establishment of conservative government

The first industries of the New South were usually processing plants for the agricultural products of the region. Above, African Americans working on a sugar plantation in Louisiana are cutting sugarcane to be processed in the plantation's refinery.

tion among white Southerners.

Northern Republicans soon reverted to denouncing the South for its crimes against black suffrage. But this "waving of the bloody shirt", which also served as a reminder of the war and northern casualties, quickly degenerated into a campaign ritual aimed at northern voters who could still be moved by sectional antagonism.

The New South

The men who came to power after Radical Reconstruction fell in one southern state after another are usually referred to as the "Redeemers." They had differing backgrounds and previous loyalties. Some were members of the Old South's ruling planter class who had warmly supported secession and now sought to reestablish the old order with as few changes as possible. Others, of middle-class origin or outlook, favored commercial and industrial interests over agrarian groups and called for a "New South," committed to

diversified economic development. A third group were professional politicians bending with the prevailing winds—like Joseph E. Brown of Georgia who had been a secessionist, a wartime governor, and a leading scalawag Republican, before becoming a Democratic "Redeemer."

Although historians have tried to assign the Redeemers a single coherent ideology or view of the world and have debated as to whether it was Old South agrarianism or New South industrialism that they endorsed, these leaders can perhaps best be understood as power brokers mediating among the dominant interest groups of the South in ways that served their own political advantage. In many ways, the "rings" that they established on the state and county level were analogous to the political machines developing at the same time in northern cities.

They did, however, agree on and endorse two basic principles: laissez-faire and white supremacy. Laissez-faire—the notion that government should be limited and should not intervene openly and directly in the economy—could unite planters, frustrated at seeing direct state support going to businessmen, and capitalist promoters who had come to realize that low taxes and freedom from government regulation were even more advantageous than state subsidies. It soon became clear that the Redeemers responded only to privileged and entrenched interest groups, especially landlords, merchants, and industrialists, and offered little or nothing to tenants, small farmers, and working people. As industrialization began to gather steam in the 1880s, Democratic regimes became increasingly accommodating to manufacturing interests and hospitable to agents of northern capital who were gaining control of the South's transportation system and its extractive industries.

White supremacy was the principal rallying cry that brought the Redeemers to power in the first place. Once in office, they found that they could stay there by charging that opponents of ruling Democratic cliques were trying to divide "the white man's party" and open the way for a return to "black domination." Appeals to racism could also deflect attention away from the economic grievances of groups without political clout.

The new governments were more economical than those of Reconstruction, mainly because they cut back drastically on appropriations for schools and other needed public services. But they were scarcely more honest—embezzlement of funds and bribery of officials continued to occur to an alarming extent. Louisiana, for example, suffered for decades from the flagrant corruption associated with a state-chartered lottery.

The Redeemer regimes of the late 1870s and '80s badly neglected the interests of small white farmers. Whites, as well as blacks, were suffering from the notorious "crop lien" system, which gave local merchants who advanced credit at high rates of interest during the growing season the right to take possession of the harvested crop on terms that buried farmers deeper and deeper in debt. As a result, increasing numbers of whites lost title to their homesteads and were reduced to tenancy. When a depression of world cotton prices added to the burden of a ruinous credit system, agrarian protesters began to challenge the ruling elite, first through the Southern Farmers' Alliance of the late 1880s and then by supporting its political descendant—the Populist party of the 1890s.

But the greatest hardships imposed by the new order were reserved for African Americans. The Redeemers promised, as part of the understanding that led to the end of federal intervention in 1877, that they would respect the rights of blacks as set forth in the Fourteenth and Fifteenth Amendments. Governor Wade Hampton of South Carolina was especially vocal in pledging that African Americans would not be reduced to second-class citizenship by the new regimes. But when blacks tried to vote Republican in the "redeemed" states, they encountered renewed violence and intimidation. "Bulldozing" African-American voters remained common practice in state elections during the late 1870s and early '80s; those blacks who withstood the threat of losing their jobs or being evicted from tenant farms if they voted for the party of Lincoln were visited at night and literally whipped into line. The message was clear—vote Democratic or vote not at all.

Furthermore, white Democrats now controlled the electoral machinery and were able to manipu-

Lynching was responsible for more than three thousand deaths between 1889 and 1918, and they were not confined to the South. During that thirty-year period, only seven states reported no lynchings.

Supreme Court Decisions Affecting Black Civil Rights, 1875–1900	
Hall v. *DeCuir* (1878)	Struck down Louisiana law prohibiting racial discrimination by "common carriers" (railroads, steamboats, buses). Court declared the law a "burden" on interstate commerce, over which states had no authority.
United States v. *Harris* (1882)	Declared federal laws to punish crimes such as murder and assault unconstitutional. Such crimes declared to be the sole concern of local government. Court ignored the frequent racial motivation behind such crimes in the South.
Civil Rights Cases (1883)	Struck down Civil Rights Act of 1875. Congress may not legislate on civil rights unless a *state* passes a discriminatory law. Court declared the Fourteenth Amendment silent on racial discrimination by private citizens.
Plessy v. *Ferguson* (1896)	Upheld Louisiana statute requiring "separate but equal" accommodations on railroads. Court declared that segregation is *not* necessarily discrimination.
Williams v. *Mississippi* (1898)	Upheld state law requiring a literacy test to qualify for voting. Court refused to find any implication of racial discrimination in the law. Using such laws, southern states rapidly disenfranchised blacks.

late the black vote by stuffing ballot boxes, discarding unwanted votes, or reporting fraudulent totals. Some states also imposed complicated new voting requirements to discourage black participation. Full-scale disfranchisement did not occur until literacy tests and other legalized obstacles to voting were imposed in the period from 1890 to 1910, but by that time less formal and comprehensive methods had already made a mockery of the Fifteenth Amendment.

Nevertheless, blacks continued to vote freely in some localities until the 1890s; a few districts even elected black Republicans to Congress during the immediate post-Reconstruction period. The last of these, Representative George H. White of North Carolina, served until 1901. His farewell address eloquently conveyed the agony of southern blacks in the era of Jim Crow (strict segregation).

> These parting words are in behalf of an outraged, heart-broken, bruised, and bleeding but God-fearing people, faithful, industrious, loyal people—rising people, full of potential force. . . . The only apology that I have to make for the earnestness with which I have spoken is that I am pleading for the life, the liberty, the future happiness, and manhood suffrage of one-eighth of the entire population of the United States.

The dark night of racism that fell on the South after Reconstruction seemed to unleash all the baser impulses of human nature. Between 1889 and 1899 an average of 187 blacks were lynched every year for alleged offenses against white supremacy. Those convicted of petty crimes against property were often little better off; many were condemned to be leased out to private contractors whose brutality rivaled that of the most sadistic slaveholders. (Annual death rates in the convict camps ranged as high as 25 percent.) Finally, the dignity of blacks was cruelly affronted by the wave of segregation laws passed around the turn of the century, which served to remind them constantly that they were deemed unfit to associate with whites on any basis that implied equality.

The North and the federal government did little or nothing to stem the tide of racial oppression in the South. A series of Supreme Court decisions between 1875 and 1896 gutted the Reconstruction amendments and the legislation passed to enforce them, leaving blacks virtually defenseless against political and social discrimination.

The career of Henry McNeal Turner sums up the black experience in the South during and after Reconstruction. Born free in South Carolina in 1834, Turner became a minister of the African Methodist Episcopal church (AME) just before the outbreak of the Civil War. During the war, he recruited African Americans for the Union army and later served as chaplain for black troops.

After the fighting was over, he went to Georgia to work for the Freedmen's Bureau but encountered racial discrimination from white Bureau officers and left government service for church work and Reconstruction politics. Elected to the 1867 Georgia constitutional convention and to the state legislature in 1868, he was one of a number of black clergymen who assumed leadership roles among the freedmen. But whites won control of the Georgia legislature and expelled all the black members. Turner's reaction was a bitter speech in which he proclaimed that white men were never to be trusted. As the inhabitant of a state in which blacks never gained the degree of power that they achieved in some other parts of the South, Turner was one of the first black leaders to see the failure of Reconstruction as the betrayal of African-American hopes for citizenship.

Becoming a bishop of the AME church in 1880, Turner emerged as the late nineteenth century's leading proponent of black emigration to Africa. Because he believed that white Americans were so deeply prejudiced against blacks that they would never grant them equal rights, Turner

became an early advocate of black nationalism and a total separation of the races. Emigration became a popular movement among southern blacks who were especially hard hit by terror and oppression just after the end of Reconstruction, but a majority of blacks in the nation as a whole and even in Turner's own church refused to give up on the hope of eventual equality. But Bishop Turner's anger and despair were the understandable responses of a proud man to the way that he and his fellow African Americans had been treated in the post–Civil War period.

By the late 1880s, the wounds of the Civil War were healing, and white Americans were seized by the spirit of sectional reconciliation. Union and Confederate veterans were tenting together and celebrating their common Americanism. "Reunion" was becoming a cultural as well as political reality. But whites could come back together only because Northerners had tacitly agreed to give Southerners a free hand in their efforts to reduce blacks to a new form of servitude. The "outraged, heart-broken, bruised, and bleeding" African Americans of the South paid the heaviest price for sectional reunion.

Henry M. Turner, who was born in freedom, became a bishop of the African Methodist Episcopal Church and was elected to the Georgia legislature.

Recommended Reading

The best one volume account of Reconstruction is Eric Foner, *Reconstruction: America's Unfinished Revolution* (1988). Two excellent short surveys are Kenneth Stampp, *The Era of Reconstruction, 1865–1877* (1965), and John Hope Franklin, *Reconstruction: After the Civil War* (1961). Both were early efforts to synthesize modern "revisionist" interpretations. W. E. B. DuBois, *Black Reconstruction in America, 1860–1880* (1935) remains brilliant and provocative. Reconsiderations of Reconstruction issues can be found in J. Morgan Kousser and James M. McPherson, eds. *Region, Race, and Reconstruction: Essays in Honor of C. Vann Woodward* (1982), and Eric Foner, *Nothing but Freedom: Emancipation and Its Legacy* (1983). Morton Keller, *Affairs of State: Public Life in Late Nineteenth Century America* (1977), provides an insightful analysis of American government and politics during Reconstruction and afterward.

Formulation and implementation of northern policies on Reconstruction are covered in Eric L. McKitrick, *Andrew Johnson and Reconstruction, 1865–1867* (1960); W. R. Brock, *An American Crisis: Congress and Reconstruction, 1865–1867* (1963); and William Gillette, *Retreat from Reconstruction, 1869–1879* (1979). Leon F. Litwack, *Been in the Storm So Long: The Aftermath of Slavery* (1979), provides a moving portrayal of the black experience of emancipation. On what freedom meant in economic terms, see Gerald David Jaynes, *Branches Without Roots: Genesis of the Black Working Class in the American South, 1862–1882* (1986). The best overview of the postwar southern economy is Gavin

CHRONOLOGY

1863 Lincoln sets forth 10 percent Reconstruction plan

1864 Wade-Davis Bill passes Congress, is pocket-vetoed by Lincoln

1865 Johnson moves to reconstruct the South on his own initiative • Congress refuses to seat representatives and senators elected from states reestablished under presidential plan (December)

1866 Johnson vetoes Freedmen's Bureau Bill (February) • Johnson vetoes Civil Rights Act; it passes over his veto (April) • Congress passes Fourteenth Amendment (June) • Republicans increase their congressional majority in the fall elections

1867 First Reconstruction Act is passed over Johnson's veto (March)

1868 Johnson is impeached; he avoids conviction by one vote (February–May) • Southern blacks vote and serve in constitutional conventions • Grant wins presidential election, defeating Horatio Seymour

1869 Congress passes Fifteenth Amendment, granting African Americans the right to vote

1870–1871 Congress passes Ku Klux Klan Acts to protect black voting rights in the South

1872 Grant relected President, defeating Horace Greeley, candidate of Liberal Republicans and Democrats

1873 Financial panic plunges nation into depression

1875 Congress passes Specie Resumption Act • "Whiskey Ring" scandal exposed

1876–1877 Disputed presidential election resolved in favor of Republican Hayes over Democrat Tilden

1877 "Compromise of 1877" results in end to military intervention in the South and fall of the last Radical governments

Wright, *Old South, New South* (1986). The best introduction to the Grant era is William S. McFeeley, *Grant: A Biography* (1981). On the end of Reconstruction and the character of the post-Reconstruction South, see two classic works by C. Vann Woodward: *Reunion and Reaction*, rev. ed. (1956) and *Origins of the New South, 1877–1913* (1951).

Additional Bibliography

The Reconstruction era is surveyed in Rembert W. Patrick, *The Reconstruction of the Nation* (1967); Avery O. Craven, *Reconstruction: The Ending of the Civil War* (1969); and Michael L. Perman, *Emancipation and Reconstruction, 1862–1879* (1987). The conflict between the President and Congress is examined in David Donald, *The Politics of Reconstruction, 1863–1867* (1965); Michael Les Benedict, *A Compromise of Principle: Congressional Republicans and Reconstruction* (1974) and *The Impeachment and Trial of Andrew Johnson* (1973). On constitutional issues, Stanley I. Kutler, *Judicial Power and Reconstruction Politics* (1968), and Harold M. Hyman, *A More Perfect Union: The Impact of the Civil War and Reconstruction on the Constitution* (1973), are useful.

Presidential Reconstruction in the South is surveyed in Dan T. Carter, *When the War Was Over: Self-Reconstruction in the South* (1985). A major aspect of Radical Reconstruction is covered in Mark W. Summers, *Railroads, Reconstruction, and the Gospel of Prosperity* (1984).

Michael Perman, *Reunion Without Compromise: The South and Reconstruction, 1865–1868* (1973), and *The Road to Redemption: Southern Politics, 1869–1879* (1984), deal authoritatively with southern politics in the postwar years. On the Freedmen's Bureau, see George R. Bentley, *A History of the Freedmen's Bureau* (1965); William McFeeley, *Yankee Stepfather: General O. O. Howard and the Freedmen* (1968); and Donald G. Nieman, *To Set the Law in Motion: The Freedmen's Bureau and Legal Rights for Blacks, 1865–1869* (1979).

On carpetbaggers, see Richard N. Current, *Those Terrible Carpetbaggers: A Reinterpretation* (1989). Among the most valuable of the many state studies of Reconstruction in the South are Joel Williamson, *After Slavery: The Negro in South Carolina, 1861–77* (1965); Elizabeth Studley Nathans, *Losing the Peace: Georgia Republicans and Reconstruction, 1865–1871* (1968); William C. Harris, *The Day of the Carpetbagger: Republican Reconstruction in Mississippi* (1979); and Thomas Holt, *Black over White: Negro Political Leadership in South Carolina During Reconstruction* (1977). Essays on black leadership in several southern states can be found in Howard N. Rabinowitz, ed., *Southern Black Leaders of the Reconstruction Era* (1982).

Howard N. Rabinowitz, *Race Relations in the Urban South, 1865–1890* (1977); C. Vann Woodward, *The Strange Career of Jim Crow*, 3d rev. ed. (1974); and Joel Williamson, *The Crucible of Race: Black-White Relations in the American South Since Emancipation* (1984) cover race relations in the postwar South. Economic and social adjustments are analyzed in Lawrence N. Powell, *New Masters: Northern Planters During the Civil War and Reconstruction* (1980); Michael Wayne, *The Reshaping of Plantation Society* (1983); Roger L.

Ransom and Richard Sutch, *One Kind of Freedom: The Economic Consequences of Emancipation* (1977); Daniel A. Novak, *The Wheel of Servitude: Black Forced Labor After Emancipation* (1978); Stephen Hahn, *The Roots of Southern Populism: Yeoman Farmers and the Transformation of the Georgia Upcountry, 1850–1896* (1983); and Charles L. Flynn, Jr., *White Land, Black Labor: Caste and Class in Late Nineteenth-Century Georgia* (1983).

American labor during Reconstruction is the subject of David Montgomery, *Beyond Equality: Labor and the Radical Republicans, 1861–1872* (1967). Liberal republicanism is examined in Ari A. Hoogenboom, *Outlawing the Spoils: A History of Civil Service Reform* (1961), and John G. Sproat, *"The Best Men": Liberal Reformers in the Gilded Age* (1968).

Keith I. Polakoff, *The Politics of Inertia* (1977), challenges C. Vann Woodward's interpretation of the Compromise of 1877. Woodward's conclusions on the Redeemer period have been confirmed or disputed in Paul M. Gaston, *The New South Creed* (1970); William Cooper, *The Conservative Regime: South Carolina, 1877–1890* (1968); Jonathan M. Weiner, *Social Origins of the New South: Alabama, 1860–1885* (1978); and J. Morgan Kousser, *The Shaping of Southern Politics: Suffrage Restriction and the Establishment of the One-Party South* (1974).

CHAPTER 17

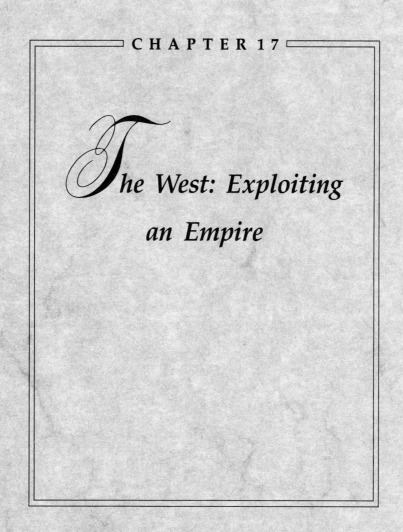

The West: Exploiting
an Empire

In the last three decades of the nineteenth century, a flood of settlers ventured into America's newest and last West. James H. Kyner, a railroad contractor in Oregon, saw in the 1880s "an almost unbroken stream of emigrants from horizon to horizon. . . . Teams and covered wagons, horsemen, little bunches of cows, more wagons, some drawn by cows, men walking, women and children riding—an endless stream of hardy, optimistic folk, going west to seek their fortunes and to settle an empire."

Prospectors poured into unsettled areas in search of "paydirt," railroads crisscrossed the continent, eastern and foreign capitalists invested in cattle and land bonanzas, and farmers took up the promise of free western lands. In 1867, Horace Greeley, editor of the New York *Tribune*, told New York City's unemployed: "If you strike off into the broad, free West, and make yourself a farm from Uncle Sam's generous domain, you will crowd nobody, starve nobody, and neither you nor your children need evermore beg for something to do."

With the end of the Civil War, white Americans again claimed a special destiny to expand across the continent. In the process, they crushed the culture of the Native Americans and ignored the special contributions of those of other nationalities, such as the Chinese miners and laborers and the Mexican herdsmen. As millions moved west, the states of Colorado, Washington, Montana, the Dakotas, Idaho, Wyoming, and Utah were carved out of the vast lands across the Mississippi. At the turn of the century, only Arizona, New Mexico, and Oklahoma remained as territories.

The West became a great colonial empire, harnessed to eastern capital and tied increasingly to national and international markets. Its raw materials, sent east by wagon, train, and ship, helped fuel eastern factories. Western economies depended to an unusual degree on the federal government, which subsidized their railroads, distributed their land, and spent millions of dollars for the upkeep of soldiers and Indians. Regional variations persisted; and Westerners remained proud of their hardy, individualistic traditions. Yet they imitated the East's social, cultural, and political patterns.

By the 1890s, the West of the buffalo and Native American was gone, replaced by cities and towns, health resorts, Paris fashions, and the latest magazines. As Francis Parkman, a New Englander who had made the dangerous crossing to Oregon in 1846, reflected sadly in 1892: "The Wild West is tamed, and its savage charms have withered."

BEYOND THE FRONTIER

The frontier line had reached the edge of the Missouri timber country by 1840. Beyond lay an enormous land of rolling prairies, parched deserts, and rugged, majestic mountains. Emerging from the timber country, travelers first encountered the Great Plains—treeless, nearly flat, an endless "sea of grassy hillocks." The Prairie Plains, the eastern part of the region, enjoyed rich soil and good rainfall; it included parts of present-day Wisconsin, Minnesota, the Dakotas, Nebraska, Kansas, Oklahoma, and Texas. To the west—covering Montana, Wyoming, Colorado, New Mexico, and Arizona—were the High Plains, rough, semiarid, rising gently to the foothills of the Rocky Mountains.

Running from Alaska to central New Mexico, the Rockies presented a formidable barrier. There were valuable beaver in the streams and gold near Pike's Peak. But most travelers hurried through the northern passes, emerging in the desolate basin of present-day southern Idaho and Utah. Native Americans lived there—the Utes, Paiutes, Bannocks, and Shoshoni—scrabbling out a bare subsistence by digging for roots, seeds, and berries. Scornful whites called them "Digger Indians," a stern judgment on people trying their best to survive. On the west, the lofty Coast ranges—the Cascades and Sierra Nevada—held back rainfall; beyond were the temperate lands of the Pacific Coast.

Early explorers like Zebulon Pike thought the country beyond the Mississippi was uninhabitable, fit only, Pike said, for "wandering and uncivilized aborigines." Mapmakers agreed; between 1825 and 1860, American maps showed this land as "The Great American Desert." As a result, settlement paused on the edge of the Plains, and most early settlers headed directly for California and Oregon.

The Plains daunted even those hurrying across them. "You look on, on, on, out into space, out

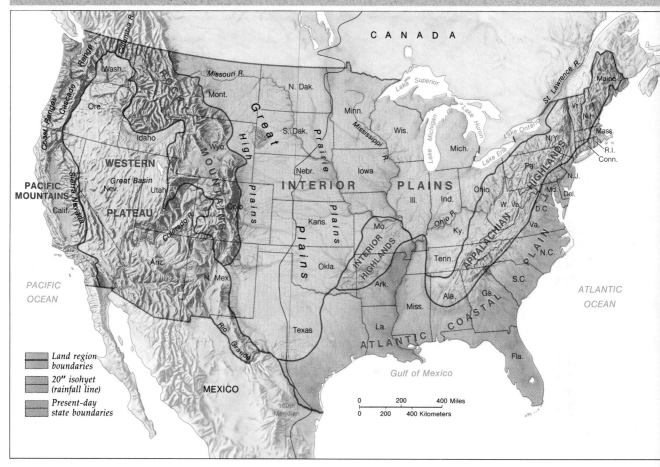

Physiographic Map of the United States

In the Great Plains and Rocky Mountains, the topography, climate, altitudes, crops, and, especially, the lack of rain led to changes in a mode of settlement that had been essentially uniform from the Atlantic Coast through Kentucky and Ohio and on to Missouri. The rectangular land surveys and the quarter-section lots that were traditional in woods and prairie could not accommodate Great Plains conditions.

almost beyond time itself,'' John Noble, a painter reared in Kansas, remarked.

You see nothing but the rise and swell of land and grass, and then more grass—the monotonous, endless prairie! A stranger traveling on the prairie would get his hopes up, expecting to see something different on making the next rise. To him the disappointment and monotony were terrible. "He's got loneliness," we would say of such a man.

Few rivers cut through the Plains; those that did raged in the winter and trickled in the summer. Rainfall usually did not reach fifteen inches a year, not enough to support extensive agricul-

ture. There was little lumber for homes and fences, and the tools of eastern settlement—the cast-iron plow, the boat, and the ax—were virtually useless on the tough and treeless Plains soil. ''East of the Mississippi,'' historian Walter Prescott Webb noted, ''civilization stood on three legs—land, water, and timber; west of the Mississippi not one but two of these legs were withdrawn—water and timber—and civilization was left on one leg—land.''

Hot winds seared the Plains in summer, and northers, blizzards, and hailstorms froze them in winter. Wildlife roamed in profusion. Antelope shared the open prairies with wolves, coyote, and millions of jack rabbits and prairie dogs. The

American bison, better known as the buffalo, grazed in enormous herds from Mexico to Canada. In 1865, perhaps fifteen million buffalo lived on the Plains, so many they seemed like "leaves in a forest" to an early observer. A single herd sighted in 1871 had four million head.

CRUSHING THE NATIVE AMERICANS

When Greeley urged New Yorkers to move West and "crowd nobody," he—like almost all his white countrymen—ignored the fact that large numbers of people already lived there. At the close of the Civil War, Native Americans inhabited nearly half the United States. By 1880, they had been driven onto smaller and smaller reservations and were no longer an independent people. A decade later, even their culture had crumbled under the impact of white domination.

In 1865, nearly a quarter of a million Native Americans lived in the western half of the country. Tribes like the Winnebago, Menominee, Cherokee, and Chippewa were resettled there, forced out of their eastern lands by advancing white settlement. Other tribes were native to the region. In the Southwest there were the Pueblo groups, including the Hopi, Zuñi, and Río Grande Pueblos. Peaceful farmers and herders, they had built up complex traditions around a settled way of life.

The Pueblo groups were cultivators of corn. They lived on the subdesert plateau of present-day western New Mexico and eastern Arizona. Harassed by powerful neighboring tribes, they built communal houses of adobe brick on high mesas or in cracks in the cliffs. More nomadic were the Camp Dwellers, the Jicarilla Apache and Navajo who roamed eastern New Mexico and western Texas. Blending elements of the Plains and Plateau environments, they lived in teepees or mud huts, grew some crops to supplement their hunting, and moved readily from place to place. The Navajo herded sheep and produced beautiful ornamental silver, baskets, and blankets. Fierce fighters, Apache horsemen were feared by whites and fellow Indians across the southwestern Plains.

Farther west were the tribes that inhabited present-day California. Divided into many small bands, they eked out a difficult existence living on roots, grubs, berries, and small game. In the Pacific Northwest, where fish and forest animals made life easier, the Klamath, Chinook, Yurok, and Shasta tribes developed a rich civilization. They built plank houses and canoes, worked extensively in wood, and evolved a complex social and political organization. Settled and determined, they resisted the invasion of the whites.

By the 1870s, most of these tribes had been destroyed or beaten into submission. The powerful Ute, crushed in 1855, ceded most of their Utah lands to the United States and settled on a small reservation near Great Salt Lake. The Navajo and Apache fought back fiercely, but between 1865 and 1873 they too were confined to reservations. The Native Americans of California succumbed to the contagious diseases carried by whites during the Gold Rush of 1849. Miners burned their villages and by 1880 there were less than twenty thousand Indians in California.

Life of the Plains Indians

Nearly two-thirds of the Native Americans lived on the Great Plains. The Plains tribes included the Sioux of present-day Minnesota and the Dakotas, the Blackfoot of Idaho and Montana, the Cheyenne, Crow, and Arapaho of the central Plains, the Pawnee of western Nebraska, and the Kiowa, Apache, and Comanche of present-day Texas and New Mexico.

Nomadic and warlike, the Plains Indians depended on the buffalo and horse. The modern horse, first brought by Spanish explorers in the 1500s, spread north from Mexico onto the Plains, and by the 1700s had changed the Plains Indians' way of life. They gave up farming almost entirely to hunt the buffalo, ranging widely over the rolling plains. They also became superb warriors and horsemen, among the best light cavalry in the world.

Equipped with stout wooden bows, three feet or less in length, Plains Indians were fierce warriors. Hiding their bodies behind their racing ponies, they drove deadly arrows clear through buffalo. Against white troops or settlers, the skillful Comanche rode 300 yards and shot twenty arrows in the time it took a soldier to load his firearm once. The introduction of the new Colt six-shooters during the 1850s gave government

The Buffalo Hunt by Charles M. Russell (below). At first the Plains Indians hunted the buffalo on foot; then, with the arrival of the horse, on horseback. After the buffalo was killed, women skinned the hide, cut up the meat, and then cured the hide as shown in the painting (right) by George Catlin. Women also decorated the teepees and preserved the meat by drying it in the sun.

troops a rapid-fire weapon but did not entirely offset the Indians' advantage.

Migratory in culture, the Plains Indians formed tribes of several thousand people but lived in smaller "bands" of three to five hundred. The Comanche, who numbered perhaps seven thousand, had thirteen bands with such names as Burnt Meat, Making Bags While Moving, and Those Who Move Often. Each band was governed by a chief and a council of elder men, and Indians of the same tribe transferred freely from band to band. Bands acted independently, making it difficult for the United States government to deal with the fragmented tribes.

The bands followed and lived off the buffalo. Buffalo provided food, clothing, and shelter; and the Indians, unlike later white hunters, used every part of the animal. The meat was dried or "jerked" in the hot Plains air. The skins made teepees, blankets, and robes. Buffalo bones became knives; tendons were made into bow strings; horns and hooves were boiled into glue. Buffalo "chips"—dried manure—were burned as fuel. All in all, the buffalo was "a galloping department store."

Warfare between tribes usually took the form of brief raids and skirmishes. Plains Indians fought few prolonged wars and rarely coveted territory. Most conflicts involved only a few warriors intent on stealing horses or "counting coups"—touching an enemy's body with the hand or a special stick. Tribes developed a fierce and trained warrior class, recognized for achievements in battle. Speaking different languages, Native Americans of various tribes were nevertheless able to communicate with one another through a highly developed sign language.

The Plains tribes divided labor tasks according to sex. Men hunted, traded, supervised ceremonial activities, and cleared ground for planting. They usually held the positions of authority, such as chief or medicine man. Women were responsible for child-rearing and artistic activity. They also performed the camp work, grew vegetables, prepared buffalo meat and hides, and gathered berries and roots. In most tribes, women played an important role in political, economic, and religious activities. Among the Navajo and Zuñi, kinship descended from the mother's side, and Navajo women were in charge of most of the family's property. In tribes like the Sioux, there was little difference in status. Men were respected for hunting and war, women for their artistic skills with quill and paint.

"As Long as Waters Run"

Before the Civil War, Americans used the land west of the Mississippi as "one big reservation." The government named the area "Indian Country," moved eastern tribes there with firm treaty guarantees, and in 1834 passed the Indian Intercourse Act, which prohibited any white person from entering Indian country without a license.

The situation changed in the 1850s. Wagon trains wound their way to California and Oregon, miners pushed into western gold fields, and there was talk of a transcontinental railroad. To clear the way for settlement, the federal government in 1851 abandoned "One Big Reservation" in favor of a new policy of "concentration." For the first time, it assigned definite boundaries to each tribe. The Sioux, for example, were given the Dakota country north of the Platte River, the Crows a large area near the Powder River, and the Cheyenne and Arapaho the Colorado foothills between the North Platte and Arkansas rivers for "as long as waters run and the grass shall grow."

The "concentration" policy lasted only a few years. Accustomed to hunting widely for buffalo, many Native Americans refused to stay within their assigned areas. White settlers poured into Indian lands, then called on the government to protect them. Indians were pushed out of Kansas and Nebraska in the 1850s, even as white reformers fought to hold those territories open for free blacks. In 1859, gold miners moved into the Pikes Peak country, touching off warfare with the Cheyenne and Arapaho.

In 1864, tired of the fighting, the two tribes asked for peace. Certain that the war was over, Chief Black Kettle led his seven hundred followers to camp on Sand Creek in southeastern Colorado. Early on the morning of November 29, 1864, a group of Colorado militia led by Colonel John M. Chivington attacked the sleeping group. "Kill and scalp all, big and little," Chivington told his men. "Nits make lice." Black Kettle tried to stop the ambush, raising first an American flag and then a white flag. Neither worked. The Native American men, women, and children were clubbed, stabbed, and scalped.

The Chivington massacre set off angry protests

Native Americans in the West: Major Battles and Reservations

"They made us many promises, more than I remember, but they never kept but one; they promised to take our land, and they took it." So said Red Cloud of the Oglala Sioux, summarizing Native American-white relations in the 1870s.

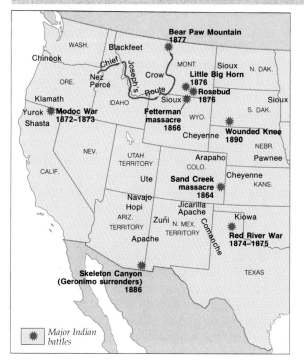

Major Indian battles

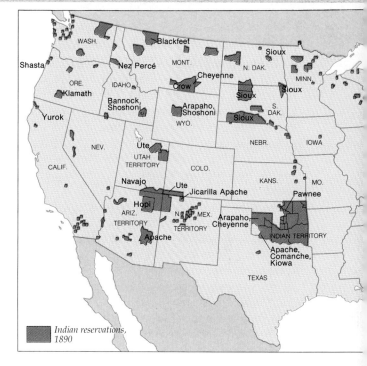

Indian reservations, 1890

in Colorado and the East. Congress appointed an investigating committee, and the government concluded a treaty with the Cheyenne and Arapaho condemning "the gross and wanton outrages." Still, the two tribes were forced to surrender their Sand Creek reservation in exchange for lands elsewhere. The Kiowa and Comanche were also ousted from areas they had been granted "forever" only a few years before. As the Sioux chief Spotted Tail said: "Why does not the Great Father put his red children on wheels so that he can move them as he will?"

Before long, the powerful Sioux were on the warpath in the great Sioux War of 1865–1867. Once again an invasion of gold miners touched off the war, which flared even more intensely when the federal government announced plans to connect the various mining towns by building the Bozeman Trail through the heart of the Sioux hunting grounds in Montana. Red Cloud, the Sioux chief, determined to stop the trail. In December 1866, pursued by an army column under Captain William J. Fetterman, he lured the incautious Fetterman deep into the wilderness,

ambushed him, and wiped out all eighty-two soldiers in his command.

The Fetterman massacre, coming so soon after the Chivington massacre, sparked a public debate over the nation's Indian policy. Like the policy itself, the debate reflected differing white views of the Native Americans. In the East, some reform, humanitarian, and church groups wanted a humane peace policy, directed toward educating and "civilizing" the tribes. Many white people, in the East and West, questioned this approach, convinced that Native Americans were savages unfit for civilization. Westerners, of course, had some reason to fear Indian attacks, and the fears often fed on wild rumors of scalped settlers and besieged forts. As a result, Westerners in general favored firm control over the Native Americans, including swift punishment of any who rebelled.

In 1867, the peace advocates won the debate. Halting construction on the Bozeman Trail, Congress created a Peace Commission of four civilians and three generals to end the Sioux War and eliminate permanently the causes of Indian wars. Setting out for the West, the Peace Commissioners agreed that only one policy offered a permanent solution: a policy of "small reservations" to isolate the Native Americans on distant lands, teach them to farm, and gradually "civilize" them.

The commissioners chose two areas to hold all the Plains Indians. The 54,000 Native Americans on the northern Plains would be moved north of the Black Hills in Dakota Territory, far from prospective white settlement. On the southern Plains, the 86,000 Native Americans would be moved into present-day Oklahoma, a region also considered difficult to farm and unattractive to whites. In both areas, tribes would be assigned specific reservations where government agents could supervise them.

The Kiowa, Comanche, Cheyenne, and Arapaho agreed to the plan in 1867, the Sioux in 1868. Extending the policy beyond the Plains, the Ute, Shoshoni, Bannock, Navajo, and Apache also accepted small reservations. "We have now selected and provided reservations for all, off the great road," an army commander wrote. "All who cling to their old hunting-grounds are hostile and will remain so till killed off."

Final Battles on the Plains

Few Native Americans settled peacefully into life on the new reservations. The reservation system not only changed their age-old customs; it chained them in a situation of poverty and isolation. Soon, young warriors and minor chiefs denounced the treaties and drifted back to the open countryside. In late 1868, warfare broke out again, and it took over a decade of violence to beat the Indians into submission. The Kiowa and Comanche rampaged through the Texas Panhandle, looting and killing, until the U.S. army crushed them in the Red River War of 1874–1875 and ended warfare in the Southwest.

On the northern Plains fighting resulted from the Black Hills Gold Rush of 1875. As prospectors tramped across Native American hunting grounds, the Sioux gathered to stop them. They were led by Rain-in-the-Face, the great war chief Crazy Horse, and the famous medicine man Sitting Bull. The army sent several columns of troops after the Indians, but one, under flamboyant Lieutenant Colonel George A. Custer, pushed recklessly ahead, eager to claim the victory. On the morning of June 25, 1876, thinking he had a small band of Native Americans surrounded in their village on the banks of the Little Bighorn River in Montana, Custer divided his column and took 265 men toward it. Instead of finding a small band, he discovered that he had stumbled on the main Sioux camp with 2500 warriors. It was the largest Native American army ever assembled in the United States.

By mid-afternoon it was over; Custer and his men were dead. Custer was largely responsible for the loss, but "Custer's Last Stand," set in blazing headlines across the country, signaled a nationwide demand for revenge. Within a few months, the Sioux were surrounded and beaten, three thousand of them surrendering in October 1876. Sitting Bull and a few followers who had fled to Canada gave up in 1881.

The Sioux War ended the major Indian warfare in the West, but occasional outbreaks occurred for several years thereafter. In 1877, the Nez Percé tribe of Oregon, a people who had warmly welcomed Lewis and Clark in 1805, rebelled against government policy. Hoping to reach Canada, Chief Joseph led the tribe on a courageous flight lasting 75 days and covering 1321 miles. They defeated the pursuing army at every turn but then ran out of food, horses, and ammunition. Surrendering, they were sent to barren lands in the Indian Country of Oklahoma, and there, most of them died from disease.

In 1890, the Teton Sioux of South Dakota, bitter and starving, became restless. Many of them turned to the "Ghost Dances," a set of dances and rites that grew from a vision of a Paiute messiah named Wovoka. Performance of the dances, Wovoka said, would bring back Native American lands and would cause the whites to disappear. All Native Americans would reunite, the earth would be covered with dust, and a new earth would come upon the old. The vanished buffalo would return in great herds.

The army intervened to stop the dancing, touching off violence that killed Sitting Bull and a number of other warriors. Frightened Native Americans fled southwest to join other Ghost Dancers under the aging chief Big Foot. Moving quickly, troops of the Seventh Cavalry, Custer's old regiment, caught up with Big Foot's band and took them to the army camp on Wounded Knee

Sitting Bull (right) led the Sioux against the U.S. Cavalry when it attacked at the Little Bighorn. U.S. troops were outnumbered almost ten to one in the battle, also known as "Custer's Last Stand." The pictogram (above) by Oglala Sioux Amos Bad Heart Bull, is a Native-American version of the conflict.

Creek in South Dakota. A Native American, it is thought, fired the first shot, returned by the army's new machine guns. Firing a shell a second, they shredded tepees and people. About two hundred men, women, and children were massacred in the snow.

The End of Tribal Life

The final step in Indian policy came in the 1870s and '80s. Some reformers had long argued against segregating the Native Americans on reservations, urging instead that the nation assimilate them individually into white culture. These "assimilationists" wanted to use education, land policy, and federal law to eradicate tribal society.

Congress began to adopt the policy in 1871 when it ended the practice of treaty-making with Native American tribes. Since tribes were no longer separate nations, they lost many of their political and judicial functions, and the power of the chiefs was weakened. In 1882, Congress created a Court of Indian Offenses to try Native Americans who broke government rules, and soon thereafter it made them answerable in regular courts for certain crimes.

While Congress worked to break down the tribes, educators trained young Native Americans to adjust to white culture. In 1879, fifty Pawnee, Kiowa, and Cheyenne youths were brought east to the new Carlisle Indian School in Carlisle, Pennsylvania. Other Native American schools soon opened, including the Haskell Institute in Kansas and numerous day schools on the western reservations. The schools taught students to fix machines and farm; they forced them to trim their long hair, made them speak English, banned the wearing of tribal paint or clothes, and forbade tribal ceremonies and dances. "Kill the Indian and save the man," said Richard H. Pratt, the army officer who founded the Carlisle School.

Land ownership was the final and most important link in the new policy. Native Americans who owned land, it was thought, would become responsible, self-reliant citizens. Deciding to give each Native American a farm, Congress in 1887 passed the Dawes Severalty Act, the most important legal development in Indian-white relations in over three centuries.

*T*om Torlino, a Navajo Indian, photographed before and after his "assimilation." Torlino attended the Carlisle Indian School in Pennsylvania.

Aiming to end tribal life, the Dawes Act divided tribal lands into small plots for distribution among members of the tribe. Each family head received 160 acres, single adults 80 acres, and children 40 acres. Once the land was distributed, any surplus was sold to white settlers, with the profits going to Native American schools. To keep the Indians' land from falling into the hands of speculators, the federal government held it in trust for twenty-five years. Finally, American citizenship was granted to Native Americans who accepted their land, lived apart from the tribe, and "adopted the habits of civilized life."

Through the Dawes Act, 47 million acres of land were distributed to Native Americans and their families. There were another 90 million acres in the reservations, and these lands, often the most fertile, were sold to white settlers. Speculators evaded the twenty-five-year rule, leasing rather than purchasing the land from the Native Americans. Many Native Americans knew little about farming. Their tools were rudimentary, and in the culture of the Plains Indians men had not ordinarily participated in farming. In 1934, the government returned to the idea of

Huge buffalo herds grazing along rail-roads in the West frequently blocked the path of passing trains. Passengers often killed for sport, shooting at the beasts with no intention of using or removing the animal carcasses. Many killed the buffalo for sport, glad to know that they were harming the Native Americans by destroying their most important resource.

tribal land ownership, but by then 138 million acres of Indian land had shrunk to 48 million acres, half of which was barren.

The final blow to tribal life came not in the Dawes Act but in the virtual extermination of the buffalo, the Plains Indians' chief resource and the basis for their unique way of life. The killing began in the 1860s as the transcontinental rail-roads pushed west, and it stepped up as settlers found they could harm the Indians by harming the buffalo. "Kill every buffalo you can," an army officer said. "Every buffalo dead is an Indian gone." Then, in 1871, a Pennsylvania tannery discovered that buffalo hides made valuable leather. Professional hunters like William F. "Buffalo Bill" Cody swarmed across the Plains, killing millions of the beasts.

Cody's exploits were celebrated in song:

Buffalo Bill, Buffalo Bill,
Never missed and never will;
Always aims and shoots to kill
And the company pays his buffalo bill.

Between 1872 and 1874, professional hunters slaughtered three million buffalo a year. In a frontier form of a factory system, riflemen, skin-ners, and transport wagons pushed through the vast herds, which shrank steadily behind them. A good hunter killed a hundred buffalo a day; skinners took off the hides, removed the tongue, hump, and tallow, and left the rest. "I have seen their bodies so thick after being skinned," a hunter said, "that they would look like logs where a hurricane had passed through a forest." Buffalo hunting became a favorite pastime. Even churches and schools contributed to the decima-tion of the herds, raising money by sponsoring hunts.

By 1883, the buffalo were almost gone. When the government set out to produce the famous "buffalo nickel," the designer had to go to the Bronx Zoo in New York City to find a buffalo.

By 1900, there were only 250,000 Native Americans in the country. (There were 600,000 within the limits of the present-day United States in 1800, and more than 5 million in 1492, when Columbus first set foot in the New World.) Most of the Indians lived on reservations. Many lived in poverty. Alcoholism and unemployment were growing problems, and Native Americans, no longer able to live off the buffalo, became wards of the state. They lost their special distinctiveness as a culture. Once possessors of the entire continent, they had been crowded into smaller and smaller areas, overwhelmed by the demand to become settled, literate, and English-speaking. "Except for the internment of the West Coast Japanese during World War II," said historian Roger L. Nichols, "Indian removal is the only example of large-scale government-enforced migration in American history. For the Japanese, the move was temporary; for the Indians it was not."

Even as the Native Americans lost their identity, they entered the romantic folklore of the West. Dime novels, snapped up by readers young and old, told tales of Indian fighting on the Plains. Buffalo Bill Cody turned it all into a profitable business. Beginning in 1883, his Wild West Show ran for over three decades, playing to millions of viewers in the United States, Canada, and Europe. It featured Plains Indians chasing buffalo, performing a war dance, and attacking a settler's cabin. In 1885, Sitting Bull himself, victor over Custer at the battle of Little Bighorn, performed in the show.

SETTLEMENT OF THE WEST

Between 1870 and 1900, white—and some black—Americans settled the enormous total of 430 million acres west of the Mississippi; they occupied more land than had been occupied by Americans in all the years before 1870.

People moved West for many reasons. Some sought adventure; others wanted to escape the drab routine of factory or city life. Many moved to California for their health. The Mormons settled Utah to escape religious persecution. Others followed the mining camps, the advancing railroads, and the farming and cattle frontier. "Most of the time we were solitary adventurers in a great land as fresh and new as a spring morning, and we were free and full of the zest of darers," said Charles Goodnight, a Texas cattleman and founder of the famous Goodnight Trail.

Whatever the specific reason, most people moved West to better their lot. On the whole, their timing was good, for as the nation's population grew, so did demand for the livestock and the agricultural, mineral, and lumber products of the expanding West. Contrary to older historical views, the West did not act as a major "safety valve," an outlet for social and economic tensions. The poor and unemployed did not have the means to move there and establish farms. "Moreover," as Douglass C. North, an economic historian, said, "most people moved West in good times . . . in periods of rising prices, of expanding demand, when the prospects for making money from this new land looked brightest; and this aspect characterized the whole pattern of settlement."

Men and Women on the Overland Trail

The first movement west aimed not for the nearby Plains but for California and Oregon on the continent's far shore. It started in the 1849 Gold Rush to California, and in the next three decades perhaps as many as half a million individuals made the long journey. Some walked; others rode horses alone or in small groups. About half joined great caravans, numbering 150 wagons or more, that inched across the 2000 miles between the Missouri River and the Pacific Coast.

More often than not, men made the decision to make the crossing, but except for the stampedes to the mines, migration usually turned out to be a family affair. Wives were consulted, though in some cases they had little real choice. They could either go along or live alone at home. While many women regretted leaving family and friends, they agreed to the trip, sometimes as eagerly as the men. "With good courage and not one sigh of regret I mounted my pony," Lydia Rudd said. "I would not be left behind," said Luzena Wilson, whose husband ached to join the Gold Rush to California. "I thought where he could go I could, and where I went I could take my two little toddling babies." Like the Wilsons, the majority of people traveled in family groups, including in-laws, grandchildren, aunts, and uncles. As one historian said: "The quest for something new would take place in the context of the very familiar."

Individuals and wagon trains set out from various points along the Missouri River. Leaving in the spring and traveling through the summer, they hoped to reach their destination before the first snowfall. During April, travelers gradually assembled in spring camp just across the Missouri

River, waiting for the new grass to ripen into forage. They packed and repacked the wagons and elected the train's leaders, who would set the line of march, look for water and campsites, and impose discipline. Some trains adopted detailed rules, fearing a lapse into savagery in the wild lands across the Missouri. "Every man to carry with him a Bible and other religious books, as we hope not to degenerate into a state of barbarism," one agreement said.

Setting out in early May, travelers divided the enormous route into manageable portions. The first leg of the journey followed the Platte River west to Fort Kearney in central Nebraska Territory, a distance of about three hundred miles. The land was even, with good supplies of wood, grass, and water. From a distance the white-topped wagons seemed driven by a common force, but in fact, internal discipline broke down almost immediately. Arguments erupted over the pace of the march, the choice of campsites, the number of guards to post, whether to rest or push on. Elected leaders quit; new ones were chosen. Every train was filled with individualists, and as the son of one train captain said, "if you think it's any snap to run a wagon train of 66 wagons with every man in the train having a different idea of what is the best thing to do, all I can say is that some day you ought to try it."

Men, women, and children had different tasks on the trail. Men concerned themselves almost entirely with hunting, guard duty, and transportation. They rose at four A.M. to hitch the wagons, and after breakfast began the day's march. At noon, they stopped and set the teams to graze while the women prepared the midday meal. The march continued until sunset. Then, while the men relaxed, the women fixed dinner and the next day's lunch, and the children kindled the fire, brought water to camp, and searched for wood or other fuel. Walking fifteen miles a day, in searing heat and mountain cold, travelers were exhausted by late afternoon. "We can all, as soon as we stop, lie down on the grass or anywhere and be asleep in less than no time almost," Rebecca Ketcham, an Oregon-bound emigrant, reported.

For women, the trail was lonely, and they worked to exhaustion. Before long, some adjusted their clothing to the harsh conditions, adopting the new bloomer pants, shortening their skirts, or wearing regular "wash dresses"—so called because they had shorter hemlines that did not drag on the wet ground on washday. Other women continued to wear their long dresses, thinking bloomers "indecent." Men hunted buffalo and antelope for fresh meat. Both men and women carried firearms in case of Indian attacks, but most emigrants saw few Indians en route. Not every one was a crack shot. "The young men of our party . . . went out this morning for the purpose of hunting buffalo," Harriet Ward noted sardonically in her diary. "They soon discovered a herd of a hundred and fifty, rushed into their midst, fired their guns without effect and finally succeeded in capturing a cow."

The first stage of the journey was deceptively easy, and travelers usually reached Fort Kearney by late May. The second leg led another 300 miles up the Platte River to Fort Laramie on the eastern edge of Wyoming Territory. The heat of June had burned the grass, and there was no wood. Anxious to beat the early snowfalls, travelers rested a day or two at the fort, then hurried on to South Pass, 280 miles to the west, the best route through the forbidding Rockies. The land was barren. It was now mid-July, but the mountain nights were so cold that ice formed in the water buckets.

Beyond South Pass, some emigrants turned south to the Mormon settlements on Great Salt Lake, but most headed 340 miles north to Fort Hall on the Snake River in Idaho. It took another three months to cover the remaining 800 miles. California-bound travelers followed the Humboldt River through the summer heat of Nevada. Well into September, they began the final arduous push: first, a 55-mile stretch of desert; then 70 difficult miles up the eastern slopes of the Sierra Nevada, hoisting wagons laboriously over massive outcrops of rock; and finally the last 100 miles down the western slopes to the welcome October greenness of the Sacramento Valley.

Under the best of conditions the trip took six months, sixteen hours a day, dawn to dusk, of hard, grueling labor. Walking halfway across the continent was no easy task, and it provided a never-to-be-forgotten experience for those who did it. The wagon trains, carrying the dreams of thousands of individuals, reproduced society in small focus: individualistic, hopeful, mobile, divided by age and sex roles, apprehensive, yet willing to strike out for the distant and new.

Blacks in Blue:
The Buffalo Soldiers in the West

On Saturday afternoons, young-sters used to sit in darkened movie theaters and cheer the victories of the United States cavalry over the Indians. Typically, the Indians were about to capture a wagon train, when army bugles suddenly sounded. Then the blue-coated cavalry charged over the hill. Few in the theaters cheered for the Indi-ans; fewer still noticed the absence of black faces among the on-charg-ing cavalry. But in fact, more than two thousand African-American cavalrymen served on the western frontier between 1867 and 1890.

Known as the "buffalo soldiers," they made up one-fifth of the U.S. cavalry.

Black troops were first used on a large scale during the Civil War (see Chapter 15). Organized in segregated units, with white offi-cers, they fought with distinction. Nearly 180,000 blacks served in the Union army; 34,000 of them died. When the war ended in 1865, Congress for the first time author-ized black troops to serve in the regular peacetime army. In addi-tion to infantry, it created two cav-alry regiments—the Ninth and

Tenth, which became known as the famous buffalo soldiers.

Like other black regiments, the Ninth and Tenth Cavalry had white officers who took special ex-aminations before they could serve. The chaplains were assigned not only to preach but to teach read-ing, writing, and arithmetic. The food was poor; racism was wide-spread. The army stocked the first black units with worn-out horses, a serious matter to men whose lives depended on the speed and stami-na of their mounts. "Since our first mount in 1867 this regiment has received nothing but broken down horses and repaired equipment," an officer said in 1870.

Many white officers refused to serve with black troops. George A. Custer, the handsome "boy gener-al," turned down a position in the Ninth and joined the new Seventh Cavalry, headed for disaster at Lit-tle Bighorn. The *Army and Navy Journal* carried ads that told a simi-lar story:

Although they were not, in fact, treated as well as the white soldiers in their regiments, many African-American cavalrymen such as those pictured here were probably drawn into service by hard-sell recruitment posters like the one shown on the opposite page.

**A FIRST LIEUTENANT
OF INFANTRY**
(white)
Stationed at a
very desirable post
in the Department of the South
desires a transfer with
an officer of the same grade
on equal terms
if in a white regiment
but if in a colored regiment
a reasonable bonus
would be expected.

There was no shortage of black troops for the officers to lead. Blacks enlisted because the army offered some advancement in a closed society. It also paid $13 a month, plus room and board.

In 1867, the Ninth and Tenth Cavalry were posted to the West, where they remained for two decades. Under Colonel Benjamin H. Grierson, a Civil War hero, the Tenth went to Fort Riley, Kansas; the regiment arrived in the midst of a great Indian war. Kiowas, Comanches, Cheyennes, Arapahoes, and Sioux were on the warpath. Troopers of the Tenth defended farms, stages, trains, and work crews building railroad tracks to the west. Cornered by a band of Cheyennes, they beat back the attack and won a new name. Earlier known as the "brunettes" or "Africans," the Cheyenne now called them the buffalo soldiers, a name that soon applied to all African soldiers in the West. (Some of the "buffalo soldiers" are shown in the photo opposite).

From 1868 to 1874, the Tenth served on the Kansas frontier. The dull winter days were filled with drills and scouting parties outside the post. In spring and summer the good weather brought forth new forays. Indian bands raided farms and ranches and stampeded cattle herds on the way north from Texas. They struck and then melted back into the reservations.

The Ninth Cavalry also had a difficult job. Commanded by Colonel Edward Hatch, who had served with Grierson in the Civil War, it was stationed in West Texas and along the Rio Grande. The summers were so hot that men collapsed with sunstroke, the winters so cold that water froze in the canteens. Native Americans from outside the area frequently raided it. From the north Kiowa and Comanche warriors rode down the Great

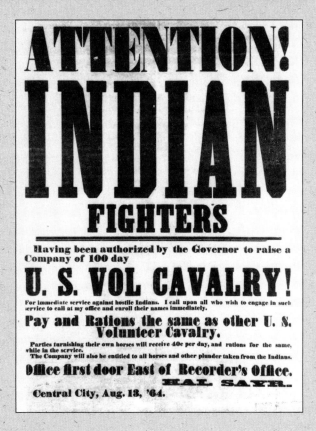

ATTENTION! INDIAN FIGHTERS

Having been authorized by the Governor to raise a Company of 100 day

U. S. VOL CAVALRY!

For immediate service against hostile Indians. I call upon all who wish to engage in such service to call at my office and enroll their names immediately.

Pay and Rations the same as other U. S. Volunteer Cavalry.

Parties furnishing their own horses will receive 40c per day, and rations for the same, while in the service.
The Company will also be entitled to all horses and other plunder taken from the Indians.

Office first door East of Recorder's Office.
HAL. SAYR.

Central City, Aug. 13, '64.

Comanche War Trail; Kickapoos crossed the Rio Grande from Mexico. Gangs of Mexican bandits and restless Civil War veterans roamed and plundered at will.

In 1874–1875, the Ninth fought in the great Red River War, in which the Kiowas and Comanches, fed up with conditions on the reservations, revolted against Grant's peace policy. Marching, fighting, then marching again, the soldiers harried and wore out the Indians, who finally surrendered in the spring of 1875. Herded into a new and desolate reservation, the Mescalero Apaches of New Mexico took to the warpath in 1877 and again in 1879. Each time it took a year of grueling warfare to effect their surrender. In 1886, black cavalrymen surrounded and captured the famous Apache chief Geronimo. In that and other campaigns, several buffalo soldiers won the Congressional Medal of Honor.

Black troops hunted Big Foot and

his band before the slaughter at Wounded Knee in 1890 (see p. 500), and they served in many of the West's most famous Indian battles. While one-third of all army recruits deserted between 1865 and 1890, the Ninth and Tenth Cavalry had few desertions. In 1880, the Tenth had the fewest desertions of any regiment in the country.

It was ironic that in the West, black men fought red men to benefit white men. Once the Indian wars ended, the buffalo soldiers worked to keep illegal settlers out of Indian or government land; much of this land was later opened to settlement. Both regiments saw action in the Spanish-American War, the Ninth at San Juan Hill, the Tenth in the fighting around Santiago. The old buffalo soldiers were forgotten in retirement, although some of them had the satisfaction of settling on the western lands they had done so much to pacify.

Land for the Taking

As railroads pushed west in the 1870s and '80s, locomotive trains replaced wagon trains, but the shift was gradual, and until the end of the century emigrants often combined both modes of travel. Into the 1890s, travelers could be seen making their way across the West by any available means. Early railroad transportation was expensive, and the average farm family could not afford to buy tickets and ship supplies. Many Europeans traveled by rail to designated outfitting places, and then proceeded West with wagons and oxen. Traffic flowed in all directions. Eager settlers heading West passed defeated ones returning East.

Why did they come? "The motive that induced us to part with the pleasant associations and the dear friends of our childhood days," explained Phoebe Judson, an early emigrant, "was to obtain from the government of the United States a grant of land that 'Uncle Sam' had promised to give to the head of each family who settled in this new country." A popular camp song reflected the same motive:

Come along, come along—don't be alarmed,
Uncle Sam is rich enough to give us all a farm.

Uncle Sam owned about 1 billion acres of land in the 1860s, much of it mountain and desert land unsuited for agriculture. By 1900, the various land laws had distributed half of it. Between 1862 and 1890, the government gave away 48 million acres under the Homestead Act of 1862, sold about 100 million acres to private citizens and corporations, granted 128 million acres to railroad companies to tempt them to build across the unsettled West, and sold huge tracts to the states.

The Homestead Act of 1862, a law of great significance, gave 160 acres of land to anyone who would pay a $10 registration and pledge to live on it and cultivate it for five years. The offer set off a mass migration of land-hungry Europeans, dazzled by a country that gave its land away. Americans also seized on the act's provisions, and between 1862 and 1900, nearly six hundred thousand families claimed free homesteads under it.

Yet the Homestead Act did not work as Congress had hoped. Few farmers and laborers had the cash to move to the frontier, buy farm equip-

*R*ailroad companies distributed elaborately illustrated brochures and broadsides to lure people to the West, where they would settle on land owned by the railroad.

ment, and wait out the year or two before the farm became self-supporting. Tailored to the timber and water conditions of the East, the act did not work as well in the semiarid West. In the fertile valleys of the Mississippi, 160 acres provided a generous farm. A farmer on the Great Plains needed either a larger farm for dry farming or a smaller one for irrigation.

The Timber Culture Act of 1873 attempted to adjust the Homestead Act to western conditions. It allowed homesteaders to claim an additional 160 acres if they planted trees on a quarter of it within four years. A successful act, it distributed 10 million acres of land, encouraged needed forestation, and enabled homesteaders to expand their farms to a workable size. Cattle ranchers lobbied for another law, the Desert Land Act of 1877, which allowed individuals to obtain 640 acres in the arid states for $1.25 an acre, provided they irrigated part of it within three years. This act invited fraud. Irrigation sometimes meant a bucket of water dumped on the ground, and ranchers used their hired hands to claim large tracts. More than 2.6 million acres were distributed, much of it fraudulently.

The Timber and Stone Act of 1878 applied only to lands "unfit for cultivation" and valuable chiefly for timber or stone. It permitted anyone in California, Nevada, Oregon, and Washington to buy up to 160 acres of forestland for $2.50 an acre. Like ranchers, lumber companies used employees to file false claims. Company agents rounded up seamen on the waterfront, marched them to the land office to file their claims, took them to a notary public to sign over the claims to the company, and then marched them back to the waterfront for payment in beer or cash. By 1900, 3.6 million acres of rich forest land had been claimed under the measure.

Speculators made ingenious use of the land laws. Sending agents in advance of settlement, they moved along choice river bottoms or irrigable areas, accumulating large holdings to be held for high prices. In the arid West, where control of water meant control of the surrounding land, shrewd ranchers plotted their holdings accordingly. In Colorado, one cattleman, John F. Iliff, owned only 105 small parcels of land, but by placing them around the few waterholes, he effectively dominated an empire stretching over 6000 square miles.

As beneficiaries of the government's policy of land grants for railway construction, the railroad companies were the West's largest landowners. Eager to have immigrants settle on the land they owned near the railroad right-of-way, and eager to boost their freight and passenger business, the companies sent agents to the East and Europe. Attractive brochures touted life in the West. The Union Pacific called the rocky Platte Valley in Nebraska "a flowery meadow of great fertility, clothed in nutritious grasses." The Burlington Railroad reminded women of the West's many unmarried men: "when a daughter of the East is once beyond the Missouri she rarely recrosses it except on a bridal tour."

Railroad lines set up Land Departments and Bureaus of Immigration. The Land Departments priced the land, arranged credit terms, and even gave free farming courses to immigrants. The Bureau of Immigration employed agents in Europe, met immigrants at eastern seaports, and ran special cars for land-seekers heading West. In 1874, the Santa Fe Railroad convinced 1900 Russian Mennonites to bring $2 million in gold drafts and settle on the fertile plains of Kansas.

Half a billion acres of western land were given or sold to speculators and corporations. At the same time, only 600,000 homestead patents were issued, covering 80 million acres. Thus, only one acre in every nine initially went to individual pioneers, the intended beneficiaries of the nation's largesse. Two-thirds of all homestead claimants before 1890 failed in their efforts to farm their new land.

Territorial Government

As new areas of the West opened, they were organized as territories under the control of Congress and the President. The territorial system started with the famous Northwest Ordinance of 1787 (see Chapter 6), which established the rules by which territories became states. Washington ran the territories like "a passive group of colonial mandates." The President appointed the governor and judges in each territory; Congress detailed their duties, set their budgets, and oversaw their activities. Territorial officials had almost absolute power over the territories.

Until they obtained statehood, then, the territories depended on the federal government for their existence. They became an important part of the patronage system, as sources of jobs for deserving politicians.

The national political parties, especially the Republicans, funneled government funds into the territorial economies, and in areas like Wyoming and the Dakotas, where resources were scarce, economic growth depended on them. Many early settlers held patronage jobs or hoped for them, traded with government-supported Native Americans, sold supplies to army troops, and speculated in government lands.

E. P. Caldwell, for example, a small-town attorney in Huron, Dakota Territory, made a living the way many Westerners did, by serving Washington and the East. His newspaper advertisement is shown on the following page.

In a large portion of the trans-Mississippi West, a generation grew up under territorial rule. Inevitably, they developed distinct ideas about politics, government, and the economy.

```
MONEY LOANED
for Eastern Capitalists
Taxes Paid for Nonresidents
INVESTMENTS CAREFULLY MADE
for Eastern Capitalists
GENERAL LAW,
Land and Collection Business
Transacted
Buy and Sell Real Estate
U.S. Land Business
Promptly Attended to
```

The Spanish-Speaking Southwest

In the nineteenth century almost all Spanish-speaking people in the United States lived in California, Arizona, New Mexico, Texas, and Colorado. Their numbers were small—California had only 8086 Mexican residents in 1900—but the influence of their culture and institutions was large. In some respects the Southwestern frontier was more Spanish-American than Anglo-American.

Pushing northward from Mexico, the Spanish gradually established the present-day economic structure of the Southwest. They brought with them techniques of mining, stock raising, and irrigated farming. After winning independence in the 1820s, the Mexicans brought new laws, ranching methods, chaps, and the burro. Both Spanish and Mexicans created the legal framework for distributing land and water, a precious resource in the Southwest. They gave large grants of land to communities for grazing, to individuals as rewards for service, and to the various Native American pueblos.

In Southern California the Californios, descendants of the original colonizers, began after the 1860s to lose their once vast landholdings to drought and mortgages. Some turned to crime and became feared bandidos; others, like José María Amador, lived in poverty and remembered better days:

> When I was but a little boy I drained the chocolate pot,
> But now I am a poor man and am condemned to slop.

In 1875, Romualdo Pacheco, an aristocratic native son, served as governor of California and then went on to Congress. But as the Californios died out, Mexican-Americans continued the Spanish-Mexican influence. In 1880, one-fourth of the residents of Los Angeles County were Spanish speaking.

In New Mexico, Spanish-speaking citizens remained the majority ethnic group until the 1940s, and the Spanish-Mexican culture dominated the territory. Contests over land grants became New Mexico's largest industry; lawyers who dealt in them amassed huge holdings. After 1888, *Las Gorras Blancas,* The White Caps, a secret organization of Spanish-Americans, attacked the movement of Anglo ranchers into the Las Vegas community land grant. Armed and hooded, they cut down fences and scattered the stock of those they viewed as intruders. Though feared, they left politely worded warnings: "This notice is with the object of requesting you to coil up your wire as soon as possible. . . . They are fences which are damaging the unhappy people . . . and if you do not do it you will suffer the consequences from us. Your Servants. The White Caps."

Throughout the Southwest, the Spanish-Mexican heritage gave a distinctive shape to society. Men headed the families and dominated economic life. Women had substantial economic rights (though few political ones), and they enjoyed a status their English-American counterparts did not have. Wives kept full control of property acquired before their marriage; they also held half-title to all property in a marriage, which later caused many southwestern states to pass community property laws.

In addition, the Spanish-Mexican heritage fostered a modified economic caste system, a strong Roman Catholic influence, and the primary use of the Spanish language. Continuous immigration from Mexico kept language and cultural ties strong. Spanish names and customs spread, even among Anglos. David Starr Jordan, arriving from Indiana to become the first president of Stanford University in California, bestowed Spanish names on streets, houses, and a Stanford dormitory. Spanish was the region's first or second language. Confronted by Sheriff Pat Garrett in a darkened room, New Mexico's famous outlaw, Billy the Kid, died saying *"Quien es? Quien es?"* ("Who is it? Who is it?").

Before the California Gold Rush of 1849, San Francisco was a sleepy little Spanish-Mexican village called Yerba Buena. Gold-seekers turned it into a boom town with an international population. Here, Spanish-Mexican rancheros, white prospectors, Chinese laborers, and a top-hatted professional gambler mingle in a San Francisco saloon.

THE BONANZA WEST

Between 1850 and 1900, wave after wave of newcomers swept across the trans-Mississippi West. There were riches for the taking, hidden in gold-washed streams, spread lushly over grass-covered prairies, or available in the gullible minds of greedy newcomers. The nineteenth-century West took shape in the search for mining, cattle, and land bonanzas that drew eager settlers from the East and around the world.

As with all bonanzas, its consequences in the West were uneven growth, boom-and-bust economic cycles, and wasted resources. Society seemed constantly in the making. People moved here and there, following river bottoms, gold strikes, railroad tracks, and other opportunities. "Instant cities" arose. San Francisco, Salt Lake City, and Denver were the most spectacular examples, but every cow town and mining camp witnessed similar phenomena of growth. Boston needed more than two centuries to attract one-third of a million people; San Francisco did the same in a little more than twenty years.

Many Westerners had left home to get rich quickly, and they adopted institutions that reflected that goal. As a contemporary poem said:

Love to see the stir an' bustle
In the busy town,
Everybody on the hustle

Saltin' profits down.
Everybody got a wad a'
Ready cash laid by;
Ain't no flies on Colorado—
Not a cussed fly.

In their lives, the West was an idea as well as a region, and the idea molded them as much as they molded it.

The Mining Bonanza

Mining was the first important magnet to attract people to the West. Many hoped to "strike it rich" in gold and silver, but at least half the newcomers had no intention of working in the mines. Instead, they provided food, clothing, and services to the thousands of miners. Leland Stanford and Collis P. Huntington, who later built the Central Pacific Railroad, set up a general store in Sacramento where they sold shovels and supplies. Stephen J. Field, later a prominent justice of the United States Supreme Court, followed the Gold Rush to California to practice law.

The California Gold Rush of 1849 began the mining boom and set the pattern for subsequent strikes in other regions. Individual prospectors made the first strikes, discovering pockets of gold along streams flowing westward from the Sierra Nevada. To get the gold, they used a simple process called placer mining, which required little skill, technology, or capital. A placer miner needed only a shovel, washing pan, and a good claim. As the placers gave out, a great deal of gold remained, but it was locked in quartz or buried deep in the earth. Mining became an expensive business, far beyond the reach of the average miner.

Large corporations moved in to dig the deep shafts and finance costly equipment. Quartz mining required heavy rock crushers, mercury vats to dissolve the gold, and large retorts to recapture it. Eastern and European financiers assumed control, labor became unionized, and mining towns took on some of the characteristics of the industrial city. Individual prospectors meanwhile dashed on to the next find. Unlike other frontiers, the mining frontier moved from west to east, as the original California miners—the "yonder-siders," they were called—hurried eastward in search of the big strike.

In 1859, fresh strikes were made near Pikes Peak in Colorado and in the Carson River Valley of Nevada. News of both discoveries set off wild migrations—one hundred thousand miners were in Pikes Peak country by June 1859. The gold there quickly played out, but the Nevada find uncovered a thick, bluish black ore that was almost pure silver and gold. A quick-witted drift-er named Henry T. P. Comstock talked his way into partnership in the claim, and word of the Comstock Lode—with ore worth $3876 a ton—flashed over the mountains.

Thousands of miners climbed the Sierra Nevada that summer. On the rough slopes of Davidson Mountain, they created Virginia City, the prototype of the tumultuous western mining town. Mark Twain was there and described the scene in *Roughing It* (1872): "The sidewalks swarmed with people. . . . Joy sat on every countenance, and there was a glad, almost fierce, intensity in every eye, that told of the money-getting schemes that were seething in every brain and the high hope that held sway in every heart."

The biggest strike was yet to come. In 1873, John W. Mackay and three partners formed a company to dig deep into the mountain, and at 1167 feet they hit the Big Bonanza, a seam of gold and silver more than 54 feet wide. It was the richest discovery in the history of mining. Between 1859 and 1879, the Comstock Lode produced gold and silver worth $306 million. Most of it went to financiers and corporations. Mackay himself became the richest person in the world, earning (according to a European newspaper) $25 a minute, $5 a minute more than Czar Alexander II of Russia.

In the 1860s and '70s, important strikes were

Miners used a "long tom" to wash placer gold from pay dirt. These prospectors, photographed in 1852, are working in a stream bed near Auburn, California.

Martha Jane Canary—Calamity Jane—in the uniform of a U.S. Army scout. She boasted of her marksmanship and her exploits as a pony express rider and a scout.

made in Washington, Idaho, Nevada, Colorado, Montana, Arizona, and Dakota. Extremely mobile, miners flocked from strike to strike, and new camps and mining towns sprang up overnight. "The miners of Idaho were like quicksilver," said Hubert Howe Bancroft, an early historian. "A mass of them dropped in any locality, broke up into individual globules, and ran off after any atom of gold in their vicinity. They stayed nowhere longer than the gold attracted them."

The final fling came in the Black Hills rush of 1874–1876. The army had tried to keep miners out of the area, the heart of the Sioux hunting grounds, and even sent a scientific party under Colonel George A. Custer to disprove the rumors of gold and stop the miners' invasion. Instead, Custer found gold all over the hills, and the rush was on. Miners, gamblers, desperadoes, and prostitutes flocked to Deadwood, the most lawless of all the mining camps. There, Martha Jane Canary—a crack shot who, as Calamity Jane, won fame as a scout and teamster—fell in love with Wild Bill Hickok; and Hickok himself—a western legend who had tamed Kansas cow towns, killed an unknown number of men, and toured in Buffalo Bill's Wild West Show—died,

shot in the back of the head. Hickok was thirty-nine.

Towns such as Deadwood, in the Dakota Territory; Virginia City, Nevada; Leadville, Colorado; and Tombstone, Arizona, demonstrated a new development process in the frontier experience. The farming frontier had developed naturally in a rural setting. On the mining frontier, the germ of a city—the camp—appeared almost simultaneously with the first "strike." Periodicals, the latest fashions, theaters, schools, literary clubs, and lending libraries came quickly to the camps, providing civilized refinements not available on other frontiers. Urbanization also created the need for municipal government, sanitation, and law enforcement.

Mining camps were governed by a simple democracy. Soon after a strike, the miners in the area met to organize a mining "district" and adopted rules governing behavior in it. Rules regulated the size and boundaries of claims, established procedures for settling disputes, and set penalties for crimes. Petty criminals were banished from the district; serious offenders were hanged. In the case of a major dispute, the whole camp gathered, chose legal counsel for both sides, and heard the evidence. If all else failed, miners formed secret vigilance committees to hang a few offenders as a lesson to the rest. Early visitors to the mining country were struck by the way miners, solitary and competitive, joined together, founded a camp, and created a society.

The camps were mostly male, made up of "men who can rough it" and a few "ladies of spirit and energy." In 1870, men outnumbered women in the mining districts by more than two to one; there were few children. Prostitutes followed the camps around the West, and "respectable" women were an object of curiosity. Four arrived in Nevada City in 1853, and as one observed: "The men stand and gaze at us with mouth and eyes wide open, every time we go out." Some women worked claims, but more often they took jobs as cooks, housekeepers, and seamstresses—for wages considerably higher than in the East. There were advantages in scarcity. "I lead a life of great variety—full of agreeable, and stirring incidents," one woman said. "I think that I should find any other country very dull after this."

In most camps, between one-quarter and one-

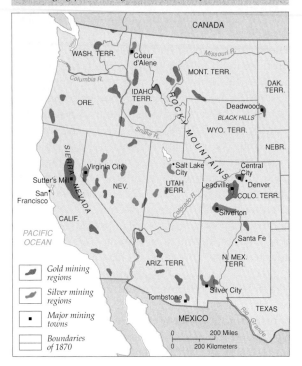

Gold mining regions

Silver mining regions

Major mining towns

Boundaries of 1870

By the 1890s, the early mining bonanza was over. All told, the western mines contributed billions of dollars to the economy. They helped finance the Civil War and provided needed capital for industrialization. The vast boost in silver production from the Comstock Lode changed the relative value of gold and silver, the base of American currency. Bitter disputes over the currency affected politics and led to the famous "battle of the standards," the presidential election of 1896 (see Chapter 20).

The mining frontier populated portions of the West and sped its process of political organization. Nevada, Idaho, and Montana were granted early statehood because of mining. Merchants, editors, lawyers, and ministers moved with the advancing frontier, establishing permanent settlements. Women in the mining camps helped to foster family life and raised the moral tone by campaigning against drinking, gambling, and prostitution. But not all the effects of the mining boom were positive. The industry also left behind painful scars in the form of invaded Indian reservations, pitted hills, and lonely ghost towns.

Gold from the Roots Up

"There's gold from the grass roots down," said California Joe, a guide in the gold districts of Dakota in the 1870s, "but there's more gold from the grass roots up." Ranchers began to recognize the potential of the vast grasslands of the West. The Plains were covered with buffalo or grama grass, a wiry variety with short, hard stems. Cattle thrived on it.

For twenty years after 1865, cattle ranching dominated the "open range," a vast, fenceless area extending from the Texas Panhandle north into Canada. The techniques of the business came from Mexico, where long before American cowboys moved herds north, their Mexican counterparts, the *vaqueros*, developed the essential techniques of branding, roundups, and roping. The cattle themselves, the famous Texas longhorns, also came from Mexico. Spreading over the grasslands of southern Texas, the longhorns multiplied rapidly. Although their meat was coarse and stringy, they fed a nation hungry for beef at the end of the Civil War.

The problem was getting the beef to eastern

half of the population was foreign-born. The lure of gold drew large numbers of Chinese, Chileans, Peruvians, Mexicans, French, Germans, and English. Experienced miners, the Latin Americans brought valuable mining techniques. At least 6000 Mexicans joined the California rush of 1849, and by 1852, there were 25,000 Chinese in California. Painstaking, the Chinese profitably worked claims others had abandoned. In the 1860s, almost one-third of the miners in the West were Chinese.

Hostility often surfaced against foreign miners, particularly the French, Latin Americans, and Chinese. In 1850, California passed a Foreign Miners' Tax that charged foreign miners a $20 monthly licensing fee. As intended, it drove out Mexican and other miners. Riots against Chinese laborers occurred in the 1870s and '80s in Los Angeles, San Francisco, Seattle, Reno, and Denver. Responding to pressure, Congress passed the Chinese Exclusion Act of 1882, which suspended immigration of Chinese laborers for ten years. The number of Chinese in the United States fell drastically.

markets, and Joseph G. McCoy, a livestock shipper from Illinois, solved it. Looking for a way to market Texas beef, McCoy conceived the idea of taking the cattle to railheads in Kansas. He talked first with the president of the Missouri Pacific, who ordered him out of his office, and then with the head of the Kansas Pacific, who laughed at the idea. The persistent McCoy finally signed a contract in 1867 with the Hannibal and St. Joseph Railroad. Searching for an appropriate rail junction, he settled on the sleepy Kansas town of Abilene, "a very small, dead place," he remembered, with about a dozen log huts and one near-bankrupt saloon.

In September 1867, McCoy shipped the first train of twenty cars of longhorn cattle. By the end of the year, a thousand carloads had followed, all headed for Chicago markets. In 1870, 300,000 head of Texas cattle reached Abilene, followed the next year—the peak year—by 700,000 head. The Alamo Saloon, crowded with tired cowboys at the end of the drive, now employed 75 bartenders, working three eight-hour shifts.

The profits were enormous. Drivers bought cheap Texas steers for $4 a head and sold them for $30 or $40 a head at the northern railhead. The most famous trail was the Chisholm, running from southern Texas through Oklahoma Territory to Ellsworth and Abilene, Kansas, on the Kansas Pacific Railroad. Dodge City, Kansas, became the prime shipping center between 1875 and 1879.

Cowboys pushed steers northward in herds of two to three thousand. Novels and films have portrayed them as white, but at least a quarter were black and possibly another quarter were Mexicans. A typical crew on the trail north might have eight men, half of them black or Mexican. Most of the trail bosses were white; they earned about $125 a month. As James "Jim" Perry, a renowned black cowboy who worked for more than twenty years as a rider, roper, and cook for the XIT ranch, said: "If it weren't for my damned old black face, I'd have been a boss long ago."

Like miners, cattlemen lived beyond the formal reach of the law and so established their own. Before each drive, Charles Goodnight drew up rules governing behavior on the trail. A cowboy who shot another was hanged on the spot. Ranchers adopted rules for cattle ownership, branding, roundups, and drives; and they formed associations to enforce them. The Wyoming Stock

Cattle Trails

Cattle raised in Texas were driven along the cattle trails to the northern railheads that carried them to market.

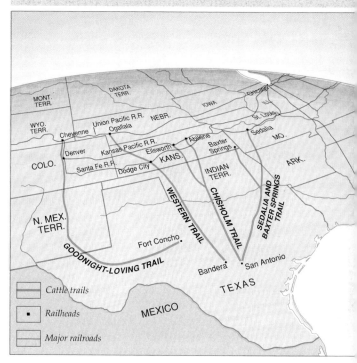

Growers' Association, the largest and most formidable, had 400 members owning 2 million cattle; its reach extended well beyond Wyoming into Colorado, Nebraska, Montana, and the Dakotas. Throughout this vast territory, the "laws" of the association were often the law of the land.

Hollywood images to the contrary, there was little violence in the booming cow towns. The number of homicides in a year never topped five in any town, and in many years no one was killed. Doc Holliday and William B. (Bat) Masterson never killed anyone. John Wesley Hardin, a legendary teenaged gunman, shot only one man, firing blindly through a hotel room wall to stop him from snoring. Famous western sheriffs had everyday duties. Wild Bill Hickok served as Abilene's street commissioner, and the Wichita city council made its lawmen, including Wyatt Earp, repair streets and sidewalks before each cattle season.

By 1880, more than six million cattle had been driven to northern markets. But the era of the great cattle drive was ending. Farmers were plant-

*N*at Love, born a slave in Tennessee in 1854, claimed to be the original "Deadwood Dick," having won the title in a cowboy contest in Deadwood, South Dakota, in 1876.

ing wheat on the old buffalo ranges; barbed wire, a recent invention, cut across the trails and divided up the big ranches. Mechanical improvements in slaughtering, refrigerated transportation, and cold storage modernized the industry. Ranchers bred the Texas longhorns with heavier Hereford and Angus bulls, and as the new breeds proved profitable, more and more ranches opened on the northern ranges.

By the mid-1880s, some 4.5 million cattle grazed the High Plains, reminding people of the once great herds of buffalo. Stories of vast profits circulated, attracting outside capital. Large investments transformed ranching into big business, often controlled by absentee owners and subject to new problems.

By 1885, experienced cattlemen were growing alarmed. A presidential order that year forced stockmen out of the Indian Territory in Oklahoma, adding two hundred thousand cattle to the overcrowded northern ranges. The winter of 1885–1886 was cold, and the following summer

was one of the hottest on record. Waterholes dried up; the grass turned brown. Beef prices fell. The *Rocky Mountain Husbandman* urged ranchers to sell: "Beef is low, very low, and prices are tending downward. . . . But for all that, it would be better to sell at a low figure, than to endanger the whole herd by having the range overstocked."

The winter of 1886–1887 was one of the worst in western history. Temperatures dropped to 45 degrees below zero, and cattle that once would have saved themselves by drifting ahead of the storms, came up against the new barbed wire fences. Herds jammed together, pawing the frozen ground or stripping bark from trees in search of food. Cattle died by the tens of thousands. In the spring of 1887, when the snows thawed, ranchers found stacks of carcasses piled up against the fences.

The melting snows did, however, produce a lush crop of grass for the survivors. The cattle business recovered, but it took different directions. Outside capital, so plentiful in the boom years, dried up. Ranchers began fencing their lands, reducing their herds, and growing hay for winter food. To the dismay of cowboys, mowing machines and hay rakes became as important as chuck wagons and branding irons. "I tell you times have changed," one cowboy said sadly.

The last roundup on the northern ranges took place in 1905. Ranches grew smaller, and some ranchers, at first in the scrub country of the Southwest, then on the Plains themselves, switched to raising sheep. By 1900, there were nearly 38 million sheep west of the Missouri River, far more than there were cattle. In Montana, there were six or seven sheep for each cow, and even Wyoming, the great center of the northern ranches, had more sheep than cows.

Ranchers and sheepherders fought bitterly to control the grazing lands, but they had one problem in common: there were troubles ahead. Homesteaders, armed with barbed wire and new strains of wheat, were pushing onto the Plains, and the day of the open range was over.

FARMING ON THE FRONTIER

Like miners and cattlemen, millions of farmers moved West in the decades after 1870 to seek crop bonanzas and new ways of life. Some real-

Agricultural Land Use in the 1880s

New farming technology and crops enabled more and more land to be distributed for productive use.

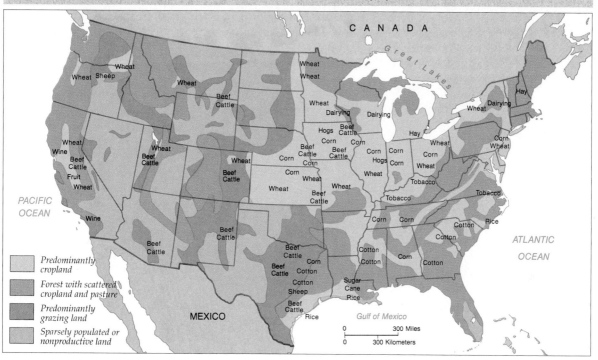

Legend:
- Predominantly cropland
- Forest with scattered cropland and pasture
- Predominantly grazing land
- Sparsely populated or nonproductive land

ized their dreams; many fought just to survive.

Said a folk song from Greer County, Oklahoma:

Hurrah for Greer County! The land of the free,
The land of the bedbug, grasshopper, and flea;
I'll sing of its praises, I'll tell of its fame,
While starving to death on my government claim.

Between 1870 and 1900, farmers cultivated more land than ever before in American history. They peopled the Plains from Dakota to Texas, pushed the Indians out of their last sanctuary in Oklahoma, and poured into the basins and foothills of the Rockies. By 1900, the western half of the nation contained almost 30 percent of the population, compared to less than 1 percent just a half-century earlier.

Sodbusters on the Plains

Unlike mining, farm settlement often followed predictable patterns, taking population from states east of the frontier line and moving gradu-

ally westward. Crossing the Mississippi, farmers settled first in South Dakota, Minnesota, western Iowa, Nebraska, Kansas, and Texas. The movement slumped during the depression of the 1870s, but then a new wave of optimism carried thousands more west. Several years of above-average rainfall convinced farmers that the Dakotas, western Nebraska and Kansas, and eastern Colorado were the "rain belt of the Plains." Between 1870 and 1900, the population on the Plains tripled.

In some areas the newcomers were blacks who had fled the South, fed up with beatings and murders, crop liens, and the "Black Codes" (see Chapter 16) that institutionalized their subordinate status. In 1879, about 6000 African Americans, known as the Exodusters, left their homes in Louisiana, Mississippi, and Texas to establish new and freer lives in Kansas, the home of John Brown and the free soil campaigns of the 1850s. Once there, they farmed or worked as laborers; women worked in the fields alongside the men or cleaned houses and took in washing to make ends meet. All told, the Exodusters homesteaded

A wagonload of sod bricks stands ready for roof repairs on this sod house in Custer County, Nebraska, 1892. Lumber was scarce and very expensive.

20,000 acres of land, and though they met prejudice, it was not as extreme as they had known at home. "I asked my wife did she know the ground she stands on," said John Solomon Lewis, a Louisianan, soon after arriving. "She said, 'No!' I said it is free ground; and she cried like a child for joy."

Other African Americans moved to Oklahoma, thinking they might establish the first African-American state. Whether headed for Oklahoma or Kansas, they picked up and moved in sizable groups that were based on family units; they took with them the customs they had known, and in their new homes they were able, for the first time, to have some measure of self-government.

For blacks and whites alike, farming on the Plains presented new problems. There was little surface water, and wells ranged between fifty and five hundred feet deep. Well drillers charged up to $2 a foot. Taking advantage of the steady Plains winds, windmills brought the water to the surface, but they too were expensive, and until 1900, many farmers could not afford them. Lumber for homes and fences was also scarce. Some settlers imported it from distant Wisconsin, but a single homestead of 160 acres cost $1000 to fence, an amount few could pay.

Unable to afford wood, farmers often started out in dreary sod houses. Cut into three-foot sections, the thick prairie sod was laid like brick, with space left for two windows and a door. Since glass was scarce, cloth hung over the windows; a blanket was hung from the ceiling to make two rooms. Sod houses were small, provided little light and air, and were impossible to keep clean. When it rained, water seeped through the roof. Yet a sod house cost only $2.78 to build.

Outside, the Plains environment sorely tested the men and women who moved there. Neighbors were distant; the land stretched on as far as the eye could see. Always the wind blew. "As long as I live I'll never see such a lonely country," a woman said of the Texas Plains; a Nebraska woman said: "These unbounded prairies have such an air of desolation—and the stillness is very oppressive."

In the winters, savage storms swept the open grasslands. Ice caked on the cattle until their heads were too heavy to hold up. Summertime temperatures stayed near 110 degrees for weeks at a time. Fearsome rainstorms, building in the summer's heat, beat down the young corn and wheat. The summers also brought grasshoppers, arriving without warning, flying in clouds so huge they shut out the sun. The grasshoppers ate everything in sight: crops, clothing, mosquito netting, tree bark, even plow handles. In the summer of 1874, they devastated the whole Plains from Texas to the Dakotas, eating everything "but the mortgage," as one farmer said.

New Farming Methods

Farmers adopted new techniques to meet these conditions. For one thing, they needed cheap and effective fencing material, and in 1874, Joseph F. Glidden, a farmer from De Kalb, Illinois, provided it with the invention of barbed wire. By 1883, his factory was turning out 600 miles of barbed wire every day, and farmers were buying it faster than it could be produced.

Dry farming, a new technique, helped compensate for the lack of rainfall. By plowing furrows twelve to fourteen inches deep, and creating a dust mulch to fill the furrow, farmers loosened the soil and slowed evaporation. Wheat farmers imported European varieties of plants that could withstand the harsh Plains winters. Hard-kerneled varieties like "Turkey Red" wheat from Russia required new milling methods, developed during the 1870s. By 1881, Minneapolis, St. Louis, and Kansas City had become milling centers for the rich "New Process" flour.

Farm technology changed long before the Civil War, but later developments improved it. In 1877, James Oliver of Indiana patented a chilled-iron plow with a smooth-surface mold board that did not clog in the thick prairie soils. The springtooth harrow (1869) sped soil preparation; the grain drill (1874) opened furrows and scientifically fed seed into the ground. The lister (1880) dug a deep furrow, planted corn at the bottom, and covered the seed—all in one operation.

The first baling press was built in 1866, and the hay loader was patented in 1876. The first successful harvester, the cord binder (1878), cut and tied bundles of grain, enabling two men and a team of horses to harvest 20 acres of wheat a day. Invented earlier, threshers grew larger; employing as many as nine men and ten horses, they threshed 300 bushels of grain a day.

In 1890, over nine hundred corporations manufactured farm machinery. Scientific agriculture flourished under new discoveries linking soil minerals and plant growth. Samuel Johnson of Yale University wrote books on *How Crops Grow* (1868) and *How Crops Feed* (1870), and one of his students pioneered work on nitrogen, the base of many modern fertilizers. The Hatch Act, passed in 1887, supported agricultural experiment stations that spread the discoveries among farmers. Four years later, these stations employed over 450 persons and distributed more than 300 published reports annually to some 350,000 readers.

In the late 1870s, huge bonanza farms rose, run by the new machinery and financed with outside capital. Oliver Dalrymple, the most famous of the bonanza farmers, headed an experiment in North Dakota's Red River Valley in 1875, then moved on to manage the Grandin Bonanza of 61,000 acres, five times the size of Manhattan Island. Dalrymple hired armies of workers, bought machinery by the carload, and planted on a scale that dazzled the West.

The bonanza farms—thanks to their size and machinery—captured the country's imagination. Using 200 pairs of harrows, 155 binders, and 16 threshers, Dalrymple produced 600,000 bushels of wheat in 1881. He and other bonanza managers profited from the economies of scale, buying materials at wholesale prices and receiving rebates from the railroads. Then a period of drought began. Rainfall dropped between 1885 and 1890, and the large-scale growers found it hard to compete with smaller farmers who diversified their crops and cultivated more intensively. Many of the large bonanzas slowly disintegrated, and Dalrymple himself went bankrupt in 1896.

Discontent on the Farm

Touring the South in the 1860s, Oliver H. Kelley, a clerk in the Department of Agriculture, was struck by the drabness of rural life. In 1867, he founded the National Grange of the Patrons of Husbandry, known simply as the Grange. The Grange provided social, cultural, and educational activities for its members. Its constitution banned involvement in politics, but Grangers often ignored the rules and supported railroad regulation and other measures.

The Grange grew rapidly during the depres-

Thirty-two horses pull a harvester-thresher combine through a wheat field in Oregon, binding and threshing the wheat in a single step. With such large-scale operations, farmers became more commercially-oriented, producing for a world market.

sion of the 1870s, and by 1875, it had over 800,000 members in 20,000 local Granges. Most were in the Midwest and South. The Granges set up cooperative stores, grain elevators, warehouses, insurance companies, and farm machinery factories. Many failed, but in the meantime the organization made its mark. Farm-oriented groups like the Farmers' Alliance, with branches in both South and West, began to attract followers. (See Chapter 20 for a more detailed discussion of the Alliance.)

Like the cattle boom, the farming boom ended sharply after 1887. A severe drought that year cut harvests, and other droughts followed in 1889 and 1894. Thousands of new farmers were wiped out on the western Plains. Between 1888 and 1892, more than half the population of western Kansas left. In the 1890s, Nebraska lost 15,000 people and 6000 farms.

Farmers grew angry and restless. They complained about declining crop prices, rising railroad rates, and heavy mortgages. In the wheat-growing Plains, the economic problems were persistent. Returning home to Iowa in 1889, the author Hamlin Garland found his farming friends caught up "in a sullen rebellion against the government and against God." "Every house I visited" he said, "had its individual message of sordid struggle and half-hidden despair. . . . All the gilding of farm life melted away."

Though many farmers were unhappy, the peopling of the West in these years transformed American agriculture. The states beyond the Mississippi became the garden land of the nation. California sent fruit, wine, and wheat to eastern markets. Under the Mormons, Utah flourished with irrigation. Texas beef stocked the country's tables, and vast wheat fields, stretching to the horizon, covered Minnesota, the Dakotas, Montana, and eastern Colorado. All produced more than Americans could consume. By 1890, American farmers were exporting large amounts of wheat and other crops.

Farmers became more commercial and scientific. They needed to know more and work harder. Mail-order houses and rural free delivery diminished their isolation and tied them ever closer to the national future. "This is a new age to the farmer," said a statistician in the Department of Agriculture in 1889. "He is now, more than ever before, a citizen of the world."

The Final Fling

As the West filled in with people, pressure mounted on the President and Congress to open the last Indian territory, Oklahoma, to settlers. In

March 1889, Congress acted and forced the Creeks and Seminoles, two tribes who had been moved into Oklahoma in the 1820s, to surrender their rights. With arrangements complete, President Benjamin Harrison announced the opening of the Oklahoma District as of noon, April 22, 1889.

Preparations were feverish all along the frontier. "From all the West," historian Ray Allen Billington noted, "the homeless, the speculators, the adventurers, flocked to the still forbidden land." On the morning of April 22, nearly 100,000 people lined the Oklahoma borders; "for miles on end horsemen, wagons, hacks, carriages, bicycles, and a host of vehicles beggaring description stood wheel to wheel awaiting the signal." Fifteen Santa Fe trains were jammed with people from platform to roof.

At noon the starting flag dropped. Bugles and cannon signaled the opening of the "last" territory. Horsemen lunged forward, overloaded wagons collided and overturned. The trains steamed slowly forward, forced by army troops to keep a pace that would not give their passengers an undue advantage.

By sunset that day, settlers claimed 12,000 homesteads, and the 1,920,000 acres of the Oklahoma District were officially settled. Homesteaders threw up shelters for the night. By evening, Oklahoma City, that morning merely a spot on the prairie with cottonwoods and grass, had 10,000 people; Guthrie to the north had 15,000. Speculators swiftly erected pay toilets, and drinking water cost as much as a beer.

The "Boomers" and "Sooners"—those who had jumped the gun—reflected the speed of western settlement. "Creation!" a character in Edna Ferber's novel *Cimarron* declared. "Hell! That took six days. This was done in one. It was History made in an hour—and I helped make it."

Between the Civil War and 1900, the West witnessed one of the greatest migrations in history. With the Native Americans driven into smaller and smaller areas, farms, ranches, mines, and cities took over the vast lands from the Mississip-

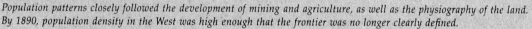

The Receding Frontier

Population patterns closely followed the development of mining and agriculture, as well as the physiography of the land. By 1890, population density in the West was high enough that the frontier was no longer clearly defined.

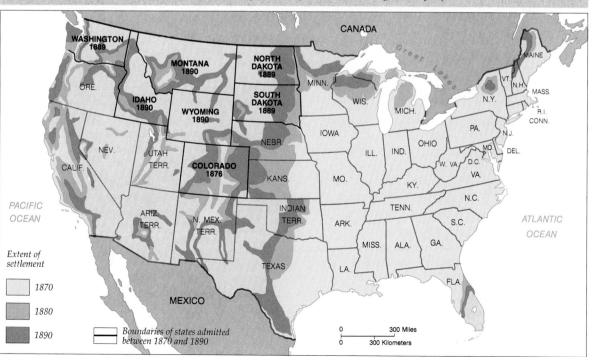

CHRONOLOGY

1849 Gold rush to California

1859 More gold and silver discoveries, in Colorado and Nevada

1862 Congress passes Homestead Act, encouraging western settlement

1864 Nevada admitted to the Union • Colonel John Chivington leads massacre of Indians at Sand Creek, Colorado

1865–1867 Sioux fight against white miners and U.S. army in Great Sioux War

1866 "Long drive" of cattle touches off cattle bonanzas

1867 Horace Greeley urges Easterners to "Go West, young man" • National Grange of the Patrons of Husbandry (the Grange) founded to enrich farmers' lives

1867–1868 Policy of "small reservations" for Indians adopted

1873 Congress passes Timber Culture Act • Big Bonanza discovered on the Comstock Lode in Nevada

1874 Joseph F. Glidden invents barbed wire • Discovery of gold in Dakota Territory sets off Black Hills Gold Rush

1876 Colorado admitted to the Union • Custer and his men defeated and killed by the Sioux at battle of Little Bighorn (June)

1883 Museum expedition discovers fewer than 200 buffalo in the West

1886–1887 Severe drought and winter damage cattle and farming bonanzas

1887 Congress passes Dawes Severalty Act, making Indians individual landowners • Hatch Act provides funds for establishment of agricultural experiment stations

1889 Washington, Montana, and the Dakotas admitted to the Union • Oklahoma Territory opened to settlement

1890 Idaho and Wyoming admitted to Union • Teton Sioux massacred at battle of Wounded Knee, South Dakota (December)

1893 Young historian Frederick Jackson Turner analyzes closing of the frontier

pi to the Pacific. The 1890 census noted that for the first time in the country's history, "there can hardly be said to be a frontier line." Picking up the theme, Frederick Jackson Turner, a young history instructor at the University of Wisconsin, examined its importance in an influential 1893 paper, "The Significance of the Frontier in American History."

"The existence of an area of free land," Turner wrote, "its continuous recession, and the advance of American settlement westward, explain American development." It shaped customs and character; gave rise to independence, self-confidence, and individualism; and fostered invention and adaptation. Historians have substantially modified Turner's thesis by pointing to frontier conservatism and imitativeness, the influence of varying racial groups, and the persistence of European ideas and institutions. Most recently, they have shown that family and community loomed as large as individualism on the frontier; men, women, and children played very much the same roles as they had back home. Yet there can be no doubt that the frontier and the West influenced American development.

Western lands attracted European, Latin American, and Asian immigrants, adding to the society's talent and diversity. The mines, forests, and farms of the West fueled the economy, sent raw materials to eastern factories, and fed the growing cities. Though defeated in warfare, Indian and Spanish influence persisted in art, architecture, law, and western folklore. The West was the first American empire, and it had a profound impact on the American mind and imagination.

Recommended Reading

The best general account of the movement west is Ray Allen Billington, *Westward Expansion* (1967), which also has a first-rate bibliography. See also Billington's *Land of Savagery, Land of Promise: The European Image of the American Frontier in the Nineteenth Century* (1981), and Frederick Merk, *History of the Westward Movement* (1978). Frederick Jackson Turner's influential interpretation of frontier development, "The Significance of the Frontier in American History," is in his *Frontier in American History* (1920). Walter Prescott Webb, *The Great Plains* (1931), offers a fascinating analysis of development on the Plains.

Howard R. Lamar, *The Far Southwest, 1846–1912* (1966), and Rodman W. Paul, *The Far West and the Great Plains in Transition, 1859–1900* (1988), are excellent surveys of the era. Paul gives a thorough survey of the mining bonanza in *Mining Frontiers of the Far West* (1963), while Fred A. Shannon provides similar coverage for agriculture in *The Farmer's Last Frontier* (1945). Lewis Atherton, *The Cattle Kings* (1961), and E. S. Osgood, *The Day of the Cattleman* (1929), cover the cattle industry. Louis B. Wright, *Culture on the Moving Frontier* (1955), argues that settlers did not give up books and other cultural assets as they moved West; Henry Nash Smith, *Virgin Land: The American West as Symbol and Myth* (1950) is superb on the literary images of the West in the nineteenth century. Patricia Nelson Limerick, *The Legacy of Conquest: The Unbroken Past of the American West* (1987), advances some important new interpretations.

Recent authors have taken fresh and stimulating looks at older or ignored questions. Robert R. Dykstra, *The Cattle Towns* (1968), examines five Kansas cattle towns, with interesting results. Gunther Barth traces the rapid rise of San Francisco and Denver in *Instant Cities* (1975), and Earl Pomeroy, *The Pacific Slope* (1965), looks at urban and other developments in the Far West. Julie Roy Jeffrey, *Frontier Women: The Trans-Mississippi West* (1979); Sandra L. Myres, *Westering Women and the Frontier Experience, 1880–1915* (1982); and Joanna L. Stratton, *Pioneer Women: Voices from the Kansas Frontier* (1981), are perceptive works on a neglected topic. John Mack Faragher, *Women and Men on the Overland Trail* (1979) and John Phillip Reid, *Law for the Elephant: Property and Social Behavior on the Overland Trail* (1980) examine social and other relationships on the trails west. Faragher's *Sugar Creek: Life on the Illinois Prairie* (1986), brilliantly explores the influence of community in western life.

Additional Bibliography

On the Native Americans, there are a number of valuable works, including William T. Hagan, *American Indians* (1961); Wilcomb E. Washburn, *The Indian in America* (1975); Russell Thornton, *American Indian Holocaust and Survival: A Population History since 1492* (1987); Frederick E. Hoxie, *A Final Promise: The Campaign to Assimilate the Indians* (1984); Robert Wooster, *The Military and United States Indian Policy, 1865–1903* (1988); Robert M. Utley, *The Last Days of the Sioux Nation* (1963), *Frontier Regulars: The United States Army and the Indian* (1973), and *The Indian Frontier of the American West, 1846–1890* (1984); Francis Paul Prucha, *American Indian Policy in Crisis* (1976); Robert A. Keller, Jr., *American Protestantism and United States Indian Policy, 1869–1882* (1983); and R. K. Andrist, *The Long Death: The Last Days of the Plains Indians* (1964). See also, Margaret Coel, *Chief Left Hand: Southern Arapaho* (1981); Loretta Fowler, *Arapahoe Politics, 1851–1978* (1982), and Albert L. Hurtado, *Indian Survival on the California Frontier* (1988). Helen Hunt Jackson, *A Century of Dishonor* (1881) is a stinging contemporary account.

Dwight W. Hoover, *The Red and the Black* (1976), and Leonard Dinnerstein, Roger L. Nichols, and David M. Reimers, *Natives and Strangers* (1979), contrast Indian policy with the treatment of other minorities. Leonard Pitt looks at *The Decline of the Californios: A Social History of the Spanish-Speaking Californians* (1966); Mario T. Garcia at the Mexican immigrants to El Paso in *Desert Immigrants* (1981);

and Gunther Barth at the treatment of the Chinese in *Bitter Strength* (1964). Also, Sucheng Chan, *This Bittersweet Soil: The Chinese in California Agriculture, 1860–1910* (1986); Sarah Deutsch, *No Separate Refuge: Culture, Class, and Gender on an Anglo-Hispanic Frontier in the American Southwest, 1880–1940* (1987); Richard Griswold del Castillo, *The Los Angeles Barrio, 1850–1890: A Social History* (1979); Albert Camarillo, *Chicanos in a Changing Society* (1979); and two studies by Arnoldo DeLeon, *The Tejano Community, 1836–1900* (1982), and *They Called Them Greasers: Anglo Attitudes Toward Mexicans in Texas* (1983).

George R. Stewart, *The California Trail* (1962) and John D. Unruh, Jr., *The Plains Across: The Overland Emigrants and the Trans-Mississippi West, 1840–1860* (1979) are good, but read some of the extraordinary diaries, including David M. Potter, ed., *The Trail to California* (1962) and Dale Morgan, ed., *Overland in 1846* (1963). A. B. Guthrie, Jr., *The Way West* (1949) is an excellent fictional account based on considerable research.

Books on the mining bonanza include Rodman W. Paul, *California Gold* (1948); Charles H. Shinn, *Mining Camps* (1885); William T. Jackson, *Treasure Hill: Portrait of a Silver Mining Camp* (1963); Odie B. Faulk, *Tombstone: Myth and Reality* (1972); D. A. Smith, *Rocky Mountain Mining Camps: The Urban Frontier* (1967); Dan DeQuille, *History of the Big Bonanza* (1876); Eliot Lord, *Comstock Mining and Miners* (1883); Joseph R. Conlin, *Bacon, Beans, and Galantines: Food and Foodways on the Western Mining Frontier* (1986); and Mark Twain, *Roughing It* (1872).

The best works on the cowboy are E. E. Dale, *Cow Country* (1942); Andy Adams, *The Log of a Cowboy* (1902); and J. B. Frantz and J. E. Choate, *The American Cowboy: The Myth and Reality* (1955). Ralph P. Bieber's edited version of Joseph G. McCoy, *Historic Sketches of the Cattle Trade of the West and the Southwest* (1940) is indispensable on the man who claimed to start the great herds north. Gene M. Gressley, *Bankers and Cattlemen* (1966), details outside investment in cattle. Roger D. McGrath, *Gunfighters, Highwaymen, and Vigilantes: Violence on the Frontier* (1984) is a recent study.

Nell Irvin Painter, *Exodusters: Black Migration to Kansas after Reconstruction* (1976), tells the story of the Exodusters. Federal land policy is surveyed in Roy M. Robbins, *Our Landed Heritage* (1942), and Paul Wallace Gates, *Fifty Million Acres* (1954). Valuable studies of farming include Gilbert C. Fite, *The Farmer's Frontier* (1966); Allan G. Bogue, *From Prairie to Corn Belt* (1963); Everett Dick, *The Sod-House Frontier* (1937); and H. M. Drache, *The Day of the Bonanza* (1964). Solon J. Buck, *The Granger Movement* (1913), studies early farm discontent and the Grange.

Patricia Nelson Limerick, *Desert Passages: Encounters with the American Deserts* (1985), examines how Americans have responded to the Great Plains. Ruth Moynihan, *Rebel for Rights: Abigail Scott Duniway* (1983), and Polly Welts Kaufman, *Women Teachers on the Frontier* (1984), examine the role of women in the West, while the impact of the West itself is treated in Vera Norwood and Janice Monk, eds., *The Desert Is No Lady: Southwestern Landscapes in Women's Writing and Art* (1987). Kathleen Underwood, *Town Building on the Colorado Frontier* (1987), is an informative study of the growth of one town.

CHAPTER 18

The Industrial Society

*I*n 1876, Americans celebrated their first century of independence. Survivors of a recent civil war, they observed the centenary proudly and rather self-consciously, in song and speech, and above all in a grand Centennial Exposition held in Philadelphia, Pennsylvania.

Spread over thirteen acres of land, the exposition focused more on the present than the past. Fairgoers strolled through exhibits of life in colonial times, then hurried off to see the main attractions: machines, inventions, and new products. They saw linoleum, a new, easy-to-clean floor covering. For the first time they tasted root beer, supplied by a young druggist named Charles Hires, and the rare banana, wrapped in foil and selling for a dime. They saw their first bicycle, an awkward high-wheeled contraption with solid tires.

A Japanese Pavilion generated widespread interest in the culture of Japan. There was also a Women's Building, the first ever in a major exposition. Inside were displayed paintings and sculpture by women artists, along with rows of textile machinery staffed by female operators.

In the entire exposition, machinery was the focus, and Machinery Hall was the most popular building. Here were the products of an ever-improving civilization. Long lines of the curious waited to see the telephone, Alexander Graham Bell's new device. ("My God, it talks!" the emperor of Brazil exclaimed.) Thomas A. Edison displayed several recent inventions, while nearby, whirring machines turned out bricks, chewing tobacco, and other products. Fairgoers saw the first public display of the typewriter, Elisha Otis's new elevator, and the Westinghouse railroad air brake.

But above all, they crowded around the mighty Corliss engine, the focal point of the exposition. A giant steam engine, it dwarfed everything in Machinery Hall, its twin vertical cylinders towering almost four stories in the air. Alone, it supplied power for the eight thousand other machines, large and small, on the exposition grounds. Poorly designed, the Corliss was soon obsolete, but for the moment it captured the nation's imagination. It symbolized swift movement toward an industrial and urban society. John Greenleaf Whittier, the aging rural poet, likened it to the snake in the Garden of Eden and refused to see it.

As Whittier feared, the United States was fast becoming an industrial society. Developments earlier in the century laid the basis, but the most spectacular advances in industrialization came during the three decades after the Civil War. At the start of the war, the country lagged well behind industrializing nations such as Great Britain, France, and Germany. By 1900, it had vaulted far into the lead, with a manufacturing output that exceeded the *combined* output of its three European rivals. Over the same years, cities grew, technology advanced, and farm production rose. Developments in manufacturing, mining, agriculture, transportation, and communication changed society.

Many Americans eagerly sought the change. William Dean Howells, a leading novelist, visited the Centennial Exposition and stood in awe be-

*T*he Corliss engine, a "mechanical marvel" at the Centennial Exposition, was a prime example of the giantism so admired by the public.

fore the Corliss. Comparing it to the paintings and sculpture on display, Howells preferred the machine: "It is in these things of iron and steel," he said, "that the national genius most freely speaks."

INDUSTRIAL DEVELOPMENT

American industry owed its remarkable growth to several considerations. It fed on an abundance of natural resources: coal, iron, timber, petroleum, waterpower. An iron manufacturer likened the nation to "a gigantic bowl filled with treasure." Labor was also abundant, drawn from American farm families and the hosts of European immigrants who flocked to American mines, cities, and factories. Nearly 8 million immigrants arrived in the 1870s and 1880s; another 15 million came between 1890 and 1914—large figures for a nation whose total population in 1900 was about 76 million people.

The burgeoning population led to expanded markets, which new devices like the telegraph and telephone helped to exploit. The swiftly growing urban populations devoured goods, and the railroads, spreading pell-mell across the land, linked the cities together and opened a national market. Within its boundaries, the United States had the largest free-trade market in the world, while tariff barriers partially protected its producers from outside competition.

Expansive market and labor conditions buoyed the confidence of investors, European and American, who provided large amounts of capital. Technological progress, so remarkable in these years, doomed some older industries (tallow, for example) but increased productivity in others, such as the kerosene industry, and created entirely new industries as well. Through inventions like the harvester and the combine, it also helped foster a firm agricultural base, on which industrialization depended.

Eager to promote economic growth, government at all levels—federal, state, and local—gave manufacturers money, land, and other resources. Other benefits, too, flowed from the American system of government: stability, commitment to the concept of private property, and initially at least, a reluctance to regulate industrial activity. Unlike their European counterparts, American manufacturers faced few legal or social barriers,

and their main domestic rivals, the southern planters, had lost political power in the Civil War.

In this atmosphere, entrepreneurs flourished. Taking steps crucial for industrialization, they organized, managed, and assumed the financial risks of the new enterprises. Admirers called them "captains of industry"; foes labeled them "robber barons." To some degree, they were both—creative *and* acquisitive. If sometimes they seemed larger than life, it was because they dealt in concepts, distances, and quantities often unknown to earlier generations.

Industrial growth, it must be remembered, was neither a simple nor steady nor inevitable process. It involved human decisions and brought with it large social benefits and costs. Growth varied from industry to industry and from year to year. It was concentrated in the Northeast, where in 1890, more than 85 percent of America's manufactured goods originated. The more sparsely settled West provided raw materials, while the South, although making major gains in iron, textiles, and tobacco, had to rebuild after wartime devastation. In 1890, the industrial production of the entire South amounted in value to about half that of the state of New York.

Still, industrial development proceeded at an extraordinary pace. Between 1865 and 1914, the real Gross National Product (GNP)–the total monetary value of all goods and services produced in a year, with prices held stable—grew at a rate of more than 4 percent a year, increasing about eightfold overall. As Robert Higgs, an economic historian, noted: "Never before had such rapid growth continued for so long."

AN EMPIRE ON RAILS

Genuine revolutions happen rarely, but a major one occurred in the nineteenth century: a revolution in transportation and communications. When the nineteenth century began, people traveled and communicated much as they had for centuries before; when it ended, the railroad, the telegraph, the telephone, and the ocean-going steamship had wrought enormous changes.

The steamship sliced in half the time of the Atlantic crossing and, not dependent on wind and tide, introduced new regularity in the movement of goods and passengers. The telegraph, flashing messages almost instantaneously along

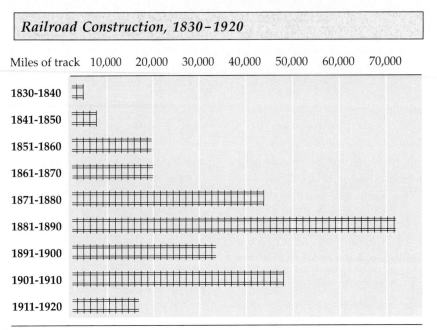

Railroad Construction, 1830–1920

Miles of track	10,000	20,000	30,000	40,000	50,000	60,000	70,000
1830-1840							
1841-1850							
1851-1860							
1861-1870							
1871-1880							
1881-1890							
1891-1900							
1901-1910							
1911-1920							

Source: U.S. Bureau of the Census. Historical Statistics of the United States, Colonial Times to 1970, *Bicentennial Edition, Washington, D.C., 1975.*

miles of wire (400,000 miles of it in the early 1880s), transformed communications, as did the telephone a little later. But the railroad worked the largest changes of all. Along with Bessemer steel, it was the most significant technical innovation of the century.

"Emblem of Motion and Power"

The railroad dramatically affected economic and social life. Economic growth would have occurred without it, of course; canals, inland steamboats, and the country's superb system of interior waterways already provided the outlines of an effective transportation network. But the railroad added significantly to the network and contributed advantages all its own.

Those advantages included more direct routes, greater speed, greater safety and comfort than other modes of land travel, more dependable schedules, a larger volume of traffic, and year-round service. A day's land travel on stagecoach or horseback might cover 50 miles. The railroad covered 50 miles in about an hour, 700 miles in a day. It went where canals and rivers did not go—directly to the loading platforms of great factories or across the arid West. As construction crews pushed tracks onward, vast areas of the continent opened for settlement.

Consequently, American railroads differed from European ones. In Europe, railroads were usually built between cities and towns that already existed; they carried mostly the same goods that earlier forms of transportation had. In the United States, they did that and more: they often created the very towns they then served, and they wound up carrying cattle from Texas, fruit from Florida, and other goods that had never been carried before.

Linking widely separated cities and villages, the railroad ended the relative isolation and self-sufficiency of the country's "island communities." It tied people together, brought in outside products, fostered greater interdependence, and encouraged economic specialization. Under its stimulus, Chicago supplied meat to the nation; Minneapolis supplied grain, and Saint Louis, beer. For these and other communities, the railroad made possible a national market and in so doing pointed the way toward mass production and mass consumption, two of the hallmarks of twentieth-century society.

It also pointed the way toward later business

development. The railroad, as Alfred D. Chandler, the historian of business, has written, was "the nation's first big business"; it worked out "the modern ways of finance, management, labor relations, competition, and government regulation."

A railroad corporation, far-flung and complex, was a new kind of business. It stretched over thousands of miles, employed thousands of people, dealt with countless customers, and required a scale of organization and decision making unknown in earlier business. Railroad managers never met most customers or even many employees; thus arose new problems in marketing and labor relations. Year by year, railroad companies consumed large quantities of iron, steel, coal, lumber, and glass, stimulating growth and employment in numerous industries.

No wonder, then, that the railroad captured so completely the country's imagination. Walt Whitman, the poet who celebrated American achievement, chanted the locomotive's praises:

Thy black cylindric body, golden brass and silvery steel . . .
Thy great protruding head-light fix'd in front,
Thy long, pale, floating vapor-pennants, tinged with delicate purple . . .
Thy knitted frame, thy springs and valves, the tremulous twinkle of thy wheels,
Thy train of cars behind, obedient, merrily following . . .
Type of the modern—emblem of motion and power —pulse of the continent . . .
Fierce-throated beauty!

For nearly a hundred years—the railroad era lasted through the 1940s—children gathered at depots, paused in the fields to wave as the fast express flashed by, listened at night to far-off whistles, and wondered what lay down the tracks. They lived in a world grown smaller.

Building the Empire

When Lee surrendered at Appomattox in 1865, the country already had 35,000 miles of track, and much of the railroad system east of the Mississippi River was in place (see Chapter 12). Farther west, the rail network stood poised on the edge of settlement. Although southern railroads were in shambles from the war, the United States had nearly as much railroad track as the rest of the world.

After the Civil War, rail construction increased by leaps and bounds. From 35,000 miles in 1865, the network expanded to 93,000 miles in 1880; 166,000 in 1890; and 193,000 in 1900—more than in all Europe including Russia. Mileage peaked at 254,037 miles in 1916, just before the industry began its long decline into the mid-twentieth century.

To build such an empire took vast amounts of capital—over $4.5 billion by 1880, before even half of it was complete. American and European investors provided some of the money; government supplied the rest. In all, local governments gave railroad companies about $300 million, and state governments added $228 million more. The federal government loaned nearly $65 million to a half dozen western railroads and donated millions of acres of the public domain. Between 1850 and 1871, some 80 railroads received more than 170 million acres of land.

Almost 90 percent of the federal land grants lay in twenty states west of the Mississippi River. Federal land grants helped build 18,738 miles of track, less than 8 percent of the system. The land was frequently distant and difficult to market. Railroad companies sometimes sold it to raise cash, but more often used it as security for bonds or loans.

Beyond doubt, the grants of cash and land promoted waste and corruption. The companies built fast and wastefully, eager to collect the subsidies that went with each mile of track. Wanting quick profits, some owners formed separate construction companies to which they awarded lavish contracts. In this way the notorious Crédit Mobilier, a construction company controlled by an inner ring on the Union Pacific, enriched its owners in the 1860s, while the Contract and Finance Company did the same on the Central Pacific. The Crédit Mobilier bribed congressmen and state legislators in order to avoid congressional investigation of its activities (see Chapter 16). The grants also enabled railroads to build into territories that were pledged to the Indians, thus contributing to the wanton destruction of Indian life.

Yet, on balance, the grants probably worked more benefits than evils. As Congress had hoped,

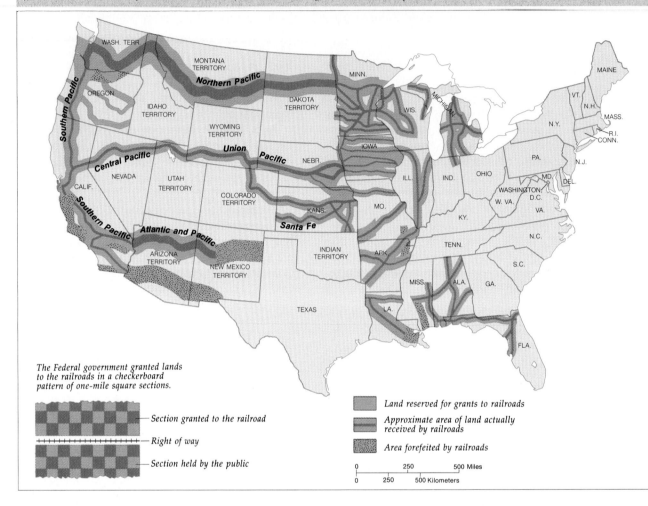

Federal Land Grants to Railroads as of 1871

Besides land, the government provided loans of $16,000 for each mile built on level land, $32,000 for each mile built on hilly terrain, and $48,000 for each mile in high mountain country.

The Federal government granted lands to the railroads in a checkerboard pattern of one-mile square sections.

— Section granted to the railroad

— Right of way

— Section held by the public

Land reserved for grants to railroads

Approximate area of land actually received by railroads

Area forfeited by railroads

the grants were the lure for railroad building across the rugged, unsettled West, where it would be years before the railroads' revenues would repay their construction. Farmers, ranchers, and merchants poured into the newly opened areas, settling the country and boosting the value of government and private land nearby. The grants seemed necessary in a nation which, unlike Europe, expected private enterprise to build the railroads. In return for government aid, Congress required the railroads to carry government freight, troops, and mail at substantially reduced rates—resulting in savings to the government of almost $1 billion between 1850 and 1945. In no other cases of federal subsidies to carriers—canals, highways, and airlines—did Congress exact specific benefits in return.

Linking the Nation via Trunk Lines

The early railroads may seem to have linked different regions, but in fact they did not. Built with little regard for through traffic, they were designed more to protect local interests than to tap outside markets. Many extended fewer than fifty miles. To avoid cooperating with other lines, they adopted conflicting schedules, built separate depots, and above all, used different gauges. Gauges, the distance between the rails, ranged from 4 feet 8½ inches, which became the standard gauge, to 6 feet. Without special equipment, trains of one gauge could not run on tracks of another.

The Civil War showed the value of fast long-distance transportation, and after 1865, railroad managers worked to provide it. In a burst of consolidation, the large companies swallowed the small; integrated rail networks became a reality. Railroads also adopted standard schedules, signals, equipment, and finally in 1886, the standard gauge. In 1866, in a dramatic innovation to speed traffic, railroad companies introduced fast freight lines that pooled cars for service between cities.

In the Northeast, four great trunk lines took shape, all intended to link eastern seaports with the rich traffic of the Great Lakes and western rivers. Like a massive river system, trunk lines drew traffic from dozens of tributaries (feeder lines) and carried it to major markets. The Baltimore and Ohio (B & O), which reached Chicago in 1874, was one; the Erie Railroad, which ran from New York to Chicago, was another. The Erie competed bitterly with the New York Central

Railroad, the third trunk line, and its owner, Cornelius Vanderbilt—the ''Commodore''—a crusty old multimillionaire from the shipping business.

Nearly seventy years old when he first entered railroading, Vanderbilt wasted no time. In 1867, he took over the New York Central and merged it with other lines to provide a track from New York City to Buffalo and Chicago. When he died in 1877, his Central operated over 4500 miles of track.

J. Edgar Thomson and Thomas A. Scott built the fourth trunk line, the Pennsylvania Railroad, which initially ran from Philadelphia to Pittsburgh. Restless and energetic, they dreamed of a rail empire stretching through the South and West. A brilliant business leader, Scott expanded the Pennsylvania system to Cincinnati, Indianapolis, Saint Louis, and Chicago in 1869, New York City in 1871, and Baltimore and Washington soon thereafter.

In the war-damaged South, consolidation took longer. As Reconstruction waned, northern and European capital rebuilt and integrated the southern lines, especially during the 1880s, when rail construction in the South led the nation. By 1900, the South had five large systems linking its

This poster advertised the Erie Railroad as a great trunk line, renowned for its "double-tracked steel rails, scenic route, and well appointed passenger cars, equipped with the celebrated Pullman hotel, drawing room and sleeping coaches."

major cities and farming and industrial regions. Four decades after the secession crisis, these systems tied the South into a national transportation network.

Over that rail system, passengers and freight moved in relative speed, comfort, and safety. Automatic couplers (1868), air brakes (1869), refrigerator cars (1867), dining cars, heated cars, electric switches, and stronger locomotives transformed railroad service. George Pullman's lavish sleeping cars became popular. Handsome depots, like New York's Grand Central and Washington's Union Station, were erected at major terminals. Passenger miles per year increased from 5 billion in 1870 to 16 billion in 1900.

In November 1883, the railroads even changed time. Ending the crazy quilt jumble of local times that caused scheduling difficulties, the American Railway Association divided the country into four time zones and adopted the modern system of standard time. Congress took thirty-five years longer; it adopted standard time in 1918, in the midst of World War I.

Rails across the Continent

The dream of a transcontinental railroad, linking the Atlantic and Pacific oceans, stretched back many years but had always been lost to sectional quarrels over the route. In 1862 and 1864, with the South out of the picture, Congress moved to build the first transcontinental. It chartered the Union Pacific Railroad Company to build westward from Nebraska and the Central Pacific Railroad Company to build eastward from the Pacific Coast. For each mile built, the two companies received from Congress twenty square miles of land in alternate sections along the track. For each mile, they also received a thirty-year loan of $16,000, $32,000, or $48,000, depending on the difficulty of the terrain over which they built.

Construction began simultaneously at Omaha and Sacramento in 1863, lagged during the war, and moved vigorously ahead after 1865. It became a race, each company vying for land, loans, and potential markets. General Grenville M. Dodge, a tough Union army veteran, served as construction chief for the Union Pacific, while Charles Crocker, a former Sacramento dry-goods merchant, led the Central Pacific crews. Dodge

organized an army of ten thousand workers, many of them ex-soldiers and Irish immigrants. Pushing rapidly westward, he encountered frequent attacks from Native Americans defending their lands, but had the advantage of building over flat prairie.

Crocker faced more trying conditions in the high Sierra Nevada along California's eastern border. After several experiments he decided that Chinese laborers worked best, and he hired six thousand of them, most brought directly from China. "I built the Central Pacific," Crocker enjoyed boasting, but the Chinese crews in fact did the awesome work. Under the most difficult conditions they dug, blasted, and pushed their way slowly east.

On May 10, 1869, the two lines met at Promontory, Utah, near the northern tip of the Great Salt Lake. Dodge's crews had built 1086 miles of track, Crocker's 689. The Union Pacific and Central Pacific presidents hammered in a golden spike (both missed it on the first try), and the dreamed-of connection was made. The telegraph flashed the news east and west, setting off wild celebrations. A photograph was taken, but it included none of the Chinese who had worked so hard to build the road; they were all asked to step aside.

The transcontinental railroad symbolized American unity and progress. Along with the Suez Canal, completed the same year, it helped knit the world together. Bret Harte, the exuberant poet of the West, wrote of Promontory:

What was it the Engines said,
Pilots touching,—head to head
Facing on the single track,
Half a world behind each back?

In the next twenty-five years, four more railroads reached the coast: the Northern Pacific (completed in 1883), running from Minnesota to Oregon; the Atchison, Topeka, and Santa Fe (1883), connecting Kansas City and Los Angeles; the powerful Southern Pacific (1883), running from San Francisco and Los Angeles to New Orleans; and James J. Hill's superbly built Great Northern Railway (1893), running from Minneapolis-Saint Paul to Seattle, Washington.

By the 1890s, business leaders talked comfortably of railroad systems stretching deep into South America and across the Bering Strait to

*A*fter the last spike was hammered in at Promontory, the pilots of the two locomotives touched and exchanged champagne toasts. The chief engineers of the two lines are seen shaking hands.

Asia, Europe, and Africa. In an age of progress, anything seemed possible. "The American," said the *Chicago Tribune*, "intelligent and self-reliant, has banished forever the impossible from his philosophy."

Problems of Growth

Overbuilding during the 1870s and '80s caused serious problems for the railroads. Lines paralleled each other, and where they did not, speculators such as Jay Gould often laid one down to force a rival line to buy it at inflated prices. While many managers worked to improve service, Gould and others bought and sold railroads like toys, watered their stock, and milked their assets. By 1885, almost one-third of railroad stock represented "water," that is, stock distributed in excess of the real value of the assets.

Competition was severe, and managers fought desperately for traffic. They offered special rates and favors: free passes for large shippers; low rates on bulk freight, carload lots, and long hauls;

and above all, rebates—secret, privately negotiated reductions below published rates. Fierce rate wars broke out frequently, convincing managers that ruthless competition helped no one. Rebates made more enemies than friends.

Managers like Albert Fink, the brilliant vice-president of the Louisville & Nashville, tried first to arrange pooling agreements, a way to control competition by sharing traffic. Fink directed the Eastern Trunk Line Association (1877), which divided westbound traffic among the four trunk lines. Similar associations pooled traffic in the South and West, but none survived the intense pressures of competition. Legally unenforceable, pools were handshake agreements among individuals who did not always keep their word. Customers grew adept at bargaining for rebates and other privileges, and railroads rarely felt able to refuse them. In the first six months of 1880, the New York Central alone granted six thousand special rates.

Failing to cooperate, railroad owners next tried to consolidate. Through purchase, lease, and merger, they gobbled up competitors and built

J.P. Morgan was a dominant figure in steel and shipping as well as in railroads. This 1902 cartoon, hostile toward his control of these industries, labels him "Alexander the Great," looking for more worlds to conquer.

"self-sustaining systems" that dominated entire regions. But many of these systems, expensive and unwieldy, collapsed in the panic of 1893. By mid-1894, a quarter of the railroads were bankrupt. The victims of the panic included such legendary names as the Erie, B & O, Santa Fe, Northern Pacific, and Union Pacific.

Needing money, railroads turned naturally to bankers, who finally imposed order on the industry. J. Pierpont Morgan, head of the New York investment house of J. P. Morgan and Company, took the lead. Massively built, with eyes so piercing they seemed like the headlights of an onrushing train, Morgan was the most powerful figure in American finance. He liked efficiency, combination, and order. He disliked "wasteful" competition. In 1885, during a bruising rate war between the New York Central and the Pennsylvania, Morgan invited the combatants to a conference aboard his palatial steam yacht, *Corsair*. Cruising on Long Island Sound, he arranged a traffic-sharing agreement and collected a million-dollar fee. Bringing peace to an industry could be profitable. It also satisfied Morgan's passion for stability.

After 1893, Morgan and a few other bankers refinanced ailing railroads, and in the process they took control of the industry. Their methods were direct: fixed costs and debt were ruthlessly cut; new stock was issued to provide capital; rates were stabilized; rebates and competition were eliminated; and control was vested in a "voting trust" of hand-picked trustees. Between 1894 and 1898, Morgan reorganized—critics said "Morganized"—the Southern Railway, the Erie, the Northern Pacific, and the B & O. In addition, he took over a half dozen other important railroads. By 1900, he was a dominant figure in American railroading.

As the new century began, the railroads had pioneered the patterns followed by most other industries. Seven giant systems controlled nearly two-thirds of the mileage, and they in turn answered to a few investment banking firms like the house of Morgan. For good and ill, a national transportation network, centralized and relatively efficient, was now in place.

AN INDUSTRIAL EMPIRE

The new industrial empire was based on steel as well as on railroads. Harder and more durable than other kinds of iron, steel wrought changes in manufacturing, agriculture, transportation, and architecture. It permitted longer bridges, taller buildings, stronger railroad track, newer weapons, better plows, heavier machinery, and faster ships. Made in great furnaces by strong men, it symbolized the tough, often brutal nature of industrial society. From the 1870s onward, steel output became the worldwide accepted measure of industrial progress, and nations around the globe vied for leadership.

The Bessemer process, developed in the late 1850s by Henry Bessemer in England and independently by William Kelly in the United States, made greater steel production possible. Both Bessemer and Kelly discovered that a blast of air forced through molten iron burned off carbon and other impurities, resulting in steel of a more uniform and durable quality. The discovery transformed the industry. While earlier methods produced amounts a person could lift, a Bessemer converter handled five tons of molten metal at a time. The mass production of steel was now possible.

Carnegie and Steel

Bessemer plants demanded extensive capital investment, abundant raw materials, and sophisticated production techniques. Using chemical and other processes, they required research departments, which became critical components of later American industries. Costly to build, they limited entry into the industry to the handful who could afford them.

Great steel districts arose in Pennsylvania, Ohio, and Alabama—in each case around large coal deposits that fueled the huge furnaces. Pittsburgh became the center of the industry, its giant mills employing thousands of workers. Output shot up. In 1874, the United States produced less than half the pig iron produced in Great Britain. By 1890, it took the lead, and in 1900, it produced four times as much as Britain.

Iron ore abounded in the fabulous deposits near Lake Superior, the greatest deposits in the world. In the mines of the Mesabi Range in Minnesota, giant steam shovels loaded ore onto railroad cars for transport to ships on the Great Lakes. Powered lifts, self-loading devices, and other innovations sped the process. "By the turn of the century," historian Peter Temin noted, "the transport of Lake ores had become an intricate ballet of large and complex machines."

Like the railroads, steel companies grew larger and larger. In 1880, only nine companies could produce more than 100,000 tons a year. By the early 1890s, several companies exceeded 250,000 tons, and two—including the great Carnegie Steel Company—produced over 1 million tons a year. As operations expanded, managers needed greater skills. Product development, marketing, and consumer preferences became important. Competition was fierce, and steel companies, like the railroads, tried secret agreements, pools, and consolidation. During the 1880s and '90s, they moved toward vertical integration, a type of organization in which a single company owns and controls the entire process from the unearthing of the raw materials to the manufacture and sale of the finished product. Such companies combined coal and iron mines, transportation companies, blast furnaces, and rolling mills into integrated networks.

Andrew Carnegie emerged as the undisputed master of the industry. Born in Scotland, he came to the United States in 1848 at the age of twelve. Settling near Pittsburgh, he went to work as a bobbin boy in a cotton mill, earning $1.20 a week. He soon took a job in a telegraph office, where in 1852 his hard work and skill caught the eye of Thomas A. Scott of the Pennsylvania Railroad. Starting as Scott's personal telegrapher, Carnegie spent a total of twelve years on the Pennsylvania, a training ground for company managers. By 1859, he had become a divisional superintendent. He was twenty-four.

Soon rich from shrewd investments, Carnegie plunged into the steel industry in 1872. On the Monongahela River south of Pittsburgh he built the giant J. Edgar Thomson Steel Works, named after the president of the Pennsylvania Railroad, his biggest customer. With his warmth and salesmanship, he attracted able partners and subordinates such as Henry Clay Frick and Charles M. Schwab, whom he drove hard and paid well. Although he had written magazine articles defending the rights of workers, Carnegie kept the wages of the laborers in his mills low, disliked unions, and, with the help of Frick, crushed a violent strike at his Homestead works in 1892 (see p. 549).

In 1878, he won the steel contract for the Brooklyn Bridge. During the next decade, as city

Of all the great industrial tycoons, Carnegie best combined intelligence, luck, and personal charm.

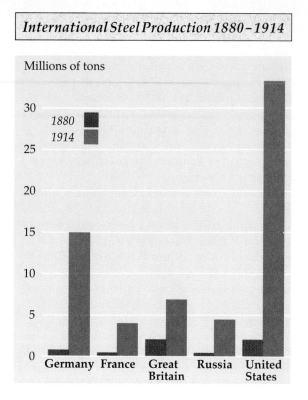

International Steel Production 1880–1914

Millions of tons

- 1880
- 1914

(Germany, France, Great Britain, Russia, United States)

Drawing other companies into the combination, Morgan on March 3, 1901, announced the creation of the United States Steel Corporation. The new firm was capitalized at $1.4 billion, the first billion-dollar company. It absorbed over 200 other companies, employed 168,000 people, and produced 9 million tons of iron and steel a year. It controlled three-fifths of the country's steel business. Soon there were other giants, including Bethlehem Steel, Republic Steel, and National Steel. As the nineteenth century ended, steel products—rare just thirty years before—had altered the landscape. Huge firms, investment bankers, and professional managers dominated the industry.

Rockefeller and Oil

Petroleum worked comparable changes in the economic and social landscape, although mostly after 1900. Distilled into oil, it lubricated the machinery of the industrial age. There seemed little use for gasoline (the internal combustion engine had only just been developed), but kerosene, another major distillate, brought inexpensive illumination into almost every home. Whale oil, cottonseed oil, and even tallow candles were expensive to burn; consequently, many people went to bed at nightfall. Kerosene lamps opened the evenings to activity, which altered the patterns of life.

Like other changes in these years, the oil boom happened with surprising speed. In the mid-1850s, petroleum was a bothersome, smelly fluid that occasionally rose to the surface of springs and streams. Clever entrepreneurs bottled it in patent medicines; a few scooped up enough to burn. Other entrepreneurs soon found that drilling reached pockets of oil beneath the earth. In 1859, Edwin L. Drake drilled the first oil well near Titusville in northwest Pennsylvania, and the "black gold" fever struck. Chemists soon discovered ways to transform petroleum into lubricating oil, grease, paint, wax, varnish, naphtha, and paraffin. Within a few years, there was a world market in oil.

At first, growth of the oil industry was chaotic. Early drillers and refiners produced for local markets, and since drilling wells and even erecting refineries cost little, competition flourished. Output fluctuated dramatically; prices rose and

building boomed, he converted the huge Homestead works near Pittsburgh to the manufacture of structural beams and angles, which went into the New York City elevated railway, the first skyscrapers, and the Washington Monument. Carnegie profits mounted: from $2 million in 1888 to $40 million in 1900. That year, Carnegie Steel alone produced more steel than Great Britain. Employing twenty thousand people, it was the largest industrial company in the world.

In 1901, Carnegie sold it. Believing that wealth brought social obligations, he wanted to devote his full time to philanthropy. He found a buyer in J. Pierpont Morgan, who in the late 1890s had put together several steel companies, including Federal Steel, Carnegie's chief rival. Carnegie Steel had blocked Morgan's well-known desire for control, and in mid-1900, when a war loomed between the two interests, Morgan decided to buy Carnegie out. In early January 1901, Morgan told Charles M. Schwab: "Go and find his price." Schwab cornered Carnegie on the golf course, Carnegie listened, and the next day handed Schwab a note, scribbled in blunt pencil, asking almost a half billion dollars. Morgan glanced at it and said: "I accept this price."

fell with devastating effect. Refineries—usually a collection of wooden shacks and tanks—were centered in Cleveland and Pittsburgh, near the original oil-producing regions.

A young merchant from Cleveland named John D. Rockefeller imposed order on the industry. "I had an ambition to build," he later recalled, and beginning in 1863, at the age of twenty-four, he built the Standard Oil Company, soon to become one of the titans of corporate business. Like Morgan, Rockefeller considered competition wasteful, small-scale enterprise inefficient, and consolidation the path of the future. Consolidation "revolutionized the way of doing business all over the world," he said. "The time was ripe for it. It had to come, though all we saw at the moment was the need to save ourselves from wasteful conditions."

Methodically, Rockefeller absorbed or destroyed competitors in Cleveland and elsewhere. As ruthless in his methods as Carnegie, he lacked the steel master's spontaneous charm. He was distant and taciturn, a man of deep religious beliefs who taught Bible classes at Cleveland's Erie Street Baptist Church. Like Carnegie, he demanded efficiency, relentless cost-cutting, and the latest technology. He attracted exceptional lieutenants—although, as one said, he could see further ahead than any of them, "and then see around the corner."

"Nothing in haste, nothing ill-done," Rockefeller often said to himself. "Your future hangs on every day that passes." Paying careful attention to detail, he counted the stoppers in barrels, shortened barrel hoops to save metal, and in one famous incident, reduced the number of drops of solder on kerosene cans from forty to thirty-nine. In large-scale production, Rockefeller realized, even small reductions meant huge savings. Research uncovered other ways of lowering costs and improving products, and Herman Frasch, a brilliant Standard chemist, solved problem after problem in the refining of oil.

In the end, Rockefeller triumphed over his competitors by marketing products of high quality at the lowest unit cost. But he employed other, less savory methods as well. He threatened rivals and bribed politicians. He employed spies to harass the customers of competing refiners. Above all, he extorted railroad rebates which lowered his transportation costs and undercut competitors. By 1879, he controlled 90 percent of

John D. Rockefeller, satirized in a 1901 Puck *cartoon, is enthroned on oil, the base of his empire; his crown is girded by other holdings.*

the country's entire oil-refining capacity.

Vertically integrated, Standard Oil owned wells, timberlands, barrel and chemical plants, refineries, warehouses, pipelines, and fleets of tankers and oil cars. Its marketing organization served as the model for the industry. Standard exported oil to Asia, Africa, and South America; and its five-gallon kerosene tin, like Coca-Cola bottles and cans during a later era, was a familiar sight in the most distant parts of the world.

To manage it all, the company developed a new plan of business organization, the trust, which had profound significance for American business. In 1881, Samuel T. C. Dodd, Standard's attorney, set up the Standard Oil Trust, with a board of nine trustees empowered "to hold, control, and manage" all Standard's properties. Stockholders exchanged their stock for trust certificates, on which dividends were paid. On January 2, 1882, the first of the modern trusts was born. As Dodd intended, it immediately centralized control of Standard's far-flung empire.

Competition had almost disappeared; profits soared. A trust movement swept the country, as industries with similar problems—whiskey, lead, and sugar, among others—followed Standard's example. The word *trust* became synonymous with monopoly, amid vehement protests from the public. *Antitrust* became a watchword for a generation of reformers from the 1880s through the era of Woodrow Wilson. But Rockefeller's purpose had been *management* of a monopoly, not monopoly itself, which he had already achieved.

During the 1890s, Rockefeller helped pioneer another form of industrial consolidation, the holding company. Taking advantage of an 1889 New Jersey law that allowed companies to purchase other companies, he moved Standard Oil to New Jersey and bought up his own subsidiaries to form a holding company. The trust, he had learned, was somewhat cumbersome, and it was under attack in Congress and the courts. Holding companies offered the next step in industrial management. They were simply large-scale mergers, in which a central corporate organization purchased the stock of the member companies and established direct, formal control.

Other companies followed suit, including American Sugar Refining, the Northern Securities Company, and the National Biscuit Company. (See Chapter 23 for further discussion of Northern Securities.) Merger followed merger. By 1900, 1 percent of the nation's companies controlled more than one-third of its industrial production. A decade later, a congressional investigation showed that two individuals, Rockefeller and Morgan, between them controlled businesses worth more than $22 billion.

In 1897, Rockefeller retired with a fortune of nearly $900 million, but for Standard Oil and petroleum in general, the most expansive period was yet to come. The great oil pools of Texas and Oklahoma had not yet been discovered. Plastics and other oil-based synthetics were several decades in the future. There were only four usable automobiles in the country, and the day of the gasoline engine, automobile, and airplane lay just ahead.

The Business of Invention

"America has become known the world around as the home of invention," boasted the Commissioner of Patents in 1892. It had not always been so; until the last third of the nineteenth century, the country had imported most of its technology. Then an extraordinary group of inventors and tinkerers—"specialists in invention," Thomas A. Edison called them—began to study the world around them. Some of their inventions gave rise to new industries; a few actually changed the quality of life.

The number of patents issued to inventors reflected the trend. During the 1850s, fewer than 2000 patents were issued each year. By the 1880s and '90s, the figure reached more than 20,000 a year. Between 1790 and 1860, the Patent Office issued just 36,000 patents; in the decade of the 1890s alone, it issued more than 200,000.

Some of the inventions transformed communications. In 1866, Cyrus W. Field improved the transatlantic cable linking the telegraph networks of Europe and the United States. By the early 1870s, land and submarine cables ran to Brazil, Japan, and the China coast; in the next two decades, they reached Africa and spread across South America. Diplomats and business leaders could now "talk" to their counterparts in Berlin or Hong Kong. Even before the telephone, the cables quickened the pace of foreign affairs, revolutionized journalism, and allowed businesses to expand and centralize.

The typewriter (1867), stock ticker (1867), cash register (1879), calculating machine (1887), and adding machine (1888) helped business transactions. High-speed spindles, automatic looms, and electric sewing machines transformed the clothing industry, which for the first time in history turned out ready-made clothes for the masses. In 1890, the Census Bureau first used machines to sort and tabulate data on punched cards, a portent of a new era of information storage and treatment.

In 1879, George Eastman patented a process for coating gelatine on photographic dry plates, which led to celluloid film and motion pictures. By 1888, he was marketing the Kodak camera, which weighed 35 ounces, took 100 exposures, and cost $25. Even though early Kodaks had to be returned to the factory, camera and all, for film

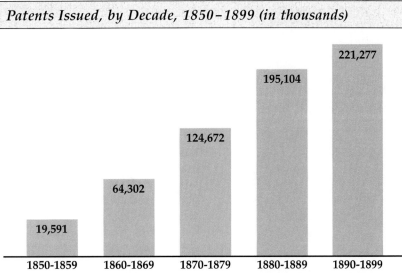

Source: U.S. Bureau of the Census. Historical Statistics of the United States, Colonial Times to 1970, Bicentennial Edition, Washington, D.C., 1975.

developing, they revolutionized photography. Now almost anyone could snap a picture.

Other innovations changed the diet. There were new processes for flour, canned meat, vegetables, condensed milk, and even beer (from an offshoot of Louis Pasteur's discoveries about bacteria). Packaged cereals appeared on breakfast tables. Refrigerated railroad cars, ice-cooled, brought fresh fruit from Florida and California to all parts of the country. In the 1870s, Gustavus F. Swift, a Chicago meatpacker, hit on the idea of using the cars to distribute meat nationwide. Setting up "dissembly" factories to butcher meat (Henry Ford later copied them for his famous "assembly" lines), he started an "era of cheap beef," as a newspaper said.

No innovation, however, rivaled the importance of the telephone and the use of electricity for light and power. The telephone was the work of Alexander Graham Bell, a shrewd and genial Scotsman who settled in Boston in 1871. Interested in the problems of the deaf, Bell experimented with ways to transmit speech electrically, and after several years developed electrified metal disks that, much like the human ear, converted sound waves to electrical impulses and back again. On March 10, 1876, he transmitted the first sentence over a telephone: "Mr. Watson, come here; I want you." Later that year, he exhibited the new device to excited crowds at the Centennial Exposition in Philadelphia.

In 1878—the year a telephone was installed in the White House—the first telephone exchange opened in New Haven, Connecticut. Fighting off competitors who challenged the patent, the young Bell Telephone Company dominated the growing industry. By 1895, there were about 310,000 phones; a decade later, there were 10 million—one for almost every ten people. American Telephone and Telegraph Company, formed by the Bell interests in 1885, became another of the vast holding companies, consolidating over a hundred local systems.

If the telephone dissolved communications barriers as old as the human race, Thomas Alva Edison, the "Wizard of Menlo Park," invented processes and products of comparable significance. Born in 1847, Edison had little formal education, although he was an avid reader. Like Carnegie, he went into the new field of telegraphy. Tinkering in his spare time, he made several important improvements, including a telegraph capable of sending four messages over a single wire. Gathering teams of specialists to work on specific problems, Edison built at Menlo Park, New Jersey, the first modern research laboratory. It may have been his most important invention.

The laboratory, Edison promised, would turn

Alexander Graham Bell (top) is seen making the first telephone call between New York City and Chicago in 1892. Thomas A. Edison (bottom) holds one of his incandescent lamps. His discovery of the "Edison effect" revealed the basic principle on which modern electronics rests.

out "a minor invention every ten days and a big thing every six months or so." In 1877, it turned out a big thing. Worried about a telephone's high cost, Edison set out to invent a "telephone repeater," which became the phonograph. Those unable to afford a phone, he thought, could record their voices for replay from a central telephone station. Using tin foil wrapped around a grooved, rotating cylinder, he shouted the verses of "Mary had a little lamb" and then listened in awe as the machine played them back. "I was never so taken aback in all my life," he later said. "Everybody was astonished. I was always afraid of things that worked the first time."

In 1896, records made of hard rubber and shellac appeared on the market; the following year, a phonograph sold for $20. In 1904, someone had the idea of recording on both sides of the disc, and the phonograph record in its modern form was born. For the first time in history, people could listen again and again to a favorite symphony or piano solo. The phonograph made human experience repeatable in a way never before possible.

In 1879 came an even larger triumph, the incandescent lamp. Sir Joseph William Swan, an English inventor, had already experimented with the carbon filament, but Edison's task involved more than finding a durable filament. He set out to do nothing less than change light. A trial-and-error inventor, Edison tested sixteen hundred materials before producing, late in 1879, the carbon filament he wanted. Then he had to devise a complex system of conductors, meters, and generators, by which electricity could be divided and distributed to homes and businesses.

With the financial backing of J. Pierpont Morgan, he organized the Edison Illuminating Company and built the Pearl Street power station in New York City, the testing ground of the new apparatus. On September 4, 1882, as Morgan and others watched, Edison threw a switch and lit the house of Morgan, the stock exchange, the *New York Times,* and a number of other buildings. Amazed, a *Times* reporter marveled that writing stories in the office at night "seemed almost like writing in daylight." Power stations soon opened in Boston, Philadelphia, and Chicago. By 1900, there were 2774 stations, lighting some 2 million electric lights around the country. In a nation alive with light, the habits of centuries changed.

A typing pool in the Audit Division of the Metropolitan Life Insurance Company, 1897. As demand for clerical workers grew, women took over many of the secretarial duties formerly performed by men. Despite their prominence in the workplace, however, the women were usually overseen by male supervisors.

suffered periodic attacks of discrimination. In 1879, the Workingmen's party of California got a provision in the state constitution forbidding corporations to employ Chinese, and in 1882, Congress prohibited the immigration of Chinese workers for ten years (see Chapter 17).

Culture of Work

Among almost all groups, industrialization shattered age-old patterns, including work habits and the culture of work, as Herbert G. Gutman, a social historian, noted. It made people adapt "older work routines to new necessities and strained those wedded to premodern patterns of labor." Adaptation was difficult and often demeaning. Virtually everyone went through it, and newcomers repeated the experiences of those who came before.

Men and women fresh from farms were not accustomed to the factory's disciplines. Now they worked indoors rather than out, paced themselves to the clock rather than the movements of the sun, and followed the needs of the market rather than the natural rhythms of the seasons. They had foremen and hierarchies and strict rules. Piece work determined wages, and always —as Morris Rosenfeld, a clothing presser, wrote —there was the relentless clock:

The Clock in the workshop,—it rests not a moment;
It points on, and ticks on: eternity-time;
Once someone told me the clock had a meaning,—
In pointing and ticking had reason and rhyme. . . .
At times, when I listen, I hear the clock plainly;—
The reason of old—the old meaning—is gone!
The maddening pendulum urges me forward
To labor and still labor on.
The tick of the clock is the boss in his anger.
The face of the clock has the eyes of the foe.
The clock—I shudder—Dost hear how it draws me?
It calls me "Machine" and it cries [to] me "Sew"!

Although immigrants comprised a good portion of the industrial work force, prejudice existed against particular groups. This 1877 cartoon from a San Francisco paper shows the workingmen's prejudice against Asians in that city.

As industries grew larger, work became more impersonal. Machines displaced skilled artisans, and the unskilled tended them for employers they never saw. Workers picked up and left their jobs with startling frequency, and factories drew on a churning, highly mobile labor supply. Historian Stephan Thernstrom, who has carefully studied the census records, found that only about half the people recorded in any census still lived in the same community ten years later. "The country had an enormous reservoir of restless and footloose men, who could be lured to new destinations when opportunity beckoned."

Thernstrom and others have also found substantial economic and social mobility. The Horatio Alger stories, of course, had always said so, and careers like Andrew Carnegie's—the impoverished immigrant boy who made good— seemed to confirm it. The actual record was considerably more limited. Most business leaders in the period came from well-to-do or middle-class families of old American stock. Of 360 iron and steel barons in Pittsburgh, Carnegie's own city, only 5 fit the Carnegie characteristics, and one of those was Carnegie himself. Still, if few workers became steel magnates, many workers made major progress during their lifetimes.

Thernstrom discovered that a quarter of the manual laborers rose to middle-class positions, and working-class children were even more likely to move up the ladder. In Boston, about half the Jewish immigrants rose from manual to middle-class jobs, and English, Irish, and Italian immigrants were not far behind.

The chance for advancement played a vital role in American industrial development. It gave workers hope, wedded them to the system, and tempered their response to the appeal of labor unions and working-class agitation. Very few workers rose from rags to riches, but a great many rose to better jobs and higher status.

Labor Unions

Weak throughout the nineteenth century, labor unions never included more than 2 percent of the total labor force nor more than 10 percent of industrial workers. To many workers, unions seemed "foreign," radical, and out of step with the American tradition of individual advancement. Craft, ethnic, and other differences fragmented the labor force, and its extraordinary mobility made organization difficult. Employers opposed unions. "I have always had one rule," said an executive of U.S. Steel. "If a worker sticks up his head, hit it."

As the national economy emerged, however, national labor unions gradually took shape. The early unions often represented skilled workers in local areas, but in 1866, William H. Sylvis, a Pennsylvania iron molder, united several unions into a single national organization, the National Labor Union. Like many of the era's labor leaders, Sylvis sought long-range humanitarian reforms, such as the establishment of workers' cooperatives, rather than specific, bread-and-butter goals. A talented propagandist, he attracted many members—some 640,000 by 1868—but he died in 1869, and the organization did not long survive him.

The year Sylvis died, Uriah S. Stephens and a group of Philadelphia garment workers founded a far more successful organization, the Noble and Holy Order of the Knights of Labor. A secret fraternal order, it grew slowly through the 1870s, until Terence V. Powderly, the new Grand Master Workman elected in 1879, ended the secrecy and embarked on an aggressive recruitment program.

Wanting to unite all labor, the Knights welcomed everyone who "toiled," regardless of skill, creed, sex, or color. Unlike most unions it organized female workers, and at its peak had sixty thousand black members.

Harking back to the Jacksonians, the Knights set the "producers" against monopoly and special privilege. As members they excluded only "nonproducers"—bankers, lawyers, liquor dealers, and gamblers. Since employers were "producers," they could join; and since workers and employers had common interests, the Knights maintained that workers should not strike. The order's platform included the eight-hour day and the abolition of child and prisoner labor, but more often it focused on uplifting, utopian reform. Powderly, the eloquent and idealistic leader, spun dreams of a new era of harmony and cooperation. He wanted to sweep away trusts and end drunkenness. Workers should pool their resources, establish worker-run factories, railroads, and mines, and escape from the wage system. "The aim of the Knights of Labor—properly understood—is to make each man his own employer," Powderly said.

Membership grew steadily—from 42,000 in 1882 to 110,000 in 1885. In March 1885, ignoring Powderly's dislike of strikes, local Knights in Saint Louis, Kansas City, and other cities won a victory against Jay Gould's Missouri Pacific Railroad, and membership soared. It soon reached almost 730,000, but neither Powderly nor the union's loose structure could handle the growth. In 1886, the wily Gould struck back, crushing the Knights on the Texas and Pacific Railroad. The defeat punctured the union's growth and revealed the ineffectiveness of its national leaders. Tens of thousands of unskilled laborers, who had recently rushed to join, deserted the ranks. The Haymarket riot (see p. 549) turned public sympathy against unions like the Knights. By 1890, the order had shrunk to 100,000 members, and a few years later it was virtually defunct.

Even as the Knights waxed and waned, another organization emerged that was to endure. Founded in 1886, the American Federation of Labor (AFL) was a loose alliance of national craft unions. Unlike the Knights, the AFL rejected industrial unions in favor of trade unions. It organized only skilled workers along craft lines, avoided politics, and worked for specific practical objectives. "I have my own philosophy and my own dreams," Samuel Gompers, the founder and longtime president, said, "but first and foremost I want to increase the workingman's welfare year by year."

Born in a London tenement in 1850, Gompers was a child of the union movement. Settling in New York, he worked as a cigarmaker, took an active hand in union activities, and experimented for a time with socialism and working-class politics. As leader of the AFL, he adopted a pragmatic approach to labor's needs. Gompers accepted capitalism and did not argue for fundamental changes in it. For labor he wanted simply a recognized place within the system and a greater share of the rewards.

Unlike Powderly, Gompers and the AFL assumed that most workers would remain workers throughout their lives. The task, then, lay in improving lives in "practical" ways: higher wages, shorter hours, and better working conditions. They offered some attractive assurances to employers. As trade unionists, they would use the strike and boycott, but only to achieve limited gains, and if treated fairly, they would provide a stable labor force. They would not oppose monopolies and trusts, as Gompers said, "so long as we obtain fair wages."

By the 1890s, the AFL was the most important labor group in the country, and Gompers, the guiding spirit, stayed its president, except for one year, until his death in 1924. Membership expanded from 140,000 in 1886, past 250,000 in 1892, to over 1 million by 1901. The AFL then included almost one-third of the country's skilled workers. By 1914, it had over 2 million members. The great majority of workers—skilled and unskilled—remained unorganized, but Gompers and the AFL had become a significant force in national life.

Few unions allowed women to join. The Knights of Labor had a Department of Woman's Work headed by Leonora M. Barry, a shrewd, enthusiastic organizer who established a dozen women's locals and investigated the condition of women's labor. The Knights welcomed housewives because they were "producers." The AFL either ignored or opposed women workers. Only two of its national affiliates—the Cigar Makers' Union and the Typographical Union—accepted women as members; others prohibited them outright, and Gompers himself often complained that women workers undercut the pay scales for

Women delegates at a national meeting of the Knights of Labor in 1886. Women belonged to separate associations affiliated with local all-male unions.

men. Working conditions improved after 1900, but even then unions were largely a man's world. In 1910, when there were 6.3 million women at work, only 125,000 of them were in unions.

The AFL did not expressly forbid black workers from joining, but member unions used high initiation fees, technical examinations, and other means to discourage black membership. The AFL's informal exclusion practices were, all in all, a sorry record, but Gompers defended his policy toward blacks, women, and the unskilled by pointing to the dangers that unions faced. Only by restricting membership, he argued, could the union succeed.

Labor Unrest

Workers used various means to adjust to the factory age. To the dismay of managers and "efficiency" experts, they often dictated the pace and quality of their work, and set the tone of the workplace. Newly arrived immigrants got jobs for friends and relatives, taught them how to deal with factory conditions, and humanized the workplace.

Workers also formed their own institutions to deal with their jobs. Overcoming differences of race or ethnic origin, they often banded together to help each other out. They joined social or fraternal organizations, and their unions did more than argue for higher wages. Unions offered companionship, news of job openings, and much-needed insurance plans for sickness, accident, or death. Workers went to the union hall to play cards or pool, sing union songs, and hear older workers tell of past labor struggles. Unions provided food for sick members, and there were dances, picnics, and parades. "The night I joined the Cattle Butchers' Union," a young Lithuanian said, "I was led into the room by a negro member. With me were Bohemians, Germans and Poles. . . . We swore to be loyal to our union above everything else except the country, the city and the State—to be faithful to each other—to protect the women workers—to do our best to understand the history of the labor movement, and to do all we could to help it on."

Many employers believed in an "iron law of wages" in which supply and demand, not the welfare of their workers, dictated wages. "If I wanted boiler iron," a steelmaker said, "I would go out on the market and buy where I could get it the cheapest, and if I wanted to employ men I would do the same thing." Wanting a docile labor force, employers fired union members, hired scabs to replace strikers, and used a new weapon, the court injunction, to quell strikes.

The injunction, which forbade workers to interfere with their employers' business, was used to break the great Pullman strike of 1894 (see Chapter 20), and the Supreme Court upheld use of the injunction in *In re Debs* (1895). Court decisions also affected the legal protection offered to workers. In *Holden* v. *Hardy* (1898), the Court upheld a law limiting working hours for miners because their work was dangerous and long hours might increase injuries. In *Lochner* v. *New York* (1905), however, it struck down a law limiting bakery workers to a sixty-hour week and ten-hour day. Because baking was safer than mining, the Court saw no need to interfere with the right of bakers to sell their labor freely.

As employers' attitudes hardened, strikes and violence broke out. The United States had the greatest number of violent confrontations between capital and labor in the industrial world. Between 1880 and 1900, there were more than

23,000 strikes involving 6.6 million workers. The railroad strike of 1877 (see "The Great Railroad Strike of 1877" on pp. 550–51) paralyzed railroads from West Virginia to California, resulted in the deaths of over 100 workers, and required federal troops to suppress it. Another outburst of labor unrest occurred during the mid-1880s; in 1886, the peak year, 610,000 workers were off the job because of strikes and lockouts.

The worst incident took place at Haymarket Square in Chicago, where workers had been campaigning for an eight-hour workday. In early May 1886, police, intervening in a strike at the McCormick Harvester works, shot and killed two workers. The next evening, May 4, labor leaders called a protest meeting at Haymarket Square near downtown Chicago. The meeting was peaceful, even a bit dull; about 3000 people were there. Police ordered them to disperse; someone threw a dynamite bomb which instantly killed 1 policeman and fatally wounded 6 others. Police fired into the crowd and killed 4 people.

No one ever discovered who threw the bomb, but many Americans—not just business leaders—demanded action against labor "radicalism." Cities strengthened their police forces and armories. In Chicago, donors helped to establish nearby Fort Sheridan and the Great Lakes Naval Training Station to curb social turmoil. Uncertain who threw the bomb, Chicago police rounded up 8 anarchists who were convicted of murder. Although there was no evidence of their guilt, 4 were hanged, 1 committed suicide, and 3 remained in jail until pardoned by the governor in 1893. Linking labor and anarchism in the public mind, the Haymarket Riot weakened the national labor movement.

Violence again broke out in the unsettled conditions of the 1890s. In 1892, federal troops crushed a strike of silver miners in the Coeur d'Alene district of Idaho. That same year, Carnegie and Henry Clay Frick, his partner and manager, lowered wages nearly 20 percent at the Homestead steel plant. The Amalgamated Iron and Steel Workers, an AFL affiliate, struck, and Frick responded by locking the workers out of the plant. The workers surrounded it, and Frick, furious, hired a small private army of Pinkerton detectives to drive them off. But alert workers spotted the detectives, pinned them down with gunfire, and forced them to surrender. Three detectives and ten workers died in the battle.

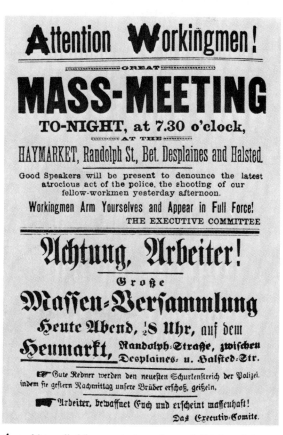

Anarchists called for a protest meeting and distributed these bilingual handbills on the day of the Haymarket Square bombing in 1886.

A few days later, the Pennsylvania governor ordered the state militia to impose peace at Homestead. On July 23, an anarchist named Alexander Berkman, who was not one of the strikers, walked into Frick's office and shot him. He fired twice, then stabbed him several times. Incredibly, Frick survived, watched the police take Berkman away, called in a doctor to bandage his wounds, and stayed in the office until closing time. "I do not think I shall die," he told reporters. "But if I do or not, the company will pursue the same policy and it will win." In late July, the Homestead works reopened under military guard, and in November the strikers gave up.

Events like those at Homestead troubled many Americans who wondered whether industrialization, for all its benefits, might carry a heavy price in social upheaval, class tensions, and even outright warfare. Most workers did not share in the immense profits of the industrial age, and as the nineteenth century came to a close, there were some who rebelled against the inequity.

The Great Railroad Strike of 1877

On May 24, 1877, in the midst of a nationwide depression, the Pennsylvania Railroad announced a 10 percent cut in pay for its employees. At the time, engineers made about $3.25 a day for twelve hours of work, conductors $2.75, firemen $1.90, and brakemen $1.75. Other railroads also cut pay; the Baltimore & Ohio announced cuts totaling 20 percent. For firemen and brakemen on the B & O, that meant a wage of $.90 a day.

The wage cuts hurt. As a worker on the B & O said: "We eat our hard bread and tainted meat two days on the sooty cars up the road, and when we come home, find our children gnawing bones and our wives complaining that they cannot even buy hominy and molasses for food."

When pay cuts on the B & O took effect on July 16, anger erupted. In Martinsburg, West Virginia, one crew walked off the job leaving their cattle train standing on the tracks; the stoppage spread to other crews. Trains backed up for two miles east and west of town, and at the request of B & O officials, the governor of West Virginia called out the state militia.

The next day, the militia stood guard as another crew took over the cattle train. Strikers boarded the train, and one of them fired a pistol at the guards. His fire was returned, and he fell, mortally wounded. The militiamen, many of them sympathetic to the strike, turned and left the yards. Alarmed, West Virginia's governor called for federal troops to protect railroad

property. President Rutherford B. Hayes hesitated, but on July 18 he issued the orders. For the first time since the 1830s, the army was ordered out in peacetime to quell a strike.

As the strike spread along the B & O, jeering crowds threw stones at passing freights. At Cumberland, Maryland, west of Martinsburg, only one freight in sixteen got through. On July 20, the governor of Maryland, too, ordered out the state militia. As one regiment emerged from the Garden Street Armory in Baltimore, the city's factories let out for the day. Homeward-bound workers pelted the bewildered soldiers with stones. Blocks away, several thousand people penned up another regiment. Shooting started, and when it end-

Violence and fires associated with the strike destroyed railyards across the country. By the end of the strike, $10 million of railroad property had been reduced to rubble.

ed, eleven civilians were dead and forty were wounded. At the request of Maryland's governor, President Hayes that night sent army units to Baltimore. Portions of two states were now under federal protection.

The strike spread westward through New York, Pennsylvania, and Ohio. In each one of those states the militia was called out. Workers on the giant Pennsylvania system stayed on the job until Robert Pitcairn, the aggressive superintendent of the Pittsburgh division, ordered double-headers—trains with two locomotives—on all eastbound freights. Double-headers pulled more freight and required fewer crewmen, but they were difficult to handle.

The morning the order took effect, Augustus Harris, a veteran flagman, refused to take out the 8:40 double-header. Workers and sympathizers blocked the 9:40 trains; incoming crews joined the shutdown. At noon, men from the steel mills mingled in the crowd.

During the night, Pennsylvania state officials ordered in two trainloads of militia from Philadelphia to clear the key Twenty-eighth Street railroad crossing. Several thousand people massed at the crossing and on the hillsides above. There were revolver shots, and the militia opened fire. Within minutes, twenty people lay dead, including a woman and three small children. Fifteen soldiers were hurt.

The strike spread. On Monday, July 23, the New York Central, a vital link between New York City and Chicago, shut down. Cleveland, Buffalo, and other cities were cut off from fuel and supplies. The next day, a general strike paralyzed Saint Louis, and strikes hit major railroads to the West. That night, all freight traffic in and out of Chi-

cago, a vital railroad hub, came to a halt.

Chicago factories closed; angry crowds paraded through the streets. Bankers and lawyers armed themselves with Springfield rifles from nearby government arsenals. On Wednesday evening, July 25, violence broke out when excited policemen fired into a crowd. Citizens' militias and working people battled across the city. Shooting continued through the next day; eighteen people died.

Determined to stop the violence, President Hayes sent six companies of soldiers to Chicago and ordered the army to open the Pennsylvania line between Philadelphia and Pittsburgh. On Saturday, July 28, the break came. Nine days after the original order, the first double-header left Pittsburgh with thirty-four cars of cattle and two cars of troops.

Within a matter of days the anger was spent and the Great Strike was over. It lasted about two weeks, touched eleven states, and affected two-thirds of the country's railroad track. According to one estimate, it involved over 80,000 railroad workers and 500,000 workers in other occupations. More than one hundred people died.

Some employers responded to the strike by tightening hiring procedures, cracking down on labor unions, and strengthening police forces. Others, eager to avert another conflict, took measures to alleviate grievances. By 1880, most of the railroads had raised pay scales to earlier levels.

Many people in America and abroad studied the significance of the strike. Did it mean, as some suggested, that war between capital and labor had begun? Did industrialization inevitably involve class dislocation, class tensions, and vio-

Here, an angry mob of civilians and strikers drags soldiers from the train at Hornellsville, New York, on July 23rd, the day the New York Central was forced to shut down.

lence? Were federal troops required to maintain peace in the new industrial society?

Answers differed. In response, there was heightened demand for government intervention to regulate railroads and thereby lessen the hardships brought on by rapid industrial growth.

Like most events, however, the strike's greatest impact was on ordinary individuals whose opinions went unrecorded. In moments of individual decision, they stranded trains in Martinsburg, closed factories in Chicago, and shut down entire railroad networks.

1859 First oil well drilled near Titusville, Pennsylvania

1866 William Sylvis establishes National Labor Union

1869 Transcontinental railroad completed at Promontory, Utah • Knights of Labor organize

1876 Alexander Graham Bell invents the telephone • Centennial Exposition held in Philadelphia

1877 Railroads cut workers' wages, leading to bloody and violent strike

1879 Thomas A. Edison invents the incandescent lamp

1882 Rockefeller's Standard Oil Company becomes nation's first trust • Edison opens first electric generating station in New York

1883 Railroads introduce standard time zones

1886 Samuel Gompers founds American Federation of Labor (AFL) • Labor protest erupts in violence in Haymarket Riot in Chicago • Railroads adopt standard gauge

1892 Workers strike at Homestead steel plant in Pennsylvania

1893 Economic depression begins

1901 J. P. Morgan announces formation of U.S. Steel Corporation, nation's first billion-dollar company

and fewer hands. Maturing quickly, the young system became a new corporate capitalism: giant businesses, interlocking in ownership, managed by a new professional class, and selling an expanding variety of goods in an increasingly controlled market. As goods spread through the society, so did a sharpened, aggressive materialism. Workers felt the strains of the shift to a new social order.

In 1902, a well-to-do New Yorker named Bessie Van Vorst decided to see what it was like to work for a living in a factory. Disguising herself in coarse woolen clothes, a shabby felt hat, a cheap piece of fur, and an old shawl and gloves, she went to Pittsburgh and got a job in a canning factory. She worked 10 hours a day, 6 days a week, including 4 hours on Saturday afternoons when she and the other women, on their hands and knees, scrubbed the tables, stands, and entire factory floor. For that she earned $4.20 a week, $3 of which went for food alone. "My hands are stiff," she said, "my thumbs almost blistered. . . . Cases are emptied and refilled; bottles are labeled, stamped and rolled away . . . and still there are more cases, more jars, more bottles. Oh! the monotony of it!" The noise around her was deafening; her head grew dazed and weary. She paused to rest. "Quickly a voice whispers in my ear: 'You'd better not stand there doin' nothin'. If *she* catches you she'll give it to you.'"

Van Vorst was lucky—when she tired of the life, she could go back to her home in New York. The working men and women around her were not so fortunate. They stayed on the factory floor, and by dint of their labor, created the new industrial society.

In the half-century after the Civil War, the United States became an industrial nation—the leading one, in fact, in the world. On one hand, industrialization meant "progress," growth, world power, and in some sense, fulfillment of the American promise of abundance. National wealth grew from $16 billion in 1860 to $88 billion in 1900; wealth per capita more than doubled. For the bulk of the population, the standard of living—a particularly American concept—rose.

But industrialization also meant rapid change, social instability, exploitation of labor, and growing disparity in income between rich and poor. Industry flourished, but control rested in fewer

Recommended Reading

Samuel P. Hays, *The Response to Industrialism: 1885–1914* (1957) is an influential interpretation of the period. A detailed survey is Edward C. Kirkland, *Industry Comes of Age: Business, Labor, and Public Policy, 1860–1897* (1967). Douglass C. North, *Growth and Welfare in the American Past: A New Economic History* (1966) is stimulating. Other valuable overviews include Stuart Bruchey's brief *Growth of the Modern Economy* (1975), W. Elliot Brownlee's more detailed *Dynamics of Ascent: A History of the American Economy* (1974), and Robert Higgs, *The Transformation of the American Economy, 1865–1914* (1971). David Montgomery, *The Fall of the House of Labor: The Workplace, the State, and American Labor Activism, 1865–1925* (1987) is an outstanding recent study of labor in the period.

For stimulating interpretations of the period, see Robert H. Wiebe, *The Search for Order, 1877–1920* (1968) and John

A. Garraty, *The New Commonwealth, 1877–1890* (1968). Sean Dennis Cashman, *America in the Gilded Age* (1984) is a recent study. Thomas C. Cochran and William Miller, *The Age of Enterprise* (1942), Alfred D. Chandler, *The Visible Hand: The Managerial Revolution in American Business* (1978), and JoAnne Yates, *Control through Communication: The Rise of System in American Management* (1989), are perceptive. The railroad empire is treated in G. R. Taylor and I. D. Neu, *The American Railroad Network, 1861–1890* (1956); John R. Stilgoe, *Metropolitan Corridor: Railroads and the American Scene* (1983); John Hoyt Williams, *A Great & Shining Road: The Epic Story of the Transcontinental Railroad* (1988); and John F. Stover, *American Railroads* (1961). On the steel industry, see Peter Temin, *Iron and Steel in Nineteenth-Century America* (1964) and Joseph F. Wall, *Andrew Carnegie* (1970).

For the techniques of selling, see Daniel J. Boorstin, *The Americans: The Democratic Experience* (1973). Two superb books by Sam B. Warner, Jr., *Streetcar Suburbs: The Process of Growth in Boston, 1870–1900* (1962) and *The Urban Wilderness: A History of the American City* (1973), examine technology and city development. The wage earner is examined in Herbert G. Gutman, *Work, Culture, and Society in Industrializing America* (1976); Walter Licht, *Working for the Railroad: The Organization of Work in the Nineteenth Century* (1983); James H. Ducker, *Men of the Steel Rails* (1983); John T. Cumbler, *Working Class Community in Industrial America: Work, Leisure and Struggle in Two Industrial Cities, 1880–1930* (1979); Tamara K. Hareven, *Family Time and Industrial Time: The Relationship Between the Family and Work in a New England Industrial Community* (1982); James R. Barrett, *Work and Community in the Jungle: Chicago's Packinghouse Workers, 1894–1922* (1987); Richard Jules Oestreicher, *Solidarity and Fragmentation: Working People and Class Consciousness in Detroit 1875–1900* (1986); and Gerald David Jaynes, *Branches Without Roots: Genesis of the Black Working Class in the American South, 1862–1882* (1986). Two books by Stephan Thernstrom: *Poverty and Progress: Social Mobility in the Nineteenth-Century City* (1964) and *The Other Bostonians: Poverty and Progress in the American Metropolis, 1880–1970* (1973), and Howard M. Gitelman, *Workingmen of Waltham: Mobility in American Urban Industrial Development 1850–1890* (1974) examine mobility. Philip S. Foner, *Women and the American Labor Movement*, 2 vols. (1979); Lois W. Banner, *Women in Modern America: A Brief History* (1974); Susan E. Kennedy, *If All We Did Was to Weep at Home* (1979); Barbara Wertheimer, *We Were There: The Story of Working Women in America* (1977); Alice Kessler-Harris, *Out to Work: A History of Wage-Earning Women in the United States* (1982); and Milton Cantor and Bruce Laurie, eds., *Class, Sex, and the Woman Worker* (1977) are excellent on the subject of women in the workplace.

Additional Bibliography

Alfred D. Chandler, *The Railroads: The Nation's First Big Business* (1965), stresses the railroads' importance; Robert Fogel, *Railroads in American Economic Growth* (1964), questions it. Julius Grodinsky, *Jay Gould* (1957) and Albro Martin, *James J. Hill and the Opening of the Northwest* (1976) are superb.

For steel, see Carnegie's *Autobiography of Andrew Carnegie* (1920); Harold C. Livesay, *Andrew Carnegie and the Rise of Big Business* (1975); and John Ingham, *The Iron Barons: A Social Analysis of an American Urban Elite, 1874–1965* (1978). For the oil industry, see Edward N. Akin, *Flagler* (1988); Carl Solberg, *Oil Power* (1976); H. F. Williamson and A. R. Daum, *The American Petroleum Industry: Age of Illumination* (1959); and Allan Nevins, *Study in Power: John D. Rockefeller*, 2 vols. (1953). Anthony F. C. Wallace, *St. Clair* (1987) and Edward J. Davies II, *The Anthracite Aristocracy* (1985) are useful on coal. For the era's most prominent financier, see Vincent P. Carosso, *The Morgans* (1987).

On technological developments, Lewis Mumford, *Technics and Civilization* (1934); Wolfgang Schivelbusch, *Disenchanted Night: The Industrialization of Light in the Nineteenth Century* (1988); Carolyn Marvin, *When Old Technologies Were New* (1988); Charles Singer et al., eds., *History of Technology*, vol. 5, *The Late Nineteenth Century, c. 1850 to c. 1900* (1958); and W. P. Strassmann, *Risk and Technological Innovation* (1959) are the places to begin. Useful studies include Matthew Josephson, *Edison* (1959); H. G. Prout, *A Life of George Westinghouse* (1921); John Brooks, *Telephone: The First Hundred Years* (1976); and Robert V. Bruce, *Alexander Graham Bell and the Conquest of Solitude* (1973).

Frank Presbrey, *The History and Development of Advertising* (1929) is the best general account; others include J. P. Wood, *The Story of Advertising* (1958); Ralph M. Hower, *History of Macy's of New York, 1858–1919* (1943); John K. Winkler, *Five and Ten: The Fabulous Life of F. W. Woolworth* (1940); and Boris Emmet and John E. Jeuck, *Catalogues and Counters: A History of Sears, Roebuck and Company* (1950). Also, David M. Potter, *People of Plenty: Economic Abundance and the American Character* (1954).

On labor, see David Brody, *Steelworkers in America: The Nonunion Era* (1960); Shelton Stromquist, *A Generation of Boomers: The Pattern of Railroad Labor Conflict in Nineteenth-Century America* (1987); Cindy Sondik Aron, *Ladies and Gentlemen of the Civil Service: Middle-Class Workers in Victorian America* (1987); Joanne J. Meyerowitz, *Women Adrift: Independent Wage Earners in Chicago, 1880–1930* (1988); Susan Levine, *Labor's True Women: Carpet Weavers, Industrialization, and Labor Reform in the Gilded Age* (1984); Mary H. Blewett, *Men, Women, and Work: Class, Gender, and Protest in the New England Shoe Industry, 1780–1910* (1988); Gerald N. Grob, *Workers and Utopia: A Study of Ideological Conflict in the American Labor Movement, 1865–1900* (1961); William H. Harris, *The Harder We Run: Black Workers Since the Civil War* (1982); N. J. Ware, *The Labor Movement in the United States, 1860–1893* (1929); Leon Fink, *Workingmen's Discovery: The Knights of Labor and American Politics* (1983); Harold C. Livesay, *Samuel Gompers and Organized Labor in America* (1978); and S. B. Kaufman, *Samuel Gompers and the Origins of the American Federation of Labor* (1973).

John Laslett, *Labor and the Left: A Study of Socialist and Radical Influences in the American Labor Movement, 1881–1924* (1970) is illuminating. Alexander Keyssar, *Out of Work* (1986) examines the issue of unemployment. Paul Avrich, *The Haymarket Tragedy* (1984) is a detailed account of that event. See also, Bruce C. Nelson, *Beyond the Martyrs: A Social History of Chicago's Anarchists* (1988). Terence V. Powderly, *Thirty Years of Labor* (1889) and Samuel Gompers, *Seventy Years of Life and Labor*, 2 vols. (1925), give the flavor of their thought.

CHAPTER 19

Toward an Urban Society:

1877–1900

One day around 1900, Harriet Vittum, a settlement house worker in Chicago, went to the aid of a young Polish girl who lived in a nearby slum. The girl, fifteen, had discovered she was pregnant and had taken poison. An ambulance was on the way, and Vittum, told of the poisoning, rushed over to do what she could.

Quickly she climbed the three flights of stairs to the floor where the girl and her family lived. Pushing open the door, she found the father, several male boarders, and two or three small boys asleep on the kitchen floor. In the next room lay the mother on the floor among several women boarders and one or two small children. Glancing out the window, Vittum saw the wall of another building so close she could reach out and touch it.

There was a third room; in it lay the fifteen-year-old girl, along with two more small children who were asleep. Looking at the scene, Vittum thought about the girl's life in the crowded tenement, with its lack of light and air. Did she have the right, Vittum asked herself, to bring the girl back "to the misery and hopelessness of the life she was living in that awful place"?

The young girl died, and in later years, Vittum often told her story; it was easy to see why. The girl's life in the slum, the children on the floor, the need to take in boarders to make ends meet, the way mothers and fathers collapsed at the end of working days that began long before sunup—all reflected the experiences of millions of people.

People poured into cities in the last part of the nineteenth century, lured by glitter and excitement, by friends and relatives who were already there, and above all, by the greater opportunities for jobs and higher wages. Between 1860 and 1910 the rural population of the United States almost doubled; the number of people living in cities increased sevenfold.

Little of the increase came from natural growth, since urban families had high rates of infant mortality, a declining fertility rate, and a high death rate from injury and disease. Many of the newcomers came from rural America, and many more came from Europe, Latin America, and Asia. In one of the most significant migrations in American history, thousands of African Americans began in the 1880s to move from the rural South to northern cities. By 1900, there were large black communities in New York, Washing-ton, D.C., Baltimore, Chicago, and other cities. Yet to come was the even greater black migration during World War I.

Two major forces reshaped American society between 1870 and 1920. One was *industrialization* (see Chapter 18); the other was *urbanization,* the headlong rush of people from their rural roots into the modern urban environment. By 1920, the city had become the center of American economic, social, and cultural life.

THE LURE OF THE CITY

William Allen White left the small Kansas town of his boyhood in 1891 to go to the "gilded metropolis" of Kansas City. White was twenty-three years old, and the experience affected him for the rest of his life. He rode the cable cars and used the newfangled telephone—"always with the consciousness that I was tampering with a miracle." He purchased a second-hand dress suit, listened to the music of a sixty-piece orchestra, attended plays, and heard James Whitcomb Riley

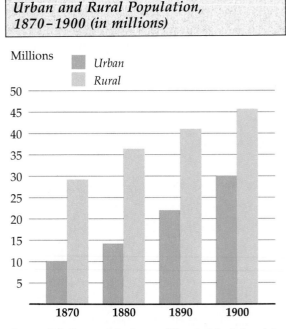

Urban and Rural Population, 1870–1900 (in millions)

Source: U.S. Bureau of the Census. Historical Statistics of the United States, Colonial Times to 1970, *Bicentennial Edition,* Washington, D.C., 1975.

recite poetry. "Life was certainly one round of joy in Kansas City," White said.

Between 1870 and 1900, the city—like the factory—became a symbol of a new America. Drawn from farms, small towns, and foreign lands, newcomers swelled the population of older cities and created new ones almost overnight. At the beginning of the Civil War, only one-sixth of the American people lived in cities of 8000 people or more. By 1900, one-third did; by 1920, one-half. "We live in the age of great cities," wrote the Reverend Samuel Lane Loomis in 1887. "Each successive year finds a stronger and more irresistible current sweeping in towards the centers of life."

The current brought growth of an explosive sort. Thousands of years of history had produced only a handful of cities with more than a half-million in population. In 1900, the United States had six such cities, including three—New York, Chicago, and Philadelphia—with a population over 1 million.

Skyscrapers and Suburbs

Like so many things in these years, the city was transformed by a revolution in technology. Beginning in the 1880s, the age of steel and glass produced the skyscraper; the streetcar produced the suburbs and new residential patterns.

On the eve of the change, American cities were a crowded jumble of small buildings. Church steeples stood out on the skyline, clearly visible above the roofs of factories and office buildings. (As late as 1890, the tallest structure in New York City was the spire of Trinity Church, only 286 feet high.) Buildings were usually made of masonry, and since the massive walls had to support their own weight, they could be no taller than a dozen or so stories. Steel frames and girders ended that limitation and allowed buildings to soar higher and higher. "Curtain walls," which concealed the steel framework, were no longer load-bearing; they were pierced by many windows that let in fresh air and light. Completed in 1885, the Home Insurance Building in Chicago was the country's first metal-frame structure.

To a group of talented Chicago architects, the new trends served as a springboard for innovative forms. The leader of the movement was Louis H. Sullivan, who had studied at the Massachusetts Institute of Technology and in Paris before settling in Chicago, attracted by the chance to rebuild the city after the great fire of 1871. In 1886, at the age of thirty, he began work on the Chicago Auditorium, one of the last great masonry buildings. "Then came the flash of imagination which saw the single thing," he later said. "The trick was turned; and there swiftly came into being something new under the sun." Sullivan's skyscrapers, the "flash of imagination," changed the urban skyline.

In the Wainwright Building in St. Louis (1890), the Schiller Building (1892) and the Carson, Pirie, and Scott department store (1899) in Chicago, and the Prudential Building in Buffalo (1895), Sullivan developed the new forms. Architects must discard "books, rules, precedents," he announced; responding to the new, they should design for a building's function. "Form follows function," Sullivan believed, and he passed the idea on to a talented disciple, Frank Lloyd Wright. The modern city should stretch to the sky. A skyscraper "must be every inch a proud and soaring thing, rising in sheer exaltation . . . from bottom to top . . . a unit without a single dissenting line."

Electric elevators carried passengers upward in the new skyscrapers. During the same years streetcars carried the people outward to expanded boundaries that transformed urban life.

Cities were no longer largely "walking cities," confined to a radius of two or three miles, the distance an individual might walk. Streetcar systems extended the radius and changed the urban map. Cable lines, electric surface lines, and elevated rapid transit brought shoppers and workers into central business districts and sped them home again. Offering the modest five-cent fare with a free transfer, these mass transit systems fostered commuting; widely separated business and residential districts sprang up. The middle class moved farther and farther out to the leafy greenness of the suburbs.

As the middle class moved out of the cities, the immigrants and working class poured in. They took over the older brownstones, row houses, and workers' cottages, turning them, under the sheer weight of numbers, into the slums of the central city. In the cities of the past, classes and occupations had been thrown together; without streetcars and subways there was no other choice. The streetcar city, sprawling and specialized, became a more fragmented and stratified society with middle-class residential rings surrounding a business and working-class core.

Tenements and Privies

In the shadow of the skyscrapers, grimy rows of tenements filled the central city. Exploring them in words and photographs, Jacob Riis described *How the Other Half Lives* (1890).

Be a little careful, please! The hall is dark and you might stumble. . . . Here where the hall turns and dives into utter darkness is . . . a flight of stairs. You can feel your way, if you cannot see it. Close? Yes! What would you have? All the fresh air that enters these stairs comes from the hall-door that is forever slamming. . . . Here is a door. Listen! That short, hacking cough, that tiny, helpless wail—what do they mean? . . . The child is dying of measles. With half a chance it might have lived; but it had none. That dark bedroom killed it.

Tenement houses on small city lots crowded people into cramped apartments. In the late 1870s, architect James E. Ware won a competition for tenement design with the "dumbbell tenement." Rising seven or eight stories in height, the dumbbell tenement packed about 30 four-room apartments on a lot only 25 by 100 feet. Between four and sixteen families lived on a floor; two toilets in the hall of each floor served their needs. Narrowed at the middle, the tenement resembled a giant dumbbell in shape. The indented middle created an air shaft between adjoining buildings that provided a little light and ventilation. In case of fire, it also carried flames from one story to the next, making these buildings notorious firetraps. In 1890, nearly half the dwellings in New York City were tenements.

That year more than 1.4 million people lived on Manhattan Island, one of whose wards had a population density of 334,000 people per square mile. Many people lived in alleys and basements so dark they could not be photographed until flashlight photography was invented in 1887. Exploring the city, William Dean Howells, the prominent author, inhaled "the stenches of the

Impoverished immigrant families often lived in tiny, windowless rooms in crowded tenement districts like New York City's lower East Side.

neglected street . . . [and] the yet fouler and dreadfuller poverty smell which breathes from the open doorways."

Howells smelled more than poverty. In the 1870s and '80s, cities stank. One problem was horse manure, hundreds of tons of it a day in every city. Another was the privy, "a single one of which," said a leading authority on public health, "may render life in a whole neighborhood almost unendurable in the summer."

Baltimore smelled "like a billion polecats," recalled H. L. Mencken, who grew up there. Said one New York City resident: "The stench is something terrible." Another wrote that "the stink is enough to knock you down." In 1880, the Chicago *Times* said that a "solid stink" pervaded the city. "No other word expresses it so well as stink. A stench means something finite. Stink reaches the infinite and becomes sublime in the magnitude of odiousness." In 1892, one neighborhood of Chicago, covering one-third of a square mile, had only three bathtubs.

Cities dumped their wastes into the nearest body of water, then drew drinking water from the same site. Many built modern, purified waterworks but could not keep pace with spiraling growth. In 1900, fewer than one in ten city dwellers drank filtered water. Factories, the pride of the era, polluted the urban air. At night, Pittsburgh looked and sounded like "Hell with the lid off," according to contemporary observers. Smoke poured from 73 glass factories, 41 iron and steel mills, and 29 oil refineries. The choking air helped prevent lung diseases and malaria—or so the city's advertising claimed.

Crime was another growing problem. The nation's homicide rate nearly tripled in the 1880s, much of the increase coming in the cities. Slum youths formed street gangs with names like the Hayes Valley gang in San Francisco or the Baxter Street Dudes, the Daybreak Boys, and the Alley Gang in New York. After remaining constant for many decades, the suicide rate rose steadily between 1870 and 1900, according to a recent study of Philadelphia. Alcoholism also rose, especially among men, though recent studies have shown that for working-class men, the urban saloon was as much a gathering spot as it was a place to drink. Nonetheless, a 1905 survey of Chicago counted as many saloons as grocery stores, meat markets, and dry goods stores combined.

Strangers in a New Land

While some of the new city dwellers came from farms and small towns, many more came from abroad. Most came from Europe, where unemployment, food shortages, and increasing threats of war sent millions fleeing across the Atlantic to make a fresh start. Often they knew someone already in the United States, a friend or relative who had written them about prospects for jobs and freer lives in a new land. Italians first came in large numbers to escape an 1887 cholera epidemic in southern Italy; tens of thousands of Jews sought refuge from the anti-Semitic massacres that swept Russia and Czarist-ruled Poland after 1880.

All told, the immigration figures were staggering. Between 1877 and 1890, more than 6.3 million people entered the United States. In one year alone, 1882, almost 789,000 people came. By 1890, about 15 percent of the population, 9 million people, were foreign-born.

Most newcomers were job seekers. Nearly two-thirds were males, and the majority were between the ages of fifteen and forty. Most were unskilled laborers. Most settled on the eastern seaboard. In 1901, the Industrial Relocation Office was established to relieve overcrowding in the eastern cities; opening Galveston, Texas, as a port of entry, it attracted many Russian Jews to Texas and the Southwest. But most immigrants preferred the shorter, more familiar journey to New York, and they tended to crowd into northern and eastern cities, settling in areas where others of their nationality or religion had settled.

They were often dazzled by what they saw. They stared at electric lights, indoor plumbing, soda fountains, streetcars, plush train seats for all classes, ice cream, lemons, and bananas. Relatives whisked them off to buy new "American" clothes and showed them the teeming markets, department stores, and Woolworth's new five and dime stores. "It seemed quite advanced compared with our home in Khelm," said a Polish girl. "There was a sense of safety and hope that we had never felt in Poland."

Cities had increasingly large foreign-born populations. In 1900, four-fifths of Chicago's population was foreign-born or of foreign-born parentage, two-thirds of Boston's, and one-half of Philadelphia's. New York City, where most im-

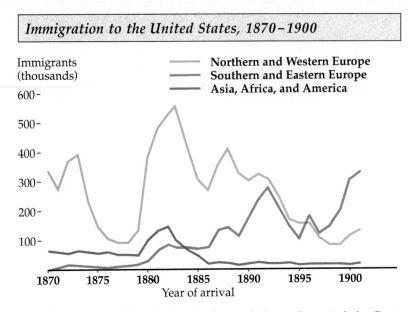

Immigration to the United States, 1870–1900

Immigrants (thousands)

Northern and Western Europe
Southern and Eastern Europe
Asia, Africa, and America

600 –
500 –
400 –
300 –
200 –
100 –

1870   1875   1880   1885   1890   1895   1900

Year of arrival

Note: For purposes of classification, *Northern and Western Europe* includes Great Britain, Ireland, Scandinavia, the Netherlands, Belgium, Luxembourg, Switzerland, France and Germany. *Southern and Eastern Europe* includes Poland, Austria-Hungary, Russia and the Baltic States, Romania, Bulgaria, European Turkey, Italy, Spain, Portugal and Greece. *Asia, Africa and America* includes Asian Turkey, China, Japan, India, Canada, the Caribbean, Latin America and all of Africa.

Source: U.S. Bureau of the Census. Historical Statistics of the United States, Colonial Times to 1970, Bicentennial Edition, Washington, D.C., 1975.

migrants arrived and many stayed, had more Italians than lived in Naples, more Germans than lived in Hamburg, and twice as many Irish as lived in Dublin. Four out of five New York City residents in 1890 were of foreign birth or foreign parentage.

Beginning in the 1880s, the sources of immigration shifted dramatically away from northern and western Europe, the chief source of immigration for over two centuries. More and more immigrants came from southern and eastern Europe: Italy, Greece, Austro-Hungary, Poland, and Russia. Between 1880 and 1910, approximately 8.4 million people came from these lands. The "new" immigrants tended to be Catholics or Jews rather than Protestants. Like their predecessors, most were unskilled rather than skilled, and they often spoke "strange" languages. Most were poor and uneducated; sticking together in closeknit communities, they clung to their native customs, languages, and religions.

More than any previous group, the so-called new immigrants troubled the mainstream society. Could they be assimilated? Did they share "American" values? Such questions preoccupied

groups like the American Protective Association, a midwestern anti-Catholic organization which expanded in the 1890s and worked to limit or end immigration. Sneering epithets became part of the national vocabulary: "wop" and "dago" for Italians, "bohunk" for Bohemians, Hungarians, and other Slavs, "grease-ball" for Greeks, and "kike" for Jews. "You don't call . . . an Italian a white man?" a congressman asked a railroad construction boss in 1890. "No, Sir," the boss replied. "An Italian is a Dago."

Anti-Catholicism and anti-Semitism flared up again, as they had in the 1850s (recall chapter 14). Edward A. Ross, a prominent sociologist, publicly decried "the lower class of Jews of Eastern Europe [who] reach here [as] moral cripples, their souls warped and dwarfed." In 1889, the head of the Fresh Air Fund, a program that sent New York City children on vacations to the suburbs, noted that "no one asked for Italian children." The Immigration Restriction League, founded in 1894, demanded a literacy test for immigrants from southern and eastern Europe. Congress passed such a law in 1896, but President Cleveland vetoed it.

In a Puck cartoon entitled "looking backward," the shadows of their immigrant origins loom over the rich and powerful who wanted to deny the "new" immigrants from central and southern Europe admission to America. The caption on the cartoon reads, "They would close to the newcomer the bridge that carried them and their fathers over."

Immigrants and the City

Industrial capitalism—the world of factories and foremen and grimy machines—tested the immigrants and placed an enormous strain upon their families. Many immigrants came from peasant societies where life proceeded according to outdoor routine and age-old tradition. In their new city homes, they found both new freedoms and new confinements, a different language, and a novel set of customs and expectations. Historians have only recently begun to discover the remarkable ways in which they learned to adjust.

Like native-born families, most immigrant families were nuclear in structure—they consisted of two parents and their children. Though variations occurred from group to group, men and women occupied roles similar to those in native families; men were wage earners, women housekeepers and mothers. Margaret Byington, who studied steelworkers' homes in Homestead in the early 1900s, learned that the father played a relatively small role in child-rearing or managing the family's finances. "His part of the problem is to earn and hers to spend." In Chicago, social reformer Jane Addams discovered that immigrant women made it "a standard of domestic virtue that a man must not touch his pay envelope, but bring it home unopened to his wife."

Although patterns varied among ethnic groups, and between economic classes within ethnic groups, immigrants tended to marry within the group more than did the native-born. In one New York community, only 2 percent of French Canadian and 7 percent of Irish working men married outside their ethnic group in 1880, compared to almost 40 percent of native-born working men. Immigrants also tended to marry at a later age than natives, and they tended to have more children, a fact that worried nativists opposed to immigration.

Immigrants shaped the city as much as it shaped them. Most of them tried to retain their traditional culture for themselves and their children while at the same time adapting to life in their new country. To do this, they spoke their native language, practiced their religious faith, read their own newspapers, and established special parochial or other schools. They observed traditional holidays and formed a myriad of social organizations to maintain ties between members of the group.

Immigrant associations—there were many of them in every city—offered fellowship in a strange land. They helped newcomers find jobs and homes; they provided important services such as unemployment and health insurance. In a Massachusetts textile town, the Irish Benevolent Society said: "We visit our sick, and bury our dead." Some groups were no larger than a neighborhood; others spread nationwide. In 1914, the Deutsch-Amerikanischer Nationalbund, the largest of the associations, had more than two million members in dozens of cities and towns. Many women belonged to and participated in the work of the immigrant associations; in addition, there were groups exclusively for women such as the Polish Women's Alliance, the Jednota Ceskyck Dam (Society of Czech Women), and the National Council of Jewish Women.

The Polish National Alliance (PNA), a typical immigrant association, was founded in 1880. Like other organizations, it helped new immigrants on their arrival, offered insurance plans, established libraries and museums, sponsored youth programs, fielded baseball teams, and organized trips back to Poland. Each year the PNA published a sought-after calendar filled with Polish holidays, information, and proverbs. Extolling Poles' contributions to their new country, it erected monuments to distinguished Americans of Polish descent.

Every major city had dozens of foreign-language newspapers, with circulations large and small. The first newspaper published in the Lithuanian language appeared in the United States, not in Lithuania. Eagerly read, the papers not only carried news of events in the homeland, but also reported on local ethnic leaders, told readers how to vote and become citizens, and gave practical tips on adjusting to life in the United States. The Swedes, Poles, Czechs, and Germans established ethnic theaters that performed national plays and music. The most famous of these, the Yiddish (Jewish) Theater, started in the 1880s in New York City and lasted more than fifty years.

The church and the school were the most important institutions in every immigrant community. East European Jews established synagogues and religious schools wherever they settled; they taught the Hebrew language and raised their children in a heritage they did not want to leave behind. Among such groups as the Irish and the Poles, the Roman Catholic Church provided spiritual and educational guidance. In the parish schools, Polish priests and nuns taught Polish-American children about Polish as well as American culture in the Polish language.

Church, school, and fraternal societies shaped the way in which immigrants adjusted to life in America. By preserving language, religion, and heritage, they also shaped the country itself.

The House That Tweed Built

Closely connected with explosive urban growth was the emergence of the powerful city political machine. As cities grew, lines of responsibility in city governments became hopelessly confused, increasing the opportunity for corruption and greed. Burgeoning populations required streets, buildings, and public services; immigrants needed even more services. In this situation, political party machines played an important role.

The machines traded services for votes. Loosely knit, they were headed by a strong, influential leader—the ''boss''—who tied together a network of ward and precinct captains, each of whom looked after his local constituents. In New York, ''Honest'' John Kelly, Richard Croker, and Charles F. Murphy led Tammany Hall, the famous Democratic party organization that dominated city politics from the 1850s to the 1930s. Other bosses included ''Hinky Dink'' Kenna and ''Bathhouse John'' Coughlin in Chicago, James McManes in Philadelphia, and Christopher A. Buckley—the notorious ''Blind Boss,'' who used an exceptional memory for voices to make up for failing eyesight—in San Francisco.

William M. Tweed, head of the famed Tweed Ring in New York, provided the model for them all. Nearly six feet tall, weighing almost three hundred pounds, Tweed rose through the ranks of Tammany Hall. He served in turn as city alderman, member of Congress, and New York State assemblyman. A man of culture and warmth, he moved easily between the rough back alleys of New York and the parlors and clubs of the city's elite. Behind the scenes he headed a ring that plundered New York for tens of millions of dollars.

The New York County Courthouse—''The House that Tweed Built''—was his masterpiece. Nestled in City Hall Park in downtown Manhattan, the three-story structure was designed to cost $250,000, but the bills ran a bit higher. Furniture, carpets, and window shades alone came to more than $5.5 million. Three tables and forty chairs cost the city $180,000. Tweed's own quarry supplied the marble; the plumber got almost $1.5

million for fixtures. Andrew Garvey, the "Prince of Plasterers," charged $500,000 for plaster work, and then $1 million to repair the same work. His total bill came to $2,870,464.06. (The *New York Times* suggested that the six cents be donated to charity.) In the end the building cost over $13 million—and in 1872, when Tweed fell, it was still not finished.

The role of the political bosses can be overemphasized. Power structures in the turn-of-the-century city were complex, involving a host of people and institutions. Banks, realtors, insurance companies, architects, and engineers, among others, played roles in governing the city. Viewed in retrospect, many city governments were remarkably successful. With populations that in some cases doubled every decade, city governments provided water and sewer lines, built parks and playgrounds, and paved streets. When it was over, Boston had the world's largest public library; New York City had the Brooklyn Bridge and Central Park, two of the finest architectural achievements of any era. By the 1890s, New York also had 660 miles of water lines, 464 miles of sewers, and 1800 miles of paved streets, far more than comparable cities in Europe.

Bosses, moreover, differed from city to city. Buckley stayed in power in San Francisco by keeping city tax rates low. "Honest" John Kelly earned his nickname serving as a watchdog over the New York City treasury. Tweed was one of the early backers of the Brooklyn Bridge. Some bosses were plainly corrupt; others believed in "honest graft," a term Tammany's George Washington Plunkitt coined to describe "legitimate" profits made from advance knowledge of city projects.

Why did voters keep the bosses in power? The answers are complex, but involve skillful political organization and the fact that immigrants and others made up the bosses' constituency. Most immigrants had little experience with democratic government and proved easy prey for well-oiled machines. For the most part, however, the bosses stayed in power because they paid attention to the needs of the least privileged city voters. They offered valued services in an era when neither government nor business lent a hand.

If an immigrant, tired and bewildered after the long crossing, came looking for a job, bosses like Tweed, Plunkitt, or Buckley found him one in city offices or local businesses. If a family's breadwin-ner died or was injured, the bosses donated food and clothing and saw to it that the family made it through the crisis. If the winter was particularly cold, they provided free coal to heat tenement apartments. They ran picnics for slum children on hot summer days and contributed to hospitals, orphanages, and dozens of worthy neighborhood causes.

Most bosses became wealthy; they were not Robin Hoods who took from the rich to give to the poor. They took for themselves as well. Reformers occasionally ousted them. Tweed fell from power in 1872, "Blind Boss" Buckley in 1891, Croker in 1894. But the reformers rarely stayed in power long. Drawn mainly from the middle and upper classes, they had little understanding of the needs of the poor. Before long, they returned to private concerns, and the bosses, who had known that they would all along, cheerily took power again.

"What tells in holdin' your grip on your district," the engaging Plunkitt once said, "is to go right down among the poor families and help them in the different ways they need help. . . . It's philanthropy, but it's politics, too—mighty good politics. . . . The poor are the most grateful people in the world."

LIFE IN AMERICA, 1877

The rise of cities and industry between 1877 and the 1890's affected all aspects of American life. Mores changed; family ties loosened. Factories turned out consumer goods, and the newly invented cash register rang up record sales. Public and private educational systems burgeoned; illiteracy declined; life expectancy increased. While many people worked harder and harder just to survive, others found they had a greater amount of leisure time. The roles of women and children changed in a number of ways, and the family took on functions it had not had before. Thanks to advancing technology, news flashed quickly across the oceans, and for the first time in history, people read of the day's events in distant lands when they opened their daily newspapers.

"We are in a period," President Rutherford B. Hayes said in 1878, "when old questions are settled, and the new ones are not yet brought forward." Old questions—questions of racial,

A man shows off his new buggy in front of a handsome Victorian house on a quiet, tree-lined street in small-town America, circa 1890.

social and economic justice, and of federal-state relations—were not settled, but people wanted new directions. Political issues lost the sharp focus of the Civil War and Reconstruction. For men and women of middle age in 1877, the issues of the Union and slavery had been the overriding public concerns throughout their adult lives. Now, with the end of Reconstruction, it seemed time for new concerns.

In 1877, the country had 47 million people. In 1900, it had grown to nearly 76 million. Nine-tenths of the population were white; just under one-tenth was black. There were 66,000 Indians, 108,000 Chinese, and 148 Japanese. The bulk of the white population, most of whom were Protestant, came from the so-called Anglo-Saxon countries of northern Europe. WASPs—White Anglo-Saxon Protestants—were the dominant members of American society.

Though the rush to the cities was about to begin, most people of 1877 still lived on farms or in small towns. Their lives revolved around the farm, the church, and the general store. In 1880, nearly 75 percent of the population lived in communities of fewer than twenty-five hundred people. In 1900, in the midst of city growth, 60 percent still did. The average family in 1880 had three children, dramatically fewer than at the beginning of the century, and life expectancy was about forty-three years. By 1900, it had risen to forty-seven years, the result of improved health care. For blacks and other minorities, who often lived in unsanitary rural areas, life expectancy was substantially lower: thirty-three years in 1900.

In small towns, houses were usually made of wooden shingles or clapboard, set back from unpaved streets, whose dusty surfaces muffled the sound of passing horses. Life was quiet. Many homes had a front porch for summertime sitting. In the backyard there were numerous outbuildings, including one—at the end of a well-worn path—with a distinctive half-moon carved in the door. There was a vegetable garden and often a chicken coop or cowshed; families—even in the cities—needed backyard produce to supplement their diets. Inside the house, life centered in the kitchen with its enormous wood or coal stove.

Meals tended to be heavy and so did people. Even breakfast had several courses and could include steak, eggs, fish, potatoes, toast, and coffee. Food prices were low. Families ate fresh homegrown produce in the summer, and "put up" their fruits and vegetables for the long winters. Toward the end of the century, eating habits changed. New, packaged breakfast cereals became popular; fresh fruit and vegetables came in on fast trains from Florida and California, and commercially canned food processing became safer and cheaper. The newfangled icebox, cooled by blocks of ice, kept food fresher and added new treats such as ice cream.

Medical science was in the midst of a major revolution. Louis Pasteur's recent discovery that germs cause infection and disease, created the new science of microbiology and led the way to the development of vaccines and other preventive measures. But tuberculosis, typhoid, diphtheria, and pneumonia—all now curable—were still the leading causes of death. Many families knew the wrenching pain of a child's death. Infant mortality declined between 1877 and 1900, but the decline was gradual; a great drop did not come until after 1920.

There were few hospitals and no hospital insurance. Most patients stayed at home, although medical practice, especially surgery, expanded rapidly. Once brutal and dangerous, surgery in these years became relatively safe and painless. Anesthetics—ether and chloroform—eliminated pain, and antiseptic practices helped prevent postoperative infections. Antiseptic practices at childbirth also cut down on puerperal fever, an infection that for centuries had killed many women and newborn infants. The new science of psychology began to explore the mind, hitherto uncharted. William James, a leading American psychologist and philosopher, laid the foundations of modern behavioral psychology, which stressed the importance of the environment on human development.

Manners and Mores

The code of Victorian morality, its name derived from the British queen who reigned throughout the period, set the tone for the era. The code prescribed strict standards of dress, manners, and sexual behavior. It was both obeyed and disobeyed, and it reflected the tensions of a generation that was undergoing a change in moral standards.

1890 Retail Prices: Food

BACON 1 lb.	15.5¢
BUTTER 1 lb.	25.5¢
EGGS 1 dozen	20.8¢
FLOUR 5 lbs.	14.5¢
MILK ½ gal. delivered	13.6¢
PORK CHOPS 1 lb.	10.7¢
POTATOES 10 lbs.	16¢
ROUND STEAK 1 lb.	12.3¢
SUGAR 5 lbs.	34.5¢

Source: U.S. Bureau of the Census, Historical Abstract of the United States, Colonial Times to 1970, Bicentennial Edition, Washington, D.C., 1975.

In 1877, children were to be seen and not heard. They spoke when spoken to, listened rather than chattered—or at least that was the rule. Older boys and girls were often chaperoned, although they could always find moments alone. They played post office and spin the bottle; they puffed cigarettes behind the barn. William Allen White, later a famous journalist, recalled the high jinks of his boyhood. He and his friends smeared their naked bodies with mud and leaped out in full view of passengers on passing trains. Counterbalancing such youthful exuberance was strong pride in virtue and self-control. "Thank heaven I am absolutely pure," Theodore Roosevelt, the future President, wrote in 1880 after proposing to Alice Lee. "I can tell Alice everything I have ever done."

Gentlemen of the middle class dressed in heavy black suits, derby hats, and white shirts with paper collars. Women wore tight corsets, long, dark dresses, and black shoes reaching well above the ankles. As with so many things, styles changed dramatically toward the end of the century, spurred in part by new sporting fads such as golf, tennis, and bicycling, which required looser clothing. By the 1890s, a middle-class woman wore a tailored suit or a dark skirt and a blouse, called a "shirtwaist," modeled after men's shirts. Her skirts still draped about the ankles, but more

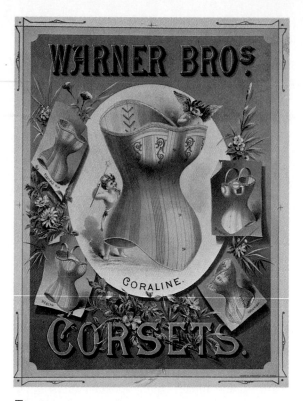

The slightest exertion on the part of women who wore the fashionable, tightly laced, steel-and-whalebone corset was likely to bring on a fainting spell.

educated and upper class, they included individuals like Thomas Nast, the famous political cartoonist, George William Curtis, editor of *Harper's Weekly*, and E. L. Godkin, editor of the influential *Nation.* Other zealous reformers campaigned for prohibition of the sale of intoxicating liquors, hoping to end the social evils that stemmed from drunkenness. In 1874, women who advocated total abstinence from alcoholic beverages formed the Women's Christian Temperance Union. Their leader, Frances E. Willard, served as president of the group from 1879 until her death in 1898. By then, the WCTU had 10,000 branches and 500,000 members.

In New York City, Anthony Comstock formed the Society for the Suppression of Vice, which supervised public morality. At his request, Congress passed the Comstock Law (1873) prohibiting the mailing or transporting of "obscene, lewd or lascivious" articles. The law was not successful; within a few years Comstock reported finding 64,094 "articles for immoral use," 700 pounds of "lead moulds for making obscene matter," 202,679 obscene photographs, and 26 "obscene pictures, framed on walls of saloons."

Leisure and Entertainment

In the 1870s, people tended to rise early. On getting up; they washed from the pitcher and bowl in the bedroom, first breaking the layer of ice if it was winter. After dressing and eating, they went off to work and school. Without large refrigerators, housewives marketed almost daily. In the evening, families gathered in the "second parlor" or living room, where the children did their lessons, played games, sang around the piano, and listened to that day's verse from the Bible.

Popular games included cards, dominoes, backgammon, chess, and checkers. Many homes had a packet of "author cards" that required knowledge of books, authors, and noted quotations. The latest fad was the stereopticon or "magic lantern," which brought three-dimensional life to art, history, and nature. Like "author cards" and other games, it was instructional as well as entertaining.

The newest outdoor game was croquet, so popular that candles were mounted on the wick-

and more she removed or loosened the corset, the dread device that squeezed skin and internal organs into fashionable eighteen-inch waistlines.

Religious and patriotic values were strong. One of the centers of community life, the church often set the tenor for family and social relationships. On Sundays, the family dressed in Sunday-best and attended a long morning service, followed by Sunday dinner, naps, reading, and another church service in the evening. In the 1880s, eight out of ten church members were Protestants; most of the rest were Roman Catholics. Evangelists like Dwight L. Moody, a former Chicago shoe salesman, and Ira B. Sankey, an organist and singer, conducted mass revival meetings across the country. Enormously successful, Moody preached to millions and sparked a spiritual awakening on American college campuses.

With slavery abolished, reformers turned their attention to new moral and political issues. One group, known as the Mugwumps, worked to end corruption in politics. Drawn mostly from the

Above, the third baseman makes a bare-handed catch as the runner slides safely into base. At right, the high-wheeled bicycles the men are riding were called "ordinaries."

ets to allow play at night. Croquet was the first outdoor game designed for play by both sexes, and it frequently served as a setting for courtship. Early manuals advised girls how to assume attractive poses while hitting the ball. A popular song of the period told of a pair seated side by side as the

mallets and balls unheeded lay . . .
and I thought to myself, is that Croquet?

Sentimental ballads such as "Silver Threads Among the Gold" (1873) remained the most popular musical form, but the insistent syncopated rhythms of ragtime were being heard, reflecting the influence of the new urban culture. By the time the strains of Scott Joplin's "Maple Leaf Rag" (1899) popularized ragtime, critics complained that "a wave of vulgar, filthy and suggestive music has inundated the land." Classical music flourished. The New England Conservatory (1867), the Cincinnati College of Music (1878), and the Metropolitan Opera (1883) were new sources of civic pride; New York, Boston, and Chicago launched first-rate symphony orchestras between 1878 and 1891.

In the hamlets and small towns of America,

traveling circuses were enormously popular. Hamlin Garland, an author who grew up in small Iowa villages, recalled how the circus came "trailing clouds of glorified dust and filling our minds with the color of romance. . . . It brought to our ears the latest band pieces and taught us the popular songs. It furnished us with jokes. It relieved our dullness. It gave us something to talk about." Larger circuses, run by entrepreneurs like P. T. Barnum and James A. Bailey, played the cities, but every town attracted its own smaller version.

Fairs, horse races, balloon ascensions, bicycle tournaments, and football and baseball contests attracted avid fans. The years between 1870 and 1900 saw the rise of organized spectator sports, a trend reflecting both the rise of the city and the new uses of leisure. Baseball's first professional team, the Cincinnati Red Stockings, appeared in 1869, and baseball soon became the preeminent national sport. Fans sang songs about it ("Take Me Out to the Ballgame"), wrote poems about it ("Casey at the Bat"), and made up riddles about it ("What has eighteen feet and catches flies?"). Modern rules were adopted. Umpires were designated to call balls and strikes; catchers wore masks and chest protectors and moved closer to the plate instead of staying back to catch the ball on the bounce. Fielders had to catch the ball on the fly rather than on one bounce in their caps. By 1890, professional baseball teams were drawing crowds of sixty thousand daily. In 1901, the American League was organized, and two years later the Boston Red Sox beat the Pittsburgh Pirates in the first modern World Series.

In 1869, Princeton and Rutgers played the first intercollegiate football game. Soon, other schools picked up the sport, and by the early 1890s, crowds of fifty thousand or more attended the most popular contests. Basketball, invented in 1891, gained a large following. Boxing, a popular topic of conversation in saloons and schoolyards, was outlawed in most states. For a time, championship prizefights were held in secret, with news of the result spread rapidly by word of mouth. Matches were long and bloody, fought with bare knuckles until the invention in the 1880s of the five-ounce boxing glove. John L. Sullivan, the Boston Strong Boy and the era's most popular champion, won the heavyweight title in 1889 in a brutal seventy-five-round victory over the stubborn Jake Kilrain.

As gas and electric lights brightened the night, and streetcars crisscrossed city streets, leisure habits changed. Delighted with the new technology, people took advantage of an increasing variety of things to do. They stayed home less often. New York City's first electric sign—"Manhattan Beach Swept by Ocean Breezes"—appeared in 1881, and people went out at night, filling the streets on their way to the theater, vaudeville shows, dance halls, or just out for an evening stroll.

Family Life

Under the impact of industrialization and urbanization, family relationships were changing. On the farm, parents and children worked more or less together, and the family was a producing unit. In factories and offices, family members rarely worked together. In working-class families, mothers, fathers, and children separated at dawn and returned, ready for sleep, at dark. Morris Rosenfeld, a clothing presser lamenting that he was unable to spend more time with his son, wrote a poem entitled "My Boy."

Steam, steel, and electricity transformed cities. In this W. Louis Sonntag, Jr. watercolor of New York City's Bowery in 1895, electric streetcars travel up and down the street while the elevated railroad rumbles overhead. Bright incandescent lamps light up the night.

I have a little boy at home,
A pretty little son;
I think sometimes the world is mine
In him, my only one. . . .

'Ere dawn my labor drives me forth;
'Tis night when I am free;
A stranger am I to my child;
And stranger my child to me.

Working-class families of the late nineteenth century, like the family of the young Polish girl that Harriet Vittum saw, often lived in complex household units—taking in relatives and boarders to pay the rent. As many as one-third of all households contained people who were not members of the immediate family. Although driven apart by the daily routine, family ties among the working-class tended to remain strong, cemented by the need to join forces in order to survive in the industrial economy.

The middle-class wife and children, however, became increasingly isolated from the world of work. Turning inward, the middle-class family became more self-contained. Older children spent more time in adolescence, and periods of formal schooling were lengthier. Families took in fewer apprentices and boarders. By the end of the century, most middle-class offspring continued to live with their parents into their late teens and twenties, a larger proportion than today.

Fewer middle-class wives participated directly in their husbands' work. As a result, they and their children occupied what contemporaries called a "separate sphere of domesticity," set apart from the masculine sphere of income-producing work. The family became a "walled garden," a place to retreat from the crass materialism of the outside world. Middle-class fathers began to move their families out of the city to the suburbs, commuting to work on the new streetcars, and leaving wives and children at home and school.

The middle-class family had once functioned in part to transmit a craft or skill, arrange marriages, and offer care for dependent kin. Now, as these functions declined, the family took on new emotional and ideological responsibilities. In a society that worried about the weakening hold of other institutions, it became more and more important as a means of social control. It also placed new burdens on wives.

"In the old days," said a woman in 1907, "a married woman was supposed to be a frump and a bore and a physical wreck. Now you are supposed to keep up intellectually, to look young and well and be fresh and bright and entertaining." Magazines like the *Ladies' Home Journal*, which started in 1889, glorified motherhood and the home, but its articles and ads featured women as homebound, child-oriented consumers. While society's leaders spoke fondly of the value of homemaking, the status of housewives declined under the factory system, which emphasized money rewards and devalued household labor.

Underlying all these changes was one of the modern world's most important trends, a major decline in fertility rates that lasted from 1800 to 1939. Though blacks, immigrants, and rural dwellers continued to have more children than white native city dwellers, the trend affected all classes and races; among white women, the birthrate fell from 7 in 1800 to just over 4 in 1880 to about 3 in 1900. People everywhere tended to marry later and have fewer children.

Since contraceptive devices were not yet widely used, the decline reflected abstinence and a conscious decision to postpone or limit families. In some cases, women decided to devote greater attention to a smaller number of children, in other cases to pursue their own careers. There was a marked increase in the number of young, unmarried women working for wages or attending school; an increase in the number of women delaying marriage or not marrying at all; and a gradual decline in rates of illegitimacy and premarital pregnancy.

In large part, the decline in fertility stemmed from people's responses to the social and economic forces around them, the rise of cities and industry. In a host of individual decisions, they decided to have fewer children, and the result reshaped some of the fundamental attitudes and institutions of American society.

Changing Views: A Growing Assertiveness among Women

In and out of the family, there was growing recognition of the self-sufficient working woman, employed in factory, telephone exchange, and business office, who was entering the work force

*W*omen operators, called "Hello Girls," were hired to work telephone switchboards after it was discovered that male operators tended to argue too much with subscribers!

contract before marriage. By 1890, many states had substantially revised the doctrine to allow wives control of their earnings and inherited property. In cases of divorce, the new laws also recognized women's rights to custody or joint custody of their children. Although divorce was still far from being socially acceptable, divorce rates more than doubled during the last third of the century. By 1905, one in twelve marriages was ending in divorce.

In the 1870s and '80s, a growing number of women were asserting their own humanness. They fought for the vote, lobbied for equal pay, and sought self-fulfillment. The new interest in psychology and medicine strengthened their causes. Charlotte Perkins Gilman, author of *Women and Economics* (1898), joined other women in questioning the ideal of womanly "innocence," which, she argued, actually meant ignorance. In medical and popular literature, menstruation, sexual intercourse, and childbirth were becoming viewed as natural functions instead of taboo topics.

Edward Bliss Foote's *Plain Home Talk of Love, Marriage, and Parentage,* a best-seller that went through many editions between the 1880s and 1900s, challenged Victorian notions that sexual intercourse was unhealthy and intended solely to produce children. In *Plain Facts for Old and Young* (1881), Dr. John H. Kellogg urged parents to recognize the early awakening of sexual feelings in their children. Still, such matters were avoided in many American homes. Rheta Childe Dorr, a journalist, remembered that when a girl reached the age of fourteen, new rules were introduced, "and when you asked for an explanation you met only embarrassed silence."

Women espoused causes with new fervor. Susan B. Anthony, a veteran of many reform campaigns, tried to vote in the 1872 presidential election and was fined $100, which she refused to pay. In 1890, she helped form the National American Woman Suffrage Association to work for the enfranchisement of women (see Chapter 22). On New York's Lower East Side, the Ladies Anti-Beef Trust Association, which formed to protest increases in the price of meat, established a boycott of butcher shops. When their demands were ignored, the women invaded the shops, poured kerosene on the meat, and set fire to it. "We don't riot," Rebecca Ablowitz told the judge.

in increasing numbers. In 1880, there were 2.6 million women gainfully employed; in 1890, 4 million. In 1882, the Census Bureau took the first census of working women; most were single and worked out of necessity rather than choice.

This "New Woman" was seen by many as a corruption of the ideal vision of the American woman, in which man worshipped "a diviner self than his own," innocent, helpless, and good. Women were to be better than the world around them. They were brought up, said Ida Tarbell, a leading political reformer, "as if wrongdoing were impossible to them."

Views changed, albeit slowly. One important change occurred in the legal codes pertaining to women, particularly in the common law doctrine of *femme couverte.* Under that doctrine, wives were chattel of their husbands; they could not legally control their own earnings, property, or children unless they had drawn up a specific

"But if all we did was to weep at home, nobody would notice it; so we have to do something to help ourselves."

Educating the Masses

Continuing a trend that stretched back one hundred years, childhood was becoming an even more distinct time of life. There was still only a vague concept of adolescence—the special nature of the teenage years—but the role of children was changing. Less and less were children perceived as "little adults," valued for the additional financial gain they might bring into the family. Now children were to grow and learn and be nurtured rather than rushed into adulthood.

As a result, schooling became more important and American educators came closer than ever before to universal education. By 1900, thirty-one states and territories (out of fifty-one) had enacted laws making school attendance compulsory, though most only required attendance until the age of fourteen. In 1870, there were only 160 public high schools; in 1900, there were 6000. In the same years, public school budgets rose from $63 million to $253 million; illiteracy declined from 20 percent to just over 10 percent of the population. Still, even as late as 1900, the average adult had only five years of schooling.

Educators saw the school as the primary means to train people for life and work in an industrializing society. Hence, teachers focused on basic skills—reading and mathematics—and on values—obedience and attentiveness to the clock. Most schools had a highly structured curriculum, built around discipline and routine. In 1892, Joseph Rice, a pediatrician, toured twelve hundred classrooms in thirty-six cities. In a typical classroom, he reported, the atmosphere was "damp and chilly," the teacher strict. "The unkindly spirit of the teacher is strikingly apparent; the pupils being completely subjugated to her will, are silent and motionless." One teacher asked her pupils, "How can you learn anything with your knees and toes out of order?"

Many children dropped out of school early, and not just to earn money. Helen Todd, a factory inspector in Chicago, found a group of young girls working in a hot, stuffy attic. When she asked why they were not in school, Tillie Isakow-sky, who was fourteen, said: "School! School is de fiercest t'ing youse kin come up against. Factories ain't no cinch, but schools is worst." A few blocks away, Todd stumbled on a thirteen-year-old boy hiding in a basement. He cried when she said he would have to go to school, blurting that "they hits ye if yer don't learn, and they hits ye if ye whisper, and they hits ye if ye have string in yer pocket, and they hits ye if yer seat squeaks, and they hits ye if ye don't stan' up in time, and they hits ye if yer late, and they hits ye if ye ferget the page." Curious, Todd asked 500 children whether they would go to school or work in a factory if their families did not need the money—412 preferred the factory.

School began early; boys attended all day, but girls often stayed home after lunch, since it was thought they needed less in the way of learning. On the teacher's command, students stood and recited from *Webster's Spellers* and *McGuffey's Readers*, the period's most popular textbooks. The work of William Holmes McGuffey, a professor

Although education was growing in importance, in most schools the emphasis continued to be on comformity and deportment, with the teacher acting as drillmaster and disciplinarian.

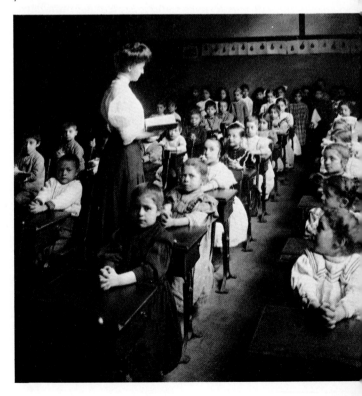

of languages at Miami University in Ohio, *McGuffey's Readers* had been in use since 1836 (see Chapter 11); 100 million copies were sold in the last half of the nineteenth century. Nearly every child read them; they taught not only reading but also ethics, values, and religion. In the *Readers*, boys grew up to be heroes, girls to be mothers, and hard work always meant success:

> *Shall birds, and bees, and ants, be wise,*
> *While I my moments waste?*
> *O let me with the morning rise,*
> *And to my duty haste.*

The South lagged far behind in education. The average family size there was about twice as large as in the North, and a greater proportion of the population lived in isolated rural areas. State and local authorities mandated fewer weeks in the average school year, and many southern states refused to adopt compulsory education laws. Most important, Southerners insisted on maintaining separate school systems to segregate the races. Supported by the United States Supreme Court decision of 1896 in *Plessy* v. *Ferguson* (see "The Shaping of Jim Crow," pp. 576–77) segregated schooling added a devastating financial burden to education in the South.

North Carolina and Alabama mandated segregated schools in 1876, South Carolina and Louisiana in 1877, Mississippi in 1878, and Virginia in 1882. A series of Supreme Court decisions in the 1880s and 90s upheld the concept of segregation. In the *Civil Rights Cases* (1883), the Court ruled that the Fourteenth Amendment barred state governments from discriminating on account of race but did not prevent private individuals or organizations from doing so. *Plessy* v. *Ferguson* (1896) established the doctrine of "separate but equal" and upheld a Louisiana law requiring different railroad cars for whites and blacks. The Court applied the doctrine directly to schools in *Cumming* v. *County Board of Education* (1899), which approved the creation of separate schools for whites, even if there were no comparable schools for blacks.

Southern school laws often implied that the schools would be "separate but equal," but they rarely were. Black schools were usually dilapidated, the teachers in them were paid considerably less than white teachers. In 1890, only 35 percent of black children attended school in the South; 55 percent of white children did. That year nearly two-thirds of the country's black population was illiterate.

Educational techniques changed after the 1870s. Educators paid more attention to early elementary education, a trend that placed young children in school and helped the growing number of mothers who worked outside the home. The kindergarten movement, started in St. Louis in 1873, spread across the country. In kindergartens, four- to six-year olds learned by playing, not by keeping their knees and toes in order. For older children, social reformers advocated "practical" courses in manual training and homemaking. "We are impatient with the schools which lay all stress on reading and writing," Jane Addams said, for "they fail to give the child any clew to the life about him."

For the first time, education became a field of university study. European theorists like Johann Friedrich Herbart, a German educator, argued that learning occurred best in an atmosphere of freedom and confidence between teachers and pupils. Teacher training became increasingly professional. Only 10 normal schools, or teacher-training institutions, existed in the United States before the Civil War. By 1900, there were 345, and one in every five elementary teachers had graduated from a professional school.

Higher Education

Nearly 150 new colleges and universities opened in the twenty years between 1880 and 1900. The Morrill Land Grant Act of 1862 gave large grants of land to the states for the establishment of colleges to teach "agriculture and the mechanic arts." The act fostered 69 "land-grant" institutions, including the great state universities of Wisconsin, California, Minnesota, and Illinois.

Private philanthropy, born of the large fortunes of the industrial age, also spurred growth in higher education. Leland Stanford gave $24 million to endow Stanford University on his California ranch, and John D. Rockefeller, founder of the Standard Oil Company, gave $34 million to found the University of Chicago. Other industrialists established Cornell (1865), Vanderbilt (1873), and Tulane (1884).

As colleges expanded, their function changed,

and their curriculum broadened. No longer did they exist primarily to train young men for the ministry. They moved away from the classical curriculum of rhetoric, mathematics, Latin, and Greek toward "reality and practicality," as President David Starr Jordan of Stanford University said. The Massachusetts Institute of Technology (M.I.T.), founded in 1861, focused on science and engineering.

Influenced by the new German universities, which emphasized specialized research, Johns Hopkins University in Baltimore opened the nation's first separate graduate school in 1876. Under President Daniel Coit Gilman, Johns Hopkins stressed the seminar and laboratory as teaching tools, bringing together student and teacher in close association. By 1900, more than nine thousand Americans had studied in Germany, and some of them returned home to become presidents of institutions such as Harvard, Yale, Columbia, the University of Chicago, and Johns Hopkins.

One of them, Charles W. Eliot, who became president of Harvard in 1869 at the age of thirty-five, moved to end, as an admirer said, the "old fogyism" that marked the institution. Revising the curriculum, Eliot set up the elective system in which students chose their own courses rather than following a rigidly prescribed curriculum. Lectures and discussions replaced rote recitation, and courses in the natural and social sciences, fine arts, and modern languages multiplied. In the 1890s, Eliot's Harvard moved to the forefront of educational innovation.

Women still had to fight for educational opportunities. Some formed study clubs, an important movement that spread rapidly between 1870 and 1900. Groups like the Decatur (Illinois) Art Class, the Boston History Class, and the Barnesville (Georgia) Shakespeare Club aimed "to enlarge the mental horizon as well as the knowledge of our members." Club members read Virgil and Chaucer, studied history and architecture, and discussed women's rights. As the Monday Club of Mount Vernon, Ohio, put it:

In ancient days when Monday came
We used our clothes to rub,
And set them boiling on the stove,
And stir them with a club.
But, Oh, our Monday Club today

Unlike these Smith College chemistry students, most women who attended college in the 1870s were urged to take home economics rather than science courses.

Is quite a different stick;
For we've abandoned household toils
And learned a better trick.

. . . .

And with it, just as Moses did,
We drive the waves apart,
And enter on the promised land
Of learning and of art.

Clubs sprang up almost everywhere there were women: in Caribou, Maine; Tyler, Texas; and Leadville, Colorado—as well as San Francisco, New York, and Boston. Although they were usually small, study clubs sparked a greater interest among women and their daughters in education and contributed to a rapid rise in the number of women entering college in the early 1900s.

Before the Civil War, only three private colleges admitted women to study with men. After the war, educational opportunities increased for women. A number of women's colleges opened, including Vassar (1865), Wellesley (1875), Smith (1875), Bryn Mawr (1885), Barnard (1889), and Radcliffe (1893). The land-grant colleges of the Midwest, open to women from the outset, spurred a nationwide trend toward coeducation, although some physicians, like Harvard Medical School's Dr. Edward H. Clarke in his popular *Sex*

An upholstery class at Booker T. Washington's Tuskegee Institute in Alabama. Although Washington emphasized the importance of learning a trade, students at Tuskegee also received instruction in the liberal arts and sciences.

in Education (1873), continued to argue that the strain of learning made women sterile. By 1900, women made up about 40 percent of college students, and four out of five colleges admitted them.

Fewer opportunities existed for blacks and other minorities. Mrs. Jane Stanford encouraged the Chinese who had worked on her husband's Central Pacific Railroad to apply to Stanford University, but her policy was unusual. Most colleges did not accept minorities, and only a few applied. W. E. B. Du Bois, the brilliant African-American sociologist and civil rights leader, attended Harvard in the late 1880s but found the society of Harvard Yard closed against him. Disdained and disdainful, he "asked no fellowship of my fellow students." Chosen as one of the commencement speakers, Du Bois picked as his topic, "Jefferson Davis," treating it, said an onlooker, with "an almost contemptuous fairness."

Black students turned to black colleges such as the Hampton Normal and Industrial Institute in Virginia and the Tuskegee Institute in Alabama. These colleges were often supported by whites who favored manual training for blacks. Booker T. Washington, an ex-slave, put into practice his educational ideas at Tuskegee, which opened in 1881. Washington began Tuskegee with limited funds, 4 run-down buildings, and only 30 students; by 1900 it was a model industrial and agricultural school. Spread over 46 buildings, it offered instruction in 30 trades to 1400 students.

Washington stressed patience, manual training, and hard work. "The wisest among my race understand," he said in a widely acclaimed speech at the Atlanta Exposition in 1895, "that the agitation of questions of social equality is the extremest folly." Blacks should focus on economic gains; they should go to school, learn skills, and work their way up the ladder. "No race," he said at Atlanta, "can prosper till it learns that there is as much dignity in tilling a field as in writing a poem. It is at the bottom of life we must begin, and not at the top." Southern whites should help out because they would then have "the most patient, faithful, law-abiding, and unresentful people that the world has seen."

Outlined most forcefully in Washington's speech in Atlanta, the philosophy became known as the Atlanta Compromise, and many whites and some blacks welcomed it. Acknowledging white domination, it called for slow progress through self-improvement, not through lawsuits or agitation. Rather than fighting for equal rights, blacks should acquire property, and show they were worthy of their rights. But Washington did believe in black equality. Often secretive in his methods, he worked behind the scenes to organize black voters and lobby against harmful laws. In his own way, he bespoke a racial pride that contributed to the rise of black nationalism in the twentieth century.

Du Bois wanted a more aggressive strategy. Born in Massachusetts in 1868, the son of poor parents, he studied at Fisk University in Tennessee and the University of Berlin before he went to Harvard. Unable to find a teaching job in a white college, he took a low-paying research position at the University of Pennsylvania. He had no office but did not need one. Du Bois used the new discipline of sociology, which emphasized factual observation in the field, to study the condition of blacks.

Notebook in hand, he set out to examine crime in Philadelphia's black seventh ward. He interviewed five thousand people, mapped and classified neighborhoods, and produced *The Philadelphia Negro* (1898), a book of nearly one thousand pages. The first study of the effect of urban life on blacks, it cited a wealth of statistics, all suggesting that crime in the ward stemmed not from inborn degeneracy but from the environment in which blacks lived. Change the environment, and people would change, too; education was a good way to go about it.

In *The Souls of Black Folk* (1903), Du Bois openly attacked Booker T. Washington and the philosophy of the Atlanta Compromise. He urged African Americans to aspire to professional careers, to fight for the restoration of their civil rights, and wherever possible, to get a college education. Calling for integrated schools with equal opportunity for all, Du Bois urged blacks to educate their "talented tenth," a highly trained intellectual elite, to lead them.

Du Bois was not alone in promoting careers in

In 1895, W. E. B. Du Bois became the first African American to receive a doctorate from Harvard.

the professions. Throughout higher education there was increased emphasis on professional training, particularly in medicine, dentistry, and law. Enrollments swelled, even as standards of admission tightened. The number of medical schools in the country rose from 75 in 1870 to 160 in 1900, and the number of medical students—including more and more women—almost tripled. Schools of nursing grew from only 15 in 1880 to 432 in 1900. Doctors, lawyers, and others became part of a growing middle class that shaped the concerns of the Progressive era (see Chapter 22).

Although fewer than 5 percent of the college-age population attended college during the 1877–1890 period, the new trends had great impact. A generation of men and women encountered new ideas that changed their views of themselves and society. Courses never before offered, like Philosophy II at Harvard, "The Ethics of Social Reform," which students called "drainage, drunkenness, and divorce," heightened interest in social problems and the need for reform. Some graduating students burned with a desire to cure society's ills. "My life began . . . at Johns Hopkins University," Frederic C. Howe, an influential reformer, recalled. "I came alive, I felt a sense of responsibility to the world, I wanted to change things."

The Shaping of Jim Crow: Plessy v. Ferguson

In a nation of laws, the interpretation of law can profoundly change people's lives. *Plessy* v. *Ferguson* (1896), one of the most important cases to reach the Supreme Court, changed the lives of millions of black and white Americans. Interpreting law in a way that lasted for more than a half century, it permitted the segregation of blacks in public facilities throughout the land.

Given the significance of the case, we know surprisingly little about Homer A. Plessy, the man behind it. He was young—we know that—and apparently he worked as a carpenter in Louisiana. According to the court records, he was "seven-eighths Caucasian," which perhaps was the reason he was chosen to test the constitutionality of a Louisiana law requiring railroad companies to segregate whites and blacks on trains in the state. It seemed a good law to test. Louisiana's own constitution forbade such discrimination; so did the federal Civil Rights Act of 1875, which guaranteed blacks "full and equal enjoyment" of public conveyances.

Whatever the details of his life, Plessy lived in a post-Reconstruction South in which racism was widespread but segregation was not. Where segregation did exist, it usually was not enacted into law. During the 1870s and 1880s, blacks and whites often ate together and worked together. "I can ride in first-class cars on the railroads and in the streets," a delighted black visitor wrote home from South Carolina in 1885. "I can go into saloons and get refreshments even as in New York. I can stop in and drink a glass of soda and be more politely waited upon than in some parts of New England."

That situation changed dramatically near the end of the century. The courts often reflect trends in the society, and whites in the North as well as the South of the 1890s had little enthusiasm for civil rights. In addition, economic depression heightened racial tensions, and the spread of colonial imperialism in Africa and Asia led to talk about "inferior" peoples, both at home and abroad. Beginning in the 1870s, the Supreme Court handed down a series of decisions that overturned much Reconstruction legislation, limited federal protection for blacks, and encouraged racial segregation.

In the *Slaughterhouse Cases* of 1873, the Supreme Court narrowed the scope of the Fourteenth Amendment protecting blacks; a decade later, in the *Civil Rights Cases* (1883), it said that Congress could not punish private individuals for acts of racial discrimination. Emboldened by such decisions,

The Louisiana segregation law tested by Homer Plessy in 1892 was representative of a growing number of such laws passed in the 1880s and '90s. Segregation legislation was neither new nor confined to the South. This 1856 engraving documents the expulsion of an African American from a railway car in Philadelphia.

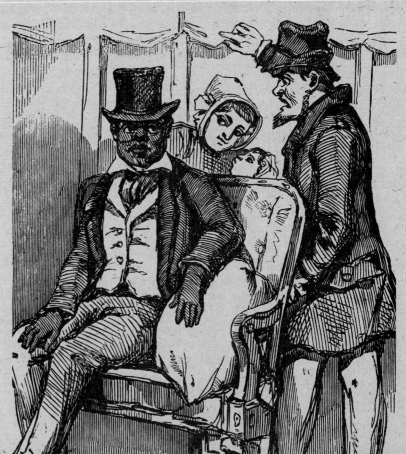

southern states passed many segregation laws, including laws requiring railroad companies to separate white and black riders. In 1890 Louisiana passed "An Act to promote the comfort of passengers" that made railroads in the state provide "equal but separate" cars.

Blacks in Louisiana protested; railroad officials, not liking the cost of the extra cars, were sympathetic. And so on June 7, 1892, to test the law, Homer A. Plessy boarded an East Louisiana Railway train in New Orleans for the thirty-mile trip to Covington. He took a seat in a car reserved for whites, refused to move when a conductor asked him to, and was arrested by a detective who was standing by for the occasion. John H. Ferguson, a local judge, ruled against Plessy's argument that the law violated his rights, and Plessy appealed to the Supreme Court.

Four years later, in a 7 to 1 decision, the Court decided against Plessy. Upholding the doctrine of "separate but equal," it held that the Louisiana law did not violate Plessy's rights. Plessy could still travel on the railroad, and there was no evidence that "the enforced separation of the two races stamps the colored race with a badge of inferiority." Justice John Marshall Harlan, the sole dissenter, scoffed at the reasoning. The Louisiana law, he said, was clearly prejudicial, designed to keep blacks from railroad cars occupied by whites. If upheld, what stood in the way of laws calling for segregation of all kinds? Laws might make blacks and whites (or for that matter, Protestants and Catholics) walk on opposite sides of the street or paint their houses different colors.

After *Plessy*, Jim Crow laws spread swiftly through the South. More and more public conveyances, schools, and restaurants were segregated. Signs saying "Whites Only" or "Colored" appeared on entrances and exits, restrooms and water fountains, waiting rooms, and even elevators. In 1905, Georgia passed the first law requiring separate public parks. In 1909, Mobile, Alabama, enacted a curfew requiring blacks to be off the streets by 10 P.M. In 1915, South Carolina forbade blacks and whites to work in the same rooms in textile factories. The Oklahoma legislature required separate telephone booths; New Orleans segregated white and black prostitutes. Atlanta had separate Bibles for black witnesses in the city courts.

Plessy v. *Ferguson* set a pattern of Court-supported Southern segregation that lasted sixty years. Generations of blacks and whites, children and adults alike, were deeply affected—sometimes traumatized—by it. The practice became a major focus of grievance in the growing movement for civil rights during the 1930s and 1940s. At last, in the 1954 case of *Brown* v. *Board of Education of Topeka* (see Chapter 29), the Supreme Court overturned *Plessy*. Ruling that segregated schools are inherently unequal, the Court's stand toppled segregation of many kinds.

Plessy v. Ferguson served to reinforce policies of racial segregation and eventually resulted in the institution of "separate but equal" facilities, which, like the one shown below, were often not equal at all.

When Henry George, one of the era's leading reformers, asked a friend what could be done about the problem of political corruption in American cities, his friend replied: "Nothing! You and I can do nothing at all. . . . We can only wait for evolution. Perhaps in four or five thousand years evolution may have carried men beyond this state of things."

This stress on the slow pace of change reflected the doctrine of Social Darwinism, based on the evolutionary theories of Charles Darwin and the writings of English social philosopher Herbert Spencer. In several influential books, Spencer applied Darwinian principles of natural selection to society, combining biology and sociology in a theory of "social selection" that explained human progress. Like animals, society evolved, slowly, by adapting to the environment. The "survival of the fittest"—a term Spencer, not Darwin, invented—preserved the strong and weeded out the weak. "If they are sufficiently complete to live, they *do* live, and it is well they should live. If they are not sufficiently complete to live, they die, and it is best they should die."

Social Darwinism had a number of influential followers in the United States, including William Graham Sumner, a professor of political and social science at Yale University. One of the country's best-known academic figures, Sumner was forceful and eloquent. In writings such as *What Social Classes Owe to Each Other* (1883) and "The Absurd Effort to Make the World Over" (1894), he argued that government action on behalf of the poor or weak interfered in evolution and sapped the species. Reform tampered with the laws of nature. "It is the greatest folly of which a man can be capable to sit down with a slate and pencil to plan out a new social world," Sumner said.

The influence of Social Darwinism on American thinking has been exaggerated, but in the powerful hands of Sumner and others it did influence some journalists, ministers, and policymakers. Between 1877 and the 1890s, however, it came under increasing attack. In fields like religion, economics, politics, literature, and law, thoughtful people raised questions about established conditions and suggested the need for reform.

Read and reread, passed from hand to hand, Henry George's nationwide best-seller, *Progress and Poverty* (1879), led the way to a more critical appraisal of American society in the 1880s and beyond. The book jolted traditional thought. "It was responsible," one historian has said, "for starting along new lines of thinking an amazing number of the men and women" who became leaders of reform.

Born in 1839, the child of a poor Philadelphia family, George had little formal schooling. As a boy he went to sea, then worked as a prospector, printer, and journalist. Self-educated as an economist, he moved to San Francisco in the late 1850s and began to study "the fierce struggle of our civilized life." Disturbed by the depression of the 1870s and labor upheavals like the great railroad strikes of 1877, George saw modern society—rich, complex, with material goods hitherto unknown—as sadly flawed.

"The present century," he wrote "has been marked by a prodigious increase in wealth-producing power. . . . It was natural to expect, and it was expected, that . . . real poverty [would become] a thing of the past." Instead, he argued

> it becomes no easier for the masses of our people to make a living. On the contrary, it is becoming harder. The wealthy class is becoming more wealthy; but the poorer class is becoming more dependent. The gulf between the employed and the employer is growing wider; social contrasts are becoming sharper; as liveried carriages appear, so do barefooted children.

George proposed a simple solution. Land, he thought, formed the basis of wealth, and a few people could grow wealthy just because the price of their land rose. Since the rise in price did not result from any effort on their part, it represented an "unearned increment," which, George argued, should be taxed for the good of society. A "single tax" on the increment, replacing all other taxes, would help equalize wealth and raise revenue to aid the poor. "Single-tax" clubs sprang up around the country, but George's solution, simplistic and unappealing, had much less impact than his analysis of the problem itself. He raised questions a generation of readers set out to answer.

The rich and poor of Victorian America: Mrs. Cornelia Ward Hall and her children (above) and a tenement mother and her children (right) trying to eke out a living by making paper roses.

New Currents in Social Thought

George's emphasis on deprivation in the environment excited a young country lawyer in Ashtabula, Ohio, Clarence Darrow. Unlike the Social Darwinists, Darrow was sure that criminals were made and not born. They grew out of "the unjust condition of human life." In the mid-1880s, he left for Chicago and a forty-year career working to convince people that poverty lay at the root of crime. "There is no such thing as crime as the word is generally understood . . . ," he told a group of startled prisoners in the Cook County jail. "If every man, woman and child in the world had a chance to make a decent, fair, honest living there would be no jails and no lawyers and no courts."

As Darrow rejected the implications of Social Darwinism, in similar fashion did Richard T. Ely and a group of young economists poke holes in traditional economic thought. Fresh from graduate study in Germany, Ely in 1884 attacked classical economics for its dogmatism, simple faith in laissez-faire, and reliance on self-interest as a guide for human conduct. The "younger" economics, he said, must no longer be "a tool in the hands of the greedy and the avaricious for keeping down and oppressing the laboring classes. It does not acknowledge laissez-faire as an excuse for doing nothing while people starve."

Accepting a post at Johns Hopkins University, Ely assigned graduate students to study labor conditions in Baltimore and other cities; one of them, John R. Commons, went on to publish a massive four-volume study, *History of Labour in the United States.* In 1885, Ely led a small band of rebels in founding the American Economic Association, which linked economics to social problems and urged government intervention in economic affairs. Social critic Thorstein Veblen saw economic laws as a mask for human greed. In *The Theory of the Leisure Class* (1899), Veblen analyzed the "predatory wealth" and "conspicuous consumption" of the business class.

Edward Bellamy dreamed of a cooperative society where poverty, greed, and crime no longer existed. A lawyer from western Massachusetts, Bellamy published *Looking Backward, 2000–1887,* in 1887 and became a national reform figure virtually overnight. The novel's protagonist, Julian West, falls asleep in 1887 and awakes in the year 2000. Wide-eyed, he finds himself in a socialist utopia; the government owns the means of production, and citizens share the material rewards. Cooperation, rather than competition, is the watchword.

The world of *Looking Backward* had limits; it was regimented, paternalistic, and filled with the gadgets and material concerns of Bellamy's own day. But it had a dramatic effect on many readers.

The book sold at the rate of ten thousand copies a week, and its followers formed Nationalist Clubs to work for its objectives. By 1890, there were such clubs in twenty-seven states, all calling for the nationalization of public utilities and a wider distribution of wealth.

Walter Rauschenbusch, a young Baptist minister, read widely from the writings of Bellamy and George, along with the works of other social reformers. When he took his first church post in Hell's Kitchen, a blighted area of New York City, he soon discovered the weight of the slum environment. "One could hear," he said, "human virtue cracking and crushing all around." In the 1890s, Rauschenbusch became a professor at the Rochester Theological Seminary, and he began to expound on the responsibility of organized religion to advance social justice.

Some Protestant sects stressed individual salvation and a better life in the next world, not in this one. Poverty was evidence of sinfulness; the poor had only themselves to blame. "God has intended the great to be great and the little to be little," said Henry Ward Beecher, the country's best-known pastor. Wealth and destitution, suburbs and slums—all formed part of God's plan.

Challenging those traditional doctrines, a number of churches in the 1880s began establishing missions in the city slums. William Dwight Porter Bliss, an Episcopal clergyman, founded the Church of the Carpenter in a working-class district of Boston. Lewis M. Pease worked in the grim Five Points area of New York; Alexander Irvine, a Jewish missionary, lived in a flophouse in the Bowery. Irvine walked his skid row neighborhood every afternoon to lend a hand to those in need. Living among the poor and homeless, the urban missionaries grew impatient with religious doctrines that endorsed the status quo.

Many of the new trends were reflected in an emerging religious philosophy known as the "Social Gospel." As the name suggests, the Social Gospel focused on society as well as individuals, on improving living conditions as well as saving souls. Sermons in Social Gospel churches called upon church members to fulfill their social obligations, and adults met before and after the regular service to discuss social and economic problems. Children were excused from sermons, organized into age groups, and encouraged to make the church a center for social as well as religious activity. Soon, churches included dining halls, gymnasiums, and even theaters.

The most active Social Gospel leader was Washington Gladden, a Congregational minister and prolific writer. Linking Christianity to the social and economic environment, Gladden spent a lifetime working for "social salvation." He saw Christianity as a fellowship of love and the church as a social agency. In *Applied Christianity* (1886) and other writings, he denounced competition, urged an "industrial partnership" between employers and employees, and called for efforts to help the poor.

The Settlement Houses

A growing number of social reformers, living in the urban slums, shared Gladden's concern. Like Tweed and Plunkitt, they appreciated the dependency of the poor; unlike them, they wanted to eradicate the conditions that underlay it. To do so, they formed settlement houses in the slums and went to live in them to experience the problems they were trying to solve.

Youthful, idealistic, and mostly middle-class, these social workers took as their model Toynbee Hall, founded in 1884 in the slums of East London to provide community services. Stanton Coit, a moody and poetic graduate of Amherst College, was the first American to borrow the settlement-house idea; in 1886, he opened the Neighborhood Guild on the Lower East Side of New York. The idea spread swiftly. By 1900, there were over 100 settlements in the country; five years later, there were over 200, and by 1910, more than 400.

The settlements included Jane Addams's famous Hull House in Chicago (1889); Robert A. Woods's South End House in Boston (1892); and Lillian Wald's Henry Street Settlement in New York (1893). These reformers wanted to bridge the socioeconomic gap between rich and poor and to bring education, culture, and hope to the slums. They sought to create in the heart of the city the values and sense of community of small-town America. Of settlement workers, Wald said in *The House on Henry Street* (1915): "We were to live in a neighborhood . . . identify ourselves with it socially, and, in brief, contribute to it our citizenship."

Jane Addams founded Chicago's Hull House in 1889. The settlement house provided recreational and day-care facilities, offered extension classes in academic, vocational, and artistic subjects, and above all, sought to bring hope to poverty-stricken slum dwellers.

Many of the settlement workers were women, some of them college graduates, who found that society had little use for their talents and energy. Jane Addams, a graduate of Rockford College in Illinois, opened Hull House on South Halsted Street in the heart of the Chicago slums. Twenty-nine years old, endowed with a forceful and winning personality, she intended "to share the lives of the poor" and humanize the industrial city. "American ideals," she said, "crumbled under the overpowering poverty of the overcrowded city."

Occupying an old rundown house, Hull House had a "plainness that just escaped barrenness and just touched the artistic." Its staff stressed education, offering classes in elementary English and Shakespeare, lectures on ethics and the history of art, and courses in cooking, sewing, and manual skills. A pragmatist, Addams believed in investigating a problem, then doing something to solve it. Noting the lack of medical care in the area, she established an infant welfare clinic and free medical dispensary. Because the tenements lacked bathtubs, she installed showers in the basement of the house and built a bathhouse for the neighbors. Because there was no local library,

she opened a reading room. Gradually Hull House expanded to occupy a dozen buildings sprawling over more than a city block.

Like settlement workers in other cities, Addams and her colleagues studied the immigrants in nearby tenements. Laboriously they identified the background of every family in a one-third square mile area around Hull House. Finding people of eighteen different nationalities, they taught them American history and the English language, yet also encouraged them—through folk festivals and art—to preserve their heritage.

In Boston, Robert Woods of South End House focused on the problem of school dropouts. He offered manual training, formed clubs to get young people off the streets, and established a cheap restaurant where the hungry could eat. Lillian Wald, the daughter of a middle-class family and herself a graduate nurse, concentrated on providing health care for the poor. In 1898, the first Catholic-run settlement house opened in New York, and in 1900, Bronson House opened in Los Angeles to work in the Mexican-American community.

Florence Kelley, an energetic graduate of Cornell University, taught night school one winter in Chicago. Watching children break under the burden of poverty, she devoted her life to the problem of child labor. Convinced of the need for political activism, she worked with Addams and others to push through the Illinois Factory Act of 1893, which mandated an eight-hour day for women in factories and for children under the age of fourteen.

The settlement house movement had its limits. Hull House, one of the best, attracted 2000 visitors a week, still just a fraction of the 70,000 people who lived within six blocks. Immigrants sometimes resented these middle-class "strangers" who told them how to live. Dressed always in a brown suit and dark stockings, Harriet Vittum, the head resident of Chicago's Northwestern University Settlement (who told the story of the suicide victim at the beginning of this chapter), was known in the neighborhood as "the police lady in brown." She once stopped a dance because it was too wild, and then watched in disgust as the boys responded by "making vulgar sounds with their lips." Though her attempts to help were sincere, in private, Vittum called the people she was trying to help "ignorant foreigners, who live in an atmosphere of low morals . . . surrounded by anarchy and crime," a situation she found hopeless at times.

Although Addams tried to offer a few programs for blacks, most white reformers did not, and after 1900 a number of black reformers opened their own settlements. Like the whites, they offered employment information, medical care, and recreational facilities, along with concerts, lectures, and other educational events. White and black, the settlement workers made important contributions to urban life.

A Crisis in Social Welfare

The depression of 1893 (see Chapter 20) jarred the young settlement workers, many of whom had just begun their work. Addams and the Hull House workers helped form the Chicago Bureau of Charities to coordinate emergency relief. Kelley, recently appointed the chief factory inspector of Illinois, worked even harder to end child labor, and in 1899, she moved to New York City to head the National Consumers League, which marshaled the buying power of women to encourage employers to provide better working conditions.

In cities and towns across the country traditional methods of helping the needy foundered in the crisis. Churches, Charity Organization Societies, and Community Chests did what they could, but their resources were limited, and they functioned on traditional lines. Many of them still tried to change rather than aid individual families, and people were often reluctant to call on them for help.

Gradually, a new class of professional social workers arose to fill the need. Unlike the church and charity volunteers, these social workers wanted not only to feed the poor but to study their condition and alleviate it. Revealingly they called themselves "case workers" and daily collected data on the income, housing, jobs, health, and habits of the poor. Prowling tenement districts, they gathered information about the number of rooms, number of occupants, ventilation, and sanitation, putting together a fund of useful data.

Studies of the poor popped up everywhere. Walter Wyckoff, a graduate of Princeton University, embarked in 1891 on what he called "an experiment in reality." For eighteen months he worked as an unskilled laborer in jobs from Connecticut to California. "I am vastly ignorant of the labor problems and am trying to learn by experience," he said as he set out. After working as a ditch digger, farmhand, and logger, Wyckoff summarized his findings in *The Workers* (1897), a book immediately hailed as a major contribution to sociology.

To investigate living issues, Wyckoff felt, one must investigate life, and so many others followed his example that sometimes it seemed the observers outnumbered those being observed. W. E. B. Du Bois did his pioneering study of urban blacks (see p. 575); Lillian Pettengill took a job as a domestic servant to see "the ups and downs of this particular dog-life from the dog's end of the chain." Others became street beggars, miners, lumberjacks, and factory laborers. Bessie and Marie Van Vorst's *The Woman Who Toils: Being the Experiences of Two Gentlewomen as Factory Girls* (1903) studied female workers, as did Helen Campbell's *Women Wage-Earners: Their Past, Their Present and Their Future* (1893), which suggested that the conditions of factory employment prepared women mainly "for the hospital, the workhouse, and the prison."

William T. Stead, a prominent British editor, visited the Chicago World's Fair in 1893 and stayed to examine the city. He roamed the flophouses and tenements and dropped in at Hull House to drink hot chocolate and talk over conditions with Jane Addams. Later he wrote an influential book *If Christ Came to Chicago* (1894), and in a series of mass meetings during 1893, he called for a civic revival. In response, Chicagoans formed the Civic Federation, a group of forty leaders who aimed to make Chicago "the best governed, the healthiest city in this country." Setting up task forces for philanthropy, moral improvement, and legislation, the new group helped spawn the National Civic Federation (1900), a nationwide organization devoted to reform of urban life.

"The United States was born in the country and moved to the city," historian Richard Hofstadter said. Much of that movement occurred during the nineteenth century when the United States was the most rapidly urbanizing nation in the western world. American cities bustled with energy; they absorbed millions of migrants who came from Europe and other distant and not-so-distant parts of the world. That migration, and the urban growth that accompanied it, reshaped American politics and culture.

By 1920, the census showed that, for the first time, most Americans lived in cities. By then, too, almost half the population was descended from people who arrived after the American Revolution. As European, African, and Asian cultures met in the American city, a culturally pluralistic society emerged. Dozens of nationalities produced a hyphenated culture whose members considered themselves Polish-Americans, African-Americans, and Irish-Americans. The melting pot sometimes softened distinctions between the various groups, but it only partially blended them into a unified society.

"Ah, Vera," said a character in Israel Zangwill's popular play, *The Melting Pot* (1908), "what is the glory of Rome and Jerusalem where all nations and races come to worship and look back, compared with the glory of America, where all races and nations come to labour and look forward!" Critics scorned the play as "romantic claptrap," and indeed it was. But the metaphor of the melting pot clearly depicted a new national image. In the decades after the 1870s a jumble of ethnic and racial groups struggled for a place in society.

That society, it is clear, experienced a crisis between 1870 and 1900. Together, the growth of cities and the rise of industrial capitalism brought jarring change, the exploitation of labor, ethnic and racial tensions, poverty, and for a few, wealth beyond the imagination. At Homestead, Pullman, and a host of other places, there was open warfare between capital and labor. As reformers struggled to mediate the situation, they turned more and more to state and federal government to look after human welfare, a tendency the Supreme Court stoutly resisted. In the midst of the crisis, the depression of the 1890s struck, adding to the turmoil and straining American institutions. Tracing the changes wrought by waves of urbanization and industrialization, Henry George described the country as "the House of Have and the House of Want," almost in paraphrase of Lincoln's earlier metaphor of the "house divided." Could this house, unlike that one, stand?

CHRONOLOGY

1862 Morrill Land Grant gives land to states for establishment of colleges

1869 Rutgers and Princeton play in nation's first intercollegiate football game • Cincinnati Red Stockings, baseball's first professional team, organized

1873 Comstock Law bans obscene articles from U.S. mail • Nation's first kindergarten opens in Saint Louis, Missouri

1874 Women's Christian Temperance Union formed to crusade against evils of liquor

1876 Johns Hopkins University opens first separate graduate school

1879 Henry George analyzes problems of urbanizing America in *Progress and Poverty* • Salvation Army arrives in United States

1880 Polish National Alliance formed to help Polish immigrants adjust to life in America

1881 Booker T. Washington opens Tuskegee Institute in Alabama • Dr. John H. Kellogg advises parents to teach their children about sex in *Plain Facts for Old and Young*

1883 Metropolitan Opera opens in New York

1885 Home Insurance Building, country's first metal-frame structure, erected in Chicago • American Economic Association formed to advocate government intervention in economic affairs

1887 Edward Bellamy promotes idea of socialist utopia in *Looking Backward, 2000–1887*

1889 Jane Addams opens Hull House in Chicago

1890 National Woman Suffrage Association and the American Woman Suffrage Association, both formed in 1869, merge to consolidate the woman suffrage movement

1894 Immigration Restriction League formed to limit immigration from southern and eastern Europe

1896 Supreme Court decision in *Plessy* v. *Ferguson* establishes constitutionality of "separate but equal" facilities • John Dewey's Laboratory School for testing and practice of new educational theory opens at University of Chicago

Recommended Reading

On urban America, see Sam Bass Warner, Jr.: *Streetcar Suburbs* (1962) and *The Urban Wilderness* (1972). Arthur M. Schlesinger, *The Rise of the City, 1878–1898* (1933) is a pioneering study; Constance M. Green, *The Rise of Urban America* (1965); Morris J. Vogel, *The Invention of the Modern Hospital: Boston 1870–1930* (1980); and Howard P. Chuda-coff, *The Evolution of American Urban Society*, rev. ed. (1981) are also valuable. See also two recent books by Jon C. Teaford, *The Unheralded Triumph: City Government in America, 1870–1900* (1984), and *City and Suburb: The Political Fragmentation of Metropolitan America, 1850–1970* (1979).

Kenneth T. Jackson, *Crabgrass Frontier: The Suburbaniza-tion of the United States* (1985) and John R. Stilgoe, *Border-land: Origins of the American Suburb, 1820–1939* (1988) are recent treatments of the growth of the suburbs. Russel B. Nye, *The Unembarrassed Muse* (1970), covers popular cul-ture; Neil Harris, *Humbug: The Art of P. T. Barnum* (1973), is superb on both Barnum and the era. For family life, see Carl N. Degler, *At Odds: Women and the Family in America from the Revolution to the Present* (1980); Joseph Kett, *Rites of Passage: Adolescence in America* (1977); Elaine Tyler May, *Great Expectations: Marriage and Divorce in Post-Victorian America* (1980); Steven Mintz, *A Prison of Expectations: The Family in Victorian Culture* (1983); Norma Basch, *In the Eyes of the Law: Women, Marriage, and Property in Nineteenth-Century New York* (1982); and Tamara K. Hareven and Maris Vinovskis, eds., *Family and Population in Nineteenth Century America* (1978). For education, see L. A. Cremin, *The Transformation of the School* (1961); Lawrence Veysey, *The Emergence of the American University* (1965); and David B. Tyack, *The One Best System* (1974).

Oscar Handlin, *The Uprooted*, 2d ed. (1973) and John Higham, *Strangers in the Land* (1955) are classic studies. Robert H. Bremner, *From the Depths: The Discovery of Poverty in the United States* (1956); Judith Ann Trolander, *Professionalism and Social Change: From the Settlement House Movement to Neighborhood Centers, 1886 to the Present* (1987); Allen F. Davis, *Spearheads for Reform: The Social Settlements and the Progressive Movement, 1890–1914* (1967); and *American Heroine: The Life and Legend of Jane Addams* (1973), examine urban reform.

Treatments of intellectual currents include Richard Hof-stadter, *Social Darwinism in American Thought*, rev. ed. (1955); Jon H. Roberts, *Darwinism and the Divine in America* (1988); Robert C. Bannister, *Sociology and Scientism* (1987); Bannister, *Social Darwinism: Science and Myth in Anglo-American Social Thought* (1979); Sidney Fine, *Laissez Faire and the General Welfare State* (1956); John L. Thomas, *Alternative America: Henry George, Edward Bellamy, Henry Demarest Lloyd and the Adversary Tradition* (1983); and Eric F. Goldman, *Rendezvous with Destiny* (1952).

Additional Bibliography

Robert H. Walker, *Life in the Age of Enterprise, 1865–1900* (1967), examines everyday life. On leisure and entertain-ment, see Gunther Barth, *City People* (1980); Lary May,

Screening Out the Past: The Birth of Mass Culture and the Motion Picture Industry (1980); and Ronald L. Davis, *A History of Music in American Life*, vol. 2 (1980). David J. Pivar, *Purity Crusade: Sexual Morality and Social Control, 1868–1900* (1973); Susan Estabrook Kennedy, *If All We Did Was to Weep at Home: A History of White Working Class Women in America* (1979); Barbara Mayer Wertheimer, *We Were There: The Story of Working Women in America* (1977); and Lois W. Banner, *Women in Modern America: A Brief History* (1974), are helpful on the topic of women in urban society.

Robert V. Bruce, *The Launching of Modern American Science, 1846–1876* (1987); Wolfgang Schivelbusch, *Disen-chanted Night* (1988); and Cecelia Tichi, *Shifting Gears: Technology, Literature, Culture in Modernist America* (1987), are helpful on science and technology. For one of the era's leading architects, see Robert Twombly, *Louis Sullivan* (1986); Joseph Siry, *Carson-Pirie-Scott* (1988); and David S. Andrew, *Louis Sullivan and the Polemics of Modern Architec-ture* (1985).

On education, see Sidney Hook, *John Dewey* (1939); Frederick Rudolph, *The American College and University* (1962); Donald Spivey, *Schooling for the New Slavery: Black Industrial Education, 1868–1915* (1978); Lawrence A. Cre-min, *American Education: The Metropolitan Experience, 1876–1950* (1988); Robert L. McCaul, *The Black Struggle for Public Schooling in Nineteenth-Century Illinois* (1987); James D. Anderson, *The Education of Blacks in the South, 1860–1935* (1988); Gerald David Jaynes, *Branches Without Roots: Gene-sis of the Black Working Class in the American South, 1862–1882* (1986); Ronald Butchart, *Northern Schools, Southern Blacks, and Reconstruction, Freedmen's Education, 1862–1875* (1980); and two books by Louis R. Harlan, *Booker T. Washington: The Making of a Black Leader, 1856–1901* (1972), and *Booker T. Washington: The Wizard of Tuskegee, 1901–1915* (1953). Charles A. Lofgren, *The Plessy Case* (1987) is a detailed study of that important decision.

For immigration and urban growth, consult Barbara Solomon, *Ancestors and Immigrants* (1956); Josef J. Barton, *Peasants and Strangers* (1975); Leonard Dinnerstein, Roger L. Nichols, and David M. Reimers, *Natives and Strangers* (1979); Oliver Zunz, *The Changing Face of Inequality* (1982); Moses Rischin, *The Promised City: New York's Jews* (1962); David Ward, *Cities and Immigrants* (1971); Thomas L. Philpott, *The Slum and the Ghetto* (1978); Terrence J. McDonald, *The Parameters of Urban Fiscal Policy: Socioeco-nomic Change and Political Culture in San Francisco, 1860–1906* (1986); Patricia Mooney Melvin, *The Organic City: Urban Definition & Community Organization, 1880–1920* (1987); Carl V. Harris, *Political Power in Birmingham, 1871–1921* (1977); Stuart Galishoff, *Newark: The Nation's Un-healthiest City, 1832–1895* (1988); William A. Bullough, *The Blind Boss and His City* (1979); and Leo Hershkowitz, *Tweed's New York: Another Look* (1977).

See also Dorothy Rose Blumberg, *Florence Kelley* (1971); Gloria Moldow, *Women Doctors in Gilded-Age Washington: Race, Gender, and Professionalization* (1987); Martha Banta, *Imaging American Women: Idea and Ideals in Cultural History* (1987); Martha Vicinus, *Independent Women: Work and Community for Single Women 1850–1920* (1985); Theodora Penny Martin, *The Sound of Our Own Voices: Women's Study Clubs, 1860–1910* (1987); Leslie Woodcock Tentler, *Wage-*

Earning Women: Industrial Work and Family Life in the United States, 1900–1930 (1979); Ruth Bordin, *Woman and Temperance: The Quest for Power and Liberty, 1873–1900* (1981); Mary A. Hill, *Charlotte Perkins Gilman: The Making of a Radical Feminist, 1860–1896* (1980); John M. O'Donnell, *The Origins of Behaviorism: American Psychology, 1870–1920* (1985); Roy M. Lubove, *The Progressives and the Slums* (1962); Martin J. Schiesl, *The Politics of Efficiency: Municipal Administration and Reform in America* (1977); and R. C. White, Jr., and C. H. Hopkins, *The Social Gospel* (1976).

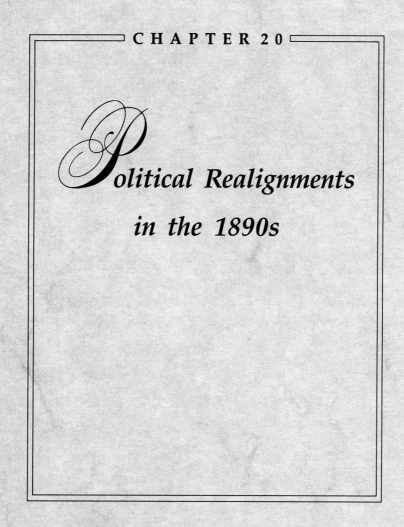

CHAPTER 20

Political Realignments in the 1890s

*I*n June 1894, Susan Orcutt, a young farm woman from western Kansas, sat down to write the governor of her state a letter. She was desperate. The nation was in the midst of a devastating economic depression, and she had no money and nothing to eat. "I take my Pen In hand to let you know that we are Starving to death," she wrote. On top of their already bad financial situation, hail had ruined the Orcutts' crops, and the head of the household could not find work. "My Husband went away to find work and came home last night and told me that we would have to Starve. [H]e has bin in ten countys and did not Get no work. . . . I havent had nothing to Eat today and It is three oclock[.]"

As bad as conditions were on the farms, they were no better in the cities. "There are thousands of homeless and starving men in the streets," reported a journalist in Chicago in the winter of 1893. "I have seen more misery in this last week than I ever saw in my life before." Charity societies and churches tried to help, but they could not handle the huge numbers of people who were in need. The records of the Massachusetts state medical examiner told a grim story:

C.W., 45   Suicide by bullet
Boston   Death May 21, 1895
    Out of work and poor, left home a.m. May 21, to collect some old bills. About noon, went to shop of one P. and demanded $5 on account of an old trade. Payment was refused. After some words, W. drew a revolver and fired at P.'s head, without effect; a second shot made a scalp wound and P. fell. W. then turned the weapon on himself and fired into his right temple, making a wound from which he died at once.

K.R., 29   Suicide by drowning
Boston   October 2, 1896
    Out of work and despondent for a long while. Body found floating in the Charles [River].

F.S., 29   Suicide by arsenic
Boston   January 1, 1896
    Much depressed for several weeks. Loss of employment. At 7:50 a.m. Jan. 1, she called her father and told him she had taken poison and wished to die.

L.M., 38   Hanging suicide
E. Boston   October 15, 1895
    Had been out of work for several weeks and was very despondent. Wife went to market at about 11 a.m. and upon returning at about 12 p.m. found him hanging from bedroom door. . . . Slipped noose about his neck and [fell] forward upon it.

R.N., 23   Suicide by bullet
                            wound of brain
Boston   June 22, 1896
    Out of work. Mentally depressed. About 3 p.m. June 21 shot himself in right temple. . . . Left a letter explaining that he killed himself to save others the trouble of caring for him.

Lasting until 1897, the depression was the decisive event of the decade. At its height, three million people were unemployed—fully 20 percent of the work force. The human costs were enormous, even among the well-to-do. "They

A run on a New York bank during the Panic of 1893. The stock market crashed on June 27, and by the end of the year, nearly 500 banks had closed.

were for me years of simple Hell," shattering "my whole scheme of life," said Charles Francis Adams, the descendant of two American presidents. "I was sixty-three years old and a tired man when at last the effects of the 1893 convulsion wore themselves out."

Like the depression of the 1930s that gave rise to the New Deal, the depression of the 1890s had profound and lasting effects. Bringing to a head many of the tensions that had been building in the society, it increased rural hostility toward the cities, brought about a bitter fight over the currency, and changed people's thinking about government, unemployment, and reform. There were outbreaks of warfare between capital and labor; farmers demanded a fairer share of economic and social benefits; the "new" immigrants came under fresh attack. The depression of the 1890s changed the course of American history, as did another event of that decade: the war with Spain in 1898 (see Chapter 21).

Under the cruel impact of the depression, ideas changed in many areas, including in politics. A realignment of the American political system, which had been developing since the end of Reconstruction, finally reached its fruition in the 1890s, establishing new patterns that gave rise to the Progressive Era and lasted well into the twentieth century.

POLITICS OF STALEMATE

Electoral politics was a major fascination of the late nineteenth century, its mass entertainment and favorite sport. Political campaigns were events that involved the whole community, even though in most states men were the only ones who could vote. During the weeks leading up to an election, there were rallies, parades, picnics, and torchlight processions. Millions of Americans read party newspapers, listened to three-hour speeches by party leaders, and in elections turned out in enormous numbers to vote. In the six presidential elections from 1876 to 1896, an average of almost 79 percent of the electorate voted, a higher percentage than voted before or after.

White males made up the bulk of the electorate; until after the turn of the century, women could vote in national elections only in Wyoming,

Utah, Idaho, and Colorado. The National Woman Suffrage Association early sued for the vote, but in 1875 the Supreme Court (*Minor* v. *Happersett*) upheld the power of the states to deny this right to women. On several occasions, Congress refused to pass a constitutional amendment for woman's suffrage, and between 1870 and 1910, nearly a dozen states defeated referenda to grant women the vote.

Black men were increasingly kept from the polls. In 1877, Georgia adopted the poll tax to make voters pay an annual tax for the right to vote. The technique, aimed at impoverished blacks, was quickly copied across the South. In 1882, South Carolina adopted the "eight box" law, copied elsewhere, that required ballots for separate offices to be placed in separate boxes, a difficult task for illiterate voters.

In 1890, Mississippi required voters to be able to read and interpret the federal Constitution to the satisfaction of registration officials, all of them white. Such literacy tests, which the Supreme Court upheld in the case of *Williams* v. *Mississippi* (1898), excluded poor white voters as well as blacks. In 1898, Louisiana got around that problem by adopting the famous "grandfather clause," which used a literacy test to disqualify black voters but permitted men who had failed the test to vote anyway if their fathers and grandfathers had voted before 1867—a time, of course, when no blacks could vote. The number of black voters decreased dramatically. In 1896, there were 130,334 registered black voters in Louisiana; in 1904, there were 1342.

The Party Deadlock

The 1870s and '80s were still dominated by the Civil War generation, the unusual group of people who rose to power in the turbulent 1850s. In both the North and South, they had ruled longer than most generations, with a consciousness that the war experience had set them apart. Five of the six presidents elected between 1865 and 1900 had served in the war, as had many civic, business, and religious leaders. In 1890, there were well over one million veterans of the Union army still alive, and Confederate veterans numbered in the hundreds of thousands.

Party loyalties—rooted in Civil War traditions,

ethnic and religious differences, and perhaps class distinctions—were remarkably strong. Voters clung to their old parties, shifts were infrequent, and there were relatively few "independent" voters. Although linked to the defeated Confederacy, the Democrats revived quickly after the war. In 1874, they gained control of the House of Representatives, which they maintained for all but four of the succeeding twenty years. The Democrats rested on a less sectional base than did the Republicans. While identification with civil rights and military rule cut Republican strength in the South, the Democratic party's principles of states' rights, decentralization, and limited government won supporters everywhere.

While Democrats wanted to keep government local and small, the Republicans pursued policies for the nation as a whole, in which government was an instrument to promote moral progress and material wealth. The Republicans passed the Homestead Act (1862), granted subsidies to the transcontinental railroads, and pushed other measures to encourage economic growth. They enacted legislation and constitutional amendments to protect civil rights. They advocated a high protective tariff as a tool of economic policy, to keep out foreign products while "infant industries" grew.

In national elections, sixteen states, mostly in New England and the North, consistently voted Republican; fourteen states, mostly in the South, consistently voted Democratic. Elections, therefore, depended on a handful of "doubtful" states, which could swing elections either way. These states—New York, New Jersey, Connecticut, Ohio, Indiana, and Illinois—received special attention at election time. Politicians lavished money and time on them; presidential candidates usually came from them. From 1868 to 1912, eight of the nine Republican presidential candidates and six of the seven Democratic candidates came from the "doubtful" states, especially New York and Ohio.

The two parties were evenly matched, and elections were closely fought. In three of the five presidential elections from 1876 to 1892, the victor won by less than 1 percent of the vote; in 1876 and 1888, the losing candidates actually had more popular votes than the winners but lost in the electoral college. Knowing that small mistakes could lose elections, politicians became extremely cautious. Only twice during these years did one party control both the presidency and the two houses of Congress—the Republicans in 1888 and the Democrats in 1892.

Historians once believed that politicians accomplished little between 1877 and 1900, but those who saw few achievements were looking in the wrong location. With the impeachment of Andrew Johnson, the authority of the presidency dwindled in relation to congressional strength. For the first time in many years, attention shifted away from Washington itself. North and South, people who were weary of the centralization brought on by war and Reconstruction looked first to state and local governments to deal with issues.

Experiments in the States

Across the country, state bureaus and commissions were established to regulate the new industrial society. Many of the early commissions were formed to oversee the railroads, at the time the nation's largest businesses. People who shipped goods over the railroads, especially farmers and merchants, wanted to end the policies of rate discrimination and other harmful practices. In 1869, Massachusetts established the first commission to regulate the railroads; by 1900, twenty-eight states had taken such action. Most of the early commissions were advisory in nature; they collected statistics and published reports on rates and practices—serving, one commissioner said, "as a sort of lens" to focus public attention. Impatient with the results, legislatures in the Midwest and on the Pacific Coast established commissions with greater powers to fix rates, outlaw rebates, and investigate rate discrimination. These commissions, experimental in nature, served as models for later policy at the federal level.

Illinois had one of the most thoroughgoing provisions. Responding to local merchants who were upset with existing railroad rate policies, the Illinois state constitution of 1870 declared railroads to be public highways and authorized the legislature to pass laws establishing maximum rates and preventing rate discrimination. In the important case of *Munn* v. *Illinois* (1877), the Supreme Court upheld the Illinois legislation, declaring that private property "affected with the public interest . . . must submit to being con-

*T*his cartoon, entitled "The Scourge of the West" (1885) satirizes railroad monopolists. The robber baron astride his iron horse brandishes his weapons—land grants and federal funds—and shoots down workers and farmers.

trolled by the public for the common good."

But the Court soon weakened that judgment. In the *Wabash* case of 1886 (*Wabash, St. Louis, & Pacific Railway Co.* v. *Illinois*), it narrowed the *Munn* rule and held that states could not regulate commerce extending beyond their borders. Only Congress could. The *Wabash* decision turned people's attention back to the federal government. It spurred Congress to pass the Interstate Commerce Act (1887), which created the Interstate Commerce Commission to investigate and oversee railroad activities. The act outlawed rebates and pooling agreements, and the ICC became the prototype of the federal commissions that today regulate many parts of the economy.

Reestablishing Presidential Power

Johnson's impeachment, the scandals of the Grant administrations, and the controversy surrounding the 1876 election (see Chapter 16) weakened the presidency. During the last two decades of the nineteenth century, presidents fought to reassert their authority, and by 1900, under William McKinley, they had succeeded to a remarkable degree. The late 1890s, in fact, marked the birth of the modern powerful presidency.

Rutherford B. Hayes entered the White House with his title clouded by the disputed election of 1876. Opponents called him "His Fraudulency"

and "Rutherfraud B. Hayes," but soon he began to reassert the authority of the presidency. Hayes worked for reform in the civil service, placed well-known reformers in high offices, and, ordering the last troops out of South Carolina and Louisiana, ended military Reconstruction. He hoped to revive the Republican party in the South by persuading business-oriented ex-Whigs to join a national party that would support their economic interests more effectively than the Democrats did. In this attempt, however, he failed. Committed to the gold standard—the only basis, Hayes thought, of a sound currency—in 1878 he vetoed the Bland-Allison Silver Purchase bill, which called for the partial coinage of silver, but Congress passed it over his veto.

James A. Garfield, a Union army hero and long-time member of Congress, succeeded Hayes. Winning by a handful of votes in 1880, he took office energetically, determined to unite the Republican party (which had been split by personality differences and disagreement over policy toward the tariff and the South), lower the tariff to cut taxes, and assert American economic and strategic interests in Latin America. Ambitious and eloquent, Garfield had looked forward to the presidency, yet within a few weeks he said to friends: "My God! What is there in this place that a man should ever want to get into it?"

Office seekers, hordes of them, evoked Garfield's anguish. Each one wanted a government job, and each one thought nothing of cornering

The Election of 1880		Popular Vote	Electoral Vote
Candidate	Party		
Garfield	Republican	4,446,158	214
Hancock	Democrat	4,444,260	155
Weaver	Greenback	305,997	0

The Election of 1884		Popular Vote	Electoral Vote
Candidate	Party		
Cleveland	Democrat	4,874,621	219
Blaine	Republican	4,848,936	182
Butler	Greenback	175,096	0
St. John	Prohibition	147,482	0

the President on every occasion. The problem of government jobs also provoked a bitter fight with the powerful senator from New York, Roscoe Conkling, who resented some of Garfield's choices. On the verge of victory over Conkling, Garfield planned to leave Washington on July 2, 1881, for a vacation in New England. Walking toward his train, he was shot in the back by Charles J. Guiteau, a deranged lawyer and disappointed office seeker. Suffering through the summer, Garfield died on September 19, 1881, and Vice-President Chester A. Arthur—an ally of Senator Conkling—became president.

Arthur was a better president than many had expected. Deftly he established his independence of Conkling. Conservative in outlook, he reversed Garfield's foreign policy initiatives in Latin America, but he approved the construction of the modern American navy. Arthur worked to lower the tariff, and in 1883, with his backing, Congress passed the Pendleton Act to reform the civil service. In part a reaction against Garfield's assassination, the act created a bipartisan Civil Service Commission to administer competitive examinations and appoint officeholders on the basis of merit. Initially, the act affected only about 14,000 of some 100,000 government offices, but it laid the basis for the later expansion of the civil service.

In the election of 1884, Grover Cleveland, the Democratic governor of New York, narrowly defeated Republican nominee James G. Blaine, largely because of the continuing divisions in the Republican party. The first Democratic president since 1861, Cleveland was slow and ponderous, known for his honesty, stubbornness, and hard work. His term in the White House from 1885 to 1889 reflected the Democratic party's desire to curtail federal activities. Cleveland vetoed more than two-thirds of the bills presented to him, more than all his predecessors combined.

Forthright and sincere, he brought a new re-

spectability to a Democratic party still tainted by its link with secession. Working long into the night, he reviewed veterans' pensions and civil service appointments. He continued Arthur's naval construction program and forced railroad, lumber, and cattle companies to surrender millions of acres of fraudulently occupied public domain. Late in 1887, he devoted his annual message to an attack on the tariff, "the vicious, inequitable, and illogical source of unnecessary taxation," and committed himself and the Democratic party to lowering the tariff.

The Republicans accused him of undermining American industries, and in 1888, they nominated for the presidency Benjamin Harrison, a defender of the tariff. Cleveland garnered ninety thousand more popular votes than Harrison but won the electoral votes of only two northern states and the South. Harrison won the rest of the North, most of the "doubtful" states, and the election.

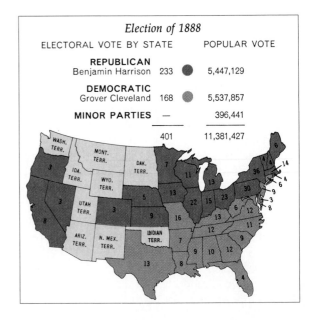

Election of 1888

ELECTORAL VOTE BY STATE	POPULAR VOTE
REPUBLICAN Benjamin Harrison 233	5,447,129
DEMOCRATIC Grover Cleveland 168	5,537,857
MINOR PARTIES —	396,441
401	11,381,427

REPUBLICANS IN POWER: THE BILLION-DOLLAR CONGRESS

Despite Harrison's narrow margin, the election of 1888 was the most sweeping victory for either party in almost twenty years; it gave the Republicans the presidency and both houses of Congress. Eager to block Republican-sponsored laws, the Democrats in Congress used minority tactics, especially the "disappearing quorum" rule, which let members of the House of Representatives join in debate but then refuse to answer the roll call to determine if a quorum was present.

For two months, the Democrats used the rule to bring Congress to a halt. The Republicans grew angry and impatient. On January 29, 1890, they fell two votes short of a quorum, and Speaker of the House Thomas B. Reed, a crusty veteran of Maine politics, made congressional history. "The Chair," he said, "directs the Clerk to record the following names of members present and refusing to vote." Democrats shouted "Czar! Czar!" a title that stuck to Reed for the rest of his life. Tumult continued for days, but in mid-February 1890, the Republicans adopted the Reed rules and proceeded to enact the party's program.

Tariffs, Trusts, and Silver

As if a dam had burst, law after law poured out of the Republican Congress during 1890. The Republicans passed the McKinley Tariff Act, which raised tariff duties about 4 percent, higher than ever before; it also included a novel reciprocity provision that allowed the president to lower duties if other countries did the same. In addition, the act used duties to promote new industries, like tinplate for packaging the new "canned" foods appearing on grocery-store shelves. A Dependent Pensions Act granted pensions to Union Army veterans, their widows, and children. The pensions were modest—$6 to $12 a month—but the number of pensioners doubled by 1893, when nearly one million individuals received about $160 million in pensions.

With little debate, the Republicans and Democrats joined in passing the Sherman Antitrust Act, the first federal attempt to regulate big business. As the initial attempt to deal with the problem of trusts and industrial growth, the act shaped all later antitrust policy. It declared illegal "every contract, combination in the form of trust or otherwise, or conspiracy, in restraint of trade or commerce." Penalties for violation were stiff, including fines and imprisonment and the dissolution of guilty trusts. Experimental in nature, the act's terms were often vague and left precise interpretation to later experience and the courts.

One of the most important laws Congress passed, the Sherman Antitrust Act made the United States virtually the only industrial nation to regulate business combinations. It tried to harness big business without harming it. Many members of Congress did not expect the new law to have much effect on businesses, and for a decade, in fact, it did not. The Justice Department rarely filed suit under it, and in the *United States* v. *E. C. Knight Co.* (1895), the first judicial interpretation of the law, the Supreme Court severely crippled it. Though the E. C. Knight Co. controlled 98 percent of all sugar refining in the country, the Court drew a sharp distinction between commerce and manufacturing, holding that the company, as a manufacturer, was not subject to the law. But judicial interpretations changed after the turn of the century, and the Sherman Antitrust Act gained fresh power.

Another measure, the Sherman Silver Purchase Act, tried to end the troublesome problem presented by silver. As one of the two most commonly used precious metals, silver had once played a large role in currencies around the world, but by the mid-1800s, it had slipped into disuse. With the discovery of the great bonanza mines in Nevada (see Chapter 17), American silver production quadrupled between 1870 and 1890, glutting the world market, lowering the price of silver, and persuading many European nations to demonetize silver in favor of the scarcer metal, gold. The United States kept a limited form of silver coinage with congressional passage of the Bland-Allison Act in 1878.

Support for silver coinage was especially strong in the South and West, where people thought it might inflate the currency, raise wages and crop prices, and challenge the hated power of the gold-oriented Northeast. Eager to avert the free coinage of silver, which would require the coinage of all silver presented at the United States mints, President Harrison and other Republican leaders pressed for a compromise that took shape in the Sherman Silver Purchase Act of 1890.

The act directed the Treasury to purchase 4.5

million ounces of silver a month and to issue legal tender in the form of Treasury notes in payment for it. The act was a compromise; it satisfied both sides. Opponents of silver were pleased that it did not include free coinage. Silverites, on the other hand, were delighted that the monthly purchases would buy up most of the country's silver production. The Treasury notes, moreover, could be cashed for either gold or silver at the bank, a gesture toward a true bimetallic system based on silver and gold.

As a final measure, Republicans in the House courageously passed a federal elections bill to protect the voting rights of blacks in the South. Although restrained in language and intent, it set off a storm of denunciation among the Democrats, who called it a "force bill" that would station army troops in the South. Because of the outcry, the bill failed in the Senate; it was the last major effort until the 1950s to enforce the Fifteenth Amendment to the Constitution.

The 1890 Elections

The Republican Congress of 1890 was one of the most important Congresses in American history. It passed a record number of significant laws that helped shape later policy, and asserted the authority of the federal government to a degree the country would not then accept. Sensing the public reaction, the Democrats labeled it the "Billion-Dollar Congress" for spending that much in appropriations and grants.

"This is a billion-dollar country," Speaker Reed replied, but the voters disagreed. The 1890 elections crushed the Republicans, who lost an extraordinary seventy-eight seats in the House. The elections also crushed Republicans in the Midwest where, again enlarging government authority, they had passed state laws prohibiting the sale of alcoholic beverages, requiring the closing of businesses on Sunday, and mandating the use of English in the public and parochial schools. Roman Catholics, German Lutherans, and other groups resented such laws, which they saw as a direct attack on their religion and personal freedoms, and they angrily deserted the Republicans.

Political veterans went down to defeat, and new leaders vaulted into sudden prominence.

Nebraska elected a Democratic governor for the first time in its history. The state of Iowa, once so staunchly Republican that a local leader had predicted that "Iowa will go Democratic when Hell goes Methodist," went Democratic in 1890.

THE RISE OF THE POPULIST MOVEMENT

The elections of 1890 drew attention to a fast growing movement among farmers that soon came to be known far and wide as Populism. The movement had begun rather quietly, in places distant from normal centers of attention, and for a time it went almost unnoticed in the press. But during the summer of 1890, wagonloads of farm families in the South and West converged on campgrounds and picnic areas to socialize and discuss common problems. They came by the thousands, weary of drought, mortgages, and low crop prices. At the campgrounds, they picnicked, talked, and listened to recruiters from an organization called the National Farmers' Alliance and Industrial Union, which promised unified action to solve agricultural problems.

Farmers were joining the Alliance at the rate of 1000 a week; the Kansas Alliance alone claimed 130,000 members in 1890. The summer of 1890 became "that wonderful picnicking, speech-making Alliance summer," a time of fellowship and spirit long remembered by farmers.

The Farm Problem

Farm discontent was a worldwide phenomenon between 1870 and 1900. With the new means of transportation and communication, farmers everywhere were caught up in a complex international market they neither controlled nor entirely understood.

American farmers complained bitterly about declining prices for their products, rising railroad rates for shipping them, and burdensome mortgages. Some of their grievances were valid. Farm profits were certainly low; agriculture in general tends to produce low profits because of the ease of entry into the industry. The prices of farm commodities fell between 1865 and 1890—corn sold at sixty-three cents a bushel in 1881 and

Selected Commodity Prices

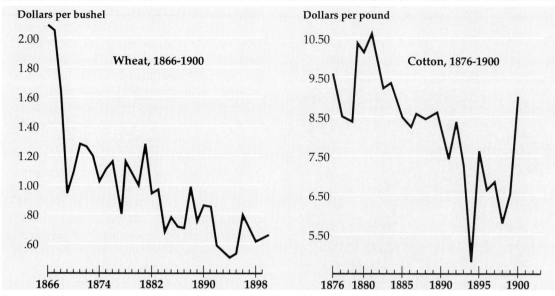

Source: U.S. Bureau of the Census. Historical Statistics of the United States, Colonial Times to 1970, *Bicentennial Edition, Washington, D.C., 1975.*

twenty-eight cents in 1890—but they did not fall as low as did other commodity prices. Despite the fact that farmers received less for their crops, their purchasing power actually increased.

Neither was the farmers' second grievance—rising railroad rates—entirely justified. Railroad rates actually fell during these years, benefiting shippers of all products. Farm mortgages, the farmers' third grievance, were common since many farmers mortgaged their property to expand their holdings or buy new farm machinery. While certainly burdensome, most mortgages did not bring hardship. They were often short, with a term of four years or less, after which farmers could renegotiate at new rates, and the new machinery the farmers bought enabled them to triple their output and increase their income.

The terms of the farm problem varied from area to area and year to year. New England farmers suffered from overworked land; farmers in western Kansas and Nebraska went broke in a severe drought that followed a period of unusual rainfall. Many southern farmers were trapped in the crop lien system that kept them in debt. They called it the "anaconda" system because of the way it coiled slowly and tightly around them.

A study of farms in the Midwest between 1860 and 1900 suggests that farm income rose substantially in the 1860s, fell during the devastating depression of the '70s, rose in the '80s, and remained roughly constant in the '90s. There were also large variations in farm profits from county to county, again indicating the absence of clear nationwide patterns. Farmers who had good land close to railroad transportation did well; others did not.

Some farmers did have valid grievances, though many understandably tended to exaggerate them. More important, many farmers were *sure* their condition had declined, and this perception—as bitterly real as any actual fact—sparked a growing anger. Equally upsetting, everyone in the 1870s and '80s seemed excited about factories, not farms. Farmers had become "hayseeds," a word that first appeared in 1889, and they watched their offspring leave for city lights and new careers. Books like *The Spider and the Fly: or, Tricks, Traps, and Pitfalls of City Life* by *One Who Knows* (1873) warned against such a move, but still the children went. A literature of disillusionment emerged, most notably Hamlin Garland's *Son of the Middle Border* (1890) and

The Grange, personified as a farmer, rouses the sleeping citizenry to the dangers of trusts in this 1880 engraving.

Main-Travelled Roads (1891), which described the drabness of farm life.

The Fast-Growing Farmers' Alliance

Originally a social organization for farmers, the Grange lost many of its members as it turned more and more toward politics in the late 1870s (see Chapter 17). In its place, a multitude of farm societies sprang into existence. By the end of the 1880s, they had formed into two major organizations: the National Farmers' Alliance, located on the Plains west of the Mississippi and known as the Northwestern Alliance; and the Farmers' Alliance and Industrial Union, based in the South and known as the Southern Alliance.

The Southern Alliance began in Texas in 1875 but did not assume major proportions until Dr. Charles W. Macune, an energetic and farsighted person, took over the leadership in 1886. Rapidly expanding, the Alliance absorbed other agricultural societies. Its agents spread across the South where farmers were fed up with crop liens, depleted lands, and sharecropping. They "seem

like unto ripe fruit," an Alliance organizer said, "you can garner them by a gentle shake of the bush." In 1890, the Southern Alliance claimed more than a million members. It welcomed to membership the farmers' "natural friends"—country doctors, school teachers, preachers, and mechanics. It excluded lawyers, bankers, cotton merchants, and warehouse operators.

An effective organization, the Southern Alliance published a newspaper, distributed Alliance material to hundreds of local newspapers, and in five years sent lecturers to forty-three states and territories where they spoke to two million farm families. It was "the most massive organizing drive by any citizen institution of nineteenth-century America." Like the Grange, the Alliance also established cooperative grain elevators, marketing associations, and retail stores—all designed to bring farmers together to make greater profits. Most of the projects were short-lived, but for a time, between 1886 and 1892, cooperative enterprises blossomed in the South.

Loosely affiliated with the Southern Alliance, a separate Colored Farmers' National Alliance and Cooperative Union enlisted black farmers in the South. Claiming over a million members, it probably had closer to 250,000, but even that figure was sizable in an era when "uppity" blacks faced not merely defeat, but death. In 1891, black cotton pickers struck for higher wages near Memphis, Tennessee. Led by Ben Patterson, a thirty-year-old picker, they walked off several plantations, but a posse hunted them down and, following violence on both sides, lynched fifteen strikers, including Patterson. The abortive strike ended the Colored Farmers' Alliance.

On the Plains, the Northwestern Alliance, a smaller organization, was formed in 1880. Its objectives were similar to those of the Southern Alliance, but it disagreed with the Southerners' emphasis on secrecy, centralized control, and separate organizations for blacks. In 1889, the Southern Alliance changed its name to the National Farmers' Alliance and Industrial Union and persuaded the three strongest state alliances on the plains—those in North Dakota, South Dakota, and Kansas—to join. Thereafter, the renamed organization dominated the Alliance movement.

The Alliance mainly sponsored social and economic programs, but it turned early to politics. In the West, its leaders rejected both the Republicans and Democrats and organized their own

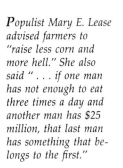

Populist Mary E. Lease advised farmers to "raise less corn and more hell." She also said " . . . if one man has not enough to eat three times a day and another man has $25 million, that last man has something that belongs to the first."

party; in June 1890, Kansas Alliance members formed the first major People's party. The Southern Alliance resisted the idea of a new party for fear it might divide the white vote, thus undercutting white supremacy. The Southerners instead followed leaders such as Benjamin F. Tillman of South Carolina who wanted to capture control of the dominant Democratic party.

Thomas E. Watson and Leonidas L. Polk, two politically minded Southerners, reflected the high quality of Alliance leadership. Georgia-born, Watson was a talented orator and organizer; he urged Georgia farmers, black and white, to unite against their oppressors. The president of the National Farmers' Alliance, Polk believed in scientific farming and cooperative action. Jeremiah Simpson of Kansas, probably the most able of the western leaders, was reflective and well-read. A follower of reformer Henry George, he pushed for major social and economic change. Also from Kansas, Mary E. Lease—Mary Ellen to her friends, "Mary Yellin'" to her opponents—helped head a movement remarkably open to female leadership. A captivating speaker, she made 160 speeches during the summer of 1890, calling on farmers to rise against Wall Street and the industrial East.

Meeting in Ocala, Florida, in 1890, the Alliance adopted the Ocala Demands, the platform it pushed for as long as it existed. First and foremost, the demands called for the creation of a "sub-treasury system," which would allow farmers to store their crops in government warehouses. In return, they could claim Treasury notes for up to 80 percent of the local market value of the crop, a loan to be repaid when the crops were sold. Farmers could thus hold their crops for the best price. The Ocala Demands also urged the free coinage of silver, an end to protective tariffs and national banks, a federal income tax, the direct election of senators by voters instead of state legislatures, and tighter regulation of railroad companies.

The Alliance strategy worked well in the elections of 1890. In Kansas, the Alliance-related People's party, organized just a few months before, elected four congressmen and a United States senator. Across the South, the Alliance won victories based on "the Alliance Yardstick," a demand that Democratic party candidates pledge support for Alliance measures. Alliance leaders claimed thirty-eight Alliance supporters elected to Congress, with at least a dozen more pledged to Alliance principles.

The People's Party

After the 1890 elections, Northern Alliance leaders urged the formation of a national third party to promote reform, although the Southerners remained reluctant, still hopeful of capturing control of the Democratic party. Plans for a new party were discussed at Alliance conventions in 1891 and the following year. In July 1892, a convention in Omaha, Nebraska, formed the new People's party. Southern Alliance leaders joined in, convinced now that there was no reason to cooperate with the Democrats who exploited Alliance popularity but failed to adopt its reforms.

In the South, some Populists had worked to unite black and white farmers. "They are in the ditch just like we are," a white Texas Populist said. Blacks and whites served on Populist election committees; they spoke from the same platforms, and they ran on the same tickets. Populist sheriffs called blacks for jury duty, an unheard-of practice in the close-of-the-century South. In 1892, a black Populist was threatened with lynching; he took refuge with Tom Watson, and two thousand white farmers, some of whom rode all night to get there, guarded Watson's house until the threat passed.

Many of the delegates at the Omaha convention had planned to nominate Leonidas L. Polk for president, but he died suddenly in June, and

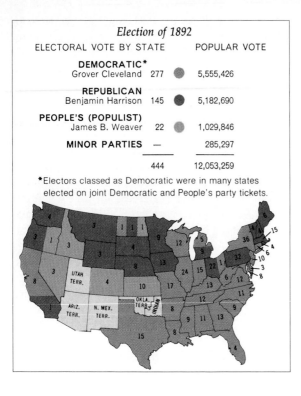

Election of 1892

ELECTORAL VOTE BY STATE			POPULAR VOTE
DEMOCRATIC* Grover Cleveland	277		5,555,426
REPUBLICAN Benjamin Harrison	145		5,182,690
PEOPLE'S (POPULIST) James B. Weaver	22		1,029,846
MINOR PARTIES	—		285,297
	444		12,053,259

*Electors classed as Democratic were in many states elected on joint Democratic and People's party tickets.

the convention turned instead to James B. Weaver of Iowa, a former congressman, Union army general, and third-party candidate for president in 1880 (on the Greenback-Labor party ticket). As its platform, the People's party adopted many of the Ocala Demands.

Weaver waged an active campaign but with mixed results. He won 1,039,000 votes, the first third-party presidential candidate ever to attract more than a million. He carried Kansas, Idaho, Nevada, and Colorado, along with portions of North Dakota and Oregon, for a total of twenty-two electoral votes. The Populists elected governors in Kansas and North Dakota, ten congressmen, five senators, and about fifteen hundred members of state legislatures.

Despite the Populists' victories, the election brought disappointment. Southern Democrats used intimidation, fraud, and manipulation to hold down Populist votes. Weaver was held to less than a quarter of the vote in every southern state except Alabama. In most of the country, he lost heavily in urban areas with the exception of some mining towns in the Far West. He also failed to win over most farmers. In no midwestern state except Kansas and North Dakota did he win as much as 5 percent of the vote.

In the election of 1892, many voters switched parties, but they tended to realign with the Democrats rather than the Populists, whose platform on silver and other issues had relatively little appeal among city dwellers or factory workers. Although the Populists did run candidates in the next three presidential elections, they had reached their peak in 1892. That year, Farmers' Alliance membership dropped for the second year in a row, and the organization, which was once the breeding ground of the People's party, was broken.

While it lived, the Alliance was one of the most powerful protest movements in American history. Catalyzing the feelings of hundreds of thousands of farmers, it attempted to solve specific economic problems, while at the same time advancing a larger vision of harmony and community, in which people who cared about each other were rewarded for what they produced.

THE CRISIS OF THE DEPRESSION

It was economic crisis, however, not harmony and community, that dominated the last decade of the century. Responding to the heady forces of industrialization, the American economy had expanded too rapidly in the 1870s and 1880s. Railroads had overbuilt, gambling on future growth. Companies had grown beyond their markets; farms and businesses had borrowed heavily for expansion.

The mood changed early in 1893. In mid-February, panic suddenly hit the New York stock market. In one day, investors dumped one million shares of a leading company, the Philadelphia and Reading Railroad, and it went bankrupt. Business investment dropped sharply in the railroad and construction industries, touching off the worst economic downturn to that point in the country's history.

Frightened, people hurriedly sold stocks and other assets to buy gold. The overwhelming demand depleted the gold reserve of the United States Treasury. Eroding almost daily, in March 1893, the Treasury's reserve slumped toward the $100 million mark, an amount that stood for the government's commitment to maintain the gold standard. On April 22, for the first time since the 1870s, it fell below $100 million.

The news shattered business confidence—the stock market broke. On Wednesday, May 3, railroad and industrial stocks plummeted, and the next day several major firms went bankrupt. When the market opened on Friday, crowds filled its galleries, anticipating a panic. Within minutes, leading stocks plunged to record lows, and there was pandemonium on the floor and in the streets outside. May 5, 1893, Wall Street's worst day until the Great Crash of 1929, became "Industrial Black Friday," "a day of terrible strain long remembered on the market."

Afterward, banks cut back on loans. Unable to get capital, businesses failed at an average rate of two dozen a day during the month of May. "The papers are full of failures—banks are breaking all over the country, and there is a tremendous contraction of credits and hoarding of money going on everywhere," an observer noted. On July 26, the Erie Railroad, one of the leading names in railroading history, failed.

August 1893 was the worst month. Across the country, factories and mines shut down. In Orange, New Jersey, Thomas A. Edison, the symbol of the country's ingenuity, laid off 240 employees at the Edison Phonograph Works. On August 15, the Northern Pacific Railroad went bankrupt; the Union Pacific and the Santa Fe soon followed. Some economists estimated unemployment at 2 million people or nearly 15 percent of the labor force. During 1893, 15,000 business firms and more than 600 banks closed.

The year 1894 was even worse. The gross national product dropped again, and by mid-year the number of unemployed stood at three million. One out of every five workers was unemployed. "Famine is in our midst," said the head of one city's relief committee. In the summer, a heat wave and drought struck the farm belt west of the Mississippi River, creating conditions unmatched until the devastating Dust Bowl of the 1930s. Corn withered in the fields. In the South, the price of cotton fell below five cents a pound, far under the break-even point.

People became restless and angry. As one newspaper said in 1896: "On every corner stands a man whose fortune in these dull times has made him an ugly critic of everything and everybody." There was even talk of revolution and bloodshed. "Everyone scolds," Henry Adams, the historian, wrote a British friend. "Everyone also knows what ought to be done. Everyone reviles everyone who does not agree with him, and everyone differs, or agrees only in contempt for everyone else. As far as I can see, everyone is right."

Coxey's Army and the Pullman Strike

Some of the unemployed wandered across the country—singly, in small groups, and in small armies. In February 1894, police ejected 600 unemployed men who stormed the State House in Boston demanding relief. During 1894, there were some 1400 strikes involving more than a half million workers.

On Easter Sunday, 1894, an unusual "army" of perhaps three hundred people left Massillon, Ohio. At its head rode "General" Jacob S. Coxey, a mild-looking, middle-aged businessman who wanted to put the nation's jobless to work build-

Armies of unemployed men following Coxey's lead, marched, and in this case, floated to Washington. The march was an indication of the strength of Populist sentiment and the widespread unrest of the decade.

*A*rmy cavalry troopers clear the way for a train to pass through the strikers' lines during the 1894 Pullman strike in Chicago.

ing roads. Coxey wanted Congress to pass the Coxey Good Roads bill, which would authorize the printing of $500 million in paper money to finance road construction. His march to Washington—"a petition in boots," he called it—drew nationwide attention. Forty-three newspaper correspondents accompanied him, reporting every detail of the march.

Other armies sprang up around the country, and all headed for Washington to persuade the government to provide jobs on irrigation, road construction, or other projects. In the West, they commandeered freight trains and headed east. Coxey himself reached Washington on May 1, 1894, after a difficult, tiring march. Police were everywhere, lining the streets and blocking the approaches to the Capitol. Coxey made it to the foot of the Capitol steps, but before he could do anything, the police were on him. He and a companion were clubbed, then arrested for trespassing. A week later, Coxey was sentenced to twenty days in jail.

The armies melted away, but discontent did not. The great Pullman strike—one of the largest strikes in the country's history—began just a few days after Coxey's arrest when the employees of the Pullman Palace Car Company, living in a company town just outside of Chicago (a town in which everything was owned and meted out by the company), struck to protest wage cuts, continuing high rents, and layoffs. On June 26, 1894, the American Railway Union (ARU) under Eugene V. Debs joined the strike by refusing to handle trains that carried Pullman sleeping cars.

Within hours, the strike paralyzed the western half of the nation. Grain and livestock could not reach markets. Factories shut down for lack of coal. The strike extended into twenty-seven states and territories, tying up the economy and renewing talk of class warfare. In Washington, President Grover Cleveland, who had been re-elected to the presidency in 1892, decided to break the strike on the grounds that it obstructed delivery of the mail.

On July 2, he secured a court injunction against the ARU, and he ordered troops to Chicago. When they arrived on the morning of Independence Day, the city was peaceful. Before long, however, violence broke out, and mobs, composed mostly of nonstrikers, overturned freight cars, looted, and burned. Restoring order, the army occupied railroad yards in Illinois, California, and other points. By late July, the strike was over; Debs was jailed for violating the injunction. Many people applauded Cleveland's action, "nominally for the expedition of the mails," a newspaper said, but "really for the preservation of society."

The Pullman strike had far-reaching consequences for the development of the labor movement. Working people resented Cleveland's actions in the strike, particularly as it became apparent that he sided with the railroads. Upholding Debs' sentence in *In re Debs* (1895), the Supreme Court endorsed the use of the injunction in labor disputes, thus giving business and government an effective antilabor weapon that hindered union growth in the 1890s. The strike's failure catapulted Debs into prominence. During his time in jail, he turned to socialism, and after his release he worked to build the Socialist party of America, which experienced some success after 1900.

The Miners of the Midwest

The plight of coal miners in the Midwest illustrated the personal and social impact of the depression. Even in the best of times, mining was a dirty and dangerous business. One miner in twelve died underground; one in three suffered injury. Mines routinely closed for as long as six months a year, and wages fell with the depression. An Illinois miner earned $.97 per ton in 1889 and only $.80 in 1896. A bituminous coal miner made $282 a year.

Midwestern mining was often a family occupation, passed down from father to son. It demanded delicate judgments about when to blast, where to follow a seam, and how to avoid rockfalls. Until 1890, English and Irish immigrants dominated the business. They migrated from mine to mine, but nearly always lived in flimsy shacks owned by the company. Time and again the miners struck for higher wages—between 1887 and 1894 there were 116 major coal strikes in Illinois, 111 in Ohio.

After 1890, immigration from southern and eastern Europe, hitherto a trickle, became a flood. Italians, Lithuanians, Poles, Slovaks, Magyars, Russians, Bohemians, and Croatians came to the mines to find work. In three years, nearly one thousand Italians settled in Coal City, Illinois; they comprised more than one-third of the population. In other mining towns, Italian and Polish miners soon comprised almost half the population.

As the depression deepened, tensions grew between miners and their employers and between "old" miners and the "new." Many "new" miners spoke no English, and often they were "birds of passage," transients who had come to the United States to make money to take back home. Lacking the skills handed down by the "old" miners, they were often blamed for accidents, and they worked longer hours for less pay. At many a tavern after work, "old" miners grumbled about the different-looking newcomers and considered ways to get rid of them.

In April 1894, a wave of wage reductions sparked an explosion of labor unrest in the mines. The United Mine Workers, a struggling union formed just four years earlier, called for a strike of bituminous coal miners, and on April 21, virtually all Midwestern and Pennsylvania miners— some 170,000 in all—quit working. The flow of crucial coal slackened; cities faced blackouts; factories closed.

The violence that soon broke out followed a significant pattern. Over the years, the English and Irish miners had built up a set of unspoken understandings with their employers. The "new" miners had not, and they were more prone to violent action to win a strike. The depression hit them especially hard, frustrating their plans to earn money and return home. In many areas, anger and frustration turned the 1894 strikes into outright war.

For nearly two weeks in June 1894 fighting rocked the Illinois, Ohio, and Indiana coalfields. Mobs ignited mine shafts, dynamited coal trains, and defied state militias. While miners of all backgrounds participated in the violence, it often divided "old" miners and "new." In Spring Valley, Illinois, exiled Italian anarchists took over the strike leadership and incited rioting despite the opposition of the "old" miners. Elsewhere, a mine fired by arsonists burned because the "new" miners prevented the "old" ones from extinguishing the blaze.

Shocked by the violence, public opinion shifted against the strikers. The strike ended in a matter of weeks, but its effects lingered. English and Irish miners moved out into other jobs or up into supervisory positions. Jokes and songs poked cruel fun at the "new" immigrants, and the Pennsylvania and Illinois legislatures adopted laws to keep them out of the mines. Thousands of "old" miners voted Populist in 1894—the Populist platform called for restrictions on immigration—in one of the Populists' few successes that year. The United Mine Workers, dominated by the older miners, began in 1896 to urge Congress to stop the "demoralizing effects" of immigration.

Occurring at the same time, the Pullman strike pulled attention away from the crisis in the coalfields, yet the miners' strike involved three times as many workers and provided a revealing glimpse of the tensions within American society. The miners of the Midwest were the first large group of skilled workers seriously affected by the flood of immigrants from southern and eastern Europe. Buffeted by depression, they reflected the social and economic discord that permeated every industry.

A Beleaguered President

Building on the Democratic party's sweeping triumph in the midterm elections of 1890, Grover Cleveland decisively defeated the Populist candidate James B. Weaver and incumbent President Benjamin Harrison in 1892. He won by nearly four hundred thousand votes, a large margin by the standards of the era, and the Democrats increased their strength in the cities and among working-class voters. For the first time since the 1850s, they controlled the White House and both branches of Congress.

Unfortunately for Cleveland, the panic of 1893 struck almost as he took office. He was sure that he knew its cause. The Sherman Silver Purchase Act of 1890, he believed, had damaged business confidence, drained the Treasury's gold reserve, and caused the panic. The solution to the depression was equally simple: repeal the act.

In June 1893, Cleveland summoned Congress into special session. India had just closed its mints to silver, and Mexico was now the only country in the world with free silver coinage. The silverites were on the defensive, although they pleaded for a compromise. Rejecting the pleas, Cleveland pushed the repeal bill through Congress, and on November 1, 1893, he signed it into law. Always sure of himself, he had staked everything on a single measure—a winning strategy if he succeeded, a devastating one if he did not.

Repeal of the Sherman Silver Purchase Act was probably a necessary action. It responded to the realities of international finance, reduced the flight of gold out of the country, and over the long run, boosted business confidence. Unfortunately, it contracted the currency at a time when inflation might have helped. It did not bring economic revival. The stock market remained listless, businesses continued to close, unemployment spread, and farm prices dropped. "We are hourly expecting the arrival of the benevolent man who is to pay ten cents a pound for cotton," a Virginia newspaper said.

The repeal battle of 1893, discrediting the conservative Cleveland Democrats who had dominated the party since the 1860s, reshaped the politics of the country. It confined the Democratic party largely to the South, helped the Republicans become the majority party in 1894, and strengthened the position of the silver Democrats in their bid for the presidency in 1896. It also focused national attention on the silver issue and thus intensified the silver sentiment Cleveland had intended to dampen. In the end, repeal did not even solve the Treasury's gold problem. By January 1894, the reserve had fallen to $65 million. A year later, it fell to $44.5 million.

In January 1894, Cleveland desperately resorted to a sale of $50 million in gold bonds to replenish the gold reserve; the following November, he again sold bonds; and in February 1895, arousing outrage among many, he agreed to a third bond sale that allowed financier J. Pierpont Morgan and other bankers to reap large profits. A fourth bond sale in January 1896 also failed to stop the drain on the reserve, although it further sharpened the silverites' hatred of President Cleveland.

Still another blow to the morale of the Democrats came in 1894 when they tried to fulfill their long-standing promise to reduce the tariff. Despite all their efforts, the Wilson-Gorman Tariff Act, passed by Congress in August 1894, contained only modest reductions in duties. It reduced the tariff on coal, iron ore, wool, and sugar, ended the McKinley Tariff Act's popular reciprocity agreements with other countries, and moved some duties higher than ever before. It also imposed a small income tax, a provision the Supreme Court overturned in 1895 (*Pollock* v. *Farmer's Loan and Trust Co.*). Very few Democrats, including Cleveland, were pleased with the measure, and the President let it become law without his signature.

Depression Politics

The Democrats were buried in the elections of 1894, which were some of the most important elections in American history. Suffering the greatest defeat in congressional history, they lost 113 House seats, while the Republicans gained 117. In twenty-four states, not a single Democrat was elected to Congress. Only one Democrat (Boston's John F. Fitzgerald, the grandfather of President John F. Kennedy) came from all of New England. The Democrats even lost some of the "Solid South," and in the Midwest, a crucial battleground of the 1890s, the party was virtually destroyed.

Wooing labor and the unemployed, the Populists made striking inroads in parts of the South and West, yet their progress was far from enough. In a year in which thousands of voters switched parties, the People's party elected only four senators and four congressmen. Southern Democrats again used fraud and violence to keep the Populists' totals down. In the Midwest, the Populists won double the number of votes they had received in 1892, yet still attracted less than 7 percent of the vote. Across the country, the discontented tended to vote for the Republicans, not the Populists, a discouraging sign for the Populist party.

For millions of people, Grover Cleveland became a scapegoat for the country's economic ills. Fearing attack, he placed new police barracks on the White House grounds. The Democratic party split, and southern and western Democrats deserted him in droves. At Democratic conventions, Cleveland's name evoked jeers. "He is an old bag of beef," Democratic Congressman "Pitchfork" Ben Tillman told a South Carolina audience, "and I am going to go to Washington with a pitchfork and prod him in his old fat ribs."

The elections of 1894 marked the end of the party deadlock that had existed since the 1870s. The Democrats lost, the Populists gained somewhat, and the Republicans became the majority party in the country. In the midst of the depression, the Republican doctrines of activism and national authority, which voters had repudiated in the elections of 1890, became more attractive. This was a development of great significance, because as Americans became more accepting of the use of government power to regulate the economy and safeguard individual welfare, the way lay open to the reforms of the Progressive Era, the New Deal, and beyond.

CHANGING ATTITUDES

The depression, brutal and far-reaching, did more than shift political alignments. Across the country, it undermined traditional views and caused people to rethink older ideas about government, the economy, and society. As men and women concluded that established ideas had failed to deal with the depression, they looked for new ones. There was, the president of the University of Wisconsin said, "a general, all-pervasive, restless discontent with the results of current political and economic thought."

In prosperous times, Americans had thought of unemployment as the result of personal failure, affecting primarily the lazy and immoral. "Let us remember," a leading Protestant minister once said, "that there is not a poor person in the United States who was not made poor by his own shortcomings." In the midst of depression, such views were harder to maintain, since everyone knew people who were both worthy *and* unemployed. Next door, a respected neighbor might be laid off; down the block, an entire factory might be shut down. People debated issues they had long taken for granted. New and reinvigorated local institutions—discussion clubs, women's clubs, reform societies, university extension centers, church groups, farmers' societies—gave people a place to discuss alternatives to the existing order. Pressures for reform increased, and demand grew for government intervention to help the poor and unemployed.

Everybody Works but Father

Women and children had been entering the labor force for years, and the depression accelerated the trend. As husbands and fathers lost their jobs,

Tiny children peddling newspapers and female domestics serving the rich —their meager earnings were desperately needed.

more and more women and children went to work. Even as late as 1901, well after the depression had ended, a study of working-class families showed that more than half the principal breadwinners were out of work. So many women and children worked that in 1905 there was a popular song, "Everybody Works but Father."

During the 1890s, the number of working women rose from 4 million to 5.3 million. Trying to make ends meet, they took in boarders and found jobs as laundresses, cleaners, or domestics. Where possible, they worked in offices and factories. Far more black urban women than white worked to supplement their husbands' meager earnings. In New York City in 1900, nearly 60 percent of all black women worked compared to 27 percent of the foreign-born and 24 percent of native-born white women. Men still dominated business offices, but during the 1890s, more and more employers noted the relative cheapness of female labor. Women telegraph and telephone operators nearly tripled in number during the decade. Women worked as clerks in the new five-and-tens and department stores, and as nurses; in 1900, half a million were teachers. They

increasingly entered office work as stenographers and typists, occupations in which they earned between $6.00 and $15.00 a week, compared to factory wages of $1.50 to $8.00 a week.

The depression also caused an increasing number of children to work. During the 1890s, the number of children employed in southern textile mills jumped more than 160 percent, and boys and girls under sixteen years of age made up nearly one-third of the labor force of the mills. Youngsters of eight and nine years worked twelve hours a day for pitiful wages. In most cases, however, children worked not in factories but in farming and city street trades like peddling and shoeshining. In 1900, the South had more than half the child laborers in the nation.

Concerned about child labor, middle-class women in 1896 formed the League for the Protection of the Family, which called for compulsory education to get children out of factories and into classrooms. The Mothers Congress of 1896 gave rise to the National Congress of Parents and Teachers, the spawning-ground of thousands of local PTAs. The National Council of Women and the General Federation of Women's Clubs took up similar issues. By the end of the 1890s, the Federation had 150,000 members who worked for various civic reforms in the fields of child welfare, education, and sanitation.

Changing Themes in Literature

The depression also gave point to a growing movement in literature toward realism and naturalism. In the years after the Civil War, literature often reflected the mood of romanticism—sentimental and unrealistic. Walt Whitman called it "ornamental confectionary" and "copious dribble," but it remained popular through the end of the century.

The novels of Horatio Alger, which provided simple lessons about how to get ahead in business and life, continued to attract large numbers of readers. A failed New York minister, Alger published some 130 novels—with titles like *Sink or Swim*, *Work and Win*, and *Struggling Upward*—which sold over 20 million copies. They told of poor youngsters who made their way to the top through hard work, thrift, honesty, and luck. Louisa May Alcott's *Little Women* (1868–69) related the daily lives of four girls in a New England family; Anna Sewell's *Black Beauty* (1877) charmed readers with the story of an abused horse that found a happy home; and Lew Wallace's *Ben Hur* (1880), one of the era's best-selling books, offered a sweeping epic of life in the Roman empire.

After the 1870s, however, a number of talented authors began to reject romanticism and escapism, turning instead to realism. Determined to portray life as it was, they studied local dialects, wrote regional stories, and emphasized the "true" relationships between people. In doing so, they reflected broader trends in the society, such as industrialism, evolutionary theory, which emphasized the effect of the environment on humans, and the new philosophy of pragmatism, which stressed the relativity of values. (See Chapter 22 for a more detailed discussion of pragmatism.)

Regionalist authors like Joel Chandler Harris and George Washington Cable depicted life in the South; Hamlin Garland described the grimness of life on the Great Plains; and Sarah Orne Jewett wrote about everyday life in rural New England.

Another regionalist, Bret Harte, achieved fame with stories that portrayed the local color of the California mining camps, particularly in his popular tale, "The Outcasts of Poker Flat."

Harte was joined by a more talented writer, Mark Twain, who became the country's most outstanding realist author. Growing up along the Mississippi River in Hannibal County, Missouri, the young Samuel Langhorne Clemens observed life around him with a humorous and skeptical eye. Adopting a pen name from the river term "mark twain" (two fathoms), he wrote a number of important works that drew on his own experiences. *Life on the Mississippi* (1883) described his career as a steamboat pilot. *The Adventures of Tom Sawyer* (1876) and *The Adventures of Huckleberry Finn* (1884) gained international prominence. In these books, Twain used dialect and common speech instead of literary language, touching off a major change in American prose style.

William Dean Howells—after Twain, the country's most famous author—came more slowly to the realist approach. At first, he wrote about the happier sides of life, but then he grew worried about the impact of industrialization. *A Traveler from Altruria* (1894), a utopian novel, described an industrial society that consumed lives. The poem, "Society" (1895), written in the midst of the depression, compared society to a splendid ball in which men and women danced on flowers covering the bodies of the poor:

> And now and then from out the dreadful floor
> An arm or brow was lifted from the rest,
> As if to strike in madness, or implore
> For mercy; and anon some suffering breast
> Heaved from the mass and sank; and as before
> The revellers above them thronged and prest.

Other writers became impatient even with realism. Pushing Darwinian theory to its limits, they wrote of a world in which a cruel and merciless environment determined human fate. Often focusing on economic hardship, naturalist writers studied the poor, the lower classes, and the criminal mind; they brought to their writing the social workers' passion for direct and honest experience.

Stephen Crane spent a night in a seven-cent lodging house on the Bowery and in "An Experiment in Misery" captured the smells and sounds of the poor. Crane depicted the carnage of war in

*I*n one of the popular literary works of the time, Mark Twain created an idyllic setting for the adventures of the irrepressible Tom Sawyer, shown here convincing a gullible friend of the joys of whitewashing a fence (at left). A powerful drawing entitled From the Depths (above) illustrated another popular work, J. Ames Mitchell's The Silent War (1906), which dealt with the class struggle.

The Red Badge of Courage (1895) and the impact of poverty in *Maggie: A Girl of the Streets* (1893). His poetry suggested the unimportance of the individual in an uncaring world:

> *A man said to the universe*
> *"Sir, I exist!"*
> *"However," replied the universe,*
> *"The fact has not created in me*
> *A sense of obligation."*

Frank Norris assailed the power of big business in two dramatic novels, *The Octopus* (1901) and *The Pit* (1903), both the story of individual futility in the face of the heartless corporations. Norris' *McTeague* (1899) studied the disintegration of character under economic pressure. Jack London, another naturalist author, traced the power of nature over civilized society in novels like *The Sea Wolf* (1904) and *The Call of the Wild* (1903), his classic tale of a sled dog that preferred the difficult life of the wilderness to the world of human beings.

Theodore Dreiser, the foremost naturalist writer, grimly portrayed a dark world in which human beings were tossed about by forces beyond their understanding or control. "My own ambition," Dreiser said, "is to represent my world, to conform to the large, truthful lines of life." In his great novel, *Sister Carrie* (1901), he followed a young farm girl who took a job in a Chicago shoe factory. He described the exhausting nature of factory work: "Her hands began to ache at the wrists and then in the fingers, and towards the last she seemed one mass of dull, complaining muscle, fixed in an eternal position, and performing a single mechanical movement."

Like other naturalists, Dreiser focused on environment and character. He thought writers should tell the truth about human affairs, not fabricate romance, and *Sister Carrie*, he said, was "not intended as a piece of literary craftsmanship, but was a picture of conditions."

THE PRESIDENTIAL ELECTION OF 1896

The election of 1896 was known as "the battle of the standards" because it focused primarily on the gold and silver standards of value in the monetary system of the nation. New voting patterns replaced old, a new majority party confirmed its control of the country, and national policy shifted to suit new realities.

The Mystique of Silver

Sentiment for free silver coinage grew swiftly after 1894, dominating the South and West, appearing even in the farming regions of New York and New England. Prosilver literature flooded the country (see "The Wonderful Wizard of Oz," pp. 608-09). Pamphlets issued by the millions argued silver's virtues.

People wanted quick solutions to the economic crisis. During 1896, unemployment shot up; farm income and prices fell to the lowest point in the decade. "I can remember back as far as 1858," an Iowa hardware dealer said in February 1896, "and I have never seen such hard times as these are." The silverites offered a solution, simple but compelling: the free and independent coinage of silver at the ratio of sixteen ounces of silver to every one ounce of gold. Free coinage meant that the United States mints would coin all the silver offered to them. Independent coinage meant that the country would coin silver regardless of the policies of other nations, nearly all of which were on the gold standard.

It is difficult now to understand the kind of faith the silverites placed in silver as a cure for the depression. But faith it was, and of a sort that some observers compared to religious fervor. Underlying it all was a belief in a quantity theory of money: the silverites believed that the amount of money in circulation determined the level of activity in the economy. If money was short, that meant there was a limit on economic activity and ultimately a depression. If the government coined silver as well as gold, that meant more money in circulation, more business for everyone, and thus prosperity. Farm prices would rise; laborers would go back to work. As one silverite said: "It means the reopening of closed factories, the relighting of fires in darkened furnaces; it means hope instead of despair; comfort in place of suffering; life instead of death."

By 1896, silver was also a symbol. It had moral and patriotic dimensions—by going to a silver standard, the United States could assert its independence in the world—and it stood for a wide range of popular grievances. For many, it reflected rural values rather than urban ones, suggested a shift of power away from the Northeast, and spoke for the downtrodden instead of the well-to-do. Silver represented the common people, as the vast literature of the movement showed.

William H. Harvey's *Coin's Financial School* (1894), the most popular of all silver pamphlets, had the eloquent Coin, a wise but unknown youth, tutoring famous people on the currency. Bankers, lawyers, and scholars came to argue for gold, but left shaken, leaning toward silver. *Coin's Financial School* sold five thousand copies a day at its peak in 1895, with tens of thousands of copies distributed free by silver organizations. It "is being sold on every railroad train by the newsboys and at every cigar store . . . ," a Mississippi congressman said. "It is being read by almost everybody."

Silver was more than just a political or economic issue. It was a social movement, one of the largest in American history, but its life span turned out to be brief. As a mass phenomenon, it flourished between 1894 and 1896, then succumbed to electoral defeat, the return of prosperity, and the onset of fresh concerns. But in its time,

The Wonderful Wizard of Oz

A restless dreamer, Frank Baum tried his hand at several careers before he gained fame and fortune as a writer of children's literature. From 1888 to 1891, he ran a store and newspaper in South Dakota, where he experienced the desolation and grayness that accompanied agrarian discontent. An avid supporter of William Jennings Bryan in the "battle of the standards," Baum wrote an enduring allegory of the silver movement, *The Wonderful Wizard of Oz.* Published in April 1900, it was an immediate success.

The book opens with a grim description of Kansas:

When Dorothy stood in the doorway and looked around, she could see nothing but the great gray prairie on every side. Not a tree nor a house broke the broad sweep of flat country that reached the edge of the sky in all directions. The sun had baked the plowed land into a gray mass, with little cracks running through it. Even the grass was not green, for the sun had burned the tops of the long blades until they were the same gray color to be seen everywhere. Once the house had been painted, but the sun blistered the paint and the rains washed it away, and now the house was as dull and gray as everything else.

Kansas had not always seemed that way. After 1854, when the Kansas-Nebraska Act opened to settlement its fifty million acres of rich grassland, people poured into the state to stake their claims. Many came from the hilly, timbered country to the east, and breaking onto the prairie, they saw "a new world, reaching to the far horizon without break of trees or chimney stack; just sky and grass and grass and sky. . . . The hush was so loud. . . . The heavens seemed nearer than ever before and awe and beauty and majesty over all."

In later years railroads crisscrossed the state, and advertisements touted the fertile soil. Land was plentiful, rainfall somehow seemed to increase each year, crop prices held at levels high enough to pay, new farming implements yielded larger crops, and property values increased.

Yet life on the prairie was never an easy matter. Flat, lonely, and windswept, the land affected people in ways that were hard to describe to the folks back East. When Aunt Em, Dorothy's aunt, came to Kansas to live, she was young and pretty, but the sun and wind soon changed her. "They had taken the sparkle from her eyes and left them a sober gray; they had taken the red from her cheeks and lips, and they were gray also." Like Aunt Em, Uncle Henry never laughed. "He worked hard from morning till night and did not know what joy was."

After 1887, a series of droughts struck Kansas, and as many as three out of four farms were mortgaged in some Kansas counties. Thousands of settlers like Aunt Em and Uncle Henry gave up and retraced their steps east; others trusted in the Farmers' Alliance and pinned their hopes on the free coinage of silver. While gold as a standard of currency symbolized the idle rich of the industrial

The Wicked Witch of the West.

Northeast, silver stood for the common folk. Added to the currency in the form of silver dollars, it meant more money, higher crop prices, and a return of prosperity.

Or so the supporters of silver coinage believed. In *The Wonderful Wizard of Oz,* Dorothy (every person) is carried by a cyclone (a victory of the silver forces at the polls) from drought-stricken Kansas to a marvelous land of riches and witches. Unlike dry, gray Kansas, Oz is beautiful, with rippling brooks, stately trees, colorful flowers, and bright-feathered birds. On arrival, Dorothy disposes of one witch, the Wicked Witch of the East (the Eastern money power and

Dorothy (wearing silver, not ruby, slippers in the original version) and her friends prepare to "follow the yellow brick road."

those favoring gold), and frees the Munchkins (the common people) from servitude. To return to Kansas, she must first go to the Emerald City (the national capital, greenback-colored).

Dorothy wears magical silver slippers and follows the yellow brick road, thus achieving a proper relationship between the precious metals, silver and gold. Like many of her countrymen, she does not at first recognize the power of the silver slippers, but a kiss from the Good Witch of the North (Northern voters) protects her on the road. Dorothy meets the Scarecrow (the farmer) who has been told he has no brain but actually possesses great common sense (no "hick" or "hayseed," he); the Tin Woodman (the industrial worker) who fears he has become heartless but discovers the spirit of love and cooperation; and the Cowardly Lion (reformers, particularly William Jennings Bryan) who turns out not to be very cowardly at all.

When the four companions reach the Emerald City, they meet the "Great and Terrible" Wizard who tells them that, to gain his help, they must destroy the Wicked Witch of the West (mortgage companies, heartless nature, and other things opposing progress there). Courageously, they set forth. Dorothy dissolves the witch with a bucket of water (what else for drought-ridden farmers?), but when they return to the Emerald City, they find that the great and powerful Wizard (the money power) is only a charlatan, a manipulator, whose power rests on myth and illusion. "'I thought Oz was a great Head,' said Dorothy. . . . 'And I thought Oz was a terrible Beast,' said the Tin Woodman. 'And I thought Oz was a Ball of Fire,' exclaimed the Lion. 'No; you are all wrong,' said the little man meekly. 'I have been making believe.'"

Dorothy unmasks the wizard, and with the help of Glinda, the Good Witch of the South (support for silver was strong in the South), uses the silver slippers to return home to Kansas. Sadly, the shoes are lost in flight. Back in Oz, the Scarecrow rules the Emerald City (the triumph of the farmers), and the Tin Woodman reigns in the West (industrialism moves West). "Oz" was a familiar abbreviation to those involved in the 16 to 1 (ounces) fight over the ratio of silver to gold.

Baum wanted to write American fairy tales to "bear the stamp of our times and depict the progressive fairies of today." The land of Oz reflected his belief in the American values of freedom and independence, love of family, self-reliance, individualism, and sympathy for the underdog. *Oz*, he said in the original introduction, "aspires to being a modernized fairy tale, in which the wonderment and joy are retained and the heartaches and nightmares are left out."

The *Oz* stories have remained popular, and they still rest on many children's bookshelves. A 1939 film starring Judy Garland as Dorothy, with Ray Bolger as the Scarecrow, Jack Haley as the Tin Woodman, Bert Lahr as the Cowardly Lion, and Frank Morgan as the Wizard was spectacularly successful. Released in the midst of another depression, the film included songs designed to escape hardship, as Dorothy once had, "Somewhere Over the Rainbow."

the silver movement bespoke a national mood and won millions of followers.

The Republicans and Gold

Scenting victory over the discredited Democrats, numerous Republicans fought for the party's presidential nomination, including "Czar" Thomas B. Reed of the Billion-Dollar Congress. Reed picked up early support but suffered from his reputation for biting wit. William McKinley of Ohio, his chief rival, soon passed him in the race for the nomination.

Able, calm, and affable, McKinley had served in the Union army during the Civil War. In 1876, he won a seat in Congress where he became the chief sponsor of the tariff act named for him. In the months before the 1896 national convention, Marcus A. Hanna, his campaign manager and trusted friend, built a powerful national organization that featured McKinley as "the Advance Agent of Prosperity," an alluring slogan in a country beset with depression. When the convention met in June, McKinley had the nomination in hand, and he backed a platform that favored the gold standard against the free coinage of silver.

Republicans favoring silver proposed a pro-silver platform, but the convention overwhelmingly defeated it. Twenty-three silverite Republicans, far fewer than prosilver forces had hoped, marched out of the convention hall. The remaining delegates waved handkerchiefs and flags and shouted "Good-bye" and "Put them out." Hanna stood on a chair screaming "Go! Go! Go!" William Jennings Bryan, who was there as a special correspondent for a Nebraska newspaper, climbed on a desk to get a better view.

The Democrats and Silver

Silver, meanwhile, had virtually captured large segments of the Democratic party in the South and West. Despite President Cleveland's opposition, more than twenty Democratic state platforms came out for free silver in 1894. Power in the party shifted to the South, where it remained for decades. The party's base narrowed; its outlook increasingly reflected southern views on silver, race, and other issues. In effect, the Demo-

crats became a sectional—no longer a national— party.

The anti-Cleveland Democrats had their issue, but they lacked a leader. Out in Nebraska, Bryan saw the opportunity to take on that role. He was barely thirty-six years old and had relatively little political experience. But he had spent months wooing support, and he was a captivating public speaker—tall, slender, and handsome, with a resounding voice that, in an era without microphones, projected easily into every corner of an auditorium. Practicing at home before a mirror, he rehearsed his speeches again and again, as his wife, Mary, a bright, sharp, and politically astute woman, listened for errors.

From the outset of the 1896 Democratic convention, the silver Democrats were in charge, and they put together a platform that stunned the Cleveland wing of the party. It demanded the free coinage of silver, attacked Cleveland's actions in the Pullman strike, and censured his gold bond sales. On July 9, as delegates debated the platform, Bryan's moment came. Striding to the stage, he stood for an instant, a hand raised for silence, waiting for the applause to die down. He would not contend with the previous speakers, he began, for "this is not a contest between persons. The humblest citizen in all the land, when clad in the armor of a righteous cause, is stronger than all the hosts of error. I come to speak to you in defense of a cause as holy as the cause of liberty —the cause of humanity."

The delegates were captivated. Like a trained choir, they rose, cheered each point, and sat back to listen for more. Easterners, Bryan said, liked to praise businessmen but forgot that plain people —laborers, miners, and farmers—were businessmen, too. Shouts rang through the hall and delegates pounded on chairs. Savoring each cheer, Bryan defended silver. Then came the famous closing: "Having behind us the producing masses of this nation and the world . . . we will answer their demand for a gold standard by saying to them: 'You shall not press down upon the brow of labor this crown of thorns, you shall not crucify mankind upon a cross of gold.'"

Bryan moved his fingers down his temples, suggesting blood trickling from his wounds. He ended with his arms outstretched as on a cross. Letting the silence hang, he dropped his arms, stepped back, then started to his seat. Suddenly, there was pandemonium. Delegates shouted and cheered. When the tumult subsided, they adopted the anti-Cleveland platform, and the next day, Bryan won the presidential nomination.

Campaign and Election

The Democratic convention presented the Populists with a dilemma. The People's party had staked everything on the assumption that neither major party would endorse silver. Now it faced a painful choice: nominate an independent ticket and risk splitting the silverite forces or nominate Bryan and give up its separate identity as a party.

The choice was unpleasant, and it shattered the People's party. Meeting late in July, the party's national convention nominated Bryan, but rather than accept the Democratic candidate for vice-president, it named Tom Watson instead. The Populists' endorsement probably hurt Bryan as much as it helped. It won him relatively few votes, since many Populists would have voted for him anyway, and it identified him as a Populist, which he was not, allowing the Republicans to accuse him of heading a ragtag army of malcontents. The squabble over Watson seemed to prove that the Democratic-Populist alliance could never stay together long enough to govern.

In August 1896, Bryan set off on a campaign that became an American legend. Much of the

Although William Jennings Bryan was acclaimed enthusiastically as he campaigned throughout the nation, he failed to win the election.

conservative Democratic eastern press had deserted him, and he took his campaign directly to the voters, the first presidential candidate in history to do so in a systematic way. By his own count, Bryan traveled 18,009 miles, visited 27 states, and spoke 600 times to a total of some 3 million people. He built skillfully on a new "merchandising" style of campaign in which he worked to educate and persuade voters.

Bryan summoned voters to an older America: a land where farms were as important as factories, where the virtues of rural and religious life outweighed the doubtful lure of the city, where common people still ruled, and opportunity existed for all. He drew on the Jeffersonian tradition of rural virtue, distrust of central authority, and abiding faith in the powers of human reason.

Urged to take the stump against Bryan, McKinley replied: "I might just as well put up a trapeze on my front lawn and compete with some professional athlete as go out speaking against Bryan." The Republican candidate let voters come to him.

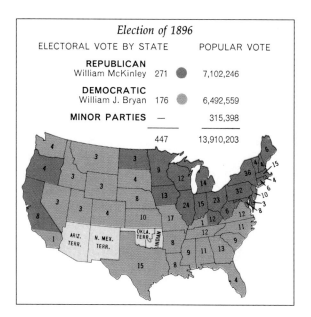

Election of 1896

ELECTORAL VOTE BY STATE		POPULAR VOTE
REPUBLICAN William McKinley	271	7,102,246
DEMOCRATIC William J. Bryan	176	6,492,559
MINOR PARTIES	—	315,398
	447	13,910,203

Railroads brought them by the thousands into McKinley's hometown of Canton, Ohio, and he spoke to them from his front porch. Through use of the press, he reached fully as many people as Bryan's more strenuous effort. Appealing to labor, immigrants, well-to-do farmers, businessmen, and the middle class, McKinley defended economic nationalism and the advancing urban-industrial society.

On election day, voter turnout was extraordinarily high, a measure of the intense interest. By nightfall, the outcome was clear: McKinley won 50 percent of the vote to Bryan's 46 percent. He won the Northeast and Midwest and carried four border states. In the cities, McKinley crushed Bryan.

The election struck down the Populists, whose totals sagged nearly everywhere. Many Populist proposals were later adopted under different leadership. The graduated income tax, crop loans to farmers, the secret ballot, and direct election of United States senators all were early Populist ideas. But the People's party never could win over a majority of the voters, and failing that, it vanished after 1896.

THE MCKINLEY ADMINISTRATION

The election of 1896 cemented the voter realignment of 1894 and initiated a generation of Republican rule. For more than three decades after 1896, with only a brief Democratic resurgence under Woodrow Wilson, the Republicans remained the country's majority party.

McKinley took office in 1897 under favorable circumstances. To everyone's relief, the economy had begun to revive. The stock market rose, factories once again churned out goods, and farmers prospered. Farm prices climbed sharply during 1897 on bumper crops of wheat, cotton, and corn. Discoveries of gold in Australia and Alaska—together with the development of a new cyanide process for extracting gold from ore—enlarged the world's gold supply, decreased its price, and inflated the currency as the silverites had hoped. For the first time since 1890, the 1897 Treasury statements showed a comfortable gold reserve.

McKinley and the Republicans basked in the glow. They became the party of progress and

The Election of 1900

Candidate	Party	Popular Vote	Electoral Vote
McKinley	Republican	7,218,039	292
Bryan	Democrat	6,358,345	155
Woolley	Prohibition	209,004	0
Debs	Socialist	86,935	0

prosperity, an image that helped them win victories until another depression hit in the 1930s. McKinley's popularity soared. Open and accessible in contrast to Cleveland's isolation, he rode the Washington streetcars, walked the streets, and enjoyed looking in department store windows. Cleveland's special police barracks vanished from the White House lawn. McKinley became the first President to ride in an automobile, reaching the speed of eighteen miles an hour.

An activist President, he set the policies of the administration. Conscious of the limits of power, he maintained close ties with Congress and worked hard to educate the public on national choices and priorities. McKinley struck new relations with the press and traveled far more than previous presidents. In some ways, he began the modern presidency.

Shortly after taking office, he summoned Congress into special session to revise the tariff. In July 1897, the Dingley Tariff passed the House and Senate. It raised average tariff duties to a record level, and as the final burst of nineteenth-century protectionism, it caused trouble for the Republican party. By the end of the 1890s, consumers, critics, and the Republicans themselves were wondering if the tariff had outlived its usefulness in the maturing American economy.

From the 1860s to the '90s, the Republicans had built their party on a pledge to *promote* economic growth through the use of state and national power. By 1900, with the industrial system firmly in place, the focus had shifted. The need to *regulate*, to control the effects of industrialism, became a central public concern of the new century. McKinley prodded the Republicans to meet that shift, but he died before his plans matured.

McKinley toyed with the idea of lowering the tariff, but one obstacle always stood in the way:

Gold triumphs over silver in this Puck *cartoon referring to the Gold Standard Act of 1900.*

the government needed revenue, and tariff duties were one of the few taxes the public would support. The Spanish-American War of 1898 (see Chapter 21) persuaded people to accept greater federal power and, with it, new forms of taxation. In 1899, McKinley spoke of lowering tariff barriers in a world that technology had made smaller. "God and man have linked the nations together . . . ," he said in his last speech at Buffalo, New York, in 1901. "Isolation is no longer possible or desirable."

In 1898 and '99, the McKinley administration focused on the war with Spain, the peace treaty that followed, and the dawning realization that the war had thrust the United States into a position of world power. In March 1900, Congress passed the Gold Standard Act, which declared gold the standard of currency and ended the silver controversy that had dominated the 1890s.

The presidential campaign of 1900 was a replay of the McKinley-Bryan fight of 1896. McKinley's running mate was Theodore Roosevelt, hero of the Spanish-American War (see Chapter 21) and former governor of New York, who was nominated for vice president to capitalize on his popularity and, his enemies hoped, to sidetrack his political career into oblivion. Bryan stressed the issues of imperialism and the trusts; McKinley stressed his record at home and abroad. The result in 1900 was a landslide.

On September 6, 1901, a few months after his second inauguration, McKinley stood in a receiving line at the Pan-American Exposition in Buffalo. Leon Czolgosz, a twenty-eight-year-old unemployed laborer and anarchist, moved through the line, and reaching the President, shot him. Surgeons probed the wound but could find nothing. A recent discovery called the X ray was on display at the exposition, but it was not used. On September 14, McKinley died, and Vice-President Theodore Roosevelt became President. A new century had begun.

As the funeral train carried McKinley's body back to Ohio, Mark Hanna, McKinley's old friend and ally, sat slumped in his parlor car. "I told William McKinley it was a mistake to nominate that wild man at Philadelphia," he mourned. "I asked him if he realized what would happen if he should die. Now look, that damned cowboy is President of the United States!"

Hanna's world had changed, and so had the nation's—not so much because "that damned cowboy" was suddenly President, but because events of the 1890s had had powerful effects. In the course of that decade, political patterns shifted, the presidency acquired fresh power, and massive unrest prompted social change. The war with Spain brought a new empire and worldwide responsibilities. Economic hardship posed questions of the most difficult sort about industrialization, urbanization, and the quality of American life. Worried, people embraced new ideas and causes. Reform movements begun in the 1890s flowered in the Progressive period after 1900.

Technology continued to alter the way Americans lived. In 1896, Henry Ford produced a two-cylinder, four-horsepower car, the first of the famous line that bore his name. In 1899, the first automobile salesroom opened in New York, and some innovative thinkers were already imagining a network of service stations to keep the new cars running. At Kitty Hawk, North Carolina, Wilbur and Orville Wright, two bicycle manufacturers, neared the birth of powered flight.

CHRONOLOGY

1876 Mark Twain publishes *The Adventures of Tom Sawyer*

1877 Disputed election of 1876 results in awarding of presidency to Republican Rutherford B. Hayes

1880 Republican James A. Garfield elected president

1881 Garfield assassinated; Vice-President Chester A. Arthur becomes president

1884 Democrat Grover Cleveland elected president, defeating Republican James G. Blaine

1887 Cleveland calls for lowering of tariff duties

1888 Republican Benjamin Harrison wins presidential election

1889 National Farmers' Alliance and Industrial Union formed to address problems of farmers

1890 Republican-dominated "Billion-Dollar" Congress enacts McKinley Tariff Act, Sherman Antitrust Act, and Sherman Silver Purchase Act • Farmers' Alliance adopts the Ocala Demands

1892 Democrat Cleveland defeats Republican Harrison for presidency • People's Party formed

1893 Financial panic touches off depression lasting until 1897 • Sherman Silver Purchase Act repealed • World Columbian Exposition opens in Chicago

1894 Coxey's army marches on Washington • Pullman employees strike

1896 Republican McKinley defeats William Jennings Bryan, Democratic and Populist candidate, in "Battle of the Standards"

1897 Gold discovered in Alaska • Dingley Tariff Act raises tariff duties

1900 McKinley reelected, again defeating Bryan • Gold Standard Act establishes gold as standard of currency

1901 McKinley assassinated; Vice-President Theodore Roosevelt assumes presidency • Naturalist writer Theodore Dreiser publishes *Sister Carrie*

The realignments that reached their peak in the 1890s seem distant, yet they are not. Important decisions in those years shaped nearly everything that came after them. In character and influence, the 1890s are as much a part of the twentieth century as of the nineteenth.

Recommended Reading

The most thorough account of the 1890s is in Harold U. Faulkner, *Politics, Reform and Expansion, 1890–1900* (1959), but see also Robert H. Wiebe, *The Search for Order, 1877–1920* (1967) and Samuel P. Hays, *The Response to Industrialism, 1855–1914* (1957). David P. Thelen, *The New Citizenship: Origins of Progressivism in Wisconsin, 1885–1900* (1972), stresses the impact of the depression on ideas and attitudes.

The best study of the 1890s depression is Charles Hoffman, *The Depression of the Nineties: An Economic History* (1970). Alexander Keyssar, *Out of Work: The First Century of Unemployment in Massachusetts* (1986) is also valuable. H. Wayne Morgan, *From Hayes to McKinley: National Party Politics, 1877–1896* (1969), and Richard J. Jensen, *The Winning of the Midwest: Social and Political Conflict, 1888–1896* (1971) are good on politics. See also, William R. Brock, *Investigation and Responsibility: Public Responsibility in the United States, 1865–1900* (1984). C. Vann Woodward examines the South in *Origins of the New South, 1877–1913* (1951).

Larzer Ziff, *The American 1890s* (1966); Henry Steele Commager, *The American Mind* (1950); and Justin Kaplan, *Mr. Clemens and Mark Twain* (1966), examine literary currents. On Populism, see John D. Hicks, *The Populist Revolt* (1931) and Lawrence Goodwyn, *Democratic Promise: The Populist Moment in America* (1976). C. Vann Woodward, *Tom Watson: Agrarian Rebel* (1938), is a superb biography. John L. Shover, *First Majority—Last Minority: The Transforming of Rural Life in America* (1976) examines conditions on the farms.

Additional Bibliography

On politics, see Morton Keller, *Affairs of State: Public Life in Late Nineteenth Century America* (1977); Paul John Kleppner, *The Cross of Culture: A Social Analysis of Midwestern Politics, 1850–1900* (1970), and *Continuity and Change in Electoral Politics, 1893–1928* (1987); Michael E. McGerr, *The Decline of Popular Politics: The American North, 1865–1928* (1986); Richard L. McCormick, *The Party Period and Public Policy: American Politics from the Age of Jackson to the Progressive Era* (1986); Samuel McSeveney, *The Politics of Depression* (1972); Robert D. Marcus, *Grand Old Party: Political Structure in the Gilded Age, 1880–1896* (1971); Ballard C. Campbell, *Representative Democracy: Public Policy and Midwestern Legislatures in the Late Nineteenth Century* (1980); Eric Anderson, *Race and Politics in North Carolina, 1872–1901: The Black Second* (1981); and R. Hal Williams, *Years of Decision: American Politics in the 1890s* (1978).

Biographies of the era's personalities include Allan Nevins, *Grover Cleveland* (1932); Paola E. Coletta, *William Jennings Bryan*, 3 vols. (1964–1969); Robert W. Cherny, *A Righteous Cause: The Life of William Jennings Bryan* (1985); LeRoy Ashby, *William Jennings Bryan* (1987); Kenneth Davison, *The Presidency of Rutherford B. Hayes* (1972); Ari Hoogenboom, *The Presidency of Rutherford B. Hayes*, (1988); Justus D. Doenecke, *The Presidencies of James A. Garfield and Chester A. Arthur* (1981); Richard E. Welch, *The Presidencies of Grover Cleveland* (1988); Homer E. Socolofsky and Allan B. Spetter, *The Presidency of Benjamin Harrison* (1987); and Lewis L. Gould, *The Presidency of William McKinley* (1981). See also Peter H. Argersinger, *Populism and Politics: William Alfred Peffer and the People's Party* (1974); and Martin Ridge, *Ignatius Donnelly* (1962).

On Populism, see Steven Hahn, *The Roots of Southern Populism* (1983); Robert C. McMath, Jr., *Populist Vanguard: A History of the Southern Farmers' Alliance* (1975); Bruce Palmer, *"Man Over Money": The Southern Populist Critique of American Capitalism* (1980); Barton C. Shaw, *The Wool-Hat Boys: Georgia's Populist Party* (1984); Norman Pollack, *The Just Polity: Populism, Law, and Human Welfare* (1987); Scott G. McNall, *The Road to Rebellion: Class Formation and Kansas Populism, 1865–1900* (1988); Lala Carr Steelman, *The North Carolina Farmers' Alliance* (1985); Worth Robert Miller, *Oklahoma Populism* (1987); Theodore R. Mitchell, *Political Education in the Southern Farmers' Alliance, 1887–1900* (1987); James E. Wright, *The Politics of Populism: Dissent in Colorado* (1974); O. Gene Clanton, *Kansas Populism: Ideas and Men* (1969); Robert W. Larson, *New Mexico Populism* (1974); Larson, *Populism in the Mountain West* (1986); and Stanley B. Parsons, *The Populist Context: Rural Versus Urban Power on a Great Plains Frontier* (1973).

Social and labor unrest is covered in Almont Lindsey, *The Pullman Strike: The Story of a Unique Experiment and of a Great Labor Upheaval* (1942); Stanley Buder, *Pullman: An Experiment in Industrial Order and Community Planning, 1880–1930* (1967); Ray Ginger, *The Bending Cross: A Biography of Eugene Victor Debs* (1969); Nick Salvatore, *Eugene V. Debs: Citizen and Socialist* (1982); Donald L. McMurry, *Coxey's Army: A Study of the Industrial Army Movement of 1894* (1929); Carlos A. Schwantes, *Coxey's Army: An American Odyssey* (1985); Shelton Stromquist, *A Generation of Boomers: The Pattern of Railroad Labor Conflict in Nineteenth-Century America* (1987); and Dorothy Schweider, *Black Diamonds: Life and Work in Iowa's Coal Mining Communities, 1895–1925* (1983). Walter T. K. Nugent, *Money and American Society* (1968), and Allen Weinstein, *Prelude to Populism: Origins of the Silver Issue, 1867–1878* (1970), explain the silver-gold controversy.

Stanley L. Jones, *The Presidential Election of 1896* (1964); Paul W. Glad, *McKinley, Bryan, and the People* (1964); and Robert F. Durden, *The Climax of Populism: The Election of 1896* (1965) examine that election.

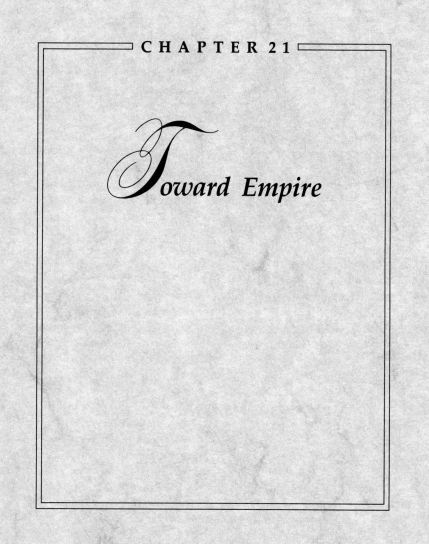

CHAPTER 21

Toward Empire

Many Americans regretted the start of the war with Spain that began in April 1898, but many others welcomed it. War was different then, shorter and more personal than the all-encompassing, lengthy, and mechanistic wars of the twentieth century. Many highly respected people believed that nations must fight every now and then to prove their power and test the national spirit.

Theodore Roosevelt, thirty-nine years old in 1898, was one of them. Nations needed to fight in order to survive, he thought. For months Roosevelt argued strenuously for war with Spain for three reasons: first, on grounds of freeing Cuba and expelling Spain from the hemisphere; second, because of "the benefit done to our people by giving them something to think of which isn't material gain"; and third, because the army and navy needed the practice.

In April 1898, Roosevelt was serving in the important post of assistant secretary of the navy. When war broke out, he quickly resigned to join the army, rejecting the advice of the secretary of the navy who warned he would only "ride a horse and brush mosquitoes from his neck in the Florida sands." The secretary was wrong—dead wrong—and later had the grace to admit it. "Roosevelt was right," he said. "His going into the Army led straight to the Presidency."

In 1898, officers supplied their own uniforms, and Roosevelt, the son of well-to-do parents, wanted his to be stylish. He wired Brooks Brothers, the expensive New York clothier, for a "regular Lieutenant-Colonel's uniform without yellow on the collar and with leggings," to be ready in a week. Joining a friend, he chose to enlist his own regiment, and after a few telephone calls to friends, and telegrams to the governors of Arizona, New Mexico, and Oklahoma asking for "good shots and good riders," he had more than enough men. The First United States Volunteer Cavalry, an intriguing mixture of Ivy League athletes and western frontiersmen, was born.

Known as the Rough Riders, it included men from the Harvard, Yale, and Princeton clubs of New York City, the Somerset Club of Boston, and New York's exclusive Knickerbocker Club. Former college athletes—football players, tennis players, and track stars—enlisted. Woodbury Kane, a wealthy yachtsman, signed up and promptly volunteered for kitchen duty.

Other volunteers came from the West—natural soldiers, Roosevelt called them, "tall and sinewy, with resolute, weather-beaten faces, and eyes that looked a man straight in the face without flinching." Among the cowboys, hunters, and prospectors, there was Bucky O'Neill, a legendary Arizona sheriff and Indian fighter, a half-dozen other sheriffs and Texas Rangers, a large number of Indians, a famous broncobuster, and an ex-marshal of Dodge City, Kansas.

Eager for war, the men trained hard, played harder, and rarely passed up a chance for an intellectual discussion—if Roosevelt's memoir of the war is to be believed. Once, he overheard Bucky O'Neill and a Princeton graduate "discussing Aryan word-roots together, and then sliding off into a review of the novels of Balzac, and a discussion as to how far Balzac could be said to be the founder of the modern realistic school of fiction." Roosevelt himself spent his spare time reading *Superiorité des Anglo-Saxons,* a French work that strove to prove the superiority of English-speaking peoples. In such a camp discipline was lax, and enlisted men got on easily with the officers.

The troops howled with joy when orders came to join the invasion army for Cuba. They won their first victories in Florida, fighting off other regiments to capture a train to take them to the wharf and then seizing the only available troopship to Cuba. The Rough Riders set sail on June 14, 1898, and Lieutenant Colonel Roosevelt, who had performed a war dance for the troops the night before, caught their mood: "We knew not whither we were bound, nor what we were to do; but we believed that the nearing future held for us many chances of death and hardship, of honor and renown. If we failed, we would share the fate of all who fail; but we were sure that we would win, that we should score the first great triumph in a mighty world-movement."

AMERICA LOOKS OUTWARD

The overseas expansion of the 1890s differed in several important respects from earlier expansionist moves of the United States. From its beginning, the American Republic had been expanding. After the first landings in Jamestown and Plymouth, settlers pushed westward: into the transAppalachian region, the Louisiana Territory,

Florida, Texas, California, Arizona, and New Mexico. Most of these lands were contiguous with existing territories of the United States, and most were intended for settlement, usually agricultural.

The expansion of the 1890s was different. It sought to gain island possessions, the bulk of them already thickly populated. The new territories were held less for settlement than as naval bases, trading outposts, or commercial centers on major trade routes. More often than not, they were viewed as colonies, not as states-in-the-making.

Historian Samuel F. Bemis described the overseas expansion of the 1890s as "the great aberration," a time when the country adopted expansionist policies that did not fit with prior experience. Other historians, pointing to expansionist tendencies in thought and foreign policy that surfaced during the last half of the nineteenth century, have found a developing pattern that led naturally to the overseas adventures of the 1890s. In this view, "the United States did not set out on an expansionist path in the late 1890s in a sudden, spur-of-the-moment fashion. The overseas empire that Americans controlled in 1900 was not a break in their history, but a natural culmination."

Catching the Spirit of Empire

Most people in most times in history tend to look inward, and Americans in these years following the Civil War were no exception. Among other things, they focused on Reconstruction, the movement westward, and simply making a living. They took seriously the well-remembered advice of George Washington's Farewell Address to "steer clear" of foreign entanglements. Throughout the nineteenth century, Americans enjoyed "free security" without fully appreciating it. Sheltered by two oceans and the British navy, they could enunciate bold policies like the Monroe Doctrine, which instructed European nations to stay out of the affairs of the Western Hemisphere, while remaining virtually impregnable to foreign attack.

In those circumstances, some people urged abolition of the foreign service, considering it an unnecessary expenditure, a dangerous profession that might lead to entanglement in the struggles

In the late 1800s, America and Russia began to make expansionist moves in the Pacific.

of the world's great powers. A New York newspaper called it a "relic of medieval, monarchical trumpery," and if not that, it certainly became at times a dumping ground of the spoils system. Presidents named ambassadors from lists of politicians, journalists, and business leaders who, though successful in their own fields, had no training in languages or diplomatic relations.

In the 1870s and after, however, Americans began to take an increasing interest in events abroad. There was a growing sense of internationalism, which stemmed in part from the telegraphs, telephones, and undersea cables that kept people better informed about political and economic developments in distant lands. Many Americans continued to be interested in expansion of the country's borders; relatively few were interested in imperialism. Expansion meant the kind of growth that had brought California and Oregon into the American system. Imperialism meant the imposition of control over other peoples through annexation, military conquest, or economic domination.

Several developments in these years combined to shift attention outward across the seas. The end of the frontier, announced officially in the census report of 1890, sparked fears about diminishing opportunities at home. Further growth, it seemed, must take place abroad, as John A. Kasson, an able and experienced diplomat, said in the *North American Review:* "We are rapidly utilizing the whole of our continental territory. We must turn our eyes abroad, or they will soon look inward upon discontent."

Factories and farms multiplied, producing more goods than the domestic market could consume. Both farmers and industrialists looked for new overseas markets, and the growing volume of exports—including more and more manufactured goods—changed the nature of American trade relations with the world. American exports of merchandise amounted to $393 million in 1870, $858 million in 1890, and $1.4 billion in 1900. In 1898, the United States exported more than it imported, beginning a trend that lasted through the 1960s.

Political leaders such as James G. Blaine began to argue for the vital importance of foreign markets to continued economic growth. Blaine, secretary of state under Garfield and again under Harrison, aggressively sought wider markets in Latin America, Asia, and Africa, using tariff reciprocity agreements and other measures. To some extent, he and others were also caught up in a worldwide scramble for empire. In the last third of the century, Great Britain, France, and Germany divided up Africa and looked covetously at Asia. The idea of imperialistic expansion was in the air, and the great powers measured their greatness by the colonies they acquired. Inevitably, some Americans—certain business interests and foreign-policy strategists, for example—caught the spirit and wanted to enter the international hunt for territory.

Intellectual currents that supported expansion drew on Charles Darwin's theories of evolution. Adherents pointed, for example, to *The Origin of Species,* which mentioned in its subtitle *The Preservation of Favoured Races in the Struggle for Life.* Applied to human and social development, biological concepts seemed to call for the triumph of the fit and the elimination of the unfit. "In this world," said Theodore Roosevelt, who thought of himself as one of the fit, "the nation that has trained itself to a career of unwarlike and isolated ease is bound, in the end, to go down before other nations which have not lost the manly and adventurous qualities."

Haeckel's Biogenetic Law, then a popular theory, suggested that the development of the individual repeated the development of the race. Primitive peoples thus were in the arrested stages of childhood or adolescence; they needed supervision and protective treatment. In a similar vein, John Fiske, a popular writer and lecturer, argued for Anglo-Saxon racial superiority, a result of the process of natural selection. The English and Americans, Fiske said, would occupy every land on the globe that was not already "civilized," bringing the advances of commerce and democratic institutions.

Such views were widespread among the lettered and unlettered alike. In Cuba, one of the Rough Riders ushered a visiting Russian prince around the trenches, informing him with ill-considered enthusiasm: "You see, Prince, the great result of this war is that it has united the two branches of Anglo-Saxon people; and now that they are together they can whip the world, Prince! they can whip the world!" Eminent scholars like John W. Burgess, a professor of political science at Columbia University, argued in similar though more dignified fashion that people of English origin were destined to impose their political institutions on the world.

The career of Josiah Strong, a Congregational minister and fervent expansionist, suggested the strength of the developing ideas. A champion of overseas missionary work, Strong traveled extensively through the West for the Home Missionary Society, and in 1885, drawing on his experiences, he published a book entitled *Our Country: Its Possible Future and Its Present Crisis.* An immediate best-seller, the book called upon foreign missions to civilize the world under the Anglo-Saxon races. Strong became a national celebrity.

Our Country argued for expanding American trade and dominion. Trade was important, because the desire for material things was one of the hallmarks of civilized people. So was the Christian religion, and by exporting both trade and religion, Americans could civilize and Christianize inferior races around the world. As Anglo-Saxons, they were members of a God-favored race destined to lead the world. Anglo-Saxons already owned one-third of the earth, Strong said, and in a famous passage he concluded that they would take more. In "the final competition of races," they would win out and "move down upon Mexico, down upon Central and South America, out upon the islands of the sea, over upon Africa and beyond."

Taken together, these developments in social, political, and economic thought prepared Americans for a larger role in the world. The change was gradual, and there was never a day when people awoke with a sudden realization of their interests overseas. But change there was, and by the 1890s, Americans were ready to reach out into the world in a more determined and deliberate fashion than ever before. For almost the first time, they felt the need for a foreign "policy."

Foreign Policy Approaches: 1867–1900

Rarely consistent, American foreign policy in the last half of the nineteenth century took different approaches to different areas of the world. In relation to Europe, seat of the dominant world powers, policymakers promoted trade and tried to avoid diplomatic entanglements. In North and South America, they based policy on the Monroe Doctrine, a recurrent dream of annexing Canada or Mexico, a hope for extensive trade, and Pan-American unity against the nations of the Old World. In the Pacific, they coveted Hawaii and other outposts on the sea lanes to China.

Secretary of State William Henry Seward, who served from 1861 to 1869, aggressively pushed an expansive foreign policy. "Give me . . . fifty, forty, thirty more years of life," he told a Boston audience in 1867, "and I will give you possession of the American continent and control of the world." Seward, it turned out, had only five more years of life, but he developed a vision of an American empire stretching south into Latin America and west to the shores of Asia. This vision included Canada and Mexico; islands in the Caribbean as strategic bases to protect a canal across the isthmus; and Hawaii and other islands as stepping-stones to Asia which Seward and many others considered a virtually bottomless outlet for farm and manufactured goods.

Seward tried unsuccessfully to negotiate a commercial treaty with Hawaii in 1867, and the

Cartoonists had a field day when Seward purchased Alaska. Here, he invites the Alaskan representative to "bring Mr. McSeal along with you to Washington."

same year he annexed the Midway Islands, a small atoll group 1200 miles northwest of Hawaii. In 1867, he concluded a treaty with Russia for the purchase of Alaska (which was promptly labeled "Seward's Folly") partly to sandwich western Canada between American territory and lead to its annexation. As the American empire spread, Seward thought, Mexico City would become its capital.

Secretary of State Hamilton Fish, an urbane New Yorker, followed Seward in 1869, serving under President Ulysses S. Grant. An avid expansionist, Grant wanted to extend American influence in the Caribbean and Pacific, though Fish, more conservative, often restrained him. They moved first to repair relations with Great Britain. The first business was settlement of the *Alabama* claims—demands that Britain pay the United States for damages to Union ships caused by Confederate vessels which, like the *Alabama*, had been built and outfitted in British shipyards (see Chapter 15). Negotiating patiently, Fish signed the Treaty of Washington in 1871, providing for arbitration of the *Alabama* issue and other nettlesome controversies. The treaty, one of the landmarks in the peaceful settlement of international disputes, marked a significant step in cementing Anglo-American relations.

Grant and Fish looked most eagerly to Latin America. In 1870, Grant became the first president to proclaim the nontransfer principle—"hereafter no territory on this continent shall be regarded as subject to transfer to a European power." Fish also promoted the independence of Cuba, restive under Spanish rule, while holding off the annexation desired by the more eager Grant. Influenced by speculators, Grant tried to annex Santo Domingo in 1869 but was thwarted by powerful Republicans in the Senate who disliked foreign involvement and feared a subsequent attempt to annex Haiti.

James G. Blaine served briefly as Garfield's secretary of state and laid extensive plans to establish closer commercial relations with Latin America. His successor, Frederick T. Frelinghuysen, changed Blaine's approach but not his strategy. Like Blaine, Frelinghuysen wanted to find Caribbean markets for American goods; he negotiated separate reciprocity treaties with Mexico, Cuba and Puerto Rico, the British West Indies, Santo Domingo, and Colombia. Using these treaties, Frelinghuysen hoped not only to obtain markets for American goods but to bind these countries to American interests.

When Blaine returned to the State Department in 1889 under President Benjamin Harrison, he moved again to expand markets in Latin America. Drawing on earlier ideas, he envisaged a hemispheric system of peaceful intercourse, arbitration of disputes, and expanded trade. He also wanted to annex Hawaii. "I think there are only three places that are of value and not already taken, that are not continental," he wrote in a letter to President Harrison in 1891. "One is Hawaii and the others are Cuba and Puerto Rico." The last two might take a generation to acquire, but "Hawaii may come up for decision at any unexpected hour and I hope we shall be prepared to decide it in the affirmative."

Harrison and Blaine toyed with naval acquisitions in the Caribbean and elsewhere, but in general they focused on Pan-Americanism and tariff reciprocity. Blaine presided over the first Inter-American Conference in Washington on October 2, 1889. Delegates from nineteen American nations were present. They negotiated several agreements to promote trade and created the International Bureau of the American Republics, later renamed the Pan-American Union, for the exchange of general information including political, scientific, and cultural knowledge. The conference, a major step in hemispheric relations, led to later meetings promoting trade and other agreements.

Reciprocity, Harrison and Blaine hoped, would divert Latin American trade from Europe to the United States. Working hard to sell the idea in Congress, Blaine lobbied for a reciprocity provision in the McKinley Tariff Act of 1890 (see Chapter 20), and once that was enacted, he negotiated important reciprocity treaties with most Latin American nations. The treaties suffered from the depression of the 1890s; nevertheless, they resulted in greater American exports of flour, grain, meat, iron, and machinery. Exports to Cuba jumped by one-third between 1891 and 1893, then dropped precipitously when the 1894 Wilson-Gorman Tariff Act ended reciprocity.

Grover Cleveland, Harrison's successor, also pursued an aggressive policy toward Latin America. In 1895, he brought the United States precariously close to war with Great Britain over a boundary dispute between Venezuela and British Guiana. Cleveland sympathized with Venezuela, and he and Secretary of State Richard Olney urged Britain to arbitrate the dispute. When Britain failed to act, Olney drafted a stiff diplomatic note affirming the Monroe Doctrine and denying European nations the right to meddle in Western Hemisphere affairs.

Four months passed before Lord Salisbury, the British foreign secretary, replied. Rejecting Olney's arguments, he sent two letters, the first bluntly repudiating the Monroe Doctrine as international law. The second letter, carefully reasoned and sometimes sarcastic, rejected Olney's arguments for the Venezuelan boundary. Enraged, Cleveland defended the Monroe Doctrine, and he asked Congress for authority to appoint a commission to decide the boundary and enforce its decision. "I am fully alive to the responsibility incurred and keenly realize all the consequences that may follow," he told Congress, plainly implying war.

Preoccupied with larger diplomatic problems in Africa and Europe, Britain changed its position. In November 1896, the two countries signed a treaty of arbitration, under which Great Britain and Venezuela divided the disputed territory. Though Cleveland's approach was clumsy—throughout the crisis, for example, he rarely consulted Venezuela—the Venezuelan incident demonstrated a growing determination to exert American power in the Western Hemisphere. Cleveland and Olney had persuaded Great Britain to recognize the United States's dominance, and they had increased American influence in Latin America. The Monroe Doctrine assumed new importance. In averting war, an era of Anglo-American friendship was begun.

The Lure of Hawaii and Samoa

The islands of Hawaii offered a tempting way station to Asian markets. In the early 1800s, they were already called the "Crossroads of the Pacific," and trading ships of many nations stopped there. In 1820, the first American missionaries arrived to convert the islanders to Christianity. Like missionaries elsewhere, they advertised Hawaii's economic and other benefits and attracted new settlers. Their children later came to dominate Hawaiian political and economic life and played an important role in annexation.

After the Civil War, the United States tightened its connections with the islands. The reciprocity treaty of 1875 allowed Hawaiian sugar to enter the United States free of duty and bound the Hawaiian monarchy to make no territorial or economic concessions to other powers. The treaty increased Hawaiian economic dependence on the United States; its political clauses effectively made Hawaii an American protectorate. In 1887, a new treaty reaffirmed these arrangements and granted the United States exclusive use of Pearl Harbor, a magnificent harbor that had early caught the eye of naval strategists.

Following the 1875 treaty, white Hawaiians became more and more influential in the islands' political life. The McKinley Tariff Act of 1890 ended the special status given Hawaiian sugar and at the same time awarded American producers a bounty of two cents a pound. Hawaiian sugar production dropped dramatically, unemployment rose, and property values fell. The following year, the weak King Kalakaua died, bringing to power a strong-willed nationalist, Queen Liliuokalani. Resentful of white minority rule, she decreed a new constitution that gave greater power to native Hawaiians.

Unhappy, the American residents revolted in early 1893 and called on the United States for help. John L. Stevens, the American minister in Honolulu, sent 150 marines ashore from the cruiser *Boston*, and within three days the bloodless revolution was over. Queen Liliuokalani surrendered "to the superior force of the United States," and the victorious rebels set up a provisional government. Stevens urged annexation, telling Washington that the "Hawaiian pear is now fully ripe, and this is the golden hour for the United States to pluck it." On February 14, 1893, Harrison's Secretary of State John W. Foster and delegates of the new government signed a treaty annexing Hawaii to the United States.

But only two weeks remained in Harrison's term, and the Senate refused to ratify the agreement. Five days after taking office, Cleveland withdrew the treaty; he then sent a representative to investigate the cause of the rebellion. The investigation revealed that the Americans' role in it had been improper, and Cleveland decided to restore the queen to her throne. He made the demand, but the provisional government in Hawaii politely refused and instead established the Republic of Hawaii, which the embarrassed Cleveland, unable to do otherwise, recognized.

The debate over Hawaiian annexation, continuing through the 1890s, foreshadowed the later debate over the treaty to end the Spanish-American War. People in favor of annexation pointed to Hawaii's strategic location, argued that Japan or other powers might seize the islands if the United States did not, and suggested that Americans had a responsibility to civilize and Christianize the native Hawaiians. Opponents warned that annexation might lead to a colonial army and colonial problems, the inclusion of a "mongrel" population in the United States, and rule over an area not destined for statehood.

Annexation came swiftly in July 1898 in the midst of excitement over victories in the Spanish-American War. The year before, President William McKinley had sent a treaty of annexation to the Senate, but opposition quickly arose, and the treaty stalled. Japan protested against it, pointing out that Japanese made up a quarter of the Hawaiian population. Japan dispatched a cruiser to Honolulu; the Navy Department sent the

The first step toward American annexation of Hawaii came in 1893 when Queen Liliuokalani (right) was removed from the throne. Hawaii finally became a part of the United States on August 12, 1898. Sanford B. Dole, president of the Republic of Hawaii and later its first governor, is shown above at the transfer of sovereignty ceremony at Iokani Palace.

battleship *Oregon* and ordered naval forces to take Hawaii if the Japanese made threatening moves.

In 1898, annexationists redoubled arguments about Hawaii's commercial and military importance. McKinley and congressional leaders switched strategies to seek a joint resolution, rather than a treaty, for annexation. A joint resolution required only a majority of both houses, while a treaty needed a two-thirds vote in the Senate. Bolstered by the new strategy, the annexation measure moved quickly through Congress, and McKinley signed it on July 7, 1898. His signature, giving the United States a naval and commercial base in the mid-Pacific, realized a goal held by policymakers since the 1860s.

While annexation of Hawaii represented a step toward China, the Samoan Islands, three thousand miles to the south, offered a strategic location astride the sea lanes of the South Pacific. Americans showed early interest in Samoa, and in 1872, a naval officer negotiated a treaty granting the United States the use of Pago Pago, a splendid harbor on one of its islands. The Senate rejected the treaty, but six years later approved a similar agreement providing for a naval station there. The agreement bound the United States to use its good offices to adjust any disputes between the Samoan chiefs and foreign governments. Great Britain and Germany also secured treaty rights in Samoa, and thereafter the three nations jockeyed for position.

The situation grew tense in 1889 when warships from all three countries gathered in a Samoan harbor. But a sudden typhoon destroyed the fleets, and tensions eased. A month later, delegates from Britain, Germany, and the United States met in Berlin to negotiate the problem. Britain and Germany wanted to divide up the islands; Secretary of State Blaine held out for some degree of authority by the indigenous population, with American control over Pago Pago.

The agreement, an uneasy one, ended in 1899 when the United States and Germany divided Samoa and compensated Britain with lands elsewhere in the Pacific. Germany claimed the two larger islands in the chain; the United States kept the harbor at Pago Pago.

The New Navy

Large navies were vital in the scramble for colonies, and in the 1870s the United States had almost no naval power. One of the most powerful fleets in the world during the Civil War, the American navy had fallen into rapid decline. By

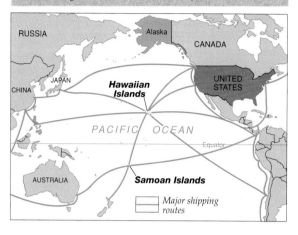

RUSSIA · Alaska · CANADA · JAPAN · CHINA · Hawaiian Islands · UNITED STATES · PACIFIC OCEAN · Equator · AUSTRALIA · Samoan Islands · Major shipping routes

1880, there were fewer than 2000 vessels, only 48 of which could fire a gun. Ships rotted, and many officers left the service. "It was easy then," said George Dewey, later a hero of the war with Spain, "for an officer to drift along in his grade, losing interest and remaining in the navy only because he was too old to change his occupation."

Conditions changed during the 1880s. A group of rising young officers, steeped in a new naval philosophy, argued for an expanded navy equipped with fast, aggressive fleets capable of fighting battles across the seas. This group had its greatest influence in a special Naval Advisory Board, formed by the secretary of the navy in 1881. Big-navy proponents pointed to the growing fleets of Great Britain, France, and Germany, arguing that the United States needed greater fleet strength to protect its economic and other interests in the Caribbean and Pacific.

In 1883, Congress authorized construction of four steel ships, marking the beginning of the new navy. Experts also worked to improve naval management and the quality of fleet personnel, and between 1885 and 1889, Congress budgeted funds for thirty additional ships. The initial building program focused on lightly armored, fast cruisers for raiding enemy merchant ships and protecting American shores, but after 1890, the program shifted to the construction of a seagoing, offensive battleship navy capable of challenging the strongest fleets of Europe.

Alfred Thayer Mahan and Benjamin F. Tracy were two of the main forces behind the new navy. Austere and scholarly, Mahan was the era's most influential naval strategist. After graduating from the Naval Academy in 1859, he devoted a lifetime to studying the influence of sea power in history; for over two decades he headed the Newport Naval War College, where officers imbibed the latest in strategic thinking. A clear, logical writer, Mahan summarized his beliefs in several major books, including *The Influence of Sea Power Upon History, 1660–1783* (1890) and *The Interest of America in Sea Power* (1897).

Mahan's reasoning was simple and, to that generation, persuasive. Industrialism, he argued, produced vast surpluses of agricultural and manufactured goods, for which markets must be found. Markets involved distant ports; reaching them required a large merchant marine and a powerful navy to protect it. Navies, in turn, needed coaling stations and repair yards. Coaling stations meant colonies, and colonies became strategic bases, the foundation of a nation's wealth and power. The bases might serve as markets themselves, but they were more important as stepping-stones to other objectives, such as the markets of Latin America and Asia.

Mahan called attention to the worldwide race for power, a race, he warned, the United States could not afford to lose. "All around us now is strife; 'the struggle of life,' 'the race of life' are phrases so familiar that we do not feel their significance till we stop to think about them. Everywhere nation is arrayed against nation; our own no less than others." To compete in the struggle, Mahan argued, the United States must expand. It needed strategic bases, a powerful, oceangoing navy, a canal across the isthmus to link the East coast with the Pacific, and Hawaii as a way station on the route to Asia.

Mahan influenced a generation of policymakers in the United States and Europe; one of them, Benjamin F. Tracy, became Harrison's secretary of the navy in 1889. Between then and 1893, Tracy organized the Bureau of Construction and Repair to design and build new ships, established the Naval Reserve in 1891, and ordered construction of the first American submarine in 1893. He also started the first heavy rapid-fire guns, smokeless powder, torpedoes, and heavy armor. Above all, Tracy joined with big-navy advocates

This 1881 cartoon depicted "our top heavy navy," a decrepit vessel sinking with idle officers.

in Congress to push for a far-ranging battleship fleet capable of attacking distant enemies. He wanted two fleets of battleships, eight in the Pacific and twelve in the Atlantic. He got four first-class battleships.

In 1889, when Tracy entered office, the United States ranked twelfth among world navies; in 1893, when he left, it ranked seventh and was climbing rapidly. "The sea," he predicted in 1891, "will be the future seat of empires. And we shall rule it as certainly as the sun doth rise." By the end of the decade, the navy had seventeen steel battleships, six armored cruisers, and many smaller craft. It ranked third in the world.

WAR WITH SPAIN

The war with Spain in 1898 built a mood of national confidence, altered older, more insular patterns of thought, and reshaped the way Americans saw themselves and the world. While its outcome pleased some people, it troubled others, and they raised questions about war itself, colonies, and subject peoples. The war left a lingering strain of isolationism and antiwar feeling that affected later policy. It also left an American empire, small by European standards, but quite new to the American experience by virtue of its overseas location. When the war ended, American possessions stretched into the Caribbean and deep into the Pacific. American influence went further still, and the United States was recognized as a "world power."

The Spanish-American War established the United States as a dominant force for the twentieth century. It brought America colonies and millions of colonial subjects; it brought the responsibilities of governing an empire and protecting it. For better or worse, it involved the country in other nations' arguments and affairs. The war strengthened the office of the presidency, swept the nation together in a tide of emotion, and confirmed the long-standing belief in the superiority of the New World over the Old. When it was over, Americans looked outward as never before, touched, they were sure, with a special destiny.

They seemed a chosen people, as Mr. Dooley, a character created by humorist Finley Peter Dunne, pointed out to his friend Hennessy over

Mr. Dooley, the irreverent Irish-American saloon keeper created by Finley Peter Dunne, often aimed his sardonic humor at the "Establishment."

the Archey Road bar. "We're a gr-reat people" said Hennessy, in his rolling Irish brogue. "We ar-re that," replied Mr. Dooley. "We ar-re that. An th' best iv it is we know we ar-re."

A War for Principle

By the 1890s, Cuba and the nearby island of Puerto Rico comprised nearly all that remained of Spain's once vast empire in the New World. Several times, Cuban insurgents had rebelled against Spanish rule, including a decade-long rebellion from 1868 to 1878 (the Ten Years' War) that failed to settle the conflict. The depression of 1893 damaged the Cuban economy, and the Wilson-Gorman Tariff of 1894 prostrated it. Duties on sugar, Cuba's lifeblood, were raised 40 percent. With the island's sugar market in ruins, discontent with Spanish rule heightened, and in late February 1895, revolt again broke out.

Recognizing the importance of the nearby United States, Cuban insurgents established a junta in New York City to raise money, buy weapons, and wage a propaganda war to sway American public opinion. Conditions in Cuba were grim. The insurgents pursued a hit-and-run, scorched-earth policy to force the Spanish to leave. Spain committed more than two hundred thousand soldiers; the Spanish commander, who had won with similar tactics in 1878, tried to pin the insurgents in the eastern part of the island where they could be cornered and destroyed.

When this strategy failed, Spain in January 1896 sent a new commander, General Valeriano Weyler y Nicolau. Relentless and brutal, Weyler gave the rebels ten days to lay down their arms. He then put into effect a "reconcentration" policy designed to move the native population into camps and destroy the rebellion's popular base. Herded into fortified areas, Cubans died by the thousands, victims of unsanitary conditions, overcrowding, and disease.

There was a wave of sympathy for the insurgents stimulated by the newspapers (see "Reporting the Spanish-American War," pp. 634–35). But "yellow" journalism did not cause the war. The conflict stemmed from larger disputes in policies and perceptions between Spain and the United States. Grover Cleveland, under whose administration the rebellion began, preferred

Spanish rule to the kind of turmoil that might invite foreign intervention. Opposed to the annexation of Cuba, he issued a proclamation of neutrality and tried to restrain public opinion. In 1896, Congress passed a resolution favoring recognition of Cuban belligerency, but Cleveland ignored it. Instead, he offered to mediate the struggle, an offer Spain declined.

Taking office in March 1897, President McKinley also urged neutrality but leaned slightly toward the insurgents. He immediately sent a trusted aide on a fact-finding mission to Cuba; the aide reported in mid-1897 that Weyler's policy had wrapped Cuba "in the stillness of death and the silence of desolation." The report in hand, McKinley offered to mediate the struggle, but concerned over the suffering, he protested against Spain's "uncivilized and inhuman" conduct. The United States, he made clear, did not contest Spain's right to fight the rebellion but insisted it be done within humane limits.

Late in 1897, a change in government in Madrid brought a temporary lull in the crisis. The new government recalled Weyler and agreed to offer the Cubans some form of autonomy. It also declared an amnesty for political prisoners and released Americans in Cuban jails. The new initiatives pleased McKinley, though he again warned Spain that it must find a humane end to the rebellion. Then, in January 1898, Spanish army officers led riots in Havana against the new autonomy policy, shaking the President's confidence in Madrid's control over conditions in Cuba.

McKinley ordered the battleship *Maine* to Havana to demonstrate strength and protect American citizens if necessary. On February 9, 1898, the *New York Journal,* a leader of the "yellow press," published a letter stolen from Enrique Dupuy de Lôme, the Spanish ambassador in Washington. The letter was a private letter to a friend, and in it de Lôme called McKinley "weak," "a would-be politician," and "a bidder for the admiration of the crowd." Many Americans were angered by the insult; McKinley himself was more worried about other sections of the letter which revealed Spanish insincerity in the negotiations. De Lôme immediately resigned and went home, but the damage was done.

A few days later, at 9:40 in the evening of February 15, an explosion tore through the hull of

MAINE EXPLOSION CAUSED BY BOMB OR TORPEDO?

Capt. Sigsbee and Consul-General Lee Are in Doubt---The World Has Sent a Special Tug, With Submarine Divers, to Havana to Find Out---Lee Asks for an Immediate Court of Inquiry---Capt. Sigsbee's Suspicions.

CAPT. SIGSBEE, IN A SUPPRESSED DESPATCH TO THE STATE DEPARTMENT, SAYS THE ACCIDENT WAS MADE POSSIBLE BY AN ENEMY.

Dr. E. C. Pendleton, Just Arrived from Havana, Says He Overheard Talk There of a Plot to Blow Up the Ship---Capt. Zalinski, the Dynamite Expert, and Other Experts Report to The World that the Wreck Was Not Accidental---Washington Officials Ready for Vigorous Action if Spanish Responsibility Can Be Shown---Divers to Be Sent Down to Make Careful Examinations.

Headlines like these in the New York World *left little doubt among readers that Spain had sunk the* Maine.

the *Maine,* riding at anchor in Havana harbor. The ship, a trim symbol of the new steel navy, sank quickly; 266 lives were lost. McKinley cautioned patience and promised an immediate investigation. Crowds gathered quietly on Capitol Hill and outside the White House, mourning the lost men. Soon there was a new slogan, "Remember the *Maine* and to Hell with Spain!"

The most recent study of the *Maine* incident blames the sinking on an accidental internal explosion, caused perhaps by spontaneous combustion in poorly ventilated coal bunkers. In 1898, Americans blamed it on Spain. Spaniards were hanged in effigy in many communities. Roosevelt, William Jennings Bryan, and others urged war, but McKinley delayed, hopeful that Spain might yet agree to an armistice and perhaps Cuban independence. "I have been through one war; I have seen the dead piled up; and I do not want to see another," he told a White House visitor.

In early March 1898, wanting to be ready for war if it came, McKinley asked Congress for $50 million in emergency defense appropriations, a request Congress promptly approved. The unanimous vote stunned Spain; allowing the President

a latitude that was highly unusual for the era, it appropriated the money "for the National defense and for each and every purpose connected therewith to be expended at the discretion of the President." In late March, the report of the investigating board blamed the sinking of the *Maine* on an external (and thus presumably Spanish) explosion. Pressures for war increased.

On March 27, McKinley cabled Spain his final terms. He asked Spain to declare an armistice, end the reconcentration policy, and—implicitly—move toward Cuban independence. When the Spanish answer came, it conceded some things, but not, in McKinley's judgment, the important ones. Spain offered a suspension of hostilities (but not an armistice) and left the Spanish commander in Cuba to set the length and terms of the suspension. It also revoked the reconcentration policy. But the Spanish response made no mention of a true armistice, McKinley's offer to mediate, or Cuba's independence.

Reluctantly McKinley prepared his war message. It was long and temperate—at seven thousand words even deliberately boring; it suggested the possibility of further negotiations. Congress heard it on April 11, 1898. On April 19, Congress passed a joint resolution declaring Cuba independent and authorizing the President to use the army and navy to expel the Spanish from it. An amendment by Colorado Senator Henry M. Teller pledged that the United States had no intention of annexing the island.

On April 21, Spain severed diplomatic relations. The following day, McKinley proclaimed a blockade of Cuba and called for 125,000 volunteers. On Monday, April 25, Congress passed a declaration of war. Late that afternoon, McKinley signed it.

Some historians have suggested that in leading the country toward war, McKinley was weak and indecisive, a victim of war hysteria in the Congress and country; others have called him a wily manipulator for war and imperial gains. In truth he was neither. Throughout the Spanish crisis, McKinley pursued a moderate middle course that sought to end the suffering in Cuba, promote Cuba's independence, and allow Spain time to adjust to the loss of the remnant of empire. He also wanted peace, as did Spain, but in the end, the conflicting national interests of the two countries brought them to war.

"A Splendid Little War"

Ten weeks after the declaration of war the fighting was over. For Americans, they were ten glorious, dizzying weeks, with victories to fill every headline and slogans to suit every taste. No war can be a happy occasion for those who fight it, but the Spanish-American War came closer than most. Declared in April, it ended in August. Relatively few Americans died, and the quick victory seemed to verify burgeoning American power, though Sherwood Anderson, the author, suggested that fighting a weakened Spain was "like robbing an old gypsy woman in a vacant lot at night after a fair." John Hay, soon to be McKinley's secretary of state, called it "a splendid little war."

At the outset, the United States was militarily unprepared. Unlike the navy, the army had not been rebuilt or modernized in structure, and it had shrunk drastically since the day thirty-three years before when Grant's great Civil War army marched 60 abreast, 200,000-strong, down Washington's Pennsylvania Avenue. In 1898, the regular army consisted of only 28,000 officers and men, most of them more experienced in quelling Indian uprisings than fighting large-scale battles. The Indian wars did produce effective, small-scale forces, well-trained and tightly disciplined, but the army was unquestionably too small for war against Spain.

When McKinley called for 125,000 volunteers, as many as 1 million young Americans responded. Ohio alone had 100,000 volunteers. Keeping the regular army units intact, War Department officials enlisted the volunteers in National Guard units that were then integrated into the national army. Men clamored to join. William Jennings Bryan, a pacifist by temperament, took command of a regiment of Nebraska volunteers; Roosevelt chafed to get to the front; and young Cordell Hull, who became secretary of state in the 1930s, was "wildly eager to leave at once." The secretary of war feared "there is going to be more trouble to satisfy those who are not going than to find those who are willing to go."

In an army inundated with men, problems of equipment and supply quickly appeared. The regulars had the new .30 caliber Krag-Jorgensen rifles, but National Guard units carried Civil War Springfield rifles that used old, black powder cartridges. The cartridges gave off a puff of smoke when fired, neatly marking the troops' position. Spanish troops were better equipped; they had modern Mausers with smokeless powder, which they used to devastating effect. Food was also a problem, as was sickness. The War Department fell behind in supplies and received many complaints about the canned beef it offered the men. Tropical disease felled many soldiers. Scores took ill after landing in Cuba and the Philippines, and it was not uncommon for half a regiment to be unable to answer the bugle call.

Americans then believed that "a foreign war should be fought by the hometown military unit acting as an extension of their community." Soldiers identified with their hometowns, dressed in the local fashion, and thought of themselves as members of a town unit in a national army. The poet Carl Sandburg, twenty years old in 1898, rushed to join the army and called his unit a "living part" of his hometown of Galesburg, Illinois. And the citizens of Galesburg, for their part, took a special interest in Sandburg's unit, in a fashion repeated in countless towns across the country.

Not surprisingly, then, National Guard units mirrored the social patterns of their communities. Since everyone knew each other, there was an easygoing familiarity, tempered by the deference that went with hometown wealth, occupation, education, and length of residence. Enlisted men resented officers who grabbed too much authority, and they expected officers and men to call each other by their first names. Sandburg knew most of the privates in his unit, had worked for his corporal, and had gone to school with the first lieutenant. "Officers and men of the Guard mingle on a plane of beautiful equality," said a visitor to one volunteer camp. "Privates invade the tents of their officers at will, and yell at them half the length of the street."

Each community thought of the hometown unit as *its* unit, an extension of itself. In later wars, the government censored news and dominated press relations; there was little censorship in the war with Spain, and the freshest news arrived in the latest letter home. Small-town newspapers printed news of the men; townswomen knit special red or white bellybands of stitched flannel, thought to ward off tropical fevers; towns sent food, clothing, and occasional-

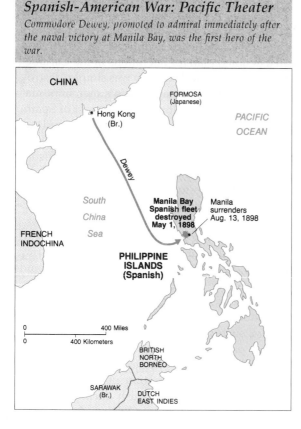

Spanish-American War: Pacific Theater

Commodore Dewey, promoted to admiral immediately after the naval victory at Manila Bay, was the first hero of the war.

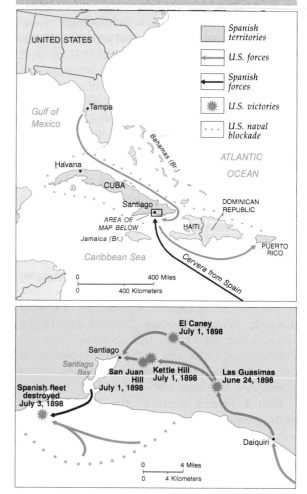

Spanish-American War: Cuban Theater

President McKinley set up a "war room" in the White House, following the action on giant war maps with red and white marking pins.

victory, quickly raised an expeditionary force. On August 13, 1898, the troops accepted the surrender of Manila, and with it, the Philippines.

McKinley and his aides were worried about Admiral Pascual Cervera's main Spanish fleet, thought to be headed across the Atlantic for an attack on Florida. On May 13, the navy found Cervera's ships near Martinique in the Caribbean but then lost them again. A few days later, Cervera slipped secretly into the harbor of Santiago de Cuba, a city on the island's southern coast. But a spy in the Havana telegraph office alerted the Americans, and on May 28, a superior American force under Admiral William T. Sampson bottled Cervera up.

In early June, a small force of Marines seized Guantanamo Bay, the great harbor on the south of the island. They established depots for the navy to refuel and pinned down Spanish troops in the area. On June 14, an invasion force of about seventeen thousand men set sail from Tampa. Seven days later, they landed at Daiquiri on Cuba's southeastern coast. All was confusion, but the Spanish offered no resistance. Helped by Cuban insurgents, the Americans immediately pushed west toward Santiago, which they hoped to surround and capture. At first, the advance was peaceful, through the lush tropical countryside.

The first battle broke out at Las Guasimas, a crossroads on the Santiago road. After a sharp fight, the Spanish fell back. On July 1, the Rough Riders, troops from the four black regiments, and the other regulars reached the strong fortifications at El Caney and San Juan Hill. Black soldiers of the Twenty-fifth Infantry charged the El Caney blockhouses, surprising the Spanish defenders with Comanche yells. For the better part of a day, the defenders fought stubbornly and held back the army's elite corps. In the confusion of battle, Roosevelt rallied an assortment of infantry and cavalry to take Kettle Hill, adjacent to San Juan Hill.

They charged directly into the Spanish guns, Roosevelt at their head, mounted on a horse, a blue polka-dot handkerchief floating from the brim of his sombrero. "I waved my hat and we went up the hill with a rush," he recalled in his autobiography. Actually it was not quite so easy. Losses were heavy; eighty-nine Rough Riders were killed or wounded in the attack. Dense foliage concealed the enemy; smokeless powder gave no clue to their position. At nightfall, the surviving Spanish defenders withdrew, and the Americans prepared for the counterattack. "We have won so far at a heavy cost," Roosevelt wrote home, "but the Spaniards fight very hard and charging these entrenchments against modern rifles is terrible. We are within measurable distance of a terrible military disaster."

American troops now occupied the ridges overlooking Santiago. They were weakened by sickness, a fact unknown to the Spanish who decided the city was lost. The Spanish command in Havana ordered Cervera to run for the open sea, although he knew the attempt to escape was hopeless. On the morning of July 3, Cervera's squadron steamed down the bay and out through the harbor's narrow channel, but the waiting American fleet closed in, and in a few hours every Spanish vessel was destroyed. Two weeks later, Santiago surrendered.

Soon thereafter, army troops, meeting little resistance, occupied Puerto Rico. Cervera had commanded Spain's only battle fleet, and when it sank, Spain was helpless against attacks on the colonies or even its own shores. The war was over. Lasting 113 days, it took relatively few lives, most of them the result of accident, yellow fever, malaria, and typhoid in Cuba. Of the 5500 Americans who died in the war, only 379 were killed in battle. The navy lost one man in the battle at Santiago Bay, and only one to heat stroke in the stunning victory in Manila Bay.

DEBATE OVER EMPIRE

Late in the afternoon of August 12, 1898, representatives of Spain and the United States met in McKinley's White House office to sign the preliminary instrument of peace. Secretary of State William R. Day beckoned a presidential aide over to a large globe, remarking: "Let's see what we get by this."

What the United States got was an expansion of its territory and an even larger expansion of its responsibilities. According to the preliminary agreement, Spain granted independence to Cuba,

A Puck *cartoon entitled "School Begins" satirizes Uncle Sam's course in civilization, in which he tells his new class that they will soon be glad for all they will learn.*

Reporting the Spanish-American War

The personalities of the "yellow journalists" attracted almost as much attention as the stories they reported. When the Journal *sent reporter Richard Harding Davis and illustrator Fredric Remington to cover the Spanish-American War, it gave the duo front-page coverage. The cartoon of William Randolph Hearst on the opposite page attacks him and the* Journal *as instigators of the declaration of war with Spain.*

The force of the newspaper is the greatest force in civilization.
Under republican government, newspapers form and express public opinion.
They suggest and control legislation. They declare wars.
They punish criminals, especially the powerful.
They reward with approving publicity the good deeds of citizens everywhere.
The newspapers control the nation because
THEY REPRESENT THE PEOPLE.

So proclaimed William Randolph Hearst, owner of the *New York Journal* in the paper's September 25, 1898, issue. Proud of the power of the press, Hearst and a handful of other publishers built newspaper empires that not only reported events but also influenced their outcomes.

Several of these empires took shape during the 1890s. The American population was growing rapidly, and so there were more people to read newspapers. In addition, more and more Americans were literate. Publishers did not hesitate to take advantage of the growing urban market. Technological improvements helped the spread of information: new machines made newspapers faster to print; larger type, a new half-tone engraving process for clearer pictures, and color cartoon supplements made them more appealing.

In 1865, there were about 500 daily newspapers in the country with a total circulation of about 2 million. By 1900, there were over 2000 dailies with a circulation of over 15 million. Papers sold for only one or two cents a copy. At that price, publishers could not make money on the paper itself, so they recouped their losses with advertising. Advertisers wanted readers, and to attract more and more of them, publishers used new methods. They lured buyers with banner headlines and front-page photographs. Stories stressed sex and scandals, and more cartoons and comic strips appeared.

One of the first publishing magnates, Joseph Pulitzer, bought the *New York World* in 1883 and within a year increased its sales from 15,000 a day to 100,000. Pulitzer had little competition until 1895 when William Randolph Hearst, an aggressive publisher from San Francisco, bought the *New York Journal.* Hearst was thirty-two. The son of a multimillionaire, he had been expelled from Harvard, had traveled widely and discovered a love for power and attention. Although he was shy and relatively inexperienced, money from his father and a desire to enter the world of newspaper publishing helped launch his career.

Fiercely competitive for "scoops" and circulation, Hearst and Pulitzer experimented with several new features: headlines that ran across the front page, profuse illustrations, a large Sunday paper with a comic section printed in color, and special sports' and women's sections. A cartoon character, "The Yellow Kid," appeared daily in both the *Journal* and the *World*, and they became known as "yellow journals." Stressing the sensational, yellow journals aimed to make news as

WAR CIRCULATION

well as report it. Hearst told his reporters: "Don't wait for things to turn up. Turn them up!"

The new journalism reached a peak in the crisis in Cuba between 1895 and 1898. When the short-lived rebellion of 1895 broke out, correspondents flocked to Cuba to cover it. Pulitzer sent the novelist Stephen Crane and printed reports from a young Englishman named Winston Churchill. Hearst sent the star *Journal* reporter Richard Harding Davis and the famous Western artist Frederic Remington to sketch scenes of Spanish cruelty. Both Hearst and Pulitzer sided with the rebels. Denouncing Spanish policy, they attacked General Valeriano Weyler—"Butcher," the *Journal* nicknamed him—and other Spanish generals.

Hearst was particularly proud of the story of Evangelina Cisneros, the seventeen-year-old niece of the rebellion's president. In August 1897, Evangelina was sentenced to twenty years in prison for aiding the rebels. Sensing the story's potential, Hearst started a letter-writing campaign to the queen of

Spain to win her release. Soon he decided on a more direct method. He sent reporter Karl Decker to Havana to rescue Evangelina. Renting the house next door to the prison, Decker broke into the prison, freed Evangelina, and disguising her as a boy, smuggled her out of Havana. On October 10, 1897, the *Journal* broke the news with the headline: "An American Newspaper Accomplishes at a Single Stroke What the Best Efforts of Diplomacy Failed Utterly to Bring About in Many Months."

Once war erupted between the United States and Spain, Hearst and his rivals stepped up their efforts. They employed hundreds of correspondents and hired a fleet of swift boats to carry stories to Florida for transmission back to New York. The correspondents both reported and fought in the war. At one point, Hearst considered sinking a ship in the Suez Canal to keep the Spanish fleet from reaching the Philippines, and from aboard a chartered steamer, he personally watched the destruction of

Cervera's fleet off Santiago. Waving a revolver, he waded ashore to capture a handful of Spanish sailors who survived the battle. The efforts paid off in newspaper sales. When Hearst bought the *Journal*, it was selling 77,000 copies a day. At the war's height, its sales had increased to over 1.5 million daily.

After the war, Hearst cartoonists like Homer Davenport turned their skillful attention to the trusts and other issues. Showing the lack of restraint that characterized "yellow journalism," the *Journal*, a Democratic newspaper, again and again criticized President McKinley, even suggesting that assassination might be in order. In September 1901, McKinley was shot, and when reports circulated that the assassin had a copy of the *Journal* in his pocket, the public turned on Hearst. The *Journal's* circulation dropped sharply. The new journalism continued into the twentieth century—Hearst himself went on to establish a famous publishing empire—but yellow journalism itself was never the same again.

This illustration by Remington, printed in the Journal *demonstrates the sensationalism that Hearst encouraged to arouse American passions, in this case against Spain.*

SPANIARDS SEARCH WOMEN ON AMERICAN STEAMERS
DRAWN BY FREDERIC REMINGTON

ceded Puerto Rico and the Pacific island of Guam to the United States, and allowed Americans to occupy Manila until the two countries reached final agreement on the Philippines. To McKinley, the Philippines were the problem. Puerto Rico was close to the mainland, and it appealed even to many of the opponents of expansion. Guam was small and unknown; it escaped attention. The Philippines, on the other hand, were huge, sprawling, and thousands of miles from America.

McKinley weighed a number of alternatives for the Philippines, but he liked none of them. He felt he could not give the islands back to Spain; public opinion would not allow it. He might turn them over to another nation, but then they would fall, as he later said, "a golden apple of discord, among the rival powers." Germany, Japan, Great Britain, and Russia had all expressed interest in acquiring them. Germany even sent a large fleet to Manila and laid plans to take the Philippines if the United States let them go.

Rejecting those alternatives, McKinley considered independence for the islands but was soon talked out of it. People who had been there, reflecting the era's racism, told him the Filipinos were not ready for independence. He thought of establishing an American protectorate but discarded the idea, convinced it would bring American responsibilities without full American control. Sifting the alternatives, McKinley decided there was only one practical policy: annex the Philippines, with an eye to future independence after a period of tutelage.

At first hesitant, American opinion was swinging to the same conclusion. Religious and missionary organizations appealed to McKinley to hold on to the Philippines in order to "Christianize" them. Some merchants and industrialists saw them as the key to the China market and the wealth of Asia. Many Americans simply regarded them as the legitimate fruits of war. In October 1898, representatives of the United States and Spain met in Paris to discuss a peace treaty. Spain agreed to recognize Cuba's independence, assume the Cuban debt, and cede Puerto Rico and Guam to the United States.

Acting on instructions from McKinley, the American representatives demanded the cession of the Philippines. "Grave as are the responsibilities and unforeseen as are the difficulties which are before us, the President can see but one plain path of duty—the acceptance of the archipelago," the instructions said. In return, the United States offered a payment of $20 million. Spain resisted but had little choice, and on December 10, 1898, the American and Spanish representatives signed the Treaty of Paris.

Submitted to the Senate for ratification, the treaty set off a storm of debate throughout the country. Industrialist Andrew Carnegie, reformer Jane Addams, labor leader Samuel Gompers, prominent Republicans like Thomas B. Reed and John Sherman, Mark Twain, William Dean Howells, and a host of others argued forcefully against annexing the Philippines. Annexation of the Philippines, the anti-imperialists protested over and over again, violated the very principles of independence and self-determination on which the country was founded.

Some labor leaders feared the importation of cheap labor from new Pacific colonies. Gompers warned about the "half-breeds and semi-barbaric people" who might undercut wages and the union movement. Other anti-imperialists argued against assimilation of different races, "Spanish-Americans," as one said, "with all the mixture of Indian and negro blood, and Malays and other unspeakable Asiatics, by the tens of millions!" Such racial views were also common among those favoring expansion, and the anti-imperialists usually focused on different arguments. If the United States established a tyranny abroad, they were sure, there would soon be tyranny at home. "This nation," declared William Jennings Bryan, "cannot endure half republic and half colony—half free and half vassal."

Charles Francis Adams, Jr., warned that the possession of colonies meant big armies, government, and debts ("an income tax looms up in the largest possible proportions," he said). Bryan scoffed at the argument that colonies were good for trade, pointing out that "It is not necessary to own people to trade with them." E. L. Godkin, the editor of *The Nation,* George F. Hoar, a leading Republican senator, and many others thought there was no way to reconcile the country's republican ideals with the practice of keeping people under heel abroad. As one of them put it: "Dewey took Manila with the loss of one man—and all our institutions."

William James, the psychologist, said the United States was about to "puke up its heritage."

Unless the Philippines were freed, Americans would rob Filipinos of "the one sacred thing in the world, the spontaneous budding of a national life." To Booker T. Washington, the country had more important things to think about at home, including its treatment of Indians and blacks. Carnegie was so upset he offered to buy Filipino independence with a personal check for $20 million. He was sure that keeping the Philippines would divert attention from industrial development to foreign adventure, would glorify physical force, and would lead to a war against the Filipinos themselves, in which American soldiers who had signed up "to fight the oppressor" would end up "shooting down the oppressed."

In November 1898, opponents of expansion formed the Anti-Imperialist League to fight against the peace treaty. Local leagues sprang up in Boston, New York, Philadelphia, and many other cities; the parent league claimed thirty thousand members and over half a million "contributors." Membership centered in New England; the cause was less popular in the West and South. It enlisted more Democrats than Republicans, though never a majority of either. The anti-imperialists were weakened by the fact that they lacked a coherent program. Some favored keeping naval bases in the conquered areas. Some wanted Hawaii and Puerto Rico but not the Philippines. Others wanted nothing at all to do with any colonies. Most simply wished that Dewey had sailed away after beating the Spanish at Manila Bay.

The treaty debate in the Senate lasted a month. Pressing hard for ratification, McKinley earlier toured the South to rally support and consulted closely with senators. Though opposed to taking the Philippines, Bryan supported ratification in order to end the war; his support influenced some Democratic votes. Still, on the final weekend before the vote, the treaty was two votes short. That Saturday night, news reached Washington that fighting had broken out between American troops and Filipino insurgents who demanded immediate independence. The news increased pressure to ratify the treaty, which the Senate did on February 6, 1899, with two votes to spare. An amendment promising independence as soon as the Filipinos established a stable government lost by one vote. The United States had a colonial empire.

Guerrilla Warfare in the Philippines

Historians rarely write of the Philippine-American War, but it was an important event in American history. The war with Spain was over a few months after it began; war with the Filipinos lasted more than three years. Four times as many American soldiers fought in the Philippines as in Cuba. For the first time, Americans fought men of a different color in an Asian guerrilla war. The Philippine-American War of 1898–1902 took a heavy toll: 4300 American lives and untold thousands of Filipino lives (estimates range from 50,000 to 200,000).

Emilio Aguinaldo, the Filipino leader, was twenty-nine years old in 1898. An early organizer of the anti-Spanish resistance, he had gone into exile in Hong Kong, from where he welcomed the outbreak of the Spanish-American War. Certain the United States would grant independence, he worked for an American victory. Filipino insurgents helped guide Dewey into Manila Bay, and Dewey himself sent a ship to Hong Kong to bring back Aguinaldo to lead a native uprising against the Spanish. On June 12, 1898, the insurgents proclaimed their independence.

Cooperating with the Americans, they drove the Spanish out of many areas of the islands. In the liberated regions, Aguinaldo established local governments with appointed provincial governors. He waited impatiently for American recognition, but McKinley and others had concluded that the Filipinos were not ready. Soon, warfare broke out between the Filipinos and Americans over the question of Filipino independence.

By late 1899 the American army had defeated and dispersed the organized Filipino army, but claims of victory proved premature. Aguinaldo and his advisers shifted to guerrilla tactics, striking suddenly and then melting into the jungle or friendly native villages. In many areas, the Americans ruled the day, the guerrillas the night. There were terrible atrocities on both sides. The Americans found themselves using brutal, Weyler-like tactics. After any attack on an American patrol, the Americans burned all the houses in the nearest district. They tortured people and executed prisoners. They established protected "zones" and herded Filipinos into them. Seizing or destroying all food outside the zones, they starved many guerrillas into submission.

Emilio Aguinaldo (seated, in vest) and his advisors in the Philippines, 1896. Aguinaldo's forces helped the Americans drive Spain out of the Philippines, expecting that the United States would recognize Filipino independence. When the United States failed to do so, Aguinaldo led his forces in warfare against the Americans.

Bryan tried to turn the election of 1900 into a debate over imperialism, but the attempt failed. For one thing, he himself refused to give up the silver issue, which cost him some support among anti-imperialists in the Northeast who were for gold. McKinley, moreover, was able to take advantage of the surging economy, and he could defend expansion as an accomplished fact. "It is no longer a question of expansion with us," he told one audience. "If there is any question at all it is a question of contraction; and who is going to contract?" Riding a wave of patriotism and prosperity, McKinley won the election handily—by an even larger margin than he had in 1896 (see Chapter 20).

In 1900, McKinley sent a special Philippine Commission under William Howard Taft, a prominent Ohio judge. Directed to establish a civil government, the commission organized municipal administrations and, in stages, created a government for the Philippines. In March 1901, five American soldiers tricked their way into Aguinaldo's camp deep in the mountains and took him prisoner. Back in Manila, he signed a proclamation urging his people to end the fighting. Some guerrillas held out for another year but

to no avail. On July 4, 1901, authority was transferred from the army to Taft, who was named civilian governor of the islands, and his civilian commission. McKinley reaffirmed his purpose to grant the Filipinos self-government as soon as they were ready for it.

Given broad powers, the Taft Commission introduced many changes. New schools provided education and vocational training for Filipinos of all social classes. The Americans built roads and bridges, reformed the judiciary, restructured the tax system, and introduced sanitation and vaccination programs. They established local governments built on Filipino traditions and hierarchies. Taft encouraged Filipino participation in government. During the following decades, other measures broadened Filipino rights; independence finally came on July 4, 1946, nearly fifty years after Aguinaldo proclaimed it.

Governing the Empire

Ruling the colonies raised new and perplexing questions. How could—and how should—the distant dependencies be governed? Did their inhabitants have the rights of American citizens? Some people contended that acquisition did not automatically incorporate the new possessions into the United States and endow them with constitutional privileges. Others argued that "the Constitution followed the flag," meaning that acquisition made the possessions part of the nation and thus entitled them to all constitutional guarantees. A third group suggested that only "fundamental" constitutional guarantees—citizenship, the right to vote, and the right to trial by jury—not "formal" privileges—the right to use American currency, the right to be taxed, and the right to run for the presidency—were applicable to the new empire.

In a series of cases between 1901 and 1904 (*De Lima* v. *Bidwell*, *Dooley* v. *U.S.*, and *Downes* v. *Bidwell*), the Supreme Court asserted the principle that the Constitution did not automatically and immediately apply to the people of an annexed territory and did not confer upon them all the privileges of United States citizenship. Instead, Congress could specifically extend such constitutional provisions as it saw fit. "Ye-es," the Secretary of War said of the Court's ambiguous rulings, "as near as I can make out the Con-

American Empire, 1900

With the Treaty of Paris, the United States gained an expanded colonial empire stretching from the Caribbean to the far Pacific. It embraced Puerto Rico, Alaska, Hawaii, part of Samoa, Guam, the Philippines, and a chain of Pacific islands.

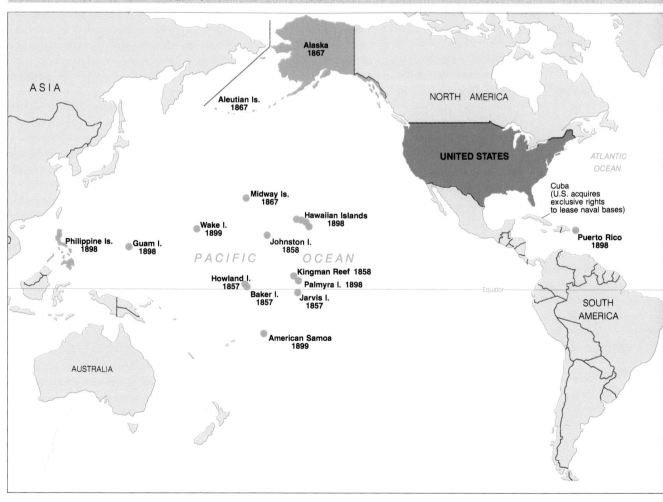

stitution follows the flag—but doesn't quite catch up with it."

Four dependencies—Hawaii, Alaska, Guam, and Puerto Rico—were organized quickly. In 1900, Congress granted territorial status to Hawaii, gave American citizenship to all citizens of the Hawaiian republic, authorized an elective legislature, and provided for a governor appointed from Washington. A similar measure made Alaska a territory in 1912. Guam and American Samoa were simply placed under the control of naval officers.

Unlike the Filipinos, Puerto Ricans readily accepted the war's outcome, and McKinley early withdrew troops from the island. The Foraker Act of 1900 established civil government in Puerto Rico. It organized the island as a territory, made its residents citizens of Puerto Rico (United States citizenship was extended to them in 1917), and empowered the president to appoint a governor general and a council to serve as the upper house of the legislature. A lower house of delegates was to be elected.

Cuba proved a trickier matter. McKinley asserted the authority of the United States over conquered territory and promised to govern the island until the Cubans had established a firm and stable government of their own. "I want you to go down there to get the people ready for a republican form of government," he instructed General Leonard Wood, commander of the army in Cuba until 1902. "I leave the details of procedure to you. Give them a good school system, try to straighten out their ports, and put them on their feet as best you can. We want to do all we can for them and to get out of the island as soon as we safely can."

Wood moved quickly to implement the instructions. Early in 1900, he completed a census of the Cuban population, conducted municipal elections, and arranged the election of delegates to a constitutional convention. The convention adopted a constitution modeled on the U.S. Constitution and, at Wood's prodding, included provisions for future relations with the United States. Known as the Platt Amendment to the new Cuban Constitution, the provisions stipulated that Cuba should make no treaties with other powers that might impair its independence, acquire no debts it could not pay, and lease naval bases like Guantanamo Bay to the United States.

Most important, the amendment empowered the United States to intervene in Cuba to maintain orderly government.

Between 1898 and 1902, the American military government worked hard for the economic and political revival of the island, though it often demonstrated a paternalistic attitude toward the Cubans themselves. It repaired the damage of the civil war, built roads and schools, and established order in rural areas. A public health campaign headed by Dr. Walter Reed, an army surgeon, wiped out yellow fever. Most troops withdrew at the end of 1899, but a small American occupation force remained until May 1902. When it sailed for home, the Cubans at last had a form of independence, but they were still under the clear domination of their neighbor to the north.

The Open Door

Poised in the Philippines, the United States had become an Asian power on the doorstep of China. Weakened by years of warfare, China in 1898 and 1899 was unable to resist foreign influence. Japan, England, France, Germany, and Russia eyed it covetously, dividing parts of the country into "spheres of influence." They forced China to grant "concessions" that allowed them exclusive rights to develop particular areas, and threatened American hopes for extensive trade with the country.

McKinley first outlined a new China policy in September 1898 when he said that Americans sought more trade, "but we seek no advantages in the Orient which are not common to all. Asking only the open door for ourselves, we are ready to accord the open door to others." In September 1899, Secretary of State John Hay addressed identical diplomatic notes to England, Germany, and Russia, and later to France, Japan, and Italy, asking them to join the United States in establishing the "Open Door." The policy urged three agreements: nations possessing a sphere of influence would respect the rights and privileges of other nations in that sphere; the Chinese government would continue to collect tariff duties in all spheres; and nations would not discriminate against other nations in levying port dues and railroad rates within their respective spheres of influence.

The nations of Europe are getting ready to cut up all of China to expand their spheres of influence, but Uncle Sam stands firm on American commitments to preserve China's sovereignty.

Under the Open Door policy, the United States would retain many commercial advantages it might lose if China were partitioned into spheres of influence. McKinley and Hay also attempted to preserve for the Chinese some semblance of national authority. Great Britain most nearly accepted the principle of the Open Door. Russia declined to approve it, and the other powers, sending evasive replies, stated they would only agree if all the other nations did. Hay turned the situation to American advantage by boldly announcing in March 1900 that all the powers had accepted the Open Door policy.

The policy's first test came just three months later with the outbreak of the Boxer Rebellion in Peking (now Beijing). In June 1900, a secret, intensely nationalistic Chinese society called the Boxers tried to oust all foreigners from their country. Overrunning Peking, they drove foreigners into their legations and penned them up for nearly two months. In the end, the United States joined Britain, Germany, and other powers in sending troops to lift the siege.

Fearing that the rebellion gave some nations, especially Germany and Russia, an excuse to expand their spheres of influence, Hay took quick action to emphasize American policy. In July, he sent off another round of Open Door notes affirming U.S. commitment to equal commercial opportunity and respect for China's indepen-

dence. While the first Open Door notes had implied recognition of China's continued independence, the second notes explicitly stated the need to preserve it. Together, the two notes comprised the Open Door policy, which became a central element in American policy in the Far East.

To some degree, the policy tried to help China, but it also led to further American meddling in the affairs of another country. Moreover, by committing itself to a policy that Americans were not prepared to defend militarily, the McKinley administration left the opportunity for later controversy with Japan and other expansion-minded powers in the Pacific.

The war with Spain over, Roosevelt and the Rough Riders sailed for home in mid-August 1898. They sauntered through the streets of New York, the heroes of the city. A few weeks later, Roosevelt bade them farewell. They presented him with a reproduction of Frederick Remington's famed bronze, *The Bronco-Buster,* and close to tears, he told them: "I am proud of this regiment beyond measure." Roosevelt later wrote an account of the war in which he played so central a role that Mr. Dooley suggested "If I was him, I'd call th' book 'Alone in Cubia.'" By then Roosevelt was already governor of New York and on his way to the White House.

CHRONOLOGY

1867 United States purchases Alaska from Russia • Midway Islands are annexed

1871 Treaty of Washington between United States and Great Britain sets precedent for peaceful settlement of international disputes

1875 Reciprocity treaty with Hawaii binds Hawaii economically and politically to United States

1878 United States acquires naval base in Samoa

1883 Congress approves funds for construction of first modern steel ships; beginning of modern navy

1887 New treaty with Hawaii gives United States exclusive use of Pearl Harbor

1889 First Inter-American Conference meets in Washington, D.C.

1893 American settlers in Hawaii overthrow Queen Liliuokalani; provisional government established

1895 Cuban insurgents rebel against Spanish rule

1898 Battleship *Maine* explodes in Havana harbor (February) • Congress declares war against Spain (April) • Commodore Dewey defeats Spanish fleet at Manila Bay (May) • United States annexes Hawaii (July) • Americans defeat Spanish at El Caney, San Juan Hill (actually Kettle Hill), and Santiago (July) • Spain sues for peace (August) • Treaty of Paris ends Spanish-American War (December)

1899 Congress ratifies Treaty of Paris • United States sends Open-Door notes to Britain, Germany, France, Russia, Japan, and Italy • Philippine-American War erupts

1900 Foraker Act establishes civil government in Puerto Rico

1901 Platt Amendment authorizes American intervention in Cuba

1902 Philippine-American War ends with American victory

Other soldiers were also glad to be home, although they were sometimes resentful of the reception they found. "The war is over now," said Winslow Hobson, a black trooper from the Ninth Ohio, "and Roosevelt . . . and others (white of course) have all there is to be gotten out of it." Bravery in Cuba and the Philippines won some recognition for black soldiers, but the war itself set back the cause of civil rights. It spurred talk about "inferior" races, at home and abroad, and united whites in the North and South. "The Negro might as well know it now as later," a black editor said, "the closer the North and South get together by this war, the harder he will have to fight to maintain a footing." A fresh outburst of segregation and lynching occurred during the decade after the war.

McKinley and the Republican party soared to new heights of popularity. Firmly established, the Republican majority dominated politics until 1932. Scandals arose about the canned beef and the conduct of the War Department, but there was none of the sharp sense of deception and betrayal that was to mark the years after World War I. In a little more than a century, the United States had grown from thirteen states stretched along a thin Atlantic coastline into a world power that reached from the Caribbean to the Pacific. As Seward and others had hoped, the nation now dominated its own hemisphere, dealt with European powers on more equal terms, and was a major power in Asia.

Recommended Reading

The best general account of the development of American foreign policy during the last part of the nineteenth century is Walter LaFeber, *The New Empire: An Interpretation of American Expansion, 1860–1898* (1963). Robert L. Beisner, *From the Old Diplomacy to the New, 1865–1900* (1975), and Charles S. Campbell, Jr., *Transformation of American Foreign Relations, 1865–1900* (1976), give useful overviews that suggest important changes that took place in the 1890s. J. A. S. Grenville and George Berkeley Young present a series of significant essays in *Politics, Strategy and American Diplomacy: Studies in Foreign Policy, 1873–1917* (1966). William Appleman Williams, *The Tragedy of American Diplomacy* (1959) examines the economic motives for expansion.

Ernest R. May analyzes the causes of the Spanish-American War in *Imperial Democracy: The Emergence of America as a Great Power* (1961); for a briefer treatment, see H. Wayne Morgan, *America's Road to Empire: The War with Spain and Overseas Expansion* (1965). Lewis L. Gould persuasively reassesses McKinley's diplomacy and wartime leadership in *The Presidency of William McKinley* (1980).

Graham A. Cosmas presents a detailed account of military organization and strategy in *An Army for Empire: The United States Army in the Spanish-American War* (1971), while Willard B. Gatewood, Jr., *"Smoked Yankees" and the Struggle for Empire: Letters from Negro Soldiers, 1898–1902* (1971), offers a fascinating glimpse of the thoughts of some black soldiers in the war. Gerald F. Linderman relates the war to the home front in *The Mirror of War: American Society and the Spanish-American War* (1974).

Additional Bibliography

On American foreign policy during this period, see David M. Pletcher, *The Awkward Years: American Foreign Relations Under Garfield and Arthur* (1962); David F. Healy, *U.S. Expansionism: The Imperialist Urge in the 1890's* (1970); Milton Plesur, *America's Outward Thrust: Approaches to Foreign Affairs, 1865–1890* (1971); Richard W. Leopold, *The Growth of American Foreign Policy* (1962); Michael H. Hunt, *Ideology and U.S. Foreign Policy* (1987); John Dobson, *America's Ascent: The United States Becomes a Great Power, 1880–1914* (1978); Michael J. Devine, *John W. Foster: Politics and Diplomacy in the Imperial Era, 1873–1917* (1981); and Tom E. Terrill, *The Tariff, Politics, and American Foreign Policy, 1874–1901* (1973).

For policies toward specific areas, see R. P. Gilson, *Samoa 1830 to 1900: The Politics of a Multi-Cultural Community* (1970); Charles S. Campbell, Jr., *Anglo-American Understanding, 1898–1903* (1957); Thomas J. McCormick, *China Market: America's Quest for Informal Empire, 1893–1901* (1967); Michael H. Hunt, *The Making of a Special Relationship: The United States and China to 1914* (1983); David L. Anderson, *Imperialism and Idealism: American Diplomats in China, 1861–1898* (1985); Marilyn B. Young, *Rhetoric of Empire: American China Policy, 1895–1901* (1968); Merze Tate, *The United States and the Hawaiian Kingdom: A Political History* (1965); and William A. Russ, Jr., *The Hawaiian Republic, 1894–98 and Its Struggle to Win Annexation* (1961).

Books on naval and military developments during these years include Walter R. Herrick, *The American Naval Revolution* (1966); William R. Braisted, *The United States Navy in the Pacific, 1897–1909* (1958); Peter Karsten, *The Naval Aristocracy* (1972); Benjamin J. Cooling, *Gray Steel and Blue Water Navy* (1979); and Kenneth J. Hagan, *American Gunboat Diplomacy and the Old Navy, 1877–1889* (1973).

For the background of the war with Spain, see David F. Trask, *The War with Spain in 1898* (1981); Julius W. Pratt, *Expansionists of 1898: The Acquisition of Hawaii and the Spanish Islands* (1936); Walter Millis, *The Martial Spirit: A Study of Our War with Spain* (1931); Philip S. Foner, *The Spanish-Cuban-American War and the Birth of American Imperialism, 1895–1902*, 2 vols. (1972); J. E. Wisan, *The Cuban Crisis as Reflected in the New York Press, 1895–1898* (1934); and Hyman G. Rickover, *How the Battleship* Maine *Was Destroyed* (1976).

Biographies of the period's leading personalities include H. Wayne Morgan, *William McKinley and His America* (1963); Margaret Leech, *In the Days of McKinley* (1959); Robert Seager, II, *Alfred Thayer Mahan* (1977); and Ronald Spector, *Admiral of the New Empire: The Life and Career of George Dewey* (1974). See also Theodore Roosevelt, *The Rough Riders* (1899); John D. Long, *The New American Navy*, 2 vols. (1903); and H. Wayne Morgan, ed., *Making Peace with Spain: The Diary of Whitelaw Reid, September-December 1898* (1965).

The course of the war itself can be followed in Frank Freidel, *The Splendid Little War* (1958); Orestes Femara, *The Last Spanish War* (1937); Frederick Funston, *Memories of Two Wars: Cuba and Philippine Experiences* (1914); Charles H. Brown, *The Correspondents' War: Journalists in the Spanish-American War* (1967); David A. Gerber, *Black Ohio and the Color Line, 1860–1915* (1976); and Herschel V. Cashin et al., *Under Fire with the Tenth U.S. Cavalry* (1899). Willard B. Gatewood, Jr., *Black Americans and the White Man's Burden, 1898–1903* (1975) is a thorough and thought-provoking study.

For the debate over expansion and the treaty with Spain, consult Richard E. Welch, Jr., *George Frisbie Hoar and the Half-Breed Republicans* (1971); E. Berkeley Tompkins, *Anti-Imperialism in the United States: The Great Debate, 1890–1920* (1970); Daniel B. Schirmer, *Republic or Empire: American Resistance to the Philippine War* (1972); Thomas J. Osborne, *"Empire Can Wait": American Opposition to Hawaiian Annexation, 1893–1898* (1981); and Göran Rystad, *Ambiguous Imperialism: American Foreign Policy and Domestic Politics at the Turn of the Century* (1975).

Policy toward Cuba and the Philippines is covered in Richard E. Welch, Jr., *Response to Imperialism: The United States and the Philippine-American War, 1899–1902* (1979); David F. Healy, *The United States in Cuba, 1898–1902* (1963), and *Drive to Hegemony: The United States in the Caribbean, 1898–1917* (1988); James H. Hitchman, *Leonard Wood and Cuban Independence, 1898–1902* (1971); John Morgan Gates, *Schoolbooks and Krags: The United States Army in the Philippines, 1898–1902* (1973); Glenn A. May, *Social Engineering in the Philippines* (1980); Stuart Creighton Miller, *"Benevolent Assimilation": The American Conquest of the Philippines, 1899–1903* (1982); Brian McAllister Linn, *The U.S. Army and Counterinsurgency in the Philippine War, 1899–1902* (1989); and Peter W. Stanley, *A Nation in the Making: The Philippines and the United States, 1899–1921* (1974).

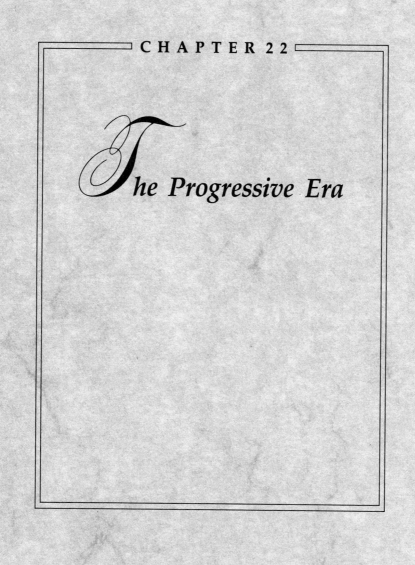

CHAPTER 22

The Progressive Era

*A*n 1902, Samuel S. McClure, the shrewd owner of *McClure's Magazine*, sensed something astir in the country that his reporters were not covering. Like *Life*, *Munsey's*, the *Ladies' Home Journal*, and *Cosmopolitan*, *McClure's* was reaching more and more people—over one-quarter of a million readers a month. Americans were snapping up the new popular magazines filled with eye-catching illustrations and up-to-date fiction. Advances in photoengraving during the 1890s dramatically reduced the cost of illustrations; at the same time, income from advertisements rose sharply. By the turn of the century, some magazines earned as much as $60,000 an issue from advertising alone, and publishers could price them as low as 10 cents a copy.

McClure was always chasing new ideas and readers, and in 1902, certain that something was happening in the public mood, he told one of his editors, thirty-six-year-old Lincoln Steffens, a former Wall Street reporter, to find out what it was. "Get out of here, travel, go—somewhere . . . ," he said to Steffens. "Buy a railroad ticket, get on a train, and there, where it lands you, there you will learn to edit a magazine."

McClure's, it turned out, had an unpaid bill from the Lackawanna Railroad, and Steffens traveled west. In Saint Louis, he came across a young district attorney named Joseph W. Folk who had found a trail of corruption linking politics and some of the city's respected business leaders. Eager for help, Folk did not mind naming names to the visiting editor from New York. "It is good business men that are corrupting our bad politicians . . . ," he stressed again and again. "It is the leading citizens that are battening on our city." Steffens's story, "Tweed Days in St. Louis," appeared in the October 1902 issue of *McClure's*.

The November *McClure's* carried the first installment of Ida Tarbell's scathing "History of the Standard Oil Company," and in January 1903, Steffens was back with "The Shame of Minneapolis," another tale of corrupt partnership between business and politics. McClure had what he wanted, and in the January issue he printed an editorial, "Concerning Three Articles in This Number of *McClure's*, and a Coincidence That May Set Us Thinking." Steffens on Minneapolis, Tarbell on Standard Oil, and an article on abuses in labor unions—all, McClure said, on different topics but actually on the same theme: corruption in American life. "Capitalists, workingmen, politicians, citizens—all breaking the law, or letting it be broken."

Readers were enthralled, and articles and books by other muckrakers—Theodore Roosevelt coined the unflattering term in 1906 to describe the practice of exposing the corruption of public and prominent figures—spread swiftly. *Collier's* had articles on questionable stock-market practices, patent medicines, and the beef

During the Progressive Era, McClures magazine was at the front of the journalistic crusade for reform, which took the form of muckraking articles by such writers as Ida Tarbell (right). Her exposé of the Standard Oil Company ran side by side with Lincoln Steffens's article on the alliances between business and corrupt political machines in several cities.

trust. Novelist Upton Sinclair tackled the meat packers in *The Jungle* (1906). In 1904, Steffens collected his *McClure's* articles in *The Shame of the Cities*, with an introduction expressing confidence that reform was possible, "that our shamelessness is superficial, that beneath it lies a pride which, being real, may save us yet."

Muckraking flourished from 1903 to 1909, and while it did, good writers and bad investigated almost every corner of American life: government, labor unions, big business, Wall Street, health care, the food industry, child labor, women's rights, prostitution, ghetto living, and life insurance. "Time was," Mr. Dooley, the fictional character of humorist Finley Peter Dunne, said to Mr. Hennessy, when magazines

> was very ca'ming to the mind. Angabel an' Alfonso dashin' f'r a marriage license. Prom'nent lady authoresses makin' pomes at the moon. . . . Th' idee ye got fr'm these here publications was that life was wan glad sweet song. . . .
>
> But now whin I pick me fav-rite magazine off th' flure, what do I find? Ivrything has gone wrong. . . . All th' pomes by th' lady authoresses that used to begin: "Oh, moon, how fair!" now begin: "Oh, Ogden Armour, how awful!" . . . Graft ivrywhere. "Graft in th' Insurance Companies," "Graft in Congress," "Graft be an Old Grafter," "Graft in Its Relations to th' Higher Life". . . .
>
> An' so it goes, Hinnissy . . . till I don't thrust anny man anny more. . . . I used to be nervous about burglars, but now I'm afraid iv a night call fr'm th' prisidint iv th' First National Bank.

The muckrakers were a journalistic voice of a larger movement in American society. Called *progressivism*, it lasted from the mid-1890s through World War I. Like muckraking itself, progressivism reflected worry about the state of society, the effects of industrialization and urbanization, social disorder, political corruption, and a host of other issues. With concerns so large, progressivism often had a sense of crisis and urgency although it was rooted in a spirit of hopefulness and confidence in human progress. For varying reasons, thousands of people became concerned about their society, and separately and together, they set out to cure some of the ills they saw around them. Known later as the "progressives," their efforts changed the nation and gave the era its name.

As McClure had hoped, Steffens *had* found something astir in the country, something so important and pervasive that it altered the course of American history in the twentieth century. This chapter will examine in detail the economic, social, and intellectual conditions that gave rise to progressivism. Chapter 23 will examine progressivism itself, in the cities, states, and nation.

THE CHANGING FACE OF INDUSTRIALISM

"Life in the States," an English visitor said in 1900, "is one perpetual whirl of telephones, telegrams, phonographs, electric bells, motors, lifts, and automatic instruments." If not quite as automated as the visitor described, conditions in America were better than just a few years before. Farms and factories were once again prosperous; in 1901, for the first time in years, the economy reached full capacity. Farm prices rose almost 50 percent between 1900 and 1910. Unemployment dropped. "In the United States of today," a Boston newspaper said in 1904, "everyone is middle class. The resort to force, the wild talk of the nineties are over. Everyone is busily, happily getting ahead."

Everyone, of course, was not middle class, nor was everyone getting ahead. "Wild talk" persisted. Many of the problems that had angered people in the 1890s continued into the new century, and millions of Americans still suffered from poverty and disease. Racism sat even more heavily on African Americans in both South and North, and there was increasing hostility against immigrants from southern and eastern Europe, Mexico, and Asia. Yet to some degree the Boston newspaper was right: economic conditions *were* better for many people, and as a result, prosperity became one of the keys to understanding the era and the nature of progressive reform.

The start of the new century was another key as well, for it influenced people to take a fresh look at themselves and their times. Excited about beginning the twentieth century, people believed that technology and enterprise would shape a better life. Savoring the word "new," they talked of the new poetry, new cinema, new history, new democracy, new woman, new art, new immigration, new morality, and new city. Magazines picked up the word; there were the *New Republic* and the *New Statesman*. Presidents Theodore Roosevelt and Woodrow Wilson called their political programs the New Nationalism and the New Freedom.

The word "mass" also cropped up frequently. Victors in the recent war with Spain, many Americans took pride in teeming cities, burgeoning corporations, and other marks of the mass society. They enjoyed the fruits of mass production, read mass-circulation newspapers and magazines, and took mass transit from the growing spiral of suburbs into the central cities.

Behind mass production lay significant changes in the nation's industrial system. Businesses grew at a rapid rate. They were large in the three decades after the Civil War, but in the years between 1895 and 1915, they became mammoth, employing thousands of workers and equipped with assembly lines to turn out huge numbers of the company's product. Inevitably, changes in management attitudes, business organization, and worker roles influenced the entire society. Inevitably, too, the growth of giant businesses gave rise to a widespread fear of "trusts" and a desire among many progressive reformers to break them up or regulate them.

The Innovative Model T

In the movement toward large-scale business and mass production, the automobile industry was one of those that led the way. In 1895, there were only four cars on the nation's roads; in 1917, there were nearly five million, and the automobile had already helped work a small revolution in industrial methods and social mores.

Mass production of automobiles began in the first years of the century. Using an assembly-line system that foreshadowed later techniques, Ransom E. Olds turned out five thousand Olds runabouts in 1904. But Olds's days of leadership were numbered. In 1903, Henry Ford and a small group of associates formed the Ford Motor Company, the firm that transformed the business.

Ford was forty years old. He had tried farming and hated it; during the 1890s, he worked as an engineer for Detroit's Edison Company but spent his spare time designing internal combustion engines and automobiles. At first, like many

(*T*op) *Assembling small parts on the Ford line. One worker could do it in twenty minutes; twenty-nine workers, properly arranged, could do it in five minutes. (Bottom) One day's output of car chassis at the Ford Highland Park plant in 1913.*

others in the industry, he concentrated on building luxury and racing cars. Racing his own cars, Ford became the "speed demon" of Detroit; in 1904, he set the world's land speed record—over ninety miles per hour—in the 999, a large red racer that shot flames from the motor.

In 1903, Ford sold the first Ford car. The price was high, and in 1905, Ford raised prices still higher. Sales plummeted. In 1907, he lowered the price; sales and revenues rose. Ford learned an important lesson of the modern economy: a smaller unit profit on a large number of sales meant enormous revenues. Early in 1908, he introduced the Model T, a four-cylinder, twenty-horsepower "Tin Lizzie," costing $850, and available only in black. Eleven thousand were sold the first year.

"I am going to democratize the automobile," Ford proclaimed. "When I'm through everybody will be able to afford one, and about everyone will have one." The key was mass production, and after many experiments, Ford copied the techniques of meat packers who moved animal carcasses along overhead trolleys from station to station. Adapting the process to automobile assembly, Ford in 1913 set up moving assembly lines in his plant in Highland Park, Michigan, that dramatically reduced the time and cost of producing cars. Emphasizing continuous movement, he strove for a nonstop flow from raw material to finished product. In 1914, he sold 248,000 Model T's.

That year, Ford workers assembled a car in ninety-three minutes, one-tenth the time it had taken just eight months before. By 1925, the Ford plant turned out 9109 Model T's, a new car for every ten seconds of the working day.

While Ford was putting more and more cars on the road, the 1916 Federal Aid Roads Act, a little-noticed measure, set the framework for road building in the twentieth century. Removing control from county governments, it required every state desiring federal funds to establish a highway department to plan routes, oversee construction, and maintain roads. In states that had such departments, the federal government paid half the cost of building the roads. Providing for a planned highway system, the act produced a national network of two-lane, all-weather intercity roads.

The Burgeoning Trusts

As businesses like Ford's grew, capital and organization became increasingly important, and the result was the formation of a growing number of trusts. Standard Oil started the trend in 1882 (see Chapter 18), but the greatest momentum came

*A*s early as 1886, cartoonist Thomas Nast attacked trusts. Here the people's welfare is sinking as the Statue of Liberty is defaced.

two decades later. Between 1898 and 1903, a series of mergers and consolidations swept the economy. Many smaller firms disappeared, swallowed up in giant corporations. By 1904, large-scale combinations of one form or another controlled nearly two-fifths of the capital in manufacturing in the country.

The result was not monopoly, but oligopoly—control of a commodity or service by a small number of large, powerful companies. Six great financial groups dominated the railroad industry; a handful of holding companies controlled utilities and steel. Rockefeller's Standard Oil owned about 85 percent of the oil business. Large companies like Standard Oil and American Tobacco

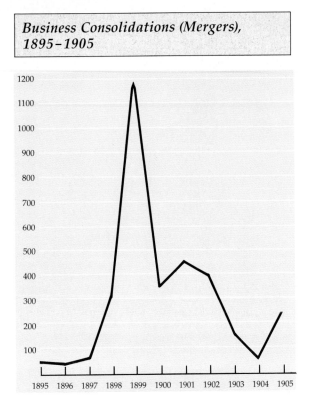

Business Consolidations (Mergers), 1895–1905

had weathered the depression of the 1890s, and after 1898, financiers and industrialists followed their example and formed the Amalgamated Copper Company, Consolidated Tobacco, U.S. Rubber, and a host of others.

By 1909, just 1 percent of the industrial firms were producing nearly half of all manufactured goods. Giant businesses reached abroad for raw materials and new markets. United Fruit, an empire of plantations and steamships in the Caribbean, exploited opportunities created by victory in the war with Spain. U.S. Steel worked with overseas companies to fix the price of steel rails, an unattainable dream just a few years before. For decades, competition had sent rail prices up and down; now they stayed at $28 a ton, and through the famous "Gary dinners" in which Elbert H. Gary of U.S. Steel brought steel executives from "competing" firms together to set prices over dinner, market conditions were fixed for wide areas of the industry.

Though the trend has been overstated, finance capitalists like J. P. Morgan tended to replace the industrial capitalists of an earlier era. Able to finance the mergers and reorganizations, invest-

ment bankers played a greater and greater role in the economy. A multibillion-dollar financial house, J. P. Morgan and Company operated a network of control that ran from New York to every industrial and financial center in the nation. Like other investment firms, it held directorships in many corporations, creating "interlocking directorates" that allowed it to control many businesses. In 1913, two banking groups—Morgan's and Rockefeller's—held 341 directorships in 112 corporations with an aggregate capital of more than $22 billion.

Massive business growth set off a decade-long debate over what government should do about the trusts. Some critics who believed that the giant companies were responsible for stifling individual opportunity and raising prices wanted to break them up into small competitive units. Others argued that large-scale business was a mark of the times; it produced more goods and better lives.

The debate over the trusts was one of the issues that shaped the Progressive Era, but it was never a simple contest between high-minded reformers and greedy business titans. Some progressives favored big business; others wanted it broken up. Business leaders themselves were divided in their viewpoints, and some welcomed reform-led assaults on giant competitors. As a rule, both progressives and business leaders drew on similar visions of the country: complex, expansive, hopeful, managerially-minded, and oriented toward results and efficiency. They both believed in private property and the importance of economic progress. In fact, in working for reform, the progressives often drew on the managerial methods of a business world they sought to regulate.

Managing the Machines

Mass production changed the direction of American industry. Size, system, organization, and marketing became increasingly important. Management focused on speed and product, not on workers. Assembly-line technology changed tasks and, to some extent, values. The goal was no longer to make a unique product that would be better than the one before. "The way to make automobiles," Ford said as early as 1903, "is to make one automobile like another automobile, to

AT NIGHT IN THE GRAND COURT.

"White City"
The Columbian Exposition of 1893

At Night in the Grand Court. *The Administration Building loomed above the gondolas and illuminated fountains that shimmered on the lagoon at the main entrance to the fair.*

On May 1, 1893, the World's Columbian Exposition opened in Chicago. A focal event of the decade, the Exposition commemorated the four-hundredth anniversary of Columbus's voyage to the New World and celebrated modern industrial progress, featuring the latest mechanical inventions in acres of white plaster buildings modeled on Greek and Roman patterns. Called the White City, the Exposition cost $31 million and attracted 27 million visitors.

Artists, architects, and engineers flocked to Chicago to participate in its creation. In contrast to the normal jumble of urban growth, the Exposition offered one of the first examples of a planned city. Ten leading architects set out to design it. Frederic Law Olmstead, the designer of New York's famed Central Park, produced his last major public landscape for it, a large lagoon and park along Lake Michigan. The Exposition touched off city-planning and "city-beautiful" movements that affected cities as far apart as Washington, Manila, and San Francisco. Chicago was transformed under the farsighted Chicago Plan (1907–1909) of Daniel H. Burnham, one of the Exposition's chief architects.

Visitors strolled amid parkways, islands, commemorative columns, and shining white palaces mirrored in wide lagoons.

Louis Sullivans's Transportation Building was unique in its deviation from the Fair's classic style of porticoes and pillars.

City-beautiful designers integrated transportation, sanitation, and urban architecture in a more "human" city; parks, playgrounds, and tree-lined boulevards proliferated.

Opening day attracted a crowd of two hundred thousand, eager to see the marvels. Jane Addams's purse was snatched; the crowd on the Midway saw the first Ferris wheel, commissioned as a feat of American engineering to rival the recently erected Eiffel Tower in Paris; visitors tasted the first grapefruit brought in on refrigerated railroad cars from Florida and California; American Bell Telephone, a fast-growing young company, offered the first long-distance calls to New York and Boston; Edison showed his latest phonographs and, more fascinating, his new Kinetoscope, a peep-show device that

In the Palace of Electricity, many fairgoers saw their first electric lamp—a great pillar of light studded with colored globes that flashed kaleidoscopic patterns.

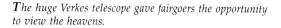

ran short motion pictures on the just-invented celluloid film. (The first Kinetoscope parlor opened the next month on Broadway in New York.)

Machinery at the Exposition went far beyond the capacity of the famous Corliss steam engine that had impressed the world when it generated the power for the Philadelphia Exposition only seventeen years earlier. A much more "up-to-date" wonder—the new magic of electricity—powered the marvels of machinery exhibited in Chicago. For the first time, visitors saw the electric dynamo and George Westinghouse's alternating-current generator. The Westinghouse Company tucked Edison's incandescent light bulbs in every nook and cranny. Opening the Exposition, President Grover Cleveland touched an ivory telegraph key and the electric current unfurled flags, lit ten thousand electric lights, and started engines throughout the grounds of the fair. In Machinery Hall, the thirty-seven steam engines started at once, producing, in a reporter's words, "a sound that will thrill every observer."

The Exposition represented "the transformation of power into beauty," one onlooker said. Elaborate in its symbolism, the White City celebrated social harmony, the union of architects, engineers, inventors, businessmen, and laborers to create the industrial society. It fused timeless classical forms with the turbulent progress of the new civilization.

For a dazzling moment in Chicago an era paid homage to its accomplishments. A moment was all it had. Three days after the opening ceremonies, the stock market broke, rallied, then broke again. The American economy, so lovingly celebrated by the White City in Chicago, was about to collapse into the worst depression in the history of the nation.

A favorite with visitors, the Midway Plaisance was the entertainment area of the fair, featuring foreign villages where a babel of tongues could be heard.

*E*ach glass car on the 264-foot high ferris wheel (above left) held sixty passengers. Several couples tried unsuccessfully to get married in the top car! "Little Egypt" (above) scored a triumph on the midway despite debate about "whether the customs of Cairo would undermine the morals of the public."

*P*hoenix House was an exquisite, small, Japanese structure, ereted by workmen sent by the emperor of Japan. The building influenced American architects, notably Frank Lloyd Wright, whose "prairie style" incorporated features of Japanese architecture.

make them all alike, to make them come through the factory just alike."

In a development that rivaled assembly lines in importance, businesses established industrial research laboratories where scientists and engineers developed new products. General Electric founded the first one in 1900, housed in a barn. It soon attracted experts who designed improvements in light bulbs, invented the cathode-ray tube, worked on early radio, and even tinkered with atomic theory. Du Pont opened its labs in 1911, Eastman Kodak in 1912, and Standard Oil in 1919. As the source of new ideas and technology, the labs altered life in the twentieth century.

Through all this, business became large-scale, mechanized, and managed. While many shops still employed fewer than a dozen workers, the proportion of such shops shrank. By 1920, close to one-half of all industrial workers worked in factories employing more than 250 people. More than one-third worked in factories that were part of multiplant companies.

Industries that processed materials—iron and steel, paper, cement, and chemicals—were increasingly continuous and automatic. In the glass industry, machines ended the domination of highly skilled and well-paid craft workers. In 1908, Irving W. Colburn invented a machine to manufacture plate glass; the Libbey-Owens-Ford Company bought the patent; and Ford soon had a glassmaking machine from which emerged every day for two years a 3½-mile ribbon of automobile window glass, eventually reaching a length of almost 2000 miles.

Workers tending such ribbons could not fall behind. Foremen still managed the laborers on the factory floor, but more and more, the rules came down from a central office where trained, professional managers supervised production flow. Systematic record keeping, cost accounting, and inventory and production controls became widespread. Workers lost control of the work pace. "If you need to turn out a little more," a manager at Swift and Company said, "you speed up the conveyor a little and the men speed up to keep pace." It worked. For that and other reasons, in the automobile industry, output per manhour multiplied an extraordinary four times between 1909 and 1919.

Folkways of the work place—workers passing job-related knowledge to each other, performing their tasks with little supervision, setting their own pace, and in effect running the shop—began to give way to "scientific" labor management. More than anyone else, Frederick Winslow Taylor, an inventive mechanical engineer, strove to extract maximum efficiency from each worker. (See "Frederick Winslow Taylor and the Rise of Scientific Management," pp. 662-63.)

Taylor proposed two major reforms. First, management must take responsibility for job-related knowledge and classify it into "rules, laws, and formulae." Second, management should control the work place "through *enforced* standardization of methods, *enforced* adoption of the best implements and working conditions, and *enforced* cooperation." Although few factories wholly adopted Taylor's principles, he had great influence, and the doctrines of scientific management spread through American industry.

Workers caught up in the changing industrial system experienced the benefits of efficiency and productivity; in some industries, they earned more. But they suffered important losses as well. Performing repetitive tasks, they seemed part of the machinery, to the pace and needs of which they moved. Bored, they might easily lose pride of workmanship, though many workers, it is clear, did not. Efficiency engineers experimented with tools and methods, a process many workers found unsettling. Yet the goal was to establish routine—to work out, as someone said of a garment worker, "one single precise motion each second, 3600 in one hour, and all exactly the same." Praising that worker, the manager said: "She is a sure machine."

Jobs became not only monotonous but dangerous. As machines and assembly lines sped up, boredom or miscalculation could bring disaster. Meat cutters sliced fingers and hands. Illinois steel mills, a magazine said, were "Making Steel and Killing Men"; one mill had forty-six deaths in 1906 alone. Injuries were part of many jobs. "The machines go like mad all day," a garment worker said, "because the faster you work the more money you get. Sometimes in my haste I get my finger caught and the needle goes right through it . . . I bind the finger up with a piece of cotton and go on working."

In March 1911, a fire at the Triangle Shirtwaist Company in New York focused nationwide attention on unsafe working conditions. When the fire

started, five hundred men and women, mostly Italians and Jews from eastern Europe, were just finishing their workday. Firefighters arrived within minutes, but they were already too late. Terrified seamstresses raced to the exits to try to escape the flames, but most exit doors were closed, locked by the company to prevent theft and shut out union organizers. Many died in the stampede down the narrow stairways or the single fire escape. Still others, trapped on the building's top stories far above the reach of the fire department's ladders, jumped to their deaths on the street below. One hundred forty-six people died.

A few days later, eighty thousand people marched silently in the rain in a funeral procession up Fifth Avenue. A quarter of a million people watched. At a mass meeting held to protest factory working conditions, Rose Schneiderman, a twenty-nine-year-old dynamic organizer for the Women's Trade Union League, told New York City's civic and religious leaders that they had not done enough, they had not cared. "We have tried you good people of the public and we have found you wanting. . . . Every week I must learn of the untimely death of one of my sister workers. Every year thousands of us are maimed. The life of men and women is so cheap and property is so sacred."

The outcry impelled New York's governor to appoint a State Factory Investigating Commission that recommended laws to shorten the work-week and improve safety in factories and stores.

Fire nets were of no avail to the Triangle workers who jumped from the upper stories to escape the flames. Speaking to a mass meeting after the fire, labor organizer Rose Schneiderman inveighed against a system that treated human beings as expendable commodities.

SOCIETY'S MASSES

Spreading consumer goods through society, mass production not only improved people's lives, but sometimes cost lives, too. Tending the machines, as Rose Schneiderman pointed out, took hard, painful labor, often under dangerous conditions. As businesses expanded, they required more and more people, and the labor force increased tremendously to keep up with the demand for workers in the factories, mines, and forests. Women, African Americans, and Mexican-Americans played larger and larger roles. Immigration soared. Between 1901 and 1910, nearly 8.8 million immigrants entered the United States; between 1911 and 1920, another 5.7 million came.

For many of these people, life was harsh, spent in crowded slums and long hours on the job. Fortunately, the massive unemployment of the 1890s was over, and in many skilled trades, like cigar making, there was plenty of work to go around. Though the economic recovery helped nearly everyone, the less skilled continued to be the less fortunate. Migrant workers, lumberjacks, ore shovelers, and others struggled to find decent-paying jobs.

Under such circumstances, many people fought to make a living, and many, too, fought to improve their lot. Their efforts, along with the efforts of the reform-minded people who came to their aid, became another important hallmark of the Progressive Era.

Better Times on the Farm

While people continued to flee the farms—by 1920, fewer than one-third of all Americans lived on farms; fewer than one-half lived in rural areas—farmers themselves prospered, the beneficiaries of greater production and expanding urban markets. Rural Free Delivery, begun in 1893, helped diminish the farmers' sense of isolation, and changed farm life. The delivery of mail to the farm door opened that door to a wider world; it exposed farmers to urban thinking, national advertising, and political events. In 1911, over one billion newspapers and magazines were delivered over RFD routes.

Parcel post (1913) permitted the sending of packages through the U.S. mail. Mail-order houses flourished; rural merchants suffered. Packages went both ways—President Woodrow Wilson's first parcel-post delivery had 8 pounds of New Jersey apples—and within a year, 300 million packages were being mailed annually. While telephones and electricity did not reach most rural areas for decades, better roads, mail-order catalogs, and other innovations knit farmers into the larger society. Early in the new century, Mary E. Lease—who in her Populist days had urged Kansas farmers to raise less corn and more Hell— moved to Brooklyn.

Farmers still had problems. Land prices rose with crop prices, and farm tenancy increased, especially in the South. Tenancy grew from one-quarter of all farms in 1880 to more than

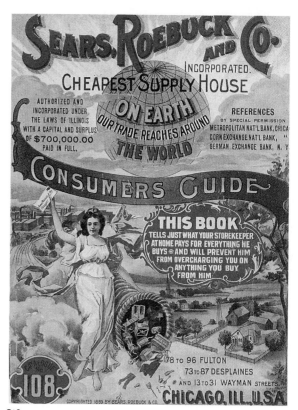

With Rural Free Delivery, people in even the most remote areas had access to the goods in the catalogs of the large mail-order houses.

one-third in 1910. In South Carolina, Georgia, Alabama, and Mississippi, nearly two-thirds of the farms were run by tenant farmers. Many southern tenant farmers were African Americans, and they suffered from farm-bred diseases. In one of the reforms of the Progressive Era, in 1909, the Rockefeller Sanitary Commission, acting on recent scientific discoveries, began a sanitation campaign that eventually wiped out the hookworm disease, and in 1912, the U.S. Public Health Service began work on rural malaria.

Women at Work

Women worked in larger and larger numbers. In 1900, more than 5 million worked—one-fifth of all adult women—and among those aged fourteen to twenty-four, the employment rate was almost one-third. Of those employed, single women outnumbered married women by seven to one, yet more than one-third of married women worked. Most women held service jobs. Only a small number held higher paying jobs as professionals or managers.

In the 1890s, women made up over one-quarter of medical school graduates. Using a variety of techniques, men gradually squeezed them out, and by the 1920s, only about 5 percent of the graduates were women. Few women taught in colleges and universities, and those who did were expected to resign if they married. In 1906, Harriet Brooks, a promising physicist at Barnard College in New York, became engaged and refused to resign; the dean told her icily that Barnard expected a married woman to "dignify her home-making into a profession, and not assume that she can carry on two full professions at a time."

More women than men graduated from high school, and with professions like medicine and science largely closed to them, they often turned to the new "business schools" that offered training in stenography, typing, and bookkeeping. In 1920, over one-quarter of all employed women held clerical jobs. Many others taught school.

In 1907 and 1908, investigators studied 22,000 women workers in Pittsburgh; 60 percent of them earned less than $7 a week, a minimum for "decent living." Fewer than 1 percent held skilled jobs; most tended machines, wrapped and labeled, or did handwork that required no particular skill. In New York, many women toiled six days a week as garment workers from eight in the morning to six in the evening, with an extra hour off on Saturdays. They earned $7 to $12 a week, nothing at all during slack season. They had to buy their own needles and thread and pay for electricity and chairs to sit on.

Critics charged that women's employment endangered the home, threatened their reproductive functions, and even, as one man said, stripped them of "that modest demeanor that lends a charm to their kind." Adding to these fears, the birth rate continued to drop between 1900 and 1920, and the divorce rate soared, in part because working-class men took advantage of the newer moral freedom and deserted their families in growing numbers. By 1916, there was one divorce for every nine marriages as compared to one for twenty-one in 1880.

David Graham Phillips, a novelist troubled by the woman's problem, depicted a husband's oppression of his wife in The Hungry Heart, published in 1909. "He kissed her, patted her cheek, went back to his work." When the wife grew restless, the husband knew why: "A few more years'll wash away the smatter she got at college,

PICKING SLATE

LAD FELL TO DEATH IN BIG COAL CHUTE

Dennis McKee Dead and Arthur Allbecker Had Leg Burned In the Lee Mines.

Wilkes-Barre
News
Jan 7, 1911

Falling into a chute at the Chauncey colliery of the George S. Lee Coal Company at Avondale, this afternoon, Dennis McKee, aged 16, of West Nanticoke, was smothered to death and

He was removed to his home at Avondale.

Both boys were employed as breaker boys, and going too close to the chutes fell in. Fellow workmen rushed to their assistance and soon

Breaker boys, who picked out pieces of slate from the coal as it rushed past, often became bent-backed after years of working fourteen hours a day in the coal mines. Accidents—and death—were common.

and this restlessness of hers will yield to nature, and she'll be content and happy in her womanhood. . . . As grandfather often said, it's a dreadful mistake, educating women beyond their sphere." Such views, mild as they were, got Phillips assassinated by a lunatic who claimed the novelist was "trying to destroy the whole ideal of womanhood."

Many children worked. In 1900, about three million children—nearly 20 percent of those between the ages of five and fifteen—held full- or almost full-time jobs. Twenty-five thousand boys under sixteen worked in mining; twenty thousand children under twelve, mainly girls, worked in southern cotton mills. Gradually the use of child labor shrank, as public indignation grew.

Determined to do something about the situation, the Women's Trade Union League (p. 660) lobbied the federal Bureau of Labor to investigate the conditions under which women and children worked. Begun in 1907, the investigation took four years and resulted in nineteen volumes of data, some of it shocking, all of it factual. In 1911, spurred by the data, the Children's Bureau was formed within the U.S. Bureau of Labor, with Grace Abbott, a social worker, at its head. It immediately began its own investigations, showing among other things the need for greater protection of maternal and infant health. In 1921, Congress passed the Sheppard-Towner Maternity and Infancy Protection Act, which helped fund maternity and pediatric clinics. Providing a precedent for the Social Security Act of 1935, it demonstrated the increasing effectiveness of women reformers in the Progressive Era.

Numerous middle-class women became involved in the fight for reform, while many others, reflecting the ongoing changes in the family (see Chapter 19), took increasing pride in homemaking and motherhood. Mother's Day, the national holiday, was formally established in 1913. With families preferring smaller numbers of children, birth control became a more acceptable practice. Margaret Sanger, a nurse and outspoken social reformer, led a campaign to give physicians broad discretion in prescribing contraceptives. When Sanger became involved in the birth-control movement, the federal Comstock Law banned the interstate transport of contraceptive devices and information (see "Margaret Sanger and the Birth Control Movement," pp. 686-87).

The Niagara Movement and the NAACP

Black women had always worked, and in far larger numbers than their white counterparts. The reason was usually economic; an African-American man or woman alone could rarely earn enough to support a family. Unlike many white women, black women tended to remain in the labor force after marriage or the start of a family. They also had less opportunity for job advancement, and in 1920, between one-third and one-half of all African-American women who were working were restricted to personal and domestic service jobs.

For the first time since their arrival in North America, the percentage of African-American women who worked would decline with the migration north during World War I (see Chapter 24), but at the turn of the century eight of every ten African Americans still lived in rural areas, mainly in the South. Most were poor sharecroppers. "Jim Crow" laws segregated many schools, railroad cars, hotels, and hospitals. Poll taxes and other devices disfranchised blacks and many poor whites. Violence was common; from 1900 to 1914, white mobs murdered over a thousand black people.

Two murders occurred near Vicksburg, Mississippi, in 1904, and they revealed a great deal about the kind of violence African Americans faced. Looking for the killer of a white planter, a mob captured a black man and woman, their guilt or innocence unknown. They were tied to trees, and their fingers and ears were cut off as souvenirs. "The most excruciating form of punishment consisted in the use of a large corkscrew in the hands of some of the mob. This instrument was bored into the flesh of the man and the woman, in the arms, legs and body, and then pulled out, the spirals tearing out big pieces of raw, quivering flesh every time it was withdrawn." Finally, both people were thrown on a fire and burned to death, "a relief," a witness said, "to the maimed and suffering victims."

Many African Americans labored in the cotton farms, railroad camps, sawmills, and mines of the South under conditions of peonage. Peons traded their lives and labor for food and shelter. Often illiterate, they were forced to sign contracts allowing planters "to use such force as he or his

The wish to have "our children . . . enjoy fairer conditions than have fallen to our lot" was the impetus behind the NAACP, which sponsored the 1917 parade in New York City, pictured at left.

agents may deem necessary to require me to remain on his farm and perform good and satisfactory services." Armed guards patrolled the camps and whipped those trying to escape. "In the woods," a peon said, "they can do anything they please, and no one can see them but God."

Few blacks belonged to labor unions, and blacks almost always earned less than whites in the same job. In Atlanta, white electricians earned $5.00 a day, blacks $3.50. Black songs like "I've Got a White Man Workin' for Me" (1901) voiced more hope than reality. The illiteracy rate among African Americans dropped from 45 percent in 1900 to 30 percent in 1910, but nowhere were they given equal school facilities, teachers' salaries, or educational materials. In 1910, scarcely eight thousand African-American youths were attending high schools in all the states of the Southeast. South Carolina spent $13.98 annually for the education of each white child, $1.13 for each black child.

African-American leaders grew increasingly impatient with this kind of treatment, and in 1905 a group of them, led by sociologist W. E. B. Du Bois, met near Niagara Falls, New York (they met on the Canadian side of the Falls, since no hotel on the American side would take them). There they pledged action in the matters of voting, equal access to economic opportunity, integration, and equality before the law. Rejecting Booker T. Washington's gradualist approach, the Niagara movement claimed for African Americans "every single right that belongs to a freefreeborn American, political, civil, and social; and until we get these rights we will never cease to protest."

The Niagara movement focused on equal rights and the education of African-American youth, of whom it said: "They have a right to know, to think, to aspire." Keeping alive a program of militant action, it spawned later civil rights movements. Du Bois was its inspiration. In *The Souls of Black Folk* (1903) and other works, he called eloquently for justice and equality. "By every civilized and peaceful method," he said, "we must strive for the right which the world accords to man."

Peace was sometimes hard to come by. Race riots broke out in Atlanta, Georgia, in 1906 and Springfield, Illinois, in 1908, the latter the home of Abraham Lincoln. Unlike the riots of the 1960s, white mobs invaded black neighborhoods, burning, looting, and killing. They lynched two blacks—one eighty-four years old—in Springfield.

William E. Walling, a wealthy southerner and settlement house worker; Mary Ovington, a white anthropology student; and Oswald Garrison Villard, grandson of the famous abolitionist William Lloyd Garrison, were outraged. Along with other reformers, white and black (among them, Jane Addams and John Dewey), they issued a call for the conference that organized the National Association for the Advancement of Colored People, which swiftly became the most important civil rights organization in the country. Created in 1910, within four years the NAACP grew to 50 branches and more than 6000 members. Walling headed it, and Du Bois, the only African American among the top officers, directed publicity and edited *The Crisis*, the voice of the organization.

Joined by the National Urban League, which was created in 1911, the NAACP pressured employers, labor unions, and the government on behalf of African Americans. It had some victories. In *Guinn* v. *United States* (1915), the Supreme Court overturned a "grandfather clause" that kept African Americans from voting in Oklahoma, and in *Buchanan* v. *Worley* (1917), it struck down a law in Louisville, Kentucky, requiring residential segregation. In 1918, in the midst of World War I, the NAACP and the National Urban League persuaded the federal government to form a special Bureau of Negro Economics within the Labor Department to look after the interests of African-American wage earners.

Despite these gains, African Americans continued to experience disenfranchisement, poor job opportunities, and segregation. As Booker T. Washington said in 1913: "I have never seen the colored people so discouraged and so bitter as they are at the present time."

"I Hear the Whistle": Immigrants in the Labor Force

While women and African Americans worked in growing numbers, much of the huge increase in the labor force in these years came from outside the country, particularly from Europe and Mexico. Between 1901 and 1920, the extraordinarily high total of 14.5 million immigrants entered the country, more than in any previous twenty-year period. Continuing the recent trend (see Chapter 19), many came from southern and eastern Europe. Still called the "new" immigrants, they met hostility from "older" immigrants of northern European stock who questioned their values, religion (often Catholic or Jewish), traditions and appearance.

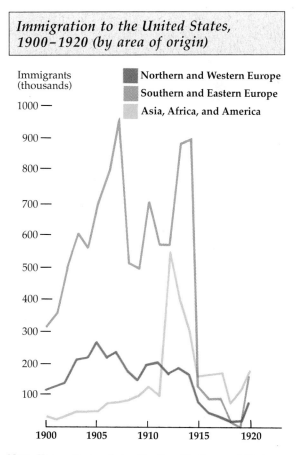

Immigration to the United States, 1900–1920 (by area of origin)

Immigrants (thousands)

- Northern and Western Europe
- Southern and Eastern Europe
- Asia, Africa, and America

Note: For purposes of classification, *Northern and Western Europe* includes Great Britain, Ireland, Scandinavia, the Netherlands, Belgium, Luxembourg, Switzerland, France and Germany. *Southern and Eastern Europe* includes Poland, Austria-Hungary, Russia and the Baltic States, Romania, Bulgaria, European Turkey, Italy, Spain, Portugal and Greece. *Asia, Africa and America* includes Asian Turkey, China, Japan, India, Canada, the Caribbean, Latin America and all of Africa.
Source: U.S. Bureau of the Census, Historical Statistics of the United States, Colonial Times to 1970, *Bicentennial Edition, Washington, D.C., 1975.*

Labor agents—called *padroni* among the Italians, Greeks, and Syrians—recruited immigrant workers, found them jobs, and deducted a fee from their wages. Headquartered in Salt Lake City, Leonidas G. Skliris, the "Czar of the Greeks," provided workers for the Utah Copper Company and the Western Pacific Railroad. In Chicago at the turn of the century, padroni employed more than one-fifth of all Italians; in New York City, they controlled two-thirds of the entire labor force.

Immigrant patterns often departed from traditional stereotypes. Immigrants, for example, moved both to and from their homelands. Fifty percent or more of some groups returned home, although the numbers varied among groups. Jews and Czechs often brought their families to resettle in America; Serbs and Poles tended to come singly, intent on earning enough money to make a fresh start at home. Many Italian men virtually commuted, "birds of passage" who returned home every slack season. However, the outbreak of World War I interrupted the practice and trapped hundreds of thousands of Italians and others who had planned to return to Europe.

Older residents lumped the newcomers together, ignoring geographic, religious, and other differences. Preserving important regional distinctions, Italians tended to settle as Calabreses, Venetians, Abruzzis, and Sicilians. Native Americans viewed them all simply as Italians. Henry Ford and other employers tried to erase the differences through English classes and deliberate "Americanization" programs. The Ford Motor Company ran a school where immigrant employees were first taught to say: "I am a good American." At the graduation ceremony, the pupils acted out a gigantic pantomime in which, clad in their old-country dress, they filed into a large "melting pot." When they emerged, they were wearing identical American-made clothes, and each was waving a little American flag.

In similar fashion, the International Harvester Corporation taught Polish laborers to speak English, but it had other lessons in view as well. According to "Lesson One," drilled into the Polish "pupils":

I hear the whistle. I must hurry.
I hear the five minute whistle.
It is time to go into the shop.
I take my check from the gate board and hang it on the department board.
I change my clothes and get ready to work.
The starting whistle blows.
I eat my lunch.
It is forbidden to eat until then.
The whistle blows at five minutes of starting time.
I get ready to go to work.
I work until the whistle blows to quit.
I leave my place nice and clean.
I put all my clothes in the locker.
I must go home.

Labor groups soon learned to counter these techniques. The Women's Trade Union League (WTUL) urged workers to ignore business-sponsored English lessons because they did not "tell the girl worker the things she really wants to know. They do not suggest that $5 a week is not a living wage. They tell her to be respectful to her employer." Designing its own educational program, the WTUL in 1912 published "New World Lessons for Old World Peoples," which provided quite a different kind of English lesson:

*T*he Pledge of Allegiance was part of the Americanization process for millions of immigrant children.

A Union girl takes me into the Union.
The Union girls are glad to see me.
They call me sister.
I will work hard for our Union.
I will come to all the Union meetings.

In another significant development, at the beginning of the twentieth century, Mexicans for the first time immigrated in large numbers, especially after a revolution in Mexico in 1910 forced many to flee across the northern border into Texas, New Mexico, Arizona, and California. Their exact numbers were unknown. American officials did not count border crossings until 1907, and even then, many migrants avoided the official immigration stations. Almost all came from the Mexican lower class, eager to escape peonage and violence in their native land. Labor agents—called *coyotes*—usually in the employ of large corporations or working for ranchers, recruited Mexican workers.

Between 1900 and 1910, the Mexican population of Texas and New Mexico nearly doubled; in Arizona, it more than doubled; in California, it quadrupled. In all four states, it doubled again between 1910 and 1920. After the turn of the century, almost 10 percent of the total population of Mexico moved to the American Southwest.

In time, these Mexican-Americans and their children transformed the Southwest. They built most of the early highways in Texas, New Mexico, and Arizona; dug the irrigation ditches that watered crops throughout the area; laid railroad track; and picked the cotton and vegetables that clothed and fed millions of Americans. Many lived in shacks and shanties along the railroad tracks, isolated in a separate Spanish-speaking world. Like other immigrant groups, they also formed enclaves in the cities, *barrios*, which became cultural islands of family life, foods, church, and festivals.

As the newcomers arrived from Europe and Mexico, nativist sentiment, which had criticized earlier waves of immigrants, intensified. Old-stock Americans sneered at their dress and language. Racial theories emphasized the superiority of northern Europeans (see Chapter 21) and the new "science" of eugenics suggested controls over the population growth of "inferior" peoples. Hostility toward Catholics and Jews was common but touched other groups as well.

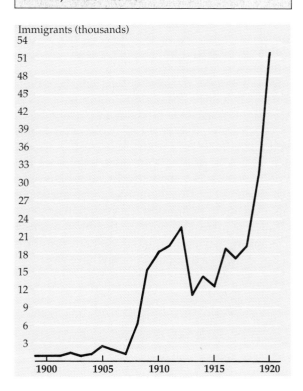

Mexican Immigration to the United States, 1900–1920

Immigrants (thousands)

In 1902, Congress enacted a law prohibiting immigration from China. Statutes requiring literacy tests designed to curtail immigration from southern and eastern Europe were vetoed by William Howard Taft in 1913, and Woodrow Wilson in 1915 and 1917. In 1917, such a measure passed despite Wilson's veto. Other measures tried to limit immigration from Mexico and Japan.

CONFLICT IN THE WORKPLACE

Assembly lines, speed-ups, long hours, and low pay produced a dramatic increase in American industrial output (and profits) after 1900; they also gave rise to numerous strikes and other kinds of labor unrest. Sometimes strikes took place through the action of unions; sometimes workers just decided they had had enough and walked off the job. Whatever the cause, strikes were frequent. In one industry, in one city—the meatpacking industry in Chicago—there were 251 strikes in 1903 alone.

Strikes and absenteeism increased after 1910; labor productivity dropped 10 percent between 1915 and 1918, the first such decline in memory. In many industries, labor turnover became a serious problem; workers changed jobs in droves. Union membership grew. In 1900, only about 1 million workers—less than 4 percent of the work force—belonged to unions. By 1920, 5 million workers belonged, increasing the unionized portion of the work force to about 13 percent.

As tensions grew between capital and labor, some people in the middle class became fearful that, unless something were done to improve the workers' situation, there might be violence or even revolution. This fear motivated some of the labor-oriented reforms of the Progressive Era. While some reform supporters genuinely wanted to improve labor's lot; others embraced reform because they were afraid of something else.

Organizing Labor

Samuel Gompers' American Federation of Labor increased from 250,000 members in 1897 to 1.7 million in 1904. By far the largest union organization, it remained devoted to the interests of skilled craftsmen. While it aimed partly at better wages and working conditions, it also sought to limit entry into the craft and protect worker prerogatives. Within limits, the AFL found acceptance among giant business corporations eager for conservative policies and labor stability.

There were 8 million female workers in 1910, but only 125,000 belonged to unions. Gompers continued to resist organizing them, saying they were too emotional and, as union organizers, "had a way of making serious mistakes." Margaret Dreier Robins, an organizer of proven skill, scoffed at that. "[T]hese men died twenty years ago and are just walking around dead!" she said.

Robins helped found the Women's Trade Union League in 1903. The WTUL led the effort to organize women into trade unions, lobby for legislation protecting female workers, and educate the public on the problems and needs of working women. It took in all working women who would join, regardless of skill (though not, at first, African-American women), and it won crucial financial support from well-to-do women like Anne Morgan, daughter of the feared financier

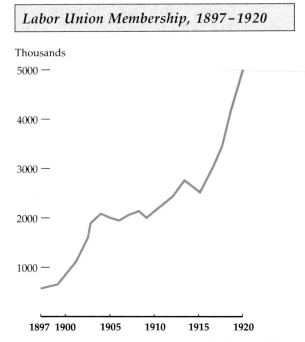

Labor Union Membership, 1897–1920

Thousands

Source: U.S. Bureau of the Census. Statistical Abstract of the United States: 1982–83 (103rd edition) Washington, D.C., 1982.

J. P. Morgan. Robins's close friend, Jane Addams (see Chapter 19), belonged, as did Mary McDowell, "The Angel of the Stockyards," who worked with slaughterhouse workers in Chicago; Julia Lathrop, who tried to improve the lot of wage-earning children; and Dr. Alice Hamilton, a pioneer in American research on the causes of industrial disease.

The WTUL never had many members—a few thousand at most—but its influence extended far beyond its membership. In 1909, it supported the "Uprising of the 20,000," a strike of shirtwaist workers in New York City. When female employees of the Triangle Shirtwaist Company tried to form a union, the company fired them, and they walked out; 20,000 men and women in 500 other shops followed. Strike meetings were conducted in three languages—English, Yiddish, and Italian —and before being forced to go back to work, the strikers won a shorter workweek and a few other gains. Sadly, the Triangle women lost out on another important demand—for unlocked shop doors and safe fire escapes. Their loss proved lethal in the famous Triangle Shirtwaist Company fire of 1911.

The WTUL also backed a strike in 1910 against

Hart, Schaffner and Marx, Chicago's largest manufacturer of men's clothing. One day, Annie Shapiro, the eighteen-year-old daughter of Russian immigrants, was told that her wages were being cut from $7 a week to $6.20. That was a large cut, and along with sixteen other young women, Shapiro refused to accept it and walked out. "We had to be recognized as people," she said later. Soon other women walked out, and the revolt spread. Managers quickly promised to restore the cuts, but as one woman said, "just then there was big noise outside and we all rushed to the windows and there we saw the police beating the strikers on our account, and when we saw that we went out."

In a matter of days, some forty thousand garment workers were on strike, about half of them women. Manufacturers hurried to negotiate, and the result was the important Hart, Schaffner agreement, which created an arbitration committee composed of management and labor to handle grievances and settle disputes. The first successful experiment in collective bargaining, the Hart, Schaffner agreement became the model for the kind of agreements that govern industrial relations today.

Another union, the Industrial Workers of the World (IWW), attracted by far the greatest attention (and fears) in these years. Unlike the WTUL, it welcomed everyone regardless of sex or race. Unlike the AFL, it tried to organize the unskilled and foreign-born laborers who worked in the mass-production industries. Founded in Chicago in 1905, it aimed to unite the American working class into a mammoth union to promote labor's interests. Its motto—"an injury to one is an injury to all"—stressed labor solidarity as had the earlier Knights of Labor. But unlike the Knights, the IWW, or Wobblies as they were often known, urged social revolution.

"It is our purpose to overthrow the capitalist system by forcible means if necessary," William D. (Big Bill) Haywood, one of its founders, said; and he went on in his speeches to say he knew of nothing a worker could do that "will bring as much anguish to the boss as a little sabotage in the right place." Joe Hill, the IWW's legendary folk poet, reminded labor of its potential strength:

> If the workers took a notion
>   They could stop all speeding trains;
> Every ship upon the ocean
>   They can tie with mighty chains.
>
> Every wheel in the creation
>   Every mine and every mill;
> Fleets and armies of the nation,
>   Will at their command stand still.

As one of the founders of the IWW, Big Bill Haywood (center) advocated the tactics of strikes and sabotage to achieve the goals of worker solidarity and eventual seizure of industry.

Frederick Winslow Taylor and the Rise of Scientific Management

Between 1880 and 1920, American businesses underwent revolutionary changes. For one thing, they grew larger and larger, employing thousands of people and turning out products sold around the world. Some grew so large they owned the mines or farms that produced the raw materials, the railroads and steamships that transported them, the factories that turned raw materials into a finished product, and the retailing system that marketed it. As businesses grew in size, they also grew more bureaucratic, with layers of people between the owners and the shop floor. In the years after 1880 a new "science" of management sprang up to help managers organize and control the giant new businesses of the industrial age.

Frederick Winslow Taylor, an ingenious inventor and engineer, was the leader in this effort. Born in Philadelphia in 1856, Taylor was headed for Harvard when his parents, afraid that studying was hurting his eyesight, urged him to drop out of school and get a job. He went to work for Midvale Steel in Philadelphia, first as a clerk and machinist, and then as subforeman in the machine shop, his first managerial post. Taylor was aggressive and ambitious, and he soon began to step up the pace in the shop. The men refused. As late as the 1880s, workers in factories like Midvale tended to make the rules themselves, regardless of orders from the top. They established their own quotas, worked at their

Frederick Winslow Taylor

own pace, and resisted attempts to hurry them up.

Impatient, Taylor tinkered with ways to improve the machinery and, before long, the factory system itself. "My head," he said, "was full of wonderful and great projects to simplify the processes, to design new machines, to revolutionize the methods of the whole establishment." Among other products, he invented high-speed tool steel for cutting hard metals, an innovation crucial to modern industry. At the same time he developed a broad plan of scientific management for every industry, certain, he said, that "the best management is a true science, resting upon clearly defined laws, rules, and principles."

Setting out to uncover those laws, he studied each job in a factory, trying to reduce it to the simplest components. How did the worker's arms move? Were there

wasted motions? Did he or she have the right tools? The right instructions? If the job involved materials, were they ready at hand, or did the worker have to reach for them? By 1889, when he left Midvale, Taylor had settled on four principles of scientific management: (1) centralized planning of the factory and its output; (2) systematic analysis of each job; (3) detailed instruction and supervision of each worker; and (4) an incentive wage scale that would get workers to follow the instructions. Managers, he said, not workers, should determine what happens on the shop floor. "In the past the man has been first; in the future the system must be first."

To prove the point Taylor told the story of "Schmidt," an ordinary laborer at the Bethlehem Steel plant. When war with Spain broke out in 1898, Bethlehem had 80,000 tons of pig iron stacked in piles in a field. With the sudden demand for arms the price soared, and Bethlehem asked Taylor to load it quickly for the market. Running a railroad track into the field, he studied what to do. Each bar of pig iron weighed 92 pounds; to load it, a worker had to pick it up, carry it up a ramp into a boxcar, stack it, and return for another bar. A worker usually loaded 12½ long tons of pig iron a day. Taylor had different ideas. Someone working efficiently, he thought, should load almost four times that much—47½ long tons (106,400 pounds)—a day.

An avid tennis player, Taylor designed this spoon-shaped raquet to give himself an advantage on the court.

That was no small difference, and when Taylor collected the men he wanted and offered them higher wages to do the job, they refused, thinking it was all just an excuse to get everyone in the factory to work harder. Starting again, Taylor chose one worker, Henry Noll, whom he made famous in his writings as "Schmidt." He had watched Noll carefully and liked the way he worked hard all day and trotted a mile home at night. Taking Noll

aside, Taylor offered him a chance to earn $1.85 a day, instead of the usual $1.15. To earn the higher wage, he just had to work exactly as he was told. Noll leaped at the chance, and after a bit, others joined him. The pig iron was soon loaded and on its way.

From his experiments with Schmidt, Taylor derived a "law of heavy laboring" that told workers when to work and when to rest. Studying the shoveling of iron ore, he came up with a "science of shoveling." He designed fifteen kinds of shovel for different conditions and prescribed the exact motions for using each one. Companies adopting his ideas were often able to lay off workers and cut costs—one company cut its shoveling crew from 600 men to 140 for the same work—but Taylor argued that those who remained earned more and were happier. "Many if not most of them were saving money," he said, "and they all lived better than they had before."

In the last years of his life Taylor spent most of his time writing, consulting, and lecturing. His book, *The Principles of Scientific Management* (1911), was read widely by managers; workers passed

copies of it around so everyone could fight Taylorism whenever it appeared. At his death in 1915 Taylor ranked with Henry Ford as an American industrial hero. Business leaders, of course, liked his efforts to increase productivity, but Taylor was also popular because he had much in common with the generation of progressivism. Like the progressives, he believed in experts, efficiency, systematic planning, and the application of science to human life. Theodore Roosevelt praised him; Milwaukee, Pittsburgh, Seattle, and Philadelphia used his ideas to streamline city government. Taylor and the progressives wanted to bring order to the industrial society. "There have been times in recent years," a leading progressive said of him, "when it seemed as though our civilization were being throttled by things, by property, by the very weight of industrial mechanism, and it is no small matter when a man arises who can show us new ways of commanding our environment."

Since Taylor's time, researchers have found that workers care about job security, working conditions, and fringe benefits, not just higher wages, as Taylor had believed. Today, more emphasis is placed on the quality of the work, not just the time on the job, and some managers have even begun encouraging the kind of decision making on the shop floor that Taylor fought so hard to get rid of at Midvale. The Japanese, recognized today as the foremost management specialists, combine Taylor's ideas about centralized planning with Midvale's way of involving workers in some decisions. Yet when people go to their jobs in industrial nations around the world, the conditions they find are still shaped by Frederick Winslow Taylor's principles of scientific management, developed more than three-quarters of a century ago.

Below are some of the Bethlehem Steel pig-iron workers who benefited from Taylor's management practices and labor-saving tools.

Elizabeth Gurley Flynn, labor's "Joan of Arc," addresses textile workers on strike at Patterson, New Jersey.

IWW leaders included "Mother" Jones, a famous veteran of battles in the Illinois coalfields; Elizabeth Gurley Flynn, a fiery young radical who joined as a teenager; and Big Bill Haywood himself, the strapping, one-eyed founder of the Western Federation of Miners.

The IWW led a number of major strikes. The Lawrence, Massachusetts (1912), and Paterson, New Jersey (1912), strikes attracted national attention: in Lawrence when the strikers sent their children, ill-clad and hungry, out of the city to stay with sympathetic families; in Paterson when they rented New York's Madison Square Garden for a massive labor pageant. IWW leaders welcomed the revolutionary tumult sweeping Russia and other countries. In the United States, they thought, a series of local strikes would bring about capitalist repression, then a general strike, and eventually a workers' commonwealth.

The IWW fell short of these objectives, but during its lifetime—from 1905 to the mid-1920s—it made major gains among immigrant workers in the Northeast, migrant farm labor on the Plains, and loggers and miners in the South and Far West. In factories like Ford's, it recruited workers resentful of the speed-ups on the assembly lines. Although IWW membership probably amounted to no more than 100,000 at any one time, workers came and left so often that its total membership may have reached as high as 1 million.

Working with Workers

Concerned about labor unrest, some business leaders used violence and police action to keep workers in line, but others turned to the new fields of applied psychology and personnel management. A school of industrial psychology emerged. As had Taylor, industrial psychologists studied workers' routines and further, they showed that output was also affected by job satisfaction. While most businesses pushed ahead with efficiency campaigns, a few established industrial-relations departments, hired public relations firms to improve their corporate image, and linked productivity to job safety and happiness.

Ivy L. Lee, a pioneer in the field of corporate public relations, advised clients like the Pennsylvania Railroad and Standard Oil on how to improve relations with labor and the public. Calling himself, a "physician to corporate bodies," Lee urged complete openness on the company's part. To please employees, companies printed newsletters and organized softball teams; they awarded prizes and celebrated retirements. Ford created a "Sociology Department" staffed by 150 experts who showed workers how to budget their incomes and care for their health. They even taught them how to shop for meat.

On January 5, 1914, Ford took another significant step. He announced the Five-Dollar Day, "the greatest revolution," he said, "in the matter of rewards for workers ever known to the industrial world." With a stroke, he doubled the wage rate for common labor, reduced the working day from nine hours to eight, and established a personnel department to place workers in appropriate jobs. The next day, ten thousand applicants stood outside the gates.

As a result, Ford had the pick of the labor force. Turnover declined; absenteeism, previously as much as one-tenth of all Ford workers every day, fell to .3 percent. Output increased; the IWW at Ford collapsed. The plan increased wages, but allowed the company greater control over a more stable labor force. Workers had to meet a behavior code in order to qualify for the Five-Dollar

Day. At first scornful of the "utopian" plan, business leaders across the country soon copied it, and on January 2, 1919, Ford announced the Six-Dollar Day.

Amoskeag

In size, system, and worker relations, the record of the Amoskeag Company textile mills was revealing. Located beside the Merrimack River in Manchester, New Hampshire, the mills—an enormous complex of factories, warehouses, canals, and machinery—had been built in the 1830s. By the turn of the century, they were producing nearly 50 miles of cloth an hour, more cloth each day than any other mills in the entire world.

The face of the mills, an almost solid wall of red brick, stretched nearly a mile in length. Archways and bridges pierced the facade. Amoskeag resembled a walled, medieval city within which workers found "a total institution, a closed and almost self-contained world." At first the mills employed young women for labor, but by 1900, more and more immigrant males staffed the machines. French Canadians, Irish, Poles, and Greeks—seventeen thousand in all—worked there, and their experiences revealed a great deal about factory work and life at the turn of the century.

The company hired and fired at will, and it demanded relentless output from the spindles and spinning frames. Yet it also viewed employees as its "children" and looked for total loyalty in return, an expectation often realized. Workers identified with Amoskeag and, decades later, still called themselves Amoskeag men and women. "We were all like a family," one said.

Most Amoskeag workers preferred the industrial world of the mills to the farms they had left behind. They did not feel displaced; they knew the pains of industrial life; and they adapted in ways that fit their own needs and traditions. Families played a large role. They neither disintegrated nor lost their relationships. French Canadians and others often came in family units. One or two family members left the farm for the mills, maintained close ties with those back home, and then sent for others creating a form of "chain migration."

Once in Manchester, families often worked in the same workrooms. Looking after each other, they asked foremen for transfers and promotions for relatives; they taught their children technical skills and how to get along with bosses and fellow workers. Although low-paid, Amoskeag employees took pride in their work, and for many of them, a well-turned out product provided dignity and self-esteem.

The company long showed a paternal interest in employee welfare, and in 1910 it inaugurated a deliberate welfare and efficiency program. The program aimed to increase productivity, accustom immigrants to industrial work, instill company loyalty, and curb labor unrest. Playgrounds and visiting nurses, home-buying plans, a cooking school, and dental service were part of the plan. The Amoskeag Textile Club held employee dinners and picnics, organized shooting clubs and a baseball team, sponsored Christmas parties for the children, and put out the *Amoskeag Bulletin,* a monthly magazine of employee news.

From 1885 to 1919, no strike touched the mills. Thereafter, however, labor unrest increased. Overproduction and foreign competition took their toll, and Amoskeag closed in 1935.

LIFE IN AMERICA, 1920

For many Americans, the quality of life improved significantly between 1900 and 1920. Jobs were relatively plentiful, and in a development of great importance, more and more people were entering the professions as doctors, lawyers, teachers, and engineers (see Chapter 23). With comfortable incomes, a growing middle class could take advantage of new life-styles, inventions, and forms of entertainment. Mass production could not have worked without mass consumption, and Americans in these years increasingly became a nation of consumers.

In 1900, business firms spent about $95 million on advertising; twenty years later they spent over $500 million. Ads and billboards touted cigarettes, cars, perfumes, and cosmetics. Advertising agencies boomed. Using new sampling techniques, they developed modern concepts of market testing and research. Sampling customer preferences affected business indirectly as well, making it more responsive to public opinion on social and political issues.

Mass production swept the clothing industry and dressed more Americans better than any people ever before. Using lessons learned in making uniforms during the Civil War, manufacturers for the first time developed standard clothing and shoe sizes that fit most bodies. Clothing prices dropped; the availability of inexpensive, "off-the-rack" clothes lessened distinctions between rich and poor. By 1900, nine of every ten men and boys wore the new "ready-to-wear" clothes.

In 1900, people employed in manufacturing earned on average $418 a year. Two decades later, they earned $1342 a year, though inflation took much of the increase. While the middle class expanded, the rich also grew richer. In 1920, the new income tax showed the first accurate tabulation of income, and it confirmed what many had suspected all along. Five percent of the population received almost one-fourth of all income.

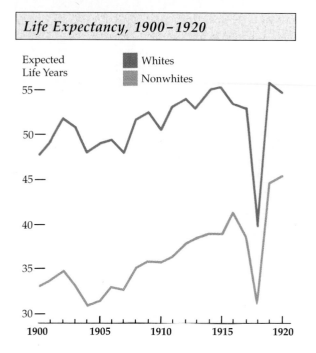

Life Expectancy, 1900–1920

An Urban Nation

In 1920, the median age of the population was only twenty-five. (It is now thirty). Immigration accounted for part of the population's youthfulness, since most immigrants were young. Thanks to medical advances and better living conditions, death rates dropped in the early years of the century; the average life span increased. Between 1900 and 1920, life expectancy rose from forty-nine to fifty-six years for white women and from forty-seven to fifty-four years for white men. It rose from thirty-three to forty-five years for blacks and other racial minorities.

Despite the increase in life expectancy, infant mortality remained high; nearly 10 percent of white babies and 20 percent of minority babies died in the first year of life. In comparison to today, fewer babies on average survived to adolescence, and fewer people survived beyond middle age. In 1900, the death rate among people between forty-five and sixty-five was more than twice the modern rate. As a result, there were relatively fewer older people—in 1900, only 4 percent of the population was older than sixty-five compared to nearly 12 percent today. Fewer children than today knew their grandparents. Still, improvements in health care helped people live longer, and as a result, the incidence of cancer and heart disease increased.

Cities grew, and by any earlier standards, they grew on a colossal scale. Downtowns became a central hive of skyscrapers, department stores, warehouses, and hotels. Strips of factories radiated from the center. As street railways spread, cities took on a systematic pattern of socioeconomic segregation, usually in rings. The innermost ring filled with immigrants, circled by a belt of working-class housing. The remaining rings marked areas of rising affluence outward toward wealthy suburbs, which themselves formed around shopping strips and grid patterns of streets that restricted social interaction.

The giants were New York, Chicago, and Philadelphia, industrial cities that turned out every kind of product from textiles to structural steel. Smaller cities like Rochester, New York, or Cleveland, Ohio, specialized in manufacturing a specific line of goods or processing regional products for the national market. Railroads instead of highways tied things together; in 1916, the rail network, the largest in the world, reached its peak—254,000 miles of track that carried over three-fourths of all intercity freight tonnage.

Step by step, cities adopted their twentieth-century forms. Between 1909 and 1915, Los Angeles, a city of three hundred thousand people, passed a series of ordinances that gave rise to modern urban zoning. For the first time, the ordinances divided a city into three districts of specified use: a residential area, an industrial area, and an area open to residence and a limited list of industries. Other cities followed. Combining several features, the New York Zoning Law of 1916 became the model for the nation; within a decade, 591 cities copied it.

Zoning ordered city development, keeping skyscrapers out of factory districts, factories out of the suburbs. It also had powerful social repercussions. In the South, zoning became a tool to extend racial segregation; in northern cities, it acted against ethnic minorities. Jews in New York, Italians in Boston, Poles in Detroit, African Americans in Chicago—zoning laws held them all at arm's length. Like other migrants, African Americans often preferred to settle together, but zoning also helped put them there. By 1920, ten districts in Chicago were more than three-quarters black. In Los Angeles, Cleveland, Detroit, and Washington, D.C., most blacks lived in only two or three wards.

THE USES OF LEISURE

Thanks to changing work rules and mechanization, many Americans benefited from more leisure time. The average workweek for manufacturing laborers fell from sixty hours in 1890 to fifty-one in 1920. By the early 1900s, white-collar workers might spend only eight to ten hours a day at work and a half day on weekends. Greater leisure time gave more people more opportunity for play and enjoyment of the arts.

People flocked to places of entertainment. Baseball entrenched itself as the national pastime. Automobiles and streetcars carried growing numbers of fans to ballparks; attendance at major-league games doubled between 1903 and 1920. Football also drew fans, although critics attacked the sport's violence and the use of "tramp athletes," nonstudents whom colleges paid to play. In 1905, the worst year, 18 players were killed and 150 seriously injured.

Alarmed, President Theodore Roosevelt—who

Annexation: Patterns of City Expansion

After 1900, dwellers in the suburban commuter belt around Chicago created by improved transit systems began to resist annexation by the city.

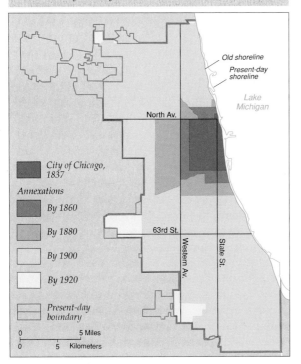

Ethnic Neighborhoods in Chicago, 1920

The ethnic groups shown here predominated in certain districts of the city, partly by choice, but also partly because of restrictive zoning practices.

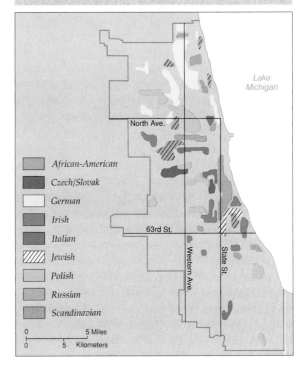

had once said, "I am the father of three boys [and] if I thought any one of them would weigh a possible broken bone against the glory of being chosen to play on Harvard's football team I would disinherit him"—called a White House conference to clean up college sports. The conference founded the Intercollegiate Athletic Association, which in 1910 became the National Collegiate Athletic Association.

Movie theaters opened everywhere. By 1910, there were 10,000 of them, drawing a weekly audience of 10 million people. Admission was usually five cents, and movies stressing laughter and pathos appealed to a mass market. In 1915, D. W. Griffith, a talented and creative director, produced the first movie spectacular *The Birth of a Nation*. Griffith adopted new film techniques, including close-ups, fade-outs, artistic camera angles, and dramatic battle scenes. (For further discussion of the film see "Changing Views of Reconstruction," pp. 476–77.)

Phonographs brought ready-made entertainment into the home. By 1901, phonograph and record companies included the Victor Talking Machine Company, the Edison Speaking Machine Company, and Columbia Records. Ornate mahogany Victrolas became standard fixtures in middle-class parlors. Early records were usually of vaudeville skits; orchestral recordings began in 1906. In 1919, 2.25 million phonographs were produced; two years later more than 100 million records were sold.

As record sales grew, families sang less and listened more. Music became a business. In 1909, Congress enacted a copyright law that provided a two-cent royalty on each piece of music on phonograph records or piano rolls. The royalty, small as it was, offered welcome income to composers and publishers, and in 1914, composer Victor Herbert and others formed the American Society of Composers, Authors and Publishers (ASCAP) to protect musical rights and royalties.

The faster rhythms of syncopated ragtime became the rage, especially after 1911 when Irving Berlin, a Russian immigrant, wrote "Alexander's Ragtime Band." Ragtime set off a nationwide dance craze. Secretaries danced on their lunch hour, the first night clubs opened, and restaurants and hotels introduced dance floors. Waltzes and polkas gave way to a host of new dances, many with animal names: the Fox Trot, Bunny Hop, Turkey Trot, Snake, and Kangaroo Dip. Partners were not permitted to dance too close; bouncers tapped them on the shoulder if they got closer than nine inches. The aging John D. Rockefeller hired a private instructor to teach him the tango, although Yale University banned that dance at its 1914 Junior Prom.

Vaudeville, increasingly popular after 1900, reached maturity around 1915. Drawing on the immigrant experience, it voiced the variety of city life and included skits, songs, comics, acrobats, and magicians. Dances and jokes showed an earthiness new to mass audiences. By 1914, stage runways extended into the crowd; performers had bared their legs and were beginning to show glimpses of the midriff. Fanny Brice, Ann Pennington, the "shimmy" queen, and Eva Tanguay—who sang "It's All Been Done Before but Not the Way I Do It"—starred in Florenz Ziegfeld's *Follies*, the peak of vaudeville.

In songs like "St. Louis Blues" (1914), W. C. Handy took the black southern folk music of the blues to northern cities. Gertrude "Ma" Rainey, the daughter of minstrels, sang in black vaudeville for nearly thirty-five years. Performing in Chattanooga, Tennessee, about 1910, she came across a twelve-year-old orphan, Bessie Smith, who became the "Empress of the Blues." Smith's voice was huge and sweeping. Recording for the "Race" division of Columbia Records, she made over eighty records that together sold nearly ten million copies.

Another musical innovation came north from New Orleans. Charles (Buddy) Bolden, a cornetist, Ferdinand "Jelly Roll" Morton, a pianist, and a youngster named Louis Armstrong played an improvisational music that had no formal name. Reaching Chicago, it became "jas," then "jass," and finally, "jazz." Jazz jumped, and jazz musicians relied on feeling and mood. A restaurant owner once asked Jelly Roll Morton to play a waltz. *"Waltz?"* Morton exclaimed. "Man, these people want to *dance!* And you talking about waltz. This is the *Roll* you're talking to."

Popular fiction reflected changing interests. Kate Douglas Wiggins' *Rebecca of Sunnybrook Farm* (1903) and Lucy M. Montgomery's *Anne of Green Gables* (1908) showed the continuing popularity of rural themes. Westerns also sold well, but readers turned more and more to detective thrillers with hard-bitten city detectives, and science fic-

Lavish production numbers and elaborate costumes were the hallmark of vaudeville's glamorous Ziegfield Follies.

tion featuring the latest dream in technology. The Tom Swift series, begun in 1910, looked ahead to spaceships, ray guns, and gravity nullifiers.

Edward L. Stratemeyer, the mind behind Tom Swift, brought the techniques of mass production to book writing. In 1906, he formed the Stratemeyer Literary Syndicate that employed a stable of writers to turn out hundreds of Tom Swift, Rover Boys, and Bobbsey Twins stories for young readers. Burt Standish, another prolific author, took the pen name of Gilbert Patten and created the character of Frank Merriwell, wholesome college athlete. As Patten said: "I took the three qualities I most wanted him to represent—frank and merry in nature, well in body and mind—and made the name Frank Merriwell." The Merriwell books sold twenty-five million copies.

Experimentation in the Arts

"There is a state of unrest all over the world in art as in all other things," the director of New York's Metropolitan Museum said in 1908. "It is the same in literature, as in music, in painting, and in sculpture."

Isadora Duncan and Ruth St. Denis transformed the dance. Departing from traditional ballet steps, both women stressed improvisation, emotion, and the human form. "Listen to the music with your soul . . . ," Duncan told her students. "Unless your dancing springs from an inner emotion and expresses an idea, it will be meaningless." Draped in flowing robes, she revealed more of her legs than some thought tasteful, while she proclaimed the "noblest art is the nude." After a triumphant performance with the New York Symphony in 1908, her ideas and techniques swept the country. Duncan died tragically in 1927, her neck broken when her long red scarf caught in the wheel of a racing car.

The lofts and apartments of New York's Greenwich Village attracted artists, writers, and poets interested in experimentation and change. To these artists, the city was the focus of national life and the sign of a new culture. Robert Henri and the realist painters—known to their critics as the Ashcan School—relished the city's excitement. They wanted, a friend said, "to paint truth and to paint it with strength and fearlessness and individuality."

To the realists, a painting carried into the future the look of life as it happened. With the same feel for the environment that many progressive reformers would show (see Chapter 23), their paintings depicted street scenes, colorful crowds, and slum children swimming in the river. In paintings like the "Cliff Dwellers," George W.

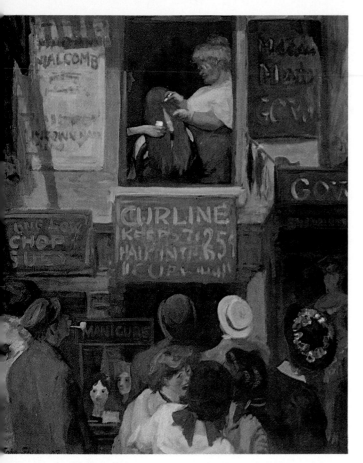

Hairdresser's Window *by John Sloan. One of the Ashcan realists, Sloan found his subject matter in the tenements, cafés, and barrooms of the modern city.*

Bellows captured the color and excitement of the tenements; John Sloan, one of Henri's most talented students, painted the vitality of ordinary people and familiar scenes.

In 1913, a show at the New York Armory presented sixteen hundred modernist paintings, prints, and sculptures. The work of Picasso, Cézanne, Matisse, Brancusi, Van Gogh, and Gauguin dazed and dazzled American observers. Critics attacked the show as worthless and depraved; a Chicago official wanted it banned from the city because the "idea that people can gaze at this sort of thing without [it] hurting them is all bosh."

The Post-Impressionists changed the direction of twentieth-century art and influenced adventuresome American painters. John Marin, Max Weber, Georgia O'Keeffe, Arthur Dove, and other modernists experimented in ways foreign to Henri's realists. Defiantly avant garde, they shook off convention and experimented with new forms. Using bold colors and abstract patterns, they worked to capture the energy of urban life. "I see great forces at work, great movements," Marin said, "the large buildings and the small buildings, the warring of the great and the small. . . . I can hear the sound of their strife, and there is a great music being played."

There was an extraordinary outburst of poetry. In 1912, Harriet Monroe started the magazine *Poetry* in Chicago, the hotbed of the new poetry; Ezra Pound and Vachel Lindsay, both daring experimenters with ideas and verse, published in the first issue. T. S. Eliot published the classic "Love Song of J. Alfred Prufrock" in *Poetry* in 1915. Attacked bitterly by conservative critics, the poem established Eliot's leadership among a group of poets, many of them living and writing in London, who rejected traditional meter and rhyme as artificial constraints. Eliot, Pound, and Amy Lowell, among others, believed that the poet's task was to capture fleeting images in verse.

Others experimenting with new techniques in poetry included Robert Frost (*North of Boston*, 1915), Edgar Lee Masters (*Spoon River Anthology*, 1915), and Carl Sandburg (*Chicago Poems*, 1916). Sandburg's poem "Chicago" celebrated the vitality of the city:

Come and show me another city with lifted head singing so proud to be alive and coarse and strong and cunning.
Fierce as a dog with tongue lapping for action, cunning as a savage pitted against the wilderness,
. . . .
Bareheaded,
Shoveling,
Wrecking,
Planning,
Building, breaking, rebuilding,
. . . .
Bragging and laughing that under his wrist is the pulse, and under his ribs the heart of the people,
                    Laughing!
Laughing the stormy, husky, brawling laughter of Youth, half-naked, sweating, proud to be Hog Butcher, Tool Maker, Stacker of Wheat, Player with Railroads and Freight Handler to the Nation.

Brooklyn Bridge *by Joseph Stella. Stella used fragments of color and dynamic patterns to capture the movement and intensity of a big city.*

Manners and morals change slowly, and many Americans overlooked the importance of the first two decades of the twentieth century. Yet sweeping change was underway; anyone who doubted it could visit a gallery, see a film, listen to music, or read one of the new literary magazines. Garrets and galleries were filled with a breathtaking sense of change. "There was life in all these new things," Marsden Hartley, a modernist painter, recalled. "There was excitement, there was healthy revolt, investigation, discovery, and an utterly new world out of it all."

The ferment of progressivism in city, state, and nation reshaped the country. In a burst of reform, people built playgrounds, restructured taxes, regulated business, won the vote for women, shortened working hours, altered political systems, opened kindergartens, and improved factory safety. They tried to fulfill the national promise of dignity and liberty.

Marsden Hartley, it turned out, had voiced a mood that went well beyond painters and poets. Across society, people in many walks of life were experiencing a similar sense of excitement and discovery. Racism, repression, and labor conflict were present, to be sure, but there was also talk of hope, progress, and change. In politics, science, journalism, education, and a host of other fields, people believed for a time that they could make a difference, and in trying to do so, they became part of the progressive generation.

Recommended Reading

There are several important analyses of the progressive era, including Robert H. Wiebe, *The Search for Order, 1877–1920* (1967); Richard Hofstadter, *The Age of Reform* (1955); Samuel P. Hays, *The Response to Industrialism* (1957); and Gabriel Kolko, *The Triumph of Conservatism* (1963). C. Vann Woodward, *Origins of the New South, 1877–1913* (1951) is a superb account of developments in the South. Lewis L. Gould, ed., *The Progressive Era* (1974), covers the period from varying perspectives; William L. O'Neill, *The Progressive Years* (1975) is a useful overview.

James T. Kloppenberg, *Uncertain Victory: Social Democracy and Progressivism in European and American Thought, 1870–1920* (1986), examines progressivism at home and abroad. C. Vann Woodward, *The Strange Career of Jim Crow* (1955), traces the civil-rights setbacks of the Progressive years. Sam Bass Warner, Jr., *Streetcar Suburbs* (1962) and *The Urban Wilderness* (1972) are excellent on the subject of urban development, including zoning and industrial growth.

Additional Bibliography

Studies of the muckrakers include David M. Chalmers, *The Social and Political Ideas of the Muckrakers* (1964); Justin Kaplan, *Lincoln Steffens* (1974); and Harold S. Wilson, *McClure's Magazine and the Muckrakers* (1970). Lincoln Steffens, *The Shame of the Cities* (1904) and *Autobiography of Lincoln Steffens* (1931) and Upton Sinclair, *The Jungle* (1906), give contemporary flavor.

Studies of youth, age, and family life include Joseph Kett, *Rites of Passage: Adolescence in America* (1977); W. Andrew Achenbaum, *Old Age in the New Land* (1978); William O'Neill, *Divorce in the Progressive Era* (1967); Carl N. Degler, *At Odds: Women and the Family in America* (1980); Michael Gordon, ed., *The American Family in Social-Historical Perspective* (1973); Tamara K. Hareven, ed., *Anonymous Americans* (1971) and *Transitions: The Family and Life Course in Historical Perspective* (1978). For birth control, see Linda Gordon, *Woman's Body, Woman's Right: A Social History of Birth Control in America* (1976) and David M. Kennedy, *Birth Control in America: The Career of Margaret Sanger* (1970).

See also Eleanor Flexner, *Century of Struggle: The Women's Rights Movement in the United States* (1959); William L. O'Neill, *Everyone Was Brave: The Rise and Fall of Feminism in America* (1969); Carole Nichols, *Votes and More for Women* (1983); Leslie Woodcock Tentler, *Wage-Earning Women: Industrial Work and Family Life in the United States,*

CHRONOLOGY

1898 Mergers and consolidations begin to sweep the business world, leading to fear of trusts

1903 Ford Motor Company formed • W. E. B. Du Bois calls for justice and equality for African Americans in *The Souls of Black Folk* • Women's Trade Union League (WTUL) formed to organize women workers

1905 Industrial Workers of the World (IWW) established • African-American leaders inaugurate Niagara movement, advocating integration and equal opportunity for African Americans

1909 Shirtwaist workers in New York City strike in the "Uprising of the 20,000" • Campaign by Rockefeller Sanitary Commission wipes out hookworm disease

1910 NAACP founded • Strike at Hart, Schaffner and Marx leads to pioneering collective bargaining agreement • National Collegiate Athletic Association formed

1911 Fire at the Triangle Shirtwaist Company kills 146 people • Irving Berlin popularizes rhythm of ragtime with "Alexander's Ragtime Band" • Frederick Winslow Taylor publishes *The Principles of Scientific Management*

1912 Harriet Monroe begins publishing magazine *Poetry* • IWW leads strikes in Massachusetts and New Jersey

1913 Ford introduces the moving assembly line in Highland Park, Michigan, plant • Mother's Day becomes national holiday

1915 D. W. Griffith produces the first movie spectacular, *The Birth of a Nation* • T. S. Eliot publishes "The Love Song of J. Alfred Prufrock"

1916 Margaret Sanger forms New York Birth Control League • Federal Aid Roads Act creates national road network • New York Zoning Law sets the pattern for zoning laws across the nation

1917 Congress passes law requiring literacy test for all immigrants

1921 Congress passes the Sheppard-Towner Act to help protect maternal and infant health

1900–1930 (1979); Sheila M. Rothman, *Woman's Proper Place* (1978); and Ellen Condliffe Lagemann, *A Generation of Women: Education in the Lives of the Progressive Reformers* (1979).

Work, workers, and the industrial society are perceptively treated in Herbert G. Gutman, *Work, Culture and Society in Industrializing America* (1977); David Montgomery, *Workers' Control in America: Studies in the History of Work, Technology, and Labor Struggles* (1979) and *The Fall of the House of Labor: The Workplace, the State, and American Labor Activism, 1865–1925* (1987); and David Brody, *Workers in Industrial America: Essays on the Twentieth Century Struggle* (1980). Stephan Thernstrom, *The Other Bostonians* (1973), is the best study of social and economic mobility.

Also on labor and laborers, Patricia A. Cooper, *Once a Cigarmaker: Men, Women, and Work Culture in American Cigar Factories, 1900–1919* (1987); Dorothy Schweider, *Black Diamonds: Life and Work in Iowa's Coal Mining Communities, 1895–1925* (1983); Cathy L. McHugh, *Mill Family: The Labor System in the Southern Cotton Textile Industry, 1880–1915* (1988); Martha Vicinus, *Independent Women: Work and Community for Single Women, 1850–1920* (1985); and Richard Jules Oestreicher, *Solidarity and Fragmentation: Working People and Class Consciousness in Detroit, 1875–1900* (1986).

Roger Burlingame, *Henry Ford* (1954) and Allan Nevins and Frank E. Hill, *Ford*, 3 vols. (1954–1963) cover Ford's career, while Alfred D. Chandler, *Strategy and Structure: Chapters in the History of American Industrial Enterprise* (1962); Bruce E. Seely, *Building the American Highway System: Engineers as Policy Makers* (1987); Martin J. Sklar, *The Corporate Reconstruction of American Capitalism, 1890–1916* (1988); Samuel Haber, *Efficiency and Uplift: Scientific Management in the Progressive Era* (1964); Daniel Nelson, *Frederick W. Taylor and the Rise of Scientific Management* (1980); and Frederick A. White, *American Industrial Research Laboratories* (1961), provide useful overviews. See also Tamara K. Hareven and Randolph Langenbach, *Amoskeag: Life and Work in an American Factory-City* (1978), and Judith Sealander, *Grand Plans: Business Progressivism and Social Change in Ohio's Miami Valley, 1890–1919* (1988).

The labor movement is covered in Harold Livesay, *Samuel Gompers and Organized Labor in America* (1978); Melvyn Dubofsky, *We Shall Be All: A History of the Industrial Workers of the World* (1969) and *"Big Bill" Haywood* (1987); Anne Huber Tripp, *The I.W.W. and the Paterson Silk Strike of 1913* (1987); Steve Golin, *The Fragile Bridge: Paterson Silk Strike of 1913* (1988); Dee Garrison, *Mary Heaton Vorse: The Life of an American Insurgent* (1989); Elizabeth Anne Payne, *Reform, Labor, and Feminism: Margaret Dreier Robins and the Women's Trade Union League* (1988); Leslie Woodcock Tentler, *Wage-Earning Women: Industrial Work and Family Life in the United States, 1900–1930* (1979); Susan Estabrook Kennedy, *If All We Did Was to Weep at Home: A History of White Working Class Women in America* (1979); and Barbara Mayer Wertheimer, *We Were There: The Story of Working Women in America* (1977).

Leonard Dinnerstein, Roger L. Nichols, and David M. Reimers, *Natives and Strangers: Ethnic Groups and the Building of America* (1979), offer a useful overview of Mexican-Americans and the "new" immigrants. See also Oscar Handlin, *The Uprooted* (1951); John Higham, *Strangers in* the Land: Patterns of American Nativism (1955); Josef J. Barton, Peasants and Strangers (1975); Donald B. Cole, Immigrant City: Lawrence, Massachusetts, 1845–1921 (1963); A. T. Lane, Solidarity or Survival? American Labor and European Immigrants, 1830–1924 (1987); and John E. Bodnar, Immigration and Industrialization (1977). Thomas Kessner, The Golden Door, Italian and Jewish Immigrant Mobility in New York City, 1880–1915 (1977), is excellent.

On Du Bois, see Elliot M. Rudwick, W. E. B. Du Bois (1968). Other useful books include George M. Frederickson, The Black Image in the White Mind (1971); Charles F. Kellogg, NAACP: A History of the National Association for the Advancement of Colored People, 1909–1920 (1967); Louis R. Harlan, Separate and Unequal: Public School Campaigns and Racism in the Southern Seaboard States, 1900–1915 (1968); William H. Harris, The Harder We Run: Black Workers Since the Civil War (1982); Allen H. Spear, Black Chicago (1967); and Idus A. Newby, Jim Crow's Defense: Anti-Negro Thought in America, 1900–1930 (1965). Leslie Fishbein, Rebels in Bohemia: The Radicals of the Masses, 1911–1917 (1982); and Dewey W. Grantham, Jr., Hoke Smith and the Politics of the New South (1958) are valuable studies.

For the ways in which Americans entertained themselves, see Gunther Barth, City People (1980); Allison Danzig, History of American Football (1956); Russel B. Nye, The Unembarrassed Muse: The Popular Arts in America (1970); John E. DiMeglio, Vaudeville U.S.A. (1973); Ronald L. Davis, A History of Music in American Life, Volume II: The Gilded Years, 1865–1920 (1980); and Robert Sklar, Movie-Made America: A Social History of the American Movies (1975).

674

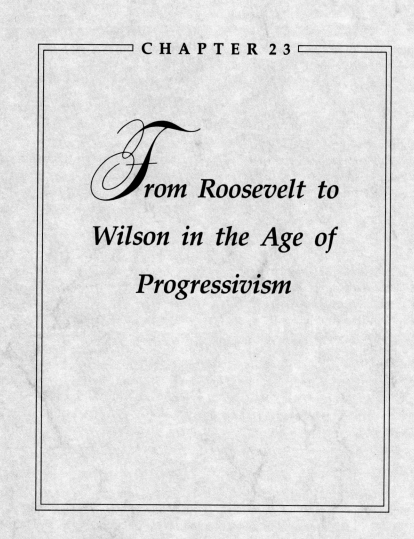

CHAPTER 23

From Roosevelt to Wilson in the Age of Progressivism

On a sunny spring morning in 1909, Theodore Roosevelt, wearing the greatcoat of a colonel of the Rough Riders, left New York for a safari in Africa. An ex-president at the age of fifty, he had turned over the White House to his chosen successor, William Howard Taft, and was now off for "the joy of wandering through lonely lands, the joy of hunting the mighty and terrible lords" of Africa, "where death broods in the dark and silent depths."

Some of Roosevelt's enemies hoped he would not return. "I trust some lion will do its duty," Wall Street magnate J. P. Morgan said. Always prepared, Roosevelt took nine extra pairs of eyeglasses, and just in case, several expert hunters accompanied him. When the nearsighted Roosevelt took aim, three others aimed at the same moment. "Mr. Roosevelt had a fairly good idea of the general direction," the safari leader said, "but we couldn't take chances with the life of a former president." Though he had built a reputation as an ardent conservationist, Roosevelt shot nine lions, five elephants, thirteen rhinoceroses, seven hippopotamuses, and assorted other game—acquiring nearly three hundred trophies in all.

It was all good fun, and afterward Roosevelt set off on a tour of Europe. He attended the funeral of the king of England with the crowned heads of Europe, dined with the king and queen of Italy—an experience he likened to "a Jewish wedding on the East Side of New York"—and happily spent five hours reviewing troops of the German empire. Less happily, he followed events back home where, in the judgment of many friends, Taft was not working out as President. Gifford Pinchot, Roosevelt's close companion in the conservation movement, came to Italy to complain personally about Taft, and at almost every stop there were letters waiting for him from other disappointed Republicans.

For his part, Taft was puzzled by it all. Honest and warmhearted, he had intended to continue Roosevelt's policies, even writing Roosevelt that he would "see to it that your judgment in selecting me as your successor and bringing about that succession shall be vindicated. . . ." But events turned out differently. The conservative and progressive wings of the Republican party split, and Taft often sided with the conservatives. Among progressive Republicans, Taft's troubles stirred talk of a Roosevelt "Back from Elba" movement, akin to Napoleon's return from exile.

Thousands gathered to greet Roosevelt on his return from Europe. He sailed into New York harbor on June 18, 1910, to the sound of naval guns and loud cheers. In characteristic fashion, he had helped make the arrangements: "If there is to be a great crowd, do arrange it so that the whole crowd has a chance to see me and that there is as little disappointment as possible." Greeting Pinchot, one of Taft's leading opponents, with a hearty "Hello, Gifford," Roosevelt slipped away to his home in Oyster Bay, New York, where other friends awaited him.

He carried with him a touching letter from Taft, received just before he left Europe. "I have had a hard time—I do not know that I have had harder luck than other Presidents, but I do know that thus far I have succeeded far less than have others. I have been conscientiously trying to carry out your policies but my method of doing so has not worked smoothly." Taft invited Teddy to spend a night or two at the White House, but Roosevelt declined—saying that ex-presidents should not visit Washington. Relations between the two friends cooled. "It is hard, very hard," Taft said in 1911, "to see a devoted friendship going to pieces like a rope of sand."

A year later, there was no longer thought of friendship, only a desperate fight between Taft and Roosevelt for the Republican presidential nomination. Taft won the nomination, but angry and ambitious, Roosevelt bolted and helped form a new party, the Progressive (or "Bull Moose") party, to unseat Taft and capture the White House. With Taft, Roosevelt, Woodrow Wilson (the Democratic party's candidate), and Socialist party candidate Eugene V. Debs all in the race, the election of 1912 became one of the most exciting in American history.

It was also one of the most important. People were worried about the social and economic effects of urban-industrial growth (see Chapter 22). The election of 1912 provided a forum for those worries, and to a degree unusual in American politics, it pitted deeply opposed candidates against one another and outlined differing views of the nation's future. In the spirited battle between Roosevelt and Wilson, it also brought to the forefront some of the currents of progressive reform.

THE SPIRIT OF PROGRESSIVISM

In one way or another, progressivism touched all aspects of society. Politically, it fostered a reform movement that sought cures for the problems of city, state, and nation. Intellectually, it drew on the expertise of the new social sciences and reflected a shift from older absolutes of class and religion to newer schools of thought that emphasized physiological explanations for behavior, the role of the environment in human development, and the relative nature of truth. Culturally, it inspired fresh modes of expression in dance, film, painting, literature, and architecture. Touching individuals in different ways, progressivism became a set of attitudes as well as a definable movement.

Though broad and diverse, progressivism as a whole had a half-dozen characteristics that gave it definition. First, the progressives acted out of concern about the effects of industrialization and the conditions of industrial life. While their viewpoints varied, they did not, as a rule, set out to harm big business, but instead sought to humanize and regulate it.

In pursuing these objectives, the progressives displayed a second characteristic, a fundamental optimism about human nature, the possibilities of progress, and the capacity of people to recognize problems and take action to solve them. Progressives believed they could "investigate, educate, and legislate"—learn about a problem, inform people about it, and with the help of an informed public, find and enforce a solution.

Third, more than many earlier reformers, the progressives were willing to intervene in people's lives, confident it was their right to do so. They knew best, some of them thought, and as a result, there was an element of coercion in a number of their ideas. Fourth, while progressives preferred if possible to use voluntary means to achieve reform, they tended to turn more and more to the authority of the state and government at all levels, to put into effect the reforms they wanted.

As a fifth characteristic, many progressives drew on a combination of evangelical Protestantism, which gave them the desire (and, they thought, the duty) to purge the world of sins such as prostitution and drunkenness; and the natural and social sciences, the theories of which made them confident that they could understand and control the environment in which people lived. Progressives tended to view the environment as a key to reform, thinking (in the way some economists, sociologists, and other social scientists were suggesting) that if they could change the environment, they could change the individual.

Finally, progressivism was distinctive because it touched virtually the whole nation. Not everyone, of course, was a progressive, and there were many who opposed or ignored the ideas of the movement. But in one way or another, a remarkable number of people were caught up in it, giving progressivism a national reach and a mass base.

That was one of the features, in fact, that set it off from populism, which had grown mostly in the rural South and West. Progressivism drew support across society. "The thing that constantly amazed me," said William Allen White, a leading progressive journalist, "was how many people were with us." Progressivism appealed to the expanding middle class, prosperous farmers, and skilled laborers; it also attracted significant support in the business community.

The progressives believed in progress and disliked waste. No single issue or concern united them all. Some progressives wanted to clean up city governments, others to clean up city streets. Some wanted to purify politics or control corporate abuses, others to eradicate poverty or prostitution. Some demanded social justice in the form of woman's rights, child labor laws, temperance, and factory safety. They were Democrats, Republicans, Socialists, and independents.

Progressives believed in a better world and in the ability of people to achieve it. They paid to people, as a friend said of social reformer Florence Kelley, "the high compliment of believing that, once they knew the truth, they would act upon it." Progress depended on knowledge. The progressives stressed individual morality and collective action, the scientific method, and the value of expert opinion. Like contemporary business leaders, they valued system, planning, management, and predictability. They wanted not only reform but efficiency. In the introduction to *The Shame of the Cities,* Steffens said the cure for American ills lay in "good conduct in the individual, simple honesty, courage, and efficiency."

Historians once viewed progressivism as the

triumph of one group in society over another. In this view, farmers took on the hated and powerful railroads; upstart reformers challenged the city bosses; business interests fought for favorable legislation; youthful professionals carved out their place in society. Now, historians stress the way progressivism brought people together rather than drove them apart. Disparate groups united in an effort to improve the well-being of many groups in society.

The Rise of the Professions

Progressivism fed on an organizational impulse that encouraged people to join forces, share information, and solve problems. Between 1890 and 1920, a host of national societies and associations took shape—nearly four hundred of them in just three decades. Groups such as the National Child Labor Committee, which lobbied for legislation to regulate the employment and working conditions of children, were formed to attack specific issues. Other groups reflected one of the most significant developments in American society at the turn of the century—the rise of the professions.

Growing rapidly in these years, the professions —law, medicine, religion, business, teaching, and social work—were the source of much of the leadership of the progressive movement. The professions attracted young, educated men and women, who in turn were part of a larger trend: a dramatic increase in the number of individuals working in administrative and professional jobs. In businesses, these people were managers, architects, technicians, and accountants. In city governments, they were experts in everything from education to sanitation. They organized and ran the urban-industrial society.

Together these professionals formed part of a new middle class, whose members did not derive their status from birth or inherited wealth, as had many members of the older middle class. Instead, they moved ahead through education and personal accomplishment. They had worked to become doctors, lawyers, ministers, and teachers. Proud of their skills, they were ambitious and self-confident, and they thought of themselves as experts who could use their knowledge for the benefit of society.

As a way of asserting their status, they formed professional societies to look after their interests and govern entry into their professions. Just a few years before, for example, a doctor had become a doctor simply by stocking up on patent medicines and hanging out a sign. The advances in medical and scientific knowledge near the turn of the century (see Chapter 19) made the practice of medicine more respectable. Doctors began to insist that they were part of a medical *profession*, with educational requirements and minimum standards for practice. In 1901, they reorganized the American Medical Association (AMA) and made it into a modern, national professional society. The AMA had 8400 members that year. A decade later, it had over 70,000, and by 1920, nearly two-thirds of all doctors belonged.

Other groups and professions showed the same pattern. Lawyers formed bar associations, created examining boards, and lobbied for regulations restricting entry into the profession. Teachers organized the National Education Association (1905) and pressed for teacher-certification and compulsory education laws. Social workers formed the National Federation of Settlements (1911); business leaders created the National Association of Manufacturers (1895) and the U.S. Chamber of Commerce (1912); and farmers joined the National Farm Bureau Federation to spread information about farming and to try to improve their lot.

Working both as individuals and groups, members of the professions had a major impact on the era, as the career of one of them, Dr. Alice Hamilton, illustrated. Hamilton early decided to devote her life to helping the less fortunate. Choosing medicine, she went to the University of Michigan Medical School, one of a shrinking number of medical schools that admitted women, and then settled in Chicago where she met Jane Addams and took a room in Hull House. Soon thereafter, she traced a local typhoid epidemic to flies carrying germs from open privies. The study won national acclaim, but Hamilton had already turned her attention to the work-related illnesses she found everywhere around Hull House.

Combining field study with meticulous laboratory techniques, she pioneered research into the causes of lead poisoning and other industrial disease. In 1908, the governor of Illinois appointed her to a Commission on Occupational Diseases; two years later, she headed a statewide survey of industrial poisons. Thanks to her work, in 1911, Illinois passed the first state law providing compensation for industrial disease caused by poisonous fumes and dust. By the end of the 1930s, all major industrial states had such laws.

One of the new professionals, Hamilton had used her education and skill to broaden knowledge of her subject, change industrial practices, and improve the lives of countless workers. "For me," she said later in a comment characteristic of the progressives, "the satisfaction is that things are better now, and I had some part in it."

The Social-Justice Movement

As Alice Hamilton's career exemplified, progressivism began in the cities during the 1890s. It first took form around settlement workers and others interested in freeing individuals from the crushing impact of cities and factories.

Ministers, intellectuals, social workers, and lawyers joined in a social-justice movement that focused national attention on the need for tenement house laws, more stringent child labor legislation, and better working conditions for women. They brought pressure on municipal agencies for more and better parks, playgrounds, day nurseries, schools, and community services. Blending private and public action, settlement leaders turned increasingly to government aid. "Private beneficence," Jane Addams said, "is totally inadequate to deal with the vast numbers of the city's disinherited."

Social-justice reformers were more interested in social cures than individual charity. Unlike earlier reformers, they saw problems as endless and interrelated; individuals became part of a city's larger patterns. With that insight, social-service casework shifted from a focus on an individual's well-being to a scientific analysis of neighborhoods, occupations, and classes.

In the spring of 1900, the Charity Organization Society of New York held a tenement-house exhibition that graphically presented the new kind of sociological data. Put together by Lawrence Veiller, a young social worker, the exhibition included over one thousand photographs, detailed maps of slum districts, statistical tables and charts, and graphic cardboard depictions of

An Infant Welfare Society nurse treats the baby of an immigrant family in Chicago. A host of medical discoveries and improvements in the quality of medical education fostered an interest in public health work among the social-justice reformers.

tenement blocks. Never before had so much information been pulled together in one place. Veiller correlated data on poverty and disease with housing conditions, and he pointed out that new slums were springing up in more areas of the city. Stirred by the public outcry, Governor Theodore Roosevelt appointed the New York State Tenement House Commission to do something about the problem.

With Veiller's success as a model, study after study analyzed the condition of the poor. Books and pamphlets like *The Standard of Living Among Working Men's Families in New York City* (1909) contained pages of data on family budgets, women's wages and working conditions, child labor, and other matters. Between 1910 and 1913, the U.S. Commissioner of Labor issued a massive nineteen-volume report on *Conditions of Women and Children Wage-Earners in the United States.*

Banding together to work for change, social-justice reformers formed the National Conference of Charities and Corrections, which in 1915 became the National Conference of Social Work. Controlled by social workers, the conference reflected the growing professionalization of reform. Through it, social workers discovered each other's efforts, shared methodology; and tried to establish themselves as a separate field within the social sciences. Once content with informal training sessions in a settlement-house living room, they now founded complete professional schools at Chicago, Harvard, and other universities. After 1909, they had their own professional magazine, the *Survey*, and instead of piecemeal reforms they aimed at a comprehensive program of minimum wages, maximum hours, workers' compensation, and widows' pensions.

The Purity Crusade

Working in city neighborhoods, social-justice reformers were often struck by the degree to which alcohol affected the lives of the people they were trying to help. Workers drank away their wages; some men spent more time at the saloon than at home. Drunkenness caused violence, and it angered employers who did not want intoxicated workers on the job. In countless ways, alcohol wasted human resources, the reformers believed, and along with business leaders, ministers, and others, they launched a crusade to remove the evils of drink from American life.

At the head of the crusade was the Women's Christian Temperance Union (WCTU), which had continued to grow since it was founded in the 1870s. By 1911, the WCTU had nearly one quarter of a million members, the largest organization of women in American history to that time. In 1893, it was joined by the Anti-Saloon League, and together the groups pressed to abolish alcohol and the places where it was consumed. By 1916, they had succeeded in nineteen states, but as drinking continued elsewhere, they pushed for a nationwide law. In the midst of the moral fervor of World War I, they succeeded, and the Eighteenth Amendment to the Constitution, prohibiting the manufacture, sale, and transportation of intoxicating liquors, took effect in January 1920.

The amendment encountered troubles later in the 1920's as the social atmosphere changed, but at the time it passed, progressives thought prohibition was a major step toward eliminating social instability and moral wrong. In a similar fashion, some progressive reformers also worked to get rid of prostitution, convinced that poverty and ignorance drove women to the trade. By 1915, nearly every state had banned brothels, and in 1910,

Congress passed the Mann Act, which prohibited the interstate transportation of women for immoral purposes. Like the campaign against liquor, the campaign against prostitution reflected the era's desire to purify and elevate, often through the instrument of government action.

Woman Suffrage, Woman's Rights

Women played a very large role in the social-justice movement. Feminists were particularly active, especially in the political sphere, between 1890 and 1914—feminists were more active then, in fact, than at any time until the 1960s. Some working-class women pushed for higher wages and better working conditions. College-educated women—five thousand a year graduated after 1900—took up careers in the professions, from which some of them supported reform. From 1890 to 1910, the work of a number of national women's organizations, including the National Council of Jewish Women, National

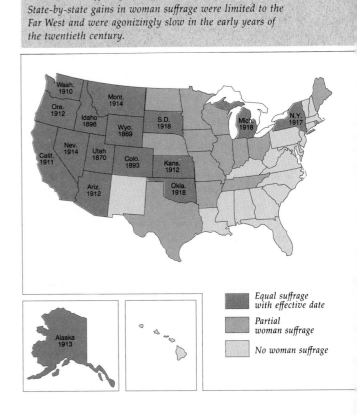

Woman Suffrage Before 1920

State-by-state gains in woman suffrage were limited to the Far West and were agonizingly slow in the early years of the twentieth century.

*W*oman suffrage was a key element in the social-justice movement. Without the right to vote, women working actively for reform had little real power to influence elected officials to support their endeavors.

Congress of Mothers, and the Women's Trade Union League, furthered the aims of the progressive movement.

The National Association of Colored Women was founded in 1895, fifteen years before the better known, male-oriented National Association for the Advancement of Colored People (NAACP). Aimed at social welfare, the women's organization was the first African-American social-service agency in the country. At the local level, African-American women's clubs established kindergartens, day nurseries, playgrounds, and retirement homes.

From 200,000 members in 1900, the General Federation of Women's Clubs grew to over 1 million by 1912. The clubs met, as they had before, for coffee and literary conversation, but they also began to look closely at conditions around them. In 1904, Mrs. Sarah P. Decker, the federation's new president, told the national convention: "Ladies, you have chosen me your leader. Well, I have an important piece of news to give

you. Dante is dead. He has been dead for several centuries, and I think it is time that we dropped the study of his *Inferno* and turned our attention to our own."

Forming an Industrial Section and a Committee on Legislation for Women and Children, the federation supported reforms to safeguard child and women workers, improve schools, ensure pure food, and beautify the community. Reluctant at first, the federation finally lent support in 1914 to woman suffrage, a cause that dated back to the first woman's rights convention in Seneca Falls, New York, in 1848. Divided over tactics since the Civil War, the suffrage movement suffered from disunity, male opposition, indecision over whether to seek action at the state or at the national level, resistance from the Catholic Church, and opposition from liquor interests, who linked the cause to prohibition.

Women in the social-justice movement needed to influence elected officials—most of them men, whom they could not reach through the vote.

Because politics was an avenue for reform, growing numbers of women activists became involved in the suffrage movement. After years of disagreement, the two major suffrage organizations, the National Woman Suffrage Association and the American Woman Suffrage Association, merged in 1890 to form the National American Woman Suffrage Association. The merger opened a new phase of the suffrage movement, characterized by unity and a tightly controlled national organization.

In 1900, Carrie Chapman Catt, a superb organizer, became president of the National American Woman Suffrage Association, which by 1920 had nearly two million members. Catt and Anna Howard Shaw, who became the association's head in 1904, believed in organization and peaceful lobbying to win the vote. Alice Paul and Lucy Burns, founders of the Congressional Union, were more militant; they interrupted public meetings, focused on Congress rather than the states, and in 1917 picketed the White House.

Significantly, Catt, Paul, and others made a major change in the argument for woman suffrage. When the campaign began in the nineteenth century, suffragists had claimed the vote as a natural right, owed to women as much as men. Now, they stressed a pragmatic argument: since women were more sensitive to moral issues than men, they would use their votes to help create a better society. They would support temperance, clean government, laws to protect workers and other reforms. This argument attracted many progressives who believed woman's suffrage would purify politics. In 1918, the House passed a constitutional amendment stating simply that the right to vote shall not be denied "on account of sex." The Senate and enough states followed, and, after three generations of suffragist efforts, the Nineteenth Amendment took effect in 1920.

The social-justice movement had the most success in passing state laws limiting the working hours of women. By 1913, thirty-nine states set maximum working hours for women or banned the employment of women at night. Illinois had a ten-hour law; California and Washington had eight-hour laws. Wisconsin, Oregon, and Kansas allowed expert commissions to set different hours depending on the degree of strain in various occupations. As early as 1900, thanks to groups such as the National Child Labor Committee, twenty-eight states had laws regulating child labor. But the courts often ruled against such laws, and families—needing extra income—sometimes ignored them. Parents sent children off to jobs with orders to lie about their ages.

In 1916, President Woodrow Wilson backed a law to limit child labor, the Keating-Owen Act, but in *Hammer* v. *Dagenhart* (1918) the Supreme Court overturned it as an improper regulation of local labor conditions. In 1919, Congress tried again in the Second Child Labor Act, and in *Bailey* v. *Drexel Furniture Company* (1922) was again struck down. Not until the 1930s did Congress succeed in passing a Court-supported national child labor law.

A Ferment of Ideas

A dramatic shift in ideas became one of the most important forces behind progressive reform. Building on the developments of the 1890s (see Chapter 19), writers in law, economics, history, sociology, psychology, and a host of other fields advanced ideas that together challenged the status quo and called for change.

Most of the ideas focused on the role of the environment in shaping human behavior. Progressive reformers accepted society's growing complexity, called for factual treatment of piecemeal problems, allowed room for new theories, and above all, rejected age-encrusted divine or natural "laws" in favor of thoughts and actions that worked.

A new doctrine, called pragmatism, emerged in this ferment of ideas. It came from William James, a brilliant Harvard psychologist who became the key figure in American thought from the 1890s to World War I. A warm, tolerant person, James was impatient with theories that made truth an abstract and stagnant thing. Truth, he believed, should work for the individual, and it worked best not in abstraction, but in action. "True ideas are those we can assimilate, validate, corroborate, and verify. False ideas are those we cannot."

People, James thought, were not only shaped by their environment; they shaped it. In *Pragmatism* (1907), a book so popular it went through many editions, he praised "tough-minded" individuals who could live effectively in a world with no easy answers. The tough-minded accepted change; they knew how to pick manageable problems, gather facts, discard ideas that did not work, and act on those that did. Ideas that worked became truth. "What is the 'cash value' of a thought, idea, or belief?" James asked. Does it work? Does it make a difference to the individual who experiences it? "The ultimate test for us of what a truth means," said James, "is the conduct it dictates."

The most influential educator of the Progressive Era, John Dewey, applied pragmatism to educational reform. A friend and disciple of William James, he argued that thought evolves in relation to the environment and that education is directly related to experience. In 1896, he and his wife founded a separate School of Pedagogy at the University of Chicago, with a laboratory in which educational theory based on the newer philosophical and psychological studies could be tested and practiced.

Dewey introduced an educational revolution that stressed children's needs and capabilities. He described his beliefs and methods in a number of books, notably *School and Society* (1899) and *Democracy and Education* (1916). New ideas in education, he said, are "as much a product of the changed social situation, and as much an effort to meet the needs of the society that is forming, as are changes in modes of industry and commerce." He opposed memorization, rote learning, and dogmatic, authoritarian teaching methods; he emphasized personal growth, free inquiry, and creativity.

Providing an overarching framework within which others could fit, William James and Dewey had a great effect on other thinkers. Edward A. Ross, a reform sociologist, in *Sin and Society* (1907) called for "pure environmentalism" and a new standard of morality. Economist Richard T. Ely (see Chapter 19) rejected the conservative "laws" of classical economics and developed theories that placed economics in a changing environment. In *The Theory of the Leisure Class* (1899) and *The Instinct of Workmanship* (1914) Thorstein Veblen argued that everything was flux, the only law was the lack of laws, and modern business was an anarchic struggle for profit. Reform, to Veblen, was not only permissible; it was essential to provide order and efficiency in an industrial and entrepreneurial system characterized by disorder.

Rejecting the older view of the law as universal and unchanging, lawyers and legal theorists instead viewed it as a reflection of the environment —an instrument for social change. Law reflected the environment that shaped it. A movement grew among judges for "sociological jurisprudence" that related the law to social reform.

In Denver, Colorado, after Judge Ben Lindsey sentenced a boy to reform school for stealing coal, the boy's mother rushed forward and, grief-stricken, beat her head against the wall. Lindsey investigated the case and he found that the father was a smelting worker dying of lead poisoning; the family needed coal for heat. From such experiences, Lindsey concluded that children were not born with a genetic tendency to crime; they were made good or bad by the environment in which they grew. Lindsey "sentenced" youthful offenders to education and good care. He worked for playgrounds, slum clearance, public baths, and technical schools. Known as the "Kids' Judge," he attracted visitors from as far away as Japan, who wanted to study and copy his methods.

Louis D. Brandeis graduated from Harvard Law School in 1878 and became a corporation lawyer and near-millionaire. But like many others, he changed his mind about social issues during the depression of the 1890s, and as the "People's Attorney," he fought corporate abuses and political corruption. In 1908 he accepted an invitation from the National Consumers' League to defend an Oregon law limiting working hours for women to ten hours a day.

Brandeis decided on a new kind of argument. With the help of Josephine Goldmark, his sister-in-law and the director of research at the National Consumers League, he compiled masses of medical and sociological data, and when he submitted to the Court a 104-page brief, only 2 pages examined traditional legal precedents. The rest included reports from factory inspectors, health and hygiene commissioners, and expert commissions—all showing that the ten-hour law was necessary to protect the health, safety, and morals of women in Oregon.

Agreeing, the Supreme Court in *Muller* v. *Oregon* (1908) upheld the Oregon statute, and the famous "Brandeis Brief," based on sociological data rather than legal precedent, influenced lawyers and courts across the country. Like so many other reform efforts during these years, it focused

Laundry owner Curt Muller (at left, arms folded) challenged an Oregon law limiting the length of the working day for women. Lawyer Louis D. Brandeis (above), used sociological data to defend the law before the Supreme Court.

on the effects of the environment, suggesting that changes in the way in which people lived and worked—through social and political reforms—could improve their condition. Sociological jurisprudence of the kind Brandeis pioneered has played a large role in legal thinking ever since, including in the Supreme Court's 1954 landmark decision to end segregation in the schools.

Socialism, a reformist political philosophy, grew dramatically before the First World War. Socialist political parties, composed of followers of Karl Marx, first appeared in New York, Chicago, Milwaukee, and other cities after the Civil War. They urged workers to join a worldwide revolution to overthrow capitalism. Such public appeals, however, drew little support. Leaders of a new Socialist Labor party, founded in 1877, tried in secret to gain control of important labor unions. That strategy also failed.

Daniel De Leon, a brilliant tactician, took over leadership of the Socialist Labor party during the 1890s, but he too lacked mass support. Arguing for a more moderate form of socialism, Eugene V. Debs, president of the American Railway Union, in 1896 formed a rival organization, the Social Democratic party. Gentle and reflective, not at all

the popular image of the wild-eyed radical, Debs was thrust into prominence by the Pullman strike (see Chapter 20). In 1901, persuading opponents of De Leon to join him, he formed the important Socialist party of America. Neither Debs nor the party ever developed a cohesive platform, nor was Debs an effective organizer. But he was eloquent, passionate, and visionary. An excellent speaker, he captivated audiences, attacking the injustices of capitalism and urging a workers' republic.

The Socialist party of America enlisted some intellectuals, factory workers, disillusioned Populists, tenant farmers, miners, and lumberjacks. By 1911, there were Socialist mayors in thirty-two cities, including Berkeley, California; Butte, Montana; and Flint, Michigan. Although its doctrines were aimed at an urban proletariat, the Socialist party drew support in rural Texas, Missouri, Arkansas, Idaho, and Washington. In Oklahoma, it attracted as much as one-third of the vote. Most Socialists who won promised progressive reform rather than threatening to overthrow capitalists.

Although torn by factions, the Socialist party doubled in membership between 1904 and 1908, then tripled in the four years after that. Running for president, Debs garnered 100,000 votes in 1900; 400,000 in 1904; and 900,000 in 1912, the party's peak year.

REFORM IN THE CITIES AND STATES

Desiring reform, the progressives realized government could be a crucial agent in accomplishing their goals. They wanted to curb the influence of "special interests" and, through such measures of political reform as the direct primary and the direct election of senators, make government follow the public will. Once it did, they welcomed government action at whatever level was appropriate.

As a result of this thinking, the use of federal power increased, as did the power and prestige of the presidency. Progressives not only lobbied for government-sponsored reform, but also worked actively in their home neighborhoods, cities, and states; much of the significant change occurred in local settings, outside the national limelight. Most important, the progressives believed in the ability of experts to solve problems. At every level—local, state, and federal—thousands of commissions and agencies took form. Staffed by trained experts, they oversaw a multitude of matters ranging from railroad rates to public health.

Interest Groups and the Decline of Popular Politics

Placing government in the hands of experts was one way to get it out of the hands of politicians and political parties. The direct primary was another way. These initiatives and others like them were part of a fundamental change in the way Americans viewed their political system.

As one sign of the change, fewer and fewer people were going to the polls. Voter turnout dropped dramatically after 1900 when the intense partisanship of the decades after the Civil War gave way to media-oriented political campaigns based largely on the personalities of the candidates. From 1876 to 1900, the average turnout in presidential elections was 77 percent. From 1900 to 1916, it was 65 percent, and in the 1920s,

it dropped to 52 percent, close to the average today. Turnout was lowest among young people, immigrants, the poor and, ironically, the newly enfranchised women.

It was particularly low in the South where conservative whites used restrictive election laws to keep blacks and others from the polls. Turnout in the South fell sharply, from an average of 64 percent in the presidential elections of the 1880s to just 20 percent in 1920 and 1924. Although the decline in the North was less sharp, the reasons for it were more complex. By the 1920s, as many as one-quarter of all eligible Northern voters never cast a ballot.

There were numerous causes for the fall-off, but among the most important was the fact that people had found another way to achieve some of the objectives they had once assigned to political parties. They had found the "interest group," a means of action that assumed importance in this era and became a major feature of politics ever after. Professional societies, trade associations, labor organizations, farm lobbies, and scores of other interest groups worked outside the party system to pressure government for things their members wanted. Social workers, women's clubs, reform groups, and others learned to apply pressure in similar ways, and the result was much significant legislation of the Progressive Era.

Reform in the Cities

During the early years of the twentieth century, urban reform movements, many of them born in the depression of the 1890s, spread across the nation. In 1894, the National Municipal League was organized, and it became the forum for debate over civic reform, changes in the tax laws, and municipal ownership of public utilities. Within a few years, nearly every city had a variety of clubs and organizations directed at improving the quality of city life.

"For two generations," Frederic C. Howe said in 1905, "we have wrought out the most admirable laws and then left the government to run itself. This has been our greatest fault." In the 1880s, reformers like Howe would call an evening conference, pass resolutions, and then go home; after 1900, they formed associations, adopted long-range policies, and hired a staff to

Margaret Sanger and the Birth-Control Movement

Margaret Higgins Sanger, founder of the American Birth Control League (1921) which later became the Planned Parenthood Federation of America.

At the start of the twentieth century, birth control was an issue fraught with social and religious controversy. Devout Christians—Protestants and Catholics—opposed it as a violation of God's law; the overseers of society's moral behavior feared it might foster promiscuity. Theodore Roosevelt said it meant "race death: a sin for which there is no atonement." The Comstock Act of 1873 banned from the U.S. mails all information on birth control, and by 1914 twenty-two states had enacted laws that hindered the dissemination of such information. That year Margaret Sanger formally launched her campaign for birth control.

Born in 1883, Sanger grew up in Corning, New York, an upstate factory town. Her father, an Irish-born stonecutter, encouraged his children to think for themselves. "Leave the world better because you, my child, have dwelt in it," he told Margaret. One of eleven children, Margaret from an early age linked poverty to large families. "Our childhood," she said, "was one of longing for things that were always denied."

Longing for excitement and romance, Sanger settled in New York City, married, and had three children. Restless, and finding her marriage confining, she discovered Greenwich Village, a favorite haunt of the period's intense young radicals. On McDougal Street in the Village, Sanger met Socialist leader Eugene V. Debs; young reporter and revolutionary, John Reed, later to be honored by the Bolsheviks and buried in the Kremlin; William D. "Big Bill" Haywood of the radical Industrial Workers of the World (IWW); and feminist and socialist agitator, Emma Goldman.

The Village was filled with people determined to improve the world. Stimulated by the exciting talk, Sanger joined the Socialist party and worked to organize women for socialism in New York City. In 1912 she marched in the IWW picket lines in the great strike at the textile mills in Paterson, New Jersey. Pursuing a nursing career, Sanger worked on the lower East Side of New York where thousands upon thousands of people were crowded into tenement houses. Struck by the ignorance of tenement women about their own bodies, she wrote in 1912 a series of newspaper articles about venereal disease and personal hygiene, entitled "What Every Girl Should Know"; the Post Office Department banned it from the mails.

That same year Sanger watched at the bedside of Sadie Sachs, a poor working woman dying from a self-induced abortion. Warned that she might not survive another pregnancy, Sachs had asked for contraceptive advice, but the doctor had suggested only that she make her husband sleep on the roof. After Sachs died, Sanger spent hours walking the streets and thinking about birth and children and poverty. She resolved that night, she later said, "to seek out the root of the evil, to do something to change the destiny of mothers whose miseries were as vast as the sky."

The answer was birth control—a term she and several friends coined in 1914. Sanger spent a year absorbing medical opinion and learning about contraceptives, and then began publishing the journal *Woman Rebel* which urged "women to look the whole world in the face with a go-to-hell look in the eyes; to have an ideal; to speak and act in defiance of convention." Aimed at the working class, the journal touched on birth control, but its chief focus was on social revolution, particularly on raising the social consciousness of working women. It ran for only seven issues before it was banned by the post office. Sanger, indicted under the

Comstock Act, fled to Europe.

There, after considerable reflection, she decided that birth control was a medical matter, not a social or revolutionary one. It belonged in the hands of physicians and their patients, with physicians free to prescribe contraception and other measures when appropriate. Women should "decide for themselves whether they shall become mothers, under what conditions, and when." Working through the National Birth Control League and other groups, Sanger broadened the movement's base beyond the socialists and feminists who had originally backed it. Settlement-house workers had been cool to birth control at first, but soon they too lent support.

Sanger returned to the United States, and the government, preoccupied with other issues, dropped the indictment against her. In October 1916, again defying the law, she opened the nation's first birth-control clinic in the teeming Brownsville section of Brooklyn,

New York. Police soon raided the clinic, and Sanger was sentenced to thirty days in jail. On appeal, the New York State Court of Appeals upheld the sentence, but in a victory for Sanger, it ruled that physicians should have greater discretion in prescribing birth control.

Late in 1916 Sanger formed the New York Birth Control League to push for legislation to give physicians even broader discretion. The league's argument that birth control would be an effective means of promoting the social welfare was a persuasive idea that convinced a wide variety of groups. Some reformers thought that smaller families would raise the standard of living of the poor. Other people thought birth control might limit the number of "undesirables" in the population. Eugenicists who wanted to improve the human species through genetic control saw it as a way to reduce the proportion of the unwanted and unfit in the society. Gradually Sanger herself reflected such arguments. "More

children from the fit, less from the unfit—that is the chief issue," she said in 1919.

In 1921 Sanger organized a nationwide movement through the American Birth Control League; it held clinics and conferences to educate the public. Although the Catholic Church remained opposed, the movement spread among Protestants, Jews, and those who did not attend church. In 1940 Eleanor Roosevelt, the popular First Lady, came out in support of family planning, and by the 1940s every state with the exception of Massachusetts and Connecticut had legalized the distribution of birth-control information.

When Margaret Sanger died in 1966, the birth-control pill had the approval of the Federal Drug Administration, and its use was widespread. The cause she had championed—once thought so shocking and radical—was won in American society.

*V*olunteers selling copies of the Birth Control League's "Birth Control Review."

achieve them. In the mid-1890s, only Chicago had an urban reform league with a full-time paid executive; within a decade, there were such leagues in every major city.

In city after city reformers reordered municipal government. Tightening controls on corporate activities, they broadened the scope of utility regulation and restricted city franchises. They updated tax assessments, often skewed in favor of corporations, and tried to clean up the electoral machinery. Devoted to efficiency, they developed a trained civil service to oversee planning and operations. The generation of the 1880s also had believed in civil service, but the goal then was mostly negative: to get spoilsmen out and "good" people in. Now the goal was efficiency and, above all, results.

In constructing their model governments, urban reformers often turned to recent advances in business management and organization. They stressed continuity and expertise, a system in which professional experts staffed a government overseen by elective officials. At the top, the elected leader surveyed the breadth of city, state, or national affairs and defined directions. Below, a corps of experts—trained in the various disciplines of the new society—funneled the definition into specific, scientifically based policies.

Reformers thus created a growing number of regulatory commissions and municipal departments. They hired engineers to oversee utility and water systems, physicians and nurses to improve municipal health, and city planners to oversee park and highway development. They created specialized "academies" to train police and firefighters. Imitated by the state and federal governments, the proliferation of experts and commissions widened the gap between voters and decision makers but dramatically improved the efficiency of government.

As cities exploded in size, they freed themselves from the tight controls of state legislatures and began to experiment with their own governments. Struggling to recover from a devastating hurricane in 1900, Galveston, Texas, pioneered the commission form of government: a form of municipal government in which commissions of appointed experts, rather than elected officials, ran the city. Wanting nonpartisan expertise, Staunton, Virginia, was the first city to hire a city manager. Other cities followed, and by 1910 over one hundred cities were using either the commission or manager type of government.

In the race for reform, a number of city mayors won national reputations—among them Seth Low in New York City and Hazen S. Pingree in Detroit—working to modernize taxes, clean up politics, lower utility rates, and control the awarding of valuable city franchises. In Toledo, Ohio, Mayor Samuel M. ("Golden Rule") Jones, a wealthy manufacturer, took billy clubs away from the police, established free kindergartens, playgrounds, and night schools, and improved wages for city workers.

In Cleveland, Ohio, Tom L. Johnson demonstrated an innovative approach to city government. A millionaire who had made his fortune manipulating city franchises, Johnson one day read Henry George's *Progress and Poverty* (see Chapter 19) and turned to reform. Elected mayor of Cleveland, he served from 1901 to 1909 and collected a group of aggressive and talented young advisers. Frederic C. Howe, Newton D. Baker, and Edward Bemis—all of whom later won national reputations—shaped Johnson's ideas on taxes, prison reform, utility regulation, and other issues facing the city.

Johnson combined shrewdness and showmanship. Believing in an informed citizenry, he held outdoor meetings in huge tents. He used colorful charts to give Cleveland residents a course in utilities and taxation. He cut down on corruption, cut off special privilege, updated taxes, and gave Cleveland a reputation as the country's best-governed city.

Finding it difficult to regulate powerful city utilities and keep their costs down, Johnson and mayors in other cities turned more and more to public ownership of gas, electricity, water, and transportation. Called "gas and water socialism," the idea spread swiftly. In 1896, fewer than half of American cities owned their own waterworks; by 1915, almost two-thirds did.

Action in the States

Reformers soon discovered, however, that many problems lay beyond a city's boundaries, and they turned for action to the state governments. From the 1890s to 1920, reformers worked to stiffen state laws regulating the labor of women and children, to create and strengthen commissions to regulate railroads and utilities, to impose corporate and inheritance taxes, to improve mental and penal institutions, and to allocate more funds for state universities, which were viewed as the training ground for the experts and educated citizenry needed for the new society.

Maryland passed the first workers' compensation law in 1902; soon most industrial states had such legislation. After 1900, many states adopted factory inspection laws, and by 1916, almost two-thirds of the states mandated insurance for the victims of factory accidents. By 1914, twenty-five states had enacted employers' liability laws.

New York was one of the states that led the way in adopting significant reforms. Around 1905, a series of dramatic investigations in the state revealed a systematic and corrupt alliance between politicians and business leaders in the gas, electricity, and insurance industries—all of which directly touched the general public. An angry public responded immediately, supporting greater state regulation and management by independent expert commissions. In 1905 and 1906, the state established regulatory boards to oversee utilities and insurance; it also outlawed corporate contributions to political campaigns and restricted business lobbying in the state legislature.

To regulate business, virtually every state created regulatory commissions empowered to examine corporate books and hold public hearings. Building on earlier experience, state commissions after 1900 were given new power to initiate actions, rather than await complaints, and in some cases to set maximum prices and rates. Dictating company practices, they pioneered regulatory methods later adopted in federal legislation of 1906 and 1910. Some business leaders supported the federal laws in order to get rid of "the intolerable supervision" of dozens of separate state commissions.

Historians have long praised the regulation movement, but the commissions did not always act wisely or even in the public interest. Elective commissions often produced commissioners who had little knowledge of corporate affairs. In addition, to win election, some promised specific rates or reforms, obligations which might bias the commission's investigative functions. Appointive commissions sometimes fared better, but they too had to oversee extraordinarily complex business-

*T*he most famous of the reform leaders in the states was Wisconsin's Robert M. "Fighting Bob" La Follette.

es like the railroads. Shaping everything from wages to train schedules, the regulatory commissions affected railroad profits and growth negatively, and in the end, damaged the railroad industry.

To the progressives, commissions offered a way to end the corrupt alliance between business and politics. There was another way, too, and that was to "democratize" government by reducing the power of politicians and increasing the influence of the electorate. To do that, progressives backed three measures to make officeholders responsive to popular will: the initiative, which allowed voters to propose new laws; the referendum, which allowed them to accept or reject a law at the ballot box; and the recall, which gave them a way to remove an elected official from office.

Oregon adopted the initiative and referendum in 1902; by 1912, twelve states had them. That year Congress added the Seventeenth Amendment to the Constitution to provide for the direct election of U.S. senators. By 1916, all but three states had direct primaries, which allowed the people, rather than nominating conventions, to choose candidates for office.

As attention shifted from the cities to the states, reform governors throughout the country earned greater visibility. Joseph Folk, Steffens's hero in

Saint Louis, became the governor of Missouri in 1904. Hiram Johnson won fame in California for his shrewd and forceful campaign against the Southern Pacific Railroad. In the East, the cause of reform was upheld by Charles Evans Hughes in New York and Woodrow Wilson, the former president of Princeton University, in New Jersey.

Robert M. La Follette became the most famous reform governor. A graduate of the University of Wisconsin, La Follette served three terms in Congress during the late 1880s. A staunch Republican, he supported the tariff and other Republican doctrines but the Democratic landslide of 1890 turned him out of office. Moving to state politics, he became interested in reform, spurred in part, as so many were, by the depression of the 1890s. In 1901, he became governor of Wisconsin. Then forty-five years old, La Follette was talented, aggressive, and a superb stump speaker.

In the following six years, he put together the "Wisconsin Idea," one of the most important reform programs in the history of state government. He established an industrial commission, the first in the country, to regulate factory safety and sanitation. He improved education, workers' compensation, public utility controls, and resource conservation. He lowered railroad rates and raised railroad taxes. Under La Follette's prodding, Wisconsin became the first state to adopt a direct primary for all political nominations. It also became the first to adopt a state income tax.

Like other progressives, La Follette drew on expert advice and relied on academic figures like Richard Ely and Edward Ross at the University of Wisconsin. La Follette supporters established the first Legislative Reference Bureau in the university's library; the bureau stocked the governor and his allies with facts and figures to support the measures they wanted. Theodore Roosevelt called La Follette's Wisconsin "the laboratory of democracy," and the "Wisconsin Idea" soon spread to many other states, including New York, California, Michigan, Iowa, and Texas.

After 1905, the progressives looked more and more to Washington. For one thing, Teddy Roosevelt was there, with his zest for publicity and alluring grin. But progressives also had a growing sense that many concerns—corporations and conservation, factory safety and child labor—crossed state lines. Federal action seemed desirable; specific reforms fit into a larger plan perhaps best seen from the nation's center. Within a few years, La Follette and Hiram Johnson became senators, and while reform went on back home, the focus of progressivism shifted to Washington.

THE REPUBLICAN ROOSEVELT

In September 1901, President William McKinley died of gunshot wounds (see Chapter 20); Vice-President Theodore Roosevelt succeeded him in the White House. McKinley and Roosevelt had moved in similar directions, and the new President initially vowed to carry on McKinley's policies. He continued some, developed others of his own, and in the end brought to them all the particular exuberance of his own personality.

At age forty-two, Roosevelt was then the youngest President in American history. In contrast to the dignified McKinley, he was open, aggressive, and high-spirited. At his desk by 8:30 every morning, he worked through the day, usually with visitors for breakfast, lunch, and dinner. Politicians, labor leaders, industrialists, poets, artists, and writers paraded through the White House.

In personal conversation Roosevelt was persuasive and charming. He read widely and he held opinions on every issue—literature, art, marriage, divorce, conservation, business, football, and even spelling. An advocate of simplified spelling, he once instructed government printers to use "thru" for "through" and "dropt" for "dropped." Public opposition forced him to withdraw the order, and shortly afterward, as he was watching a naval review in Long Island Sound, a launch marked "Pres Bot" steamed by. Roosevelt laughed with delight.

If McKinley cut down on presidential isolation, Roosevelt virtually ended it. The presidency, he thought, was "the bully pulpit," a forum of ideas and leadership for the nation. The President was "a steward of the people bound actively and affirmatively to do all he could for the people." Self-confident, Roosevelt enlisted talented associates, including Elihu Root, secretary of war and later secretary of state; William Howard Taft, secretary of war; Gifford Pinchot, the nation's chief forester and leading conservationist; and Oliver Wendell Holmes, Jr., whom he named to the Supreme Court.

In 1901, Roosevelt invited Booker T. Washing-

Theodore Roosevelt is shown here addressing a group of African-American businessmen in 1910. Booker T. Washington is seated next to Roosevelt.

ton, the prominent African-American educator, to dinner at the White House. Many Southerners protested—"a crime equal to treason," a newspaper said—and they protested again when Roosevelt appointed several African Americans to important federal offices in South Carolina and Mississippi. At first Roosevelt considered building a biracial, "black-and-tan" southern Republican party, thinking it would foster racial progress and his own renomination in 1904. He denounced lynching and ordered the Justice Department to act against peonage.

But Roosevelt soon retreated. In some areas of the South, he supported "lily-white" Republican organizations, and his policies often reflected his own belief in African-American inferiority. He said nothing when a race riot broke out in Atlanta in 1906, although twelve persons died. He joined others in blaming African-American soldiers stationed near Brownsville, Texas, after a night of violence there in August 1906. Acting quickly and on little evidence, he discharged "without honor" three companies of African-American troops. Six of the soldiers who were discharged held the Congressional Medal of Honor.

Busting the Trusts

"There is a widespread conviction in the minds of the American people that the great corporations known as trusts are in certain of their features and tendencies hurtful to the general welfare,"

Roosevelt reported to Congress in 1901. Like most people, however, the President wavered on the trusts. Large-scale production and industrial growth, he believed, were natural and beneficial; they needed only to be controlled. Still he distrusted the trusts' impact on local enterprise and individual opportunity. Distinguishing between "good" and "bad" trusts, he pledged to protect the former while controlling the latter.

At first, Roosevelt hoped the combination of investigative journalism and public opinion would be enough to uncover and correct business evils, and in public he both praised and attacked the trusts. Mr. Dooley poked fun at his wavering: "'Th' trusts,' says he, 'are heejous monsthers built up be th' enlightened intherprise iv th' men that have done so much to advance progress in our beloved country,' he says. 'On wan hand I wud stamp thim undher fut; on th' other hand not so fast.'"

In 1903, Roosevelt asked Congress to create a Department of Commerce and Labor, with a Bureau of Corporations empowered to investigate corporations engaged in interstate commerce. Congress balked; Roosevelt called in reporters, and in an off-the-record interview, charged that John D. Rockefeller had organized the opposition to the measure. The press spread the word, and in the outcry that followed, the proposal passed easily in a matter of weeks. Roosevelt was delighted. With the new Bureau of Corporations publicizing its findings, he thought, the glare of publicity would eliminate most corporate abuses.

A 1904 cartoon depicts TR as "Jack the Giant-Killer," battling the Wall Street titans. Actually, Roosevelt dissolved relatively few trusts.

Roosevelt also undertook direct legal action. On February 18, 1902, he instructed the Justice Department to bring suit against the Northern Securities Company for violation of the Sherman Antitrust Act. It was a shrewd move. A mammoth holding company, Northern Securities controlled the massive rail networks of the Northern Pacific, Great Northern, and Chicago, Burlington & Quincy railroads. Some of the most prominent names in business were behind the giant company—J. P. Morgan and Company; the Rockefeller interests; Kuhn, Loeb and Company; and railroad operators James J. Hill and Edward H. Harriman.

Shocked by Roosevelt's action, Morgan charged that the President had not acted like a "gentleman," and Hill talked glumly of having "to fight for our lives against the political adventurers who have never done anything but pose and draw a salary." Morgan rushed to Washing-

ton to complain and to ask whether there were plans to "attack my other interests," notably U.S. Steel. "No," Roosevelt replied, "unless we find out they have done something that we regard as wrong."

In 1904, the Supreme Court, in a five to four decision, upheld the suit against Northern Securities and ordered the company dissolved. Roosevelt was jubilant, and he followed up the victory with several other antitrust suits. In 1902, he had moved against the beef trust, an action applauded by western farmers and urban consumers alike. After a lull, he initiated suits in 1906 and 1907 against the American Tobacco Company, the Du Pont Corporation, the New Haven Railroad, and Standard Oil.

But Roosevelt's policies were not always clear, nor his actions always consistent. He invited Morgan to the White House to confer with him and allowed the president of National City Bank to preview a draft of the President's third annual message to Congress. Roosevelt also asked for (and received) business support in his bid for reelection in 1904. Large donations came in from industrial leaders, and Morgan himself later testified that he gave $150,000 to Roosevelt's campaign. In 1907, acting in part to avert a threatened financial panic, the President permitted Morgan's U.S. Steel to absorb the Tennessee Coal and Iron Company, an important competitor.

Roosevelt, in truth, was not a "trust-buster," although he was frequently called that. William Howard Taft, his successor in the White House, initiated forty-three antitrust indictments in four years—nearly twice as many as the twenty-five Roosevelt initiated in the seven years of his presidency. Instead, Roosevelt used antitrust threats to keep businesses within bounds. Regulation, he believed, was a better way to control large-scale enterprise.

"Square Deal" in the Coalfields

A few months after announcing the Northern Securities suit, Roosevelt intervened in a major labor dispute involving the anthracite coal miners of northeastern Pennsylvania. Led by John Mitchell, a moderate labor leader, the United Mine Workers demanded wage increases, an eight-hour workday, and company recognition of the union. The coal companies refused, and in May 1902, 140,000 miners walked off the job. The mines closed.

As the months passed and the strike continued, coal prices rose. With winter coming on, schools, hospitals, and factories ran short of coal. Public opinion turned against the companies. Morgan and other industrial leaders privately urged them to settle, but George F. Baer, head of one of the largest companies, refused: "The rights and interests of the laboring man," Baer said, "will be protected and cared for—not by the labor agitators, but by the Christian men to whom God in his infinite wisdom has given the control of the property interests of this country."

Roosevelt was furious. Complaining of the companies' arrogance, he invited both sides in the dispute to an October 1902 conference at the White House. There, Mitchell took a moderate tone and offered to submit the issues to arbitration, but the companies again refused to budge. Roosevelt ordered the army to prepare to seize the mines and then leaked word of his intent to Wall Street leaders.

Alarmed, Morgan and others again urged settlement of the dispute, and at last the companies retreated. They agreed to accept the recommendations of an independent commission the President would appoint. In late October, the strikers returned to work, and in March 1903, the commission awarded them a 10 percent wage increase and a cut in working hours. It recommended, however, against union recognition. The coal companies, in turn, were encouraged to raise prices to offset the wage increase.

More and more, Roosevelt saw the federal government as an honest and impartial "broker" between powerful elements in society. Rather than leaning toward labor, he pursued a middle way to curb corporate and labor abuses, abolish privilege, and enlarge individual opportunity. Conservative by temperament, he sometimes backed reforms in part to head off more radical measures.

During the 1904 campaign, Roosevelt called his actions in the coal miners' strike a "square deal" for both labor and capital, a term that stuck to his administration. His actions stood in powerful contrast to Grover Cleveland's in the 1894 Pullman strike (see Chapter 20). Roosevelt was not the first President to take a stand for labor, but he was the first to bring opposing sides in a labor dispute to the White House to settle it. He was the first to threaten to seize a major industry, and he was the first to appoint an arbitration commission whose decision both sides agreed to accept.

Another Term

In the election of 1904, the popular Roosevelt soundly drubbed his Democratic opponent, Alton B. Parker of New York, and the Socialist party candidate, Eugene V. Debs of Indiana. Roosevelt attracted a large campaign chest and won votes everywhere. In a landslide victory, he received 57 percent of the vote to Parker's 38 percent, and on election night, he savored the public's confidence. Overjoyed, he pledged that "under no circumstances will I be a candidate for or accept another nomination," a statement he later regretted.

Following his election, Roosevelt in late 1904 laid out a reform program that included railroad regulation, employers' liability for federal employees, greater federal control over corporations, and laws regulating child labor, factory inspection, and slum clearance in the District of Columbia. He turned first to railroad regulation. In 1903, he had worked with Congress to pass the Elkins Act to prohibit railroad rebates and increase the powers of the Interstate Commerce Commission (ICC). The Elkins Act, a moderate law, was framed with the consent of railroad leaders. In 1904 and 1905, the President wanted much more, and he urged Congress to empower the ICC to set reasonable and nondiscriminatory rates and prevent inequitable practices.

Widespread demand for railroad regulation strengthened Roosevelt's hand. In the Midwest and Far West, the issue was a popular one, and

The Election of 1904			
Candidate	Party	Popular Vote	Electoral Vote
T. Roosevelt	Republican	7,626,593	336
Parker	Democrat	5,082,898	140
Debs	Socialist	402,489	0
Swallow	Prohibition	258,596	0

reform Governors La Follette in Wisconsin and Albert B. Cummins in Iowa urged federal action. Roosevelt maneuvered cannily. As the legislative battle opened, he released figures showing that Standard Oil had reaped $750,000 a year from railroad rebates. He also skillfully traded congressional support for a strong railroad measure in return for his promise to postpone a reduction of the tariff, a stratagem that came back to plague President Taft.

Triumph came with passage of the Hepburn Act of 1906. A significant achievement, the act strengthened the rate-making power of the Interstate Commerce Commission. It increased membership on the ICC from five to seven, empowered it to fix reasonable maximum railroad rates, and broadened its jurisdiction to include oil-pipeline, express, and sleeping-car companies. ICC orders were binding, pending any court appeals, thus placing the burden of proof of injustice upon the companies. Delighted, Roosevelt viewed the Hepburn Act as a major step in his plan for continuous, expert federal control over industry.

Soon he was dealing with two other important bills, these aimed at regulating the food and drug industries. Muckraking articles had touched frequently on filthy conditions in meat-packing houses, but Upton Sinclair's *The Jungle* (1906) set off a storm of indignation. Ironically, Sinclair had set out to write a novel about the packinghouse workers, the "wage slaves of the Beef Trust," hoping to do for wage slavery what Harriet Beecher Stowe had done for chattel slavery. But readers largely ignored his story of the workers and seized instead on the graphic descriptions of the things that went into their meat:

> There would be meat stored in great piles in rooms; and the water from leaky roofs would drip over it, and thousands of rats would race about on it. It was too dark in these storage places to see well, but a man could run his hand over these piles of meat and sweep off handfuls of the dried dung of rats. These rats were nuisances, and the packers would put poisoned bread out for them; they would die, and then rats, bread, and meat would go into the hoppers together.

Sinclair was disappointed at the reaction. "I aimed at the public's heart," he later said, "and by accident I hit it in the stomach." He had, indeed. After reading *The Jungle*, Roosevelt or-

Early twentieth-century meat processing scenes like this are idyllic compared to those described in Upton Sinclair's The Jungle, *which became the most successful of the muckraking books.*

dered an investigation. The result, he said, was "hideous," and he threatened to publish the entire "sickening report" if Congress did not act. Meat sales plummeted in the United States and Europe. Demand for reform grew. Alarmed, the meat packers themselves supported a reform law, which they hoped would be just strong enough to still the clamor. The Meat Inspection Act of 1906, stronger than the packers wanted, set rules for sanitary meat packing and government inspection of meat products.

A second measure, the Pure Food and Drug Act, passed more easily. Samuel Hopkins Adams, a muckraker, exposed the dangers of patent medicines in several sensational articles in *Collier's*. Patent medicines, Adams pointed out, contained mostly alcohol, drugs, and "undiluted fraud." Dr. Harvey W. Wiley, the chief chemist in the Department of Agriculture, led a "poison squad" of young assistants who experimented with the medicines. With evidence in hand, Wiley pushed for regulation; Roosevelt and the recently reorganized American Medical Association joined the fight, and the act passed on June 30, 1906. Requiring manufacturers to list certain ingredients on the label, it represented a pioneering effort to ban the manufacture and sale of adulterated, misbranded, or unsanitary food or drugs.

An expert on birds, Roosevelt loved nature and the wilderness, and some of his most enduring accomplishments came in the field of conservation. Working closely with Gifford Pinchot, Chief of the Forest Service, he established the first comprehensive national conservation policy. He undertook a major reclamation program, created the federal Reclamation Service, and strengthened the forest preserve program in the Department of Agriculture. Broadening the concept of conservation, he placed power sites, coal lands, and oil reserves as well as national forests in the public domain.

When Roosevelt took office in 1901, there were 45 million acres in government preserves. In 1908, there were almost 195 million. That year, he called a National Conservation Congress attended by forty-four governors and hundreds of experts. Roosevelt formed the National Commission on the Conservation of Natural Resources to look after waters, forests, lands, and minerals. With Pinchot as head, it drew up an inventory of the nation's natural resources.

As 1908 approached, Roosevelt became increasingly strident in his demand for sweeping reforms. He attacked "malefactors of great wealth," urged greater federal regulatory powers, criticized the conservatism of the federal courts, and called for laws protecting factory workers. Many business leaders blamed him for a severe financial panic in the autumn of 1907, and conservatives in Congress stiffened their opposition. Divisions between Republican conservatives and progressives grew.

Immensely popular, Roosevelt prepared in 1908 to turn over the White House to William

*N*aturalist John Muir (shown here with TR) influenced the conservation policies of Roosevelt and played a role in the establishment of many national parks.

Howard Taft, his close friend and colleague. "The Roosevelt policies will not go out with the Roosevelt administration," a party leader said. "If Taft weakens, he will annihilate himself." As expected, Taft soundly defeated the Democratic standard-bearer William Jennings Bryan, who was making his third try for the presidency. The Republicans retained control of Congress. Taft prepared to move into the White House, ready and willing to carry on the Roosevelt legacy.

THE ORDEAL OF WILLIAM HOWARD TAFT

The Republican national convention that nominated Taft had not satisfied either Roosevelt or Taft. True, Taft won the presidential nomination as planned, but conservative Republicans beat back the attempts of progressive Republicans to influence the convention. They named a conservative, James S. Sherman, for vice-president, and built a platform that reflected conservative views on labor, the courts, and other issues. Taft wanted a pledge to lower the tariff but got only a promise

The Election of 1908

Candidate	Party	Popular Vote	Electoral Vote
Taft	Republican	7,676,258	321
Bryan	Democrat	6,406,801	162
Debs	Socialist	420,380	0
Chafin	Prohibition	252,821	0

of revision, which might lower—or raise—it. La Follette, Cummins, Jonathan P. Dolliver of Iowa, Albert J. Beveridge of Indiana, and other progressive Republicans were openly disappointed.

Taking office in 1909, Taft felt "just a bit like a fish out of water." The son of a distinguished Ohio family, and a graduate of Yale Law School, he became an Ohio judge, solicitor general of the United States, and a judge of the federal circuit court. In 1900, McKinley asked him to head the Philippine Commission, charged with the difficult and challenging task of forming a civil government in the Philippines. Later Taft was named the first governor general of the Philippines. In 1904, Roosevelt appointed him secretary of war. In all these positions, Taft made his mark as a skillful administrator. He worked quietly behind the scenes, avoided controversy, and shared none of Roosevelt's zest for politics. A good-natured man, Taft had personal charm and infectious humor. He fled from fights rather than seeking them out and disliked political maneuvering, preferring instead quiet solitude. "I don't like politics," he said. "I don't like the limelight."

Weighing close to three hundred pounds, Taft enjoyed conversation, golf and bridge, good food, and plenty of rest. Compared to the hard-working Roosevelt and Wilson, he was lazy. He was also honest, kindly, and amiable, and in his own way he knew how to get things done. Reflective, he preferred the life of a judge, but his wife, Helen H. Taft, who enjoyed politics, prodded him toward the White House. When a Supreme Court appointment opened in 1906, Taft reluctantly turned it down. "Ma wants him to wait and be president," his youngest son said.

Taft's years as President were not happy. Mrs. Taft's health soon collapsed, and as it turned out, Taft presided over a Republican party torn with tensions that Roosevelt had either brushed aside or concealed. The tariff, business regulation, and other issues split conservatives and progressives and Taft often wavered or sided with the conservatives. Taft revered the past and distrusted change; although an ardent supporter of Roosevelt, he never had Roosevelt's faith in the ability of government to impose reform and alter individual behavior. He named five corporation attorneys to his cabinet, leaned more to business than to labor, and spoke of a desire to "clean out the unions."

At that time and later, Taft's reputation suffered by comparison to the flair of Roosevelt and the moral majesty of Woodrow Wilson. He deserved better. Taft was an honest and sincere President, who—sometimes firm, sometimes befuddled—faced a series of important and troublesome problems during his term of office.

Party Insurgency

Taft started his term with an attempt to curb the powerful Republican Speaker of the House, Joseph "Uncle Joe" Cannon of Illinois. Using the powers of his position, Cannon had been setting House procedures, appointing committees, and virtually dictating legislation. Straightforward and crusty, he often opposed reform. In March 1909, thirty Republican congressmen joined Taft's effort to curb Cannon's power, and the President sensed success. But Cannon retaliated and, threatening to block all tariff bills, forced a compromise. Taft stopped the anti-Cannon campaign in return for Cannon's pledge to help with tariff cuts.

Republicans were divided over the tariff, and there was a growing party insurgency against high rates. The House quickly passed a bill providing for lower rates, but in the Senate, protectionists raised them. Senate leader Nelson

A 1910 cartoon shows Taft snarled in the intricacies of office as his disapproving mentor looks on.

"GOODNESS GRACIOUS! I MUST HAVE BEEN DOZING!"

W. Aldrich of Rhode Island introduced a revised bill that added over eight hundred amendments to the rates approved in the House. It placed no duties on curling stones, false teeth, canary-bird seed, and hog bristles, which brought a chuckle from Mr. Dooley. "Th' new Tariff Bill," he said, "put these familyar commodyties within th' reach iv all."

Angry, La Follette and other Republicans attacked the bill as the child of special interests. In speeches on the Senate floor they called themselves "progressives," invoked Roosevelt's name, and urged Taft to defeat the high-tariff proposal. Caught between protectionists and progressives, Taft wavered, then tried to compromise. In the end, he backed Aldrich. The Payne-Aldrich Act, passed in November 1909, called for higher rates than the original House bill, though it lowered them from the Dingley Tariff of 1897 (see Chapter 20). An unpopular law, Payne-Aldrich helped discredit Taft and revealed the tensions in the Republican party.

Republican progressives and conservatives drifted apart. Thin-skinned, Taft resented the persistent pinpricks of the progressives who criticized him for virtually everything he did. He tried to find middle ground but leaned more and more toward the conservatives. During a nationwide speaking tour in the autumn of 1909, he praised Aldrich, scolded the low-tariff insurgents, and called the Payne-Aldrich Act "the best bill that the Republican party ever passed." Traveling through the Midwest, he pointedly ignored La Follette, Cummins, and other progressive Republicans.

By early 1910, progressive Republicans in Congress no longer looked to Taft for leadership. As before, they challenged Cannon's power, and Taft wavered. In an outcome embarrassing to the President, the progressives won, managing to curtail Cannon's authority to dictate committee assignments and schedule debate. In progressive circles there was growing talk of a Roosevelt return to the White House.

The Ballinger-Pinchot Affair

The conservation issue dealt another blow to relations between Roosevelt and President Taft. In 1909, Richard A. Ballinger, Taft's secretary of the interior, offered for sale a million acres of public land that Pinchot, who had stayed on as Taft's chief forester, had withdrawn from sale. Pinchot, fearing that Ballinger would hurt conservation programs, protested and, seizing on a report that Ballinger had helped sell valuable Alaskan coal lands to a syndicate that included J. P. Morgan, asked Taft to intervene. After investigating, Taft supported Ballinger on every count, although he asked Pinchot to remain in office.

Pinchot refused to drop the matter. Behind the scenes, he provided material for two anti-Ballinger magazine articles, and he wrote a critical public letter that Senator Dolliver of Iowa read to the Senate. Taft had had enough. He fired the insubordinate Pinchot which, though appropriate, again lost support for Taft. Although a conservationist himself, the President had fired one of the nation's leading conservationists. Newspapers followed the controversy for months, and muckrakers assailed the administration's "surrender" to Morgan and other "despoilers of the national heritage."

The Ballinger-Pinchot controversy obscured Taft's important contributions to conservation. He won from Congress the power to remove lands from sale, and he used it to conserve more land than Roosevelt did. Still, the controversy tarred Taft, and it upset his old friend Roosevelt. Pinchot hurried to Italy where Roosevelt was on tour; he talked again with Roosevelt within days of the ex-president's arrival home in June 1910.

Taft's Final Years

Interested in railroad regulation, Taft backed a bill in 1910 to empower the ICC to fix maximum railroad rates. Progressive Republicans favored that plan but attacked Taft's suggestion of a special Commerce Court to hear appeals from ICC decisions because most judges were traditionally conservative in outlook and usually rejected attempts to regulate railroad rates. They also thought the railroads had been consulted too closely in drawing up the bill. Democratic and Republican progressives tried to amend the bill to strengthen it; Taft made support of it a test of party loyalty.

The Mann-Elkins Act of 1910 gave something to everyone. It gave the ICC power to set rates, stiffened long- and short-haul regulations, and placed telephone and telegraph companies under ICC jurisdiction. These provisions delighted progressives. The act also created a Commerce Court, pleasing conservatives. In a trade-off, conservative Republican Senate leaders pledged their support for a statehood bill for Arizona and New Mexico, which were both predicted to be Democratic. In return, enough Democratic senators promised to vote for the Commerce Court provision to pass the bill. While pleased with the act, Taft and the Republican party lost further ground. In votes on key provisions of the Mann-Elkins Act, Taft raised the issue of party regularity, and progressive Republicans defied him.

Withholding patronage, Taft attempted to defeat the progressive Republicans in the 1910 elections. He helped form antiprogressive organizations, and he campaigned against progressive Republican candidates for the Senate. In California, he opposed Hiram Johnson, the progressive Republican champion; in Wisconsin, the home of La Follette, he sent Vice-President James S. Sherman to take control of the state convention. Progressive Republicans retaliated by organizing a nationwide network of anti-Taft Progressive Republican Clubs.

The 1910 election results were a major setback for Taft and the Republicans—especially conservative Republicans. A key issue in the election, the high cost of living, gave an edge to the progressive wings in both major parties, lending support to their attack on the tariff and the trusts. In party primaries, progressive Republicans overwhelmed most Taft candidates, and in the general election, they tended to fare better than the conservatives, which increased progressive influence in the Republican party.

For Republicans of all persuasions, however, it was a difficult election. The Democrats swept the urban-industrial states from New York to Illinois. New York, New Jersey, Indiana, and even Taft's Ohio elected Democratic governors. For the first time since 1894, Republicans lost control of both the House and the Senate. In all, they lost fifty-eight seats in the House and ten in the Senate. Disappointed, Taft called it "not only a landslide, but a tidal wave and holocaust all rolled into one general cataclysm."

Despite the defeat, Taft pushed through several important measures before his term ended. With the help of the new Democratic House, he backed laws to regulate safety in mines and on railroads, create a Children's Bureau in the federal government, establish employers' liability for all work done on government contracts, and mandate an eight-hour workday for government workers.

In 1909, Congress initiated a constitutional amendment authorizing an income tax which, along with woman suffrage, was one of the most significant legislative measures of the twentieth century. The Sixteenth Amendment took effect early in 1913. A few months later, an important progressive goal was realized when the direct election of senators was ratified as the Seventeenth Amendment to the Constitution.

An ardent supporter of competition, Taft relentlessly pressed a campaign against trusts. The Sherman Antitrust Act, he said in 1911, "is a good law that ought to be enforced, and I propose to enforce it." That year, the Supreme Court in cases against Standard Oil and American Tobacco established the "rule of reason," which allowed the Court to determine whether a business presented "reasonable" restraint on trade. Taft thought the decisions gave the Court too much discretion, and he pushed ahead with the antitrust effort.

In October 1911, he sued U.S. Steel for its acquisition of the Tennessee Coal and Iron Company in 1907. Roosevelt had approved the acquisition (see p. 692), and the suit seemed designed to impugn his action. Enraged, he attacked Taft, and Taft, for once, fought back. He accused Roosevelt of undermining the conservative tradition in the country and began working to undercut the influence of the progressive Republicans. Increasingly now, Roosevelt listened to anti-Taft Republicans who urged him to run for President in 1912. In the following months, he sounded Republican sentiment for a presidential bid. In February 1912, he announced: "My hat is in the ring."

Differing Philosophies in the Election of 1912

Delighted Democrats looked on as Taft and Roosevelt fought for the Republican nomination. As the incumbent President, Taft controlled the party machinery, and when the Republican convention met in June 1912, he took the nomination. In early July, the Democrats met in Baltimore and, confident of victory for the first time in two decades, struggled through forty-six ballots before finally nominating Woodrow Wilson, the reform-minded governor of New Jersey.

A month later some of the anti-Taft and progressive Republicans—now calling themselves the Progressive party—whooped it up in Chicago. Roosevelt was there to give a stirring "Confession of Faith" and listen to the delegates sing:

> Thou wilt not cower in the dust,
>   Roosevelt, O Roosevelt!
> Thy gleaming sword shall never rust,
>   Roosevelt, O Roosevelt!

Naming Roosevelt for President, the Progressive—soon known as the "Bull Moose"—party convention set the stage for the first important three-cornered presidential contest since 1860.

Saddened, Taft was out of the running before the campaign even began. "I think I might as well give up so far as being a candidate is concerned," he said in July. "There are so many people in the country who don't like me." Taft stayed at home and made no speeches before the election. Roosevelt campaigned strenuously, even completing one speech after being shot in the chest by an anti-third-term fanatic. "I have a message to deliver," he said, "and will deliver it as long as there is life in my body."

Roosevelt's message involved a program he called the New Nationalism. An important phase in the shaping of twentieth-century American political thought, it demanded a national approach to the country's affairs and a strong President to deal with them. The New Nationalism called for efficiency in government and society. It exalted the executive and the expert, urged social-justice reforms to protect workers, women, and children, and accepted "good" trusts. The New Nationalism encouraged large concentrations of labor and capital, serving the nation's interests under a forceful federal executive.

For the first time in the history of a major political party, the Progressive campaign enlisted women in its organization. Jane Addams, the well-known settlement worker, seconded Roosevelt's nomination at Chicago, and she and other women played a leading role in his campaign. Some labor leaders, who saw potential for union growth, and some business leaders, who saw relief from destructive competition and labor strife, supported the new party.

Wilson, in contrast, set forth a program called the New Freedom that emphasized business competition and small government. A states' rights Democrat, he wanted to rein in federal authority, using it only to sweep away special privilege, release individual energies, and restore competition. Drawing on the thinking of Louis D. Brandeis, the brilliant shaper of reform-minded law, he echoed the Progressive party's social-justice objectives, while continuing to attack Roosevelt's planned state. For Wilson, the vital issue was not a planned economy but a free one. "The history of liberty is the history of the limitation of governmental power . . . ," he said in October 1912. "If America is not to have free enterprise, then she can have freedom of no sort whatever."

In the New Nationalism and New Freedom, the election of 1912 offered competing philosophies of government. Both Roosevelt and Wilson saw the central problem of the American nation as economic growth and its effect on individuals and society. Both focused on the government's relation to business; both believed in bureaucratic reform; and both wanted to use government to protect the ordinary citizen. But Roosevelt welcomed federal power, national planning, and business growth; Wilson distrusted them all.

On election day, Wilson won 6.3 million votes

Election of 1912

	ELECTORAL VOTE BY STATE		POPULAR VOTE
DEMOCRATIC Woodrow Wilson	435	●	6,296,547
PROGRESSIVE (BULL MOOSE) Theodore Roosevelt	88	●	4,118,571
REPUBLICAN William H. Taft	8	●	3,486,720
MINOR PARTIES	—		1,135,697
	531		15,037,535

To overcome his image as an austere scholar, Wilson campaigned vigorously in 1912, "stumping" the country from the rear of a train.

to 4.1 million for Roosevelt (who had recovered quickly from his wound) and 900,000 for Eugene V. Debs, the Socialist party candidate. Taft, the incumbent President, finished third with 3.5 million votes; he carried only Vermont and Utah for 8 electoral votes. The Democrats also won outright control of both houses.

WOODROW WILSON'S NEW FREEDOM

If under Roosevelt social reform took on the excitement of a circus, "under Wilson it acquired the dedication of a sunrise service." Born in Virginia in 1856, and raised in the South, Wilson was the son of a Presbyterian minister. As a young man, he wanted a career in public service, and he trained himself carefully in history and oratory. At age sixteen he became intrigued by the English parliamentary system, a fascination that shaped his scholarly career and perhaps his diplomacy in the First World War (see Chapter 24). A moralist, he reached judgments easily. Once reached, almost nothing shook them. Opponents called him stubborn and smug. "He gives me the creeps," a Maryland ward boss said. "The time I met him, he said something to me, and I didn't know whether God or him was talking."

After graduating from Princeton University

and the University of Virginia Law School, Wilson found that practicing law bored him. Shifting to history, from 1890 to 1902 he served as professor of jurisprudence and political economy at Princeton. In 1902, he became president of the university. Eight years later, he was governor of New Jersey, where he led a campaign to reform election procedures, abolish corrupt practices, and strengthen railroad regulation.

Wilson's rise was rapid, and he knew relatively little about national issues and personalities. But he learned fast, and in some ways the lack of experience served him well. He had few political debts to repay, and he brought fresh perspectives to older issues. Ideas intrigued Wilson; details bored him. Although he was outgoing at times, he could also be cold and aloof, and aides soon learned that he preferred loyalty and flattery to candid criticism.

Prone to self-righteousness, Wilson often turned differences of opinion into bitter personal quarrels. Like Roosevelt, he believed in strong presidential leadership. A scholar of the party system, he cooperated closely with Democrats in Congress, and his legislative record placed him among the most effective Presidents in terms of passing bills that he supported. Forbidding in individual conversation, Wilson could move crowds with graceful oratory. Unlike Taft, and to a greater degree than Roosevelt, he could inspire.

His inaugural address was eloquent. "The Nation," he said, "has been deeply stirred, stirred by a solemn passion, stirred by the knowledge of wrong, of ideals lost, of government too often debauched and made an instrument of evil. The feelings with which we face this new age of right and opportunity sweep across our heartstrings like some air out of God's own presence."

The New Freedom in Action

On the day of his inauguration, Wilson called Congress into special session to lower the tariff. When the session opened on April 8, 1913, Wilson himself was there, the first President since John Adams in 1801 to appear personally before Congress. In forceful language, he urged Congress to reduce tariff rates.

As the bill moved through Congress, Wilson showed exceptional skill. He worked closely with congressional leaders, and when lobbyists threatened the bill in the Senate, he appealed for popular support. The result was a triumph for Wilson and the Democratic party. The Underwood Tariff Act passed in 1913. The first tariff cut in nineteen years, it lowered rates about 15 percent and removed duties from sugar, wool, and several other consumer goods.

To make up for lost revenue, the act also levied a modest, graduated income tax, authorized under the just-ratified Sixteenth Amendment. Marking a significant shift in the American tax structure, it imposed a 1 percent tax on individuals and corporations earning more than $4000 annually and an additional 1 percent tax on incomes over $20,000. Above all, the act reflected a new unity within the Democratic party which, unlike its experience under Grover Cleveland, had worked together to pass a difficult tariff law.

Wilson himself emerged as an able leader. "At a single stage," a foreign editor said, "[he went] from the man of promise to the man of achievement." Encouraged by his success, Wilson decided to keep Congress in session through the hot Washington summer. Now he focused on banking reform, and the result in December 1913 was the Federal Reserve Act, the most important domestic law of his administration.

Meant to provide the United States with a sound yet flexible currency, the act established the country's first efficient banking system since Andrew Jackson killed the Second Bank of the United States in 1832 (see Chapter 10). It created twelve regional banks, each to serve the banks of its district. The regional banks answered to a Federal Reserve Board, appointed by the President, which governed the nationwide system.

A compromise law, the act blended public and private control of the banking system. Private bankers owned the federal reserve banks but answered to the presidentially appointed Federal Reserve Board. The reserve banks were authorized to issue currency and through the discount rate—the interest rate at which they loaned money to member banks—could raise or lower the amount of money in circulation. Monetary affairs no longer depended solely on the price of gold. Within a year, nearly half the nation's banking resources were in the Federal Reserve System.

The Clayton Antitrust Act (1914) completed Wilson's initial legislative program. Like previous antitrust measures, it reflected confusion over how to discipline a growing economy without

putting a brake on output. In part it was a response to the revelations of the Pujo Committee of the House, publicized by Brandeis in a disquieting series of articles, "Other People's Money." In its investigation of Wall Street, the committee discovered a pyramid of money and power capped by the Morgan-Rockefeller empire that, through "interlocking directorates," controlled companies worth $22 billion, over one tenth of the national wealth.

The Clayton Act outlawed such directorates and prohibited unfair trade practices. It forbade pricing policies that created monopoly, and it made corporate officers personally responsible for antitrust violations. Delighting Samuel Gompers and the labor movement, the act declared that unions were not conspiracies in restraint of trade, outlawed the use of injunctions in labor disputes unless necessary to protect property, and approved lawful strikes and picketing. To Gompers's dismay, the courts continued to rule against union activity.

A related law established a powerful Federal Trade Commission to oversee business methods. Composed of five members, the commission could demand special and annual reports, investigate complaints, and order corporate compliance, subject to court review. At first, Wilson opposed the commission concept, which was an approach more suitable to Roosevelt's New Nationalism, but he changed his mind and, along with Brandeis, called it the cornerstone of his antitrust plan. To reassure business leaders, he appointed a number of conservatives to the new commission and to the Federal Reserve Board.

In November 1914, Wilson proudly announced the completion of his New Freedom program. Tariff, banking, and antitrust laws promised a brighter future, he said, and it was now "a time of healing because a time of just dealing." Many progressives were aghast. To think society's ills were so easily cured, the *New Republic* said, "casts suspicion either upon his own sincerity or upon his grasp of the realities of modern social and industrial life."

Retreat and Advance

Distracted by the start of war in Europe, Wilson gave less attention to domestic issues for over a year. When he returned to concern with reform, he adopted more and more of Roosevelt's New Nationalism and blended it with the New Freedom to set it off from his earlier policies.

One of Wilson's problems was the Congress. To his dismay, the Republicans gained substantially in the 1914 elections. Reducing the Democratic majority in the House, they swept key industrial and farm states. At the same time, a recession struck the economy, which had been hurt by the outbreak of the European war in August 1914. Some business leaders blamed the tariff and other New Freedom laws. On the defensive, Wilson soothed business sentiment and invited bankers and industrialists to the White House. He allowed companies fearful of antitrust actions to seek advice from the Justice Department.

Preoccupied with such problems, Wilson blocked significant action in Congress through most of 1915. He refused to support a bill providing minimum wages for women workers, sidetracked a child-labor bill on the ground that it was unconstitutional, and opposed a bill to establish long-term credits for farmers. He also refused to endorse woman suffrage, arguing that the right to vote was a state, not a federal matter.

Wilson's record on race disappointed African Americans and many progressives. He had appealed to African-American voters during the 1912 election, and a number of African-American leaders campaigned for him. Soon after the inauguration, Oswald Garrison Villard, a leader of the NAACP, proposed a National Race Commission to study the problem of race relations. Initially sympathetic, Wilson rejected the idea because he feared he might lose southern Democratic votes in Congress. A Virginian himself, he appointed many Southerners to high office, and for the first time since the Civil War, southern views on race dominated the nation's capital.

At one of Wilson's first cabinet meetings, the postmaster general proposed the segregation of all African Americans in the federal service. No one dissented, including Wilson. Several government bureaus promptly began to segregate workers in offices, shops, restrooms, and restaurants. Employees who objected were fired. African-American leaders protested, and they were joined by progressive leaders and clergymen. Surprised at the protest, Wilson backed quietly away from the policy, although he continued to insist that segregation benefited African Americans.

As the year 1916 began, Wilson made a dramatic switch in focus and again pushed for substantial reforms. The result was a virtual river of reform laws, which was significant because it began the second, more national-minded phase of the New Freedom. With scarcely a glance over his shoulder, Wilson embraced important portions of Roosevelt's New Nationalism campaign.

In part, he was motivated by the approaching presidential election. A minority President, Wilson owed his victory in 1912 to the split in the Republican party, now almost healed. Roosevelt was moving back into Republican ranks, and there were issues connected with the war in Europe that he might use against Wilson (see Chapter 24). Moreover, many progressives were voicing disappointment with Wilson's limited reforms and his failure to support more advanced reform legislation such as farm credits, child labor, and woman's suffrage.

Moving quickly to patch up the problem, Wilson named Brandeis to the Supreme Court in January 1916. Popular among progressives, Brandeis was also the first person of Jewish faith to serve on the Court. When conservatives in the Senate tried to defeat the nomination, Wilson stood firm and won, earning further praise from progressives, Jews, and others. In May, he reversed his stand on farm loans and accepted a rural credits bill to establish farm-loan banks backed by federal funds. The Federal Farm Loan Act of 1916 created a Federal Farm Loan Board to give farmers credit similar to the Federal Reserve's benefits for trade and industry.

Wilson was already popular within the labor movement. Going beyond Roosevelt's policies, which had sought a balance between business and labor, he defended union recognition and collective bargaining. In 1913, he appointed William B. Wilson, a respected leader of the United Mine Workers, as the first head of the Labor Department, and he strengthened the department's Division of Conciliation. In 1914, in Ludlow, Colorado, state militia and mine guards fired machine guns into a tent colony of coal strikers, killing twenty-six men, women, and children. Outraged, Wilson stepped in and used federal troops to end the violence while negotiations to end the strike went on.

In August 1916, a threatened railroad strike again revealed Wilson's sympathies with labor. Like Roosevelt, he invited the two sides to the

White House where he urged the railroad companies to grant an eight-hour day and labor leaders to abandon the demand for overtime pay. Labor leaders accepted the proposal; railroad leaders did not. "I pray God to forgive you, I never can," Wilson said as he left the room. Soon he signed the Adamson Act (1916) that imposed the eight-hour day on interstate railways and established a federal commission to study the railroad problem. Ending the threat of a strike, the act marked a milestone in the expansion of the federal government's authority to regulate industry.

With Wilson leading the way, the flow of reform legislation continued until the election. The Federal Workmen's Compensation Act established workers' compensation for government employees. The Keating-Owen Act, the first federal child-labor law, prohibited the shipment in interstate commerce of products manufactured by children under the age of fourteen. It too expanded the authority of the federal government, though it was soon struck down by the Supreme Court. The Warehouse Act, similar to the subtreasury proposal the Populists urged in the 1890s (see Chapter 20), authorized licensed warehouses to issue negotiable receipts for farm products deposited with them.

In September, Wilson signed the Tariff Commission Act creating an expert commission to recommend tariff rates. The same month, the Revenue Act of 1916 boosted income taxes and furthered tax reform. Four thousand members of the National American Woman Suffrage Association cheered when Wilson finally came out in support of woman suffrage. Two weeks later he endorsed the eight-hour day for all the nation's workers.

The 1916 presidential election was close, but Wilson won it on the issues of peace and progressivism (see Chapter 24). By the end of 1916, he and the Democratic party had enacted most of the important parts of Roosevelt's Progressive party platform of 1912. To do it, Wilson abandoned portions of the New Freedom and accepted much of the New Nationalism, including greater federal power and commissions governing trade and tariffs. In mixing the two programs, he blended some of the competing doctrines of the Progressive Era, established the primacy of the federal government, and foreshadowed the pragmatic outlook of Franklin D. Roosevelt's New Deal.

Expecting eviction from company housing, striking miners in Ludlow built a tent colony. Guards hired to break the strike sprayed the tents with gunfire then set the colony afire.

The election of 1916 showed how deeply progressivism had reached into American society. Candidates were vying for the reform-minded vote; the party of Grover Cleveland had become the party of Woodrow Wilson and, soon thereafter, of Franklin D. Roosevelt. "We have in four years," Wilson said that fall, "come very near to carrying out the platform of the Progressive party as well as our own; for we are also progressives."

In retrospect, however, 1916 also marked the beginning of progressivism's sad decline into the 1920s. At most, the years of progressive reform lasted from the 1890s to 1921, and in large measure they were compressed into a single decade between 1906 and American entry into World War I. Many problems the progressives addressed, they did not solve; and some important ones, like race, they did not even tackle. Yet their regulatory commissions, direct primaries, city improvements, and child-labor laws marked an era of important and measured reform.

The institution of the presidency expanded. From the White House radiated executive departments that guided a host of activities. Independent commissions, operating within flexible laws, supplemented executive authority.

These developments owed a great deal to both Roosevelt and Wilson. To manage a complex society, TR developed a simple formula: expert advice; growth-minded policies; a balancing of business, labor, and other interests; the use of publicity to gather support; and stern but often

CHRONOLOGY

1894 National Municipal League formed to work for reform in cities

1900 Galveston, Texas, is first city to try commission form of government

1901 Theodore Roosevelt becomes President • Robert M. La Follette elected reform governor of Wisconsin • Doctors reorganize the American Medical Association • Socialist party of America organized

1902 Roosevelt sues the Northern Securities Company for violation of Antitrust Act • Coal miners in northeastern Pennsylvania strike • Maryland is first state to pass workers' compensation law • Oregon adopts the initiative and referendum

1904 Roosevelt elected President

1906 Hepburn Act strengthens ICC • Upton Sinclair attacks meat-packing industry in *The Jungle* • Congress passes Meat Inspection Act and Pure Food and Drug Act

1908 Taft elected President • Supreme Court upholds Oregon law limiting working hours for women in *Muller* v. *Oregon*

1909 Payne-Aldrich Tariff Act divides Republican party

1910 Mann-Elkins Act passed to regulate railroads • Taft fires Gifford Pinchot, head of U.S. Forest Service • Democrats sweep midterm elections

1912 Progressive party formed; nominates Roosevelt for President • Woodrow Wilson elected President

1913 Underwood Tariff Act lowers rates • Federal Reserve Act reforms U.S. banking system • Sixteenth Amendment authorizes Congress to collect taxes on incomes

1914 Clayton Act strengthens antitrust legislation

1916 Wilson wins reelection

1918 Supreme Court strikes down federal law limiting child labor in *Hammer* v. *Dagenhart*

1920 Nineteenth Amendment gives women the right to vote.

permissive oversight of the economy. TR strengthened the executive office, and he called upon the newer group of professional, educated, public-minded citizens to help him. "I believe in a strong executive," he said; "I believe in power."

At first, Wilson had different ideas, wanting to dismantle much of Roosevelt's governing apparatus. But driven by outside forces and changes in his own thinking, Wilson soon moved in directions similar to those Roosevelt had championed. Starting out to disperse power, he eventually consolidated it. Against his earlier policies, Wilson created a Federal Trade Commission to oversee business, a Tariff Commission to regulate overseas trade, and a powerful Federal Reserve Board to control money and banking.

Through such movements, government at all levels accepted responsibility for the welfare of various elements in the social order. A reform-minded and bureaucratic society took shape, in which men and women, labor and capital, political parties and social classes competed for shares in the expansive framework of twentieth-century life. But there were limits to reform. As both TR and Wilson found, the new government agencies, understaffed and underfinanced, depended on the responsiveness of those they sought to regulate.

Soon there was a far darker cloud on the horizon. The spirit of progressivism rested upon a belief in human potential, peace, and progress. After Napoleon's defeat in 1815, a century of peace began in western Europe, and as the decades passed, war seemed a dying institution. "It looks as though this were going to be the age of treaties rather than the age of wars," an American said in 1912, "the century of reason rather than the century of force." It was not to be. Two years later, the most devastating of wars broke out in Europe, and in 1917, Americans were fighting on the battlefields of France.

Recommended Reading

George Mowry, *The Era of Theodore Roosevelt* (1958) and Arthur S. Link, *Woodrow Wilson and the Progressive Era* (1954), trace the social and economic conditions of the period. See also Henry F. Pringle's biography, *Theodore Roosevelt* (1931), John M. Blum's perceptive and brief *The Republican Roosevelt* (1954), and William H. Harbaugh's thoughtful *The Life and Times of Theodore Roosevelt*, rev. ed. (1975). Donald E. Anderson, *William Howard Taft* (1973) and Paolo E. Coletta, *The Presidency of William Howard Taft* (1973), study Taft. The definitive biography of Wilson is Arthur S. Link, *Wilson*, 5 vols. (1947–1965).

Samuel P. Hays offers an influential interpretation of progressivism in *Conservation and the Gospel of Efficiency* (1959). Albro Martin, *Enterprise Denied: Origins of the Decline of American Railroads, 1897–1917* (1971), argues persuasively that reformers damaged as well as regulated. Intellectual currents are traced in Charles Forcey, *The Crossroads of Liberalism* (1961); social justice reforms in Harold U. Faulkner, *The Quest for Social Justice, 1898–1914* (1931); and the important tax issue in Clifton K. Yearley, *The Money Machines* (1970).

Additional Bibliography

On specific issues, see O. E. Anderson, *The Health of a Nation: Harvey W. Wiley and the Fight for Pure Food* (1958); James G. Burrow, *Organized Medicine in the Progressive Era: The Move Toward Monopoly* (1977); Morris J. Vogel, *The Invention of the Modern Hospital: Boston, 1870–1930* (1980); Craig West, *Banking Reform and the Federal Reserve, 1863–1923* (1977); Eugene Nelson White, *The Regulation and Reform of the American Banking System. 1900–1929* (1983); Aileen Kraditor, *The Ideas of the Woman Suffrage Movement. 1890–1920* (1981); Christine A. Lunardini, *From Equal Suffrage to Equal Rights: Alice Paul and the National Woman's Party, 1910–1928* (1986); David W. Southern, *The Malignant Heritage: Yankee Progressives and the Negro Question. 1901–1914* (1968); James H. Timberlake, *Prohibition and the Progressive Crusade* (1963); and Walter I. Trattner, *Crusade for the Children* (1970).

See also, Paul Russell Cutright, *Theodore Roosevelt: The Making of a Conservationist* (1985); Ruth Rosen, *The Lost Sisterhood: Prostitution in America, 1900–1918* (1982), and *Women and Temperance* (1980); David J. Pivar, *Purity Crusade* (1973); and Norman H. Clark, *Deliver Us from Evil: An Interpretation of American Prohibition* (1976). Peter J. Coleman, *Progressivism and the World of Reform* (1987) takes a comparative look at progressivism.

On politics, see George E. Mowry, *Theodore Roosevelt and the Progressive Movement* (1946); Richard L. McCormick, *The Party Period and Public Policy: American Politics from the Age of Jackson to the Progressive Era* (1986); Michael E. McGerr, *The Decline of Popular Politics: The American North, 1865–1928* (1986); Kenneth W. Hechler, *Insurgency: Personalities and Politics of the Taft Era* (1940); David Sarasohn, *The Party of Reform: Democrats in the Progressive Era* (1989); Norman M. Wilensky, *Conservatives in the Progressive Era: The Taft Republicans of 1912* (1965); George Juergens, *News from the White House: The Presidential-Press Relationship in the Progressive Era* (1981); and L. J. Holt, *Congressional Insurgents and the Party System, 1909–1916* (1967).

Helpful biographies include Edmund Morris, *The Rise of Theodore Roosevelt* (1979); William Manners, *TR and Will* (1969); G. Wallace Chessman, *Theodore Roosevelt and the Politics of Power* (1969); John M. Blum, *Woodrow Wilson and the Politics of Morality* (1962), John M. Mulder, *Woodrow Wilson: The Years of Preparation* (1978); Kendrick A. Clements, *Woodrow Wilson* (1987); Henry F. Pringle, *Life and Times of William Howard Taft*, 2 vols. (1939); David P. Thelen, *Robert M. La Follette and the Insurgent Spirit* (1976); Fred Greenbaum, *Robert Marion La Follette* (1975); Philippa

Strum, *Louis D. Brandeis* (1984); Alpheus Thomas Mason, *Brandeis: A Free Man's Life* (1946); and Harold W. Currie, *Eugene V. Debs* (1976).

On urban reform, see John D. Buenker, *Urban Liberalism and Progressive Reform* (1973); Roy M. Lubove, *The Progressive and the Slums* (1962); and Martin J. Schiesl, *The Politics of Efficiency: Municipal Administration and Reform in America, 1880–1920* (1977). Also, Robert M. Crunden, *Ministers of Reform: The Progressives' Achievements in American Civilization, 1889–1920* (1982); James T. Patterson, *America's Struggle Against Poverty, 1900–1980* (1981); and Stephen Skowronek, *Building a New American State: The Expansion of National Administrative Capacities, 1877–1920* (1982). Bradley R. Rice, *Progressive Cities: The Commission Government Movement in America, 1901–1920* (1977) is helpful.

Books on specific cities include Melvin Holli, *Reform in Detroit: Hazen S. Pingree and Urban Politics* (1969); Carl V. Harris, *Political Power in Birmingham, 1871–1921* (1977); James B. Crooks, *Politics and Progress: The Rise of Urban Progressivism in Baltimore, 1895–1911* (1968); Zane L. Miller, *Boss Cox's Cincinnati* (1968); and Jack Tager, *The Intellectual as Urban Reformer: Brand Whitlock and the Progressive Movement* (1968).

Statewide movements are covered in George E. Mowry's influential study, *The California Progressives* (1951); Spencer C. Olin, Jr., *California's Prodigal Sons: Hiram Johnson and the Progressives, 1911–1917* (1968); David P. Thelen, *The New Citizenship: Origins of Progressivism in Wisconsin, 1885–1900* (1972); Herbert Margulies, *The Decline of the Progressive Movement in Wisconsin, 1890–1920* (1968); Ransom E. Noble, Jr., *New Jersey Progressivism Before Wilson* (1946); John F. Reynolds, *Testing Democracy: Electoral Behavior and Progressive Reform in New Jersey, 1880–1920* (1988); James Wright, *The Progressive Yankees: Republican Reformers in New Hampshire, 1906–1916* (1987); Robert F. Wesser, *Charles Evans Hughes: Politics and Reform in New York, 1905–1910* (1967); Richard L. McCormick, *From Realignment to Reform: Political Change in New York State, 1893–1910* (1981); Sheldon Hackney, *Populism to Progressivism in Alabama* (1969); Richard M. Abrams, *Conservatism in a Progressive Era: Massachusetts Politics, 1900–1912* (1964); and H. L. Warner, *Progressivism in Ohio, 1897–1917* (1964).

For intellectual currents, see Bruce Kuklick, *The Rise of American Philosophy* (1977); John M. O'Donnell, *The Origins of Behaviorism: American Psychology, 1870–1920* (1985); Aileen S. Kraditor, *The Radical Persuasion, 1890–1917: Aspects of the Intellectual History and the Historiography of Three American Radical Organizations* (1981); L. Glen Seretan, *Daniel DeLeon: The Odyssey of an American Marxist* (1979); Elliott Shore, *Talkin' Socialism* (1988); John Thompson, *Closing the Frontier: Radical Response in Oklahoma, 1889–1923* (1986); Gary Marks, *Unions in Politics* (1989); and Nick Salvatore, *Eugene V. Debs: Citizen and Socialist* (1982).

Contemporary accounts include Herbert Croly, *The Promise of American Life* (1909); Walter Lippmann, *Drift and Mastery* (1914); William Allen White, *The Old Order Changeth* (1910) and *The Autobiography of William Allen White* (1946); and Charles Seymour, ed., *The Intimate Papers of Colonel House*, 4 vols. (1926–1928).

CHAPTER 24

The Nation at War

On the morning of May 1, 1915, the German government took out the following important advertisement in the *New York World* as a warning to Americans and other voyagers setting sail for England:

NOTICE—

Travellers intending to embark on the Atlantic voyage are reminded that a state of war exists between Germany and her allies and Great Britain and her allies; that the zone of war includes the waters adjacent to the British Isles; that, in accordance with formal notice given by the Imperial German Government, vessels flying the flag of Great Britain, or of any of her allies, are liable to destruction in those waters and that travellers sailing in the war zone on ships of Great Britain or her allies do so at their own risk.

At 12:30 that afternoon, the British steamship *Lusitania* set sail from New York to Liverpool. Secretly, it carried a load of ammunition as well as passengers.

The steamer was two hours late in leaving, but it held several speed records and could easily make up the time. The passenger list of 1257 was the largest since the outbreak of war in Europe. Alfred G. Vanderbilt, the millionaire sportsman, was aboard; so were Charles Frohman, a famous New York theatrical producer, and Elbert Hubbard, a popular writer who jested that a submarine attack might help sell his new book. While some passengers chose the *Lusitania* for speed, others liked the modern staterooms, more comfortable than the older ships of the competing American Line.

Six days later, the *Lusitania*, back on schedule, reached the coast of Ireland. German U-boats were known to patrol these dangerous waters. When the war began in 1914, Great Britain imposed a naval blockade of Germany. In return, Germany in February 1915 declared the area around the British Isles a war zone; all enemy vessels, armed or unarmed, were at risk. Germany had only a handful of U-boats, but the submarines were a new and frightening weapon. On behalf of the United States, President Woodrow Wilson protested the German action, and on February 10 he warned Germany of its "strict accountability" for any American losses resulting from U-boat attacks.

Off Ireland, the passengers lounged on the deck of the *Lusitania*. As if it were peacetime, the ship sailed straight ahead, with no zigzag maneuvers to throw off pursuit. But the submarine U-20 was there, and the commander, seeing a large ship, fired a single torpedo. Seconds after it hit, a boiler exploded and blew a hole in the *Lusitania*'s side. The ship listed immediately, hindering the launching of lifeboats, and in eighteen minutes it sank. Nearly 1200 people died, including 128 Americans. As the ship's bow lifted and went under, the U-20 commander for the first time read the name: *Lusitania*.

The sinking, the worst since the *Titanic* went down with 1500 people in 1912, horrified Americans. Theodore Roosevelt called it "an act of piracy" and demanded war. On the French front, the Germans had just introduced poison gas, another alarming new weapon, and there were reports of German atrocities in Belgium. Still, most Americans wanted to stay out of war; like Wilson, they hoped negotiations could solve the problem. "There is such a thing," Wilson said a few days after the sinking, "as a man being too proud to fight. There is such a thing as a nation being so right that it does not need to convince others by force."

In a series of diplomatic notes, Wilson demanded a change in German policy. The first *Lusitania* note (May 13, 1915) called on Germany to abandon unrestricted submarine warfare, disavow the sinking, and compensate for lost American lives. Germany sent an evasive reply, and Wilson drafted a second *Lusitania* note (June 9) insisting on specific pledges. Fearful that the demand would lead to war, Secretary of State William Jennings Bryan resigned rather than sign the note. Wilson sent it anyway and followed with a third note (July 21)—almost an ultimatum —warning Germany that the United States would view similar sinkings as "deliberately unfriendly."

Unbeknownst to Wilson, Germany had already ordered U-boat commanders not to sink passenger liners without warning. In August 1915, a U-boat mistakenly torpedoed the British liner *Arabic*, killing two Americans. Wilson protested, and Germany, eager to keep the United States out of the war, backed down. The *Arabic* pledge (September 1) promised that U-boats would stop and warn liners, unless they tried to resist or escape. Germany also apologized for American deaths on the *Arabic*, and for the rest of 1915, U-boats hunted freighters, not passenger liners.

Although Wilson's diplomacy had achieved his immediate goal, the *Lusitania* and *Arabic* crises contained the elements that led to war. Trade and travel tied the world together, and Americans no longer hid behind safe ocean barriers. New weapons, such as the submarine, strained old rules of international law. But while Americans sifted the conflicting claims of Great Britain and Germany, they hoped for peace. A generation of progressives, inspired with confidence in human progress, did not easily accept war.

Wilson also hated war, but he found himself caught up in a worldwide crisis that demanded the best in American will and diplomacy. In the end, diplomacy failed, and in April 1917, the United States entered a war that changed the nation's history.

A NEW WORLD POWER

As they had in the late nineteenth century, Americans after 1900 continued to pay relatively little attention to foreign affairs. Newspapers and magazines ran stories every day about events abroad, but people paid closer attention to what was going on at home. As Walter Lippmann, one of this century's most outstanding political commentators, once said: "I cannot remember taking any interest whatever in foreign affairs until after the outbreak of the First World War."

For Americans at the time, foreign policy was something to be left to the president in office, an attitude the presidents themselves favored. Foreign affairs became an arena in which they could exert a free hand largely unchallenged by Congress or the courts, and Roosevelt, Taft, and Wilson all took advantage of the opportunity to do so.

The foreign policy they pursued from 1901 to 1920 was aggressive and nationalistic. During these years, the United States intervened in Europe, the Far East, and Latin America. It dominated the Caribbean.

In 1898, the United States left the peace table possessing the Philippines, Puerto Rico, and Guam. Holding distant possessions required a colonial policy; it also required a change in foreign policy, reflecting an outward approach. From the Caribbean to the Pacific, policymakers paid attention to issues and countries they had earlier ignored. Like other nations in these years, the United States built a large navy, protected its colonial empire, and became increasingly involved in international affairs.

The nation also became more and more involved in economic ventures abroad. Turning out

With the sinking of the Lusitania, *the American people learned first-hand of the horrors of total war. President Wilson's decision to protest the incident through diplomacy kept the United States out of the war—but only temporarily.*

goods from textiles to steel, mass-production industries sold products overseas, and financiers invested in Asia, Africa, Latin America, and Europe. During the years between the Spanish-American War and World War I, investments abroad rose from $445 million to $2.5 billion. While investments and trade never wholly dictated American foreign policy, they fostered greater involvement in foreign lands.

"I Took the Canal Zone"

Convinced that the United States should take a more active international role, Theodore Roosevelt spent his presidency preparing the nation for world power. Along with Secretary of War Elihu Root, he modernized the army, using lessons from the war with Spain. Roosevelt and Root established the Army War College, imposed stiff tests for the promotion of officers, and in 1903 created a general staff to oversee military planning and mobilization. Determined to end dependence on the British fleet, Roosevelt doubled the navy's strength during his term in office.

Stretching his authority to the limits, Roosevelt took steps to consolidate the country's new position in the Caribbean and Central America. European powers, which had long resisted American initiatives there, now accepted American supremacy. Preoccupied with problems in Europe and Africa, Great Britain agreed to United States plans for an isthmian canal in Central America and withdrew much of its military force from the area.

Roosevelt wanted a canal to link the Atlantic and Pacific oceans across the isthmus connecting North and South America. When the war with Spain started in 1898, it took the battleship *Oregon* seventy-one days to sail from San Francisco around Cape Horn to its battle station in the Atlantic; years later, naval experts still shuddered at the thought. Secretary of State John Hay negotiated with Britain the Hay-Pauncefote Treaty of 1901 that permitted the United States to construct and control an isthmian canal, providing it would be free and open to ships of all nations.

Delighted, Roosevelt began selecting the route. One route, fifty miles long, wandered through the rough, swampy terrain of the Panama region of Colombia. A French company had recently

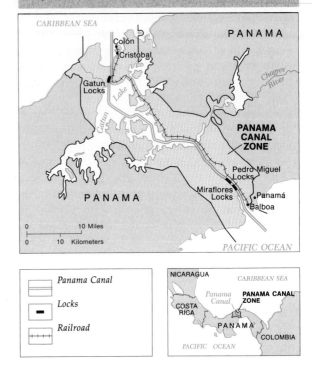

The Panama Canal Zone

Construction of the canal began in 1904, and despite landslides, steamy weather, and yellow fever, work was completed in 1914.

tried and failed to dig a canal there. Northwest of Panama, another route ran through mountainous Nicaragua. Although two hundred miles in length, it followed natural waterways, a factor that would make construction easier.

An Isthmian Canal Commission investigated both routes in 1899 and recommended the shorter route through Panama. Roosevelt backed the idea, and he authorized Hay to negotiate an agreement with the Colombian chargé d'affaires, Tomas Herrán. The Hay-Herrán Convention (1903) gave the United States a ninety-nine-year lease, with option for renewal, on a canal zone six miles in width. In exchange, the United States agreed to pay Colombia a one-time fee of $10 million and an annual rental of $250,000.

To Roosevelt's dismay, the Colombian Senate rejected the treaty, in part because it infringed upon Colombian sovereignty. The Colombians also wanted more money. Calling them "jack rabbits" and "contemptible little creatures," Roosevelt considered seizing Panama, then hinted he would welcome a Panamanian revolt from Colombia. In November 1903, the Panamanians took the hint, and Roosevelt moved quickly to support them. Sending the cruiser *Nashville* to prevent Colombian troops from putting down the revolt, he promptly recognized the new Republic of Panama.

Two weeks later, the Hay–Bunau-Varilla Treaty with Panama granted the United States control of a canal zone ten miles wide across the Isthmus of Panama. In return, the United States guaranteed the independence of Panama and agreed to pay the same fees offered Colombia. Using giant steam shovels and thousands of laborers from Jamaica, engineers cut their way across the isthmus. On August 15, 1914, the first ocean steamer sailed through the completed canal, which had cost $375 million to build.

Roosevelt's actions angered many Latin Americans. Trying to soothe feelings, Wilson agreed in 1914 to pay Colombia $25 million in cash, give it preferential treatment in using the canal, and express "sincere regret" over American actions. Roosevelt was furious, and his friends in the Senate blocked the agreement. Colombian-American relations remained strained until 1921, when the two countries signed a treaty that included Wilson's first two provisions but omitted the apology.

For his part, Roosevelt took great pride in the canal, calling it "by far the most important action in foreign affairs." Defending his methods, he said in 1911: "If I had followed traditional conservative methods, I would have submitted a dignified state paper of 200 pages to Congress and the debate on it would have been going on yet; but I took the Canal Zone and let Congress debate; and while the debate goes on the Canal does also."

The Roosevelt Corollary

With interests in Puerto Rico, Cuba, and the canal, the United States developed a Caribbean policy to ensure its dominance in the region. It established protectorates over some countries and subsidized others to keep them dependent. When necessary, the United States purchased islands to keep them out of the hands of other powers, as in the case of the Danish West Indies

A cartoon from Judge *entitled "The World's Constable." The Roosevelt Corollary claimed the right of the U.S. to exercise "an international police power."*

(now the Virgin Islands), bought in 1917 to prevent the Germans from acquiring them.

From 1903 to 1920, the United States intervened often in Latin America to protect the canal, promote regional stability, and exclude foreign influence. One problem worrying American policymakers was the scale of Latin American debts to European powers. Many countries in the Western Hemisphere owed money to European governments and banks, and often these nations were poor, prone to revolution, and unable to pay. The situation invited European intervention. In 1902, Venezuela defaulted on debts; England, Germany, and Italy sent Venezuela an ultimatum and blockaded its ports. American pressure forced a settlement of the issue, but the general problem remained.

Roosevelt was concerned about it, and in 1904, when the Dominican Republican defaulted on its debts, he was ready with a major announcement. Known as the Roosevelt Corollary of the Monroe Doctrine, the policy warned Latin American nations to keep their affairs in order or face American intervention.

Applying the new policy immediately, Roosevelt in 1905 took charge of the Dominican Republic's revenue system. American officials collected customs and saw to the payment of debt. Within two years, Roosevelt also established protectorates in Cuba and Panama. In 1912, the United States Senate added the Lodge Corollary, which warned foreign corporations not to purchase harbors and other sites of military significance in Latin America. Continued by Taft, Wilson, and other presidents, the Roosevelt Corollary guided American policy in Latin America until the 1930s, when Franklin D. Roosevelt's Good Neighbor policy replaced it.

Ventures in the Far East

The Open Door policy toward China (see Chapter 21) and possession of the Philippine Islands shaped American actions in the Far East. Congress refused to arm the Philippines, and the islands were vulnerable to the growing power of Japan. Roosevelt wanted to balance Russian and Japanese power, and he was not unhappy at first when war broke out between them in 1904. As Japan won victory after victory, however, Roosevelt grew worried. Acting upon a request from Japan, he offered to mediate the conflict, and both Russia and Japan accepted: Russia because it was losing, and Japan because it was financially drained.

In August 1905, Roosevelt convened a peace conference at Portsmouth, New Hampshire. The conference ended the war, but Japan emerged as the dominant force in the Far East. Adjusting policy, Roosevelt sent Secretary of War Taft to Tokyo to negotiate the Taft-Katsura Agreement (1905), which recognized Japan's dominance over Korea in return for its promise not to invade the Philippines. Giving Japan a free hand in Korea violated the Open Door policy, but Roosevelt argued that he had little choice.

Relations between Japan and the United States were again strained in 1906 when the San Francisco school board ordered the segregation of Japanese, Chinese, and Korean children into a separate Oriental school. A year later, the California legislature considered a bill limiting the immigration of Japanese laborers into the state. As resentment mounted in Japan, Roosevelt intervened to persuade the school board to rescind its order, while at the same time he got from Japan the "Gentlemen's Agreement" (1907) promising to stop the flow of Japanese agricultural laborers into the United States.

In case Japan viewed his policy as a sign of weakness, Roosevelt sent sixteen battleships of the new American fleet around the world, including a stop in Tokyo in October 1908. Critics at home predicted dire consequences, and European naval experts felt certain Japan would attack the fleet. Instead, the Japanese welcomed it, even posting ads to sell the sailors Mitsukoshi washing powder to "rid yourselves of the seven blemishes on the way home." For the moment, Japanese-American relations improved, and in 1908 the two nations, in an exchange of diplomatic notes, reached the comprehensive Root-Takahira Agreement in which they promised to maintain the status quo in the Pacific, uphold the Open Door, and support Chinese independence.

In later years, tensions again grew in the Far East. Anger mounted in Japan in 1913 when the California legislature prohibited Japanese residents from owning property in the state. At the start of the First World War, Japan seized some German colonies, and in 1915 it issued the Twenty-One Demands insisting on authority over China. Coveting an Asian empire, Japan eyed American possessions in the Pacific.

Taft and Dollar Diplomacy

In foreign as well as domestic affairs, President Taft tried to continue Roosevelt's policies. For secretary of state he chose Philander C. Knox, Roosevelt's attorney general, and together they pursued a policy of "dollar diplomacy" to promote American financial and business interests abroad. The policy had profit-seeking motives, but it also aimed to substitute economic ties for military alliances with the idea of increasing American influence and bringing lasting peace.

Intent, like Roosevelt, on supremacy in the Caribbean, Taft worked to replace European loans with American ones, thereby reducing the danger of outside meddling. In 1909, he asked American bankers to assume the Honduran debt in order to fend off English bondholders. A year later, he persuaded them to take over the assets of the National Bank of Haiti, and in 1911 he helped Nicaragua secure a large loan in return for American control of Nicaragua's National Bank. When Nicaraguans revolted against the agreement, Taft sent marines to put them down. A marine detachment remained in the country intermittently until the 1930s.

In the Far East, Knox worked closely with Willard Straight, an agent of American bankers, who argued that dollar diplomacy was the financial arm of the Open Door. Straight had close ties to Edward H. Harriman, the railroad magnate, who wanted to build railroads in Manchuria. Roosevelt had tacitly promised Japan he would keep American investors out of the area, and Knox's plan reversed the policy. Trying to organize an international syndicate to loan China money to purchase the Manchurian railroads, Knox approached England, Japan, and Russia. In January 1910, all three turned him down.

The outcome was a blow to American policy and prestige in Asia. Russia and Japan found reasons to cooperate with each other, and staked out spheres of influence in violation of the Open Door. Japan resented Taft's initiatives in Manchuria, and China's distrust of the United States deepened. Instead of cultivating friendship, as Roosevelt had envisioned, Taft had started an intense rivalry with Japan for commercial advantage in China.

FOREIGN POLICY UNDER WILSON

When he took office in 1913, Woodrow Wilson knew little about foreign policy. As a Princeton professor, he had studied Congress and the presidency, but his books made only passing reference to foreign issues, and during the 1912 campaign he mentioned foreign policy only when it affected domestic concerns. "It would be the irony of fate if my administration had to deal chiefly with foreign affairs," he said to a friend just before becoming president. And so it was. During his two terms, Wilson faced crisis after crisis in foreign affairs, including the outbreak of World War I.

A supremely self-confident man, Wilson conducted his own diplomacy. He composed important diplomatic notes on his own typewriter, sent personal emissaries abroad, and carried on major negotiations without the knowledge of his secretaries of state. Failing to find the right persons for key diplomatic posts, he filled these positions with party regulars like James W. Gerard, his

ambassador to Germany, for whom he had contempt. On Gerard's dispatches, Wilson penciled notes: "Ordinarily our Ambassador ought to be backed up as [a matter] of course, but—this ass? It is hard to take it seriously." Or, the next day: "Who can fathom this? I wish they would hand this idiot his passports!"

The idealistic Wilson believed in a principled, ethical world in which militarism, colonialism, and war were brought under control. He stressed moral purposes over material interests and said during one crisis: "The force of America is the force of moral principle." Rejecting the policy of dollar diplomacy, Wilson initially chose a course of moral diplomacy, designed to bring right to the world, preserve peace, and extend to other peoples the blessings of democracy.

Conducting Moral Diplomacy

William Jennings Bryan, whom Wilson appointed as secretary of state, was also an amateur in foreign relations. Trusting in the common people, Bryan was skeptical of experts in the State Department. To key posts abroad he appointed "deserving Democrats," believing they could do the job as well as career diplomats. Bryan was a fervent pacifist, and like Wilson, he believed in the American duty to "help" less-favored nations.

In 1913 and 1914, he embarked on an idealistic campaign to negotiate treaties of arbitration throughout the world. Known as "cooling-off" treaties, they provided for submitting all international disputes to permanent commissions of investigation. Neither party could declare war or increase armaments until the investigation ended, usually within one year. The idea drew on the era's confidence in commissions and the sense that human reason, given time for emotions to fade, could settle problems without war. Bryan negotiated cooling-off treaties with thirty nations, including Great Britain, France, and Italy. Germany refused to sign one. Based on a generous idea, the treaties were naive, and they did not work.

Wilson and Bryan promised a dramatic new approach in Latin America, concerned not with the "pursuit of material interest" but with "human rights" and "national integrity." Signaling

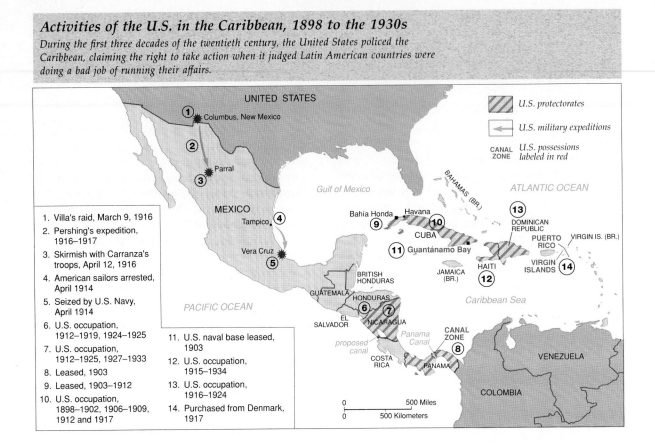

Activities of the U.S. in the Caribbean, 1898 to the 1930s

During the first three decades of the twentieth century, the United States policed the Caribbean, claiming the right to take action when it judged Latin American countries were doing a bad job of running their affairs.

Legend:
- U.S. protectorates
- U.S. military expeditions
- U.S. possessions labeled in red

1. Villa's raid, March 9, 1916
2. Pershing's expedition, 1916–1917
3. Skirmish with Carranza's troops, April 12, 1916
4. American sailors arrested, April 1914
5. Seized by U.S. Navy, April 1914
6. U.S. occupation, 1912–1919, 1924–1925
7. U.S. occupation, 1912–1925, 1927–1933
8. Leased, 1903
9. Leased, 1903–1912
10. U.S. occupation, 1898–1902, 1906–1909, 1912 and 1917
11. U.S. naval base leased, 1903
12. U.S. occupation, 1915–1934
13. U.S. occupation, 1916–1924
14. Purchased from Denmark, 1917

the change, in 1913 they negotiated the treaty with Colombia apologizing for Roosevelt's Panamanian policy. Yet in the end, Wilson, distracted by other problems and impatient with the results of his idealistic approach, continued the Roosevelt-Taft policies. He defended the Monroe Doctrine, gave unspoken support to the Roosevelt Corollary, and intervened in Latin America more than had either Roosevelt or Taft.

In 1914, Wilson negotiated a treaty with Nicaragua to grant the United States exclusive rights to build a canal and lease sites for naval bases. This treaty made Nicaragua an American satellite. In 1915, he sent marines into Haiti to quell a revolution; they stayed until 1934. In 1916, he occupied the Dominican Republic, establishing a protectorate that lasted until 1924. By 1917, American troops "protected" Nicaragua, Haiti, the Dominican Republic, and Cuba—four nations that were U.S. dependencies in all but name.

Troubles across the Border

Wilson's moral diplomacy encountered one of its greatest challenges across the border in Mexico. Porfirio Díaz, president of Mexico for thirty-seven years, was overthrown in 1911. Díaz had encouraged foreign investments in Mexican mines, railroads, oil, and land; by 1913, Americans had invested over $1 billion. But most Mexicans remained poor and uneducated, and Díaz's overthrow led to a decade of violence that tested Wilson's policies and brought the United States close to war with Mexico.

A liberal reformer, Francisco I. Madero, followed Díaz as president in 1911. But Madero could not keep order in the troubled country, and opponents of his reforms undermined him. With support from wealthy landowners, the army, and the Catholic Church, General Victoriano Huerta ousted Madero in 1913, threw him in jail, and arranged his murder. Most European nations immediately recognized Huerta, but Wilson, calling him a "butcher," refused to do so. Instead, he announced a new policy toward revolutionary regimes in Latin America. To win American recognition, they must not only exercise power but reflect "a just government based upon law, not upon arbitrary or irregular force."

On that basis, Wilson withheld recognition from Huerta and maneuvered to oust him. Early in 1914, he stationed naval units off Mexico's ports to cut off arms shipments to the Huerta regime. The action produced trouble. On April 9, 1914, several American sailors, who went ashore in Tampico to purchase supplies, were arrested. They were promptly released, but the American admiral demanded an apology and a twenty-one-gun salute to the American flag. Huerta agreed— if the Americans also saluted the Mexican flag.

Wilson asked Congress for authority to use military force if needed; then, just as Congress acted, he learned that a German ship was landing arms at Vera Cruz on Mexico's eastern coast. With Wilson's approval, American warships shelled the harbor, and marines went ashore.

Against heavy resistance, they took the city. Outraged, Mexicans of all factions denounced the invasion, and for a time the two countries hovered on the edge of war.

Retreating hastily, Wilson explained that he desired only to help Mexico. Argentina, Brazil, and Chile came to his aid with an offer to mediate the dispute, and tensions eased. In July 1914, weakened by an armed rebellion, Huerta resigned. Wilson recognized the new government, headed by Venustiano Carranza, an associate of Madero. Early in 1916, Francisco ("Pancho") Villa, one of Carranza's generals, revolted. Hoping to goad the United States into an action that would help him seize power, he raided border towns, injuring American civilians. In January, he removed seventeen Americans from a train in Mexico and murdered them. Two months later he invaded Columbus, New Mexico, killing sixteen Americans and burning the town.

Stationing militia along the border, Wilson ordered General John J. Pershing on a punitive expedition to seize Villa in Mexico. Pershing led six thousand troops deep into Mexican territory.

*T*he goal of his policy in Latin America, Wilson once said, was "to teach the South American republics to elect good men." In the cartoon, Wilson shakes his finger at Mexico in obvious disapproval of the Mexican revolution and Huerta's government. The punitive expedition that Wilson eventually ordered into Mexico to seize rebel "Pancho" Villa, included the last mounted cavalry charge of the U.S. Army.

At first, Carranza agreed to the drive, but as the Americans pushed farther and farther into his country, he changed his mind. As the wily Villa eluded Pershing, Carranza protested bitterly, and Wilson, worried about events in Europe, ordered Pershing home.

Wilson's policy had laudable goals; he wanted to help the Mexicans achieve political and agrarian reform. But his motives and methods were condescending. Wilson tried to impose gradual, progressive reform on a society sharply divided along class and other lines. With little forethought, he interfered in the affairs of another country, and in doing so he revealed the themes —moralism, combined with pragmatic self-interest and a desire for peace—that also shaped his policies in Europe.

TOWARD WAR

In May 1914, Colonel Edward M. House, Wilson's close friend and adviser, sailed to Europe on a fact-finding mission. Tensions there were rising. "The situation is extraordinary," he reported to Wilson. "It is jingoism [extreme nationalism] run stark mad. . . . There is too much hatred, too many jealousies."

Large armies dominated the European continent. A web of alliances entangled nations, maximizing the risk that a local conflict could produce a wider war. In Germany, the ambitious Kaiser Wilhem II coveted a world empire to match those of Britain and France. Germany had military treaties with Turkey and Austria-Hungary, a sprawling Central European country of many nationalities. Linked in another alliance, England, France, and Russia agreed to aid each other in case of attack.

On June 28, 1914, a Bosnian assassin linked to Serbia murdered Archduke Franz Ferdinand, heir to the Austro-Hungarian throne. Within weeks Germany, Turkey, and Austria-Hungary (the Central Powers) were at war with England, France, and Russia (the Allied Powers). Americans were shocked at the events. "I had a feeling that the end of things had come . . . ," one of Wilson's cabinet members said. "I stopped in my

European Alliances and Battlefronts, 1914–1917

Allied forces suffered early defeats on the Eastern Front (Tannenberg) and in the Dardanelles (Gallipoli). In 1917, the Allies were routed on the southern flank (Caporetto); the Western Front then became the critical theater of the war. (See map on p. 723.)

tracks, dazed and horror-stricken." Wilson immediately proclaimed neutrality and asked Americans to remain "impartial in thought as well as in action."

The war, he said, was one "with which we have nothing to do, whose causes cannot touch us." In private, Wilson was stunned. A man who loved peace, he had long admired the British parliamentary system, and he respected the leaders of the British Liberal party, who supported social programs akin to his own. "Everything I love most in the world," he said, "is at stake."

The Neutrality Policy

In general, Americans accepted neutrality. They saw no need to enter the conflict, especially after the Allies in September 1914 halted the first German drive toward Paris. America resisted involvement in other countries' problems and had a tradition of freedom from foreign entanglements.

For the nation's large number of progressives, there were additional reasons to resist. War violated the very spirit of progressive reform. Why demand safer factories in which people could work and then kill them by the millions in war? To many progressives, moreover, England represented international finance, an institution they detested. Germany, on the other hand, had pioneered some of their favorite social reforms.

Furthermore, progressives and others tended to put the blame for war on the greed of "munition manufacturers, stockbrokers, and bond dealers" eager for wartime profits. "Do you want to know the cause of the war?" Henry Ford, who was no progressive, asked. "It is capitalism, greed, the dirty hunger for dollars." Above all, progressives were sure that war would end reform. It consumed money and attention; it inflamed emotions.

As a result, Jane Addams, Florence Kelley, Frederic C. Howe, Lillian Wald, and other progressives fought to keep the United States out of war. In late 1915, they formed the American Union Against Militarism, to throw, they said, "a monkey wrench into the machinery" of war. Throughout 1915 and 1916, *La Follette's Magazine*, the voice of the progressive leader, railed against the Morgans, Rockefellers, Du Ponts, and "the thirty-eight corporations most benefited by war

Although reports of German atrocities shocked Americans, most still adhered to the attitude expressed in the cartoon below: "Don't mix in a family quarrel."

orders." In 1915, Addams and Wald helped organize the League to Limit Armament, and shortly thereafter, Addams and Carrie Chapman Catt formed the Woman's Peace Party to organize women against the war.

The war's outbreak also tugged at the emotions of millions of immigrant Americans. Those who came from the British Isles tended to support the Allies; those from Ireland tended to support Germany, hoping that Britain's wartime troubles might free their homeland from British domination. The large population of German-Americans often sympathized with the Central Powers. But many people thought that, in a nation of immigrants, a policy of neutrality would be wise from a domestic point of view as well as from the viewpoint of foreign policy.

At the deepest level, a majority in the country, bound by common language and institutions, sympathized with the Allies and blamed Germany for the war. Like Wilson, many Americans admired English literature, customs, and law; they remembered Lafayette and the times when France had helped the United States in its early years. Germany, on the other hand, seemed arrogant and militaristic. When the war began, it invaded Belgium to strike at France and violated a treaty which the German chancellor called "just a scrap of paper." Many Americans resented the violation, and they liked it even less when

German troops executed Belgian civilians who resisted.

Both sides sought to sway American opinion, and fierce propaganda campaigns flourished. The German Literary Defense Committee distributed over a million pamphlets during the first year of the war. German propaganda tended to stress strength and will; Allied propaganda called on historical ties and took advantage of German atrocities, both real and alleged. In the end, the propaganda probably made little difference. Ties of heritage and the course of the war, not propaganda, decided the American position. At the outset, no matter which side they cheered for, Americans of all persuasions preferred simply to remain at peace.

Freedom of the Seas

The demands of trade tested American neutrality and confronted Wilson with difficult choices. Under international law, neutral countries were permitted to trade in nonmilitary goods with all belligerent countries. But Great Britain controlled the seas, and it intended to cut off shipments of war materials to the Central Powers.

As soon as war broke out, Britain blockaded German ports and limited the goods Americans could sell to Germany. American ships had to carry cargoes to neutral ports from which, after examination, they could be carried to Germany. As time passed, Britain stepped up the economic sanctions by forbidding the shipment to Germany of all foodstuffs and most raw materials, seizing and censoring mail, and "blacklisting" American firms that dealt directly with the Central Powers. British ships often stopped American ships and confiscated cargoes.

Again and again Wilson protested against such infringements on neutral rights. Sometimes Britain complied, sometimes not, and Wilson often grew angry. But needing American support and supplies, Britain pursued a careful strategy to disrupt German-American trade without disrupting Anglo-American relations. After forbidding cotton shipments to Germany in 1915, it agreed to buy enough cotton to make up for the losses. When necessary, it also promised to reimburse American businesses after the war's end.

Other than the German U-boats, there were no constraints on trade with the Allies, and a flood of Allied war orders fueled the American economy. England and France bought huge amounts of arms, grain, cotton, and clothing. To finance the purchases, the Allies turned to American bankers for loans. By 1917, loans to Allied governments exceeded $2 billion, while loans to Germany came to only $27 million.

In a development that influenced Wilson's policy, the war produced the greatest economic boom in the nation's history. Loans and trade drew the United States ever closer to the Allied cause. And even though Wilson often protested English maritime policy, the protests involved American goods and money whereas Germany's submarine policy threatened American lives.

The U-Boat Threat

A relatively new weapon, the *Unterseeboot*, or submarine, strained the guidelines of international law. Traditional law required a submarine to

A new and terrifying weapon of the war was the German U-boat, which attacked silently and without warning.

surface, warn the target to stop, send a boarding party to check papers and cargo, then allow time for passengers and crew to board lifeboats before sinking the vessel. Flimsy and slow, submarines could ill-afford to surface while the prey radioed for help. If they did surface, they might be rammed or blown up by deck guns.

When Germany announced the submarine campaign in February 1915, Wilson protested sharply, calling the sinking of merchant ships without checking cargo "a wanton act." The Germans promised not to sink American ships—an agreement that lasted until 1917—and thereafter the issue became the right of Americans to sail on the ships of belligerent nations. In March, an American citizen aboard the British liner *Falaba* perished when the ship was torpedoed off the Irish coast. Bryan urged Wilson to forbid Americans to travel in the war zones, but the President, determined to stand by the principles of international law, refused.

Wilson reacted more harshly in May and August of 1915 when U-boats sank the *Lusitania* and *Arabic*. He demanded that the Germans protect passenger vessels and pay for American losses. At odds with Wilson's understanding of neutrality, Bryan resigned as secretary of state and was replaced by Robert Lansing, a lawyer and counselor in the State Department. Lansing brought a very different spirit to the job. He favored the Allies and believed that democracy was threatened in a world dominated by Germany. He urged strong stands against German violations of American neutrality.

In February 1916, Germany declared unrestricted submarine warfare against all *armed* ships. Lansing protested and told Germany it would be held strictly accountable for American losses. A month later, a U-boat torpedoed the unarmed French channel steamer, *Sussex*, without warning, injuring several Americans. Arguing that the sinking violated the *Arabic* pledge, Lansing urged Wilson to break relations with Germany. Wilson rejected the advice, but on April 18 sent an ultimatum to Germany, stating that unless the Germans immediately called off attacks on cargo and passenger ships, the United States would sever relations.

The kaiser, convinced he did not yet have enough submarines to risk war, yielded. In the *Sussex* pledge of May 4, 1916, he agreed to

Roosevelt's campaign for preparedness became a personal attack on Wilson, whom TR called a coward and a weakling.

Wilson's demands and promised to shoot on sight only ships of the enemy's navy. But he attached the condition that the United States compel the Allies to end their blockade and comply with international law. Wilson accepted the pledge but turned down the condition.

The *Sussex* pledge marked the beginning of a short period of friendly relations between Germany and the United States. The agreement applied not only to passenger liners, but to *all* merchant ships, belligerent or not. There was one problem: Wilson had taken such a strong position that if Germany renewed submarine warfare on merchant shipping, war was likely. Most Americans, however, viewed the agreement as a diplomatic stroke for peace by Wilson, and the issues of peace and preparedness dominated the presidential election of 1916.

"He Kept Us Out of War"

The "preparedness" issue pitted antiwar groups against those who wanted to prepare for war. The American Rights Committee, the National Security League, and other groups urged stepped-up military measures in case of war. In the summer of 1915, they persuaded the War Department to hold a training camp in Plattsburg, New York, in which regular army officers trained 1200 civilian volunteers in modern warfare. The following summer 16,000 volunteers participated in such training camps.

Bellicose as always, Teddy Roosevelt led the preparedness campaign. He called Wilson "yellow" for not pressing Germany harder and scoffed at the popular song, "I Didn't Raise My Boy to Be a Soldier," which he compared to singing "I Didn't Raise My Girl to Be a Mother." Defending the military's state of readiness, Wilson refused to be stampeded just because "some amongst us are nervous and excited." In fact, when government revenue dropped in 1915, he cut military appropriations.

Wilson's position was attacked from both sides as preparedness advocates charged cowardice, while pacifists denounced any attempt at military readiness. The difficulty of his situation, plus the growing U-boat crisis, soon changed Wilson's mind. In mid-1915, he asked the War Department to increase military planning, and he quietly notified congressional leaders of a switch in policy. Later that year, Wilson approved large increases in the army and navy, a move that upset many peace-minded progressives. In January 1916, he toured the country to promote preparedness, and in June, with an American flag draped over his shoulder, he marched in a giant preparedness parade in Washington.

For their standard-bearer in the presidential election of 1916, the Republicans nominated Charles Evans Hughes, a moderate justice of the Supreme Court. Hughes seemed to have all the qualifications for victory. A former reform governor of New York, he could lure back the Roosevelt progressives, while at the same time appealing to the Republican conservatives. To woo the Roosevelt wing, Hughes called for a tougher line against Germany, thus allowing the Democrats to label him the "war" candidate. Even so, Roosevelt and others considered Hughes a "bearded iceberg," a dull campaigner who wavered on important issues.

The Democrats renominated Wilson in a convention marked by spontaneous demonstrations for peace. Determined to outdo Republican patriotism, Wilson himself had ordered the convention's theme to be "Americanism." The delegates were to sing "America" and "The Star-Spangled Banner," and to cheer any mention of America and the flag. They did it all dutifully but then

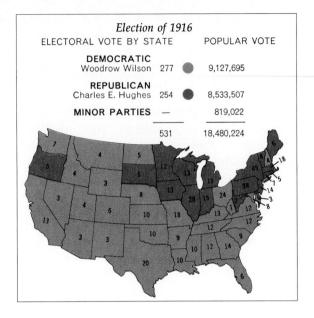

Election of 1916

broke into spontaneous applause at the mention of Wilson's careful diplomatic moves. As the keynote speaker reviewed them, the delegates shouted: "What did we do? What did we do?" The speaker shouted back: "We didn't go to war! We didn't go to war!"

Picking up the theme, perhaps with reservation, Wilson said in October: "I am not expecting this country to get into war." The campaign slogan, "He kept us out of war" was repeated again and again, and just before the election, the Democrats took full-page ads in leading newspapers:

> You Are Working—Not Fighting!
> Alive and Happy—Not Cannon Fodder!
> Wilson and Peace with Honor?
> or
> Hughes with Roosevelt and War?

On election night, Hughes had swept most of the East, and Wilson retired at 10 P.M., thinking he had lost. During the night, the results came in from California, New Mexico, and North Dakota; all supported Wilson—California by a mere 3773 votes. Wilson won with 9.1 million votes against 8.5 million for Hughes. Holding the Democratic South, he carried key states in the Midwest and West and took large portions of the labor and progressive vote. Women—who were then allowed to vote in presidential elections in twelve states—also voted heavily for Wilson.

The Final Months of Peace

Just before election day, Great Britain further limited neutral trade, and there were reports from Germany of a renewal of unrestricted submarine warfare. Fresh from his victory, Wilson redoubled his efforts for peace. Aware that time was running out, he hoped to start negotiations to end the bloodshed and create a peaceful postwar world.

In December 1916, he sent messages to both sides asking them to state their war aims. Should they do so, he pledged the "whole force" of the United States to end the war. The Allies refused, although they promised privately to negotiate if the German terms were reasonable. The Germans replied evasively and in January 1917 revealed their real objectives. Close to forcing Russia out of the war, Germany sensed victory and wanted territory in eastern Europe, Africa, Belgium, and France.

On January 22, in an eloquent speech before the Senate, Wilson called for a "peace without victory." Outlining his own ambitious aims, he urged respect for all nations, freedom of the seas, arms limitations, and a league of nations to keep the peace. "Only a peace between equals can last, only a peace the very principle of which is equality and a common participation in a common benefit." The speech made a great impression on many Europeans, but it was too late. The Germans had decided a few weeks before to unleash the submarines and gamble on a quick end to the war. Even as Wilson spoke, U-boats were in the Atlantic west of Ireland, preparing to attack.

On January 31, the German ambassador in Washington informed Lansing that beginning February 1, U-boats would sink on sight all ships—passenger or merchant, neutral or belligerent, armed or unarmed—in the waters around England and France. Staking everything on a last effort, the Germans calculated that if they could sink 600,000 tons of shipping a month, they could defeat England in six months. As he had pledged in 1916, Wilson broke off relations with Germany, although he still hoped for peace.

On February 25 the British government privately gave Wilson a telegram intercepted from Arthur Zimmermann, the German foreign minister, to the German ambassador in Mexico. A day later, Wilson asked Congress for authority to arm merchant ships to deter U-boat attacks. When La Follette and a handful of others threatened to filibuster, Wilson divulged the contents of the

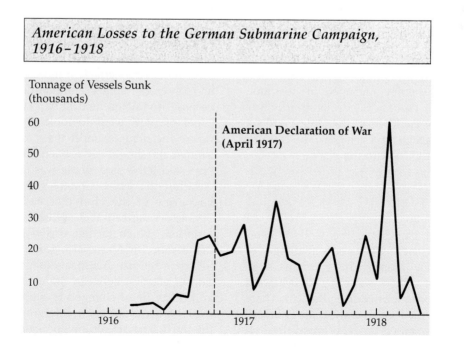

American Losses to the German Submarine Campaign, 1916–1918

Zimmermann telegram. It proposed an alliance with Mexico in case of war with the United States, offering financial support and recovery of Mexico's "lost territory" in New Mexico, Texas, and Arizona.

Spurred by a wave of public indignation toward the Germans, the House passed Wilson's measure, but La Follette and others still blocked action in the Senate. On March 9, 1917, Wilson ordered merchant ships armed on his own authority. Three days later, he announced the arming, and on March 13, the navy instructed all vessels to fire on submarines. Between March 12 and March 21, U-boats sank five American ships, and Wilson decided to wait no longer.

He called Congress into special session and at 8:30 in the evening on April 2, 1917, asked for a declaration of war. "It is a fearful thing to lead this great peaceful people into war, into the most terrible and disastrous of all wars, civilization itself seeming to be in the balance. But the right is more precious than peace, and we shall fight for the things which we have always carried nearest our hearts,—for democracy, . . . for the rights and liberties of small nations, for a universal dominion of right by such a concert of free peoples as shall bring peace and safety to all nations and make the world itself at last free."

Congressmen broke into applause and crowded the aisles to congratulate Wilson. "My message today was a message of death for our young men," he said afterward. "How strange it seems to applaud that."

Pacifists in Congress continued to hold out, and for four days they managed to postpone action. Finally, on April 6, the declaration of war passed, with fifty members of the House and six Senators voting against it. Even now, the country was divided over entry into the war.

OVER THERE

With a burst of patriotism, the United States entered a war its new allies were in danger of losing. That same month, the Germans sank 881,000 tons of Allied shipping, the highest amount for any one month during the war. There were mutinies in the French army; a costly British drive in Flanders stalled. In November, the Bolsheviks seized power in Russia, and led by V. I.

Lenin, they soon signed a separate peace treaty with Germany (see the map on p. 716), freeing German troops to fight in the West. German and Austrian forces routed the Italian army on the southern flank, and the Allies braced for a spring 1918 offensive.

Mobilization

The United States was not prepared for war. Some Americans hoped the declaration of war itself might daunt the Germans; there were those who thought that naval escorts of Allied shipping would be enough. Others hoped money and arms supplied to the Allies would be sufficient to produce victory without sending troops. "Good Lord!" an influential senator exclaimed just after war was declared. "You're not going to send soldiers over there, are you?"

Bypassing older generals, Wilson named "Black Jack" Pershing, leader of the Mexican campaign, to head the American Expeditionary Force (AEF). Pershing inherited an army unready for war. In April 1917, it had 200,000 officers and men, equipped with 300,000 old rifles, 1500 machine guns, 55 out-of-date airplanes, and 2 field radio sets. Its most recent battle experience had been chasing Pancho Villa around northern Mexico. It had not caught him.

The armed forces had just two war plans: War Plan Orange, for a defensive war against Japan in the Pacific, and War Plan Black, to counter a possible German attack in the Caribbean. Wilson had ordered military commanders not to plan because it violated neutrality. "When the Acting Chief of Staff went to look at the secret files where the plans to meet the situation that confronted us should have been found," Pershing later said, "the pigeonhole was empty."

Although some in Congress preferred a voluntary army of the kind that had fought in the Spanish-American War, Wilson turned to conscription, which he felt was both efficient and democratic. In May 1917, Congress passed the Selective Service Act, providing for the registration of all men between the ages of twenty-one and thirty (later changed to eighteen and forty-five). Early in June, 9.5 million men registered for the draft. The act ultimately registered 24.2 million men, about 2.8 million of whom were inducted into the army. Defending the draft, Wilson said it was not really a draft at all, but a "selection from a nation which has volunteered in mass."

The draft included black men as well as white and four African-American regiments were among the first sent into action. Despite their contributions, however, no black soldiers were allowed to march in the victory celebrations that eventually took place in Paris. Nor were they included in a French mural of the different races in the war, even though black servicemen from English and French colonies were represented.

War in the Trenches

World War I may have been the most terrible war of all time, more terrible even than World War II and its vast devastation. After the early offensives, the European armies dug themselves into trenches only hundreds of yards apart in places. Artillery, poison gas, hand grenades, and a new weapon—rapid-fire machine guns—kept them pinned down.

Even in moments of respite, the mud, rats, cold, fear, and disease took a heavy toll. Deafening bombardments shook the earth, and there was a high incidence of shell shock. From time to time, troops went "over the top" of the trenches in an effort to break through the enemy's lines, but the costs were enormous. The German offensive at Verdun in 1916 killed 600,000 men; the British lost 20,000 on the first day of an offensive on the Somme.

The first American soldiers reached France in June 1917. By March of the following year, 300,000 Americans were there, and by war's end, 2 million men had crossed the Atlantic. No troop ships were sunk, a credit to the British and American navies. In the summer of 1917, Admiral William S. Sims, a brilliant American strategist, pushed through a convoy plan that used Allied destroyers to escort merchant vessels across the ocean. At first resisted by English captains who

The Western Front: U.S. Participation, 1918

The turning point of the war came in July, when the German advance was halted at the Marne. The "Yanks," now a fighting force, were thrown into the breach. They played a dramatic role in stemming the tide and mounting the counteroffensives that ended the war.

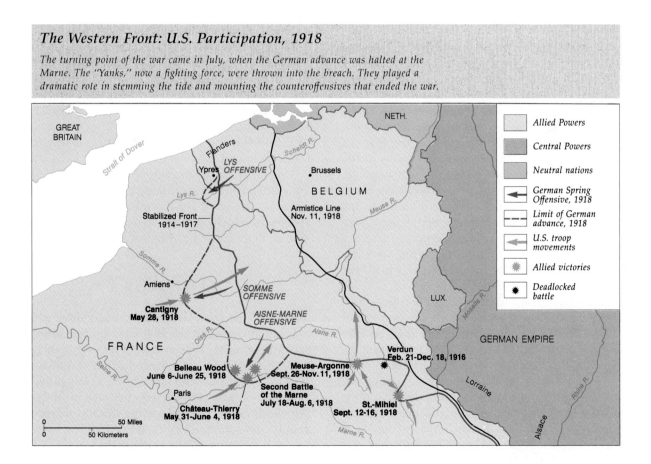

German prisoners and American wounded returning from the front lines of the Meuse-Argonne. More Americans died in that campaign than in the rest of the war.

liked to sail alone, the plan soon cut shipping losses in half.

As expected, on March 21, 1918, the Germans launched a massive assault in western Europe. Troops from the Russian front added to the force, and by May they had driven Allied forces back to the Marne River, just fifty miles from Paris. There, the Americans saw their first action. The American forces blocked the Germans at the town of Château-Thierry, and four weeks later forced them out of Belleau Wood, a crucial stronghold. On July 15, the Germans threw everything into a last drive for Paris, but they were halted at the Marne, and in three days of battle they were finished. "On the 18th," the German chancellor said, "even the most optimistic among us knew that all was lost. The history of the world was played out in three days."

With the German drive stalled, the Allies counterattacked along the entire front. On September 12, 1918, half a million Americans and a smaller contingent of French drove the Germans from the St. Mihiel salient, twelve miles south of Verdun. Two weeks later, 896,000 American soldiers attacked between the Meuse River and the Argonne Forest. Focusing their efforts on a main railroad supply line for the German army in the West, American troops broke through in early Novem-

ber, cut the line, and drove the Germans back along the whole front.

The German high command knew that the war was lost. On October 6, 1918, Germany appealed to Wilson for an armistice, and by the end of the month, Turkey, Bulgaria, and Austria-Hungary were out of the war. At 4 A.M. on November 11, Germany signed the armistice. The AEF lost 48,909 dead and 230,000 wounded; losses to disease brought the total of dead to over 112,000.

The American contribution, although small in comparison to the enormous costs to European nations, was vital. Fresh, enthusiastic American troops raised Allied morale; they helped turn the tide at a crucial point in the war.

OVER HERE

Victory at the front depended on economic and emotional mobilization at home. Consolidating federal authority, Wilson moved quickly in 1917 and 1918 to organize war production and distribution. An idealist who knew how to sway public opinion, he also recognized the need to enlist American emotions. To him, the war for people's minds, the "conquest of their convictions," was as vital as events on the battlefield.

*T*he use of machine guns by both sides in World War I forced the infantry into the trenches, greatly reducing its mobility and causing heavy casualties whenever troops advanced.

The Conquest of Convictions

A week after war was declared, Wilson formed the Committee on Public Information (CPI) and asked George Creel, an outspoken progressive journalist, to head it. Creel hired other progressives like Ida Tarbell and Ray Stannard Baker, and recruited thousands of people in the arts, advertising, and film industries to publicize the war. He worked out a system of voluntary censorship with the press, plastered walls with colorful posters, and issued more than seventy-five million pamphlets.

Creel also enlisted 75,000 "four-minute men" to give quick speeches at public gatherings and places of entertainment on "Why We Are Fighting" and "The Meaning of America." At first, they were instructed to stress facts and stay away from emotions, particularly hatred, but by the beginning of 1918, the instructions shifted; the Germans were to be depicted as bloodthirsty Huns bent on world conquest. Exploiting a new medium, the CPI promoted films like *The Prussian Cur* and *The Kaiser, the Beast of Berlin*. Creel secretly subsidized several prowar groups and formed the CPI's Division of Industrial Relations to rally labor to the war.

Helped along by the propaganda campaign, anti-German sentiment spread rapidly. Many schools stopped offering instruction in the German language—California's state education board called it a language "of autocracy, brutality, and hatred." Sauerkraut became "liberty cabbage," saloon-keepers removed pretzels from the bar. Orchestral works by Bach, Beethoven, and Brahms vanished from some symphonic programs, and the New York Philharmonic agreed not to perform the music of living German composers. Government agents harassed Karl Muck, the German conductor of the Boston Symphony, imprisoned him for over a year, and then after the war ended, deported him. German-Americans and antiwar figures were badgered, beaten, and in some cases killed.

Vigilantism, sparked often by superpatriotism of a ruthless sort, flourished. Frequently it focused on radical antiwar figures like Frank Little, an IWW official in Butte, Montana, who was taken from his boardinghouse in August 1917, tied to the rear of an automobile, and dragged through the streets until his kneecaps were scraped off. Little was then hanged from a railroad trestle. In April 1918, a Missouri mob seized Robert Prager, a young man whose sole crime was being born in Germany. They bound him with an American flag, paraded him through town, and then lynched him. A jury acquitted the mob's members—who wore red, white, and blue ribbons to court—as one juror shouted: "Well, I guess nobody can say we aren't loyal now."

Rather than curbing the repression, Wilson encouraged it. "Woe be to the man or group of men that seeks to stand in our way," he told peace advocates soon after the war began. At his request, Congress passed the Espionage Act of 1917, which imposed sentences of up to twenty years in prison for persons found guilty of aiding the enemy, obstructing recruitment of soldiers, or encouraging disloyalty. It allowed the postmaster general to remove from the mails materials that incited treason or insurrection. The Trading-with-the-Enemy Act of 1917 authorized the government to censor the foreign-language press.

In 1918, Congress passed the Sedition Act, imposing harsh penalties on anyone using "disloyal, profane, scurrilous, or abusive language" about the government, flag, or armed forces uniforms. In all, over fifteen hundred persons were arrested under the new laws. People indicted or imprisoned included a Californian who laughed at rookies drilling at an army camp, a woman who greeted a Red Cross solicitor in a "hostile" way, and an editor who printed the sentence: "We must make the world safe for democracy even if we have to 'bean' the Goddess of Liberty to do it."

The sedition laws clearly went beyond any clear or present danger. There were, to be sure, German spies in the country, Germans who wanted to encourage strikes in American arms factories. Moreover, the United States government and other national leaders were painfully aware of how divided Americans had been about entering the war. They set out to promote unity —by force, if necessary—in order to convince Germany that the nation was united behind the war.

But none of these matters warranted a nationwide program of repression. Conservatives took advantage of wartime feelings to try to stamp out American socialists, who in fact were vulnerable because, unlike their European counterparts, they continued to oppose the war even after their country had entered it. Using the sedition laws, conservatives harried the Socialist party and another favorite target, the Industrial Workers of the World (see Chapter 22). In 1921, ill and facing imprisonment, Big Bill Haywood, one of the IWWs best-known members fled to the Soviet Union where he died a few years later.

Wilson's postmaster general banned from the mails more than a dozen socialist publications, including the *Appeal to Reason* which went to over half a million people weekly. In 1918, Eugene V. Debs, the Socialist party leader, delivered a speech denouncing capitalism and the war. He was convicted for violation of the Espionage Act and spent the war in a penitentiary in Atlanta. Nominated as the Socialist party candidate in the presidential election of 1920, Debs—prisoner 9653—won nearly a million votes, but the Socialist movement never fully recovered from the repression of the war.

In fostering hostility towards anything that smacked of dissent, the war also gave rise to the great "Red Scare" that began in 1919 (see Chapter 25). Pleased at first with the Russian revolution, Americans in general turned quickly against it, especially after Lenin and the Bolsheviks

*E*ugene V. Debs, serving time in an Atlanta penitentiary for speaking out against the war, is shown here after receiving word of his nomination for the presidency. Debs campaigned in 1920 from behind bars.

seized control late in 1917. The Americans feared Lenin's anticapitalist program, and they denounced his decision in early 1918 to make peace with Germany because it freed German troops to fight in France.

Once again, Wilson himself played a prominent role in the development of anti-Bolshevik sentiment. In the summer of 1918, he sent fifteen thousand American troops into the Soviet Union, where they joined other Allied soldiers. Ostensibly, the troops were there to protect Allied supplies from the Germans and to rescue a large number of Czechs who wanted to return home to fight Germany. But the underlying reason for their presence was that Wilson and others hoped to bring down the fledgling Bolshevik government, fearful it would spread revolution around the world.

Besides sending troops, Wilson joined in an economic blockade of Russia, sent weapons to anti-Bolshevik insurgents, and refused to recognize Lenin's government. He also blocked Russian participation in the peace conference that ended the war. American troops remained in

Russia until April 1920, and on the whole, American willingness to interfere soured Russian-American relations for decades to come.

A Bureaucratic War

Quick, effective action was needed to win the war. To meet the need, Wilson and Congress set up an array of new federal agencies, nearly five thousand in all. Staffed largely by businessmen, the agencies drew on funds and powers of a hitherto unknown scope. At night, the secretary of the treasury sat in bed, a yellow pad on his knees, adding up the money needed to finance the war. "The noughts attached to the many millions were so boisterous and prolific," he later said, "that, at times, they would run clear over the edge of the paper."

By the time the war was over, the "noughts" had boisterously added up to $32 billion in direct war expense—in an era when the entire federal budget rarely exceeded $1 billion. To raise the money, the administration sold about $23 billion in "Liberty Bonds" and, using the new Sixteenth Amendment (see Chapter 23), boosted taxes on corporations and personal incomes. The taxes brought in another $10 billion to help pay for the war.

At first Wilson tried to organize the wartime economy along decentralized lines, almost in the fashion of his early New Freedom thinking. But that proved unworkable, and he moved instead to a series of highly centralized planning boards, each with broad authority over a specific area of the economy. There were boards to control virtually every aspect of transportation, agriculture, and manufacturing. Though only a few of them were as effective as Wilson had hoped, they did coordinate the war effort to some degree.

The War Industries Board, one of the most powerful of the new agencies, oversaw the production of all American factories. Headed by millionaire Bernard M. Baruch, a Wall Street broker and speculator, it determined priorities, allocated raw materials, and fixed prices. It told manufacturers what they could and could not make. The WIB set the output of steel and regulated the number of stops on elevators. Working closely with business, Baruch for a time acted as the dictator of the American economy.

Celebrities were recruited to drum up financial support for the war and to improve civilian morale. Here, film actor Douglas Fairbanks calls for the purchase of war bonds at a rally on Wall Street.

Herbert Hoover, the hero of a campaign to feed starving Belgians, headed a new Food Administration, and he set out with customary energy to supply food to the armies overseas. Appealing to the "spirit of self-sacrifice," Hoover convinced people to save food by observing "meatless" and "wheatless" days. He fixed prices to boost production, bought and distributed wheat, and encouraged people to plant "victory gardens" behind homes, churches, and schools. He sent half a million persons door-to-door to get housewives to sign cards pledging their cooperation. One householder—Wilson—set an example by grazing sheep on the White House lawn.

At another new agency, the Fuel Administration, Harry A. Garfield, the president of Williams College, introduced daylight saving time, rationed coal and oil, and imposed gasless days when motorists could not drive. To save coal, he shut down nonessential factories one day a week, and in January 1918, he closed all factories east of the Mississippi for four days to divert coal to

ℳeasuring the Mind

From 1870 to 1920, scientists and physicians explored new ideas about the mind. In Europe, the Viennese psychiatrist Sigmund Freud studied the unconscious, which, he thought, shaped human behavior. Russia's Ivan Pavlov tested the conditioned reflex in mental activity (Pavlov's dogs), and in the United States William James, the psychologist and philosopher, examined emotions and linked psychology to everyday problems.

As one way of understanding *the mind*, psychologists studied the mental processes of a great many minds, a task to which the relatively new science of statistics lent a hand. Testing large samples of subjects, they developed the concept of the "normal" and "average," helpful boundaries used to determine an individual's place in the population. In 1890, the psychologist James McKeen Cattell tested one hundred freshmen at the University of Pennsylvania for vision and hearing, sensitivity to pain, reaction time, and memory. He called these examinations by a new name—"mental tests"—and the idea spread. In 1895, the American Psychological Association (APA) set up a special committee to promote the nationwide collection of mental statistics.

Work was underway on both sides of the ocean, and in 1905 Alfred Binet and Theodore Simon, two French psychologists, devised a metric intelligence scale. Seizing on the idea that until maturity, intelligence increases with age, they tested children of various ages to find an average level of perfor-

Administered to soldiers in groups, the IQ test was used in World War I to classify recruits and determine which of them were "officer material." The results of the tests not only raised questions about the mental abilities and backgrounds of the men, but also about the possible biases in the tests themselves.

mance for each age. Once they had determined the average, they could compare any child's test performance with it and thus distinguish between the child's "mental age" and chronological age. In 1912, William Stein, a German psychologist, introduced the "Intelligence Quotient," found by dividing a person's mental age by the chronological age. In 1916, Lewis M. Terman of Stanford University improved Binet's test, and the term I.Q. became part of the American vocabulary.

Employers and educators, however, remained skeptical of measuring intelligence. Thus, when the United States entered World War I, psychologists at once saw the op-

portunity to overcome the doubts and prove their theories. Huge numbers of men needed to be recruited, classified, and assigned to units quickly. Why not use the new mental tests? APA leaders formed twelve committees, including one on the Psychological Examination of Recruits, to explore the military uses of psychology.

Preferring to issue promotions on the basis of seniority, the army resisted the "mental meddlers," but the APA persuaded the War Department to make use of the tests. In early 1918, psychological examiners were posted at all training camps to administer the Alpha Test to literates and the Beta Test (with instructions given in pantomime) to illiterates and those who did not understand English. At the start of each Alpha Test, the examiners put the men at ease by explaining that the army was "not looking for crazy people. The aim is to help find out what we are best fitted to do." On the Beta Test, which was made up largely of pictures, the examiners were reminded that Beta men "sometimes sulk and refuse to work."

On the basis of the tests, the examiners classified recruits as "superior," "average," or "inferior." From the "superior" category, they selected men for officer training, a helpful winnowing process in an army that expanded quickly from 9000 officers to 200,000. That task done, they distributed the remaining "superior," "average," and "inferior" men among each military unit. In all, the examiners tested 1.7 million men—by far the largest testing program in human history to that time. To some degree the tests served their purpose, but they also seemed to raise questions about the education and mental ability of many American men.

For one thing, there was the extent of illiteracy—nearly one-quarter of the draft-age men in 1918 could neither read nor write. (One-third, incidentally, were physically unfit for service.) There was also the limited schooling of the recruits, most of whom had left school between the fifth and seventh grades. More alarming, according to the test results, 47 percent of the white draftees and 89 percent of the black draftees had a "mental age" of twelve years or under, which classified them as "feeble-minded." Did that mean half or more of the American population was feebleminded?

The tests also turned up racial and national distinctions—or so some of the examiners concluded.

Men of "native" backgrounds and "old" immigrant stock (from northern Europe and the British Isles) tended to score well and fall in the "superior" category; "new" immigrants (from central and southern Europe) tended to score less well and rank as "inferior." Among Russian, Polish, and Italian draftees, more than half were classified as "inferior." Such results came as no surprise to those who had long doubted the intelligence of the "new" immigrants, nor did the fact that 80 percent of the African Americans taking the Alpha Test scored in the inferior range.

Some observers, however, wondered what the tests really measured. The APA examiners claimed they measured "native intelligence," but questions about Edgar Allan Poe's poem "The Raven" or the paintings of Rosa Bonheur, a French artist of the mid-nineteenth century, required answers that native intelligence alone could not supply. When blacks and whites scored comparably on the early Beta Test, the examiners decided that something must be wrong with the test, so they changed the questions until the scores showed the expected racial differences. Most of those taking the Beta Test had never taken a written test before; many had probably never held a pencil.

Still skeptical, the army discontinued the tests the moment the war ended, but what the army rejected, the nation adopted. Businesses, government, and above all, educational institutions found greater and greater uses for intelligence testing. In 1926, the College Entrance Examination Board (CEEB) administered the first Scholastic Aptitude Test (SAT), designed to test "intelligence" and predict performance in college. In 1935, it established scoring ranges from 200 to 800, with the average score set at 500. During World War II SAT tests were widely used. In 1947, the CEEB became part of a new Educational Testing Service that spurred an educational revolution by making intelligence instead of social or economic standing the main criterion of college admissions.

Before long, intelligence testing —the measuring of minds— touched every aspect of American life. Shaping lives and careers, it pushed some people forward and held others back, in the military, industry, the civil service, and higher education. "Intelligence tests. . ." an expert said in 1971, "have more and more become society's instrument for the selection of human resources."

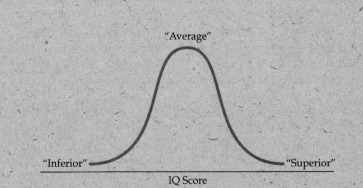

munitions ships stranded in New York harbor. A fourth agency, the Railroad Administration, dictated rail traffic over nearly 400,000 miles of track—standardizing rates, limiting passenger travel, and speeding arms shipments. The War Shipping Board coordinated shipping, the Emergency Fleet Corporation supervised shipbuilding, and the War Trade Board oversaw foreign trade.

As never before, the government intervened in American life. When strikes threatened the telephone and telegraph companies, the government simply seized and ran them. Businessmen, paid a nominal dollar a year, flocked to Washington to run the new agencies, and the partnership between government and business grew closer. As government expanded, business expanded as well, responding to wartime contracts. Industries like steel, aluminum, and cigarettes boomed, and corporate profits increased threefold between 1914 and 1919.

Labor in the War

The war also brought organized labor into the partnership with government, although the results were more limited than in the business-government alliance. Samuel Gompers, president of the AFL, served on Wilson's Council of National Defense, an advisory group formed to unify business, labor, and government. Gompers hoped to trade labor peace for labor advances, and he formed a War Committee on Labor to enlist workers' support for the war. With the blessing of the Wilson administration, membership in the AFL and other unions grew from about 2.7 million in 1916 to more than 4 million in 1919.

Hoping to encourage production and avoid strikes, Wilson adopted many of the objectives of the social-justice reformers. He supported an eight-hour day in war-related industries and improved wages and working conditions. In May 1918, he named Felix Frankfurter, a brilliant young law professor, to head a new War Labor Board. The agency standardized wages and hours, and at Wilson's direction, it protected the right of labor to organize and bargain collectively. Although it did not forbid strikes, it used various tactics to discourage them. It enforced decisions in well-publicized cases; when the Smith and Wesson arms factory in Massachusetts and the Western Union telegraph company disobeyed the WLB's union rules, the union took them over.

The WLB also ordered that women be paid equal wages for equal work in war industries. In 1914, the flow of European immigrants suddenly stopped because of the war, and in 1917, the draft began to take large numbers of American men. The result was a labor shortage, filled by women, African Americans, and Mexican-Americans. One million women worked in war industries. Some of them took jobs previously held by men, but for the most part, they moved from one set of "women's jobs" into another. From the beginning of the war to the end, the number of women in the work force held steady at about eight million, and unlike the experience in World War II, large numbers of housewives did not leave the home for machine shops and arms plants.

Still, there were some new opportunities and in some cases higher pay. In food, airplane, and electrical plants, women made up one-fifth or more of the work force. As their wages increased, so did their expectations; some became more militant, and conflict grew between them and male co-workers. To set standards for female employment, a Women's Bureau was established in the Department of Labor, but the government's influence varied. In the federally run railroad industry, women often made wages equal to those of men; in the federally run telephone industry, they did not.

Looking for more people to fill wartime jobs, corporations found another major source among southern blacks. Beginning in 1916, northern labor agents traveled across the South, promising jobs, high wages, and free transportation. Soon the word spread, and the movement northward became a flood. Between 1916 and 1918, over 450,000 African Americans left the Old South for the booming industrial cities of Saint Louis, Chicago, Detroit, and Cleveland. In the decade before 1920, Detroit's black population grew by over 600 percent, Cleveland's by over 300 percent, and Chicago's by 150 percent.

Most of the newcomers were young, unmarried, and skilled or semiskilled. The men found jobs in factories, railroad yards, steel mills, packing houses, and coal mines; black women worked in textile factories, department stores, and restaurants. In their new homes, African Americans

Housewives did not leave home for the factory en masse in 1917 as they later did during World War II, but many women already employed outside the home found new, well-paying opportunities in jobs previously held by men.

found greater racial freedom but also different living conditions. If the South was often hostile, the North could be impersonal and lonely. Accustomed to the pace of the farm—ruled by the seasons and the sun—those blacks who were able to enter the industrial sector now worked for hourly wages in mass-production industries, where time clocks and foremen dictated the daily routine.

Racial tensions increased, resulting in part from growing competition for housing and jobs. In mid-1917, a race war in East Saint Louis, Illinois, killed nine whites and about forty blacks. In July 1919, the month President Wilson returned from the peace conference in Paris, a race riot in Washington, D.C., killed six people. Riots in Chicago that month killed thirty-eight—fifteen whites and twenty-three blacks—and there were later outbreaks in New York City and Omaha. Lynch mobs killed forty-eight blacks in 1917, sixty-three in 1918, and seventy-eight in 1919. Ten of the victims in 1919 were war veterans, several still in uniform.

Blacks were more and more inclined to fight back. Two hundred thousand blacks served in France—forty-two thousand as combat troops. Returning home, they expected better treatment. "I'm glad I went," a black veteran said. "I done my part and I'm going to fight right here till Uncle Sam does his." Roscoe Jameson, Claude McKay, and other black poets wrote biting poetry, some of it—like Fenton Johnson's "The New Day"—drawn from the war experience:

> For we have been with thee in No Man's Land,
> Through lake of fire and down to Hell itself;
> And now we ask of thee our liberty,
> Our freedom in the land of Stars and Stripes.

"Lift Ev'ry Voice and Sing," composed in 1900, became known as the "Negro National Anthem." Parents bought black dolls for their children, and W. E. B. Du Bois spoke of a "New Negro," proud and more militant: "We return. We return from fighting. We return fighting."

Eager for cheap labor, farmers and ranchers in the Southwest persuaded the federal government to relax immigration restrictions, and between 1917 and 1920 over 100,000 Mexicans migrated into Texas, Arizona, New Mexico, and California. The Mexican-American population grew from 385,000 in 1910 to 740,000 in 1920. Tens of thousands of Mexican-Americans moved to Chicago, Saint Louis, Omaha, and other northern cities to take wartime jobs. Often scorned and insecure, they created urban *barrios*, similar to the Chinatowns and Little Italys around them.

Like most wars, World War I affected patterns at home as much as abroad. Business profits grew, factories expanded, and industries turned out huge amounts of war goods. Government authority swelled, and people came to expect different things of their government. Labor made some gains, as did women and blacks. Society assimilated some of the shifts, but social and economic tensions grew, and when the war ended, they spilled over in the strikes and violence of the Red Scare that followed.

The United States emerged from the war the strongest economic power in the world. In 1914, it was a debtor nation, and American citizens owed foreign investors about $3 billion. Five years later, the United States had become a creditor nation. Foreign governments owed over $10 billion, and foreign citizens owed American investors nearly $3 billion. The war marked a shift in economic power rarely equaled in history.

The 369th infantry regiment returning from the war on the SS Stockholm *in February 1919. They were awarded the Croix de Guerre for bravery in the Meuse-Argonne.*

THE TREATY OF VERSAILLES

Long before the fighting ended, Wilson began to formulate plans for the peace. Like many others, he was disconcerted when the new Bolshevik government in Russia began revealing the terms of secret agreements among Britain, France, and czarist Russia to divide up Germany's colonies. To try to place the war on a higher plane, he appeared before Congress on January 8, 1918, and outlined terms for a far-reaching, nonpunitive settlement. Wilson's Fourteen Points were generous and farsighted, but they failed to satisfy wartime emotions that sought vindication.

England and France distrusted Wilsonian idealism as the basis for peace. They wanted Germany disarmed and crippled; they wanted its colonies; and they were skeptical of the principle of self-determination. As the end of the war neared, the Allies, who had in fact made secret commitments with one another, balked at making the Fourteen Points the basis of peace. When Wilson threatened to negotiate a separate treaty with Germany, however, they accepted.

Wilson had won an important victory, but difficulties lay ahead. As Georges Clemenceau, the seventy-eight-year-old French premier, said: "God gave us the Ten Commandments, and we broke them. Wilson gives us the Fourteen Points. We shall see."

A Peace at Paris

Unfortunately, Wilson made a grave error just before the peace conference began. He appealed to voters to elect a Democratic Congress in the November 1918 elections, saying that any other result would be "interpreted on the other side of the water as a repudiation of my leadership." Many Republicans were furious, especially those who had supported the Fourteen Points; Wilson's problems worsened when the Democrats went on to lose both the House and Senate.

Wilson's opponents immediately announced that voters had rejected his policies, as he had suggested they could. In fact, the Democratic losses stemmed largely from domestic problems, such as the price of wheat and cotton. But they hurt Wilson, who had alienated some important Republican party leaders. Soon, he would be negotiating with European leaders buoyed by rousing victories at their own polls.

Two weeks after the elections, Wilson announced that he would attend the peace conference. This was a dramatic break from tradition, and his personal involvement drew attacks from Republicans. They renewed criticism when he named the rest of the delegation: Secretary of State Lansing, Colonel House, General Tasker H. Bliss, a military expert, and Henry White, a career diplomat. Wilson named no member of the Senate, and the only Republican in the group was White.

In selecting the delegation, Wilson passed over Henry Cabot Lodge, the powerful Republican senator from Massachusetts who opposed the Fourteen Points and would soon head the Senate Foreign Relations Committee. He also decided not to appoint Elihu Root or ex-President Taft, both of them enthusiastic internationalists. Never good at accepting criticism or delegating authority, Wilson wanted a delegation he could control —an advantage at the peace table but not in any battle over the treaty at home.

Upon his arrival, Wilson received a tumultuous welcome in England, France, and Italy. Never before had such crowds acclaimed a democratic political figure. In Paris, two million people lined the Champs-Elysées, threw flowers at him, and

Woodrow Wilson's Fourteen Points, 1918: Success and Failure in Implementation

1. Open covenants of peace openly arrived at	Not fulfilled
2. Absolute freedom of navigation upon the seas in peace and war	Not fulfilled
3. Removal of all economic barriers to the equality of trade among nations	Not fulfilled
4. Reduction of armaments to the level needed only for domestic safety	Not fulfilled
5. Impartial adjustment of colonial claims	Not fulfilled
6. Evacuation of all Russian territory; Russia to be welcomed into the society of free nations	Not fulfilled
7. Evacuation and restoration of Belgium	**Fulfilled**
8. Evacuation and restoration of all French lands; return of Alsace-Lorraine to France	**Fulfilled**
9. Readjustment of Italy's frontiers along lines of Italian nationality	Compromised
10. Self-determination for the former subjects of the Austro-Hungarian Empire	Compromised
11. Evacuation of Rumania, Serbia, and Montenegro; free access to the sea for Serbia	Compromised
12. Self-determination for the former subjects of the Ottoman Empire; secure sovereignty for Turkish portion	Compromised
13. Establishment of an independent Poland, with free and secure access to the sea	**Fulfilled**
14. Establishment of a League of Nations affording mutual guarantees of independence and territorial integrity	Not fulfilled

Sources: Data from G. M. Gathorne-Hardy, The Fourteen Points and the Treaty of Versailles (Oxford Pamphlets on World Affairs, no. 6, 1939), pp. 8–34; Thomas G. Paterson et al., American Foreign Policy, A History Since 1900, 2d ed., Vol. 2, pp. 282–93.

shouted "Wilson *le Juste* [the just]" as his carriage drove by. Overwhelmed, Wilson was sure that the people of Europe shared his goals and would force their leaders to accept *his* peace. He was wrong. Like their leaders, many people on the Allied side hated Germany and wanted victory unmistakably reflected in the peace.

Opening in January 1919, the Peace Conference at Paris continued until May. Although twenty-seven nations were represented, the "Big Four" dominated it: Wilson; Clemenceau of France, tired and stubborn, determined to end the German threat forever; David Lloyd George, the crafty British prime minister who had pledged to squeeze Germany "until the pips squeak"; and the Italian prime minister, Vittorio Orlando. A clever negotiator, Wilson traded various "small" concessions for his major goals—national self-determination, a reduction in tensions, and a League of Nations to enforce the peace.

Wilson had to surrender some important principles. Departing from the Fourteen Points by violating the principle of self-determination, the treaty created two new independent nations—Poland and Czechoslovakia—with large German-speaking populations. It divided up the German colonies in Asia and Africa. Instead of a peace without victory, it made Germany accept

responsibility for the war and demanded enormous reparations—which eventually totaled $33 billion. It made no mention of disarmament, free trade, or freedom of the seas. Instead of an open covenant openly arrived at, the treaty was drafted behind closed doors.

But Wilson deflected some of the most extreme Allied demands, and he won his coveted Point 14, a League of Nations, designed "to achieve international peace and security." The League included a general Assembly; a smaller Council composed of the United States, Great Britain, France, Italy, Japan, and four nations to be elected by the Assembly; and a court of international justice. League members pledged to submit to arbitration every dispute threatening peace and to enjoin military and economic sanctions against nations resorting to war. Article X, for Wilson the heart of the League, obliged members to look out for one another's independence and territorial integrity.

The draft treaty in hand, Wilson returned home in February 1919 to discuss it with Congress and the people. Most Americans, the polls showed, favored the League; thirty-three governors endorsed it. But over dinner with the Senate and House Foreign Relations Committees, Wilson learned of the strength of congressional

Signing the Treaty at Versailles, June 28, 1919. Although the United States played a major role in drafting the treaty, the Senate never ratified the document. Instead, the U.S. made a separate peace with Germany in 1921.

opposition to it. On March 3, Senator Lodge produced a "round robin" signed by thirty-seven senators declaring they would not vote for the treaty without amendment. Should the numbers hold, Lodge had enough votes to defeat it.

Returning to Paris, Wilson attacked his critics, while he worked privately for changes to improve the chances of Senate approval. In return for major concessions, the Allies amended the League draft treaty, agreeing that domestic affairs remained outside League jurisdiction (exempting the Monroe Doctrine) and allowing nations to withdraw after two years' notice. On June 28, 1919, they signed the treaty in the Hall of Mirrors at Versailles, and Wilson started home for his most difficult fight.

Rejection in the Senate

There were ninety-six senators in 1919, forty-nine of them Republicans. Fourteen Republicans, led by William E. Borah of Idaho, were the "irreconcilables" who opposed the League on any grounds. "If the Savior of man," Borah said,

"would revisit the earth and declare for a League of Nations, I would be opposed to it." Frank B. Kellogg of Minnesota led a group of twelve "mild reservationists" who accepted the treaty but wanted to insert several reservations that would not greatly weaken it. Finally, there were the Lodge-led "strong reservationists," twenty-three of them in all, who wanted major changes that the Allies would have to approve.

With only four Democratic senators opposed to the treaty, the Democrats and Republicans willing to compromise had enough votes to ratify it, once a few reservations were inserted. Biding for time to allow public opposition to grow, Lodge scheduled lengthy hearings and spent two weeks reading the 268-page treaty aloud. Democratic leaders urged Wilson to appeal to the Republican "mild reservationists," but he refused. "Anyone who opposes me in that I'll crush!"

Fed up with Lodge's tactics, Wilson set out in early September to take the case directly to the people. Crossing the Midwest, his speeches aroused little emotion, but on the Pacific Coast he won ovations, which heartened him. On his way back to Washington, he stopped in Pueblo, Colorado, where he delivered one of the most eloquent speeches of his career. People wept as he talked of Americans who died in battle and the hope that they would never fight again in foreign lands. That night Wilson felt ill. He returned to Washington, and on October 2, Mrs. Wilson found him lying unconscious on the floor of the White House, the victim of a stroke that paralyzed his left side.

After the stroke, Wilson could not work more than an hour or two at a time. No one was allowed to see him except family members, his secretary, and his physician. For over seven months, he did not meet with the cabinet. Secretary of State Lansing convened cabinet meetings, but when Wilson learned of them, he ordered Lansing to stop and then cruelly forced him to resign. Focusing his remaining energy on the fight over the treaty, Wilson lost touch with other issues, and critics charged that his wife, Edith Bolling Wilson, ran the government.

On November 6, 1919, while Wilson convalesced, Lodge finally reported the treaty out of committee, along with "Fourteen Reservations," one for each of Wilson's points. The most important reservation stipulated that implementation of Article X, Wilson's key article, required the

Europe after the Treaty of Versailles, 1919

The treaty changed the map of Europe, creating a number of new and reconstituted nations. (Note boundary changes from prewar map on p. 716.)

action of Congress before any American intervention abroad.

The next day, the President's floor leader in the Senate told him that the Democrats could not pass the treaty without reservations. "Is it possible?" Wilson asked sadly. "It might be wise to compromise," the senator said. "Let Lodge compromise!" Wilson replied. When Mrs. Wilson urged her husband to accept the Lodge reservations, he said: "Better a thousand times to go down fighting than to dip your colors to dishonorable compromise."

On November 19, the treaty—with the Lodge reservations—failed, 39 to 55. Following Wilson's instructions, the Democrats voted against it. A motion to approve without the reservations lost 38 to 53, with only one Republican voting in favor. The defeat brought pleas for compromise, but neither Wilson nor Lodge would back down. When the treaty with reservations again came up for vote on March 19, 1920, Wilson ordered the Democrats to hold firm against it. Although

twenty-one of them defied him, enough obeyed his orders to defeat it, 49 to 35, seven votes short of the necessary two-thirds majority.

To Wilson, walking now with the help of a cane, one chance remained: the presidential election of 1920. For a time, he thought of running for a third term himself, but his party shunted him aside. The Democrats nominated Governor James M. Cox of Ohio, along with the young and popular Franklin D. Roosevelt, assistant secretary of the navy, for vice-president. Wilson called for "a great and solemn referendum" on the treaty. The Democratic platform endorsed the treaty but agreed to accept reservations that clarified the American role in the League.

On the Republican side, Senator Warren G. Harding of Ohio, who had nominated Taft in 1912, won the presidential nomination. Harding waffled on the treaty, but it made little difference. Voters wanted a change. Harding won in a landslide, taking 61 percent of the vote and beating Cox by seven million votes. Without a peace treaty, the United States remained technically at war, and it was not until July 1921, almost three years after the last shot was fired, that Congress passed a joint resolution ending the war.

After 1919 there was disillusionment. World War I was feared before it started, popular while it lasted, and hated when it ended. To a whole generation that followed, it appeared futile, killing without cause, sacrificing without benefit. Books, plays, and movies—Hemingway's *A Farewell to Arms*, John Dos Passos's *Three Soldiers* (1921), Laurence Stallings and Maxwell Anderson's *What Price Glory?* (1924), among others—showed it as waste, horror, and death.

The war and its aftermath damaged the humanitarian, progressive spirit of the early years of the century. It killed "something precious and perhaps irretrievable in the hearts of thinking men and women." Progressivism survived well into the 1920s and the New Deal, but it no longer

The Election of 1920

Candidate	Party	Popular Vote	Electoral Vote
Harding	Republican	16,133,314	404
Cox	Democrat	9,140,884	127
Debs	Socialist	913,664	0

CHRONOLOGY

1901 Hay-Pauncefote Treaty with Great Britain empowers United States to build isthmian canal

1904 Theodore Roosevelt introduces corollary to Monroe Doctrine

1904–1905 Russo-Japanese War

1905 Taft-Katsura Agreement recognizes Japanese power in Korea

1908 Root-Takahira Agreement vows to maintain status quo in the Pacific • Roosevelt sends the fleet around the world

1911 Revolution begins in Mexico

1913–1914 Bryan negotiates "cooling-off" treaties to end war

1914 World War I begins • U.S. Marines take Vera Cruz • Panama Canal completed

1915 Japan issues Twenty-One Demands to China (January) • Germany declares waters around British Isles a war zone (February) • *Lusitania* torpedoed (May) • Bryan resigns; Robert Lansing becomes secretary of state (June) • *Arabic* pledge restricts submarine warfare (September)

1916 Germany issues *Sussex* pledge (March) • General John J. Pershing leads unsuccessful punitive expedition into Mexico to seize Pancho Villa (April) • Wilson wins reelection

1917 Wilson calls for "peace without victory" (January) • Germany resumes unrestricted U-boat warfare (February) • United States enters World War I (April) • Congress passes Selective Service Act (May) • First American troops reach France (June) • War Industries Board established (July)

1918 Wilson outlines Fourteen Points for peace (January) • Germany asks for peace (October) • Armistice ends the war (November)

1919 Peace negotiations begin in Paris (January) • Treaty of Versailles defeated in Senate

1920 Warren G. Harding elected President

had the old conviction and broad popular support. Bruising fights over the war and the League drained people's energy and enthusiasm.

Confined to bed, Woodrow Wilson died in Washington in 1924, three years after Harding, the new President, promised "not heroics but healing; not nostrums but normalcy; not revolution but restoration." Nonetheless, the "war to end all wars," and the spirit of Woodrow Wilson left an indelible imprint on the country.

Recommended Reading

American foreign policy between 1901 and 1921 has been the subject of considerable study. Richard W. Leopold, *The Growth of American Foreign Policy* (1962) is balanced and informed. Howard K. Beale, *Theodore Roosevelt and the Rise of America to World Power* (1956), traces foreign policy during the early years; Robert E. Osgood, *Ideals and Self-Interest in America's Foreign Relations* (1953), and William Appleman Williams, *Roots of the Modern American Empire* (1969), explore the forces underlying American foreign policy.

David McCullough gives a lively account of the building of the Panama Canal in *The Path Between the Seas* (1977). For American policy toward Latin America, see Dana G. Munro's detailed account, *Intervention and Dollar Diplomacy in the Caribbean, 1900–1920* (1964). Arthur S. Link examines Wilson's foreign policy in his exceptional five-volume biography, *Wilson* (1947–1965) and in *Woodrow Wilson: Revolution, War, and Peace* (1979). N. Gordon Levin, Jr., *Woodrow Wilson and World Politics: America's Response to War and Revolution* (1968), places Wilson in the larger context of world events.

Ernest R. May studies American policy before the war in *The World War and American Isolation, 1914–1917* (1959). Bradford Perkins, *The Great Rapprochement: England and the United States, 1895–1914* (1968), examines the growing friendship between the two countries. Studies of events at home during the war include David M. Kennedy, *Over Here* (1980); Robert D. Cuff, *The War Industries Board* (1973); and Maurine W. Greenwald, *Women, War, and Work* (1980).

Woodrow Wilson and the Lost Peace (1944) and *Woodrow Wilson and the Great Betrayal* (1945) by Thomas A. Bailey are dated but thorough on Wilson's efforts at Versailles. Arthur Walworth, *America's Moment, 1918: American Diplomacy at the End of World War I* (1977), also examines Wilson's attempt to create a peaceful world order.

Additional Bibliography

For background to American policy in these years, see Richard D. Challener, *Admirals, Generals, and American Foreign Policy, 1898–1914* (1973); Michael Pearlman, *To Make Democracy Safe for America: Patricians and Preparedness in the Progressive Era* (1984); Lloyd C. Gardner, *Safe for*

Democracy: The Anglo-American Response to Revolution, 1913–1923 (1984); William C. Widenor, Henry Cabot Lodge and the Search for an American Foreign Policy (1980); and Paul P. Abrahams, The Foreign Expansion of American Finance and Its Relationship to the Foreign Economic Policies of the United States, 1907–1921 (1976). David H. Burton, Theodore Roosevelt, Confident Imperialist (1968); Frederick Marks III, Velvet on Iron: The Diplomacy of Theodore Roosevelt (1979); and C. E. Neu, An Uncertain Friendship: Theodore Roosevelt and Japan, 1906–1909 (1967), trace Roosevelt's policies.

On Taft and Wilson, see Ralph E. Minger, William Howard Taft and United States Foreign Policy (1975); Walter V. Scholes and Marie V. Scholes, The Foreign Policies of the Taft Administration (1970); Frederick S. Calhoun, Power and Principle: Armed Intervention in Wilsonian Foreign Policy (1986); Kendrick A. Clements, William Jennings Bryan: Missionary Isolationist (1983); Robert W. Cherny, A Righteous Cause: The Life of William Jennings Bryan (1985); Robert H. Ferrell, Woodrow Wilson and World War I (1985); and John Morton Blum, Woodrow Wilson and the Politics of Morality (1956). For relations with Latin America, see Dexter R. Perkins, The United States and the Caribbean, rev. ed. (1966); Richard L. Lael, Arrogant Diplomacy: U.S. Policy toward Colombia, 1903–1922 (1987); David Healy, Drive to Hegemony: The United States in the Caribbean, 1898–1917 (1988); and two books by Lester D. Langley: Struggle for the American Mediterranean (1975) and The United States and the Caribbean, 1900–1970 (1980).

On Mexico, see Peter Calvert, The Mexican Revolution, 1910–1914 (1968); Lloyd Gardner, Wilson and Revolutions, 1913–1921 (1976); and Robert E. Quirk, An Affair of Honor: Woodrow Wilson and the Occupation of Veracruz (1962). Several books deal with policies in the Far East, including Charles Vevier, United States and China, 1906–1913 (1955); Charles S. Campbell, Special Business Interests and the Open Door Policy (1951); Warren I. Cohen, America's Response to China, 2d ed. (1980); Raymond A. Esthus, Theodore Roosevelt and Japan (1966); and Jerry Israel, Progressivism and the Open Door: America and China, 1905–1921 (1971).

Historians have long debated the reasons for America's entry into the war; see, for example, Charles Seymour, American Diplomacy During the World War (1934) and American Neutrality, 1914–1917 (1935); Patrick Devlin, Too Proud to Fight: Woodrow Wilson's Neutrality (1974); David M. Smith, Robert Lansing and American Neutrality (1958); Ross Gregory, The Origins of American Intervention in the First World War (1971); John W. Coogan, The End of Neutrality: The United States, Britain, and Maritime Rights, 1899–1915 (1981); and Jeffrey J. Safford, Wilsonian Maritime Diplomacy (1978).

The war at home is followed in Valerie Jean Conner, The National War Labor Board: Stability, Social Justice, and the Voluntary State in World War I (1983); Neil A. Wynn, From Progressivism to Prosperity: World War I and American Society (1986); John Whiteclay Chambers II, To Raise an Army: The Draft Comes to Modern America (1987); Paul L. Murphy, World War I and the Origin of Civil Liberties in the United States (1979); John G. Clifford, The Citizen Soldiers (1972); William Preston, Jr., Aliens and Dissenters: Federal Suppression of Radicals, 1903–1933 (1963); H. C. Peterson and Gilbert C. Fite, Opponents of War, 1917–1918 (1957); Carol S. Gruber, Mars and Minerva: World War I and the Uses of Higher Learning in America (1975); and Stephen Vaughn, Holding Fast the Inner Lines: Democracy, Nationalism, and the Committee on Public Information (1980). John A. Thompson, Reformers and War: American Progressive Publicists and the First World War (1987) examines the war's effects on reform journalists.

On military intervention, see Harvey DeWeerd, President Wilson Fights His War (1968); E. M. Coftman, The War to End All Wars (1968); Frank E. Vandiver, Black Jack: The Life and Times of John J. Pershing, 2 vols. (1977); Russell F. Weigley, The American Way of War (1973); Laurence Stallings, The Doughboys (1963); and Arthur E. Barbeau and Henri Florette, The Unknown Soldiers: Black American Troops in World War I (1974).

The Treaty of Versailles and the struggle for ratification are covered in Arno J. Mayer, Politics and Diplomacy of Peacemaking (1967); Charles L. Mee, Jr., The End of Order, Versailles, 1919 (1980); Lloyd E. Ambrosius, Woodrow Wilson and the American Diplomatic Tradition: The Treaty Fight in Perspective (1987); Arthur Walworth, Wilson and His Peacemakers: American Diplomacy at the Paris Peace Conference, 1919 (1986); Warren F. Kuehl, Seeking World Order (1969); L. W. Martin, Peace Without Victory (1958); and Ralph A. Stone, The Irreconcilables (1970).

Wesley M. Bagby, The Road to Normalcy (1962); Seward W. Livermore, Politics Is Adjourned: Woodrow Wilson and the War Congress, 1916–1918 (1966); and David Burner, The Politics of Provincialism: The Democratic Party in Transition, 1918–1932 (1967) are excellent studies of domestic politics of the era.

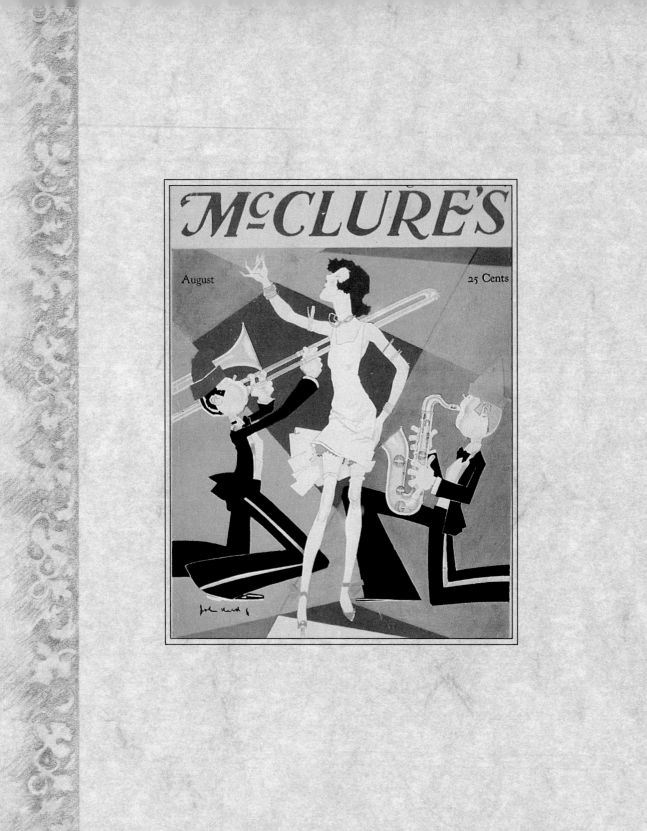

CHAPTER 25

Transition to Modern America

he moving assembly line that Henry Ford perfected in 1913 for manufacture of the Model T marked only the first step toward full mass production and the beginning of America's worldwide industrial supremacy. A year later, Ford began buying large plots of land along the Rouge River southeast of Detroit, Michigan. He already had a vision of a vast industrial tract where machines, moving through a sequence of carefully arranged manufacturing operations, would transform raw materials into finished cars, trucks, and tractors. The key would be control over the flow of goods at each step along the way—from lake steamers and railroad cars bringing in the coal and iron ore, to overhead conveyor belts and huge turning tables carrying the moving parts past the stationary workers on the assembly line. "Everything must move," Ford commanded, and by the mid-1920s at River Rouge, as the plant became known, it did.

Ford began fulfilling his industrial dream in 1919 when he built a blast furnace and foundry to make engine blocks for both the Model T and his tractors. By 1924, more than forty thousand workers were turning out nearly all the metal parts used in making Ford vehicles. One tractor factory was so efficient that it took just over twenty-eight hours to convert raw ore into a new farm implement.

Visitors from all over the world came to marvel at River Rouge. Some were disturbed by the jumble of machines (by 1926, there were forty-three thousand in operation) and the apparent congestion on the plant floor, but industrial experts recognized that the arrangement led to incredible productivity because "the work moves and the men stand still." A trained engineer summed it up best when he wrote that a visitor to the plant "sees each unit as a carefully designed gear which meshes with other gears and operates in synchronism with them, the whole forming one huge, perfectly-timed, smoothly-operating industrial machine of almost unbelieveable efficiency."

In May 1927, after producing over fifteen million Model Ts, Ford closed the assembly line at Highland Park. For the next six months, his engineers worked on designing a more compact and efficient assembly line at River Rouge for the Model A, which went into production in Novem-

*O*n the Assembly line at Ford's River Rouge plant, workers performed repetitive tasks on the car chassis that rushed by at a rate of six feet per minute.

ber. By then, River Rouge had more than justified Ford's vision. "Ford had brought together everything at a single site and on a scale no one else had ever attempted," concluded historian Geoffrey Perrett. "The Rouge plant became to a generation of engineers far more than a factory. It was a monument."

Mass production, born in Highland Park in 1913 and perfected at River Rouge in the 1920s, became the hallmark of American industry. Other carmakers copied Ford's methods and soon his emphasis on the flow of parts moving past stationary workers became the standard in nearly every American factory. The moving assembly line—with its emphasis on uniformity, speed, precision, and coordination—took away the last vestiges of craftsmanship and turned workers into near robots. It led to amazing efficiency that produced both high profits for manufacturers and low prices for buyers. By the mid-1920s, the cost of the Model T had dropped from $950 down to only $290.

Most important, mass production led to a consumer-goods revolution. American factories turned out a flood of automobiles and electric appliances that made life easier and more pleasant for the vast majority of the American people. The result was the creation of a new America, one in which individualism was sacrificed to conformity as part of the price to be paid for a new era of abundance.

The twenties, often seen as a time of escape and frivolity before the onset of the Depression, actually marked a beginning, a time when the American people learned to adapt to life in the city, when they decided (wisely or not) to center their existence upon the automobile, and when they rejected their rural past while still longing for the old values it had created. It is in the 1920s that we can find the roots of modern America—the America we know today.

THE SECOND INDUSTRIAL REVOLUTION

The first Industrial Revolution in the late nineteenth century had catapulted the United States into the forefront among the world's richest and most highly developed nations. With the advent of the new consumer-goods industries, the American people by the 1920s enjoyed the highest standard of living of any nation on earth. After a brief postwar depression, 1922 saw the beginning of a great boom that peaked in 1927 and lasted until 1929. In this brief period, American industrial output nearly doubled, and the gross national product rose by 40 percent. Most of this explosive growth took place in industries producing consumer goods—automobiles, appliances, furniture, and clothing. Equally important, the national per-capita income increased by 30 percent to $681 in 1929. American workers became the highest paid in history and thus were able to buy the flood of new goods they were turning out on the assembly lines.

The key to the new affluence lay in technology. The moving assembly line pioneered by Ford became a standard feature in nearly all American plants. Electric motors replaced steam engines as the basic source of energy in factories; by 1929, 70 percent of all industrial power came from electricity. Efficiency experts broke down the

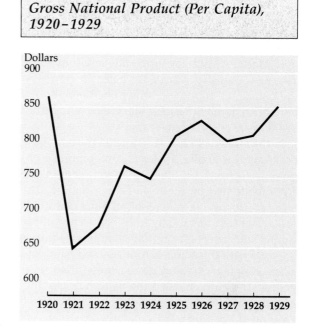

Gross National Product (Per Capita), 1920–1929

industrial process into minute parts using time and motion studies and then showed managers and workers how to maximize the output of their labor. Production per man-hour increased an amazing 75 percent over the decade; in 1929, a work force no larger than that of 1919 was producing almost twice as many goods.

The Automobile Industry

The nature of the consumer-goods revolution can best be seen in the automobile industry, which became the nation's largest in the 1920s. Rapid growth was its hallmark. In 1920, there were 10 million cars in the nation; by the end of the decade, 26 million were on the road. Production jumped from less than 2 million units a year to over 5 million by 1929.

The automobile boom, at its peak from 1922 to 1927, depended on the apparently insatiable appetite of the American people for cars. But as the decade continued, the market became saturated as more and more of those who could afford the new luxury had become car owners. Marketing became as crucial as production. Automobile makers began to rely heavily on advertising and annual model changes, seeking to make customers dissatisfied with their old vehicles and eager to order new ones. Despite these efforts, sales slumped in 1927 when Ford stopped making the Model T, picked up again the next year with the new Model A, but began to slide again in 1929. The new industry revealed a basic weakness in the consumer-goods economy; once people had bought an item with a long life, they would be out of the market for a few years.

In the affluent 1920s, few noticed the emerging economic instability. Instead, contemporary observers focused on the stimulating effect the automobile had on the rest of the economy. The mass production of cars required huge quantities of steel; entire new rolling mills had to be built to supply sheet steel for car bodies. Rubber factories boomed with the demand for tires, and paint and glass suppliers had more business than ever before. The auto changed the pattern of city life, leading to a suburban explosion. Real estate developers, no longer dependent on street cars and railway lines, could now build houses in ever wider concentric circles around the central cities.

The automobile had a profound effect on all aspects of American life in the 1920s. Filling stations appeared on the main streets, replacing the smithies and stables of the past. In Kansas City, Jess D. Nichols built the first shopping center, Country Club Plaza, and thus set an example quickly followed by other suburban developers.

Even in smaller communities, the car ruled. In Muncie, Indiana, site of a famous sociological survey in the 1920s, one elder replied when asked what was taking place, "I can tell you what's happening in just four letters: A-U-T-O!" A nation that had always revered symbols of movement, from the Mayflower to the covered wagon, now had a new icon to worship.

Patterns of Economic Growth

Automobiles were the most conspicuous of the consumer products that flourished in the 1920s but certainly not the only ones. The electrical industry grew almost as quickly. Central power stations, where massive steam generators converted coal into electricity, brought current into the homes of city and town dwellers. Two-thirds of all American families enjoyed electricity by the end of the decade, and they spent vast sums on washing machines, vacuum cleaners, refrigerators, and ranges. The new appliances eased the burdens of the housewife and ushered in an age of leisure.

Radio broadcasting and motion-picture production also boomed in the 1920s. The early success of KDKA in Pittsburgh stimulated the growth of more than eight hundred independent radio stations, and by 1929, NBC had formed the first successful radio network. Five nights a week, "Amos 'n Andy," a comic serial featuring two "blackface" vaudevillians, held the attention of millions of Americans. The film industry thrived in Hollywood, reaching its maturity in the mid-1920s when in every large city there were huge theaters seating as many as four thousand people. With the advent of the "talkies" by 1929, average weekly movie attendance climbed to nearly one hundred million.

Other industries prospered as well. Production of light metals such as aluminum and magnesium grew into a major business. Chemical engineering came of age with the invention of synthetics, ranging from rayon for clothing to cellophane for packaging. Americans found a whole new spectrum of products to buy—cigarette lighters, wristwatches, heat-resistant glass cooking dishes, and rayon stockings to name just a few.

The corporation continued to be the dominant economic unit in the 1920s. Growing corporations now had hundreds of thousands of stockholders; and one individual or family rarely held more than 5 percent of the stock. The enormous profits generated by these corporations enabled their managers to finance growth and expansion internally, thus freeing companies from their earlier dependence on investment bankers like J. P. Morgan. Voicing a belief in social responsibility and enlightened capitalism, the new professional class operated independently, free from outside restraint. In the final analysis, the corporate managers were accountable only to other managers.

Another wave of mergers accompanied the growth of corporations during the 1920s. From 1920 to 1928, some eight thousand mergers took place as more and more small firms proved unable to compete effectively with the new giants. By the end of the decade, the two hundred largest nonfinancial corporations owned almost

General Electric presents
the first
All-steel Refrigerator

A new small-family model at the very low price of

$215

ANOTHER chapter has been added to the achievements of the engineers and scientists of the General Electric Research Laboratories. The same group of men who, after fifteen years of painstaking endeavor, perfected the hermetically sealed mechanism of the General Electric Refrigerator, have now designed and built the first all-steel refrigerator cabinet. This marks the first major improvement made during thirty years, in the design and construction of household cabinets. It means that new and even greater value has been built into the already unrivaled General Electric Refrigerator.

NEW DESIGN—MADE IN A NEW WAY...General Electric has made a large investment in new machinery. Giant presses had to be designed and built to cut the steel, bend it into shape and weld together the folded forms. But it has achieved its purpose. Its aim was, by mass production, to build the best

• • •

All steel, with electrically welded joints. Bronze hardware, bolted right into the steel. Under-formed door edges, gaskets to protect cost interiors, and many other unique features.

refrigerator ever produced and offer it to the small families of America at a price easily within their reach—$215 at the factory.

$215—WITH CONVENIENTLY SPACED PAYMENTS ...The new all-steel General Electric makes safe refrigeration possible for every home. Only a small down payment is required. The balance can conveniently be paid over a period of time.

FIRST PUBLIC SHOWING MARCH 22...The only way to appreciate the durability and the beauty of this refrigerator is to see it. You will then readily understand why General Electric announces it so proudly and why it has been called "the refrigerator of the future." On display by dealers everywhere on and after Friday, March 22nd. Be sure to be among the first to see it. Write for a descriptive booklet to Section Z-4 Electric Refrigeration Department of General Electric Company, Hanna Building, Cleveland, Ohio.

GENERAL ⊛ ELECTRIC
ALL-STEEL REFRIGERATOR

For "a dollar down and a dollar a week" Americans of the 1920s could purchase the latest household electrical appliance—a washing machine, for example, or a refrigerator like the one shown here.

half of the country's corporate wealth. The oligopoly in the automobile industry set an example for other areas. The greatest abuses took place in public utilities where promoters like Samuel Insull built vast paper empires by gaining control of operating power companies and then draining them of their assets.

The most distinctive feature of the new consumer-oriented economy was the emphasis on marketing. Advertising earnings rose from $1.3 billion in 1915 to $3.4 billion in 1926. Skillful practitioners like Edward Bernays and Bruce Barton sought to control public taste and consumer spending by identifying the good life with the possession of the latest product of American industry, whether it be a car, a refrigerator, or a brand of cigarettes. Chain stores advanced rapidly at the expense of small retail shops. A&P dominated the retail food industry, growing from 400 stores in 1912 to 15,500 by 1932. Woolworth's "five and tens" spread almost as rapidly, while such drugstore chains as Rexall and Lig-

getts—both owned by one huge holding company—opened outlets in nearly every town and city in the land.

Uniformity and standardization, the characteristics of mass production, now prevailed. The farmer in Kansas bought the same kind of car, the same groceries, and the same pills as the factory worker in Pennsylvania. Sectional differences in dress, food, and furniture began to disappear. Even the regional accents that distinguished Americans in different parts of the country were threatened with extinction by the advent of radio and films which promoted a standard national dialect devoid of any local flavor.

Economic Weaknesses

The New Era, as businessmen labeled the decade, was not as prosperous as it first appeared. The revolution in consumer goods disguised the decline of many traditional industries in the 1920s. Railroads, overcapitalized and poorly managed, suffered from internal woes and from competition with the growing trucking industry. The coal industry was also troubled, with petroleum and natural gas beginning to replace coal as a fuel. The use of cotton textiles declined with the development of rayon and other synthetic fibers. The New England mills moved south in search of cheap labor, leaving behind thousands of unemployed workers and virtual ghost towns in the nation's oldest industrial center.

Hardest hit of all was agriculture. American farmers had expanded production to meet the demands of World War I, when they fed their own nation and most of Europe as well. A sharp cutback of exports in 1919 caused a rapid decline in prices. By 1921, farm exports had fallen by more than $2 billion. Throughout the 1920s, the farmers' share of the national income dropped until by 1929, the per-capita farm income was only $273, compared to the national average of $681.

Workers were better off than farmers in the 1920s, but they did not share fully in the decade's affluence. The industrial labor force remained remarkably steady for a period of economic growth; technical innovations meant that the same number of workers could produce far more than before. Most new jobs appeared in the lower-paying service industry. During the decade, factory wage rates rose only a modest 11 percent; by 1929, nearly half of all American families had an income of less than $1500. At the same time, however, conditions of life improved. Prices remained stable, even dropping somewhat in the early twenties, so that workers enjoyed a gain in real wages.

Organized labor proved unable to advance the interests of workers in the 1920s. Conservative leadership in the AFL neglected the task of organizing the vast number of unskilled laborers in the mass-production industries. Aggressive management weakened the appeal of unions by portraying them as radical organizations after a series of strikes in 1919. Many businessmen used the injunction and "yellow-dog" contracts— which forbade employees to join unions—to establish open shops and deny workers the benefits of collective bargaining. Other employers wooed their workers away from unions using techniques of welfare capitalism, spending money to improve plant conditions and winning employee loyalty with pensions, paid vacations, and company cafeterias. The net result was a decline in union membership from a postwar high of five million to less than three million by 1929.

Black workers remained on the bottom, both economically and socially. Nearly half a million African Americans had migrated northward from the rural South during World War i. Some found jobs in northern industries, but many more worked in menial service areas, collecting garbage, washing dishes, and sweeping floors. Yet even these jobs offered them a better life than they found on the depressed southern farms, where millions of African Americans still lived in poverty, and so the migration continued. The black ghettos in northern cities grew rapidly in the 1920s; Chicago's African-American population doubled during the decade, while New York's rose from 152,467 to 327,706, with most African Americans living in Harlem.

Middle- and upper-class Americans were the groups who thrived in the 1920s. The rewards of this second Industrial Revolution went to the managers—the engineers, bankers, and executives—who directed the new industrial economy. Corporate profits nearly doubled in ten years, and income from dividends rose 65 percent,

nearly six times the rate of workers' wages. Bank accounts, reflecting the accumulated savings of the upper-middle and wealthy classes, rose from $41.1 billion to $57.9 billion. These were the people who bought the fine new houses in the suburbs and who could afford more than one car. Their conspicuous consumption helped fuel the prosperity of the 1920s, but their disposable income eventually became greater than their material wants. The result was speculation, as those with idle money began to invest heavily in the stock market to reap gains from the industrial growth.

The economic trends of the decade had both positive and negative implications for the future. On the one hand, there was the solid growth of new consumer-based industries. Automobiles and appliances were not passing fancies; their production and use became a part of the modern American way of life, creating a high standard of living that roused the envy of the rest of the world. The future pattern of American culture— cars and suburbs, shopping centers and skyscrapers—was determined by the end of the 1920s.

But at the same time, there were ominous signs of danger. The unequal distribution of wealth, the saturation of the market for consumer goods, and the growing speculation all created economic instability. The boom of the twenties would end in a great crash; yet the achievements of the decade would survive even that dire experience to shape the future of American life.

THE NEW URBAN CULTURE

The city replaced the countryside as the focal point of American life in the 1920s. The 1920 census revealed that for the first time, slightly more than half of the population lived in cities (defined broadly to include all places of more than 2500 people). During the decade, the metropolitan areas grew rapidly as both whites and blacks from rural areas came seeking jobs in the new consumer industries. Between 1920 and 1930, cities with populations of 250,000 or more had added some 8 million people to their ranks. New York alone grew by nearly 25 percent, while Detroit more than doubled its population during the decade.

The skyscraper soon became the most visible

Its 102 stories rising 1250 feet into the sky (222 feet were added in 1950), the Empire State Building had space for 25,000 tenants.

feature of the city. Faced with inflated land prices, builders turned upward—developing a distinctively American architectural style in the process. New York led the way with the ornate Woolworth Building in 1913. The sleek 102-story Empire State Building, completed in 1930, was for years the tallest building in the world. Other cities erected their own jagged skylines. By 1929, there were 377 buildings over 20 stories tall across the nation. Most significantly, the skyscraper came to symbolize the new mass culture. "The New York skyscrapers are the most striking manifestation of the triumph of numbers," wrote one French observer. "One cannot understand or like them

without first having tasted and enjoyed the thrill of counting or adding up enormous totals and of living in a gigantic, compact and brilliant world."

In the metropolis, life was different. The old community ties of home, church, and school were absent, but there were important gains to replace them—new ideas, new creativity, new perspectives. Some city dwellers became lost and lonely without the old institutions; others thrived in the urban environment.

Women and the Family

The urban culture of the 1920s witnessed important changes in the American family. This vital institution began to break down under the impact of economic and social change. A new freedom for women and children seemed to be emerging in its wake.

Women had already begun to leave the home in the early twentieth century as the second Industrial Revolution opened up new jobs for them. World War I sped up the process, but in the 1920s there was no great permanent gain in the number of working women. Although two million more women were employed in 1930 than in 1920, this represented an increase of only 1 percent. Most women workers, moreover, had low-paying jobs, ranging from stenographers to maids. The number of women doctors actually decreased, and even though women earned nearly one-third of all graduate degrees, only 4 percent of the full professors were female. For the most part, the professions were reserved for men, with women relegated to such stereotypical fields as teaching and nursing.

To be sure, women had won the right to vote in 1920, but the Nineteenth Amendment proved to have less impact than its proponents had hoped. Once achieved, it robbed women of a unifying cause, and the exercise of the franchise itself did little to change the prevailing sex roles in society. Men remained the principal breadwinners in the family; women cooked, cleaned, and reared the children. "The creation and fulfillment of a successful home," a *Ladies Home Journal* writer advised women, "is a bit of craftsmanship that compares favorably with building a beautiful cathedral."

The feminist movement, however, still showed

One of the hard-won rights that women finally realized in 1920 was the right to vote, celebrated here in a cover from Leslie's Illustrated Weekly Newspaper.

signs of vitality in the 1920s. Social feminists pushed for humanitarian reform, and were successful in gaining enactment of the Sheppard-Towner Act of 1921, which provided for federal aid to establish state programs for maternal and infant health care. Although the failure to enact the child-labor amendment in 1925 marked the beginning of a decline in humanitarian reform, for the rest of the decade women's groups continued to work for good-government measures, for the inclusion of women on juries, and for consumer legislation.

One group of activists, led by Alice Paul's National Women's Party (NWP), lobbied for full equality for women under the law. In 1923, the NWP succeeded in having an Equal Rights Amendment introduced in Congress. The amendment stated: "Men and women shall have equal rights throughout the United States and every place subject to its jurisdiction." Most other women's organizations, notably the League of Women Voters, opposed the amendment because it threatened gender-specific legislation like the Sheppard-Towner Act that women had fought so hard to enact. The drive for the ERA in the twenties failed.

Growing assertiveness had a profound impact on feminism in the 1920s. Instead of crusading for social progress, young women concentrated on individual self-expression by rebelling against Victorian restraints. In the larger cities, some quickly adopted what critic H. L. Mencken called the flapper image, portrayed most strikingly by artist John Held, Jr. Cutting their hair short, raising their skirts above the knee, and binding their breasts, "flappers" set out to compete on equal terms with men on the golf course and in the speakeasy. Young women delighted in shocking their elders—they rouged their cheeks and danced the Charleston. For the first time, women smoked cigarettes and drank alcohol in public. The flappers assaulted the traditional double standard in sex, demanding that equality with men should include sexual fulfillment before and during marriage. New and more liberal laws led to a sharp rise in the divorce rate; by 1928, there were 166 divorces for every 1000 marriages, compared to only 81 in 1900.

The sense of woman's emancipation was heightened by a continuing drop in the birthrate and the abundance of consumer goods. With fewer children to care for and with washing machines and vacuum cleaners to ease their household labor, it seemed that women of the 1920s would have more leisure time. Yet appearances were deceptive. Advertisers eagerly sought out women as buyers of labor-saving consumer

"It's broccoli dear." "I say it's spinach, and I say the hell with it." This New Yorker *cartoon captures perfectly the spirit of the '20s.*

Mexican–American
Experience in the Southwest

❦   ❦   ❦

Mission San Carlos Borromeo de Carmelo, *painted by Oriana Day, depicts the most beautiful of the California missions. Founded in 1770 by Father Junipero Serra, it was secularized in 1834 when the Mexican government turned over the mission to the* rancheros.

From California to Texas in the early 1820s, one could enter the northern fringes of a rich civilization born out of three centuries of contact between the Spanish and the Indians. Already, a distinctly Mexican culture was emerging from the blend of European and native societies. By the early 1830s this borderlands Hispanic society flourished among forty thousand people thinly spread from the Rio Grande Valley in Texas to northern California.

After the annexation of Texas and the acquisition of California by the United States in the mid-nineteenth century, Mexicans in America fared poorly in encounters with Anglo society. Sought after as cheap labor in agriculture, mining, and industry, Hispanic Americans shouldered the burden of economic growth in the Southwest but did not share materially in the fruits of the region.

In the 1870s, railroads constructed largely by Mexican labor unleashed forces that changed the face of the Southwest. Trains brought white settlers

Standing with friends and relatives at the ranch of the bride's family in Karnes County, Texas (1909), Eufracio and Eufemia Zambrano Rodriguez celebrate their wedding (above). At left John Sloan's Mother and Daughter, painted in Santa Fe in 1919, shows an older woman clad in traditional black garb and a younger woman in modern dress.

At right, refugees in the El Paso, Texas area are shown after fleeing the Mexican Revolution. This photo was taken by El Paso photographer Otis Aultman around 1911.

to previously isolated areas and carried their products to nationwide markets. Owners of farms, mines, and factories all wanted cheap labor and they looked to Mexico where many of the same forces of modernization and change produced a great migration to the United States between 1880 and 1930. Facing overpopulation, loss of land, and unemployment, many Mexicans crossed the border. There was a ready demand for unskilled hands. Confined to "Mexican work"—the most menial tasks—they were paid "peon's wages," well below those for whites performing comparable duties, with little opportunity for advancement.

What began as a temporary expedient among unemployed Mexicans became a permanent pattern of immigration. The economic dislocation and social upheaval attendant upon the Mexican revolution that started in 1910 increased the trend. Fanning out across the country as migrant farm workers and following the rail lines to urban factory jobs, Mexicans now came to the United States to stay.

Increased Mexican immigration became the focus

At left, Christian Soldiers, *painted by John Sloan in 1930, depicts the annual Corpus Christi procession in Santa Fe, with St. Francis Cathedral in the background. The older women, again, appear in the black dress of Spanish tradition. Below, Cesar Chavez speaks at an AFL/CIO/United Farm Workers convention.*

of nativism, racism, and violence that often accompanied the cyclical downswings of the American economy. Many Anglos already worried about the burgeoning Mexican population they considered incapable of assimilation into American society. Such concerns only grew with the influx of refugees fleeing the instability of revolutionary Mexico.

Between 1913 and 1917, xenophobia, a brief recession, and World War I combined to produce what historian Ricardo Romo has called "the brown scare." Wild rumors circulated about uprisings planned in the *barrios* (neighborhoods) and of Mexican plots to recapture the Southwest. Skirmishes along the border lent credence to even the most outlandish fears. In Los Angeles, the police called out reinforcements to patrol the barrio, put controls on the sale of liquor and guns to Hispanics, and recruited an army of white vigilantes, "just in case."

Settlement followed two basic patterns. In the cities, Mexican-Americans congregated in ghettos where housing was substandard and rents low enough for the poorest paid factory workers. Though impoverished, the barrio did provide a social anchor for the Hispanic community in the United States. They clung to their traditional culture: religious ceremonies for the living and the dead, unique foods and festivals, and a brightly hued palette of artistic expression. In rural areas, some Mexicans settled in small farming towns, working for wages or as tenant farmers; many migrated seasonally with the harvests without even the security of a permanent home. Paid by volume of produce, instead of by the hour, entire families worked the fields just to make enough to survive.

The coming of the Great Depression witnessed another phase in the boom and bust cycle for Mexican-Americans. As the economy flagged, unemployment and nativist sentiment rose apace. Hispanics from agricultural regions, hit hard by the Depression, flocked to the cities in search of jobs, only to find higher living costs and relief programs stretched to the limits. Mexican immigration slowed to a trickle. Meanwhile, federal and local authorities cooperated in an informal "send-the-Mexicans-back-to-Mexico" program, sending back hundreds of thousands of Mexicans for "repatriation." Although the government emphasized the voluntary nature of this operation, many American citizens

The mosaic of Hispanic and Anglo cultures in the Southwest is symbolized in San Antonio's Fiesta by a Mexican-American in charro *costume parading the Stars and Stripes and by young bike riders eyeing a barrio mural of Aztec warriors, painted by teenagers.*

Lauro Cavazos, Jr., United States Secretary of Education under both Presidents Ronald Reagan and George Bush, was the first Hispanic American cabinet officer in America's history. Cavazos taught at the Medical College of Virginia and Tufts University School of Medicine and served as dean at Tufts and president of Texas Tech University. In 1983, he was named Hispanic Educator of the year, in Texas.

were caught up among the "illegals" and temporary laborers who were returned to Mexico.

In the 1930s, industrial unions provided urban Chicanos, as Mexican-Americans came to be called, with an opportunity to join the mainstream of American labor. Unfortunately, New Deal legislation gave no protection to agricultural workers. Undaunted, farm workers tried to organize and bargain collectively, and various small farm unions gained modest increases in pay and improved benefits for migrants.

World War II brought still more Chicanos to cities and opened new occupational opportunities. On the land, conditions remained much the same. During and after the war, the aggressive antiunion policies of the farm owners, the contract labor system, and the prevalence of undocumented laborers thwarted efforts to organize farm workers. Not until the 1960s did Cesar Chavez lead the United

Farm Workers in a boycott so effective that it forced the California growers to accept the union (see Chapter 31).

In the 1960s and '70s, the Hispanic community in the Southwest made strides in their struggle for equal protection and equal opportunity in employment, education, and housing, but Mexican immigration reemerged as a troublesome issue in the 1980s. Faced with an increasing number of illegal aliens entering the country Congress, in 1986, granted amnesty to those who could prove they had been living in the United States before January 1, 1982. In return, the new legislation imposed heavy penalties on employers who hired illegal immigrants. These new rules seemed to have little effect on the growth of the Hispanic population, which increased from 14 to 20 million in the 1980s, with Mexican-Americans forming the largest component by far.

products, but wives exercised purchasing power only as delegated by their husbands. In addition, many women were not in the position to put the new devices to use—one-fourth of the homes in Cleveland lacked running water in the twenties, and three-quarters of the nation's families did not have washing machines. The typical childless woman spent between forty-three and fifty hours a week on household duties; for mothers, the average work week was fifty-six hours, far longer than that of their husbands. And despite the talk of the "new woman," the flappers fell victim to the sex-role conditioning of their parents. Boys continued to play with guns and grew up to head their families; girls played with dolls and looked forward to careers as wives and mothers. "In the 1920s, as in the 1790s," concluded historian June Sochen, "marriage was the only approved state for women."

The family, however, did change. It became smaller as new techniques of birth control enabled couples to limit their offspring. More and more married women took jobs outside the home, bringing in an income and gaining a measure of independence (although their rate of pay was always lower than that for men). Young people, who had once joined the labor force when they entered their teens, now discovered adolescence as a stage of life. A high-school education was no longer uncommon, and college attendance increased.

Prolonged adolescence led to new strains on the family in the form of youthful revolt. Freed of the traditional burden of earning a living at an early age, youths in the 1920s went on a great spree. Heavy drinking, casual sexual encounters, and a constant search for excitement became the hallmarks of the upper-class youth immortalized by F. Scott Fitzgerald. "I have been kissed by dozens of men," one of his characters commented. "I suppose I'll kiss dozens more." The theme of rebellion against parental authority, which runs through all aspects of the 1920s, was at the heart of the youth movement.

The Roaring Twenties

Frivolity and excitement ran high in the cities as both crime waves and highly publicized sports events flourished. Prohibition ushered in such distinctive features of the decade as speakeasies, bootleggers, and bathtub gin. Crime rose sharply as middle- and upper-class Americans willingly broke the law to gain access to alcoholic beverages. City streets became the scene of violent shoot-outs between rival bootleggers; by 1929, Chicago had witnessed over five hundred gangland murders. Underworld czars like Al Capone controlled illicit empires; Capone's produced revenue of $60 million a year.

Sports became a national mania in the 1920s as people found more leisure time. Golf boomed, with some 2-million men and women playing on nearly five thousand courses across the country. Spectator sports attracted even more attention. Boxing drew huge crowds to see fighters like Jack Dempsey and Gene Tunney. Baseball attendance soared. More than 20 million fans attended games in 1927, the year Babe Ruth became a national idol by hitting sixty home runs. On college campuses, football became more popular than ever. Universities vied with each other in building massive stadiums, seating upward of 70,000 people.

In what Frederick Lewis Allen called "the ballyhoo years," the popular yearning for excitement led people to seek vicarious thrills in all kinds of ways—applauding Charles Lindbergh's solo flight across the Atlantic, cheering Gertrude Ederle's swim across the English Channel, and flocking to such bizarre events as six-day bicycle races, dance marathons, and flagpole-sittings. It was a time of pure pleasure-seeking, when people sought to escape from the increasingly drab world of the assembly line by worshiping heroic individuals.

Sex became another popular topic in the 1920s as Victorian standards began to crumble. Sophisticated city dwellers seemed to be intent on exploring a new freedom in sexual expression. Plays and novels focused on adultery, and the new urban tabloids—led by the *New York Daily News*—delighted in telling their readers about love nests and kept women. The popular songs of the decade, like "Hot Lips" and "Burning Kisses," were less romantic and more explicit than those of years before. Hollywood exploited the obsession with sex by producing movies with such provocative titles as *Up in Mable's Room, A Shocking Night,* and *Women and Lovers.* Theda Bara and Clara Bow, the "vamp" and the "it" girl, set

In this George Bellows painting, Argentina's Luis Firpo knocks Jack Dempsey out of the ring. Dempsey came back to win the fight in the second round.

the model for feminine seductiveness while Rudolph Valentino became the heartthrob of millions of American women. Young people embraced the new permissiveness joyfully, with the automobile giving couples an easy way to escape parental supervision.

There is considerable debate, however, over the extent of the sexual revolution in the '20s. Later studies by Dr. Alfred C. Kinsey showed that premarital intercourse was twice as common among women born after 1900 than for those born before the turn of the century. But a contemporary survey of over two thousand middle-class women by Katherine B. Davis found that only 7 percent of those who were married had had sexual relations before marriage and that only 14 percent of the single women had engaged in intercourse. Actual changes in sexual behavior are beyond the historian's reach, hidden in the privacy of the bedroom, but the old Victorian prudishness was a clear casualty of the 1920s. Sex was no longer a taboo subject, at least in urban areas; men and women now could discuss it openly and many of them did.

The Literary Flowering

The greatest cultural advance of the 1920s was visible in the outpouring of literature. The city gave rise to a new class of intellectuals—writers who commented on the new industrial society. Many had been uprooted by World War I. They were bewildered by the rapidly changing social patterns of the 1920s and appalled by the materialism of American culture. Some fled to Europe to live as expatriates, congregating in Paris cafes to bemoan the loss of American innocence and purity. Others stayed at home, observing and condemning the excesses of a business civilization. All shared a sense of disillusionment and wrote pessimistically of the flawed promise of American life. Yet, ironically, their body of writing revealed a profound creativity that suggested America was coming of age intellectually.

The exiles included the poets Ezra Pound and T. S. Eliot and the novelist Ernest Hemingway. Pound discarded rhyme and meter in a search for clear, cold images that conveyed reality. Like many of the writers of the 1920s, he reacted against World War I, expressing a deep regret for the tragic waste of a whole generation in defense of a "botched civilization."

Eliot, who was born in Missouri but became a British citizen, displayed even more profound despair. In *The Waste Land,* which appeared in 1922, he evoked images of fragmentation and sterility that had a powerful impact on the other disillusioned writers of the decade. He reached the depths in *The Hollow Men* (1925), a biting description of the emptiness of modern man.

Ernest Hemingway sought redemption from the modern plight in the romantic individualism of his heroes. Preoccupied with violence, he wrote of men alienated from society who found a sense of identity in their own courage and quest for personal honor. His own experiences, ranging from driving an ambulance in the war to stalking lions in Africa, made him a legendary figure; his greatest impact on other writers, however, came from his sparse, direct, and clean prose style.

The writers who stayed home were equally disdainful of contemporary American life. F. Scott Fitzgerald chronicled American youth in *This Side of Paradise* (1920) and *The Great Gatsby* (1925), writing in bittersweet prose about "the beautiful and the damned." Amid the glitter of life among the wealthy on Long Island's North Shore came the haunting realization of emptiness and lack of human concern.

Sinclair Lewis became the most popular of the

*T*he novels and short stories of Edith Wharton (above) are noted for their careful structure and penetrating social satire.

T. S. Eliot, whose long poem The Wasteland *owed much to Ezra Pound's critical eye, set the standard by which modern American poetry was judged in the mid-twentieth century.*

critical novelists. *Main Street*, published in 1920, satirized the values of small-town America as dull, complacent, and narrow-minded; *Babbitt*, which appeared two years later, poked fun at the commercialism of the 1920s, portraying George Babbitt as the stereotype of the lazy, smug, middle class businessman who hailed the decade as a New Era.

Most savage of all was H. L. Mencken, the Baltimore newspaperman and literary critic who founded *American Mercury* magazine in 1923. Declaring war on the "homo boobiens," Mencken mocked everything he found distasteful in America from the Rotary Club to the Ku Klux Klan. "From Boy Scouts, and from Home Cooking, from Odd Fellows' funerals, from Socialists, from Christians—Good Lord, deliver us," he pleaded. It was not difficult to discover what Mencken disliked (including Jews, as his recently published diary makes clear); the hard part was finding out what he affirmed, other than wit and a clever turn of phrase. A born cynic, he served as a zealous guardian of public rationality in an era of excessive boosterism.

The cultural explosion of the 1920s was surprisingly broad. It included novelists like Sherwood Anderson and John Dos Passos, who described the way the new machine age under-

THE RURAL COUNTERATTACK

The shift of population from the countryside to the city led to heightened social tensions in the 1920s. Intent on preserving traditional social values, rural Americans saw in the city all that was evil in contemporary life. Saloons, whorehouses, little Italys and little Polands, Communists cells, free love, and atheism—all were identified with the city. Accordingly, the countryside struck back at the newly dominant urban areas, aiming to restore the primacy of the Anglo-Saxon and predominantly Protestant culture they revered. This counterattack won considerable support in the cities from those so recently uprooted from their rural backgrounds.

Other factors contributed to the intensity of the counterattack. The war had unleashed a nationalistic spirit that craved unity and conformity. In a nation where one-third of the people were foreign-born, the attack on immigrants and the call for 100 percent Americanism took on a frightening zeal. When the war was over, groups like the American Legion tried to root out "un-American" behavior and insisted on cultural as well as political conformity. The prewar progressive reform spirit added to the social tension. Stripped of much of its former idealism, progressivism focused on such social problems as drinking and illiteracy to justify repressive measures like Prohibition and immigration restriction. The result was tragic. Amid the emergence of a new urban culture, the movements aimed at preserving the values of an earlier America succeeded only in complicating life in an already difficult period of cultural transition.

The "Red Scare"

The first and most intense outbreak of national alarm came in 1919. The heightened nationalism of World War I, aimed at achieving unity at the expense of ethnic diversity, found a new target in bolshevism. The Russian Revolution and the triumph of Marxism frightened many Americans. A growing turn to communism among American radicals (especially the foreign-born) accelerated these fears. Although the numbers involved were tiny—at most there were sixty thousand Communists in the United States in 1919—they were

highly visible. Located in the cities, their influence appeared to be magnified with the outbreak of widespread labor unrest.

A general strike in Seattle, a police strike in Boston, and a violent strike in the iron and steel industry thoroughly alarmed the American people in the spring and summer of 1919. A series of bombings led to panic. First the mayor of strike-bound Seattle received a small brown package containing a homemade bomb; then an alert New York postal employee detected sixteen bombs addressed to a variety of famous citizens (including John D. Rockefeller); and finally, on June 2, a bomb shattered the front of Attorney General A. Mitchell Palmer's home. Although the man who delivered it was blown to pieces, authorities quickly identified him as an Italian anarchist from Philadelphia.

In the ensuing public outcry, Attorney General Palmer led the attack on the alien threat. A Quaker and progressive, Palmer abandoned his earlier liberalism to launch a massive roundup of foreign-born radicals. In a series of raids that began on November 7, federal agents seized suspected anarchists and Communists and held them for deportation with no regard for due process of law. In December, 249 aliens—including such well-known radical leaders as Emma Goldman and Alexander Berkman—were sent to Russia aboard the *Buford*, dubbed the "Soviet Ark" by the press. Nearly all were innocent of the charges against them. A month later, Palmer rounded up nearly 4,000 suspected Communists in a single evening. Federal agents broke into homes, meeting halls, and union offices without search warrants. Many native-born Americans were caught in the dragnet and spent several days in jail before being released; aliens rounded up were deported without hearings or trials.

For a time, it seemed that this Red Scare reflected the prevailing views of the American people. Instead of condemning their government's action, citizens voiced their approval and even urged more drastic steps. One patriot said his solution to the alien problem was simple: "S.O.S.—ship or shoot." General Leonard Wood, the former army chief of staff, favored placing Bolsheviks on "ships of stone with sails of lead," while evangelist Billy Sunday preferred to take "these ornery, wild-eyed Socialists" and "stand them up before a firing squad and save

With flagrant disregard for due process of law and basic civil liberties, Attorney General A. Mitchell Palmer in 1919 ordered raids on "dangerous aliens" and "foreign subversives."

eleven thousand strong, was placed on duty to prepare for imminent disaster. When no bombings or violence took place on May Day, the public began to react against Palmer's hysteria. Despite a violent explosion on Wall Street in September that killed thirty-three people, the Red Scare died out by the end of 1920. Palmer passed into obscurity, the tiny Communist party became torn with factionalism, and the American people tried hard to forget their loss of balance.

Yet the Red Scare exerted a continuing influence on American society in the 1920s. The foreign-born lived in the uneasy realization that they were viewed with hostility and suspicion. Two Italian aliens in Massachusetts, Nicola Sacco and Bartolomeo Vanzetti, were arrested in May 1920 for a payroll robbery and murder. They faced a prosecutor and jury who condemned them more for their ideas than for any evidence of

Ben Shahn's The Passion of Sacco and Vanzetti (1931–1932) depicts the members of the committee who investigated the trial and confirmed its fairness.

space on our ships." Inflamed by public statements like these, a group of legionnaires in Centralia, Washington, dragged a radical from the town jail, castrated him, and hanged him from a railway bridge. The coroner's report blandly stated that the victim "jumped off with a rope around his neck and then shot himself full of holes."

The very extremism of the Red Scare led to its rapid demise. In early 1920, courageous government officials from the Department of Labor insisted on due process and full hearings before anyone else was deported. Prominent public leaders began to speak out against the acts of terror. Charles Evans Hughes, the defeated GOP candidate in 1916, offered to defend six Socialists expelled from the New York legislature; Ohio Senator Warren G. Harding, the embodiment of middle-class values, expressed his opinion that "too much has been said about bolshevism in America." Finally, Palmer himself, with evident presidential ambition, went too far. In April 1920, he warned of a vast revolution to occur on May 1; the entire New York City police force, some criminal conduct and a judge who referred to them as "those anarchist bastards." Despite a worldwide effort that became the chief liberal cause of the 1920s, the courts rejected all appeals. Sacco and Vanzetti, a shoemaker and a fish peddler, died in the electric chair on August 23, 1927. Their fate symbolized the bigotry and intolerance that lasted through the twenties and made this decade one of the least attractive in American history.

Prohibition

In December 1917, Congress adopted the Eighteenth Amendment, prohibiting the manufacture and sale of alcoholic beverages. A little over a year later, Nebraska was the necessary thirty-sixth state to ratify, and Prohibition became the law of the land.

As implemented under the Volstead Act, beginning January 16, 1920, it was illegal for anyone to make, sell, or transport any drink that contained more than one-half of 1 percent alcohol by volume. Prohibition was the result of both a rural effort of the Anti-Saloon League, backed by Methodist and Baptist clergymen, and the urban Progressive concern over the social disease of drunkenness, especially among industrial workers. The moral issue had already led to the enactment of Prohibition laws in twenty-six states by 1920; the real tragedy would occur in the effort to extend this "noble experiment" to the growing cities, where it was deeply resented by ethnic groups like the Germans and the Irish and was almost totally disregarded by the well-to-do and the sophisticated.

Prohibition did in fact lead to a decline in drinking. Americans consumed much less alcohol in the twenties than in the prewar years. Rural areas became totally dry, and in the cities, the consumption of alcoholic beverages dropped sharply among the lower classes, who could not afford the high prices for bootleg liquor. Among the middle class and the wealthy, however, drinking became fashionable. Bootleggers supplied whiskey, which quickly replaced lighter spirits such as wine and beer. The alcohol was either smuggled from abroad (a $40-million per year business by 1924) or illicitly manufactured in America. Such exotic products as Jackass Bran-

*A*lthough federal agents captured many illegal stills and much bootleg whiskey during Prohibition, there were too few agents to police the thousands of violators.

dy, Soda Pop Moon, and Yack Yack Bourbon were common—and all could be fatal. Despite the risk of illness or death from extraordinarily high alcohol content or poorly controlled distillation, Americans consumed some 150 million quarts of liquor a year in the twenties. Bootleggers took in nearly $2 billion annually, about 2 percent of the gross national product.

Urban resistance to Prohibition finally led to its repeal in 1933. But in the intervening years, it damaged American society by breeding a profound disrespect for the law. The flamboyant excesses of bootleggers were only the more obvious evils spawned by Prohibition. In city after city, police openly tolerated the traffic in liquor, and judges and prosecutors agreed to let bootleggers pay merely token fines, creating almost a system of licenses. Prohibition satisfied the countryside's desire for vindication, yet rural and urban America alike suffered from this overzealous attempt to legislate morals.

The Ku Klux Klan

The most ominous expression of protest against the new urban culture was the rebirth of the Ku Klux Klan. On Thanksgiving night in 1915, on Stone Mountain in Georgia, Colonel William J. Simmons and thirty-four followers founded the modern Klan. Only "native born, white, gentile Americans" were permitted to join "the Invisible Empire, Knights of the Ku Klux Klan." Membership grew slowly during World War I, but after 1920, fueled by postwar fears and shrewd promotional techniques, the Klan mushroomed. In villages, towns, and small cities across the nation, Anglo-Saxon Protestant men flocked into the newly formed chapters, seeking to relieve their anxiety over a changing society by embracing the Klan's unusual rituals and by demonstrating their hatred against blacks, aliens, Jews, and Catholics.

The Klan of the 1920s, unlike the night riders of the post–Civil War era, was not just antiblack; the threat to American culture, as Klansmen perceived it, came from aliens—Italians and Russians, Jews and Catholics. They attributed much of the tension and conflict in society to the prewar flood of immigrants, foreigners who spoke different languages, worshiped in strange churches, and lived in distant, threatening cities. The Klansmen struck back by coming together and enforcing their own values. They punished blacks who did not know their place, women who practiced the new morality, and aliens who refused to conform. Beating, flogging, burning with acid—even murder—were condoned. They also tried more peaceful methods of coercion, formulating codes of behavior and seeking communitywide support.

The Klan entered politics, at first hesitantly, then with growing confidence. The KKK gained control of the legislatures in Texas, Oklahoma, Oregon, and Indiana; in 1924, it blocked a resolution of censure at the Democratic National Convention. With an estimated five million members by the mid-1920s, the Klan seemed to be fully established.

Its appeal lay in the sanctuary it offered to insecure and anxious people. Protestant to the core, the members found in the local Klavern a reassurance missing in their churches. The poor and ignorant became enchanted with the titles, ranging from Imperial Wizard to Grand Dragon, and gloried in the ritual that centered around the letter "K." Thus each Klan had its own Klalendar, held its weekly Klonklave in the local Klavern, and followed the rules set forth in the Kloran. Members found a sense of identity in the group

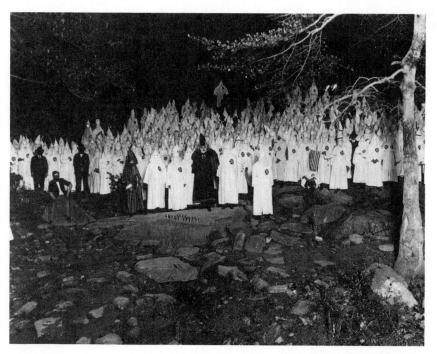

A KKK initiation ceremony. Only native-born white Americans "who believe in the tenets of the Christian religion" were admitted into the Klan.

Marcus Garvey: Racial Redemption and Black Nationalism

World War I brought blacks to Northern cities in unprecedented numbers. In the postwar economic slump, the scramble for jobs aggravated existing racial tensions and violence erupted in cities across the country. Urban slums, job discrimination, disenfranchisement, segregation—black disillusionment with white America gave powerful resonance to the message of racial redemption preached by Marcus Garvey, a Jamaican black nationalist.

Garvey's upbringing under the color-based caste system of the Brit-ish-ruled West Indies convinced him that only black racial solidarity could overturn the traditions that pitted blacks against each other, locked out of the privileges of white society. Studying in London in 1912, he espoused black nation-alism and dreamed of an independent black Africa; from Booker T. Washington he adopted the doc-trine of economic self-help. He molded these ideas into a vision of the black race redeemed through his new organization, the United Negro Improvement Association (UNIA). Its purpose was racial uni-ty; its program included the strengthening of self-identity and racial pride, education, international commerce, industry, and the re-construction of an independent black Africa.

In 1916, Garvey toured the Unit-ed States. American blacks re-sponded so strongly to his message of racial redemption and black na-tionalism that he decided to move UNIA headquarters to Harlem. With a new weekly, the *Negro world*, Garvey advanced his crusade for pride in black heritage and sep-aratism. The paper extolled the beauty of black skin color and Afri-can features; his editorials echoed B. T. Washington's message of eco-nomic self-reliance, but with a new militant tone. "Up, you mighty race," he exhorted, "you can ac-complish what you will."

In 1919, Garvey put his principles into practice, opening a consulting firm to assist black en-trepreneurs and launching a steam-ship company. With the Black Star Line, Garvey hoped to demonstrate black competence in business, to enhance black pride, and to strengthen the bonds among blacks worldwide. The idea caught the popular imagination, though American black leadership was skeptical. A company brochure of-fered every black investor the promise of easy dividends and an opportunity to climb the ladder of success for only $5 per share. In November 1919, the BSL launched its first of three ships and stock sales soared.

Spirits were high at the first in-ternational convention of UNIA in 1920. Several thousand delegates from all 48 states and more than 20 foreign countries came to New York. After leading the opening-day parade, which stretched for several miles through the streets of Harlem, Garvey delivered the key-note address before a crowd of 25,000 at Madison Square Garden. His message was black nationalism and separatism:

We are the descendents of a suffering people. We are the descendents of a people determined to suffer no longer. We shall now organize the 400,000,000 Negroes of the world into a vast organization to plant the banner of freedom on the great continent of Africa. . . . If Europe is for Europeans, then Africa

Marcus Garvey's advocacy of black nationalism and independent black entrepreneurship were, in part, discredited by his trial and conviction for mail fraud.

shall be for the black peoples of the world. We say it; we mean it.

Garvey's ill-fated plans for African redemption began with his Liberian Rehabilitation Project. The black African republic welcomed his offer of financial and technical assistance through the UNIA, and in late 1920 Garvey began to raise money for a reconstruction loan. In subsequent months, however, he diverted much of the proceeds to keep the ailing BSL afloat. With large capital outlays, poor management, and high operating costs, Garvey's dream of a maritime empire verged on financial collapse.

The "establishment" black press accused Garvey of adventurism, opportunism, and diversion from the real paths of progress. His views on the Ku Klux Klan made him even more controversial. While deploring Klan terror and violence, Garvey voiced appreciation of Klan candor on race relations:

I regard the Klan, the Anglo-Saxon Clubs, and White American societies as better friends of the race than all other groups of hypocritical whites put together. I like honesty and fair play. You may call me a Klansman if you will, but potentially every white man is a Klansman, as far as the Negro in competition with whites socially, economically, and politically is concerned, and there is no use lying about it.

So stark a statement of racial separatism and suspicion of whites appalled other black leaders and Garvey found himself under attack from all sides. W. E. B. Du Bois called Garvey "the most dangerous enemy of the Negro race," but he was uncertain if Garvey were "a lunatic or a traitor."

Garvey's battle with black leaders was but one of his challenges. In May 1923, he and three of his associates went on trial for mail fraud in the sale of BSL stock. Defending himself, Garvey used the courtroom as much to preach his philosophy as to plead his case. Although the government documented the BSL's record of mismanagement and overspending, the legal issue was Garvey's intent; had he and his associates sold BSL stock knowing the company was insolvent? E. D. Cronon, Garvey's most meticulous biographer, finds the evidence equivocal. Garvey's business acumen was questionable and his bookkeeping atrocious, but neither he nor his executives drew large salaries from the BSL or lived lavishly at company expense. The BSL, concludes Cronon, may have been "ill-advised and even foolish," but not willfully fraudulent. The jury, unmoved by Garvey's eloquence, found him guilty while acquitting his codefendants; the judge, a white member of the NAACP, sentenced Garvey to the maximum 5-year term.

A federal appeals court upheld Garvey's conviction and on February 8, 1925, he began serving his term in the federal penitentiary at Atlanta. Ironically, once he was behind bars, Garvey gained the support of many of his erstwhile detractors who protested the severity of white justice. Under mounting pressure, President Coolidge commuted Garvey's sentence late in 1927. Immediate deportation followed, as required by U.S. immigration law.

Garvey tried in vain to revitalize the UNIA in Jamaica, but with the onset of the Great Depression, American blacks concentrated more on survival than on racial redemption. Garvey slipped into obscurity and died in 1940 at the age of 52.

His movement inspired blacks disgusted by the hypocrisy of American democracy and frustrated by the failure of gradualism to improve their lot. He gave them an alternative to the litigation and legislation approach of the more conservative black establishment. Although his projects offered no lasting solutions to the problems of race relations, his stress on pride of heritage and ties to Africa influenced many black Americans in succeeding generations.

activities, whether they were peaceful picnics, ominous parades in white robes, or fiery cross-burnings at night.

Although it was a male organization, the Klan did not neglect the family. There was a Women's Order, a Junior Order for boys, and a Tri-K Klub for girls. Members had to be born in America, but foreign-born Protestants were allowed to join a special Krusaders affiliate. Only blacks, Catholics, Jews, and prostitutes were beyond redemption to these lonely and anxious men who came together to chant:

> United we stick
> Divided we're stuck.
> The better we stick
> The better we Klux!

The Klan fell even more quickly than it rose. Its more violent activities—which included kidnapping, lynching, setting fire to synagogues and Catholic churches, and in one case, murdering a priest—began to offend the nation's conscience. Misuse of funds and sexual scandals among Klan leaders, notably in Indiana, repelled many of the rank and file; effective counterattacks by traditional politicians ousted the KKK from control in Texas and Oklahoma. Membership declined sharply after 1925; by the end of the decade, the Klan had virtually disappeared. But its spirit lived on, testimony to the recurring demons of nativism and hatred that have surfaced periodically throughout the American experience.

Immigration Restriction

The nativism that permeated the Klan found its most successful outlet in the immigration legislation of the 1920s. The sharp increase in immigration in the late nineteenth century had led to a broad-based movement. Spearheaded by organized labor and by New England aristocrats like Henry Cabot Lodge, the movement acted to restrict the flow of people from Europe. In 1917, over Wilson's veto, Congress enacted a literacy test which reduced the number of immigrants allowed into the country. The war caused a much more drastic decline—from an average of 1 million a year between 1900 and 1914 to only 110,000 in 1918.

After the armistice, however, rumors began to spread of an impending flood of people seeking to escape war-ravaged Europe. Kenneth Roberts, a popular historical novelist, warned that all Europe was on the move, with only the limits of available steamship space likely to stem the flow. Worried congressmen spoke of a "barbarian horde" and a "foreign tide" that would inundate the United States with "dangerous and deadly enemies of the country." Even though the actual number of immigrants, 810,000 in 1920 (less than the prewar yearly average), did not match these projections, Congress responded in 1921 by passing an emergency immigration act. The new quota system restricted immigration from Europe to 3 percent of the number of nationals from each country living in the United States in 1910.

The 1921 act failed to satisfy the nativists. The quotas still permitted more than 500,000 Europeans to come to the United States in 1923, nearly half of them from southern and eastern Europe. The declining percentage of Nordic immigrants alarmed writers like Madison Grant, who warned the American people that the Anglo-Saxon stock that had founded the nation was about to be overwhelmed by lesser breeds with inferior genes. "These immigrants adopt the language of the native American, they wear his clothes and are beginning to take his women, but they seldom adopt his religion or understand his ideals," Grant wrote.

Psychologists, relying on primitive IQ tests used by the army in World War I, confirmed this judgment (see "Measuring the Mind," pp. 728–29). One senator claimed that all the nation's ills were due to an "intermingled and mongrelized people" as he demanded that racial purity replace the older reliance on the melting pot. In 1924, Congress adopted the National Origins Quota Act which limited immigration from Europe to 150,000 a year; allocated most of the available slots to immigrants from Great Britain, Ireland, Germany, and Scandinavia; and banned all Asian immigrants. The measure passed Congress with overwhelming rural support.

The new restrictive legislation marked the most enduring achievement of the rural counterattack. Unlike the Red Scare, Prohibition, and the Klan, the quota system would survive until the 1960s, enforcing a racist bias that excluded Asians and limited the immigration of Italians, Greeks, and Poles to a few thousand a year while permitting a steady stream of Irish, English, and Scandinavian immigrants. The large corporations, no longer dependent on armies of unskilled immigrant workers, did not object to the 1924 law; the machine had replaced the immigrant on the assembly line. Yet even here the victory was not complete. A growing tide of Mexican laborers, exempt from the quota act, flowed northward across the Rio Grande to fill the continuing need for unskilled workers on the farms and in the service trades. The Mexican immigrants, as many as 100,000 a year, marked the strengthening of an element in the national ethnic mosaic that would grow in size and influence until it became a major force in modern American society.

The Fundamentalist Controversy

The most famous of all attacks on the new urban culture was the Scopes trial held in Dayton, Tennessee. There in 1925, William Jennings Bryan, who had unsuccessfully run for president several times in previous decades, engaged in a crusade against the theory of evolution, appearing as a chief witness against John Scopes. Scopes, a high-school biology teacher, had initiated the case by deliberately violating a new Tennessee law that forbade the teaching of Darwin's theory.

In the trial, Bryan testified under oath that he believed Jonah had been swallowed by a big fish and declared, "It is better to trust in the Rock of Ages than in the age of rocks." Chicago defense attorney Clarence Darrow succeeded in making Bryan look ridiculous. The court found Scopes guilty but let him off with a token fine; Bryan, exhausted by his efforts, died a few days later. H. L. Mencken, who covered the trial in person, rejoiced in the belief that fundamentalism was dead.

In reality, however, traditional rural religious beliefs were stronger than ever. As middle- and upper-class Americans drifted into a genteel Christianity which stressed good works and respectability, the Baptist and Methodist churches continued to hold on to the old faith. In addition, aggressive fundamentalist sects such as the Churches of Christ, the Pentecostals, and Jehovah's Witnesses grew rapidly. While church membership increased from 41.9 million in 1916 to 54.5 million in 1926, the number of churches actually declined during the decade. More and more rural dwellers drove their cars into town

GATHERING DATA FOR THE TENNESSEE TRIAL

Religious fundamentalism, which enjoyed a resurgence after World War I, clashed with current scientific theory in the Scopes trial.

instead of going to the local crossroads chapel.

Many of those who came to the city in the twenties brought their religious beliefs with them and found new outlets for their traditional ideas. Thus evangelist Aimee Semple McPherson enjoyed amazing success in Los Angeles with her "Four-Square Gospel," building the Angelus Temple to seat over 5000 worshipers. And in Fort Worth, the Reverend J. Frank Norris erected a 6000-seat sanctuary for the First Baptist Church, bathing it in spotlights so that it could be seen for 30 miles across the north Texas prairie.

Far from dying out, as divinity professor Thomas G. Oden noted, biblical fundamentalism retained "remarkable grass-roots strength among the organization men and the industrialized mass society of the 20th century." The rural counterattack, while challenged by the city, did enable some older American values to survive in the midst of the new mass-production culture.

POLITICS OF THE TWENTIES

The tensions between the city and the countryside also shaped the course of politics in the 1920s. On the surface, it was a Republican decade. The GOP controlled the White House from 1921 to 1933 and had majorities in both houses of Congress from 1918 to 1930. The Republicans used their return to power after World War I to halt further reform legislation and to establish a friendly relationship between government and business. Important shifts were taking place, however, in the American electorate. The Democrats, although divided into competing urban and rural wings, were laying the groundwork for the future by winning over millions of new voters, especially among the ethnic groups in the cities. The rising tide of urban voters indicated a fundamental shift away from the Republicans toward a new Democratic majority.

Harding, Coolidge, and Hoover

The Republicans regained the White House in 1920 with the election of Warren G. Harding of Ohio. A dark-horse contender, Harding won the GOP nomination when the convention deadlocked and he became the compromise choice. Handsome and dignified, Harding reflected both the virtues and blemishes of small-town America. Originally a newspaper publisher in Marion, he had made many friends and few enemies throughout his career as a legislator, lieutenant governor, and finally, after 1914, a United States senator. Conventional in outlook, Harding was a genial man who lacked the capacity to govern and who, as president, broadly delegated power.

He made some good cabinet choices, notably Charles Evans Hughes as secretary of state and Herbert C. Hoover as secretary of commerce, but two corrupt officials—Attorney General Harry Daugherty and Secretary of the Interior Albert Fall—sabotaged his administration. Daugherty became involved in a series of questionable deals that led ultimately to his forced resignation; Fall was the chief figure in the Teapot Dome scandal. Two oil promoters gave Fall nearly $400,000 in loans and bribes; in return, he helped them secure leases on naval oil reserves in Elk Hills, California, and Teapot Dome, Wyoming. The scandal came to light after Harding's death from a heart attack in 1923. Fall eventually served a year in jail, and the reputation of the Harding administration never recovered.

Vice President Calvin Coolidge assumed the

Attorney General Daugherty struggles to keep the scandals of the Harding administration hidden in the closet.

presidency upon Harding's death, and his honesty and integrity quickly reassured the nation. Coolidge, born in Vermont of old Yankee stock, had first gained national attention in 1919 as governor of Massachusetts when he had dealt firmly with a Boston police strike by declaring, "There is no right to strike against the public safety by anybody, anywhere, any time." A reserved, reticent man, Coolidge became famous for his epigrams, which contemporaries mistook for wisdom. "The business of America is business," he proclaimed. "The man who builds a factory builds a temple; the man who works there worships there." Consistent with this philosophy, he believed his duty was simply to preside benignly, not govern the nation. "Four fifths of all our troubles in this life would disappear," he said, "if we would just sit down and be still." Calvin Coolidge, one observer noted, "aspired to become the least President the country ever had; he attained his desire." Satisfied with the prosperity of the mid-twenties, the people responded favorably. Coolidge was elected to a full term by a wide margin in 1924.

When Coolidge announced in 1927 that he did not "choose to run," Herbert Hoover became the Republican choice to succeed him. By far the ablest GOP leader of the decade, Hoover epitomized the American myth of the self-made man. Orphaned as a boy, he had worked his way through Stanford University and had gained both wealth and fame as a mining engineer. During World War I, he had displayed admirable administrative skills in directing Wilson's food program at home and relief activities abroad. Sober, intelligent, and immensely hard-working, Hoover embodied the nation's faith in individualism and free enterprise.

As secretary of commerce under Harding and Coolidge, he had sought cooperation between government and business. He used his office to assist American manufacturers and exporters in expanding their overseas trade, and he strongly supported a trade association movement to encourage cooperation rather than cutthroat competition among smaller American companies. He did not view business and government as antagonists. Instead, he saw them as partners, working together to achieve efficiency and affluence for all Americans. His optimistic view of the future led him to declare in his speech accepting the Republican presidential nomination in 1928 that "we in America today are nearer to the final triumph over poverty than ever before in the history of any land."

Republican Policies

During the 1920 campaign, Warren Harding urged a return to "not heroism, but healing, not nostrums, but normalcy." Misreading his speechwriter's "normality," he coined a new word that became the theme for the Republican administrations of the '20s. Aware that the public was tired of zealous reform-minded presidents like Teddy Roosevelt and Woodrow Wilson, Harding and his successors sought a return to traditional Republican policies. In some areas they were successful, but in others the Republican leaders were forced to adjust to the new realities of a mass-production society. The result was a mixture of tradition-

al and innovative measures that was neither wholly reactionary nor entirely progressive.

The most obvious attempt to go back to the Republicanism of William McKinley came in tariff and tax policy. Fearful of a flood of postwar European imports, Congress passed an emergency tariff act in 1921 and followed it a year later with the protectionist Fordney-McCumber Tariff Act. The net effect was to raise the basic rates substantially over the moderate Underwood Tariff schedules of the Wilson period.

Secretary of the Treasury Andrew Mellon, a wealthy Pittsburgh banker and industrialist, worked hard to achieve a similar return to normalcy in taxation. Condemning the high wartime tax rates on businesses and wealthy individuals, Mellon pressed for repealing an excess-profits tax on corporations and slashing personal rates on the very rich. Using the new budget system adopted by Congress in 1921, he reduced government spending from its World War I peak of $18 billion to just over $3 billion by 1925, thereby creating a slight surplus. Congress responded in 1926 by cutting the highest income-tax bracket to a modest 20 percent.

The revenue acts of the 1920s greatly reduced the burden of taxation; by the end of the decade, the government was collecting one-third less than it had in 1921, and the number of people paying income taxes dropped from over 6.5 million to 4 million. Yet the greatest relief went to the wealthy. The public was shocked to learn in the 1930s that J. P. Morgan and his nineteen partners had paid no income tax at all during the depths of the Depression.

The growing crisis in American farming during the decade forced the Republican administrations to seek new solutions. The end of the European war led to a sharp decline in farm prices and a return to the problem of overproduction. Southern and western lawmakers formed a farm bloc in Congress to press for special legislation for American agriculture. The farm bloc supported the higher tariffs, which included protection for constituents' crops, and helped secure passage of legislation to create federal supervision over stockyards, packinghouses, and grain trading.

This special-interest legislation failed to get at the root of overproduction, however. Farmers then supported more controversial measures designed to raise domestic crop prices by having the

CHRONOLOGY

1919 U.S. agents arrest 1700 in Red Scare raids • Congress passes Volstead Act over Wilson's veto (October)

1920 Budget Bureau set up to oversee federal spending • Nineteenth Amendment passed, granting women the right to vote • Transcontinental airmail service inaugurated (September) • WWJ-Detroit broadcasts first commercial radio program (November)

1921 Congress enacts quotas for European immigrants

1923 Newspapers expose KKK graft, torture, murder • Henry Luce begins publishing *Time* magazine (March)

1924 Senate probes Teapot Dome scandal • Veterans' World War I bonus bill passed

1925 John Scopes convicted of teaching theory of evolution in violation of Tennessee law (July)

1926 First Martha Graham modern dance recital (April)

1927 Charles Lindbergh completes first nonstop transatlantic flight from New York to Paris (May) • Coolidge vetoes farm price-control bill • Sacco and Vanzetti executed (August) • The movie *The Jazz Singer* features singing-talking soundtrack

government sell the surplus overseas at low world prices. Coolidge vetoed the legislation on grounds that it involved unwarranted government interference in the economy.

Yet the government's role in the economy increased rather than lessened in the 1920s. Republicans widened the scope of federal activity and nearly doubled the ranks of government employees. Herbert Hoover led the way in the Commerce Department, establishing new bureaus to help make American industry more efficient in housing, transportation, and mining. Under his leadership, the government encouraged corporations to develop welfare programs that undercut trade unions, and he tried to mini-

mize labor disturbances by devising new federal machinery to mediate disputes. Instead of going back to the laissez-faire tradition of the nineteenth century, the Republican administrations of the twenties were pioneering a close relationship between government and private business.

The Divided Democrats

While the Republicans ruled in the 1920s, the Democrats seemed bent on self-destruction. The Wilson coalition fell apart in 1920 as pent-up dissatisfaction stemming from the war enabled Harding to win by a landslide. The pace of the second Industrial Revolution and the growing urbanization split the party in two. One faction was centered in the rural South and West. Traditional Democrats who had supported Wilson stood for Prohibition, fundamentalism, the Klan, and other facets of the rural counterattack against the city. In contrast, a new breed of Democrat was emerging in the metropolitan areas of the North and Midwest. Immigrants and their descendants began to become active in the Democratic party. Catholic or Jewish in religion and strongly opposed to Prohibition, they had little in common with their rural counterparts.

The split within the party surfaced dramatically at the national convention in New York in 1924. Held in Madison Square Garden, a hall built in the 1890s and too small and cramped for the more than one thousand delegates, the convention soon degenerated into what one observer described as a "snarling, cursing, tenuous, suicidal, homicidal roughhouse." City slickers mocked the "rubes and hicks" from the "sticks"; populist orators struck back by denouncing the city as "wanting in national ideals, devoid of conscience . . . rooted in corruption, directed by greed and dominated by selfishness." An urban resolution to condemn the Ku Klux Klan led to a

The Election of 1924			
Candidate	Party	Popular Vote	Electoral Vote
Coolidge	Republican	15,717,553	382
Davis	Democrat	8,386,169	136
LaFollette	Progressive	4,814,050	13

spirited response from the rural faction and its defeat by a single vote. Then for nine days, in the midst of a stifling heat wave, the delegates divided between Alfred E. Smith, the governor of New York, and William G. McAdoo of California, Wilson's secretary of the treasury. When it became clear that neither the city nor the rural candidate could win a majority, both men withdrew; on the 103rd ballot, the weary Democrats finally chose John W. Davis, a former West Virginia congressman and New York corporation lawyer, as their compromise nominee.

In the ensuing election, the conservative Davis had difficulty in distinguishing his views from those of Republican President Calvin Coolidge. For the discontented, Senator Robert LaFollette of Wisconsin offered an alternative by running on an independent Progressive party ticket. Coolidge won easily, receiving 15 million votes to 8 million for Davis and nearly 5 million for LaFollette. Davis had made the poorest showing of any Democratic candidate in the twentieth century.

Yet the Democrats were in far better shape than this setback indicated. Beginning in 1922, the party had made heavy inroads into the GOP majority in Congress. The Democrats took seventy-eight seats away from Republicans in that election, many of them in the cities of the East and Midwest. In New York alone, they gained thirteen new congressmen, all but one in districts with heavy immigrant populations. Even in 1924, the Republican vote in large cities declined as many urban voters chose LaFollette in the absence of an attractive Democratic candidate. By 1926, the Democrats were within one vote of controlling the Senate and had picked up nine more seats in the House in metropolitan areas. The large cities were swinging clearly into the Democratic column; all the party needed was a charismatic leader who could fuse the older rural elements with the new urban voters.

The Election of 1928

The selection of Al Smith as the Democratic candidate in 1928 indicated the growing power of the city. Born on the lower east side of Manhattan of mixed Irish-German ancestry, Smith was the prototype of the urban Democrat. He was Catholic; he was associated with a big-city machine; he

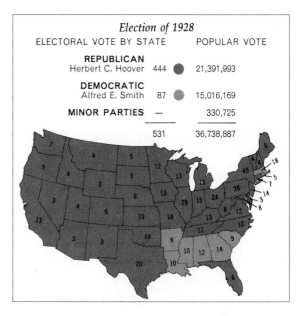

Election of 1928

ELECTORAL VOTE BY STATE		POPULAR VOTE
REPUBLICAN Herbert C. Hoover	444	21,391,993
DEMOCRATIC Alfred E. Smith	87	15,016,169
MINOR PARTIES	—	330,725
	531	36,738,887

was a "wet" who wanted to end Prohibition. Starting out in the Fulton Fish Market as a boy, he had joined Tammany Hall and gradually climbed the political ladder, rising from subpoena server to state legislator to governor, a post he held with distinction for nearly a decade. Rejected by rural Democrats in 1924, he still had to prove that he could unite the South and West behind his leadership. His lack of education, poor grammar, and distinctive New York accent all hurt him, as did his eastern provincialism. When reporters asked him about his appeal in the states west of the Mississippi, he replied, "What states *are* west of the Mississippi?"

The choice facing the American voter in 1928 seemed unusually clear-cut. Herbert Hoover was a Protestant, a dry, and an old-stock American who stood for efficiency and individualism; Smith was a Catholic, a wet, and a descendant of immigrants who was closely associated with big-city politics. Just as Smith appealed to new voters in the cities, so Hoover won the support of many old-line Democrats who feared the city, Tammany Hall, and the pope.

Yet beneath the surface, as Allan J. Lichtman points out, there were "striking similarities between Smith and Hoover." Both were self-made men who embodied the American belief in freedom of opportunity and upward mobility. Neither advocated any significant degree of economic change nor any redistribution of national

The happy warrior, Al Smith, in his familiar brown derby, campaigning from a train platform in 1928.

Republican candidate Herbert Hoover campaigned on a platform that stressed continued economic prosperity.

wealth or power. Though religion proved to be the most important issue in the minds of the voters, hurting Smith far more than Prohibition or his identification with the city, the Democratic candidate's failure to spotlight the growing cracks in prosperity or to offer alternative economic policies ensured his defeat.

The 1928 election was a dubious victory for the Republicans. Hoover won easily, defeating Smith by more than six million votes and carrying such traditionally Democratic states as Oklahoma, Texas, and Florida. But Smith succeeded for the first time in winning a majority of votes for the Democrats in the nation's twelve largest cities. A new Democratic electorate was emerging, consisting of Catholics and Jews, Irish and Italians, Poles and Greeks. Now the task was to unite the traditional Democrats of the South and West with the urban voters of the Northeast and Midwest.

The growing influence of the city on politics of the 1920s reflected the sweeping changes taking place throughout the decade in American social and economic development. Al Smith, despite his defeat in 1928, symbolized the emergence of the city as the center of twentieth century American life. An older nation founded on rural values had given way to a new urban society in which the production and use of consumer goods led to a very different life-style. Just as nineteenth-century American culture had revolved around the farm and the railroad, modern America focused on the automobile and the city. Yet despite the genuine economic progress achieved in the twenties, the decade ended in a severe depression that lasted all through the 1930s. Only after World War II would the American people finally enjoy an abundance and prosperity rooted in the urban transformation that began in the 1920s.

Recommended Reading

William Leuchtenburg provides the best overview of the 1920s in *The Perils of Prosperity, 1914–1932* (1958). He stresses the theme of rural-urban conflict and claims that the achievements of the decade were more significant than its failures. The essays in John Braeman, Robert H. Bremner, and David Brody, eds., *Change and Continuity in Twentieth Century America: The 1920s* (1968) illuminate important aspects of the period.

A fully detailed account of economic developments in the decade is George Soule, *Prosperity Decade* (1947). Two classic studies, Frederick Lewis Allen, *Only Yesterday* (1931) and Helen Lynd and Robert Lynd, *Middletown* (1929), offer valuable insights into social and cultural trends. The most recent overview of the decade is Geoffrey Perrett, *America in the Twenties* (1982).

The spirit of rural discontent with the new urban society is captured best in Lawrence Levine, *Defender of the Faith* (1965), an account of the last ten years of William Jennings Bryan's life. For changing political alignments of the 1920s, see David Burner, *The Politics of Provincialism* (1968).

Additional Bibliography

General surveys of the 1920s include Ellis W. Hawley, *The Great War and the Search for a Modern Order* (1979) and Donald McCoy, *Coming of Age* (1973). Books on economic themes are John B. Rae, *The American Automobile* (1965); James J. Flink, *The Car Culture* (1975) and *The Automobile Age* (1988); Allen Nevins and Frank E. Hill, *Ford: Expansion and Challenge, 1915–1933* (1957); James Prothro, *The Dollar Decade* (1954); Otis A. Pease, *The Responsibilities of American Advertising* (1959); Roland Marchand, *Advertising the American Dream, 1920–1940* (1985); and Alfred D. Chandler, Jr., *Strategy and Structure* (1962). The best books on labor are Irving Bernstein, *The Lean Years* (1960) and Robert H. Zieger, *Republicans and Labor, 1919–1929* (1969). James Shideler discusses the postwar agricultural depression in *Farm Crisis* (1957).

Social history is covered in Preston Slosson, *The Great Crusade and After* (1930); Paul Carter, *Another Part of the Twenties* (1976); Elizabeth Stevenson, *Babbitts and Bohemians* (1967); and Paula S. Fass, *The Damned and the Beautiful* (1977).

The role of women in the 1920s is examined in William Chafe, *The American Woman* (1972); J. Stanley Lemons, *The Woman Citizen* (1973); Susan D. Becker, *The Origins of the Equal Rights Amendment* (1981); Dorothy M. Brown, *Setting a Course* (1987); Nancy Cott, *The Grounding of American Feminism* (1987); and Winifred D. Wandersee, *Women's Work and Family Values, 1920–1940* (1981). For blacks in the 1920s, see Nathan Huggins, *Harlem Renaissance* (1971); Gilbert Osofsky, *Harlem* (1966); and David Levering Lewis, *When Harlem Was in Vogue* (1981), a lively account of black culture. The career of Marcus Garvey is traced in E. David Cronon, *Black Moses* (1955) and Judith Stein, *The World of Marcus Garvey* (1986). Ricardo Romo explores one aspect of Mexican-American experience in *East Los Angeles: History of a Barrio* (1983).

Frederick Hoffman, *The Twenties* (1955) and Alfred Kazin, *On Native Grounds* (1942) survey the literary trends during the decade. Other studies of this subject are Roderick Nash, *The Nervous Generation* (1969); Robert Crunden, *From Self to Society* (1972); Malcolm Cowley, *Exile's Return* (1934); and Edmund Wilson, *Shores of Light* (1952). Biographies of major literary figures of the period include William Manchester, *Disturber of the Peace* (1951) on H. L. Mencken; Arthur Mizener, *The Far Side of Paradise* (1951) on F. Scott Fitzgerald; Mark Shorer, *Sinclair Lewis* (1961); and Carlos Baker, *Hemingway* (1956).

Studies of political fundamentalism include Robert K. Murray, *Red Scare* (1955); William Young and David E. Kaiser, *Postmortem: New Evidence in the Case of Sacco and Vanzetti* (1985); and Stanley Coben, *A. Mitchell Palmer* (1963) on the postwar panic over radicalism; Andrew Sinclair, *Prohibition* (1962) and Herbert Asbury, *The Great Illusion* (1950) on the noble experiment; David Chalmers, *Hooded Americans* (1965), Arnold S. Rice, *The Ku Klux Klan in American Politics* (1962), and Kenneth T. Jackson, *The Ku Klux Klan in the City* (1967) on the KKK; Robert A. Divine, *American Immigration Policy* (1957) and John Higham, *Strangers in the Land* (1955) on nativism and immigration restriction; and Norman Furniss, *The Fundamentalist Controversy* (1954) and Ray Ginger, *Six Days or Forever?* (1956) on the attack on Darwinism and the Scopes trial.

For political developments during the 1920s, see Robert Murray, *The Harding Era* (1969) and *The Politics of Normalcy* (1973); Burl Noggle, *Teapot Dome* (1962); Francis Russell, *The Shadow of Blooming Grove: Warren G. Harding and His Times* (1968); Joan H. Wilson, *Herbert Hoover* (1975); Martin L. Fausold, *The Presidency of Herbert Hoover* (1985); and David Burner, *Herbert Hoover: A Public Life* (1979). Allan Lichtman, *Prejudice and the Old Politics* (1979) and Kristi Andersen, *The Creation of a Democratic Majority, 1928–1936* (1979) offer contrasting interpretations of the election of 1928.

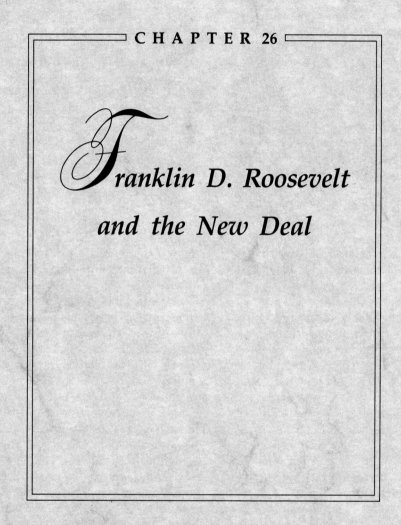

CHAPTER 26

Franklin D. Roosevelt and the New Deal

he prosperity of the twenties came to an abrupt halt in October 1929. The stock market, which had boomed during the decade, suddenly faltered. Investors who had borrowed heavily to take part in the speculative mania that had swept Wall Street suddenly were forced to sell their securities to cover their loans. The wave of selling triggered an avalanche. On October 24, later known as Black Thursday, nearly 13 million shares were traded as highfliers like RCA and Westinghouse lost nearly half their value. In the afternoon, a group of New York bankers, led by the House of Morgan, pooled their resources and began to buy stocks to stem the decline. The stock market rallied for the next two days, but on Tuesday, October 29, the downslide resumed. Frightened sellers dumped over 16 million shares and the industrial average fell by forty-three points. The panic ended in November, with stocks at 1927 levels. For the next four years, there was a steady drift downward, until by 1932, prices were 80 percent below their 1929 highs.

The Great Depression which followed the crash of 1929 was the most devastating economic blow ever suffered by the nation. It lasted for more than ten years, dominating every aspect of American life during the 1930s. Unemployment rose to 12 million by 1932, and though it dipped midway through the decade, it still stood at 10 million by 1939. Children grew up thinking that economic deprivation was the norm rather than the exception in America. Year after year, people kept looking for a return to prosperity, but the outlook remained dismal. Intractable and all-encompassing, the Depression loosened its grip on the nation only after the outbreak of World War II. And even then, it left enduring psychological scars—never again would the Americans who lived through it be quite so optimistic about their economic future.

The Depression led to a profound shift in American political loyalties. The Republicans, dominant since the 1890s, gave way to a new Democratic majority. The millions of immigrants who had come to the United States before World War I became more active politically, as did their children who were beginning to reach voting age. The result was the election of Franklin D. Roosevelt to the presidency and the development of the New Deal, a broad program of relief, recovery, and reform that greatly increased the role of government in American life.

THE GREAT DEPRESSION

The economic collapse altered American attitudes. In the twenties, optimism had prevailed as people looked forward to an ever-increasing flow of consumer goods and a better way of life. But after 1929, despair set in. Factories closed, machines fell silent, and millions upon millions of people walked the streets, looking for jobs that did not exist.

The Great Bull Market

The consumer-goods revolution contained the seeds of its own collapse. The steady expansion of the automobile and appliance industries led gradually to a saturation of the market. Each year after 1924, the rate of increase in the sale of cars and refrigerators and ranges slowed, a natural consequence as more and more people already owned these durable goods. Production began to falter, and in 1927, the nation underwent a mild recession. The sale of durable goods declined, and construction of houses and buildings fell slightly. If corporate leaders had heeded these warning signs, they might have responded by raising wages or lowering prices, both effective ways to stimulate purchasing power and sustain the consumer-goods revolution. Or if government officials had recognized the danger signals and forced a halt in installment-buying and slowed bank loans, the nation might have experienced a sharp but brief depression.

Neither government nor business leaders were so farsighted. The Federal Reserve Board lowered the discount rate, charging banks less for loans in an attempt to stimulate the economy. Much of this additional credit, however, went not into solid investment in factories and machinery but instead into the stock market, touching off a new wave of speculation that obscured the growing economic slowdown and ensured a far greater crash to come.

Individuals with excess cash began to invest heavily in the stock market, betting that the

The 1920s was a get-rich-quick era in which millions of Americans either played or watched the stock market—from corporate managers to floor sweepers.

already impressive rise in security prices would bring them even greater windfall profits. The market had advanced in spurts during the decade; the value of all stocks listed on the New York Stock Exchange rose from $27 billion in 1925 to $67 billion in early 1929. The strongest surge began in the spring of 1928, when investors ignored the declining production figures in the belief that they could make a killing in the market. People took their savings and bet on speculative stocks. Corporations used their large cash reserves to supply money to brokers who in turn loaned it to investors on margin; in 1929, for example, the Standard Oil Company of New Jersey loaned out $69 million a day in this fashion.

Investors could now play the market on credit, buying stock listed at $100 a share with $10 down and $90 on margin, the broker's loan for the balance. If the stock advanced to $150, the investor could sell and reap a gain of 500 percent on the $10 investment. And in the bull-market climate of the twenties, everyone was sure that the market would go up.

By 1929, it seemed that the whole nation was engaged in speculation. In city after city, brokers opened branch offices, each complete with a stock ticker and a huge board covered with the latest Wall Street quotations. People crowded into the customers' rooms in the offices, filling the seats and greeting the latest advances of their favorite stocks with shouts of approval. So great was the public's interest in the stock market that

newspapers carried the stock averages on their front pages.

In reality, though, more people were spectators than speculators; fewer than 3 million Americans owned stocks in 1929, and only about 500,000 were active buyers and sellers. But the bull market became a national obsession, assuring everyone that the economy was healthy and preventing any serious analysis of its underlying flaws. When the market soared to over $80 billion in total value by mid-summer, *The Wall Street Journal* discounted any possibility of a decline, proclaiming, "The outlook for the fall months seems brighter than at any time."

The great crash in October 1929 put a sudden and tragic end to the speculative mania. The false confidence that had kept the economy from collapsing in 1927 evaporated overnight. Suddenly, corporations and financial institutions were no longer willing to provide capital for stock-market purchases. More important, investors and bankers cut off consumer credit as well, drying up buying power and leading to a sharp decline in the sales of consumer goods. Factories began to cut back production, laying off some workers and reducing hours for others. The layoffs and cutbacks lowered purchasing power even further, so fewer people bought cars and appliances. More factory layoffs resulted, and some plants closed entirely, leading to the availability of even less money for the purchase of consumer goods.

This downward economic spiral continued for four years. By 1932, unemployment had swelled to 25 percent of the work force. Steel production was down to 12 percent of capacity, and the vast assembly lines in Detroit produced only a trickle of cars each day. The Gross National Product fell to 67 percent of the 1929 level. The bright promise of mass production had ended in a nightmare.

The basic explanation for the Great Depression lies in the fact that U.S. factories produced more goods than the American people could consume. The problem was not that the market for such products was fully saturated. In 1929, there were still millions of Americans who did not own cars or radios or refrigerators, but many of them could not afford the new products. There were other contributing causes—unstable economic conditions in Europe, the agricultural decline since 1919, corporate mismanagement, and excessive speculation—but it all came down to the fact that people did not have enough money to buy the consumer products coming off the assembly lines. Installment sales helped bridge the gap, but by 1929 the burden of debt was just too great.

The new economic system had failed to distribute wealth more broadly. Too much money had gone into profits, dividends, and industrial expansion, and not enough had gone into the hands of the workers, who were also consumers. Factory productivity had increased 43 percent during the decade, but the wages of industrial workers had only gone up 11 percent (see Chapter 25). If the billions that went into stock-market speculation had been used instead to increase wages—which would then have increased consumer purchasing power—production and consumption could have been brought into balance. Yet it is too much to expect that the prophets of the New Era could have foreseen this flaw and corrected it. They were pioneering a new industrial system, and only out of the bitter experience of the Depression would they discover the full dynamics of the consumer-goods economy.

Effect of the Depression

It is difficult to measure the human cost of the Great Depression. The material hardships were bad enough. Men and women lived in lean-tos made of scrap wood and metal, and families went without meat and fresh vegetables for months, existing on a diet of soup and beans. The psychological burden was even greater: Americans suffered through year after year of grinding poverty with no letup in sight. The unemployed stood in line for hours waiting for relief checks, veterans sold apples or pencils on street corners, their manhood—once prized so highly by the nation —now in question. People left the city for the countryside but found no salvation on the farm. Crops rotted in the fields because prices were too low to make harvesting worthwhile; sheriffs fended off angry crowds as banks foreclosed long-overdue mortgages on once-prosperous farms.

Few escaped the suffering. African Americans who had left the poverty of the rural South for factory jobs in the North were among the first to be laid off. Mexican-Americans, who had flowed in to replace European immigrants, met with competition from angry citizens, now willing to do stoop labor in the fields and work as track layers on the railroads. Immigration officials used technicalities to halt the flow across the Rio Grande and even to reverse it; nearly a half million Mexicans were deported in the 1930s, including families with children born in the United States.

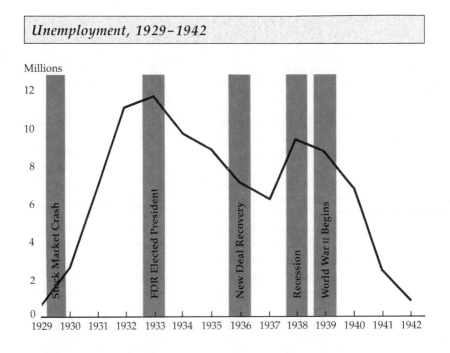

Unemployment, 1929–1942

Unemployment devastated thousands, who turned to selling apples or advertising their labor. The suddenly homeless gathered in hobo camps, like the New York City "Hooverville" at left, while others crowded together on The Park Bench, *as shown in this detail of the painting by Reginald Marsh (above).*

The poor—black, brown, and white—survived because they knew better than most Americans how to exist in poverty. They stayed in bed in cold weather, both to keep warm and to avoid unnecessary burning up of calories; they patched their shoes with pieces of rubber from discarded tires, heated only the kitchens of their homes, and ate scraps of food that others would reject.

The middle class, which had always lived with high expectations, was hit hard. Professionals and white-collar workers refused to ask for charity even while their families went without food;

one New York dentist and his wife turned on the gas and left a note saying, "We want to get out of the way before we are forced to accept relief money." People who fell behind in their mortgage payments lost their homes and then faced eviction when they could not pay the rent. Health care declined. Middle-class people stopped going to doctors and dentists regularly, unable to make the required cash payment in advance for services rendered.

Even the well-to-do were affected, giving up many of their former luxuries and weighed down with guilt as they watched former friends and business associates join the ranks of the impoverished. "My father lost everything in the Depression" became an all too-familiar refrain among young people who dropped out of college.

Many Americans sought escape in movement. Men, boys, and some women, rode the rails in search of jobs, hopping freights to move south in the winter or west in the summer. On the Missouri Pacific alone, the number of vagrants increased from just over 13,000 in 1929 to nearly 200,000 in 1931. One town in the Southwest hired special policemen to keep vagrants from leaving the boxcars. Those who became tramps had to keep on the move, but they did find a sense of community in the hobo jungles that sprang up along the major railroad routes. Here a man could find a place to eat and sleep, and people with whom to share his misery. Louis Banks, a black veteran, told interviewer Studs Terkel what these informal camps were like:

Black and white, it didn't make any difference who you were, 'cause everybody was poor. All friendly, sleep in a jungle. We used to take a big pot and cook food, cabbage, meat and beans all together. We all set together, we made a tent. Twenty-five or thirty would be out on the side of the rail, white and colored: They didn't have no mothers or sisters, they didn't have no home, they were dirty, they had overalls on, they didn't have no food, they didn't have anything.

FIGHTING THE DEPRESSION

The Great Depression presented an enormous challenge for American political leadership. The inability of the Republicans to overcome the economic catastrophe provided the Democrats with the chance to regain power. Although they failed to achieve full recovery before the outbreak of World War II, the Democrats did succeed in alleviating some of the suffering and establishing political dominance.

Hoover and Voluntarism

Herbert Hoover was the Depression's most prominent victim. When the economic downturn began in late 1929, he tried to rally the nation with bold forecasts of better days ahead. His repeated assertion that prosperity was just around the corner bred cynicism and mistrust. Expressing complete faith in the American economic system, Hoover blamed the depression on foreign causes, especially unstable European banks. The President rejected proposals for bold governmental action and relied instead on voluntary cooperation within business to halt the slide. He called the leaders of industry to the White House and secured their agreement to maintain prices and wages at high levels. Yet within a few months, employers were reducing wages and cutting prices in a desperate effort to survive.

Hoover also believed in voluntary efforts to relieve the human suffering brought about by the Depression. He called on private charities and local governments to help feed and clothe those in need. But when these sources were exhausted, he rejected all requests for direct federal relief, asserting that such handouts would undermine the character of proud American citizens.

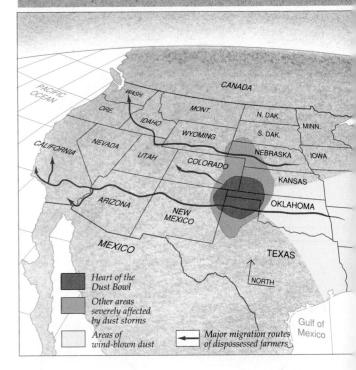

The Dust Bowl

In the Plains States, farms already burdened with the economic hardship of the Depression were plagued by drought and dust storms. Farm families were forced to leave their homes to find work farther west.

Heart of the Dust Bowl

Other areas severely affected by dust storms

Areas of wind-blown dust

Major migration routes of dispossessed farmers

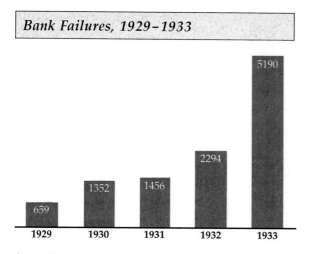

Bank Failures, 1929–1933

- 1929: 659
- 1930: 1352
- 1931: 1456
- 1932: 2294
- 1933: 5190

Source: Data compiled from C. D. Bremer, American Bank Failures *(New York: Columbia University Press, 1935), p. 42.*

As the Depression deepened, Hoover reluctantly began to move beyond voluntarism to undertake more sweeping governmental measures. A new Federal Farm Board loaned money to aid cooperatives and bought up surplus crops in the open market in a vain effort to raise farm prices. At Hoover's request, Congress cut taxes in an attempt to restore public confidence and adopted a few federal public-works projects, such as Boulder Dam, to provide jobs for idle men.

To help imperiled banks and insurance companies, Hoover proposed the Reconstruction Finance Corporation which Congress established in early 1932. The RFC loaned government money to financial institutions to save them from bankruptcy. Hoover's critics, however, pointed out that while he favored aid to business, he still opposed measures such as direct relief and massive public works that would help the millions of unemployed.

By 1932, Hoover's efforts to overcome the Depression had clearly failed. The Democrats had gained control of the House of Representatives in the 1930 elections and were pressing the President to take bolder action, but Hoover stubbornly resisted. His public image suffered its sharpest blow in the summer of 1932 when he ordered General Douglas MacArthur to clear out the "bonus army." This ragged group of some twenty-two thousand World War I veterans had come to Washington in the summer of 1932 to lobby for Congress to pay a bonus for military service due them in 1945 immediately. After the

Senate rejected the bonus bill, some of the veterans stayed in Washington, living in ramshackle huts in Anacostia Flats along the Potomac. Mounted troops drove the bonus army out of the capital, blinding the veterans with tear gas and burning their shacks.

Meanwhile, the nation's banking structure approached collapse. Bank failures rose steadily in 1931 and 1932 as customers responded to rumors of bankruptcy by rushing in to withdraw their deposits, thereby causing a bank's failure. The banking crisis completed the nation's disenchantment with Hoover; the people were ready for a new leader in the White House.

The Emergence of Roosevelt

The man who stepped forward to meet this national need was Franklin D. Roosevelt. Born into the old Dutch colonial aristocracy of New York, FDR was a distant cousin of the Republican Teddy. He grew up with all the advantages of wealth—private tutors, his own sailboat and pony, frequent trips to Europe, and education at Groton and Harvard. His strong-willed mother smoothed all the obstacles in the path of her only child and gave him a priceless sense of inner security. After graduation from Harvard, he briefly attended law school but left to plunge into politics. He served in the New York legislature and then went to Washington as assistant secretary of the navy under Wilson, a post he filled capably during World War I. He met with defeat in 1920 as the Democratic vice-presidential candidate and had begun a banking career when an attack of polio crippled him in the summer of 1921. Refusing to give in, he fought back bravely, and though he never again walked unaided, he reentered politics in the mid-twenties and was elected governor of New York in 1928.

Roosevelt's dominant trait was his ability to persuade and convince other people. He possessed a marvelous voice, deep and rich, a winning smile, and a bouyant confidence that he could easily transmit to others. Some felt he was too vain and superficial as a young man, but his bout with polio gave him both an understanding of human suffering and a broad political appeal as a man who had faced heavy odds and overcome them. He understood the give-and-take of politics, knew how to use flattery to win over

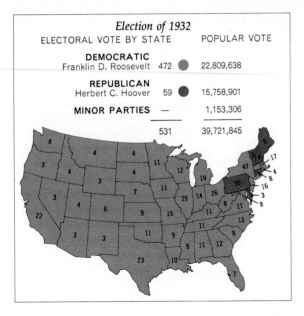

Election of 1932

ELECTORAL VOTE BY STATE   POPULAR VOTE

DEMOCRATIC
Franklin D. Roosevelt   472   22,809,638

REPUBLICAN
Herbert C. Hoover   59   15,758,901

MINOR PARTIES   —   1,153,306

531   39,721,845

Presidential Voting in Chicago by Ethnic Groups, 1924–1932 (Percent Democratic)			
	1924	1928	1932
Czechoslovakians	40	73	83
Poles	35	71	80
Lithuanians	48	77	84
Yugoslavs	20	54	67
Italians	31	63	64
Germans	14	58	69
Jews	19	60	77

Source: John M. Allswang, A House for All Peoples: Ethnic Politics in Chicago, 1890–1936 (Lexington: University Press of Kentucky, 1971).

doubters, and was especially effective in exploiting the media, whether in bantering with newspaper reporters or reaching out to the American people on the radio. Although his mind was quick and agile, he had little patience with philosophical nuances; he dealt with the appearance of issues, not their deeper substance, and he displayed a flexibility toward political principles that often dismayed even his warmest admirers.

Roosevelt took advantage of the opportunity offered by the Depression. With the Republicans discredited, he cultivated the two wings of the divided Democrats, appealing to both the traditionalists from the South and West and the new urban elements in the North. After winning the party's nomination in 1932, he broke with tradition by flying to Chicago and accepting in person, telling the cheering delegates, "I pledge you—I pledge myself to a new deal for the American people."

In the fall, he defeated Herbert Hoover in a near landslide for the Democrats. Roosevelt tallied 472 electoral votes as he swept the South and West and carried nearly all the large industrial states as well. Farmers and workers, Protestants and Catholics, immigrants and native-born rallied behind the new leader who promised to restore prosperity. Roosevelt not only met the challenge of the Depression but also solidified the shift to the Democratic party and created an enduring coalition that would dominate American politics for a half century.

The Hundred Days

When Franklin Roosevelt took the oath of office on March 4, 1933, the nation's economy was on the brink of collapse. Unemployment stood at nearly thirteen million, one-fourth of the labor force; banks were closed in thirty-eight states. On inauguration morning, the governors of New York and Illinois closed the banks in the nation's two largest cities, thus bringing the country's financial transactions to a halt. Speaking from the steps of the Capitol, FDR declared boldly, "First of all, let me assert my firm belief that the only thing we have to fear is fear itself—nameless, unreasoning, unjustified terror." Then he announced that he would call Congress into special session and request "broad executive power to wage a war against the emergency, as great as the power that would be given to me if we were in fact invaded by a foreign foe."

Within the next ten days, Roosevelt won his first great New Deal victory by saving the nation's banks. On March 5, he issued a decree closing the banks and called Congress back into session. His aides drafted new banking legislation and presented it to Congress on March 9; a few hours later, both houses passed it, and FDR signed the new legislation that evening. The measure provided for government supervision and aid to the banks. Strong ones would be reopened with federal support, weak ones closed, and those in difficulty bolstered by government loans.

On March 12, FDR addressed the nation by radio in the first of his fireside chats. In conversational tones, he told the public what he had done.

With his fireside chats, FDR became the first president to use radio to reach and reassure the American people.

Some banks would begin to reopen the next day, with the government standing behind them. Other banks, once they became solvent, would open later, and the American people could safely put their money back into these institutions. The next day, March 13, the nation's largest and strongest banks opened their doors; at the end of the day, customers had deposited more cash than they withdrew. The crisis was over; gradually other banks opened, and the runs and failures ceased.

"Capitalism was saved in eight days," boasted one of Roosevelt's advisers. Most surprising was the conservative nature of FDR's action. Instead of nationalizing the banks, he had simply thrown the government's resources behind them and preserved private ownership. Though some other New Deal measures would be more radical, Roosevelt set a tone in the banking crisis. He was out to reform and restore the American economic system, not change it drastically. He drew upon the Progressive tradition and his experience with World War I mobilization to fashion a moderate program of governmental action.

For the next three months, until it adjourned in June, Congress responded to a series of presidential initiatives. During these "Hundred Days," Roosevelt sent fifteen major requests to Congress and received back fifteen pieces of legislation. A few created permanent agencies that have become a part of American life: the Tennessee Valley Authority (TVA) proved to be the most successful and enduring of all Roosevelt's New Deal measures. This innovative effort at regional planning resulted in the building of a series of dams in seven states along the Tennessee River to control floods, ease navigation, and produce electricity. This last feature created cheap and abundant power that helped transform the poverty-stricken upper South into a relatively prosperous industrial area.

Other New Deal agencies were temporary in nature, designed to meet the specific economic problems of the Depression. None were completely successful; the Depression would continue for another six years, immune even to Roosevelt's magic. But psychologically the nation turned the corner in the spring of 1933. Under FDR, the government seemed to be responding to the economic crisis, enabling people for the first time since 1929 to look to the future with hope.

Roosevelt and Recovery

Two major New Deal programs launched during the Hundred Days were aimed at industrial and agricultural recovery. The first was the National

Recovery Administration (NRA), FDR's attempt to achieve economic advance through planning and cooperation between government, business, and labor. In the midst of the Depression, businessmen were intent on stabilizing production and raising prices for their goods. Spokesmen for labor were equally determined to spread work through maximum hours and to put a floor under workers' income with minimum wages.

The NRA hoped to achieve both goals by permitting companies in each major industry to cooperate in writing codes of fair competition which would set realistic limits on production, allocate percentages to individual producers, and set firm guidelines for prices. Section 7a of the enabling act mandated protection for labor in all the codes by establishing maximum hours, minimum wages, and the guarantee of collective bargaining by unions. No company could be compelled to join, but the New Deal sought complete participation by appealing to patriotism. Each firm that took part could display a blue eagle and stamp this symbol on its products. With energetic Hugh Johnson in charge, the NRA quickly enrolled the nation's leading companies and unions. By the summer of 1933, more than 500 industries had adopted codes that covered 2.5 million workers.

Although the NRA quickly bogged down in a bureaucratic morass, the NRA blue eagle became a widely respected symbol of a business's patriotism.

The NRA quickly bogged down in a huge bureaucratic morass. The codes proved to be too detailed to enforce easily. Written by the largest companies, these rules favored big business at the expense of smaller competitors. Labor quickly became disenchanted with Section 7a. The minimum wages were often near starvation level, while business got around the requirement for collective bargaining by creating company unions that did not represent the real needs of workers. After a brief upsurge in the spring of 1933, industrial production began to sag as disillusionment with the NRA grew. By 1934, more and more businessmen were complaining about the new agency, calling it the "National Run Around." When the Supreme Court finally invalidated the NRA in 1935 on constitutional grounds, few mourned its demise. The idea of trying to overcome the Depression by relying on voluntary cooperation between competing businessmen and labor leaders had collapsed in the face of individual self-interest and greed.

The New Deal's attempt at farm recovery fared a little better. Henry A. Wallace, FDR's secretary of agriculture, came up with an answer to the farmers' old dilemma of overproduction. The government would act as a clearinghouse for producers of major crops, arranging for them to set production limits for wheat, cotton, corn, and other leading crops. Under the Agricultural Adjustment Act (AAA) passed by Congress in May 1933, the government would allocate acreage among individual farmers, encouraging them to take land out of production by paying them subsidies (raised by a tax on food processors). Unfortunately, Wallace preferred not to wait until the 1934 planting season to implement this program, and so farmers were paid in 1933 to plow under crops they had already planted and to kill livestock they were raising. Faced with the problem of hunger in the midst of plenty, the New Deal seemed to respond by destroying the plenty.

The AAA program worked better in 1934 and 1935 as land removed from production led to smaller harvests and rising farm prices. Farm income rose for the first time since World War I, increasing from $2 billion in 1933 to $5 billion by 1935. Severe weather, especially dust-bowl conditions in the Great Plains, contributed to the crop-limitation program, but most of the gain in farm income came from subsidy payments themselves rather than from higher market prices.

On the whole, large farmers benefited most from the program. Possessing the capital to buy machinery and fertilizer, they were able to farm more efficiently than before on fewer acres of land. Small farmers, tenants, and sharecroppers did not fare as well, receiving very little of the government payments and often being driven off the land as owners took the acreage previously cultivated by tenants and sharecroppers out of production. Some three million people left the land in the thirties, crowding into the cities where they swelled the relief rolls. In the long run, the New Deal reforms improved the efficiency of American agriculture, but at a real human cost.

The Supreme Court eventually found the AAA unconstitutional in 1936, but Congress reenacted it in modified form that year and again in 1938. The system of allotments, now financed directly by the government, became a standard feature of the farm economy. Other New Deal efforts to assist the rural poor, notably the Farm Security Administration (FSA), sought to loan tenants and sharecroppers money to acquire land of their own, but the sums appropriated by Congress were too modest. The FSA was able to extend loans to fewer than 2 percent of the nation's tenant farmers. "Obviously," the FSA director informed Roosevelt, "this . . . program can be regarded as only an experimental approach to the farm tenancy problem." The result of the New Deal for American farming was to hasten its transformation into a business in which only the efficient and well-capitalized would thrive.

Roosevelt and Relief

The New Deal was far more successful in meeting the most immediate problem of the 1930s—relief for the millions of unemployed and destitute citizens. Roosevelt never shared Hoover's distaste for direct federal support; on May 12, 1933, in response to FDR's March request, Congress authorized the RFC to distribute $500 million to the states to help individuals and families in need.

Roosevelt brought in Harry Hopkins to direct the relief program. A former social worker who seemed to live on black coffee and cigarettes, Hopkins set up a desk in the hallway of the RFC building and proceeded to spend over $5 million

"Hunger is not debatable," said Harry Hopkins, the brash but selfless New Dealer who distributed $5 million of relief in his first two hours in office.

in less than two hours. By the end of 1933, Hopkins had cut through red tape to distribute money to nearly one-sixth of the American people. The relief payments were modest in size, but they enabled millions to avoid starvation and stay out of humiliating breadlines.

Another, more imaginative early effort was the Civilian Conservation Corps (CCC), which was Roosevelt's own idea. The CCC enrolled youth from city families on relief and sent them to the nation's parks and recreational areas to build trails and improve public facilities. Ultimately, more than two million young people served in the CCC, contributing both to their families' incomes and to the nation's welfare.

Hopkins realized the need to do more than just keep people alive, and he soon became an advocate of work relief. Hopkins argued that the government should put the jobless to work, not just to encourage self-respect, but also to enable them to earn enough to purchase consumer goods and thus stimulate the entire economy. A Public Works Administration (PWA) headed by Secretary of the Interior Harold Ickes had been authorized in 1933, but Ickes, intent on the quality of the projects rather than human needs, failed to put many people to work. In the fall of 1933, Roosevelt created the Civil Works Administration (CWA) and charged Hopkins with getting people off the unemployment lines and relief rolls and back to work. Hopkins had over four million men and women at work by January 1934, building roads, schools, playgrounds, and athletic fields. Many of the workers were unskilled, and some of the projects were shoddy, but the CWA at least enable people to work and earn enough money to survive the winter. Roosevelt, appalled at the huge expenditures involved, shut down the CWA in 1934 and forced Hopkins to return to federal relief payments as the only source of aid to the jobless.

The final commitment to the idea of work relief came in 1935 when Roosevelt established the Works Progress Administration (WPA) to spend nearly $5 billion authorized by Congress for emergency relief. The WPA, under Hopkins, put the unemployed on the federal payroll so that they could earn enough to meet their basic needs and help stimulate the stagnant economy. Conservatives complained that the WPA amounted to nothing more than hiring the jobless to do make-work tasks with no real value. But Hopkins cared less about what was accomplished than about helping those who had been unemployed for years to get off the dole and gain self-respect by working again.

In addition to funding the usual construction and conservation projects, the WPA tried to preserve the skills of American artists, actors, and writers. The Federal Theatre Project produced plays, circuses, and puppet shows that enabled entertainers to practice their crafts and to perform before people who often had never seen a professional production before. Similar projects for writers and artists led to a series of valuable state guidebooks and to murals that adorned public buildings across the land. A separate National Youth Administration (NYA) found part-time jobs for young people still in school and developed projects—ranging from automobile repairing in New York City to erecting tuberculosis isolation units in Arizona—for 2.5 million young adults.

The WPA helped ease the burden for the unemployed, but it failed to overcome the Depression. Rather than spending too much, as his

Federal work relief programs helped millions maintain their self-respect. Workers in the CCC (below) received $30 a month for planting trees and digging drainage ditches. Artists and writers found work with the WPA (right).

critics charged, Roosevelt's greatest failure was not spending enough. The WPA never employed at any one time more than 3 million of the 10 million jobless. The wages, although larger than relief payments, were still pitifully low, averaging only $52 a month. Thus the WPA failed to prime the American economy by increasing consumer purchasing power. Factories remained closed and machinery idle because the American people still did not have the money, either from relief or the WPA, to buy cars, radios, appliances, and the other consumer goods that had been the basis for the prosperity of the 1920s. By responding to basic human needs, Roosevelt had made the Depression bearable. The New Deal's failure, however, to go beyond relief to achieve prosperity led to a growing frustration and the appearance of more radical alternatives that challenged the conservative nature of the New Deal and forced FDR to shift to the left.

As the Depression continued, it became apparent that the stopgap measures of the New Deal would have to be replaced by more sweeping reforms.

ROOSEVELT AND REFORM

In 1935, the focus of the New Deal shifted from relief and recovery to reform. During his first two years in office, FDR had concentrated on fighting the Depression by shoring up the sagging American economy. Only a few new agencies, notably TVA, sought to make permanent changes in national life. Roosevelt was developing a "broker-state" concept of government, responding to pressures from organized elements such as corporations, labor unions, and farm groups while ignoring the needs and wants of the dispossessed who had no clear political voice. The early New Deal tried to assist bankers and industrialists, large farmers, and members of the labor unions, but it did little to help unskilled workers and sharecroppers.

The continuing depression and high unemployment began to build pressure for more sweeping changes. Roosevelt faced the choice of either providing more radical programs, ones designed to end historical inequities in American life, or deferring to others who put forth solutions to the nation's ills. Bolstered by an impressive Democratic victory in the 1934 congressional elections, Roosevelt responded by embracing a reform program that marked the climax of the New Deal.

Angry Voices

The signs of discontent were visible everywhere by 1935. In the upper Midwest, progressives and agrarian radicals, led by Minnesota Governor Floyd Olson, were calling for government action to raise farm and labor income. "I am a radical in the sense that I want a definite change in the system," Olson declared. "I am not satisfied with patching." Upton Sinclair, the muckraking novelist, nearly won the governorship of California in 1934 running on the slogan "End Poverty in California," while in the East a violent strike in the textile industry shut down plants in twenty states. The most serious challenge to Roosevelt's leadership, however, came from three demagogues who captured national attention in the mid-thirties.

The first was Father Charles Coughlin, a Roman Catholic priest from Detroit, who had originally supported FDR. Speaking to a rapt nationwide radio audience in his rich, melodious voice, Coughlin appealed to the discontented with a strange mixture of crank monetary schemes and anti-Semitism. He broke with the New Deal in late 1934, denouncing it as the "Pagan Deal," and founded his own National Union for Social Justice. Increasingly vitriolic, he called for monetary inflation and the nationalization of the banking

Eleanor Roosevelt and the Quest for Social Justice

A modest, self-effacing woman with tremendous popular appeal, Eleanor Roosevelt played the traditional role of first lady, graciously hosting such gatherings as the one shown above. She also took on less traditional roles, fighting actively for social justice.

Eleanor Roosevelt entered public life as a reformer long before she became the First Lady. Although she loved and admired her uncle Theodore, her side of the Roosevelt family was more active in New York society than politics. In a family environment where the social graces were highly prized, Eleanor grew up shy and insecure. She turned to voluntary social work for fulfillment, where her relationships were based on common interests and ideals rather than social stand-

ing. Before her marriage to Franklin Roosevelt in 1905, she had been active in the New York settlement-house movement and the Consumers' League. Like many reformers of her day, she found her sense of social justice upset by the existence of poverty and inequality. Avoiding politics, which she then considered a "sinister affair," she limited her activities to nonpartisan reform and relief organizations.

After her marriage, she curtailed her social work, placing her re-

sponsibilities as a wife and mother first, as she believed a woman should. Though always a supportive partner, Mrs. Roosevelt did not develop a taste for politics despite her husband's tenure in the New York State Senate and later as assistant secretary of the navy during World War I. But when FDR was stricken with polio in 1921, she was determined that he return to political life as soon as possible; such a goal, she thought, was the best antidote to his pain and depression. While she worked tirelessly to speed his physical recovery, she also struck out on her own to keep the Roosevelt name alive in New York politics. In the newly formed League of Women Voters, the Women's City Club, the Non-Partisan Legislative Committee, and the New York State Democratic party, Eleanor Roosevelt brought her reformer's impulse to politics. In these organizations she formed the nucleus of an "old-girls' network" that she would employ extensively during the New Deal years. Her newly acquired political and organizational skills as well as her knowledge and speeches served her husband well in his gubernatorial and presidential campaigns.

In a speech delivered in 1928, Mrs. Roosevelt commented on the need to "bring government closer to the people" and to "develop the human side of government." Focusing on those whose needs were greatest, Eleanor Roosevelt was an advocate for the dispossessed. She advanced their interests within the administration, working hardest for women and African Americans, whose voices were least often heard.

FDR appealed to the "forgotten man"; his wife concerned herself with the "forgotten woman." She worked with Harry Hopkins to achieve equity for women on relief and to create more jobs for women under the auspices of the CWA and the WPA. With Frances Perkins, she arranged to establish camps for unemployed girls patterned after the CCC while she continued to work with the Women's Trade Union League to guarantee women equal pay for equal work on federal projects. In her syndicated newspaper column "My Day," she often dealt with the problems faced by women during the Depression. She even held press conferences to which only women reporters were invited to ensure employment for at least a handful of female journalists.

The First Lady's office became, in effect, a clearinghouse for federally sponsored programs for women, and her endorsement often meant the difference between success or failure. She took advantage of her position to expedite the programs she thought most important. She saw to it that whenever possible, women administrators were hired to supervise projects for women, but there were precious few programs for women to be administered. Although Mrs. Roosevelt was instrumental in the few gains made by women through the New Deal, her advocacy could not overcome the sexual stereotypes that continued to limit the role of women in the work force.

She worked equally hard for African Americans, but with little more to show for her efforts. "We can have no group beaten down, underprivileged," said the First Lady in a radio address in 1934, "without reaction on the rest." In one sentence, she captured the essence of her appeal for justice and equality for blacks. Social justice was not merely desirable for blacks; it was necessary to ensure the vitality of American democracy. She spoke eloquently in favor of equal opportunity for blacks and sought their inclusion in New Deal programs. She worked with Hopkins to include more blacks in federal projects and lobbied within the administration for the appointment of black men and women to administer the programs designed specifically for them. Publicly, she endeavored to set an example by addressing black audiences throughout the country, presiding over a more egalitarian White House, and resigning her membership in the DAR over the Marian Anderson incident (see p. 787).

In her struggle against racial discrimination, Mrs. Roosevelt sometimes found her desires to be in conflict with her husband's attempts to keep the coalition of Democratic voters intact. His fear of alienating southern supporters caused him to temporize on the antilynching bill and abolition of the poll tax, both of which he considered desirable but not "must" legislation. Mrs. Roosevelt's support of these measures, however, put the Roosevelt name behind them. In her efforts to secure passage of the legislation, she arranged for meetings between FDR and Walter White of the NAACP. She briefed White to prepare him for FDR's objections in his conference with the President. When she asked FDR if he minded her public support of the antilynching bill, he replied, "Certainly not. . . . I can always say, 'Well, that is my wife; I can't do anything about her.'" Thus it appears that the President and Mrs. Roosevelt were of one mind, but she was able to support a cause that he felt it impolitic to advocate himself.

This distinction between the First Lady's activities as a representative of the Roosevelt administration and her actions as a private citizen was often a difficult one to establish. It is even harder to assess accurately her impact on the policies of the New Deal. Eleanor Roosevelt was revered by millions of Americans who saw in her the very essence of American ideals. Her support of women and blacks was instrumental in swaying their support to the Roosevelt coalition. Still, the telling fact remains that the plight of the two groups to which she devoted the lion's share of her attention during the Depression—women and blacks—was only slightly relieved. This is not to minimize her achievements. As the self-appointed conscience of the Roosevelt administration, she exposed the areas where the New Deal had not been realized. Her accessibility to the public and her willingness to serve its interests gave encouragement to those who had lost all hope. Her courage and vitality in the pursuit of human rights and equality made her the embodiment of reform and social justice in the New Deal.

system in his weekly radio sermons to an audience of more than thirty million.

A more benign but equally threatening figure appeared in California. Dr. Francis Townsend, a sixty-seven-year-old physician, came forward in 1934 with a scheme to assist the elderly, who were suffering greatly during the Depression. The Townsend Plan proposed giving everyone over the age of sixty a monthly pension of $200 with the proviso that it must be spent within thirty days. Although designed less as an old-age pension plan than as a way to stimulate the economy, the proposal understandably had its greatest appeal among the elderly. They embraced it as a holy cause, joining Townsend Clubs across the country. Despite the criticism from economists that the plan would transfer over half the national income to less than 10 percent of the population, more than ten million people signed petitions endorsing the Townsend Plan, and few politicians dared oppose it.

The third new voice of protest was that of Huey Long, the flamboyant senator from Louisiana. Like Coughlin, an original supporter of the New Deal, Long turned against FDR and by 1935 had become a major political threat to the President. A shrewd, ruthless, yet witty man, Long had a remarkable ability to mock those in power. The Kingfish (a nickname he borrowed from "Amos 'n Andy") announced a nationwide "Share the Wealth" movement in 1934. He spoke grandly of taking from the rich to make "Every Man a King," guaranteeing each American a home worth $5000 and an annual income of $2500. To finance the plan, Long advocated seizing all fortunes of more than $5 million and levying a tax of 100 percent on incomes over $1 million. By 1935, Long claimed to have founded twenty-seven thousand Share the Wealth Clubs and had a mailing list of over 7 million people, including workers, farmers, college professors, and even bank presidents. Threatening to run as a third-party candidate in 1936, Long generated fear among Democratic leaders that he might attract 3 or 4 million votes, possibly enough to swing the election to the Republicans. Although an assassin killed Huey Long in Louisiana in late 1935, his popularity showed the need for the New Deal to do more to help those still in distress.

Social Security

When the new Congress met in January 1935, Roosevelt was ready to support a series of reform measures designed to take the edge off national dissent. The recent elections had increased Democratic congressional strength significantly, with the Republicans losing thirteen seats in the House and retaining less than one-third of the Senate. Many of the Democrats were to the left of Roosevelt, favoring increased spending and more sweeping federal programs. "Boys—this is our hour," exulted Harry Hopkins. "We've got to get everything we want . . . now or never." Congress quickly appropriated $4.8 billion for the WPA and was prepared to enact virtually any proposal that Roosevelt offered.

The most significant reform enacted in 1935 was the Social Security Act. The Townsend move-

Despite the administration's boosterism, many felt that Social Security could not fulfill its promises.

ment had reminded Americans that the United States, alone among modern industrial nations, had never developed a welfare system to aid the aged, the disabled, and the unemployed. A cabinet committee began studying the problem in 1934, and President Roosevelt sent its recommendations to Congress the following January.

The proposed legislation had three major parts. First, it provided for old-age pensions financed equally by a tax on employers and workers, without government contributions. In addition, it gave states federal matching funds to provide modest pensions for the destitute elderly. Second, it set up a system of unemployment compensation on a federal-state basis, with employers paying a payroll tax and with each state setting benefit levels and administering the program locally. Finally, it provided for direct federal grants to the states, on a matching basis, for welfare payments to the blind, handicapped, needy elderly, and dependent children.

Although there was criticism from conservatives who mourned the passing of traditional American reliance on self-help and individualism, the chief objections came from those who argued that the administration's measure did not go far enough. Democratic leaders, however, defeated efforts to incorporate Townsend's proposal for $200-a-month pensions and increases in unemployment benefits. Congress then passed the Social Security Act by overwhelming margins.

Critics began to point out its shortcomings as they have ever since. The old-age pensions were paltry. Designed to begin in 1942, they ranged from $10 to $85 a month. Not everyone was covered; those who most needed protection in their old age, such as farmers and domestic servants, were not included. The regressive feature of the act was even worse. All participants, regardless of income or economic status, paid in at the same rate, with no supplement from the general revenue. The trust fund also took out of circulation money that was desperately needed to stimulate the economy in the 1930s.

Other portions of the act were equally open to question. The cumbersome unemployment system offered no aid to those currently out of work, only to people who would lose their jobs in the future, and the benefits (depending on the state) ranged from barely adequate to substandard. The outright grants to the handicapped and dependent children were minute in terms of the need; in New York City, for example, a blind person received only $5 a week in 1937.

The conservative nature of the legislation reflected Roosevelt's own fiscal orthodoxy, but even more it was a product of his political realism. Despite the severity of the Depression, he realized that establishing a system of federal welfare went against deeply rooted American convictions. He insisted on a tax on participants to give those involved in the pension plan a vested interest in Social Security. He wanted them to feel that they had earned their pensions and that in the future no one would dare take them away. "With those taxes in there," he explained privately, "no damned politician can ever scrap my social security program." Above all, FDR had succeeded in establishing the principle of governmental responsibility for the aged, the handicapped, and the unemployed. Whatever the defects of the legislation, Social Security stood as a landmark of the New Deal, creating a system to provide for the welfare of individuals in a complex industrial society.

Labor Legislation

The other major reform achievement in 1935 was passage of the National Labor Relations Act. Senator Robert Wagner of New York introduced legislation in 1934 to outlaw company unions and other unfair labor practices in order to ensure collective bargaining for unions. FDR, who had little knowledge of labor-management relations and apparently little interest in them, opposed the bill. In 1935, however, Wagner began to gather broad support for his measure, which passed the Senate in May with only twelve opposing votes, and the President, seeing passage as likely, gave it his approval. The bill moved quickly through the House, and Roosevelt signed it into law in July.

The Wagner Act, as it became known, created a National Labor Relations Board to preside over labor-management relations and enable unions to engage in collective bargaining with federal support. The act outlawed a variety of union-busting tactics and in its key provision decreed that whenever the majority of a company's workers voted for a union to represent them, management would be compelled to negotiate with the union on all matters of wages, hours, and working conditions. With this unprecedented government sanction, labor unions could now proceed to recruit the large number of unorganized workers throughout the country. The Wagner Act, the most far-reaching of all New Deal measures, led to the revitalization of the American labor movement and a permanent change in labor-management relations.

Three years later, Congress passed a second law which had a lasting impact on American workers—the Fair Labor Standards Act. A long-sought goal of the New Deal, this measure aimed to establish both minimum wages and maximum hours of work per week. Since labor unions usually were able to negotiate adequate levels of pay and work for their members, the act was aimed at unorganized workers and met with only grudging support from unions. Southern conservatives opposed it strongly, both on ideological grounds (it meant still greater government involvement in private enterprise) and because it threatened the low southern wages that had attracted northern industry since Reconstruction.

Roosevelt finally succeeded in winning passage of the Fair Labor Standards Act in 1938, but only at the cost of exempting many key industries from its coverage. The act provided for a minimum wage of forty cents an hour by 1940 and a standard workweek of forty hours, with time and a half for overtime. Despite its loopholes, the legislation did lead to pay raises for the twelve million workers earning less than forty cents an hour. More important, like Social Security it set up a system—however inadequate—which Congress could build upon in the future to reach more generous and humane levels.

Other New Deal reform measures met with a mixed reception in Congress. Proposals to break up the huge public-utility holding companies created by promoters in the 1920s and to levy a "soak-the-rich" tax on the wealthy stirred up bitter debate, and these bills were passed only in greatly weakened form. Roosevelt was more successful in passing a banking act that made important reforms in the Federal Reserve System. He also gained congressional approval of the Rural Electrification Administration (REA), which helped to bring electricity to the 90 percent of Ameri-

can farms that still did not have it in the 1930s.

All in all, Roosevelt's record in reform was similar to that in relief and recovery—modest success but no sweeping victory. A cautious and pragmatic leader, FDR moved far enough to the left to overcome the challenges of Coughlin, Townsend, and Long without venturing too far from the mainstream. His reforms improved the quality of life in America significantly, but he made no effort to correct all the nation's social and economic wrongs.

IMPACT OF THE NEW DEAL

The New Deal had a broad influence on the quality of life in the United States in the 1930s. Government programs reached into areas hitherto untouched. Many of them brought about long overdue improvements, but others failed to make any significant dent in historic inequities. The most important advances came with the dramatic growth of labor unions; the conditions for working women and minorities in nonunionized industries showed no comparable advance.

Rise of Organized Labor

Trade unions were weak at the onset of the Depression, with a membership of fewer than three million workers. Most were in the American Federation of Labor (AFL), composed of craft unions which served the needs of skilled workers. The nation's basic industries like steel and automobiles were unorganized; the great mass of unskilled workers thus fared poorly in terms of wages and working conditions. Section 7a of the NRA had led to some growth in AFL ranks, but the Federation's conservative leaders, eager to cooperate with business, failed to take full advantage of the opportunity to organize the mass-production industries.

John L. Lewis, head of the United Mine Workers, took the lead in forming the Committee on Industrial Organization (CIO) in 1935. The son of a Welsh coal miner, Lewis was a dynamic and ruthless man. He had led the mine workers since 1919 and was determined to spread the benefits of unions throughout industry. Lewis first battled with the leadership of the AFL, and then—after

*U*nion members in some companies resorted to sit-down strikes to achieve union recognition—as they did at General Motors in 1936 (right). In other cases, strikers met with brute force as depicted in Philip Evergood's 1937 painting, The American Tragedy (above) of the Republic Steel strike.

being expelled—he renamed his group the Congress of Industrial Organizations and announced in 1936 that he would use the Wagner Act to extend collective bargaining to the nation's auto and steel industries.

Within five years, Lewis had scored a remarkable series of victories. Some came easily. The big steel companies, led by U.S. Steel, surrendered without a fight in 1937; management realized that with federal support the unions were in a strong position. There was greater resistance in the automobile industry. When General Motors, the first target, resisted, the newly created United Automobile Workers (UAW) developed an effective strike technique. In late December, 1936, GM workers in Flint, Michigan, simply sat down in the factory, refusing to leave until the company recognized their union, and threatening to destroy the valuable tools and machines if they were removed forcibly. When the Michigan governor refused to call out the National Guard to break the strike, General Motors conceded defeat in the sit-down strike and signed a contract with the UAW. Chrysler quickly followed suit, but Henry Ford refused to give in and fought the UAW, hiring strikebreakers and beating up organizers. In 1941, however, Ford finally recognized the UAW. Smaller steel companies, led by Republic Steel, engaged in even more violent resistance; in one incident in 1937, police shot ten strikers. The companies eventually reached a settlement with the steelworkers' union in 1941.

By the end of the 1930s, the CIO had some five million members, slightly more than the AFL. The successes were remarkable—in addition to the auto-making and steel unions, organizers for the CIO and the AFL had been successful in the textile, rubber, electrical, and metal industries. For the first time, unskilled as well as skilled were unionized. Women and African Americans benefited from the creation of the CIO, not because the union followed enlightened policies, but simply because they made up a substantial proportion of the unskilled work force that the CIO organized.

Yet despite these impressive gains, only 28 percent of all Americans (excluding farm workers) belonged to unions by 1940. Millions in the restaurant, retail, and service trades remained unorganized, working long hours for very low wages. Employer resistance and traditional hostility to unions blocked further progress, as did the aloof attitude of President Roosevelt, who commented to labor and management, "A plague on both your houses" during the steel strike. The Wagner Act had helped open the way, but labor leaders like Lewis, Philip Murray of the Steel Workers Organizing Committee, and Walter Reuther of the United Automobile Workers deserved most of the credit for union achievements.

The New Deal Record on Help to Minorities

The Roosevelt administration's attempts to aid the downtrodden were least effective with African Americans and other racial minorities. The Depression had hit blacks with special force. Sharecroppers and tenant farmers had seen the price of cotton drop from eighteen to six cents a pound, far below the level to sustain a family on the land. In the cities, the saying "First Fired, Last Hired" proved all too true; by 1933, over 50 percent of urban blacks were unemployed. Hard times sharpened racial prejudice. "No Jobs for Niggers Until Every White Man Has a Job" became a rallying cry for whites in Atlanta.

The New Deal helped African Americans survive the Depression, but it never tried to confront squarely the racial injustice built into the federal relief programs. Although the programs served blacks as well as whites, in the South the weekly payments blacks received were much smaller. In the early days, NRA codes permitted lower wage scales for blacks, while the AAA led to the eviction of thousands of Negro tenants and sharecroppers. African-American leaders referred to the NRA as standing for "Negro Robbed Again" and dismissed the AAA as "a continuation of the same old raw deal." Nor did later reform measures help very much. Neither the minimum wage nor Social Security covered those working as farmers or domestic servants, categories that comprised 65 percent of all African-American workers. Thus an NAACP official commented that Social Security "looks like a sieve with the holes just large enough for the majority of Negroes to fall through."

Despite this bleak record, African Americans rallied behind Roosevelt's leadership, abandoning their historic ties to the Republican party. In 1936, over 75 percent of those African Americans who voted supported FDR. In part, this switch came in response to Roosevelt's appointment of a number of prominent African Americans to high-ranking government positions, such as William H. Hastie in the Interior Department and Mary McLeod Bethune (founder and president of Bethune-Cookman College) in the National Youth Administration. Eleanor Roosevelt spoke out eloquently throughout the decade against racial discrimination, most notably in 1939 when the Daughters of the American Revolution refused to let African-American contralto Marian Anderson sing in Constitution Hall. The First Lady and Interior Secretary Harold Ickes arranged for the singer to perform at the Lincoln Memorial, where seventy-five thousand people

*W*ith the Statue of Lincoln as a backdrop, African-American contralto Marian Anderson sang on the steps of the Lincoln Memorial in a concert given April 9, 1939.

gathered to hear her on Easter Sunday.

Perhaps the most influential factor in the African Americans' political switch was the color-blind policy of Harry Hopkins. He had more than one million blacks working for the WPA by 1939, many of them in teaching and artistic positions as well as in construction jobs. Overall, the New Deal provided assistance to 40 percent of the nation's blacks during the Depression. Uneven as his record was, Roosevelt had still done more to aid this oppressed minority than any previous president since Lincoln. One African-American newspaper commented that while "relief and WPA are not ideal, they are better than the Hoover bread lines and they'll have to do until the real thing comes along."

The New Deal did far less for Mexican-Americans. Engaged primarily in agricultural labor, these people found their wages in California fields dropping from thirty-five to fourteen cents an hour by 1933. The pool of unemployed migrant labor expanded rapidly with dust-bowl conditions in the Great Plains and the subsequent flight of "Okies" and "Arkies" to the cotton fields of Arizona and the truck farms of California. The Roosevelt administration cut off any further influx from Mexico by barring entry of any immigrant "likely to become a public charge"; local authorities rounded up and shipped migrants back to Mexico to reduce the welfare rolls.

The New Deal relief program did aid many thousands of Mexican-Americans in the Southwest in the 1930s, although migrant workers had difficulty meeting state requirements. The WPA hired Mexican-Americans for a variety of construction and cultural programs, but after 1937 such employment was denied to aliens. Overall, the pattern was one of great economic hardship and relatively little federal assistance for Mexican-Americans.

The American Indian, after decades of neglect, fared slightly better under the New Deal. Roosevelt appointed John Collier, a social worker who championed Indian rights, to serve as commissioner of Indian affairs. In 1934, Congress passed the Indian Reorganization Act, a reform measure designed to stress tribal unity and autonomy instead of attempting (as previous policy had done) to transform Indians into self-sufficient farmers by granting them small plots of land (see Chapter 17). Collier employed more Native Americans in the Indian Bureau, supported educational programs on the reservations, and encouraged tribes to produce native handiwork such as blankets and jewelry. Despite modest gains however, the nation's one-third of a million Indians remained the most impoverished citizens in America.

Women at Work

The decade witnessed no significant gain in the status of American women. In the midst of the Depression, there was little concern expressed for protecting or extending their rights. The popular idea that women worked for "pin money" while men were the breadwinners for their families led employers to discriminate in favor of men when cutting the work force. Working women "are holding jobs that rightfully belong to the God-intended providers of the household," declared a Chicago civic group. More than three-fourths of the nation's school boards refused to hire wives,

Government employment was one of the few areas in which working women made advances in the 1930s. Secretary of Labor Frances Perkins, shown here inspecting the Golden Gate Bridge, was the first woman cabinet member, one of a number of women appointed by FDR to posts previously held only by men.

and more than half of them fired women teachers who married. Federal regulations prohibited more than one member of a family from working in the civil service, and almost always it was the wife who had to defer to her husband. A Gallup poll revealed that 82 percent of the people disapproved of working wives, with 75 percent of the women polled agreeing.

Many of the working women in the 1930s were either single or the sole supporters of an entire family. Yet their wages remained lower than those for men, and their unemployment rate ran higher than 20 percent throughout the decade. Women over forty found it particularly hard to find or retain jobs during the Depression. The New Deal offered little encouragement. NRA codes sanctioned lower wages for women, permitting laundries, for example, to pay them as little as fourteen cents an hour. The minimum wage did help those women employed in industry, but too many worked as maids and waitresses—jobs not covered by the law—to have much overall effect. Despite these hardships, the num-

ber of married women and women between the ages of twenty-five and forty in the labor force increased during the 1930s. Relatively few women worked in heavy industry, where unemployment was greatest; most were employed in the clerical and service sectors, areas of traditional female employment, in which jobs were more plentiful.

The one area of advance in the 1930s came in government. Eleanor Roosevelt set an example which encouraged millions of American women. Instead of presiding sedately over the White House, she traveled continually around the country, always eager to uncover wrongs and bring them to the President's attention (see "Eleanor Roosevelt and the Quest for Social Justice," pp. 780–81). Frances Perkins, the secretary of labor, became the first woman cabinet member, and FDR appointed women as ambassadors and federal judges for the first time.

Women also were elected to office in larger numbers in the thirties. Hattie W. Caraway of Arkansas succeeded her husband in the Senate,

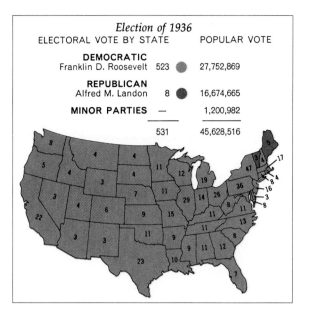

ELECTORAL VOTE BY STATE		POPULAR VOTE
DEMOCRATIC Franklin D. Roosevelt	523	27,752,869
REPUBLICAN Alfred M. Landon	8	16,674,665
MINOR PARTIES	—	1,200,982
	531	45,628,516

winning a full term in 1934. That same year voters elected six women to the House of Representatives. Public service, however, was one of the few professions open to women. The nation's leading medical and law schools discouraged women from applying, and the percentage of female faculty members in colleges and universities continued to decline in the 1930s. In sum, a decade that was grim for most Americans was especially hard on American women.

END OF THE NEW DEAL

The New Deal reached its high point in 1936, when Roosevelt was overwhelmingly reelected and the Democratic party strengthened its hold on Congress. This political triumph was deceptive. In the next two years, Roosevelt met with a series of defeats in Congress. Yet despite these setbacks, he remained a popular political leader who had restored American self-confidence as he strove to meet the challenges of the Depression.

The Election of 1936

Franklin Roosevelt enjoyed his finest political hour in 1936. A man who loved the give-and-take of politics, FDR faced challenges from both the left and the right as he sought reelection. Father Coughlin and Gerald L. K. Smith, who inherited Huey Long's following after the senator's assassination in 1935, organized a Union party, with North Dakota Progressive Congressman William Lemke heading the ticket. At the other extreme, a group of wealthy industrialists formed the Liberty League to fight what they saw as the New Deal's assault on property rights. The Liberty League attracted prominent Democrats, including Al Smith, but in 1936 it endorsed the Republican presidential candidate, Governor Alfred M. Landon of Kansas. A moderate, colorless figure, Landon disappointed his backers by refusing to campaign for repeal of the popular New Deal reforms.

Roosevelt ignored Lemke and the Union party, focusing attention instead on the assault from the right. Democratic spokesmen condemned the Liberty League as a "millionaire's union" and reminded the American people of how much Roosevelt had done for them in fighting unemployment and providing relief. In his speeches, FDR condemned the "economic royalists" who were "unanimous in their hatred for me." "I welcome their hatred," he declared, and promised that in his second term these forces would meet "their master."

This frank appeal to class sympathies proved enormously successful. Roosevelt won easily, receiving five million more votes than he had gotten in 1932 and outscoring Landon in the electoral college by 523 to 8. The Democrats did almost as well in Congress, piling up margins of 331 to 89 in the House and 76 to 16 in the Senate (with 4 not aligned with either major party).

Equally important, the election marked the stunning success of a new political coalition that would dominate American politics for the next three decades. FDR, building on the inroads into the Republican majority that Al Smith had begun in 1928, carried urban areas by impressive margins, winning 3.6 million more votes than his opponents in the nation's twelve largest cities. He held on to the traditional Democratic votes in the South and West and added to them by appealing strongly to the diverse religious and ethnic groups in the northern cities—Catholics and Jews, Italians and Poles, Irish and Slavs. The strong support of labor, together with three-quarters of the black vote, indicated that the

Major New Deal Agencies

AAA—*Agricultural Adjustment Administration 1933*
Attempted to regulate agricultural production through farm subsidies; reworked after the Supreme Court ruled its key regulatory provisions unconstitutional in 1936; coordinated agricultural production during World War II, after which it was disbanded.

CCC—*Civilian Conservation Corps 1933*
Young men between the ages of eighteen and twenty-five volunteered to be placed in camps to work on regional environmental projects mainly west of the Mississippi; they received $30 a month of which $25 was sent home; disbanded during World War II.

CWA—*Civil Works Administration 1933*
Emergency work-relief program that put over four million people to work during the extremely cold winter of 1933–34, after which FDR disbanded it.

FSA—*Farms Security Administration 1937*
Granted loans to small farmers and tenants for rehabilitation and purchase of small-sized farms; Congress slashed its appropriations during World War II when many poor farmers entered the armed forces or migrated to urban areas.

FCC—*Federal Communications Commission 1934*
Regulatory agency with wide discretionary powers established to oversee wired and wireless communication; reflected growing importance of radio in everyday lives of Americans during the Depression; today it regulates television as well as radio.

FDIC—*Federal Deposit Insurance Corporation 1933*
Federal guarantee of savings bank deposits initially of up to $2,500, raised to $5,000 in 1934, and frequently thereafter; continues today with a limit of $100,000.

FERA—*Federal Emergency Relief Administration 1933*
Combined cash relief to needy families with work relief; super seded in early 1935 by the extensive work relief projects of the WPA and unemployment insurance established by Social Security (see below).

FHA—*Federal Housing Administration 1934*
Expanded private home ownership among moderate income families through federal guarantees of private mortgages, the reduction of down payments from 30 to 10 percent, and the extension of repayment from twenty to thirty years; continues to function today.

NLRB—*National Labor Relations Board 1935*
Established by Wagner Act; greatly enhanced power of American labor by instituting legal and procedural apparatus for overseeing collective bargaining; continues to arbitrate labor-management disputes today.

nation's new alignment followed economic as well as cultural lines. The poor and the oppressed, who in the Depression years included many middle-class Americans, became attached to the Democratic party, leaving the GOP in a minority position, limited to the well-to-do and rural and small-town Americans of native stock.

The Supreme Court Fight

FDR proved to be far more adept at winning electoral victories than in achieving his goals in Congress. In 1937, he attempted to use his recent success to overcome the one obstacle remaining in his path—the Supreme Court. During his first term, the Court had ruled several New Deal programs unconstitutional, most notably the NRA and the AAA. Only three of the nine justices were sympathetic to the need for emergency measures in the midst of the Depression. Two others were unpredictable, sometimes approving New Deal measures and sometimes opposing them. Four justices were bent on using the Constitution to block Roosevelt's proposals. All were elderly men, and one, Willis Van Devanter, had planned to retire in 1932 but remained on the Court because he believed Roosevelt to be "unfitted and unsafe for the Presidency."

When Congress convened in 1937, the Presi-

NRA—*National Recovery Administration 1933*
Attempt to combat the Depression through national economic planning by establishing and administering a system of industrial codes to control production, prices, labor relations, and trade practices among leading business interests; ruled unconstitutional by Supreme Court in 1936.

NYA—*National Youth Administration 1935*
Established by the WPA (see below) to reduce competition for jobs by supporting education and training of youth; paid grants to over two million high school and college students in return for work performed in their schools; also trained another 2.6 million out-of-school youths at skilled labor to prepare them for later employment in the private sector; disbanded during World War II.

PWA—*Public Works Administration 1933*
Financed construction of over 34,000 federal and nonfederal construction projects at a cost of over $6 billion; initiated the first federal public housing program, made the federal government the nation's leading producer of power, and advanced conservation of the nation's natural resources; only three counties in the entire nation did not experience a PWA project; discontinued in 1939 due to its ineffectiveness at reducing unemployment and promoting private investment.

REA—*Rural Electrification Administration 1935*
Transformed American rural life by making electricity available at low rates to American farm families in areas private power companies refused to service; closed cultural gap between rural and urban everyday life by making modern amenities, such as radio, available in the countryside; in 1933 only one in ten farms had electricity, in 1941 four in ten, by the early-1950s nine in ten—by the 1960s all but the most remote rural areas had electric power.

SEC—*Securities and Exchange Commission 1934*
Continues today to regulate trading practices in stocks and bonds according to federal laws.

SSB—*Social Security Board 1935*
Guaranteed retirement payments for enrolled workers beginning at age 65, set up federal-state system of unemployment insurance and care for dependent mothers and children, the handicapped, and public health; continues today.

TVA—*Tennessee Valley Authority 1933*
Attempt at regional planning, included provisions for environmental and recreational design, architectural, educational, and health projects as well as its controversial public power projects; continues today to meet the Tennessee Valley's energy and flood control needs.

WPA—*Works Progress Administration 1935*
Massive work-relief program, funded projects ranging from construction to acting; disbanded by FDR during World War II.

---

dent offered a startling proposal to overcome the Court's threat to the New Deal. Instead of seeking a constitutional amendment either to limit the Court's power or to clarify the constitutional issues, FDR chose an oblique attack. Declaring that the Court was falling behind schedule because of the age of its members, he asked Congress to appoint a new justice for each member of the Court over the age of seventy, up to a maximum of six.

Although this "court-packing" scheme, as critics quickly dubbed it, was perfectly legal, it outraged not only conservatives but liberals as well, who realized it could set a dangerous precedent for the future. Republicans wisely kept

silent, letting prominent Democrats such as Senator Burton Wheeler of Montana lead the fight against Roosevelt's plan. Despite all-out pressure from the White House, resistance in the Senate blocked early action on the proposal.

The Court defended itself well. Chief Justice Charles Evans Hughes testified tellingly to the Senate Judiciary Committee, pointing out that in fact the Court was up-to-date and not behind schedule as Roosevelt charged. The Court then surprised observers with a series of rulings approving such controversial New Deal measures as the Wagner Act and Social Security. In the midst of the struggle, Justice Van Devanter resigned, enabling FDR to make his first appointment to the Court since taking office in 1933. Feeling that he had proved his point, the President allowed his Court-packing plan to die in the Senate.

During the next few years, four more vacancies occurred, and Roosevelt was able to appoint such distinguished jurists as Hugo Black, William O. Douglas, and Felix Frankfurter to the Supreme Court. Yet the price was high. The Court fight had badly weakened the President's relations with Congress, opening up deep rifts with members of his own party. Many senators and representatives who had voted reluctantly for Roosevelt's measures during the depths of the Depression now felt free to oppose any further New Deal reforms.

The New Deal in Decline

The legislative record during Roosevelt's second term was meager. Aside from the minimum wage and a maximum-hour law passed in 1938, Congress did not extend the New Deal into any new areas. Attempts to institute national health insurance met with stubborn resistance, as did efforts by civil-rights advocates to pass antilynching legislation. Disturbed by this growing congressional resistance, Roosevelt set out in the spring of 1938 to defeat a number of conservative Democratic congressmen and senators, primarily in the South. His targets gleefully charged the President with interference in local politics; only one of the men he sought to defeat lost in the primaries. The failure of this attempted purge further undermined Roosevelt's strained relations with Congress.

The worst blow came in the economic sector. The slow but steady improvement in the economy suddenly gave way to a sharp recession in the late summer of 1937. In the next ten months, industrial production fell by one-third, and nearly four million workers lost their jobs. Critics of the New Deal quickly labeled the downturn "the Roosevelt recession," and businessmen claimed it reflected a lack of confidence in FDR's leadership.

Actually, Roosevelt was at fault. In an effort to reduce expanding budget deficits, he had cut back sharply on WPA and other government programs after the election. Federal contributions to the consumer purchasing power fell from $4.1 billion in 1936 to less than $1 billion in 1937. For several months, Roosevelt refused to heed calls from economists to renew heavy government spending. Finally, in April 1938, Roosevelt asked Congress for a $3.75-billion relief appropriation, and the economy began to revive. But FDR's premature attempt to balance the budget had meant two more years of hard times and had marred his reputation as the energetic foe of the Depression.

The political result of the attempted purge and the recession was a strong Republican upsurge in the elections of 1938. The GOP won an impressive 81 seats in the House and 8 more in the Senate, as well as 13 governorships. The party many thought dead suddenly had new life. The Democrats still held a sizable majority in Congress, but their margin in the House was particularly deceptive. There were 262 Democratic representatives to 169 Republicans, but 93 southern Democrats held the balance of power. More and more often after 1938, anti-New Deal Southerners voted with Republican conservatives to block social and economic reform measures. Thus not

*F*DR's battle with the Supreme Court provoked both sympathy and contempt among political cartoonists of the day. In the cartoon on the right, the NRA blue eagle lies dead, nailed to the wall by the Supreme Court. The cartoon on the left, entitled "That's the kind of sailor he is," satirizes FDR's Court-packing scheme.

only was the New Deal over by the end of 1938, but a new bipartisan conservative coalition that would prevail for a quarter century had formed in Congress.

Evaluation of the New Deal

The New Deal lasted a brief five years, and most of its measures came in two legislative bursts in the spring of 1933 and the summer of 1935. Yet its impact on American life was enduring. Nearly every aspect of economic, social, and political development in the decades that followed bore the imprint of Roosevelt's leadership.

The least impressive achievement of the New Deal came in the economic realm. Whatever credit Roosevelt is given for relieving human suffering in the depths of the Depression must be balanced against his failure to achieve recovery in the 1930s. The moderate nature of his programs, especially the unwieldy NRA, led to slow and halting industrial recovery. Although much of the advances that were made came as a result of government spending, FDR never embraced the concept of planned deficits, striving instead for a balanced budget. As a result, the nation had barely reached the 1929 level of production a

decade later, and there were still nearly ten million men and women unemployed.

Equally important, Roosevelt refused to make any sweeping changes in the American economic system. Aside from the TVA, there were no broad experiments in regional planning and no attempt to alter free enterprise beyond imposing some limited forms of governmental regulation. The New Deal did nothing to alter the basic distrubution of wealth and power in the nation. The outcome was the preservation of the traditional capitalist system with a thin overlay of federal control.

More significant change occurred in American society. With the adoption of Social Security, the government acknowledged for the first time its responsibility to provide for the welfare of those unable to care for themselves in an industrial society. The Wagner Act helped stimulate the growth of labor unions to balance corporate power, and the minimum-wage law provided a much-needed floor for many workers.

Yet the New Deal tended to help only the more vocal and organized groups, such as union members and commercial farmers. Those without effective voices or political clout—African Americans, Mexican-Americans, women, sharecroppers, restaurant and laundry workers—received little help from the New Deal. For all the appealing rhetoric about the "forgotten man," Roosevelt did little more than Hoover in responding to the long-term needs of the dispossessed.

The most lasting impact of the Roosevelt leadership came in politics. Taking advantage of the emerging power of ethnic voters and capitalizing on the frustration growing out of the Depression, FDR proved to be a genius at forging a new coalition. He overcame the friction between rural and urban Democrats that had prolonged Republican supremacy in the 1920s and attracted new groups to the Democratic party, principally African Americans and organized labor. His political success led to a major realignment that lasted long after he left the scene.

His political achievement also reveals the true nature of Roosevelt's success. He was a brilliant politician who recognized the essence of leadership in a democracy—appealing directly to the people and giving them a sense of purpose. He succeeded in infusing them with the same indomitable courage and jaunty optimism that had marked his own battle with polio. Thus despite his limitations as a reformer, Roosevelt proved to be the leader the American people needed in the 1930s—a president who provided the psychological lift that helped them endure and survive the Great Depression.

Recommended Reading

The best overall account of political developments in the 1930s is William Leuchtenburg, *Franklin D. Roosevelt and the New Deal* (1963). Leuchtenburg offers a balanced treatment but concludes by defending Roosevelt's record. For a more critical view, see James MacGregor Burns, *Roosevelt: The Lion and the Fox* (1956), which portrays FDR as an overly cautious political leader, and Robert A. McElvaine, *The Great Depression: America, 1929–1941* (1984), which laments the New Deal's failure to make more sweeping changes in American life. An exhaustive study of the New Deal through 1936 is Arthur M. Schlesinger, Jr., *The Age of Roosevelt*, 3 vols. (1957–1960), written from a sympathetic point of view. The best critique of Roosevelt's policies is the brief but perceptive book by Paul Conkin, *The New Deal* (1967).

Additional Bibliography

General accounts of the 1930s include Broadus Mitchell, *Depression Decade* (1947) on economic developments; Dixon Wecter, *The Age of the Great Depression* (1948) on

social themes; John Braeman, Robert H. Bremner, and David Brody, eds., *The New Deal*, 2 vols. (1975), a collection of essays on both national and state trends; Joseph P. Lash, *Dealers and Dreamers* (1988), a sympathetic view of key New Deal figures; and Harvard Sitkoff, ed., *Fifty Years Later—The New Deal Evaluated* (1985), a scholarly reappraisal.

Books on the Great Depression include John Kenneth Galbraith, *The Great Crash* (1955); Robert Sobel, *The Great Bull Market* (1968); Michael A. Bernstein, *The Great Depression* (1987); and Studs Terkel, *Hard Times* (1970). Harris Warren, *Herbert Hoover and the Great Depression* (1959); Jordan Schwartz, *Interregnum of Despair* (1970); and Albert Romasco, *The Poverty of Abundance* (1965) all deal with Hoover's failure to stem the Depression.

Frank Freidel, *Franklin D. Roosevelt*, 4 vols. (1952–1976) is the most comprehensive biography of FDR, but the most recent volume only covers through mid-1933. Other biographical accounts of value are Rexford G. Tugwell, *The Democratic Roosevelt* (1957); Kenneth Davis, *FDR: The New Deal Years, 1933–1937* (1986); and Alfred B. Rollins, *Roosevelt and Howe* (1962). The rich memoir literature for the New Deal includes Frances Perkins, *The Roosevelt I Knew* (1946); Raymond Moley, *The First New Deal* (1966); and Samuel I. Rosenman, *Working with Roosevelt* (1952). For biographies of Eleanor Roosevelt, see Joseph Lash, *Eleanor and Franklin* (1971); Lois Scharf, *Eleanor Roosevelt* (1987); and Tamara K. Hareven, *Eleanor Roosevelt* (1968). Susan Ware traces the role of women in the New Deal in *Beyond Suffrage* (1981). J. Joseph Huthmacher has written a fine biography of a major New Deal figure, *Senator Robert Wagner and the Rise of Urban Liberalism* (1968).

Recent biographies of important New Deal leaders include John Kennedy Ohl, *Hugh S. Johnson and the New Deal* (1986); Roy Talbert, Jr., *FDR's Utopian: Arthur Morgan of the TVA* (1987); Graham White and John Maze, *Harold Ickes and the New Deal* (1985); and George McJimsky, *Harry Hopkins* (1987).

The transition from Hoover and the beginning of the New Deal is traced in Elliot Rosen, *Hoover, Roosevelt, and the Brain Trust* (1977). The best of many books dealing with farm problems in the 1930s are Richard Kirkendall, *Social Scientists and Farm Politics in the Age of Roosevelt* (1966); Paul Conkin, *Tomorrow A New World* (1959); Van Perkins, *Crisis in Agriculture* (1969); Sidney Baldwin, *Poverty and Politics* (1968); Theodore Saloutos, *The American Farmer and the New Deal* (1982); Janet Poppendieck, *Breadlines Knee-Deep in Wheat* (1986) and two books on the impact of drought on Great Plains farmers, Donald Worster, *Dust Bowl* (1979) and James N. Gregory, *American Exodus* (1989), on the Okie Migration to California. Searle F. Charles traces Harry Hopkins' role in the New Deal in *Minister of Relief* (1963), while William McDonald describes the WPA's cultural activities in detail in *Federal Relief Administration and the Arts* (1969). For labor developments, see Sidney Fine, *Sit Down: The General Motors Strike of 1936–37* (1969); John Barnard, *Walter Reuther and the Rise of the Auto Workers* (1983); and Robert H. Zieger, *John L. Lewis* (1988). Irving Bernstein surveys the impact of the Depression on workers in two books, *The Turbulent Years* (1970) and *A Caring Society* (1985).

Among the many books surveying the various New Deal programs, the most useful are John Salmond, *The Civilian Conservation Corps, 1933–1942* (1967); William R. Brock, *Welfare, Democracy, and the New Deal* (1988); William R. Childs, *Trucking and the Public Interest* (1985); Albert Romasco, *The Politics of Recovery* (1983); Thomas K. Mc-Craw, *TVA and the Power Fight, 1933–1939* (1971); and Jane D. Mathews, *The Federal Theatre, 1935–1939* (1967). Two other important books on the New Deal are Otis L. Graham, Jr., *An Encore for Reform* (1967) and Ellis Hawley, *The New Deal and the Problem of Monopoly, 1933–1939* (1965).

Studies by critics of the New Deal include George Wolfskill, *Revolt of the Conservatives* (1962); T. Harry Williams, *Huey Long* (1969); Abraham Holtzman, *The Townsend Movement* (1963); Charles Tull, *Father Coughlin and the New Deal* (1965); Sheldon Marcus, *Father Coughlin* (1973); Glen Jeansonne, *Gerald L. K. Smith: Minister of Hate* (1988); and Alan Brinkley, *Voices of Protest: Huey Long, Father Coughlin, and the Great Depression* (1982). For intel-lectual radicalism in the 1930s, see Daniel Aaron, *Writers on the Left* (1960); Terry A. Cooney, *The Rise of the New York Intellectuals* (1986); Richard Pells, *Radical Visions and American Dreams* (1973).

Raymond Wolters offers a critical view of Roosevelt's policies toward blacks in *Negroes and the Great Depression* (1970); Harvard Sitkoff is more positive in *A New Deal for Blacks* (1978). Nancy Weiss traces the shift of blacks to the Democratic party in *Farewell to the Party of Lincoln* (1984). Abraham Hoffman deals with the repatriation issue in *Unwanted Mexican-Americans in the Great Depression* (1974). For the impact of the Depression on women, see William H. Chafe, *The American Woman* (1972); Susan Ware, *Holding Their Own* (1982); and Lois Sharf, *To Work and to Wed* (1980).

Leonard Baker describes Roosevelt's attempt to pack the Supreme Court in *Back to Back* (1967). The best account of the waning of the reform impulse in Congress is James T. Patterson, *Congressional Conservatism and the New Deal* (1967).

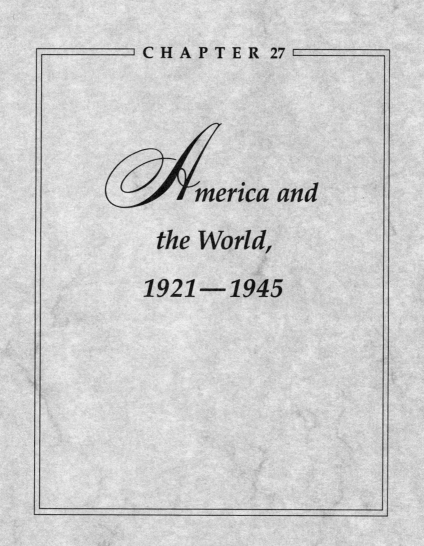

CHAPTER 27

*America and
the World,
1921—1945*

On August 27, 1928, U.S. Secretary of State Frank B. Kellogg, French Foreign Minister Aristide Briand, and representatives of twelve other nations met in Paris to sign a treaty outlawing war. Several hundred spectators crowded into the ornate clock room of the Quai d'Orsay to watch the historic ceremony. Six huge kleig lights illuminated the scene so that photographers could record the moment for a world eager for peace. Briand opened the ceremony with a speech in which he declared, "Peace is proclaimed," and then Kellogg signed the document with a foot-long gold pen given to him by the citizens of Le Havre as a token of Franco-American friendship. In the United States, a senator called the Kellogg-Briand Treaty "the most telling action ever taken in human history to abolish war."

In reality, the Pact of Paris was the result of a determined American effort to avoid involvement in the European alliance system. In June 1927, Briand had sent a message to the American people inviting the United States to join with France in signing a treaty to outlaw war between the two nations. The invitation struck a sympathetic response, especially among pacifists who had advocated the outlawing of war throughout the 1920s, but the State Department feared correctly that Briand's true intention was to establish a close tie between France and the United States. The French had already created a network of alliances with the smaller countries of Eastern Europe; and antiwar treaty with the United States would at least ensure American sympathy, if not involvement, in case of another European war. Kellogg delayed several months and then outmaneuvered Briand by proposing that the pledge against war not be confined just to France and the United States, but instead be extended to all nations. An unhappy Briand, who had wanted a bilateral treaty with the United States, had no choice but to agree, and so the diplomatic charade finally culminated in the elaborate signing ceremony in Paris.

Eventually the signers of the Kellogg-Briand Treaty included nearly every nation in the world, but the effect was negligible. All promised to renounce war as an instrument of national policy, except of course, as the British made clear in a reservation, in matters of self-defense. Enforcement of the treaty relied solely on the moral force of world opinion. The Pact of Paris was, as one senator shrewdly commented, only "an international kiss."

Unfortunately, the Kellogg-Briand Pact was symbolic of American foreign policy in the years after World War I. Instead of asserting the role of leadership its resources and power commanded, the United States kept aloof from other nations. America went its own way, extending trade and economic dominance but refusing to take the lead in maintaining world order. This retreat from responsibility seemed unimportant in the 1920s when exhaustion from World War I ensured relative peace and tranquillity. But in the '30s, when threats to world order arose in Europe and Asia, the American people retreated even deeper, searching for an isolationist policy that would spare them the agony of another great war.

There was no place to hide in the modern world. The Nazi onslaught in Europe and the Japanese expansion in Asia finally led to American entry into World War II in late 1941, at a time when the chances for an Allied victory seemed most remote. With incredible swiftness, the nation mobilized its military and industrial strength. American armies were soon fighting on

"Married Again" is the caption of this 1928 cartoon depicting the hopeful promise of the Kellog-Briand Treaty. The wicked world is once again pledging fidelity to peace "forever and ever."

three continents, the U.S. Navy controlled the world's oceans, and the nation's factories were sending a vast stream of war supplies to more than twenty Allied countries.

When victory came in 1945, the United States was by far the most powerful nation in the world. But instead of the enduring peace that might have permitted a return to a less active foreign policy, the onset of the Cold War with the Soviet Union brought on a new era of tension and conflict. This time the United States could not retreat from responsibility. World War II was a coming of age for American foreign policy.

RETREAT, REVERSAL, AND RIVALRY

"The day of the armistice America stood on the hilltops of glory, proud in her strength, invincible in her ideals, acclaimed and loved by a world free of an ancient fear at last," wrote journalist George Creel in 1920. "Today we writhe in a pit of our own digging; despising ourselves and despised by the betrayed peoples of earth." The bitter disillusionment Creel described ran through every aspect of American foreign policy in the 1920s. In contrast to diplomatic actions under Wilsonian idealism, American diplomats in the twenties made loans, negotiated treaties and agreements, and pledged the nation's good faith, but were careful not to make any binding commitments on behalf of world order. The result was neither isolation nor involvement but rather a cautious middle course that managed to alienate friends and encourage foes.

Retreat in Europe

The United States emerged from World War I as the richest nation on earth, displacing England from its prewar position of economic primacy. The Allied governments owed the United States a staggering $10 billion in war debts, money they had borrowed during and right after the conflict. Each year of the 1920s saw the nation increase its economic lead as the balance of trade tipped heavily in America's favor. The war-ravaged countries of Europe borrowed enormous amounts from American bankers to rebuild their economies; Germany alone absorbed over $3 billion in American investments during the decade. By 1929, American exports totaled more than $7 billion a year, three times the prewar level, and American overseas investment had risen to $17.2 billion.

The European nations could no longer compete on equal terms. The high American tariff, first imposed in 1922 and then raised again in 1930, frustrated attempts by England, France, and a defeated Germany to earn the dollars necessary to meet their American financial obligations. The Allied partners in World War I asked Washington to cancel the $10 billion in war debts, particularly after they were forced to scale down their demands for German reparations payments. American leaders from Wilson to Hoover indignantly refused this request, claiming that the ungrateful Allies were trying to repudiate their sacred obligations.

Only a continuing flow of private American capital to Germany allowed the payment of reparations to the Allies and the partial repayment of the Allies war debts in the 1920s. The financial crash of 1929 halted the flow of American dollars across the Atlantic and led to subsequent default on the debt payments, with accompanying bitterness on both sides of the ocean.

Political relations fared little better. The United States never joined the League of Nations, nor did it take part in the attempts by England and France to negotiate European security treaties. American observers attended League sessions and occasionally took part in economic and cultural missions in Geneva. But the Republican administrations of the twenties refused to compromise American freedom of action by embracing collective security, the principle on which the League was founded. And FDR, always realistic, made no effort to renew Wilson's futile quest. Thus the United States remained aloof from the European balance of power and refused to stand behind the increasingly shaky Versailles settlement.

The United States government ignored the Soviet Union throughout the 1920s. American businesses, however, exported large quantities of heavy machinery to Russia as part of her rapid industrialization. When that trade began to slump after 1930, business leaders hoped to revive it by calling on Washington to extend diplomatic recognition to the Bolshevik regime which had come to power in the Russian Revolution of 1917. In 1933, Franklin Roosevelt finally ended the long estrangement by signing an agreement opening up diplomatic relations between the two countries. The Soviets soon went back on promises to stop all subversive activity in the United States and to settle prerevolutionary debts, but even if they rarely understood one another, at least the two nations had opened a channel of communication.

Cooperation in Latin America

United States policy in the Western Hemisphere was both more active and more enlightened than in Europe. The State Department sought new ways in the 1920s to pursue traditional goals of political dominance and economic advantage in Latin America. The outcome of World War I lessened any fears of European threats to the area and thus enabled the United States to dismantle the interventions in the Caribbean carried out by Roosevelt, Taft, and Wilson (see Chapter 24). At the same time, both Republican and Democratic administrations worked hard to extend American trade and investment in the nations to the south.

Under Harding, Coolidge, and Hoover, American marines were withdrawn from Haiti and the Dominican Republic, and in 1924 the last detachment left Nicaragua, ending a twelve-year occupation. Renewed unrest there the next year, however, led to a second intervention in Nicaragua, which did not end until the early 1930s.

Showing a new sensitivity, the State Department released the Clark Memorandum in 1930, a policy statement repudiating the controversial Roosevelt Corollary to the Monroe Doctrine. Under the Monroe Doctrine, the United States had no right to intervene in neighboring states, declared Under Secretary of State J. Reuben Clark, although he asserted a traditional claim to protect American lives and property under international law.

When FDR took office in 1933, relations with Latin America were far better than they had been under Wilson, but American trade in the hemisphere had fallen drastically as the Depression worsened. Roosevelt moved quickly to solidify the improved relations and gain economic bene-

fits. With his usual flair for the dramatic, he proclaimed a policy of the "good neighbor" and then proceeded to win goodwill by renouncing the imperialism of the past.

In 1933, Secretary of State Cordell Hull signed a conditional pledge of nonintervention at a Pan-American conference in Montevideo, Uruguay. A year later, the United States renounced its right to intervene in Cuban affairs under the Platt Amendment and loosened its grip on Panama. By 1936, American troops were no longer occupying any Latin American nation. FDR personally cemented the new policy by traveling to Buenos Aires to sign an agreement that forbade intervention "directly or indirectly, and for whatever reason" in the internal affairs of a Central or South American state.

The United States had not changed its basic goal of political and economic dominance in the hemisphere; rather, the new policy of benevolence reflected Roosevelt's belief that cooperation and friendship were more effective tactics than threats and armed intervention. Mexico tried his patience in 1938 by nationalizing its oil resources; with admirable restraint, the President finally negotiated a settlement in 1941 on terms favorable to Mexico. Yet this economic loss was more than offset by the new trade opportunities opened up by the Good Neighbor policy. American commerce with Latin America increased fourfold in the 1930s, and investment rose substantially from its Depression low. Most important, FDR succeeded in forging a new policy of regional collective security. As the ominous events leading to World War II unfolded in Europe and Asia, the nations of the Western Hemisphere looked to the United States for protection against external danger.

Rivalry in Asia

In the years following World War I, the United States and Japan were on a collision course in the Pacific. The Japanese, lacking the raw materials to sustain their developing industrial economy, were determined to expand onto the Asian mainland. They had taken Korea by 1905, and during World War I had extended their control over the mines, harbors, and railroads of Manchuria, the industrial region of northeast China. The American Open Door policy remained the primary obstacle to complete Japanese dominion over China. The United States thus faced the clear-cut choice of either abandoning China or forcefully opposing Japan's expansion. American efforts to avoid making this painful decision postponed the eventual showdown but not the growing rivalry.

The first attempt at a solution came in 1921 when the United States convened the Washington Conference which included delegates from the United States, Japan, Great Britain and six other nations. The major objective was a political settlement of the tense Asian situation, but the most pressing issue was a dangerous naval race between Japan and the United States. Both nations were engaged in extensive shipbuilding programs begun during the war. Great Britain was forced to compete in order to preserve its traditional control of the sea; even so, projected construction indicated that both the United States and Japan would overtake the British navy by the end of the decade. Japan, spending nearly one-third of its total budget on naval construction, was eager for an agreement; in the United States, growing congressional concern over appropriations suggested the need for slowing the naval buildup.

In his welcoming address at the Washington Conference, Secretary of State Charles Evans Hughes outlined a specific plan for naval disarmament, calling for the scrapping of sixty-six battleships—thirty American, nineteen British, and seventeen Japanese. Three months later, delegates signed a Five Power Treaty embodying the main elements of Hughes' proposal: limitation of capital ships (battleships and aircraft carriers) in a ratio of 5–5–3 for the United States, Britain, and Japan respectively and 1.67–1.67 for France and Italy. England reluctantly accepted equality with the United States, while Japan agreed to the lower ratio only in return for an American pledge not to fortify Pacific bases such as the Philippines and Guam. The treaty cooled off the naval race even though it did not include cruisers, destroyers, or submarines.

The Washington Conference produced two other major agreements, the Nine Power Treaty and the Four Power Treaty. The first simply pledged all of the countries involved to uphold the Open Door policy, while the other compact replaced the old Anglo-Japanese alliance with a new Pacific security pact signed by the United States, Great Britain, Japan, and France. Neither document contained any enforcement provision beyond a promise to consult in case of a violation. In essence, the Washington treaties formed a parchment peace, a pious set of pledges that attempted to freeze the status quo in the Pacific.

This compromise lasted less than a decade. In September 1931, Japanese forces overran Manchuria, violating the Nine Power Treaty and the Kellogg-Briand Pact in a brutal act of aggression. The United States, paralyzed by the Depression, responded feebly. Secretary of State Henry L. Stimson sent an observer to Geneva to assure cooperation with the League of Nations, which was content to investigate the "incident." In January 1932, Stimson fell back on moral force, issuing notes vowing that the United States would not recognize the legality of the Japanese seizure of Manchuria. Despite ultimate concurrence by the League on nonrecognition, the Japanese ignored the American moral sanction and incorporated the former Chinese province, now renamed Manchukuo, into their rapidly expanding empire.

Aside from the good-neighbor approach in the Western Hemisphere, American foreign policy faithfully reflected the prevailing disillusionment with world power that gripped the country after World War I. The United States avoided taking any constructive steps toward preserving world order, preferring instead the empty symbolism of the Washington treaties and the Kellogg-Briand Pact.

ISOLATIONISM

The retreat from an active world policy in the 1920s turned into a headlong flight back to isolationism in the '30s. Two factors were responsible. First, the Depression made foreign policy seem remote and unimportant to most Americans. As unemployment increased and the economic crisis intensified after 1929, many people grew apathetic about events abroad. Second, the danger of war abroad, when it did finally penetrate the American consciousness, served only to strengthen the desire to escape involvement.

Three powerful and discontented nations were on the march in the 1930s—Germany, Italy, and

Millions of Germans idolized Adolf Hitler, portrayed in this captured German painting as a white knight. After the painting came into American hands, a GI slashed Hitler's face to indicate his displeasure with the mystique of the Führer.

Japan. In Germany, Adolf Hitler came to power in 1933 as the head of a National Socialist, or Nazi, movement. A shrewd and charismatic leader, Hitler capitalized on both domestic discontent and bitterness over World War I. Blaming the Jews for all of Germany's ills and asserting the supremacy of the "Aryan" race of blond, blue-eyed Germans, he quickly imposed a totalitarian dictatorship in which the Nazi party ruled and the führer was supreme. At first, his foreign policy seemed harmless, but as he consolidated his power, the ultimate threat to world peace became clearer. Hitler took Germany out of the League of Nations, reoccupied the Rhineland, and formally denounced the Treaty of Versailles. His boasts of uniting all Germans into a Greater Third Reich that would last a thousand years filled his European opponents with terror, blocking any effective challenge to his regime.

In Italy, another dictator, Benito Mussolini, had come to power in 1922. Emboldened by Hitler's success, he embarked on an aggressive foreign policy in 1935. His invasion of the independent African nation of Ethiopia led its emperor, Haile Selassie, to call upon the League of Nations for support. With England and France far more concerned about Hitler, the League's half-hearted measures utterly failed to halt Mussolini's conquest. "Fifty-two nations had combined to resist aggression," commented historian A. J. P. Taylor; "all they accomplished was that Haile Selassie lost all his country instead of only half." Collective security had failed its most important test.

Japan formed the third element in the threat to world peace. Militarists began to dominate the government in Tokyo by the mid-1930s, using tactics of fear and even assassination against their liberal opponents. By 1936, Japan had left the League of Nations and had repudiated the Washington treaties. A year later, its armies began an invasion of China that marked the beginning of the Pacific phase of World War II.

The resurgence of militarism in Germany, Italy, and Japan undermined the Versailles settlement and threatened to destroy the existing balance of power. England and France in Europe proved as powerless as China in Asia to stop the tide of aggression. In 1937, the three totalitarian nations signed an anti-Comintern pact completing a Berlin-Rome-Tokyo axis. Their alliance ostensibly was aimed at the Soviet Union, but in fact it threatened the entire world. Only a determined

*B*enito Mussolini, dictator of Italy, marches in Munich (1938) with his partner in the Rome-Berlin axis. Although Mussolini was a powerful, aggressive tyrant, he was clearly subordinate to Hitler, who dominated the partnership.

American response could unite the other nations against this Axis threat. Unfortunately, the United States deliberately abstained from assuming this role of leadership until it was nearly too late.

The Lure of Pacifism and Neutrality

The growing danger of war abroad led to a rising American desire for peace and noninvolvement. Memories of World War I contributed heavily. The novel *All Quiet on the Western Front,* as well as the movie based on it, reminded people of the brutality of war. Historians began to treat the Great War as a mistake, criticizing Wilson for failing to preserve American neutrality and claiming that the clever British had duped the United States into entering the war. Walter Millis advanced this thesis in a popular book, *America's Road to War, 1914–1917,* published in 1935. It was hailed as a vivid description of the process by which "a peace-loving democracy, muddled but excited, misinformed and whipped to a frenzy, embarked upon its greatest foreign war."

American youth made clear their determination not to repeat the mistakes of their elders. Pacifism swept across college campuses. A Brown University poll indicated 72 percent of the students opposed military service in wartime. At Princeton, undergraduates formed the Veterans of Future Wars, a parody on veterans' groups, to demand a bonus of $1000 apiece before they marched off to a foreign war! In April 1934, students and professors alike walked out of class to attend massive antiwar rallies, which became an annual rite of spring in the 1930s. Amid demonstrators carrying signs reading "Abolish the R.O.T.C." and "Build Schools—Not Battleships," pacifist orators urged students to sign a pledge not to support their country "in any war it might conduct."

The pacifist movement found a scapegoat in the munitions industry. The publication of several books exposing the unsavory business tactics of large arms dealers such as Krupp in Germany and Vickers in Britain led to a demand to curb these "merchants of death." Senator Gerald Nye of North Dakota headed a special Senate committee which spent two years investigating American munitions dealers. The committee revealed the enormous profits such firms as Du Pont reaped from World War I, but Nye went further, charging that bankers and munitions makers were responsible for American intervention in 1917. No proof was forthcoming, but the public—prepared to believe the worst of businessmen during the Depression—accepted the "merchants-of-death" thesis.

The Nye Committee's revelations culminated in neutrality legislation. In 1935, Senator Nye and another Senate colleague introduced measures to ban arms sales and loans to belligerents and to prevent Americans from traveling on belligerent ships. By outlawing the activities that led to World War I, they hoped the United States could avoid involvement in the new conflict. This "never-again" philosophy proved irresistible. In August 1935, Congress passed the first of three neutrality acts. The 1935 law banned the sale of arms to nations at war and warned American citizens not to sail on belligerent ships. In 1936, a second act added a ban on loans, and in 1937, a third neutrality act made these prohibitions permanent and required, on a two-year trial basis, that all trade other than munitions be conducted on a cash-and-carry basis.

President Roosevelt played a passive role in the adoption of the neutrality legislation. At first opposed to the arms embargo, he finally approved it for six months in 1935 in a compromise designed to save important New Deal legislation in Congress. Yet he also appeared to share the isolationist assumption that a European war would have no impact on vital national interests. He termed the first neutrality act "entirely satisfactory" when he signed it. Others in the administration criticized the mandatory nature of the new law, pointing out that it prevented the United States from distinguishing between aggressors and their victims. Privately, Roosevelt expressed some of the same reservations, but publicly he bowed to the prevailing isolationism. He signed the subsequent neutrality acts without protest, and during the 1936 election, he delivered an impassioned denunciation of war. "I hate war," he told an audience in Chautauqua, New York. "I have passed unnumbered hours, I shall pass unnumbered hours, thinking and planning how war may be kept from this nation."

Yet FDR did take a few steps to try to limit the nation's retreat into isolationism. His failure to invoke the neutrality act after the Japanese invasion of China in 1937 enabled the hard-pressed Chinese to continue buying arms from the United States. In January 1938, he used his influence to block a proposal by Indiana Congressman Louis Ludlow to require a nationwide referendum before Congress could declare war. FDR's strongest public statement came earlier, in Chicago in October 1937, when he denounced "the epidemic of world lawlessness" and called for an international effort to "quarantine" this disease. When reporters asked him if his call for "positive efforts to preserve peace" signaled a repeal of the neutrality acts, however, Roosevelt quickly reaffirmed this isolationist legislation. Whatever his private yearning for cooperation against aggressors, the President had no intention of challenging the prevailing public mood of the 1930s.

War in Europe

The neutrality legislation played directly into the hands of Adolf Hitler. Bent on the conquest of Europe, he could now proceed without worrying about American interference. In March 1938, he seized Austria in a bloodless coup. Six months later, he was demanding the Sudetenland, a province of Czechoslovakia with a large German population. When the British and French leaders agreed to meet with Hitler at Munich, FDR voiced his approval. Roosevelt carefully kept the United States aloof from the subsequent surrender of the Sudetenland. At the same time, he gave his tacit approval of the Munich agreement by telling the British prime minister that he shared his "hope and belief that there exists today the greatest opportunity in years for the establishment of a new order based on justice and on law."

Six months after the meeting at Munich, Hitler violated his promises by seizing nearly all of Czechoslovakia. In the United States, Roosevelt permitted the State Department to press for neutrality revision. The administration proposal to repeal the arms embargo and place *all* trade with belligerents, including munitions, on a cash-and-carry basis soon met stubborn resistance from isolationists. They argued that cash-and-carry would favor England and France, who controlled the sea. The House rejected the measure by a narrow margin, and the Senate's Foreign Relations Committee voted 12 to 11 to postpone any action on neutrality revision.

In July 1939, Roosevelt finally abandoned his aloof position and held a meeting with Senate leaders to plead for reconsideration. Warnings of the imminence of war in Europe by both the President and the secretary of state failed to impress the isolationists. Senator William Borah, who had led the fight against the League of Nations in 1919, responded that he felt the chances for war in Europe were remote. After canvassing the senators present, Vice-President John Nance Garner bluntly told FDR that the neutrality revision was dead. "You haven't got the votes," Garner commented, "and that's all there is to it."

On September 1, 1939, Hitler began World War II by invading Poland. England and France responded two days later by declaring war, although there was no way they could prevent the German conquest of Poland. Russia had played a key role, refusing Western overtures for a common front against Germany and finally signing a nonaggression treaty with Hitler in late August. The Nazi-Soviet Pact enabled Germany to avoid a two-front war; the Russians were rewarded with a generous slice of eastern Poland.

President Roosevelt reacted to the outbreak of

Hitler sent his armies into Poland with tremendous force and firepower, devastating the country. When Jews, such as these residents of the Warsaw Ghetto, fell into the hands of the Nazi occupiers, they were deported to slave labor camps that soon became the sites of mass extermination.

war by proclaiming American neutrality, but the successful aggression by Nazi Germany brought into question the isolationist assumption that American well-being did not depend upon the European balance of power. Strategic as well as ideological considerations began to undermine the earlier belief that the United States could safely pursue a policy of neutrality and noninvolvement. The long retreat from responsibility was about to end as Americans came to realize that their own democracy and security were at stake in the European war.

THE ROAD TO WAR

For two years, the United States tried to remain at peace while war raged in Europe and Asia. In contrast to Wilson's attempt to be impartial during most of World War I, however, the American people displayed an overwhelming sympathy for the Allies and total distaste for Germany and Japan. Roosevelt made no secret of his preference for an Allied victory, but a fear of isolationist criticism compelled him to move slowly, and often deviously, in adopting a policy of aid for England and France.

From Neutrality to Undeclared War

Two weeks after the outbreak of war in Europe, Roosevelt called Congress into special session to revise the neutrality legislation. He wanted to repeal the arms embargo in order to supply weapons to England and France, but he refused to state this aim openly. Instead he asked Congress to replace the arms embargo with cash-and-carry regulations. Belligerents would be able to purchase war supplies in the United States, but they would have to pay cash and transport the goods in their own ships. Public opinion strongly supported the President, and Congress passed the revised neutrality policy by heavy margins in early November 1939.

A series of dramatic German victories had a profound impact on American opinion. Quiet during the winter of 1939–1940, the Germans struck with lightning speed and devastating effect in the spring. In April, they seized Denmark and Norway, and on May 10, 1940, they unleashed the *blitzkreig* (lightning war) on the western front. Using tanks, armored columns, and dive bombers in close coordination, the German army cut deep into the Allied lines, dividing the British and

Employing typical blitzkrieg tactics, a motorized division of German troops drives through a ravaged town, their way into enemy territory cleared by repeated bombings.

French forces. Within three weeks, the British were driven off the continent. In another three weeks, France fell to Hitler's victorious armies.

Americans were stunned. Hitler had taken only six weeks to achieve what Germany had failed to do in four years of fighting in World War I. Suddenly they realized that they did have a stake in the outcome; if England fell, Hitler might well gain control of the British navy. The Atlantic would no longer be a barrier; instead, it would be a highway for German penetration of the New World.

Roosevelt responded by invoking a policy of all-out aid to the Allies, short of war. In a speech at Charlottesville, Virginia, in June (just after Italy entered the war by invading France), he denoun-

ced Germany and Italy as representing "the gods of force and hate" and vowed that "the whole of our sympathies lies with those nations that are giving their life blood in combat against these forces." It was too late to help France, but in early September, FDR announced the transfer of fifty old destroyers to England in exchange for rights to build air and naval bases on eight British possessions in the Western Hemisphere. Giving warships to a belligerent nation was clearly a breach of neutrality, but Roosevelt stressed the importance of guarding the Atlantic approaches, calling the destroyers-for-bases deal "the most important action in the reinforcement of our national defense that has been taken since the Louisiana Purchase."

Isolationists cried out against this departure from neutrality. A bold headline in the St. Louis *Post-Dispatch* read, "Dictator Roosevelt Commits Act of War." A group of Roosevelt's opponents in the Midwest formed the America First Committee to protest the drift toward war. Such diverse individuals as aviator-hero Charles Lindbergh, conservative Senator Robert A. Taft of Ohio, socialist leader Norman Thomas, and liberal educator Robert M. Hutchins condemned FDR for involving the United States in a foreign conflict. Voicing belief in a "Fortress America," they denied that Hitler threatened American security and claimed that the nation had the strength to defend itself regardless of what happened in Europe.

To support the administration's policies, opponents of the isolationists organized the Committee to Defend America by Aiding the Allies. Eastern Anglophiles, moderate New Dealers, and liberal Republicans made up the bulk of the membership, with Kansas newspaper editor William Allen White serving as chairman. The White Committee, as it became known, advocated unlimited assistance to England short of war, although some of its members privately favored entry into the conflict. Above all, the interventionists challenged the isolationist premise that events in Europe did not affect American security. "The future of western civilization is being decided upon the battlefield of Europe," White declared.

In the ensuing debate, the American people gradually came to agree with the interventionists. The battle of Britain helped. "Every time Hitler bombed London, we got a couple of votes," noted one interventionist. Frightened by the events in Europe, Congress approved large sums for preparedness, increasing the defense budget from $2 billion to $10 billion during 1940. Roosevelt courageously asked for a peacetime draft, the first in American history, to build up the army; in September, Congress agreed.

The sense of crisis affected domestic politics. Roosevelt ran for an unprecedented third term in 1940 because of the European war; the Republicans nominated Wendell Willkie, a former Democratic businessman who shared FDR's commitment to aid for England. Both candidates made appeals to peace sentiment during the campaign, but Roosevelt's decisive victory made it clear that the nation supported his increasing departure from neutrality.

After the election, FDR took his boldest step. Responding to British Prime Minister Winston Churchill's warning that England was running out of money, the President asked Congress to approve a new program to lend and lease goods and weapons to countries fighting against aggressors. Roosevelt's call for America to become "the great arsenal of democracy" seemed straightforward enough, but he acted somewhat deviously by naming the program lend-lease and by comparing it to loaning a neighbor a garden hose to put out a fire.

Isolationists angrily denounced lend-lease as both unnecessary and untruthful. "Lending war equipment is a good deal like lending chewing gum," commented Senator Taft. "You don't want it back." In March 1941, however, Congress voted by substantial margins to authorize the President to "sell, transfer title to, exchange, lease, lend, or otherwise dispose of" war supplies to "any country the President deems vital to the defense of the United States." The accompanying $7-billion appropriation ended the "cash" part of cash-and-carry and ensured Britain full access to American war supplies.

The Election of 1940

Candidate	Party	Popular Vote	Electoral Vote
Roosevelt	Democrat	27,263,448	449
Willkie	Republican	22,336,260	82

The "carry" problem still remained. German submarines were sinking over five hundred thousand tons of shipping a month. England desperately needed the help of the American navy in escorting convoys across the U-boat-infested waters of the North Atlantic. Roosevelt, fearful of isolationist reaction, responded with naval patrols in the western half of the ocean. Hitler placed his submarine commanders under strict restraints to avoid drawing America into the European war. Nevertheless, incidents were bound to occur. In September 1941, after a U-boat narrowly missed torpedoing an American destroyer tracking it, Roosevelt denounced the German submarines as the "rattlesnakes of the Atlantic" and issued orders for the navy to convey British ships halfway across the ocean.

Undeclared naval war quickly followed. On October 17, 1941, a German submarine damaged the U.S. destroyer *Kearney;* ten days later, another U-boat sank the *Reuben James,* killing more than one hundred American sailors. FDR issued orders for the destroyers to shoot U-boats on sight. He also asked Congress to repeal the "carry" section of the neutrality laws and permit American ships to deliver supplies to England. In mid-November, Congress approved these moves by slim margins. Now American merchant ships as well as destroyers would become targets for German attacks. By December, it seemed only a matter of weeks—or months at most—until repeated sinkings would lead to a formal declaration of war against Germany.

In leading the nation to the brink of war in Europe, Roosevelt opened himself to criticism from both sides in the domestic debate. Interventionists felt that he had been too cautious in dealing with the danger to the nation from Nazi Germany. Isolationists were equally critical of the President, claiming that he had misled the American people by professing peace while plotting for war. Roosevelt was certainly less than candid, relying on executive discretion to engage in highly provocative acts in the North Atlantic. He agreed with the interventionists that in the long run American security would be threatened by a German victory in Europe. But he also was aware that a poll taken in September 1941 showed that nearly 80 percent of the American people wanted to stay out of World War II. Realizing that leading a divided nation into war would be disastrous,

Kneeling at the Capitol Plaza in Washington, women from various mothers' groups conduct a pray-in to protest the passage of the Lend-Lease Act.

FDR played for time, inching the country toward war while waiting for the Axis nations to make the ultimate move. Japan finally obliged at Pearl Harbor.

Showdown in the Pacific

Japan had taken advantage of the war in Europe to expand further in Asia. Although successful after 1937 in conquering the populous coastal areas of China, the Japanese had been unable to defeat Chiang Kai-shek, whose forces retreated into the vast interior of the country. The German defeat of France and the Netherlands in 1940, however, left their colonial possessions in the East Indies and Indochina vulnerable and defenseless. Japan now set out to incorporate these territories—rich in oil, tin, and rubber—into a Greater East Asia Co-Prosperity Sphere.

The Roosevelt administration countered with economic pressure. Japan was heavily dependent upon the United States for shipments of petroleum and scrap metal. In July 1940, President Roosevelt signed an order setting up a licensing and quota system for the export of these crucial materials to Japan and banned the sale of aviation gasoline altogether. With Britain fighting for survival and France and the Netherlands occupied by Germany, the United States was now employ-

ing economic sanctions to defend Southeast Asia against Japanese expansion.

Tokyo appeared to be unimpressed. In early September, Japanese troops occupied strategic bases in the northern part of French Indochina. Later in the month, Japan signed the Tripartite Pact with Germany and Italy, a defensive treaty that confronted the United States with a possible two-ocean war. The new Axis alignment confirmed American suspicions that Japan was part of a worldwide totalitarian threat. Roosevelt and his advisers, however, saw Germany as the primary danger; thus they pursued a policy of all-out aid to England while hoping that economic measures alone would deter Japan.

The embargo on aviation gasoline, extended to include scrap iron and steel in late September 1940, was a burden Japan could bear, but a possible ban on all oil shipments was a different matter. Japan lacked petroleum reserves of its own and was entirely dependent on imports from the United States and the Dutch East Indies. In an attempt to ease the economic pressure through negotiation, Japan sent a new envoy to Washington in the spring of 1941. But these talks quickly broke down. Tokyo wanted nothing less than a free hand in China and an end to American sanctions, while the United States insisted on an eventual Japanese evacuation of all China.

In July 1941, Japan invaded southern Indochina, beginning the chain of events that led to war. Washington knew of this aggression before it occurred. Naval intelligence experts had broken the Japanese diplomatic code and were intercepting and reading all messages between Tokyo and the Japanese embassy in Washington. President Roosevelt responded on July 25, 1941, with an order freezing all Japanese assets in the United States. This step, initially intended only as a temporary warning to Japan, soon became a permanent embargo due to positive public reaction and State Department zeal. Trade with Japan, including the vital oil shipments, came to a complete halt. When the Dutch government-in-exile took similar action, Japan faced a dilemma: in order to have oil shipments resumed, Tokyo would have to end its aggression; the alternative would be to seize the needed petroleum supplies in the Dutch East Indies, an action that would mean war.

After one final diplomatic effort failed, General Hideki Tojo, an army militant, became the new premier of Japan. To mask its war preparations, Tokyo sent yet another envoy to Washington with new peace proposals. Code-breaking enabled American diplomats to learn that the Japanese terms were unacceptable even before they were formally presented. Army and navy leaders urged President Roosevelt to seek at least a temporary settlement with Japan to give them time to prepare American defenses in the Pacific. Secretary of State Cordell Hull, however, refused to allow any concession; on November 26, he sent a stiff ten-point reply to Tokyo that included a demand for Japanese withdrawal from China.

The Japanese response came two weeks later. On the evening of December 6, 1941, the first thirteen parts of the reply to Hull's note arrived in Washington, with the fourteenth part to follow the next morning. Naval intelligence actually decoded the message faster than the Japanese embassy clerks. A messenger delivered the text to President Roosevelt late that night; after glancing at it, he commented, "This means war." The next day, December 7, the fourteenth part arrived, revealing that Japan totally rejected the American position.

Officials in Washington immediately sent warning messages to American bases in the Pacific, but they failed to arrive in time. At 7:55 in the morning, just before 1 P.M. in Washington, squadrons of Japanese carrier-based planes caught the American fleet at Pearl Harbor totally by surprise. In little more than an hour, they crippled the American Pacific fleet and its major base, sinking eight battleships and killing more than twenty-four hundred American sailors.

In Washington, the Japanese envoys had re-

American ships were destroyed in the surprise attack of Pearl Harbor, December 7, 1941. Caught completely off guard, U.S. forces still managed to shoot down 29 enemy planes.

quested a meeting with Secretary Hull at 1 P.M. Just before the meeting news arrived of the attack on Pearl Harbor. An irate Cordell Hull read the note the Japanese handed him and then, unable to restrain himself any longer, burst out, "In all my fifty years of public service, I have never seen a document that was more crowded with infamous falsehoods and distortions—on a scale so huge that I never imagined until today that any government was capable of uttering them."

Speaking before Congress the next day, President Roosevelt termed December 7 "a date which will live in infamy" and asked for a declaration of war on Japan. With only one dissenting vote, both branches did so. On December 11, Germany and Italy declared war against the United States; the nation was now fully involved in World War II.

The whole country united behind Roosevelt's leadership to seek revenge for Pearl Harbor and to defeat the Axis threat to American security. After the war, however, critics charged that FDR had entered the conflict by a back door, claiming that the President had deliberately exposed the Pacific fleet to attack. Subsequent investigations uncovered negligence in both Hawaii and Washington but no evidence to support the conspiracy charge. Commanders in Hawaii, like most military experts, believed that the Japanese would not launch an attack on a base four thousand miles away from Japan. FDR, like too many Americans, had badly underestimated the daring and skill of the Japanese; he and the nation alike paid a heavy price for this cultural and racial prejudice. But there was no plot. Roosevelt could not have known that Hitler, so restrained in the Atlantic, would reverse his policy and foolishly declare war against the United States after Pearl Harbor. Perhaps the most frightening aspect of the whole episode is that it took the shock of the Japanese sneak attack to make the American people aware of the extent of the Axis threat to their well-being and lead them to end the long American retreat from responsibility.

TURNING THE TIDE AGAINST THE AXIS

In the first few months after the United States entered the war, the outlook for victory was bleak. In Europe, Hitler's armies controlled virtually the entire continent, from Norway in the north to Greece in the south. Despite the nonaggression pact, German armies had penetrated deep into Russia after an initial invasion in June 1941. Although they had failed to capture either Moscow or Leningrad, the Nazi forces had conquered the Ukraine and by the spring of 1942 were threatening to sweep across the Volga and seize the vital oil fields in the Caucasus. In North Africa, General Erwin Rommel's Afrika Korps had pushed the British back into Egypt and threatened the Suez Canal (see the map on the facing page).

The situation was no better in Asia. The Pearl Harbor attack had enabled the Japanese to move unopposed across Southeast Asia. Within three months they had conquered Malaya and the Dutch East Indies, with its valuable oil fields, and were pressing the British back both in Burma and New Guinea. American forces under General Douglas MacArthur had tried vainly to block the Japanese conquest of the Philippines. MacArthur finally escaped by torpedo boat to Australia; the American garrison at Corregidor surrendered after a long siege, the survivors then enduring the cruel death march across the Bataan peninsula. With the American navy still recovering from the devastation at Pearl Harbor, Japan controlled the western half of the Pacific (see the map on p. 816).

Over the next two years, the United States and its allies would finally halt the German and Japanese offensives in Europe and Asia. But then they faced the difficult process of driving back the enemy, freeing the vast conquered areas, and finally defeating the Axis powers on their home territory. It would be a difficult and costly struggle that would require great sacrifice and heavy losses; World War II would test American will and resourcefulness to the hilt.

Wartime Partnerships

The greatest single advantage that the United States and its partners possessed was their willingness to form a genuine coalition to bring about the defeat of the Axis powers. Although there were many strains within the wartime alliance, it did permit a high degree of coordination. In striking contrast was the behavior of Germany and Japan, each fighting a separate war without any attempt at cooperation.

The United States and Britain achieved a com-

World War II in Europe and North Africa

The tide of battle shifted in this theater during the winter of 1942–1943. The massive German assault on the eastern front was turned back by the Russians at Stalingrad, and the Allied forces recaptured North Africa.

Legend:
- Axis Powers before World War II
- Extent of Axis control early Nov. 1942
- Allies
- Neutral nations
- Allied troop movements
- Major battles

ICELAND

FINLAND

NORWAY

SWEDEN

EST.

Leningrad besieged Sept. 1941– Jan. 19, 1944

Moscow

LAT. Sept. 1944

LITH.

SOVIET UNION

Northern Ireland

North Sea

DEN.

East Prussia (Ger.)

Stalingrad Aug. 21, 1942– Jan. 31, 1943

GREAT BRITAIN

IRELAND

Berlin surrendered May 2, 1945

Warsaw

Aug. 1943

Volga R.

London

Elbe R.

Rhine

NETH.

POLAND

July 1944

Ukraine

ATLANTIC OCEAN

Apr. 1945

BELG.

D-Day June 6, 1944

FRANCE

GERMANY

Battle of the Bulge Dec. 16, 1944– Jan. 31, 1945

Czechoslovakia

Oder R.

March 1944

Caucasus

Normandy

Paris liberated Aug. 1944

Austria

HUNG.

Dec. 1944

ROM.

Aug. 1944

VICHY FRANCE occupied Nov. 1942

SWITZ.

Aug. 1944

Black Sea

Danube R.

YUGO.

BULG.

PORT.

SPAIN

ITALY

Rome liberated June 4, 1944

ALB. (It.)

TURKEY

GREECE

SYRIA

Rhodes (It.)

Cyprus (Br.)

LEB.

Sicily

July 1943

Crete (Greece)

Mediterranean Sea

PALESTINE (Br.)

TRANSJORDAN

Nov. 1942

Sp. Morocco

ALGERIA

Kasserine Pass Feb. 14–22, 1943

MOROCCO

FRENCH NORTH AFRICA (Vichy France)

Joined Allies Nov. 1942

TUNISIA

Nov. 1942

Suez Canal

El Alamein Oct. 23–Nov. 5, 1942

0   200   400 Miles

0   200   400 Kilometers

LIBYA (It.)

EGYPT

Nile R.

plete wartime partnership. Prewar military talks led to the formation of a Combined Chiefs of Staff, headquartered in Washington, which directed Anglo-American military operations. The close cooperation between President Roosevelt and Prime Minister Churchill ensured a common

strategy. The leaders decided at the outset that a Germany victory posed the greater danger and thus gave priority to the European theater in the conduct of the war. In a series of meetings in December 1941, Roosevelt and Churchill signed a Declaration of the United Nations, eventually

"*I*nside the Vicious Heart"

The liberation of the Nazi death camps near the end of World War II was not a priority objective; nor was it a planned operation. Convinced that military victory was the surest way to end Nazi oppression, Allied strategists organized their campaigns without specific reference to the camps; they staged no daring commando raids to rescue the survivors of Nazi genocide. It was by chance that Allied forces first stumbled upon the camps, and the GIs who threw open the gates to that living hell were totally unprepared for what they found.

Not until November, 1944, did the U.S. Army discover its first camp, Natzwiller-Struthof, abandoned by the Germans months before. Viewing Natzwiller from a distance, Milton Bracker of the *New York-Times* noted its deceptive similarity to an American Civilian Conservation Corps camp: "The sturdy green barracks buildings looked exactly like those that housed forestry trainees in the U.S. during the early New Deal."

As he toured the grounds, however, he faced a starker reality and slowly came to think the unthink-

able. In the crematorium, he reported, "I cranked the elevator tray a few times and slid the furnace tray a few times, and even at that moment, I did not believe what I was doing was real."

"There were no prisoners," he wrote, "no screams, no burly guards, no taint of death in the air as on a battlefield." Bracker had to stretch his imagination to its limits to comprehend the camp's silent testimony to Nazi barbarism. U.S. military personnel who toured Natzwiller shared this sense of the surreal. In their report to headquarters, they carefully qualified every observation. They described "what appeared to be a disinfection unit," a room "allegedly used as a lethal gas chamber," "a cellar room with a special type elevator," and "an incinerator room with equipment obviously intended for the burning of human bodies." They saw before them the evidence of German atrocities, but the truth was so horrible, they could not quite bring themselves to draw the obvious conclusions.

Inside the Vicious Heart, Robert Abzug's recent study of the liberation of the concentration camps, refers to this phenomenon as "double vision." Faced with a revelation so terrible, witnesses could not fully comprehend the evidence of mass murder without meaning or logic. But as the Allied armies advanced into Germany, the shocking evidence mounted. On April 4, 1945, the Fourth Armored Division of the Third Army unexpectedly discovered Ohrdruf, a relatively small concentration camp. Ohrdruf's liberation had a tremendous

*P*hotos of the death camps, such as these, made the almost unimaginable atrocities of the Führer's regime real to Americans at home.

impact on American forces. It was the first camp discovered intact, with its grisly array of the dead and dying. Inside the compound, corpses were piled in heaps in the barracks. An infantryman recalled, "I guess the most vivid recollection of the whole camp is the pyre that was located on the edge of the camp. It was a big pit, where they stacked bodies—stacked bodies and wood and burned them."

On April 12, Generals Eisenhower, Bradley, and Patton toured Ohrdruf. The generals, professional soldiers familiar with the devastation of battle, had never seen its like. Years later, Bradley recalled, "The smell of death overwhelmed us even before we passed through the stockade. More than 3,200 naked, emaciated bodies had been flung into shallow graves. Others lay in the street where they had fallen."

Eisenhower ordered every available armed forces unit in the area to visit Ohrdruf. "We are told that the American soldier does not know what he is fighting for," said Eisenhower. "Now at least he will know what he is fighting against." He urged government officials and journalists to visit the camps and tell the world. In an official message Eisenhower summed it up:

> We are constantly finding German camps in which they have placed political prisoners where unspeakable conditions exist. From my own personal observation, I can state unequivocally that all written statements up to now do not paint the full horrors.

On April 11, the Timberwolf Division of the Third Army uncovered Nordhausen. They found 3000 dead and only 700 survivors. The scene sickened battle-hardened veterans.

> The odors, well there is no way to describe the odors. . . . Many of the boys I am talking about now—these were tough soldiers, there were combat men who had been all the way through the invasion—were ill and vomiting, throwing up, just at the sight of this. . . .

For some, the liberation of Nordhausen changed the meaning of the war.

> I must also say that my fellow GIs, most thought that any stories they had read in the paper . . . were either not true or at least exaggerated. And it did not sink in, what this was all about, until we got into Nordhausen.

If the experience at Nordhausen gave many GIs a new sense of mission in battle, it also forced them to distance themselves from the realities of the camps. Only by closing off their emotions could they go about the grim task of sorting out the living from the dead and tending to the survivors. Margaret Bourke-White, whose *Life* magazine photographs brought the horrors of the death camps to millions on the home front, recalled working "with a veil over my mind."

> People often ask me how it is possible to photograph such atrocities. In photographing the murder camps, the protective veil was so tightly drawn that I hardly knew what I had taken until I saw prints of my own photographs.

By the end of 1945, most of the liberators had come home and returned to civilian life. Once home, their experiences produced no common moral responses. No particular pattern emerged in their occupational, political, and religious behavior, beyond a fear of the rise of postwar totalitarianism shared by most Americans. Few spoke publicly about their role in the liberation of the camps; most found that after a short period of grim fascination, their friends and families preferred to forget. Some had nightmares, but most were not tormented by memories. For the liberators the ordeal was over. For the survivors of the hell of the camps, liberation was but the first step in the tortuous process of rebuilding broken bodies and shattered lives.

subscribed to by twenty-six countries, that pledged them to fight together until the Axis powers were defeated.

Relations with the other members of the United Nations coalition in World War II were not quite so harmonious. The decision to defeat Germany first displeased the Chinese, who had been at war with Japan since 1937. Roosevelt tried to appease Chiang Kai-shek with a trickle of supplies, flown in at great risk by American airmen over the Himalayas from India. France posed a more delicate problem. FDR virtually ignored the Free French government in exile under General Charles de Gaulle. Roosevelt preferred to deal with the Vichy regime, despite its collaboration with Germany, because it still controlled the French fleet and retained France's overseas territories.

The greatest strain of all within the wartime coalition was with the Soviet Union. Although Roosevelt had ended the long period of nonrecognition in 1933, close ties had failed to develop. The Russian refusal to pay prerevolutionary debts, together with continued Soviet support of domestic Communist activity in the United States in the 1930s, intensified American distaste for Stalin's regime. The great Russian purge trials and the temporary Nazi-Soviet alliance from 1939 to 1941, along with deep-seated cultural and ideological differences, made wartime cooperation difficult.

Ever the pragmatist, Roosevelt tried hard to break down the old hostility and establish a more cordial relationship with Russia during the war. Even before Pearl Harbor, he extended lend-lease aid to Russia, and after American entry into the war, this economic assistance grew rapidly, limited only by the difficulty in delivering the supplies. Eager to keep Russia in the war, the President promised a visiting Russian diplomat in May 1942 that the United States would create a second front in Europe by the end of that year, a pledge he could not fulfill. In January 1943, Roosevelt joined with Churchill at the Casablanca conference to declare a policy of unconditional surrender, vowing that the Allies would fight until the Axis nations were completely defeated.

Despite these promises, the Soviet Union bore the brunt of battle against Hitler in the early years of the war, fighting alone against more than two hundred German divisions. The United States

and England, grateful for the respite to build up their forces, could do little more than offer promises of future help and send lend-lease supplies. The result was a rift that never fully healed—one that did not prevent the defeat of Germany but did ensure future tensions and uncertainties between the Soviet Union and the Western nations.

Halting the German Blitz

From the outset, the United States favored an invasion across the English Channel. Army planners, led by Chief of Staff George C. Marshall and his protégé, Dwight D. Eisenhower, were convinced that such a frontal assault would be the quickest way to win the war. Roosevelt concurred, in part because it fulfilled his second-front commitment to the Soviets.

The initial plan, drawn up by Eisenhower, called for a full-scale invasion of Europe in the spring of 1943, with provision for a temporary beachhead in France in the fall of 1942 if necessary to keep Russia in the war. Marshall surprised everyone by placing Eisenhower, until then a

American troops entering Palermo, Sicily, on July 23, 1943. Italy soon capitulated, but the Allies' Italian campaign bogged down under fierce German resistance.

relatively junior general, in charge of implementing the plan.

But the British, remembering the heavy casualties of trench warfare in World War I, preferred a perimeter approach, with air and naval attacks around the edge of the continent until Germany was properly softened up for the final invasion. Their strategists assented to the basic plan but strongly urged that a preliminary invasion of North Africa be launched in the fall of 1942. Roosevelt, too, wanted American troops engaged in combat against Germany before the end of 1942 to offset growing pressure at home to concentrate on the Pacific; hence, after he overruled objections from his military advisers, American and British troops landed on the Atlantic and Mediterranean coasts of Morocco and Algeria in November 1942.

The British launched an attack against Rommel at El Alamein in Egypt and soon forced the Afrika Korps to retreat across Libya to Tunisia. Eisenhower, delayed by poor roads and bad weather, was slow in bringing up his forces, and in their first encounter with Rommel at the Kasserine Pass in the desert south of Tunis, inexperienced American troops suffered a humiliating defeat. General George Patton quickly rallied the demoralized soldiers, and by May 1943, Germany had been driven from Africa, leaving behind nearly three hundred thousand troops.

During these same months, the Red Army had broken the back of German military power in the battle of Stalingrad. Turned back at the critical bend in the Volga, Hitler had poured in division after division in what was ultimately a losing cause; never again would Germany be able to take the offensive in Europe.

At Churchill's insistence, FDR agreed to follow up the North African victory with the invasion first of Sicily and then Italy in the summer of 1943. Italy dropped out of the war when Mussolini fled to Germany, but the Italian campaign proved to be a strategic dead end. Germany sent in enough divisions to establish a strong defensive line in the mountains south of Rome; American and British troops were forced to fight their way slowly up the peninsula, suffering heavy casualties.

More important, these Mediterranean operations delayed the second front, postponing it eventually to the spring of 1944. Meanwhile, the Soviets began to push the Germans out of Russia and looked forward to the liberation of Poland, Hungary, and Romania, where they could establish "friendly" Communist regimes. Having borne the brunt of the fighting against Nazi Germany, Russia was ready to claim its reward— the postwar domination of Eastern Europe.

Checking Japan in the Pacific

Both the decision to defeat Germany first and the vast expanses of the Pacific dictated the nature of the war against Japan. The United States conducted amphibious, island-hopping campaigns rather than attempting to reconquer the Dutch East Indies, Southeast Asia, and China. There would be two separate American operations. One, led by Douglas MacArthur based in Australia, would move from New Guinea back to the Philippines, while the other, commanded by Admiral Chester Nimitz from Hawaii, was directed at key Japanese islands in the Central Pacific. The original plan called for the two offensives to come together for the final invasion of the Japanese home islands.

Success in the Pacific depended above all else on control of the sea. The devastation at Pearl Harbor gave Japan the initial edge, but fortunately the United States had not lost any of its four aircraft carriers. In the battle of the Coral Sea in May 1942, American naval forces blocked a Japanese thrust to outflank Australia. The turning point came one month later at Midway. A powerful Japanese task force threatened to seize this remote American outpost over a thousand miles west of Pearl Harbor; Japan's real objective was the destruction of what remained of the American Pacific fleet. Superior American air power enabled Nimitz's forces to engage the enemy at long range. Japanese fighters shot down thirty-five of forty-one attacking torpedo bombers, but a second wave of dive bombers scored hits on three Japanese carriers. The battle of Midway ended with the loss of four Japanese aircraft carriers compared to just one American. It was the first defeat the modern Japanese navy had ever suffered, and it left the United States in control of the Central Pacific.

Encouraged by this victory, American forces launched their first Pacific offensive in the Solomon Islands, east of New Guinea, in August

World War II in the Pacific

The tide of battle turned in the Pacific the same year as in Europe. The balance of sea power shifted back to the United States from Japan after the naval victories of 1942.

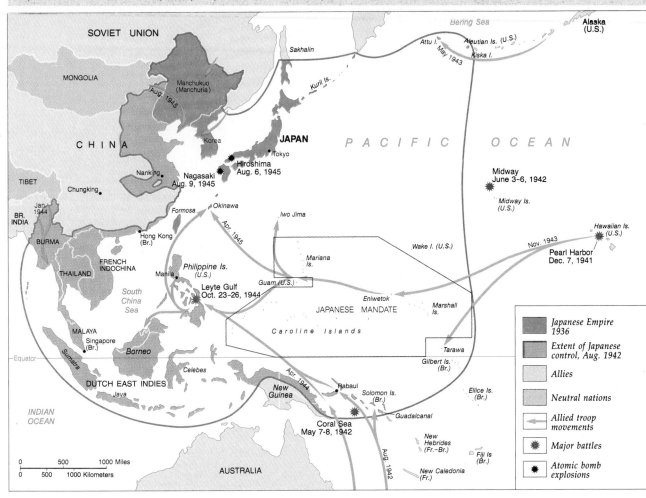

1942. Both sides suffered heavy losses, but six months later the last Japanese were driven from the key island of Guadalcanal. At the same time, MacArthur began the long, slow, and bloody job of driving the Japanese back along the north coast of New Guinea.

By early 1943, the defensive phase of the war with Japan was over. The enemy surge had been halted in both the Central and the Southwest Pacific, and the United States was preparing to penetrate the Gilbert, Marshall, and Caroline islands and recapture the Philippines. Just as Russia had broken German power in Europe, so the United States, fighting alone except for Australia and New Zealand, had halted the Japanese.

And, like the Soviet plans for Eastern Europe, America expected to reap the rewards of victory by dominating the Pacific in the future.

THE HOME FRONT

World War II had a greater impact than the Depression on the future of American life. While American soldiers and sailors fought abroad, the nation underwent sweeping social and economic changes at home.

American industry made the nation's single most important contribution to victory. Even though over fifteen million Americans served in

*A*merican war production was twice that of all the Axis countries. Here, Boeing aircraft workers celebrate the completion of their five-thousandth bomber.

the armed forces, it was the nearly sixty million who worked on farms and factories who achieved the miracle of production that ensured the defeat of Germany and Japan. The manufacturing plants that had run at half-capacity through the 1930s now hummed with activity. In Detroit, automobile assembly lines were converted to produce tanks and airplanes; Henry Ford built the giant Willow Run factory, covering sixty-seven acres, where forty-two thousand workers turned out a B-24 bomber every hour. Henry J. Kaiser, a California industrialist who constructed huge West Coast shipyards to meet the demand for cargo vessels and landing craft, operated on an equally large scale. His Richmond, California, plant lowered the time to build a merchant ship from 105 to 14 days. In part, America won the battle of the Atlantic by building ships faster than German U-boats could sink them.

This vast industrial expansion, however, created many problems. In 1942, President Roosevelt appointed Donald Nelson, a Sears, Roebuck executive, to head a War Production Board (WPB). A jovial, easy-going man, Nelson soon was outmaneuvered by the army and the navy, which preferred to negotiate directly with large corporations. The WPB allowed business rapid deprecia-

tion, and thus huge tax credits, for new plants and awarded lucrative cost-plus contracts for urgently needed goods. Shortages of such critical materials as steel, aluminum, and copper led to an allocation system based on military priorities. Rubber, cut off by the Japanese conquest of Southeast Asia, was particularly scarce; the administration finally began gasoline-rationing in 1943 to curb pleasure-driving and prolong tire life. The government itself built fifty-one synthetic rubber plants, which by 1944 were producing nearly one million tons for the tires of American airplanes and military vehicles. All in all, the nation's factories turned out twice as many goods as did German and Japanese industry combined.

Roosevelt revealed the same tendency toward compromise in directing the economic mobilization as he did in shaping the New Deal. When the Office of Price Administration—which tried to curb inflation by controlling prices and rationing scarce goods like sugar, canned food, and shoes —clashed with the WPB, FDR appointed James Byrnes to head an Office of Economic Stabilization. Byrnes, a former South Carolina senator and Supreme Court justice, used political judgement to settle disputes between agencies and keep all groups happy. The President was also forced to

During and immediately after the war, ration stamps were issued for scarce food items, shoes, tires, and gasoline.

compromise with Congress, which pared down the administration's requests for large tax increases. Half the cost of the war was financed by borrowing; the other half came from revenues. A $7-billion revenue increase in 1942 included so many first-time taxpayers that in the following year the Treasury Department instituted a new practice—withholding income taxes from workers' wages.

The result of this wartime economic explosion was a growing affluence. Despite the federal incentives to business, heavy excess-profit taxes and a 94 percent tax rate for the very rich kept the wealthy from benefiting unduly. The huge increase in federal spending, from $9 billion in 1940 to $98 billion in 1944, spread through American society. A government agreement with labor unions in 1943 held wage rates to a 15 percent increase, but the long hours of overtime resulted in doubling and sometimes tripling the weekly paychecks of factory workers. Farmers shared in the new prosperity as their incomes quadrupled between 1940 and 1945. For the first time in the twentieth century, the lowest fifth of wage earners increased their share of the national income in relation to the more affluent; their income rose by 68 percent between 1941 and 1945, compared to a 20 percent increase for the well-to-do. Most important, this rising income

ensured postwar prosperity. Workers and farmers saved their money, channeling much of it into government war bonds, waiting for the day when they could buy the cars and home appliances they had done without during the long years of depression and war.

A Nation on the Move

The war led to a vast migration of the American population. Young men left their homes for training camps and then for service overseas. Defense workers and their families, some nine million people in all, moved to work in the new booming shipyards, munitions factories, and aircraft plants. Norfolk, Virginia; San Diego, California; Mobile, Alabama, and other centers of defense production grew by more than 50 percent in just a year or two. Rural areas lost population while coastal regions, especially along the Pacific and the Gulf of Mexico, drew millions of people. The location of army camps in the South and West created boom conditions in the future Sunbelt, as did the concentration of aircraft factories and shipyards in this region. California had the greatest gains, adding nearly two million to its population in less than five years.

This movement of people caused severe social problems. Housing was in short supply. Migrating workers crowded into house trailers and boardinghouses, bringing unexpected windfalls to landlords. In one boom town, a reporter described an old Victorian house that had five bedrooms on the second floor. "Three of them," he wrote, "held two cots apiece, the two others held three cots." But the owner revealed that "the third floor is where we pick up the velvet. . . . We rent to workers in different shifts . . . three shifts a day . . . seven bucks a week apiece."

Family life suffered under these crowded living conditions. An increase in the number of marriages, as young people searched for something to hang on to in the midst of wartime turmoil, was offset by a rising divorce rate. The baby boom that would peak in the 1950s began during the war and brought its own set of problems. Only a few publicly funded day-care centers were available, and working mothers worried about their "latch-key children." Schools in the boom areas were unable to cope with the influx of new students; a teacher shortage, intensified by the lure of higher wages in war industries, compounded the educational crisis.

Despite these problems, women found the war a time of economic opportunity. The demand for workers led to a dramatic rise in female employment, from 14 million working women in 1940 to 19 million by 1945. Most of the new women workers were married and many were middle-aged, thus broadening the composition of the female work force, which in the past had been composed primarily of young, single women. Women entered industries once viewed as exclusively male; by the end of the war, they worked alongside men tending blast furnaces in steel mills and welding hulls in shipyards. Few challenged the traditional view of sex roles, yet the wartime experience helped temporarily undermine the concept that woman's only proper place was in the home. Women enjoyed the hefty weekly paychecks, which rose by 50 percent from 1941 to 1943, and they took pride in their contributions to the war effort. "To hell with the life I have had," commented a former fashion designer. "This war is too damn serious, and it is too damn important to win it."

African Americans shared in the wartime migration, but their social and economic gains were limited by racial prejudice. Nearly one million served in the armed forces, but relatively few saw combat. The army placed black soldiers in segregated units, usually led by white officers, and used them for service and construction tasks. The navy was even worse, relegating them to menial jobs until late in the war. African Americans were denied the chance to become petty officers, Secretary of the Navy Frank Knox explained, because experience had shown that "men of the colored race . . . cannot maintain discipline among men of the white race."

African-American civilians fared a little better. In 1941, black labor leader A. Philip Randolph threatened a massive march on Washington to force President Roosevelt to end racial discrimination in defense industries and government employment and to integrate the armed forces. FDR compromised, persuading Randolph to call off the march and drop his integration demand in return for an executive order creating a Fair Employment Practices Committee (FEPC) to ban racial discrimination in war industries. As a re-

"Rosie the Riveter," a song extolling women workers, was very popular during the war. This photograph from Life *is by Margaret Bourke-White.*

sult, African-American employment by the federal government rose from 60,000 in 1941 to 200,000 by the end of the war. The FEPC proved less successful in the private sector. Weak in funding and staff, the FEPC was able to act on only one-third of the eight thousand complaints it received. The nationwide shortage of labor was more influential than the FEPC in accounting for the rise in black employment during wartime. African-Americans moved from the rural South to northern and western cities, finding jobs in the automobile, aircraft, and shipbuilding industries.

This movement of an estimated seven hundred thousand people helped transform black/white relations from a regional issue into a national concern that could no longer be ignored. The limited housing and recreational facilities for both black and white war workers created tensions that led to urban race riots. On a hot Sunday evening in June 1943, blacks and whites began exchanging insults and then blows near Belle Island recreation park in Detroit. The next day, a full-scale riot broke out in which twenty-three blacks and nine whites died. The fighting

The migration of African Americans from the South to northern cities was recorded in a series of sixty tempera panels by Jacob Lawrence, a black artist. The paintings are done in sharp primary colors and a forceful but simple design. They form a continuous narrative of visual history and African-American experience.

raged for twenty-four hours until National Guard troops were brought in to restore order. Later that summer, only personal intervention by New York Mayor Fiorello LaGuardia quelled a Harlem riot that took the lives of six blacks.

These outbursts of racial violence fueled the resentments that would grow into the postwar civil rights movement. For most African Americans, despite economic gains, World War II was a reminder of the inequality of American life. "Just carve on my tombstone," remarked one black soldier in the Pacific, "here lies a black man killed fighting a yellow man for the protection of a white man."

One-third of a million Mexican-Americans served in the armed forces and shared some of the same experiences as African Americans. Although they were not as completely segregated, many served in the Eighty-eighth Division, made up largely of Mexican-American officers and troops, which earned the nickname "Blue Devils" in the Italian campaign. At home, Spanish-speaking people left the rural areas of Texas, New Mexico, and California for jobs in the cities, especially in aircraft plants and petroleum refineries. Despite low wages and union resistance, they improved their economic position substantially. But they still faced discrimination based

African-American Migration from the South, 1940–1950

Movement was from the Southeast to the Mid-Atlantic and New England states and from the south central states to the Midwest and Far West.

both on skin color and language, most notably in the Los Angeles "zoot-suit" riots in 1943 when white sailors attacked Mexican-American youths dressed in their distinctive long jackets and flared pants tightly pegged at the ankles. The racial prejudice heightened feelings of ethnic identity and led returning Mexican-American veterans to form organizations such as the American G.I. Forum to press for equal rights in the future.

A tragic counterpoint to the voluntary movement of American workers in search of jobs was the forced relocation of 120,000 Japanese-Americans from the West Coast. Responding to racial fears in California after Pearl Harbor, President Roosevelt approved an Army order in February 1942 to move all Japanese-Americans on the West Coast to concentration camps in the interior. More than two-thirds of those detained were *Nisei*, native-born Americans whose only crime was their Japanese ancestry. Forced to sell their farms and businesses at distress prices, the Japanese-Americans lost not only their liberty but also most of their worldly goods. Herded into ten hastily built detention centers in seven western and southern states, they lived as prisoners in tar-papered barracks behind barbed wire, guarded by armed troops.

Appeals to the Supreme Court proved fruitless; in 1944, six justices upheld relocation on grounds of national security in wartime. Beginning in 1943, individual Nisei could win release by pledging their loyalty and finding a job away from the West Coast. Some 35,000 left the camps during the next two years, including over 13,000 who joined the armed forces. The all-Nisei 442nd Combat Team served gallantly in the European theater, losing over five hundred men in battle and winning more than one thousand citations for bravery. One World War II veteran remembers that when his unit was in trouble, the commander would issue a familiar appeal, "Call in the Japs."

For other Nisei, the experience was bitter. More than five thousand renounced their American citizenship and chose to live in Japan at the war's end. The government did not close down the last detention center until March 1946. Japanese-Americans never experienced the torture and mass death of the German concentration camps, but their treatment was a disgrace to a nation fighting for freedom and democracy. Finally in

A bewildered nisei toddler, tagged like a piece of luggage and guarded by a GI, waits to be taken to a detention camp.

1988, Congress voted an indemnity of $1.2 billion for the estimated 60,000 surviving Japanese-Americans detained during World War II. Susumi Emori, who had been moved with his wife and four children from his farm in Stockton, California to a camp in Arkansas, felt vindicated. "It was terrible," he said, with tears in his eyes," but it was a time of war. Anything can happen. I didn't blame the United States for that."

Win-the-War Politics

Franklin Roosevelt used World War II to strengthen his leadership and maintain Democratic political dominance. As war brought about prosperity and removed the economic discontent that had sustained the New Deal, FDR announced that "Dr. New Deal" had given way to "Dr. Win-the-War." Congress, already controlled by a conservative coalition of southern Democrats and northern Republicans, had almost slipped into GOP hands in 1942. With a very low voter turnout, due in part to the large numbers of men in service and uprooted workers who failed to meet residency requirements for voting, the Republicans won forty-four new seats in the House and nine in the Senate and elected governors in New York and California as well.

The Election of 1944			
Candidate	Party	Popular Vote	Electoral Vote
Roosevelt	Democrat	25,611,936	432
Dewey	Republican	22,013,372	99

In 1944, Roosevelt responded to the Democratic slippage by dropping Henry Wallace, his liberal and visionary vice-president, for Harry Truman, a moderate and down-to-earth Missouri senator who was acceptable to all factions of the Democratic party. Equally important, FDR received increased political support from organized labor, which had grown in membership during the war from ten to fifteen million. The newly organized Political Action Committee (PAC) of the CIO, headed by Sidney Hillman, conducted massive door-to-door drives to register millions of workers and their families.

The Republicans nominated Thomas E. Dewey, who had been elected governor of New York after gaining fame as a prosecutor of organized crime. Dewey, moderate in his views, played down opposition to the New Deal and instead tried to make Roosevelt's age and health the primary issues, along with the charge that the Democrats were soft on communism.

Despite his abrasive campaign style, Dewey did not advocate a return to isolationism. The Republican party was trying hard to shake the obstructionist image it had gained during the League of Nations fight in 1919; it went on record in 1943 as favoring American postwar cooperation for world peace. Indeed, Dewey pioneered a bipartisan approach to foreign policy. He accepted wartime planning for the future United Nations and kept the issue of an international organization out of the campaign.

Reacting to the issues of his age and health, especially after a long bout with influenza in the spring, FDR disregarded the advice of his doctors and took a five-hour, rain-soaked drive through the streets of New York City in an open car just before the election. His vitality impressed the voters, and in November 1944 he swept back into office for a fourth term, although the margin of 3.6 million votes was his smallest yet. The campaign, however, had taken its toll. The President,

suffering from high blood pressure and congestive heart failure, had only a few months left to lead the nation.

VICTORY

World War II ended with surprising swiftness. By 1943, the Axis tide had been turned in Europe and Asia, and it did not take long for Russia, the United States, and England to mount the offensives that drove Germany and Japan back across the vast areas they had conquered and set the stage for their final defeat.

The long-awaited second front finally came on June 6, 1944. For two years, the United States and England concentrated on building up an invasion force of nearly three million troops and a vast armada of ships and landing craft to carry them across the English Channel. In hopes of catching Hitler by surprise, Eisenhower chose the Normandy peninsula, where the absence of good harbors had led to lighter German fortifications. Allied aircraft bombed the roads, bridges, and rail lines of northern France for six weeks preceding the assault in order to block the movement of German reinforcements once the invasion began.

D-day was originally set for June 5, but bad weather forced a delay. Relying on a forecasted break in the storm, Eisenhower gambled on going ahead on June 6. During the night, three divisions parachuted down behind the German defenses; at dawn, the British and American troops fought their way ashore at five points along a sixty-mile stretch of beach, encountering stiff German resistance at several points. By the end of the day, however, Eisenhower had won his beachhead; a week later, more than one-third of a million men were slowly pushing back the German forces through the hedgerows of Normandy. The breakthrough came on July 25 when General Omar Bradley decimated the enemy with a massive artillery and aerial bombardment at Saint-Lô, opening a gap for General George Patton's Third Army. American tanks raced across the French countryside, trapping thousands of Germans and liberating Paris by August 25. Allied troops reached the Rhine River by September, but a shortage of supplies, especially gasoline, forced a three-month halt.

Hitler took advantage of this breathing spell to

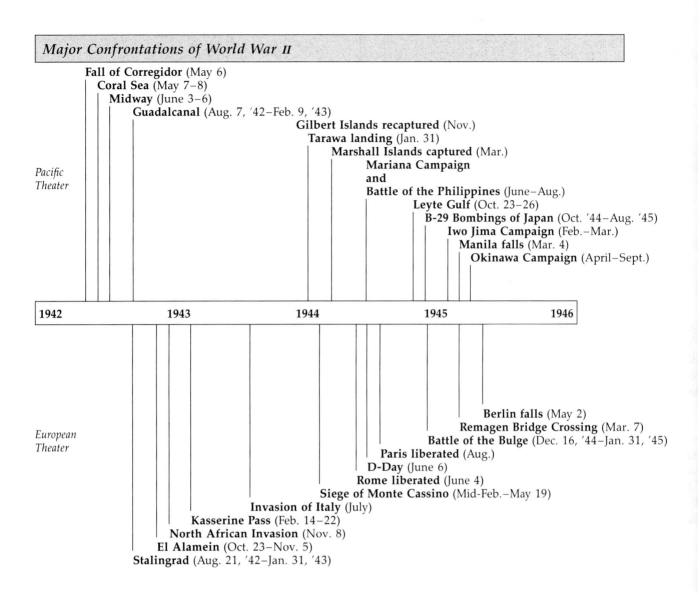

Major Confrontations of World War II

Pacific Theater

Fall of Corregidor (May 6)
Coral Sea (May 7–8)
Midway (June 3–6)
Guadalcanal (Aug. 7, '42–Feb. 9, '43)
Gilbert Islands recaptured (Nov.)
Tarawa landing (Jan. 31)
Marshall Islands captured (Mar.)
Mariana Campaign
and
Battle of the Philippines (June–Aug.)
Leyte Gulf (Oct. 23–26)
B-29 Bombings of Japan (Oct. '44–Aug. '45)
Iwo Jima Campaign (Feb.–Mar.)
Manila falls (Mar. 4)
Okinawa Campaign (April–Sept.)

1942 1943 1944 1945 1946

European Theater

Berlin falls (May 2)
Remagen Bridge Crossing (Mar. 7)
Battle of the Bulge (Dec. 16, '44–Jan. 31, '45)
Paris liberated (Aug.)
D-Day (June 6)
Rome liberated (June 4)
Siege of Monte Cassino (Mid-Feb.–May 19)
Invasion of Italy (July)
Kasserine Pass (Feb. 14–22)
North African Invasion (Nov. 8)
El Alamein (Oct. 23–Nov. 5)
Stalingrad (Aug. 21, '42–Jan. 31, '43)

deliver a daring counterattack. In mid-December, the remaining German armored divisions burst through a weak point in the Allied lines in the Ardennes Forest, planning a breakout to the coast that would have cut off nearly one-third of Eisenhower's forces. A combination of tactical surprise and bad weather, which prevented Allied air support, led to a huge bulge in the American lines. But an airborne division dug in at the key crossroads of Bastogne, in Belgium, and held off a much larger German force. Allied reinforcements and clearing weather then combined to end the attack. By committing nearly all his reserves to the Battle of the Bulge, Hitler had delayed Eisenhower's advance into Germany, but he also had

fatally weakened German resistance in the West.

The end came quickly. A massive Russian offensive began in mid-January and swept across the Oder River toward Berlin. General Bradley's troops, finding a bridge left virtually intact by the retreating Germans, crossed the Rhine on March 7. Eisenhower overruled the British, who favored one concentrated drive on Berlin. Instead the Allied forces advanced on a broad front, capturing the industrial Ruhr basin and meeting the Russians at the Elbe by the last week in April. With the Red Army already in the suburbs of Berlin, Adolf Hitler committed suicide on April 30. A week later, on May 7, 1945, Eisenhower accepted the unconditional surrender of all

German forces. Just eleven months and a day after the landings in Normandy, the Allied forces had brought the war in Europe to a successful conclusion.

War Aims and Wartime Diplomacy

The American contribution to Hitler's defeat was relatively minor compared to the damage inflicted by the Soviet Union. At the height of the German invasion of Russia, more than 300 Soviet divisions had been locked in battle with 250 German ones, a striking contrast to the 58 divisions the United States and Britain used in the Normandy invasion. As his armies overran Poland and the Balkan countries, Joseph Stalin was determined to retain control over this region, which had been the historic pathway for Western invasion into Russia. Delay in opening the second front and an innate distrust of the West convinced the Soviets that they should maximize their territorial gains by imposing Communist regimes on Eastern Europe.

American postwar goals were quite different. Now believing that the failure to join the League of Nations in 1919 had led to the coming of World War II, the American people and their

The nation's grief at FDR's death is mirrored in the face of this serviceman as the President's funeral cortege passes.

leaders vowed to put their faith in a new attempt at collective security. At Moscow in 1943, Secretary of State Cordell Hull had won Russian agreement to participate in a future world organization at the war's end. The first wartime Big Three conference brought together Roosevelt, Churchill, and Stalin at Teheran, Iran, in late 1943. Stalin reaffirmed this commitment and also indicated to President Roosevelt that Russia would enter the war against Japan once Germany was defeated.

By the time the Big Three met again at Yalta, in February 1945, the military situation favored the Russians. While British and American forces were still recovering from the Battle of the Bulge, the Red Army was advancing to within fifty miles of Berlin. Stalin drove a series of hard bargains. He refused to give up his plans for Communist domination of Poland and the Balkans, although he did agree to Roosevelt's request for a Declaration of Liberated Europe, which called for free elections without providing for any method of enforcement or supervision. More important for the United States, Stalin promised to enter the Pacific war three months after Germany surrendered. In return, Roosevelt offered extensive concessions in Asia, including Russian control over Manchuria. While neither a sellout nor a betrayal, as some critics have charged, Yalta was a significant diplomatic victory for the Soviets—one that reflected Russia's major contribution to a victory in Europe.

For the President, the long journey to Yalta proved to be too much. His health continued to fail after his return to Washington. In early April, FDR left the capital for Warm Springs, Georgia, where he had always been able to relax. He was sitting for his portrait at midday on April 12, 1945, when he suddenly complained of a "terrific headache," then slumped forward and died.

The nation mourned a man who had gallantly met the challenge of depression and global war. Unfortunately, FDR had taken no steps to prepare his successor for the difficult problems that lay ahead. The defeat of Nazi Germany dissolved the one strong bond between the United States and the Soviet Union. With very different histories, cultures, and ideologies, the two nations were bound to drift apart. It was now up to the inexperienced Harry Truman to manage the growing rivalry that was destined to develop into the future cold war.

Triumph and Tragedy in the Pacific

The total defeat of Germany in May 1945 turned all eyes toward Japan. Although the Combined Chiefs of Staff had originally estimated that it would take eighteen months after Germany's surrender to conquer Japan, American forces moved with surprising speed. Admiral Nimitz swept through the Gilbert, Caroline, and Marshall islands in 1944, securing bases for further advances and building airfields for American B-29s to begin a deadly bombardment of the Japanese home islands. General MacArthur cleared New Guinea of the last Japanese defender in early 1944 and began planning his long-heralded return to the Philippines. American troops landed on the island of Leyte on October 20, 1944, and Manila fell by the end of the year. The Japanese navy, in a Pacific version of the Battle of the Bulge, launched a daring three-pronged attack on the American invasion fleet in Leyte Gulf. The U.S. Navy rallied to blunt all three Japanese thrusts, sinking four carriers and ending any further Japanese naval threat.

The defeat of Japan was now only a matter of time. The United States had three possible ways to proceed. The military favored a full-scale invasion, beginning on the southernmost island of Kyushu in November 1945 and culminating with an assault on Honshu (the main island of Japan) and a climactic battle for Tokyo in 1946; casualties were expected to run into the hundreds of thousands. Diplomats suggested a negotiated peace, urging that the United States modify the unconditional-surrender formula to permit Japan to retain the institution of the emperor. At Potsdam, Churchill and Truman did issue a call for surrender, warning Japan it faced utter destruction, but they made no mention of the emperor.

The third possibility involved the highly secret Manhattan Project. Since 1939, the United States had spent $2 billion to develop an atomic bomb based on the fission of radioactive uranium and plutonium. Scientists, many of them refugees from Europe, worked at the University of Chicago; Oak Ridge, Tennessee; Hanford, Washington; and a remote laboratory in Los Alamos, New Mexico, to perfect this deadly new weapon. In the New Mexico desert on July 16, 1945, they successfully tested the first atomic bomb, creating a fireball brighter than several suns and a telltale

mushroom cloud that rose some 40,000 feet above an enormous crater in the desert floor.

Informed of this achievement upon his arrival at Potsdam, President Truman authorized the army air force to use the atomic bomb against Japan. Truman had been unaware of the existence of the Manhattan Project before he became president on April 12. Now he simply followed the

These traumatized victims of the first A-bomb blast August 6, 1945, over Hiroshima are seeking first aid a few hours after the explosion.

recommendation of a committee headed by Secretary of War Henry L. Stimson to drop the bomb on a Japanese city. The committee discussed but rejected the possibility of inviting the Japanese to observe a demonstration shot at a remote Pacific site and even ruled out the idea of giving advance notice of the bomb's destructive power. Neither Truman nor Stimson had any qualms about the decision to drop the bomb without warning. They viewed it as a legitimate wartime measure, one designed to save the lives of hundreds of thousands of Americans—and Japanese—that would be lost in a full-scale invasion.

Weather conditions on the morning of August 6 dictated the choice of Hiroshima as the bomb's target. The explosion incinerated four square miles of the city, instantly killing more than sixty thousand. Two days later, Russia entered the war against Japan, and the next day, August 9, the United States dropped a second bomb on Nagasaki. There were no more atomic bombs available, but no more were needed. The emperor personally broke a deadlock in the Japanese cabinet and persuaded his ministers to surrender unconditionally on August 14, 1945. Three weeks later, Japan signed a formal capitulation agreement on the decks of the battleship *Missouri* in Tokyo Bay to bring World War II to its official close.

Many years later, scholars charged that Truman had more in mind than defeating Japan when he decided to use the atomic bomb. Citing Air Force and Naval officers who claimed Japan could be defeated by a blockade or by conventional air attacks, these revisionists suggested that the real reason for dropping the bomb was to impress the Soviet Union with the fact that the United States had exclusive possession of the ultimate weapon. The available evidence indicates that while Truman and his associates were aware of the possible effect on the Soviet Union, their primary motive was to end World War II as quickly and effortlessly as possible. The saving of American lives, along with a desire for revenge for Pearl Harbor, were uppermost in the decision to bomb Hiroshima and Nagasaki. Yet in using the atomic bomb to defeat Japan, the United States virtually guaranteed a postwar arms race with the Soviet Union.

The second great war of the twentieth century has had a lasting impact on American life. For the first time, the nation's military potential had been reached. In 1945, the United States was unquestionably the strongest country on the earth, with eleven million men and women in uniform, a vast array of shipyards, aircraft plants, and munitions factories in full production, and a monopoly over the atomic bomb. For better or worse, the nation was now launched on a global career. In the future, the United States would be involved in all parts of the world, from Western Europe to remote jungles in Asia, from the nearby Caribbean to the distant Persian Gulf. And despite its enormous strength in 1945, the nation's new world role would encompass failure and frustration as well as power and dominion.

The legacy of war was equally strong at home. Four years of fighting brought about industrial recovery and unparalleled prosperity. The old pattern of unregulated free enterprise was as much a victim of the war as of the New Deal; big government and huge deficits had now become the norm as economic control passed from New York and Wall Street to Washington and Pennsylvania Avenue. The war led to far-reaching changes in American society that would only become apparent decades later. Such distinctive patterns of recent American life as the baby boom and the growth of the Sunbelt can be traced back to wartime origins. The Second World War was a watershed in twentieth-century America, ushering in a new age of global concerns and domestic upheaval.

Recommended Reading

The best general account of American attitudes toward the world in the 1920s can be found in Warren I. Cohen, *Empire Without Tears* (1987). Robert Dallek provides a thorough account of FDR's diplomacy in *Franklin D. Roosevelt and American Foreign Policy, 1932–1945* (1979). For a more critical view, see Robert A. Divine, *Roosevelt and World War II* (1969).

Two good books on the continuing controversy over Pearl Harbor are Roberta Wohlstetter, *Pearl Harbor: Warning and Decision* (1962), and Gordon W. Prange, *At Dawn We Slept* (1981). Both authors deny the charge that Roosevelt deliberately exposed the naval base to attack.

In his brief overview of wartime diplomacy, *American Diplomacy During the Second World War*, 2nd ed. (1985), Gaddis Smith stresses the tensions within the victorious coalition. The two best accounts of the home front are Richard Polenberg, *War and Society* (1972) and John W. Blum, *V Was for Victory* (1976).

Additional Bibliography

On American foreign policy in the period between the wars, see Selig Adler, *The Isolationist Impulse* (1957); Arnold A. Offner, *The Origins of the Second World War* (1975); Robert H. Ferrell, *Peace in Their Time* (1952); Charles Chatfield, *For Peace and Justice* (1971); Charles DeBenedetti, *Origins of the Modern American Peace Movement, 1915–1929* (1978); Michael J. Hogan, *Informal Entente* (1977); Melvin P. Leffler, *The Elusive Quest* (1978); Akira Iriye, *After Imperialism* (1965); Roger Dingman, *Power in the Pacific* (1976); Thomas H. Buckley, *The United States and the Washington Conference, 1921–1922* (1970); and Robert F. Smith, *The United States and Revolutionary Nationalism in Mexico, 1916–1932* (1972).

For foreign policy during the Hoover years, see Robert H. Ferrell, *American Diplomacy in the Great Depression* (1957); Alexander DeConde, *Herbert Hoover's Latin American Policy* (1951); and Armin Rappaport, *Henry L. Stimson and Japan* (1963). Diplomatic developments in the 1930s under FDR are covered in Dorothy Borg, *The United States and the Far Eastern Crisis of 1933–1938* (1964); Stephen E. Pelz, *Race to Pearl Harbor* (1974); Bryce Wood, *The Making of the Good Neighbor Policy* (1961); Irwin F. Gellman, *Good Neighbor Diplomacy* (1979); Dick Steward, *Trade and Hemisphere* (1979); Manfred Jonas, *Isolationism in America, 1935–1941* (1966); Robert A. Divine, *The Illusion of Neutrality* (1962); and Wayne S. Cole, *Senator Gerald Nye and American Foreign Relations* (1963).

Examinations of Roosevelt's policies during World War II include Robert Sherwood, *Roosevelt and Hopkins* (1948); James M. Burns, *Roosevelt: Soldier of Freedom* (1970); and Wayne S. Cole, *Roosevelt and the Isolationists* (1983). For details of the American entry into the war; see William L. Langer and S. Everett Gleason, *The Challenge to Isolation* (1950) and *The Undeclared War* (1953); Robert A. Divine, *The Reluctant Belligerent*, 2nd ed. (1979); Bruce Russett, *No Clear and Present Danger* (1972); Wayne S. Cole, *America First* (1953); Warren F. Kimball, *The Most Unsordid Act: Lend-Lease, 1939–1941* (1969); David Reynolds, *The Creation of the Anglo-American Alliance, 1937–1941* (1982); Saul Friedlander, *Prelude to Downfall: Hitler and the United States* (1967); Waldo Heinrichs, *Threshold of War* (1988); Patrick J. Hearden, *Roosevelt Confronts Hitler* (1987); Herbert Feis, *The Road to Pearl Harbor* (1950); Paul W. Schroeder, *The Axis Alliance and Japanese-American Relations: 1941* (1958); Jonathan Utley, *Going to War with Japan, 1937–1941* (1985); Akira Iriye, *The Origins of the Second World War in Asia and the Pacific* (1987); Dorothy Borg and Shumpei Okamoto, eds., *Pearl Harbor as History* (1973); and Harry Elmer Barnes, ed., *Perpetual War for Perpetual Peace* (1953).

Military and strategic aspects of World War II are covered in A. Russell Buchanan, *The United States and World War II*, 2 vols. (1964); Chester Wilmot, *The Struggle for Europe* (1952); Eric Larrabee, *Commander in Chief: Franklin Delano Roosevelt, His Lieutenants, Their War* (1987); John Dower, *War Without Mercy: Race and Power in the Pacific War* (1986); Michael Sherry, *The Rise of American Air Power* (1987); David Eisenhower, *Eisenhower: At War, 1943–1945* (1986); Kent Roberts Greenfield, *American Strategy in World War II* (1963); and Mark A. Stoler, *The Politics of the Second Front, 1941–1943* (1977). For wartime diplomacy, see Herbert Feis, *Churchill, Roosevelt and Stalin* (1957); William H. McNeill, *America, Britain, and Russia, 1941–1946* (1953); Michael Schaller, *The U.S. Crusade in China, 1936–1945* (1979); Akira Iriye, *Power and Culture* (1981); Julian G. Hurstfield, *America and the French Nation, 1939–1945* (1986); Russell Buhite, *Decision at Yalta* (1986); Diane Clemens, *Yalta* (1970); Ralph B. Levering, *American Opinion and the Russian Alliance, 1939–1945* (1976); and Warren F. Kimball, ed., *Churchill and Roosevelt: The Complete Correspondence*, 3 vols. (1984).

On the atomic bomb, see Richard G. Hewlett and Oscar E. Anderson, *The New World, 1939–1946* (1962); Richard Rhodes, *The Making of the Atomic Bomb* (1987); Gar Alperovitz, *Atomic Diplomacy* (1965); Martin Sherwin, *A World Destroyed* (1975); Herbert Feis, *The Atomic Bomb and the End of World War II* (1966); and Robert J. C. Butow, *Japan's Decision to Surrender* (1954). Social developments during World War II are examined in Roger Daniels, *Concentration Camps, USA* (1971); Peter Irons, *Justice at War* (1984); Karen Anderson, *Wartime Women* (1981); Susan Hartmann, *The Home Front and Beyond* (1982); Ruth Milkman, *Gender at Work* (1987); Sherna Berger Gluck, *Rosie the Riveter Revisited* (1987); Neil A. Wynn, *The Afro-Americans and the Second World War* (1976); and Mauricio Mazon, *The Zoot-Suit Riots* (1984). Harold G. Vatter surveys wartime economic trends in *The U.S. Economy in World War II* (1986).

The American relationship to the Holocaust can be traced in David Wyman, *The Abandonment of the Jews* (1985); Monty M. Penkower, *The Jews Were Expendable* (1983); and Robert Abzug, *Inside the Vicious Heart* (1985). For a realistic assessment of the brutality of World War II, see Paul Fussell, *Wartime* (1989).

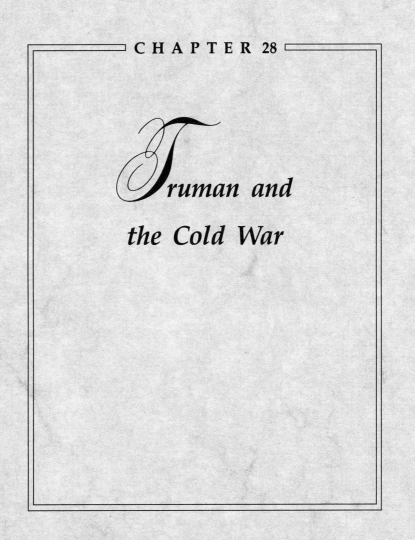

CHAPTER 28

*Truman and
the Cold War*

*A*am getting ready to go see Stalin and Churchill," President Truman wrote to his mother in July 1945, "and it is a chore." On board the cruiser *Augusta*, the new President continued to complain about the upcoming Potsdam Conference in his diary. "How I hate this trip!" he confided. "But I have to make it win, lose or draw and we must win. I am giving nothing away except to save starving people and even then I hope we can only help them to help themselves."

Halfway around the world, Joseph Stalin left Moscow a day late because of a slight heart attack. The Russian leader hated to fly, so he traveled by rail. Moreover, he ordered the heavily guarded train to detour around Poland for fear of an ambush, further delaying his arrival. When he made his entrance into Potsdam, a suburb of Berlin miraculously spared the total destruction that his forces had created in the German capital, he was ready to claim the spoils of war.

These two men, one the veteran revolutionary who had been in power for two decades, the other an untested leader in office for barely three months, symbolized the enormous differences that now separated the wartime allies. Stalin was above all a realist. Brutal in securing total control at home, he was more flexible in his foreign policy, bent on exploiting Russia's victory in World War II rather than aiming at world domination. Cunning and caution were the hallmarks of his diplomatic style. Small in stature, ungainly in build, he radiated a catlike quality as he waited behind his unassuming facade, ready to dazzle an opponent with his "brilliant, terrifying tactical mastery." Truman, in contrast, personified traditional Wilsonian idealism. Lacking Roosevelt's guile, the new President placed his faith in international cooperation. Like many Americans, he believed implicitly in his country's innate goodness. Self-assured to the point of cockiness, he came to Potsdam clothed in the armor of self-righteousness.

Truman and Stalin met for the first time on July 17, 1945. "I told Stalin that I am no diplomat," the President recorded in his diary, "but usually said yes and no to questions after hearing all the argument." The Russian dictator's reaction to Truman remains a mystery, but Truman felt that

President Truman, Churchill, and Stalin relax in the palace garden before the meeting at Potsdam, July 25, 1945. The conference revealed the growing divergence among the wartime allies that soon led to the onset of the Cold War.

the first encounter went well. "I can deal with Stalin," he wrote. "He is honest—but smart as hell."

Together with Winston Churchill and his replacement, Clement Attlee, whose Labour party had just triumphed in British elections, Truman and Stalin clashed for the next ten days over such difficult issues as reparations, the Polish border, and the fate of Eastern Europe. Truman presented the ideas and proposals formulated by his advisers; he saw his task as essentially procedural, and when he presided, he moved the agenda along in brisk fashion. After he had "banged through" three items one day, he commented, "I am not going to stay around this terrible place all summer, just to listen to speeches. I'll go home to the Senate for that." In an indirect, roundabout way, he informed Stalin of the existence of the atomic bomb, tested successfully in the New Mexico desert just before the conference began. Truman offered no details, and the impassive Stalin asked for none, commenting only that he hoped the United States would make "good use of it against the Japanese."

Reparations proved to be the crucial issue at Potsdam. The Russians wanted to rebuild their war-ravaged economy with German industry; the United States feared it would be saddled with the entire cost of caring for the defeated Germans. A compromise was finally reached. Each side would take reparations primarily from its own occupation zone, a solution that foreshadowed the future division of Germany. "Because they could not agree on how to govern Europe," wrote historian Daniel Yergin, "Truman and Stalin began to divide it." The other issues were referred to the newly created Council of Foreign Ministers, which would meet in the fall in London.

The conference thus ended on an apparent note of harmony; beneath the surface, however, the bitter antagonism of the Cold War was festering. America and Russia, each distrustful of the other, were preparing for a long and bitter confrontation. A dozen years later, Truman reminisced to an old associate about Potsdam. "What a show that was!" Describing himself as "an innocent idealist" surrounded by wolves, he claimed that all the agreements reached there were "broken as soon as the unconscionable Russian Dictator returned to Moscow!" He added ruefully, "And I liked the little son of a bitch."

THE COLD WAR BEGINS

The conflict between the United States and the Soviet Union began gradually. For two years, the nations tried to adjust their differences over the division of Europe, postwar economic aid, and the atomic bomb through discussion and negotiation. The Council of Foreign Ministers provided the forum. Beginning in London during the fall of 1945 and meeting with their Russian counterparts in Paris, New York, and Moscow, American diplomats searched for a way to live in peace with a suspicious Soviet Union.

The Division of Europe

The fundamental disagreement was over who would control postwar Europe. In the east, the Red Army had swept over Poland and the Balkans, laying the basis for Soviet domination there. American and British forces had liberated Western Europe from Scandinavia to Italy. The Russians, mindful of past invasions from the west across the plains of Poland, were intent on imposing Communist governments loyal to Moscow in the Soviet sphere. The United States, on the other hand, upheld the principle of national self-determination, insisting that the people in each country should freely choose their postwar rulers. The Soviets saw this demand for free elections as subversive, since they knew that popularly chosen regimes would be unfriendly to Russia. Suspecting American duplicity, Stalin brought down an "Iron Curtain" (Churchill's phrase) from the Baltic to the Adriatic as he created a series of satellite governments.

Germany was the key. The temporary zones of occupation gradually hardened into permanent lines of division. Ignoring the Potsdam Conference agreement that the country be treated as an economic unit, the United States and Great Britain were by 1946 refusing to permit the Russians to take reparations from the industrial western zones. The initial harsh occupation policy gave way to more humane treatment of the German people and a slow but steady economic recovery. The United States and England merged their zones and championed the idea of the unification of all Germany. Russia, fearing a resurgence of German military power, responded by intensify-

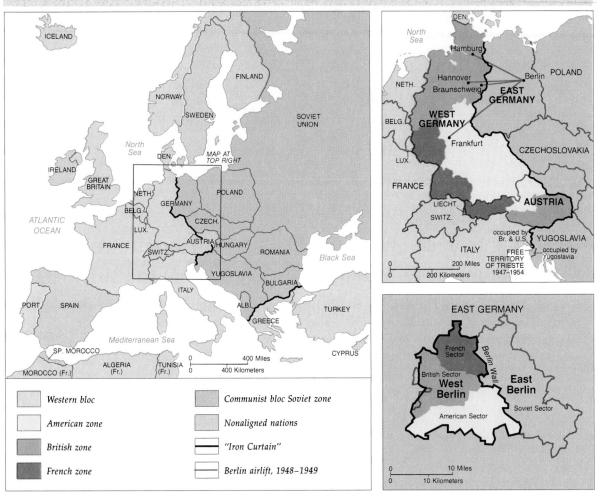

Europe After World War II

The heavy black line splitting Germany shows in graphic form the division of Europe between the Western and Soviet spheres of influence. The two power blocs faced each other across an "iron curtain."

Legend:

- Western bloc
- American zone
- British zone
- French zone
- Communist bloc Soviet zone
- Nonaligned nations
- "Iron Curtain"
- Berlin airlift, 1948–1949

ing the communization of its zone, which included the jointly occupied city of Berlin. By 1947, England, France, and the United States were laying plans to transfer their authority to an independent West Germany.

The Soviet Union consolidated its grip on Eastern Europe in 1946 and 1947. One by one, Communist regimes replaced coalition governments in Poland, Hungary, Rumania, and Bulgaria. Moving cautiously to avoid provoking the West, Stalin used communism as a means to dominate half of Europe, both to protect the security of the Soviet state and to advance its international power. The climax came in March 1948 when a coup in Czechoslovakia overthrew a democratic government and gave the Soviets a strategic foothold in Central Europe.

The division of Europe was an inevitable after-effect of World War II. Both sides were intent on imposing their values in the areas liberated by their troops. The Russians were no more likely to withdraw from Eastern Europe than the United States and Britain were from Germany, France, and Italy. A frank recognition of competing spheres of influence might have avoided further escalation of tension. But the Western nations, remembering Hitler's aggression in the 1930s, began to see Stalin as an equally dangerous threat to their well-being. Instead of accepting him as a cautious leader bent on protecting Russian security, they perceived him as an aggressive dictator leading a Communist drive for world domination.

Withholding Economic Aid

The Second World War had inflicted enormous damage on Russia. The brutal fighting had taken between fifteen and twenty million Russian lives, destroyed over thirty thousand factories, and torn up 40,000 miles of railroad track. The industrialization that Stalin had achieved at such great sacrifice in the 1930s had been badly set back; even agricultural production had fallen by half during the war. Outside aid and assistance were vital for the reconstruction of the Soviet Union.

American leaders knew of Russia's plight and hoped to use it to good advantage. Wartime ambassador Averell Harriman wrote in 1944 that economic aid was "one of the most effective weapons at our disposal" in dealing with Russia. President Truman was convinced that economically "we held all the cards and the Russians had to come to us."

There were two possible forms of postwar assistance: loans and lend-lease. In January 1945, the Soviets requested a $6 billion loan to finance postwar reconstruction. Despite initial American encouragement, President Roosevelt deferred action on this request; as relations with Russia cooled, the chances for action dimmed. "Our experience," commented Harriman in April 1945, had "incontrovertibly proved it was not possible to bank goodwill in Moscow." By the war's end, the loan request, though never formally turned down, was dead.

Lend-lease proved no more successful. In the spring of 1945, Congress instructed the administration not to use lend-lease for postwar reconstruction. President Truman went further, however, by signing an order on May 11, 1945, terminating all shipments to Russia, including those already at sea. The State Department saw the action as applying "leverage against the Soviet Union"; Stalin termed it "brutal." Heeding Russian protests, Truman resumed lend-lease shipments, but only until the war was over in August. After that, all lend-lease ended.

Deprived of American assistance, the Russians were forced to rebuild their economy through reparations. American and British resistance prevented them from taking reparations in Western Germany, but the Soviets systematically removed factories and plants from other areas they controlled, including their zone of Germany, Eastern Europe, and Manchuria. Slowly the Russian economy recovered from the war, but the bitterness over the American refusal to extend aid convinced Stalin of Western hostility and thus deepened the growing antagonism between the Soviet Union and the United States.

The Atomic Dilemma

Overshadowing all else was the atomic bomb. Used by the United States with deadly success at Hiroshima and Nagasaki, the new weapon raised problems that would have been difficult for even friendly nations to resolve. Given the uneasy state of Soviet-American relations, the effect was disastrous.

The wartime policy followed by Roosevelt and Churchill ensured a postwar nuclear arms race. Instead of informing their major ally of the developing atomic bomb, they kept it a closely guarded secret. Stalin learned of the Manhattan Project through espionage and responded by starting a Soviet atomic program in 1943. By the time Truman informed Stalin of the weapon's existence at Potsdam, the Russians were well on the way to making their own bomb.

After the war, the United States developed a disarmament plan that would turn control of fissionable material, then the processing plants, and ultimately the American stockpile of bombs over to an international agency. When President Truman appointed financier Bernard Baruch to present this proposal to the United Nations, Baruch insisted on changing it in several important ways, adding sanctions against violators and exempting the international agency from the UN veto. Ignoring scientists who pleaded for a more cooperative position, Baruch followed instead the advice of Army Chief of Staff Dwight D. Eisenhower, who cited the rapid demobilization of American armed forces (from nearly 12 million in 1945 to less than 2 million in 1947) to argue that "we cannot at this time limit our capability to produce or use this weapon." In effect, the Baruch Plan, with its multiple stages and emphasis on inspection, would preserve the American atomic monopoly for the indefinite future.

The Soviets responded predictably. Diplomat Andrei Gromyko presented a simple plan calling for a total ban on the production and use of the new weapon as well as the destruction of all existing bombs. The Russian proposal was founded on the same perception of national self-interest as the Baruch Plan. Though Russia had also demobilized rapidly, it still had nearly three million men under arms in 1947 and wished to use its conventional strength to the utmost by outlawing the atomic bomb.

No agreement was possible. Neither the United States nor the Soviet Union could abandon its position without surrendering a vital national interest. Wanting to preserve its monopoly, America stressed inspection and control; hoping to neutralize the U.S. advantage, Russia advocated immediate disarmament. The nuclear dilemma, inherent in the Soviet-American rivalry, blocked any national settlement. Instead, the two superpowers agreed to disagree. Trusting neither each other nor any form of international cooperation, each concentrated on taking maximum advantage of its wartime gains. Thus the Russians exploited the territory they had conquered in Europe while the United States retained its economic and strategic advantages over the Soviet Union. The result was the Cold War.

CONTAINMENT

A major departure in American foreign policy occurred in January 1947 when General George C. Marshall, the wartime army chief of staff, became secretary of state. Calm, mature, and orderly of mind, Marshall had the capability—honed in World War II—to think in broad, strategic terms. An extraordinarily good judge of ability, he relied on gifted subordinates to handle the day-to-day implementation of his policies. In the months after taking office, he came to rely on two men in particular: Dean Acheson and George Kennan.

Acheson, an experienced Washington lawyer and bureaucrat, was appointed undersecretary of state and given free rein by Marshall to conduct American diplomacy. In appearance, he seemed more British than American, with his impeccable Ivy League clothes and bushy mustache. A man of keen intelligence, he had a carefully cultivated reputation for arrogance and a low tolerance for mediocrity. As an ardent Anglophile, he wanted to see the United States take over a faltering Britain's role as the supreme arbiter of world affairs. Recalling the lesson of Munich, he opposed appeasement and advocated a policy of negotiating only from strength.

Marshall's other mainstay was George Kennan, who headed the newly created Policy Planning Staff. A career foreign-service officer, Kennan had become a Soviet expert, mastering Russian history and culture as well as speaking the language fluently. He served in Moscow after U.S. recognition in 1933 and again during World War II, developing there a profound distrust for the Soviet regime. In a crucial telegram in 1946, he warned that the Kremlin believed "that there can be no compromise with rival power" and advocated a policy of containment, arguing that only strong and sustained resistance could halt the outward flow of Russian power. As self-assured as Acheson, Kennan believed that neither Congress nor public opinion should interfere with the conduct of foreign policy by the experts.

In the spring of 1947, a sense of crisis impelled Marshall, Acheson, and Kennan to set out on a new course in American diplomacy. Dubbed "containment," after an article by Kennan in *Foreign Affairs*, the new policy both consolidated the evolving postwar anticommunism and established guidelines that would shape America's role in the world for more than two decades. What Kennan proposed was "a long-term, patient but firm, and vigilant containment of Russian expansive tendencies." Such a policy of halting Soviet aggression would not lead to any immediate victory, Kennan warned. In the long run, however, he felt that the United States could force the Soviet Union to adopt more reasonable policies and live in peace with the United States.

The Truman Doctrine

The initial step toward containment came in response to an urgent British request. Since March 1946, England had been supporting the Greek government in a bitter civil war against

Communist guerrillas. On February 21, 1947, the British informed the United States that they could no longer afford to aid Greece or Turkey, the latter under heavy pressure from the Soviets for access to the Mediterranean. Believing that the Russians were responsible for the strife in Greece (in fact, they were not), Marshall, Acheson, and Kennan quickly decided that the United States would have to take over Britain's role in the eastern Mediterranean.

Worried about congressional support, especially since the Republicans had gained control of Congress in 1946, Marshall called a meeting with the legislative leadership in late February. He outlined the problem, and then Acheson took over to describe "a highly possible Soviet breakthrough" that "might open three continents to Soviet penetration." Comparing the situation in Greece to one rotten apple spoiling an entire barrel, Acheson warned that "the corruption of Greece would infect Iran and all to the east. It would also carry infection to Africa through Asia Minor and Egypt, and to Europe through Italy and France." Claiming that the Soviets were "playing one of the greatest gambles in history," Acheson concluded that "we and we alone were in a position to break up the play."

The bipartisan group of congressional leaders was deeply impressed. Finally, Republican Senator Arthur M. Vandenberg spoke up, saying he would support the President, but adding that to ensure public backing, Truman would have to "scare hell" out of the American people.

The President followed the senator's advice. On March 12, 1947, he asked Congress for $400 million for military and economic assistance to Greece and Turkey. In stating what would become known as the Truman Doctrine, he made clear that more was involved than just these two countries—the stakes in fact were far higher. "It must be the policy of the United States," Truman told the Congress, "to support free peoples who are resisting attempted subjugation by armed minorities or by outside pressure." After a brief debate, both the House and the Senate approved the program by margins of better than three to one.

The Truman Doctrine marked an informal declaration of cold war against the Soviet Union. Truman used the crisis in Greece to secure congressional approval and build a national consen-

*C*ritics expressed doubts about the Truman Doctrine, as in this cartoon, but the national mood was shifting toward approval of the containment policy.

sus for the policy of containment. In less than two years, the civil war in Greece ended, but the American commitment to oppose Communist expansion, whether by internal subversion or external aggression, placed the United States on a collision course with the Soviet Union around the globe.

The Marshall Plan

Despite American interest in controlling Soviet expansion into Greece, Western Europe was far more vital to U.S. interests than was the eastern Mediterranean. Yet by 1947 many Americans felt that Western Europe was open to Soviet penetration. The problem was economic in nature. Despite $9 billion in piecemeal American loans, England, France, Italy, and the other European countries had great difficulty in recovering from World War II. Food was scarce, with millions existing on less than fifteen hundred calories a day; industrial machinery was broken down and obsolete; and workers were demoralized by years of depression and war. The cruel winter of 1947, the worst in fifty years, compounded the problem. Resentment and discontent led to growing

A Greek Orthodox priest blesses a much-needed truckload of American flour brought to Athens under the Marshall Plan. The plan was an economic, social, and political success, creating an enormous reservoir of European goodwill toward the United States.

Communist voting strength, especially in Italy and France. If the United States could not reverse the process, it seemed as though all Europe might drift into the Communist orbit.

In the weeks following proclamation of the Truman Doctrine, American officials dealt with this problem. Secretary of State Marshall, returning from a frustrating Council of Foreign Ministers meeting in Moscow, warned that "the patient is sinking while the doctors deliberate." Acheson believed that it was time to extend American "economic power" in Europe both "to call an effective halt to the Soviet Union's expansionism" and "to create a basis for political stability and economic well-being." The experts drew up a plan for the massive infusion of American capital to finance the economic recovery of Europe. Speaking at a Harvard commencement on June 5, 1947, Marshall presented the broad outline. He offered extensive economic aid to all the nations of Europe if they could reach agreement on ways to achieve "the revival of a working economy in the world so as to permit the emergence of political and social conditions in which free institutions can exist."

The fate of the Marshall Plan depended on the reaction of the Soviet Union and the U.S. Congress. Marshall had taken, in the words of one American diplomat, "a hell of a gamble" by including Russia in his offer of aid. At a meeting of the European nations in Paris in July 1947, the Soviet foreign minister ended the suspense by abruptly withdrawing. Neither the Soviet Union nor its satellites would take part, apparently because Moscow saw the Marshall Plan as an American attempt to weaken Soviet control over Eastern Europe. The other European countries then made a formal request for $17 billion in assistance over the next four years.

Congress responded cautiously to this proposal, appointing a special joint committee to investigate. The administration lobbied vigorously, pointing out that the Marshall Plan would help the United States by stimulating trade with Europe as well as checking Soviet expansion. It was the latter argument, however, that proved decisive. When the Czech coup touched off a war scare in March 1948, Congress quickly approved the Marshall Plan by heavy majorities. Over the next four years, the huge American investment paid rich dividends, generating a broad industrial revival in Western Europe that became self-sustaining by the 1950s. The threat of Communist domination faded, and a prosperous Europe proved to be a bonanza for American farmers, miners, and manufacturers.

The Western Military Alliance

The third and final phase of containment came in 1949 with the establishment of the North Atlantic Treaty Organization (NATO). NATO grew out of European fears of Russian military aggression. Recalling Hitler's tactics in the 1930s, the people of Western Europe wanted assurance that the United States would protect them from attack as they began to achieve economic recovery. American diplomats were sympathetic. "People could not go ahead and make investments for the future," commented Averell Harriman, "without some sense of security."

England, France, and the Low Countries (Belgium, the Netherlands, and Luxembourg) began the process in March 1948 when they signed the Brussels Treaty, providing for collective self-defense. In January 1949, President Truman called for a broader defense pact including the United States; ten European nations, from Norway in the north to Italy in the south, joined the United States and Canada in signing the North Atlantic Treaty in Washington on April 4, 1949. This historic departure from the traditional policy of isolation—the United States had not signed such a treaty since the French alliance in the eighteenth century—caused extensive debate, but the Senate ratified it in July by a vote of 82 to 13.

There were two main features of NATO. First, the United States committed itself to the defense of Europe in the key clause which stated that "an armed attack against one or more shall be considered an attack against them all." In effect, the United States was extending its atomic shield over Europe. The second feature was designed to reassure worried Europeans that the United States would honor this commitment. In late 1950, President Truman appointed General Dwight D. Eisenhower to the post of NATO supreme commander and authorized the stationing of four American divisions in Europe to serve as the nucleus of the NATO army. The threat of American troop involvement in any Russian assault would deter the Soviet Union from making such an attack.

The Western military alliance escalated the developing Cold War. Whatever its advantage in building a sense of security among worried Europeans, it represented an overreaction to the Soviet danger. Americans and Europeans alike were attempting to apply the lesson of Munich to the Cold War. But Stalin was not Hitler, and the Soviets were not the Nazis. There was no evidence of any Russian plan to invade Western Europe, and in the face of the American atomic bomb, none was likely. NATO only intensified Russian fears of the West and thus increased the level of international tension.

The Berlin Blockade

The main Russian response to containment came in 1948 at the West's most vulnerable point. American, British, French, and Soviet troops each occupied a sector of Berlin, but the city was located over one hundred miles within the Russian zone of Germany (see the map of postwar Europe on p. 832). Stalin decided to test his opponents' resolve by cutting off all rail and highway traffic to Berlin on June 20, 1948.

The timing was very awkward for Harry Truman. He had his hands full resisting efforts to force him off the Democratic ticket, and he faced a difficult reelection effort against a strong Republican candidate, Governor Thomas E. Dewey of New York. Immersed in election-year politics, Truman was caught unprepared by the Berlin blockade. The alternatives were not very appealing. The United States could withdraw its forces and lose not just a city, but the confidence of all Europe; it could try to send in reinforcements and fight for Berlin; or it could sit tight and attempt to find a diplomatic solution. Truman made the basic decision in characteristic fashion, telling the military that there would be no thought of pulling out. "We were going to stay, period," an aide reported Truman as saying.

In the next few weeks, the President and his advisers developed ways to implement this decision. Rejecting proposals for provoking a showdown by sending an armored column down the main highway, the administration adopted a two-phase policy. The first part was a massive airlift of food, fuel, and supplies for both the 10,000 troops and the 2 million civilians in Berlin. A fleet of fifty-two C-54s and eighty C-47s began making two daily round-trip flights to Berlin, carrying 2500 tons every twenty-four hours. Then, to guard against Soviet interruption of the airlift, Truman transferred sixty American B-29s, planes

Changing Views of the Cold War:
The Debate Among Historians

The outbreak of the Cold War between the United States and the Soviet Union was the subject of intense and bitter controversy among American historians. One group blamed the conflict solely on the Soviet Union, claiming that the Russians were bent on world domination; opponents argued that the United States had provoked the Cold War through attempts to establish a Pax Americana after World War II.

The scholarly debate followed the course of the Cold War itself. When the diplomatic contest between the United States and Russia was at its height in the 1950s, American historians maintained that the Cold War was clearly the result of Soviet aggression. This orthodox view was that American actions stemmed from an attempt to absorb the lessons of the 1930s, when the Western democracies had failed to halt the aggression of Germany and Japan until it was almost too late. Citing Munich and the folly of appeasement, historians asserted that Stalin and the Soviet Union were pursuing the same kind of expansionist policies in Europe that Hitler and Nazi Germany had been guilty of in the 1930s. Some saw the Russians as aiming at dominance in Europe; others believed the Soviets desired world domination. The most influential of these writers, former State Department official Herbert Feis, found the origin of the Cold War in the failure of Franklin D. Roosevelt to prepare the American people for the postwar expansion of the Soviet Union.

According to this orthodox view, the Russians nearly achieved their aggressive plan. Weak American diplomacy enabled Stalin to establish an Iron Curtain over Eastern Europe, and by 1947 there was a growing danger of Communist penetration into such Western European countries as Italy and France. Then in the spring of 1947, American policy suddenly met the challenge. According to Joseph Jones in *The Fifteen Weeks,* the president and the secretary of state reversed American policy at the last minute with the Truman Doctrine and the Marshall Plan. These two measures, along with NATO in 1949, formed the essence of containment, the American determination to preserve a favorable balance of power in Europe to check the Russian drive for world control.

This highly nationalistic view of how the Cold War began prevailed through the early 1960s. It justified heavy American military expenditures by portraying the United States as the protector of the free world. The belated and defensive American response to Soviet aggression also fit neatly into a familiar pattern. Three times in the twentieth century—in 1917, in 1941, and again in 1947—the United States had reluctantly acted to preserve a decent and civilized world.

In the next decade, however, two

developments undermined this complacent explanation. First, the escalation of the Vietnam War in 1965 led to a new mood of doubt and dissent over American foreign policy. As the wisdom of U.S. intervention in Vietnam came into question, historians began to probe the roots of the Cold War to find out why Americans had ended up fighting an unpopular war in Southeast Asia. Second, the State Department archives and the private papers of American diplomats were opened for historical research in the 1960s, providing scholars with a behind-the-scenes view of policymaking that often contradicted the accepted version.

The early revisionists, notably Denna F. Fleming and Gar Alperovitz, tended to blame the Cold War on the transfer of power from Roosevelt to Truman and particularly on the decision to drop the atomic bomb. According to this view, Roosevelt tried hard to cooperate with the Soviets, relying on his personal ties with Stalin to ensure postwar cooperation. FDR understood the historic Russian concern over security, which led to an insistence on friendly regimes in Eastern Europe. Truman, however, lacking Roosevelt's experience in foreign policy, immediately antagonized the Russians by challenging their control over Poland and the Balkans. According to Alperovitz, Truman even tried to use the atomic bomb to force a Russian retreat in Eastern Europe, and his decision to use this dread weapon was based as much on a desire to overwhelm the Soviets as to defeat Japan.

Later revisionists gave greater weight to economic factors in accusing the United States of starting the Cold War. Writers such as Gabriel Kolko argued that it was an American need to dominate world

Kruschev and Eisenhower face each other in this British cartoon entitled "Handshake."

markets that lay behind the refusal to accept Soviet control of Eastern Europe. A capitalist system that needed to expand overseas to overcome its own inherent weaknesses prevented the United States from reaching a territorial settlement with Russia that could have led to a peaceful world. Thus a powerful and expansionist United States, not an insecure Soviet Union, was responsible for the Cold War.

In the 1970s, as détente mellowed Soviet-American relations, a more balanced view of the origins of the diplomatic conflict emerged. Writers like John Lewis Gaddis and Daniel Yergin, who became known as postrevisionists, began to treat the Cold War as a historical event that transcended simple accusations of national guilt. Rather than challenging the revisionists completely, they tried to incorporate their views into a broader explanation that stressed the inevitability of the Cold War.

The postrevisionists based their explanation on the confusion and misunderstanding prevalent at the end of World War II. The United States, misled by the experience with Hitler in the 1930s, mistook

Stalin's attempt to bolster Russian security in Eastern Europe for a design for world conquest. When Truman responded with containment, which was essentially an effort to preserve the balance of power in postwar Europe, the Russians thought that America and its allies were bent on encircling and eventually destroying the Soviet Union. A vicious cycle then began, with each nation perceiving every step taken by the other as a threat to its existence. Neither the United States nor the Soviet Union alone was guilty of beginning the Cold War; both must share responsibility for this tragedy.

The postrevisionist explanation is very close to an early explanation for the Cold War advanced by historian William H. McNeill. Writing in 1950, McNeill pointed out that throughout history, victorious coalitions had split apart as soon as the common enemy was overcome. The defeat of the Axis had created a vacuum of power in which the United States and the Soviet Union were bound to clash to determine who would control the future of Europe.

Yet even this view does not explain why the competition between the two nations became so intense. Other wartime alliances dissolved without creating such a fierce rivalry. Here is where the atomic bomb played a key role. The existence of a new weapon of vast destructive power added an unknown element to the international arena, one that was beyond all previous experience. The very survival of the two antagonists became a genuine matter of concern in the nuclear age. Thus Hiroshima not only ended the Second World War; it also created the unstable diplomatic climate that gave rise to the Cold War.

capable of delivering atomic bombs, to bases in England. The President was bluffing; the B-29s were not equipped with atomic bombs, but at the time, the threat was effective.

For a few weeks, the world teetered on the edge of war. Stalin did not attempt to disrupt the flights to Berlin, but he rejected all American diplomatic initiatives. Although at any time the Russians could have halted it by jamming radar or shooting down the defenseless cargo planes, the airlift gradually increased to more than 4000 tons a day. Governor Dewey patriotically supported the President's policy, thus removing foreign policy from the presidential campaign. Yet for Truman, the tension was fierce. In early September, he asked his advisers to brief him "on bases, bombs, Moscow, Leningrad, etc." "I have a terrible feeling afterward that we are very close to war," he confided in his diary. "I hope not."

Slowly the tension eased. The Russians did not shoot down any planes, and the daily airlift climbed to nearly 7000 tons. Truman, a decided underdog, won a surprising second term in November over a complacent Dewey (see p. 847), in part because the Berlin crisis had rallied the nation behind his leadership. In early 1949, the

Soviets gave in, ending the blockade in return for another meeting of the Council of Foreign Ministers on Germany—a conclave that proved as unproductive as all the earlier ones.

The Berlin crisis marked the end of the initial phase of the Cold War. The airlift had given the United States a striking political victory, showing the world the triumph of American ingenuity over Russian stubbornness. Yet it could not disguise the fact that the Cold War had cut Europe in two. Behind the Iron Curtain, the Russians had consolidated control over the areas won by their troops in the war, while the United States had used the Marshall Plan to revitalize Western Europe. But a divided continent was a far cry from the wartime hopes for a peaceful world. And the rivalry that began in Europe would soon spread into a worldwide contest between the superpowers.

THE COLD WAR EXPANDS

The rivalry between the United States and the Soviet Union grew in the late 1940s and early 1950s. Both sides ended the postwar demobiliza-

The Berlin airlift of 1948–1949 broke the Soviet blockade. Called "Operation Vittles," it provided food and fuel for West Berliners. Here children wait for the candy that American pilots dropped in tiny handkerchief parachutes.

tion and began to rebuild their military forces with new methods and new weapons. Equally significant, the diplomatic competition spread from Europe to Asia as each of the superpowers sought to enhance its influence in the Orient. By the time Truman left office in early 1953, the Cold War had taken on global proportions.

The Military Dimension

After World War II, American leaders were intent on reforming the nation's military system in light of their wartime experience. Two goals were uppermost. First, nearly everyone agreed in the aftermath of Pearl Harbor that the United States' armed services should be unified into an integrated military system. The developing Cold War reinforced this decision. Without unification, declared George Marshall in 1945, "there can be little hope that we will be able to maintain through the years a military posture that will secure for us a lasting peace." Equally important, planners realized, was the need for new institutions to coordinate military and diplomatic strategy so that the nation could cope effectively with threats to its security.

In 1947, Congress responded by passing the National Security Act. It established a Department of Defense, headed by a civilian secretary of cabinet rank presiding over three separate services—the army, the navy, and the new air force. In addition, the act created the Central Intelligence Agency (CIA) to coordinate the intelligence-gathering activities of various government agencies. Finally, the act provided for a National Security Council (NSC)—composed of the service secretaries, the secretary of defense, and the secretary of state—to advise the president on all matters regarding the nation's security.

Despite the appearance of equality among the services, the air force quickly emerged as the dominant power in the atomic age, based on its capability both to deter an enemy from attacking and to wage war if deterrence failed. President Truman, intent on cutting back defense expenditures, favored the air force in his 1949 military budget, allotting this branch over one-half the total sum. After the Czech coup and the resulting war scare, Congress granted an additional $3 billion to the military. The appropriation included funds for a new B-36 to replace the B-29 as the nation's primary strategic bomber.

American military planners received even greater support in the fall of 1949 when the Soviet Union exploded its first atomic bomb. President Truman appointed a high-level committee to explore mounting an all-out effort to build a hydrogen bomb to maintain American nuclear supremacy.

Some scientists had technical objections to the H-bomb, which was still far from being perfected, while others opposed the new weapon on moral grounds, claiming that its enormous destructive power (intended to be one thousand times greater than the atomic bomb) made it unthinkable. George Kennan suggested a new effort at international arms control with the Soviets, but Dean Acheson—who succeeded Marshall as secretary of state in early 1949—felt it was imperative that the United States develop the hydrogen bomb before the Soviet Union. When Acheson presented the committee's favorable report to the President in January 1950, Truman took only seven minutes to decide to go ahead with the awesome new weapon.

At the same time, Acheson ordered the Policy Planning Staff (now headed by Paul Nitze after Kennan resigned in protest) to draw up a new statement of national defense policy. NSC-68, as the document eventually became known, was based on the premise that the Soviet Union sought "to impose its absolute authority over the rest of the world" and thus "mortally challenged" the United States. Rejecting such options as appeasement or a return to isolation, Nitze advocated a massive expansion of American military power so that the United States could halt and overcome the Soviet threat. Contending that the nation could afford to spend "upward of 50 percent of its gross national product" for security, NSC-68 proposed increasing defense spending from $13 to $45 billion annually. Approved in principle by the National Security Council in April 1950, NSC-68 stood as a symbol of the Truman administration's determination to win the Cold War regardless of cost.

The Cold War in Asia

The Soviet-American conflict developed more slowly in Asia. At Yalta, the two superpowers had agreed to a Far Eastern balance of power, with the Russians dominating Northeast Asia and the Americans in control of the Pacific, including both Japan and its former island empire.

The United States moved quickly to consolidate its sphere of influence. General Douglas MacArthur, in charge of Japanese occupation, denied the Soviet Union any role in the reconstruction of Japan. Instead, he supervised the transition of the Japanese government into a constitutional democracy, shaped along Western lines, in which Communists were barred from all government posts. The Japanese willingly renounced war in their new constitution, relying instead on American forces to protect their security. American policy was equally nationalistic in the Pacific. A trusteeship arrangement with the United Nations merely disguised the fact that the United States held full control over the Marshall, Mariana, and Caroline islands. American scientists conducted atomic bomb tests at Bikini atoll in 1946, and by 1949, MacArthur was declaring that the entire Pacific "had become an Anglo-Saxon lake and our line of defense runs through the chain of islands fringing the coast of Asia."

As defined at Yalta, China lay between the Soviet and American spheres. When World War II ended, the country was torn between Chiang Kai-shek's Nationalists in the South and Mao Tse-tung's Communists in the North. Chiang had many advantages, including American political and economic backing and official Soviet recognition. But corruption was widespread among the Nationalist leaders, and a raging inflation that soon reached 100 percent a year devastated the Chinese middle classes and thus eroded Chiang's base of power. Mao used tight discipline and patriotic appeals to strengthen his hold on the peasantry and extend his influence. When the Soviets abruptly vacated Manchuria in 1946, after stripping it of virtually all the industrial machinery Japan had installed, Mao inherited control of this rich northern province. Ignoring American advice, Chiang rushed north to occupy Manchurian cities, overextending his supply lines and exposing his forces to Communist counterattack.

American policy sought to prevent a Chinese civil war. Before he became secretary of state, George Marshall undertook the difficult task of forming a coalition government between Chiang

*D*uring World War II, Mao Tse-tung (center), leader of the Communist forces in China, fought the Japanese, sometimes alongside American GIs. Later, Mao triumphed over the Nationalists and created a Marxist China.

and Mao. For a few months in early 1946, Marshall appeared to have succeeded, but Chiang's attempts to gain control of Manchuria doomed the agreement. In reality, there was no basis for compromise. Chiang insisted he "was going to liquidate Communists," while Mao was trying to play the United States against Russia in his bid for power. By 1947, as China plunged into full-scale civil war, the Truman administration had given up any meaningful effort to influence the outcome. Political mediation had failed, military intervention was out of the question so soon after World War II, and a policy of continued American economic aid served only to appease domestic supporters of Chiang Kai-shek; 80 percent of the military supplies ended up in Communist hands.

The Chinese conflict climaxed at the end of the decade. Mao's forces drove the Nationalists out of Manchuria in late 1948 and advanced across the Yangtze by mid-1949. Acheson released a lengthy White Paper justifying American policy in China on the grounds that the civil war there "was beyond the control of the government of the

United States." An American military adviser concurred, telling Congress that the Nationalist defeat was due to "the world's worst leadership" and "a complete loss of will to fight." Republican senators, however, disagreed, blaming American diplomats for sabotaging the Nationalists and terming the White Paper "a 1054-page whitewash of a wishful, do-nothing policy." While the domestic debate raged over responsibility for the loss of China, Chiang's forces fled the mainland for sanctuary on Formosa Taiwan in December 1949. Two months later, Mao and Stalin signed a Sino-Soviet treaty of mutual assistance that clearly placed China in the Russian orbit.

The American response to the Communist triumph in China was twofold. First, the State Department refused to recognize the legitimacy of the new regime in Peking, maintaining instead formal diplomatic relations with the Nationalists on Formosa. Citing the Sino-Soviet alliance, Assistant Secretary of State Dean Rusk called the Peking regime "a colonial Russian government" and declared, "It is not the Government of China. It does not pass the first test. It is not Chinese." Then, to compensate for the loss of China, the United States focused on Japan as its main ally in Asia. The State Department encouraged the buildup of Japanese industry, and the Pentagon expanded American bases on the Japanese home islands and Okinawa. A Japanese-American security pact led to the end of American occupation by 1952. The Cold War had now split Asia in two.

The Korean War

The showdown between the United States and the Soviet Union in Asia came in Korea. Traditionally the cockpit of international rivalry in Northeast Asia, Korea had been divided at the thirty-eighth parallel in 1945. The Russians occupied the industrial North, installing a Communist government under the leadership of Kim Il-Sung. In the agrarian South, Syngman Rhee, a conservative nationalist, emerged as the American-sponsored ruler. Neither regime heeded a UN call for elections to unify the country. The two superpowers pulled out most of their occupation forces by 1949. The Russians, however, helped train a well-equipped army in the North, while the United States—fearful that Rhee would seek

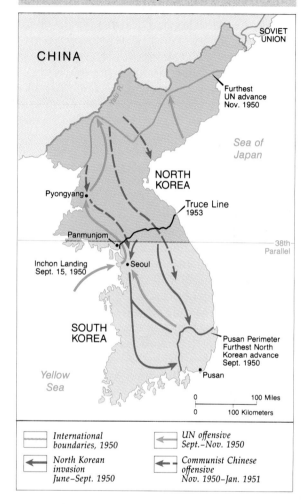

The Korean War, 1950–1953

After a year of rapid movement up and down the Korean peninsula, the fighting stalled just north of the 38th parallel. The resulting truce line has divided North and South Korea ever since the July 1953 armistice.

unification through armed conquest—gave much more limited military assistance to South Korea.

On June 25, 1950, the North Korean army suddenly crossed the thirty-eighth parallel in great strength. The Soviet role in this act of aggression is shrouded in mystery. Presumably Stalin ordered the attack in an attempt to expand the Soviet sphere in Asia and to counter the American buildup of Japan. Yet there is also evidence to suggest that Kim Il-Sung acted on his own, confident that the Russians would have no choice but to back his move.

There was nothing ambiguous about the American response. President Truman saw the invasion as a clear-cut case of Soviet aggression reminiscent of the 1930s. "Communism was acting in Korea just as Hitler, Mussolini, and the Japanese had acted ten, fifteen, and twenty years earlier," he commented in his memoirs. Following the advice of Acheson, the President convened the UN Security Council and, taking advantage of a temporary Soviet boycott, secured a resolution condemning North Korea as an aggressor and calling on the member nations to engage in a collective-security action. Within a few days, American troops from Japan were in combat in South Korea. The conflict, which would last for more than three years, was technically a police action fought under UN auspices; in reality, the United States was at war with a Soviet satellite in Asia.

In the beginning, the fighting went badly as the North Koreans continued to drive down the peninsula. But by August, American forces had halted the Communist advance near Pusan. In September, General MacArthur changed the whole complexion of the war by carrying out a brilliant amphibious assault at Inchon, on the waist of Korea, cutting off and destroying most of the North Korean army in the South. Encouraged by this victory, Truman began to shift from his original goal of restoring the thirty-eighth parallel, to a new one, the unification of Korea by military force.

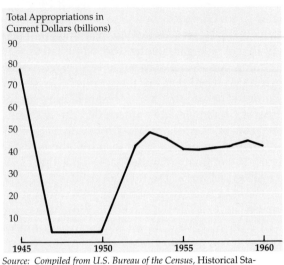

National Defense Outlays, 1945–1960

Total Appropriations in Current Dollars (billions)

Source: Compiled from U.S. Bureau of the Census, Historical Statistics of the United States, Colonial Times to 1970, *Bicentennial Edition, Washington, D.C., 1975.*

The administration ignored warnings from Peking against an American invasion of North Korea; "I should think it would be sheer madness for the Chinese to intervene," commented Dean Acheson. MacArthur was even more confident. "We are no longer fearful of their intervention," he told Truman at a Wake Island conference in mid-October. Noting that the Chinese had no air force, the general prophesied that if they crossed the Yalu River into Korea, "there would be the greatest slaughter."

Rarely has an American president received worse advice than Truman did from Acheson and MacArthur. The UN forces crossed the thirty-eighth parallel in October, advanced confidently to the Yalu in November, and then were completely routed by a massive Chinese counterattack that drove them out of all North Korea by December. MacArthur finally stabilized the fighting near the thirty-eighth parallel, but when Truman decided to give up his attempt to unify Korea, the general protested to Congress, calling for a renewed offensive and proclaiming, "There is no substitute for victory."

Truman courageously relieved the popular hero of the Pacific of his command on April 11, 1951. At first, MacArthur seemed likely to force the President to back down. Huge crowds came forward to welcome him home and hear him call

President Truman and General MacArthur at Wake Island in October 1950 when hopes were high for total victory in Korea.

After the Chinese onslaught of November 1950, U.S. Marines retreated to the sea along icy roads in near-zero weather. They faced three Chinese divisions in the bloody struggle but managed to bring out their wounded and their equipment.

for victory over the Communists in Asia. At a special congressional hearing, the administration struck back effectively by warning that MacArthur's strategy would expose all Europe to Soviet attack. General Omar Bradley, Truman's chief military adviser, succinctly pointed out that a "showdown" with communism in Asia would be "the wrong war, at the wrong place, at the wrong time, and with the wrong enemy."

Congress and the American people came to accept MacArthur's recall. The Korean War settled into a stalemate near the thirty-eighth parallel as truce talks with the Communists bogged down for the rest of Truman's term in office. The President could take heart from the fact that he had achieved his primary goal, defense of South Korea and the principle of collective security. Yet by taking the gamble to unify Korea by force, he had confused the American people and humiliated the United States in the eyes of the world.

In the last analysis, the most significant result of the Korean conflict was the massive American rearmament it brought about. The war led to the implementation of NSC-68—the army expanded to 3.5 million troops, the defense budget increased to $50 billion a year by 1952, and the

United States acquired distant military bases from Saudi Arabia to Morocco. American was now committed to waging a global contest against the Soviet Union with arms as well as words.

THE COLD WAR AT HOME

The Cold War cast a long shadow over American life in the late 1940s and early 1950s. Harry Truman tried to carry on the New Deal reform tradition he had inherited from FDR, but the American people were more concerned about events abroad. The Republican party used growing dissatisfaction with both postwar economic adjustment and fears of Communist penetration of the United States to revive its sagging fortunes and regain control of the White House in 1952 for the first time in twenty years.

Truman's Troubles

Matching his foreign policy successes with equal achievements at home was not easy for Harry S. Truman. As a loyal supporter of Franklin D.

Roosevelt's New Deal programs during his Senate career, Truman had earned a reputation for being a hard-working, reliable, and intensely partisan legislator. But he was relatively unknown to the general public and his background as a Missouri county official associated with Kansas City machine politics did little to inspire confidence in his ability to lead the nation. Surprisingly well read—especially in history and biography—Truman possessed sound judgment, the ability to reach decisions quickly, and a fierce and uncompromising sense of right and wrong.

Two weaknesses marred his performance in the White House. One was a fondness for old friends, which resulted in the appointment of many Missouri and Senate cronies to high office. Men like Attorney General Tom Clark, Secretary of the Treasury Charles Snyder, and White House military aide Harry Vaughn brought little credit to the Truman administration, while the loss of such effective public servants as Secretary of the Interior Harold Ickes and Labor Secretary Frances Perkins hurt it. The President's other serious limitation was his lack of political vision. Failing to pursue a coherent legislative program of his own, he tried to perpetuate FDR's New Deal, and as a result, engaged in a running battle with Congress.

The postwar mood was not conducive to an extension of New Deal reforms. Americans were weary of shortages and sacrifices; they wanted the chance to buy the consumer goods denied them under wartime conditions. But in the rush to convert industry from producing planes and tanks to cars and appliances, problems soon emerged. Prices and wages rose quickly as Congress voted to end wartime controls. With prices going up 25 percent in two years, workers demanded higher wages to offset the loss of overtime pay. A wave of labor unrest swept over the country in the spring of 1946, culminating in two critical strikes: a walkout by coal miners that threatened to close down much of American industry, and a paralyzing strike by railroad workers.

President Truman was caught in the middle. Sensitive to union demands, he permitted businessmen to negotiate large pay increases for their workers and then pass on the cost to consumers in the form of higher prices. He criticized Congress for weakening wartime price controls, but he failed to offer anything else to curb inflation.

Housewives blamed him for the rising price of food, while organized labor condemned Truman as the country's "No. 1 Strikebreaker" when he asked Congress for power to draft striking railway workers into the army.

In the face of this rising discontent, Truman's efforts to extend the New Deal met with little success. Congress ignored his September 1945 call for a series of measures to ensure economic security and enacted only the Employment Act of 1946. While this measure created the Council of Economic Advisers to assist the President and asserted the principle that the government was responsible for the state of the economy, it failed to include Truman's original goal of mandatory federal planning to achieve full employment.

The Republicans took advantage of growing public dissatisfaction with postwar economic woes to attack the Democrats. "To err is Truman," the GOP proclaimed, and then adopted a very effective two-word slogan for the 1946 congressional elections, "Had enough?" The American people, weary of inflation and labor unrest, responded by electing Republican majorities in both the House and Senate for the first time since 1930.

Truman Vindicated

The President's relations with Congress became even stormier after the GOP victory in the 1946 election. Truman successfully vetoed two GOP measures to give large tax cuts to the wealthy, but Congress overrode his veto of the Taft-Hartley Act in 1947. Designed to correct the imbalance in labor-management relations created by the Wagner Act, the Taft-Hartley Act outlawed specific unfair labor union activities—including the closed shop and secondary boycotts—and it permitted the President to invoke an eighty-day cooling-off period to delay strikes that might endanger national health or safety. Despite Truman's claim that it was a "slave-labor" bill, unions were able to survive its provisions.

President Truman's political fortunes reached their lowest ebb in early 1948. Former Vice President Henry A. Wallace, claiming to represent the New Deal, announced his third-party (Progressive) candidacy in the presidential contest that year. Worried Democratic party leaders sought to persuade Truman to step aside and allow General Dwight D. Eisenhower to become the Democratic candidate. When Eisenhower turned down bids from both parties, the Democrats reluctantly nominated Truman. His prospects for victory in the fall, however, looked very dim—especially after disgruntled Southerners bolted the Democratic party in protest over a progressive civil rights platform. The Dixiecrats, as they became known, nominated Strom Thurmond, the governor of South Carolina, on a States' Rights party ticket.

The defection of the Dixiecrats in the South and Wallace's liberal followers in the North led political experts to predict an almost certain Republican victory. Governor Thomas E. Dewey of New York, the GOP candidate, was so certain of winning that he waged a cautious and bland campaign designed to give him a free hand once he was in the White House. With nothing to lose, Truman barnstormed around the country denouncing the ''do-nothing'' Republican Eightieth Congress. The President's ''give-'em hell'' tactics reminded voters of how much they owed the Democrats for helping them survive the Depression. To the amazement of the pollsters, Truman won a narrow but decisive victory in November. The old Roosevelt coalition—farmers, organized labor, urban ethnic groups, and blacks—had held together, enabling Truman to remain in the

A jubilant Harry Truman, on the morning after his 1948 election win, displays the headline blazoned on the front page of the Chicago Tribune—*a newspaper that believed the pollsters.*

White House and the Democrats to regain control of Congress.

There was one more reason for Truman's win in 1948. During this election, held at the height of the Berlin crisis, the GOP failed to challenge Truman's conduct of the Cold War. Locked in a tense rivalry with the Soviet Union, the American people saw no reason to reject a President who had countered aggression overseas with the Truman Doctrine and the Marshall Plan. The Republicans, committed to support the bipartisan policy of containment, had allowed the Democrats to preempt the foreign policy issue. Until they found a way to challenge Truman's Cold War policies, GOP leaders had little chance to regain the White House.

The Loyalty Issue

Despite Truman's surprising victory in 1948, there was one area on which the Democrats were vulnerable. The fear of communism abroad that had led to the bipartisan containment policy could be used against them at home by politicians who were more willing to exploit the public's deep-seated anxiety.

Fear of radicalism had been a recurrent feature of American life since the early days of the

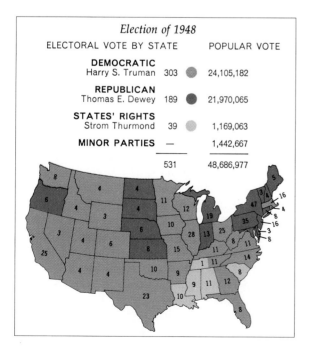

Election of 1948

	ELECTORAL VOTE BY STATE		POPULAR VOTE
DEMOCRATIC Harry S. Truman	303		24,105,182
REPUBLICAN Thomas E. Dewey	189		21,970,065
STATES' RIGHTS Strom Thurmond	39		1,169,063
MINOR PARTIES	—		1,442,667
	531		48,686,977

Republic. Federalists had tried to suppress dissent with the Alien and Sedition Acts in the 1790s; the Know-Nothings had campaigned against foreigners and Catholics in the 1850s, and the Red Scare after World War I had been directed against both aliens and radicals. The Cold War heightened the traditional belief that subversion from abroad endangered the Republic. Bold rhetoric from members of the Truman administration, portraying the men in the Kremlin as inspired revolutionaries bent on world conquest, frightened the American people. They viewed the Soviet Union as a successor to Nazi Germany—a totalitarian police state that threatened the basic liberties of a free people.

A series of revelations of Communist espionage activities reinforced these fears. Canadian officials uncovered a Soviet spy ring in 1946, and the House Un-American Activities Committee held hearings indicating that Communist agents had flourished in the Agriculture and Treasury departments in the 1930s.

The most famous disclosure came in August

The conviction of Alger Hiss (below) convinced many Americans that internal subversion threatened the nation's survival.

1948, however, when Whittaker Chambers, a repentant Communist, accused Alger Hiss of having been a Soviet spy in the 1930s. When Hiss, who had been a prominent State Department official, denied the charges, Chambers led investigators to a hollowed-out pumpkin on his Maryland farm. Inside the pumpkin were microfilms of confidential government documents. Chambers claimed that Hiss had passed these State Department materials to him in the late 1930s. Although the statute of limitations prevented a charge of treason against Hiss, he was convicted of perjury in January 1950 and sentenced to a five-year prison term.

Although Truman tried to dismiss the loyalty issue as a "red herring," he felt compelled to take protective measures, thus lending substance to the charges of subversion. In March 1947, he had initiated a loyalty program, ordering security checks of government employees in order to root out Communists. Originally intended to remove subversives for whom "reasonable grounds exist for belief that the person involved is disloyal," within four years the Loyalty Review Board was dismissing workers as security risks if there was "reasonable doubt" of their loyalty. Thousands of government workers lost their jobs, charged with guilt by association with radicals or with membership in left-wing organizations. Often those who were charged had no chance to face their accusers.

In 1948, the Justice Department further heightened fears of subversion. It charged eleven officials of the Communist party with advocating the violent overthrow of the government. After a long trial, the jury found them guilty, and the party officials received prison sentences and heavy fines; in 1951, the Supreme Court upheld these convictions as constitutional.

Such repressive measures failed, however, to reassure the nation. Events abroad intensified the sense of danger. The Communist triumph in China in the fall of 1949 came as a shock; soon there were charges that "fellow travelers" in the State Department were responsible for "the loss of China." In September 1949, when the Truman administration announced that the Russians had detonated their first atomic bomb, the ending of America's nuclear monopoly was blamed on Soviet espionage. In early 1950, Klaus Fuchs—a British scientist who had worked on the wartime

*T*hree days before Julius and Ethel Rosenberg were executed for treason, their two young sons, ten and six years old, marched to the White House to plead executive clemency for their parents.

*S*enator Joseph McCarthy maintained a steady stream of unsubstantiated charges, always ready to make new accusations of communist infiltration before the preceding ones could be proven untrue.

Manhattan Project—admitted giving the Russians vital information about the A-bomb.

A few months later, the government charged American Communists Ethel and Julius Rosenberg with conspiracy to transmit atomic secrets to the Soviet Union. In 1951, a jury found the Rosenbergs guilty of treason, and Judge Irving Kaufman sentenced them to die for what he termed their "loathsome offense." Despite their insistent claims of innocence and worldwide appeals on their behalf, the Rosenbergs were electrocuted on June 19, 1953. Thus by the early 1950s, nearly all the ingredients were at hand for a new outburst of hysteria—fear of Russia, evidence of espionage, and a belief in a vast unseen conspiracy. The only element missing was a leader to release this new outburst of intolerance.

McCarthyism in Action

On February 12, 1950, Senator Joseph R. McCarthy of Wisconsin delivered a routine Lincoln's Birthday speech in Wheeling, West Virginia. This little known Republican suddenly attracted national attention when he declared, "I have here in

my hand a list of 205—a list of names that were made known to the secretary of state as being members of the Communist party and who nevertheless are still working and shaping policy in the State Department." The charge that there were Communists in the State Department—repeated on different occasions with the number changed to 57, then 81—was never substantiated. But McCarthy's Wheeling speech triggered a four-and-a-half-year crusade to hunt down alleged Communists in government. The stridency and sensationalism of the senator's accusations soon won the name "McCarthyism."

McCarthy's basic technique was the multiple untruth. He leveled a bevy of charges of treasonable activities in government. While officials were refuting his initial accusations, he brought forth a steady stream of new ones, so that the corrections never caught up with the latest blast. He failed to unearth a single confirmed Communist in government, but he kept the Truman administration in turmoil. Drawing on an army of informers, primarily disgruntled federal workers with grievances against their colleagues and superiors, he charged government agencies with harboring and protecting Communist agents, and he accused the State Department of deliberately losing the Cold War. His briefcase bulged with documents, but he did very little actual research, relying instead on reports (often outdated) from earlier congressional investigations. He exploited the press with great skill, combining current accusations with promises of future disclosures to guarantee headlines.

The secret of McCarthy's power was the fear he engendered among his Senate colleagues. In 1950, Maryland Senator Millard Tydings, who headed a committee critical of McCarthy's activities, failed to win reelection when McCarthy opposed him; after that, other senators ran scared. McCarthy delighted in making sweeping, startling charges of Communist sympathies against prominent public figures. A favorite target was patrician Secretary of State Dean Acheson, whom McCarthy ridiculed as the "Red Dean," with his "cane, spats and tea-sipping little finger"; he even went after General George Marshall, claiming that the wartime army chief of staff was an agent of the Communist conspiracy. Nor were fellow Republicans immune. One GOP senator was described as "a living miracle in that he is without question the only man who has lived so long with neither brains nor guts."

These attacks on the wealthy, famous, and privileged won McCarthy a devoted national following, though at the height of his influence in early 1954 he gained the approval of only 50 percent of the respondents in a Gallup poll. McCarthy drew a disproportionate backing from working-class Catholics and ethnic groups, especially the Irish, Poles, and Italians, who normally voted Democratic. He offered a simple solution to the complicated Cold War: defeat the enemy at home rather than continue to engage in costly foreign aid programs and entangling alliances abroad. Above all, McCarthy appealed to conservative Republicans in the Midwest who shared his right-wing views and felt cheated by Truman's upset victory in 1948. Even GOP leaders who viewed McCarthy's tactics with distaste, such as Robert A. Taft of Ohio, quietly encouraged him to attack the vulnerable Democrats.

The Republicans in Power

In 1952, the GOP capitalized on a growing sense of national frustration to capture the presidency. The stalemate in Korea and the second Red Scare created a desire for political change; revelations of scandals by several individuals close to Truman intensified the feeling that someone needed to clean up "the mess in Washington." In Dwight D. Eisenhower, the Republican party found the

McCarthy's relentless barrage of accusations went on for four years, but when he began to attack the upper echelon of the U.S. Army, McCarthy (left) was finally brought down. Millions of Americans tuned in to watch the televised hearings as Army counsel Joseph Welch (right) destroyed the credibility of McCarthy's panel of informers.

perfect candidate to explore what one senator called K_1C_2—Korea, communism, and corruption.

Immensely popular because of his amiable manner, winning smile, and heroic stature, Eisenhower alone appeared to have the ability to unite a divided nation. In the 1952 campaign, Ike displayed hidden gifts as a politician in running against Adlai Stevenson, the eloquent Illinois governor whose appeal was limited to diehard Democrats and liberal intellectuals. Eisenhower allowed his young running mate, Senator Richard M. Nixon of California, to hammer away at the Democrats on the Communist and corruption issues, but he himself delivered the most telling blow of all on the Korean War. Speaking in Detroit in late October, just after the fighting had intensified again in Korea, Ike promised if elected he would go personally to the battlefield in an attempt "to bring the Korean War to an early and honorable end."

"That does it—Ike is in," several reporters exclaimed after they heard this pledge. The hero of World War II had clinched his election by committing himself to end an unpopular war. Ten days later, he won the presidency handily, carrying thirty-nine states, including four in the formerly solid Democratic South. The Republican party, however, did not fare as well in Congress; it gained just a slight edge in the House and controlled the Senate by only one seat.

Once elected, Eisenhower moved quickly to fulfill his campaign pledge. He spent three days in early December touring the battlefront in Korea, quickly ruling out the new offensive the military favored. "Small attacks on small hills," he later wrote, "would not end the war." Instead he turned to diplomacy, relying on subtle hints to China on the possible use of nuclear weapons to break the stalemated peace talks. These tactics, together with the death of Joseph Stalin in early March, finally led to the signing of an armistice on July 27, 1953, which ended the fighting but left Korea divided—as it had been before the war—near the thirty-eighth parallel.

The new President was less effective in dealing with the problem raised by Senator Joseph McCarthy's continuing witchhunt. Instead of toning down his anti-Communist crusade after the Republican victory in 1952, McCarthy used his new position as chairman of the Senate Committee on

The Election of 1952			
Candidate	Party	Popular Vote	Electoral Vote
Eisenhower	Republican	33,936,137	442
Stevenson	Democrat	27,314,649	89

Government Operations as a base for ferreting out Communists on the federal payroll. He made a series of charges against the foreign affairs agencies and demanded that certain books be purged from American information libraries overseas. Eisenhower's advisers urged the President to use his own great prestige to stop McCarthy. But Ike refused such a confrontation, saying, "I will not get into a pissing contest with a skunk." Eisenhower preferred to play for time, hoping that the American people would eventually come to their senses.

The Wisconsin senator finally overreached himself. In early 1954, he uncovered an Army dentist suspected of disloyalty and proceeded to attack the upper echelons of the United States Army, telling one much-decorated general that he was "not fit to wear the uniform." The controversy culminated in the televised Army-McCarthy hearings. For six weeks, the senator revealed his crude, bullying behavior to the American people. Viewers were repelled by his frequent outbursts that began with the insistent cry, "Point of order, Mr. Chairman, point of order," and by his attempt to slur the reputation of a young lawyer associated with Army counsel Joseph Welch. This last maneuver led Welch to condemn McCarthy for his "reckless cruelty" and ask rhetorically, as millions watched on television, "Have you no sense of decency, sir?"

Courageous Republicans, led by Senators George Aiken of Vermont and Margaret Chase Smith of Maine, joined with Democrats to bring about the Senate's censure of McCarthy in December 1954, by a vote of 67 to 22. Once rebuked, McCarthy fell quickly from prominence. He died three years later virtually unnoticed and unmourned.

Yet his influence was profound. Not only did he paralyze national life with what a Senate subcommittee described as "the most nefarious campaign of half-truth and untruth in the history of the Republic," but he also helped impose a

1945 Truman meets Stalin at Potsdam Conference (July) • World War II ends with Japanese surrender (August)

1946 Winston Churchill gives "Iron Curtain" speech

1947 Truman Doctrine announced to Congress (March) • George Marshall outlines Marshall Plan (June) • Truman orders loyalty program for government employees (March)

1948 Soviets begin blockade of Berlin (June) • Truman scores upset victory in presidential election

1949 NATO treaty signed in Washington (April) • Soviet Union tests its first atomic bomb (August)

1950 Truman authorizes building of hydrogen bomb (January) • Senator Joseph McCarthy claims Communists in government (February) • North Korea invades South Korea (June)

1951 Truman recalls MacArthur from Korea

1952 Dwight D. Eisenhower elected president

1953 Julius and Ethel Rosenberg executed for atomic-secrets spying (June) • Korean War truce signed at Panmunjom (July)

By the early 1950s, the Cold War had become an enduring reality of American life. The initial disagreements between the United States and the Soviet Union had settled down into a deadly rivalry with no end in sight. Thus World War II had led to neither the era of peace and tranquility that so many had looked forward to nor to the period of American world dominance that some thought possible. Although the United States emerged from the war more powerful than at any time in the nation's history, it faced a seemingly endless struggle against a determined and dangerous foe. And as the second Red Scare had so vividly demonstrated, it was a contest that was bound to affect every aspect of American life in the postwar era.

Recommended Reading

The Cold War has spawned a vast array of books, some enduring in nature and many that are already outdated. The best general guide to American diplomacy since World War II is Walter LaFeber, *America, Russia and the Cold War, 1945–1984* (1985). LaFeber, who writes from a moderately revisionist perspective, is more concerned with explaining the course of American foreign policy than in criticizing it. On the much-debated question of the origins of the Cold War, the best balanced account is Daniel Yergin, *Shattered Peace* (1977), a book which characterizes American policy as flawed by misunderstanding rather than by ill-will.

The classic account of containment is still the lucid recollection of its chief architect, George Kennan, *Memoirs, 1925–1950* (1967). John L. Gaddis uses Kennan's ideas as a point of departure for his account of the changing nature of American Cold War policy in *Strategies of Containment* (1982). For developments in the Far East, consult the perceptive book by Akira Iriye, *The Cold War in Asia* (1974).

The best book on the Truman period is Alonzo L. Hamby, *Beyond the New Deal* (1973), which focuses on Truman's attempts to preserve and extend the liberal reform tradition. Of the many books on the postwar Red Scare, Earl Latham's *The Communist Controversy in Washington* (1966) is the most thorough and reliable.

Additional Bibliography

Surveys of American foreign policy since 1945 include Stephen Ambrose, *Rise to Globalism*, 5th ed. (1987); John Spanier, *American Foreign Policy Since World War II*, 9th ed. (1983); Ralph Levering, *The Cold War, 1945–1972* (1982); and James A. Nathan and James K. Oliver, *United States Foreign Policy and World Order*, 2d ed. (1981). For perceptive essays on the Cold War, see John Lewis Gaddis, *The Long Peace* (1987) and Thomas G. Paterson, *Meeting the Communist Threat* (1988). Adam B. Ulam provides a perceptive

political and cultural conformity that froze dissent for the rest of the 1950s. Long after McCarthy's passing, the nation tolerated loyalty oaths for teachers, the banning of left-wing books in public libraries, and the blacklisting of entertainers in radio, television and films. Freedom of expression was inhibited, and the opportunity to try out new ideas and approaches was lost as the United States settled into a sterile Cold War consensus.

While Dwight Eisenhower could claim that his policy of giving McCarthy enough rope to hang himself had worked, it is possible that a bolder and more forthright presidential attack on the senator might have spared the nation some of the excesses of the second Red Scare.

summary of Soviet-American relations for this period in *The Rivals* (1971). For a good critique, see John C. Donovan, *The Cold Warriors* (1974).

Gar Alperovitz began the revisionist controversy over the origins of the Cold War in *Atomic Diplomacy* (1965), which focuses on Truman's use of the atomic bomb as a veiled diplomatic weapon. Other revisionist accounts include Lloyd Gardner, *Architects of Illusion* (1970); Joyce Kolko and Gabriel Kolko, *The Limits of Power* (1972); Thomas G. Paterson, *Soviet-American Confrontation* (1973); and Lawrence Wittner, *American Intervention in Greece, 1943* (1982). For a brief, moderate revisionist view, see Thomas G. Paterson, *On Every Front* (1979). Robert Tucker offers a shrewd assessment of revisionism in *The Radical Left and American Foreign Policy* (1971). Post revisionist studies include John L. Gaddis, *The United States and the Origins of the Cold War* (1972); Vojtech Mastny, *Russia's Road to the Cold War* (1979); Robert L. Messer, *The End of an Alliance* (1982); and James L. Gormly, *The Collapse of the Grand Alliance, 1945–1948* (1987). For a lively account of the Potsdam Conference, see Charles L. Mee, *Meeting at Potsdam* (1975).

The foreign policy of the Truman administration is covered in Harry S. Truman, *Memoirs*, 2 vols. (1955, 1956) and two works by Robert J. Donovan: *Conflict and Crisis* (1977) and *Tumultuous Years* (1982). See also Forrest Pogue, *George C. Marshall: Statesman, 1945–1949* (1987); Gaddis Smith, *Dean Acheson* (1972); David S. McLellan, *Dean Acheson* (1976); and Dean Acheson, *Present at the Creation* (1969). For military policy, see Walter Millis, ed., *The Forrestal Diaries* (1951); Richard F. Haynes, *The Awesome Power* (1973); Lawrence S. Kaplan, *NATO and the United States* (1988); Warner R. Schilling, et al., *Strategy, Politics and Defense Budgets* (1962); and Thomas H. Etzold and John L. Gaddis, eds., *Containment* (1976). Studies of special interest include Gregg Herken, *The Winning Weapon* (1980) on atomic diplomacy under Truman; Michael Hogan, *The Marshall Plan* (1987), a standard account; Howard Jones, *"A New Kind of War"* (1989), on the Truman Doctrine; and Avi Shlaim, *The United States and the Berlin Blockade, 1948* (1983).

For the Cold War in the Far East, consult Mark S. Gallicchio, *The Cold War Begins in Asia* (1988); Michael Schaller, *The American Occupation of Japan* (1985); Dorothy Borg and Waldo Heinrichs, eds., *The Uncertain Years: Chinese-American Relations, 1947–1950* (1980); Russell D. Buhite, *Soviet-American Relations in Asia, 1945–1954* (1982); William W. Streck, *The Road to Confrontation* (1981); Nancy B. Tucker, *Patterns in the Dust* (1983); Robert M. Blum, *Drawing the Line* (1982); and June M. Grasso, *Harry Truman's Two-China Policy, 1948–1950* (1987). Books on the Korean War include David Rees, *Korea: The Limited War and American Politics* (1968); Charles W. Dobbs, *The Unwanted Symbol* (1981); Bruce Cumings, *The Origins of the Korean War* (1981); John W. Spanier, *The Truman-MacArthur Controversy and the Korean War* (1959), Rosemary Foot, *The Wrong War* (1985), Roy E. Appleman, *Disaster in Korea: The Chinese Confront MacArthur* (1989); and Burton Kaufman, *The Korean War* (1986).

Biographies of Truman include Merle Miller, *Plain Speaking* (1973); Margaret Truman, *Harry S. Truman* (1973); Richard L. Miller, *Truman: The Rise to Power* (1986); Robert H. Ferrell, *Harry S. Truman and the Modern American Presidency* (1982); Roy Jenkins, *Truman* (1986); William E. Pemberton, *Harry S. Truman: Fair Dealer and Cold Warrior* (1989); and two volumes by Robert J. Donovan: *Conflict and Crisis* (1977) and *Tumultuous Years* (1982). Studies of specific policies include Barton J. Bernstein, ed., *Politics and Policies of the Truman Administration* (1970); R Alton Lee, *Truman and Taft-Hartley* (1966); Susan M. Hartmann, *Truman and the 80th Congress* (1971); Donald R. McCoy, *The Presidency of Harry S. Truman* (1984); and Monte M. Poen, *Harry S. Truman and the Medical Lobby* (1979).

Three studies of the 1948 election are Irwin Ross, *The Loneliest Campaign* (1968); Norman D. Markowitz, *The Rise and Fall of the People's Century: Henry A. Wallace and American Liberalism, 1941* (1973); and Allen Yarnell, *Democrats and Progressives* (1973). For Republican leaders, see two perceptive biographies, James T. Patterson, *Mr. Republican* (1968) on Senator Robert A. Taft, and Richard N. Smith, *Thomas E. Dewey and His Times* (1982).

The relationship of the Truman administration to the Communist issue is covered in Allan D. Harper, *The Politics of Loyalty* (1970); Athan G. Theoharis, *Seeds of Repression* (1971); and Richard Freeland, *The Truman Doctrine and the Origins of McCarthyism* (1972). Other works on the second Red Scare are Stanley Kutler, *The American Inquisition* (1982); Ronald Radosh and Joyce Milton, *The Rosenberg File* (1983); Victor Navasky *Naming Names* (1980); Allen Weinstein, *Perjury: The Hiss-Chambers Case* (1978); and William L. O'Neil, *A Better World* (1982), which examines its impact on American intellectuals. Among the many books on McCarthyism, the best are Thomas C. Reeves, *The Life and Times of Joe McCarthy* (1982); Richard H. Rovere, *Senator Joe McCarthy* (1959); Michael P. Rogin, *The Intellectuals and McCarthy* (1967); Robert Griffith, *The Politics of Fear* (1970); Richard M. Fried, *Men Against McCarthy* (1976); William Ewald, *Who Killed Joe McCarthy?* (1984); Ellen W. Schrecker, *No Ivory Tower: McCarthyism in the Universities* (1986); and David Oshinsky, *A Conspiracy So Immense: The World of Joe McCarthy* (1983).

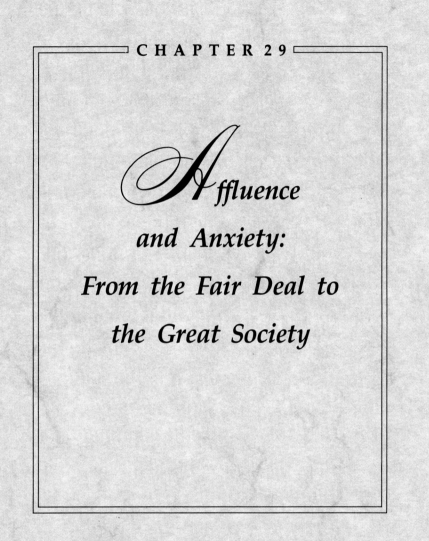

CHAPTER 29

Affluence and Anxiety: From the Fair Deal to the Great Society

On May 7, 1947, William Levitt announced plans to build 2000 rental houses in a former potato field on Long Island, thirty miles from midtown Manhattan. Using mass production techniques he had learned while erecting navy housing during the war, Levitt quickly built 4000 homes and rented them to young veterans eager to leave crowded city apartments or their parents' homes to begin raising families. A change in government financing regulations led him to begin offering his houses for sale in 1948 for a small amount down and a low monthly payment. Young couples, many of them the original renters, quickly bought the first 4000; by the time Levittown—as he called the new community—was completed in 1951, it contained over 17,000 homes. So many babies were born in Levittown that it soon became known as "Fertility Valley" and "The Rabbit Hutch."

Levitt eventually built two more Levittowns, one in Pennsylvania and one in New Jersey; each contained the same curving streets, neighborhood parks and playgrounds, and community swimming pools as did the first development. Some observers denounced Levittown, seeing it as a symbol of conformity and materialism, but William Levitt had tapped the postwar desire of young Americans to move to the suburbs and raise their children outside the central city.

The secret of Levittown's appeal was the basic house, a 720-square-foot Cape Cod design built on a concrete slab. It had a kitchen, two bedrooms and bath, a living room complete with a fireplace and sixteen-foot picture window, and an expansion attic with room for two more bedrooms. Levitt built only one interior, but there were four different facades to break the monotony. The original house sold for $6990 in 1948; even the improved model, a ranch-style house, sold for less than $10,000 in 1951.

Levitt's houses were ideal for young people just starting out in life. They were cheap, comfortable, and efficient, and each home came with a refrigerator, cooking range, and washing machine. Despite the conformity of the houses, the three Levittowns were surprisingly diverse communities; residents had a wide variety of religious, ethnic, and occupational backgrounds. African Americans, however, were rigidly excluded. In time, as the more successful families moved on to larger homes in more expensive neighborhoods, the Levittowns became enclaves for lower-middle-class families.

Levittown symbolized the most significant social trend of the postwar era in the United States—the flight to the suburbs. The residential areas surrounding cities like New York and Chicago nearly doubled in the 1950s. While central cities remained relatively stagnant during the decade, suburbs grew by 46 percent; by 1960, some sixty million people, one-third of the nation, lived in suburban rings around the cities. This massive shift in population from the central city was accompanied by a baby boom that started during World War II. Young married couples began to have three, four, or even five children (compared with only one or two children in American families during the 1930s). These larger families led to a 19 percent growth in the nation's population between 1950 and 1960, the greatest increase in growth rate since 1910.

The economy boomed as residential construction soared. By 1960, one-fourth of all existing homes were less than ten years old and factories

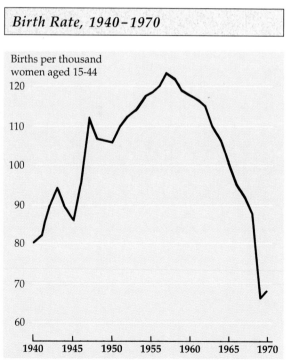

Birth Rate, 1940–1970

Births per thousand women aged 15-44

Source: Compiled from U.S. Bureau of the Census, Historical Statistics of the United States, Colonial Times to 1970, Bicentennial Edition, Washington, D.C., 1975.

Shoppers in a New York City department store in 1951 besiege the salesclerks at the electric mixer counter. Consumers were starved for home appliances, which had been unaffordable before the war and unavailable during the war.

were turning out large quantities of appliances and television sets for the new households. A multitude of new consumer products—ranging from frozen foods to filter cigarettes, from high fidelity phonographs to cars equipped with automatic transmissions and tubeless tires—appeared in stores and showrooms. In the suburbs, the supermarket replaced the corner grocer, carrying a vast array of items that enabled homemakers to provide their families with a more varied diet.

A new affluence replaced the poverty and hunger of the Great Depression for most Americans, but many could not forget the haunting memories of the thirties. The obsession with material goods took on an almost desperate quality, as if a profusion of houses, cars, and home appliances could guarantee that the nightmare of depression would never return. Critics were quick to disparage the quality of life in suburban society. They condemned the conformity, charging the newly affluent with forsaking traditional American individualism to live in identical houses, drive look-alike cars, and accumulate the same material possessions. Folksinger Malvina Reynolds caught the essence of postwar suburbia in her 1963 song:

> *Little boxes on the hillside,*
> *Little boxes made of ticky tacky*
> *Little boxes on the hillside,*
> *Little boxes all the same.*

> *There's a green one and a pink one*
> *And a blue one and a yellow one*
> *And they're all made out of ticky tacky*
> *And they all look just the same.*

("Little Boxes," words and music by Malvina Reynolds. Copyright © 1962 Schroder Music Co. [ASCAP]. Used by permission. All rights reserved.)

Events abroad added to the feeling of anxiety in the postwar years. Nuclear war became a frighteningly real possibility. The rivalry with the Soviet Union had led to the second Red Scare, with charges of treason and disloyalty being leveled at loyal Americans. Many Americans joined with Senator Joseph McCarthy in searching for the Communist enemy at home rather than abroad. Loyalty oaths and book-burning revealed how insecure Americans had become in the era of the Cold War. Thus beneath the bland surface of suburban affluence, a dark current of distrust and insecurity marred the picture of a nation fulfilling its economic destiny.

THE POSTWAR BOOM

For fifteen years following World War II, the nation witnessed a period of unparalleled economic growth. A pent-up demand for consumer goods fueled a steady industrial expansion. And heavy government spending during the Cold War added an extra stimulus to the economy, offsetting brief recessions in 1949 and 1953 and moderating a steeper one in 1957–1958. By the end of the fifties, the American people had achieved an affluence that finally erased the lingering memories of the Great Depression.

Postwar Prosperity

The economy began its upward surge as the result of two long-term factors. First, American consumers—after being held in check by depression and then by wartime scarcities—finally had a chance to indulge their suppressed appetites for material goods. At the war's end, personal savings in the United States stood at more than $37 billion, providing a powerful stimulus to consumption. Initially, American factories could not turn out enough automobiles and appliances to satisfy the horde of buyers. By 1950, however, production lines had finally caught up with the demand. In that year, Americans bought more than six million cars, and the gross national product (GNP) reached $318 billion (50 percent higher than in 1940).

A suburban Sunday in the 1950s. The family car, laden with shiny chrome and elongated tailfins, became an essential part of suburban life.

The Cold War provided the additional stimulus the economy needed when postwar expansion slowed. The Marshall Plan and other foreign-aid programs financed a heavy export trade. Then the outbreak of the Korean War helped overcome a brief recession and ensured continued prosperity as the government spent massive amounts on guns, planes, and munitions. In 1952, the nation spent $44 billion, two-thirds of the federal budget, on national defense. Although Eisenhower managed to bring about some modest reductions, defense spending continued at a level of $40 billion throughout the decade.

The nation achieved a level of affluence in the 1950s that made the persisting fear of another Great Depression seem irrational. The baby boom and the spectacular growth of suburbia served as great stimulants to the consumer-goods industries. Manufacturers turned out an ever-increasing number of refrigerators, washing machines, and dishwashers to equip the kitchens of Levittown and its many imitators across the country. The automobile industry thrived with suburban expansion as two-car families became more and more common. In 1955, in an era when oil was abundant and gasoline sold for less than 30¢ a gallon, Detroit sold a record 8 million cars. The electronics industry boomed. Consumers were eager to acquire the latest marvel of home entertainment—the television set.

In addition, commercial enterprises snapped up office machines and the first generation of computers; industry installed electronic sensors and processors as it underwent extensive automation, and the military displayed an insatiable appetite for electronic devices for its planes and ships. As a result, American industry averaged more than $10 billion a year in capital investment, and the number of persons employed rose above the long-sought goal of sixty million nationwide.

Yet the economic abundance of the 1950s was not without its problems. While some sections of the nation (notably the emerging Sunbelt areas of the South and West) benefited enormously from the growth of the aircraft and electronics industries, older manufacturing regions, such as New England, did not fare as well. The steel industry increased its capacity during the decade, but it began to fall behind the rate of national growth. Agriculture continued to experience bumper

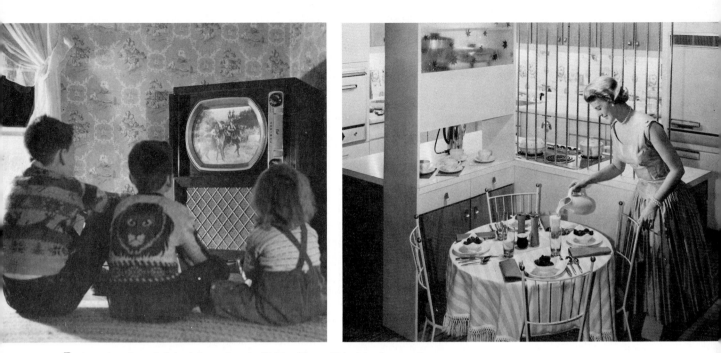

*P*ostwar Americans indulged themselves in flights of fancy. Television became the new entertainment medium and the advertising industry conjured up images of the ideal home-maker in her dream kitchen.

crops and low prices, so that rural regions, like the vast areas of the Plains states, failed to share in the general affluence. Unemployment persisted despite the boom, rising to over 7 percent in a sharp recession that hit the country in the fall of 1957 and lasted through the summer of 1958. The rate of economic growth slowed in the second half of the decade, causing concern about the continuing vitality of the American economy.

None of these flaws, however, could disguise the fact that the nation was prospering to an extent no one dreamed possible in the 1930s. The GNP grew to $440 billion by 1960, more than double the 1940 level. More important, workers now labored fewer than forty hours a week; they rarely worked on Saturdays, and nearly all enjoyed a two-week paid vacation each year. By the mid-1950s, the average American family had twice as much real income to spend as its counterpart had possessed in the boom years of the 1920s. From 1945 to 1960, per-capita disposable income rose by $500—to $1845—for every man, woman, and child in the country. The American people, in one generation, had moved from poverty and depression to the highest standard of living the world had ever known.

Life in the Suburbs

Sociologists had difficulty describing the nature of suburban society in the fifties. Some saw it as classless, while others noted the absence of both the very rich and the very poor and consequently labeled it "middle class." Rather than forming a homogeneous social group, though, the suburbs contained a surprising variety of people, whether classified as "upper lower," "lower middle," and "upper middle" or simply as blue collar, white collar, and professional. Doctors and lawyers often lived in the same developments as shoe salesmen and master plumbers. The traditional distinctions of ancestry, education, and size of residence no longer differentiated people as easily as they had in the past.

Yet suburbs could vary widely, from working-class communities clustered near factories built in the countryside to old, elitist areas like Scarsdale, New York, and Shaker Heights, Ohio. Most were almost exclusively white and Christian, but suburbs like Great Neck on Long Island and Richmond Heights outside Miami enabled Jews and blacks to take part in the flight from the inner city.

Life in all these suburban communities depended on the automobile. Highways and expressways allowed fathers to commute to jobs in the cities, often an hour or more away. Children might ride buses to and from school, but mothers had to drive them to piano lessons and Little League ball games. Two cars became a necessity for almost every suburban family, thus helping spur the boom in automobile production. In 1948, only 59 percent of American families owned a car; just a few years later, nearly every family above the poverty line had at least one vehicle, and many had several.

In the new drive-in culture, people shopped at the stores that first grew up in "miracle miles" along the highways and later at the shopping centers that began to dot the countryside by the mid-1950s. There were only eight shopping centers in the entire country in 1946; hundreds appeared over the next fifteen years, including Poplar Plaza in Memphis, with one large department store, 30 retail shops, and parking for over 500 cars. In 1956, the first enclosed air-conditioned mall, the Southdale Shopping Center, opened outside Minneapolis.

Despite the increased mobility provided by the car, the home became the focus for activities and aspirations. The postwar shortage of housing which often forced young couples to live with their parents or in-laws created an intense demand for new homes in the suburbs. When questioned, prospective buyers expressed a desire for "more space," for "comfort and roominess," and for "privacy and freedom of action" in their new residences. Men and women who moved to the suburbs prized the new kitchens with their built-in dishwashers, electric ovens, and gleaming counters; the extra bedrooms that ensured privacy from and for the children; the large garages that could be converted into recreation rooms; and the small, neat lawns that gave them an area for outdoor activities as well as a new way to compete with their neighbors. "Togetherness" became the code word of the fifties. Families did things together, whether gathering around the TV sets that dominated living rooms, attending community activities, or taking vacations in the huge station wagons of the era.

But there were some less attractive consequences of the new suburban lifestyle. The extended family, where several generations had lived in close proximity, was a casualty of the

Married Women in the Labor Force	
Year	Percentage (as percentage of all married women)
1950	24.8
1951	26.7
1952	26.8
1953	27.7
1954	28.1
1955	29.4
1956	30.2
1957	30.8
1958	31.4
1959	32.3
1960	31.7

Source: Compiled from U.S. Bureau of the Census, Historical Statistics of the United States, Colonial Times to 1970, Bicentennial Edition, Washington, D.C., 1975.

boom in small, detached homes. As Kenneth Jackson has noted, suburban life "ordained that most children would grow up in intimate contact only with their parents and siblings." Grandparents, aunts and uncles, cousins, and more distant relatives would become remote figures, seen only on special occasions.

The nuclear family, typical of the suburb, did nothing to encourage the development of feminism. The end of the war saw many women who had entered the work force return to the home, where the role of wife and mother continued to be viewed as the ideal for women in the 1950s. Trends toward getting married earlier and having larger families reinforced the pattern of women devoting all their efforts to housework and child-raising rather than acquiring professional skills and pursuing careers outside the home. Adlai Stevenson, extolling "the humble role of housewife," told Smith College graduates that there was much they could do "in the living room with a baby in your lap or in the kitchen with a can opener in your hand." Dr. Benjamin Spock's 1946 bestseller, Baby and Child Care, became a fixture in millions of homes, while the traditional women's magazines like McCall's and Good Housekeeping thrived by featuring articles on natural childbirth and inspirational pieces such as "Homemaking Is My Vocation."

Nonetheless, the number of working wives

doubled between 1940 and 1960. By the end of the fifties, 40 percent of American women, and nearly one-third of all wives, had jobs outside the home. The heavy expenses involved in rearing and educating children led wives and mothers to seek ways to augment the family income, inadvertently preparing the way for a new demand for equality in the 1960s.

THE GOOD LIFE?

Consumerism became the dominant social theme of the 1950s. Yet even with an abundance of creature comforts and added hours of leisure time, the quality of life left many Americans anxious and dissatisfied.

Areas of Greatest Growth

Organized religion flourished in the climate of the 1950s. Ministers, priests, and rabbis all commented on the rise in church and synagogue attendance in the new communities. Will Herberg claimed that religious affiliation had become the primary identifying feature of modern American life, dividing the nation into three separate segments—Protestant, Catholic, and Jewish.

Some observers condemned the bland, secular nature of suburban churches, which seemed to be an integral part of the consumer society. "On weekdays one shops for food," wrote one critic, "on Saturdays one shops for recreation, and on Sundays one shops for the Holy Ghost." But the popularity of religious writer Norman Vincent Peale, with his positive gospel that urged people to "start thinking faith, enthusiasm and joy," suggested that the new churches filled a genuine if shallow human need. At the same time, the emergence of neo-orthodoxy in Protestant seminaries (notably through the ideas of Reinhold Niebuhr) and the rapid spread of radical forms of fundamentalism (such as the Assemblies of God) indicated that millions of Americans still were searching for a more personal religious faith.

Schools provided an immediate problem for the growing new suburban communities. The unprecedented increase in the number of school-age children, from twenty to thirty million in the first eight grades, overwhelmed the resources of many local districts, leading to demands for

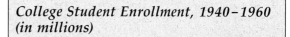

College Student Enrollment, 1940–1960 (in millions)

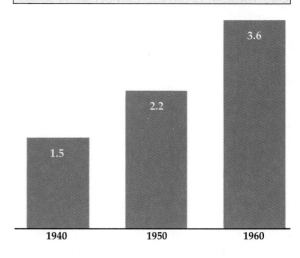

1940   1950   1960

federal aid. Congress granted limited help for areas affected by defense plants and military bases, but Eisenhower's reluctance to unbalance the budget—along with traditional adherence to state control over public education—blocked further federal assistance prior to 1957 when the government reacted to *Sputnik* (see p. 865).

Equally important, a controversy arose over the nature of education in the 1950s. Critics of "progressive" education called for sweeping educational reforms and a new stress on traditional academic subjects. Suburban communities often had bitter fights; affluent parents demanded kindergarten enrichment programs and grade-school foreign-language instruction while working-class people resisted such costly innovations. The one thing all seemed to agree on was the desirability of a college education. The number of young people attending colleges increased from 1.5 million in 1940 to 3.6 million in 1960, leading to rapid expansion of university enrollment.

The largest advances were made in the exciting new medium of television. From a shaky start just after the war, TV boomed in the fifties, pushing radio aside and undermining many of the nation's magazines. By 1957, three networks controlled the airwaves, reaching 40 million sets over nearly 500 stations. Advertisers soon took charge of the new medium, using techniques first pioneered in radio—including pretaped commercials, quiz shows, and soap operas.

ℛise of a New Idiom in Modern Painting:
Abstract Expressionism

In the 1950s, New York replaced Paris as the Western world's capital of avant-garde art. The artists at the center of this phenomenon were the Abstract Expressionists—notably Jackson Pollock, Mark Rothko, Robert Motherwell, Willem De Kooning, Barnett Newman, Adolph Gottlieb, and Franz Kline.

These artists did not share a common style or motif of painting. Rather they shared a mutual conception of what constituted art: a portrayal of individual feelings and psychological traumas through improvised visual expressions.

The Abstract Expressionists abandoned representational art—the use of figures—and geometric design for a freer use of color and line. They strove to express transcendental themes by capturing a moment in their own lives rather than depicting a figure or a premeditated idea. Their work, wrote art critic Harold Rosenberg, "was not a picture but an event."

The careers of Jackson Pollock and Mark Rothko exemplify the

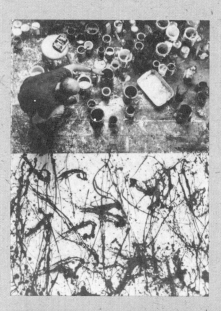

Pollack began each painting without a preconceived plan, spontaneously dripping pigment across a canvas on the floor until the composition began to suggest its own development. His Convergence (1952), a typically complex work of varied colors, is shown below.

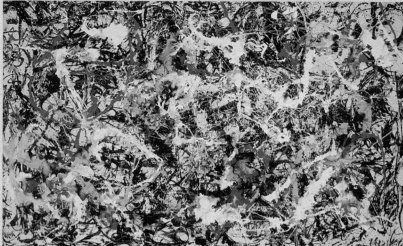

common and contrasting themes that characterized the Abstract Expressionists. Jackson Pollock was born in Cody, Wyoming in 1912. Mark Rothko was born nine years earlier in Dvinsk, Russia, emigrated to the United States as a boy, and was reared in Portland, Oregon. By the early 1930s, both painters had settled in New York City, the crucible of avant-garde American painting during the Great Depression.

The New Deal's Federal Art Project under the Work's Progress Administration (WPA) contributed to the development of a self-conscious artistic community in New York. The Project also provided Pollock and Rothko their first opportunities to paint full-time. Like many artists of their generation, they adopted leftist political concerns. Their early 1930s works in Social Realism—a style of monumental narrative painting that emphasized social themes and collective action—reflected these beliefs.

In the late 1920s and 1930s, several important museums opened in New York. Among them, the Museum of Modern Art, opened in 1929, displayed works by such masters as Pablo Picasso. These collections gave New York artists the opportunity to study first-hand the leaders of the dominant movements in twentieth-century European art. Pollock, for instance, studied Wassily Kandinsky's Expressionist works while working as a custodian at the Museum of Non-Objective Art (today's Solomon R. Guggenheim Museum). Also, prominent European artists—

such as Andre Breton, Mark Chagall, Andre Masson, Piet Mondrian, and Yves Tanguy, to name a few—fled to New York to escape fascist regimes. The arrival of the Europeans provided "American painters," noted critic Clement Greenberg, "the sense, wholly new in this country, of being in the center of art in their time."

The presence of these artists had a major impact on Pollock and Rothko. With the onset of World War II, they abandoned their leftist politics and what they now considered the provincialism of Social Realism. Inspired by Cubism's radical abstraction of figures and Surrealism's juxtaposition of ordinary objects and symbols in psychologically provocative ways, Pollock and Rothko each began to experiment. Both became intrigued, for instance, with the Surrealists' use of automatism—a form of free-association in painting—to probe the unconscious.

The Depression and World War II compelled American artists to explore ways to confront the national consciousness forged by these two momentous events. This search for a new idiom evolved into Abstract Expressionism. Like other artists in their circle, Pollock's and Rothko's work in the early 1940s focused on archetypal myths—present in the unconscious of the individual and basic to human experience—as a source for examining universal psychological themes. Such fundamental concepts would transcend the cultural and social differences that separated individuals in complex modern societies like the United States.

The absence of any new generation of European talent after World War II augmented the growing self-assurance of American artists. In the late forties, Rothko and Pollock led the transition into the new genre of Abstract Expressionism. Pollock and Rothko abandoned all references to natural forms and mythological themes in favor of individual emotional experience. Their canvases became immense, creating a visual environment that enveloped the viewer.

Pollock physically involved himself in the painting process by using the floor of his studio as an easel. This allowed him to traverse the canvas while he cathartically dripped paint. Although Rothko worked more conventionally, his visions were as radical as Pollock's. Rothko painted introspective, floating color-masses that captured the somber mood of his more conventional 1930s paintings. Their shared commitment "to work from within" rather than "go to a subject matter outside from themselves," as Pollock put it, conceptually linked their very different visions.

In other areas of postwar culture —such as method acting, Beat literature, and be-bop jazz—American artists also experimented with extemporaneous expression in search of a new formal vocabulary that reflected existential concerns. Poet Robert Creeley commented that the horrors of World War II and the spectre of nuclear apocalypse had "shaken" the arts, leading both the Beats and Abstract Expressionists to conclude that cultural expression "had to be reformed" in postwar America.

Avant-garde painters, like many other artists and intellectuals in the fifties, abhorred the dominance of middle-class cultural values and social conformity that stifled individualism and led to alienation. And although the avant-garde painters avoided political interpretations of their work, there was an intellectual agreement between their aesthetic concerns—which emphasized freedom—and the emerging Cold War ethos condemning totalitarianism. According to art historian Serge Guilbaut, the

Rothko, Mark. Number 10 *1950. 7'6⅜" × 57⅛", Collection, The Museum of Modern Art, New York. Gift of Phillip Johnson.*

Abstract Expressionists became the "protégé of the new liberalism," that sought to defend freedom from the "authoritarianism of the left and the right."

Whatever their social message, these artists tapped feelings that produced moving paintings but sometimes had tragic impact on their lives. After 1953, Pollock's work declined as he turned to alcohol. Following much personal anguish, he died in a possibly suicidal 1956 automobile accident. Mark Rothko battled serious bouts of depression throughout his career; he took his own life in 1970.

Pollock, Rothko, and the other Abstract Expressionists collectively left an enduring legacy. Their paintings stand as both a striking aesthetic commentary on culture in the Cold War and as testimony to the emergence of the United States as the center of avant-garde art and New York City as its capital.

I Love Lucy *starred Lucille Ball and her husband Desi Arnaz; they also produced the show together. Lucy was an immediate hit with audiences and Ball's sense of comedy made the show one of the most enduring in television history.*

At first, the insatiable demand for programs encouraged a burst of creativity. Playwrights such as Reginald Rose, Rod Serling, and Paddy Chayefsky wrote a series of notable dramas for *Playhouse 90, Studio One,* and the *Goodyear Television Playhouse.* Broadcast live from cramped studios, these productions thrived on tight dramatic structures, movable scenery, and frequent close-ups of the actors.

Advertisers, however, quickly became disillusioned with the live anthology programs, which usually dealt with controversial subjects or focused on ordinary people and events. In contrast, sponsors wanted shows that stressed excitement, glamor, and instant success. Aware that audiences were fascinated by contestants with unusual expertise (a shoemaker answering tough questions on operas, a grandmother stumping experts on baseball), producers began giving away huge cash prizes on *The $64,000 Question* and *Twenty-one.* In 1959, the nation was shocked when Charles Van Doren, a Columbia University professor, confessed that he had been given the answers in advance to win $129,000 on *Twenty-one.* The three networks quickly dropped all the big-prize quiz programs, replacing them with comedy, action, and adventure shows such as *The Untouchables* and *Bonanza.* Despite its early promise of artistic innovation, television had become a technologically sophisticated but safe conveyor of the consumer culture.

Critics of the Consumer Society

One striking feature of the 1950s was the abundance of self-criticism. A number of widely read books explored the flaws in the new suburbia. John Keats' *The Crack in the Picture Window* described the endless rows of tract houses "vomited up" by developers as "identical boxes spreading like gangrene." Their occupants—whom he dubbed the Drones, the Amiables, and the Fecunds—lost any sense of individuality in their obsession with material goods.

Richard and Katherine Gordon were more concerned about the psychological toll of suburban life in their 1960 book *The Split Level Trap.* They labeled the new life-style "Disturbia" and bemoaned the "haggard" men, "tense and anxious" women, and the "gimme" kids it produced. The most sweeping indictment came in William H. Whyte's *The Organization Man* (1956), based on a study of the Chicago suburb of Park Forest. Whyte perceived a change from the old Protestant ethic, with its emphasis on hard work and personal responsibility, to a new social ethic, where everything centered on "the team" and the ultimate goal was "belongingness." The result was a stifling conformity and the loss of personal identity.

The most influential social critic of the fifties was Harvard sociologist David Riesman. His book *The Lonely Crowd* appeared in 1950 and set

Novelist Jack Kerouac and his fellow "beat" poets bemoaned the moral bankruptcy of popular culture. Their conversational writing styles and intensely personal subject matter influenced other poets.

the tone for intellectual commentary about suburbia for the rest of the decade. Riesman described the shift from the "inner-directed" Americans of the past who had relied on such traditional values as self-denial and frugality to the "other-directed" Americans of the consumer society who constantly adapted their behavior to conform to social pressures. The consequences—a decline in individualism and a tendency for people to become acutely sensitive to the expectations of others—produced a bland and tolerant society of consumers lacking creativity and a sense of adventure.

C. Wright Mills was a far more caustic, though less popular, commentator on American society in the 1950s. Anticipating government statistics that revealed that white-collar workers (sales clerks, office workers, bank tellers) now outnumbered blue-collar workers (miners, factory workers, millhands), Mills described the new middle class in ominous terms in his books *White Collar* (1951) and *Power Elite* (1956). The corporation

was the villain for Mills, depriving office workers of their own identities and imposing an impersonal discipline through manipulation and propaganda. The industrial assembly line had given way to an even more dehumanizing workplace, the modern office. "At rows of blank-looking counters sat rows of blank-looking girls with blank, white folders in their blank hands, all blankly folding blank papers."

This disenchantment with the consumer culture reached its most eloquent expression with the "beats," literary groups that rebelled against the materialistic society of the 1950s. Jack Kerouac's novel *On the Road,* published in 1957, set the tone for the new movement. The name came from the quest for beatitude, a state of inner grace sought in Zen Buddhism. Flouting the respectability of suburbia, the 'beatniks"—as middle-America termed them—were easily identified by their long hair, bizarre clothing, and penchant for sexual promiscuity and drug experimentation. They were conspicuous dropouts from a society they found senseless. Poet Lawrence Ferlinghetti, who held forth in the City Lights Bookshop in San Francisco (a favorite resort of the beats), summed it up this way: "I was a wind-up toy someone had dropped wound up into a world already running down."

Despite the disapproval they evoked from mainstream Americans, the beat generation had only compassion for their detractors. "We love everything," Kerouac proclaimed, "Bill Graham, the Big Ten, Rock and Roll, Zen, apple pie, Eisenhower—we dig it all." Yet as highly visible nonconformists in an era of stifling conformity, the beats demonstrated a style of social protest that would flower into the counterculture of the sixties.

The Reaction to *Sputnik*

The profound insecurity that underlay American life throughout the fifties burst into view in October 1957, when the Soviets sent the satellite *Sputnik* into orbit around the earth. The public's reaction to this impressive scientific feat was panic. The declining rate of economic growth; the recession of 1957–1958; the growing concern that American schools, with their frills and frivolities and their emphasis on social adjustment,

*F*earing that losing the space race might mean losing the Cold War, the United States quickly geared up to compete with the Soviet Union in space.

eign-language programs in the nation's schools and colleges. Soon American students were hard at work mastering the "new physics" and the "new math."

The belief persisted, however, that the faults lay deeper, that in the midst of affluence and abundance Americans had lost their competitive edge. Economists pointed to the higher rate of Soviet economic growth, and social critics bemoaned a supermarket culture that stressed consumption over production, comfort over hard work. Disturbed by the charge that the nation had lost its sense of purpose, President Eisenhower finally appointed a Commission on National Goals "to develop a broad outline of national objectives for the next decade and longer." Ten prominent citizens from all walks of life, led by Henry W. Wriston of Brown University, issued a report which called for increased military spending abroad, greater economic growth at home, broader educational opportunities, and more government support for both scientific research and the advancement of the arts. The consensus seemed to be that rather than a change of direction, all the United States needed was a renewed commitment to the pursuit of excellence.

FAREWELL TO REFORM

It is not surprising that the spirit of reform underlying the New Deal failed to flourish in the postwar years. Growing affluence took away the sense of grievance and the cry for change that was so strong in the thirties. Eager to enjoy the new prosperity after years of want and sacrifice, the American people turned away from federal regulation and welfare programs.

Truman and the Fair Deal

Harry Truman tried to capitalize on his upset victory in 1948 to offer a broad program of reform to the nation on January 5, 1949. Venturing beyond earlier proposals by FDR to increase the minimum wage and broaden Social Security coverage, he called for a "Fair Deal," a reform package that comprised a new program of national medical insurance, federal aid to education, enactment of a Fair Employment Practices Com-

were lagging behind their Russian counterparts —all contributed to a conviction that the nation had somehow lost its previously unquestioned primacy in the eyes of the world.

In the late 1950s, the President and Congress moved to restore national confidence. Eisenhower appointed James R. Killian, president of the Massachusetts Institute of Technology, as his special assistant for science and technology and to oversee a crash program in missile development. The House and Senate followed by creating the National Aeronautics and Space Administration (NASA) in 1958. Congress appropriated vast sums to allow the agency to compete with the Russians in the space race. Soon a new group of heroes, the astronauts, began the training that led to suborbital flights and eventually to John Glenn's five-hour flight around the globe in 1962. (See the picture essay on the Space Program following p. 915.)

Congress also sought to match the Soviet educational advances by passing the National Defense Education Act (NDEA). This legislation authorized federal financing of scientific and for-mission (FEPC) to prevent economic discrimination against blacks, and an overhaul of the farm subsidy program.

The Fair Deal was never enacted. Except for raising the minimum wage to seventy-five cents an hour and broadening Social Security to cover ten million more Americans, Congress refused to pass any of Truman's health, education, or civil rights measures. The nation's doctors waged an effective campaign against the President's health-insurance plan, and southern senators blocked any action on FEPC. Aid to education, repeal of Taft-Hartley, and the new farm program all failed to win congressional approval. In part, Truman was to blame for trying to secure too much too soon; if he had selected one or two measures and given them priority, he might have been more successful. More important, however, was the fact that despite the Democratic victory in 1948, Congress remained under the control of a bipartisan conservative coalition of northern Republicans and southern Democrats, the same alignment that had halted Roosevelt's reforms after 1938.

Although his legislative failure became certain in 1950 when war once again subordinated domestic issues to foreign policy, President Truman deserves credit for maintaining and consolidating the New Deal. His spirited leadership prevented any Republican effort to repeal the gains of the 1930s. Moreover, even though he failed to get any new measures enacted, he broadened the reform agenda and laid the groundwork for future advances in health care, aid to education, and civil rights.

Eisenhower's Modern Republicanism

The American people found that moderation was the keynote of the Eisenhower presidency. His major goal from the outset was to restore calm and tranquility to a badly divided nation. Unlike FDR and Truman, Eisenhower had no commitment to social change or economic reform. Ike was a fiscal conservative who was intent on balancing the budget. Yet unlike some Republicans of the extreme right wing, he had no plans to dismantle the social programs of the New Deal. He sought instead to keep military spending in check, to encourage as much private initiative as

Eisenhower neither enacted nor repealed any major reform legislation during his presidency. His landslide victories in 1952 and 1956 reflected the country's satisfaction with the status quo.

possible, and to reduce federal activities to the bare minimum. Defining his position as "Modern Republicanism," he claimed that he was "conservative when it comes to money and liberal when it comes to human beings."

On domestic issues, Eisenhower preferred to delegate authority and to play a passive role. He concentrated his own efforts on the Cold War abroad. The men he chose to run the nation reflected his preference for successful corporation executives. Thus George Humphrey, an Ohio industrialist, carried out a policy of fiscal stringency as secretary of the treasury, while Charles E. Wilson (the former head of General Motors) sought to keep the Pentagon budget under control as secretary of defense. Neither man was wholly successful, and both were guilty of tactless public statements. Humphrey warned that unless Congress showed budgetary restraint "we're gonna have a depression which will curl your hair," and Wilson gained notoriety by proclaiming "what was good for our country was good for General Motors, and vice versa."

Eisenhower was equally reluctant to play an active role in dealing with Congress. A fervent believer in the separation of powers, Ike did not wish to engage in intensive lobbying. He left congressional relations to aides such as Sherman Adams, a former New Hampshire governor who served as White House chief of staff. Adams's skill at resolving problems at lower levels insulated Eisenhower from many of the nation's pressing domestic problems.

Relations with Congress were weakened further by Republican losses in the midterm election of 1954. The Democrats regained control of both houses and kept it throughout the 1950s. The President had to rely on two Texas Democrats, Senate Majority Leader Lyndon B. Johnson and House Speaker Sam Rayburn, for legislative action; at best, it was an awkward and uneasy relationship.

The result was a very modest legislative record. Eisenhower did continue the basic social measures of the New Deal. In 1954, he signed bills extending Social Security benefits to more than 7 million Americans, raising the minimum wage to $1 an hour, and adding 4 million workers to those eligible for unemployment benefits. He consolidated the administration of welfare programs by creating the Department of Health, Education and Welfare in 1953. Oveta Culp Hobby, the first woman to hold a cabinet post in a Republican administration, headed the new department. But Ike steadfastly opposed Democratic plans for compulsory health insurance—which he condemned as the "socialization of medicine" —and comprehensive federal aid to education, preferring to leave everything except school construction in the hands of local and state authorities. This lack of presidential support and the continuing grip of the conservative coalition in Congress blocked any further reform in the 1950s.

The one significant legislative achievement of the Eisenhower years came with the passage of the Highway Act of 1956. After a twelve-year delay, Congress appropriated funds for a 41,000-mile interstate highway system consisting of multilane divided expressways that would connect

The Election of 1956			
Candidate	Party	Popular Vote	Electoral Vote
Eisenhower	Republican	35,585,245	457
Stevenson	Democrat	26,030,172	73

the nation's major cities. Justified on grounds of national defense, the 1956 act pleased a variety of highway users: the trucking industry, automobile clubs, organized labor (eager for construction jobs), farmers (needing to speed their crops to market), and state highway officials (anxious for the 90 percent funding contributed by the federal government). Eisenhower's insistence that general revenue funds not be used to provide the federal share—estimated at $25 billion—of the total cost led to the creation of a highway trust fund raised by taxes on fuel, tires, and new cars and trucks. Built over the next twenty years, the interstate highway system had a profound influence on American life. It stimulated the economy and shortened travel time dramatically, while at the same time intensifying the nation's dependence on the automobile and distorting metropolitan growth patterns into long strips paralleling the new expressways.

Overall, the Eisenhower years marked an era of political moderation. The American people, enjoying the abundance of the 1950s, seemed quite content with legislative inaction. The President was sensitive to the nation's economic health; when recessions developed in 1953 and again in 1957 after his landslide reelection victory, he quickly abandoned his goal of a balanced budget in favor of a policy advocating government spending to restore prosperity. These steps, along with modest increases in New Deal welfare programs, led to a steady growth in the federal budget from $29.5 billion in 1950 to $76.5 in 1960. Eisenhower was able to balance the budget in only three of his eight years in office, and the $12-billion deficit in 1959 was larger than any ever before recorded in peacetime. In this manner, Eisenhower was able to maintain the New Deal legacy of federal responsibility for social welfare and the state of the economy while at the same time, he successfully resisted demands for more extensive government involvement in American life.

THE STRUGGLE OVER CIVIL RIGHTS

Despite President Eisenhower's reluctance to champion the cause of reform, powerful pressures for change forced long overdue action in one area of American life—the denial of basic rights to the nation's black minority. In the midst of the Cold War, the contradiction between the denunciation of the Soviet Union for its human-rights violations and the second-class status of African Americans began to arouse the national conscience. Fighting for freedom against Communist tyranny abroad, Americans had to face the reality of the continued denial of freedom to a submerged minority at home.

African Americans had benefited economically from World War II, but they were still a seriously disadvantaged group. Those who had left the South for better opportunities in northern and western cities were concentrated in blighted and segregated neighborhoods, working at low-paying jobs, suffering economic and social discrimination, and failing to share fully in the postwar prosperity.

In the South, conditions were much worse. State laws forced blacks to live almost totally segregated from white society. Not only did African Americans attend separate (and almost always inferior) schools, but they also were rigidly segregated in all public facilities. They were forced to use separate waiting rooms in train stations, separate seats on all forms of transportation, separate drinking fountains, and even separate telephone booths. "Segregation was enforced at all places of public entertainment, including libraries, auditoriums, and circuses," Chief Justice Earl Warren noted. "There was segregation in the hospitals, prisons, mental institutions, and nursing homes. Even ambulance service was segregated."

Civil Rights as a Political Issue

Truman was the first president to attempt to alter the historic pattern of racial discrimination in the United States. In 1946, he appointed a presidential commission on civil rights. A year later, in a sweeping report entitled "To Secure These Rights," the commission recommended the reinstatement of the wartime Fair Employment Prac-

tices Committee (FEPC), the establishment of a permanent civil rights commission, and the denial of federal aid to any state that condoned segregation in schools and public facilities. The President's ten-point legislative program in 1948 included some of these measures, notably the establishment of a permanent FEPC and a civil rights commission. But southern resistance blocked any action by Congress, and the inclusion of a strong civil rights plank in the 1948 Democratic platform led to the walkout of some southern delegations and a separate States' Rights (Dixiecrat) ticket in several states of the South that fall.

African-American voters in the North responded by backing Truman overwhelmingly over Dewey in the 1948 election. The African-American vote in key cities—Los Angeles, Cleveland, and Chicago—ensured the Democratic victory in California, Ohio, and Illinois. Truman responded by including civil rights legislation in his Fair Deal program in 1949. Once again, however, determined southern opposition blocked congressional action on both a permanent FEPC and an anti-lynching measure.

Even though President Truman had been unable to secure any significant legislation, he had succeeded in adding civil rights to the liberal agenda. From this time forward, it would be an integral part of the Democratic reform program. And Truman was able to use his executive power to assist African Americans. He strengthened the civil rights division of the Justice Department, which aided black groups in their efforts to challenge school segregation and restrictive housing covenants in the courts. Most important, in 1948 Truman issued an order calling for the desegregation of the armed forces. The navy and the air force quickly complied, but the army resisted until the personnel needs of the Korean War finally overcame the military's objections. By the end of the 1950s, the armed forces had become far more integrated than American society at large.

Desegregating the Schools

The nation's schools soon became the primary target of civil rights advocates. The NAACP concentrated first on universities, successfully waging an intensive legal battle to win admission for

Linda Brown (left). Her parents were the plaintiffs in the Brown v. Board of Education of Topeka *landmark Supreme Court case. Thurgood Marshall (above), a leading African-American civil rights lawyer, was chief counsel for the Browns.*

qualified African Americans to graduate and professional schools. Led by Thurgood Marshall, NAACP lawyers then took on the broader issue of segregation in the country's public schools. Challenging the 1896 Supreme Court decision (*Plessy v. Ferguson*) that upheld the constitutionality of separate but equal public facilities, (see "The Shaping of Jim Crow," pp. 576-77), Marshall argued that even substantially equal but separate schools did profound psychological damage to African-American children and thus violated the Fourteenth Amendment.

The Supreme Court was unanimous in its 1954 decision in the case of *Brown* v. *Board of Education of Topeka*. Chief Justice Earl Warren, recently appointed by President Eisenhower, wrote the landmark opinion which flatly declared that "separate educational facilities are inherently unequal." To divide grade-school children "solely because of their race," Warren argued, "generates a feeling of inferiority as to their status in the community that may affect their hearts and minds in a way unlikely ever to be undone."

Despite this sweeping language, Warren realized that it would be difficult to change historic patterns of segregation quickly. Accordingly, in 1955 the Court ruled that implementation should proceed "with all deliberate speed" and left the details to the lower federal courts.

The process of desegregating the schools proved to be agonizingly slow. Officials in the border states quickly complied with the Court's ruling, but states deeper in the South responded with a policy of massive resistance. Local white citizens' councils organized to fight for retention of racial separation; 101 representatives and senators signed a Southern Manifesto in 1956 that denounced the *Brown* decision as "a clear abuse of judicial power." School boards, encouraged by this show of defiance, found a variety of ways to evade the Court's ruling. The most successful was the passage of pupil-placement laws. These laws enabled local officials to assign individual students to schools on the basis of scholastic aptitude, ability to adjust, and "morals, conduct, health and personal standards." These stalling tactics led to long disputes in the federal courts; by the end of the decade, less than 1 percent of the black children in the Deep South attended school with whites.

A conspicuous lack of presidential support further weakened the desegregation effort. Dwight Eisenhower was not a racist, but he believed that people's attitudes could not be changed by "cold lawmaking"—only "by appealing to reason, by prayer, and by constantly working at it through our own efforts." Quietly and unobtrusively, he worked to achieve desegregation in federal facilities, particularly in veterans' hospitals, navy yards, and the District of Columbia school system. Yet he refrained from endorsing the *Brown* decision, which he told an aide he believed had *"set back* progress in the South *at least fifteen years."*

Southern leaders mistook Ike's silence for tacit support of segregation. In 1957, Governor Orville Faubus of Arkansas called out the national guard to prevent the integration of Little Rock's Central High School on grounds of a threat to public order. After 270 armed troops turned back 9 young African-American students, a federal judge ordered the guardsmen removed; but when the blacks entered the school, a mob of 500 jeering whites surrounded the building. Eisenhower, who had told Faubus that "the Federal Constitution will be upheld by me by every legal means at my command," sent in 1000 paratroopers to ensure the rights of the 9 students to attend Central High. The children finished the school year under armed guard. Then Little Rock authorities closed Central High School for the next two years; when it reopened, there were only 3 African Americans in attendance.

Despite the snail's pace of school desegregation, the *Brown* decision led to other advances. In 1957, the Eisenhower administration proposed the first general civil rights legislation since Reconstruction. Strong southern resistance and compromise by both the administration and Senate Democratic leader Lyndon B. Johnson of Texas weakened the bill considerably. The final act, however, did create a permanent Commission for Civil Rights, one of Truman's original goals. It also provided for federal efforts aimed at "securing and protecting the right to vote." A second civil rights act in 1960 slightly strengthened the voting-rights section.

*A*ngry whites taunt one of the black students trying to pass through the lines of Arkansas National Guardsmen to enroll in Little Rock's Central High School in 1957.

Like the desegregation effort, the attempt to ensure African-American voting rights in the South was still largely symbolic. Southern registrars used a variety of devices, ranging from intimidation to unfair tests, to deny African Americans suffrage. Yet the actions of Congress and the Supreme Court marked a vital turning point in national policy toward racial justice.

The Beginnings of Black Activism

The most dynamic force for change came from African Americans themselves. The shift from legal struggles in the courts to protest in the streets began with an incident in Montgomery, Alabama. On December 1, 1955, Rosa Parks—a black seamstress who had been active in the local NAACP chapter—violated a city ordinance by refusing to give up her seat to a white person on a local bus. After her arrest, African Americans

*R*osa Parks's refusal to give up her seat to a white man on a Montgomery, Alabama, bus led to a citywide bus boycott that brought its leader, Rev. Martin Luther King, Jr., to prominence.

gathered to protest and found a young, eloquent leader in Martin Luther King, Jr. The son of a successful Atlanta preacher, King had studied theology at Boston University and only recently had taken his first church in Montgomery. He agreed to lead a massive boycott of the city's bus system, which depended heavily on African-American patronage.

The Montgomery bus boycott started out with a modest goal. Instead of challenging the legality of segregated seating, King simply asked that seats be taken on a first-come, first-served basis, with African Americans being seated from the back and the whites from the front of each bus. As the protest continued, however, and as they endured both legal harassment and sporadic acts of violence, the protesters began to be more assertive. An effective system of car pools enabled them to avoid using the city buses. Soon they were insisting on a complete end to segregated seating as they sang their new song of protest:

Ain't gonna ride them buses no more
Ain't gonna ride no more
Why in the hell don't the white folk know
That I ain't gonna ride no more.

The boycott ended in victory a year later when the Supreme Court ruled the Alabama segregated-seating law unconstitutional. King had won far more than this limited dent in the wall of segregation, however. He had emerged as the charismatic leader of a new civil rights movement—a man who won acclaim not only at home but around the world. He visited Third World leaders in Africa and Asia and paid homage to India's Mahatma Gandhi, who had influenced his reliance on civil disobedience. He led a triumphant Prayer Pilgrimage to Washington in 1957 on the third anniversary of the *Brown* decision, stirring the crowd of thirty thousand with his ringing demand for the right to vote. His cry, "Give us the ballot," boomed in salvos that civil rights historian Taylor Branch likened to "cannon bursts in a diplomatic salute." His remarkable voice became familiar to the entire nation. Unlike many African-American preachers, he never shouted, yet he captured his audience by presenting his ideas with both passion and a compelling cadence. "Though still a boy to many of his older listeners," Branch noted, "he had the commanding air of a burning sage."

Even more important, he had a strategy and message that fitted perfectly with the plight of his followers. Drawing on sources as diverse as Gandhi and Henry David Thoreau, King came out of the bus boycott with the concept of passive resistance. "If cursed," he had told protesters in Montgomery, "do not curse back. If struck, do not strike back, but evidence love and goodwill at all times." The essence of his strategy was to use the apparent weakness of southern blacks—their lack of power—and turn it into a conquering weapon. His message to southern whites was clear and unmistakable: "We will match your capacity to inflict suffering with our capacity to endure suffering. We will meet your physical force with soul force. We will not hate you, but we will not obey your evil laws. We will soon wear you down by pure capacity to suffer."

His ultimate goal was to unite the broken community through bonds of Christian love. He hoped to use nonviolence to appeal to middle-class white America, "to the conscience of the great decent majority who through blindness, fear, pride or irrationality have allowed their consciences to sleep." The result, King prophesied, would be to enable future historians to say of the effort, "There lived a great people—a black

Lunch counter sit-ins proved an effective tactic in the hard-fought effort to desegregate public facilities in southern cities.

people—who injected new meaning and dignity into the veins of civilization."

A year after the successful bus boycott, King founded the Southern Christian Leadership Conference (SCLC) to direct the crusade against segregation. Then in February 1960 another spontaneous event sparked a further advance for passive resistance. Four African-American students from North Carolina Agricultural and Technical College sat down at a dime-store lunch counter in Greensboro, North Carolina, and refused to move after being denied service. Other students, both whites and blacks, joined in similar "sit-ins" across the South, as well as "kneel-ins" at churches and "wade-ins" at swimming pools. By the end of the year, some fifty thousand young people had succeeded in desegregating public facilities in over a hundred southern cities. Several thousand of the demonstrators were arrested and put in jail, but the movement gained strength, leading to the formation of the Student Nonviolent Coordinating Committee (SNCC) in April 1960. From this time on, SCLC and SNCC, with their tactic of direct, though peaceful, confrontation, would replace the NAACP and its reliance on court action in the forefront of the civil rights movement. The change would eventually lead to dramatic success for the movement, but it also ushered in a period of heightened tension and social turmoil in the 1960s.

KENNEDY AND THE NEW FRONTIER

On Monday evening, September 26, 1960, John F. Kennedy and Richard M. Nixon faced each other in the nation's first televised debate between two presidential candidates. Kennedy, as the relatively unknown Democratic challenger, had proposed the debates; Nixon, confident of his mastery of television, had accepted even though, as Eisenhower's vice-president and early front-runner in the election, he had more to lose and less to gain.

Nixon arrived at the Chicago studio looking tired and ill at ease. The Republican candidate was still recovering from a knee injury which had slowed his campaign and left him pale and weak as he pursued a hectic catch-up schedule. The TV cameras were merciless, highlighting his heavy jowls and accentuating his pallor. In contrast, Kennedy, tanned from open-air appearances in California and rested by a day spent free from other campaign activities, looked fresh and robust.

Before a nationwide audience estimated at seventy-seven million, the Democratic challenger took the initiative, accusing the Republicans of letting the country drift at home and abroad. "I think it's time America started moving again," Kennedy declared. Nixon agreed that the problems facing the nation were serious, claiming

*B*oth candidates performed well in the televised Kennedy-Nixon debates, but Nixon lost the advantage of greater name recognition, while Kennedy won supporters with his healthier appearance and more confident manner.

only that he had better solutions. For more than an hour, the two candidates answered questions from a panel of journalists. Radiating confidence and self-assurance, Kennedy used a flow of statistics and details to create the image of a man deeply knowledgeable about all aspects of government. On the defensive, Nixon fought back by citing Eisenhower's record of peace and prosperity, but he appeared tense and uncomfortable in front of the cameras.

Polls taken over the next few weeks revealed a sharp swing to Kennedy. Many Democrats and independents who had thought him too young or too inexperienced were impressed by his performance. Nixon suffered more from his unattractive image than from what he said; those who heard the debate on radio thought that the Republican candidate more than held his own. In the three additional debates held during the campaign, Nixon improved his performance notably by wearing makeup to soften his appearance and by taking the offensive from Kennedy on the issues. But the damage had been done. A postelection poll revealed that of 4 million voters who were influenced by the debates, 3 million voted for Kennedy.

The televised debates were only one of many factors influencing the outcome of the 1960 election. In essence, Kennedy won because he took full advantage of all his opportunities. Lightly regarded by Democratic leaders, he won the nomination by appealing to the rank and file in the primaries, but then astutely chose Lyndon Johnson of Texas as his running mate to blunt Nixon's southern strategy.

During the fall campaign, Kennedy exploited the national mood of frustration that had followed *Sputnik.* At home, he promised to stimulate the lagging economy and carry forward long-overdue reforms in education, health care, and civil rights under the banner of the "New Frontier." Abroad, he pledged a renewed commitment to the Cold War, vowing that he would lead the nation to victory over the Soviet Union. He met the issue of his Catholicism head on, telling a group of Protestant ministers in Houston that as president he would always place country above religion. In the shrewdest move of all, he won over African-American voters by helping to secure the release of Martin Luther King, Jr., from a Georgia jail where the civil rights leader was being held on a trumped-up charge.

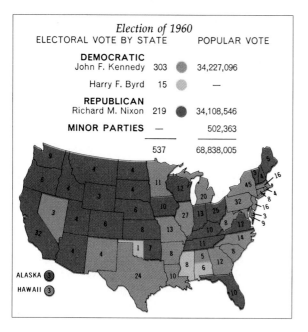

Election of 1960

ELECTORAL VOTE BY STATE			POPULAR VOTE
DEMOCRATIC			
John F. Kennedy	303		34,227,096
Harry F. Byrd	15		—
REPUBLICAN			
Richard M. Nixon	219		34,108,546
MINOR PARTIES	—		502,363
	537		68,838,005

ALASKA 3
HAWAII 3

The Democratic victory in 1960 was paper-thin. Kennedy's edge in the popular vote was only two-tenths of 1 percent, and his wide margin in the electoral college (303 to 219) was tainted by voting irregularities in several states—notably Illinois and Texas—which went Democratic by very slender majorities. Yet even though he had no mandate, Kennedy's triumph did mark a sharp political shift. In contrast to the aging Eisenhower, Kennedy symbolized youth, energy, and ambition. His mastery of the new medium of television reflected his sensitivity to the changes taking place in American life in the sixties. He came to office promising reform at home and advance abroad. Over the next five years, he and Lyndon Johnson achieved many of their goals only to find the nation caught up in new and even greater dilemmas.

The New Frontiersmen

The election of John F. Kennedy marked the arrival of a new generation of leadership. For the first time, people born in the 20th century who had entered political life after World War II were in charge of national affairs. Kennedy himself had first been elected to Congress in 1946 at the age of 29 and then had won a Senate seat in 1952. Although he had not sponsored any significant legislation as a senator, he championed the traditional Democratic reforms during his presidential campaign, labelling them the New Frontier. Above all, he had criticized the Republicans for allowing sluggish economic growth and failing to deal with such pressing social problems as health care and education. His call to get the nation moving again was particularly attractive to young people, who had shunned political involvement during the Eisenhower years.

The new administration reflected Kennedy's aura of youth and energy. Major cabinet appointments went to activists—notably Connecticut Governor Abraham Ribicoff as secretary of health, education, and welfare; labor lawyer Arthur J. Goldberg as secretary of labor; and Arizona Congressman Stuart Udall as secretary of the interior. The most controversial choice was Robert F. Kennedy, the President's brother, as attorney general. Critics scoffed at his lack of legal experience, leading JFK to note jokingly that he wanted to give Bobby "a little experience before he goes out to practice law." In fact, the President prized his brother's loyalty and shrewd political advice.

Equally important were the members of the White House staff who handled domestic affairs.

With their gala dinners and balls, the Kennedys brought a glamorous tone to the White House. Here, at an April 1962 party for Nobel Prize laureates, poet Robert Frost greets the couple.

Like their counterparts in foreign policy, these New Frontiersmen—Kenneth O'Donnell, Theodore Sorensen, Richard Goodwin, and Walter Heller—prided themselves on being tough-minded and pragmatic. In contrast to Eisenhower, Kennedy relied heavily on academics and intellectuals to help him infuse the nation with energy and a new sense of direction.

Kennedy's greatest asset was his own personality. A cool, attractive, and intelligent man, he possessed a sense of style that endeared him to the American public. He invited artists and musicians as well as corporate executives to White House functions; and his speeches were filled with references to Emerson and Shakespeare. He seemed to be a new Lancelot, bent on calling forth the best in national life; admirers likened his inner circle to King Arthur's court at Camelot. Reporters loved him, both for his fact-filled and candid press conferences and for his witty comments. Thus, after an embarrassing foreign policy failure, when his standing in the polls actually went up, he remarked, "It's just like Eisenhower. The worse I do, the more popular I get."

The Congressional Obstacle

Neither Kennedy's wit nor charm proved strong enough to break the logjam in Congress. Since the late 1940s, a series of reform bills ranging from health care to federal aid to education had been stalled on Capitol Hill. Despite his own triumph, however, the election of 1960 clouded the outlook for the New Frontier program. The Democrats had lost twenty seats in the House and two in the Senate; even though they retained majorities in both branches, a conservative coalition of northern Republicans and southern Democrats opposed all efforts at reform.

The situation was especially critical in the House, where 101 southern representatives held the balance of power between 160 northern Democrats and 174 Republicans. Aided by Speaker Sam Rayburn, Kennedy was able to enlarge the Rules Committee and overcome a traditional conservative roadblock, but the narrowness of the vote, 217 to 212, revealed how difficult it would be to enact reform measures. "There is no sense in raising hell and then not being successful," JFK noted ruefully after Catholic objections

to his aid to education bill—which excluded federal money for church schools—led to its defeat in the House. Discouraged, the President gave up the fight for health care in the Senate; he settled instead for a modest increase in the minimum wage and the passage of manpower training and area-redevelopment legislation.

Kennedy had no more success in enacting his program in 1962 and 1963. The conservative coalition stood firmly against education and health-care proposals. Shifting ground, the President did win approval for a trade expansion act in 1962 designed to lower tariff barriers, but no significant reform legislation was passed. Although the composition of Congress was his main obstacle, Kennedy's greater interest in foreign policy and his distaste for legislative infighting contributed to the outcome. JFK did not enjoy "blarneying with pompous congressmen and simply would not take the time to do it," one observer noted. As a result, the New Frontier languished in Congress.

Economic Advance

Kennedy gave a higher priority to the sluggish American economy. During the last years of Eisenhower's administration, the rate of economic growth had slowed to just over 2 percent annually, while unemployment rose to new heights with each recession. JFK was determined to recover quickly from the recession he had inherited and to stimulate the economy to achieve a much higher rate of long-term growth. In part, he wanted to redeem his campaign pledge to get the nation moving again; he also felt that the United States had to surpass the Soviet Union in economic vitality.

Kennedy received conflicting advice from the experts. Those who claimed the problem was essentially a technological one urged manpower-training and area-redevelopment programs to modernize American industry. Others called for long-overdue federal spending to rebuild the nation's public facilities—from parks and playgrounds to decaying bridges and courthouses in the cities. Kennedy sided with the first group, largely because Congress was opposed to massive spending on public works.

The actual stimulation of the economy, howev-

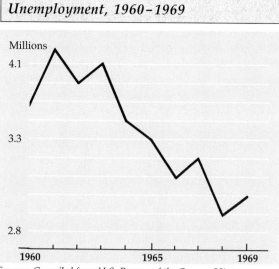

Unemployment, 1960–1969

Millions

4.1

3.3

2.8

1960   1965   1969

Source: Compiled from U.S. Bureau of the Census, Historical Statistics of the United States, Colonial Times to 1970, *Bicentennial Edition, Washington, D.C., 1975.*

er, came not from social programs but from greatly increased appropriations for defense and space. A $6 billion increase in the arms budget in 1961 gave the economy a great lift, and Kennedy's decision to send an astronaut to the moon eventually cost $25 billion. (See photo essay on the space race following p. 915.) By 1962, over half the federal budget was devoted to space and defense; aircraft and computer companies in the South and West benefited, but unemployment remained uncomfortably high in the older industrial areas of the Northeast and Midwest.

The administration's desire to keep the inflation rate low led to a serious confrontation with the business community. Kennedy relied on informal wage and price guidelines to hold down the cost of living. But in April 1962, just after the President had persuaded the steelworkers' union to accept a new contract with no wage increases and only a few additional benefits, U.S. Steel head Roger Blough informed Kennedy that his company was raising steel prices by $6 a ton. Outraged, the President publicly called the increase "a wholly unjustifiable and irresponsible defiance of the public interest" and accused Blough of displaying "contempt for the interests of 185 million Americans." Privately, Kennedy was even blunter. He confided to aides, "My father always told me that all businessmen were sons-of-bitches, but I never believed it till now."

Roger Blough soon gave way. The President's tongue-lashing, along with a cutoff in Pentagon steel orders and the threat of an antitrust suit, forced him to reconsider. When several smaller steel companies refused to raise their prices in hopes of expanding their share of the market, U.S. Steel rolled back its prices. The business community deeply resented the President's action, and when the stock market, which had been rising steadily since 1960, suddenly fell sharply in late May 1962, analysts were quick to label the decline "the Kennedy market."

Troubled by his strained relations with business and by the continued lag in economic growth, the President decided to adopt a more unorthodox approach in 1963. Walter Heller, chairman of the Council of Economic Advisers, had been arguing for a major cut in taxes since 1961 in the belief that it would stimulate consumer spending and give the economy the jolt it needed. The idea of a tax cut and resulting deficits during a period of prosperity went against economic orthodoxy, but Kennedy finally gave his approval. In January 1963, the President proposed a tax reduction of $13.5 billion, asserting that "the unrealistically heavy drag of federal income taxes on private purchasing power" was the "largest single barrier to full employment." When finally enacted by Congress in 1964, the massive tax cut led to the longest sustained economic advance in American history.

Kennedy's economic policy was far more successful than his legislative efforts. Although the rate of economic growth doubled to 4.5 percent by the end of 1963 and unemployment was reduced substantially, the cost of living rose only 1.3 percent a year. Personal income went up 13 percent in the early 1960s, but the greatest gains came in corporate profits—up 67 percent in this period. Yet critics pointed to the Kennedy administration's failure to close the glaring loopholes in the tax laws that benefited the rich and its lack of effort to help those at the bottom by forcing redistribution of national wealth. Despite the overall economic growth, the public sector continued to be neglected. "I am not sure what the advantage is," complained economist John Kenneth Galbraith, "in having a few more dollars to spend if the air is too dirty to breathe, the water too polluted to drink, the commuters are losing out in the struggle to get in and out of the cities, the streets are filthy, and the schools so bad that the young, perhaps wisely, stay away."

Moving Slowly on Civil Rights

Kennedy faced a genuine dilemma over the issue of civil rights. Despite his own lack of a strong record while in the Senate, he had portrayed himself during the 1960 campaign as a crusader for African-American rights. He had promised to launch an attack on segregation in the Deep South and had endeared himself to people across the nation when he helped win Martin Luther King's release from a Georgia jail. Kennedy's fear of alienating the large bloc of southern Democrats, however, forced him to downplay civil rights legislation.

The President's solution was to defer congressional action in favor of executive leadership in this area. He directed his brother, Attorney General Robert Kennedy, to continue and expand the Eisenhower administration's efforts to achieve voting rights for southern blacks. To register previously disfranchised citizens, the Justice Department worked with the civil rights movement —notably the Student Non-Violent Coordinating Committee (SNCC)—in the Deep South. In two years, the Kennedy administration increased the number of voting-rights suits fivefold. Yet the attorney general could not force the FBI to provide protection for the civil rights volunteers who risked their lives by encouraging African Americans to register. "SNCC's only contact with federal authority," noted one observer, "consisted of the FBI agents who stood by taking notes while local policemen beat up SNCC members."

Other efforts had equally mixed results. Vice-President Lyndon Johnson headed a presidential Commission on Equal Employment Opportunities that worked with defense industries and other government contractors to increase jobs for African Americans. But a limited budget and a reliance on voluntary cooperation prevented any dramatic gains; African American employment improved only in direct proportion to economic growth in the early 1960s.

Kennedy did succeed in appointing a number of African Americans to high government positions: Robert Weaver became chief of the federal housing agency, and Thurgood Marshall, who pleaded the *Brown* v. *Topeka* school desegregation case before the Supreme Court, was named to the United States Circuit Court. On the other hand, among his judicial appointments, Kennedy included one Mississippi jurist who referred to African Americans in court as "niggers" and once compared them to "a bunch of chimpanzees."

The civil rights movement refused to accept Kennedy's indirect approach. In May 1961, the Congress of Racial Equality (CORE) sponsored a "freedom ride" in which a biracial group attempted to test a 1960 Supreme Court decision outlawing segregation in all bus and train stations used in interstate commerce. When they arrived in Birmingham, Alabama, the freedom riders were attacked by a mob of angry whites. "It's the most horrible thing I've ever seen," a Justice Department official reported. "It's terrible, terrible." The attorney general quickly dispatched several hundred federal marshals to protect the freedom riders, but the President, deeply involved in the Berlin crisis, was more upset at the distraction the protesters created. Kennedy directed one of his aides to get in touch with the leaders of CORE. "Tell them to call it off," he demanded. "Stop them."

In September, after the attorney general finally convinced the Interstate Commerce Commission to issue an order banning segregation in interstate terminals and buses, the freedom rides ended. The Kennedy administration then sought to prevent further confrontations by involving civil rights activists in its voting drive.

A pattern of belated reaction to southern racism marked the basic approach of the Kennedys. When James Meredith courageously sought admission to the all-white University of Mississippi in 1962, the President and the attorney general worked closely with Mississippi Governor Ross Barnett to avoid violence. A transcript of Robert Kennedy's conversation with Governor Barnett on September 25 indicates that the attorney general's concerns were for the legal rather than the moral issues involved:

RFK: *I think the problem is that the federal courts have acted and when there is a conflict between your state and the federal courts under arrangements made some years ago—*

BARNETT: *The institution is supported by the taxpayers of this state and controlled by the Trustees.*

RFK: *Governor, you are a part of the United States.*

BARNETT: . . . I am going to treat you with every courtesy, but I won't agree to let that boy get to Ole Miss. I will never agree to that. I would rather spend my whole life in a penitentiary than do that.

RFK: I have a responsibility to enforce the laws of the United States.

BARNETT: I appreciate that. You have a responsibility. Why don't you let the NAACP run their own affairs and quit cooperating with that crowd? . . .

Despite Barnett's later promise of cooperation, the night before Meredith enrolled at the University of Mississippi, a mob attacked the federal marshals and National Guard troops sent to protect him. The violence left 2 dead and 375 injured, including 166 marshals and 12 guardsmen, but Meredith attended the university and eventually graduated.

In 1963, Kennedy sent the deputy attorney general to face down Governor George C. Wallace, an avowed segregationist who had promised "to stand in the schoolhouse door" to prevent the integration of the University of Alabama. After a brief confrontation, Wallace yielded to federal authority, and two African-American students peacefully desegregated the state university.

"I Have a Dream"

Martin Luther King, Jr., finally forced Kennedy to abandon his cautious tactics and come out openly in behalf of racial justice. In the spring of 1963, King began a massive protest in Birmingham, one of the South's most segregated cities. Public marches and demonstrations aimed at integrating public facilities and opening up jobs for African Americans quickly led to police harassment and many arrests, including that of King himself. Police Commissioner Eugene "Bull" Connor was determined to crush the civil rights movement; King was equally determined to prevail. Writing from his cell in Birmingham, he vowed an active campaign to bring the issue of racial injustice to national attention. When several Alabama clergymen asked him to open negotiations rather than provoke violence, King responded from jail, "Nonviolent direct action seeks to create such a crisis and foster such a tension that a community which has constantly refused to negotiate is forced to confront the issue."

Bull Connor played directly into King's hands. On May 3, as six thousand children marched in place of the jailed protesters, authorities broke up a demonstration with clubs, snarling police dogs, and high-pressure water hoses strong enough to

The attempts of African Americans to end discrimination and secure their civil rights met violent resistance in Birmingham, Alabama, where police used snarling dogs, fire hoses, clubs, and electric cattle prods to turn back the unarmed demonstrators.

The 1963 march on Washington gave the civil rights movement a national focus.

event was Martin Luther King's eloquent description of his dream for America. It concluded:

> *When we let freedom ring, when we let it ring from every village and every hamlet, from every state and every city, we will be able to speed up that day when all God's children, black men and white men, Jews and Gentiles, Protestants and Catholics, will be able to join hands and sing, in the words of that old Negro spiritual. "Free at last! Free at last! Thank God almighty, we are free at last!"*

By the time of Kennedy's death in November 1963, his civil rights legislation was well on its way to passage in Congress. Yet even this achievement did not fully satisfy his critics. For two years, they had waited for him to deliver on his campaign promise to wipe out housing discrimination "with a stroke of the pen." When the executive order on housing was finally issued in November 1962, it proved disappointing; it ignored all past discrimination and applied only to homes and apartments financed by the federal government. For many, Kennedy had raised hopes for racial equality that he never fulfilled.

But unlike Eisenhower, he had provided presidential leadership for the civil rights movement. His emphasis on executive action gradually paid off, especially in extending voting rights. By early 1964, 40 percent of southern blacks had the franchise, compared to only 28 percent in 1960. Moreover, Kennedy's sense of caution and restraint, painful and frustrating as it was to African-American activists, had proved well-founded. Avoiding an early, and possibly fatal, defeat in Congress, he had waited until a national consensus emerged and then had carefully channeled it behind effective legislation. Behaving very much the way Franklin Roosevelt did in guiding the nation into World War II, Kennedy chose to be a fox rather than a lion on civil rights.

The Supreme Court and Reform

The most active impulse for social change in the early 1960s came from a surprising source: the usually staid and conservative Supreme Court. Under the leadership of Earl Warren, a pragmatic jurist more noted for his political astuteness than his legal scholarship, the Court ventured into new areas. A group of liberal judges—especially

take the bark off a tree. With a horrified nation watching scene after scene of this brutality on television, the Kennedy administration quickly intervened to arrange a settlement with the Birmingham civic leaders that ended the violence and granted the protesters most of their demands.

More important, Kennedy finally ended his long hesitation and sounded the call for action. "We are confronted primarily with a moral issue," he told the nation on June 11. "It is as old as the Scriptures and is as clear as the American Constitution." Eight days later, the administration sponsored civil rights legislation providing equal access to all public accommodations as well as an extension of voting rights for African Americans.

Despite pleas from the government for an end to demonstrations and protests, the movement's leaders decided to keep pressure on the administration. They scheduled a massive march on Washington for August 1963. The President and the attorney general persuaded the sponsors to tone down their rhetoric—notably one speech by a SNCC leader that termed the Kennedy legislation "too little, too late." On August 28, more than two hundred thousand marchers gathered for a day-long rally in front of the Lincoln Memorial where they listened to hymns, speeches, and prayers for racial justice. The climax of the

William O. Douglas, Hugo Black, and William J. Brennan, Jr.—argued for social reform, while advocates of judicial restraint (such as John Marshall Harlan and Felix Frankfurter) fought stubbornly against the new activism.

In addition to ruling against segregation, the Warren Court in the Eisenhower years had angered conservatives by protecting the constitutional rights of victims of McCarthyism. In *Yates* v. *U.S.* (1956), the judges reversed the conviction of fourteen Communist leaders, claiming that government prosecutors had failed to prove that the accused had actually organized a plot to overthrow the government. Mere advocacy of revolution, the Court said, did not justify conviction. In 1957, the Court issued a series of rulings that led dissenting Justice Tom Clark to protest what he saw as giving defendants "a Roman holiday for rummaging through confidential information as well as vital national secrets."

The resignation of Felix Frankfurter in 1962 enabled President Kennedy to appoint Secretary of Labor Arthur Goldberg, a committed liberal, to the Supreme Court. With a clear majority now favoring judicial intervention, the Warren Court issued a series of landmark decisions designed to extend to state and local jurisdictions the traditional rights afforded the accused in federal courts. Thus, in *Gideon* v. *Wainwright* (1963), *Escobedo* v. *Illinois* (1964), and *Miranda* v. *Arizona* (1966), the majority decreed that defendants had to be provided lawyers, had to be informed of their constitutional rights, and could not be interrogated or induced to confess to a crime without defense counsel being present. In effect, the Court extended to the poor and the ignorant those constitutional guarantees that had always been available to the rich and to the legally informed—notably hardened criminals.

The most far-reaching Warren Court decisions came in the area of legislative reapportionment—a "political thicket" that Justice Frankfurter had always refused to enter. In 1962, the Court ruled in *Baker* v. *Carr* that Tennessee had to redistribute its legislative seats to give citizens in Memphis equal representation. Subsequent decisions reinforced the ban on rural overrepresentation as the Court proclaimed that places in all legislative bodies, including the House of Representatives, be allocated on the basis of "people, not land or trees or pastures." The principle of "one man, one vote" greatly increased the political power of cities at the expense of rural areas; it also involved the Court directly in the reapportionment process, frequently forcing judges to draw up new legislative and congressional districts.

The activism of the Supreme Court stirred up a storm of criticism. The rulings that extended protection to criminals and those accused of subversive activity led some Americans to charge that the Court was encouraging crime and weakening national security. The John Birch Society, an extreme anti-Communist group, demanded the impeachment of Chief Justice Warren. Decisions banning school prayers and permitting pornography incensed many conservative Americans, who saw the Court as undermining moral values. "They've put the Negroes in the schools," complained one southern congressman, "and now they've driven God out." Legal scholars worried more about the weakening of the Court's prestige as it became more directly involved in the political process. On balance, however, the Warren Court helped achieve greater social justice by protecting the rights of the underprivileged and by permitting dissent and free expression to flourish.

The liberal political activism of the Supreme Court during the 1960s drew sharp criticism and led to demands for the impeachment of Chief Justice Earl Warren.

"LET US CONTINUE"

The New Frontier came to a sudden and violent end on November 22, 1963, when Lee Harvey Oswald assassinated John F. Kennedy as the President rode in a motorcade in downtown Dallas. The shock of losing the young president, who had become a symbol of hope and promise for a whole generation, stunned the entire world. The American people were bewildered by the rapid sequence of events: the brutal killing of their beloved president; the televised slaying of Oswald by Jack Ruby in the basement of the Dallas police station; the composure and dignity of Kennedy's widow, Jacqueline, at the ensuing state funeral; and the hurried Warren Commission report, which identified Oswald as the lone assassin. Afterward, critics would charge that Oswald had been part of a vast conspiracy, but at the time the prevailing national reaction was a numbing sense of loss.

Vice President Lyndon B. Johnson moved quickly to fill the vacuum left by Kennedy's death. Sworn in on board Air Force One as he returned to Washington, he soon met with a stream of world leaders to reassure them of American political stability. Five days after the tragedy in Dallas, Johnson spoke eloquently to a special joint session of Congress. Recalling JFKs summons in his inaugural address, "Let us begin," the new President declared, "Today in the moment of new resolve, I would say to all my fellow Americans, 'let us continue.'" Asking Congress to enact Kennedy's tax and civil rights bills as a tribute to the fallen leader, LBJ concluded, "Let us here highly resolve that John Fitzgerald Kennedy did not live or die in vain."

Johnson in Action

Lyndon Johnson suffered from the inevitable comparison with his young and stylish predecessor. LBJ was acutely aware of his own lack of polish; he sought to surround himself with Kennedy advisers and insiders, hoping that their learning and sophistication would rub off on him. Johnson's assets were very real—he possessed an intimate knowledge of Congress, an incredible energy and determination to succeed, and a fierce ego. When a young marine officer tried to direct him to the proper helicopter, saying, "This one is yours," Johnson replied, "Son, they are all my helicopters."

Moments after this photograph was taken in Dallas police headquarters, accused presidential assassin Lee Harvey Oswald was fatally shot.

Aboard Air Force One on the return from Dallas to Washington, D.C., Judge Sarah Hughes administers the presidential oath of office to Lyndon Johnson.

LBJ's height and intensity gave him a powerful presence; he dominated any room he entered, and he delighted in using his physical power of persuasion. One Texas politician explained why he had given in to Johnson: "Lyndon got me by the lapels and put his face on top of mine and he talked and talked and talked. I figured it was either getting drowned or joining."

Yet LBJ found it impossible to project his intelligence and vitality to large audiences. Unlike Kennedy, he wilted before the camera, turning his televised speeches into stilted and awkward performances. Trying to belie his reputation as a riverboat gambler, he came across like a foxy grandpa, clever, calculating and not to be trusted. He lacked Kennedy's wit and charm, and reporters delighted in describing the way he berated his aides or shocked the nation by baring his belly to show the scar from a recent operation.

Whatever his shortcomings in style, however, Johnson possessed far greater ability than Kennedy in dealing with Congress. He entered the White House with more than thirty years experience in Washington as a legislative aide, congressman, and senator. His encyclopedic knowledge of the legislative process and his shrewd manipulation of individual senators had enabled him to become the most influential Senate majority leader in history. Famed for "the Johnson treatment," a legendary ability to use personal persuasion to reach his goals, Johnson in fact relied more on his close ties with the Senate's power brokers—or "whales," as he called them—than on his exploitation of the "minnows."

Above all, Johnson sought consensus. Indifferent to ideology, he had moved easily from New Deal liberalism to oil-and-gas conservatism as his career advanced. He had carefully cultivated Richard Russell of Georgia, leader of the Dixie bloc, but he also had taken Hubert Humphrey, a Minnesota liberal, under his wing. He had performed a balancing act on civil rights, working with the Eisenhower administration on behalf of the 1957 Voting Rights Act, yet carefully weakening it to avoid alienating southern Democrats. When Kennedy dashed Johnson's own intense presidential ambitions in 1960, LBJ had gracefully agreed to be his running mate and had endured the humiliation of the vice presidency loyally and silently. Suddenly thrust into power, Johnson used his gifts wisely. Citing his favorite scriptural passage from Isaiah, "Come now, and let us reason together, saith the Lord," he concentrated on securing passage of Kennedy's tax and civil rights bills in 1964.

The tax cut came first. Aware of the power wielded by Senate Finance Committee Chairman Harry Byrd, a Virginia conservative, Johnson astutely lowered Kennedy's projected $101.5 billion budget for 1965 to $97.9 billion. Although Byrd voted against the tax cut, he let the measure out of his committee, telling Johnson, "I'll be working for you behind the scenes." In February, Congress reduced personal income taxes by more than $10 billion, touching off a sustained economic boom. Consumer spending increased by an impressive $43 billion in the next eighteen months, and new jobs opened up at the rate of one million a year.

Johnson was even more influential in passing the Kennedy civil rights measure. Staying in the background, he encouraged liberal amendments that strengthened the bill in the House. With Hubert Humphrey leading the floor fight in the Senate, Johnson refused all efforts at compromise, counting on growing public pressure to force northern Republicans to abandon their traditional alliance with southern Democrats. Everett M. Dirksen of Illinois, the GOP leader in the Senate, met repeatedly with Johnson at the White House. When LBJ refused to yield, Dirksen finally announced, "The time has come for equality of opportunity in sharing in government, in education, and in employment," and led a Republican vote to end a fifty-seven-day filibuster.

The 1964 Civil Rights Act, signed on July 2, made illegal the segregation of African Americans in public facilities, established an Equal Employment Opportunity Commission to lessen racial discrimination in employment, and protected the voting rights of African Americans. An amendment sponsored by segregationists in an effort to weaken the bill added sex to the prohibition of discrimination in Title VII of the act; in the future, women's groups would use this clause to secure government support for greater equality in employment and education.

The Election of 1964

Passage of two key Kennedy measures within six months did not satisfy Johnson. Having established the theme of continuity, he now set out to win the presidency in his own right. Eager to surpass Kennedy's narrow victory in 1960, he hoped to win by a great landslide.

Searching for a cause of his own, LBJ found one in the issue of poverty. Beginning in the late 1950s, economists had warned that the prevailing affluence only disguised a persistent and deep-seated problem of poverty. John Kenneth Galbraith had urged a policy of increased public spending to help the poor, but Kennedy ignored Galbraith's advice. In 1962, however, Michael Harrington's book *The Other America* attracted national attention. Writing with passion and eloquence, Harrington claimed that nearly one-fifth of the nation, some thirty-five million Americans, lived in poverty.

Three groups predominated among the poor— African Americans, the aged, and households headed by women. The problem, Harrington contended, was that the poor were invisible, living in slums or depressed areas like Appalachia and cut off from the educational facilities, medical care, and employment opportunities afforded more affluent Americans. Moreover, poverty was a vicious cycle. The children of the poor were trapped in the same culture of poverty as their parents, living without hope or knowledge of how to enter the mainstream of American life.

Johnson quickly took over proposals that Kennedy had been developing and made them his own. In his State of the Union address in January 1964, LBJ announced, "This administration, today, here and now, declares unconditional war on poverty in America." Over the next eight months, Johnson fashioned a comprehensive poverty program under the direction of R. Sargent Shriver, Kennedy's brother-in-law. The President added $500 million to existing programs to come up with a $1 billion effort which Congress passed in August 1964.

The new Office of Economic Opportunity (OEO) set up a wide variety of programs, ranging from Head Start for preschoolers to the Job Corps for high-school dropouts in need of vocational training. The emphasis was on self-help, with the government providing money and know-how so that the poor could reap the benefits of neighborhood day-care centers, consumer-education classes, legal-aid services, and adult remedial-reading programs. The level of funding was never high enough to meet the OEOs ambitious goals,

*T*hrough Head Start, the government offered preschool classes to children from families that might otherwise be unable to afford such programs.

and a controversial attempt to include representatives of the poor in the Community Action Program led to bitter political feuding with city and state officials. Nonetheless, the war on poverty, along with the economic growth provided by the tax cut, helped reduce the ranks of the poor by nearly ten million between 1964 and 1967.

For Johnson, the new program established his reputation as a reformer in an election year. He still faced two challenges to his authority. The first was Robert F. Kennedy, the late president's brother who continued as attorney general but who wanted to become vice-president and Johnson's eventual successor in the White House. Desperate to prove his ability to succeed without Kennedy help, LBJ commented, "I don't need that little runt to win," and chose Hubert Humphrey as his running mate.

The second challenge was the Republican candidate, Senator Barry Goldwater, an outspoken conservative from Arizona. An attractive and articulate man, Goldwater openly advocated a rejection of the welfare state and a return to unregulated free enterprise. To Johnson's delight, Goldwater chose to place ideology ahead of political expediency. The senator spoke out boldly against the Tennessee Valley Authority, denounced Social Security, and advocated a hawkish foreign policy. "In Your Heart, You Know He's Right," read the Republican slogan, leading the

Candidate	Party	Popular Vote	Electoral Vote
Johnson	Democrat	43,126,584	486
Goldwater	Republican	27,177,838	52

Democrats to reply, "Yes, Far Right," and in reference to a careless Goldwater comment about using nuclear weapons, Johnson backers punned, "In Your Heart, You Know He Might."

Johnson stuck carefully to the middle of the road, embracing the liberal reform program—which he now called "The Great Society"—while stressing his concern for balanced budgets and fiscal orthodoxy. The more Goldwater sagged in the polls, the harder Johnson campaigned, determined to achieve his treasured landslide. On election day, LBJ did even better than FDR had in 1936, receiving 61.1 percent of the popular vote and an overwhelming majority in the electoral college; Goldwater carried only Arizona and five states of the Deep South. Equally important, the Democrats achieved huge gains in Congress, controlling the House by a margin of 295 to 140 and the Senate by 68 to 32. Kennedy's legacy and Goldwater's candor had enabled Johnson to break the conservative grip on Congress for the first time in a quarter of a century.

The Triumph of Reform

LBJ moved quickly to secure his legislative goals. Despite solid majorities in both Houses, including seventy freshman Democrats who had ridden into office on his coattails, Johnson knew he would have to enact the Great Society as swiftly as possible. "You've got to give it all you can, that first year," he told an aide. "Doesn't matter what kind of majority you come in with. You've got just one year when they treat you right, and before they start worrying about themselves."

Johnson gave two traditional Democratic reforms—health care and education—top priority. Aware of strong opposition to a comprehensive medical program, LBJ settled for Medicare, which mandated health insurance under the Social Security program for Americans over age sixty-five, with a supplementary Medicaid program for the

*T*hroughout his presidency, LBJ had great success at persuading Congress to enact the legislation he favored, from the bill authorizing the "war on poverty," passed in 1964, to the acts promoting fair housing and protecting national resources, passed in 1968.

indigent. To symbolize the end of a long struggle, Johnson flew to Independence, Missouri, so that Truman could witness the ceremonial signing of the Medicare law which had its origins in Truman's 1949 health insurance proposal.

LBJ overcame the religious hurdle on education by supporting a child-benefit approach, allocating federal money to advance the education of students in parochial as well as public schools. The Elementary and Secondary Education Act of 1965 provided over $1 billion in federal aid, the largest share going to school districts with the highest percentage of impoverished pupils. During his administration, federal aid to education increased sharply.

Civil rights proved to be the most difficult test of Johnson's leadership. Martin Luther King, concerned that three million southern blacks were still denied the right to vote, in early 1965 chose Selma, Alabama, as the site for a test case.

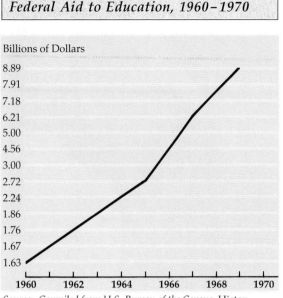

Federal Aid to Education, 1960–1970

Billions of Dollars

8.89	
7.91	
7.18	
6.21	
5.00	
4.56	
3.00	
2.72	
2.24	
1.86	
1.76	
1.67	
1.63	

1960   1962   1964   1966   1968   1970

Source: Compiled from U.S. Bureau of the Census, Historical Statistics of the United States, Colonial Times to 1970, Bicentennial Edition, Washington, D.C., 1975.

The white authorities in Selma, led by Sheriff James Clark, used cattle prods and bullwhips to break up the demonstrations. Over two thousand African Americans were jailed. Johnson intervened in March, after TV cameras showed Sheriff Clark's deputies brutally halting a march from Selma to Montgomery. The President ordered the Alabama National Guard to federal duty to protect the demonstrators, had the Justice Department draw up a new voting-rights bill, and personally addressed the Congress on civil rights. "I speak tonight for the dignity of man and the destiny of democracy," he began. Calling the denial of the right to vote "deadly wrong," LBJ issued a compelling call to action. "Their cause must be our cause too. Because it is not just Negroes, but really it is all of us who must overcome the crippling legacy of bigotry and injustice."

Five months later, Congress passed the Voting Rights Act of 1965. Once again Johnson had worked with Senate Republican leader Dirksen to break a southern filibuster and assure passage of a measure. The act banned literacy tests in states and counties in which less than half the population had voted in 1964 and provided for federal registrars in these areas to assure African Americans the franchise.

The results were dramatic. In less than a year, 166,000 African Americans were added to the voting rolls in Alabama, while African-American registration went up 400 percent in Mississippi. By the end of the decade, the percentage of eligible African-American voters who had registered had risen from 40 to 65 percent. For the first time since Reconstruction, African Americans were playing an active and effective role in southern politics.

Before the Eighty-ninth Congress ended its first session in the fall of 1965, it had passed eighty-nine bills. These included measures to create two new cabinet departments (Transportation, and Housing and Urban Affairs); acts to provide for highway safety and to ensure clean air and water; and large appropriations for higher education, public housing, and the continuing war on poverty. In nine months, Johnson had enacted the entire Democratic reform agenda, moving the nation beyond the New Deal by mandating federal concern for health, education, and the quality of life in both city and country.

The man responsible for this great leap forward, however, had failed to win the public adulation he so deeply desired. His legislative skills had made the most of the opportunities offered by the 1964 Democratic landslide, but the people did not respond to Johnson's leadership with the warmth and praise they had showered on Kennedy. Reporters continued to portray him as a crude wheeler-dealer; as a maniac who drove around Texas back roads at ninety miles an hour, one hand on the wheel and the other holding a glass of beer; or as a bully who picked up his dog by the ears. No one was more aware of this lack of affection than LBJ himself. His public support, he told an aide, is "like a Western river, broad but not deep."

Johnson's realization of the fleeting nature of his popularity was all too accurate. The dilemmas of the Cold War began to divert his attention from domestic concerns and eventually, in the case of Vietnam, would overwhelm him. Yet his legislative achievements were still remarkable. In one brief outburst of reform, he had accomplished more than any president since FDR.

Difficulties abroad would dim the luster of the Johnson presidency, but they could not diminish the lasting impact of the Great Society on Ameri-

African-American Voter Registration Before and After the Voting Rights Act of 1965

State	1960	1966	Increase	Percentage of Increase over 1960
Alabama	66,000	250,000	184,000	278.8
Arkansas	73,000	115,000	42,000	57.5
Florida	183,000	303,000	120,000	65.6
Georgia	180,000	300,000	120,000	66.7
Louisiana	159,000	243,000	84,000	52.8
Mississippi	22,000	175,000	153,000	695.4
North Carolina	210,000	282,000	72,000	34.3
South Carolina	58,000	191,000	133,000	229.3
Tennessee	185,000	225,000	40,000	21.6
Texas	227,000	400,000	173,000	76.2
Virginia	100,000	205,000	105,000	105.0

Source: Compiled from U.S. Bureau of the Census, Statistical Abstract of the United States: 1982-83, 103rd edition, Washington, D.C., 1982.

can life. Federal aid to education, the enactment of Medicare and Medicaid and above all, the civil rights acts of 1964 and 1965, changed the nation irrevocably. The aged and the poor now were guaranteed access to medical care, communities saw an infusion of federal funds to improve local education and African Americans could now begin to attend integrated schools, enjoy public facilities and gain political power by exercising the right to vote. But even at this moment of triumph for liberal reform, new currents of dissent and rebellion were brewing.

Recommended Reading

Two excellent books survey the social, cultural, and political trends in the United States during the postwar period. In *One Nation Divisible* (1980), Richard Polenberg analyzes class, ethnic, and racial changes, while William Leuchtenburg offers a fine overview of American life since 1945 in *A Troubled Feast*, updated ed. (1983).

Richard Pells provides a sweeping survey of the American intellectual community's response to the Cold War in *The Liberal Mind in a Conservative Age* (1985). The most incisive account of suburban life is Kenneth A. Jackson, *Crabgrass Frontier* (1986).

Charles Alexander provides a balanced view of the Eisenhower years in *Holding the Line* (1975), portraying the Republican president as an able chief executive who was well suited to the times. For the 1960s, the best general account is Jim F. Heath, *Decade of Disillusionment* (1975), which stresses the continuity in policy between the Ken-

nedy and Johnson administrations. Herbert Parmet provides a balanced account of the Kennedy administration in *JFK: The Presidency of John F. Kennedy* (1983), while Eric Goldman offers a sympathetic view of the Johnson years in *The Tragedy of Lyndon Johnson* (1969).

Taylor Branch gives a comprehensive account of the genesis of the civil rights movement in *Parting the Waters: America in the King Years, 1954–1963* (1988). Three fine biographies—David L. Lewis' *King* (1970), Stephen B. Oates' *Let the Trumpet Sound* (1982) and David Garrow's, *Bearing the Cross* (1986)—present perceptive portraits of Martin Luther King, Jr., the movement's most influential leader.

Additional Bibliography

Books on social and cultural trends in the 1950s include Bernard Rosenberg and D. M. White, eds., *Mass Culture* (1957); Douglas Miller and Marion Novak, *The Fifties: The Way We Really Were* (1977); Robert H. Bremer and Gary Reichard, eds., *Reshaping America* (1982); William O'Neill, *American High* (1986); J. Ronald Oakley, *God's Country* (1986); Paul Carter, *Another Part of the Fifties* (1983); David Potter, *People of Plenty* (1954); Herbert Gans, *The Levittowners* (1967); Scott Donaldson, *The Suburban Myth* (1969); Diane Ravitch, *The Troubled Crusade* (1983), on education; Serge Guilbaut, *How New York Stole the Idea of Modern Art* (1983); Irving Sandler, *The Triumph of American Painting* (1970); Will Herberg, *Protestant, Catholic, Jew* (1955); Lawrence Lipton, *The Holy Barbarians* (1959); Eric Barnouw, *The Image Empire* (1970); and Kent Anderson, *Television Fraud* (1978). For the role of women in the postwar years, see Eugenia Kaledin, *Mothers and More* (1984) and Leila Rupp and Verta Taylor, *Survival in the Doldrums* (1987).

CHRONOLOGY

1946 Republicans win control of both houses of Congress in November elections

1947 Truman orders loyalty program for government employees (March) • William Levitt announces first Levittown (May)

1948 Truman orders end to segregation in armed forces (July) • Truman scores upset victory in presidential election

1949 Minimum wage raised from forty to seventy-five cents an hour

1950 Senator Joseph McCarthy claims Communists in government

1952 Republican Dwight Eisenhower elected president

1953 Julius and Ethel Rosenberg executed for atomic-secrets spying (June)

1954 Supreme Court orders schools desegregated in *Brown* v. *Board of Education of Topeka* (May)

1955 Dr. Jonas Salk reports success of antipolio vaccine (April) • African Americans begin boycott of Montgomery, Alabama, bus company (December)

1956 Eisenhower reelected in landslide victory

1957 Congress passes first Civil Rights Act since Reconstruction (August) • Soviets launch *Sputnik* (October)

1960 African-American college students stage sit-in in Greensboro, North Carolina (February)

1961 Kennedy commits U.S. to landing an astronaut on the moon by 1969 (May)

1962 James Meredith is first African American to enroll at University of Mississippi (September)

1963 Kennedy assassinated, Lyndon B. Johnson sworn in as president (November)

1964 President Johnson declares war on poverty (January) • Johnson wins presidency in landslide victory (November)

1965 Martin Luther King, Jr. leads Selma-Montgomery march (March) • Medicare legislation provides aged with medical care (July)

Paul Boyer examines the initial response of the American people to the nuclear age in *By the Bomb's Early Light* (1985). On *Sputnik* and the beginning of the space program, see Lloyd Swenson et al., *This New Ocean* (1966); Clayton Koppes, *JPL and the American Space Program* (1982); and Walter A. MacDougall, *The Heavens and the Earth* (1985).

Truman's contributions to the civil rights movement are surveyed critically in Harry C. Berman, *The Politics of Civil Rights in the Truman Administration* (1970) and more sympathetically in Donald R. McCoy and Richard T. Ruetten, *Quest and Response* (1973). Other important books on civil rights are Richard Dalfiume, *Desegregation of the U.S. Armed Forces* (1969); Richard Kluger, *Simple Justice* (1975) on the *Brown* decision; Benjamin Muse, *Ten Years of Prelude* (1964); Steven Lawson, *Black Ballots* (1977) on the voting rights issue; Robert F. Burk, *The Eisenhower Administration and Civil Rights* (1985); Juan Williams, *Eyes on the Prize* (1986); and Numan V. Bartley, *The Rise of Massive Resistance* (1969) on the southern reaction.

Herbert Parmet began the scholarly reappraisal of Dwight Eisenhower in *Eisenhower and the American Crusades* (1973). Stephen E. Ambrose portrays Ike sympathetically in his two-volume biography, *Eisenhower* (1983, 1984); for a more critical view, see Piers Brendon, *Ike: His Life and Times* (1986). Other useful books on the Eisenhower years include Fred Greenstein, *The Hidden Hand Presidency* (1982); Elmo Richardson, *The Presidency of Dwight D. Eisenhower* (1979); Robert F. Burk, *Dwight D. Eisenhower* (1986); Barbara R. Clowse, *Brainpower and the Cold War* (1981); Garry Wills, *Nixon Agonistes* (1971); John Bartlow Martin, *Adlai Stevenson and the World* (1977); James L. Sundquist, *Politics and Policy: The Eisenhower, Kennedy and Johnson Years* (1968); Gary W. Reichard, *The Reaffirmation of Republicanism: Eisenhower and the 83rd Congress* (1975); and Mark Rose, *Interstate* (1979). For economic developments during the 1950's, consult Edward S. Flash, *Economic Advice and Presidential Leadership* (1965); Harold G. Vatter, *The U.S. Economy in the 1950's* (1962); and two books by John Kenneth Galbraith: *American Capitalism* (1952) and *The Affluent Society* (1958).

Kennedy's career before he became president is discussed in James MacGregor Burns, *John Kennedy*, 2d ed. (1961); Joan Blair and Clay Blair, Jr., *The Search for JFK* (1976); Herbert Parmet, *Jack* (1980); and Arthur M. Schlesinger, Jr., *A Thousand Days* (1965). Favorable evaluations of the Kennedy presidency include Theodore Sorensen, *Kennedy* (1965); Arthur M. Schlesinger, Jr., *Robert Kennedy and His Times* (1978); Richard Goodwin, *Remembering America* (1988); Benjamin Bradlee, *Conversations with Kennedy* (1975); and Lewis J. Paper, *The Promise and the Performance* (1975). For a more critical view, see Bruce Miroff, *Pragmatic Illusions* (1976); Henry Fairlie, *The Kennedy Promise* (1973); David Burner, *John F. Kennedy and a New Generation* (1988); and Garry Wills, *The Kennedy Imprisonment* (1981), the latter dealing with Robert and Edward Kennedy as well. William Manchester, *Death of a President* (1967), gives the standard view of JFKs assassination; the best of the many dissenting accounts is Edward J. Epstein, *Inquest* (1966).

British journalist Louis Heren offers an objective and lucid survey of the Johnson presidency in *No Hail, No Farewell* (1970); Vaughn Bornet gives a fuller account in *The Presidency of Lyndon Johnson* (1983). The best brief biography is Paul Conkin, *Big Daddy from the Pedernales* (1986). Other books on LBJ include the President's memoirs, *The Vantage Point* (1971); Harry McPherson, *A Political Education* (1972); Robert Novak and Rowland Evans, *Lyndon B. Johnson* (1966); Doris Kearns, *Lyndon Johnson and the American Dream* (1976); Merle Miller, *Lyndon* (1980); and two books that focus on his Texas background, Alfred Steinberg, *Sam Johnson's Boy* (1965) and Ronnie Dugger, *The Politician* (1982). The most detailed account of Johnson's early career is Robert Caro's critical volume *The Path to Power* (1982); for a briefer but more astute assessment of Johnson's complex character, see George Reedy, *Lyndon Johnson: A Memoir* (1982). Two books edited by Robert A. Divine, *Exploring the Johnson Years* (1981) and *The Johnson Years, Volume Two* (1987) contain essays surveying major themes of the Johnson administration.

For political developments in the first half of the sixties, see Theodore White, *The Making of the President* (1961), the first in a series of election books; Sidney Kraus, *The Great Debates* (1962) on the Nixon-Kennedy TV debates; and two memoirs by prominent Democrats, Larry O'Brien, *No Final Victories* (1974) and Hubert H. Humphrey, *The Education of a Public Man* (1976); and a first-rate biography, Carl Solberg, *Hubert Humphrey* (1984).

Books on economic developments include Seymour Harris, *Economics of the Kennedy Years* (1964); Hobart Rowen, *The Free Enterprisers* (1964); and Jim F. Heath, *John F. Kennedy and the Business Community* (1969). Among studies of the Supreme Court are Alexander Bickel, *Politics and the Warren Court* (1965); Richard C. Cortner, *The Apportionment Cases* (1970); Anthony Lewis, *Gideon's Trumpet* (1965); and G. Edward White, *Earl Warren* (1982).

Victor S. Navasky's account of Robert Kennedy as attorney general, *Kennedy Justice* (1971) is quite critical. More sympathetic books on the same topic are Arthur Schlesinger, Jr., *Robert Kennedy and His Times* (1976); Carl Brauer, *John F. Kennedy and the Second Reconstruction* (1977); and Harris Wofford, *Of Kennedys and Kings* (1980). For civil rights developments under Johnson, consult Benjamin Muse, *The American Negro Revolution* (1969); David Garrow, *Protest at Selma* (1976); Michal Belknap, *Federal Law and Southern Order* (1987); and Doug McAdams, *Freedom Summer* (1988).

The Great Society, particularly in regard to welfare and the war on poverty, can be traced in Allen J. Matusow, *The Unraveling of America* (1984); Marshall Kaplan and Peggy Cuciti, eds., *The Great Society and Its Legacy* (1986); John C. Donovan, *The Politics of Poverty* (1973); Gilbert Steiner, *The State of Welfare* (1971); Sar Levitan, *The Great Society's Poor Law* (1969); James T. Patterson, *America's Struggle Against Poverty* (1982); and Julie Roy Jeffrey, *Education for the Children of the Poor* (1976).

Robert H. Bremner, Gary Reichard and Richard J. Hopkins, eds., *American Choices* (1986) contains essays on public policy issues of the 1960s. For environmental concerns, see Samuel P. Hays, *Beauty, Health and Permanence* (1987) and Lewis L. Gould, *Lady Bird Johnson and Beautification* (1987).

CHAPTER 30

Vietnam and the Escalating Cold War, 1953–1968

O n November 20, 1953, French planes dropped over eighteen hundred elite paratroopers into Dien Bien Phu, a remote heart-shaped valley in North Vietnam. This move was the latest effort by France to crush the rebellion of the Viet Minh, a Communist movement led by Ho Chi Minh, which had been fighting for the independence of Vietnam since 1946. The paratroopers quickly gained control of Dien Bien Phu with only minor casualties, built airstrips to receive supplies and reinforcements, and then prepared for the expected onslaught from the Viet Minh. The French hoped to engage the elusive guerrilla forces in a pitched battle using the superior French firepower to gradually sap the strength of the Viet Minh insurgency.

By March 1954, the French garrison, now composed of 13,000 troops, was in a desperate position. The Viet Minh had moved 50,000 troops into the hills surrounding Dien Bien Phu and had brought in heavy Russian artillery supplied by China and American weapons captured in Korea. Vietnamese soldiers wearing woven helmets and rubber tire sandals carried the disassembled pieces of cannons and mortars through the jungle to the hilltops overlooking the French positions in the valley below. The French seemed to have ignored the classic Chinese military advice, "Never fight on a terrain which looks like a tortoise turned upside down."

When the first attack began in mid-March, the Viet Minh quickly overran three French outposts at Dien Bien Phu and wiped out two entire battalions in the first few days of fighting. Surprisingly accurate antiaircraft fire made it increasingly difficult for the French planes to bring in supplies and reinforcements. What had begun as an attempt to decimate the Viet Minh had turned into a showdown battle in which France's control of Indochina was thrown into jeopardy.

In desperation, the French sent a high official to Washington in late March to seek American military help in relieving their beseiged garrison. Although the United States had begun extending military and financial assistance to France in Indochina in May 1950, President Dwight D. Eisenhower in 1954 was not prepared to commit American forces to bail out the French. Instead, he and Secretary of State John Foster Dulles sought only to prevent Indochina from falling

*H*oping to maintain colonial rule in Indochina, France dropped paratroopers into the valley of Dien Bien Phu to prepare a decisive attack against Vietnamese guerrilla forces.

under Communist control by trying to arrange for diplomatic and political support for the French effort among other Western nations. Although Admiral Arthur Radford, chairman of the Joint Chiefs of Staff, came forward with a bold plan for an American air strike to relieve the pressure at Dien Bien Phu, neither the President nor his other military advisers were ready to involve American forces in another Asian war so soon after Korea.

While political leaders searched for a negotiated settlement, the Viet Minh tightened the vise on Dien Bien Phu. The French were in a hopeless tactical position. Their garrison was more than 200 miles behind the enemy's lines and was being pounded relentlessly by artillery shells. By mid-April, a devastating five-night attack had

Ho Chi Minh and members of the Vietnam Workers' party discuss strategy during the Dien Bien Phu campaign.

On May 7, the Viet Minh attackers overcame the last stronghold at Dien Bien Phu. A French officer saw a white flag on a Viet Minh rifle only 50 feet away. "You're not going to shoot anymore?" asked a Viet Minh soldier. "No, I am not going to shoot anymore," the Frenchman replied. And then, writes historian Bernard Fall, "all around them, as on some gruesome Judgment Day, mudcovered soldiers, French and enemy alike, began to crawl out of their trenches and stand erect as firing ceased everywhere."

At an international conference held in Geneva a few months later, Indochina was divided at the seventeenth parallel. Ho Chi Minh gained control of North Vietnam, while the French continued to rule in the South, with provision for a general election within two years to unify the country. The election was never held, largely because Eisenhower feared it would result in an overwhelming mandate for Ho. Instead the United States gradually took over from the French, sponsoring a new government in Saigon headed by Ngo Dinh Diem, a Vietnamese nationalist from a northern Catholic family. While Eisenhower can be given credit for refusing to engage American forces on behalf of French colonialism in Indochina, his determination to resist Communist expansion had committed the United States to a long and eventually futile struggle to prevent Ho Chi Minh from achieving his long-sought goal of a unified, independent Vietnam.

EISENHOWER WAGES THE COLD WAR

Dwight D. Eisenhower came into the presidency in 1952 unusually well-prepared to lead the nation at the height of the Cold War. His long years of military service had exposed him to a wide variety of international issues, both in Asia and in Europe, and to an even broader array of world leaders, such as Winston Churchill and Charles de Gaulle. He was not only an experienced military strategist, but a gifted politician and diplomat as well. He was blessed with a sharp, pragmatic mind and organizational genius that enabled him to plan and carry out large enterprises, grasping the precise relationship between the parts and the whole. Above all, he had a serene confidence in his own ability. At the end

closed the last remaining airstrip, limiting supplies to those dropped by air and preventing even the evacuation of the wounded. When the French government made a last minute appeal for Radford's air strike, President Eisenhower used characteristically indirect means to turn it down. Fearful that an air attack would lead to an intervention by American ground forces, Ike insisted that both Congress and American allies in Europe approve the use of American forces in advance. Congressional leaders, recalling the recent Korean debacle, were reluctant; the British were appalled and ruled out any joint action.

The President used these objections to turn down intervention in Indochina in 1954. Much later, just before the American involvement in the Vietnam War in the 1960s, he stated his reasons more candidly. "The jungles of Indochina would have swallowed up division after division of United States troops," he explained. Equally important, he believed that U.S. involvement in France's war would have compromised the American "tradition of anticolonialism. . . . The standing of the United States as the most powerful of the anticolonial powers is an asset of incalculable value to the Free World," he concluded.

of his first day in the White House, he confided in his diary: "Plenty of worries and difficult problems. But such has been my portion for a long time—the result is that this just seems like a continuation of all I've been doing since July 1941."

Eisenhower chose John Foster Dulles as his secretary of state. The myth soon developed that Ike had given Dulles free rein to conduct American diplomacy. Appearances were deceptive. Eisenhower preferred to work behind the scenes. He let Dulles make the public speeches and appearances before congressional committees, where the secretary's hardline views placated GOP extremists. But Dulles carefully consulted with the President before every appearance, meeting frequently with Eisenhower at the White House and telephoning him several times a day. Ike respected his secretary of state's broad knowledge of foreign policy and his skill in conducting American diplomacy, but he made all the major decisions himself. "There's only one man I know who has seen *more* of the world and talked with more people and *knows* more than he does," Ike said of Dulles, "and that's me."

From the outset, Eisenhower was determined to bring the Cold War under control. Ideally, he wanted to end it, but as a realist, he would settle for a relaxation of tensions with the Soviet Union. In part, he was motivated by a deeply held budgetary concern. Defense spending had increased from $13 billion to $50 billion under Truman; Ike was convinced that the nation was in danger of going bankrupt unless military spending was reduced. As president, he inaugurated a "new look" for American defense, cutting back on the army and navy and relying even more heavily than Truman had on the air force and its nuclear striking power. As a result, the defense budget dropped below $40 billion annually. In 1954, Dulles announced reliance on massive retaliation—in fact a continuance of Truman's policy of deterrence. Rather than becoming involved in limited wars such as Korea, the United States would consider the possibility of using nuclear weapons to halt any Communist aggression that threatened vital U.S. interests anywhere in the world.

While he permitted Dulles to make his veiled nuclear threats, Eisenhower's fondest dream was to end the arms race. Sobered by the development of the hydrogen bomb, successfully tested by the United States in November 1952 and by the Soviet Union in August 1953, the President began a new effort at disarmament with the Russians. Yet before this initiative could take

Below, Secretary of State John Foster Dulles is shown reporting to President Eisenhower and the nation after a European tour in 1955. At right, cartoonist Herblock, a sharp critic of Dulles's hard line, depicts him in a Superman suit pushing Uncle Sam to the brink of nuclear war.

effect, Ike had to weather a series of crises around the world that tested his skill and patience to the utmost.

Containing China

The Communist government in Peking posed a serious challenge for the Eisenhower administration. Senate Republicans, led by William Knowland of California, blamed the Democrats for the "loss" of China. They viewed Mao as a puppet of the Soviet Union and insisted that the United States recognize the Nationalists on Formosa as the only legitimate government of China. While State Department experts realized that there were underlying tensions between China and Russia, Mao's intervention in the Korean War had convinced most Americans that the Chinese Communists were an integral part of a larger Communist effort at world domination. Thus Truman and Acheson had abandoned any hope of trying to exploit differences between Mao and Stalin by wooing China away from the Soviet Union.

Eisenhower and Dulles chose to accentuate the potential conflict between Russia and China. By taking a strong line against China, the U.S. could make the Chinese realize that Russia was unable to protect their interests; at the same time, such a hawkish policy would please Congressional conservatives like Knowland. Ultimately Eisenhower and Dulles hoped that a policy of firmness would not only contain Communist Chinese expansion in Asia, but also drive a wedge between Moscow and Peking.

A crisis in the Formosa Straits provided the first test of the new policy. In the fall of 1954, Communist China threatened to seize coastal islands, notably Quemoy and Matsu, occupied by the Nationalists. Fearful that seizure of these offshore islands would be the first step toward an invasion of Formosa, Eisenhower permitted Dulles to sign a security treaty with Chiang Kai-shek committing the United States to defend Formosa. When the Communists began shelling the offshore islands, Eisenhower persuaded Congress to pass a resolution authorizing him to use force to defend Formosa and "closely related localities."

Despite repeated requests, however, the President refused to say whether he would use force to repel a Chinese attack on Quemoy or Matsu.

Instead he and Dulles hinted at the use of nuclear weapons, carefully stating that their action would depend on whether they considered an attack on the offshore islands part of a larger offensive aimed at Formosa. The Chinese leaders, unsure whether Eisenhower was bluffing, decided not to test American resolve. The shelling ended in 1955, and when the Communists resumed it again in 1958, another firm but equally ambiguous American response forced them to desist. The apparent refusal of the Soviet Union to come to China's aid in these crises with the United States contributed to a growing rift between these two Communist nations by the end of the 1950s. Unfortunately, the Eisenhower administration failed to take full advantage of the opportunity that it had helped to create.

Turmoil in the Middle East

The gravest crisis for Eisenhower came in the Middle East when Egyptian leader Gamal Nasser seized the Suez Canal in July 1956. England and France were ready to use force immediately; their citizens owned the canal company, and their economies were dependent on the canal for the flow of oil from the Persian Gulf. President Eisenhower, however, was staunchly opposed to intervention, preferring to seek a diplomatic solution with Nasser, who kept the canal running smoothly. For three months, Dulles did everything possible to restrain the European allies, but finally they decided to take a desperate gamble— they invaded Egypt and seized the canal, relying on the United States to prevent any Russian interference.

Eisenhower was furious when England and France launched their attack in early November. Campaigning for reelection against Adlai Stevenson on the slogan of keeping the peace, Ike had to abandon domestic politics to deal with the threat of war. "The White House crackled with barracks-room language," reported one observer; the President told an aide that the Western allies had made "a complete *mess* and *botch* of things." Unhesitatingly, he instructed Dulles to sponsor a UN resolution calling for British and French withdrawal from Egypt. Yet when the Russians supported the American proposal and went further, threatening rocket attacks on British and

*T*he ships scuttled by British and French forces during the Suez crisis formed an effective physical blockade of the canal and gave their invading forces control of the traffic flowing through the waterway.

French cities and even offering to send "volunteers" to fight in Egypt, Eisenhower made it clear that he would not tolerate Soviet interference. He put the Strategic Air Command on alert and said of the Russians, "If those fellows start something, we may have to hit 'em—and, if necessary, with everything in the bucket."

Just after noon on election day, November 6, 1956, British Prime Minister Anthony Eden called the President to inform him that England and France were ending their invasion. Eisenhower breathed a sigh of relief. American voters rallied behind Ike, electing him to a second term by a near landslide. As a result of the Suez crisis, the United States replaced England and France as the main Western influence in the Middle East. With Russia strongly backing Egypt and Syria, the Cold War had found yet another battleground.

Two years later, Eisenhower found it necessary to intervene in the strategic Middle Eastern country of Lebanon. Political power in this neutral nation was divided between Christian and Moslem elements. When the outgoing Christian president, Camille Chamoun, broke with tradition by seeking a second term, Moslem groups (aided by Egypt and Syria) threatened to launch a rebellion. At first, Eisenhower turned down Chamoun's request for American intervention to avert a civil war, but after an unexpected nationalist coup overthrew the pro-Western government of Iraq, Ike decided to act in order to uphold the U.S. commitment to political stability in the Middle East.

American Marines from the Sixth Fleet moved swiftly ashore on July 15, 1958, securing the Beirut airport and preparing the way for a force of some fourteen thousand troops airlifted from bases in Germany. The military wanted to occupy the entire country, but Eisenhower insisted on limiting American forces to the area of Beirut. The mission of the troops, he argued, was "not primarily to fight," but simply to show the flag. Lebanese political leaders quickly agreed on a successor to Chamoun, and American soldiers left the country before the end of October. This restrained use of force achieved Eisenhower's primary goal of quieting the explosive Middle East. It also served, as Secretary of State Dulles pointed out, "to reassure many small nations that they could call on us in a time of crisis."

Covert Actions

Amid these dangerous crises, the Eisenhower administration worked behind the scenes in the 1950s to expand the nation's global influence. In 1953, the CIA was instrumental in overthrowing a popularly elected government in Iran and placing the Shah in full control of that country. American oil companies were rewarded with lucrative concessions, and Eisenhower felt that he had gained a valuable ally on the Russian border. But these short-run gains created a deep-seated animosity among Iranians that would haunt the United States in the future.

Closer to home, in Latin America, Eisenhower once again relied on covert action. In 1954, the CIA masterminded the overthrow of a leftist regime in Guatemala. The immediate advantage was in denying the Soviets a possible foothold in the Western Hemisphere, but Latin Americans resented the thinly disguised interference of the United States in their internal affairs. More important, when Fidel Castro came to power in Cuba in 1959, the Eisenhower administration—after a brief effort at conciliation—adopted a hard line that helped drive Cuba into the Soviet orbit and led to new attempts at covert action.

Eisenhower's record as a Cold Warrior was thus mixed. His successful ending of the Korean War and his peacekeeping efforts in Indochina and Formosa and in the Suez crisis are all to his credit. Yet his reliance on coups and subversion directed by the CIA in Iran and Guatemala reveal Ike's corrupting belief that the ends justified the means. And despite the 1952 campaign call for the liberation of Eastern Europe, Eisenhower accepted Soviet domination of this region, refusing to act on behalf of East German protesters in 1953 or Hungarian freedom fighters in 1956.

Nevertheless, Eisenhower did display an admirable ability to stay calm and unruffled in moments of great tension, reassuring the nation and the world. And above all, he could boast, as he did in 1962, of his ability to keep the peace. "In those eight years," he reminded the nation, "we lost no inch of ground to tyranny. One war was ended and incipient wars were blocked."

Waging Peace

Eisenhower hoped to ease Cold War tensions by ending the nuclear arms race. The advent of the hydrogen bomb intensified his concern over nuclear warfare; by 1955, both the United States and the Soviet Union had added this dread new weapon to their arsenals. With new long-range ballistic missiles being perfected, it was only a matter of time before Russia and the United States would be capable of destroying each other completely. Peace, as Winston Churchill noted, now depended on a balance of terror.

Throughout the fifties, Eisenhower sought a way out of the nuclear dilemma. In April 1953, shortly after Stalin's death, he gave a speech in which he called on the Russians to join him in a new effort at disarmament, pointing out that "every warship launched, every rocket fired signifies, in the final sense, a theft from those who hunger and are not fed, those who are cold and are not clothed." When the Soviets ignored this appeal, the President tried again in December 1953. Addressing the UN General Assembly, he outlined an "atoms-for-peace" plan whereby the United States and the Soviet Union would donate fissionable material to a new UN agency to be used for peaceful purposes. Despite Ike's appeal "to serve the needs rather than the fears of mankind," the Russians again rebuffed him. Undaunted, Eisenhower tried once more. At the Geneva summit conference in 1955, Ike proposed to Nikita Khrushchev, just emerging as Stalin's successor after a two-year struggle for power, a way to break the disarmament deadlock. "Open skies," as reporters dubbed the plan, would overcome the traditional Russian objection to on-site inspection by having both superpowers open their territory to mutual aerial surveillance. Unfortunately, Khrushchev dismissed open skies as "a very transparent espionage device," and the Geneva Conference ended without any significant breakthrough in the Cold War.

After his reelection in 1956, the President made a new effort to initiate nuclear arms control. Concern over atmospheric fallout from nuclear testing had led presidential candidate Adlai Stevenson to propose a mutual ban on such experiments. At first, Eisenhower rejected the test-ban idea, arguing it could be effective only as part of a comprehensive disarmament agreement,

From *Straight Herblock* (Simon & Schuster, 1964)

Cartoonist Herblock's view of the Khrushchev-Eishenhower meetings.

missile gap would open up by the early 1960s—a time when the Russians might have such a commanding lead in ICBMs that they could destroy America with a first strike. Despite the President's belief that the American missile program was in good shape, he allowed a major increase in defense spending to speed up the building of American ICBMs and the new Polaris submarine-launched intermediate range missile (IRBM).

Nikita Khruschev took full advantage of the furor over *Sputnik* to put the United States on the defensive. "We will bury capitalism," he boasted, telling Americans, "Your grandchildren will live under communism." The most serious threat of all came in November 1958 when the Russian leader declared that within six months he would sign a separate peace treaty with East Germany, calling for an end to American, British, and French occupation rights in Berlin.

Eisenhower met the second Berlin crisis as firmly as Truman had the first. He refused to abandon the city, but also tried to avoid a military showdown. Prudent diplomacy forced Khrushchev to extend his deadline indefinitely. After a trip to the United States, culminating in a personal meeting with Eisenhower at Camp David, the Russian leader agreed to attend a summit conference in Paris in May 1960.

This much-heralded meeting never took place. On May 1, two weeks before the leaders were to convene in Paris, the Soviets shot down an American U-2 plane piloted by Francis Gary Powers. The United States had been overflying Russia since 1956 in these high-altitude spy planes, gaining vital information about the Soviet missile program which showed there was little basis for the public fear that the Russians had opened up a dangerous missile gap. After initially denying any knowledge, Eisenhower took full responsibility for the Powers' overflight and Khrushchev responded with a scathing personal denunciation and a refusal to meet with the American president.

Eisenhower deeply regretted the breakup of the Paris summit, telling an aide that "the stupid U-2 mess" had destroyed all his efforts for peace. Sadly he concluded that "he saw nothing worthwhile left for him to do now until the end of his presidency." Khrushchev marked time for the next nine months, waiting for the American people to choose a new president. Eisenhower

but the Russians supported it. Finally, in 1958, the President changed his mind after American and Soviet scientists developed a system to detect nuclear testing in the atmosphere without on-site inspection. In October 1958, Eisenhower and Khrushchev each voluntarily suspended further weapons tests pending the outcome of a conference held at Geneva to work out a test-ban treaty. Although the Geneva Conference failed to make progress, neither the United States nor the Soviet Union resumed testing for the remainder of Ike's term in office.

The suspension of testing halted the pollution of the world's atmosphere, but it did not lead to the improvement in Soviet-American relations that Eisenhower sought. Instead, the Soviet feat in launching *Sputnik*, the first artificial satellite to orbit the earth, served to intensify the Cold War. Fearful that the Russians were several years ahead of the United States in the development of intercontinental ballistic missiles (ICBMs), Democrats criticized Eisenhower for not spending enough on defense and warned that a dangerous did make a final effort at peace, however. Three days before leaving office, he delivered a farewell address in which he gave a somber warning about the danger of massive military spending. "In the councils of government, we must guard against the acquisition of unwarranted influence, whether sought or unsought, by the military-industrial complex," he declared. "The potential for the disastrous rise of misplaced power exists and will persist."

Rarely has an American president been more prophetic. In the next few years, the level of defense spending would skyrocket as the Cold War escalated under his successors in the White House. The military-industrial complex reached its acme of power in the 1960s when the United States realized the full implications of Truman's doctrine of containment. Eisenhower had succeeded in keeping the peace for eight years, but he had failed to halt the momentum of the Cold War he had inherited from Harry Truman. Ike's efforts to ease tension with the Soviet Union were dashed by his own distrust of communism and by Khrushchev's belligerent rhetoric and behavior. Still, he had begun to relax tensions, a process that would survive the troubled sixties and, after several false starts, would finally begin to erode the Cold War by the end of the 1980s.

KENNEDY INTENSIFIES THE COLD WAR

John F. Kennedy was determined to succeed where he felt Eisenhower had failed. Critical of his predecessor for holding down defense spending and apparently allowing the Soviet Union to open up a dangerous lead in ICBMs, Kennedy sought to warn the nation of its peril and lead it to victory in the Cold War.

In his inaugural address, the young President sounded the alarm. Ignoring the domestic issues aired during the campaign, he dealt exclusively with the world. "Let every nation know, whether it wishes us well or ill, that we shall pay any price, bear any burden, meet any hardship, support any friend, oppose any foe," Kennedy declared, "to assure the survival and success of liberty. We will do all this and more."

From the day he took office, John F. Kennedy gave foreign policy top priority. In part, this

In his inaugural address, Kennedy called upon the American people to "Ask not what your country can do for you: ask what you can do for your country."

decision reflected the perilous world situation, the immediate dangers ranging from the unresolved Berlin crisis, through a developing civil war in Vietnam, to the emergence of Fidel Castro as a Soviet ally in Cuba. But it also corresponded to Kennedy's personal priorities. As a congressman and senator, he had been an intense Cold Warrior, supporting containment after World War II, lamenting the loss of China, and accusing the Eisenhower administration of allowing the Russians to open up a dangerous missile gap. Bored by committee work and legislative details, he had focused on foreign policy in the Senate, gaining a seat on the Foreign Relations Committee and publishing a book of speeches, *The Strategy of Peace,* in early 1960.

His appointments reflected his determination to win the Cold War. His choice of Dean Rusk, an experienced but unassertive diplomat, to head the State Department indicated that Kennedy planned to be his own secretary of state. He surrounded himself with young, pragmatic advisers who prided themselves on toughness: McGeorge Bundy, dean of Harvard College, became national security adviser; Walt W. Rostow, an MIT economist, was Bundy's deputy; and Robert McNamara, the youthful president of the Ford Motor Company, took over as secretary of defense.

These New Frontiersmen, later dubbed "the best and the brightest" by journalist David Halberstam, all shared a hard-line view of the Soviet Union and the belief that American security depended upon superior force and the willingness to use it. Walt Rostow summed up their view of the contest with Russia best when he wrote, "The cold war comes down to this test of whether we and the democratic world are fundamentally tougher and more purposeful in the defense of our vital interests than they are in the pursuit of their global ambitions."

Flexible Response

The first goal of the Kennedy administration was to build up the nation's armed forces. During the 1960 campaign, Kennedy had warned that the Soviets were opening a missile gap. In fact, due largely to Eisenhower's foresight, the United States had a significant lead in nuclear striking power by early 1961, with a fleet of over 600 B-52 bombers, 2 Polaris submarines, and 16 Atlas ICBMs capable of delivering more than 2000 warheads against Russian targets. Nevertheless, the new administration, intent on putting the Soviets on the defensive, authorized the construction of an awesome nuclear arsenal that included 1000 Minuteman solid-fuel ICBMs (five times the number Eisenhower had felt necessary) and 32 Polaris submarines carrying 656 missiles. The United States thus opened a missile gap in reverse, creating the possibility of a successful American first strike.

At the same time, the Kennedy administration augmented conventional military strength. Secretary of Defense McNamara developed plans to add five combat-ready army divisions, three tactical air wings, and a ten-division strategic reserve. These vast increases led to a $6 billion jump in the defense budget in 1961 alone. The President took a personal interest in counterinsurgency. He expanded the Special Forces unit at Fort Bragg, North Carolina, and insisted, over army objections, that it adopt a distinctive green beret as a symbol of its elite status.

The purpose of this buildup was to create an

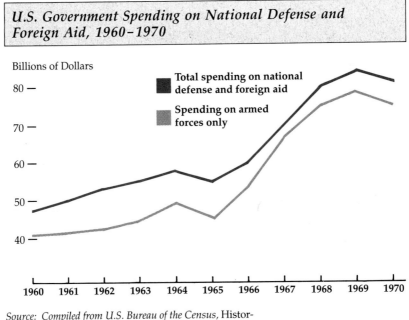

U.S. Government Spending on National Defense and Foreign Aid, 1960–1970

Billions of Dollars

Total spending on national defense and foreign aid

Spending on armed forces only

Source: Compiled from U.S. Bureau of the Census, Historical Statistics of the United States, Colonial Times to 1970, Bicentennial Edition, Washington, D.C., 1975.

alternative to Eisenhower's policy of massive retaliation. Instead of responding to Communist moves with nuclear threats, the United States could now call on a wide spectrum of force— ranging from ICBMs to Green Berets. Thus, as Robert McNamara explained, the new strategy of flexible response meant that the United States could "choose among several operational plans. We shall be committed only to a system that gives us the ability to use our forces in a controlled and deliberate way." The danger was that such a powerful arsenal might tempt the new administration to test its strength against the Soviet Union.

Crisis over Berlin

The first confrontation came in Germany. Since 1958, Soviet Premier Khrushchev had been threatening to sign a peace treaty that would put access to the isolated western zones of Berlin under the control of East Germany. The steady flight of skilled workers to the West through the Berlin escape route weakened the East German regime dangerously, and the Soviets felt they had to resolve this issue quickly.

At a summit meeting in Vienna in June 1961, Kennedy and Khrushchev focused on Berlin as the key issue. Pointing out that sixteen years had passed since the end of World War II, the Russian leader called the current situation "intolerable" and announced that the Soviet Union would proceed with an East German peace treaty. Kennedy was equally adamant, defending the American presence in Berlin and refusing to give up occupation rights which he considered crucial to the defense of Western Europe. In their last session, the failure to reach agreement took on an ominous tone. "I want peace," Khrushchev declared, "but, if you want war, that is your problem." "It is you, not I," the young President replied, "who wants to force a change." When the Soviet leader said he would sign a German peace treaty by December, Kennedy added, "It will be a cold winter."

The climax came sooner than either man expected. On July 25, Kennedy delivered an impassioned televised address to the American people in which he called the defense of Berlin "essential" to "the entire Free World." Announcing a series of arms increases, including $3 billion more in defense spending and a nationwide

Entrance and egress between East and West Berlin was controlled by a series of checkpoints. "Checkpoint Charlie" was the gateway between the American and Soviet zones.

program of fallout shelters, the President took the unprecedented step of calling more than 150,000 reservists and National Guardsmen to active duty. Above all, he sought to convince Khrushchev of his determination and resolve. "I hear it said that West Berlin is militarily untenable," he commented. "And so was Bastogne. And so, in fact, was Stalingrad. Any dangerous spot is tenable if men—brave men—will make it so."

Aware of superior American nuclear striking power, Khrushchev settled for a stalemate. On August 13, the Soviets sealed off their zone of the city. They began the construction of the Berlin Wall to stop the flow of brains and talent to the West. For a brief time, Russian and American tanks maneuvered within sight of each other at Checkpoint Charlie (where the American and Soviet zones met), but by fall, the tension gradually eased. The Soviets signed a separate peace treaty that did not affect U.S. occupation rights; Berlin—like Germany and, indeed, all of Europe —remained divided between the East and the West. Neither side could claim a victory, but Kennedy felt that at least he had proved to the world America's willingness to honor its commitments.

Containing Fidel Castro

Two weeks before Kennedy's inauguration, Nikita Khrushchev gave a speech in Moscow in which

*C*old War allies, Soviet Premier Nikita Khrushchev (left) and Cuban Premier Fidel Castro (right).

Courtesy the National Library of Wales.

*T*o his great embarrassment, Kennedy's handling of the Bay of Pigs invasion backfired like the exploding Cuban cigar.

he declared Soviet support for "wars of national liberation." The Russian leader's words were actually aimed more at China than the United States; the two powerful Communist nations were now rivals for influence in the Third World. But the new American President, ignoring the growing Sino-Soviet split, concluded that the United States and Russia were locked in a struggle for the hearts and minds of the uncommitted in Asia, Africa, and Latin America.

Calling for a new policy of nation-building, Kennedy advocated financial and technical assistance designed to help Third World nations achieve economic modernization and stable, pro-Western governments. Measures ranging from the formation of the idealistic Peace Corps to the ambitious Alliance for Progress—a massive economic aid program for Latin America—were part of this effort. Unfortunately, Kennedy relied even more on counterinsurgency and the Green Berets to beat back the Communist challenge in the Third World.

Kennedy's determination to check global Communist expansion reached a peak of intensity in Cuba. In the 1960 campaign, pointing to the growing ties between the Soviet Union and Fidel Castro's regime, he had accused the Republicans of permitting a "Communist satellite" to arise on "our very doorstep." Kennedy had even issued a

statement backing "anti-Castro forces in exile," calling them "fighters for freedom" who held out hope for "overthrowing Castro."

In reality, the Eisenhower administration had been training a group of Cuban exiles in Guatemala since March 1960 as part of a CIA plan to topple the Castro regime. Many of the new President's advisers had doubts about the proposed invasion. Some saw little chance for success because the operation depended heavily on a broad uprising of the Cuban people. Others—notably Senator William Fulbright of Arkansas, chairman of the Foreign Relations Committee—viewed it as an immoral act that would discredit the United States. "The Castro regime is a thorn in the flesh," Fulbright argued, "but it is not a dagger in the heart." The President, however, committed by his own campaign rhetoric and assured of success by the military, decided to go ahead.

On April 17, 1961, fourteen hundred Cuban exiles moved ashore at the Bay of Pigs on the southern coast of Cuba. Even though the United States had masterminded the entire operation, Kennedy insisted on covert action, even canceling at the last minute a planned American air strike on the beachhead. With air superiority, Castro's well-trained forces had no difficulty in quashing the invasion. They killed nearly five hundred exiles and forced the rest to surrender within forty-eight hours.

Aghast at the swiftness of the defeat, President Kennedy took personal responsibility for the failure. In his address to the American people, however, he showed no remorse for arranging the violation of a neighboring country's sovereignty, only regret at the outcome. Above all, he expressed renewed defiance, warning the Soviets that "our restraint is not inexhaustible." He went on to assert that the United States would resist "Communist penetration" in the Western Hemisphere, terming it part of the "primary obligations . . . to the security of our nation." For the remainder of his presidency, Kennedy continued to harass the Castro regime, imposing an economic blockade on Cuba, supporting a continuing series of raids by exile groups operating out of Florida, and failing to stop the CIA from experimenting with bizarre plots to assassinate Fidel Castro.

At the Brink

The climax of Kennedy's crusade came in October 1962 with the Cuban missile crisis. Throughout the summer and early fall, the Soviets engaged in a massive arms buildup in Cuba, ostensibly to protect Castro from an American invasion. In the United States, Republican candidates in the 1962 congressional elections called for a firm American response; Kennedy contented himself with a stern warning against the introduction of any offensive weapons, believing that their presence would directly threaten American security. Khrushchev publicly denied any such intent, but secretly he took a daring gamble, building twenty-four medium-range (1000-mile) and eighteen intermediate-range (2000-mile) missile sites in Cuba. Later he claimed his purpose was purely defensive, but most likely he was responding to the pressures from his own military to close the enormous strategic gap in nuclear striking power that Kennedy had opened.

On October 14, 1962, American U-2 planes finally discovered the missile sites that were nearing completion. As soon as he learned of the Russian action, Kennedy decided to seek a showdown with Khrushchev. Insisting on absolute secrecy, he convened a special group of advisers to consider the way to respond.

An initial preference for an immediate air strike gradually gave way to discussion of either a full-scale invasion or a naval blockade. The President and his advisers ruled out diplomacy, rejecting a proposal to offer the withdrawal of obsolete American Jupiter missiles from Turkey in return for a similar Russian pullout in Cuba. Kennedy finally agreed to a two-step procedure. He would proclaim a quarantine of Cuba to prevent the arrival of new missiles and threaten a nuclear confrontation to force the removal of those already there. If the Russians did not cooperate, then the United States would invade Cuba and dismantle the missiles by force.

On the evening of October 22, the President informed the nation of the existence of the Soviet missiles and his plans to remove them. He spared no words in blaming Khrushchev for "this clandestine, reckless and provocative threat to world peace," and he made it clear that any missile attack from Cuba would lead to "a full retaliatory response upon the Soviet Union."

For the next six days, the world hovered on the brink of nuclear catastrophe. Khrushchev replied defiantly, accusing Kennedy of pushing mankind "to the abyss of a world nuclear-missile war." In the Atlantic, some sixteen Soviet ships continued on course toward Cuba, while the American navy was deployed to intercept them 500 miles from the island. In Florida, nearly one-quarter of a million men were being concentrated in the largest invasion force ever assembled in the continental United States.

The first break came at midweek when the Soviet ships suddenly halted to avert a confrontation at sea. "We're eyeball to eyeball," commented Secretary of State Dean Rusk, "and I think the other fellow just blinked." Kennedy was relieved on Friday when Khrushchev sent him a long, rambling letter offering a face-saving way out— Russia would remove the missiles in return for an American promise never to invade Cuba. The President was ready to accept when a second Russian message raised the stakes by insisting that the American Jupiter missiles be withdrawn from Turkey. Kennedy refused to bargain; Khrushchev had endangered world peace by putting the missiles in Cuba secretly, and he must take them out immediately. Nevertheless, while the military went ahead with plans for the invasion of Cuba, the President, heeding his brother's advice, decided to make one last appeal for peace.

Ignoring the second Russian message, he sent a cable to Khrushchev accepting his original offer.

On Saturday night, October 27, Robert Kennedy—the President's brother and most trusted adviser—met with Soviet ambassador Anatoly Dobrynin to make it clear that this was the last chance to avert nuclear confrontation. "We had to have a commitment by tomorrow that those bases would be removed," Robert Kennedy recalled telling him. "He should understand that if they did not remove those bases, we would remove them." Then the President's brother calmly remarked that if Khrushchev did not back down, "there would be not only dead Americans but dead Russians as well."

In reality, John F. Kennedy was not quite so ready to risk nuclear war. Secretary of State Dean Rusk more recently revealed that the President had instructed him to propose a deal through the United Nations involving "the removal of both the Jupiters and the missiles in Cuba." "I am not," Kennedy told Rusk, "going to go to war over missiles in Turkey."

President Kennedy never had to make this final concession. At nine the next morning, Khrushchev agreed to remove the missiles in return for Kennedy's promise not to invade Cuba. The crisis was over.

On the surface, Kennedy appeared to have won a striking personal and political victory. His party successfully overcame the Republican challenge in the November elections and his own popularity reached new heights in the Gallup poll. The American people, on the defensive since Sputnik, suddenly felt that they had proved their superiority over the Russians; they were bursting with national pride. Arthur Schlesinger, Kennedy's confidant and later his biographer, claimed that the Cuban crisis showed the "whole world . . . the ripening of an American leadership unsurpassed in the responsible management of power. . . . It was this combination of toughness and restraint, of will, nerve and wisdom, so brilliantly controlled, so matchlessly calibrated, that dazzled the world."

The Cuban missile crisis had more substantial results as well. Shaken by their close call, Kennedy and Khrushchev agreed to install a "hot line" to speed direct communication between Washington and Moscow in an emergency. Long-stalled negotiations over the reduction of nuclear testing suddenly resumed, leading to the limited test ban treaty of 1963, which outlawed tests in the atmosphere while still permitting them underground. Above all, Kennedy displayed a new maturity as a result of the crisis. In a speech at American University in June 1963, he shifted from the rhetoric of confrontation to that of conciliation. Speaking of the Russians, he said, "Our most basic common link is the fact that we all inhabit this planet. We all breathe the same air. We all cherish our children's future. And we are all mortal."

Despite these hopeful words, the missile crisis also had an unfortunate consequence. Those who believed that the Russians understood only the language of force were confirmed in their penchant for a hard line. Hawks who had backed Kennedy's military buildup felt that events had justified a policy of nuclear superiority. The Russian leaders drew similar conclusions. Aware that the United States had a four-to-one advantage in nuclear striking power during the Cuban crisis, one Soviet official told his American counterpart, "Never will we be caught like this again." After 1962, the Soviets embarked on a crash program to build up their navy and to overtake the American lead in nuclear missiles. Within five years, they had the nucleus of a modern fleet and had surpassed the United States in ICBMs. Kennedy's fleeting moment of triumph thus ensured the escalation of the arms race. His legacy was a bittersweet one of short-term success and long-term anxiety.

JOHNSON ESCALATES THE VIETNAM WAR

Lyndon Johnson stressed continuity in foreign policy just as he had in enacting Kennedy's domestic reforms. He not only inherited the policy of containment from his fallen predecessor, but he shared the same Cold War assumptions and convictions. And feeling less confident about dealing with international issues, he tended to rely heavily on Kennedy's advisers—notably Secretary of State Rusk, Secretary of Defense McNamara, and McGeorge Bundy (the national security adviser until he was replaced in 1966 by the even more hawkish Walt Rostow).

Johnson had broad exposure to national security affairs. He had served on the Naval Affairs Committee in the House before and during World War II and as Senate majority leader he had been briefed and consulted regularly on the crises of the 1950s. A confirmed Cold Warrior, he took to heart the supposed lesson of Munich; he was convinced that wars came from weakness, not from strength.

He had also seen in the 1940s the devastating political impact on the Democratic party of the Communist triumph in China. "I am not going to lose Vietnam," he told the American ambassador to Saigon just after taking office in 1963. "I am not going to be the President who saw Southeast Asia go the way China went."

Aware of the problem Castro had caused John Kennedy, LBJ moved firmly to contain communism in the Western Hemisphere. When a military junta overthrew a leftist regime in Brazil, Johnson offered covert aid and open encouragement. He was equally forceful in compelling Panama to restrain rioting aimed at the continued American presence in the Canal Zone.

In 1965, to block the possible emergence of a Castro-type government, LBJ sent twenty thousand American troops to the Dominican Republic. Johnson's flimsy justifications—ranging from the need to protect American tourists to a dubious list of suspected Communists among the rebel leaders—served only to alienate liberal critics in the United States, particularly Senate Foreign Relations Committee Chairman J. William Fulbright, a former Johnson favorite. The intervention ended in 1966 with the election of a conservative government. Senator Fulbright, however, continued his criticism of Johnson's foreign policy by publishing *The Arrogance of Power*, a biting analysis of the fallacies of containment. Fulbright's defection symbolized a growing gap between the President and liberal intellectuals; the more LBJ struggled to uphold the Cold War policies he had inherited from Kennedy, the more he found himself under attack from Congress, the media, and the universities.

Civil War in Vietnam

It was Vietnam rather than Latin America that became Lyndon Johnson's obsession and led ultimately to his political downfall. He inherited both the problem of civil war in South Vietnam and the American commitment to Diem's regime in Saigon from Eisenhower and Kennedy.

The American decision to back Ngo Dinh Diem (see p. 893) had prevented the holding of elections throughout Vietnam in 1956, as called for in the Geneva accords. Instead, Diem sought to establish a separate government in the South with large-scale American economic and military assistance. By the time Kennedy entered the White House, however, the Communist government in North Vietnam, led by the venerable Ho Chi Minh, was directing the efforts of Viet Cong rebels in the South. As the guerrilla war intensified in the fall of 1961, the President sent two trusted advisers, Walt Rostow and General Maxwell Taylor, to South Vietnam. They returned favoring the dispatch of eight thousand American combat troops. "As an area for the operation of U.S. troops," reported General Taylor, "SVN [South Vietnam] is not an excessively difficult or unpleasant place to operate. . . . The risks of backing into a major Asian war by way of SVN, are present but are not impressive."

The President decided against sending in combat troops in 1961, but he authorized substantial increases in economic aid to Diem and in the size of the military mission in Saigon. The number of American advisers in Vietnam grew from fewer than one thousand in 1961 to over sixteen thousand by late 1963. The flow of supplies and the creation of "strategic hamlets," fortified villages designed to protect the peasantry from the Viet Cong, slowed the Communist momentum. American helicopters gave government forces mobility against the Viet Cong for the first time, but by 1963, the situation had again become critical. Diem had failed to win the support of his own people; Buddhist monks set themselves aflame in public protests against him; and even Diem's own generals plotted his overthrow.

President Kennedy was in a quandary. He realized that the fate of South Vietnam would be determined not by America but by the Vietnamese. "In the final analysis," he said in September 1963, "it is their war. They are the ones who have to win it or lose it." But at the same time, Kennedy was not prepared to accept the possible loss of all Southeast Asia. Saying it would be "a great mistake" to withdraw from South Vietnam, he told reporters, "Strongly on our mind is what happened in the case of China at the end of World War II, where China was lost. We don't want that." Although aides later claimed he planned to pull out after the 1964 election, Kennedy raised the stakes by tacitly approving a coup that led to Diem's overthrow and death on November 1, 1963. The resulting power vacuum in Saigon made further American involvement in Vietnam almost certain.

The Vietnam Dilemma

Lyndon Johnson had little choice but to continue Kennedy's policy in Vietnam. The crisis created by Diem's overthrow only three weeks before Kennedy's assassination led to a vacuum of power in Saigon that prevented the new President from conducting a thorough review and reassessment of the strategic alternatives in Southeast Asia. In 1964, seven different governments ruled South Vietnam; the government changed hands three times within one month. According to an American officer, the atmosphere in Saigon "fairly smelled of discontent," with "workers on strike, students demonstrating, [and] the local press pursuing a persistent campaign of criticism of the new government."

Resisting pressure from the Joint Chiefs of Staff for direct American military involvement, LBJ continued Kennedy's policy of economic and technical assistance. He sent in seven thousand more military advisers and an additional $50 million in aid. While he insisted it was still up to the Vietnamese themselves to win the war, he expanded American support for covert operations, including amphibious raids on the North.

These undercover activities led directly to the Gulf of Tonkin affair. On August 2, 1964, North Vietnamese torpedo boats attacked the *Maddox*, an American destroyer engaged in electronic intelligence-gathering in the Gulf of Tonkin. The attack was prompted by the belief that the American ship had been involved in a South Vietnamese raid nearby. The *Maddox* escaped unscathed, but to show American resolve, the navy sent in another destroyer, the *C. Turner Joy*. On the evening of August 4, the two destroyers, responding to sonar and radar contacts, opened fire on North Vietnamese gunboats in the area. Johnson ordered retaliatory air strikes on North Vietnamese naval bases. Later investigation suggested that the North Vietnamese gunboats had not launched a second attack on the American ships.

The next day the President asked Congress to pass a resolution authorizing him to take "all necessary measures to repel any armed attack against the forces of the United States and to prevent further aggression." He did not in fact need this authority; he had already ordered the retaliatory air strike without it. Later, critics charged that LBJ wanted a blank check from Congress to carry out the future escalation of the Vietnam War, but such a motive is unlikely. He had already rejected immediate military intervention. In part, he wanted the Gulf of Tonkin Resolution to demonstrate to North Vietnam the American determination to defend South Vietnam at any cost. "The challenge we face in Southeast Asia today," he told Congress, "is the same challenge that we have faced with courage and that we have met with strength in Greece and Turkey, in Berlin and Korea." He also wanted to preempt the Vietnam issue from his Republican opponent, Barry Goldwater, who had been advocating a tougher policy. By taking a firm stand on the Gulf of Tonkin incident, Johnson could both impress the North Vietnamese and outmaneuver a political rival at home.

Congress responded with alacrity. The House acted unanimously, while only two senators voted against the Gulf of Tonkin Resolution. Johnson appeared to have won a spectacular victory. His standing in the Gallup poll shot up from 42 to 72 percent, and he had effectively blocked Goldwater from exploiting Vietnam as a campaign issue.

In the long run, however, this easy victory proved costly. Having used force once against North Vietnam, LBJ was more likely to do so in the future. And although he apparently had no intention of widening the conflict in August 1964, the congressional resolution was phrased broadly enough to enable him to use whatever level of force he wished—including unlimited military intervention. Above all, when he did wage war in Vietnam, he left himself open to the charge of deliberately misleading Congress. Presidential credibility proved to be Johnson's ultimate Achilles' heel; his political downfall began with the Gulf of Tonkin Resolution.

The Space Race: Commitment to the Future

❧   ❧   ❧

The flag of the United States stands on lunar soil, amid the footprints of Neil Armstrong and Edwin Aldrin, astronauts on the Apollo 11 *moon trip.*

"These are extraordinary times," said President John F. Kennedy in a special message to Congress on May 25, 1961, "and we face an extraordinary challenge." The contest was with the Soviet Union, and outer space was the field of honor. Russia had stolen a march on the United States, sending a man into orbit before an American had even reached outer space. "Now is the time," Kennedy observed, "time for this nation to take a clearly leading role in space achievements." Project Apollo, its goal a manned lunar landing within the decade, was our answer to the challenge.

Man had always looked to the heavens with awe and wonder, but the American space program was not the product of romantic or scientific curiosity. Clearly, there was a race, a "space race," and America's preeminence in world affairs was at stake.

Russia and the United States had been competing in rocket technology since World War II. As the disaffected allies marched into Germany, each sought to gain the secrets of the German V-2, the first supersonic ballistic missile. Although the Soviet zone of occupation contained the primary V-2 plant, the U.S. Army's *Operation Paperclip* brought to the United States most of the top personnel of the

*S*putnik I *on its support stand before launching. The first news of* Sputnik *was not carried in Soviet newspapers until two days after the launch.*

*T*he Mercury-Redstone rocket (below) fails its first test, November 21, 1960. It later successfully carried astronauts Alan B. Shepard, Jr. and Virgil I. (Gus) Grissom into space.*

German Rocket program. Wernher von Braun and more than one hundred other German scientists and engineers were recruited for the army missile program. American military rocketry continued to receive priority over civilian space projects in the 1950s. President Eisenhower's fiscal conservatism and his low estimate of the significance of space exploration prevailed until the successful launch of the Soviet satellite *Sputnik I* on October 4, 1957.

While Eisenhower publicly dismissed *Sputnik* as an event of only "scientific interest" and denied the existence of a "space race," American confidence was shaken. Both houses of Congress established Space Committees; Eisenhower created the National Aeronautics and Space Administration (NASA); and the satellite program planned new *Explorers, Pioneers,* and other unmanned experiments. In the fall of 1958, Project Mercury, the United States' first manned space program, was announced.

Meanwhile, the Soviets pursued a variety of outer space objectives. Soviet spacecraft orbited the moon and photographed its dark side. *Sputnik V* launched two dogs into orbit and returned them safely to earth. But despite these Soviet successes, Eisenhower rejected NASA's proposed lunar mission, judging its benefits too narrowly scientific and its cost far too high. He continued to advocate a slow and steady program, with little sense of urgency.

John Kennedy pointed to Eisenhower's lack of initiative in space programs in his 1960 presidential

Twenty-three days before astronaut Alan B. Shepard, Jr., rode into space on the Mercury-Redstone rocket, Soviet cosmonaut Yuri A. Gagarin (above) orbited the earth once.

The historic first walk by Apollo 11 astronauts Neil A. Armstrong and Edwin E. Aldrin, Jr., on July 20, 1969. Shown here is the lunar landing Nodule and Roving Vehicle (moon buggy) at Hadley Base.

Tethered to a twenty-five-foot umbilical cord (above), astronaut Edward H. White II "walks" in space on June 3, 1965. By the end of 1966 the United States had flown ten manned missions; the Soviets had flown none.

campaign. "We are in a strategic space race with the Russians," he said in a campaign statement, "and we are losing." Referring to space as America's New Frontier, Kennedy created a slogan for his administration. But it took two unsettling events in April 1961 to gain his endorsement of Project Apollo.

On April 12, Soviet Cosmonaut Yuri Gagarin's first successful manned orbit of the earth put America even further behind in the space race. Despite the Kennedy rhetoric about closing the gap, the Soviet lead seemed greater than ever. Then, less than one week after the Gagarin flight, the American-sponsored invasion of Cuba at the Bay of Pigs collapsed. Just as the Soviets gained worldwide

acclaim in space, the United States was humiliated in Cuba, and—as Kennedy well knew—the prestige lost was not merely a matter of public relations but a real factor in world affairs. The combination of these events led the President, already predisposed toward space exploration, to look to NASA for a way to redeem America's tarnished image. Kennedy had three criteria in mind: the project would have to be spectacular, achievable within the decade, and a guaranteed American "first." Project Apollo fit the bill. "If we can get to the moon before the Russians," said Kennedy, "then we should." Eight years and nearly $24 billion later, on July 20, 1969, the Kennedy program came to fruition. Astronaut

*P*resident John F. Kennedy and Dr. Wernher von Braun. After World War II, German engineer von Braun was instrumental in developing the rocketry that launched the space and moon missions.

*D*espite the controversy over the billions of dollars spent on the race to the moon, Americans have always gathered to watch rocket launchings. Through television coverage, millions of other people worldwide have followed the American space program.

*O*n March 1, 1962, New York City sponsored a traditional ticker-tape parade for astronaut John H. Glenn, Jr., the first American to orbit the earth. After leaving the space program, Glenn was elected to the U.S. Senate.

Neil Armstrong stepped out onto the surface of the moon and uttered the first words ever spoken on earth's natural satellite. "That's one small step for a man," he said, "one giant leap for mankind."

Although the American space program was active before 1961, the Kennedy decision to send men to the moon marked the beginning of the program's heyday. Gemini, Apollo, Skylab, and the Space Shuttle were all products of the space race. Generally successful except for the 1986 *Challenger* disaster, American space projects have nonetheless had their detractors. Even at the time of its inception, many questioned the wisdom of spending billions on a race in space when millions of Americans were ill-fed, ill-housed, and under-educated. Even winning the race to the moon was a dubious victory, since the Soviets apparently never intended to achieve this feat themselves. But the American space effort did achieve Kennedy's primary goal—renewing a sense of national pride and restoring America's reputation for technological leadership.

Highlights of America's Longest War: Vietnam, 1950–1975

Date	Event	Significance
May 1950	Truman authorizes $10 million in aid to the French in Indochina fighting a war against guerrilla forces led by Ho Chi Minh.	Beginning of the American involvement in Vietnam.
May 1954	Fall of Dien Bien Phu.	End of French dominance in Indochina.
July 1954	Geneva Conference.	Division of Vietnam at 17th parallel. Ho's forces gain control of North Vietnam.
Oct. 1954	Eisenhower backs Diem regime in Saigon, capital of South Vietnam.	U.S. replaces France as chief Western supporter of South Vietnam.
Nov. 1961	Kennedy sends thousands of military "advisers" to Vietnam.	The way is opened for an American combat role in Vietnam.
Nov. 1963	Overthrow and assassination of Ngo Dinh Diem after Kennedy gives tacit approval to coup.	Political vacuum of power created in Saigon.
Aug. 1964	Congress passes Gulf of Tonkin Resolution.	President Johnson is given authority to use unlimited military force in Vietnam.
Feb. 1965	U.S. begins bombing of North Vietnam. It proves ineffective.	Johnson commits U.S. prestige to prevent defeat of South Vietnam.
July 1965	Johnson announces decision to send 50,000 ground troops to Vietnam.	U.S. involvement escalates in an effort to compel a diplomatic settlement.
Jan. 1968	American ground troops reach the 500,000 mark. Viet Cong launch Tet offensive.	Public support for Vietnam War erodes in United States.
March 1968	Johnson announces he will not run for reelection.	End of American escalation in Vietnam.
May 1968	Paris peace talks begin.	U.S. and North Vietnam quickly deadlock on peace terms.
June 1969	Nixon announces withdrawal of 25,000 American troops from Vietnam.	Beginning of policy of Vietnamization.
April 1970	Nixon orders invasion of Cambodia.	Widening of war to include all Indochina.
May 1972	Nixon authorizes mining of Haiphong harbor and intensified bombing of North Vietnam.	U.S. attempts to pressure North Vietnam into agreeing to peace terms.
Jan. 1973	Cease-fire agreements signed in Paris. U.S. agrees to remove its troops within 60 days.	End of direct American military involvement in Vietnam.
Jan. 1975	North Vietnam invades South Vietnam.	U.S. unwilling to try again to rescue South Vietnam.
April 1975	Fall of Saigon.	Abrupt withdrawal of U.S. from South Vietnam.

Escalation

The full-scale American involvement in Vietnam began in 1965 in a series of steps designed primarily to prevent a North Vietnamese victory. With the political situation in Saigon growing more hopeless every day, the President's advisers urged the bombing of the North as the only conceivable solution. American air attacks would serve several purposes: they would block North Vietnamese infiltration routes, make Hanoi pay a heavy price for its role, and lift the sagging morale of the South Vietnamese. But most important, as McGeorge Bundy reported after a visit to Pleiku (site of a Viet Cong attack on an American base which took nine lives), "Without new U.S. action defeat appears inevitable—probably not in a matter of weeks or perhaps even months, but within the next year or so." Johnson responded in February 1965 by ordering a long-planned aerial bombardment of a set of selected North Vietnamese targets.

The air strikes, aimed at impeding the Communist supply line and damaging Hanoi's economy, proved ineffective. In April, Johnson authorized the use of American combat troops in South Vietnam, but restricted them to defensive operations intended to protect American air bases. The Joint Chiefs then pressed the President for both unlimited bombing of the North and the aggressive use of American ground forces in the South. In mid-July, Secretary of Defense McNamara recommended sending 100,000 combat troops to Vietnam, more than doubling the American forces there. He felt this escalation would lead to a "favorable outcome," but also told the President that an additional 100,000 soldiers might be needed in 1966 and that American battle deaths could rise as high as 500 a month (by early 1968, they hit a peak of over 500 a week).

At the same time, other advisers, most notably Under Secretary of State George Ball, spoke out against military escalation in favor of a political settlement. Warning that the United States was likely to suffer France's fate in Vietnam, "national humiliation," Ball told the President that he had "serious doubt that an army of westerners can successfully fight Orientals in an Asian jungle."

Lyndon Johnson was genuinely torn, asking his advisers at one point: "Are we starting something that in two to three years we simply can't finish?" But he finally decided he had no choice but to

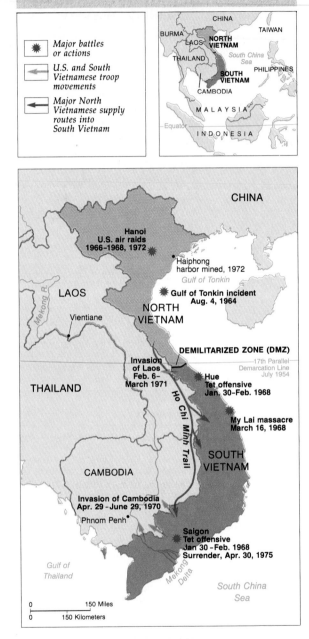

Southeast Asia and the Vietnam War
American combat forces in South Vietnam rose from 16,000 in 1963 to 500,000 in 1968, but a successful conclusion to the war was no closer.

persevere in Vietnam. Although he insisted on paring down McNamara's troop request, LBJ settled on a steady military escalation designed to compel Hanoi to accept a diplomatic solution. In late July, the President permitted a gradual increase in the bombing of North Vietnam and

The Strategists

Although the United States conducted thousands of air strikes over North Vietnam and committed half a million troops to the South, it failed to win the advantage. North Vietnamese regulars and Viet Cong guerrillas were better able to use the jungle terrain to advantage than their American adversaries. At right, cartoonist Bill Mauldin depicts Johnson's two options—all-out war or complete pullout—as equally precarious.

allowed American ground commanders to conduct offensive operations in the South. Most ominously, he approved the immediate dispatch of 50,000 troops to Vietnam and the future commitment of 50,000 more.

These July decisions formed "an open-ended commitment to employ American military forces as the situation demanded," writes historian George Herring, and they were "the closest thing to a formal decision for war in Vietnam." Convinced that withdrawal would destroy American credibility before the world and that an invasion of the North would lead to World War III, Johnson opted for large-scale but limited military intervention. Moreover, LBJ feared the domestic consequences of either extreme. A pullout could cause a massive political backlash at home, as conservatives condemned him for betraying South Vietnam to communism. All-out war, however, would mean the end of his social programs. Once Congress focused on the conflict, he explained to biographer Doris Kearns, "that bitch of a war" would destroy "the woman I really loved

—the Great Society." So he settled for a limited war, committing a half-million American troops to battle in Southeast Asia, all the while pretending it was a minor engagement and refusing to ask the American people for the support and sacrifice required for victory.

Lyndon Johnson was not solely responsible for the Vietnam War. He inherited both a policy that assumed that Vietnam was a vital national interest, and a deteriorating situation in Saigon that demanded a more active American role. Truman, Eisenhower, and Kennedy had taken the United States deep into the Vietnam maze; it was Johnson's fate to have to find a way out. But LBJ must bear full responsibility for the way he tried to resolve his dilemma. The failure to confront the people with the stark choices the nation faced in Vietnam, the insistence on secrecy and deceit, the refusal to acknowledge that he had committed the United States to a dangerous military involvement—these were Johnson's sins in Vietnam. His lack of self-confidence in foreign policy and fear of domestic reaction led directly to his undoing.

$\mathcal{S}$urviving Vietnam

*T*he stark, black, angled wall that forms the Vietnam Veterans' Memorial is engraved from top to bottom along its entire length with the names of U.S. personnel killed or thought to be missing in Vietnam.

Vietnam ranks after World War II as America's second most expensive war. Between 1950 and 1975, the United States spent $123 billion on combat in Southeast Asia. More importantly, Vietnam ranks —after our Civil War and World Wars I and II—as the nation's fourth deadliest war, with 57,661 Americans killed in action.

Yet, when the last U.S. helicopter left Saigon, Americans suffered what historian George Herring terms "collective amnesia." Everyone, even those who had fought in 'Nam, seemed to want to forget Southeast Asia. It took nearly ten years for the government to erect a national monument to honor those who died in Vietnam. The Vietnam Veterans Memorial in Washington, D.C., was dedicated in November 1982; on its polished black granite walls are carved the names of the dead and missing in action. And only in 1981 did collections of oral histories of some of those who served in Vietnam begin to appear: Al Santoli's well-documented *Everything We Had: An Oral History of the Vietnam War by Thirty-three American Soldiers Who Fought It*, and Mark Baker's *Nam: The Vietnam War in the Words of the Men and Women Who Fought There*. Both books demonstrate that in the steaming jungles of Vietnam one thing mattered most: survival.

One Vietnam veteran expressed the general feeling of men in combat: "War is not killing. Killing is the easiest part. . . . Sweating twenty-four hours a day, seeing guys drop all around you from heatstroke, not having food, not having water, sleeping only three hours a night for weeks at a time, that's what war is. Survival."

During his term President Kennedy ordered a more than tenfold increase in the number of U.S. advisers in Vietnam. Yet, for the ten to twelve thousand predominantly career soldiers there by December of 1962, Vietnam seemed a nice little nine-to-five war. Recalls radio technician Jan Barry of the army's 18th Aviation Company, "If we wanted to go out and chase people around and shoot at them . . . we had a war going. If we didn't . . . they left us alone." In those early days, even the Special Forces Green Berets "used to stop at four-thirty and have a happy hour and get drunk," says Barry, adding that "there was no war after four-thirty. On Saturdays, no war. On Sundays, no war. On holidays, no war. That's right, a nine-to-five war."

Within two years, however, the Joint Chiefs of Staff and President Johnson committed 50,000 American troops to combat in Vietnam, and the nice little war turned grim. By mid-1967, in fact, more than 400,000 Americans were fighting in Vietnam. As many as 300 died each week. Combat, recalls 26th Marine Division scout-sniper James Hebron, turned out "totally different" from what he had expected when he had joined the corps at age seventeen early in 1967. "There was no romance at all," says Hebron. During one combat period, Hebron's Bravo Company went without a hot meal for seven months. During that same operation, he notes, "I didn't brush my teeth for two months," explaining that "they sent toothbrushes . . . we had to use them to clean our rifles."

The Screaming Eagles of the elite 101st Airborne Division arrived in Vietnam shortly before the Tet offensive of January 1968. Lieutenant Robert Santos, destined to become one of the division's most decorated men, told his platoon, "two things can happen to you. You can get wounded and go home early. Or you can die." He added that the "best way to go home is whole. If you stick with me . . . and learn from the [more experienced men] you won't get wounded. You won't die." Santos and his men earned a basketful of medals for valor in combat. Lieutenant Santos explains those medals in grim terms: "My responsibility was to kill and in the process of killing to be so good at it that I indirectly saved my men's lives." So, notes Santos, "You come home with the high body count, high kill ratio," but, he concludes, "there's nothing, nothing, that's very satisfying about that."

Few who served in Vietnam survived unscathed, whether psychologically or physically. One of the 303,600 Americans wounded during the long war was 101st Airborne platoon leader James Bombard, first shot and then blown up by a mortar round during the bitter Tet fighting at Hue in February 1968. He describes his traumatic experience as

> feeling the bullet rip into your flesh, the shrapnel tear the flesh from your bones and the blood run down your leg. . . . To put your hand on your chest and to come away with your hand red with your own blood, and to feel it running out of your eyes and out of your mouth, and seeing it spurt out of your guts, realizing you were dying. . . . I was ripped open from the top of my

> head to the tip of my toes. I had forty-five holes in me.

Somehow Bombard survived Vietnam.

The fighting continued for four years after President Nixon took office. Robert Rawls served as a rifleman with the 1st Cavalry Division from early 1969 to early 1970. He recalls:

> We got fire fights after fire fights. My first taste of death. After fire fights you could smell it. They brought the [dead men] back wrapped in ponchos. . . . [T]hey just threw them up on the helicopter and [piled empty, reusable supply cases] on top of them. You could see the guys' feet hanging out. . . . I had nightmares. . . . I can still see those guys.

As the war dragged on, pacifist frustration at home paralleled the bitterness of those who had fought in Vietnam. John Muir's experience is typical. Early in the war, Muir had served as a rifleman with the 1st Marine Division during the battle of Dong Ha. Muir's single company fought continuously for four days and four nights, frequently in hand-to-hand combat, against two divisions of the North Vietnamese Army. When the marines were relieved, only ninety-one men—all wounded—were still able to fight at all. Muir's squad, however, had been wiped out: he had ended up throwing rocks at his attackers.

"It was a major battle," recalls Muir. "We did a fine job there. If it had happened in World War II, they still would be telling stories about it. But it happened in Vietnam, so nobody knows about it."

Withdrawing U.S. forces from Vietnam ended only the combat. Returning veterans fought government disclaimers concerning the toxicity of the defoliant Agent Orange. VA hospitals across the na-

tion still contain thousands of para- and quadriplegic Vietnam veterans, as well as the maimed from earlier wars. Throughout America the "walking wounded" find themselves still embroiled in the psychological aftermath of Vietnam. To this day, says former 1st Infantry Division combat medic David Ross, "If I'm walking someplace and there's grass, I find myself sometimes doing a shuffle and looking down at the ground. . . . I'm looking for a wire or a piece of vine that looks too straight, might be a [land mine] trip wire. Some of the survival habits you pick up stay residual for a long time."

Stalemate

For the next three years, Americans waged an intensive war in Vietnam and succeeded only in preventing a Communist victory. In the air, American bombing of the North proved ineffective. The rural, undeveloped nature of the North Vietnamese economy meant there were few industrial targets; a political refusal to bomb the main port of Haiphong allowed Soviet and Chinese arms to flow freely into the country. Nor were the efforts at interdiction any more successful. American planes pounded the Ho Chi Minh trail that ran down through Laos and Cambodia, but the North Vietnamese used the jungle panoply effectively to hide their shipments and massive manpower to repair damaged roads and bridges. In fact, the American air attacks, with their inadvertent civilian casualties, gave North Vietnam a powerful propaganda weapon, which it used to sway world opinion against the United States.

The war in the South went no better. Despite the steady increase in American ground forces, from 184,000 in late 1965 to more than 500,000 by early 1968, the Viet Cong still controlled much of the countryside. The search-and-destroy tactics employed by the American commander, General William Westmoreland, proved ill-suited. The Viet Cong, aided by North Vietnamese regulars, were waging a war of insurgency, avoiding fixed positions and striking from ambush. In a vain effort to destroy the enemy, Westmoreland used superior American firepower wantonly, devastating the countryside, causing many civilian casualties, and driving the peasantry into the arms of the guerrillas. Inevitably, these tactics led to the slaughter of innocent civilians, most notably at the hamlet of My Lai. In March 1968, an American company led by Lieutenant William Calley, Jr., killed over 200 unarmed villagers.

The main premise of Westmoreland's strategy was to wage a war of attrition that would finally reach a "crossover point" when Communist losses each month would be greater than the number of new troops they could recruit. He hoped to lure the Viet Cong and the North Vietnamese regulars into pitched battles where American firepower would inflict heavy casualties. But soon it was the Communists who were deciding where and when the fighting would take place, provok-

ing American attacks in remote areas of South Vietnam that favored the defenders and made Westmoreland pay heavily in American lives for the Communist losses. In late 1967, the North Vietnamese began a borders strategy designed to lure the bulk of American troops into battle in the Central Highlands and the areas bordering on Laos and Cambodia. The main attack came against the Marines at Khe Sahn in the northern interior, drawing more than 40 percent of all American infantry and armor battalions into the two northernmost provinces of South Vietnam.

The Viet Cong then used the traditional lull in the fighting at Tet, the lunar New Year, to launch a surprise attack in the heavily populated cities. Beginning on January 30, 1968, the VC struck at 36 of the 44 provincial capitals; the most daring raid came at the American embassy compound in Saigon. Although the guerrillas were unable to penetrate the embassy proper, for six hours television cameras caught the dramatic battle that ensued in the courtyard before military police finally overcame the attackers. Prompt response by American and South Vietnamese forces quickly repulsed the Tet offensive everywhere except Hue, the old imperial capital, which was only retaken after three weeks of heavy fighting had left this beautiful city, in the words of one observer, "a shattered, stinking hulk, its streets choked with rubble and rotting bodies."

Tet proved to be the turning point of the Vietnam War. Although the Communists suffered a major military defeat, losing an estimated 50,000 men, they scored an impressive political victory. For months, President Johnson had been telling the American people that the war was almost over and victory in sight; suddenly it appeared to be nearly lost. CBS-TV newscaster Walter Cronkite took a quick trip to Saigon to find out what had happened. Horrified at what he saw, he exclaimed to his guides, "What the hell is going on? I thought we were winning the war." He returned home to tell the American people, "It seems now more certain than ever that the bloody experience of Vietnam is to end in a stalemate."

President Johnson reluctantly came to the same conclusion after the Joint Chiefs of Staff requested an additional 205,000 troops to achieve victory in Vietnam following the Tet offensive. He began to listen to his new secretary of defense,

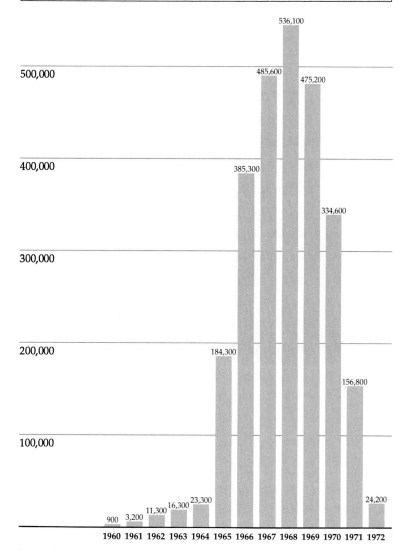

U.S. Troop Levels in Vietnam (as of Dec. 31 of each year)

536,100

500,000   485,600
                                                              475,200

400,000   385,300

                                                                     334,600

300,000

200,000   184,300

                                                                            156,800

100,000

              23,300   24,200
        16,300
     11,300
900 3,200

1960 1961 1962 1963 1964 1965 1966 1967 1968 1969 1970 1971 1972

Source: U.S. Department of Defense

Clark Clifford, who replaced Robert McNamara in January 1968. In mid-March, after receiving advice from the Wise Men, a group of experienced Cold Warriors that included such illustrious figures as Dean Acheson and Omar Bradley, the President decided to limit the bombing of North Vietnam in an effort to open up peace negotiations with Hanoi. In a speech to the nation on Sunday evening, March 31, 1968, Johnson outlined his plans for a new effort at ending the war peacefully, and then concluded by saying, as proof of his sincerity, "I shall not seek, and I will not accept, the nomination of my party for another term as your President."

In the twenty-four years since the seige of Dien Bien Phu, American policy had gone full cycle in Vietnam. Even though Eisenhower had decided against using force to rescue the French, his commitment to the Diem regime in Saigon had led eventually to American military involvement on a massive scale. Three years of inconclusive

*B*y 1968, the war had brought neither side to victory and had resulted only in the vast destruction of people, land, and property, especially in South Vietnam where most of the fighting took place.

fighting and a steadily mounting loss of American lives had disillusioned the American people and finally cost Lyndon Johnson the presidency. And the full price the nation would have to pay for its folly in Southeast Asia was still unknown —the Vietnam experience would continue to cast a shadow over American life for years to come.

The failure in Vietnam reflected the difficulty the United States faced in pursuing containment on a global scale. The policies that had worked well in Europe in the 1940s had little relevance to a very different situation in Southeast Asia. Intent on halting the spread of Communism, American leaders never grasped the political realities in Vietnam. The United States ended up backing a series of corrupt regimes in Saigon while the Viet Cong won the struggle for the hearts and minds of the Vietnamese people. More than anything else, the Vietnam War revealed the need for a thorough reexamination of the basic premises of American foreign policy in the Cold War.

Recommended Reading

The best introduction to the Vietnam War is the balanced survey by George Herring, *America's Longest War*, 2nd ed. (1985). Lloyd Gardner offers a persuasive analysis of the early American involvement through 1954 in *Approaching Vietnam* (1988), while George McT. Kahin, *Intervention* (1986) is excellent on what led to the escalation of the 1960s.

Stephen E. Ambrose exemplifies the recent reevaluation of Dwight D. Eisenhower by historians in the second volume of his biography, *Eisenhower: The President* (1985). For an equally favorable analysis, see Robert A. Divine, *Eisenhower and the Cold War* (1981).

Roger Hilsman, *To Move a Nation* (1967), is by far the most complete and analytical study of Kennedy's foreign policy.

Additional Bibliography

H. W. Brands gives a good overview of Eisenhower's foreign policy team in *Cold Warriors* (1988). Other books on Ike's foreign policy include Emmet J. Hughes, *The Ordeal of Power* (1962), a revealing memoir; Peter Lyon, *Eisenhower: Portrait of the Hero* (1974), a critical biography; William B. Ewald, *Eisenhower the President* (1981), a sympathetic account; and Blanche W. Cook, *The Declassified Eisenhower* (1981), a critique of his diplomacy. Eisenhower's two volumes of memoirs, *Mandate for Change* (1963) and *Waging Peace* (1966) are full and revealing accounts.

The best accounts of early American involvement in Vietnam are Andrew Rotter, *The Path to Vietnam* (1988), on events before 1954; Ellen J. Hammer, *The Struggle for Indochina, 1940–1955* (1966); Melvin Gurtov, *The First Vietnamese Crisis* (1967); Bernard B. Fall, *Hell in a Very Small Place* (1966), on the siege of Dien Bien Phu; and Melanie Billings-Yun, *Decision Against War* (1988) on Eisenhower and Dien Bien Phu. On Latin America, the best accounts are Richard Immerman, *The CIA in Guatemala* (1982) and Stephen Rabe, *Eisenhower and Latin America* (1988). For information on specific topics, see Chester Cooper, *The Lion's Last Roar* (1978) and Donald Neff, *Warriors at Suez* (1981) on the Suez crisis; David A. Mayers, *Cracking the Monolith* (1986) and Gordon Chang, *Friends and Enemies: The United States, China, and the Soviet Union, 1948–1972* (1990) on policy toward Communist China; Robert A. Divine, *Blowing on the Wind* (1978) and Richard Hewlett and Jack Holl, *Atoms for Peace and War, 1953–1961* (1989) on nuclear issues; Michael R. Beschloss, *May-Day* (1986) on the U-2 crisis; and Burton Kaufman, *Trade and Aid* (1982) on foreign economic policy.

Kennedy's foreign policy is subjected to critical scrutiny in Richard J. Walton, *Cold War and Counter-revolution* (1972) and Louise FitzSimmons, *The Kennedy Doctrine* (1972); the most recent scholarly reappraisal is Thomas Paterson, ed. *Kennedy's Quest for Victory* (1989). Philip Geyelin analyzes LBJs foreign-policy weaknesses in *Lyndon B. Johnson and the World* (1966), while Walt W. Rostow defends both the Kennedy and Johnson records in *The*

Diffusion of Power (1972). Concerning nuclear weapons in the 1960s, consult Michael Mandelbaum, *The Nuclear Question* (1979); Desmond Ball, *Politics and Force Levels* (1981); Harland B. Moulton, *Nuclear Superiority and Parity* (1972); and two broader studies of the arms race since 1945, McGeorge Bundy, *Danger and Survival* (1989) and Ronald Powaski, *March to Armageddon* (1987).

On Latin America, Theodore Draper, *Castro's Revolution* (1962); Richard E. Welch, *Response to Revolution* (1985); Trumbull Higgins, *The Perfect Failure* (1987); Peter Wyden, *The Bay of Pigs* (1979); Elie Abel, *The Missile Crisis* (1966); Robert F. Kennedy, *Thirteen Days* (1968); Graham Allison, *The Essence of Decision* (1971); Raymond Garthoff, *Reflections on the Cuban Missile Crisis* (1987); James G. Blight and David A. Welch, *On the Brink* (1989); and Herbert Dinerstein, *The Making of the Missile Crisis* (1976) all deal with aspects of the Cuban problem. Books on Johnson's intervention in the Dominican Republic include John B. Martin, *Overtaken by Events* (1966); Jerome Slater, *Intervention and Negotiation* (1970); Abraham Lowenthal, *The Dominican Intervention* (1972); and Piero Gleijeses, *The Dominican Crisis* (1976).

Kennedy's handling of a key European problem is traced in Norman Gelb, *The Berlin Wall* (1986) and Honore Catudel, *Kennedy and the Berlin Wall Crisis* (1980). For African policy, see Richard D. Mahoney, *JFK: Ordeal in Africa* (1983) and Thomas J. Noer, *Cold War and Black Liberation* (1985).

Stanley Karnow offers a broad view of the Vietnam War in *Vietnam: A History* (1983). Other general accounts of the war in Vietnam include Guenther Lewy, *American in Vietnam* (1978); Gabriel Kolko, *Anatomy of a War* (1986); Chester Cooper, *The Lost Crusade* (1970); Leslie H. Gelb and Richard K. Betts, *The Irony of Vietnam* (1979); and David Halberstam, *The Best and the Brightest* (1972). For Kennedy's role, see William J. Rust, *Kennedy in Vietnam* (1985) and Ellen J. Hammer, *A Death in November* (1987). Neil Sheehan, ed., *The Pentagon Papers* (1971) contains important documents on the war.

Lyndon Johnson's Vietnam decisions and their consequences are traced in two books by Larry Berman, *Planning a Tragedy* (1982) and *Lyndon Johnson's War* (1989); two books on the Gulf of Tonkin incident, Joseph C. Goulden, *Truth is the First Casualty* (1969) and Anthony Austin, *The President's War* (1971); Kathleen Turner, *Lyndon Johnson's Dual War* (1985), on LBJ and the media; Townsend Hoopes, *The Limits of Intervention* (1969); Don Oberdorfer, *Tet!* (1971); and Herbert Y. Schandler, *The Unmaking of a President* (1977), on Johnson's change of heart in 1968.

Analyses of the military issues involved in the Vietnam War include Bruce Palmer, Jr., *The 25-Year War* (1984); Harry G. Summers, Jr., *On Strategy* (1982); Timothy Lomperis, *The War Nobody Lost—and Won* (1984); Mark Clodfelter, *The Limits of Air Power: The American Bombing of North Vietnam* (1989); and James W. Gipson, *The Perfect War*

CHRONOLOGY

1954 Fall of Dien Bien Phu to Viet Minh ends French control of Indochina

1955 Eisenhower meets Khrushchev at Geneva summit

1956 England and France touch off Suez crisis

1957 Russia launches *Sputnik* satellite

1959 Fidel Castro takes power in Cuba

1960 America U-2 spy plane shot down over Russia

1961 JFK establishes Peace Corps (March) • U.S.-backed Bay of Pigs invasion crushed by Cubans (April)

1962 Cuban missile crisis takes world to brink of nuclear war

1963 United States, Great Britain, and USSR sign Limited Nuclear Test Ban Treaty (August) • JFK assassinated; Lyndon B. Johnson sworn in as president (November)

1964 Congress overwhelmingly passes Gulf of Tonkin Resolution

1965 LBJ commits 50,000 American troops to combat in Vietnam

1967 Israel wins Six Day War in Middle East

1968 Viet Cong launch Tet offensive (January) • Johnson announces he will not seek reelection (March)

(1986). Neil Sheehan, *A Bright Shining Lie* (1988) explores the war through the eyes of John Paul Vann.

Biographies and memoirs relating to foreign policy include Warren Cohen, *Dean Rusk* (1980); Thomas J. Schoenbaum, *Waging Peace and War: Dean Rusk* (1988); Chester Bowles, *Promises to Keep* (1971); George Ball, *The Past Has Another Pattern* (1982); Glen T. Seaborg, *Kennedy, Khrushchev and the Test Ban* (1982) and *Stemming the Tide* (1987); and Thomas Powers, *The Man Who Kept the Secrets* (1979), which uses the career of Richard Helms to illuminate the history of the CIA.

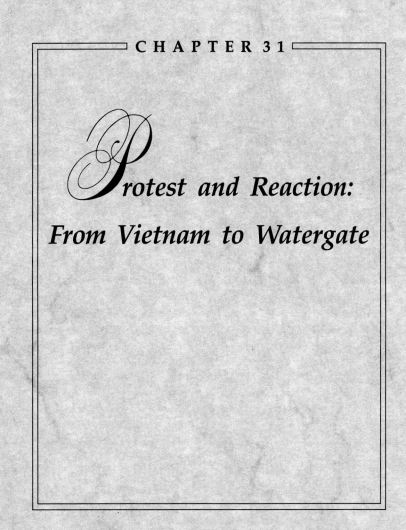

CHAPTER 31

Protest and Reaction:
From Vietnam to Watergate

e are the people of this generation, bred in at least modest comfort, housed now in universities, looking uncomfortably to the world we inherit." So began the preamble to the Port Huron Statement, a manifesto of the newly reorganized Students for a Democratic Society (SDS), which became the call to arms for the vanguard of an entire generation. Like most revolutions, this one started out small. Only fifty-nine delegates attended the convention held at a union summer camp in Port Huron, Michigan, in June 1962. The two main organizers, Al Haber and Tom Hayden, recent graduates of the University of Michigan, hoped to transform their small student-protest group into the vehicle that would rid American society of poverty, racism, and violence.

Their timing was perfect. College enrollments were climbing rapidly as a result of the post-World War II baby boom and growing affluence. There were twenty-seven million young people between the ages of fourteen and twenty-four in 1960; before the end of the decade, more than half the American population would be under age thirty. And many, repelled by the crass materialism of American life—with its endless suburbs and shopping centers—were ready to embrace a new life-style based on the belief that "man is sensitive, searching, poetic, and capable of love." They were ready to create what Jack Newfield called "a new adversary culture based on community and psychic liberation. Drugs, rock music, underground papers, long hair, colorful dress and liberated sex," he explained, "are all part of it."

In some ways, the sixty-six-page proposal adopted at Port Huron was prosaic, repeating many conventional liberal reforms, such as expanded public housing and broader health-insurance programs. But it offered a startling new approach by advocating "participatory democracy" as its main tactic for social change. "We seek the establishment of a democracy of individual participation" in order to achieve two goals: "that the individual share in those social decisions determining the quality and direction of his life" and "that society be organized to encourage independence in men." In contrast to both traditional liberalism and old-fashioned socialism, the SDS sought salvation through the individual rather than the group. Personal control of one's life and destiny, not the creation of new bureaucracies, was the hallmark of the New Left.

In the next few years, the SDS grew phenomenally. Its 10 original campus chapters swelled to 151 by 1966; the Port Huron Statement, despite its length, was distributed across the nation—20,000 copies by 1964; 40,000 two years later. Spurred on by the Vietnam War and massive campus unrest, the SDS could count more than 100,000 followers and was responsible for disruptions at nearly 1000 colleges in 1968. Yet its very emphasis on the individual and its fear of bureaucracy left it leaderless and subject to division and disunity. By 1970, a split between factions, some of which were given to violence, led to its complete demise.

The meteoric career of the SDS symbolized the turbulence of the 1960s. For a brief time, it seemed as though the nation's youth had gone berserk, indulging in a wave of experimentation with drugs, sex, and rock music. Older Americans felt that all the nation's traditional values, from the Puritan work ethic to the family, were under attack.

Not all American youth joined in the cultural insurgency, however. In small towns and among blue-collar families in the cities, young people went to Friday-night high-school football games, cheered John Wayne as he wiped out the Viet Cong in the movie, *The Green Berets,* and attended church with their parents on Sunday. The rebellion was generally limited to children of the upper middle class, products of "economic surplus and spiritual starvation." But like the flappers of the 1920s, they set the tone for an entire era and left a lasting impression on American society.

YEARS OF TURMOIL

The agitation of the 1960s was at its height from 1965 to 1968, the years that marked the escalation of the Vietnam War. Disturbances on college campuses reflected growing discontent in other parts of society, from the ghettos of the cities to the lettuce fields of the Southwest. All who felt disadvantaged—students, African Americans, Hispanics, Native Americans, women, hippies—took to the streets to give vent to their feelings.

Feeling powerless but determined to gain the "Establishment's" attention, students—largely from upper-middle and middle class backgrounds—began their crusade against poverty, racism, and war by "taking it to the streets."

The Student Revolt

The first sign of student rebellion came in the fall of 1964 at the prestigious University of California at Berkeley. A small group of radical students resisted university efforts to deny them a place to solicit volunteers and funds for off-campus causes. Forming the Free Speech Movement (FSM), they struck back by occupying administration buildings and blocking the arrest of a nonstudent protester. For the next two months, the campus was in turmoil. The administration overreacted, calling in the police; the faculty, predictably, condemned the radicals' tactics but supported their goals; the rest of the student body, distraught at the size, complexity, and impersonality of the university, rallied behind the FSM.

In the end, the protesters won the rights of free speech and association that they championed, and youth everywhere had a new model for effective direct action. The hero was Mario Savio, a student who had eloquently summed up the cause by likening the university to a great machine and telling others "you've got to put your bodies upon the gears, and upon the wheels, upon the levers, upon all the apparatus, and you've got to make it stop."

The Free Speech Movement at Berkeley offered many insights into the causes of campus unrest. It was fueled in part by student suspicion of an older, Depression-born generation that viewed affluence as the answer to all problems. The catchphrase of the movement was coined by activist Jack Weinberg in the midst of the turmoil: "Don't trust anyone over thirty." Unable to exert much influence on the power structure that directed the consumer society, the students turned on the university. They viewed higher education as the faithful servant of the corporate and political elite as it trained hordes of technicians to operate the new computers, harbored the research laboratories that perfected dreadful weapons, and regimented its students with IBM punch cards. The feeling of powerlessness that underlay the Berkeley riots was best revealed by the protester carrying the sign that read, "I am a UC student. Please don't bend, fold, spindle or mutilate me."

War, racism, and poverty were the three great evils that student radicals addressed. Many were involved first in the civil-rights cause. But as African Americans began to take over the leadership in this area by 1965, white militants found a new issue—the Vietnam War. The first student teach-ins began at the University of Michigan in March 1965; soon they spread to campuses across the nation. More than twenty thousand protesters, under SDS auspices, gathered in Washington in April to listen to entertainers Joan Baez and Judy Collins sing antiwar songs and hear journalist I. F. Stone and Senator Ernest Gruening of Alaska, who voted against the Gulf of Tonkin Resolution, denounce Johnson's war. "End the War in Vietnam Now, Stop the Killing," read the signs.

One of the great ironies of the Vietnam War was the system of student draft deferments, which enabled most of those enrolled in college to avoid military service. As a result, the children of the well-to-do, who were more likely to attend college, were able to escape the draft. Those too poor to attend college served in Vietnam in much larger numbers. One survey revealed that men from disadvantaged families, including a disproportionately large African-American and Hispanic representation, were twice as likely to be drafted and engage in combat in Vietnam as those from more privileged backgrounds. Consequently, a sense of guilt led many college activists who were safe from Vietnam because of their student status, to take the lead in denouncing an unjust war.

As the fighting in Southeast Asia intensified in 1966 and 1967, the protests grew larger and the slogans more extreme. "Hey, Hey, LBJ, How Many Kids Have You Killed Today?" chanted students as they proclaimed, "Hell, No, We Won't Go!" At the Pentagon in October 1967, over one hundred thousand demonstrators—mainly students, but housewives, teachers, and young professionals as well—confronted a cordon of military policemen guarding the heart of the nation's war machine. From the windows above, Secretary of Defense McNamara and his generals looked down on the protesters. "The troops you employ belong to us and not to you," an SDS leader shouted up to them through his bullhorn. "They don't belong to the generals."

The climax came in the spring of 1968. Driven both by opposition to the war and concern for social justice, the SDS and African-American radicals at Columbia University joined forces in April. They seized five buildings, effectively paralyzing one of the country's leading colleges. After eight days of tension, the New York City police regained control. In the melee, more than 200 students were injured and 700 were arrested. The brutal repression quickened the pace of protest elsewhere. Students held sit-ins at more than forty colleges, ranging from Cheyney State in

In a scene that was repeated many times across the nation, unarmed protestors face a cordon of military police during a peace march in Washington, D.C.

Pennsylvania to Northwestern in Illinois. Violent marches and arrests took place at sixty others.

The students failed to stop the war, but they did succeed in gaining a voice in their education. University administrations allowed undergraduates to sit on faculty curriculum-planning committees and gave up their once rigid control of dormitory and social life. But the students' greatest impact lay outside politics and the campus. They spawned a cultural uprising that transformed the manners and morals of America.

The Cultural Revolution

In contrast to the elitist political revolt of the SDS, the cultural rebellion by youth in the sixties was pervasive. Led by college students, young people challenged the prevailing adult values, in clothing, hairstyles, sexual conduct, work habits, and music. Blue jeans and love beads took the place of business suits and wristwatches; long hair and unkempt beards for men, bare feet and bralessness for women became the new uniform of protest. Families gave way to communes; once quiet and conservative neighborhoods like San Francisco's Haight-Ashbury district became havens for runaways and drug users, the "flower children" of the sixties.

Theorists quickly emerged to extol the new way of life. Theodore Roszak gloried in the rejection of modern science and technology in his influential book, *The Making of a Counter Culture* (1969). "In its place," he wrote, "there must be a new culture in which the non-intellective capacities of personality . . . become the arbiters of the true, the good and the beautiful." Yale law school professor Charles Reich portrayed the emergence of a new world of love, beauty, and racial harmony in his rhapsodic work, *The Greening of America* (1970). He dubbed the new society "Consciousness III." Herbert Marcuse, the visionary Marxist who became the guru of the new culture, called for people to overcome capitalist repression and live by an "aesthetic ethos."

Music became the touchstone of the new departure. Folk singers like Joan Baez and Bob Dylan, popular for their songs of social protest in the mid-sixties, gave way first to rock groups such as the Beatles, whose lyrics were often suggestive of drug use, and finally to "acid rock" as symbolized by the Grateful Dead. The climactic event of

*T*he cultural revolution climaxed in August 1969 at the Woodstock music festival, billed as "Three Days of Peace and Music." Despite rainy weather, food and water shortages, and massive traffic jams, the three-day happening inspired visions of a "Woodstock nation."

the decade came at the Woodstock concert at Bethel in upstate New York when four hundred thousand young people indulged in a three-day orgy of rock music, drug experimentation, and public sexual activity.

Former Harvard psychology professor Timothy Leary encouraged youth to join him in trying out the drug scene. Millions accepted his invitation, "Tune in, turn on, drop out," literally, as they experimented with marijuana and with LSD—a new and dangerous chemical hallucinogen. Yippie leader Jerry Rubin praised drugs for leading to "the total end of the Protestant ethic: screw work, we want to know ourselves."

The Yippies, led by Rubin and Abbie Hoffman, represented the ultimate expression of cultural insurgency. Shrewd buffoons who mocked the consumer culture, they delighted in capitalizing on the mood of social protest to win attention. Once, when testifying before a congressional committee investigating internal subversion, Rubin dressed as a revolutionary war soldier; Hoffman appeared in the gallery of the New York Stock Exchange in 1967, raining money down on the cheering brokers below. The Yippies succeeded in revealing the hypocrisy in American society, but in the process they fragmented the protest movement; serious radicals dismissed them as parasites.

"Black Power"

The civil rights movement, which had spawned the mood of protest in the sixties, fell on hard times later in the decade. The legislative triumphs of 1964 and 1965 were relatively easy victories over southern bigotry; now the movement faced the far more complex problem of achieving economic equality in the cities of the North, where more than half of the nation's African Americans lived. Mired in poverty, crowded into ghettos from Harlem in New York City to Watts in Los Angeles, blacks had actually fallen further behind whites in disposable income since the beginning of the integration effort. The civil rights movement had raised the expectations of urban African Americans for improvement; frustration mounted as they failed to experience any significant economic gain.

The first sign of trouble came in the summer of 1964, when African-American teenagers in Har-

lem and Rochester, New York, rioted. The next summer, a massive outburst of rage and destruction swept over Watts as the inhabitants burned buildings and looted stores. Riots in the summer of 1966 were less destructive, but in 1967 the worst ones yet took place in Newark and Detroit, where forty-three were killed and hundreds were injured. The mobs attacked the shops and stores, expressing a burning grievance against a consumer society from which they were excluded by their poverty. One participant in the Detroit mayhem likened it to "an outing," with the whole family taking part. "The rebellion—it was caused by the commercials," he explained. "I mean you saw all those things you'd never been able to get—go out and get 'em. Men's clothing, furniture, appliances, color TV. All that crummy TV glamour just hanging out there."

The civil rights coalition fell apart, a victim of both its legislative success and economic failure. Black militants took over the leadership of the Student Nonviolent Coordinating Committee (SNCC); they disdained white help and even reversed Martin Luther King's insistence on nonviolence. The split over tactics became public during a Mississippi Freedom March in 1966 in which King pleaded for a continuation of peaceful protest. SNCC's new leader, Stokely Carmichael, disagreed, telling blacks that they should seize power in those parts of the South where they outnumbered whites. "I am not going to beg the white man for anything I deserve," he said, "I'm going to take it." A few days later, in Greenwood, Mississippi, Carmichael raised the cry of "black power" to the cheers of six hundred marchers.

The slogan, which marked a radical change from King's call for peaceful integration of the races, caught on quickly. SNCC spoke of the need for African Americans to form "our own institutions, credit unions, co-ops, political parties" and even write "our own history." Others went further than calls for ethnic separation. H. Rap Brown, who replaced Carmichael as the leader of SNCC in 1967, told an African-American crowd in Cambridge, Maryland, to "get your guns" and "burn this town down," while Huey Newton, one of the founders of the militant Black Panther party, proclaimed, "We make the statement, quoting from Chairman Mao, that Political Power comes through the Barrel of a Gun."

King suffered the most from this extremism. He

Violence broke out in cities across the country as black frustration with poverty and a lack of progress toward economic gain peaked. The assassination of Martin Luther King, Jr., triggered a series of outbreaks across the country, the worst being in Washington, D.C. The violence in many instances was of such magnitude that the army or national guard was called upon to guard the streets and restore order.

tried to keep control of the civil rights movement by leading a campaign for better housing for African Americans in Chicago, only to meet with indifference from the ghetto-dwellers and bitter hostility from the city's political machine and working-class whites. His denunciation of the Vietnam War cost him the support of the Johnson administration and alienated him from the more conservative civil rights groups like the NAACP and the Urban League. He finally seized on poverty as the proper enemy for attack, but before he could lead his Poor People's March on Washington in 1968, he was assassinated in Memphis in early April.

Both blacks and whites realized that the nation had lost its most eloquent spokesman for racial harmony. His tragic death elevated King to the status of a martyr, but it also led to one last outbreak of urban violence. African Americans exploded in angry riots in 125 cities across the nation; in Chicago and Baltimore, army units were needed to restore order in the ghettos. The worst rioting took place in Washington, D.C., where buildings were set on fire within a few blocks of the White House. "It was as if the city were being abandoned to an invading army," wrote a British journalist. "Clouds of smoke hung

over the Potomac, evoking memories of the London blitz. . . ."

Yet there was a positive side to the emotions engendered by black nationalism. Leaders began to urge African Americans to take pride in their ethnic heritage, to embrace their blackness as a positive value. Sales of hair-straighteners, long a staple in African-American barber and beauty shops, plummeted; African Americans began to wear Afro hairstyles and dress in dashikis, stressing their African roots. Students began to demand new black-studies programs in the colleges; the word Negro—identified with white supremacy of the past—virtually disappeared from usage overnight, replaced by the favored "Afro-American" or "black." Singer James Brown best expressed the sense of racial identity: "Say It Loud—I'm Black and I'm Proud."

Ethnic Nationalism

Other groups quickly emulated the African-American phenomenon. American Indians decried the callous use of their identity as football mascots; in response, universities such as Stanford changed their symbols. Puerto Ricans demanded that their history be included in school and college texts. Polish, Italian, and Czech groups insisted on respect for their nationalities. Congress acknowledged these demands with passage of the Ethnic Heritage Studies Act of 1972. Instead of trying to melt all groups down into a standard American type, Congress now gave what one sponsor of the measure called "official recognition to ethnicity as a positive constructive force in our society today." Some $15 million was appropriated to subsidize ethnic-studies courses in schools and colleges across the nation.

Mexican-Americans were in the forefront of the ethnic groups that became active in the 1970s. The primary impulse came from the efforts of César Chávez to organize the poorly paid grape pickers and lettuce workers in California into the National Farm Workers Association (NFWA). Building on the earlier efforts of Filipinos who had organized some field workers, Chávez appealed to ethnic nationalism in mobilizing Mexican-American field hands to strike against grape growers in the San Joaquin Valley in 1965. The NFWA's main demand, a wage of $1.40 an hour, was relatively modest, but Chávez's techniques were more radical. Rallying Mexican farm workers with a red flag featuring a bold thunderbird (a cultural symbol), he soon won the attention of the media. A national boycott of grapes by Mexican-Americans and their sympathizers among the young people of the counter-culture led to a series of hard-fought victories over the growers. The five-year struggle resulted in a union victory in 1970, but at an enormous cost—95 percent of the farm workers involved had lost their homes and their cars. Undaunted, Chávez turned next to the lettuce fields, and although he met with resistance from both the growers and the Teamster's Union, he succeeded in raising the hourly wage of farm workers in California to $3.53 by 1977 (it had been $1.20 in 1965).

Chávez's efforts helped spark an outburst of ethnic consciousness among Mexican-Americans that swept through the urban barrios of the Southwest. Aware that a majority of their compatriots were functionally illiterate as a result of language difficulties and inferior schools, Mexican-American leaders campaigned for bilingual programs and improved educational opportunities. Young activists began to call themselves Chicanos, which had previously been a derogatory term, and to take pride in their cultural heritage; in 1968, they succeeded in establishing the first Mexican-American studies program at California State College at Los Angeles. Campus leaders called for reform, urging high-school students to insist on improvements. "If you are a student at Lincoln [high school] you should be angry!" declared activist Raúl Ruiz in 1967. "You should demand! You should protest! You should organize for better education! This is your right! This is your life!" Heeding such appeals, nearly ten thousand students at East Los Angeles high schools walked out of class in March 1968. These walkouts sparked similar movements in San Antonio, Texas, and Phoenix, Arizona, and led to significant reforms, such as the introduction of bilingual programs in grade schools and the hiring of more Chicano teachers at all levels.

The Chicano movement had a broad cultural impact. In California and Texas, Mexican-Americans began forming paramilitary organizations known as the Brown Berets. This militancy led inevitably to suspicion and hostility on the part of whites as well as to police harassment, which served only to intensify the Brown Berets' radical stance. At the same time, other Chicanos succeeded in compelling the Frito-Lay Company to replace their Frito Bandito, a threatening cartoon character who stole corn chips, with Frito Amigo, who gave them away to children. A more significant cultural milestone came in 1967 with the founding of *El Grito: A Journal of Contemporary Mexican-American Thought*, which published scholarly articles on Chicano history and culture.

Women's Liberation

Active as they were in the civil rights and antiwar movements, women soon learned that the male leaders of these causes were little different from corporate executives—they expected women to fix the food and type the communiqués while the men made the decisions. Or as a protest leader once said, perhaps in jest, "The position of women in our movement should be prone." Understandably, women soon realized that they could only achieve respect and equality by mounting their own protest.

In some ways, the position of women in Ameri-

In addition to expressing concern about unequal wages and opportunities, many women felt suffocated and unfulfilled by their traditional roles in society.

the 1960s. The beginning of the effort to raise women's consciousness was her 1963 book, *The Feminine Mystique.* Calling the American home "a comfortable concentration camp," she attacked the prevailing view that women were completely contented with their housekeeping and child-rearing tasks, claiming that housewives had no self-esteem and no sense of identity. "I'm a server of food and putter on of pants and a bedmaker," a mother of four told Friedan, "somebody who can be called on when you want something. But who am I?"

The 1964 Civil Rights Act helped women attack economic inequality head-on by making it illegal to discriminate in employment on the basis of sex. Women filed suit for equal wages, demanded that companies provide day care for their infants and preschool children, and entered politics to lobby against laws which—in the guise of protection of a weaker sex—were unfair to women. As the women's liberation movement grew, its advocates began to attack laws banning abortion and waged a campaign to toughen the enforcement of rape laws. They even attacked the hallowed Miss America contest for its sexist tone.

The women's movement met with many of the same obstacles as other protest groups in the '60s. The moderate leadership of the National Organization for Women (NOW), founded by Betty Friedan in 1966, soon was challenged by those with more extreme views. Ti-Grace Atkinson and Susan Brownmiller attacked revered institutions

can society was worse in the 1960s than it had been in the '20s. After forty years, there was a lower percentage of women enrolled in the nation's colleges and professional schools. There was a great upsurge in female employment (nearly two-thirds of all new jobs in the sixties went to women), but women with college degrees earned only half as much as similarly trained men. Women were still relegated to stereotyped occupations like nursing and teaching; there were few female lawyers and even fewer women doctors. And sex roles, as portrayed on television commercials, continued to call for the husband to be the breadwinner and the wife to be the homemaker.

Betty Friedan was one of the first to seize upon the sense of grievance and discrimination that developed among white, middle-class women in

Married Working Women, 1960-1969

Year	Percent (as percentage of all married women)
1960	31.7
1961	34.0
1962	33.7
1963	34.6
1964	35.3
1965	35.7
1966	36.5
1967	37.8
1968	39.1
1969	40.4

Source: Compiled from U.S. Bureau of the Census, Historical Statistics of the United States, Colonial Times to 1970, *Bicentennial Edition, Washington, D.C., 1975.*

—the family and the home—and even denounced sexual intercourse with men calling it a method of male domination. Many women were repelled by the harsh rhetoric of the extremists and expressed satisfaction with their lives. "Where do they get the lunatic idea that women had rather work for a boss than stay home and run their own domain?" asked one female critic. But despite these disagreements, most women supported the effort to achieve equal status with men, and in 1972 Congress responded by approving the Equal Rights Amendment to the Constitution. This measure, first introduced in Congress in 1923, at last could be sent to the state legislatures for their votes, the final step in the process of ratification.

THE ELECTION OF 1968

The turmoil of the sixties reached a crescendo in 1968 as the American people responded to the two dominant events of the decade—the war in Vietnam and the cultural insurgency at home. To add to the chaos, this election year witnessed a series of bizarre events, including the assassination of a leading candidate, a riot-plagued political convention, and the emergence of the most effective third-party candidate in fifty years.

The Democrats Divide

Lyndon Johnson's withdrawal from the presidential race after the Tet offensive set the tone for the 1968 election. LBJ's decision had come in response to political as well as military realities. By 1966, the antiwar movement had spread from the college campuses to Capitol Hill. Chairman J. William Fulbright gave the protests a new respectability when his Senate Foreign Relations Committee held probing hearings on the war, broadcast on television to the entire country. Housewives and middle-class professionals began attending the antiwar rallies; respected commentators and academics such as Walter Lippmann and Professor Hans Morgenthau came out against the Vietnam War, suggesting it was foolish and unproductive. Johnson began to feel like a prisoner in the White House, since in his infrequent public appearances he was hounded by

larger and larger groups of antiwar demonstrators, whose taunts and jeers wounded him.

The essentially leaderless protest against the war took on a new quality on January 3, 1968, when Senator Eugene McCarthy, a Democrat from Minnesota, announced that he was challenging LBJ for the party's presidential nomination. McCarthy at first seemed an unlikely candidate. Intellectual, cool, aloof, and almost arrogant, he was motivated primarily by a belief that Kennedy and Johnson had abused the power of the presidency. McCarthy raised the banner of idealism, telling audiences, "Whatever is morally necessary must be made politically possible."

It was his stance against the war, however, that attracted the support of American youth. College students flocked to his campaign, shaving their beards and cutting their hair to be "clean for Gene." In the New Hampshire primary in early March, the nation's earliest political test, McCarthy shocked the political experts by coming within a few thousand votes of defeating President Johnson.

McCarthy's strong showing in New Hampshire led Robert Kennedy, who had been weighing the risks in challenging Johnson, to enter the presidential race. Despite facing the obvious charge of opportunism, Kennedy had a much better chance than did McCarthy to defeat LBJ and win in the fall. Elected senator from New York in 1964, Bobby Kennedy had become an effective spokesman for the disadvantaged, as well as an increasingly severe critic of the Vietnam War. Unlike McCarthy, whose appeal was largely limited to upper-middle-class whites and college students, Kennedy attracted strong support among blue-collar workers, African Americans, Chicanos, and other minorities who formed the nucleus of the continuing New Deal coalition. Moreover, in contrast to McCarthy, whose cool wit and lack of passion bothered even his staunchest admirers, Kennedy provoked an intense emotional loyalty among his followers.

Lyndon Johnson's dramatic withdrawal caused an uproar in the Democratic party. With Johnson's tacit backing and strong support from party regulars and organized labor, Vice President Hubert H. Humphrey immediately declared his candidacy. Humphrey, a classic Cold War liberal who had worked equally hard for social reform at home and American expansion abroad, was total-

In 1967, British cartoonist Leslie Illingworth showed LBJ caught in "The Time Machine," fated to be ground down despite his panic-stricken and exhausting scramble.

where except in Oregon, but his narrow victory in California ended in tragedy when a Palestinian immigrant, Sirhan Sirhan, assassinated him in a Los Angeles hotel.

With his strongest opponent struck down, Hubert Humphrey had little difficulty turning back the challenges from Eugene McCarthy and George McGovern, a last-minute replacement for Kennedy, at the Chicago convention. Backed by that city's political boss, Mayor Richard Daley, the vice-president relied on party leaders to defeat an antiwar resolution and win the nomination on the first ballot by a margin of more than two to one. Those hoping for change had to be content with one small victory—the abolition of the unit rule among state delegations, which would make open conventions possible in the future.

Humphrey's triumph was marred by violence outside the heavily guarded convention hall. Radical groups had urged their members to come to Chicago to agitate; the turnout was relatively small but included many who were ready to provoke the authorities in their despair over the convention's outcome. Epithets and cries of "pigs" brought about a savage response from Daley's police, who shared their mayor's contempt for the protesters. "The cops had one thing on their mind," commented journalist Jimmy Breslin. "Club and then gas, club and then gas, club and then gas."

ly unacceptable to the antiwar movement. Accordingly, he decided to avoid the primaries and work for the nomination within the framework of the party.

Kennedy and McCarthy, the two antiwar candidates, were thus left to compete in the spring primaries, requiring agonizing choices among those who desired change. Kennedy won every-

Alarmed by antiwar demonstrators drawn to the Democratic convention, Chicago Mayor Richard Daley erected barbed wire fences in an attempt to control access to the convention hall.

The bitter fumes of tear gas hung in the streets for days afterward; the battered heads and bodies of demonstrators and innocent bystanders alike flooded the city's hospital emergency rooms. What an official investigation later termed a "police riot" marred Humphrey's nomination and made a sad mockery out of his call for "the politics of joy." The Democratic party itself had become the next victim of the Vietnam War.

The Republican Resurgence

The primary beneficiary of the Democratic debacle was Richard Nixon. Written off as politically dead after his unsuccessful race for governor of California in 1962, Nixon had slowly rebuilt his place within the party by working loyally for Barry Goldwater in 1964 and for GOP congressional candidates two years later. Positioning himself squarely in the middle, with Governor

Nelson Rockefeller of New York to his left and Governor Ronald Reagan, who had inherited Goldwater's following, to his right, he quickly became the front-runner for the Republican nomination. At the GOP convention in Miami Beach —blissfully tranquil compared to the Democrats' experience in Chicago—Nixon won an easy first-ballot nomination and chose Maryland Governor Spiro Agnew as his running mate. Agnew, little-known on the national scene, was a former Rockefeller backer who had won the support of conservatives by taking a strong stand against African-American rioters.

In the fall campaign, Nixon opened up a wide lead by avoiding controversy and reaping the benefit of discontent with the Vietnam War. He exploited television skillfully, appearing before carefully arranged panels to answer friendly questions. He played the peace issue shrewdly, appearing to advocate an end to the conflict without ever taking a definite stand. The United States should "end the war and win the peace," he declared, hinting that he had a secret formula for peace but never revealing what it was. Above all, he chose the role of reconciler for a nation torn by emotion, a leader who promised to bring a divided country together again.

Humphrey, in contrast, found himself hounded by antiwar demonstrators who heckled him constantly. He walked a tightwire, desperate for the continued support of President Johnson but handicapped by LBJ's stubborn refusal to speed up the diplomatic preliminaries to full-scale peace talks and to end all bombing of North Vietnam. His campaign gradually gained momentum, however, as he picked up support from union leaders and from African Americans who remembered his strong stand on civil rights. When he broke with Johnson in late September by announcing in Salt Lake City that if elected he would "stop the bombing of North Vietnam as an acceptable risk for peace," he began to close in on Nixon.

Unfortunately for Humphrey, a third-party candidate cut deeply into the normal Democratic majority. George Wallace had first gained national attention as the racist governor of Alabama whose motto was, "Segregation now . . . segregation tomorrow . . . segregation forever." In 1964, he had shown surprising strength in Democratic primaries in northern states. His appeal was to blue-collar workers and white ethnics —Poles, Italians, Greeks—who believed that many of the gains made by African Americans during the 1960s had come at their expense.

By attacking both black leaders and their liberal white allies, Wallace appealed to the sense of powerlessness among the urban working classes. "Liberals, intellectuals and long hairs have run the country for too long," Wallace told his followers. "When I get to Washington," he promised, "I'll throw all these phonies and their briefcases into the Potomac."

Running on the ticket of the American Independent Party with General Curtis LeMay—whose solution to the Vietnam War was to "nuke 'em back to the Stone Age"—as his running mate, Wallace was a close third in the September polls, gaining support from more than 20 percent of the electorate. But as the election neared, his following declined. Humphrey continued to gain, especially after Johnson agreed in late October to end all bombing of North Vietnam. By the first week in November, the outcome was too close for the experts to call.

Nixon won the election with the smallest share of the popular vote of any winning candidate since 1916. But he swept a broad band of states from Virginia and the Carolinas through the Midwest to the Pacific for a clear-cut victory in the electoral college. Humphrey held on to the urban Northeast, scoring well only among African Americans and manual laborers. Wallace took just five states in the Deep South, but his heavy inroads into blue-collar districts in the North shattered the New Deal coalition.

The election marked a repudiation of the politics of protest and the cultural insurgency of the mid-sixties. The combined popular vote for Nixon and Wallace, 56.5 percent of the electorate, signified that there was a silent majority that was fed up with violence and confrontation. A growing concern over psychedelic drugs, rock music, long hair, and sexual permissiveness had offset the usual Democratic advantage on economic issues and led to the election of a Republican president. Or as Richard Scammon put it, most of the voters were made up of "the unyoung, the unblack, and the unpoor." By voting for Nixon and Wallace, the American people were sending out a message: they wanted a return to traditional values and an end to the war in Vietnam.

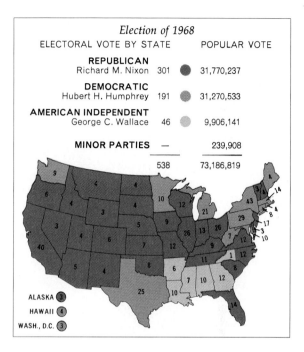

NIXON IN POWER

The man who took office as the thirty-sixth president of the United States on January 20, 1969, seemed to be a new Nixon. Gone were the fiery rhetoric and the penchant for making enemies. In their place, observers found an air of moderation and restraint. He appeared to have his emotions under firm control. The scars of too many political battles had given him a veneer of toughness, even of indifference. But beneath the surface, he remained bitter, hurt, and sensitive to criticism.

An innately shy man, Nixon hoped to enjoy the power of the presidency in splendid solitude. Described by Barry Goldwater as "the most complete loner I've ever known," Nixon assembled a powerful White House staff whose main task was to isolate him from Congress, the press, and even his own cabinet. Loyal subordinates like H. R. Haldeman and John Ehrlichman took charge of domestic issues, often making decisions without even consulting Nixon, who once said that "the country could run itself domestically without a President." Foreign policy was Nixon's great passion, and here he relied heavily on Henry Kissinger, his national security adviser, to formulate policy, leaving Secretary of State William

*T*hroughout his career, Richard Nixon projected a double image: that of a knowledgeable leader, skilled in foreign policy and that of the devious, somewhat paranoid "Tricky Dick."

Rogers to keep the State Department bureaucrats busy with minor details.

The Nixon White House soon could be likened to a fortress under siege. Distrusting everyone, from the media to members of his own party, the President sought to rule the nation without help from either Congress or his cabinet. An almost paranoid belief that he was surrounded by enemies led Nixon to authorize wiretapping and covert surveillance to plug news leaks to the press and to preserve secrecy. In his quest for privacy, the President cut himself off from the nation and thus sowed the seeds of his downfall.

Reshaping the Great Society

Nixon began his first term on a hopeful note, promising the nation peace and respite from the chaos of the sixties. Rejecting the divisions that had split Americans apart, he promised in his inaugural address to "bring us together." "We

cannot learn from one another until we stop shouting at one another—until we speak quietly enough so that our words can be heard as well as our voices."

Nixon's moderation promised a return to the politics of accommodation that had characterized the Eisenhower era. Faced with a Democratic Congress, Nixon, like Ike, appeared ready to accept the main outlines of the welfare state. Instead of any massive overthrow of the Great Society, he focused on making the federal bureaucracy function more efficiently.

Daniel Patrick Moynihan, a Democrat who had helped LBJ design his reforms, joined the White House staff as urban affairs adviser and created the Family Assistance Plan as a way to overhaul the clumsy welfare system. Instead of piecemeal handouts, each poor family would receive an annual payment of $1600, a variation of a guaranteed annual wage, which had long been a goal of liberals. Democrats, however, quickly criticized Moynihan's plan for the low level of payments and a provision requiring heads of poor households, mainly women, to register for employment as a condition for receiving the payment. Despite its many attractive features, including substantial aid to the working poor, the Family Assistance Plan failed to win congressional approval.

Nixon was more successful with his effort to shift responsibility for social problems from Washington to state and local authorities. He developed the concept of revenue sharing, by which federal funds would be dispersed to state, county, and city agencies to meet local needs. Conservatives, who objected to separating the pain of collecting public funds from the pleasure of disbursing them, opposed the plan, but in 1972 Congress finally approved a measure to share $30.1 billion with local governments, over a five-year period. An accompanying ceiling of $2.5 billion a year on federal welfare payments, however, meant that much of the revenue-sharing payments had to be allocated by cities and states to programs previously paid for by the federal government.

In the area of civil rights, Nixon made a shrewd political move. Action by Congress and the outgoing Johnson administration had ensured that massive desegregation of southern schools, delayed for over a decade by legal action, would finally begin just as Nixon took office. Nixon and his attorney general, John Mitchell, decided to shift the responsibility for this process to the courts. In the summer of 1969, the Justice Department asked a federal judge to delay the integration of thirty-three school districts in Mississippi. The Supreme Court quickly ruled against the Justice Department, declaring that "the obligation of every school district is to terminate dual school systems at once." Thus, in the minds of southern white voters, it was the hated Supreme Court, not Richard Nixon, who had forced them to integrate their schools.

Nixon used similar tactics in his attempt to reshape the Supreme Court along more conservative lines. His appointment of Warren Burger, an experienced federal judge with moderate views, to replace the retiring Earl Warren as Chief Justice, met with little objection. But when the President nominated Clement Haynesworth of South Carolina to fill another vacancy on the Court, liberal Democrats led an all-out attack. The Senate, troubled by conflict-of-interest charges against Haynesworth, who in fact had a sound record as a federal judge, rejected the appointment. Seventeen Republicans voted with the majority.

Nixon then responded by offering the name of G. Harrold Carswell, a Florida jurist whose legal record was so bad that one senator finally defended him on the dubious grounds that "there are lots of mediocre judges." When the senators rejected Carswell by a narrow margin, Nixon denounced them for insulting "millions of Americans who live in the South." Once again, the President had used the Supreme Court to enhance his political appeal to Southerners.

Nixon finally filled the Court position with Harry Blackmun, a reputable conservative from Minnesota, who easily won confirmation. Subsequently, the President appointed Lewis Powell, a distinguished Virginia lawyer, and William Rehnquist, a rigidly conservative Justice Department attorney from Arizona, to the Supreme Court. Surprisingly, the Burger Court, despite its more conservative make-up, did not engage in any massive overturn of the Warren Court's decisions. It continued to uphold the legality of desegregation, ruling in 1971 that busing was a necessary and proper way of achieving integrated schools. In other rulings, it restricted the government's right to wiretap suspected subversives, overturned state laws prohibiting abortion, and insisted that the death penalty be invoked only under very limited and precise circumstances.

The moderation of the Supreme Court and the legislative record of the Nixon administration indicated that the nation was not yet ready to abandon the reforms adopted in the 1960s. The pace of change slowed down in areas such as civil rights and welfare, but the commitment to social justice was still clear.

Nixonomics

The economy posed a more severe test for Richard Nixon. He inherited a growing inflation that accompanied the Vietnam War, the product of Lyndon Johnson's unsuccessful attempt to wage the war without raising taxes. The budget deficit was a staggering $25 billion in 1968 and the inflation rate had risen to 5 percent. Strongly opposed to the idea of federal controls, Nixon rejected suggestions of national guideposts to hold down wages and prices. Instead, he opted for a reduction in government spending while encouraging the Federal Reserve Board to curtail the money supply, forcing interest rates to rise and slowing the rate of business expansion.

The result was disastrous. Inflation continued, reaching nearly 6 percent by the end of 1970, the highest rate since the Korean War. At the same time the economy underwent its first major recession since 1958. The stock market tumbled; the Dow-Jones average fell from over 900 to just above 600, the sharpest drop in thirty years. Unemployment rose to 6 percent by the end of 1970, and business failures jumped alarmingly.

The collapse of the Penn Central Railroad was the most spectacular bankruptcy in the nation's history. Democrats quickly coined a new word, "Nixonomics," to describe the disaster. According to Democratic Chairman Larry O'Brien, it meant that "all the things that should go up—the stock market, corporate profits, real spendable income, productivity—go down, and all the things that should go down—unemployment, prices, interest rates—go up."

Conditions seemed to worsen in 1971. Inflation continued unabated, and the nation's balance of trade became negative as imports exceed-

The Pentagon Papers Affair

On June 13, 1971, the *New York Times* published an extraordinary front-page story on the history of America's war in Vietnam. The feature was based on the findings of a top-secret Defense Department study—the so-called Pentagon Papers. It was the first in a series of articles detailing the way successive Presidents had embroiled the United States in war in Southeast Asia.

The appearance of the *Times* special led to a dramatic showdown between the press and the government; immediately after the story broke, the Nixon administration fought hard to prevent any further release of classified material. And in the wake of the whole affair, the Nixon White House developed a siege mentality—an attitude that contributed in the long run to the Watergate break-in and cover-up.

In the summer of 1967, Secretary of Defense Robert McNamara commissioned a review of America's Vietnam policy since World War II. A team of analysts led by Leslie Gelb, a civilian Pentagon official, collected and commented on thousands of documents. Over the course of two years, scores of individuals contributed to this history, which ultimately ran to more than 7000 pages in 47 volumes.

The man responsible for leaking this classified study was Daniel Ellsberg, a talented defense analyst who had worked on the project briefly. He became so disillusioned with the Vietnam War that he felt compelled to share the disturbing material in the Papers with the American people. Gaining access to the manuscript at the Rand Corporation, Ellsberg photocopied thou-

sands of pages from the Papers and offered them to several Senators. When they showed little interest in the documents, Ellsberg went to the press. In March 1971, Neil Sheehan of the *New York Times* agreed to take the documents and use them to write a special series on the war.

When the story broke on June 13, the Nixon administration moved quickly to enjoin any fur-

ther disclosure of the Papers. In seeking an injunction against the *Times*, the White House claimed that the Papers' release had "prejudiced the defense interests of the United States" and that continued publication would "result in irreparable injury" to the nation.

The administration's action was surprising. Traditionally, under the First Amendment there had been few, if any, instances of "prior re-

Daniel Ellsberg after the opening session of his trial. Ellsberg was indicted for espionage, theft, and conspiracy, but the case was dismissed on the grounds of government misconduct.

With frustration over the "Establishment's" handling of the Vietnam War at a high, Ellsberg's leak reinforced the public suspicion that government actions were based on deceit.

straint" (efforts to block publication in advance). Moreover, the contents of the Papers pertained to the policies of previous Presidents, and some members of the White House staff believed they could use the Papers to embarrass the Democrats, who had, after all, led the United States into Vietnam. But President Nixon and National Security Adviser Henry Kissinger saw in the release of the Papers a massive breach of security—a signal to foreign governments that the United States could not be trusted to keep sensitive undertakings with other nations confidential. Unknown to the public, Kissinger was then conducting three sensitive negotiations: with China, on opening up relations; with the Soviet Union, on limiting strategic arms; and with North Vietnam, on ending the war. He and Nixon saw in the release of the Pentagon Papers a threat to the very essence of their secretive approach to diplomacy.

The battle in court lasted more than two weeks. Initially, the administration claimed that the top-secret classification of the Papers was reason enough to prohibit further disclosure, since the Espionage Act forbade the publication of classified material. Before the Supreme Court, however, government attorneys singled out the release of just a few portions of the study that they claimed posed a risk to national security.

The administration's case suffered from several crucial weaknesses. Part of the problem lay in the classification system. In the case of Vietnam, so much material had already been released, in many cases by government officials from the President on down, that the distinction between classified and non-classified had long since lost any meaning. There can be no doubt that the material in the Papers embarrassed many American policymakers. But the government failed to prove to the Court that publication of stories based on the Papers or even of the documents themselves would harm the national security.

Equally important, the government's effort came too late to be effective. Ellsberg also gave the Papers to the Washington *Post*, which began publishing them on July 18. The administration responded with legal action, but the dam had burst. By the time the Court ruled, some 20 newspapers, including the Boston *Globe* and the St. Louis *Post-Dispatch*, were publishing various portions of the Papers.

On June 30, the Supreme Court voted 6 to 3 to dismiss the government's case. In the view of the majority, the government had failed to carry the heavy burden of proof necessary to overcome the presumption against "prior restraint." Yet the press's victory was limited, since each of the nine justices pre-

sented his own opinion—several of which were as critical of the newspapers as they were of the government. The Court did not hold that the First Amendment prevented *any* injunction against publication. As one expert explained, the court battle over the Papers proved "that there *can* be prior restraint of publication while a case is being reviewed in the courts."

Although the publication of the Papers did not lead to the dire consequences its lawyers had predicted in their arguments before the Court, the White House remained resentful about the whole affair. President Nixon still believed that there were too many leaks to the press and he set out to solve the problem by organizing investigative working groups, later known as "plumbers." Loyal only to the President, these men were willing to go beyond the law to insure secrecy. The President also approved a revision of the classification system to allow his administration to operate in even greater secrecy. Most significant of all, a siege mentality now pervaded the White House. Fearful of the antiwar movement and increasingly wary of the press, the Nixon administration initiated an unprecedented series of steps that culminated in the Watergate scandal.

ed exports by a substantial margin, leading to a weakening of the dollar abroad.

In mid-August, Nixon acted suddenly and boldly to halt the economic decline. Abandoning his earlier resistance to controls, he announced a ninety-day freeze on wages and prices to be followed by federally imposed guidelines in both areas. The new secretary of the treasury, Democrat John Connally, carried out a devaluation of the dollar which, along with a 10 percent surtax on all imports, led to a greatly improved balance of trade. The sudden Nixon economic reversal quickly ended the recession. Industrial production increased by over 5 percent in the first quarter of 1972 and the Dow-Jones average broke the 1000 barrier for the first time.

Building a Republican Majority

"The Great Nixon Turnaround," as historian Lloyd Gardner termed it, came too late to help the Republicans in the 1970 congressional elections. From the time he took office in 1969, the President was obsessed with the fact that he had received only 43 percent of the popular vote in 1968. He owed his election to the third-party candidacy of George Wallace. The Republicans were still a minority party, and to be reelected in 1972, Nixon would need to win over southern whites and blue-collar workers who had followed Wallace out of the Democratic party.

Attorney General John Mitchell, who had been Nixon's campaign manager in 1968, had devised a southern strategy to help achieve a Republican majority by 1972. The administration's well-publicized objection to school desegregation in the South and the attempt to put Haynesworth and Carswell on the Court were part of this design. Kevin Phillips, one of Mitchell's aides, urged the Nixon administration to direct its appeal to "middle Americans"—southern whites, Catholic ethnic groups, blue-collar workers, and, above all, the new suburbanites of the South and West. In his 1969 book, *The Emerging Republican Majority*, Phillips argued that the GOP's future lay in the Sunbelt. "From space-center Florida across the booming Texas plains to the Los Angeles-San Diego suburban corridor," he contended, "the nation's fastest-growing areas are strongly Republican and conservative."

Nixon unleashed his vice president, Spiro Agnew, the former governor of Maryland, in an attempt to exploit the social issue in the 1970 election. Blaming all social problems—from drug abuse and sexual permissiveness to crime in the streets—on Democratic liberals and their allies in the media, Agnew delivered a series of scathing speeches. He denounced intellectuals as "an effete corps of impudent snobs," branded television commentators as "a tiny and closed fraternity of privileged men," and damned the press in general as "nattering nabobs of negativism." Despite howls of protest, Agnew proved to be an effective political weapon, as blue-collar workers began displaying on their cars bumper stickers with the proud assertion, "Spiro Is My Hero."

The Democrats struck back by changing their tactics. Warned by Richard Scammon and Ben Wattenberg in *The Real Majority* (1970) that most voters were not young, black, or poor, Democratic candidates were careful to stress economic issues, blaming the Republicans for both inflation and recession. On the social issue, they joined in the chorus against crime, pornography, and drugs. Running for the Senate in Minnesota, Hubert Humphrey reversed his previous stand and came out against gun control; in Illinois, Adlai Stevenson III campaigned for reelection wearing an American flag in his lapel.

The outcome was a standoff. Agnew's attacks helped the GOP to limit the usual off-year losses in the House to nine seats, while the Republicans actually gained two votes in the Senate. But the Democrats did well in state elections and proved once again that economic issues were crucial in American politics. Nixon and the Republicans still did not command a national majority.

In Search of Détente

Richard Nixon gave foreign policy top priority, and he proved surprisingly adept at it. In Kissinger, he had a White House specialist who had devoted his life to the study of diplomacy. A refugee from Nazi Germany, Kissinger had become a professor of government at Harvard, the author of several influential books, and an acknowledged authority on international affairs. Nixon and Kissinger approached foreign policy from a similar realistic perspective. "They recog-

Kissinger's search for détente began with a calculated decision to improve relations with China, a rival with whom the USSR shared a long, fortified border. In a highly publicized state visit, Nixon and Chinese leaders were seen sharing banquets and touring the Great Wall of China.

nized a cold and logical world without fated allies or enemies—only interested parties," commented one close observer. Instead of viewing the Cold War as an ideological struggle for survival with communism, they saw it as a traditional great-power rivalry, one to be managed and controlled rather than to be won.

Kissinger and Nixon had a grand design. Realizing that recent events, especially the Vietnam War and the rapid Soviet arms buildup of the 1960s, had eroded America's position of primacy in the world, they planned a strategic retreat. There were five major centers of power by the 1970s—the United States, the Soviet Union, China, Japan, and the NATO countries of Western Europe. Russia had great military strength, but its economy was weak and it had a dangerous rival in China. Kissinger planned to use American trade—notably grain and high technology—to induce Soviet cooperation, while at the same time improving U.S. relations with China. With the Soviet Union neutralized, the United States would then focus on its economic rivalry with Japan and the countries of Western Europe.

Nixon and Kissinger shrewdly played the Chi-

na card as their first step toward achieving détente—that is, a relaxation of tension—with the Soviet Union. In the summer of 1971, the administration revealed that Kissinger had secretly gone to China and had made the arrangements for a state visit by President Nixon. The following February, accompanied by a planeload of reporters and television camera crews, Nixon made a triumphal tour of China, meeting with the Communist leaders and ending more than two decades of Sino-American hostility. The problem of Taiwan prevented full-scale diplomatic relations, but Nixon agreed to establish an American liaison mission in Beijing as a first step toward ultimate recognition.

The Soviets, who viewed China as a dangerous adversary along a 2000-mile frontier in Asia, responded by agreeing to reach an arms-control pact with the United States. The Strategic Arms Limitation Talks (SALT) had been underway since 1969. During a visit to Moscow in May 1972, President Nixon signed two vital documents with Soviet leader Leonid Brezhnev. The first limited the two superpowers to two hundred antiballistic missiles (ABMs) apiece; the second froze the

A triumphant Kissinger (left) and Nixon (right) clink glasses to celebrate the signing of two vital arms agreements with Soviet leader Leonid Brezhnev (center) in Moscow on May 26, 1972.

number of offensive ballistic missiles for a five-year period. SALT I recognized the existing Soviet lead in missiles, but the American deployment of multiple warheads that could each be individually targeted (MIRV), ensured a continuing American strategic advantage.

The SALT I agreements were most important as a symbolic first step toward control of the nuclear-arms race. They signified that the United States and Russia were trying to achieve a settlement of their differences by peaceful means. The sale of American grain to Russia, along with proposed trade agreements to share more advanced American computer technology with the Soviets, seemed to promise a genuine relaxation of the dangerous tensions of the Cold War.

Ending the Vietnam War

Vietnam remained the one foreign-policy challenge that Nixon could not overcome. He had a three-part plan to end the conflict—renewed bombing, a hard line in negotiations with Hanoi, and the gradual withdrawal of American troops. The last tactic, known as Vietnamization, proved the most successful. The plan involved training the troops of South Vietnam to take over the American combat role. The number of American soldiers in Vietnam dropped from 543,000 in early 1969 to under 30,000 by 1972; domestic opposition to the war declined sharply with the

accompanying drop in casualties and reductions in the draft call.

The call for renewed bombing proved the most controversial part of the plan. As early as the spring of 1969, Nixon secretly ordered raids on Communist supply lines in neutral Cambodia. Then in April 1970, he ordered both air and ground strikes into Cambodia. These relieved pressure on hard-pressed South Vietnamese forces but caused a massive outburst of antiwar protests at home. Students demonstrated against the invasion of Cambodia on campuses across the nation. Tragedy struck at Kent State University in Ohio in early May. After rioters had firebombed an ROTC building, the governor sent in national guard troops who were taunted and harassed by irate students. The guardsmen then opened fire, killing four students and wounding eleven more. The victims were innocent bystanders; two were young women caught in the fusillade on their way between classes. A week later, two African-American student demonstrators were killed at Jackson State College in Mississippi; soon riots and protests raged on more than four hundred campuses across the country in what one educator called "the most disastrous month of May in the history of American higher education."

Nixon had little sympathy for the demonstrators, telling aides that they were "bums" who were intent on "blowing up the campuses." The "silent majority" to whom he appealed seemed to agree; one poll showed that most Americans blamed the students, not the national guard, for the deaths at Kent State. Construction workers showed their support for the President by attacking student protesters in New York City and then marching on City Hall shouting, "All the way, U.S.A." An "Honor America Day" program, held in Washington, D.C., on July 4 attracted 250,000 people who heard Billy Graham and Bob Hope endorse the President's policies. Nixon's Cambodian invasion did little to shorten the Vietnam War, but the public reaction reinforced the President's resolve not to surrender.

The third tactic, negotiation with Hanoi, finally proved successful. Beginning in the summer of 1969, Kissinger held a series of secret meetings with North Vietnam's foreign minister, Le Duc Tho. In the summer and fall of 1972, after heavy American B-52 raids on North Vietnam had halted a Communist thrust into the South, the two sides were near agreement. South Vietnamese objections blocked a settlement before the 1972 election. When the North Vietnamese tried to make last-minute changes, Nixon ordered a series of savage B-52 raids on Hanoi that finally led to the signing of a truce on January 27, 1973. In return for the release of all American prisoners

of war, the United States agreed to remove its troops from South Vietnam within sixty days. The political clauses allowed the North Vietnamese to keep their troops in the South, thus virtually guaranteeing future control of all Vietnam by the Communists.

The agreement was, in fact, a disguised surrender, but finally the American combat role in the Vietnam War was over. After eight years of fighting, the loss of more than fifty-seven thousand American lives, and the expenditure of over $150 billion, the United States had emerged from the quagmire in Southeast Asia. Yet known only to a few insiders around the President, the nation was already deeply enmeshed in another dilemma—what Gerald R. Ford termed "the long national nightmare" of Watergate.

THE CRISIS OF DEMOCRACY

"The illegal we do immediately; the unconstitutional takes a little longer," Henry Kissinger once said jokingly of the Nixon administration. Unfortunately, he was far closer to the truth than anyone realized.

The renewed bombing of North Vietnam ordered by Nixon in hopes of ending the conflict precipitated student protests at many campuses. At Kent State, demonstrators and bystanders were shot by Ohio national guardsmen (left). An end to U.S. armed intervention in the war was finally negotiated by Henry Kissinger and Le Duc Tho in 1973 (right).

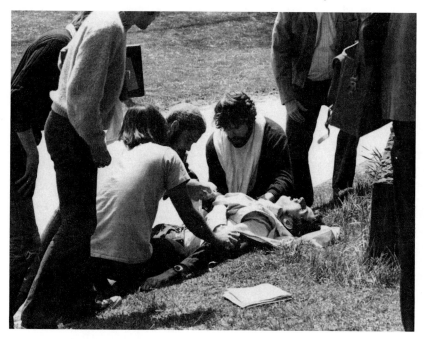

The Politics of Deceit

Richard Nixon's consuming distrust of even his own associates quickly led to a series of underhanded and illegal activities. In the spring of 1969, he ordered the bombing of Cambodia without informing Congress. When details began to leak to the press, the President ordered wiretaps on the telephones of both reporters and members of Kissinger's National Security Council staff. A year later, White House aide Tom Charles Huston drew up a proposal for a new secret committee of FBI and CIA officials to coordinate undercover federal operations. The Huston plan contemplated—in the name of national security—wiretapping, electronic eavesdropping, and "surreptitious entries"—a bureaucratic euphemism for burglaries and break-ins. Only the opposition of FBI director J. Edgar Hoover, who feared a threat to his own agency's independence, blocked implementation of this illegal scheme.

When the *New York Times* and the *Washington Post* began publishing the Pentagon Papers (see "The Pentagon Papers Affair," pp. 932-33), a classified Defense Department study of the Vietnam War, Nixon decided to take drastic measures to plug any further leaks of secret documents. His aides created a self-styled "plumbers" unit within the White House directed by G. Gordon Liddy, a former FBI agent, and E. Howard Hunt, a veteran of the CIA. Charged with preserving secrecy and discrediting those who kept the press informed, Hunt and Liddy set out to embarrass Daniel Ellsberg, the Defense Department official who had leaked the Pentagon Papers. In a vain effort to find damaging information, they went so far as to break into the office of Ellsberg's psychiatrist in Los Angeles.

Elsewhere in the White House, aides John Dean and Charles Colson were busy preparing an enemies list, which contained the names of several hundred prominent Americans, ranging from movie stars like Jane Fonda and Paul Newman to journalists and educators such as columnist James Reston and Kingman Brewster, president of Yale University. The White House labored under a siege mentality that seemed to justify any and all measures necessary to defeat its opponents, who were thought to include the media, the intellectual community, and virtually all minority groups.

Nixon went to great lengths to guarantee his reelection in 1972. A Committee to Re-elect the President (CREEP) was formed, headed by Attorney General John Mitchell. Specialists in dirty tricks, notably Donald Segretti, harassed Democratic contenders, while G. Gordon Liddy, of the White House plumbers, developed an elaborate plan to spy on the opposition. Liddy's scheme included bugging the Democratic national headquarters in the Watergate complex in Washington. In the early morning hours of June 17, James McCord and four other men working under the direction of Hunt and Liddy were caught by police during a break-in at the Watergate. The continuing abuse of power had finally culminated in an illegal act which soon threatened to bring down the entire Nixon administration.

The Election of 1972

The irony of the Watergate break-in was that by the time it occurred, Nixon's election was assured. Aided by Segretti's dirty tricks, which included issuing phony press releases and campaign documents to embarrass such prominent contenders as Edmund Muskie and Hubert Humphrey, the Democrats destroyed themselves. First Muskie, the front-runner, replying in the New Hampshire primary to a Segretti-inspired letter accusing him of prejudice against French Canadians, lost his composure. Then a lone assassin, Arthur Bremer, shot and seriously wounded George Wallace, who was succeeding in his promise to "rattle the eye teeth of the Democratic party" in the spring primaries. Paralyzed, Wallace was forced to drop out of the race, leaving Nixon with a complete monopoly over the political right.

Senator George McGovern of South Dakota then became the leading Democratic candidate. Aided by rules that he had helped write, which opened up the party convention to women, youth, and minorities, McGovern emerged as the Democratic nominee. He ran on a platform that advocated a negotiated settlement in Vietnam, the right to abortion, and tolerance of diverse life-styles. The South Dakota senator hoped to unite the New Left with traditional Democratic voters, but his strong stand against the Vietnam War and in favor of income redistribution at home was perceived as "anti-establishment" by

The unceremonious dumping of vice presidential nominee Thomas Eagleton (left) tarnished McGovern's image and cost him support.

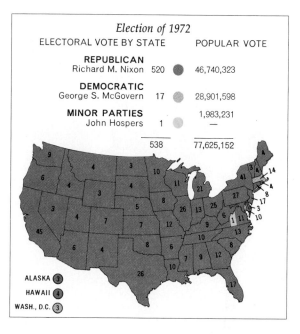

Election of 1972

ELECTORAL VOTE BY STATE			POPULAR VOTE
REPUBLICAN Richard M. Nixon	520		46,740,323
DEMOCRATIC George S. McGovern	17		28,901,598
MINOR PARTIES John Hospers	1		1,983,231 —
	538		77,625,152

ALASKA 3
HAWAII 4
WASH., D.C. 3

middle-class America and greatly strengthened Nixon's appeal.

McGovern quickly lost what little strength he had by his inept handling of the vice-presidential nomination. Originally selecting Missouri Senator Thomas Eagleton, McGovern dumped him for R. Sargent Shriver of Maryland when it was disclosed that Eagleton had undergone psychiatric treatment for depression. Integrity had been McGovern's strongest point; when he dropped Eagleton from the ticket despite a promise to stand behind him "1000 percent," that quality was called into question. Under the slogan, "Come Home, America," McGovern attempted to wage a crusade against the war and on behalf of reform, but his stiff speaking style and his self-righteous manner appealed only to those already committed to his cause.

Instead of focusing on his own record in office, Richard Nixon shrewdly let McGovern's apparent extremism and New Left support become the main issue in the campaign. Staying carefully aloof from partisanship, Nixon let others campaign for him, relying heavily on the recent improvement in the economy and his foreign-policy triumphs with China and Russia to sway the nation's voters.

The result was a stunning victory. Nixon won a popular landslide with 60.8 percent of the vote—

second only to Lyndon Johnson's record in 1964 —and an even more decisive sweep of the electoral college, taking every state but Massachusetts. The very low turnout and Democratic control of both Houses of Congress suggests that the election was primarily a repudiation of McGovern and the radicalism he appeared to stand for, rather than an endorsement of Richard Nixon. The voting patterns did suggest, however, the beginning of a major political realignment, as only blacks, Jews, and low-income voters continued to vote overwhelmingly Democratic. The GOP made significant gains in the South and West, thus giving substance to Kevin Phillips' prediction of an emerging Republican majority based in the Sunbelt.

The Watergate Scandal

Only Richard Nixon knew how fragile his victory was in 1972. The President apparently had no foreknowledge of the Watergate break-in, but he was deeply implicated in the attempt to cover up the involvement of White House aides in the original burglary. On June 23, only six days after the crime, he ordered the CIA to keep the FBI off the case, on the specious grounds that it involved national security. The President even urged his aides to lie under oath, if necessary. "I don't give a [expletive deleted] what happens," Nixon said

H. R. Haldeman, President Nixon's chief of staff, is sworn in before giving testimony to the Senate committee investigating Watergate charges. Haldeman was later convicted of conspiracy, obstruction of justice, and perjury.

to John Mitchell. "I want you all to stonewall it, let them plead the Fifth Amendment, cover-up, or anything else. . . ."

In the short run, the cover-up, directed by White House counsel John Dean, worked. Hunt and Liddy were convicted for their roles in the Watergate break-in, but they carefully avoided implicating either CREEP or Nixon's inner circle of advisers. Despite some very revealing stories by reporters Bob Woodward and Carl Bernstein in the *Washington Post,* the public was kept ignorant of the true dimensions of the Watergate affair.

The first thread unraveled when federal judge John Sirica, known for his firmness toward criminals, sentenced the burglars to long jail terms. James McCord was the first to crack, informing Sirica that he had received money from the White House and had been promised a future pardon in return for his silence. By April 1973, Nixon was forced to fire John Dean, who refused to become the scapegoat for the cover-up, and to allow Haldeman and Ehrlichman, who were deeply implicated, to resign. The Senate then appointed a special committee to investigate the Watergate episode, with North Carolina Democrat Sam Ervin as chairman. In a week of dramatic testimony, John Dean revealed the President's personal involvement in the cover-up. Still, it was basically

a matter of whose word was to be believed, that of the President or of a discredited aide, and Nixon hoped to weather the storm.

The existence of tapes of conversations in the Oval Office, recorded regularly since 1970, finally brought Nixon down. At first the President tried to invoke executive privilege to withhold the tapes. When Archibald Cox, appointed as Watergate special prosecutor, demanded the release of the tapes, Nixon responded by firing Cox. When Attorney General Eliot Richardson refused to remove Cox, Nixon fired him too. But the new Watergate prosecutor, Leon Jaworski, continued to press for the tapes. Nixon tried to release only a few of the less damaging ones, but the Supreme Court ruled unanimously in June 1974 that the tapes had to be turned over to Judge Sirica.

By that time the House Judiciary Committee, acting on evidence compiled by the staff of the Ervin committee, voted three articles of impeachment, charging Nixon with obstruction of justice, abuse of power, and contempt of Congress. Faced with the release of tapes which directly implicated him in the cover-up, the President finally chose to resign on August 9, 1974.

Nixon's resignation proved to be the culmination of the Watergate scandal. The entire episode revealed both the weaknesses and strengths of the American political system. Most regrettable was the abuse of presidential authority—a reflection both of the growing power of the modern presidency and of the fatal flaws in Richard Nixon's character. Unlike such previous executive-branch scandals as the Whiskey Ring and Teapot Dome, Watergate involved a lust for power rather than for money. Realizing that he had reached the White House almost by accident, Nixon did everything possible to retain his hold on his office. He used the plumbers to maintain executive secrecy, he directed the Internal Revenue Service and the Justice Department to punish his enemies and reward his friends, and he created CREEP to keep himself free from dependency on the Republican Party in his quest for reelection.

But Watergate also demonstrated the vitality of a democratic society. The press, particularly Woodward and Bernstein, showed how investigative reporting could unlock even the most closely guarded executive secrets. Judge Sirica proved that an independent judiciary was still the best bulwark for individual freedom. And Congress rose to the occasion, both by carrying out a successful investigation of executive misconduct and by following a scrupulous and nonpartisan impeachment process that left Nixon with no chance to escape his ultimate fate.

The nation survived the shock of Watergate with its institutions intact. Attorney General John Mitchell and twenty-five presidential aides were sentenced to jail terms. Congress, in decline since Lyndon Johnson's exercise of executive dominance, was rejuvenated, with its members now intent on extending congressional authority into all areas of American life.

There was, however, one lasting casualty. The people's faith in politicians was severely shaken. The events of the 1960s and the early '70s, ranging from the Vietnam War to Watergate, from ghetto riots to violent antiwar demonstrations, had left the American people in a mood of cynicism and despair. Nixon had broken the slender bond of trust between those who govern and those who are governed. After the Watergate experience, the ultimate challenge facing presidential aspirants was to offer the kind of inspired leadership that would rekindle the flagging democratic spirit.

An embattled Richard Nixon waves goodbye after resigning the presidency on August 9, 1974.

Recommended Reading

The fullest account of the student protests is Todd Gitlin, *The Sixties* (1987). Gitlin, a sociologist and former SDS leader, offers a sympathetic analysis of the motives and aspirations of the youthful protesters. For other views, see James Miller, *"Democracy Is in the Streets"* (1987), which focuses on the original SDS leadership, and Irwin Unger, *The Movement* (1974), a more critical study of the New Left.

Garry Wills provides the most revealing portrait of the career and character of Richard Nixon in *Nixon Agonistes* (1970). Wills concentrates on the prepresidential years; for Nixon in office, the best accounts are two memoirs: William Safire, *Before the Fall* (1975), a speechwriter's account that focuses on domestic policy; and Henry Kissinger's two volumes, *The White House Years* (1979), and *Years of Upheaval* (1982), for foreign policy developments.

The best books on Watergate are still the two contemporary accounts by Bob Woodward and Carl Bernstein. *All the President's Men* (1974) tells how these two reporters penetrated the cover-up; in *The Final Days* (1976), they detail Nixon's fall from power.

CHRONOLOGY

1963 Betty Friedan publishes *The Feminine Mystique*

1966 National Organization for Women (NOW) formed

1967 Riots in Detroit kill 43, injure 2000, leave 5000 homeless

1968 Martin Luther King, Jr., assassinated in Memphis, Tennessee (April) • Robert F. Kennedy assassinated in Los Angeles, California (June)

1970 U.S. Forces invade Cambodia (April) • Ohio National Guardsmen kill four students at Kent State University (May)

1971 *New York Times* publishes the Pentagon Papers (June) • Nixon announces wage-and-price freeze (August)

1972 President Nixon visits China (February) • U.S. and USSR sign SALT I accords in Moscow (May) • White House "Plumbers" unit breaks into Democratic headquarters in Watergate complex (June) • Richard Nixon wins reelection in landslide victory over McGovern

1973 U.S. and North Vietnam sign truce (January) • Vice President Spiro Agnew resigns (October)

1974 Supreme Court orders Nixon to surrender White House tapes (June) • Richard M. Nixon resigns presidency (August)

Additional Bibliography

Books on the New Left include S. Kirkpatrick Sale, *SDS* (1973); Jack Newfield, *A Prophetic Minority* (1966); Christopher Lasch, *The Agony of the American Left* (1969); Edward J. Bacciocco, *The New Left in America* (1974); Todd Gitlin, *The Whole World Is Watching* (1981); W.J. Rorabaugh, *Berkeley at War* (1989); and David Caute, *The Year of the Barricades* (1988), which places the 1968 American protests in a global context. For other aspects of the youth rebellion, see Paul Goodman, *Growing Up Absurd* (1960); Kenneth Keniston, *Young Radicals* (1968); and Lewis Feuer, *The Conflict of Generations* (1972). Representative books reflecting the views of the counterculture are Charles

Reich, *The Greening of America* (1970); Herbert Marcuse, *An Essay on Liberation* (1969); and Theodore Roszak, *The Making of a Counter Culture* (1969).

The transition from the quest for integration to the assertion of black power is traced in James C. Harvey, *Black Civil Rights During the Johnson Administration* (1973), Clayborne Carson, *In Struggle* (1981); Steven F. Lawson, *In Pursuit of Power* (1985); and Stokely Carmichael and C. V. Hamilton, *Black Power* (1967). For the urban riots of the sixties, see Robert Conot, *Rivers of Blood, Years of Darkness* (1967) on Watts; John Hersey, *The Algiers Hotel Incident* (1968) on Detroit; and James W. Button, *Black Violence* (1978), which shows the impact of the riots on federal policy. Bernard Schwartz traces a key Supreme Court decision on school busing in *"Swann's" Way* (1986). The growing self-consciousness of other minorities is described in Michael Novak, *The Rise of the Unmeltable Ethnics* (1973); Matt Meier and Feliciano Rivera, *The Chicanos* (1972); and Rodolfo Acuña, *Occupied America: A History of Chicanos*, 2d ed. (1981). For the emerging feminist movement, see two books by William Chafe, *The American Woman* (1972) and *Women and Equality* (1977); Patricia G. Zelman, *Women, Work, and National Policy* (1982); Cynthia Harrison, *On Account of Sex: The Politics of Women's Issues, 1945–1968* (1988); and Sara Evans, *Personal Politics* (1979).

The tumultuous election of 1968 is described in Theodore White, *The Making of the President, 1968* (1969) and Lewis Chester, Godfrey Hodgson, and Bruce Page, *American Melodrama* (1969). For Wallace's role, see Jody Carlson, *George C. Wallace and the Politics of Powerlessness, 1964–1976* (1981). Fawn Brodie traces Nixon's prepresidential career critically in *Richard Nixon* (1981); Stephen Ambrose offers a more balanced view in *Nixon: The Education of a Politician, 1913–1962* (1987). Other important books on Nixon include Jules Witcover, *The Resurrection of Richard Nixon* (1970); Rowland Evans and Robert Novak, *Nixon in the White House* (1971); and the President's two volumes of memoirs, *RN* (1978) and *In the Arena* (1990). For Nixon's domestic policies, see Leonard Silk, *Nixonomics* (1972); Daniel Moynihan, *Politics of a Guaranteed National Income* (1973); and two books on the Supreme Court nomination controversies by Richard Harris, *Justice* (1970) and *Decision* (1971).

The major shifts in American politics in the late 1960s are described in Richard N. Scammon and Ben J. Wattenberg, *The Real Majority* (1970); S. Kirkpatrick Sale, *Power Shift* (1975); David L. Broder, *The Party's Over* (1971); Samuel Lubell, *The Hidden Crisis in American Politics* (1970); and Frederick G. Dutton, *The Changing Sources of Power* (1971).

Henry Brandon, *The Retreat of American Power* (1973); Tad Szulc, *The Illusion of Peace* (1978); Robert S. Litwak, *Détente and the Nixon Doctrine* (1984); and Stanley Hoffman, *Primacy or World Order* (1978) all describe Nixon's foreign policy and the search for détente. For the changing nature of relations with the Soviet Union in the 1970s, see Raymond L. Garthoff, *Détente and Confrontation* (1985) and Adam Ulam, *Dangerous Relations* (1983). The most balanced account of Kissinger's contributions to American foreign policy is Robert D. Schulzinger, *Henry Kissinger: Doctor of Diplomacy* (1989). Books that focus on Kissinger's role include Marvin Kalb and Bernard Kalb, *Kissinger* (1974), a sympathetic view; Roger Morris, *Uncertain Greatness* (1977), a critical analysis; Seymour Hersh, *The Price of Power* (1983), a savage indictment; and Seyom Brown, *The Crises of Power* (1979), a balanced account. For SALT, see John Newhouse, *Cold Dawn* (1973). Robert Sutter traces the new U.S. policy toward Beijing in *China Watch* (1978). William Shawcross, a British journalist, blames Kissinger for the secret bombing of Cambodia in *Sideshow* (1979).

Books on the antiwar movement and the violent protests in 1970 include Alexander Kendrick, *The Wound Within* (1974); Thomas Powers, *The War at Home* (1973); John Mueller, *War, Presidents and Public Opinion* (1973); I. F. Stone, *The Killings at Kent State* (1971); Noam Chomsky, *American Power and the New Mandarins* (1977); Melvin Small, *Johnson, Nixon and the Doves* (1988); Charles DeBenedetti, *An American Ordeal* (1990); and Lawrence M. Baskir and William A. Strauss, *Chance and Circumstance* (1978), a study of the impact of the draft on American youth.

For the last phases of the Vietnam conflict, see Frank Snepp, *Decent Interval* (1977); Arnold R. Isaacs, *Without Honor* (1983); and Nguyen Tien Hung and Jerrold Schecter, *The Palace File* (1986). Myra MacPherson surveys the impact of the war on an entire generation in *Long Time Passing* (1984). The different lessons drawn from the Vietnam experience are expounded in Earl C. Ravenal, *Never Again* (1978) and Norman Podhoretz, *Why We Were in Vietnam* (1982).

The election of 1972 is dealt with uncritically by Theodore White in *The Making of the President, 1972* (1973) and entertainingly by Hunter S. Thompson in *Fear and Loathing: On the Campaign Trail '72* (1973).

General accounts of Watergate include Theodore White, *Breach of Faith* (1975); Jonathan Schell, *Time of Illusion* (1976); and J. Anthony Lukas, *Nightmare* (1976). For the abuse of power that reached its culmination in the Watergate affair, see Arthur M. Schlesinger, Jr., *The Imperial Presidency* (1973); David Wise, *The American Police State* (1976); and Athan Theoharis, *Spying on Americans* (1978). Bruce Oudes reprints many illuminating private memos from the Nixon presidential papers in *From the President* (1989). Among the many memoirs by Watergate participants, the most revealing is John Dean, *Blind Ambition* (1976).

944

CHAPTER 32

The Troubled Seventies

O n October 6, 1973, Egypt and Syria launched a surprise attack on Israel. The invasion, which came while the Israelis were observing the Jewish holy day of atonement, Yom Kippur, caught American leaders completely off-guard. After recovering from the initial shock, President Nixon and Henry Kissinger, who had become secretary of state in September, expected Israel to repel the Arab invaders and display the same military dominance it had used to win the Six Day War in 1967. In that conflict, Israel had devastated its Arab neighbors, taking possession of the Golan Heights from Syria, the Sinai peninsula from Egypt, and Jerusalem and the West Bank from Jordan. Instead of increasing Israeli security, however, these conquests had only added to Middle East tensions. They unified the Arab countries, who now called for the return of their lands, and increased Egyptian and Syrian dependence on the Soviet Union for arms and political support.

Henry Kissinger saw the outbreak of the Yom Kippur War as an opportunity to shift American policy from its traditional pro-Israeli position to a more neutral stance. He wanted the United States to play the role of honest broker between Israel and its Arab neighbors. To achieve that position, Kissinger was hoping that the Yom Kippur War would end without a clear-cut victory for either side, permitting the United States to step in and arrange a diplomatic settlement.

Events nearly betrayed Kissinger's strategy. The initial Egyptian and Syrian attacks proved surprisingly successful, finally leading Nixon and Kissinger to approve a massive resupply of Israel in mid-October. But when the Israeli counterattack drove the Syrians back toward Damascus and trapped an entire Egyptian army near the Suez Canal, the secretary intervened diplomatically to prevent a victory for Israel that would preclude American mediation. Joint Soviet-American efforts to arrange a cease-fire nearly broke down in the face of Israeli militancy. When the Soviets threatened to send in troops to save Egypt, President Nixon, on Kissinger's advice, ordered a worldwide nuclear alert that helped defuse the crisis. The fighting finally ended in late October; Israel had repulsed the Arab attack but had been stopped short of complete victory.

Kissinger's apparent diplomatic triumph, how-

"Hat in Hand" shows an unaccustomed posture for Uncle Sam following the Arab oil embargo.

ever, was offset by an unforeseen consequence of the Yom Kippur War. On October 17, the Arab members of the Organization of Petroleum Exporting Countries (OPEC) announced a 5 percent cut in oil production, with additional cuts of 5 percent each month until Israel gave up the lands it had seized in 1967. President Nixon announced a $2.2 billion aid package for Israel on October 19, and the next day Saudi Arabia cut off oil shipments to the United States and to the Netherlands, the European nation that had most strongly supported American policy in the Middle East.

The Arab oil embargo had a disastrous impact on the American economy. First, it produced a worldwide shortage of oil. Arab producers cut production by 25 percent from the September 1973 level, leading to a curtailment of 10 percent in the world supply. For the United States, which imported one-third of its daily consumption, this meant a loss of nearly two million barrels a day. Increased imports from Iran, Libya, and Nigeria helped offset the Arab embargo, but American consumers began to panic. Long lines formed at automobile service stations as motorists kept filling their tanks in fear of running out of gas.

A dramatic increase in oil prices proved to be a far more significant result of the embargo. The relatively low price of oil had been creeping upward in the early 1970s as demand began to match supply; after the Arab embargo began, OPEC, led by the Shah of Iran, raised crude oil prices fourfold. In the United States, gasoline prices at the pumps nearly doubled in a few weeks time, while the cost of home heating fuel rose even more sharply.

President Nixon responded with a series of temporary measures, including pleas to turn down thermostats in homes and offices, close service stations on weekends to curb pleasure driving, and reduce automobile speed limits to fifty miles per hour. He also outlined a plan for American energy independence. Designed to end reliance on imported oil, the plan encouraged conservation and the use of alternative sources of energy, such as coal and nuclear power. When the Arab oil embargo ended in March, after Kissinger negotiated an Israeli pullback in the Sinai, the American public relaxed. Gasoline once again became plentiful, thermostats were raised, and people rekindled their love affair with the automobile.

But the energy crisis did not end with the lifting of the embargo. The Arab action marked the beginning of a new era in American history. The United States, with only 6 percent of the world's population, had been using nearly 40 percent of the earth's energy supplies. The nation's vast reserves of petroleum and natural gas had fueled American economic expansion through World War II, and then oil imports had sustained postwar growth with artificially low energy costs. In 1970, domestic oil production began to decline; the embargo served only to highlight the fact that the nation was now dependent on other countries, notably those in the Persian Gulf, for its economic well-being.

The consequences soon became clear. The growing shortage of oil and natural gas led to a steady increase in energy costs which contributed heavily to inflation. The revenues sent to OPEC members further weakened the American economy, leading to periodic recessions, higher interest rates, and the slowing of economic growth. A nation that based its way of life on abundance and expansion suddenly was faced with the reality of limited resources and economic stagna-

tion. A land of plenty now had to face the challenge of scarcity.

ENERGY AND THE ECONOMY

The energy crisis that began with the Arab oil embargo in 1973 had a profound impact. The price American consumers paid for oil went up sixfold during the 1970s. The result was rampant inflation, rising unemployment, and an end to the postwar era of rapid economic growth.

The Oil Shocks

Cheap energy had been the underlying force behind the amazing expansion of the American economy after World War II. The world price of oil had actually declined in the 1950s and '60s as huge new fields in the Middle East and North Africa began to produce. The GNP had more than doubled between 1950 and 1973; the American people had come to base their way of life on gasoline prices that averaged about $.35 a gallon. The huge gas-guzzling cars, the flight to the suburbs, the long drives to work each day, the detached houses heated by fuel oil and natural gas and cooled by central air conditioning represented a dependence on inexpensive energy that everyone took for granted.

The first great oil shock of the '70s came with the Yom Kippur War and the resulting Arab oil embargo. Few had noticed a gradual increase in OPEC prices in the early 1970s; the world level had risen from $1.80 a barrel to $3.07 by mid-1973, but the regulated domestic price had remained stable at the $3.00 mark. Global demand for oil, intensified by the explosive economic development of Western Europe and Japan as well as the United States, had now caught up with oil production. In the ensuing shortfall, the OPEC nations quickly raised prices, first to over $5.00 a barrel, then to $11.65.

The effect on the American economy was devastating. In 1979, consumers had to pay an additional $16.4 billion to cover the cost of imported oil. Gasoline prices jumped from $.35 to $.65 a gallon; the cost of manufacturing went up proportionately, while utility rates rose sharply as a result of the higher cost of fuel oil and natural

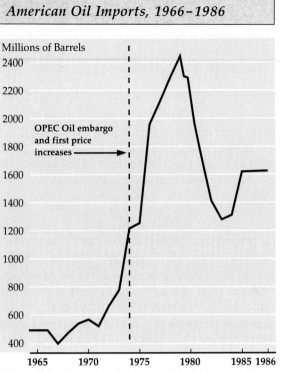

American Oil Imports, 1966–1986

Millions of Barrels

OPEC Oil embargo and first price increases →

Source: *U.S. Bureau of the Census. Statistical Abstract of the United States: 1989, (109th edition) Washington, D.C., 1989.*

gas. Suddenly Americans faced drastic and unexpected increases in such everyday expenses as driving to work and heating their homes.

The result was a sharp decline in consumer spending and the worst recession since World War II. The GNP dropped by 6 percent in 1974 and unemployment rose to over 9 percent, the highest level since the Great Depression of the 1930s. Detroit was hit the hardest. Buyers shied away from big cars with their low gas mileage, but many were skeptical of the first generation of American-made small cars, notably the Ford Pinto and the Chevrolet Vega. Sales declined by 20 percent, and by the fall of 1974, Detroit's big three automakers had laid off more than 225,000 workers.

President Gerald R. Ford, who followed Richard Nixon into the White House (see p. 962), was concerned at first with inflation; he responded belatedly to the economic crisis by proposing a tax cut to stimulate consumer spending. Congress passed a $22.8 billion reduction in taxes in early 1975 which included rebates averaging $130 for each individual taxpayer, an across-the-board cut

in personal income tax rates, and an increase in investment tax credits for business. With this stimulus, the economy gradually recovered by 1976, but the resulting budget deficits helped keep inflation above 5 percent and prevented a return to full economic health.

The next administration, headed by Jimmy Carter of Georgia (see pp. 963-65), had little more success in achieving a rapid rate of economic growth. Continued federal deficits and relatively high interest rates kept the economy sluggish throughout 1977 and '78. Then in 1979, the outbreak of the Iranian Revolution and the overthrow of the shah touched off another oil shock. Although the cutoff of Iranian oil led to a shortfall of only 3 percent of the world's oil supply, the members of the OPEC cartel took advantage of the situation to raise prices by a staggering $21 a barrel over the next eighteen months. The price of oil, which had actually declined in relation to industrial prices in the mid-1970s, now shot up to over $30 a barrel. Gasoline prices climbed to more than $1 a gallon at American service stations, and an even greater wave of inflation than the 1973 increase occurred.

The American people panicked. When lines began to form at gas stations in California and Florida in early May 1979, drivers started filling their tanks every day or two. Soon stations were jammed and supplies ran short as the nation's normal inventory shifted from underground storage reservoirs to motorists' gas tanks. Service stations began closing on weekends, and in state after state, governors experimented with plans regulating gasoline purchases. The long lines frustrated American drivers; incidents of violence began to mount and the public took out its fury on the Carter administration. In June, the President's staff warned him of the danger in the "worsening short-term energy crisis." "Nothing else has so frustrated, confused, angered the American people," Carter was told, "or so targeted their distress at you personally."

By the fall of 1979, world supply had caught up with demand, and the oil scare ended. But the price of gasoline remained at over a dollar a gallon, and the inflation rate began to reach double-digit levels again. The twin oil shocks of the seventies had left the economy battered and had undermined the average American's faith in the future.

The age of cheap and abundant oil was ending. As prices climbed and supplies dwindled, Americans found themselves waiting in long gas lines.

The Search for an Energy Policy

The oil shocks of 1973 and 1979 were but two symptoms of a much deeper energy crisis. Put simply, the United States was running out of the fossil fuels on which it had relied for its economic growth in the past. Domestic oil production peaked in 1970 and declined every year thereafter; there were more ample reserves of natural gas, but both fuels were nonrenewable sources of energy that would eventually be exhausted. American political leaders had to devise a national policy to meet not only the temporary shortfalls of the seventies but also the long-term energy problem inherent in past reliance on fossil fuels.

The success of the environmental movement in the late 1960s and early '70s compounded the problem. Efforts to protect the environment and curtail pollution of the nation's air and water had led to significant legislative restrictions on American industry. Congress created the Environmental Protection Agency in 1970 to monitor industry and passed a Clean Air Act that encour-

aged public utilities to shift from using coal, which polluted the atmosphere, to clean-burning fuel oil and natural gas to generate electricity. The observance of Earth Day in April 1970, complete with a massive parade up New York City's Fifth Avenue, and outrage over an oil spill in the Santa Barbara channel, reflected national concern about the environment.

The energy crunch pitted the environmentalists and advocates of economic growth in direct confrontation with each other. Those who put ecology first lost out. In the mid-1970s, Congress authorized construction of the Alaskan pipeline over environmentalists' objections and ordered public utilities to resume burning coal to produce electricity. By the end of the decade, groups such as the Sierra Club and Friends of the Earth had failed in their efforts to halt the gradual relaxation of environmental regulations that prohibited strip-mining of coal and offshore drilling for oil.

The nation's leaders had an even more difficult time devising a coherent and workable long-term national energy policy. Gerald Ford placed a high premium on expanding production as a means of overcoming the shortage. The Republicans advocated removing price controls on oil and natural

Participants in the Earth Day celebrations of April 22, 1970 displayed a new consciousness—concern for the condition of the environment.

gas to give wildcatters the incentive to bring in new supplies of these fuels. Greater production of coal, expanded nuclear power plants, and new technology to explore the possibilities of synthetic fuels and solar energy were all parts of the Republican approach to the energy problem.

The Democrats, in contrast, stressed price controls and conservation. In Congress, Democratic leaders were intent on shielding American consumers from the full brunt of the world price increase. They wanted to continue an elaborate system of price controls instituted by Nixon in 1973, and they favored stand-by plans for gas rationing over reliance on the marketplace as a better way to allocate scarce supplies. Democratic conservation measures included plans for tax breaks for those who insulated their homes, pressure on automakers to improve gas mileage for cars, and large appropriations for mass-transit systems for American cities.

The nation failed to adopt either the Republican or the Democratic energy plans; instead, Congress tried to muddle through with elements of both approaches. Thus, on the production front, Ford was able to win approval for building the Alaskan pipeline, which made an additional 1.5 million barrels of oil a day available to American consumers. Carter placed a strong emphasis on reviving the lagging American coal industry. Congress continued the price controls on domestic oil for another forty months in late 1975, and in its most significant step toward conservation, mandated annual increases in automobile gasoline mileage that forced Detroit to produce more fuel-efficient cars. Since nearly 10 percent of the world's oil production was burned up every day on American highways, this one congressional act would result eventually in substantial gasoline savings.

The overall outcome, however, was a patchwork that fell far short of a coherent national strategy for solving the energy problem. Neither Ford's appeal for decontrol nor Carter's call for a national conservation effort that would be "the moral equivalent of war" worked. Oil imports actually increased by 50 percent between 1973 and 1979, rising from 6 million to 9 million barrels a day, an amount nearly half of the nation's daily petroleum usage. When the oil shock of 1979–1980 revealed how vulnerable the American economy was to OPEC, Carter re-

*D*espite the environmental risk, construction of an Alaskan pipeline to tap that state's rich oil fields went forward in the mid-1970s.

versed his policy and asked Congress to decontrol the price of domestic oil.

The Great Inflation

The gravest consequence of the oil shocks was inflation. The startling increase in price levels in the 1970s stemmed from many causes. The Vietnam War, particularly Johnson's early attempts to avoid a tax increase to pay for the fighting, created budget deficits that grew from $63 billion for the entire decade of the sixties to a total of $420 billion in the seventies. A worldwide shortage of food, resulting from both rapid population increases and poor harvests around the globe in the mid-1970s, triggered a 20 percent rise in American food prices in 1973 alone. But above all else, it was the sixfold increase in petroleum prices that raised the cost of every economic activity, from transportation to farming, from manufacturing to mining, that was the primary source of the great inflation of the 1970s.

The impact on consumers was staggering. The

price of an automobile jumped 72 percent between 1973 and 1978, while the cost of new homes went up 67 percent in the same period. During the decade, the price of a hamburger doubled, milk went from $.28 to $.59 a quart, and the cost of a loaf of bread—the proverbial staff of life—rose from $.24 to $.89. Corresponding wage increases failed to do more than keep most Americans even; for the first time since World War II, real wages did not increase in the 1970s, and in 1980, the real income of the average American family fell by 5.5 percent.

Curbing inflation proved to be beyond the power of the federal government. President Ford's early efforts to roll back prices by rhetoric—including the WIN (Whip Inflation Now) buttons—were a casualty of the 1974 recession. President Carter proved equally powerless. His attempts to cut back on government spending in order to balance the budget were more than offset by the price rises of 1979 and 1980 that followed the second oil shock. Finally, in October 1979, the Federal Reserve Board, led by Carter appointee Paul Volcker, began a sustained effort to halt inflation by mandating increased bank reserves to curtail the supply of money in circulation. The new tight money policy served only to heighten inflation in the short run by driving interest rates up to record levels. By the spring of 1980, the prime interest rate reached 20 percent.

The Shifting American Economy

Inflation and the oil shocks helped bring about significant changes in American business and industry in the 1970s. The most obvious result was the slowing of the rate of economic growth, with the GNP advancing only 3.2 percent for the decade, compared to 3.7 percent in the 1960s. More important, American industry began to lose its position of primacy in world markets. In 1959, U.S. firms had been the leaders in eleven of thirteen major industrial sectors, ranging from manufacturing to banking. By 1976, American companies led in only seven areas, and in all but one category—aerospace—U.S. corporations had declined in relation to Japanese and Western European competitors.

The most serious losses came in the heavy industries where the United States had once led

the world. In 1946, American firms had produced 60 percent of the world's iron and steel; by 1978, they accounted for only 16 percent. New steel producers in Western Europe, Japan, and the Third World, using more advanced technology and aided by government subsidies, were producing steel far more efficiently than their American counterparts. As a result, by the end of the 1970s, 20 percent of all iron and steel used in the United States was imported; American firms were closing down their obsolete mills in the East and Midwest, idling thousands of workers.

Foreign competition did even more damage in the automobile industry. The oil shocks led to a consumer demand for small, efficient cars. German and Japanese automakers seized the opportunity to expand their once small volume of sales in the United States. By 1977, imported cars had captured 18.3 percent of the American market, with Japan leading the way with its well-built and fuel-saving Toyotas, Datsuns, and Hondas. In response, Detroit spent $70 billion retooling to produce a new fleet of smaller, lighter, front-wheel-drive cars; but American manufacturers barely survived the foreign invasion. Only government-backed loans helped the Chrysler Corporation stave off bankruptcy.

In other areas, American corporations fared much better. The multinationals that had emerged in the boom years of the 1960s contin-

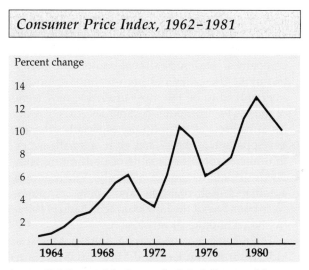

Consumer Price Index, 1962–1981

Percent change

Source: U.S. Bureau of the Census. Statistical Abstract of the United States: 1982–83 *(103rd edition) Washington, D.C., 1982.*

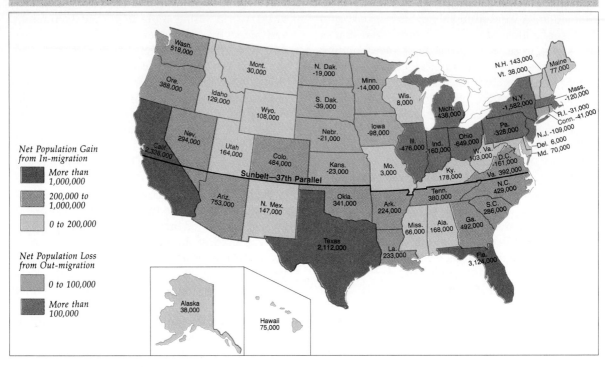

Migration to the Sunbelt, 1970–1981

Florida, California, and Texas gained the most people in the 1970s; New York, Ohio, and Illinois suffered the heaviest losses.

Net Population Gain from In-migration
- More than 1,000,000
- 200,000 to 1,000,000
- 0 to 200,000

Net Population Loss from Out-migration
- 0 to 100,000
- More than 100,000

Wash. 518,000
Mont. 30,000
N. Dak. -19,000
Minn. -14,000
N.H. 143,000
Vt. 38,000
Maine 77,000
Ore. 388,000
Idaho 129,000
S. Dak. -39,000
Wis. 8,000
Mich. 438,000
N.Y. -1,582,000
Mass. -120,000
Wyo. 108,000
Iowa -98,000
Ohio -649,000
Pa. -328,000
R.I. -31,000
Conn. -41,000
N.J. -109,000
Nev. 294,000
Nebr. -21,000
Ill. -476,000
Ind. -160,000
Del. 6,000
Md. 70,000
Calif. 2,338,000
Utah 164,000
Colo. 484,000
Kans. -23,000
Mo. 3,000
Ky. 178,000
W. Va. 103,000
D.C. -161,000
Va. 392,000
Sunbelt—37th Parallel
N.C. 429,000
Ariz. 753,000
N. Mex. 147,000
Okla. 341,000
Ark. 224,000
Tenn. 380,000
S.C. 286,000
Texas 2,112,000
Miss. 66,000
Ala. 168,000
Ga. 492,000
La. 233,000
Fla. 3,124,000

Alaska 38,000
Hawaii 75,000

ued to thrive. IBM sold computers all over the globe, while Pepsi-Cola outmaneuvered its traditional rival to penetrate the Iron Curtain. The growth of conglomerates—huge corporations that combined many dissimilar industrial concerns—accelerated as companies like Gulf & Western and the Transamerica Corporation diversified by buying up Hollywood studios, insurance companies, and recreational-equipment manufacturers. The growth of high-technology industries proved to be the most profitable new trend of the 1970s. Computer companies and electronics firms grew at a rapid rate, especially after the development of the silicon chip, a small, wafer-thin microprocessor capable of performing complex calculations almost instantly. Video games, automated cash registers, and home computers were but a few of the new products made possible by the technological revolution.

The result was a geographic shift of American industry from the East and Midwest to the Sunbelt. Electronics manufacturers flourished in California, Texas, and North Carolina, where they grew up around major universities. The absence of well-entrenched labor unions, the availability of skilled labor, and the warm, attractive climate of the southern and western states lured many new concerns to the Sunbelt. At the same time, the decline of the steel and auto industries was leading to massive unemployment and economic stagnation in the northern industrial heartland. The one exception was New England, where the rise of new scientific companies around Boston helped offset the earlier decline of the textile industry.

The overall pattern was one of an economy in transition. The oil shocks had caused serious problems of inflation, slower economic growth, and rising unemployment rates. But American business still displayed the enterprise and the ability to develop new technologies that gave promise of economic vitality in the 1980s.

A TIME OF SOCIAL CHANGE

The 1970s and the 1980s witnessed a series of significant shifts in American society that paralleled the economic changes brought about by inflation and the oil shocks. The nation's population in 1980 stood at just over 226 million, up 11.4 percent from 1970, the smallest rate of increase since the census of 1940. The vast majority—nearly 186 million—was white, while blacks were the largest ethnic minority—26.5 million.

A People on the Move

The most striking finding of the 1980 census was that for the first time in American history more than half of the population lived in the South and West; the Sunbelt had boomed. The boom in the Sunbelt, best defined as a broad band running across the country below the 37th parallel from the Carolinas to southern California, had begun to flourish with the buildup of military bases and defense plants during World War II. Rapid population growth continued with the onset of the Cold War as this area received more than its share of defense spending, and then accelerated even more in the 1970s, when new high technology firms and more established companies were attracted by the economic inducements, lower labor costs, and favorable climate of the Sunbelt states. Florida, Texas, and California led the way, each gaining more than two million new residents during the decade.

The cities of the North suffered the most from this mass exodus. New York City, which almost went bankrupt midway through the decade, lost nearly a million people between 1970 and 1980. Midwestern cities like Cleveland and Saint Louis were equally hard hit, each losing a quarter of its population in just ten years as whites led the move either to the Sunbelt or to nearby suburbs. The central cities of the North and Midwest lost many of their best-educated and most affluent citizens, leaving them with large low-income populations—comprised mainly of minority groups—with very expensive social needs.

Another striking population trend was the nationwide rise in the number of the elderly. At the beginning of the century, only 4.1 percent of the population was age sixty-five or older; by 1980, those over sixty-five made up 11.3 percent, and people over seventy-five were the single fastest growing age group of all. (The 1990 census is expected to show that there are 31.6 million people aged sixty-five or older, more Americans than were alive during the Civil War.) Major advances in medicine increased life expectancy

In the late 1970s and early '80s, the population shift from the North to the Sunbelt generated prosperity in southern cities like Houston (below), and left pockets of low-income people in desolate, poverty-stricken areas like the South Bronx in New York City (left).

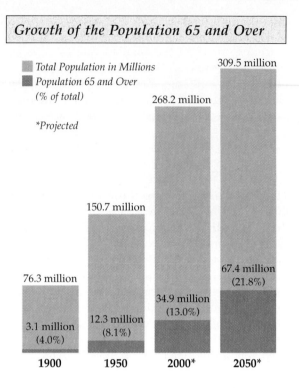

Life Expectancy at Birth: 1850–1985

Age (years)

75-
70-
65-
60-
55-
50-
45-
40-
35-

1850   1880   1910   1940   1970 1985

Growth of the Population 65 and Over

Total Population in Millions
Population 65 and Over
(% of total)

*Projected

309.5 million

268.2 million

150.7 million

76.3 million

67.4 million
(21.8%)

34.9 million
(13.0%)

12.3 million
(8.1%)

3.1 million
(4.0%)

1900   1950   2000*   2050*

from sixty-three in the 1930s to seventy-five by the late 1980s. Six of every ten older Americans were women, and they tended to be worse off economically. Yet only 12.4 percent of the elderly were below the poverty line; the annual cost of living increases in Social Security payments spared them from the worst ravages of inflation. With 65 percent of those between sixty-five and seventy-four voting regularly, compared to only 46 percent of the whole population, the elderly had considerable political clout, as they later demonstrated in 1989 by forcing Congress to eliminate the catastrophic health care surtax to be paid only by those over 65.

The postwar increase in the divorce rate continued unabated. In the 1950s, marriages outnumbered divorces by five to one; by 1980, the ratio was down to two to one. Marital breakup lost its stigma; for many, marriage ceased to be a sacred institution. The rise in the divorce rate resulted in a tremendous increase in what the census dubbed "one-parent households," reflecting a sharp decline in traditional family units. The number of one-parent families—nearly always a case of the mother rearing the children alone—rose by 79 percent during the 1970s. By the end of the decade, 22 percent of all American children were

reared in homes with only one parent; in the case of black children, the figure was 56 percent.

A more traditional American process, that of immigration, underwent a surprising shift in the 1970s. A nation that had been built on a predominantly European influx suddenly found itself adding millions of Asians (see "Asian Americans: Climbing 'The Mountain of Gold,'" pp. 960-61) and Latin Americans to its population, with very few newcomers arriving from Europe. More than 5 million immigrants entered the United States in the 1970s, with the annual rate rising to over 700,000 by the end of the decade. In 1978, Mexico provided the most, 92,000 legal entrants and probably as many more illegal ones, with Vietnam close behind at 88,000 followed by the Philippines with 37,000 and Cuba with 30,000. In contrast, only 14,200 immigrants came from England, 7400 from Italy and a mere 982 from Ireland. The newcomers from Asia and Latin America filled the traditional economic role of the immigrant, working at the dirty and difficult jobs that most Americans shunned, often for low wages and without receiving any government assistance. Their cultural, linguistic, and ethnic differences, however, created an assimilation problem at least as great as that of the "new" immigrants from southern and eastern Europe in the late nineteenth century.

Although the 1980 census revealed many departures from past experience, it also reaffirmed some traditional American patterns. In the face of inflation and unemployment, the American people continued to be prosperous. The median family income rose to $21,023, with just 11 percent of the population living below the government's official poverty line. Not only were Americans living longer, but thanks to Medicare, Medicaid, and private health plans, they were receiving better medical care than ever before, with health expenditures rising to $476 per person. A declining birthrate lowered enrollments in elementary and secondary schools, leading to better teacher-student ratios, while college attendance continued to climb. By 1981, there were nearly 12 million college students, compared to only a million and a half in 1941. Now more than 20 percent of the nation's young people received a college degree, compared to 12 percent of their parents' generation.

The overall picture was of a society in transition. The rising figures of crime, teenage pregnancy, and drug use were balanced by better health and educational opportunities than any previous generation had enjoyed. Pockets of poverty, notably in the older industrial states, were matched by boom areas. America was still the land of opportunity for immigrants, even if they came now from Mexico and Vietnam, rather than Poland and Italy. And despite the ravages of inflation and the shock of the energy crunch, people continued to look to the future, aware of the new age of limitations in which they lived, but confident that they could still achieve the American dream.

The Changing Role of Women

The entry of women into the work force accelerated in the 1970s, climbing to a new high. Some 10 million women took jobs in the period from 1965 to 1975, compared to 7 million men. By the end of the decade, 52 percent of all adult women were working, and their ranks included 6 million more working wives than in 1970.

Women scored some impressive breakthroughs. They began to enter corporation boardrooms, became presidents of major universities, and were admitted to West Point and Annapolis. Equally important, they entered the blue-collar work force in factory and construction jobs that had been traditionally held by men. The appointment of Sandra Day O'Connor to the Supreme Court in 1981 marked a historic first. Yet despite the growing number of female elected officials, doctors, and lawyers, the vast majority of working women still suffered from economic discrimination. The Equal Pay Act, passed by Congress in 1972, and a number of lawsuits which forced corporations to pay women equal wages for equal work, helped close the gap, but the sex differential still remained. The median pay for women rose from 60 percent of that for men in the 1970s to 65 percent in the 1980s. The greatest gains came among young women entering the labor market; for women between twenty and twenty-four years of age, wages went up from 78 percent to 86 percent of men's earnings. And by 1986, 1 out of 4 new graduates in high-paying fields such as law, medicine, and business were women, compared to only 1 in 20 two decades earlier.

Women had fewer children in the 1970s than in earlier decades. The birthrate, which had peaked at over 3.5 births for every woman of childbearing age in the late 1950s, dropped to less than 2 by the mid-1970s. This trend toward smaller families was related to the great increase in working wives, an increase that was intensified by the economic pressures caused by inflation in the 1970s. Many women who pursued careers put off childbearing, waiting until they had established themselves professionally, while others simply decided to forgo children entirely. The drop in the birthrate also reflected the later age of marriage in the seventies, as well as the ever larger number of single women.

The women's movement sought two different but related objectives in the 1970s. The first was ratification of the Equal Rights Amendment. Approved by Congress in 1972, the amendment stated simply, "Equality of rights under the law shall not be denied or abridged by the United States or any state on account of sex." Within a year, twenty-two states had approved the amendment, but the efforts gradually faltered and finally stalled just three states short of ratification. The opposition came in part from working-class women who feared, as one union leader explained, that those employed as "maids, laundry

*T*he Equal Rights Amendment, first introduced in 1923, was approved by Congress in 1972 and then was sent to the states for ratification. Activists for and against the ERA campaigned intensely, but when ratification narrowly failed, the amendment (but not the issue of women's rights) gradually slipped off the national agenda.

workers, hospital cleaners, or dishwashers" would lose the protection of state laws that regulated wages and hours of work for women. Right-wing activist Phyllis Schlafly led an organized effort to defeat ERA, claiming that the amendment would lead to unisex toilets, homosexual marriages, and the drafting of women. The National Organization for Women (NOW) fought back, persuading Congress to extend the time for ratification by three years and waging intense campaigns for approval in Florida and Illinois. But the deadline for ratification finally passed on June 30, 1982, with the ERA forces still three states short. NOW leader Eleanor Smeal vowed a continuing struggle: "The crusade is not over. We know that we are the wave of the future."

The women's movement had greater success in its fight for reproductive rights, but there were setbacks as well. Heartened by the 1973 Supreme Court decision, *Roe* v. *Wade*, which struck down state laws banning abortions, feminists worked hard to extend the right of women to choose whether to carry through a pregnancy. Right-to-life groups, backed by the Catholic church, fundamentalist Protestants, and many conservatives, sought to deny the use of public funds to pay for abortions, thereby limiting the exercise of this right to those women who could afford it. With the strong support of President Carter, Congress passed the Hyde amendment, which forbade the use of federal money to pay for abortions, and in

1981, the Supreme Court upheld this legislation. Despite this setback, pro-choice groups organized privately funded family-planning agencies and abortion clinics to give poor women the opportunity to exercise more reproductive control. These efforts were threatened by a 1989 Supreme Court decision, *Webster* v. *Reproductive Health Services*, which upheld a Missouri law restricting abortion clinics. *Webster* aroused pro-choice activists, however, who began to wage intense, state-by-state campaigns to defend the constitutional right to abortion they had won in *Roe* v. *Wade*.

Advance and Retreat for African Americans

For middle-class African Americans, the 1970s were a decade of progress; they began to reap the gains of the affirmative-action programs spawned by LBJ's Great Society. By 1976, one-third of all African-American workers held white-collar jobs —double the rate of 1960—and nearly 30 percent earned more than $12,000 a year. Education proved the key to African-American advances. Graduates of the nation's colleges and universities had relatively easy entry into higher paying jobs in banks, corporations, and government agencies. With more than one million blacks enrolled in college by 1980, the opportunities for

Occupations by Sex and Race, 1972 and 1987

Title of Occupation	Total Employed (millions) 1972	Total Employed (millions) 1987	1972 percentage Female	1972 percentage Nonwhite	1987 percentage Female	1987 percentage Nonwhite
Professional						
Accountants	0.7	1.3	21.7	4.3	45.7	10.9
Computer specialists	0.2	0.7	16.8	5.5	34.1	9.2
Engineers	1.1	1.7	0.8	3.4	6.9	6.1
Lawyers and judges	0.3	0.7	3.8	1.9	19.7	5.4
Physicians/dentists	0.6	0.7	9.3	6.3	17.3	8.0
Professors	0.5	0.7	28.0	7.2	37.1	7.7
Writers/artists/ entertainers	0.8	1.8	31.7	4.8	45.9	8.6
White Collar						
Real estate agents	0.3	0.8	36.7	2.6	48.7	5.2
Bookkeepers	1.5	2.0	97.9	3.6	92.4	9.4
Secretaries	2.9	4.1	99.1	5.2	99.1	11.6
Blue Collar						
Craft workers	10.8	13.5	3.6	6.9	8.5	15.3
Laborers (nonfarm)	4.2	4.7	6.3	20.2	17.1	27.1
Transport equipment operators	3.2	3.5	4.2	14.8	10.1	22.7
Farm and Service						
Farmers and farm managers	1.6	1.3	5.9	3.3	14.9	2.9
Service (nonprivate household)	9.5	12.2	57.0	10.5	65.2	26.4
Service (private household)	1.4	0.9	97.6	40.6	96.3	35.4

Sources: *U.S. Bureau of the Census,* Statistical Abstract of the United States: 1982–83, *103rd edition, Washington, D.C., 1982 and* Statistical Abstract of the United States: 1989, *109th edition, Washington, D.C., 1989.*

a middle-class style of life were greatly increased.

Many well-educated and affluent African Americans tended to behave like whites in similar circumstances. Some joined the flight to the suburbs, leaving the central city in even larger proportions than whites. Others flocked to the Sunbelt, reversing the historic movement of rural blacks from the South to the North. In the 1970s, many young African Americans, trained as doctors, lawyers, or business executives, returned to the cities of the South to pursue their careers. A 1978 survey by *Ebony* magazine identified Atlanta, Dallas, and Houston among the ten most attractive American cities for African Americans. Atlanta and New Orleans both had black mayors

by the end of the decade and, in fact, the South had become the most thoroughly integrated of all the nation's regions.

Yet despite these gains, there were also setbacks for African Americans in the 1970s. The whole affirmative-action process was brought into question by the case of Allen Bakke, a white applicant to the medical school of the University of California at Davis. Bakke claimed that his rights had been violated when his application was rejected, because his credentials were better than those of several minority applicants who were awarded some of the 16 places reserved for "disadvantaged students" in the class of 100. When the highest state court in California ruled

*T*o minorities, the affirmative action guidelines set by the Supreme Court in the Alan Bakke case were too restrictive.

in favor of Bakke in 1976, the university appealed the verdict to the Supreme Court.

The Court issued its long-awaited ruling on June 28, 1978. By a five-to-four margin, the justices ruled in favor of Bakke, asserting that the use of "explicit racial classification" had denied him equal protection under the Fourteenth Amendment. At the same time, however, by a similar five-to-four vote, the Court upheld the principle of affirmative action, claiming that universities could make race "simply one element" in their effort to select a diverse student body.

In subsequent decisions, the Court upheld an affirmative-action program designed by Kaiser Aluminum to help advance minority workers and ordered American Telephone and Telegraph to hire more African Americans and women to make up for past discrimination. It was Justice Harry A. Blackmun, a Nixon appointee, who explained the Court's position best by declaring,

"in order to get beyond racism, we must first take account of race."

The plight of lower-class African Americans, however, revealed that affirmative action had only a limited impact on their economic status. The median income for African-American families had fallen in relation to that of whites, dropping from 60 percent in the 1960s to 56 percent in 1988. Although nearly one hundred thousand African Americans joined in a reverse migration to the Sunbelt in the 1980s, the great majority still lived in the crowded ghettoes of cities in the North and West. New York had the largest concentration of African Americans, 2.9 million, with California just behind at 2.1 million. Unemployment rates for blacks remained over 10 percent, more than double that for whites, and among black teenagers, the level was a staggering 40 percent. As a result, African Americans were unable to translate their political and civil rights gains into meaningful economic advances.

The Emerging Hispanics

People with Spanish surnames, labeled Hispanics in the census, were the fastest growing ethnic group in the United States in the 1970s and 1980s. By 1989, there were 20 million Hispanics in the country, up from 14 million in 1980. The Census Bureau identified four major categories: 12.6 million people of Mexican origin, 2.5 million people from Central and South America, 2.3 million of Puerto Rican descent, and 1.07 million of Cuban origin.

Mexican-Americans, the largest group, were concentrated in the Southwest—5.9 million in California and 3.7 million in Texas. Cubans predominated in Florida, especially around Miami, and Puerto Ricans were centered in the Northeast, particularly in New York City. These varied Hispanic groups had several features in common. All were relatively youthful, with a median age of twenty-two; most were relatively poor, with one-fourth falling below the poverty line; and the great majority worked in either blue-collar or menial service jobs.

In the 1970s, Chicanos, as Mexican-American activists preferred to call themselves, became vocal in expressing their grievances. They succeeded in winning a federal mandate for bilingual education, compelling elementary schools in states like Texas and California to teach Chicano schoolchildren in Spanish as well as in English. Mexican-American political leaders became active in local politics, leading the Democratic and Republican parties to bid for their votes. In Texas, José Angel Gutiérrez founded a third party, La Raza Unida. Although La Raza failed to win statewide influence, Gutiérrez succeeded in the early 1970s in gaining control of first the school board and then the city government of Crystal City, a South Texas community with a heavy Mexican population.

The entry of several million illegal immigrants from Mexico, once derisively called "wetbacks" and now known as "undocumented aliens," created a substantial social problem for the nation and especially for the Southwest. Critics charged that the flagrant violation of the nation's border with Mexico had led to an "invisible subculture outside the boundaries of law and legitimate institutions." They argued that these aliens took jobs away from American citizens, kept wages artificially low, and received extensive welfare benefits for which they were ineligible.

Defenders of the "illegals" contended that the nation gained from the abundant supply of work-

ers who were willing to do the back-breaking jobs in fields and factories shunned by most Americans. Moreover, these illegal aliens usually paid sales and withholding taxes but rarely used government services for fear of being deported. Whichever view is correct, by 1980 there was an exploited class of illegal aliens living on the edge of poverty. The *Wall Street Journal* summed it up best by observing, "The people who benefit the most from this situation are certainly the employers, who have access to an underground market of cheap, productive labor, unencumbered by minimum wage laws, union restrictions or pension requirements."

Concern over economic competition from an estimated four million Mexican "illegals" led Congress to pass a major immigration reform bill in 1986. To discourage employers from hiring undocumented Mexican workers, the legislation imposed fines and possible prison sentences on those who knowingly employed illegal immigrants. Mexican-American groups feared that these sanctions would discourage businesses from hiring anyone of Mexican descent, but they approved of an amnesty provision that enabled any alien who had been living in the United States before January 1, 1982, to become a legal

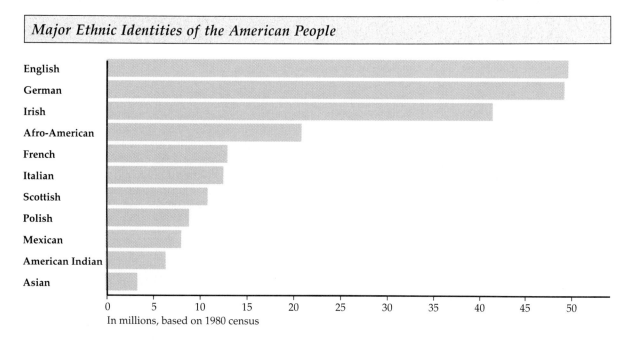

Major Ethnic Identities of the American People

In millions, based on 1980 census

Source: U.S. Bureau of the Census

Asian Americans:
Climbing "The Mountain of Gold"

Asian-American businesses play an important role in improving the neighborhoods in which they are established.

During his 1985 State of the Union Address before Congress and a nationwide television audience of millions, President Ronald Reagan unexpectly introduced twenty-one-year-old West Point cadet Jean Nguyen, characterizing her as "an American hero." A decade earlier, when Saigon fell to the Communists, eleven-year-old Nguyen had escaped Vietnam by boat across the "sea of heartbreak" to seek refuge in the United States. She spoke no English when she arrived. Nguyen grew up in Milton, Pennsylvania, finished high school at the top of her class, and was recommended for admission to West Point. In May, 1985, of 1,008 graduating cadets, Jean Nguyen would be one of 107 women receiving a commission as second lieutenant in the United States Army.

Lt. Nguyen's remarkable acculturation reflects the experience of thousands of Asian immigrants in the United States, which many recent arrivals refer to as "the mountain of gold." Asian Americans, reports sociologist Peter I. Rose, are part of "the most upwardly mobile group in the country. They have caught up to and are even surpassing the Joneses and the Smiths, as well as the Cohens and the Levines." Rose finds that the Asian American climb to success is powered by values similar to those of their Jewish American compatriots: they maintain a deep sense of ethnic identification and filial respect, and they place heavy emphasis on the benefits of education for future goals.

Between 1970 and 1990, the number of immigrants from Asia—Chinese, Japanese, Koreans, Filipinos, Laotians, Vietnamese, East Indians, and other nationalities—increased almost fourfold. Of America's estimated 246 million people, Asian Americans comprise about 6.5 million, or nearly 3 percent of the population. Their educational and economic achievements, however, are highly disproportionate to their relatively small numbers.

Approximately 75 percent of this group graduate from high school, compared to 69 percent of whites, 51 percent of blacks, and 43 percent of Hispanics. Nearly 33 percent of Asian Americans over twenty-five years of age have at least four years of college, compared to 17 percent of whites. They totaled nearly 11 percent of Harvard's 1985 freshman class. Translated into economic terms, in 1980 the median income for Asian American families was almost $2,000 more than the median income for white families.

But life for Asians in the United States has not always been so rosy. No people who came of their own volition to America, says one noted sociologist, "ever suffered as much discrimination or ostracism" as the Chinese and Japanese. Although tens of thousands of Chinese laborers were imported to build the first transcontinental railroad (1862–69), by 1882 Congress had passed the Chinese Exclusion Act, barring them from the United States. Only in 1943 did Congress relent, giving a wartime ally an immigration quota of 105 persons a year. In the case of Japanese immigrants, the U.S. twice pressured Japan into stopping all immigration to America, and the discriminatory 1924 National Origins Quota Act ruled that Japanese in the United States were "aliens ineligible to citizenship." Then, after Japan attacked Pearl Harbor and the United States declared war, all West Coast Japanese immigrants *and* their American-born children (by law American citizens) were thrown into concentration camps for most of the duration of World War II.

Not until the mid-1960s did

America really open the Golden Door. President Lyndon B. Johnson signed into law the first nondiscriminatory immigration legislation, the 1965 Immigration and Nationality Act. This new law dramatically affected Asian immigration, increasing it more than tenfold from 157,000 in the decade between 1951 and 1960 to 1,633,800 in the following decade. The end of U.S. involvement in Vietnam in 1975 fueled this increase with the passage of the humanitarian 1977 Indochinese Act and an unprecedented resettlement program for those fleeing Communist regimes in Cambodia, Laos, and Vietnam. But by March 1982 when 589,000 homeless refugees had been resettled in the United States, the Reagan administration began restricting Indochinese immigration.

Not all Asian Americans have climbed the golden mountain. Some are mired in poverty and illiteracy, and many report being depressed, especially refugees from Indochina. The Vietnamese American median income in mid-1985 was $12,800, well below the white median of $20,835, and far, far below the Japanese American median of $27,350. Many refugees have had great problems learning to read and write English. Some escapees from Indochina are from preliterate cultures. The Laotian Hmong people, for example, had no written alphabet until the 1950s. Of 8000 Hmong resettled in Minnesota's Ramsey County in the late 1970s, nearly half were not literate enough to hold jobs by mid-1985. Still, their artisans sold more than $300,000 worth of folk art—mainly needlework—in Minneapolis between 1983 and 1986.

Recent arrivals have experienced instances of racial prejudice and there have been some violent anti-Asian incidents. In a hail of bricks and bottles thrown by their Chicano neighbors, eighteen Asian refugee families fled a dilapidated Denver housing project; Hmong refugees have been beaten in Philadelphia; tension between black and Korean Americans surfaced in New York City, Los Angeles, and Washington, D.C.; in Louisiana's Plaquemines Parish, Vietnamese American fisherman were denied docking rights; the Ku Klux Klan burned three Vietnamese American fishing boats and firebombed one house in Seadrift, Texas.

But for each such incident, there are tens of thousands of examples of acceptance of Asian Americans: from the world renowned, like conductor Seiji Ozawa of the Boston Symphony Orchestra and architect I. M. Pei; to the little known, like Dr. Thieu Bui, who chose to practice medicine in an Arkansas town (Wilmot, population 1202) left without a physician; to the unknown hard-working Asian Americans who have revitalized decaying neighborhoods in New York City's Lower East Side, the North Beach section of San Francisco, and the Koreatown section of Los Angeles.

Prototypical of the Asian American ethos is the story of Korean Americans Woon Ho Park and his wife Jinsoo, who came to the United States to make a better life for their three sons. Settling in Kansas City, they found that language problems made it impossible to pursue their previous careers in law and teaching. Woon took a job in a plastics factory and Jinsoo in a restaurant; both have worked twelve to fourteen hours a day since 1974. Their eldest son is now an industrial engineer, the second is in medical school, and the third is in high school. Woon still works one shift in the plastics factory, but the Parks now own the restaurant.

Climbing "the mountain of gold" has not been easy for Asian Americans. But overall their remarkable acculturation reflects President Reagan's characterization of Lieutenant Jean Nguyen, that "anything is possible in America if we have the faith, the will, and the heart."

resident. This trade-off between amnesty and employer sanctions led to widespread use of forged documents by illegal immigrants both to gain employment and to secure resident status, but did little to reduce the flow of Mexican workers across the border.

Instead, worsening economic conditions in Mexico, as well as civil war in Nicaragua and El Salvador, intensified Latin American immigration into the United States. By 1989, there were 20 million Americans with Spanish surnames, which made Hispanics second only to the 28.9 million African Americans among the nation's ethnic and racial groups. Despite many individual success stories, Hispanics, like African Americans, tended to form an underclass that did not share fully in all the benefits of the American way of life. In the late twentieth century, as in the nineteenth, the "melting pot" was an inadequate description of the nation's ethnic mosaic.

POLITICS AFTER WATERGATE

The energy crisis and the economic dislocations of the mid-1970s could not have come at a worse time. Watergate had a paralyzing impact on the American political system. An awareness that the Cold War had led to an imperial presidency created a growing demand to weaken the power of the president and strengthen congressional authority. The result was increasing tension between the White House and Capitol Hill, preventing the strong, effective leadership needed to meet the unprecedented problems of the 1970s.

The Ford Administration

Gerald R. Ford had the distinction of being the first president who had not been elected to national office. Richard Nixon had appointed him to the vice presidency to succeed Spiro Agnew, who had been forced to resign in order to avoid prosecution for accepting bribes while he was governor of Maryland. Ford, a longtime Michigan congressman who had risen to the post of House minority leader, was a popular choice. Amiable and unpretentious, he seemed ready to restore public confidence in the presidency when he replaced Nixon in August 1974.

Ford's honeymoon lasted only a month. On

*T*he transfer of presidential power from Richard Nixon to Gerald Ford took place on August 9, 1974, shortly after this photo was taken.

September 8, 1974, he shocked the nation by announcing that he had granted Richard Nixon a full and unconditional pardon for all federal crimes he "committed or may have committed or taken part in" during his presidency. Some critics charged darkly that Nixon and Ford had made a secret bargain; others pointed out how unfair it was for Nixon's aides to serve their prison terms while the chief criminal went free. Ford apparently acted in an effort to end the bitterness over Watergate, but his attempt backfired, eroding public confidence in his leadership and linking him indelibly with the scandal.

Ford soon found himself fighting an equally difficult battle in behalf of the beleaguered CIA. The Watergate scandal and the Vietnam fiasco had eroded public confidence in the government and lent credibility to a startling series of disclosures about past covert actions. The President allowed the CIA to confirm some of these charges, notably the way the agency, at the direction of Johnson and Nixon, had begun extensive domestic surveillance of anti-war protesters in violation of its charter. Then Ford made things worse by blurting out to the press the juiciest item of all—the CIA had been involved in plots to assassinate foreign leaders.

Senate and House select committees appointed to investigate the CIA now focused on the assassination issue, eventually charging that the agency was involved in no less than eight separate attempts to kill Fidel Castro. The chairman of the Senate committee, Frank Church of Idaho, worried that the revelations would damage the reputations of Democratic Presidents Kennedy and Johnson, tried to put all the blame on the CIA, likening it to "a rogue elephant on the rampage."

In late 1975, President Ford finally moved to limit the damage to the CIA. He appointed George Bush, then a respected former Republican congressman, as the agency's new director and gave him the authority both to reform the CIA and to strengthen its role in shaping national security policy. Most notably, Ford issued an executive order outlawing assassination as an instrument of American foreign policy. The congressional investigating committees tried to secure legislation that would give Congress prior approval of all covert activities and would make the CIA budget public (it was estimated to run as high as $10 billion a year), but Ford was able to block these proposals. Instead, Congress settled for the creation of permanent House and Senate intelligence committees to exercise general oversight over covert CIA operations.

Ford proved less successful in his dealings with Congress on other issues. Though he prided himself on his good relations with members of both houses, he opposed such Democratic measures as federal aid to education and control over strip-mining. In a little more than a year, he vetoed thirty-nine separate bills. In fact, Ford, who as a congressman had opposed virtually every Great Society measure, proved far more conservative than Nixon in the White House. He urged federal agencies to do nothing to disturb "maximum freedom for private enterprise," and he openly opposed school busing, to the dismay of civil rights advocates.

The 1976 Campaign

Ford's weak record and the legacy of Watergate made the Democratic nomination a prize worth fighting for in 1976. A large field of candidates entered the contest, but a virtual unknown, former Georgia Governor James Earl Carter, quickly became the front-runner. Aware of the voters'

disgust with politicians of both parties, Jimmy Carter ran as an outsider, portraying himself as a Southerner who had no experience in Washington and one who could thus give the nation fresh and untainted leadership. As one astonished Democrat, Averell Harriman, exclaimed, "Carter? How can Carter be nominated? I don't know him and don't know anyone who does."

Appearing refreshingly candid, Carter claimed to be an honest man, ready to deal fairly with the American people. On television, the basic Carter commercial showed him at his Georgia peanut farm, dressed in blue jeans, looking directly into the camera and saying, "I'll never tell a lie."

Carter swept through the primaries and won the Democratic nomination easily, naming Senator Walter Mondale of Minnesota as his running mate. Victory in November seemed assured. Ford had barely beaten back a determined challenge from former California Governor Ronald Reagan, who was the idol of the right wing. The polls gave Carter a thirty-three-point lead when the campaign began, but he quickly lost ground as he began to hedge on the issues. President Ford counterattacked, saying of his Democratic opponent, "he wavers, he wanders, he wiggles and he waffles." But Ford, who had developed a reputation as a bumbler from both his uninspired leadership and occasional physical stumbles on golf courses and airport ramps, reinforced his own image of ineptitude. In a televised debate, responding to a question about Iron Curtain countries, he declared that "there is no Soviet domination of Eastern Europe."

Carter won an extremely narrow victory in 1976. Despite Watergate and Ford's weak record, the Democratic candidate took only 49.98 percent of the popular vote. Ford swept nearly the entire West, but Carter carried the South and key northern industrial states like New York and Ohio. Far more than most recent elections, the outcome turned on class and racial factors. "The affluent,

The Election of 1976

Candidate	Party	Popular Vote	Electoral Vote
Carter	Democrat	40,830,763	297
Ford	Republican	39,147,793	240
McCarthy	Independent	756,631	

the well-educated, the suburbanites largely went for Ford"; commented one observer, "the socially and economically disadvantaged for Carter." The black vote clinched the victory for the Democrats. Carter received over 90 percent of the votes of African Americans, and their ballots provided the margin of victory in Ohio, Pennsylvania, and seven southern states.

Disenchantment with Carter

The new President, described by an associate as "superficially self-effacing but intensely shrewd," was an ambitious and intelligent politician. He had a rare gift for sensing what people wanted and appearing to give it to them. Liberals thought he clearly stood with them; conservatives were equally convinced that he was on their side. He was especially adept at utilizing symbols. He emerged from airplanes carrying his own garment bag; after his inauguration he walked up Pennsylvania Avenue hand-in-hand with his wife Rosalynn and daughter Amy. "Look," he seemed to be saying, "I am just an ordinary citizen who happens to be in the White House."

The substance, however, failed to match the style. He had no discernible political philosophy, no clear sense of direction. He sought the White House convinced that he was brighter and better than his competitors, but once there he had no cause or mission to fulfill. He called himself a populist, but that label meant little more than an appeal to the common man, a somewhat ironic appeal, given Carter's personal wealth. "The idea of a millionaire populist has always amused me," commented his attorney general, fellow Georgian Griffin Bell, "since the two persuasions seem contradictory."

The makeup of his administration reflected the conflicting tendencies that would eventually prove destructive. In the White House, he surrounded himself with close associates from Georgia, fellow outsiders like presidential adviser Hamilton Jordan and press secretary Jody Powell. Yet he picked established Democrats for key cabinet positions; Cyrus Vance, a New York lawyer, as secretary of state; Joseph Califano, a former aide to Lyndon Johnson, to head HEW; and Michael Blumenthal, the president of the Bendix Corporation, as secretary of the treasury. In the lower ranks, however, he selected liberal activists, followers of George McGovern, Edward M. (Ted) Kennedy, and Ralph Nader, people who were intent on regulating business and preserving the environment. The result was bound to be tension and conflict, as the White House staff and the federal bureaucracy worked at cross purposes, one group seeking change while the other attempted to protect the President.

Lacking both a clear set of priorities and a coherent political philosophy, the Carter administration had little chance to succeed. The President strove hard for a balanced budget but was forced to accept mounting deficits. Federal agencies fought to save the environment and help consumers but served only to anger industry. For example, head of the highway safety program Joan Claybrook, a former associate of Ralph Nader, recalled 12.9 million automobiles in 1977. Her predecessor in 1976 had recalled only 3.4 million.

In the crucial area of social services, Joseph Califano failed repeatedly in his efforts to carry out long-overdue reforms. His attempts to overhaul the nation's welfare program, which had become a $30-billion annual operation serving some thirty million Americans, won little support from the White House. Carter's unwillingness to take the political risks involved in revamping the overburdened Social Security system by reducing benefits and raising the retirement age blocked Califano's efforts. And the HEW secretary finally gave up his attempt to draw up a workable National Health Insurance plan when he was caught in the crossfire between President Carter and Senator Ted Kennedy.

Informed by his pollsters in 1979 that he was losing the nation's confidence, Carter sought desperately to redeem himself. After a series of meetings at Camp David with a wide variety of advisers, he gave a speech in which he seemed to blame his failure on the American people, accusing them of creating "a crisis of confidence . . . that strikes at the very heart and soul and spirit of our national will." Then a week after what his critics termed the "national malaise" speech, he requested the resignation of Califano and Treasury Secretary Blumenthal. But neither the attempt to pin responsibility on the American people nor the firing of cabinet members could hide the fact that Carter, despite his good intentions and hard work, had failed to provide the bold leadership the nation needed.

*D*espite his intelligence, integrity, and hard work, Jimmy Carter suffered a crisis in leadership. The electorate perceived him as ineffectual at solving problems and indecisive at setting priorities.

FROM DÉTENTE TO RENEWED COLD WAR

America's political position in the world declined sharply in the 1970s. In part, the fault was internal. The Vietnam War left the American people convinced that the nation should never again intervene abroad and Watergate discredited strong presidential leadership, shifting power over foreign policy to Congress. The new national consensus was symbolized by the War Powers Act, passed in 1973, which required the President to consult with Congress before sending American troops into action overseas. At the same time, external events and developments, notably the control over oil exercised by OPEC and the threats posed by revolutionary nationalism in the Middle East and Latin America, further weakened American foreign policy. No longer able to dominate the international scene, the United States began to play the role of spectator, and at times even of victim.

American diplomats tried three different strategies in the '70s in an effort to adjust to the new realities of power. During the Ford presidency, Secretary of State Kissinger continued the policy of détente. Aware that the Soviet Union had neutralized America's traditional nuclear advantage, Kissinger sought to use both economic incentives and Russian fear of China to moderate Soviet policy. In the Carter administration, American foreign policy oscillated between two poles. While Secretary of State Cyrus Vance tried to maintain elements of détente, including a new strategic arms limitation treaty [SALT II], and President Carter called for an American crusade on behalf of human rights in the world, National Security Adviser Zbigniew Brzezinski advocated more hawkish policies which stressed the Soviet arms buildup and the need for confrontation. By the late 1970s, Brzezinski's hard line had triumphed over both Vance's version of détente and Carter's initial concern for human rights.

Retreat in Asia and Africa

It was Gerald Ford's fate to reap where Nixon had sown. In 1974, Congress cut in half the administration's request for $1.4 billion in military aid to South Vietnam. A year later, when a North Vietnamese offensive proved surprisingly successful, Ford was unable to get Congress to grant any additional aid. Bereft of American assistance and weakened by internal corruption, the South Vietnamese government was unable to stop the advance on Saigon in April 1975. American forces concentrated on evacuating 150,000 loyal South Vietnamese, but many more were left behind when the last helicopter left the roof of the embassy in Saigon. Bitter and frustrated, the American people dejectedly watched the televised scene as the North Vietnamese celebrated their conquest of the South. After a quarter century of futile effort, the United States finally had to admit defeat in the nation's longest and most humiliating foreign war.

Less than a month later, Ford had a chance to remind the world of American power. The Khmer Rouge government of Cambodia seized an American freighter, the *Mayaguez*, and imprisoned its

Through television, millions of Americans watched the fall of Saigon. Here, thousands of South Vietnamese seek refuge in the U.S. embassy compound.

intervention. Covert action by the CIA proved ineffective, but the government of Angola turned out to be neutral, relying on technical assistance from the United States to complement military aid from Russia. Most Americans were relieved that the United States did not intervene militarily in Angola, not sharing Kissinger's belief that the nation had been "traumatized by Vietnam as we were by Munich."

Accommodation in Latin America

President Carter was more successful than Ford in adjusting to the growing nationalism in the world, particularly in Central America, where the United States had imposed order for most of the twentieth century by backing reactionary regimes.

The first test came in Panama. Resentment over American ownership of the Panama Canal had led Lyndon Johnson to enter into negotiations aimed at the eventual return of the waterway to Panama. Carter completed the long diplomatic process in 1977 by signing two treaties. One restored sovereignty in the 500-square-mile canal zone to Panama, while the other provided for gradual Panamanian responsibility for operating the canal, with appropriate safeguards for its use and defense by the United States. In negotiating these treaties, Carter was trying both to right an ancient wrong and create stability in a highly volatile region; the Pentagon had warned him that without Panama's cooperation, one hundred thousand American troops would be needed to defend the canal.

The real struggle over the treaties took place in the Senate. Conservative Republicans expressed outrage over what they termed a "giveaway" of the Panama Canal. "It's ours. We stole it fair and square," claimed California Senator S. I. Hayakawa. Intensive personal lobbying by President Carter, as well as bipartisan support from influential Republicans such as Gerald Ford and Henry Kissinger, finally led to Senate ratification with just one vote to spare, thus paving the way for the return of the canal to Panama by the year 2000.

Carter was less successful, however, in dealing with a growing problem of left-wing uprisings in Central America. In mid-1979, dictator Anastasio Somoza capitulated to the Sandinista forces in

crew. When the Communists ignored the initial American protest, Ford authorized an armed attack on Cambodia by two thousand Marines from bases in Thailand. By the time the American forces landed on a small offshore island, Cambodia had freed the crewmen. The nation took pride in the President's resort to force, but forty Americans paid for his decision with their lives.

Events in Africa, however, proved that caution and restraint were still the hallmark of American foreign policy in the 1970s. The new nation of Angola had won its independence from Portugal in 1974, only to be caught up in a civil war between rival forces. The United States and China backed one group in this small country, but the Soviet Union, using several thousand Cuban troops, helped put a rival faction into power.

Despite repeated pleas from Ford and Kissinger, Congress refused to sanction American

Estimated Total Costs of U.S. Wars, 1775–1985
(in millions of dollars)

	Wartime Costs	Veterans' Benefit Costs	Interest Payments on War Loans	Estimated Long-term Costs
American Revolution	100–140	28	20	170
War of 1812	87	20	14	120
Mexican War	82	26	10	120
Civil War (Union side only)*	2,300	3,289	1,200	6,800
Spanish-American War	270	2,111	60	2,400
World War I	23,700	13,856	11,100	57,600
World War II	260,000	65,231	200,000	625,200
Korean Conflict	50,000	11,391	unknown	61,400
Vietnam Conflict	140,600	13,173	unknown	153,800

* Costs to the Confederate side are estimated at $1 billion.

Source: U.S. Bureau of the Census, Statistical Abstract of the United States: 1984, 104th edition, Washington, D.C., 1983.

Nicaragua. Despite American attempts to moderate the Sandinista revolution, the new regime moved steadily to the left, developing close ties with Castro's Cuba. In neighboring El Salvador, a growing leftist insurgency against a repressive regime put the United States in an awkward position. Unable to find a workable alternative between the extremes of reactionary dictatorship and radical revolution in Central America, Carter tried to use American economic aid to encourage the military junta in El Salvador to carry out democratic reforms. But after the guerrillas launched a major offensive in January 1981, he authorized large-scale military assistance to the government for its war against the insurgents, setting a precedent for the future.

The Quest for Peace in the Middle East

The inconclusive results of the 1973 Yom Kippur War gave Henry Kissinger the opportunity to play the role of peacemaker in the troubled Middle East. Shuttling back and forth between Cairo and Jerusalem, and then to Damascus, the secretary of state finally succeeded in arranging a pullback of Israeli forces in both the Sinai and the Golan Heights. Although he failed to achieve his goal of

an Arab-Israeli settlement, Kissinger had succeeded in demonstrating that the United States could play the role of neutral mediator between the Israelis and Arabs. And equally important, he had detached Egypt from dependence on the Soviet Union, thereby weakening Russian influence in the Middle East.

Jimmy Carter tried at first to bring the Soviets back into the Middle Eastern peacemaking process by proposing a big power settlement. In November 1977, however, Egyptian President Anwar Sadat stunned the world by traveling to Jerusalem in an effort to reach agreement directly with Israel. The next year, Carter abandoned his efforts to work with the Russians and instead invited both Sadat and Israeli Prime Minister Menachem Begin to negotiate under his guidance at Camp David. For thirteen days, President Carter met with Sadat and Begin, finally emerging with the ambiguous Camp David accords. A framework for negotiations, rather than an actual peace settlement, the Camp David agreements dealt gingerly with the problem of Palestinian autonomy in the West Bank and Gaza Strip areas.

In 1979, Israel and Egypt signed a peace treaty which provided for the gradual return of the entire Sinai to Egypt but left the fate of the Palestine Arabs vague and unsettled. By excluding both the Palestine Liberation Organization

Jimmy Carter sits between President Sadat and Prime Minister Begin just after the 1978 signing of the Camp David accords that set the stage for a peace treaty between Egypt and Israel. Carter's personal triumph in bringing the two leaders together was soon offset by the public perception that his responses to the Iranian Revolution were misguided.

(PLO) and the Soviet Union from the negotiations, the United States alienated Egypt from the other Arab nations and drove the more radical states closer to the Soviet Union.

Any sense of progress in the Middle East as a result of Camp David was quickly offset in 1979 with the outbreak of the Iranian Revolution. Under Nixon and Kissinger, the United States had come to depend heavily on the shah and his powerful army for defense of the vital Persian Gulf. Carter continued the close relationship with the shah, despite growing signs of domestic discontent with his leadership. In a visit to Teheran in late 1977, the President praised the shah for making Iran "an island of stability" and for personally deserving "the respect and the admiration and love which your people give to you." Yet little more than a year later, Iran was in chaos as the exiled Ayatollah Ruhollah Khomeini led a fundamentalist Moslem revolt against the shah.

Unaware of the deep resentment most Iranians felt toward the shah—a resentment based both on dislike of sweeping modernization programs and police-state rule—the Carter administration misjudged the nature of the Iranian Revolution.

At first, the United States encouraged the shah to remain in Iran, but when he decided to leave the country in January 1979, Carter tried to work with a moderate regime rather than encourage an army coup. With Khomeini's return from exile, Moslem militants quickly came to power in Teheran. In October 1979, Carter permitted the exiled shah to enter the United States for medical treatment. Irate mobs in Iran denounced the United States and on November 4, militants seized the U.S. embassy in Teheran and took fifty-eight Americans prisoner.

The prolonged hostage crisis revealed the extent to which American power had declined in the 1970s. Carter relied first on diplomacy and economic reprisals in a vain attempt to free the hostages. American allies in Western Europe and Japan, dependent on Middle Eastern oil, quickly disassociated themselves from the United States, while Khomeini offset the American economic embargo by signing trade agreements with the Soviet Union. In an attempt to impress the Iranians, the United States concentrated its naval forces in the Indian Ocean. In his State of the Union message in January 1980, the President enunciated a new Carter Doctrine, telling the world that the United States would fight to protect the vital oil supplies of the Persian Gulf. "Twin threats to the flow of oil—from regional instability and now potentially from the Soviet Union—require that we firmly defend our vital interest when threatened."

Carter was unable to back up these brave words with meaningful action. Plans for a rapid deployment force were prepared, but it would be several years before these mobile troops could be deployed. In April 1980, the President authorized a desperate rescue mission that ended in failure when several helicopters broke down in the Iranian desert. The mission was aborted, an accident cost the lives of eight crewmen, and Secretary of State Cyrus Vance—who had opposed the rescue attempt—resigned in protest. The hostage crisis dragged on through the summer and fall of 1980, a symbol of American weakness that proved to be a powerful political handicap to Carter in the upcoming presidential election.

The Cold War Resumes

The policy of détente was already in trouble when Carter took office in 1977. Congressional refusal to relax trade restrictions on the Soviet Union had doomed Kissinger's attempts to win political concessions from the Soviets through economic incentives. The Kremlin's repression of the growing dissident movement, led by nuclear physicist Andrei Sakharov, and its harsh policy restricting the emigration of Soviet Jews had caused many Americans to doubt the wisdom of seeking accommodation with the Soviet Union.

President Carter's emphasis on human rights appeared to the Russians to be a direct repudiation of détente. In his inaugural address, Carter reaffirmed his concern over the mistreatment of human beings anywhere in the world, declaring "our commitment to human rights must be absolute." It was easier said than done. Carter did withhold aid from authoritarian governments in Chile and Argentina, but equally repressive regimes in South Korea and the Philippines continued to receive generous American support. Human rights proved, in the words of one presidential aide, "absolute in principle but flexible in application." The Soviets, however, were dis-

Americans were shocked by the anger Iranian mobs directed toward the U.S. embassy staff in Teheran, and were frustrated by the United States' inability to rescue the hostages.

turbed by the principle, particularly after Carter received Soviet exiles in the White House.

Secretary of State Vance concentrated on continuing the main pillar of détente, the strategic arms limitation talks (SALT). In 1974, President Ford had met with Brezhnev in Vladivostok and reached tentative agreement on the outline of SALT II. The chief provision was for a ceiling of 2400 nuclear launchers by each side, a level which would not require either Russia or the United States to give up any existing delivery vehicles. In March 1977, Vance went to Moscow to propose a drastic reduction in this level; the Soviets, already angry over human rights, rejected the American proposal as an attempt to overcome the Russian lead in land-based ICBMs.

Zbigniew Brzezinski, Carter's national security adviser, worked from the outset to reverse the policy of détente. Commenting that he was "the first Pole in 300 years in a position to really stick it to the Russians," he favored confrontation with the Kremlin. Although Carter signed a SALT II treaty with Russia in 1979, lowering the ceiling on nuclear delivery systems to 2250, growing opposition in the Senate played directly into Brzezinski's hand. He prevailed on the President to advocate adoption of a new MX missile to replace the existing Minuteman ICBMs, which some experts thought were now vulnerable to a Soviet first strike. This new weapons system, together with the planned Trident submarine,

Soviet tanks rolled into Afghanistan in December 1979, dealing a mortal blow to East-West détente.

ensured that regardless of SALT, the nuclear arms race would be speeded up in the 1980s.

Brzezinski also was successful in persuading the President to use China to outmaneuver the Soviets. After a trip to China in 1978, Brzezinski arranged for the sale of advanced technology to China (including items denied the Russians), and the possibility of resuming full diplomatic relations was explored. Finally, on January 1, 1979, the United States and China exchanged ambassadors, thereby completing the reconciliation that Nixon had begun in 1971. The new relationship between China and the United States presented the Soviet Union with the problem of defending itself against two distinct enemies.

The Cold War, in abeyance for nearly a decade, resumed with full fury in December 1979 when the Soviet Union invaded Afghanistan. Although this move was designed to ensure a regime friendly to the Soviet Union, it appeared to many as the beginning of a Soviet thrust toward the Indian Ocean and the Persian Gulf. Carter responded to this aggression with a series of stern acts: the United States banned the sale of high technology to Russia, embargoed the export of grain, resumed draft registration, and even boycotted the 1980 Moscow Olympics. These Ameri-

can moves did not halt the invasion of Afghanistan; instead, they put the United States and Russia back on a collision course. .

The results doomed détente. Aware that he could not get a two-thirds vote in the Senate, Carter withdrew the SALT II treaty. Right-wing groups in the United States began to warn of Soviet military superiority and call for a massive American arms build-up. The hopeful phrases of détente gave way to belligerent rhetoric as groups like the Committee on the Present Danger called for an all-out effort against the Soviet Union. Jimmy Carter, who had come into office hoping to advance human rights and control the nuclear arms race, now found himself a victim of the renewed Cold War.

National frustration over the hostages in Iran and the Soviet invasion of Afghanistan, coupled with anxiety over the energy crunch and rampant inflation, eroded public confidence in the Carter administration. A leader who had benefited from Vietnam and Watergate had now been betrayed by events. Despite his substantial achievements—the Camp David agreements, the Panama Canal treaties, improved relations with Third World countries—Carter had to take the blame for developments overseas that were beyond his control. By mid-1980 the President's overall approval rating fell to 23 percent in the Gallup poll (and to 18 percent in foreign policy). The American people, disillusioned by the failures of Nixon, Ford, and Carter, yearned for new political leadership to meet the challenges facing the nation at home and abroad.

Recommended Reading

The best account of the impact of the Yom Kippur War on American foreign policy is the second volume of Henry Kissinger's memoirs, *Years of Upheaval* (1982). Edward R. F. Sheehan is critical of American policy in the Middle East in *The Arabs, Israelis and Kissinger* (1976); William B. Quandt provides a more balanced account in *Decade of Decisions* (1977).

Richard Barnet gives a thorough description of the impact of the energy crisis and foreign industrial competition on the American economy in the 1970s in *The Lean Years* (1980). Two superior collections of essays on the impact of the oil shocks are Robert Stobaugh and Daniel Yergin, eds., *Energy Future* (1980) and Daniel Yergin and Martin Hillenbrand, eds., *Global Insecurity* (1982).

Additional Bibliography

Additional information on economic themes can be found in John Blair, *The Control of Oil* (1976); Peter R. Odell, *Oil and World Power*, 5th ed. (1979); and in Richard Barnet and Ronald Muller, *Global Reach* (1974), on the rise of the multinationals. The fate of affirmative action in the 1970s is traced in Allan P. Sindler, *Bakke, Defunis, and Minority Admissions* (1978) and J. Harvie Wilkinson, III, *From Brown to Bakke* (1979). Steven F. Lawson, *In Pursuit of Power* (1985) and Manning Marable, *Black American Politics* (1985) deal with the growing importance of the black vote in the 1970s. Arthur Corwin examines problems of Mexican immigration critically in *Immigrants—and Immigrants* (1978). Changes in immigration policy and the new influx from Third World countries is covered in David Reimers, *Still the Golden Door* (1985). For the women's movement, see Jo Freeman, *The Politics of Women's Liberation* (1979); Susan M. Hartmann, *From Margin to Mainstream* (1989); Winifred D. Wandersee, *On the Move: American Women in the 1970s* (1988); and Mary Frances Berry, *Why ERA Failed* (1986).

For the Ford administration, the most useful books are Richard Reeves, *A Ford, Not a Lincoln* (1975); Clark Mollenhoff, *The Man Who Pardoned Nixon* (1976); Robert Hartmann, *Palace Politics* (1980), an insider's view by a disgruntled aide; and the President's own memoir, Gerald R. Ford, *A Time to Heal* (1979). The impact of post-Watergate reforms on the CIA can be traced in Loch Johnson, *A Season of Inquiry* (1985); James Colby, *Honorable Men* (1978); and Stansfield Turner, *Secrecy and Democracy* (1985). On the election of 1976, see Jules Witcover, *Marathon* (1977) and Elizabeth Drew, *American Journal* (1977).

Books on the Carter administration include James Wooten, *Dasher* (1978) and Betty Glad, *Jimmy Carter* (1980), which focus on Carter's political career; Charles O. Jones, *The Trusteeship Presidency* (1988), on Carter's troubled relations with Congress; Haynes Johnson, *In the Absence of Power* (1980), a journalists's view of the Carter presidency. Four memoirs offer the best insight into domestic developments during the Carter years: Joseph Califano, *On Governing America* (1981), critical of the President; Griffin Bell, *Taking Care of the Law* (1982), a defensive view by the attorney general; Jody Powell, *The Other Side of the Story* (1984), the press secretary's attack on the media; and Rosalynn Carter, *First Lady from Plains* (1984), a revealing account by the President's wife.

The conflict over foreign policy within the Carter administration can be seen clearly in the memoirs of the leading figures. Cyrus Vance defends his record as secretary of state in *Hard Choices* (1984); national security adviser Zbigniew Brzezinski is critical of Carter's handling of foreign policy in *Power and Principle* (1983); and Jimmy Carter focuses primarily on his Camp David triumph in *Keeping Faith* (1982). The best survey of the Carter administration's diplomacy is Gaddis Smith, *Morality, Reason and Power* (1985); see also, Donald S. Spencer, *The Carter Implosion* (1989), a critical account, and David S. McLellan, *Cyrus Vance* (1985). For the Panama Canal treaties, see

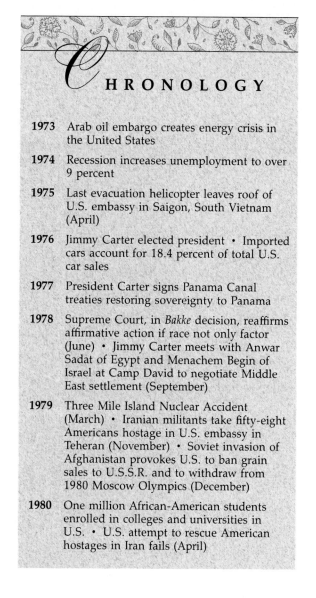

CHRONOLOGY

1973 Arab oil embargo creates energy crisis in the United States

1974 Recession increases unemployment to over 9 percent

1975 Last evacuation helicopter leaves roof of U.S. embassy in Saigon, South Vietnam (April)

1976 Jimmy Carter elected president • Imported cars account for 18.4 percent of total U.S. car sales

1977 President Carter signs Panama Canal treaties restoring sovereignty to Panama

1978 Supreme Court, in *Bakke* decision, reaffirms affirmative action if race not only factor (June) • Jimmy Carter meets with Anwar Sadat of Egypt and Menachem Begin of Israel at Camp David to negotiate Middle East settlement (September)

1979 Three Mile Island Nuclear Accident (March) • Iranian militants take fifty-eight Americans hostage in U.S. embassy in Teheran (November) • Soviet invasion of Afghanistan provokes U.S. to ban grain sales to U.S.S.R. and to withdraw from 1980 Moscow Olympics (December)

1980 One million African-American students enrolled in colleges and universities in U.S. • U.S. attempt to rescue American hostages in Iran fails (April)

Walter LaFeber, *The Panama Canal* (1978), the broadest account; J. Michael Hogan, *The Panama Canal in American Politics* (1986); and George D. Moffett, *The Limits of Victory* (1985). Other books on foreign policy issues of the 1970s are Strobe Talbott, *Endgame* (1979), on the negotiation of SALT II; Roy Rowan, *The Four Days of the Mayaguez* (1975), and John Stockwell, *In Search of Enemies* (1976), an exposé of CIA activities in Angola.

The best accounts of U.S. relations with the Shah and the Iranian revolution are Barry Rubin, *Paved with Good Intentions* (1980) and James A. Bill, *The Eagle and the Lion* (1988). For the hostage crisis, see Michael Ledeen and William Lewis, *Debacle* (1981), a journalistic account, and two books by members of Carter's White House staff, Hamilton Jordan, *Crisis* (1983) and Gary Sick, *All Fall Down* (1985).

CHAPTER 33

The Reagan Era
and Beyond

he Republican National Committee sponsored a televised address by Hollywood actor Ronald Reagan on behalf of Barry Goldwater's presidential candidacy in October 1964. Reagan's speech had originally been aired on a Los Angeles station; the resulting outpouring of praise and campaign contributions led to its national rebroadcast.

In contrast to Goldwater's strident rhetoric, Reagan used relaxed, confident, and persuasive terms to put forth the case for a return to individual freedom. Instead of the usual choice between increased government activity and less governmental involvement, often couched in terms of the left and the right, Reagan presented the options of either going up or down—"up to the maximum of human freedom consistent with law and order, or down to the ant heap of totalitarianism." Then, borrowing a phrase from FDR, he told his audience: "You and I have a rendezvous with destiny. We can preserve for our children this the last best hope of man on earth or we can sentence them to take the first step into a thousand years of darkness."

Although this speech did not rescue Goldwater's unpopular candidacy, it marked the beginning of Ronald Reagan's remarkable political career. A year later, a group of wealthy friends persuaded him, largely on the basis of the success of "the speech," to run for the California governorship. Reagan proved to be a masterful candidate. His friendly, relaxed manner and his mastery of television enabled him to present his strongly conservative message without appearing to be a rigid ideologue of the right. He sounded so reasonable and convincing as he sketched out a vision of recapturing traditional American values in an age of protest and ever growing governmental activity that he won handily. Reagan's views addressed rising middle-class suburban resentment over high taxes, expanding welfare programs, and bureaucratic regulation. For a generation increasingly disenchanted with professionals in politics, he offered himself as a "civilian politician" who embodied the feelings and frustrations of most Americans in the modern consumer culture.

In two terms as governor, Reagan displayed natural ability as a political leader. Instead of insisting on implementing all of his conservative beliefs, he proved surprisingly flexible. Faced with a Democratic legislature, he yielded on raising taxes and increasing state spending while managing to trim the welfare rolls. Symbolic victories were his specialty; in one example he managed to confront campus radicals and fire Clark Kerr, chancellor of the University of California, while at the same time generously funding higher education.

By the time Reagan left the governor's office in 1974, many signs pointed to a growing public frustration both with liberal reliance on government to solve most of the nation's problems and with increasing permissiveness in American society. In a popular rebellion against escalating property taxes in 1978, California's voters passed Proposition 13, which called for a 57 percent cut in taxes and resulted in a gradual reduction in social services. Concern over greater acceptance of homosexuality in society and rising abortion and divorce rates impelled religious groups to engage in political activity to defend traditional family values. Jerry Falwell, a successful Virginia radio and television evangelist, founded the Moral Majority, a fundamentalist group dedicated to preserving the "American way of life." The Moral Majority held workshops and seminars to teach its followers how to become active in local politics, and it also issued "morality ratings" for congressmen and senators.

Conservatives proved far more skillful than liberals in mastering new political techniques. They developed direct-mail lists to elicit campaign contributions from millions of small givers; they used polls to single out the most effective issues to exploit; they perfected the system of telephone banks to get out the vote on behalf of conservative candidates on election day. Reforms in campaign financing that stemmed from Watergate helped conservatives far more than they did liberals. Republicans especially benefited from a provision permitting PACs (political action committees) to raise and spend unlimited sums on behalf of favored candidates.

The population shift of the 1970s, especially the rapid growth of the Sunbelt region in the South and West (see Chapter 32), added momentum to the conservative upsurge. Those moving to the Sunbelt tended to be white, middle- and upper-class suburbanites—mainly skilled workers, young professionals, and business executives who were attracted both by economic opportunity and by a political climate stressing low taxes, less government regulation, and more reliance on the marketplace. In the West, the newcomers supported the dominant Republicans, while in the South, they could choose between a growing Republican party and conservative, "boll weevil" Democrats who advocated stronger national defense abroad and less government intrusion at home. The political impact of population shifts from East to West and North to South during the 1970s was reflected in the congressional gains (seventeen seats) by Sunbelt and Far West states after the 1980 census.

Conservatives also succeeded, for the first time since World War II, in making their cause intellectually respectable. Scholars and academics on the right flourished in new "think tanks," such as the American Enterprise Institute in the nation's capital. Writer William Buckley and economist Milton Friedman proved to be effective advocates of conservative causes in print and on television. Neo-conservatism, led by Norman Podhoretz's magazine *Commentary*, became fashionable among many intellectuals who were former liberal stalwarts. They denounced liberals for being too soft on the Communist threat abroad and too willing to compromise high standards at home in the face of demands for equality from African Americans, women, and the disadvantaged. Scholars and political leaders, such as Daniel Patrick Moynihan, Nathan Glazer, and Daniel Bell, called for a reaffirmation of capitalism and a new emphasis on what was right about America rather than an obsessive concern with social ills.

By the end of the 1970s, Ronald Reagan was recognized as the nation's most effective spokesman for the conservative resurgence. His personal charm softened the hard edges of his right-wing call to arms, and his conviction that America could regain its traditional self-confidence by reaffirming basic ideals had a broad appeal to a nation shaken by inflation at home and humiliation abroad. In 1976, Reagan had barely lost to Gerald Ford at the Republican convention; four years later, he overcame an early upset by George Bush in Iowa to win the GOP presidential nomination handily.

In his acceptance speech at the Republican convention in Detroit, he set forth the themes which endeared him to conservatives—less gov-

ernment, balanced budget, family values, and peace through increased military spending. Unlike Barry Goldwater, who frightened people with his rigid ideology, Reagan offered reassurance and hope for the future. He spoke of restoring to the federal government "the capacity to do the people's work without dominating their lives." As historian Robert Dallek has pointed out, Reagan "assured his listeners that he was no radical idealist courting defeat, but a sensible, thoroughly likeable American with a surefire formula for success that would please everyone." In Ronald Reagan, the Republicans had found the perfect candidate to exploit both the American people's frustration with the domestic and foreign policy failures of the 1970s and the growing conservative mood of the nation.

THE CONSERVATIVE RESURGENCE: REPUBLICANS IN POWER

The liberal Democratic political coalition, originally created by Franklin D. Roosevelt in the Great Depression, finally split apart by the end of the 1970s. The Watergate scandal gave the Democrats a brief reprieve, but by the end of the decade, the Republicans were using the conservative upsurge to make inroads into such normally Democratic groups of voters as Jews, Southerners, and blue-collar workers. Yet the continuing appeal of the New Deal legacy prevented a total political realignment.

The Reagan Victory

In 1980, Jimmy Carter, the politician who had so skillfully used the Watergate trauma to win the presidency, found himself in trouble. Inflation, touched off by the second oil shock of the 1970s, reached double-digit figures—13.3 percent in 1979 and 12.4 percent in 1980. The Federal Reserve Board's effort to shrink the money supply had led to a recession, with unemployment reaching 7.8 percent by July 1980. What Ronald Reagan dubbed the "misery index," the combined rate of inflation and unemployment, hit 28 percent early in 1980 and stayed above 20 percent throughout the year.

Foreign policy proved almost as damaging to Carter. The Soviet invasion of Afghanistan eroded hopes for continued détente; the hostage crisis in Iran highlighted the nation's sense of helplessness in the face of flagrant violations of its sovereignty. In the short run, Carter used that crisis to beat back the challenge to his renomination by fellow Democrat Edward Kennedy; the President stayed in the White House during the spring primaries, reminding the voters of his devotion to duty. The Democrats rallied behind Carter, although the delegates to the party's convention displayed a notable lack of enthusiasm in renominating him.

Ronald Reagan, in the meantime, chose George Bush as his running mate. In the fall campaign, the Republican candidates hammered away at the state of the economy and the world. Reagan scored heavily among traditionally Democratic blue-collar groups by blaming Carter for inflation, which robbed workers of any gain in real wages. Reagan also accused Carter of allowing the Soviets to outstrip the United States militarily and promised a massive buildup of American forces if he were elected. Although Republican strategists feared that Carter might spring an "October surprise"—a negotiated release of the American hostages at the height of the campaign—the Iranian situation actually helped Reagan by accentuating U.S. weakness in the world. Carter's position was further hurt by the independent candidacy of liberal Republican John Anderson of Illinois, who appealed to voters disenchanted with Carter but not yet ready to embrace Reagan.

The President struck back by claiming that Reagan was too reckless to conduct American foreign policy in the nuclear age. Charging that this election would decide "whether we have peace or war," Carter tried to portray his Republican challenger as a warmonger. The attack backfired. In a televised debate arranged late in the campaign, Reagan assured the American people of his devotion to peace, leaving Carter with the onus of trying to land a low blow. At the end of the confrontation, Reagan scored impressively when he summed up the country's dire economic condition by suggesting voters ask themselves simply, "Are you better off now than you were four years ago? Is it easier for you to go and buy things in the stores than it was four years ago?" On election day, the American people an-

Carter's administration negotiated for the release of the American hostages in Iran until the final minutes of Carter's term. After 444 days in captivity, the hostages were freed on January 20, 1981, the day of Ronald Reagan's inauguration.

swered with a resounding "no." Reagan carried forty-four states and gained 51 percent of the popular vote. Carter won only six states and 41 percent of the popular vote, while John Anderson received the remaining 8 percent but failed to carry a single state. Reagan clearly benefited from the growing political power of the Sunbelt; he carried every state west of the Mississippi and in the South lost only Georgia, Carter's home state. Even more impressive were his inroads into the old New Deal coalition. Reagan received 50.5 percent of the blue-collar vote and 46 percent of the Jewish vote, the best showing by a Republican since 1928. Only one group remained loyal to Carter; African-American voters gave him 85 percent of their ballots.

Even more surprising were the Republican gains in Congress. For the first time since 1954, the GOP gained control of the Senate, 53 to 46, and the party picked up 33 seats in the House to narrow the Democratic margin from 114 to 50. Liberals were the chief losers in Congress. Such prominent Democratic senators as George McGovern and Frank Church met with defeat, victims of a vendetta waged by the Moral Majority.

The meaning of the election was less clear than its outcome. Nearly all observers agreed that the voters had rendered an adverse judgment on the Carter administration. But most experts did not

The Election of 1980			
Candidate	Party	Popular Vote	Electoral Vote
Reagan	Republican	43,899,248	489
Carter	Democratic	35,481,435	49
Anderson	Independent	5,719,437	—

assess the outcome to be as major a realignment in American politics equivalent to the Democratic victory of FDR in 1932. Voters in 1980 expressed a distaste for current economic conditions, not a strongly held ideological preference. The fact that the Democrats still held a sizable majority in the House was seen as proof of their party's continuing strength. Political scientist Walter Dean Burnham termed the result "a conservative revitalization," but one that stopped short of making the GOP the dominant party.

Journalist Theodore White disagreed, viewing the outcome as a repudiation of the Democratic coalition that had dominated American politics since the days of Franklin D. Roosevelt and the New Deal. White may well have been right. In the eight presidential elections from 1952 to 1980, Republican candidates received 52.3 percent of the popular vote, compared to 47.7 percent for the Democrats; Republicans won four elections (1952, 1956, 1972, and 1980) by landslides, one (1968) narrowly, and lost two close races (1960 and 1976). Only in 1964 did the Republicans lose by a wide margin. The movement of the populations from the Northeast and Midwest to the South and West, along with the flight from the city, helped the Republicans far more than the Democrats. The Reagan victory in 1980 signalled a partial political realignment, ending a half-century of Democratic dominance.

Cutting Spending and Taxes

When Ronald Reagan took office in January, 1981, the ravages of inflation had cut $1400 in purchasing power from the median family income during the 1970s. High interest rates, with the prime hovering near 20 percent, led to a decline in home building and auto sales. The government's share of the GNP had risen from 18.5 percent to over 23 percent since 1960, while the value of the dollar had dropped to just 36

cents over the same period. The new President blamed what he termed "the worst economic mess since the Great Depression" on high federal spending and excessive taxation. "Government is not the solution to our problems," Reagan announced in his inaugural address, "government is the problem."

The President embraced the concept of supply-side economics as the proper remedy for the nation's economic ills. In sharp contrast to the prevailing Keynesian theory, with its reliance on government spending to boost consumer demand, Reagan favored a reduction in both federal expenditures and revenues. Supply-side economists believed that the private sector, freed of the ever increasing burden of government spending, would shift its resources from tax shelters to productive investment, leading to an economic boom that would provide enough new income to offset the lost revenue. Although many other economists worried that the 30 percent cut in income taxes that Reagan favored would lead to staggering deficits, the President was confident that his program would both stimulate the economy and reduce the role of government. As he explained in a televised speech to the nation on February 5, 1981, "Our aim is to increase our national wealth so all will have more, not just to redistribute what we already have, which is just a sharing of scarcity. We can begin to reward hard work and risk-taking by forcing government to live within its means."

Many economists were as mystified by supply-side policy as John Q. Public. Some labeled it "voodoo economics."

BOB ZSCHIESCHE
Courtesy Our Folks

In pursuing his economic goals, Reagan relied on a mixed team of advisers. Neither his secretary of the treasury, Donald Regan, a Wall Street operator of conventional, if flexible, economic views, nor his chairman of the Council of Economic Advisers, Murray Weidenbaum, an academic expert who advocated government deregulation of business, shared the President's faith in the supply-side theory. His new director of the Office of Management and Budget, David Stockman, was a former Michigan congressman who had become a convert to supply-side economics. Reagan entrusted Stockman with the primary responsibility for carrying out his policies of cutting government spending and sharply reducing taxes. Intelligent, combative, and shrewd, Stockman blended a missionary concern over bloated social programs with an insider's knowledge of how Congress worked. At the same time, Reagan supported the efforts of Paul Volker, the banker Carter had appointed to head the Federal Reserve Board, to stem inflation by restricting the money supply, and even appointed him to a second four-year term in 1983.

The President and his budget director made spending the first target. Quickly deciding not to attack such popular middle-class entitlement programs as Social Security and Medicare, and sparing critical social services for the "truly deserving needy," the so-called "safety net," they concentrated on slashing $41.4 billion from the budget by cutting heavily into such other social services as food stamps, and by reducing public service jobs, student loans, and support for urban mass transit. Reagan used his charm and powers of persuasion to woo conservative Democrats from the West and South, especially the "boll weevil" group led by Congressman Phil Gramm of Texas. Appearing before a joint session of Congress only weeks after an attempt on his life, Reagan won a commanding 253 to 176 margin of victory for his budget in the House, and an even more lopsided vote of 78 to 20 in the Senate in May. A month later, after Democrats attempted to increase appropriations in committee, the President won a final showdown in the House. Reagan thus emerged from the budget struggle victorious, telling a Los Angeles audience that he had achieved "the greatest reduction in government spending that has ever been attempted."

The President proved equally successful in reducing taxes. Adopting a proposal originally put forth by Senator William Roth of Delaware and Congressman Jack Kemp of New York, he advocated a cut of 10 percent in personal income taxes for three consecutive years. When the Democrats countered with a two-year plan that would only reduce taxes 15 percent, Reagan compromised with 5 percent the first year, but insisted on the full 10 percent for the second and third years. Despite fears of the large deficit that would result from the loss of revenue, the President once again overcame Democratic resistance in Congress. In July, the House accepted the 25 percent cut by a vote of 238 to 195 and the Senate approved it overwhelmingly, 89 to 11. Concessions to special interests offered by both sides, notably lower corporate rates and tax breaks for the oil industry and savings and loan associations, added to the loss of revenue. But regardless of the economic consequences, Reagan had demonstrated beyond any doubt his ability to wield presidential power effectively. As *Time* magazine commented, no president since FDR had "done so much of such magnitude so quickly to change the economic direction of the country."

Limiting the Role of Government

Reagan met with only mixed success in his other efforts to restrict governmental activity and reduce federal regulation of the economy. The concept of cutting back on the scope of federal agencies and limiting their impact on American business was a central tenet of the president's political philosophy. The goal of deregulation led to the appointment of men and women who shared his belief in relying on the marketplace rather than the bureaucracy to direct the nation's economy. Thus James Watt, the secretary of the interior, outraged environmentalists by opening up federal land to coal and timber production, halting the growth of national parkland and making more than a billion acres available for offshore oil drilling. Ann Gorsuch Burford proved equally controversial as the head of the Environmental Protection Agency (EPA), with critics charging her with a failure to force corporations to observe EPA regulations. Though both Watt and Burford were eventually forced to resign, the Reagan administration continued its policy of freeing business from governmental intervention long after their departures.

Transportation Secretary Drew Lewis proved to be the most effective cabinet member in the administration's first two years. He helped relieve the troubled American automobile industry of many of the regulations adopted in the 1970s to reduce air pollution and increase passenger safety. At the same time, he played a key role in the behind-the-scenes negotiations that led Japan to agree in the spring of 1981 to restrict its automobile exports to the United States for the next three years. This unilateral Japanese action enabled the Reagan administration to help Detroit's carmakers without openly violating its free market position by endorsing protectionist measures.

Lewis gained notoriety in opposing a strike by the air controllers' union (PATCO) in the summer of 1981. The President, denouncing PATCO for threatening to interrupt "the protective services which are government's reason for being," fired the striking workers, decertified the union, and ordered Lewis to hire and train thousands of new air controllers at a cost of $1.3 billion. For the Reagan administration, the price was worth paying to prove that no group of government employees had the right to defy the public interest.

The Reagan administration was less successful in trying to cut back on the entitlement programs that it viewed as the primary cause of the growing budget deficits. Social Security was the greatest offender. The decision to index old-age pensions to the cost of living in the 1970s led to a 500 percent increase in benefits over the decade and threatened to bankrupt the system's trust fund by the end of the century. Buoyed by his May budget victory in Congress, Reagan permitted the Health and Human Services Department to propose a major reduction in future benefits. In late May, the Republican Senate rejected this proposal by a stinging 96 to 0 vote and the Democrats quickly charged that Reagan was trying to balance the budget on the backs of the elderly. Chastened by this sharp rebuff, the President finally took the issue of Social Security reform out of politics by appointing a bipartisan commission to recommend ways to protect the system's endangered trust fund. In March 1983, Congress finally approved a series of changes that guaranteed the solvency of Social Security by gradually raising the retirement age, delaying cost-of-living in-

creases for six months, and taxing pensions paid to the well-to-do elderly.

The administration's record in dealing with civil rights and women's concerns proved surprisingly clumsy and divisive. In regard to federal appointments, Reagan showed far less interest than Carter in advancing minority representation. In contrast to the 12 percent African-American representation in major government positions under the Democrats, the Republican figure was only 4.1 percent. Women were also slighted, falling from 12.1 percent under Carter to 8 percent under Reagan; the percentage of Hispanics dropped only slightly, from 4.1 percent to 3.8 percent.

Although feminist groups were disappointed by the administration's strong rhetorical attacks on legalized abortion and its lack of support for the Equal Rights Amendment, which ran out of time for consideration by the states in June 1982, the appointment of Sandra Day O'Connor to the Supreme Court pleased them. By this one shrewd move, Reagan was able both to fulfill a campaign pledge and make a symbolic gesture to women. At the same time, the President also buttressed the conservative tilt of the Court. His appointments to the lower federal courts were a better indication of his administration's relatively low regard for women. Of the first 72 Reagan nominees to the federal judiciary, only 3 were women; 69 were men, only one of them black.

The administration's civil rights record proved especially revealing. Aware of how few African Americans had supported the GOP in 1980, Reagan made no effort to reward this group with government jobs or favors. Instead, the Justice Department actively opposed busing to achieve school integration and affirmative action measures that resulted in minority hiring quotas. In an especially inept move, the administration announced in January 1982, that it would reverse the traditional IRS rules denying tax-exempt status to private schools and colleges that engaged in racial segregation. After a storm of protest, Reagan declared that he would ask Congress to enact a law denying tax exemption for private institutions guilty of discrimination, explaining somewhat lamely that he only wanted to end the arbitrary use of bureaucratic authority by the IRS.

The Republicans failed to take the lead in renewing the original Voting Rights Act of 1965.

Chief Justice Warren Burger swears in Sandra Day O'Connor, the first woman to become a Supreme Court justice, in September 1981.

After opposing key amendments designed to strengthen the historic legislation that had finally enabled African Americans to participate fully in southern politics, Reagan belatedly endorsed and signed a measure to extend the Voting Rights Act for 25 years.

Despite these lapses, in its first two years the Reagan administration had achieved most of its goals in the domestic area. The President had not only succeeded in cutting domestic spending and taxes, but he had reduced the degree of government involvement in everyday American life. The cuts in social programs helped achieve this goal, as did the efforts at deregulation by James Watt and Drew Lewis. For the first time since LBJ's Great Society, the rate of government growth had been slowed and more reliance placed on business to regulate itself.

REAGAN AND THE WORLD

Ronald Reagan was even more determined to reverse the course of American policy abroad than at home. He believed that under Carter, American prestige and standing in the world had dropped to an all-time low. Intent on restoring traditional American pride and self-respect, Reagan's mission was to strengthen America's defenses and recapture world supremacy from the Soviet Union.

In reality, the new President was simply continuing the hard line that Carter had begun to take after the invasion of Afghanistan. The Democrats had begun a massive military buildup in 1979 that included plans for cruise missiles in Europe, a rapid deployment force in the Middle East, and a 5-percent increase in the defense budget.

Under Reagan, the Pentagon flourished. Secretary of Defense Caspar Weinberger, once known as a budget cutter, presented a plan that would more than double defense spending, taking it from $171 billion in 1981 to a projected $367.5 by 1986. The emphasis was on new weapons, ranging from the B-1 bomber and the controversial MX nuclear missile to the expansion of the navy from 456 to 600 ships. Despite growing opposition in Congress, by 1985 the Defense budget grew to over $300 billion at the very time the administration was cutting back on domestic spending.

Reagan was less than successful in resolving a recurring problem that had plagued the Carter administration—internal feuding between the secretary of state and the national security adviser in the White House. The appointment of Alexander Haig to head the State Department was a clear attempt to restore the dominant role of the secretary of state. Haig, a former general, NATO commander, Kissinger aide, and White House chief of staff under Nixon, was a well-known and forceful figure compared to Richard Allen, the conservative but relatively obscure national security adviser. Haig soon proved to be too outspoken and domineering for Reagan's White House staff, and after William Clark replaced Allen in the National Security Council post, the friction became intense. Finally, in mid-1982, Reagan replaced Haig as secretary of state with George Shultz, a professional economist with extensive government experience, whose low-key and relaxed style brought an air of calm reassurance to the conduct of American foreign policy. Shultz, however, proved more than able to hold his own in bureaucratic infighting with the White House staff, defense secretary Weinberger, and the administration's most outspoken hard-liner, UN Ambassador Jeane Kirkpatrick.

Despite the steady increase in defense spending and the formation of a smoothly functioning foreign policy team, Reagan soon found that his diplomatic goals were more difficult to achieve than the budgetary and tax measures he had pushed through Congress so speedily.

Challenging the "Evil Empire"

The belief that the Soviet Union was a deadly enemy that threatened the well-being and security of the United States was the central tenet of Reagan's approach to foreign policy. He saw the Russians as bent on world revolution, ready "to commit any crime, to lie, to cheat" to advance their cause. Citing what he called a "record of tyranny," Reagan denounced the Russians before the UN in 1982, claiming that "Soviet-sponsored guerrillas and terrorists are at work in Central and South America, in Africa, the Middle East, in the Caribbean and in Europe, violating human rights and unnerving the world with violence."

Given this view of Russia as "the focus of evil in the modern world," it is not surprising that the new President continued the hard line that Carter had adopted after the invasion of Afghanistan. Abandoning détente, Reagan proceeded to implement a 1979 decision to place 572 Pershing II and cruise missiles in Western Europe within range of Moscow and other Russian population centers to match Soviet deployment of medium range missiles aimed at NATO countries.

Strong protests from the Soviet Union, as well as growing uneasiness in Europe and an increasingly vocal nuclear freeze movement at home, led the Reagan administration to offer two new arms control initiatives by 1982. The first, called a "zero-option," proposed cancelling the placement of all 572 American medium-range missiles in return for Russian removal of their missiles targeted on Western Europe. Secondly, in a new series of strategic arms talks, dubbed START, Reagan proposed that the two superpowers cut their nuclear warheads by one-third, with no more than half of those remaining to be land-

Military Power: United States vs. USSR, 1983–1984

	United States	Soviet Union
Intercontinental Ballistic Missiles (ICBMs)	1,045	1,398
Submarine-launched Ballistic Missiles (SLBMs)	568	980
Long-range Strategic Bombers	272	143
Total Delivery Vehicles (ICBMs, SLBMs, Bombers)	1,885	2,521
Nuclear Warheads (ICBMs and SLBMs)	7,297	8,342
Destructive Power (in millions of tons of TNT)	2,202	5,111
Anti-Ballistic Missile Launchers (ABM)	0	32
Aircraft Carriers	14	5
Armed Forces Personnel	2,136,400	5,050,000
Related Forces		
NATO/French vs. Warsaw Pact Armed Forces	2,855,000	1,081,000
British/French SLBMs/IRBMs vs. USSR IRBMs/MRBMs	162	400
(IRBM = Intermediate-range Ballistic Missiles MRBM = Medium-range Ballistic Missiles)		

Source: The Military Balance 1983–1984, *The International Institute for Strategic Studies, London, 1983.*

"QUICK—GIMME A HUNDRED TWENTY BILLION QUARTERS!"

President Reagan steadfastly defended SDI ("star wars") against critics who questioned its huge, open-ended cost and scientists who called its feasibility into question.

based. The Russians quickly turned down both proposals. They did not wish to trade medium-range missiles already in place for cancellation of American weapons not yet deployed, nor did they consider a plan that focused primarily on land-based strategic weapons fair, since only 25 percent of American warheads were on such launchers, compared to 72 percent of the Soviet arsenal. Yet Reagan's proposals succeeded in blunting both the nuclear freeze movement at home and European doubts about Reagan's commitment to nuclear disarmament.

After Russian Foreign Minister Andrei Gromyko rejected an American offer to deploy only a portion of the 572 Pershing II and cruise missiles, the United States began putting these weapons in bases in Great Britain and Germany in November 1983. The Soviets, claiming that this move gave them only ten minutes warning time in case of an American attack, responded by breaking off the START negotiations in Geneva.

The nuclear arms race had now reached a more dangerous level than ever before. The United States stepped up research and development of the Strategic Defense Initiative (SDI), an anti-missile system based on the use of lasers and particle beams to destroy incoming missiles in outer space. SDI was quickly dubbed "star wars" by the media. Critics doubted that SDI could be perfected, but warned that even if it were, the result would be to escalate the arms race by forcing the Russians to build more offensive missiles in order to overcome the American de-

fense system. The Reagan administration, however, defended "star wars" as a legitimate attempt to free the United States from the deadly trap of deterrence, with its reliance on the threat of nuclear retaliation to keep the peace. Meanwhile, the Soviet Union kept deploying larger and more accurate land-based ICBMs. Although both sides continued to observe the unratified SALT II agreements, the fact remained that between them the two super powers had nearly fifty thousand warheads in their nuclear arsenals.

Reagan's reliance on harsh rhetoric and an arms buildup, reminiscent of Dean Acheson's policy of negotiating only from strength, had failed to force the Soviets to retreat. At the same time, the illness and death of Brezhnev in 1982, followed in rapid succession by the deaths of his aged successors, Yuri Andropov and Konstantin Chernenko, prevented any meaningful negotiations with the Soviet Union. The selection of Mikhail Gorbachev, a younger and more dynamic Soviet leader, led to a summit meeting in Geneva in November 1985. Reagan and Gorbachev failed to break the nuclear deadlock, but the two leaders did agree to begin a new effort at

President Reagan and Soviet leader Mikhail Gorbachev greet each other at the 1985 summit meeting in Geneva.

arms control, providing a glimmer of hope for future progress on the grimmest of all issues facing humanity.

Turmoil in the Middle East

Reagan tried to continue Carter's basic policy in the turbulent Middle East. In April 1982, the Israelis honored a Camp David pledge by making their final withdrawal from the Sinai. Reagan hoped to achieve the other Camp David objective of providing a homeland for the Palestinian Arabs on the West Bank, but Israel instead continued to extend Jewish settlements into this disputed area. The threat of the Palestine Liberation Organization (PLO), based in southern Lebanon and frequently raiding across the border into Israel, seemed to be the major obstacle to further progress.

On June 6, 1982, with tacit American encouragement, Israel's Prime Minister Menachem Begin began an invasion of southern Lebanon designed to secure Israel's northern border and destroy the PLO. The United States made no effort to halt this offensive, but did join with France and Italy in sending a multinational force to permit the PLO to evacuate to Tunisia. Reagan then tried to achieve an overall Arab-Israeli settlement by proposing the creation of a Palestinian homeland on the West Bank in close association with Jordan.

Unfortunately, Reagan's diplomacy soon became enmeshed in the Lebanese civil war, raging since 1975. Neither the PLO nor Syria, which occupied portions of Lebanon, would back his West Bank plan, and soon American marines, sent to Lebanon as part of the multinational force to restore order, were caught up in the renewed hostilities between Moslem and Christian militia. The Moslems perceived the marines as aiding the Christian-dominated government of Lebanon instead of acting as neutral peacekeepers, and began firing on the vulnerable American troops.

In the face of growing congressional demands for the withdrawal of the marines, Reagan declared that they were there to protect Lebanon from the designs of Soviet-backed Syria. But

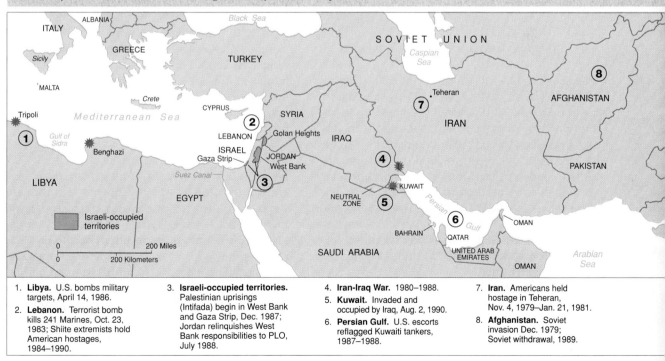

Trouble Spots in the Middle East

Armed conflict and terrorist attacks in this region intensified in the early and mid-1980s.

1. **Libya.** U.S. bombs military targets, April 14, 1986.
2. **Lebanon.** Terrorist bomb kills 241 Marines, Oct. 23, 1983; Shiite extremists hold American hostages, 1984–1990.
3. **Israeli-occupied territories.** Palestinian uprisings (Intifada) begin in West Bank and Gaza Strip, Dec. 1987; Jordan relinquishes West Bank responsibilities to PLO, July 1988.
4. **Iran-Iraq War.** 1980–1988.
5. **Kuwait.** Invaded and occupied by Iraq, Aug. 2, 1990.
6. **Persian Gulf.** U.S. escorts reflagged Kuwaiti tankers, 1987–1988.
7. **Iran.** Americans held hostage in Teheran, Nov. 4, 1979–Jan. 21, 1981.
8. **Afghanistan.** Soviet invasion Dec. 1979; Soviet withdrawal, 1989.

Marines attempt to clean up the destruction of their barracks in Beirut after a terrorist bomb blast that killed 239. Barely a week later, marines took part in the invasion of Grenada in the Caribbean.

finally, after a Moslem terrorist drove a truck loaded with explosives into the American barracks, killing 239 marines, the President had no choice but to pull out. The last American unit left Beirut in late February 1984. Despite his good intentions, Reagan had experienced a humiliation similar to Carter's in Iran—one that left Lebanon in shambles and the Arab-Israeli situation worse than ever.

Confrontation in Central America

Reagan faced a difficult situation in Central America (see Chapter 32). In an area marked by great extremes of wealth, with a small landowning elite and a mass of peasants mired in dire poverty, the United States sought moderate, middle-class regimes to support. Washington usually ended up backing repressive, right-wing dictatorships rather than the more leftist groups who raised the radical issues of land reform and redistribution of wealth. Yet it was often oppression by United States–supported regimes that drove those seeking political change to embrace revolutionary tactics.

This is precisely what happened in Nicaragua, where the Sandinista coalition finally succeeded in overthrowing the repressive Somoza regime in 1979. In an effort to strengthen the many middle-class elements in the original Sandinista govern-

ment and to avoid forcing Nicaragua into the Cuban and Soviet orbit, Carter extended American economic aid.

The Reagan administration quickly reversed this policy. Alexander Haig cut off all aid to Nicaragua in the spring of 1981, accusing the Sandinistas of driving out the moderates, welcoming Cuban advisers and Soviet military assistance, and serving as a supply base for leftist guerrillas in nearby El Salvador. The new policy became self-fulfilling, as Nicaragua became even more dependent on Cuba and the Soviet Union.

The United States and Nicaragua were soon on a collision course. In a speech to Congress in April 1983, the President declared that "the national security of all the Americas is at stake in Central America," and asked for the money and authority to "hold the line against externally supported aggression." But when Congress, fearful of repeating the Vietnam fiasco, proved reluctant to seek a military solution, Reagan opted for covert action. The CIA began supplying the Contras, exiles fighting against the Sandinistas from bases in Honduras and Costa Rica. Despite Democratic objections, the U.S.-backed rebels tried to disrupt the Nicaraguan economy, raiding villages, blowing up oil tanks and even mining harbors. The Contras succeeded only in turning Nicaragua into an armed camp, as the Sandinistas went on a war footing, building the largest military force in Central America. Then, in 1984, Congress passed the Boland Amendment prohibiting any United States agency from spending money in Central America. The withdrawl of U.S. financial backing left the Contras stranded in a fight that might not have escalated without U.S. funding in the first place.

The situation in El Salvador proved little better. There a guerrilla war had broken out in the 1970s between left-wing groups and a reactionary regime dominated by wealthy landowners. Reagan stepped up support for a government headed by middle-of-the-roader José Napoleón Duarte, granting $25 million in additional economic aid and sending in a team of American military advisers. The Reagan administration, ignoring charges that right-wing death squads, which were not under Duarte's control, had killed forty thousand civilians, did all it could to help the Duarte government, which did succeed in winning a decisive election victory over the extreme

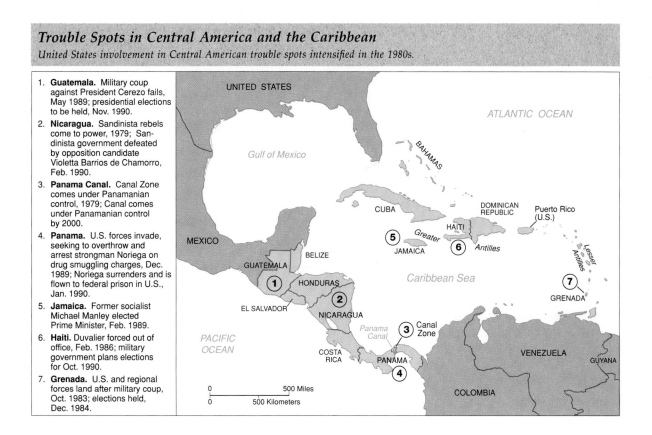

Trouble Spots in Central America and the Caribbean

United States involvement in Central American trouble spots intensified in the 1980s.

1. **Guatemala.** Military coup against President Cerezo fails, May 1989; presidential elections to be held, Nov. 1990.
2. **Nicaragua.** Sandinista rebels come to power, 1979; Sandinista government defeated by opposition candidate Violetta Barrios de Chamorro, Feb. 1990.
3. **Panama Canal.** Canal Zone comes under Panamanian control, 1979; Canal comes under Panamanian control by 2000.
4. **Panama.** U.S. forces invade, seeking to overthrow and arrest strongman Noriega on drug smuggling charges, Dec. 1989; Noriega surrenders and is flown to federal prison in U.S., Jan. 1990.
5. **Jamaica.** Former socialist Michael Manley elected Prime Minister, Feb. 1989.
6. **Haiti.** Duvalier forced out of office, Feb. 1986; military government plans elections for Oct. 1990.
7. **Grenada.** U.S. and regional forces land after military coup, Oct. 1983; elections held, Dec. 1984.

right in 1984 and began modest reforms in an effort to undercut the appeal of the guerrillas.

The only clear-cut triumph that Reagan achieved in the hemisphere came in the Caribbean. In October 1983, a military coup led to the death of the prime minister of Grenada, a friend of Fidel Castro, who was subsequently replaced by an even more radical regime. The Reagan administration, already upset by Grenada's close ties to Cuba and the construction of a large airfield on this small Caribbean island, decided to intervene to prevent the Communists from acquiring a strategic military base.

Nearly two thousand American marines invaded Grenada on October 25, 1983. After brief but strong resistance from 800 Cuban workers and troops on the island, the American forces claimed a victory that cost 18 lives. The administration proudly displayed pictures of captured Soviet arms to justify the resort to force; American medical students, shown on television kissing the ground as they returned to the United States, enabled the administration to label the operation a "rescue mission."

Aside from Grenada, however, the Reagan administration had little to show for its massive military buildup. In the Middle East, its well-intentioned use of marines had ended in disaster, while its determined opposition to left-wing groups in Central America had at best achieved a stalemate. Relations with the Soviet Union had fallen into one of the deepest chills of the entire Cold War with the nuclear arms race more intense than ever.

Yet Reagan appeared to succeed in his effort to restore American pride and self-confidence. Public opinion polls showed strong support for the President's hard line. And Russian behavior, notably the callous shooting down of a Korean civilian airliner in September 1983, underscored the administration's depiction of the Soviet Union as a dangerous and untrustworthy adversary. Most Americans seemed to agree with the President's 1980 statement: "Let us not delude ourselves. The Soviet Union underlies all the unrest that is going on. If they weren't engaged in this game of dominoes, there wouldn't be any hot spots in the world."

What Price Prosperity?

The sweeping reductions in domestic spending and income taxes that Reagan achieved in 1981 gave rise to conflicting economic expectations. Supply-side economists believed that the tax relief granted investors would lead to rapid business growth, which would raise more than enough new revenue to offset the lower rates. The administration's critics, on the other hand, were sure that heavy defense spending coupled with tax reductions would create massive deficits and result in economic stagnation.

Both groups proved to be wrong. Over the next seven years, the nation experienced both recession and rapid growth, deficits as well as prosperity, and best of all, an unexpected easing of inflation. Even though Reagan was unable to reach all of his goals, the combination of lowered inflation and renewed economic growth gave him an enormous political advantage.

Reaganomics

The supply-side theory became the first economic casualty of the 1980s. The naive belief that a combination of cuts in social spending and sharply reduced taxes could unleash an economic boom that would avoid huge deficits was the victim of both Reagan's insistence on huge increases in defense spending (projected at more than one trillion dollars over five years) and the Federal Reserve Board's tight money policy. It was the latter that touched off a recession that began in the fall of 1981 and steadily worsened throughout 1982, until factory utilization fell to under 70 percent and unemployment reached a postwar high of 10.4 percent in October 1982.

Reagan responded by refusing to give up his income tax cuts. With the first major 10 percent reduction due to come in July 1982, he claimed that his policies had not yet been given a chance. But he did prove flexible in other ways, slightly moderating the defense buildup, accepting fewer cuts in social programs than he proposed, and finally agreeing to a $98 billion increase in miscellaneous federal taxes under the guise of tax reform in order to hold the projected 1983 deficit under $100 billion. In addition, in early 1983 he accepted a Democratic proposal for spending

$4.6 billion on an emergency jobs program to relieve unemployment. But at the same time he refused to cancel the final 10 percent cut in income taxes in mid-1983. Instead he declared that all signs pointed to "a strong recovery," adding, "Our economic game plan is working."

Whether by design or good luck, the President's optimism proved justified. In the second quarter of 1983, the economy came to life, with the GNP expanding at an annual rate of 9.7 percent. The final 10 percent tax cut in July stimulated consumer spending, along with moderating inflation which kept prices from rising so quickly. The long-depressed automobile industry, helped by Japan's voluntary quotas on car exports, began to boom, with annual sales reaching 13.6 million in 1984. The American people went on a great buying spree with consumer installment debt increasing as much in the first six months of 1983 as in all of 1982. Even the dormant stock market came to life; the Dow Jones industrial average went over the 1200 mark and set new record highs in 1983.

Best of all, inflation remained under control as the economy expanded. The recession had driven the increase in the cost of living down from 7 percent to just under 4 percent in 1982; it dropped to 3.8 percent in 1983, the lowest rate

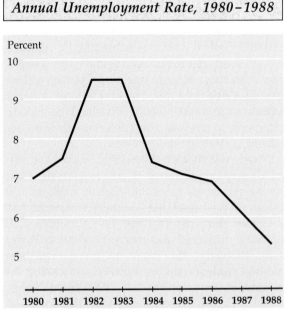

Annual Unemployment Rate, 1980–1988

Source: Economic Report of the President, 1989, *p. 344.*

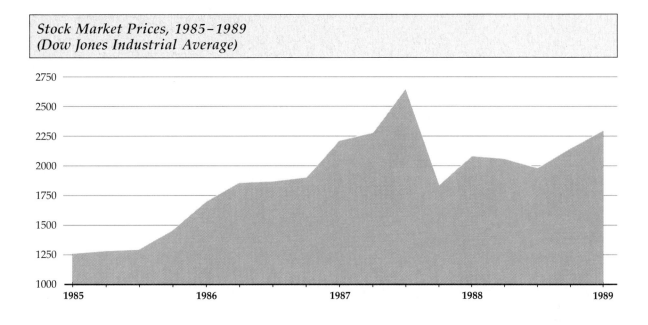

since 1972. At the same time, interest rates, which had been hovering around 16.5 percent in 1982, fell to 10.5 percent and remained below 11 percent, enabling consumers to buy goods and corporations to expand their inventories much more easily. A combination of long-term Federal Reserve policy, the impact of the recession and a worldwide decline in energy and food prices enabled the Reagan administration to take credit for solving the problem that had proved fatal for Carter and the Democrats.

The Twin Deficits

Two problems emerged in the mid-1980s to cloud Reagan's claims of economic recovery. The first was the growing federal budget deficit. The 1982 recession undercut the rosy assumptions of the supply-siders. As the economy weakened and unemployment increased, tax revenues fell below projections while government spending on unemployment insurance and other social programs climbed. The deficit reached $207.8 billion in 1983, triple the pre-Reagan high of $66 billion in 1976.

Even more frightening, some economists were predicting that at current spending and tax rates, the deficit would rise to over $300 billion a year by the end of the decade. The result, many feared,

would be soaring interest rates as the government competed with the private sector for the limited amount of investment capital in the nation. In fact, a slumping world economy led to a massive infusion of foreign investment which kept the prime rate from rising above 11 percent.

When the deficit continued to climb during the economic recovery of the mid-1980s, Congress finally came forward with what appeared to be a drastic solution. Republican Senators Phil Gramm of Texas and Warren Rudman of New Hampshire joined with Democrat Ernest Hollings of South Carolina to set a series of budgetary ceilings designed to eliminate the deficit entirely by 1991. If Congress and the administration exceeded these limits each year, then there would be automatic, across-the-board reductions in both defense and domestic spending. After the Supreme Court invalidated the compulsory feature, the revised Gramm-Rudman-Hollings Balanced Budget Act did succeed in halting the deficit spiral. As altered by Congress in 1986 and 1987, Gramm-Rudman, as it became known, stretched out the goal of ending the deficit until 1993 and called simply for reductions of $23 billion in the 1987 and 1988 budgets and a cut of $36 billion for 1989. The President and Congress, thanks in part to temporary revenue gains from a 1986 tax reform bill, were able to lower the deficit from the all-time high of $221 billion in 1986 to a

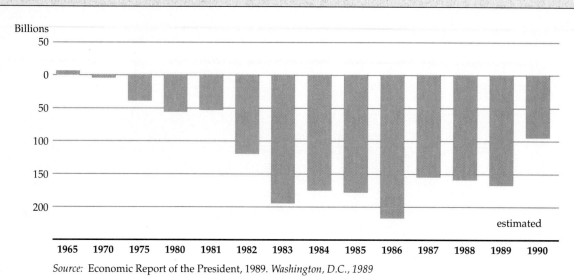

**U.S. Budget Deficits, 1965–1988
(1989–1990 est.)**

Billions

	50												

1965 1970 1975 1980 1981 1982 1983 1984 1985 1986 1987 1988 1989 1990

estimated

Source: Economic Report of the President, 1989. *Washington, D.C., 1989*

more manageable $155 billion by 1988. Even more important, the deficit as a percentage of the GNP fell from over 5 percent to close to 3 percent, a level common in many industrial nations.

In essence, Gramm-Rudman was a political compromise. The price Reagan had to pay for Democratic help in resolving his budgetary crisis was to stop the increase in defense spending; the Pentagon budget, which went from less than $200 billion to just under $300 billion in three years, was frozen for the rest of the decade. But at the same time, by agreeing to sizable budget deficits for the next few years, the Democrats who controlled Congress had to give up any hope of expanding existing social programs or enacting new ones, such as a comprehensive national health plan.

Concern over another alarming deficit—in the balance of overseas trade—became an equally important issue in the mid-1980s. American exports had been falling steadily since the 1970s as a result of the decline in traditional manufacturing industries—iron and steel, electronics, and automobiles. The Japanese had been the biggest gainers as they dominated the American market in consumer goods such as television sets and VCRs. Even the American advantage in high technology was threatened by the mid-1980s as

Japan began to capture the lead in the manufacture of semi-conductors, once an American monopoly.

A sharp rise in the value of the dollar, beginning in 1983, accentuated the problem by making American goods too expensive in foreign markets. The result was a trade deficit that grew from a modest $31 billion in 1981 to an alarming $171 billion by 1987. American trade with Japan alone was running $60 billion in the red by 1986, while commerce with newly industrialized countries such as Taiwan, South Korea, and Singapore showed a deficit of over $30 billion. In late 1985, the Reagan administration joined with the governments of Japan and Western Europe to devalue the dollar. The resulting decline in the dollar stimulated American exports and helped reduce the trade deficit to more manageable proportions by 1989, although it still remained over $100 billion a year.

The only way the United States could equalize the balance of international payments was to import even more capital from abroad. Led by the Japanese, foreign investors poured large sums into the United States, buying real estate, office buildings, and even banks. As a result, in 1985, the United States, a creditor nation since World War I, suddenly became a debtor, owing the rest

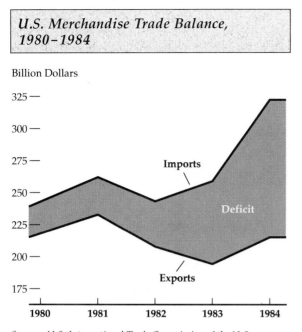

U.S. Merchandise Trade Balance, 1980–1984

Billion Dollars

Source: U.S. International Trade Commission of the U.S. Department of Commerce.

of the world more each year than it received from previous foreign investments. In fact, by the end of 1988, the United States had become the world's leading debtor at $532.5 billion, a sum surpassing the combined foreign debt of Brazil and Mexico.

The twin deficits had led to a dangerous financial dependence on other nations. In the 1980s, the American people had begun living beyond their means. Just as the government incurred large deficits rather than raising taxes to pay for the huge defense buildup, so consumers had cut back on personal saving in order to buy imported cars, television sets, and VCRs, encouraging further foreign investment. By 1988, foreigners held $400 billion in U.S. Treasury securities (almost 20 percent of the national debt), had invested another $300 billion in American industry, and owned 21 percent of the nation's banking assets. "The United States," commented one expert, "has lost control of its financial markets to foreigners." By the end of the decade, the American people would have to send $60 billion a year overseas just to pay the interest on these public and private obligations. Reaganomics had succeeded in continuing America's traditional high standard of living, but with a very high price—massive borrowing that mortgaged the nation's future.

The Politics of Prosperity

"Are you better off now than you were four years ago?" Reagan had asked voters at the end of his 1980 debate with Jimmy Carter. By the mid-1980s, he appeared to have delivered on his implicit promise to stem inflation and revive the stagnant American economy. Yet not everyone benefited equally from Reaganomics.

The gains were impressive. The 1982 recession halted the inflationary spiral, and thanks in part to a sharp decline in oil prices, inflation remained below 4 percent for the rest of the decade. Meanwhile, the recovery that began in the final quarter of 1982 led to the creation of 16 million new jobs and a drop in the unemployment rate to just over 5 percent. The best measure of living standards, the median per capita family income, rose slowly but steadily, going up 6.4 percent from 1980 to 1987 and 9.6 percent after the 1982 recession.

Despite these gains, the average American family was no better off by the end of the Reagan years than it had been in 1973. Measured in 1987 dollars, family income which had declined during the years of inflation, had just reached the level it enjoyed before the oil shocks hit so hard. Moreover, not everyone fared equally well. Those in the top 20 percent in terms of family income benefited the most, increasing their incomes at the rate of 1.9 percent a year from 1982 to 1987, compared to only 1.4 percent a year for those in the lowest fifth. The drop in the marginal tax rate, from a high of 70 percent down to 33 percent as a result of the 1981 tax cut and the 1986 tax reform act, gave upper-income Americans a much larger degree of tax relief than those in the lower brackets. Those near the bottom were helped by the Reagan administration's willingness to preserve basic social programs, the so-called "safety net," as well as by the fact that the 1986 tax reform dropped six million taxpayers from the rolls. But the lower middle class did not fare as well, gaining little from the income tax changes and seeing their weekly take-home pay drop as a result of rising Social Security taxes. The rich got richer, the poor stayed poor, while middle America struggled to make ends meet.

The most depressing development was the relatively bleak outlook for the next generation. Young people could no longer look forward to

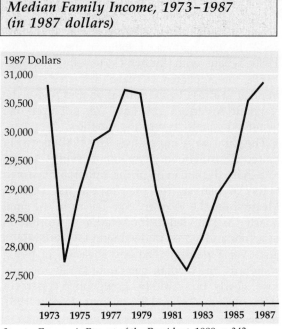

Median Family Income, 1973–1987 (in 1987 dollars)

1987 Dollars

31,000
30,500
30,000
29,500
29,000
28,500
28,000
27,500

1973　1975　1977　1979　1981　1983　1985　1987

Source: Economic Report of the President, 1989, *p. 342.*

living better than their parents. Home ownership among those aged 25 to 35 declined because of the rise in interest rates and real estate; in 1949, mortgage payments on the median-priced home took only 14 percent of the average worker's monthly salary, but by 1984, the figure was a staggering 44 percent.

Despite these mixed results, the Republicans were remarkably successful in persuading American voters that the Reagan administration had cured the nation's economic woes. The waning of inflation, which had been the most frightening development of the 1970s, along with the fact that wealthy Americans were far more likely to cast ballots than poorer ones, helps explain this seeming contradiction between public support of Reagan and the reality of Reaganomics. Even so, the GOP success was largely confined to the presidential level.

In the 1982 elections, the Democrats were able to take advantage of the recession to make substantial gains. With unemployment reaching the 10 percent level for the first time since the Great Depression, Republicans lost 26 seats in the House and saw the Democratic party gain control of the governorships and legislatures in 34 of the 50 states. The GOP, however, was able to maintain its eight-vote margin in the Senate.

The economic boom that began in 1983 came at just the right time for the Republican party. By early 1984, with personal income rising at an annual rate of 10.3 percent from January to June and unemployment shrinking rapidly, Democratic prospects dimmed for the 1984 election. After a long, bruising primary battle, Walter Mondale, former Minnesota senator and Carter's vice president, won the Democratic nomination. In a bold break with tradition, he chose a woman as a

"NOW DO YOU BELIEVE I'VE GOT HIM UNDER CONTROL?"

GENE BASSET
Courtesy Atlanta Journal

This cartoon shows ringmaster Ronald Reagan taming the wild beast of inflation despite the skepticism of the "expert."

*W*alter Mondale and Geraldine Ferraro campaigning in 1984. Ferraro was the first woman selected by a major party as a vice-presidential candidate.

running mate, Congresswoman Geraldine Ferraro of New York.

When the Republicans renominated Reagan and Bush, the campaign quickly came down to one issue—leadership. The GOP claimed that Reagan had overcome the problems that overwhelmed Carter, notably inflation at home and disrespect abroad. Asserting that he wanted to "make America great again," the President told voters if they reelected him, "You ain't seen nothin' yet."

Mondale and Ferraro, in contrast, accused Reagan of helping the rich at the expense of the poor, saddling future generations with huge deficits and risking war in the Middle East and Central America. In a surprise move, the Democratic candidate announced he intended to raise taxes to curb the deficit and then accused Reagan of harboring a "secret plan" to increase taxes himself.

Mondale had little success in his attempts to focus attention on Reagan's failures as a leader until a televised debate in early October. Stiff and strangely inarticulate, Reagan stumbled badly, which raised the issue of his age and competence. But in a second debate two weeks later, Reagan improved his performance and buried the age issue by turning to Mondale and saying, "I am not going to exploit for political purposes my opponent's youth and inexperience."

The outcome was an even greater Reagan landslide than in 1980. With a solid base in the South and West, Reagan cut deeply into the normally Democratic states of the Northeast and the swing states of the Midwest to take the electoral votes of all but Minnesota and the District of Columbia. Exit surveys revealed that economic issues were uppermost in the minds of voters; in the midst of a strong economic recovery, Reagan won a majority among all voters earning more than $12,500 a year. More than two-thirds of the white males in the nation voted for Reagan, who won even a majority of the blue-collar and women's vote. Despite Ferraro's presence on the ballot, a higher percentage of women voted for Reagan in 1984 than in 1980. Of all the traditional Democratic groups, only African Americans proved loyal to the party, giving Mondale 90 percent of their votes.

The 1984 election was far more of a triumph for Reagan than for his party. In Congress, the GOP gained only 14 seats, leaving the Democrats firmly in control of the House, while in the

The Election of 1984			
Candidate	Party	Popular Vote	Electoral Vote
Reagan	Republican	54,451,521	525
Mondale	Democratic	37,565,334	13

Three Mile Island and Chernobyl: The Promise and Peril of Nuclear Power

In March 1979, it appeared to the world that its worst nightmares about nuclear power might come true when a near-meltdown occurred at a nuclear power plant outside of Harrisburg, Pennsylvania. An accident of even greater proportions, the explosion of a reactor in the Soviet Ukraine on April 26, 1986, stirred their fears again. Three Mile Island and Chernobyl became household words that cast doubt on the viability of nuclear power.

In the 1960s, the United States and other industrialized nations had turned to nuclear power to fulfill the need for clean, inexpensive, and renewable energy free of foreign control. By 1979, there were 72 power plants operating in the U.S., and they generated 12.5 percent of the nation's electricity. Another 92 plants were under construction, and 30 more were in the planning stage. The Soviet Union had also embarked on a nuclear program. By 1984, Russia had built 43 plants that supplied 10 percent of that country's electrical needs. Advocates insisted that nuclear power plants posed no serious danger to public health, and in both countries the industry expected to play an ever larger part in meeting the growing demand for electricity.

The accident at Three Mile Island (TMI) caught the American people by surprise and touched off a strong reaction against reliance on nuclear power. Early reports on the meltdown were sketchy. It was not clear what exactly had gone wrong, except that one unit of the TMI facility had released some radioactivity into the environment. State officials and company representatives assured the anxious public that radiation levels outside were not—repeat, not—dangerous.

Inside TMI, the water system used to cool the reactor core had broken down, and company employees, scientists, and industry experts fought to get the cooling water moving again. The problem had begun at 4:00 A.M. when a relief valve failed to close after the reactor had shut down. During the next

A Soviet worker measures radiation at Chernobyl just after the disaster. High levels of radiation persist, resulting in dire health problems and economic devastation in surrounding areas.

two hours, the coolant level in the reactor core dropped significantly. And even though the chain reaction inside the reactor had stopped, the radioactive materials within continued to release tremendous quantities of heat—about 6 percent of normal reactor power.

By Friday, the crisis had become intense. Radiation readings outside the plant had risen (but were not yet dangerous). Governor Richard Thornburgh advised that those most susceptible to radiation, namely pregnant women and preschool-age children living within a 5-mile radius of TMI, ought to leave. Taking no chances, more than forty thousand people streamed out of the area that afternoon and evening. The main news of the day, however, was an announcement that a hydrogen bubble had formed above the reactor core, and that as long as it was present, there existed the possibility of the ultimate catastrophe—a meltdown. The danger was real, but remote; press reports, however, were alarmist, and a cloud of fear, confusion, and uncertainty enveloped the nation.

Over the weekend, while teams of experts worked to bring the reactor under control, news reports questioned whether the hydrogen bubble was explosive. On Sunday afternoon, President Jimmy Carter paid a visit to the site in an effort to calm the public. By Monday, the bubble had shrunk dramatically, and by Tuesday, the immediate danger had passed. The crisis was contained; a meltdown did not occur, and the radiation released posed a minimal health risk.

Soviet citizens living near the Chernobyl nuclear power station were not as lucky. The Chernobyl plant housed four reactors. On April 26, 1986, while conducting a safety test in Unit IV, plant personnel violated regulations, removing all of the control rods from the reactor core. The core temperature shot up, triggering an uncontrolled nuclear reaction and steam buildup. At 1:23 A.M., the reactor exploded, destroying the concrete shield above it and causing approximately thirty fires in the immediate vicinity.

The Soviets' first priority was to extinguish the flames in order to prevent the damage from affecting the other three reactors. Firefighting crews accomplished this task by 5 A.M., but at tremendous human cost; many later died from overexposure to radiation.

Over the course of the next ten days, Soviet officials worked to cool off the damaged core. In the meantime, the damaged reactor spewed a radioactive cloud of dust into the air—a plume that eventually spread over the Ukraine, Scandinavia, and much of Central and Eastern Europe.

Estimating the human cost of the Chernobyl disaster is difficult even today. The Kremlin reported that 237 persons were hospitalized for significant radiation exposure, and that thirty-one died in the immediate aftermath of the accident. In 1990, however, a Moscow newspaper claimed that at least 250 people had died during the accident or the subsequent rescue and cleanup operations. A more important—and controversial—question is the number of individuals who will ultimately die of cancer or various defects as a consequence of Chernobyl. According to a report by the U.S. Nuclear Regulatory

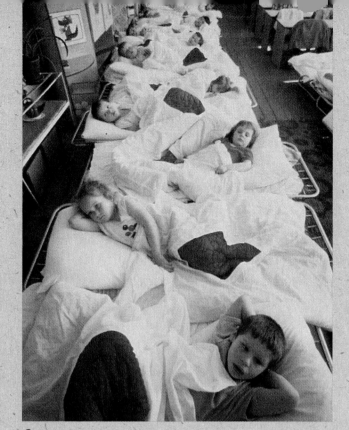

Children hospitalized for radiation sickness following the Chernobyl explosion.

Commission, the risk of cancer for those living within twenty miles of the plant is high. Dr. Robert Peter Gale, an American physician invited by the Soviets to help treat the first victims, estimates that over the next fifty years, fifty thousand lives may be lost due to cancer contracted in the wake of Chernobyl.

The two crises affected the American and Soviet nuclear power industries in strikingly similar ways. Both the American and Soviet governments stepped up their regulation of nuclear facilities rather than totally abandoning their programs. By the end of the 1980s, nuclear power plants still generated over 17 percent of America's electricity and 11 percent of the Soviet Union's.

Although nuclear power remains an important energy source in both countries, it has also lost much of its luster. In the U.S., every nuclear reactor order since 1974 has either

been canceled or postponed indefinitely. The Soviet Union has likewise scrapped some of its plans to build new stations. And in both countries, TMI and Chernobyl have left a legacy of fear that has eroded popular support for nuclear power.

Nuclear power has not, in all likelihood, been permanently discredited. Consumption of electricity in the United States has risen by one-third since the 1973 Arab oil embargo, and it promises to rise in the future. Except in certain regions where hydroelectric power, natural gas, and possibly solar energy are readily available, Americans will have to choose between coal, oil, and nuclear power. Growing environmental concern over acid rain and global warming tend to weigh against the burning of fossil fuels. In this context, the nuclear alternative may regain some of the credibility it has lost as a consequence of TMI and Chernobyl.

Senate, the Republicans lost two places, narrowing their majority to 54–46. Despite minor gains at the state level, the GOP failed to achieve the party realignment it sought. Republicans were encouraged by a strong showing among the young, with Reagan taking 56 percent of the vote of the baby boomers (those aged 25 to 34) and 60 percent of the post-boomers (those aged 18 to 24). The nation seemed to be dividing politically along economic lines, with the wealthy and affluent who fared best from Reagan's economic policies supporting the President while a growing underclass of African Americans, Hispanics, and the working poor were voting solidly Democratic. Middle-class Americans who held the balance revealed their mixed feelings by backing a Republican for President and Democratic candidates for the House and Senate.

SOCIAL DILEMMAS

Two complex social issues arose in the 1980s that went against the grain of the general sense of well-being in the Reagan years. A massive viral epidemic and a new drug crisis threatened the social fabric of the United States, yet the administration failed to respond promptly or effectively to either one.

The AIDS Epidemic

The outbreak of AIDS (acquired immune deficiency syndrome) in the early 1980s took most Americans by surprise. Even health experts had difficulty grasping the nature and extent of the new public health threat. Doctors first noticed a few cases of a rare form of pneumonia and an unusual type of skin cancer in male patients in New York and San Francisco in 1981. The Center for Disease Control noted the phenomenon in a June 1981 bulletin, but it was several years before researchers finally identified it as a hitherto unknown virus that had spread from Central Africa by way of Haiti and had found its first American victims primarily among gay men.

Initially, AIDS was perceived as only a threat to gay men, a group that had fought hard in the 1970s to gain a larger degree of societal freedom and approval. With a growing sense of urgency as the death toll mounted, gay men began to confine themselves to trusted partners.

It soon became apparent, however, that AIDS could not be so easily contained. It began to appear among intravenous drug users who shared the same needles and eventually among hemophiliacs and others receiving frequent blood transfusions. The possibility of a contaminated national blood supply terrified middle-class America, as did the possibility of the spread of AIDS to heterosexuals.

Scientists tried to reassure the public by explaining that the virus could be spread only by the exchange of bodily fluids, primarily blood and semen, and not by casual contact. The death of movie star Rock Hudson in the summer of 1985 intensified the sense of national panic. Controversy soon developed over proposals for mandatory blood tests for suspected carriers and the segregation of AIDS victims. The integrity of hospital blood supplies caused the most realistic concern; in 1985, a new test finally gave reassurance that transfusions could be performed safely.

The Reagan administration proved slow and halting in its approach to the AIDS epidemic. The lack of sympathy for gays and a need to reduce the deficit worked against any large increase in health spending; what little money was devoted to AIDS went almost entirely for research rather than for educational measures to slow its spread. The only real leadership came from Surgeon General C. Everett Koop who surprised his conservative backers in 1986 by coming out boldly with proposals for sex education, the use of condoms to ensure "safe sex," and confidential blood testing to help contain the disease.

While the administration dallied, the grim toll mounted. Since the average time between the initial infection and the first symptoms was five years and could be as long as fourteen years, efforts at prevention had little immediate impact. In November 1983, there were 2803 known cases and 1416 deaths; by the time Rock Hudson died in mid-1985, over 12,000 cases and more than 6000 deaths had been reported.

Growing public concern finally led to action. In 1987, Ronald Reagan appointed a special presidential commission headed by Admiral James Watkins, a former chief of naval operations, to study the AIDS epidemic. The Watkins report in 1988 criticized the administration's AIDS efforts

Surgeon General C. Everett Koop presents his "Understanding AIDS" campaign at a press conference in 1988. Immersing himself in the battle against the epidemic that was barely known when he first took office, Koop has been a steadfast supporter of AIDS education. Conservatives who would have expected a less explicit approach from the Fundamentalist Koop have been shocked by his directness: "You can't teach children about AIDS until you have taught them something about their own sexuality."

as "inconsistent" and recommended a new effort that included antidiscrimination legislation and explicit prevention education. Koop responded by sending out a pamphlet entitled "Understanding AIDS" to 107 million households, while in the fall, Congress voted to spend $1.3 billion to fight AIDS, with much of the money going for confidential testing and counseling and home care for victims.

Despite these new efforts, the epidemic continued to grow. In 1987, there were 50,000 cases; by mid-1989, the count had reached 100,000. The "gay" disease had spread far beyond that one group in society; by the end of the decade, most of the new victims were drug users among the urban poor, many of them racial minorities, betrayed by their reliance on tainted needles. The social cost was tragic—as just one example, babies of drug users born with the virus were frequently abandoned in city hospitals, which were already burdened with staggering health costs at a time of declining tax revenues. Most frightening of all was the time bomb ticking away in those exposed to the virus in the 1980s, which made the experts' forecast of as many as 500,000 cases by the mid-1990s all too believable. With no cure in sight, AIDS promised to be the most deadly disease in American history.

The War on Drugs

The 1980s witnessed the rapid spread of cocaine use in America, leading to a growing sense of social crisis by the end of the decade. Cocaine

had long been viewed as a relatively harmless recreational drug used by only a few people— rock musicians, Hollywood producers, and the very wealthy. By the end of the 1970s, the snorting of the pure white powder distilled from the leaves of coca plants grown in the foothills of the Andes had spread throughout the upper middle class. Bankers, lawyers, and doctors began to use it occasionally to achieve a moment of ecstasy, striving for what has been called "the illusion of instant happiness." The costs, however, were very high—$100 for a few snorts, and the danger of dying from an overdose or figuratively blowing one's mind. "Chronic cocaine use," warned one expert, "is the same as putting one's car in neutral with the brakes on and pressing the accelerator to the floor for hours— eventually, the engine will burn out." Nevertheless, the number of users reached over four million by 1982.

In the mid-1980s, cocaine suddenly was perceived as a danger to American society. The deaths of several celebrities from cocaine overdoses, notably movie star John Belushi and Maryland basketball player Len Bias, alarmed the public. More ominously, Jamaican drug gangs began to sell crack, a cheap cocaine derivative that could be smoked in a pipe to give a very intense high. Dealers sold this new form of cocaine for as little as $10 a dose, opening up a vast new market among the poor in the urban ghettoes. The phenomenon of teenage pushers selling small vials of crack first appeared in Miami and Los Angeles and soon spread to inner-city districts in New York, Houston, and

Community efforts to eradicate crack use and the crime that accompanies it have met with little success in the inner cities and ghettos.

Detroit. By 1986, an estimated 5.8 million people were using cocaine at least once a month and over 600,000 were confirmed addicts.

Despite its relatively low cost, crack led to an explosion of urban crime. The brief, intense high lasted only a few minutes, leading users to keep smoking more, desensitizing their nervous systems and thus forcing them to use still larger amounts to achieve the by-now indispensable euphoria. Needing as much as $1000 of crack each day to sustain their habits, users began to go on literal crime sprees to gain the necessary funds. By 1987, over 70 percent of all those arrested for burglary in Manhattan tested positive for cocaine.

The Reagan administration tried several approaches to the problem posed by cocaine. In 1982, the First Lady, Nancy Reagan, chose drug education as her special project. Using the slogan "Just Say No," she urged schools, churches, and civic groups to inform young people about the dangers of cocaine. Her program helped educate the middle class but had little impact on the crack smokers in the ghetto.

In the mid-1980s, the administration began to place greater emphasis on interdiction, using agents of the Drug Enforcement Agency (the DEA—a body created by Nixon in 1973) the Customs Bureau, and the Coast Guard to try to seal off the nation's borders. An international cartel of drug dealers, led by a group of Colombi-

ans, overcame this effort by saturating the nation with cocaine, losing only a fraction to the hard-pressed DEA. In reality, the Reagan administration was unwilling to devote the personnel and resources that truly effective interdiction would require; with one eye on the deficit, Washington was content with a few highly publicized skirmishes in what it termed the War on Drugs.

The very nature of the cocaine industry frustrated a third, and potentially most promising, countermeasure—wiping out the coca fields and processing plants in South America. The administration relied on diplomatic efforts in cooperation with the governments of Colombia, Bolivia, and Peru to curb the trade in cocaine, but with little success. Colombian processors set up new labs almost as soon as old ones were destroyed; well-publicized campaigns against growing coca, such as Operation Blast Forward in Bolivia in 1986, barely made a dent in crop production. South American farmers could make five times as much money growing coca leaves as food crops; it was estimated that Bolivia received $600 million a year in hard currency from the drug trade, compared to profits of only $400 million from tin and other legal exports.

By the time Ronald Reagan left office, the problem remained as serious as ever, despite actions by Congress in 1986 and 1988 to allocate more funds for drug education and enforcement, to legalize the death sentence for some drug-related killings, and to create a new federal drug czar. Latin America was producing nearly 400 tons of cocaine a year, five times the amount consumed in the United States; the wholesale price of a kilogram of the white powder in Miami and Los Angeles had dropped from $50,000 to less than $15,000 between 1982 and 1987. A government report in mid-1989 claimed that overall use of drugs, including heroin and marijuana, had declined 25 percent since 1985, while the number of people using cocaine at least once a week had risen from 647,000 to 862,000.

Only one thing had changed dramatically—public awareness. A Gallup poll taken in the summer of 1989 showed that for the first time in recent history, the American people regarded illegal drugs as their greatest concern. Twenty-seven percent of those polled placed drugs highest on the national agenda, a result which George Gallup found "virtually unprecedented," since,

Global Drug Traffic

Despite unprecedented public concern over the drug problem, the United States remains one of the world's largest markets for illegal drugs.

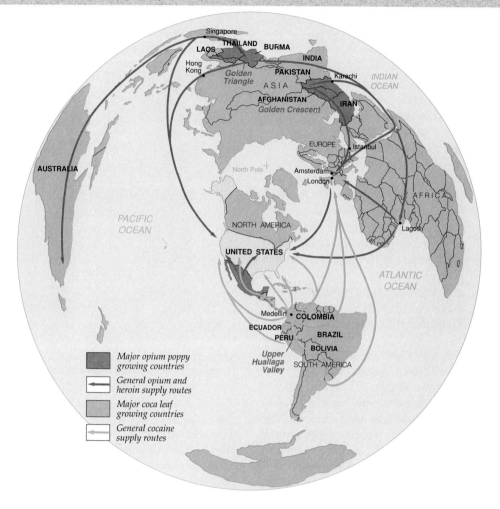

in the past, social issues had always come in behind economic and international concerns. Ronald Reagan thus bequeathed his successor a social problem that transcended even the Cold War and the state of the national economy in the minds of the American people.

THE REAGAN LEGACY

Ronald Reagan's second term in the White House proved much less successful than his first. Dubbed the "teflon president" for the way his charm and good luck enabled him to avoid being held responsible for administration failures, Rea-

gan suddenly was forced to face intense criticism and growing public disenchantment. Yet in the end he was able to rescue his troubled presidency and maintain the Republican hold on the White House.

The Changing Palace Guard

Ronald Reagan had always been unusually dependent on aides and assistants. He saw his own role as one above the heat of bureaucratic battle —providing the nation with a set of goals and a vision of the future. As the great communicator, he would build the public consensus and let others manage the more mundane task of turning his dreams into reality.

His initial success depended heavily on the very effective White House team of James Baker, Edwin Meese, and Michael Deaver. Baker, a Texan with extensive Washington experience, became the chief-of-staff, managing the White House and directing legislative strategy. Shrewd and pragmatic, he outmaneuvered Californian Meese, who accepted the role of counselor to the President, where he advised Reagan on policy but had little to do with its implementation. The final member of the trio, Mike Deaver, had the full confidence of Nancy Reagan and applied himself full time to the goal of enhancing her husband's political image. Although Deaver and Meese were close to Reagan personally, it was Baker, the newcomer with keen political instincts and experience in dealing with Congress, who was mainly responsible for the administration's stunning early successes.

The President's laid-back style was misleading. Some thought he was little more than an actor playing the role of president, content to perform the ceremonial duties of a head-of-state while letting others run the country. Although it is true he preferred to be presented with solutions rather than problems, it was Reagan's determination to cut taxes, reduce domestic spending and rebuild America's defenses that gave shape and coherence to his administration's policies. Critics made fun of his "three-by-five" index cards, suggesting Reagan was so ill-informed that aides had to be sure he had essential information in front of him before he appeared in public. In reality, he had perfected a very effective shorthand system using four-by-six cards, which enabled him to give speeches and public statements without reading from a manuscript text. In the White House, he thrived on the interplay between Baker, Meese, and Deaver, letting them present various alternatives and then instinctively suggesting viable compromises. Neither brilliant nor well-read, Reagan had a quick mind and a remarkable feel for the public's emotions that enabled him to perform very effectively as a detached but charismatic chief executive.

An abrupt change in the White House staff in 1985 nearly proved disastrous for Reagan. Tired from the constant infighting, Baker agreed to Secretary of the Treasury Donald Regan's sugges-

As chief of staff, Donald Regan used his position to control access to the President who relied heavily on him until the Iran-Contra scandal drove Regan from the White House.

tion that the two men swap jobs. A self-made Wall Street operator, Regan possessed a confident, abrasive manner and a determination to assert his authority as White House chief-of-staff. When Meese became attorney general and Deaver left the government later in 1985, Regan took advantage of the President's passive nature, extending his own control and thus ending the give-and-take in the oval office that had allowed Reagan to shape the final policy choices during his first term. Lacking Baker's sensitivity to congressional concerns and Deaver's careful nurturing of Reagan's public image, Don Regan soon brought the administration into deep political trouble.

At first, Regan and Baker were able to score a major victory. Intent on lowering tax rates on the wealthy still more while capitalizing on growing congressional demands for a simpler and fairer revenue system, the two men pressed for a major overhaul of the income tax. Making the necessary compromises with reformers in Congress, they shaped the 1986 Tax Reform Act. It cut the top rate from 50 to 28 percent while wiping out most shelters by severely restricting the tax breaks for losses in real estate ventures and many other speculative enterprises. An alternative minimum tax would end the injustice of many wealthy individuals paying no tax at all, while the new rates exempted six million people at the lower end from any tax liability at all. Although corporate rates were also cut, changes in depreciation and tax credits led to a short-term increase of $120 billion in business payments. This helped offset the loss from reductions in individual rates and thus did not add to the budget deficit.

The administration had only partial success in another area—altering the makeup of the federal judiciary. Long unhappy with judges who sought to carry out social change with their decisions, Reagan hoped to fill the federal benches with conservative judges who would simply follow the law and let Congress and state legislatures decide on policy issues. The administration was able to fill the appeals courts with sympathetic judges, most of them wealthy, white males. And in 1986, after a brief skirmish with the Senate, Reagan succeeded in replacing outgoing Chief Justice Warren Burger with the court's strongest conservative, William Rehnquist. Equally conservative appeals court judge Antonin Scalia joined the Supreme Court at the same time. But in 1987, when the President nominated Robert Bork, an outspoken opponent of judicial activism, to fill the next vacancy, Democrats drew the line. Opposition from labor and civil rights groups finally led the Senate to reject Bork's nomination by a vote of 58 to 42. It was a bittersweet victory, however, as Reagan responded by appointing the moderately conservative, but far more diplomatic, Anthony Kennedy to the Court.

The Bork defeat was especially hard on Attorney General Ed Meese, who had been directing the administration's fight against judicial activism. But by then Meese himself had become an embarrassment to Reagan by symbolizing what came to be known as the "sleaze factor." During the hearing on his nomination to the post of Attorney General, charges of loose financial dealings and unethical conduct in office had raised doubts about his judgment. In 1987, charges that he was involved with Wedtech, a defense firm

found guilty of fraud, led to the appointment of a special prosecutor. Although the prosecutor found no evidence that the attorney general had broken the law, he admitted that some of Meese's dealings had the "appearance" of impropriety. The Meese affair was one of a number of episodes that stained the administration's reputation. In December 1987 Deaver was found guilty of lying to Congress about his lobbying activities. Scandals at the Pentagon, involving high officials and members of Congress, and at HUD (Housing and Urban Development) came to light in 1989. These events as well as the earlier EPA scandals involving Ann Gorsuch, left the Reagan administration with the appearance of tolerating corruption at the highest levels of government.

The "sleaze factor," however, was not the highest price that Reagan had to pay for his detached style of leadership. His inattention to detail nearly proved fatal to his presidency when he allowed trusted subordinates to subvert the will of Congress and flout the Constitution in a way the nation had not seen since the days of Watergate.

Trading Arms for Hostages

The Iran-Contra affair began in mid-1985. Robert McFarlane, a retired Marine officer who had replaced William Clark as national security adviser in 1984, began a new initiative in 1985 designed to restore American influence in the troubled Middle East. Concerned over the fate of six Americans held hostage in Lebanon by groups thought to be loyal to Ayatollah Khomeini, McFarlane proposed trading American anti-tank missiles to Iran in return for the hostages' release. Although he realized that the President was primarily concerned with the fate of the hostages, particularly CIA officer William Buckley, McFarlane's primary goal in proposing the exchange was to establish good relations with moderate elements in Iran, anticipating the aged Khomeini's death. The Iranians, desperate for weapons in the war they had been waging against Iraq since 1980, seemed willing to comply.

McFarlane soon found himself in over his head. He relied heavily on a young Marine lieutenant colonel assigned to the National Security Council, Oliver North, and North in turn sought the assistance of CIA Director William Casey. A veteran of the Office of Strategic Services in World War II, Casey saw the Iran initiative as an opportunity to use the NSC to mount the kind of covert operation denied the CIA under the post-1975 congressional oversight policy. By early 1986, when John Poindexter, a naval officer with little political experience, replaced a burned-out McFarlane as national security adviser, Casey was able to persuade the President, over the strenuous objections of both Secretary of State Shultz and Secretary of Defense Weinberger, to go ahead with shipments of both TOW anti-tank missiles and HAWK anti-aircraft missiles to Iran.

The concept of trading arms for hostages was fatally flawed. As Shultz and Weinberger pointed out, the Reagan administration, in an effort to help end the war between Iran and Iraq, had imposed an arms embargo on Iran and had tried to prevent U.S. allies from sending weapons there. Although one hostage had been released after an initial shipment of TOW anti-tank missiles to Iran by way of Israel, the shipments of additional TOWs directly from the United States, as well as HAWK anti-aircraft missiles, had led to the release of only two more hostages. Meanwhile, terrorist groups in Iran had seized several more Americans; by 1987, there were nine Americans being held hostage in Lebanon. As one observer commented, "As soon as Iran realized how highly we valued getting those hostages back, they apparently kept a good supply of hostages to ensure that we would do their bidding."

The arms deal with Iran was bad policy, but what came next was criminal. Ever since the Boland Amendment in late 1984 had cut off congressional funding, the Reagan administration had been searching for ways to supply the Contras. Reagan sought aid from friendly foreign governments, notably Saudi Arabia and Brunei, while Oliver North was put in charge of soliciting donations from wealthy, right-wing Americans. In early 1986, North had what he later described as a "neat idea" (apparently shared by Casey as well)—he could use the enormous profits from the sale of weapons to Iran (charging as much as $10,000 for a TOW that cost the U.S. only $3500) to finance the Contra campaign in Nicaragua. Despite the appeal of using Khomeini's money to pay the Contras and topple the Sandinistas,

North's ploy was clearly not only illegal but unconstitutional, since it meant usurping the congressional power of the purse.

Unlike the policy of trading arms for hostages, the diversion of the profits to the Contras was a closely held secret never debated among Reagan's advisers. Apparently, only North, Casey, and Poindexter were aware of this illegal activity until November 1986, when the press finally learned of the Iranian arms sales. While Attorney General Meese conducted an internal investigation, North hurriedly destroyed most of the incriminating documents, but overlooked one key memo that revealed the Contra diversion.

The political fallout was very heavy. The administration, having learned from the Watergate coverup, tried to control the damage by breaking the bad news itself. Meese disclosed the illegal Contra funding while Reagan appointed John Tower to head a blue ribbon commission to find out what had gone wrong in the National Security Council. Every effort was made to protect Reagan himself. Meese blamed Poindexter and North, who both were dropped from the NSC; the Tower Commission put the responsibility on White House Chief-of-Staff Donald Regan, who at the insistence of Nancy Reagan was forced to resign. Despite these efforts to protect the President's reputation, a CBS–*New York Times* poll taken in December 1986 revealed that Reagan's popularity had dropped from 67 percent to 46

*D*espite Oliver North's questionable conduct, the public elevated him to near-heroic status during the televised Iran-Contra hearings. The bemedaled marine testified that he believed his deeds were justified as a defense of democracy.

percent in just a month, the steepest decline ever recorded.

The vital question of whether Ronald Reagan had approved of the Contra diversion was never answered satisfactorily. The Tower Commission, painting a very unflattering picture of a disengaged president, unaware of what his aides were doing, concluded that he neither knew of nor consented to this illegal move. Public opinion polls indicated that most Americans suspected the President was at least aware of the Contra diversion. In the absence of firm evidence, however, they were willing to give Reagan the benefit of the doubt. A protracted congressional hearing in the summer of 1987 did little to clear up the confusion. Oliver North used his televised appearances to win public sympathy if not approval. Poindexter insisted under oath that he had never informed the President that he and North had used the profits from arms sales to Iran to fund the Contras in defiance of Congress. The only other man who knew what had actually happened was William Casey; his death from a brain tumor in mid-1987 left the mystery unsolved.

While Reagan escaped from the Iran-Contra affair without being held fully responsible for it, his presidency was in serious trouble. In Congress, the Democrats, who gained control of the Senate as well as the House in the 1986 elections, began to override his vetoes, reject his nominees (notably Robert Bork), and bring a total halt to even humanitarian aid to the Contras, whose cause now became hopeless. Ronald Reagan was still in the White House, but his reliance on others to conduct the affairs of state had robbed him of his power to lead the nation.

Reagan the Peacemaker

By the end of 1987, Ronald Reagan and his resourceful new chief-of-staff, former GOP Senate Majority Leader Howard Baker, made a remarkable recovery. Stepping into the foreign affairs arena, Reagan, with strong pressure from his wife, shed his image as a hawk and set out to reverse the course of Soviet-American relations.

The timing was fortunate. Mikhail Gorbachev was equally intent on improving relations as part of his new policy of *perestroika* (restructuring the Soviet economy) and *glasnost* (political openness). Soviet economic performance had been deteriorating steadily under Brezhnev and his successors (Japan replaced the Soviet Union as the world's second largest producer of goods and services in the early 1980s), and the bloody war in Afghanistan, where the U.S. covertly supplied the Mujadeen guerrillas fighting against the Soviet invaders, had become a major liability. Gorbachev needed a breathing spell in the arms race and a reduction in Cold War tensions in order to carry out his sweeping changes at home.

The first meeting between the two leaders, at Geneva in 1985, had gone well, but had not led to any significant agreements. A hurried summit at Reykjavik, Iceland, in October 1986, just before the Iran-Contra affair had become public, nearly led to an historic breakthrough. The two men reached general agreement on the long disputed issue of Intermediate Nuclear Forces in Europe (INF), and then Reagan turned to a more sweeping proposal to ban all nuclear ballistic missiles over a ten year period. Gorbachev went even further, suggesting the abolition of all nuclear weapons within a decade. Reagan, failing to understand the significant difference between all ballistic missiles and all nuclear weapons (American bombers and cruise missiles with nuclear warheads were considered necessary to balance off the large Soviet advantage in conventional forces), quickly agreed, telling Gorbachev that ridding the world of all nuclear weapons had "always been my goal."

Before shocked arms control experts could alert the President to his mistake, the whole deal collapsed when Gorbachev renewed his insistence that the United States give up its plans to develop "star wars," the Strategic Defense Initiative. Reagan, who viewed SDI as a way to render America invulnerable to nuclear attack, refused to concede and the summit broke up without any agreement.

The apparent failure at Reykjavik, however, did not halt the new momentum toward peace; both leaders needed a foreign policy triumph too much not to continue the dialogue. Throughout 1987, experts worked out the details of an INF agreement built on the original Reagan "zero option." What was once considered a propaganda ploy now became the basis for the most significant achievement in disarmament since

*R*eagan and Gorbachev in Red Square. During the summits between the two leaders, the American public grew to admire the Soviet premier for his policies of perestroika (restructuring) and glasnost (openness).

arsenals, but the pictures of Reagan and Gorbachev strolling amiably about Red Square in front of Lenin's tomb, saluting tourists and taking turns kissing babies, gave rise to the hope that an end to the Cold War was finally in sight.

When Reagan returned home, his popularity soared to 70 percent, higher than it had been before the Iran-Contra affair. He had not only succeeded in making a major breakthrough in the nuclear arms race, but he could claim that his policies had led to a moderation in Soviet behavior. During the President's last year in office, the Soviets cooperated with the United States in pressuring Iran and Iraq to end their long war and opening negotiations to remove fifty thousand Soviet-supplied Cuban troops from Angola. Most impressive of all, Gorbachev moved to end the invasion of Afghanistan that had renewed the Cold War in 1979. The first Soviet units pulled out in April 1988, with the final evacuation due to be completed early the next year. By the time Reagan left office in January 1989, he had scored a series of foreign policy triumphs that offset his dismal Iran-Contra fiasco and thus helped redeem his presidency.

The Election of 1988

Despite the President's comeback, the outlook for the Democrats in 1988 was promising. Ronald Reagan would not be on the ballot. The Iran-Contra affair and the looming budget deficit undercut the Republican appeal to peace and prosperity, and most observers thought George Bush, the likely GOP nominee, would be a weak candidate. Michael Dukakis, the successful governor of Massachusetts, emerged from the grueling primary contests as the clear-cut winner. With the selection of moderate Texas Senator Lloyd Bentsen as his vice presidential running mate, Dukakis left the convention at Atlanta confident of victory, with polls showing him ahead by 17 points.

SALT I in 1972. Meeting in Washington in December 1987, Reagan and Gorbachev agreed to remove and destroy all intermediate range missiles (approximately 3 percent of the total arsenal) and to permit on-site inspection to verify this process. Thus, not only did Reagan succeed where Carter had failed in ending the Russian deployment of sophisticated SS-20 missiles targeted at Western Europe, but he could claim that his policy of building up America's defenses and talking tough to the Russians had paid off handsomely.

A fourth Reagan-Gorbachev summit in Moscow in mid-1988 did not achieve any further progress toward the goal of reducing the nuclear

The Election of 1988

Candidate	Party	Popular Vote	Electoral Vote
Bush	Republican	48,886,097	426
Dukakis	Democratic	41,809,074	112

*A*lthough the selection of Dan Quayle as Bush's running mate (left) was criticized by many, the Republicans waged a successful campaign, addressing the American spirit of voluntarism, presenting Dukakis as a governor soft on crime, and promising "no new taxes." Dukakis and Bentsen's (right) unsuccessful strategy stressed competency over patriotic fervor.

Bush quickly regained the lead, despite the controversial choice of Indiana Senator Dan Quayle as his running mate. The Republicans waged a ruthless attack on Dukakis, portraying him as soft on crime and defense, and turning the presidential contest away from potentially embarrassing issues such as the budget deficit and the Iran-Contra affair. Above all, the GOP candidate repeatedly promised not to raise taxes, reiterating his favorite line: "read my lips—no new taxes."

Dukakis fought back, gaining the edge over Bush in the first of two televised debates, but failing to close the narrow gap separating the two candidates in the polls. In the second debate in mid-October, Bush scored an impressive victory. Despite a last-minute surge by Dukakis that rallied traditional Democratic voters with the populist slogan, "I'm on your side," the vice president, with the South secure, concentrated on holding his slim leads in crucial states such as California and Ohio.

The election's outcome confirmed the pollsters' projections. Bush won overwhelmingly in the South, carried most of the West, and defeated Dukakis in such key industrial states as Michigan and Pennsylvania. His victory reflected the continuing GOP dominance of the electoral college, as well as the natural advantage of an incumbent at a time when the economy was healthy and the world at relative peace. Yet Dukakis could take some comfort in blocking a Republican landslide that might have hurt the Democrats in Congress. Indeed, the voters seemed almost schizoid, choosing a Republican president but increasing the Democratic margins in both the House and Senate. Bush would be the first new president since John F. Kennedy to enter the White House while his party lost ground in Congress.

The election of 1988 indicated that, at least on the presidential level, a significant change had taken place in American politics in 1980. Bush consolidated the GOP's grip on the electoral college, winning in the Sun Belt states, which would be due to gain at least 15 more congressional seats and electoral votes after the 1990 census reapportionment. He held much of Reagan's inroads into the working-class vote, scoring 49 percent compared to Reagan's 55 percent among blue collar voters. At the same time, racial polarization in politics continued, with Dukakis getting 88 percent of the African-American vote and 69 percent of the Hispanic ballots.

With Bush in office, major Reagan initiatives would continue, notably the shift away from the welfare state, a lower tax burden on the wealthy, more emphasis on the free market through deregulation, and a strong national defense. At the same time, Bush would have to confront the consequences of Reagan's policies, particularly the large budget deficit, the trade imbalance, the growing opposition to heavy defense spending, and the failure of the Contras to overthrow the Sandinista regime. Above all, he faced the challenge of meeting the high expectations that Reagan and Gorbachev had raised, not only in the United States but throughout the world, to end the Cold War and bring the frightening nuclear arms race under control. Winning the election had proved relatively easy; the real test of Bush's leadership still lay ahead.

A WORLD IN FLUX

Many people expected the Bush administration to reflect the reputation of the new President—bland and cautious, lacking in vision but safely predictable. A startling series of events abroad during his first year in office gave Bush the opportunity to preside over the end of the Cold War. At home, however, he was compelled to deal with issues he inherited from the Reagan years.

The Politics of Postponement

Promised new initiatives in education, health care, and environmental protection were postponed as Bush faced three pressing domestic problems. First, the nation's savings-and-loan industry, based on U.S. government-insured deposits, was in grave trouble as a result of lax regulation and unwise, even possibly fraudulent, loan policies. Second, Congress began to probe into a scandal in the Department of Housing and Urban Development (HUD) in which former secretary Samuel Pierce and members of his staff had allowed favored operators to gain huge profits from urban renewal projects. Most serious of all was the continuing budget deficit. Despite Gramm-Rudman, the nation continued to spend beyond its means, with deficits still running around $150 billion a year.

The President and Congress finally did reach agreement on two outstanding issues. In August, Congress passed an administration bill to close or merge more than 700 ailing savings-and-loans at a cost of $157 billion over a ten-year period. The proposal included a restructuring of the federal regulatory system and bond provisions to keep

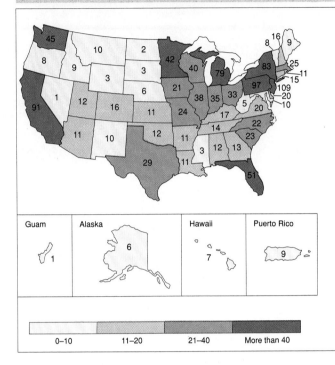

Hazardous Waste Sites, 1988

Part of the legacy left to President George Bush was a nation badly in need of cleanup due to the relaxation of environmental regulations since the 1970s.

Guam | Alaska | Hawaii | Puerto Rico

| 0–10 | 11–20 | 21–40 | More than 40 |

the thrift bailout from adding to the deficit. At first hailed as a victory for Bush, the savings-and-loan bailout soon proved that critics were right in warning that the eventual cost would be far greater than the administration's $157 billion estimate.

Action on the budget proved more difficult. After an early bipartisan agreement to keep the 1991 deficit below $100 billion broke down, the President and Congress allowed Gramm-Rudman to go into effect in October, requiring across-the-board cuts in both defense and domestic spending (but not in entitlements like Social Security and Medicare). Bush held out against any tax increases; Congress insisted on keeping domestic programs intact. In November, the two sides finally compromised on a budget just under the Gramm-Rudman deficit limit of $110 billion for 1991, with $4.6 billion of cuts in both domestic and defense spending, along with an additional $2.9 billion in minor tax changes.

Both the administration and the Democratic-controlled Congress continued to engage in an elaborate charade, since actual spending was expected to raise the deficit far above the projected $105 billion level. And without the Social Security trust fund, the true deficit was likely to run well over $200 billion.

After Bush called for spending $7.5 billion on a renewed war on drugs in September, Congress approved a higher level of spending—$8.8 billion for greater efforts at interdiction and more extensive educational and treatment programs. But even this was an increase of only $3.2 billion in actual expenditures for the war on drugs. While Bush claimed that his new effort would eradicate drug use in America "neighborhood by neighborhood, block by block," critics claimed it was inadequate to meet the challenge. "What we need is another D-Day," declared Democratic Senator Joseph Biden of Delaware, "not another Vietnam, not a limited war, fought on the cheap and destined for stalemate and human tragedy."

The End of the Cold War

Abroad, the Bush administration faced an unprecedented year of change that appeared to mark the end of the post–World War II era. In country after country, Communism gave way to freedom as the Cold War seemed to fade away more quickly than anyone had dared hope.

The first attempt at internal liberation proved tragically abortive. In May, students in China began a month-long demonstration for freedom in Beijing's Tiananmen Square that attracted worldwide attention. Watching American television coverage of Gorbachev's visit to China in mid-May, Americans were fascinated to see the Chinese students call for democracy with a hunger strike and a hand-crafted replica of the Statue of Liberty. But on the evening of June 4, the Chinese leaders sent tanks and troops to Tiananmen Square to crush the student demonstration. By the next day, full-scale repression swept over China; several hundred protesters were killed

Fed up with the corruption that accompanied the economic benefits of Chinese leader Deng Xiaoping's reforms, Chinese students demonstrated for democracy. The nonviolent protest in Tiananmen square evoked a suprisingly passive government response at first, but after a short time, military action was called for to break the students' resistance. Tanks, armored personnel carriers, and trucks cleared the square after firing randomly on unarmed students.

and thousands were injured. Chinese leaders Deng Xiaoping and Li Peng imposed martial law to quell the dissent and shatter American hopes for a democratic China.

President Bush responded cautiously. While he did suspend sales of military equipment to China and stopped all government-to-government trade, he neither imposed stiffer sanctions nor engaged in harsh rhetoric. Bush wanted to preserve American influence with the Chinese government. Hence, despite official statements denouncing the crackdown, Bush permitted National Security Adviser Brent Scowcroft to undertake a secret mission to Beijing to maintain a working relationship with the Chinese leaders.

A far more promising trend toward freedom began in Europe in mid-1989. In June, Lech Walesa and his Solidarity movement came to power in free elections in Poland. Soon the winds of change were sweeping over the former Iron Curtain countries. A new regime in Hungary opened its borders to the West in September,

allowing thousands of East German tourists in Hungary to flee to freedom. One by one, the repressive governments of East Germany, Czechoslovakia, Bulgaria, and Rumania fell. Most fell peacefully; only in Rumania did brutal violence break out, leading to the execution of its dictator, Nicolae Ceaucescu. The most heartening scene of all took place in East Germany in early November when the new Communist leaders suddenly announced the opening of the Berlin Wall. Workers quickly demolished a 12-foot high section of this despised physical symbol of the Cold War, joyously singing a German version of "For He's a Jolly Good Fellow."

Most people realized it was Mikhail Gorbachev who was responsible for the liberation of Eastern Europe. In late 1988, he signaled the spread of his reforms to the Soviet satellites by announcing that the Brezhnev doctrine, which called for Soviet control of Eastern Europe, was now replaced with "the Sinatra doctrine," which meant the people of this region could now do things

The Iron Curtain Rises

Free elections in Poland in June 1989 triggered the domino effect in the liberation of Eastern Europe. Changes in policy have come quickly, but it is already clear that the restructuring of social and economic institutions will take much longer.

1. **Latvia and Estonia** begin process of separation from Soviet Union, April 1990.
2. **Lithuania** declares independence, March 1990; Moscow calls move illegal.
3. **Poland.** Solidarity Party sweeps elections, June 1989.
4. **East Germany.** Communist government opens borders and Berlin Wall is breached, Nov. 1989; leadership resigns, Dec. 1989; free elections held, March 1990.
5. **Czechoslovakia.** Communist leadership ousted, Nov. 1989; famed dissident playwright Vaclav Havel named president, Dec. 1989.
6. **Hungary.** Free election sweeps non-Communists into power, April 1990.
7. **Romania.** Communist dictator Ceausescu overthrown and executed, Dec. 1989; Salvation Front led by dissident former Communists wins elections, May 1990.
8. **Bulgaria.** Government disavows "dominant role" for Communist Party; pledges free elections and new constitution in 1990.
9. **Yugoslavia.** Government decides to hold free elections, Dec. 1989.
10. **Albania.** Communist Party still retains Leninist orientation.

"their way." It was Gorbachev's refusal to use armed force to keep repressive regimes in power that permitted the long-delayed liberation of the captive peoples of Central and Eastern Europe.

The American response to these startling developments was slow and restrained. Fearful that any attempt to take credit would endanger Gorbachev's position in the Soviet Union, Bush favored a low-key approach. In part, this was the result of being caught by surprise. "We freely admit that events are happening so fast," one Bush adviser admitted, "that we can't keep pace with them or even comprehend them at times." The President did agree to meet with Gorbachev at a hastily-called summit conference at Malta in December 1989, which signified American approval for the new order emerging in Europe and speeded up nuclear and conventional arms control talks already under way. Bush was particularly cautious on the issue of German reunification, but in early 1990, he called for a substantial reduction of both American and Soviet troops in Europe.

Bush's most dramatic move, however, came in Latin America, not in Europe. In December 1989, twenty-six thousand American troops invaded Panama and quickly installed a new government friendly to the United States. Despite the death of twenty-three Americans and several hundred Panamanians, this action won approval from the people of both countries when it resulted in the capture of drug trafficking General Manuel Noriega. By taking such bold and decisive action in Panama, Bush was able to shake his reputation for caution. In early 1990, he received an 80 percent public approval rating, the highest accorded to any American president since John F. Kennedy. With the Cold War waning and the United States firmly in control of the Western Hemisphere, the American people were pleased with the political state of the world.

At the beginning of the last decade of the 20th century, George Bush was in an enviable position. While he still had to resolve long-standing domestic issues like the deficit and the war on drugs, Bush had the chance to work on such neglected but important areas as protection of the environment and overhaul of the educational system. Less ideological and confrontational than

*J*ubilant citizens from both East and West Germany joined to bring down the Berlin Wall in November 1989. Observers around the world cheered the triumph of freedom.

his predecessor, he sought common ground with the Democratic Congress and set forth a new agenda of constructive change in American political life. The lessening of Cold War tensions promised significantly lower levels of defense spending and thus the possibility of a "peace dividend" that would both reduce the deficit and pay for long-deferred social programs.

The outlook abroad was even brighter. Bush might have the chance to proclaim not merely the end of the Cold War, but the ultimate triumph of the policy of containment. For more than four decades, American leaders had resisted Communist aggression in the hope that people everywhere would have the right to choose their rulers and live in freedom. This transformation had taken far longer than George Kennan had predicted back in the late 1940s, but under Gorbachev, the Soviet Union appeared to be undergoing fundamental changes that ended the Soviet threat to American security. The new international order that was emerging in the 1990s might have dangers of its own—notably in German reunification and continued Japanese economic supremacy. But as the Cold War eased, people everywhere could look forward to the end of both the nuclear arms race and its risk of total

1980	Ronald Reagan wins presidency in landslide
1981	American hostages in Iran released after 444 days in captivity (January) • Reagan breaks air controllers' strike by decertifying their union (August) • Sandra Day O'Connor becomes first woman U.S. Supreme Court justice (September)
1982	Equal Rights Amendment fails state ratification (June) • Unemployment reaches postwar record high of 10.4 percent (October)
1983	Soviets shoot down Korean airliner (September) • Terrorist bomb kills 239 marines in Beirut barracks (October) • U.S. invades Grenada (October)
1984	Russia boycotts summer Olympics in Los Angeles (July) • Ronald Reagan reelected president (November)
1985	Mikhail Gorbachev becomes leader of the Soviet Union (March) • United States becomes debtor nation for first time since 1914
1986	Congress passes major tax reform legislation (September) • Iran-Contra affair made public (November)
1987	Reagan and Gorbachev sign INF treaty at Washington summit
1988	George Bush defeats Michael Dukakis decisively in presidential election
1989	Supreme Court retreats on abortion issue in *Webster* decision • Bush orders U.S. invasion of Panama (December)

destruction. In that sense, George Bush had an opportunity unlike that of any other American president since World War II to lay the foundation for a truly peaceful world.

Recommended Reading

The best introduction to Ronald Reagan is Garry Wills, *Reagan's America* (1987), a provocative analysis of the various images of American life that the future President used as substitutes for reality. Robert Schieffer and Gary Paul Gates offer a critical overview of the Reagan administration in *The Acting President* (1989). Focusing on Reagan's detached style of leadership, they concentrate on the people to whom he delegated authority.

The best account by an insider, and the only one to give a positive view of the Reagan presidency, is Martin Anderson, *Revolution* (1988).

Additional Bibliography

Theodore White offers a stimulating account of the political changes in the 1970s that led to Reagan's election to the presidency in *America in Search of Itself* (1982). Books on the 1980 election include Elizabeth Drew, *Portrait of an Election* (1981); Jack W. Germond and Jules Witcover, *Blue Smoke and Mirrors* (1981); and Thomas Ferguson and Joel Rogers, eds., *The Hidden Election of 1980* (1981). For the conservative resurgence see Peter Steinfels, *The Neo-Conservatives* (1979); Sidney Blumenthal, *The Rise of the Counter-Establishment* (1986), a critical account; and F. Clifton White and William Gil, *Why Reagan Won: The Conservative Movement, 1964–1981* (1982), a more sympathetic view.

Lou Cannon, *Reagan* (1982) offers the most thorough biography of the President. For more interpretive accounts, see Robert Dallek, *Ronald Reagan* (1984) and Michael Paul Rogin, *Ronald Reagan: The Movie* (1987). Reagan's early successes in cutting taxes and domestic spending can be traced in Rowland Evans and Robert Novak, *The Reagan Revolution* (1981); Lawrence Barrett, *Gambling with History* (1983); Fred Greenstein, ed., *The Reagan Presidency* (1983); and John L. Palmer and Isabel V. Sawhill, eds., *The Reagan Experiment* (1982). C. Brandt Short traces the conservation debate in *Ronald Reagan and the Public Lands* (1989).

The fullest account of the 1984 election is Peter Goldman and Tony Fuller, *The Quest for the Presidency 1984* (1985), but see also Elizabeth Drew, *Campaign Journal* (1985); Jack W. Germond and Jules Witcover, *Wake Us When It's Over* (1985); and Geraldine Ferraro, *My Story* (1985). Thomas Ferguson and Joel Rogers analyze the political realignment of the 1980s in *Right Turn* (1985).

Memoirs by White House staffers, many containing revelations embarrassing to the administration, include David Stockman, *The Triumph of Politics* (1986), critical of Reaganomics; Michael Deaver, *Behind the Scenes* (1987); Larry Speakes, *Speaking Out* (1988); and Donald Regan, *For the Record* (1988), a particularly vengeful account by the former White House chief-of-staff.

William G. Hyland provides an overview of American diplomacy in the 1980s in *The Reagan Foreign Policy* (1987) as does Coral Bell in *The Reagan Paradox* (1990). Reagan's first secretary of state, Alexander M. Haig, Jr., gives his views in *Caveat* (1984). On Central America, see the essays edited by Kenneth M. Coleman and George C. Herring, *The Central American Crisis* (1985) and two books on Nicaragua, Robert Pastor, *Condemned to Repetition* (1988) and Roy Gutman, *Banana Diplomacy* (1988). Paul B. Stares traces the development of the Strategic Defense Initiative in *Space and National Security* (1987). The best studies of arms control in the 1980s are two books by Strobe Talbott, *Deadly Gambits* (1984), on the failure of Reagan's early efforts, and *The Master of the Game* (1988), on the role of Paul Nitze.

The Reagan administration's attempts to deal with the cocaine problem are traced in Elaine Shannon, *Desperados* (1988) and James A. Inciardi, *The War on Drugs* (1986). The best account of the impact of AIDS on American life in the 1980s is Randy Shilts, *And the Band Played On* (1987). For economic developments, see Michael J. Boskin, *Reagan and the Economy* (1987), a spirited defense of Reaganomics, and Clyde V. Prestowitz, Jr., *Trading Places* (1988), critical of the Reagan administration's handling of the Japanese trade offensive.

The fullest account of the Iran-Contra affair is Jane Mayer and Doyle McManus, *Landslide* (1988). For views of insiders, see *Perilous Statecraft* (1988) by Michael A. Ledeen, one of the original conspirators, and *Men of Zeal* (1988) by William S. Cohen and George J. Mitchell, the two Maine senators who served on the congressional investigating committee. Bob Woodward traces CIA Director William Casey's role in the Iran-Contra affair, as well as other covert activities of the 1980s, in *Veil* (1987).

The best assessment of the overall impact of the Reagan presidency on American life can be found in the essays edited by Sidney Blumenthal and Thomas Byrne Edsall, *The Reagan Legacy* (1988). For the election of 1988, see Jack W. Germond and Jules Witcover, *Whose Broad Stripes and Bright Stars?* (1989).

APPENDIX

The Declaration of Independence

*Constitution of the United States of America
and Amendments*

Choosing the President

Cabinet Members

Supreme Court Justices

Admission of States into the Union

Growth of U.S. Population, 1790–1987

*U.S. Population Projections by Region and State,
1988, 1990, 2000, 2010*

The Declaration of Independence

In Congress, July 4, 1776

The Unanimous Declaration
of the Thirteen United States of America,

When, in the course of human events, it becomes necessary for one people to dissolve the political bonds which have connected them with another, and to assume, among the powers of the earth, the separate and equal station to which the laws of nature and of nature's God entitle them, a decent respect to the opinions of mankind requires that they should declare the causes which impel them to the separation.

We hold these truths to be self-evident: That all men are created equal; that they are endowed by their Creator with certain unalienable rights; that among these are life, liberty, and the pursuit of happiness; that, to secure these rights, governments are instituted among men, deriving their just powers from the consent of the governed; that whenever any form of government becomes destructive of these ends, it is the right of the people to alter or to abolish it, and to institute new government, laying its foundation on such principles, and organizing its powers in such form, as to them shall seem most likely to effect their safety and happiness. Prudence, indeed, will dictate that governments long established should not be changed for light and transient causes; and accordingly all experience hath shown that mankind are more disposed to suffer, while evils are sufferable, than to right themselves by abolishing the forms to which they are accustomed. But when a long train of abuses and usurpations, pursuing invariably the same object, evinces a design to reduce them under absolute despotism, it is their right, it is their duty, to throw off such government, and to provide new guards for their future security. Such has been the patient sufferance of these colonies; and such is now the necessity which constrains them to alter their former systems of government. The history of the present King of Great Britain is a history of repeated injuries and usurpations, all having in direct object the establishment of an absolute tyranny over these states. To prove this, let facts be submitted to a candid world.

He has refused his assent to laws, the most wholesome and necessary for the public good.

He has forbidden his governors to pass laws of immediate and pressing importance, unless suspended in their operation till his assent should be obtained; and, when so suspended, he has utterly neglected to attend to them.

He has refused to pass other laws for the accommodation of large districts of people, unless those people would relinquish the right of representation in the legislature, a right inestimable to them, and formidable to tyrants only.

He has called together legislative bodies at places unusual, uncomfortable, and distant from the depository of their public records, for the sole purpose of fatiguing them into compliance with his measures.

He has dissolved representative houses repeatedly, for opposing, with many firmness, his invasions on the rights of the people.

He has refused for a long time, after such disolutions, to cause others to be elected; whereby the legislative powers, incapable of annihilation, have returned to the people at large for their exercise; the state remaining, in the mean time, exposed to all the dangers of invasions from without and convulsions within.

He has endeavored to prevent the population of these states; for that purpose obstructing the laws for naturalization of foreigners; refusing to pass others to encourage their migration hither, and raising the conditions of new appropriations of lands.

He has obstructed the administration of justice, by refusing his assent to laws for establishing judiciary powers.

He has made judges dependent on his will alone, for the tenure of their offices, and the amount and payment of their salaries.

He has erected a multitude of new offices, and sent hither swarms of officers to harass our people and eat out their substance.

He has kept among us, in times of peace, standing armies, without the consent of our legislatures.

He has affected to render the military independent of, and superior to, the civil power.

He has combined with others to subject us to a jurisdiction foreign to our constitution, and unacknowledged by our laws, giving his assent to their acts of pretended legislation:

For quartering large bodies of armed troops among us;

For protecting them, by a mock trial, from punishment for any murder which they should commit on the inhabitants of these states;

For cutting off our trade with all parts of the world;

For imposing taxes on us without our consent;

For depriving us, in many cases, of the benefits of trial by jury;

For transporting us beyond seas, to be tried for pretended offenses;

For abolishing the free system of English laws in a neighboring province, establishing therein an arbitrary government, and enlarging its boundaries, so as to render it at once an example and fit instrument for introducing the same absolute rule into these colonies;

For taking away our charters, abolishing our most

valuable laws, and altering fundamentally the forms of our governments;

For suspending our own legislatures, and declaring themselves invested with power to legislate for us in all cases whatsoever.

He has abdicated government here, by declaring us out of his protection and waging war against us.

He has plundered our seas, ravaged our coasts, burned our towns, and destroyed the lives of our people.

He is at this time transporting large armies of foreign mercenaries to complete the works of death, desolation, and tyranny already begun with circumstances of cruelty and perfidy scarcely paralleled in the most barbarous ages, and totally unworthy the head of a civilized nation.

He has constrained our fellow-citizens, taken captive on the high seas, to bear arms against their country, to become the executioners of their friends and brethren, or to fall themselves by their hands.

He has excited domestic insurrection among us, and has endeavored to bring on the inhabitants of our frontiers the merciless Indian savages, whose known rule of warfare is an undistinguished destruction of all ages, sexes, and conditions.

In every stage of these oppressions we have petitioned for redress in the most humble terms; our repeated petitions have been answered only by repeated injury. A prince, whose character is thus marked by every act which may define a tyrant, is unfit to be the ruler of a free people.

Nor have we been wanting in our attentions to our British brethren. We have warned them, from time to time, of attempts by their legislature to extend an unwarrantable jurisdiction over us. We have reminded them of the circumstances of our emigration and settlement here. We have appealed to their native justice and magnanimity; and we have conjured them, by the ties of our common kindred, to disavow these usurpations, which would inevitably interrupt our connections and correspondence. They, too, have been deaf to the voice of justice and of consanguinity. We must, therefore, acquiesce in the necessity which denounces our separation, and hold them, as we hold the rest of mankind, enemies in war, in peace friends.

We, therefore, the representatives of the United States of America, in General Congress assembled, appealing to the Supreme Judge of the world for the rectitude of our intentions, do, in the name and by the authority of the good people of these colonies, solemnly publish and declare, that these United Colonies are, and of right ought to be, FREE AND INDEPENDENT STATES; that they are absolved from all allegiance to the British crown, and that all political connection between them and the state of Great Britain is, and ought to be, totally dissolved; and that, as free and independent states, they have full power to levy war, conclude peace, contract alliances, establish commerce, and do all other acts and things which independent states may of right do. And for the support of this declaration, with a firm reliance on the protection of Divine Providence, we mutually pledge to each other our lives, our fortunes, and our sacred honor.

JOHN HANCOCK

BUTTON GWINNETT
LYMAN HALL
GEO. WALTON
WM. HOOPER
JOSEPH HEWES
JOHN PENN
EDWARD RUTLEDGE
THOS. HEYWARD, JUNR.
THOMAS LYNCH, JUNR.
ARTHUR MIDDLETON
SAMUEL CHASE
WM. PACA
THOS. STONE
CHARLES CARROLL OF CARROLLTON
GEORGE WYTHE
RICHARD HENRY LEE
TH. JEFFERSON
BENJ. HARRISON

THOS. NELSON, JR.
FRANCIS LIGHTFOOT LEE
CARTER BRAXTON
ROBT. MORRIS
BENJAMIN RUSH
BENJA. FRANKLIN
JOHN MORTON
GEO. CLYMER
JAS. SMITH
GEO. TAYLOR
JAMES WILSON
GEO. ROSS
CAESAR RODNEY
GEO. READ
THO. M'KEAN
WM. FLOYD
PHIL. LIVINGSTON
FRANS. LEWIS
LEWIS MORRIS

RICHD. STOCKTON
JNO. WITHERSPOON
FRAS. HOPKINSON
JOHN HART
ABRA. CLARK
JOSIAH BARTLETT
WM. WHIPPLE
SAML. ADAMS
JOHN ADAMS
ROBT. TREAT PAINE
ELBRIDGE GERRY
STEP. HOPKINS
WILLIAM ELLERY
ROGER SHERMAN
SAM'EL HUNTINGTON
WM. WILLIAMS
OLIVER WOLCOTT
MATTHEW THORNTON

The Constitution of the United States of America

Preamble

We the people of the United States, in order to form a more perfect union, establish justice, insure domestic tranquillity, provide for the common defense, promote the general welfare, and secure the blessings of liberty to ourselves and our posterity, do ordain and establish this Constitution for the United States of America.

Article I

Section 1   All legislative powers herein granted shall be vested in a Congress of the United States, which shall consist of a Senate and a House of Representatives.

Section 2   The House of Representatives shall be composed of members chosen every second year by the people of the several States, and the electors in each State shall have the qualifications requisite for electors of the most numerous branch of the State Legislature.

No person shall be a Representative who shall not have attained to the age of twenty-five years, and been seven years a citizen of the United States, and who shall not, when elected, be an inhabitant of that State in which he shall be chosen.

Representatives and direct taxes shall be apportioned among the several States which may be included within this Union, according to their respective numbers, *which shall be determined by adding to the whole number of free persons, including those bound to service for a term of years and excluding Indians not taxed, three-fifths of all other persons.* The actual enumeration shall be made within three years after the first meeting of the Congress of the United States, and within every subsequent term of ten years, in such manner as they shall by law direct. The number of Representatives shall not exceed one for every thirty thousand, but each State shall have at least one Representative; *and until such enumeration shall be made, the State of New Hampshire shall be entitled to choose three, Massachusetts eight, Rhode Island and Providence Plantations one, Connecticut five, New York six, New Jersey four, Pennsylvania eight, Delaware one, Maryland six, Virginia ten, North Carolina five, South Carolina five, and Georgia three.*

When vacancies happen in the representation from any State, the Executive authority thereof shall issue writs of election to fill such vacancies.

The House of Representatives shall choose their Speaker and other officers; and shall have the sole power of impeachment.

Section 3   The Senate of the United States shall be composed of two Senators from each State, *chosen by the legislature thereof,* for six years; and each Senator shall have one vote.

Passages no longer in effect are printed in italic type.

Immediately after they shall be assembled in consequence of the first election, they shall be divided as equally as may be into three classes. The seats of the Senators of the first class shall be vacated at the expiration of the second year, of the second class at the expiration of the fourth year, and of the third class at the expiration of the sixth year, so that one-third may be chosen every second year; and if vacancies happen by resignation or otherwise, during the recess of the legislature of any State, the Executive thereof may make temporary appointments until the next meeting of the legislature, which shall then fill such vacancies.

No person shall be a Senator who shall not have attained to the age of thirty years, and been nine years a citizen of the United States, and who shall not, when elected, be an inhabitant of that State for which he shall be chosen.

The Vice-President of the United States shall be President of the Senate, but shall have no vote, unless they be equally divided.

The Senate shall choose their other officers, and also a President *pro tempore,* in the absence of the Vice-President, or when he shall exercise the office of President of the United States.

The Senate shall have the sole power to try all impeachments. When sitting for that purpose, they shall be on oath or affirmation. When the President of the United States is tried, the Chief Justice shall preside: and no person shall be convicted without the concurrence of two-thirds of the members present.

Judgment in cases of impeachment shall not extend further than to removal from the office, and disqualification to hold and enjoy any office of honor, trust or profit under the United States: but the party convicted shall nevertheless be liable and subject to indictment, trial, judgment and punishment, according to law.

Section 4   The times, places and manner of holding elections for Senators and Representatives shall be prescribed in each State by the legislature thereof; but the Congress may at any time by law make or alter such regulations, except as to the places of choosing Senators.

The Congress shall assemble at least once in every year, and such meeting *shall be on the first Monday in December, unless they shall by law appoint a different day.*

Section 5   Each house shall be the judge of the elections, returns and qualifications of its own members, and a majority of each shall constitute a quorum to do business; but a smaller number may adjourn from day to day, and may be authorized to compel the attendance of absent members, in such manner, and under such penalties, as each house may provide.

Each house may determine the rules of its proceedings, punish its members for disorderly behavior, and with the concurrence of two-thirds, expel a member.

Each house shall keep a journal of its proceedings, and

from time to time publish the same, excepting such parts as may in their judgment require secrecy; and the yeas and nays of the members of either house on any question shall, at the desire of one-fifth of those present, be entered on the journal.

Neither house, during the session of Congress, shall, without the consent of the other, adjourn for more than three days, nor to any other place than that in which the two houses shall be sitting.

Section 6   The Senators and Representatives shall receive a compensation for their services, to be ascertained by law and paid out of the treasury of the United States. They shall in all cases except treason, felony and breach of the peace, be privileged from arrest during their attendance at the session of their respective houses, and in going to and returning from the same; and for any speech or debate in either house, they shall not be questioned in any other place.

No Senator or Representative shall, during the time for which he was elected, be appointed to any civil office under the authority of the United States, which shall have been created, or the emoluments whereof shall have been increased, during such time; and no person holding any office under the United States shall be a member of either house during his continuance in office.

Section 7   All bills for raising revenue shall originate in the House of Representatives; but the Senate may propose or concur with amendments as on other bills.

Every bill which shall have passed the House of Representatives and the Senate, shall, before it become a law, be presented to the President of the United States; if he approve he shall sign it, but if not he shall return it with objections to that house in which it originated, who shall enter the objections at large on their journal, and proceed to reconsider it. If after such reconsideration two-thirds of that house shall agree to pass the bill, it shall be sent, together with the objections, to the other house, by which it shall likewise be reconsidered, and, if approved by two-thirds of that house, it shall become a law. But in all such cases the votes of both houses shall be determined by yeas and nays, and the names of the persons voting for and against the bill shall be entered on the journal of each house respectively. If any bill shall not be returned by the President within ten days (Sundays excepted) after it shall have been presented to him, the same shall be a law, in like manner as if he had signed it, unless the Congress by their adjournment prevent its return, in which case it shall not be a law.

Every order, resolution, or vote to which the concurrence of the Senate and House of Representatives may be necessary (except on a question of adjournment) shall be presented to the President of the United States; and before the same shall take effect, shall be approved by him, or being disapproved by him, shall be repassed by two-thirds of the Senate and House of Representatives, according to the rules and limitations prescribed in the case of a bill.

Section 8   The Congress shall have power

To lay and collect taxes, duties, imposts, and excises, to pay the debts and provide for the common defense and general welfare of the United States; but all duties, imposts and excises shall be uniform throughout the United States;

To borrow money on the credit of the United States;

To regulate commerce with foreign nations, and among the several States, and with the Indian tribes;

To establish an uniform rule of naturalization, and uniform laws on the subject of bankruptcies throughout the United States;

To coin money, regulate the value thereof, and of foreign coin, and fix the standard of weights and measures;

To provide for the punishment of counterfeiting the securities and current coin of the United States;

To establish post offices and post roads;

To promote the progress of science and useful arts by securing for limited times to authors and inventors the exclusive right to their respective writings and discoveries;

To constitute tribunals inferior to the Supreme Court;

To define and punish piracies and felonies committed on the high seas and offenses against the law of nations;

To declare war, grant letters of marque and reprisal, and make rules concerning captures on land and water;

To raise and support armies, but no appropriation of money to that use shall be for a longer term than two years;

To provide and maintain a navy;

To make rules for the government and regulation of the land and naval forces;

To provide for calling forth the militia to execute the laws of the Union, suppress insurrections, and repel invasions;

To provide for organizing, arming, and disciplining the militia, and for governing such part of them as may be employed in the service of the United States, reserving to the States respectively the appointment of the officers, and the authority of training the militia according to the discipline prescribed by Congress;

To exercise exclusive legislation in all cases whatsoever, over such district (not exceeding ten miles square) as may, by cession of particular States, and the acceptance of Congress, become the seat of government of the United States, and to exercise like authority over all places purchased by the consent of the legislature of the State, in which the same shall be, for erection of forts, magazines, arsenals, dock-yards, and other needful buildings;—and

To make all laws which shall be necessary and proper for carrying into execution the foregoing powers, and all other powers vested by this Constitution in the government of the United States, or in any department or officer thereof:

Section 9   *The migration or importation of such persons as any of the States now existing shall think proper to admit shall not be prohibited by the Congress prior to the year 1808; but a tax or duty may be imposed on such importation, not exceeding $10 for each person.*

The privilege of the writ of habeas corpus shall not be suspended, unless when in cases of rebellion or invasion the public safety may require it.

No bill of attainder or ex post facto law shall be passed.

No capitation, or other direct, tax shall be laid, unless in proportion to the census or enumeration herein before directed to be taken.

No tax or duty shall be laid on articles exported from any State.

No preference shall be given by any regulation of commerce or revenue to the ports of one State over those of another; nor shall vessels bound to, or from, one State, be obliged to enter, clear, or pay duties in another.

No money shall be drawn from the treasury, but in consequence of appropriations made by law; and a regular statement and account of the receipts and expenditures of all public money shall be published from time to time.

No title of nobility shall be granted by the United States: and no person holding any office of profit or trust under them, shall, without the consent of the Congress, accept of any present, emolument, office, or title, of any kind whatever, from any king, prince, or foreign state.

Section 10   No State shall enter into any treaty, alliance, or confederation; grant letters of marque and reprisal; coin money; emit bills of credit; make anything but gold and silver coin a tender in payment of debts; pass any bill of attainder, ex post facto law, or law impairing the obligation of contracts, or grant any title of nobility.

No State shall, without the consent of Congress, lay any imposts or duties on imports or exports, except what may be absolutely necessary for executing its inspection laws: and the net produce of all duties and imposts, laid by any State on imports or exports, shall be for the use of the treasury of the United States; and all such laws shall be subject to the revision and control of the Congress.

No State shall, without the consent of Congress, lay any duty of tonnage, keep troops or ships of war in time of peace, enter into any agreement or compact with another State, or with a foreign power, or engage in war, unless actually invaded, or in such imminent danger as will not admit of delay.

Article II

Section 1   The executive power shall be vested in a President of the United States of America. He shall hold his office during the term of four years, and, together with the Vice-President, chosen for the same term, be elected as follows:

Each State shall appoint, in such manner as the legislature thereof may direct, a number of electors, equal to the whole number of Senators and Representatives to which the State may be entitled in the Congress; but no Senator or Representative, or person holding an office of trust or profit under the United States, shall be appointed an elector.

The electors shall meet in their respective States, and vote by ballot for two persons, of whom one at least shall not be an inhabitant of the same State with themselves. And they shall make a list of all the persons voted for, and of the number of votes for each; which list they shall sign and certify, and transmit sealed to the seat of government of the United States,

directed to the President of the Senate. The President of the Senate shall, in the presence of the Senate and House of Representatives, open all the certificates, and the votes shall then be counted. The person having the greatest number of votes shall be the President, if such number be a majority of the whole number of electors appointed; and if there be more than one who have such majority, and have an equal number of votes, then the House of Representatives shall immediately choose by ballot one of them for President; and if no person have a majority, then from the five highest on the list said house shall in like manner choose the President. But in choosing the President the votes shall be taken by States, the representation from each State having one vote; a quorum for this purpose shall consist of a member or members from two-thirds of the States, and a majority of all the States shall be necessary to a choice. In every case, after the choice of the President, the person having the greatest number of votes of the electors shall be the Vice-President. But if there should remain two or more who have equal votes, the Senate shall choose from them by ballot the Vice-President.

The Congress may determine the time of choosing the electors and the day on which they shall give their votes; which day shall be the same throughout the United States.

No person except a natural-born citizen, *or a citizen of the United States at the time of the adoption of this Constitution,* shall be eligible to the office of President; neither shall any person be eligible to that office who shall not have attained to the age of thirty-five years, and been fourteen years a resident within the United States.

In case of the removal of the President from office or of his death, resignation, or inability to discharge the powers and duties of the said office, the same shall devolve on the Vice-President, and the Congress may by law provide for the case of removal, death, resignation, or inability, both of the President and Vice-President, declaring what officer shall then act as President, and such officer shall act accordingly, until the disability be removed, or a President shall be elected.

The President shall, at stated times, receive for his services a compensation, which shall neither be increased nor diminished during the period for which he shall have been elected, and he shall not receive within that period any other emolument from the United States, or any of them.

Before he enter on the execution of his office, he shall take the following oath or affirmation:—"I do solemnly swear (or affirm) that I will faithfully execute the office of the President of the United States, and will to the best of my ability preserve, protect and defend the Constitution of the United States."

Section 2   The President shall be commander in chief of the army and navy of the United States, and of the militia of the several States, when called into the actual service of the United States; he may require the opinion, in writing, of the principal officer in each of the executive departments, upon any subject relating to the duties of their respective offices, and he shall have power to grant reprieves and pardons for offenses against the United States, except in cases of impeachment.

He shall have power, by and with the advice and

consent of the Senate, to make treaties, provided two-thirds of the Senators present concur; and he shall nominate, and by and with the advice and consent of the Senate, shall appoint ambassadors, other public ministers and consuls, judges of the Supreme Court, and all other officers of the United States, whose appointments are not herein otherwise provided for, and which shall be established by law: but Congress may by law vest the appointment of such inferior officers, as they think proper, in the President alone, in the courts of law, or in the heads of departments.

The President shall have power to fill up all vacancies that may happen during the recess of the Senate, by granting commissions which shall expire at the end of their next session.

Section 3   He shall from time to time give to the Congress information of the state of the Union, and recommend to their consideration such measures as he shall judge necessary and expedient; he may, on extraordinary occasions, convene both houses, or either of them, and in case of disagreement between them, with respect to the time of adjournment, he may adjourn them to such time as he shall think proper; he shall receive ambassadors and other public ministers; he shall take care that the laws be faithfully executed, and shall commission all the officers of the United States.

Section 4   The President, Vice-President and all civil officers of the United States shall be removed from office on impeachment for, and on conviction of, treason, bribery, or other high crimes and misdemeanors.

Article III

Section 1   The judicial power of the United States shall be vested in one Supreme Court, and in such inferior courts as the Congress may from time to time ordain and establish. The judges, both of the Supreme and inferior courts, shall hold their offices during good behavior, and shall, at stated times, receive for their services a compensation which shall not be diminished during their continuance in office.

Section 2   The judicial power shall extend to all cases, in law and equity, arising under this Constitution, the laws of the United States, and treaties made, or which shall be made, under their authority;—to all cases affecting ambassadors, other public ministers and consuls;—to all cases of admiralty and maritime jurisdiction;—to controversies to which the United States shall be a party;—to controversies between two or more States;—*between a State and citizens of another State;*—between citizens of different States,—between citizens of the same State claiming lands under grants of different States, and between a State, or the citizens thereof, and foreign states, citizens or subjects.

In all cases affecting ambassadors, other public ministers and consuls, and those in which a State shall be party, the Supreme Court shall have original jurisdiction. In all

the other cases before mentioned, the Supreme Court shall have appellate jurisdiction, both as to law and fact, with such exceptions, and under such regulations, as the Congress shall make.

The trial of all crimes, except in cases of impeachment, shall be by jury; and such trial shall be held in the State where said crimes shall have been committed; but when not committed within any State, the trial shall be at such place or places as the Congress may by law have directed.

Section 3   Treason against the United States shall consist only in levying war against them, or in adhering to their enemies, giving them aid and comfort. No person shall be convicted of treason unless on the testimony of two witnesses to the same overt act, or on confession in open court.

The Congress shall have power to declare the punishment of treason, but no attainder of treason shall work corruption of blood, or forfeiture except during the life of the person attainted.

Article IV

Section 1   Full faith and credit shall be given in each State to the public acts, records, and judicial proceedings of every other State. And the Congress may by general laws prescribe the manner in which such acts, records, and proceedings shall be proved, and the effect thereof.

Section 2   The citizens of each State shall be entitled to all privileges and immunities of citizens in the several States.

A person charged in any State with treason, felony, or other crime, who shall flee from justice, and be found in another State, shall on demand of the executive authority of the State from which he fled, be delivered up, to be removed to the State having jurisdiction of the crime.

No person held to service or labor in one State, under the laws thereof, escaping into another, shall, in consequence of any law or regulation therein, be discharged from such service or labor, but shall be delivered up on claim of the party to whom such service or labor may be due.

Section 3   New States may be admitted by the Congress into this Union; but no new State shall be formed or erected within the jurisdiction of any other State; nor any State be formed by the junction of two or more States, or parts of States, without the consent of the legislatures of the States concerned as well as of the Congress.

The Congress shall have power to dispose of and make all needful rules and regulations respecting the territory or other property belonging to the United States; and nothing in this Constitution shall be so construed as to prejudice any claims of the United States, or of any particular State.

Section 4   The United States shall guarantee to every State in this Union a republican form of government, and shall protect each of them against invasion; and on application of the legislature, or of the executive (when the legislature cannot be convened), against domestic violence.

Article V

The Congress, whenever two-thirds of both houses shall deem it necessary, shall propose amendments to this Constitution, or, on the application of the legislatures of two-thirds of the several States, shall call a convention for proposing amendments, which, in either case, shall be valid to all intents and purposes, as part of this Constitution, when ratified by the legislatures of three-fourths of the several States, or by conventions in three-fourths thereof, as the one or the other mode of ratification may be proposed by the Congress; provided *that no amendments which may be made prior to the year one thousand eight hundred and eight shall in any manner affect the first and fourth clauses in the ninth section of the first article;* and that no State, without its consent, shall be deprived of its equal suffrage in the Senate.

Article VI

All debts contracted and engagements entered into, before the adoption of this Constitution, shall be as valid against the United States under this Constitution, as under the Confederation.

This Constitution, and the laws of the United States which shall be made in pursuance thereof; and all treaties made, or which shall be made, under the authority of the United States, shall be the supreme law of the land; and the judges in every State shall be bound thereby, anything in the Constitution or laws of any State to the contrary notwithstanding.

The Senators and Representatives before mentioned, and the members of the several State legislatures, and all executive and judicial officers, both of the United States and of the several States, shall be bound by oath or affirmation to support this Constitution; but no religious test shall ever be required as a qualification to any office or public trust under the United States.

Article VII

The ratification of the conventions of nine States shall be sufficient for the establishment of this Constitution between the States so ratifying the same.

Done in Convention by the unanimous consent of the States present, the seventeenth day of September in the year of our Lord one thousand seven hundred and eighty-seven and of the Independence of the United States of America the twelfth. In witness whereof we have hereunto subscribed our names.

GEORGE WASHINGTON
President and Deputy from Virginia

New Hampshire
JOHN LANGDON
NICHOLAS GILMAN

Massachusetts
NATHANIEL GORHAM
RUFUS KING

Connecticut
WILLIAM S. JOHNSON
ROGER SHERMAN

New York
ALEXANDER HAMILTON

New Jersey
WILLIAM LIVINGSTON
DAVID BREARLEY
WILLIAM PATERSON
JONATHAN DAYTON

Pennsylvania
BENJAMIN FRANKLIN
THOMAS MIFFLIN
ROBERT MORRIS
GEORGE CLYMER
THOMAS FITZSIMONS
JARED INGERSOLL
JAMES WILSON
GOUVERNEUR MORRIS

Delaware
GEORGE READ
GUNNING BEDFORD, JR.
JOHN DICKINSON
RICHARD BASSETT
JACOB BROOM

Maryland
JAMES MCHENRY
DANIEL OF ST. THOMAS JENIFER
DANIEL CARROLL

Virginia
JOHN BLAIR
JAMES MADISON, JR.

North Carolina
WILLIAM BLOUNT
RICHARD DOBBS SPRAIGHT
HU WILLIAMSON

South Carolina
J. RUTLEDGE
CHARLES COTESWORTH PINCKNEY
CHARLES PINCKNEY
PIERCE BUTLER

Georgia
WILLIAM FEW
ABRAHAM BALDWIN

Amendments to the Constitution

Amendment I

Congress shall make no law respecting an establishment of religion, or prohibiting the free exercise thereof; or abridging the freedom of speech, or of the press; or the right of the people peaceably to assemble, and to petition the government for a redress of grievances.

Amendment II

A well-regulated militia being necessary to the security of a free State, the right of the people to keep and bear arms shall not be infringed.

Amendment III

No soldier shall, in time of peace, be quartered in any house without the consent of the owner, nor in time of war, but in a manner to be prescribed by law.

Amendment IV

The right of the people to be secure in their persons, houses, papers, and effects, against unreasonable searches and seizures, shall not be violated, and no warrants shall issue but upon probable cause, supported by oath or affirmation, and particularly describing the place to be searched, and the persons or things to be seized.

Amendment V

No person shall be held to answer for a capital, or otherwise infamous crime, unless on a presentment or indictment of a grand jury, except in cases arising in the land or naval forces, or in the militia, when in actual service in time of war or public danger; nor shall any person be subject for the same offense to be twice put in jeopardy of life or limb; nor shall be compelled in any criminal case to be a witness against himself, nor be deprived of life, liberty, or property, without due process of law; nor shall private property be taken for public use without just compensation.

Amendment VI

In all criminal prosecutions, the accused shall enjoy the right to a speedy and public trial, by an impartial jury of the State and district wherein the crime shall have been committed, which district shall have been previously ascertained by law, and to be informed of the nature and cause of the accusation; to be confronted with the witnesses against him; to have compulsory process for obtaining witnesses in his favor, and to have the assistance of counsel for his defense.

Amendment VII

In suits at common law, where the value in controversy shall exceed twenty dollars, the right of trial by jury shall be preserved, and no fact tried by a jury shall be otherwise reexamined in any court of the United States, than according to the rules of the common law.

Amendment VIII

Excessive bail shall not be required, nor excessive fines imposed, nor cruel and unusual punishments inflicted.

Amendment IX

The enumeration in the Constitution, of certain rights, shall not be construed to deny or disparage others retained by the people.

Amendment X*

The powers not delegated to the United States by the Constitution, nor prohibited by it to the States, are reserved to the States respectively, or to the people.

Amendment XI [Adopted 1798]

The judicial power of the United States shall not be construed to extend to any suit in law or equity, commenced or prosecuted against one of the United States by citizens of another State, or by citizens or subjects of any foreign state.

Amendment XII [Adopted 1804]

The electors shall meet in their respective States, and vote by ballot for President and Vice-President, one of whom, at least, shall not be an inhabitant of the same State with themselves; they shall name in their ballots the person voted for as President, and in distinct ballots the person voted for as Vice-President, and they shall make distinct lists of all persons voted for as President, and of all persons voted for as Vice-President, and of the number of votes for each, which lists they shall sign and certify, and transmit sealed to the seat of government of the United States, directed to the President of the Senate;—the President of the Senate shall, in the presence of the Senate and House of Representatives, open all the certificates and the votes shall then be counted;—the person having the greatest number of votes for President shall be the President, if such number be a majority of the whole number of electors appointed; and if no person have such majority,

*The first ten Amendments (the Bill of Rights) were adopted in 1791.

then from the persons having the highest numbers not exceeding three on the list of those voted for as President, the House of Representatives shall choose immediately, by ballot, the President. But in choosing the President, the votes shall be taken by States, the representation from each State having one vote; a quorum for this purpose shall consist of a member or members from two-thirds of the States, and a majority of all the States shall be necessary to a choice. And if the House of Representatives shall not choose a President whenever the right of choice shall devolve upon them, before *the fourth day of March* next following, then the Vice-President shall act as President, as in the case of the death or other constitutional disability of the President.

The person having the greatest number of votes as Vice-President shall be the Vice-President, if such number be a majority of the whole number of electors appointed; and if no person have a majority, then from the two highest numbers on the list the Senate shall choose the Vice-President; a quorum for the purpose shall consist of two-thirds of the whole number of Senators, and a majority of the whole number shall be necessary to a choice. But no person constitutionally ineligible to the office of President shall be eligible to that of Vice-President of the United States.

Amendment XIII [Adopted 1865]

Section 1   Neither slavery nor involuntary servitude, except as a punishment for crime whereof the party shall have been duly convicted, shall exist within the United States, or any place subject to their jurisdiction.

Section 2   Congress shall have power to enforce this article by appropriate legislation.

Amendment XIV [Adopted 1868]

Section 1   All persons born or naturalized in the United States, and subject to the jurisdiction thereof, are citizens of the United States and of the State wherein they reside. No State shall make or enforce any law which shall abridge the privileges or immunities of citizens of the United States; nor shall any State deprive any person of life, liberty, or property, without due process of law; nor deny to any person within its jurisdiction the equal protection of the laws.

Section 2   Representatives shall be apportioned among the several States according to their respective numbers, counting the whole number of persons in each State, excluding Indians not taxed. But when the right to vote at any election for the choice of Electors for President and Vice-President of the United States, Representatives in Congress, the executive and judicial officers of a State, or the members of the legislature thereof, is denied to any of the male inhabitants of such State, being twenty-one years of age and citizens of the United States, or in any way abridged, except for participation in rebellion, or other crime, the basis of representation therein shall be reduced in the proportion which the number of such male citizens shall bear to the whole number of male citizens twenty-one years of age in such State.

Section 3   No person shall be a Senator or Representative in Congress, or Elector of President and Vice-President, or hold any office, civil or military, under the United States, or under any State, who, having previously taken an oath, as a member of Congress, or as an officer of the United States, or as a member of any State legislature, or as an executive or judicial officer of any State, to support the Constitution of the United States, shall have engaged in insurrection or rebellion against the same, or given aid or comfort to the enemies thereof. Congress may, by a vote of two-thirds of each house, remove such disability.

Section 4   The validity of the public debt of the United States, authorized by law, including debts incurred for payment of pensions and bounties for services in suppressing insurrection or rebellion, shall not be questioned. But neither the United States nor any State shall assume or pay any debt or obligation incurred in aid of insurrection or rebellion against the United States, or any claim for the loss of emancipation of any slave; but all such debts, obligations, and claims shall be held illegal and void.

Section 5   The Congress shall have power to enforce, by appropriate legislation, the provisions of this article.

Amendment XV [Adopted 1870]

Section 1   The right of citizens of the United States to vote shall not be denied or abridged by the United States or by any State on account of race, color, or previous condition of servitude.

Section 2   The Congress shall have power to enforce this article by appropriate legislation.

Amendment XVI [Adopted 1913]

The Congress shall have power to lay and collect taxes on incomes, from whatever source derived, without apportionment among the several States, and without regard to any census or enumeration.

Amendment XVII [Adopted 1913]

Section 1   The Senate of the United States shall be composed of two Senators from each State, elected by the people thereof, for six years; and each Senator shall have one vote. The electors in each State shall have the qualifications requisite for electors of [voters for] the most numerous branch of the State legislatures.

Section 2   When vacancies happen in the representation of any State in the Senate, the executive authority of such State shall issue writs of election to fill such vacancies: Provided, that the Legislature of any State may empower the executive thereof to make temporary appointments until the people fill the vacancies by election as the Legislature may direct.

Section 3 This amendment shall not be so construed as to affect the election or term of any Senator chosen before it becomes valid as part of the Constitution.

Amendment XVIII [Adopted 1919; Repealed 1933]

Section 1 After one year from the ratification of this article the manufacture, sale, or transportation of intoxicating liquors within, the importation thereof into, or the exportation thereof from the United States and all territory subject to the jurisdiction thereof, for beverage purposes, is hereby prohibited.

Section 2 The Congress and the several States shall have concurrent power to enforce this article by appropriate legislation.

Section 3 This article shall be inoperative unless it shall have been ratified as an amendment to the Constitution by the legislatures of the several States, as provided by the Constitution, within seven years from the date of the submission thereof to the States by the Congress.

Amendment XIX [Adopted 1920]

Section 1 The right of citizens of the United States to vote shall not be denied or abridged by the United States or by any State on account of sex.

Section 2 The Congress shall have power to enforce this article by appropriate legislation.

Amendment XX [Adopted 1933]

Section 1 The terms of the President and Vice-President shall end at noon on the 20th day of January, and the terms of Senators and Representatives at noon on the 3d day of January, of the years in which such terms would have ended if this article had not been ratified; and the terms of their successors shall then begin.

Section 2 The Congress shall assemble at least once in every year, and such meeting shall begin at noon on the 3d day of January, unless they shall by law appoint a different day.

Section 3 If, at the time fixed for the beginning of the term of the President, the President-elect shall have died, the Vice-President-elect shall become President. If a President shall not have been chosen before the time fixed for the beginning of his term, or if the President-elect shall have failed to qualify, then the Vice-President-elect shall act as President until a President shall have qualified; and the Congress may by law provide for the case wherein neither a President-elect nor a Vice-President-elect shall have qualified, declaring who shall then act as President, or the manner in which one who is to act shall be selected, and such persons shall act accordingly until a President or Vice-President shall have qualified.

Section 4 The Congress may by law provide for the case of the death of any of the persons from whom the House of Representatives may choose a President whenever the right of choice shall have devolved upon them, and for the case of the death of any of the persons from whom the Senate may choose a Vice-President whenever the right of choice shall have devolved upon them.

Section 5 Sections 1 and 2 shall take effect on the 15th day of October following the ratification of this article.

Section 6 This article shall be inoperative unless it shall have been ratified as an amendment to the Constitution by the Legislatures of three-fourths of the several States within seven years from the date of its submission.

Amendment XXI [Adopted 1933]

Section 1 The eighteenth article of amendment to the Constitution of the United States is hereby repealed.

Section 2 The transportation or importation into any State, Territory, or Possession of the United States for delivery or use therein of intoxicating liquors, in violation of the laws thereof, is hereby prohibited.

Section 3 This article shall be inoperative unless it shall have been ratified as an amendment to the Constitution by conventions in the several States, as provided in the Constitution, within seven years from the date of submission thereof to the States by the Congress.

Amendment XXII [Adopted 1951]

Section 1 No person shall be elected to the office of President more than twice, and no person who has held the office of President, or acted as President, for more than two years of a term to which some other person was elected President shall be elected to the office of President more than once. But this article shall not apply to any person holding the office of President when this article was proposed by the Congress, and shall not prevent any person who may be holding the office of President, or acting as President, during the term within which this article becomes operative from holding the office of President or acting as President during the remainder of such term.

Section 2 This article shall be inoperative unless it shall have been ratified as an amendment to the Constitution by the legislatures of three-fourths of the several States within seven years from the date of its submission to the States by the Congress.

Amendment XXIII [Adopted 1961]

Section 1 The District constituting the seat of Government of the United States shall appoint in such manner as the Congress may direct:

A number of electors of President and Vice-President equal to the whole number of Senators and Representatives in Congress to which the District would be entitled if it were a State, but in no event more than the least populous State; they shall be in addition to those appointed by the States, but they shall be considered for the purposes of the election of President and Vice-President, to be electors appointed by a State; and they shall meet in the District and perform such duties as provided by the twelfth article of amendment.

Section 2 The Congress shall have the power to enforce this article by appropriate legislation.

Amendment XXIV [Adopted 1964]

Section 1 The right of citizens of the United States to vote in any primary or other election for President or Vice-President, for electors for President or Vice-President, or for Senator or Representative in Congress, shall not be denied or abridged by the United States or any State by reason of failure to pay any poll tax or other tax.

Section 2 The Congress shall have the power to enforce this article by appropriate legislation.

Amendment XXV [Adopted 1967]

Section 1 In case of the removal of the President from office or of his death or resignation, the Vice-President shall become President.

Section 2 Whenever there is a vacancy in the office of the Vice-President, the President shall nominate a Vice-President who shall take office upon confirmation by a majority vote of both Houses of Congress.

Section 3 Whenever the President transmits to the President pro tempore of the Senate and the Speaker of the House of Representatives his written declaration that he is unable to discharge the powers and duties of his office, and until he transmits to them a written declaration to the contrary, such powers and duties shall be discharged by the Vice-President as Acting President.

Section 4 Whenever the Vice-President and a majority of either the principal officers of the executive departments or of such other body as Congress may by law provide, transmit to the President pro tempore of the Senate and the Speaker of the House of Representatives their written declaration that the President is unable to discharge the powers and duties of his office, the Vice-President shall immediately assume the powers and duties of the office as Acting President.

Thereafter, when the President transmits to the President pro tempore of the Senate and the Speaker of the House of Representatives his written declaration that no inability exists, he shall resume the powers and duties of his office unless the Vice-President and a majority of either the principal officers of the executive department[s] or of such other body as Congress may by law provide, transmit within four days to the President pro tempore of the Senate and the Speaker of the House of Representatives their written declaration that the President is unable to discharge the powers and duties of his office. Thereupon Congress shall decide the issue, assembling within forty-eight hours for that purpose if not in session. If the Congress, within twenty-one days after receipt of the latter written declaration, or, if Congress is not in session, within twenty-one days after Congress is required to assemble, determines by two-thirds vote of both Houses that the President is unable to discharge the powers and duties of his office, the Vice-President shall continue to discharge the same as Acting President; otherwise, the President shall resume the powers and duties of his office.

Amendment XXVI [Adopted 1971]

Section 1 The right of citizens of the United States, who are eighteen years of age or older, to vote shall not be denied or abridged by the United States or by any State on account of age.

Section 2 The Congress shall have power to enforce this article by appropriate legislation.

Admission of States into the Union

State	Date of Admission	State	Date of Admission
1. Delaware	December 7, 1787	26. Michigan	January 26, 1837
2. Pennsylvania	December 12, 1787	27. Florida	March 3, 1845
3. New Jersey	December 18, 1787	28. Texas	December 29, 1845
4. Georgia	January 2, 1788	29. Iowa	December 28, 1846
5. Connecticut	January 9, 1788	30. Wisconsin	May 29, 1848
6. Massachusetts	February 6, 1788	31. California	September 9, 1850
7. Maryland	April 28, 1788	32. Minnesota	May 11, 1858
8. South Carolina	May 23, 1788	33. Oregon	February 14, 1859
9. New Hampshire	June 21, 1788	34. Kansas	January 29, 1861
10. Virginia	June 25, 1788	35. West Virginia	June 20, 1863
11. New York	July 26, 1788	36. Nevada	October 31, 1864
12. North Carolina	November 21, 1789	37. Nebraska	March 1, 1867
13. Rhode Island	May 29, 1790	38. Colorado	August 1, 1876
14. Vermont	March 4, 1791	39. North Dakota	November 2, 1889
15. Kentucky	June 1, 1792	40. South Dakota	November 2, 1889
16. Tennessee	June 1, 1796	41. Montana	November 8, 1889
17. Ohio	March 1, 1803	42. Washington	November 11, 1889
18. Louisiana	April 30, 1812	43. Idaho	July 3, 1890
19. Indiana	December 11, 1816	44. Wyoming	July 10, 1890
20. Mississippi	December 10, 1817	45. Utah	January 4, 1896
21. Illinois	December 3, 1818	46. Oklahoma	November 16, 1907
22. Alabama	December 14, 1819	47. New Mexico	January 6, 1912
23. Maine	March 15, 1820	48. Arizona	February 14, 1912
24. Missouri	August 10, 1821	49. Alaska	January 3, 1959
25. Arkansas	June 15, 1836	50. Hawaii	August 21, 1959

Choosing the President

Presidential Election Year	Elected to Office			
	President	Party	Vice President	Party
1789	George Washington		John Adams	Parties not yet established
1792	George Washington		John Adams	Federalist
1796	John Adams	Federalist	Thomas Jefferson	Democratic-Republican
1800	Thomas Jefferson	Democratic-Republican	Aaron Burr	Democratic-Republican
1804	Thomas Jefferson	Democratic-Republican	George Clinton	Democratic-Republican
1808	James Madison	Democratic-Republican	George Clinton	Democratic-Republican
1812	James Madison	Democratic-Republican	Elbridge Gerry	Democratic-Republican
1816	James Monroe	Democratic-Republican	Daniel D. Tompkins	Democratic-Republican
1820	James Monroe	Democratic-Republican	Daniel D. Tompkins	Democratic-Republican
1824	John Quincy Adams Elected by House of Representatives because no candidate received a majority of electoral votes.	National Republican	John C. Calhoun	Democratic
1828	Andrew Jackson	Democratic	John C. Calhoun	Democratic
1832	Andrew Jackson	Democratic	Martin Van Buren	Democratic
1836	Martin Van Buren	Democratic	Richard M. Johnson First and only Vice President elected by the Senate (1837), having failed to receive a majority of electoral votes.	Democratic

Major Opponents		Electoral Vote		Popular Vote
For President	Party			
		Washington	69	Electors selected
		J. Adams	34	by state legislatures
George Clinton	Democratic-Republican	Washington	132	Electors selected
		J. Adams	77	by state legislatures
		Clinton	50	
Thomas Pinckney	Federalist	J. Adams	71	Electors selected
Aaron Burr	Democratic-Republican	Jefferson	68	by state legislatures
		Pinckney	59	
John Adams	Federalist	Jefferson	73	Electors selected
Charles Cotesworth Pinckney	Federalist	J. Adams	65	by state legislatures
Charles Cotesworth Pinckney	Federalist	Jefferson	162	Electors selected
		Pinckney	14	by state legislatures
Charles Cotesworth Pinckney	Federalist	Madison	122	Electors selected
		Pinckney	47	by state legislatures
George Clinton	Eastern Republican			
De Witt Clinton	Democratic-Republican (antiwar faction) and Federalist	Madison	128	Electors selected
		Clinton	89	by state legislatures
Rufus King	Federalist	Monroe	183	Electors selected
		King	34	by state legislatures
		Monroe	231	Electors selected
		J. Q. Adams	1	by state legislatures
Andrew Jackson	Democratic	J. Q. Adams	84	113,122
Henry Clay	Democratic-Republican	Jackson	99	151,271
		Clay	37	47,531
William H. Crawford	Democratic-Republican	Crawford	41	40,856
John Quincy Adams	National Republican	Jackson	178	642,553
		J. Q. Adams	83	500,897
Henry Clay	*National Republican	Jackson	219	701,780
William Wirt	Anti-Masonic	Clay	49	482,205
		Wirt	7	100,715
		*Floyd (Ind. Dem.)	11	*Delegates chosen by South Carolina legislature
Daniel Webster	Whig	Van Buren	170	764,176
Hugh L. White	Whig	W. Harrison	73	550,816
William Henry Harrison	Anti-Masonic	White	26	146,107
		Webster	14	41,201
		*Mangum (Ind. Dem.)	11	*Delegates chosen by South Carolina legislature

Presidential Election Year	Elected to Office			
	President	Party	Vice President	Party
1840	William Henry Harrison	Whig	John Tyler	Whig
1844	James K. Polk	Democratic	George M. Dallas	Democratic
1848	Zachary Taylor	Whig	Millard Fillmore	Whig
1852	Franklin Pierce	Democratic	William R. King	Democratic
1856	James Buchanan	Democratic	John C. Breckinridge	Democratic
1860	Abraham Lincoln	Republican	Hannibal Hamlin	Republican
1864	Abraham Lincoln	National Union/ Republican	Andrew Johnson	National Union/ Democratic
1868	Ulysses S. Grant	Republican	Schuyler Colfax	Republican
1872	Ulysses S. Grant	Republican	Henry Wilson	Republican
1876	Rutherford B. Hayes Contested result settled by special election commission in favor of Hayes	Republican	William A. Wheeler	Republican
1880	James A. Garfield	Republican	Chester A. Arthur	Republican
1884	Grover Cleveland	Democratic	Thomas A. Hendricks	Democratic
1888	Benjamin Harrison	Republican	Levi P. Morton	Republican

Major Opponents		Electoral Vote		Popular Vote
For President	*Party*			
Martin Van Buren	Democratic	W. Harrison	234	1,274,624
James G. Birney	Liberty	Van Buren	60	1,127,781
Henry Clay	Whig	Polk	170	1,338,464
James G. Birney	Liberty	Clay	105	1,300,097
		Birney	—	62,300
Lewis Cass	Democratic	Taylor	163	1,360,967
Martin Van Buren	Free-Soil	Cass	127	1,222,342
		Van Buren	—	291,263
Winfield Scott	Whig	Pierce	254	1,601,117
John P. Hale	Free-Soil	Scott	42	1,385,453
		Hale	—	155,825
John C. Fremont	Republican	Buchanan	174	1,832,955
Millard Fillmore	American (Know-Nothing)	Fremont	114	1,339,932
		Filmore	8	871,731
John Bell	Constitutional Union	Lincoln	180	1,865,593
Stephen A. Douglas	Democratic	Breckinridge	72	848,356
John C. Breckinridge	Democratic	Douglas	12	1,382,713
		Bell	39	592,906
George B. McClennan	Democratic	Lincoln	212	2,218,388
		McClennan	21	1,812,807
		*Eleven secessionist states did not participate		
Horatio Seymour	Democratic	Grant	286	3,598,235
		Seymour	80	2,706,829
		*Texas, Mississippi, and Virginia did not participate		
Horace Greeley	Democratic and Liberal Republican	Grant	286	3,598,235
		Greeley	80*	2,834,761
Charles O'Conor	Democratic	*Greeley died before the Electoral College met. His electoral votes were divided among the four minor candidates.		
James Black	Temperance			
Samuel J. Tilden	Democratic	Hayes	185	4,034,311
Peter Cooper	Greenback	Tilden	184	4,288,546
Green Clay Smith	Prohibition	Cooper	—	75,973
Winfield S. Hancock	Democratic	Garfield	214	4,446,158
James B. Weaver	Greenback	Hancock	155	4,444,260
Neal Dow	Prohibition	Weaver	—	305,997
James G. Blaine	Republican	Cleveland	219	4,874,621
John P. St. John	Prohibition	Blaine	182	4,848,936
Benjamin F. Butler	Greenback	Butler	—	175,096
		St. John	—	147,482
Grover Cleveland	Democratic	B. Harrison	233	5,447,129
Clinton B. Fisk	Prohibition	Cleveland	168	5,537,857
Alson J. Streeter	Union Labor			

Presidential Election Year	Elected to Office			
	President	Party	Vice President	Party
1892	Grover Cleveland	Democratic	Adlai E. Stevenson	Democratic
1896	William McKinley	Republican	Garret A. Hobart	Republican
1900	William McKinley	Republican	Theodore Roosevelt	Republican
1904	Theodore Roosevelt	Republican	Charles W. Fairbanks	Republican
1908	William Howard Taft	Republican	James S. Sherman	Republican
1912	Woodrow Wilson	Democratic	Thomas R. Marshall	Democratic
1916	Woodrow Wilson	Democratic	Thomas R. Marshall	Democratic
1920	Warren G. Harding	Republican	Calvin Coolidge	Republican
1924	Calvin Coolidge	Republican	Charles G. Dawes	Republican
1928	Herbert C. Hoover	Republican	Charles Curtis	Republican
1932	Franklin D. Roosevelt	Democratic	John N. Garner	Democratic
1936	Franklin D. Roosevelt	Democratic	John N. Garner	Democratic
1940	Franklin D. Roosevelt	Democratic	Henry A. Wallace	Democratic
1944	Franklin D. Roosevelt	Democratic	Harry S Truman	Democratic

Major Opponents		Electoral Vote		Popular Vote
For President	Party			
Benjamin Harrison	Republican	Cleveland	277	5,555,426
James B. Weaver	Populist	B. Harrison	145	5,182,600
John Bidwell	Prohibition	Weaver	22	1,029,846
William Jennings Bryan	Democratic, Populist, and National Silver Republican	McKinley	271	7,102,246
		Bryan	176	6,492,559
Joshua Levering	Prohibition			
John M. Palmer	National Democratic			
William Jennings Bryan	Democratic and Fusion Populist	McKinley	292	7,218,039
		Bryan	155	6,358,345
Wharton Barker	Anti-Fusion Populist	Woolley	—	209,004
Eugene V. Debs	Social Democratic	Debs	—	86,935
John G. Woolley	Prohibition			
Alton B. Parker	Democratic	T. Roosevelt	336	7,626,593
Eugene V. Debs	Socialist	Parker	140	5,082,898
Silas C. Swallow	Prohibition	Debs	—	402,489
		Swallow	—	258,596
William Jennings Bryan	Democratic	Taft	321	7,676,258
		Bryan	162	6,406,801
Eugene V. Debs	Socialist	Debs	—	420,380
Eugene W. Chafin	Prohibition	Chafin	—	252,821
William Howard Taft	Republican	Wilson	435	6,296,547
Theodore Roosevelt	Progressive (Bull Moose)	T. Roosevelt	88	4,118,571
		Taft	8	3,486,720
Eugene V. Debs	Socialist			
Eugene W. Chafin	Prohibition			
Charles E. Hughes	Republican	Wilson	277	9,127,695
Allen L. Benson	Socialist	Hughes	254	8,533,507
J. Frank Hanly	Prohibition			
Charles W. Fairbanks	Republican			
James M. Cox	Democratic	Harding	404	16,133,314
Eugene V. Debs	Socialist	Cox	127	9,140,884
		Debs	—	913,664
John W. Davis	Democratic	Coolidge	382	15,717,553
Robert M. LaFollette	Progressive	Davis	136	8,386,169
		LaFollette	13	4,814,050
Alfred E. Smith	Democratic	Hoover	444	21,391,993
Norman Thomas	Socialist	Smith	87	15,016,169
Herbert C. Hoover	Republican	F. Roosevelt	472	22,809,638
Norman Thomas	Socialist	Hoover	59	15,758,901
Alfred M. Landon	Republican	F. Roosevelt	523	27,752,869
William Lemke	Union	Landon	8	16,674,665
Wendell L. Willkie	Republican	F. Roosevelt	449	27,263,448
		Willkie	82	22,336,260
Thomas E. Dewey	Republican	F. Roosevelt	432	25,611,936
		Dewey	99	22,013,372

Presidential Election Year	Elected to Office			
	President	Party	Vice President	Party
1948	Harry S Truman	Democratic	Alben W. Barkley	Democratic
1952	Dwight D. Eisenhower	Republican	Richard M. Nixon	Republican
1956	Dwight D. Eisenhower	Republican	Richard M. Nixon	Republican
1960	John F. Kennedy	Democratic	Lyndon B. Johnson	Democratic
1964	Lyndon B. Johnson	Democratic	Hubert H. Humphrey	Democratic
1968	Richard M. Nixon	Republican	Spiro T. Agnew	Republican
1972	Richard M. Nixon	Republican	Spiro T. Agnew	Republican
1976	Jimmy Carter	Democratic	Walter Mondale	Democratic
1980	Ronald Reagan	Republican	George Bush	Republican
1984	Ronald Reagan	Republican	George Bush	Republican
1988	George H. Bush	Republican	J. Danforth Quayle	Republican

Major Opponents		Electoral Vote		Popular Vote
For President	*Party*			
Thomas E. Dewey	Republican	Truman	303	24,105,182
J. Strom Thurmond	States' Rights	Dewey	189	21,970,065
	Democratic	Thurmond	39	1,169,063
Henry A. Wallace	Progressive	H. Wallace	—	1,157,326
Adlai E. Stevenson	Democratic	Eisenhower	442	33,936,137
		Stevenson	89	27,314,649
Adlai E. Stevenson	Democratic	Eisenhower	457	35,585,245
		Stevenson	73	26,030,172
Richard M. Nixon	Republican	Kennedy	303	34,227,096
		Nixon	219	34,108,546
		H. Byrd (Ind. Dem.)	15	—
Barry M. Goldwater	Republican	Johnson	486	43,126,584
		Goldwater	52	27,177,838
Hubert H. Humphrey	Democratic	Nixon	301	31,770,237
George C. Wallace	American	Humphrey	191	31,270,533
	Independent	G. Wallace	46	9,906,141
George S. McGovern	Democratic	Nixon	520	46,740,323
		McGovern	17	28,901,598
		Hospers (Va.)	1	—
Gerald R. Ford	Republican	Carter	297	40,830,763
Eugene McCarthy	Independent	Ford	240	39,147,793
		E. McCarthy	—	756,631
Jimmy Carter	Democratic	Reagan	489	43,899,248
John B. Anderson	Independent	Carter	49	35,481,435
Ed Clark	Libertarian	Anderson	—	5,719,437
Walter Mondale	Democratic	Reagan	525	54,451,521
David Bergland	Libertarian	Mondale	13	37,565,334
Michael Dukakis	Democratic	Bush	426	47,917,341
Ron Paul	Libertarian	Dukakis	112	41,013,030
Lenora Fulani	New Alliance Party	Paul	—	409,412
		Fulani	—	201,430

Cabinet Members

The Washington Administration

Secretary of State	Thomas Jefferson	1789–1793
	Edmund Randolph	1794–1795
	Timothy Pickering	1795–1797
Secretary of Treasury	Alexander Hamilton	1789–1795
	Oliver Wolcott	1795–1797
Secretary of War	Henry Knox	1789–1794
	Timothy Pickering	1795–1796
	James McHenry	1796–1797
Attorney General	Edmund Randolph	1789–1793
	William Bradford	1794–1795
	Charles Lee	1795–1797
Postmaster General	Samuel Osgood	1789–1791
	Timothy Pickering	1791–1794
	Joseph Habersham	1795–1797

The John Adams Administration

Secretary of State	Timothy Pickering	1797–1800
	John Marshall	1800–1801
Secretary of Treasury	Oliver Wolcott	1797–1800
	Samuel Dexter	1800–1801
Secretary of War	James McHenry	1797–1800
	Samuel Dexter	1800–1801
Attorney General	Charles Lee	1797–1801
Postmaster General	Joseph Habersham	1797–1801
Secretary of Navy	Benjamin Stoddert	1798–1801

The Jefferson Administration

Secretary of State	James Madison	1801–1809
Secretary of Treasury	Samuel Dexter	1801
	Albert Gallatin	1801–1809
Secretary of War	Henry Dearborn	1801–1809
Attorney General	Levi Lincoln	1801–1805
	Robert Smith	1805
	John Breckinridge	1805–1806
	Caesar Rodney	1807–1809
Postmaster General	Joseph Habersham	1801
	Gideon Granger	1801–1809
Secretary of Navy	Robert Smith	1801–1809

The Madison Administration

Secretary of State	Robert Smith	1809–1811
	James Monroe	1811–1817
Secretary of Treasury	Albert Gallatin	1809–1813
	George Campbell	1814
	Alexander Dallas	1814–1816
	William Crawford	1816–1817
Secretary of War	William Eustis	1809–1812
	John Armstrong	1813–1814
	James Monroe	1814–1815
	William Crawford	1815–1817
Attorney General	Caesar Rodney	1809–1811
	William Pinkney	1811–1814
	Richard Rush	1814–1817
Postmaster General	Gideon Granger	1809–1814
	Return Meigs	1814–1817
Secretary of Navy	Paul Hamilton	1809–1813
	William Jones	1813–1814
	Benjamin Crowninshield	1814–1817

The Monroe Administration

Secretary of State	John Quincy Adams	1817–1825
Secretary of Treasury	William Crawford	1817–1825
Secretary of War	George Graham	1817
	John C. Calhoun	1817–1825
Attorney General	Richard Rush	1817
	William Wirt	1817–1825
Postmaster General	Return Meigs	1817–1823
	John McLean	1823–1825
Secretary of Navy	Benjamin Crowninshield	1817–1818
	Smith Thompson	1818–1823
	Samuel Southard	1823–1825

The John Quincy Adams Administration

Secretary of State	Henry Clay	1825–1829
Secretary of Treasury	Richard Rush	1825–1829
Secretary of War	James Barbour	1825–1828
	Peter Porter	1828–1829
Attorney General	William Wirt	1825–1829
Postmaster General	John McLean	1825–1829
Secretary of Navy	Samuel Southard	1825–1829

The Jackson Administration

Secretary of State	Martin Van Buren	1829–1831
	Edward Livingston	1831–1833
	Louis McLane	1833–1834
	John Forsyth	1834–1837
Secretary of Treasury	Samuel Ingham	1829–1831
	Louis McLane	1831–1833
	William Duane	1833
	Roger B. Taney	1833–1834
	Levi Woodbury	1834–1837
Secretary of War	John H. Eaton	1829–1831
	Lewis Cass	1831–1837
	Benjamin Butler	1837
Attorney General	John M. Berrien	1829–1831
	Roger B. Taney	1831–1833
	Benjamin Butler	1833–1837
Postmaster General	William Barry	1829–1835
	Amos Kendall	1835–1837
Secretary of Navy	John Branch	1829–1831
	Levi Woodbury	1831–1834
	Mahlon Dickerson	1834–1837

The Van Buren Administration

Secretary of State	John Forsyth	1837–1841
Secretary of Treasury	Levi Woodbury	1837–1841
Secretary of War	Joel Poinsett	1837–1841
Attorney General	Benjamin Butler	1837–1838
	Felix Grundy	1838–1840
	Henry D. Gilpin	1840–1841
Postmaster General	Amos Kendall	1837–1840
	John M. Niles	1840–1841
Secretary of Navy	Mahlon Dickerson	1837–1838
	James Paulding	1838–1841

The William Harrison Administration

Secretary of State	Daniel Webster	1841
Secretary of Treasury	Thomas Ewing	1841
Secretary of War	John Bell	1841
Attorney General	John J. Crittenden	1841
Postmaster General	Francis Granger	1841
Secretary of Navy	George Badger	1841

The Tyler Administration

Secretary of State	Daniel Webster	1841–1843
	Hugh S. Legaré	1843
	Abel P. Upshur	1843–1844
	John C. Calhoun	1844–1845
Secretary of Treasury	Thomas Ewing	1841
	Walter Forward	1841–1843
	John C. Spencer	1843–1844
	George Bibb	1844–1845
Secretary of War	John Bell	1841
	John C. Spencer	1841–1843
	James M. Porter	1843–1844
	William Wilkins	1844–1845
Attorney General	John J. Crittenden	1841
	Hugh S. Legaré	1841–1843
	John Nelson	1843–1845
Postmaster General	Francis Granger	1841
	Charles Wickliffe	1841
Secretary of Navy	George Badger	1841
	Abel P. Upshur	1841
	David Henshaw	1843–1844
	Thomas Gilmer	1844
	John Y. Mason	1844–1845

The Polk Administration

Secretary of State	James Buchanan	1845–1849
Secretary of Treasury	Robert J. Walker	1845–1849
Secretary of War	William L. Marcy	1845–1849
Attorney General	John Y. Mason	1845–1846
	Nathan Clifford	1846–1848
	Isaac Toucey	1848–1849
Postmaster General	Cave Johnson	1845–1849
Secretary of Navy	George Bancroft	1845–1846
	John Y. Mason	1846–1849

The Taylor Administration

Secretary of State	John M. Clayton	1849–1850
Secretary of Treasury	William Meredith	1849–1850
Secretary of War	George Crawford	1849–1850
Attorney General	Reverdy Johnson	1849–1850
Postmaster General	Jacob Collamer	1849–1850
Secretary of Navy	William Preston	1849–1850
Secretary of Interior	Thomas Ewing	1849–1850

The Fillmore Administration

Secretary of State	Daniel Webster Edward Everett	1850–1852 1852–1853
Secretary of Treasury	Thomas Corwin	1850–1853
Secretary of War	Charles Conrad	1850–1853
Attorney General	John J. Crittenden	1850–1853
Postmaster General	Nathan Hall Sam D. Hubbard	1850–1852 1852–1853
Secretary of Navy	William A. Graham John P. Kennedy	1850–1852 1852–1853
Secretary of Interior	Thomas McKennan Alexander Stuart	1850 1850–1853

The Pierce Administration

Secretary of State	William L. Marcy	1853–1857
Secretary of Treasury	James Guthrie	1853–1857
Secretary of War	Jefferson Davis	1853–1857
Attorney General	Caleb Cushing	1853–1857
Postmaster General	James Campbell	1853–1857
Secretary of Navy	James C. Dobbin	1853–1857
Secretary of Interior	Robert McClelland	1853–1857

The Buchanan Administration

Secretary of State	Lewis Cass Jeremiah S. Black	1857–1860 1860–1861
Secretary of Treasury	Howell Cobb Philip Thomas John A. Dix	1857–1860 1860–1861 1861
Secretary of War	John B. Floyd Joseph Holt	1857–1861 1861
Attorney General	Jeremiah S. Black Edwin M. Stanton	1857–1860 1860–1861
Postmaster General	Aaron V. Brown Joseph Holt Horatio King	1857–1859 1859–1861 1861
Secretary of Navy	Isaac Toucey	1857–1861
Secretary of Interior	Jacob Thompson	1857–1861

The Lincoln Administration

Secretary of State	William H. Seward	1861–1865
Secretary of Treasury	Samuel P. Chase William P. Fessenden Hugh McCulloch	1861–1864 1864–1865 1865
Secretary of War	Simon Cameron Edwin M. Stanton	1861–1862 1862–1865
Attorney General	Edward Bates James Speed	1861–1864 1864–1865
Postmaster General	Horatio King Montgomery Blair William Dennison	1861 1861–1864 1864–1865
Secretary of Navy	Gideon Welles	1861–1865
Secretary of Interior	Caleb B. Smith John P. Usher	1861–1863 1863–1865

The Andrew Johnson Administration

Secretary of State	William H. Seward	1865–1869
Secretary of Treasury	Hugh McCulloch	1865–1869
Secretary of War	Edwin M. Stanton Ulysses S. Grant Lorenzo Thomas John M. Schofield	1865–1867 1867–1868 1868 1868–1869
Attorney General	James Speed Henry Stanbery William M. Evarts	1865–1866 1866–1868 1868–1869
Postmaster General	William Dennison Alexander Randall	1865–1866 1866–1869
Secretary of Navy	Gideon Welles	1865–1869
Secretary of Interior	John P. Usher James Harlan Orville H. Browning	1865 1865–1866 1866–1869

The Grant Administration

Secretary of State	Elihu B. Washburne Hamilton Fish	1869 1869–1877
Secretary of Treasury	George S. Boutwell William Richardson Benjamin Bristow Lot M. Morrill	1869–1873 1873–1874 1874–1876 1876–1877
Secretary of War	John A. Rawlins William T. Sherman William W. Belknap Alphonso Taft James D. Cameron	1869 1869 1869–1876 1876 1876–1877
Attorney General	Ebenezer Hoar Amos T. Ackerman G. H. Williams Edwards Pierrepont Alphonso Taft	1869–1870 1870–1871 1871–1875 1875–1876 1876–1877
Postmaster General	John A. J. Creswell James W. Marshall Marshall Jewell James N. Tyner	1869–1874 1874 1874–1876 1876–1877

Secretary of Navy	Adolph E. Borie	1869
	George M. Robeson	1869–1877
Secretary of Interior	Jacob D. Cox	1869–1870
	Columbus Delano	1870–1875
	Zachariah Chandler	1875–1877

The Hayes Administration

Secretary of State	William B. Evarts	1877–1881
Secretary of Treasury	John Sherman	1877–1881
Secretary of War	George W. McCrary	1877–1879
	Alex Ramsey	1879–1881
Attorney General	Charles Devens	1877–1881
Postmaster General	David M. Key	1877–1880
	Horace Maynard	1880–1881
Secretary of Navy	Richard W. Thompson	1877–1880
	Nathan Goff, Jr.	1881
Secretary of Interior	Carl Schurz	1877–1881

The Garfield Administration

Secretary of State	James G. Blaine	1881
Secretary of Treasury	William Windom	1881
Secretary of War	Robert T. Lincoln	1881
Attorney General	Wayne MacVeagh	1881
Postmaster General	Thomas L. James	1881
Secretary of Navy	William H. Hunt	1881
Secretary of Interior	Samuel J. Kirkwood	1881

The Arthur Administration

Secretary of State	F. T. Frelinghuysen	1881–1885
Secretary of Treasury	Charles J. Folger	1881–1884
	Walter Q. Gresham	1884
	Hugh McCulloch	1884–1885
Secretary of War	Robert T. Lincoln	1881–1885
Attorney General	Benjamin H. Brewster	1881–1885
Postmaster General	Timothy O. Howe	1881–1883
	Walter Q. Gresham	1883–1884
	Frank Hatton	1884–1885
Secretary of Navy	William H. Hunt	1881–1882
	William E. Chandler	1882–1885

| Secretary of Interior | Samuel J. Kirkwood | 1881–1882 |
| | Henry M. Teller | 1882–1885 |

The First Cleveland Administration

Secretary of State	Thomas F. Bayard	1885–1889
Secretary of Treasury	Daniel Manning	1885–1887
	Charles S. Fairchild	1887–1889
Secretary of War	William C. Endicott	1885–1889
Attorney General	Augustus H. Garland	1885–1889
Postmaster General	William F. Vilas	1885–1888
	Don M. Dickinson	1888–1889
Secretary of Navy	William C. Whitney	1885–1889
Secretary of Interior	Lucius Q. C. Lamar	1885–1888
	William F. Vilas	1888–1889
Secretary of Agriculture	Norman J. Colman	1889

The Benjamin Harrison Administration

Secretary of State	James G. Blaine	1889–1892
	John W. Foster	1892–1893
Secretary of Treasury	William Windom	1889–1891
	Charles Foster	1891–1893
Secretary of War	Redfield Proctor	1889–1891
	Stephen B. Elkins	1891–1893
Attorney General	William H. H. Miller	1889–1891
Postmaster General	John Wanamaker	1889–1893
Secretary of Navy	Benjamin F. Tracy	1889–1893
Secretary of Interior	John W. Noble	1889–1893
Secretary of Agriculture	Jeremiah M. Rusk	1889–1893

The Second Cleveland Administration

Secretary of State	Walter Q. Gresham	1893–1895
	Richard Olney	1895–1897
Secretary of Treasury	John G. Carlisle	1893–1897
Secretary of War	Daniel S. Lamont	1893–1897
Attorney General	Richard Olney	1893–1895
	James Harmon	1895–1897
Postmaster General	Wilson S. Bissell	1893–1895
	William L. Wilson	1895–1897

Secretary of Navy	Hilary A. Herbert	1893–1897
Secretary of Interior	Hoke Smith	1893–1896
	David R. Francis	1896–1897
Secretary of Agriculture	Julius S. Morton	1893–1897

The McKinley Administration

Secretary of State	John Sherman	1897–1898
	William R. Day	1898
	John Hay	1898–1901
Secretary of Treasury	Lyman J. Gage	1897–1901
Secretary of War	Russell A. Alger	1897–1899
	Elihu Root	1899–1901
Attorney General	Joseph McKenna	1897–1898
	John W. Griggs	1898–1901
	Philander C. Knox	1901
Postmaster General	James A. Gary	1897–1898
	Charles E. Smith	1898–1901
Secretary of Navy	John D. Long	1897–1901
Secretary of Interior	Cornelius N. Bliss	1897–1899
	Ethan A. Hitchcock	1899–1901
Secretary of Agriculture	James Wilson	1897–1901

The Theodore Roosevelt Administration

Secretary of State	John Hay	1901–1905
	Elihu Root	1905–1909
	Robert Bacon	1909
Secretary of Treasury	Lyman J. Gage	1901–1902
	Leslie M. Shaw	1902–1907
	George B. Cortelyou	1907–1909
Secretary of War	Elihu Root	1901–1904
	William H. Taft	1904–1908
	Luke E. Wright	1908–1909
Attorney General	Philander C. Knox	1901–1904
	William H. Moody	1904–1906
	Charles J. Bonaparte	1906–1909
Postmaster General	Charles E. Smith	1901–1902
	Henry C. Payne	1902–1904
	Robert J. Wynne	1904–1905
	George B. Cortelyou	1905–1907
	George von L. Meyer	1907–1909
Secretary of Navy	John D. Long	1901–1902
	William H. Moody	1902–1904
	Paul Morton	1904–1905
	Charles J. Bonaparte	1905–1906
	Victor H. Metcalf	1906–1908
	Truman H. Newberry	1908–1909
Secretary of Interior	Ethan A. Hitchcock	1901–1907
	James R. Garfield	1907–1909
Secretary of of Agriculture	James Wilson	1901–1909

Secretary of Labor and Commerce	George B. Cortelyou	1903–1904
	Victor H. Metcalf	1904–1906
	Oscar S. Straus	1906–1909
	Charles Nagel	1909

The Taft Administration

Secretary of State	Philander C. Knox	1909–1913
Secretary of Treasury	Franklin MacVeagh	1909–1913
Secretary of War	Jacob M. Dickinson	1909–1911
	Henry L. Stimson	1911–1913
Attorney General	George W. Wickersham	1909–1913
Postmaster General	Frank H. Hitchcock	1909–1913
Secretary of Navy	George von L. Meyer	1909–1913
Secretary of Interior	Richard A. Ballinger	1909–1911
	Walter L. Fisher	1911–1913
Secretary of Agriculture	James Wilson	1909–1913
Secretary of Labor and Commerce	Charles Nagel	1909–1913

The Wilson Administration

Secretary of State	William J. Bryan	1913–1915
	Robert Lansing	1915–1920
	Bainbridge Colby	1920–1921
Secretary of Treasury	William G. McAdoo	1913–1918
	Carter Glass	1918–1920
	David F. Houston	1920–1921
Secretary of War	Lindley M. Garrison	1913–1916
	Newton D. Baker	1916–1921
Attorney General	James C. McReynolds	1913–1914
	Thomas W. Gregory	1914–1919
	A. Mitchell Palmer	1919–1921
Postmaster General	Albert S. Burleson	1913–1921
Secretary of Navy	Josephus Daniels	1913–1921
Secretary of Interior	Franklin K. Lane	1913–1920
	John B. Payne	1920–1921
Secretary of Agriculture	David F. Houston	1913–1920
	Edwin T. Meredith	1920–1921
Secretary of Commerce	William C. Redfield	1913–1919
	Joshua W. Alexander	1919–1921
Secretary of Labor	William B. Wilson	1913–1921

The Harding Administration

Secretary of State	Charles E. Hughes	1921–1923
Secretary of Treasury	Andrew Mellon	1921–1923
Secretary of War	John W. Weeks	1921–1923
Attorney General	Harry M. Daugherty	1921–1923
Postmaster General	Will H. Hays	1921–1922
	Hubert Work	1922–1923
	Harry S. New	1923
Secretary of Navy	Edwin Denby	1921–1923
Secretary of Interior	Albert B. Fall	1921–1923
	Hubert Work	1923
Secretary of Agriculture	Henry C. Wallace	1921–1923
Secretary of Commerce	Herbert C. Hoover	1921–1923
Secretary of Labor	James J. Davis	1921–1923

The Coolidge Administration

Secretary of State	Charles E. Hughes	1923–1925
	Frank B. Kellogg	1925–1929
Secretary of Treasury	Andrew Mellon	1923–1929
Secretary of War	John W. Weeks	1923–1925
	Dwight F. Davis	1925–1929
Attorney General	Henry M. Daugherty	1923–1924
	Harlan F. Stone	1924–1925
	John G. Sargent	1925–1929
Postmaster General	Harry S. New	1923–1929
Secretary of Navy	Edwin Denby	1923–1924
	Curtis D. Wilbur	1924–1929
Secretary of Interior	Hubert Work	1923–1928
	Roy O. West	1928–1929
Secretary of Agriculture	Henry C. Wallace	1923–1924
	Howard M. Gore	1924–1925
	William M. Jardine	1925–1929
Secretary of Commerce	Herbert C. Hoover	1923–1928
	William F. Whiting	1928–1929
Secretary of Labor	James J. Davis	1923–1929

The Hoover Administration

Secretary of State	Henry L. Stimson	1929–1933
Secretary of Treasury	Andrew Mellon	1929–1932
	Ogden L. Mills	1932–1933
Secretary of War	James W. Good	1929
	Patrick J. Hurley	1929–1933
Attorney General	William D. Mitchell	1929–1933
Postmaster General	Walter F. Brown	1929–1933
Secretary of Navy	Charles F. Adams	1929–1933
Secretary of Interior	Ray L. Wilbur	1929–1933
Secretary of Agriculture	Arthur M. Hyde	1929–1933
Secretary of Commerce	Robert P. Lamont	1929–1932
	Roy D. Chapin	1932–1933
Secretary of Labor	James J. Davis	1929–1930
	William N. Doak	1930–1933

The Franklin D. Roosevelt Administration

Secretary of State	Cordell Hull	1933–1944
	E. R. Stettinius, Jr.	1944–1945
Secretary of Treasury	William H. Woodin	1933–1934
	Henry Morgenthau, Jr.	1934–1945
Secretary of War	George H. Dern	1933–1936
	Henry A. Woodring	1936–1940
	Henry L. Stimson	1940–1945
Attorney General	Homer S. Cummings	1933–1939
	Frank Murphy	1939–1940
	Robert H. Jackson	1940–1941
	Francis Biddle	1941–1945
Postmaster General	James A. Farley	1933–1940
	Frank C. Walker	1940–1945
Secretary of Navy	Claude A. Swanson	1933–1940
	Charles Edison	1940
	Frank Knox	1940–1944
	James V. Forrestal	1944–1945
Secretary of Interior	Harold L. Ickes	1933–1945
Secretary of Agriculture	Henry A. Wallace	1933–1940
	Claude R. Wickard	1940–1945
Secretary of Commerce	Daniel C. Roper	1933–1939
	Harry L. Hopkins	1939–1940
	Jesse Jones	1940–1945
	Henry A. Wallace	1945
Secretary of Labor	Frances Perkins	1933–1945

The Truman Administration

Secretary of State	James F. Byrnes	1945–1947
	George C. Marshall	1947–1949
	Dean G. Acheson	1949–1953
Secretary of Treasury	Fred M. Vinson	1945–1946
	John W. Snyder	1946–1953

Secretary of War	Robert P. Patterson	1945–1947
	Kenneth C. Royall	1947
Attorney General	Tom C. Clark	1945–1949
	J. Howard McGrath	1949–1952
	James P. McGranery	1952–1953
Postmaster General	Frank C. Walker	1945
	Robert E. Hannegan	1945–1947
	Jesse M. Donaldson	1947–1953
Secretary of Navy	James V. Forrestal	1945–1947
Secretary of Interior	Harold L. Ickes	1945–1946
	Julius A. Krug	1946–1949
	Oscar I. Chapman	1949–1953
Secretary of Agriculture	Clinton P. Anderson	1945–1948
	Charles F. Brannan	1948–1953
Secretary of Commerce	Henry A. Wallace	1945–1946
	W. Averell Harriman	1946–1948
	Charles W. Sawyer	1948–1953
Secretary of Labor	Lewis B. Schwellenbach	1945–1948
	Maurice J. Tobin	1948–1953
Secretary of Defense	James V. Forrestal	1947–1949
	Louis A. Johnson	1949–1950
	George C. Marshall	1950–1951
	Robert A. Lovett	1951–1953

The Eisenhower Administration

Secretary of State	John Foster Dulles	1953–1959
	Christian A. Herter	1959–1961
Secretary of Treasury	George M. Humphrey	1953–1957
	Robert B. Anderson	1957–1961
Attorney General	Herbert Brownell, Jr.	1953–1958
	William P. Rogers	1958–1961
Postmaster General	Arthur E. Summerfield	1953–1961
Secretary of Interior	Douglas McKay	1953–1956
	Fred A. Seaton	1956–1961
Secretary of Agriculture	Ezra T. Benson	1953–1961
Secretary of Commerce	Sinclair Weeks	1953–1958
	Lewis L. Strauss	1958–1959
	Frederick H. Mueller	1959–1961
Secretary of Labor	Martin P. Durkin	1953
	James P. Mitchell	1953–1961
Secretary of Defense	Charles E. Wilson	1953–1957
	Neil H. McElroy	1957–1959
	Thomas S. Gates, Jr.	1959–1961
Secretary of Health, Education and Welfare	Oveta Culp Hobby	1953–1955
	Marion B. Folsom	1955–1958
	Arthur S. Flemming	1958–1961

The Kennedy Administration

Secretary of State	Dean Rusk	1961–1963
Secretary of Treasury	C. Douglas Dillon	1961–1963
Attorney General	Robert F. Kennedy	1961–1963
Postmaster General	J. Edward Day	1961–1963
	John A. Gronouski	1963
Secretary of Interior	Stewart L. Udall	1961–1963
Secretary of Agriculture	Orville L. Freeman	1961–1963
Secretary of Commerce	Luther H. Hodges	1961–1963
Secretary of Labor	Arthur J. Goldberg	1961–1962
	W. Willard Wirtz	1962–1963
Secretary of Defense	Robert S. McNamara	1961–1963
Secretary of Health, Education and Welfare	Abraham A. Ribicoff	1961–1962
	Anthony J. Celebrezze	1962–1963

The Lyndon Johnson Administration

Secretary of State	Dean Rusk	1963–1969
Secretary of Treasury	C. Douglas Dillon	1963–1965
	Henry H. Fowler	1965–1969
Attorney General	Robert F. Kennedy	1963–1964
	Nicholas Katzenbach	1965–1966
	Ramsey Clark	1967–1969
Postmaster General	John A. Gronouski	1963–1965
	Lawrence F. O'Brien	1965–1968
	Marvin Watson	1968–1969
Secretary of Interior	Stewart L. Udall	1963–1969
Secretary of Agriculture	Orville L. Freeman	1963–1969
Secretary of Commerce	Luther H. Hodges	1963–1964
	John T. Connor	1964–1967
	Alexander B. Trowbridge	1967–1968
	Cyrus R. Smith	1968–1969
Secretary of Labor	W. Willard Wirtz	1963–1969
Secretary of Defense	Robert F. McNamara	1963–1968
	Clark Clifford	1968–1969
Secretary of Health, Education and Welfare	Anthony J. Celebrezze	1963–1965
	John W. Gardner	1965–1968
	Wilbur J. Cohen	1968–1969
Secretary of Housing and Urban Development	Robert C. Weaver	1966–1969
	Robert C. Wood	1969
Secretary of Transportation	Alan S. Boyd	1967–1969

The Nixon Administration

Secretary of State	William P. Rogers	1969–1973
	Henry A. Kissinger	1973–1974
Secretary of Treasury	David M. Kennedy	1969–1970
	John B. Connally	1971–1972
	George P. Shultz	1972–1974
	William E. Simon	1974
Attorney General	John N. Mitchell	1969–1972
	Richard G. Kelindienst	1972–1973
	Elliot L. Richardson	1973
	William B. Saxbe	1973–1974
Postmaster General	Winton M. Blount	1969–1971
Secretary of Interior	Walter J. Hickel	1969–1970
	Rogers Morton	1971–1974
Secretary of Agriculture	Clifford M. Hardin	1969–1971
	Earl L. Butz	1971–1974
Secretary of Commerce	Maurice H. Stans	1969–1972
	Peter G. Peterson	1972–1973
	Frederick B. Dent	1973–1974
Secretary of Labor	George P. Shultz	1969–1970
	James D. Hodgson	1970–1973
	Peter J. Brennan	1973–1974
Secretary of Defense	Melvin R. Laird	1969–1973
	Elliot L. Richardson	1973
	James R. Schlesinger	1973–1974
Secretary of Health, Education and Welfare	Robert H. Finch	1969–1970
	Elliot L. Richardson	1970–1973
	Caspar W. Weinberger	1973–1974
Secretary of Housing and Urban Development	George Romney	1969–1973
	James T. Lynn	1973–1974
Secretary of Transportation	John A. Volpe	1969–1973
	Claude S. Brinegar	1973–1974

The Ford Administration

Secretary of State	Henry A. Kissinger	1974–1977
Secretary of Treasury	William E. Simon	1974–1977
Attorney General	William Saxbe	1974–1975
	Edward Levi	1975–1977
Secretary of Interior	Rogers Morton	1974–1975
	Stanley K. Hathaway	1975
	Thomas Kleppe	1975–1977
Secretary of Agriculture	Earl L. Butz	1974–1976
	John A. Knebel	1976–1977
Secretary of Commerce	Frederick B. Dent	1974–1975
	Rogers Morton	1975–1976
	Elliot L. Richardson	1976–1977
Secretary of Labor	Peter J. Brennan	1974–1975
	John T. Dunlop	1975–1976
	W. J. Usery	1976–1977
Secretary of Defense	James R. Schlesinger	1974–1975
	Donald Rumsfeld	1975–1977
Secretary of Health, Education and Welfare	Caspar Weinberger	1974–1975
	Forrest D. Mathews	1975–1977
Secretary of Housing and Urban Development	James T. Lynn	1974–1975
	Carla A. Hills	1975–1977
Secretary of Transportation	Claude Brinegar	1974–1975
	William T. Coleman	1975–1977

The Carter Administration

Secretary of State	Cyrus R. Vance	1977–1980
	Edmund Muskie	1980–1981
Secretary of Treasury	W. Michael Blumenthal	1977–1979
	G. William Miller	1979–1981
Attorney General	Griffin Bell	1977–1979
	Benjamin R. Civiletti	1979–1981
Secretary of Interior	Cecil D. Andrus	1977–1981
Secretary of Agriculture	Robert Bergland	1977–1981
Secretary of Commerce	Juanita M. Kreps	1977–1979
	Philip M. Klutznick	1979–1981
Secretary of Labor	F. Ray Marshall	1977–1981
Secretary of Defense	Harold Brown	1977–1981
Secretary of Health, Education and Welfare	Joseph A. Califano	1977–1979
	Patricia R. Harris	1979
Secretary of Health and Human Services	Patricia R. Harris	1979–1981
Secretary of Education	Shirley M. Hufstedler	1979–1981
Secretary of Housing and Urban Development	Patricia R. Harris	1977–1979
	Moon Landrieu	1979–1981
Secretary of Transportation	Brock Adams	1977–1979
	Neil E. Goldschmidt	1979–1981
Secretary of Energy	James R. Schlesinger	1977–1979
	Charles W. Duncan	1979–1981

The Reagan Administration

Secretary of State	Alexander M. Haig	1981–1982
	George Shultz	1982–1989
Secretary of Treasury	Donald Regan	1981–1985
	James Baker	1985–1988
	Nicholas Brady	1988–1989
Attorney General	William French Smith	1981–1985
	Edwin Meese	1985–1988
	Richard Thornburgh	1988–1989
Secretary of Interior	James Watt	1981–1983
	William P. Clark	1983–1985
	Donald Hodel	1985–1989
Secretary of Agriculture	John Block	1981–1985
	Richard Lyng	1985–1989
Secretary of Commerce	Malcolm Baldrige	1981–1987
	C. William Verity	1987–1989
Secretary of Labor	Raymond Donovan	1981–1985
	William Brock	1985–1987
	Ann D. McLaughlin	1987–1989
Secretary of Defense	Caspar Weinberger	1981–1987
	Frank Carlucci	1987–1989
Secretary of Health and Human Services	Richard Schweiker	1981–1983
	Margaret Heckler	1983–1985
	Otis R. Bowen	1985–1989
Secretary of Education	Terrel Bell	1981–1985
	William J. Bennett	1985–1988
	Lauro F. Cavazos	1988–1989
Secretary of Housing and Urban Development	Samuel Pierce	1981–1989
Secretary of Transportation	Drew Lewis	1981–1983
	Elizabeth Dole	1983–1987
	James H. Burnley	1987–1989
Secretary of Energy	James Edwards	1981–1982
	Donald Hodel	1982–1985
	John Herrington	1985–1989

The Bush Administration

Secretary of State	James Baker	1989–
Secretary of Treasury	Nicholas Brady	1989–
Attorney General	Richard Thornburgh	1989–
Secretary of Interior	Manuel Lujan	1989–
Secretary of Agriculture	Clayton Yeutter	1989–
Secretary of Commerce	Robert Mosbacher	1989–
Secretary of Labor	Elizabeth Dole	1989–
Secretary of Defense	Richard Cheney	1989–
Secretary of Health and Human Welfare	Louis Sullivan	1989–
Secretary of Housing and Urban Development	Jack Kemp	1989–
Secretary of Transportation	Samuel Skinner	1989–
Secretary of Energy	James Watkins	1989–
Secretary of Veterans Affairs	Edwin Derwinski	1989–

Supreme Court Justices

Name	Terms of Service[1]	Appointed by	Name	Terms of Service[1]	Appointed by
John Jay	1789–1795	Washington	Howell E. Jackson	1893–1895	B. Harrison
James Wilson	1789–1798	Washington	Edward D. White	1894–1910	Cleveland
John Rutledge	1790–1791	Washington	Rufus W. Peckham	1896–1909	Cleveland
William Cushing	1790–1810	Washington	Joseph McKenna	1898–1925	McKinley
John Blair	1790–1796	Washington	Oliver W. Holmes	1902–1932	T. Roosevelt
James Iredell	1790–1799	Washington	William R. Day	1903–1922	T. Roosevelt
Thomas Johnson	1792–1793	Washington	William H. Moody	1906–1910	T. Roosevelt
William Paterson	1793–1806	Washington	Horace H. Lurton	1910–1914	Taft
John Rutledge[2]	1795	Washington	Charles E. Hughes	1910–1916	Taft
Samuel Chase	1796–1811	Washington	Willis Van Devanter	1911–1937	Taft
Oliver Ellsworth	1796–1800	Washington	Joseph R. Lamar	1911–1916	Taft
Bushrod Washington	1799–1829	J. Adams	**Edward D. White**	1910–1921	Taft
Alfred Moore	1800–1804	J. Adams	Mahlon Pitney	1912–1922	Taft
John Marshall	1801–1835	J. Adams	James C. McReynolds	1914–1941	Wilson
William Johnson	1804–1834	Jefferson	Louis D. Brandeis	1916–1939	Wilson
Brockholst Livingston	1807–1823	Jefferson	John H. Clarke	1916–1922	Wilson
Thomas Todd	1807–1826	Jefferson	**William H. Taft**	1921–1930	Harding
Gabriel Duvall	1811–1835	Madison	George Sutherland	1922–1938	Harding
Joseph Story	1812–1845	Madison	Pierce Butler	1923–1939	Harding
Smith Thompson	1823–1843	Monroe	Edward T. Sanford	1923–1930	Harding
Robert Trimble	1826–1828	J. Q. Adams	Harlan F. Stone	1925–1941	Coolidge
John McLean	1830–1861	Jackson	**Charles E. Hughes**	1930–1941	Hoover
Henry Baldwin	1830–1844	Jackson	Owen J. Roberts	1930–1945	Hoover
James M. Wayne	1835–1867	Jackson	Benjamin N. Cardozo	1932–1938	Hoover
Roger B. Taney	1836–1864	Jackson	Hugo L. Black	1937–1971	F. Roosevelt
Philip P. Barbour	1836–1841	Jackson	Stanley F. Reed	1938–1957	F. Roosevelt
John Cartron	1837–1865	Van Buren	Felix Frankfurter	1939–1962	F. Roosevelt
John McKinley	1838–1852	Van Buren	William O. Douglas	1939–1975	F. Roosevelt
Peter V. Daniel	1842–1860	Van Buren	Frank Murphy	1940–1949	F. Roosevelt
Samuel Nelson	1845–1872	Tyler	**Harlan F. Stone**	1941–1946	F. Roosevelt
Levi Woodbury	1845–1851	Polk	James F. Byrnes	1941–1942	F. Roosevelt
Robert C. Grier	1846–1870	Polk	Robert H. Jackson	1941–1954	F. Roosevelt
Benjamin R. Curtis	1851–1857	Fillmore	Wiley B. Rutledge	1943–1949	F. Roosevelt
John A. Campbell	1853–1861	Pierce	Harold H. Burton	1945–1958	Truman
Nathan Clifford	1858–1881	Buchanan	**Frederick M. Vinson**	1946–1953	Truman
Noah H. Swayne	1862–1881	Lincoln	Tom C. Clark	1949–1967	Truman
Samuel F. Miller	1862–1890	Lincoln	Sherman Minton	1949–1956	Truman
David Davis	1862–1877	Lincoln	**Earl Warren**	1953–1969	Eisenhower
Stephen J. Field	1863–1897	Lincoln	John Marshall Harlan	1955–1971	Eisenhower
Salmon P. Chase	1864–1873	Lincoln	William J. Brennan, Jr.	1956–1990	Eisenhower
William Strong	1870–1880	Grant	Charles E. Whittaker	1957–1962	Eisenhower
Joseph P. Bradley	1870–1892	Grant	Potter Stewart	1958–1981	Eisenhower
Ward Hunt	1873–1882	Grant	Byron R. White	1962–	Kennedy
Morrison R. Waite	1874–1888	Grant	Arthur J. Goldberg	1962–1965	Kennedy
John M. Harlan	1877–1911	Hayes	Abe Fortas	1965–1970	Johnson
William B. Woods	1881–1887	Hayes	Thurgood Marshall	1967–	Johnson
Stanley Matthews	1881–1889	Garfield	**Warren E. Burger**	1969–1986	Nixon
Horace Gray	1882–1902	Arthur	Harry A. Blackmun	1970–	Nixon
Samuel Blatchford	1882–1893	Arthur	Lewis F. Powell, Jr.	1971–1988	Nixon
Lucious Q. C. Lamar	1888–1893	Cleveland	William H. Rehnquist	1971–1986	Nixon
Melville W. Fuller	1888–1910	Cleveland	John Paul Stevens	1975–	Ford
David J. Brewer	1890–1910	B. Harrison	Sandra Day O'Connor	1981–	Reagan
Henry B. Brown	1891–1906	B. Harrison	**William H. Rehnquist**	1986–	Reagan
George Shiras, Jr.	1892–1903	B. Harrison	Antonin Scalia	1986–	Reagan
			Anthony Kennedy	1988–	Reagan

Chief Justices in bold type

[1]The date on which the justice took his judicial oath is here used as the date of the beginning of his service, for until that oath is taken he is not vested with the prerogatives of his office. Justices, however, receive their commissions ("letters patent") before taking their oath—in some instances, in the preceding year.
[2]Acting Chief Justice; Senate refused to confirm appointment.

Growth of U.S. Population, 1790–1987

Census	Population	Percentage of Increase over Preceding Census	Population per Square Mile
1790	3,929,214		4.5
1800	5,308,483	35.1	6.1
1810	7,239,881	36.4	4.3
1820	9,638,453	33.1	5.5
1830	12,866,020	33.5	7.3
1840	17,069,453	32.7	9.7
1850	23,191,876	35.9	7.9
1860	31,443,321	35.6	10.6
1870	39,818,449	26.6	13.4
1880	50,155,783	26.0	16.9
1890	62,947,714	25.5	21.2
1900	75,994,575	20.7	25.6
1910	91,972,266	21.0	30.9
1920	105,710,620	14.9	35.5
1930	122,775,046	16.1	41.2
1940	131,669,275	7.2	44.2
1950	150,697,361	14.5	50.7
[1]1960	178,464,236	18.4	59.9
1970	204,765,770	14.7	68.8
1980	226,504,825	10.6	76.1
‡1987	243,396,000	7.5	81.8

[1]Not including Alaska (pop. 226,167) and Hawaii (632,772).
‡As of July 1, 1987.

U.S. Population Projections by Region and State, 1988, 1990, 2000, 2010

DIVISION, AND STATE	Total (thousands)				Percent Change		
	1988	1990	2000	2010	1980–1990	1990–2000	2000–2010
U.S.	245,529	249,891	267,747	282,055	10.3	7.1	5.3
Northeast	12,906	13,078	13,775	14,243	5.9	5.3	3.4
ME	1,193	1,212	1,271	1,308	7.8	4.9	2.9
NH	1,088	1,142	1,333	1,455	24.1	16.7	9.1
VT	552	562	591	608	9.9	5.1	2.9
MA	5,849	5,880	6,087	6,255	2.5	3.5	2.8
RI	989	1,002	1,049	1,085	5.8	4.6	3.4
CT	3,235	3,279	3,445	3,532	5.5	5.1	2.5
Mid-Atlantic	37,372	37,499	38,035	38,253	1.9	1.4	.6
NY	17,755	17,773	17,986	18,139	1.2	1.2	.8
NJ	7,756	7,899	8,546	8,980	7.3	8.2	5.1
PA	11,860	11,827	11,503	11,134	−.3	−2.7	−3.2
Eastern North-Central	41,923	42,055	41,746	41,111	.9	−.7	−1.5
OH	10,779	10,791	10,629	10,397	−.1	−1.5	−2.2
IN	5,531	5,550	5,502	5,409	1.1	−.9	−1.7
IL	11,584	11,612	11,580	11,495	1.6	−.3	−.7
MI	9,231	9,293	9,250	9,097	.3	−.5	−1.7
WI	4,797	4,808	4,784	4,713	2.2	−.5	−1.5
Western North-Central	17,652	17,722	17,850	17,907	3.1	.7	.3
MN	4,271	4,324	4,490	4,578	6.1	3.8	2.0
IA	2,803	2,758	2,549	2,382	−5.3	−7.6	−6.6
MO	5,132	5,192	5,383	5,521	5.6	3.7	2.6
ND	669	660	629	611	1.1	−4.7	−3.0
SD	707	708	714	722	2.5	.8	1.2
NE	1,593	1,588	1,556	1,529	1.2	−2.0	−1.7
KS	2,477	2,492	2,529	2,564	5.4	1.5	1.4
South Atlantic	42,337	43,742	50,002	55,110	18.4	14.3	10.2
DE	649	666	734	790	12.0	10.2	7.7
MD	4,599	4,729	5,274	5,688	12.1	11.5	7.8
DC	617	614	634	672	−3.8	3.2	6.0
VA	5,977	6,157	6,877	7,410	15.2	11.7	7.8
WV	1,886	1,856	1,722	1,617	−4.8	−7.3	−6.1
NC	6,512	6,690	7,483	8,154	13.7	11.8	9.0
SC	3,464	3,549	3,906	4,205	13.7	10.1	7.6
GA	6,384	6,663	7,957	9,045	22.0	19.4	13.7
FL	12,249	12,818	15,415	17,530	31.5	20.3	13.7
Eastern South-Central	15,408	15,597	16,285	16,847	6.3	4.4	3.5
KY	3,738	3,745	3,733	3,710	2.3	−.3	−.6
TN	4,891	4,972	5,266	5,500	8.3	5.9	4.5
AL	4,119	4,181	4,410	4,609	7.4	5.5	4.5
MS	2,661	2,699	2,877	3,028	7.1	6.6	5.3
Western South-Central	27,388	27,937	30,632	32,961	17.6	9.6	7.6
AR	2,400	2,427	2,529	2,624	6.1	4.2	3.7
LA	4,507	4,513	4,516	4,545	7.3	.1	.6
OK	3,288	3,285	3,376	3,511	8.6	2.8	4.0
TX	17,192	17,712	20,211	22,281	24.5	14.1	10.2
Mountain	13,517	13,995	16,022	17,679	23.1	14.5	10.3
MT	811	805	794	794	2.4	−1.4	.1
ID	1,009	1,017	1,047	1,079	7.7	3.0	3.0
WY	505	502	489	487	6.9	−2.6	−.4
CO	3,350	3,434	3,813	4,098	18.8	11.0	7.5
NM	1,557	1,632	1,968	2,248	25.3	20.5	14.3
AZ	3,542	3,752	4,618	5,319	38.0	23.1	15.2
UT	1,722	1,776	1,991	2,171	21.6	12.1	9.0
NV	1,021	1,076	1,303	1,484	34.4	21.1	13.8
Pacific	37,027	38,265	43,400	47,943	20.3	13.4	10.5
WA	4,564	4,657	4,991	5,282	12.7	7.2	5.8
OR	2,733	2,766	2,877	2,991	5.0	4.0	4.0
CA	28,074	29,126	33,500	37,347	23.1	15.0	11.5
AK	554	576	687	765	43.4	19.2	11.4
HI	1,101	1,141	1,345	1,559	18.2	17.9	15.9

Source: U.S. Bureau of the Census, *Current Population Reports*, series P–25, No. 1017.

Credits

Text Photos

Positions of the photographs are indicated in abbreviated form as follows: top **T**, bottom **B**, center **C**, left **L**, right **R**. All photographs not credited are the property of HarperCollins.

Front Matter, p. xxxvii © Earth Satellite Corporation GEOPIC ®

936 UPI/Bettmann Newsphotos   937L Paul Fusco/Magnum
Photos   937R UPI/Bettmann Newsphotos   939 Leonard
Freed/Magnum Photos   940 James Pickerell   941 Roland
Freeman/Magnum Photos

Chapter 32

949T Tony Korody/Sygma   949B Michael Abramson/Gamma-Liaison
950 Doug Wilson/Black Star   953L Joe Rodriguez/Black Star
953R Dan Connolly/Gamma-Liaison   956L Dennis Brack/
Black Star   956R D. Goldberg/Sygma   958 Martin A.
Levick/Black Star   960 Bob Sacha   961 Larry Barns/Black Star
962 AP/Wide World   965 SIPA-Press   966 Nik Wheeler/
Black Star   968 William Karel/Sygma   969 Ledru/Sygma
970 SIPA/Black Star

Chapter 33

972 Pete Souza/The White House   976 Mark Sherman/Bruce Coleman
Inc.   977 Bob Zschiesche/Courtesy Our Folks   980 Michael
Evans/The White House   982T Marlette/*The Cincinnati
Reader*   982B J. Langeuin/Sygma   984 Stuart Franken/Sygma
990 Reprinted by permission of United Feature Syndicate,
Inc.   991 Alan Tannenbaum/Sygma   992 SIPA-Press
993, 995 AP/Wide World   996 Andrew Hoolbroke/Black
Star   998 Bill Fitz-Patrick/The White House   1000 Arthur
Grace/Sygma   1002 UPI/Bettmann Newsphotos   1003L Larry
Downing/Woodfin Camp & Associates   1003R Steve Liss/
Gamma-Liaison   1005 Reuters/UPI/Bettmann Newsphotos
1007 Juergen Mueller-Sceck/Stern/Black Star

Picture Essays

The page number after which each essay falls is indicated below the
essay's title.

Picture Essay 3
"White City" The Columbian Exposition of 1893
following p. 650

1 Culver Pictures
2 T Chicago Historical Society B Chicago Historical Society
3 L Culver Pictures R Culver Pictures
4 T Culver Pictures CL Chicago Historical Society CR Brown Brothers B
Culver Pictures

Picture Essay 4
Mexican-American Experience in the Southwest
following p. 746

1 The Fine Arts Museum of San Francisco, Gift of Mrs. Eleanor Martin
2 TL Kraushaar Galleries, New York TR The University of Texas Institute
of Texan Cultures at San Antonio B Otis A. Aultman Collection, Southwest Collection, El Paso Public Library
3 L Kraushaar Galleries, New York R Bob Fitch/Black Star
4 TL Jose Azel/Contact Press Images TR, B Wide World Photos

Picture Essay 5
The Space Race: Commitment to the Future
following p. 906

1 NASA
2 L Sovfoto R © 1957 by The New York Times Company, Reprinted by
permission B NASA
3 ALL NASA
4 TL M. Naythons/Gamma-Liaison TR Wide World Photos B Ralph
Morse/LIFE Magazine © 1962, Time Warner Inc.

Literary

In addition, the authors and publisher acknowledge with gratitude permission to reprint, quote from, or adapt the following materials. (The
numbers shown below refer to pages of this text.)

520 Hamlin Garland, *a Son of the Middle Border*. P.F. Collier & Son,
1914.   543 From *The Price* by Arthur Miller. Copyright © 1968, 1969
by Arthur Miller and Ingeborg M. Miller, trustee. All rights reserved/
Reprinted by permission of Viking Penguin Inc. and International Cre-
ative Management, Inc.   588 From Archives of the Commonwealth,
Boston. Records of the Medical Examiner 1895. In the Executive Office of
Public Safety, Medical Examiner Records. As cited in *Out of Work: The
First Century of Unemployment in Massachusetts* by Alexander Keyssar,
Cambridge University Press 1986.   661 Joe Hill, "Workers of the World,
Awaken!" cited in *American Folksongs of Protest* by John Greenway. Uni-
versity of Pennsylvania Press, 1953.   667 (Map) Adapted from *Historic
City: The Settlement of Chicago*, City of Chicago, department of
Planning.   670 From "Chicago" in *Chicago Poems* by Carl Sandburg,
copyright 1916 by Holt, Rinehart and Winston, Inc.; renewed 1944 by
Carl Sandburg. Reprinted by permission of Harcourt Brace Jovanovich,
Inc.   694 Upton Sinclair, *The Jungle*, 1906.   731 "The New Day" by
Fenton Johnson cited in *The Book of American Negro Poetry*, ed. by James
Weldon Johnson. New York: Harcourt Brace and Company, 1931.   772
Studs Terkel, *Hard Times*. New York: Pantheon Books, 1970, p. 41.
880 From *I Have a Dream* by Martin Luther King, Jr. Copyright © 1963
by Martin Luther King, Jr. Reprinted by permission of Joan Daves.

Index

Automobile industry, 648, 741–42; assembly line production in, 648, 740; and foreign competition, 951, 979, 986; oligopoly in, 743; organization of workers in, 651, 785–86; output controls for, 651; pollution controls in, 979; response of, to energy crisis, 950; safety recalls in, 964; shift to smaller cars in, 950; strikes in, 786

Ayer, N. W., and Son, 541

Babbitt (Lewis), 749
Babcock, Orville E., 483
Baby and Child Care (Spock), 860
Baby boom, 818–19, 856, 858, 918
"Back from Elba" movement, 656
Baer, George F., 693
Baez, Joan, 920–21
Bailey, James A., 567
Bailey v. *Drexel Furniture Company* (1922), 682
Baker, Howard, 1001
Baker, James, 998
Baker, Mark, 910
Baker, Newton D., 688
Baker, Ray Stannard, 725
Baker v. *Carr* (1962), 881
Bakke, Allen, 957
Baling press, 519
Ball, George, 908
Ballinger, Richard A., 697
Ballinger-Pinchot affair, 697
Baltimore, Maryland: railroads in, 531; tenements in, 558–59
Baltimore and Ohio (B&O) Railroad, 531, 534, 550
Bancroft, Hubert Howe, 513
Banks/Banking: under the Federal Reserve system, 768, 951, 986–87; gold standard as issue, 591, 598, 602, 607, 610, 612; during Great Depression, 773–74; and savings-and-loan industry, 1004–1005; post-World War I, 743. *See also* Money
Banks, Louis, 772
Bannock Indians, 494, 500
Baptist church, 759
Bara, Theda, 747
Barbed wire: invention of, 519; use of, in West, 516
Barnard College, 573, 654
Barnett, Ross, 878–79
Barnum, P. T., 567
Barrios, 731
Barry, Jan, 910
Barry, Leonora M., 547
Barton, Bruce, 743
Baruch, Bernard, 727, 833–34
Baruch Plan, 833–34
Baseball, 567, 667, 747
Basketball, 568
Battle of the standards, 514
Baum, Frank, 608–609
Bay of Pigs invasion, 902
Beatles, the, 921
Beatniks, 865
Beats, 863, 865
Beecher, Henry Ward, 580
Begin, Menachem, 967, 982
Belknap, William E., 483
Bell, Alexander Graham, 526, 539
Bell, Daniel, 975
Bell, Griffin, 964
Bell Telephone Company, 539
Bellamy, Edward, 579–80
Belleau Wood, 724

Bellows, George W., 669–70
Belushi, John, 995
Bemis, Edward, 688
Bemis, Samuel F., 619
Ben Hur (Wallace), 605
Bentsen, Lloyd, 1002
Berkman, Alexander, 549, 752
Berlin: blockade of, 837, 840; construction of wall in, 901; crisis in (1958), 898; crisis in (1961), 898, 901; opening of wall in, 1006
Berlin, Irving, 668
Berlin-Rome-Tokyo axis, 802–803
Bernays, Edward, 743
Bernstein, Carl, 940–41
Bessemer, Henry, 534
Beta Test, 729
Bethlehem Steel, 536, 662
Bethune, Mary McLeod, 786
Bethune-Cookman College, 786
Beveridge, Albert J., 696
Bias, Len, 995
Biden, Joseph, 1005
Big Bonanza, 512
Big Foot, Chief of Teton Sioux, 500, 502, 507
Big Three Conferences, 824
Billington, Ray Allen, 521
Billy the Kid. *See* Bonney, William
Binet, Alfred, 728
Biogenetic Law, 620
Birmingham, Alabama, segregation in, 879–80
Birth control, 686–87. *See also* Abortion
Birth control pill, 687
Birth of a Nation, 476–77, 668
Birthrate: baby boom following World War II, 818–19, 856, 858, 918; decline in, 746, 955. *See also* Birth control
Black, Hugo, 790, 881
Black Beauty (Sewell), 605
Black Codes, 466–67, 474, 517
Blackfoot Indians, 496
Black Hills, 500
Black Hills Gold Rush (1875), 500, 513
Black Kettle, Chief, 498
Blackmun, Harry, 931, 958
Black nationalism, 923
Black Panther party, 922
Black power, 922–23
Black Reconstruction in America (Du Bois), 476–77
Blaine, James G., 482, 592, 620, 622, 624
Bland-Allison Silver Purchase Act (1878), 591, 593
Bliss, Tasker H., 732
Bliss, William Dwight Porter, 580
Blough, Roger, 877
Blues, 750
Blumenthal, Michael, 964
Boland Amendment, 984, 1000
Bolden, Charles (Buddy), 668
Bolger, Ray, 609
Bolsheviks, seizure of power of, in Russia, 722, 726
Bombard, James, 911
Bonanza farms, 519
Bonanza mines, 593
Bonheur, Rosa, 729
Bonney, William (Billy the Kid), 510
Bonus marches, 773
Bootlegging, 754
Borah, William, 734, 804
Bork, Robert, 999
Boston, 623
Boston: immigrants in, 559; settlement houses in, 580–81
Boulder Dam, 773

Bourke-White, Margaret, 813
Bow, Clara, 747
Boxer Rebellion, 641
Boxing, 568, 747
Boyington, Margaret, 561
Bozeman Trail, 499
Bracker, Milton, 812
Bradley, Omar, 813, 823, 845, 913
Branch, Taylor, 872
Brandeis, Louis, 683, 699, 701–702
Brandeis Brief, 683
Brazil: overthrow of military junta in, 905
Bremer, Arthur, 938
Brennan, William J., Jr., 881
Breslin, Jimmy, 927
Breton, Andre, 863
Brewster, Kingman, 938
Brezhnev, Leonid, 935, 982, 1001
Brezhnev doctrine, 1006
Briand, Aristide, 798
Brice, Fanny, 668
British Guiana, boundary dispute between Venezuela and, 622
British West Indies, U.S. trade with, 622
Bronson House, 581
Brooks, Harriet, 654
Brown, H. Rap, 922
Brown, James, 923
Brown, Joseph E., 486
Brown Berets, 924
Brownmiller, Susan, 925–26
Brown v. *Board of Education of Topeka* (1954), 577, 870, 878
Bruce, Blanche K., 478
Brussels Treaty (1948), 837
Bryan, Mary, 610
Bryan, William Jennings: crusade of, against evolution, 759; in election of 1896, 610–612; in election of 1900, 613, 638; in election of 1908, 695; and issue of coinage, 608–609; as secretary of state, 708, 713–15, 718; and the Spanish-American War, 628–29, 636–37
Bryn Mawr College, 573
Brzezinski, Zbigniew, 965
Buchanan v. *Worley* (1917), 657
Buckley, Christopher A. ("Blind Boss"), 562–63
Buckley, William, 975, 999
Buffalo Bill's Wild West Show, 504
Buffalo hunting, 494, 496, 498, 503–504
Buffalo soldiers, 506–507
Bui, Dr. Thieu, 961
Bulgaria, communism in, 832; end of repression in, 1005
Bulge, Battle of the, 823
Bull Moose party, 699
Bundy, McGeorge, 900, 904, 908
Burchfield, Charles, 750
Bureau of Construction and Repair, 625
Burford, Ann Gorsuch, 978, 999
Burger, Warren, 931, 999
Burgess, John W., 476–77, 620
Burlington Railroad, 509
Burnham, Walter Dean, 977
Burns, Lucy, 682
Bush, George, 963, 975, 991; and China, 1005; domestic programs of, 1004–1005; in election of 1988, 1002–1004; foreign policy of, 1005; as president, 1004, 1008
Bush-Gorbachev summit at Malta, 1007
Business, conglomerates in, 952; growth of, in 1920s, 724–25; in World War I, 730–31; in World War II, 816–18. *See also* Commerce; Industry; Trusts
Byington, Margaret, 561
Byrd, Harry, 883
Byrnes, James, 817

International Bureau of the American Republics, 622
International Business Machines (IBM), 952
International Harvester Corporation, 658
Internationalism, 981–84
Interstate Commerce Act (1887), 591
Interstate Commerce Commission (ICC), 591, 693, 878
Interventionists, versus isolationists, in World War II, 806–807
Inventions, 538–41
Iowa, farming in, 517
Iran, 897; revolution in, 948, 968; hostage crisis, 968, 976; overthrow of Shah in, 968–69; war with Iraq, 999–1000, 1002
Iran-Contra affair, 999–1002
Iraq, and war with Iran, 999–1000, 1002
Irish Benevolent Society, 561
Iron Curtain, 831
Irvine, Alexander, 580
Isakowsky, Tillie, 571
Isolationism, 801–802; versus interventionists in World War II, 804; in 1930s, 801–805; World War II as end to, 806
Israel: and Camp David accords, 967; Middle East policy in, 946; Six Day War in, 946; Yom Kippur War in, 946–47, 967
Isthmian Canal Commission, 710
Italy: immigration from, 559, 601; and World War II, 801–802, 808

Jackson, Kenneth, 860
Jackson State College, student killings at, 936
Jameson, Roscoe, 731
James, William, 565, 636, 682, 728
Japan: attack of, on Pearl Harbor, 809–10; bombing of, in World War II, 826; competition between automobile industry of, with U.S., 979; expansion of, in Asia, as cause of World War II, 798, 800–801, 808; "Gentlemen's Agreement" with, 712; invasion of China by, 801–802, 804; in 1930s, 800–801; leaving of League of Nations by, 802; occupation of, after World War II, 842; relations with U.S. in early 1900s, 712–13; "Twenty-One Demands" of, 712; and U.S. annexation of Hawaii, 623–24; and war with Russia, 712; and World War II, 802, 808–10, 815–16, 825–26
Japanese-Americans, forced relocation of, 821
Jaworski, Leon, 940
Jazz, 668, 750
Jednota Ceskyck Dam, 562
Jehovah's Witnesses, 759
Jewett, Sarah Orne, 605
Jicarilla Apache Indians, 496
Jim Crow laws, 474, 476–77, 488, 572, 576–77, 655
Jingoism, 716
Job Corps program, 884
John Birch Society, 881
Johns Hopkins University, 573, 575, 579
Johnson, Andrew: early career of, 464; effort to impeach, 470–71, 479, 590–91; in election of 1864, 465; as president, 464–66, 473; reconstruction plan of, 465–66
Johnson, Fenton, 731
Johnson, Hiram, 690, 698
Johnson, Hugh, 776
Johnson, James Weldon, 750
Johnson, Lyndon B.: assumption of presidency, 882; avoidance of tax increase, 950; and civil rights, 467, 871, 885–86; decision not to run in 1968, 913, 926; domestic programs of, 883; in

election of 1964, 883–85; foreign policy of, 904–14; Great Society program of, 885–87; as president, 882–83, 961; as senator, 868; and Vietnam War, 904–14; as vice-president, 874, 878, 883
Johnson, Samuel, 519
Johnson, Tom L., 688
Jones, Joseph, 838
Jones, "Mother" Mary, 664
Jones, Samuel M., 688
Joplin, Scott, 567
Jordan, David Starr, 510, 573
Jordan, Hamilton, 964
Joseph, Chief of Nez Percé, 500
Judges. See individual judges by name; Supreme Court, U.S.
Judson, Phoebe, 508
Julian, George, 469
Jungle, The (Sinclair), 647, 694

Kaiser, Henry J., 817
Kaiser Aluminum, 958
Kalakaua (King of Hawaii), 623
Kandinsky, Wassily, 862
Kane, Woodbury, 618
Kansas: farming in, 517; People's party in, 597; settlement of, 498, 517
Kansas City, 519, 556
Kansas-Nebraska Act (1854), 608
Kansas Pacific Railroad, 515
Kasson, John A., 620
Kaufman, Irving, 849
Kearney, 807
Kearns, Doris, 909
Keating-Owen Act (1916), 682, 703
Keats, John, 864
Kelley, Florence, 581–82, 677, 717
Kelley, Oliver H., 519
Kellogg, Frank B., 734, 798
Kellogg, John H., 570
Kellogg-Briand Treaty (1928), 798
Kellogg's, 541
Kelly, "Honest" John, 562–63
Kelly, William, 534
Kemp, Jack, 978
Kenna, "Hinky Dink," 562
Kennan, George, 834–35, 841, 1007
Kennedy, Anthony, 999
Kennedy, Edward (Ted), 964, 976
Kennedy, Jacqueline, 882
Kennedy, John F.: assassination of, 882; and the Bay of Pigs invasion, 902; and Berlin crisis, 899, 901; cabinet and advisers of, 875–76, 899–900; civil rights under, 878–80; and the Cold War, 899–904; and Cuban Missile Crisis, 902–904; debate with Nixon, 873–74; domestic program of, 876–77; in election of 1960, 873–75; foreign policy of, 899–904; and nuclear weapons, 900–901; as senator, 899; and Vietnam War, 905
Kennedy, Robert: assassination of, 927; as attorney general, 875, 878–79, 904; in election of 1968, 926–27; as senator, 926
Kent State University, student killings at, 936
Kerouac, Jack, 865
Kerr, Clark, 974
Ketcham, Rebecca, 505
Keynesian theory, 977
Khomeini, Ayatollah Ruhollah, 968, 999–1000
Khrushchev, Nikita, 897–98; and the Berlin crisis, 901; and the Cuban missile crisis, 902–904; support of, for wars of national liberation, 901–902

Kickapoo Indians, 507
Killian, James R., 866
Kilrain, Jake, 568
Kim Il-Sung, 843
King, Martin Luther, Jr.: assassination of, 923; as civil rights leader, 872, 879–80, 885–86, 922–23
Kinsey, Dr. Alfred C., 748
Kiowa Indians, 496, 499–500, 502, 507
Kirkpatrick, Jeane, 981
Kissinger, Henry: under Ford, 965; under Nixon, 929–30, 933–37, 946–47
Kitty Hawk, North Carolina, 613
Klamath Indians, 496
Kline, Franz, 862
Knights of Labor, 661
Knights of the White Camelia, 480
Knowland, William, 895
Know-Nothing (American) party, 848
Knox, Frank, 819
Knox, Philander C., 712–13
Kolko, Gabriel, 839
Koop, C. Everett, 994
Korea, communism in, 843–45
Korean airliner, shooting down of, by Soviets, 985
Korean War, 843–45, 858
Kuhn, Loeb and Company, 692
Ku Klux Klan: after Civil War, 462, 476–77, 480–82; modern, 749, 755, 758, 961
Ku Klux Klan Acts (1870–71), 481
Kyner, James H., 494

Labor: African Americans in, 544, 604, 655–56; child, 543–45, 571, 581–82, 603–605, 655, 682; culture of, 545–46; immigrant, 494, 514, 544, 559, 657–58; and New Deal legislation, 783–84; women in, 543–45, 569–71, 582, 603–605, 653–55, 730, 745, 788, 819, 860, 925, 955; during World War I, 730–31; during World War II, 818. See also Labor unions
Labor agents, recruitment of immigrants by, 658–59
Labor Department, creation of, 702
Labor unions: African Americans as members of, 547–48, 680, 786; Clayton Act support for, 701; collective bargaining, 776, 783, 785; decline in membership, 744; formation of national, 546–48; growth in membership, 660; Mexican-Americans as members of, 924; under National Labor Relations Act, 784; under New Deal, 784–86; in 1920s, 744; role of, in strikes, 547–49, 659–60; social functions of, 548; under Taft-Hartley Act, 846; women as members of, 547, 660, 786
Ladies Anti-Beef Trust Association, 570
Ladies' Home Journal, 569, 646, 745
La Follette, Robert, 721; as governor, 690, 694, 698, 696–97; as presidential candidate, 763; as senator, 690, 763
La Follette's Magazine, 717
LaGuardia, Fiorello, 820
Lahr, Bert, 609
Laissez-faire policies, 486, 579
Land-grant colleges, 572
Landon, Alfred M., 789
Land ownership: by Native Americans, 502–503; by railroads, 509, 529; speculation, 502, 509
Lansing, Robert, 718–19, 721, 732, 734
Laos, 912, 961
La Raza Unida, 959
Lathrop, Julia, 660

president, 690; on Wisconsin Idea, 690; on World War I, 720
Roosevelt Corollary, to the Monroe Doctrine, 711–12, 714, 800
Root, Elihu, 690, 710
Root-Takahira Agreement (1908), 712
Rosenberg, Ethel, 849
Rosenberg, Harold, 862
Rosenberg, Julius, 849
Rosenfeld, Morris, 545, 568
Rose, Peter I., 960
Rose, Reginald, 864
Ross, David, 911
Ross, Edward A., 560, 683, 690
Rostow, Walt, 900, 905
Roszak, Theodore, 921
Rotary Club, 749
Rotary press, 541
Rothko, Mark, 862–63
Roth, William, 978
Roughing It (Twain), 512
Rough Riders, 618, 620, 631–33, 641
Rubin, Jerry, 922
Ruby, Jack, 882
Rudd, Lydia, 504
Rudman, Warren, 987–88
Ruiz, Raúl, 924
"Rule of reason," 698
Rumania, communism in, 832; end of repression in, 1005–1006
Rural Electrification Administration (REA), 784
Rural free delivery (RFD), 520, 653
Rusk, Dean, 843, 899–900, 903–904
Russell, Richard, 883
Russia: Bolshevik seizure of power in, 722, 726; revolution in, 726–27, 752; and war with Japan, 712; in World War I, 716, 722, 732. *See also* Soviet Union
Rutgers University, 568
Ruth, Babe, 747

Sacco, Nicola, 753–54
Sachs, Sadie, 686
Sadat, Anwar, 967
St. Denis, Ruth, 669
St. Louis, Missouri, 519; African Americans in, 730; industry in, 528; population decline of, 953; railroads in, 531
Sakharov, Andrei, 969
Salisbury, Lord Robert Arthur Talbot Gascayne-Cecil, 622
SALT (Strategic Arms Limitation Talks), 935, 965, 969–70, 982, 1002
Salt Lake City, Utah, 511
Samoa, U.S. interest in, 624
Sampson, William T., 632
Sandburg, Carl, 629, 670
Sand Creek reservation, 499
Sandinistas, 966–67, 984, 1000
San Francisco, 511; Haight-Ashbury in, 921; machine politics in, 562; racial segregation in, 712; riots against foreign workers in, 514
Sanger, Margaret, 655, 686–87
Sanitary conditions, in cities, 559
Sankey, Ira B., 566
Santa Fe Railroad, 509, 534, 599
Santo Domingo: attempt at annexation of, 622; U.S. trade with, 622
Santoli, Al, 910
Santos, Robert, 911
Saudi Arabia, 845
Savings-and-loan industry, 1004–1005
Savio, Mario, 919
Scalawags, 474, 476–77

Scalia, Antonin, 999
Scammon, Richard, 929, 934
Schiller Building, 557
Schlafly, Phyllis, 956
Schlesinger, Arthur M., Sr., 904
Schneiderman, Rose, 652
Scholastic Aptitude Test (SAT), 729
School and Society (Dewey), 683
Schools. *See* Education
Schurz, Carl, 482
Schwab, Charles M., 535–36
Science, changes in, in response to Sputnik, 866
Scientific management, principles of, 651, 662–63
Scopes, John, trial of, 759
Scott, Thomas A., 531, 535
Scowcroft, Brent, 1005
Sears, Richard W., 542
Sears, Roebuck, 541–42
Seattle, Washington, riots against foreign workers in, 514
Sea Wolf, The (London), 606
Secession, Lincoln's theory on, 464
Second Child Labor Act (1919), 682
Sedition Act (1918), 725
Segregation, 473–74, 488, 572, 576–77, 869; ending, 870, 872; in South, zoning as tool of, 667. *See also* Civil rights; Jim Crow laws
Segretti, Donald, 938
Selassie, Haile, 802
Selective Service Act (1917), 722
Seminole Indians, 521
Seneca Falls convention, 681
Separate but equal doctrine, 572, 577. *See also* Plessy v. Ferguson
Serling, Rod, 864
Seward, William Henry, as secretary of state, 621, 642
"Seward's Folly," 621
Sewell, Anna, 605
Seventeenth Amendment, 689, 698
Seymour, Horatio, 479
Sex in Education (Clarke), 574
Sex roles, changes in, in 1920s, 745
Sexual revolution, in the 1920s, 748
Shame of the Cities (Steffens), 647, 677
Sharecropping, 473
"Share the Wealth" movement, 782
Shasta Indians, 496
Shaw, Anna Howard, 682
Sheehan, Neil, 932
Sheppard-Towner Act (1921), 655, 746
Sherman, James S., 695, 698
Sherman, John, 479, 636
Sherman, William T., 472
Sherman Antitrust Act (1890), 593, 692, 698
Sherman Silver Purchase Act (1890), 593, 602
Shopping center, first, 742
Shoshoni Indians, 494, 500
Shriver, R. Sargent, 884, 939
Shultz, George, 981, 1000
Sierra Club, 949
"Significance of the Frontier in American History." *See* Turner, Frederick Jackson
Silver coinage: issue of, 593, 602, 607, 610; platforms for free, 598, 610
Simmons, William J., 754
Simon, Theodore, 728
Simpson, Jeremiah, 597
Sims, William S., 723
Sin and Society (Ross), 683
Sinclair, Upton, 647, 694, 779
"Single-tax" clubs, 578
Sink or Swim (Alger), 605
Sino-Soviet treaty, 843

Sioux Indians, 496, 498–500, 507, 513
Sioux War of 1865–67, 499
Sioux War of 1876, 500
Sirhan, Sirhan B., 927
Sirica, John, 940–41
Sister Carrie (Dreiser), 607
Sit-ins, by African Americans, 873
Sitting Bull, 500, 504
Six-day war in Israel. *See* Yom Kippur War
Six-Dollar Day, 665
Sixteenth Amendment, 698, 701, 727
Skliris, Leonidas G., 658
Skyscrapers, 557, 744–45
Slaughterhouse cases of 1875, 576
Sloan, John, 670
Smeal, Eleanor, 956
Smith, Alfred E., 763–64, 789
Smith, Bessie, 668
Smith, Gerald L. K., 788–89
Smith, Margaret Chase, 852
Smith College, 573
Snyder, Charles, 846
Sochen, June, 747
Social Darwinism, 578–79
Social Democratic party, 684
Social Gospel movement, 580
Socialism, 684–85
Socialist Labor Party, 684–85
Socialist party of America, 601, 684, 686, 726
Social-justice movement, 679–82
Social reform: and the Great Society, 885–87; under New Deal, 779–84; under Roosevelt (Theodore), 699; under Wilson, 671–74
Social Security, 782–83, 792, 954; creation of, 782–83; under Eisenhower, 868; exempt workers, 786; Goldwater on, 884; Medicare and Medicaid under, 885, 887; under Reagan, 978–79; Supreme Court rulings on, 790; under Truman, 866
Social Security Act (1935), 782–83
Social workers, 582, 679
Society for the Suppression of Vice, 566
Society of Czech Women, 562
Sodbusters, 517–19
Solidarity movement in Poland, 1005
Somme River, 723
Somoza, Anastasio, 966–67, 984
Son of the Middle Border (Garland), 595
Sorensen, Theodore, 876
Souls of Black Folk (Du Bois), 575, 656
South: reconstruction in, 462–71, 474–78. *See also* Civil rights; Civil War; Confederate States of America; Jim Crow laws
South Carolina: adoption of "eight box" law, 589; Civil War damage in, 471; education in, 572; Klan violence in, 480; Jim Crow laws in, 577; reconstruction government in, 475, 482
South Dakota. *See* Dakotas
South End House, 580–81
Southeast Asia, communism in, 892, 905–906, 912, 937, 966. *See also* Vietnam War
South Korea, U.S. foreign aid to, 969. *See also* Korea
South Pass, 505
Southern Alliance, 596; adoption of Ocale Demands, 597; and formation of third political party, 597
Southern Christian Leadership Conference (SCLC), 873
Southern Manifesto, 870
Southern Pacific Railroad, 532
Southern Railway, 534
Soviet Union: Afghanistan invasion, 970, 976, 980, 1002; and the arms race, 981–82; in Berlin crisis of 1961, 901; and Chernobyl disaster, 992–93; and China, 842, 895, 966; commu-

icans in, 515; ranching in, 514–16; settlement of, 494–96, 504–510; and transportation, 504–505
Western Federation of Miners, 664
Western Pacific Railroad, 658
Westinghouse, George, 541
Westinghouse air brake, 526, 541
Westinghouse Electric Company, 541, 768
Westmoreland, William, 912
Weyler y Nicolau, Valeriano, 627, 635
Wharton, Edith, 750
What Price Glory? (Stallings, Anderson), 735
What Social Classes Owe to Each Other (Sumner), 578
Wheeler, Burton, 790
Whiskey Ring, 483, 941
White Caps, 510
White Collar (Mills), 865
White, George, 488, 630
White, Henry, 732
White, Theodore, 977
White, Walter, 781
White, William Allen, 556, 565, 677, 806
White League, 481–82
White Shadows (McKay), 750
White supremacy, 481, 486–87
Whitman, Walt, 529, 605
Whittier, John Greenleaf, 526
Whyte, William H., 864
Wiggins, Kate Douglas, 668
Wild West Show, 504
Wiley, Harvey W., 694
Wilhelm II (King of Germany), 716
Willard, Frances E., 566
Williams College, 727
Williams v. *Mississippi* (1898), 589
Willkie, Wendell, 807
Wilson, Charles E., 867
Wilson, Edith Bolling, 734–35
Wilson, Luenza, 504
Wilson, William B., 702
Wilson, Woodrow, 612, 690; on *Birth of a Nation*, 476–77; cabinet of, 702; on child labor, 682; death of, 736; in election of 1912, 699; foreign policy of, 709, 711, 713–16, 726; fourteen points of, 732–36; as governor of New Jersey, 700; illness of, 734–35; inauguration of, 700; on labor issues, 702–703; on literacy tests, 659; New Freedom program of, 699–700; as president, 700, 761; on racial issues, 702; relations with Congress, 700–701; on woman suffrage, 703; and World War I, 708–709, 716, 718–20, 722–23, 725, 733

Wilson-Gorman Tariff Act (1894), 602, 627
Winnebago Indians, 496
WIN (Whip Inflation Now) program, 951
Wisconsin Idea, 690
Woman Rebel, 686
Woman's Peace party, 717
Woman's rights movement: in 1920s, 745–47; in 1950s, 860–61; in 1960s, 924–26; in 1980s, 979
Woman suffrage movement, 681–82
Woman Who Toils (Van Vorst and Van Vorst), 582
Women: African-American, 655; changes in legal codes pertaining to, 570; changing roles of, 955–56; college education for, 573, 680, 925; education of, 925; effect of New Deal on, 787–88; in election of 1912, 699; in government, 788, 980; in labor force, 543–45, 569–71, 582, 603–605, 653–55, 730, 745, 788, 819, 860, 925, 955; in labor unions, 547, 660, 786; laws prohibiting discrimination against, 925; life expectancy of, 954; in Mexican-American families, 510; in mining camps, 513–14; in Native American culture, 498; professional opportunities for, 544; in social reform movements, 655, 680; and study clubs, 573; suffrage for, 570, 589, 681–82, 720, 745; in temperance movement, 566
Women and Economics (Gilman), 570
Women's Bureau, establishment of, in Department of Labor, 730
Women's Christian Temperance Union (WCTU), 566, 680
Women's City Club, 780
Women's rights movement: in 1920s, 746; in 1960s, 924–26; in 1970s, 955–56; in 1980s, 980. *See also* Feminist movement
Women's Trade Union League (WTUL), 652, 655, 658–60, 681, 781
Women Wage-Earners (Campbell), 582
Wonderful Wizard of Oz (Baum), 608–609
Wood, Leonard, 640, 702
Woods, Robert A., 580–81
Woodstock, 921–22
Woodward, Bob, 940–41
Woolworth, F. W., 541
WoolworthUs, 745
Work. *See* Labor
Work and Win (Alger), 605
Workers' compensation law, passage of first, 689
Workers, The (Wyckoff), 582
Working conditions, 543–45, 552, 859; for children, 655; for women, 655
Workingmen's parties, in California, 545

Works Progress Administration (WPA), 778–79, 862
World War I: battles of, 723–24; causes of, 716; and debts of Allied governments to U.S., 799; draft in, 722–23; peace terms, 732–36; submarine warfare in, 708–709, 718–22; U.S. entrance, 709, 721; U.S. mobilization for, 722–23; and U.S. neutrality, 717
World War II: bombing of Pearl Harbor, 809–10; concentration camps, 812–13; in Europe, 804–805, 814–15; home front, 816–22; impact of, 826–27; in Pacific, 809–10, 815–16, 826; and politics, 821–22; submarine warfare in, 807; U.S. entrance into, 810; victory, 822–24; and Yalta conference, 824
Wounded Knee, massacre at, 500, 502, 507
Wovoka (Paiute messiah), 500
Wright, Frank Lloyd, 557
Wright, Orville, 613
Wright, Wilbur, 613
Wriston, Henry W., 866
Wyckoff, Walter, 582
Wyoming: admission to union, 494; ranching in, 514–16; territory of, 509; women suffrage in, 589
Wyoming Stock Growers' Association, 515

Yale University, 519, 573, 578
Yalta Conference (1945), 824, 842
Yates v. *U.S.* (1956), 881
Yellow-dog contracts, 744
Yellow fever, 640
Yellow journalism, 627, 634–35
Yergin, Daniel, 831, 839
Yiddish (Jewish) Theater, 562
Yippies, 922
Yom Kippur War, 946–47, 967
Yurok Indians, 496

Zangwell, Israel, 583
Zen Buddhism, 865
Zero-option arms control initiative, 981, 1001–1002
Ziegfeld, Florenz, 668
Zimmermann, Arthur, 721
Zoning, development of, 666–67
Zoot-suit riots (1943), 821
Zuñi Indians, 496, 498